UNITED STATES ARMY IN WO

The Mediterranean Theater of Operations

# SICILY AND THE SURRENDER OF ITALY

*by*
*Lieutenant Colonel Albert N. Garland*
*and*
*Howard McGaw Smyth*
*Assisted by*
*Martin Blumenson*

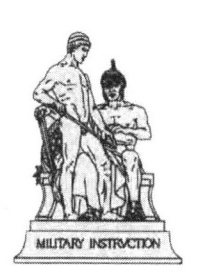

*CENTER OF MILITARY HISTORY*

*UNITED STATES ARMY*

*WASHINGTON, D.C., 1993*

Library of Congress Catalog Card Number: 64-60002

First Printed 1965—CMH Pub 6-2-1

# UNITED STATES ARMY IN WORLD WAR II
Stetson Conn, General Editor

*Advisory Committee*
(As of 15 June 1963)

| | |
|---|---|
| Fred C. Cole<br>Washington and Lee University | Maj. Gen. Hugh M. Exton<br>U.S. Continental Army Command |
| William R. Emerson<br>Yale University | Maj. Gen. Tom R. Stoughton<br>Industrial College of the Armed Forces |
| Earl Pomeroy<br>University of Oregon | Brig. Gen. Ward S. Ryan<br>U.S. Army War College |
| Theodore Ropp<br>Duke University | Col. Elias C. Townsend<br>U.S. Army Command and General Staff College |
| Bell I. Wiley<br>Emory University | Col. Vincent J. Esposito<br>United States Military Academy |

C. Vann Woodward
Yale University

*Office of the Chief of Military History*

Brig. Gen. Hal C. Pattison, Chief of Military History

| | |
|---|---|
| Chief Historian | Stetson Conn |
| Acting Chief, Histories Division | Lt. Col. Paul W. Phillips |
| Chief, Editorial and Graphics Division | Lt. Col. James R. Hillard |
| Editor in Chief | Joseph R. Friedman |

. . . to Those Who Served

# Foreword

This volume, the second to be published in the Mediterranean Theater of Operations subseries, takes up where George F. Howe's *Northwest Africa: Seizing the Initiative in the West* left off. It integrates the Sicilian Campaign with the complicated negotiations involved in the surrender of Italy.

The Sicilian Campaign was as complex as the negotiations, and is equally instructive. On the Allied side it included American, British, and Canadian soldiers as well as some Tabors of Goums; major segments of the U.S. Army Air Forces and of the Royal Air Force; and substantial contingents of the U.S. Navy and the Royal Navy. Opposing the Allies were ground troops and air forces of Italy and Germany, and the Italian Navy. The fighting included a wide variety of operations: the largest amphibious assault of World War II; parachute jumps and air landings; extended overland marches; tank battles; precise and remarkably successful naval gunfire support of troops on shore; agonizing struggles for ridge tops; and extensive and skillful artillery support. Sicily was a testing ground for the U.S. soldier, fighting beside the more experienced troops of the British Eighth Army, and there the American soldier showed what he could do.

The negotiations involved in Italy's surrender were rivaled in complexity and delicacy only by those leading up to the Korean armistice. The relationship of tactical to diplomatic activity is one of the most instructive and interesting features of this volume. Military men were required to double as diplomats and to play both roles with skill.

The authors were uniquely qualified to undertake this difficult volume. Rare indeed is the collaboration of an authority on Italian, German, and diplomatic history with an experienced infantry officer who is a Master of Arts in history.

Washington, D. C.  
15 June 1963

HAL C. PATTISON  
Brigadier General, USA  
Chief of Military History

# The Authors

Lt. Col. Albert Nutter Garland received a B.S. degree in education and an M.A. degree in history from Louisiana State University and has taught in New Orleans private schools and at Louisiana Polytechnic Institute. A Regular Army officer with more than 20 years of active service, he served during World War II as a rifle company commander with the 84th Infantry Division and participated in the Northern France, Ardennes-Alsace, and Central Europe Campaigns. Since 1945 he has served in Alaska and Taiwan and in numerous assignments in the States. Colonel Garland was a member of OCMH from 1958 to 1962 and is now Assistant Editor of *Military Review*, the U.S. Army's professional magazine, which is published at the Command and General Staff College, Fort Leavenworth, Kansas.

Howard McGaw Smyth, a graduate of Reed College, received the M.A. degree in history from Stanford and the Ph.D. degree from Harvard University. He has taught, chiefly in the field of modern European history, at Reed, Princeton, Union College, American University, and the University of California, where he devoted himself to work in the history of modern Italy. He served a term as a member of the Board of Editors of the *Journal of Modern History*.

During World War II he served for a time in the Office of Strategic Services and then in the Department of State, working on problems relating to Italy in the Division of Territorial Studies and the Division of Southern European Affairs. Dr. Smyth was a member of the staff of OCMH from 1946 to 1952 when he joined the staff of the Historical Office, Department of State, where he is now Editor in Chief, *Documents on German Foreign Policy, 1918–1945*.

# Preface

With the expulsion of German and Italian armed forces from North Africa in May 1943, Allied forces in the Mediterranean prepared to jump ninety miles across the sea to strike Sicily and thus launch the first blow against Europe's "soft underbelly." This is the story of that jump, a story which includes the high-level decisions of President Franklin D. Roosevelt, Prime Minister Winston S. Churchill, and the Combined Chiefs of Staff at the Casablanca Conference, the planning in Washington, London, and in the theater, and the subsequent fighting on the island.

Before landing in Sicily, the Allies had hoped that a successful island campaign, coming hard on the heels of Allied victories in North Africa, would cause Italy to abrogate its Pact of Steel with Germany and pull out of the war. How this Allied hope was fulfilled—the politico-military diplomatic negotiations, the ambiguities, the frustrations, the culmination in Italian surrender— is also part of the story.

A wealth of Allied documentary material, of captured German and Italian records, and of primary and secondary published material dealing with the period has been available to the authors in their attempt to reconstruct the crucial events of the spring and summer of 1943. Although their narrative focuses on American participation in these events, it does not neglect the important role played by Great Britain. The enemy side of the campaign and the Axis strategies and policies are also presented in full measure.

This volume itself has an interesting history. It was begun some years ago by Dr. Smyth when Maj. Gen. Harry J. Malony was Chief of Military History and it is a pleasure to testify to the stimulation and guidance which he offered; to acknowledge the assistance and encouragement given by Dr. George F. Howe and Dr. Sidney T. Mathews, colleagues in the then Mediterranean Section; to recall the helpful critical comment proferred from time to time by Dr. Hugh M. Cole, then Chief of the European Section. Mr. Detmar Finke and Mr. Israel Wice were unflagging in their aid in the search for materials.

At a later stage Colonel Garland joined the staff of OCMH and took over the responsibility for the work. The volume thus is a product of joint authorship. Colonel Garland tells the story of the Sicilian Campaign. Dr. Smyth narrates the story of the Italian surrender. The combined work submitted by the authors ran to excessive length and Mr. Blumenson was called in to assist in condensing and revising portions of the manuscript. He contributed materially to its final structure and form.

In the later stages of the work this volume benefited from the assistance rendered by many individuals. Conspicuous among these have been Mr. Charles MacDonald, Chief of the General Histories Branch of the Office of the Chief of Military History, who guided the project during its last four years, and Mrs. Magna E. Bauer, of the same branch, whose exhaustive research in German and Italian records provided the authors with an invaluable series of studies on the enemy's defense of Sicily.

The authors have also benefited from the help of other colleagues in OCMH, notably Brig. Gen. William H. Harris, Col. Leonard G. Robinson, Lt. Col. Joseph Rockis, Dr. John Miller, jr., Lt. Col. William Bell, and Lt. Col. James Schnabel. Many thanks are due also to David Jaffé, senior editor of the volume; B. C. Mossman, chief cartographer; Mrs. Loretto Stevens, assistant editor; and Mrs. Norma Sherris, photographic editor.

During the research stage, invaluable help was provided by Mr. Sherrod East, Chief Archivist, World War II Division, National Archives and Records Service, and certain of his assistants, Mrs. Lois Aldridge, Mrs. Hazel Ward, and Mrs. Frances J. Rubright. Without their willing and cheerful aid, this project might well never have been completed.

Although these individuals contributed much to the final product, the language used, the interpretations placed on the events, the conclusions reached, are the authors' own. No one else bears this responsibility.

Washington, D.C.  
15 June 1963

ALBERT N. GARLAND  
Lieutenant Colonel, Infantry  
HOWARD McGAW SMYTH

# Contents

## PART ONE

## Background and Plans

| Chapter | | Page |
|---|---|---|
| I. | ALLIED STRATEGY IN THE MEDITERRANEAN | 1 |
| | *Casablanca: The Decision for Sicily* | 1 |
| | *TRIDENT: Beyond Sicily* | 12 |
| | *Algiers — And Italy?* | 23 |
| | *The Surrender Problem* | 25 |
| II. | THE AXIS ON THE DEFENSIVE | 27 |
| | *The Italo-German Alliance* | 27 |
| | *The Disintegration of Fascism* | 39 |
| | *The Allied Threat* | 44 |
| III. | PREPARATIONS AND PRELIMINARIES | 52 |
| | *The Beginnings* | 52 |
| | *The Plan* | 58 |
| | *Other Factors* | 63 |
| IV. | THE AXIS SITUATION | 69 |
| | *Pantelleria* | 69 |
| | *Growing German Strength* | 73 |
| | *The Defenses of Sicily* | 75 |
| V. | FINAL ALLIED PREPARATIONS | 88 |
| | *Missions and Forces* | 88 |
| | *Seventh Army Plans* | 96 |
| | *Naval and Air Plans* | 105 |
| | *The Final Days* | 108 |

## PART TWO

## Operations and Negotiations

| VI. | THE ASSAULT | 115 |
|---|---|---|
| | *The Airborne Operations* | 115 |
| | *The Seaborne Operations* | 119 |

| Chapter | | Page |
|---|---|---|
| VII. | THE FIRST DAY | 147 |
| | *The Axis Reaction* | 147 |
| | *The Battle* | 150 |
| | *The Beaches* | 156 |
| VIII. | THE AXIS THREAT | 163 |
| IX. | AIRBORNE REINFORCEMENT | 175 |
| X. | THE BEACHHEAD SECURE | 185 |
| | *Straightening Out the Sag* | 185 |
| | *On to the Yellow Line* | 189 |
| XI. | CONTINUING THE CAMPAIGN: THE DECISIONS | 202 |
| | *Sixth Army and OB SUED* | 202 |
| | *The Allied Problem: How to Continue* | 205 |
| | *Comando Supremo and OKW* | 211 |
| XII. | SEVENTH ARMY CHANGES DIRECTIONS | 218 |
| | *The Eighth Army Attempt To Break Through* | 218 |
| | *The II Corps Front* | 219 |
| | *Agrigento* | 224 |
| | *Army Directive of 15 July 1943* | 230 |
| | *Discord and Harmony* | 234 |
| XIII. | THE DRIVE TO THE CLIMAX | 239 |
| | *The Feltre Conference* | 239 |
| | *Planning the Western Sweep* | 244 |
| | *The Pounce on Palermo* | 250 |
| | *Denouement* | 254 |
| XIV. | THE CLIMAX | 258 |
| | *Sardinia Versus the Mainland* | 258 |
| | *The Overthrow of Mussolini* | 263 |
| | *Allied Reaction* | 268 |
| | *Rome: Open City* | 278 |
| XV. | DISSOLUTION OF THE ROME-BERLIN AXIS | 281 |
| | *Badoglio's First Moves* | 281 |
| | *Friction Along the Alps* | 288 |
| | *The Italian Course is Changed* | 295 |
| XVI. | THE DRIVE TO THE EAST | 300 |
| | *Developing an East Front* | 300 |
| | *Axis Reactions* | 306 |
| | *Nicosia* | 309 |
| | *Along the North Coast* | 316 |

| Chapter | | Page |
|---|---|---|
| XVII. | THE BATTLE OF TROINA | 324 |
| XVIII. | BREAKING THE SAN FRATELLO LINE | 348 |
| XIX. | EVACUATION | 368 |
| | *The Tarvis Conference* | 368 |
| | *The Italian Dilemma* | 371 |
| | *The Decision to Evacuate Sicily* | 374 |
| | *Allied Reaction* | 378 |
| | *The Evacuation Begins* | 382 |
| XX. | BROLO | 388 |
| XXI. | THE END OF THE CAMPAIGN | 406 |
| | *The Race to Messina* | 406 |
| | *Conclusions* | 417 |
| | *Patton* | 425 |

## PART THREE

## The Surrender

| | | |
|---|---|---|
| XXII. | THE QUADRANT CONFERENCE AND THE QUEBEC MEMORANDUM | 435 |
| | *Strategic Issues at Quebec* | 435 |
| | *The Mission of General Castellano* | 440 |
| | *The Quebec Memorandum* | 446 |
| | *Approval of the Long Terms* | 448 |
| XXIII. | THE SURRENDER PRELIMINARIES | 451 |
| | *The Zanussi Mission* | 451 |
| | *Castellano at Lisbon* | 455 |
| | *Zanussi's Negotiations in Lisbon and Algiers* | 461 |
| | *Thoughts in Rome* | 465 |
| XXIV. | THE ITALIAN DECISION | 469 |
| | *ACHSE* | 469 |
| | *The Parleys at Cassibile* | 474 |
| | *The Decision at Rome* | 479 |
| XXV. | THE ARMISTICE | 482 |
| | *The Signature* | 482 |
| | *Planning GIANT II* | 485 |
| | *Second Thoughts in Rome* | 489 |

| Chapter | Page |
|---|---|
| XXVI. THE RENUNCIATION | 497 |
|     *"Innocuous"* | 498 |
|     *The Announcement* | 505 |
| XXVII. THE SURRENDER | 510 |
|     *Badoglio's Announcement* | 510 |
|     *Flight of the King and High Command* | 513 |
|     *Interpretations* | 519 |
| XXVIII. THE DISSOLUTION | 522 |
|     *German Reaction* | 522 |
|     *The Battle for Rome* | 524 |
|     *Dissolution of the Italian Armed Forces* | 532 |
|     *Mussolini* | 536 |
| XXIX. THE SECOND CAPITULATION | 540 |
|     *Mission to Brindisi* | 540 |
|     *The Long Terms* | 543 |
|     *Malta* | 549 |
|     *Epilogue* | 552 |

*Appendix*

| | |
|---|---|
| A. COMPOSITION OF AMERICAN FORCES | 555 |
| B. THE QUEBEC MEMORANDUM | 556 |
| C. SHORT (MILITARY) TERMS IN GENERAL EISENHOWER'S POSSESSION ON 6 AUGUST 1943 | 558 |
| D. ADDITIONAL CONDITIONS (LONG TERMS) SIGNED ON 29 SEPTEMBER 1943 | 559 |
| BIBLIOGRAPHICAL NOTE | 565 |
| GLOSSARY | 571 |
| BASIC MILITARY MAP SYMBOLS | 575 |
| INDEX | 579 |

# Maps

| No. | | Page |
|---|---|---|
| 1. | British Eighth Army Operations, 10 July 1943 | 122 |
| 2. | The Seizure of Agrigento, 3d Infantry Division, 14-17 July 1943 | 227 |
| 3. | 15th Army Group Front, 23 July 1943 | 305 |
| 4. | II Corps Advance, 24-31 July 1943 | 312 |
| 5. | The Capture of Troina, 1st Infantry Division, 1-6 August 1943 | 335 |
| 6. | The Fight for San Fratello, 3d Infantry Division, 8 August 1943 | 362 |
| 7. | 15th Army Group Gains, 24 July-10 August 1943 | 381 |
| 8. | Brolo and the Naso Ridge, 3d Infantry Division, 11-12 August 1943 | 395 |

*Maps I-VIII are in accompanying map envelope*

  I. The Battleground and the Enemy, 10 July 1943

|  |  | Page |
|---|---|---|
| II. | The Final Landing Plan | |
| III. | The Seventh Army Assault, 10 July 1943 | |
| IV. | Counterattack at Gela, 11 July 1943 | |
| V. | Seventh Army Advance, 11–12 July 1943 | |
| VI. | The Seventh Army Changes Direction, 13–18 July 1943 | |
| VII. | The Seventh Army Clears Western Sicily, 19–23–July 1943 | |
| VIII. | The Race to Messina, 13–17 August 1943 | |

## Illustrations

| | Page |
|---|---|
| President Franklin D. Roosevelt and Prime Minister Winston S. Churchill | 9 |
| Allied Leaders in the Sicilian Campaign | 13 |
| Churchill Addressing the U.S. Congress, May 1943 | 20 |
| Adolf Hitler and Benito Mussolini | 28 |
| King Victor Emmanuel III | 30 |
| Generale d'Armata Ugo Cavallero | 31 |
| Feldmarschall Albert Kesselring and General der Infanterie Enno von Rintelen with Prince Umberto Di Savoia | 34 |
| Generale d'Armata Vittorio Ambrosio | 36 |
| Generale di Corpo d'Armata Giacomo Carboni | 37 |
| Count Dino Grandi | 40 |
| Count Galeazzo Ciano | 41 |
| General Sir Bernard L. Montgomery and Lt. Gen. George S. Patton, Jr., in Sicily | 55 |
| Lt. Gen. Sir Miles C. Dempsey | 62 |
| Lt. Gen. Sir Oliver Leese | 63 |
| Pantelleria Under Attack | 71 |
| Generale di Corpo d'Armata Comandante Designato D'Armata Mario Roatta | 77 |
| Generale d'Armata Alfredo Guzzoni | 77 |
| Generalleutnant Eberhard Rodt | 80 |
| Feldmarschall Wolfram Freiherr von Richthofen | 80 |
| Generalmajor Paul Conrath | 80 |
| Generalleutnant Fridolin von Senger und Etterlin | 81 |
| Col. Ernst Guenther Baade | 81 |
| General der Panzertruppen Hans Valentin Hube | 81 |
| Looking South From the Heights of Enna | 85 |
| Gela Beach | 90 |
| Lt. Gen. Omar N. Bradley and Maj. Gen. Terry de la Mesa Allen | 93 |
| Maj. Gen. Troy H. Middleton | 94 |
| Maj. Gen. Matthew B. Ridgway | 94 |
| Maj. Gen. Lucian K. Truscott, Jr. | 94 |
| Maj. Gen. Manton S. Eddy | 95 |
| Maj. Gen. Hugh J. Gaffey | 95 |

|  | Page |
|---|---|
| Lt. Col. William O. Darby, Leader of Force X | 95 |
| Ponton Causeway From an LST to Shore | 104 |
| Landing Craft Massed in Bizerte Harbor for the Invasion of Sicily | 109 |
| Paratroopers Preparing To Emplane for Sicily | 116 |
| Glider Casualty | 116 |
| Ponte Dirillo Crossing Site | 118 |
| USS *Boise* Bombarding Coastal Defenses in Gela Landing Area | 121 |
| Licata and Beach Areas to the East | 124 |
| The Right Flank Beach at Licata | 126 |
| Highway 115 | 127 |
| A Shore-to-Shore LCT at Licata Beach | 130 |
| Army Donkeys Wading Ashore at Licata | 130 |
| Bringing Up Supplies by Cart at Licata Beach | 132 |
| Knocked-Out Italian Railway Battery on Licata Mole | 132 |
| Enemy Defense Positions Along Coast Road East of Licata | 134 |
| Road Junction Y | 137 |
| Italian Prisoners Taken at Gela on D-day | 138 |
| The Coast Line West of Scoglitti | 140 |
| Landing Heavy Equipment at Scoglitti | 145 |
| Looking Down the Niscemi Road to Piano Lupo | 151 |
| American Troops in Gela on D Plus 1 | 153 |
| Paratroopers Moving In on the Ridge at Abbio Priolo | 166 |
| American Ships Under Air Attack | 167 |
| Col. James M. Gavin in Biazzo Ridge Area | 169 |
| Wrecked German Tanks Dot Gela Plain | 171 |
| The *Robert Rowan* Exploding Off the Coast at Gela | 178 |
| Airborne Reinforcements in a C–47 Heading for Sicily | 180 |
| Paratroop Reinforcements Moving Through Vittoria | 183 |
| Ponte Olivo Airfield | 186 |
| Tank-Mounted Troops Rolling Through Palma | 193 |
| Canicattì Under Artillery Fire | 198 |
| Butera | 221 |
| Agrigento and the Surrounding High Ground | 225 |
| A Dukw Hauling Supplies in Porto Empedocle | 229 |
| Signal Corps Troops in Caltanissetta | 234 |
| Caltanissetta, Southwest Corner of the Enna Loop | 247 |
| General Ridgway and Staff Near Ribera | 250 |
| Mortar Squad Preparing To Attack Santo Stefano | 251 |
| The 2d Armored Division Rolls Into Palermo | 252 |
| Maj. Gen. Geoffrey Keyes and Italian Generale di Brigata Giuseppe Molinero After Surrender of Palermo | 253 |
| Maresciallo d'Italia Pietro Badoglio | 264 |
| Southern Approach to Enna | 302 |
| Leonforte | 303 |

|                                                                                      | Page |
|--------------------------------------------------------------------------------------|------|
| Caronia Valley                                                                       | 310  |
| Gangi, With Mount Etna in Distance                                                   | 311  |
| Coast Road Patrol Passing the Bombed-Out Castelbuono Railroad Station, 24 July 1943  | 316  |
| Demolished Bridge Along Highway 117                                                  | 322  |
| Troina Ridge From the High Ground Near Cerami                                        | 326  |
| Looking West From the Town of Troina                                                 | 327  |
| Goumiers Moving Toward Capizzi                                                       | 330  |
| Forward Observation Post Directing Fire on Troina                                    | 332  |
| Artillery in Position Near Cerami                                                    | 332  |
| Half-Track Squeezing Through a Narrow Street in Cerami                               | 334  |
| Maj. Gen. Clarence R. Huebner and General Allen, 8 August 1943                       | 346  |
| Provisional Pack Train and Mounted Troops                                            | 349  |
| Enemy Field of Fire Over Furiano River Crossing Site From San Fratello Ridge         | 350  |
| Looking South Over the Furiano River Valley                                          | 351  |
| Highway 113                                                                          | 354  |
| Looking North Over the San Fratello – Cesarò Ròad                                    | 355  |
| San Fratello Ridge                                                                   | 356  |
| Sant'Agata From the Seaward Side of San Fratello Ridge                               | 364  |
| Treating a Wounded Soldier                                                           | 366  |
| San Marco D'Alunzio                                                                  | 367  |
| Axis Second Echelon Leaders at Tarvis                                                | 370  |
| Smoke Pall Covers Parts of Messina After Bombing Attack                              | 377  |
| Randazzo From the Southern Approach                                                  | 383  |
| Destroyed Bridge Along Highway 116                                                   | 384  |
| Americans and British Meet at Randazzo                                               | 386  |
| Pillbox Overlooking Highway 113                                                      | 390  |
| Cape Orlando                                                                         | 391  |
| Brolo Beach From the East                                                            | 392  |
| Enemy View of Landing Area at Brolo                                                  | 394  |
| Setting a Machine Gun Position on Monte Cipolla                                      | 397  |
| Lt. Col. Lyle A. Bernard and His Radioman in Command Post Atop Monte Cipolla         | 400  |
| The Objective, Messina                                                               | 407  |
| Troops Moving Around Blown-Out Section of Cliffside Road                             | 408  |
| The Bridge That Was "Hung in the Sky"                                                | 409  |
| General Dwight D. Eisenhower and General Montgomery Observing the Effect of Artillery Fire on the Italian Mainland | 415  |
| Secret Emissaries to Lisbon                                                          | 456  |
| The Tiber River at Fumicino                                                          | 487  |
| The "Rescue" of Mussolini                                                            | 538  |
| Signing Surrender Document Aboard H.M.S. *Nelson*                                    | 550  |

# The U.S. Army Center of Military History

The Center of Military History prepares and publishes histories as required by the U.S. Army. It coordinates Army historical matters, including historical properties, and supervises the Army museum system. It also maintains liaison with public and private agencies and individuals to stimulate interest and study in the field of military history. The Center is located at 1099 14th Street, N.W., Washington, D.C. 20005–3402.

# CHAPTER I

# Allied Strategy in the Mediterranean

*Casablanca: The Decision for Sicily*

At a series of meetings held in Casablanca, French Morocco, in January 1943, the United States and Great Britain decided to attack the island of Sicily. The decision made by President Franklin D. Roosevelt and Prime Minister Winston S. Churchill, in concert with their principal military advisers, the Combined Chiefs of Staff, started a chain of events which led ultimately to invasion of the mainland of Italy, collapse of the Italian Fascist regime, and the surrender of Italy.

The Casablanca Conference set up the initial Allied move to return to the continent of Europe by way of the Mediterranean. It marked a continuation of the indirect approach toward the center of Axis might started by the Anglo-American landings in French North Africa two months before, in November 1942.

In retrospect, the decision taken at Casablanca appears as an essential link in an apparently consistent over-all Allied strategy for World War II in the Mediterranean: first, to expel Italo-German forces from North Africa; second, to attack Sicily as a steppingstone to the Italian mainland; third, to invade the mainland and eliminate Italy from the war; and finally, to contain and wear down German forces in Italy as a prelude to the main attack across the English Channel into northwest Europe.

In reality this was not the case. There was no broad plan at the outset to eliminate Italy first as the weaker of the Axis partners.[1] Actually, Allied strategy in the Mediterranean—after the decision of July 1942 to invade North Africa—evolved as a series of *ad hoc* decisions, each setting forth objectives limited by available resources and the conditions of the time.

At Casablanca, for the first time, the strategic initiative passed to the Allies. Hitherto the Allies could do little more than react to Axis movements: resist the submarine warfare against their sea lines of communications; hold the thin line in Egypt protecting the Suez Canal; attack Germany from the air for lack of other avenues to the enemy heartland; support the Soviet Union; contain the Japanese in the Pacific. But between July 1942 and January 1943 the pattern had begun to change: there was the Russian breakthrough behind Stalingrad; British victory at El 'Alamein; Anglo-American occupation of French Northwest Africa. Though each of these was essentially a defensive action, by the time Allied lead-

---

[1] Although something similar had been suggested in Anglo-American discussions in mid-1942. See Robert E. Sherwood, *Roosevelt and Hopkins: An Intimate History* (New York: Harper & Brothers, 1950, rev. ed.), p. 459; Maurice Matloff and Edwin M. Snell, *Strategic Planning for Coalition Warfare, 1941–1942*, UNITED STATES ARMY IN WORLD WAR II (Washington, 1953), pp. 285–86.

ers convened at Casablanca the balance had shifted. For the first time the Allies had a considerable degree of freedom in selecting their next move or their next objective.

The instrument of discussion and decision at Casablanca—the Combined Chiefs of Staff (CCS)—represented a new institution in the evolution of warfare. A body composed of the service chiefs of staff of the United States and Great Britain, it had taken form within a month after Pearl Harbor.[2] Despite the fact that this combined directorate helped make possible an extraordinary integration of Anglo-American effort, serious differences on strategy did emerge between the U.S. Joint Chiefs and the British Chiefs of Staff.

These differences reflected the dissimilar geographic positions, the unequal war potentials, and the divergent historical experiences of the two countries. Even the English language as used in America and Britain is not identical, and occasionally problems of verbal expression superimposed themselves on divergent concepts arising from diverse national outlooks.

A basic Allied strategic plan for the global conduct of the war began to appear at the ARCADIA Conference in Washington, December 1941, when the Combined Chiefs of Staff came into being. Here the Anglo-American decision was made, or reaffirmed, that the main weight of America's effort would be directed toward Europe to achieve, in co-operation with Great Britain and the USSR, the defeat of Germany. Against Japan, a limited and essentially defensive action would be conducted until after victory in Europe.[3]

Though the American Government would threaten at times to turn its effort against Japan, the Allies fought a genuinely coalition war, one great group of powers against another. And though the Americans might have preferred to turn their major energies toward avenging Pearl Harbor, they had to retain a British base from which to mount an attack against the European continent; and they realized the value of the eastern land

---

[2] Matloff and Snell, *Strategic Planning for Coalition Warfare, 1941–1942,* pp. 97ff; see also Gordon A. Harrison, *Cross-Channel Attack* (Washington, 1951), ch. I, and Forrest C. Pogue, *The Supreme Command* (Washington, 1954), pp. 37–41, both in UNITED STATES ARMY IN WORLD WAR II; John Ehrman, *Grand Strategy,* vol. V, *August 1943–September 1944* (London: Her Majesty's Stationery Office, 1956), pp. 15–24.
Members of the CCS were: Field Marshal Sir Alan Brooke, Chief of the Imperial General Staff; Admiral of the Fleet Sir Dudley Pound, the First Sea Lord; Air Chief Marshal Sir Charles Portal, Chief of the Air Staff; General George C. Marshall, Chief of Staff, U.S. Army; Admiral Ernest J. King, Chief of Naval Operations and Commander in Chief, U.S. Fleet; Lt. Gen. Henry H. Arnold, commanding general of the U.S. Army Air Forces and Marshall's Deputy Chief of Staff for Air. Until March 1942, Admiral Harold R. Stark was Chief of Naval Operations and a member of the Joint and Combined Chiefs. Admiral William D. Leahy became a member in the summer of 1942 in his capacity as Chief of Staff to President Roosevelt. Because the CCS sat in Washington, Field Marshal Sir John Dill, personal representative of Mr. Churchill as Minister of Defence, represented the British Chiefs during the intervals between formal conferences. The main planning bodies of the Joint Chiefs were the Joint Staff Planners and the Joint Strategic Survey Committee, the latter established in early November 1942 to study long-range policies and strategy.

[3] Harrison, *Cross-Channel Attack,* p. 8; Ray S. Cline, *Washington Command Post: The Operations Division,* UNITED STATES ARMY IN WORLD WAR II (Washington, 1953), p. 144; Dwight D. Eisenhower, *Crusade in Europe* (New York: Doubleday and Company, Inc., 1948), pp. 27–28.

front in absorbing much of the strength of Germany's ground forces.

How was Germany to be defeated? General George C. Marshall, Chief of Staff of the U.S. Army, asked this question of Brig. Gen. Dwight D. Eisenhower soon after the latter reported to the War Department in December 1941. As chief of the War Plans Division, which in March 1942 was reorganized to become the Operations Division (OPD), Eisenhower had the task of formulating the basic plan. In the early spring of 1942 Eisenhower considered a variety of plans for defeating the Axis in Europe: plans for attacking through Norway; plans for working through the Iberian Peninsula; even plans for the use of sea and air power only. The Mediterranean route was also briefly considered, this when the British situation in the Middle East was relatively good. But the domination of the central Mediterranean by Axis air forces ruled out detailed planning for an attempt to attack Italy from Gibraltar.[4]

By early April 1942 OPD had developed the basic American strategic concept.[5] Rejecting the Mediterranean route for a number of cogent reasons—the great distance from North African bases to the German industrial centers; the improbability of achieving a decisive result by first eliminating Italy from the war; the disadvantage of attacking Germany over the great natural barrier of the Alps; the inability to concentrate the full power of the United States and of Great Britain in the Mediterranean—OPD came out strongly for a cross-Channel attack. Only in England could the Allied military resources be effectively concentrated for the main blow against the Axis. No natural barriers comparable to the Alps protected Germany from attack from the west. Furthermore, England was closer to the great American ports on the Atlantic seaboard.

After getting the concurrence of the other two members of the Joint Chiefs—Admiral Ernest J. King, Chief of Naval Operations, and Lt. Gen. Henry H. Arnold, commander of the Army Air Forces—then President Roosevelt's acceptance, General Marshall in the second week of April presented the concept to the British Chiefs. The British agreed enthusiastically, and the idea took concrete form under the code name ROUNDUP, which projected a full-scale attack across the Channel into northern France in the spring of 1943.

General Marshall and his colleagues adhered consistently to this concept, which was based on a number of assumptions that in the spring of 1942 were little more than mere hopes. Could the Soviet armies resist under Adolf Hitler's second summer onslaught? Could the Anglo-American coalition relieve the pressure on Russia's ground forces?[6] When President Roosevelt pressed for any action which would assist the Russians in some manner, however minor, the outcome was the July 1942 decision in favor of TORCH, an Allied invasion of French Northwest

---

[4] Eisenhower, *Crusade in Europe*, pp. 18, 41–43. For a full account of the development of OPD, see Cline, *Washington Command Post*, pp. 76–87.

[5] The Operations Division set forth this concept in the so-called Marshall Memorandum. See Matloff and Snell, *Strategic Planning for Coalition Warfare, 1941–1942*, pp. 177–87; Harrison *Cross-Channel Attack*, p. 15; Cline, *Washington Command Post*, pp. 143–54.

[6] Harrison, *Cross-Channel Attack*, pp. 29–30. The project for an emergency cross-Channel operation was termed SLEDGEHAMMER.

Africa. An emergency decision designed to help the Russians, it also had the virtue of getting American troops into battle quickly and giving them combat experience.

The landings in North Africa in November 1942 created a new situation. The American Joint Chiefs of Staff felt that the TORCH decision had undermined the basic strategy agreed upon in April, for the North African operations meant such an investment of resources that a cross-Channel operation became improbable in 1943. Even the decision to concentrate first against Germany rather than against Japan was thrown open to question. The TORCH decision necessitated a reconsideration of fundamental policies.

Thinking about the next step beyond TORCH began even before the successful execution of that operation in November 1942. During the planning phase for TORCH, Allied leaders hoped and believed that the North African expedition would culminate in a campaign of no more than a few weeks. Prime Minister Churchill forecast "a peaceful occupation for liberation purposes of French North Africa and the next step will be to build up the attack on Sicily and Italy as well as on Rommel's back at Tripoli." [7]

But Churchill also envisaged a left hook after the Allied jab with the right: a new expedition to Norway which would eliminate Axis aerial interference with the convoys to Russia and bring visible evidence to the Soviet Government that the Western Powers were waging war against the Germans.[8]

By November 1942, British thinking tended to favor continued Mediterranean operations. At the very time the Allied landings in North Africa were taking place, Churchill informed the British Chiefs of Staff that he foresaw for 1943 efforts to pin down enemy forces in northwest Europe by threatening a cross-Channel attack; by invading Italy or southern France, preferably the latter; and by pressure "to bring in Turkey and operate overland with the Russians into the Balkans." [9]

Toward the end of the same month, he felt that the paramount task was to conquer North Africa and use the bases established there to strike at the Axis underbelly. The second immediate objective, he considered, should be either Sardinia or Sicily. Churchill considered Sicily by far the greater prize.[10] Accordingly, the British Joint Planners already had code names, appreciations, and outline plans for attacking the major Italian islands: BRIMSTONE for Sardinia; HUSKY for Sicily.

Elated by the initial successes gained by the North African venture, President Roosevelt supported British inclinations toward a Mediterranean strategy. On 18 November, the President proposed to Churchill a survey of all possible insular and peninsular invasion targets along the southern fringe of the European continent: Sardinia, Sicily, Italy, Greece, and the Balkans.[11]

Roosevelt's thoughts did not reflect a unified outlook in the American camp.

---

[7] Ltr, Prime Minister to Harry Hopkins, 4 Sep 42, as quoted in Winston S. Churchill, "The Second World War," vol. IV, *The Hinge of Fate* (Boston: Houghton Mifflin Company, 1950), p. 541.

[8] Churchill, *Hinge of Fate*, pp. 569-71.
[9] *Ibid.*, p. 649.
[10] *Ibid.*, pp. 654-55.
[11] Harrison, *Cross-Channel Attack*, p. 35.

Maj. Gen. Thomas T. Handy of OPD saw the continuation of operations in the Mediterranean beyond North Africa as logistically unfeasible and strategically unsound. He recommended either the continuation of ROUNDUP as originally planned or turning the weight of America's resources against Japan.[12]

In the middle of December 1942, General Marshall still hoped for a cross-Channel attack in 1943—a modified ROUNDUP. Marshall wanted to turn back to the main road immediately after what he considered the North African detour. According to a private conversation reported by Field Marshal Sir John Dill, Marshall was "more and more convinced that we should be in a position to undertake a modified 'Round-up' before the summer if, as soon as North Africa is cleared of Axis forces, we start pouring forces into England instead of sending them to Africa for the exploitation of 'Torch.' Such an operation would, he [Marshall] feels, be much more effective than either 'Brimstone' or 'Husky,' less costly in shipping, more satisfying to the Russians, engage more German air forces, and be the most effective answer to any German attack through Spain."[13]

Churchill's and Marshall's views were colored by early successes in Africa. The race for Tunisia was on. Until Christmas of 1942, the Allies hoped to seize Tunisia quickly. But it soon became clear that the North African campaign would be long and hard and that the next operations beyond North Africa would follow not in the spring, but in the summer of 1943. Furthermore, the Axis reaction required more Allied resources than initially allotted and outgrew the proportions contemplated in the TORCH planning phase.

In this new situation the U.S. Joint Chiefs felt the need for a long-range view in order to guide American mobilization and the allocation of men and material. Early in December they had proposed a strategy of three basic elements: a balanced build-up in the United Kingdom for a cross-Channel attack in 1943; a great air offensive against Germany from bases in England, North Africa, and the Middle East; and a massive air bombardment of Italy "with a view to destroying Italian resources and morale and eliminating her from the war."[14] They made no reference to further operations in the Mediterranean.

Meanwhile, Allied Force Headquarters (AFHQ) in the Mediterranean, commanded by Lt. Gen. Dwight D. Eisenhower, had begun to consider possible alternatives beyond TORCH. It looked at Sardinia as a possible next step after North Africa, and made this proposal to the chiefs in London and Washington.[15]

---

[12] *Ibid.*, pp. 35–36. For U.S. War Department planning in this period see Matloff and Snell, *Strategic Planning for Coalition Warfare, 1941–1942*, Chapter XVII.

[13] Churchill, *Hinge of Fate*, pp. 658–59.

[14] Harrison, *Cross-Channel Attack*, p. 36; Matloff and Snell, *Strategic Planning for Coalition Warfare, 1941–1942*, pp. 376–77.

[15] AFHQ JPS P/24 (Final), 4 Dec 42, sub: Appreciation and Outline Plan for Assault on Sardinia, 0100/12A/101, II. See also the collection of AFHQ JPS planning papers in the Salmon Files, 5-B-2, item 6, OCMH. (The Salmon Files consist of a body of papers and other materials collected at AFHQ by Col. E. Dwight Salmon.) See also 0100/12A/101, I and 0100/12A/102, I; Harry C. Butcher, *My Three Years With Eisenhower* (New York: Simon and Schuster, 1946), p. 218, entry for 9 Dec 42.

Unless otherwise indicated, all file numbers in this volume are those used by the World War II Records Division, National Archives and Records Service (NARS). (See Bibliographical Note.)

The British Chiefs gave greater support to this proposal than the American Joint Chiefs who gave it only limited encouragement.[16]

The British were thinking of what would later be termed a peripheral strategy to defeat Germany: continue the build-up in the United Kingdom; initiate operations in the Mediterranean against Sicily, Sardinia, Italy, and the Balkans; and hold back the effort against Japan. The Americans, by contrast, were eager to initiate direct action against Germany by means of a power thrust across the English Channel. If no offensive action against Germany were possible in the near future, the Americans were ready to consider increasing their allocations to the Pacific theaters for more powerful blows against the Japanese. In the view of Admiral King, the defeat of Japan would be infinitely more difficult once the Japanese had consolidated their conquests.[17]

After studying the British views, General Marshall concluded that the British Chiefs wanted the build-up in the United Kingdom but not the cross-Channel operation until a serious crack in German morale appeared. Opposed to any offensive action that might result in a heavy loss of resources inimical to the cross-Channel thrust, in particular the loss of shipping, Marshall did not entirely rule out operations in the eastern Mediterranean—near Palestine, Iraq, or Cyprus —in order to retain Turkish good will and perhaps even to induce Turkish support of the Allies. But he opposed an invasion of Sardinia, which, he felt, would be too costly in terms of shipping.[18]

Neither Americans nor British had as yet mentioned the possibility of a return to the Continent by the Mediterranean route, though both agreed that the elimination of Italy from the war was a desirable aim. A seed of serious disagreement on the price to pay for this goal— a difference which would emerge full-blown at the next major conference in May 1943 (TRIDENT)—already was apparent in early January. The Americans obviously were willing to pay only a small price. Although they accepted the need of putting pressure on Italy to bring about Italian collapse, they believed that air operations from North Africa would be enough, and they rejected the idea of ground operations on the Italian mainland. The British were not averse to paying a higher price to knock Italy out of the war. They were interested in eliminating Italy as a means of diminishing German strength. Churchill noted that the North African campaign had compelled the Germans to shift eleven divisions to southern France, thus weakening the forty-division force that garrisoned and protected the Channel areas of northern France and the Netherlands. He predicted that the Germans would probably need to move four to six divisions into Italy against the threat of Allied invasion of Sardinia and other vulnerable targets in the Mediterranean. Dispersing German strength and stretching the German defensive line in Europe

---

[16] Min, 48th Mtg JCS, 29 Dec 42; Br JP 4, 14 Jan 43, sub: Merits of BRIMSTONE and HUSKY (arguing that "an earlier BRIMSTONE would probably contribute as much as a later HUSKY"), 0100/12A/177; AFHQ JPS P/49 (Second Draft), 23 Jan 43, 0100/12A/103, II.

[17] Matloff and Snell, *Strategic Planning for Coalition Warfare, 1941–1942*, p. 377; Min, 49th Mtg JCS, 5 Jan 43; Arthur Bryant, *The Turn of the Tide* (New York: Doubleday and Company, 1957), p. 441n.

[18] Min, 49th Mtg JCS, 5 Jan 43.

would, of course, facilitate Allied re-entry into the Continent by way of northern France.[19] Carrying the thought further, some British planners explored the possibilities of "an offensive aimed at the collapse of Italy, and subsequently developed against the Balkans." One conclusion was that "the loss of either Sardinia or Sicily would almost certainly lead to the collapse of Italy." It would then be necessary for Germany to fill the vacuum by increasing the German commitment in Italy and the Balkans to the extent of twenty to thirty additional divisions.[20]

Immediately before departing for Casablanca, President Roosevelt called his Joint Chiefs to the White House on 7 January 1943 to determine whether they had formulated what might be considered an American position. Acting as spokesman, General Marshall admitted that though the Joint Chiefs regarded a cross-Channel strategy more favorably than a Mediterranean course of action, the question remained open. He summarized the British position as he understood it—to maintain the momentum of the North African campaign even at the expense of a build-up in the United Kingdom, and to attempt to bring about the collapse of Italy in order to force the commitment of additional German military units to replace Italian troops in Italy and the occupied countries.

General Marshall saw the issue primarily in logistical terms. He declared his willingness to take tactical risks, but he preferred not to gamble with shipping. Heavy shipping losses in an operation such as an invasion of Sardinia, he said, might destroy the opportunity to close with the main enemy in the near future. If he had to choose between Sardinia and Sicily, Marshall would favor the latter. Sicily was a more desirable, though probably a more difficult objective because it had more and better airfields. But any operation in the Mediterranean, Marshall believed, would impose a limit on the resources that could be sent to the United Kingdom. Admiral King added his explicit preference for Sicily over Sardinia, if a choice had to be made, for his primary concern was the protection of sea lanes of communications in the Mediterranean. Allied possession of Sicily would insure a sheltered corridor between the island and the African north coast. All the Joint Chiefs were agreed in opposing the concept of invading the southern shore of the European continent. When they indicated that Sardinia looked like a blind alley, the President summed up their feeling by saying that if the Allies took Sardinia, they could shout "Hooray," and then ask, "Where do we go from here?" The only argument in favor of invading Sardinia, Marshall remarked, was Eisenhower's suggestion that the operation could be mounted from outside the Mediterranean, perhaps one division coming directly from the United States, several from England.[21]

The American party, with the exception of Admiral William D. Leahy, who was ill, arrived in Casablanca on 13 January. Before meeting formally with the British, the Joint Chiefs again came to-

---

[19] Harrison, *Cross-Channel Attack*, p. 37; Notes by Minister of Defence, 3 Dec 42, as quoted in Churchill, *Hinge of Fate*, pp. 657–58.

[20] This argument is developed in an unofficial British planning paper, dated 19 January 1943, subject: Development of the Mediterranean Offensive, 0100/12A/177.

[21] Min of Mtg at White House, 7 Jan 43, OPD Exec 10, item 45.

gether to try to work out a clear-cut American position. Concerned with the diversion of resources in the struggle against Germany and Japan, Admiral King urged the formulation of an over-all strategy which would enable the Americans to resist expected British pressure in favor of an invasion of Sardinia. But General Marshall made no real effort to unite the American Joint Chiefs except to emphasize the necessity of a cross-Channel invasion. Lt. Gen. Brehon B. Somervell, Commanding General, Services of Supply, estimated that once the Mediterranean was cleared of enemy forces the Allies would save 1,825,000 tons of shipping in the first five months. King supported the estimate and spoke in favor of opening the Mediterranean to eliminate the long voyage around Africa and the Cape of Good Hope. Saving cargo space, the Americans believed, was much more important than eliminating Italy from the war, an aim which they were sure the British would favor.

Lt. Gen. Mark W. Clark, Eisenhower's deputy commander in chief in the Mediterranean, who was asked to consult with the Joint Chiefs, estimated that an operation against either Sardinia or Corsica could not be undertaken before the summer of 1943 because an all-out offensive against the Axis forces in Tunisia could not be mounted until the middle of March. To expel the Axis from North Africa by spring, the Allies would have to build up a force of half a million men. Might it be better, after North Africa had been cleared, to use critical shipping space to move part of that force elsewhere? Or should the force be used in operations launched directly from North Africa? If, as AFHQ calculated, four divisions plus service troops and air force units were needed for occupation and other purposes, Clark said, it would be necessary to keep 250,000 men in North Africa. An excess of some three American divisions and the entire British First Army would then remain in the theater at the conclusion of the North African campaign.

The main concerns of the U.S. Joint Chiefs before their meetings with the British at Casablanca were three: the shortage of shipping; how to use excess forces in the theater at the end of the Tunisia Campaign; and apprehension that the British would insist on invading Sardinia.[22]

Somewhat ironically, the main concern of the British Chiefs was their apprehension that the Americans would prefer the invasion of Sardinia over that of Sicily. Field Marshall Sir Alan Brooke, Chief of the Imperial General Staff, who spoke for the British when the conference opened on 14 January, indicated a lessening of anxiety with respect to Spain, which was increasingly likely to remain neutral, and at the other end of the Mediterranean a more positive hope that Turkey, though not expected to undertake an active campaign in the Balkans, might grant the Allies air bases from which to launch attacks against the German oil supply in Rumania. In the center of the Mediterranean area, Brooke suggested, the Allies had their major opportunity—to knock Italy out of the war; to force Germany to disperse her resources, and thereby to give positive aid to the Russians. As for the cross-Channel operation, Brooke estimated that the Allied build-up in England would total thirteen British and nine American

---

[22] Min, 50th Mtg JCS, 13 Jan 43.

PRESIDENT ROOSEVELT AND PRIME MINISTER CHURCHILL at Casablanca, surrounded by members of the Combined Chiefs of Staff and other high-ranking military advisers.

divisions by August 1943; these would comprise a force large enough to take advantage of a break in German morale.

Brooke the next day, 15 January, again urged the elimination of Italy from the war. He presented several choices of invasion: Sardinia, Sicily, Crete, and the Dodecanese. The threat to all these islands would compel Germany to take defensive measures or face the prospect of relinquishing them. With Italy out of the war, Germany would have to make larger commitments of military forces to hold Italy and the Balkans. The British favored Sicily as the best invasion target but did not advocate going beyond it unless Italy collapsed completely. "We should be very careful about accepting any invitation to support an anti-Fascist insurrection," General Brooke warned. "To do so might merely immobilize a considerable [Allied military] force to no purpose." [23]

Relieved that the British were not interested in occupying Italy, and beginning to feel that he was fighting a losing battle for a cross-Channel attack in 1943, General Marshall did not oppose an operation against Sicily. One of the strongest reasons was his appreciation of the need to use the excess of Allied troops that would remain in North Africa after Tunisia was clear of Axis forces. He therefore urged that operations undertaken in the Mediterranean be conducted with troops already in the theater. Yet he returned to a question more fundamental than the immediate issue—what

[23] Quote is from Min, 58th Mtg CCS, 16 Jan 43; see also Min, 55th Mtg CCS, 14 Jan and 57th Mtg CCS, 15 Jan 43; Bryant, *Turn of the Tide*, pp. 445–46, 448.

about an over-all strategy? "Was an operation against Sicily merely a means toward an end, or an end in itself? Is it to be part of an integrated plan to win the war or simply taking advantage of an opportunity?"

The questions were asked, but they were not answered. Perhaps they could not be. Perhaps the Americans had, as Churchill remarked with some annoyance, an "undue liking for logical clear-cut decisions," whereas the British were basically inclined toward an opportunistic approach to strategy.[24]

Despite their differences, the British and Americans reached agreement on the fourth day of the conference, 18 January. They decided then to invade Sicily following completion of the Tunisian campaign. As General Marshall explained, although the Americans preferred a cross-Channel attack in 1943, they were willing to accept an invasion of Sicily because of the large number of troops which would become available in North Africa, the great economy in shipping tonnage to be obtained (the major consideration), and the possibility of eliminating Italy from the war and thereby forcing Germany to assume responsibility for Italian commitments.[25]

On the question of alternative operations, General Marshall reiterated American opposition to an invasion of Sardinia because that island offered merely an air advantage whereas either Sicily or the cross-Channel operation might produce decisive results. Though invading Sicily would be more difficult than invading Sardinia, Marshall was more concerned with the security of Mediterranean shipping and with the immediate effects of operations against Germany, however indirect, than he was with eliminating Italy from the war. General Brooke, though stating his general agreement, insisted that plans be prepared for other operations on which the Allies could fall back in case of absolute necessity. The British and the Americans could not resolve differences of opinion, and in the end the decision for Sicily was the only concrete achievement of the Casablanca Conference affecting Mediterranean strategy.

In discussing the date of the projected invasion of Sicily, the British mentioned 22 August as coinciding with the favorable phase of the moon, though they were willing to settle on another, possibly earlier, date. Favorable lunar conditions actually represented a compromise between the divergent requirements of the Navy and of the airborne units—airborne troops needed a brief period of moonlight for their drops, the fleet required total darkness to cover its approach toward the Sicilian shore. When Admiral King proposed 25 July as another suitable date, the CCS quickly approved. The CCS also decided that General Eisenhower was to command the operation, General Sir Harold R. L. G. Alexander was to be the deputy commander in chief and in charge of the ground warfare, Admiral Sir Andrew B. Cunningham was

---

[24] Quotes are in Min, 58th Mtg CCS, 16 Jan 43, and Churchill, *Hinge of Fate*, p. 651. See also Min, JCS Mtg with the President, 16 Jan 43, Casablanca Conf Book, p. 61.

[25] Min, 2d Anfa Mtg, 18 Jan 43, Casablanca Conf Book, pp. 146–47. See also Richard M. Leighton and Robert W. Coakley, *Global Logistics and Strategy, 1940–1943* (Washington, 1955), ch. XXV, and Maurice Matloff, *Strategic Planning for Coalition Warfare, 1943–1944* (Washington, 1959), ch. I, both volumes in UNITED STATES ARMY IN WORLD WAR II; Bryant, *Turn of the Tide*, pp. 449–50; James Leasor, *The Clock With Four Hands* (New York: Reynal and Co., 1949), pp. 233–36.

to command the naval forces, and Air Chief Marshal Sir Arthur Tedder was to be the air commander.[26]

General Eisenhower was "infuriated" with the new command establishment and planned to combat actively "intrusion of the British Committee system" into the Allied Force Headquarters "scheme of things." He drafted a cable to the Combined Chiefs demanding a continuation of the centralization of command in his own person, which he felt had worked so well during the early stages of TORCH. The cable was never dispatched. At the insistence of Maj. Gen. Walter B. Smith, his chief of staff, General Eisenhower tore up the draft; Smith felt this was no time to be "creating any fuss." Thus, General Eisenhower found himself lifted to a supreme command with actual operations to be conducted by a committee of commanders over which he presided.[27]

From even immediate retrospect, the decision for Sicily represented a compromise between American and British views.

The purposes of the invasion were to secure the Mediterranean sea lanes, to divert pressure from the Russian front, and to intensify pressure on Italy. There was no agreement on the matter of the Mediterranean versus cross-Channel strategy, no agreement on what to do beyond Sicily, no agreement even that knocking Italy out of the war was the immediate objective of Anglo-American strategy— merely hope that the limited insular operations might, in conjunction with air bombardment, force Italy from the war. Even the expression of this hope reflected a difference that was later to emerge as a head-on clash. In the session of 18 January, General Marshall remarked "that he was most anxious not to become committed to interminable operations in the Mediterranean." He wished northern France to be the scene of the main effort against Germany. Air Chief Marshall Sir Charles Portal, chief of the British Air Staff, replied that "it was impossible to say exactly where we should stop in the Mediterranean since we hoped to knock Italy out altogether."[28]

Toward the end of the Casablanca Conference President Roosevelt, in a seemingly offhand manner, announced to the press the unconditional surrender formula to be imposed upon Germany, Italy, and Japan. The phrase was not made on the spur of the moment, for Mr. Roosevelt had discussed the matter with his Joint Chiefs on 7 January. He had told them of his intention to speak with Mr. Churchill on the advisability of informing Marshal Joseph Stalin (who had declined two invitations to confer with the American and British leaders) that the United Nations would prosecute the

---

[26] AFHQ IN Msg 466, 23 Jan 43, AFHQ CofS Log, Army War College; Min, 66th Mtg CCS, 22 Jan 43; Min, 69th Mtg CCS, 23 Jan 43; CCS 170/2, Final Report to the President and Prime Minister, and CCS 163, System of Air Command in the Mediterranean, 20 Jan 43, all in Smith Papers (Smith Papers are in Army War College and NARS); George F. Howe, *Northwest Africa: Seizing the Initiative in the West*, UNITED STATES ARMY IN WORLD WAR II (Washington, 1957), pp. 353-55.

[27] Diary of the Office of the Commander in Chief, bk. VII, p. A-598. The Diary of the Office of the Commander in Chief (hereafter cited as Diary Office CinC) was kept by Comdr. Harry C. Butcher, USNR, for General Eisenhower. It includes summaries of the Supreme Commander's activities, memoranda written for the diary, many of the top secret letters which came to or were sent by the Supreme Commander, and copies of plans, intelligence estimates, and the like. Edited portions of this diary appeared in Butcher's *My Three Years With Eisenhower*.

[28] Min, 60th Mtg CCS, 18 Jan 43.

war until they reached Berlin and that their only terms would be unconditional surrender. Mr. Roosevelt's original thought was to assure the Soviet Government that the Anglo-American allies would make no separate peace in the west. Sometime before 20 January, he had proposed to Churchill that they make a public announcement. At Casablanca some thought was given to excluding Italy in the hope that the omission would encourage Italian collapse. When the Prime Minister on 20 January wired a report of the conference to the War Cabinet in London, he asked its views on an official statement. The Cabinet discussed the matter and expressed a desire for even greater rigor. In view of the misgivings that might arise in Turkey and the Balkans if Italy were excepted, the Cabinet recommended that unconditional surrender be applied to all three chief enemy powers alike. Although Churchill personally had no reservations on the unconditional surrender formula or on application of it to Italy, he was nevertheless surprised at the President's public announcement; but, recovering quickly, he indicated his full support.[29]

### TRIDENT: Beyond Sicily

The CCS at Casablanca were hopeful that an amphibious invasion of Sicily and a subsequent ground campaign on that island, together with intensified air bombardment of the Italian mainland, would produce Italian collapse. But after the conference, as planners in Washington, London, and Algiers began to consider the Sicilian decision, the question arose not only how to use the Allied forces in the Mediterranean if the Sicilian Campaign did indeed precipitate Italian collapse, but also what to do if it did not.

An Italian collapse would leave Germany facing three alternatives, all of them favorable to the Allies: (1) occupation of Italy, Sicily, and perhaps Sardinia; (2) withdrawal from Italy but reinforcement of the Balkans; and (3) occupation of both Italy and the Balkans. The Allies regarded the latter as the most improbable of the three alternatives, for they felt that Germany did not have the resources to undertake so large an enterprise while at the same time trying to stabilize the Russian front.

If the invasion of Sicily did not lead to Italian collapse, the Allies could move into three areas, each with disadvantages as well as benefits. The invasion of the Continent through southern France could be undertaken with profit only in conjunction with an assault from the United Kingdom; immediate preparatory steps would be the conquest of Sardinia, Corsica, and possibly of the Italian Riviera for air bases. An invasion of the Italian mainland would bring the difficult problem of maintaining internal security and perhaps even of establishing civil administration throughout the country; nor was a crossing of the Alps enticing. Entrance into the Balkans would threaten Rumanian oil, perhaps induce Turkey to enter the war on the Allied side, and possibly force the Germans to abandon Greece and the Aegean Islands; but several subsidiary operations were necessary first—the capture of Crete and occupation of the toe and heel of Italy to insure control of the

---
[29] Min of Mtg at White House, 7 Jan 43, OPD Exec 10, item 45; Matloff, *Strategic Planning for Coalition Warfare, 1943–1944*, pp. 37–38; Sherwood, *Roosevelt and Hopkins*, pp. 696–97; Churchill, *Hinge of Fate*, pp. 684–88.

ALLIED LEADERS IN THE SICILIAN CAMPAIGN. *General Eisenhower meets in North Africa with (foreground, left to right): Air Chief Marshal Sir Arthur Tedder, General Sir Harold R. L. G. Alexander, Admiral Sir Andrew B. Cunningham, and (top row): Mr. Harold Macmillan, Maj. Gen. Walter Bedell Smith, and unidentified British officers.*

Strait of Messina and to open up the Adriatic.[30]

Top Allied commanders in the Mediterranean were in general agreement except Air Chief Marshal Tedder, who felt that the planners had not properly evaluated the benefits to be realized from an invasion of the Italian mainland. North Italy in particular was attractive, he believed, for the air bases that would permit intensification of the air offensive. Italy, Tedder declared on 26 March 1943, was "the backdoor of Germany's vitals," and he called for a fuller examination of this target area.[31]

Embarked on an examination of what might be required if Italy did not collapse during or after the Sicilian Campaign,

[30] See AFHQ JPS P/55, Action in the Mediterranean in the Event of the Collapse of Italy, 7 Mar 43, job 10A, reel 13C.

[31] Comment appended to document cited above, n. 30.

AFHQ planners continued to feel that the Allies ought to seize Sardinia and Corsica. Conquest of all three islands "and the subsequent bombing offensive against Italy which can be conducted from bases in these islands" might be sufficient to drive Italy out of the war. If not, air action from these islands could cover amphibious operations launched either through Genoa into the Lombard plain or into the Rome-Naples area. Invading Italy directly from Sicily, without the prior conquest of Sardinia and Corsica, as a means of forcing Italian collapse was a possibility not even considered.[32]

Though General Eisenhower agreed with his planners and though he kept open the possibility of moving into the Balkans, he was convinced that the best strategy for the Allies was a cross-Channel blow—a main assault against Germany from England and through northern France. Yet even as he asked General Marshall for his views on the best courses of action in various assumed situations—that Sicily would prove difficult to conquer; that the Sicilian operation would proceed according to plan and without great difficulties; and that the Sicilian defenses would collapse suddenly—Eisenhower outlined his own ideas on possible Mediterranean operations. Seeing Sardinia and Corsica as immediate objectives after Sicily, he indicated that General Henri Philippe Giraud, commander of the Free French forces in North Africa, had specifically requested permission to take Corsica, a request Eisenhower favored granting. More important, the long-range implication of taking the major Tyrrhenian islands, Eisenhower thought, was the need to invade the Italian mainland immediately thereafter, particularly since the Italian west coast seemed very weakly defended. The major objection to an Italian campaign appeared to be the great material investment required, not only to support the troops but to nourish the Italian population. The main advantage to be gained was the basing of bombers within better range of such critical targets as the Ploesti oil fields. Or, Eisenhower suggested, the attack on the southern shore of Europe could be shifted eastward in the Mediterranean, an attractive course in view of Turkey's neutrality, but disadvantageous because of the lengthening of Allied sea communications. Yet in the final analysis, if Mediterranean operations interfered with the build-up required for the cross-Channel attack, Eisenhower favored calling a halt to further offensive warfare in the Mediterranean.[33]

To AFHQ planners, a campaign on the Italian mainland seemed heavily weighted on the side of disadvantage. If Italy remained in the war or if Germany strongly reinforced the Italian peninsula, the Allies might find themselves committed to a major campaign necessitating heavy garrison requirements, heavy shipping and economic commitments, and heavy military forces—even though the campaign were limited to the toe and heel areas. Since the AFHQ planners were unable to gauge in advance the state of Italian morale at the end of the Sicilian Campaign, they preferred the insular operations, particularly because only comparatively limited forces would be needed. This would give the Allies full

[32] AFHQ JPS P/70 (First Draft), Action Against Italy After Operation HUSKY, 21 Apr 43, job 10C, reel 138E.

[33] Ltr, Eisenhower to Marshall, 19 Apr 43, Diary Office CinC, bk. V, pp. A-332–A-333.

liberty of action to strike, at the conclusion of Husky, in whatever direction seemed advisable at that time.[34]

Tedder continued to disagree. The difficulties of a Sardinian operation, he said, were consistently being glossed over and the air advantages of Sardinia grossly exaggerated. He insisted that he perceived a great benefit to be obtained from establishing air bases in central Italy for bombing targets in Germany.[35]

Though Brig. Gen. Lowell S. Rooks, the AFHQ G-3, presented on 8 May an outline plan for an invasion of Sardinia and proposed that the operation be entrusted to the Fifth U.S. Army, now commanded by General Clark and engaged in occupation and training duties in French Morocco, Eisenhower refrained from issuing a directive.[36] He awaited guidance from the CCS, but until the British and Americans came closer in their strategic thinking, the CCS could give no advice or instruction.

British planners in London believed that upon the collapse of Italy Germany would withdraw its military forces at least as far to the north as the Pisa-Ravenna line to cover the Po valley, thus permitting the Allies to land directly in southern and central Italy without great difficulty. They also envisaged the possibility of offensive action in the Balkans. They therefore recommended a series of expeditions to exploit Italian collapse—not against determined German resistance, but rather to follow the expected German withdrawal everywhere in the Mediterranean. After these advances and occupations, the Allies could then face the problem of choosing the route for the decisive strike against the enemy heartland.

The British were not thinking of deploying great armies on the Continent, where the decisive strike would be made. They were thinking rather of the large-scale employment of air power, of cutting the German lines of economic supply, of drawing in new allies such as Turkey, of aiding patriot forces in Yugoslavia, of stimulating political revolt in Hungary. As a consequence, logistical problems were no more important than other factors of politico-strategic planning. Furthermore, the British had no liking for far-reaching plans. They wished instead to retain a freedom of choice and the ability to adjust to new opportunities as they arose.[37]

The effect of this thinking on a cross-Channel attack was to reduce it to a moderate-scale operation, one of many which might be executed if the situation appeared favorable. If, for example, the Allies decided to invade southern France, then a limited cross-Channel operation might have value as a holding attack to divert German ground and air forces from the main invasion area.

Specifically, the big prize for the British was eliminating Italy from the war. They therefore excluded immediate operations against the Dodecanese "since the capture

---

[34] AFHQ JPS P/74 (Final), Availability of Forces in the Mediterranean, 3 May 43, job 10A, reel 18C; Memo for AFHQ CofS, sub: Opns After Husky, Incl A to CCS 223, 14 May 43, Trident Conf Book, pp. 38-42.

[35] Ltr, Tedder to Eisenhower, 8 May 43, Incl B to CCS 223, Trident Conf Book, p. 43.

[36] Memo, AFHQ G-3 for AFHQ CofS, sub: Plan for Opn Brimstone, 7 May 43, Incl A to CCS 223, 14 May 43, Trident Conf Book, pp. 38-42; AFHQ JPS P/69, Outline Plan for Operation Brimstone, 8 May 43, job 10A, reel 18C; draft directive to CG Fifth U.S. Army, 8 May 43, job 10C, reel 138E.

[37] Br JP (43) 99 (Final), 3 May 43, Report by the Joint Planning Staff, Mediterranean Strategy—If Italy Collapses, job 10A, reel 21C.

of these islands would have no immediate effect on the collapse of Italy."[38]

If Italy did not fall after Sicily, was Sardinia and Corsica or the Italian mainland the better invasion target in order to produce Italian surrender? If Italy did not sue for peace during the Sicilian Campaign, the British planners recommended invading the toe of Italy (Operation BUTTRESS) as soon as possible after Sicily. Whereas AFHQ planners tended to think of the insular operations as necessary preliminaries to the Italian mainland, the British considered the problem as a choice between the islands and the mainland.

Both invasion targets imposed difficulties. An amphibious operation against a defended shore would not be easy, particularly because of shortages of landing craft. Escort carriers would be needed to provide air cover for the landings, and these could be had only at the expense of requirements in the Atlantic. Considerable quantities of shipping would also be necessary. But, as the British put it, "In the long run, the War in Europe would thus be shortened and the switch over of our European resources to the War against Japan would be brought correspondingly closer."[39]

In the spring of 1943, while considering the choice of immediate targets after Sicily, the British planners preferred the Italian mainland over Sardinia and Corsica. Operations on the mainland, they believed, would more likely lead to Italian collapse that year and would open a land front capable of attracting and containing more Axis forces. Capture of Sardinia and Corsica, on the other hand, would increase the weight of Allied aerial pressure on Italy, but not until the spring of 1944. The British, therefore, favored an operation (BUTTRESS) against the toe of Italy before completion of the Sicilian Campaign or as soon thereafter as possible, with the initial objective to capture Reggio di Calabria across the Strait of Messina and to open a land front on the European continent. The campaign on the Italian mainland was to develop toward Crotone in the Italian instep (GOBLET) and toward the heel (MUSKET) with Bari and Naples as eventual objectives. If opposition seemed strong enough to deny the Allies the heel, Sardinia could be an alternative target.[40]

Although considerable long-range politico-strategic speculation took place in London in the spring of 1943, the focus was on immediate and short-range possibilities. The next Allied task, according to the British view, was to force Italy out of the war, and the best way to assure this was by invading the mainland as soon as possible and at the nearest point. No grand design for winning the war by the Mediterranean route was even implied. British long-range planning faded out at the Alps or on the fringes of the Balkan peninsula.[41]

---

[38] Br JP (43) 174, 3 May 43, Operations Against Italy, job 10A, reel 21C.
[39] Ibid.
[40] Ibid.
[41] See Notes on Visit to United Kingdom, Operations in 1943, dated 24 April 1943, job 10A, reel 18C, a record left by a high-ranking but otherwise unidentified officer at AFHQ on concepts being formulated in London.
In the spring of 1944, Mr. Churchill frankly told Maj. Gen. Albert C. Wedemeyer "that if we had been able to persuade the Chiefs of Staff, the Allies would have gone through Turkey and the Balkans from the South and into Norway on the North, thus surrounding the enemy and further dispersing his forces." Ltr, Wedemeyer to Handy, 13 Apr 44, OPD Exec 3, item 18. See also Churchill's instructions to General Sir Hastings L. Ismay, 17 Apr 43, in Churchill, Hinge of Fate, pp. 951-52.

In contrast, the Americans felt that the single route by which a great Allied army might penetrate the shore defenses of the Continent and break through to the vital area of German power was by way of northern France, and this General Marshall emphasized when he replied to General Eisenhower's request of 19 April for his views. Yet General Marshall admitted that plans to seize Sardinia or Corsica or both had to be available for immediate implementation if the Sicilian Campaign went according to plan or if the Italians suddenly collapsed. An all-out invasion of Italy, Marshall believed, would have such an effect on shipping as virtually to put a stop to serious offensive operations elsewhere in the world. "The decisive effort," Marshall was sure, "must be made against the Continent from the United Kingdom sooner or later." [42]

American planners in Washington were searching for a grand design by which to reach the heartland of Europe. Visualizing large-scale armies re-entering the Continent to engage the Axis armies in decisive battle, they wanted a basic overall plan to which could be fitted such matters as war production, the raising of forces, and the movement of those forces to the theaters of war. Hence they regarded approaches to the Continent in terms of where these approaches would lead. They were concerned about the stretch of road beyond the point where British thinking stopped. Having gained a beachhead on the Continent, could the Allies develop it into a base capable of supporting a feasible and effective drive into Germany?

In assessing Mediterranean possibilities in terms of a decisive blow to be struck against Germany, the American planners examined the Iberian Peninsula, southern France, Italy, Yugoslavia, Greece, the Aegean Islands, and Turkey as possible entrances into the Continent. But none offered the possibility of a strong base backing a good route for a great Allied movement into Germany.

To invade Europe by way of Italy and southern France seemed the best of the Mediterranean approaches, and these possibilities the American planners studied with care. They soon concluded that there seemed little point in considering anything beyond the initial move into Italy. Collapse or unconditional surrender of Italy, they recognized, would make it necessary for Germany to divert some fifteen divisions to replace Italian troops in occupied areas; the Italian Fleet would probably be lost to the Germans, as would certain industrial and agricultural products of marginal significance; and the Allies would gain an area from which to conduct air operations against German industrial centers. But the planners calculated that these disadvantages to Germany would in part be offset by certain advantages. Germany would regain the use of rolling stock required to supply Italy with some twelve million tons of coal annually, and would probably seize a large part of the Italian railroad cars. It would save not only coal but also bread grains and other materials provided to the Italian ally. The loss of Italy to the Germans, therefore, would be a decidedly mitigated one. Although occupation of Italy after its collapse would give the Allies a small quantity of critical nonferrous metals and some supplemental supplies of certain agri-

---

[42] Msg, Marshall to Eisenhower, CM-OUT 11068, 27 Apr 43, OPD Cable File, Out, 1 Jan 43–30 Apr 43.

cultural products, as well as enhanced safety of ship transport through the Mediterranean, they would be burdened with a heavy occupational and administrative force of some fifteen divisions. It would drain shipping resources, for an estimated one and a half million dead-weight tons of merchant shipping would be needed to maintain the Italian economy at a minimum level, a requirement the Allies would find very difficult to meet. Political and psychological gains were speculative and incapable of precise measurement, whereas the burden of supporting an Italy pried loose from the Axis was a tangible consequence—a huge subtraction from Allied shipping and manpower resources.[43]

The American Chiefs wanted a definite commitment and a definite date for a cross-Channel attack as the main effort of the Allies in Europe.[44] While rejecting the Mediterranean as unsuitable for a main effort, the American Chiefs did not rule out limited operations in this area. A blow against the Dodecanese, they admitted, would be most suitable for bringing Turkey into the war as an ally. Occupation of the toe and heel of Italy, they estimated, would be the best way to compel the dispersion of Axis forces, divert German divisions from the Russian front, and "best satisfy a situation whereby a limited scale operation might force Italy out of the war." But because operations against Sardinia and Corsica would be limited in size and scope, the U.S. Chiefs judged such a course as the least objectionable—in general, the most acceptable alternative if political pressure impelled the Allies to take some action between the completion of the Sicilian Campaign and the inception of the cross-Channel endeavor. In any case, a choice among the three possible acceptable limited operations, the U.S. Chiefs felt, ought to be postponed as long as possible in order to better assess the motives impelling additional operations in the Mediterranean.[45]

Thus, on the question of what to do after Sicily, a gap still existed between American and British views. The British wanted to put all resources available in 1943 into the Mediterranean and to force Italy out of the war by invading Calabria, the toe of the Italian mainland, at its nearest point to Sicily, and eventually to secure the airfields of central Italy and those in the north. But they did not foresee the movement of large Allied armies from the Mediterranean into the heartland of the Continent to meet the Germans directly. The Americans wished precisely what British planning avoided—a grand scale re-entry into the Continent, which meant a main effort across the Channel and through northern France. They did not wish to win the fight on points, they wanted a knockout. Opposed to the occupation of Italy because Italy was not a vital area and because an Italian invasion would involve a huge shipping commitment, the Americans envisaged Mediterranean opera-

[43] JCS 288/1, 8 May 43, sub: Invasion of the European Continent From Bases in the Mediterranean in 1943-44.

[44] Matloff, *Strategic Planning for Coalition Warfare, 1943-1944*, pp. 120-25. See also Ernest J. King and Walter Muir Whitehill, *Fleet Admiral King, A Naval Record* (New York: W. W. Norton & Company, Inc., 1952), p. 435; William D. Leahy, *I Was There* (New York: Whittlesey House, 1950), p. 157.

[45] JCS 293, 7 May 43, sub: Limited Opns in the Mediterranean, and JCS 305, 12 May 43, sub: Strategic Analysis of the Seizure and Occupation of the Toe of Italy.

tions beyond Sicily as involving limited objectives and sustained by limited resources. Seizing Sardinia and Corsica, perhaps even the heel of Italy, might be sound, but a landing on the toe of Italy seemed unwise.

As for the unconditional surrender formula, which was to have an indirect effect on the combat not only in Sicily but beyond, President Roosevelt had reiterated in February the remark he had first made at Casablanca the previous month. In March, when British Foreign Secretary Anthony Eden came to Washington to discuss political matters, the phrase again came under consideration. President Roosevelt once more declared that "he wanted no negotiated armistice after the collapse." The Allies, he said, "should insist on total surrender with no commitments to the enemy as to what we would do or what we would not do after this action." [46]

Soon after Eden's departure the State Department submitted several memorandums to the White House dealing not only with the treatment of Italy but also with the Allied military government to be established there. Unconditional surrender was the implicit assumption in all the State Department's papers. Thus, the department recommended the removal of "the entire fascist party leadership from local party secretaries to the top." Yet the department recommended that local technical and professional officials be retained in the lower ranks, responsible to the military administration. President Roosevelt was dissatisfied. With the advice of Harry Hopkins he revised this to read: "On the basis of unconditional surrender, the entire fascist party membership from the highest to the lowest should be removed from any post of government authority." Although the State Department suggested "some special treatment" of the power of Crown, the President simply deleted the statement.[47] Not only was Roosevelt preparing to demand unconditional surrender, he was also ready to assume the responsibility, through military government, for the domestic regeneration of the country.

All these matters came under examination at the next formal meetings of the CCS, held at Washington between 12 and 25 May 1943 and called the TRIDENT Conference—where "the movements of the land, sea, and air forces of the American and British Allies combined . . . [were] translated into firm commitments." [48]

Mr. Churchill and the British Chiefs of Staff sailed on the *Queen Mary* on 4 May for the United States. During the voyage the British leaders worked out their final paper proposing the seizure of a beachhead on the toe of Italy, followed by an assault in the heel, and finally an advance up the Italian boot. Soon after the Prime Minister and his party of about one hundred persons reached Washington by special train from New York, the British delegation delivered the paper to the U.S. Joint Chiefs of Staff as the basis for discussion.[49]

As Churchill stepped off the train in the U.S. capital, he was in fine fettle.

---

[46] Sherwood, *Roosevelt and Hopkins*, pp. 715, 792–93; Cordell Hull, *The Memoirs of Cordell Hull* (New York: Macmillan, 1948), vol. II, p. 1571.

[47] Sherwood, *Roosevelt and Hopkins*, pp. 721–24.

[48] Quote from *Biennial Report of the Chief of Staff of the United States Army, July 1, 1943 to June 30, 1945, to the Secretary of War* (Washington, 1945), p. 10.

[49] Churchill, *Hinge of Fate*, p. 785.

CHURCHILL *addressing the Congress of the United States, May 1943.*

He was big and magnificent, Washington loved him, and the whole nation admired his courage. Invited to speak before the Congress, he made an impression there that no foreigner since Lafayette had equaled. His straightforward, simple words, his great speaking voice, came at a time for rejoicing, for his visit coincided with the final Allied victory in Tunisia. There was much to cheer about, and there was no one who could better lead the cheering.

It was one thing for Churchill to speak to the public in generalities. It was another matter for him to match his persuasive powers and oratorical talents against the careful calculations of the American Joint Chiefs of Staff. At the plenary opening session of TRIDENT, held in the White House on the afternoon of 12 May, the Prime Minister sketched out the British view for the full employment of all Allied resources in the Mediterranean in 1943 and the relegation of a cross-Channel attack to the indefinite future. Admitting the need to find employment for the large Allied forces in the Mediterranean theater, President Roosevelt drew back from the idea of putting large military forces into Italy. Mr. Churchill expressed a lack of enthusiasm for Roosevelt's proposal for reconstituting Italy, stating that he did not feel an occupation of the country would be necessary. If the Italians collapsed, the United Nations could occupy the necessary ports and air bases from which to conduct operations against the Balkans and southern Europe, but they could let an Italian government control the country, subject to United Nations supervision.[50]

When the Combined Chiefs met to work out a program in detail, the Americans suggested that winning the war against Japan and the European Axis were aspects of a single problem. The Americans still favored the basic goal of defeating Germany first, but to them that meant a determined attack against Germany on the Continent at the earliest possible date. A strategy of nibbling at the periphery of German power, the Americans implied, was equivalent to repudiating the idea of first defeating Germany. And in that event, though they did not state it, the inference was clear— the Americans would consider seriously concentrating the greater part of their resources against Japan.[51]

The American position clearly set the limits to the discussions at TRIDENT. If the British had had any thought of candidly proposing to discard the cross-Channel concept in favor of a Mediterranean strategy, they abandoned the notion at the outset. The official discussions accepted in principle the American frame of reference—all proposed operations were to be weighed in terms of a cross-Channel attack.

The British nevertheless insisted that the main Allied task in 1943 was the elimination of Italy from the war. The continuance of Mediterranean operations and the intensification of the Allied bomber offensive, the British felt, were the only methods of giving effective aid to the Russians that year.[52] When General Marshall suggested that air power could hasten the collapse of Italy, General Brooke voiced doubt that air bombardment alone would be enough. Admirals King and Leahy cautioned against diverting to, or maintaining in, the Mediterranean forces that could be used in a cross-Channel operation. Suspicious that the British were not really converted to the cross-Channel idea, the Americans stated that U.S. ground and naval forces in the Mediterranean would not be used east of Sicily.[53] The British protested that a premature attempt to land in France would court disaster. The Americans continued to argue that further ground operations in the Mediterranean would delay the invasion of northwest Europe and prolong the war. Reassured by British declarations accepting the cross-Channel concept, the Americans agreed to consider Mediterranean operations beyond Sicily as preliminary steps for re-entry into northern France.[54]

By the end of the first week the issue was clear: would Mediterranean operations facilitate and expedite the main at-

---

[50] Min, 1st White House CCS Mtg, 12 May 43, TRIDENT Conf Book, pp. 253-61; Leasor, *The Clock With Four Hands*, pp. 239-41; Bryant, *Turn of the Tide*, p. 503.

[51] Annex A, Global Strategy of the War: Views of the U.S. Chiefs of Staff, appended to Min, 83d Mtg CCS, 13 May 43.

[52] Memo by Br COS, Conduct of the War in 1943, 12 May 43, TRIDENT Conf Book, pp. 336-41.

[53] CCS 219, Memo by U.S. CofS, 14 May 43, sub: Conduct of the War in 1943-44.

[54] Min, 84th and 85th CCS Mtgs, 14 and 15 May 43.

tack based on the United Kingdom?[55] As the CCS debated the question during the second week of the conference, the Americans proposed halting ground force operations at the Messina Strait, the British persisted in their desire to eliminate Italy as a requisite preliminary for the main attack into northern France. Where the discussion concerned a course of action for the immediate future, the British made some telling arguments and presented their case skillfully. The Americans couched their views chiefly in negative terms, but held out for a cross-Channel attack in April 1944.[56] The British pointed out the loss of deception that would result from discontinuing operations in the Mediterranean and concentrating forces in the United Kingdom; the threat that could be created against southern France; and other benefits implicit in their concept. Eliminating Italy from the war might even make the difference, they claimed, between success and failure in the invasion of northwest Europe in 1944. The British believed that continued operations in the Mediterranean need not detract from the build-up in the United Kingdom.[57]

By 18 May the Americans were coming around to the modified British position. General Brooke emphasized the low cost of the Mediterranean strategy, a loss of only three and one-half or four divisions from the build-up of forces in the United Kingdom. General Marshall still had doubts, for he feared that Mediterranean operations might exceed in magnitude those now visualized because a drive in Italy might generate its own momentum and draw in increasing numbers of troops.[58] Finally, the American Chiefs accepted the elimination of Italy as a prerequisite for a cross-Channel attack, although they insisted on holding Mediterranean operations to a role subordinate to re-entry into northern France in the spring of 1944. The date originally proposed for the cross-Channel attack was 1 April 1944, the conclusion of the fourth phase of the Allied bomber offensive against Germany and the earliest practicable date from the point of view of weather. But when General Brooke noted that 1 May or 1 June would coincide more nearly with the spring thaw and the opening of operations on the Russian front, the CCS readily accepted a postponement.[59]

Final agreement came on 19 May. The CCS decided to launch the cross-Channel attack on 1 May 1944 and to eliminate Italy from the war immediately. For the latter purpose, General Eisenhower could use only those forces already in the Mediterranean, less seven divisions to be withdrawn on 1 November 1943 and transferred to the United Kingdom.[60] The Mediterranean strategic plan transmitted by the CCS to General Eisenhower directed the Allied commander "to plan such operations in exploitation of HUSKY [the invasion of Sicily] as are best cal-

---

[55] AFHQ's views as embodied in a memorandum, 7 May 1943, to which Tedder had added his dissent, were circulated for the information of the CCS. This paper advocated Sardinia and Corsica as the next objectives; Tedder recommended the Italian mainland. CCS 227, 16 May 43.

[56] CCS 235, 18 May 43, Defeat of the Axis Powers in Europe: Defeat of Germany From the U.K.

[57] CCS 234, 17 May 43, Defeat of the Axis Powers in Europe: British Plan for the Defeat of the Axis Powers in Europe.

[58] Min, 87th Mtg CCS, 18 May 43; see also Bryant, *Turn of the Tide*, pp. 507–08.
[59] Min, 88th Mtg CCS, 19 May 43.
[60] Min, 89th Mtg CCS, 19 May 43.

culated to eliminate Italy from the war and to contain the maximum number of German forces." Which of the various possible plans beyond Sicily would be adopted and exactly how far along the southern approaches the Allies would go were matters that the CCS reserved for future determination.[61]

TRIDENT, as it turned out, was only one stage in the protracted Anglo-American struggle to reach agreement on a Mediterranean versus a cross-Channel strategy.

### Algiers—And Italy?

Keenly disappointed because the TRIDENT Conference did not commit the Allies to an invasion of the Italian mainland and still confident that an attack on Italy, if properly pushed, might be decisive enough to make unnecessary General Marshall's direct attack on Germany, Churchill decided to press his case in another quarter. Since General Eisenhower now had the responsibility of formulating specific plans designed to knock out Italy, Churchill determined to fly to Algiers, there to attempt to influence the planning in favor of the Italian mainland instead of Sardinia and Corsica. He made no secret to Mr. Roosevelt of his hopes and intentions. Lest he appear to exert undue influence on the Allied field commander, Churchill requested that General Marshall accompany him. General Marshall did so, along with General Brooke and General Sir Hastings L. Ismay.[62]

Churchill had wanted for some weeks to consult with General Eisenhower. He apparently hoped that a powerful blow against Italy might start in the unstable Mediterranean-Balkan region a kind of chain reaction, the ultimate results of which, together with Russian pressure, might render Germany incapable of continuing the war. General Brooke, and apparently Churchill too, subscribed to the belief that only the armies of Soviet Russia could yield decisive results in continental warfare; an Anglo-American force would be, in comparison, only a drop in the bucket. Brooke therefore urged that Allied strategy be directed toward diverting German strength from the Russian front so as to enable the Soviets to inflict a decisive defeat on the Germans. Naval blockade and aerial bombardment, in Brooke's opinion, were the prime Allied weapons. Tremendous losses sustained in a ground campaign, he maintained, would be useless, and a land front in Italy was about the size he thought appropriate for the Allies.[63]

The formal meetings of what became known as the Algiers Conference opened on 29 May 1943 in General Eisenhower's villa as ten British officers, including Brooke, Alexander, Cunningham, and

---

[61] CCS 242/6, 25 May 43, Final Report to the President and Prime Minister, and Memo by CCS, Opns in Mediterranean To Eliminate Italy From the War, both in TRIDENT Conf Book, p. 174; see also Bryant, *Turn of the Tide*, pp. 512-16.

[62] Min, 6th White House Mtg CCS, item 6, 25 May 43, TRIDENT Conf Book, p. 310; Churchill, *Hinge of Fate*, pp. 810-11; Bryant, *Turn of the Tide*, p. 516.

[63] Min of Mtg at Eisenhower's Villa, 29 May 43, TRIDENT Conf Book, p. 469; Sherwood, *Roosevelt and Hopkins*, p. 727; Leahy, *I Was There*, pp. 156-57; Churchill, *Hinge of Fate*, pp. 782-83, 939; Bryant, *Turn of the Tide*, pp. 494-95, 520-21; Eisenhower, *Crusade in Europe*, pp. 167-68; Matloff, *Strategic Planning for Coalition Warfare, 1943-1944*, pp. 152-53.

Tedder, and four American officers, Marshall, Eisenhower, Smith, and Rooks, met with Mr. Churchill. General Marshall came right to the point. When, he asked, should Eisenhower submit his plan for eliminating Italy from the war? He suggested that Eisenhower set up two headquarters in different places, each with its own staff, one to prepare operations against Sardinia and Corsica, the other operations against the mainland. As soon as the situation in Sicily became clearer, the choice could be made and the appropriate air and naval elements shifted to the force charged with executing the plan.

Mr. Churchill expressed the thought that the Sicilian Campaign—now less than six weeks away—might proceed too rapidly, thereby causing an embarrassing interlude of Allied inactivity. Eisenhower quickly replied that he would be willing to go straight into Italy if Sicily fell easily. But beyond that, the same factors of uncertainty that had precluded a firm choice of plan at TRIDENT—the strength of Italian resistance and German intentions—still obtained at Algiers. All agreed that it would be unwise to attack the Italian mainland against strong resistance. After considerable discussion on the opposition to be met in Sicily, including Churchill's guess that the campaign would end by 15 August, Eisenhower summarized three possibilities: (1) if the enemy collapsed quickly in Sicily, immediate operations should be undertaken against the Italian mainland; (2) if the enemy offered prolonged resistance on Sicily, no Allied resources would be available for immediate post-Sicily operations; (3) if resistance was stubborn but could be overcome by the middle of August, no decision could be made in advance. The best idea, Eisenhower said, was for him to designate two separate headquarters to plan for the alternative courses of action.[64]

This was the extent of the decision reached at Algiers, even though Churchill began to talk of Rome as the most productive Allied objective in the theater. "The capture of Rome, with or without the elimination of Italy from the war," he concluded, "would be a very great achievement for our Mediterranean forces."[65]

Not only the ancient capital but the prospect of sweet revenge on Mussolini, once greatly admired by Churchill but now the object of his distaste, fascinated the Prime Minister. Control of the Adriatic ports would also make it possible to supply the patriot bands in the Balkans, particularly in Yugoslavia, and to foment revolt in Greece and Albania. And Turkey—this time surely the conditions would be ripe for Turkey's entrance into the war.[66]

One other matter came under discussion at Algiers: the bombing of Rome. Because daylight precision bombardment was quite accurate, the Allies could bomb railroad marshaling yards with little risk of damaging the city and no danger of hitting the Vatican. A tenable objection no longer existed. The conferees agreed that the marshaling yards were an important target, and they decided to re-

[64] Min of Mtg at Eisenhower's Villa, 29 May 43, TRIDENT Conf Book, pp. 469–75.
[65] Churchill, *Hinge of Fate*, p. 822; Min of Mtg at Eisenhower's Villa, 31 May 43, TRIDENT Conf Book, pp. 478–81; *ibid.*, 3 Jun 43, p. 502; see also Butcher, *My Three Years With Eisenhower*, pp. 317–18.
[66] Background Notes by the Prime Minister and Minister of Defence, 31 May 43, TRIDENT Conf Book, pp. 491–92.

quest permission from their respective governments to authorize General Eisenhower to bomb them at a time best suited to advance the Sicilian Campaign.[67]

## The Surrender Problem

And what if Italy surrendered? How were the Allies to accept an Italian surrender and validate it? This was as much a political as a military problem.

The first set of armistice terms for use in Italy emerged from the planning for the conquest of Sicily. As early as 29 April, General Eisenhower had forwarded a set of terms to Washington for approval by the Combined Chiefs of Staff. The twenty-one clauses of this instrument provided in detail for full use by the Allies of all material resources in Sicily for further prosecution of the war. With a few minor changes, the terms had been approved by the CCS on 10 May.[68] Though surrender was to be unconditional, the terms did not deal with the sovereignty of the Italian state or the question of the continuance of the Italian monarchy. In formulating the paper, General Eisenhower had been considering a situation in Sicily where the enemy field commander might wish to surrender the whole island.

At about the same time, the U.S. Joint Chiefs began to study the problem of Italian surrender from a broader viewpoint. The Joint War Plans Committee (JWPC) assumed that civil war, collapse, or unconditional surrender might occur in Italy.[69] Civil war was the most unlikely. But if a revolution developed, the Allies could establish ground and air forces in Italy to support the revolutionists, give economic assistance, and secure from the revolutionary government military bases useful in the further prosecution of the war. Collapse might arise from Italian military reverses, from German refusal of further military assistance, from destruction caused by Allied air attacks, from a loss of faith by the Italian people in their leadership. In this situation, the Germans would probably withdraw from Italy. The Allies might then occupy a defensive line in north Italy, establish air bases in Italy, provide garrisons to maintain order, and give economic assistance. The Italian Government might surrender—but this was scarcely to be expected from Mussolini, who was publicly branded in the Allied camp as a war criminal. Yet the Italian Government might nevertheless try to negotiate for an armistice.[70]

To the British planners, the Italian alternatives seemed clearly collapse or surrender. In the event of collapse, a draft declaration of the United Nations to Italy, setting forth the general purposes of continuing the war against Germany from Italian soil, might be sufficient. In the event of surrender, the sovereign government of Italy would have to make a legal guarantee that all opposition against

---

[67] Min of Mtg at Eisenhower's Villa, 3 Jun 43, TRIDENT Conf Book, pp. 499–501; Butcher, *My Three Years With Eisenhower*, pp. 322–23; Wesley Frank Craven and James Lea Cate, eds., "The Army Air Forces in World War II," vol. II, *Europe: TORCH to POINTBLANK, August 1942 to December 1943* (Chicago: The University of Chicago Press, 1949), pp. 463–65.

[68] Msgs 7990, 7991, 7992, 7993 (NAF 212), Eisenhower to AGWAR, Salmon Files 5–B–1, VIIg, OCMH; CCS 205/2, 10 May 43.

[69] The JWPC was created just shortly before the TRIDENT Conference. See Matloff, *Strategic Planning for Coalition Warfare, 1943–1944*, pp. 106–11.

[70] JCS 302, 11 May 43, Collapse or Unconditional Surrender of Italy.

United Nations military operations would cease, and that the Allies could make full use of Italian territory, facilities, and resources to prosecute the war against Germany. For this contingency, the British proposed a formal list of armistice terms totaling forty-five articles, which formed the basis of what later became known as the Long Terms.[71]

The British submitted to the CCS the draft of their armistice terms on 16 June, and requested that if approved the terms be submitted to the Soviet Union and to the other governments at war with Italy. The U.S. Joint Chiefs referred the British draft to the Civil Affairs Division (CAD) for study, and the CAD recommended withholding concurrence because the British draft instrument "does not constitute an unconditional surrender." The CAD proposed that, after surrender, the Italian Government cease to exist, at least for the period of the war against the Axis—that it be superseded by an Allied military government functioning throughout Italy, except over the Vatican City.[72] The U.S. Joint Chiefs accepted the recommendation (after the concurrence of the State and Treasury Departments) on 29 June, and presented it, with minor modifications, as a substitute for the British proposal.

When the CCS on 2 July—a week before the invasion of Sicily—considered the problem of Italian surrender, a gap existed between British and American views, a gap so wide that no reconciliation of views was immediately possible. The CCS decided to refer both British and American proposals to a newly established Combined Civil Affairs Committee (CCAC).[73]

When the CCAC took up the problem on 10 July, the British members requested instructions from their capital. On this point the Anglo-American machinery for directing the war stalled. For, seventeen days later, though the Sicilian Campaign was by then well under way, the British representatives were still waiting to receive the views of their government.[74]

A remarkably skillful and successful organization in formulating a military strategy, the CCS could not draw up an Anglo-American political program. Planning the Italian surrender, like the strategic planning to achieve it, had to await further developments and the outcome of the combat in Sicily.

---

[71] CCS 258, an. 11, 16 Jun 43.

[72] JCS 373, 23 Jun 43, Surrender Terms for Italy and Draft Declaration and Proclamation, Report by the Civil Affairs Division.

The CAD was established on 1 March 1943 to formulate and co-ordinate U.S. military policy concerning the administration and government of captured or liberated countries. The division served as the central office and clearinghouse where occupation plans (including surrender and related documents) were drawn up.

[73] Min, 100th CCS Mtg, 2 Jul 43, Supplementary.

The CCAC was constituted on 3 July 1943 in Washington as an agency of the CCS. Its membership was made up of one representative each of the U.S. Army, the U.S. Navy, the U.S. State Department, the British Foreign Office, two representatives of the British Joint Staff Mission, and two additional civilians designated respectively by the U.S. and British Governments. See CCS 190/6/D, 3 Jul 43, Charter, Combined Civil Affairs Committee. The first formal CCAC meeting was held 15 July 1943.

[74] CCS Memo, 27 Jul 43, Supplementary Status of Papers.

## CHAPTER II

# The Axis on the Defensive

*The Italo-German Alliance*

Germany and Italy, bound together in the Pact of Steel of May 1939, had nothing even remotely resembling the Combined Chiefs of Staff. They determined their strategy according to a method that was considerably different from and much less cohesive than the *modus operandi* of the English-speaking Allies. The Italo-German alliance, termed by the treaty a pact between the National Socialist and the Fascist regimes, was essentially a personal union of the two dictators, Adolf Hitler and Benito Mussolini, each the Head of Government of his state and each the supreme commander of his armed forces. Whatever agreements were reached, whatever tensions developed were ultimately determined by the personal relations between the two individuals.

Hitler directed and controlled all the executive departments in Germany. After he assumed command of the German armed forces (*Wehrmacht*) in 1938, the Armed Forces Supreme Command (*Oberkommando der Wehrmacht*, or OKW) emerged as the over-all organ of command. Under OKW each military service had its own commander and staff—Grossadmiral Karl Doenitz heading the *Oberkommando der Kriegsmarine* (OKM) after early 1943, Reichsmarschall Hermann Goering controlling the *Oberkommando der Luftwaffe* (OKL), and Hitler himself at the head of the Army, the *Oberkommando des Heeres* (OKH).[1]

With Generalfeldmarschall Wilhelm Keitel as chief of OKW and Generaloberst Alfred Jodl head of the operations branch (*Wehrmachtfuehrungsstab* or *WFSt*), Hitler directed German strategy during the first two years of the war through the OKW. After Hitler relieved Feldmarschall Walter von Brauchitsch in 1941 and assumed personal command of the Army, he used the OKH to direct the forces fighting in Russia. He then used the OKW to direct the forces elsewhere—in Finland, Norway, France, the Balkans, and the Mediterranean.

The geographical bifurcation in the chain of command, illogical while the Axis was on the offensive, became an

---

[1] MS #P-049, *Die Strategie der deutschen obersten Fuehrung im zweiten Vierteljahr 1943*, also known as: OKW Activities, Project #35, Strategy of the German Armed Forces High Command, April–June 1943 (General der Artillerie Walter Warlimont), pp. 49–50 (See Bibliographical Note.); War Department Technical Manual E 30-451, Handbook on German Military Forces (15 March 1945), pp. 1–15; The German General Staff Corps, a study produced in the German Military Documents Section, Alexandria, by a combined British, Canadian, and U.S. staff, April 1946; General Heinz Guderian, *Panzer Leader*, translated by Constantine Fitzgibbon (New York: E. P. Dutton & Co., Inc., 1952), pp. 47–63, 84–88, 430–44, 454–65; Walter Goerlitz, *History of the German General Staff, 1657–1945*, translated by Brian Battershaw (New York: Fredrick A. Praeger, 1953), chs. X–XIV.

HITLER AND MUSSOLINI *with Italian Honor Guard in the Brenner Pass.*

acute problem when the Axis had to assume the defensive after November 1942. There was no over-all organ of command, no chief of staff who could plan total German strategy, who could view the requirements of each service and each theater in terms of available resources. Conflicting demands for resources could be resolved ultimately only by Hitler himself. Becoming more and more jealous and suspicious of the generals, he made it increasingly difficult for men of independent minds to serve him.[2]

[2] MS #P-049 (Warlimont), pp. 50–52; Pogue, *Supreme Command,* pp. 175–76.

Mussolini's powers in Italy were almost as great. The King, Victor Emmanuel III, was the head of the state, to whom the officers and men of the Royal Army, Navy, and Air Force were bound by oath. Mussolini, the Duce of the Fascist party, whose members, both civilians and uniformed militia, had sworn personal allegiance to him, was the Head of the Government (*Capo del Governo*). With all the powers of that office as enumerated by the Fascist constitutional laws of 1925–26, he had complete control of the executive branch of the government.

After 1939, Mussolini served simultaneously as Minister of War, of the Navy, and of the Air Force. The undersecretaries of the Navy and Air Force were at the same time chiefs of staff of their respective armed forces, while the War Ministry had both an undersecretary and a chief of the Army General Staff. Mussolini maintained close control over the Italian armed forces through their respective ministries.

Because the Italian constitution vested the power of command over the Army and Navy (and by implication over the Air Force) in the King alone, Mussolini in 1938 secured for himself the military rank of Marshal of the Empire, the same title as that held by the King. With Italy's entrance into the war in June 1940, Mussolini gained the command prerogative by having the King delegate to him the command of all forces operating on all fronts.[3]

Like Hitler, Mussolini had served in a humble position in World War I, was fascinated by military glory and display, had a keen, retentive mind, and had read much military literature. But while Hitler after 1942 tended increasingly to intrude on the lower levels of command, dictating the movements of even a single division, and eventually depriving his field commanders of the freedom to maneuver, Mussolini was not interested in details. Exercising his command at the strategic level only, Mussolini was amenable to argument and he operated with the advice of and through his professional officer corps.[4]

Before 1941 the Armed Forces General Staff (*Stato Maggiore Generale*), known as the *Comando Supremo*, had only seven members, exercised no command, had no direct dealings with other staffs, and served primarily as an advisory body for Mussolini as Head of Government. Each military service had its own staff, the *Stato Maggiore Regio Esercito* or *Superesercito* for the Army; the *Stato Maggiore Regia Marina* or *Supermarina* for the Navy; and the *Stato Maggiore Regia Aeronautica* or *Superaereo* for the Air Force.[5] After 1941, when Mussolini ousted Maresciallo d'Italia Pietro Badoglio as chief of *Comando Supremo* and appointed Generale d'Armata Ugo Cavallero his successor, the *Comando Supremo* went through a radical reorganization. The staff developed intelligence and operation sections, the service chiefs of staff became directly subordinate to the chief of *Comando Supremo*, and that body grew into a huge organization that acted not only as Mussolini's command organ but also as the group that coöperated with the OKW. Through its operations section, the *Comando Supremo* controlled the operational theaters: North Africa, Russia, Greece, and the Balkans; *Superesercito*, the Army Gen-

---

[3] Carmelo Carbone, *La posizione giuridica del comandante supremo in guerra* (Rome: Ugo Pinnarò Editore, 1946), p. 18; Quirino Armellini, *Diario di guerra: Nove mesi al Comando Supremo* (Cernusco sul Naviglio: Garzanti, 1946), pp. 1-2, 5, 9, 12; *The Ciano Diaries, 1939-1943*, edited by Hugh Gibson, with an introduction by Sumner Welles (Garden City, N.Y.: Doubleday and Company, 1946), pp. 250, 256, 261; Emilio Faldella, *L'Italia nella seconda guerra mondiale* (Rocca San Casciano (Forlì): Cappelli, 1959), p. 123.

[4] Mario Roatta, *Otto milioni di baionette: L'esercito italiano in guerra dal 1940 al 1944* (Milan: Arnoldo Mondadori Editore, 1946), pp. 21-30; Siegfried Westphal, *Heer in Fesseln: Aus den Papieren des Stabschefs von Rommel, Kesselring und Rundstedt* (Bonn: Athenaeum-Verlag, 1950), pp. 210-11.

[5] See Howard McGaw Smyth, "The Command of the Italian Armed Forces in World War II," *Military Affairs*, XV, No. 1 (Spring, 1951), 39-43.

KING VICTOR EMMANUEL III

eral Staff, retained the direction of the ground troops in Italy and in occupied France and of the antiaircraft defenses within Italy.[6]

On matters of interest to both powers, Italy and Germany depended on the older and more traditional methods of co-operation between states allied in war: ministerial correspondence, military attaché reports, periodic conferences between Hitler and Mussolini (who were accompanied by members of the OKW and of the *Comando Supremo*), personal letters (usually drafted in the appropriate offices), and liaison officers. But the important matters were decided by the dictators.

Though Hitler had great admiration and friendship for Mussolini, it is more than doubtful that Mussolini reciprocated this feeling. As the war progressed and German predominance grew, Mussolini found Hitler's ascendancy galling.[7]

Nazi and Fascist party leaders for the most part had considerable liking for each other, and the Nazi *Weltanschauung* tended constantly to distort favorably the picture of Italy's military capabilities. Professional military elements in both nations, however, remained generally unaffected by the mystical-mythological exuberance of the parties, and the German and Italian Armies each retained its own traditional view of the other. The Germans had a rather low estimate of Italian capabilities. They remembered not only that Italy had abandoned, then turned against the Central Powers in World War I, but also that the essential function of the Italian Army since the establishment of the Kingdom of Italy had been the defense of the Alps against the enemy to the north.[8]

When Italy entered World War II, Mussolini announced that Italy would

---

[6] Cavallero was promoted to Maresciallo d'Italia on 1 July 1942. See Ugo Cavallero, *Comando Supremo: Diario 1940-43 del Capo di S.M.G.* (Bologna: Cappelli, 1948), pp. 101-03; Roatta, *Otto milioni*, pp. 141-42; U.S. Mil Attaché Rpt 17965, Rome, 10 Jun 41, G-2 files; Giuseppe Castellano, *Come firmai l'armistizio di Cassibile* (Milan: Arnoldo Mondadori Editore, 1945), p. 10.

[7] *The Goebbels Diaries 1942-1943*, edited, translated, and with an introduction by Louis P. Lochner (Garden City, N.Y.: Doubleday and Company, 1948), pp. 469, 481; Dr. Henry Picker, *Hitlers Tischgespraeche im Fuehrerhauptquartier 1941-1942* (Bonn: Athenaeum-Verlag, 1951), pp. 41, 76-77, 109, 120-22, 235; Mario Donosti, *Mussolini e l'Europa: La politica estera fascista* (Rome: Leonardo, 1945), pp. 81-82; *Ciano Diaries*, pp. 383, 402, 435, 439, 463-64, 467, 509, 539, 580.

[8] Roatta, *Otto milioni*, p. 11.

fight a "parallel war" with Germany. Since both powers had the same enemies, each would fight for its own objectives within its own sphere. Mussolini wished no German forces in the Mediterranean, which he regarded as an Italian theater. Though Hitler never appreciated the significance of the Mediterranean, his respect for Italian prestige and his unwillingness to intrude there led in great measure to his neglect of opportunities for striking decisive blows at Britain during the winter of 1940–41.[9]

After the Germans managed in the summer of 1940 to restrain Mussolini from invading Yugoslavia, the Italian leader attacked Greece, a move that surprised and annoyed the Germans. Before long, Mussolini had to appeal for German assistance, and after receiving frantic calls for help the Germans dispatched units to the Mediterranean.[10]

GENERAL CAVALLERO

The dominant position of Germany and the subordinate place of Italy in the alliance was, therefore, a fact as early as Italy's first winter in the war. Mussolini and the *Comando Supremo* were never thereafter able to establish a parity in conference with the Germans.[11]

---

[9] Howe, *Northwest Africa*, p. 6; Raymond de Belot, Rear Admiral, French Navy (Ret.), *The Struggle for the Mediterranean, 1939–1945*, translated by James A. Field, Jr. (Princeton: Princeton University Press, 1951), p. 50.
The relations of Germany and Italy in this early period are well portrayed in *Documents on German Foreign Policy, 1918–1945*, issued by the Department of State, Series D, vol. X, June 23–August 31, 1940 (Washington, 1957); vol. XI, September 1, 1940–January 31, 1941 (Washington, 1960); and vol. XII, February 1–June 22, 1941 (Washington, 1962).

[10] For the Italian plan to attack Yugoslavia see *Documents on German Foreign Policy*, vol. X, No. 343, pp. 481–83, with Rintelen's report of 9 August; No. 367, pp. 512–13, Ambassador Mackensen's memorandum of 19 August; and No. 388, pp. 538–39, Mussolini's letter to Hitler of 24 August. For the Italian attack on Greece and Hitler's attitude see vol. XI, No. 246, pp. 411–22, a record of the discussion between Hitler and Mussolini at Florence on 28 October, and No. 477, pp. 817–23, the record of Hitler's discussion with Alfieri, the Italian Ambassador, on 8 December. For Mussolini's calls for help see No. 538, pp. 911–14, and No. 541, pp. 916–17.

[11] After Italy's entrance into the war Marshal Badoglio met with Marshal Keitel on seemingly equal terms on the one occasion at Innsbruck 14 and 15 November 1940. See *Documents on German Foreign Policy*, vol. XI, No. 400, p. 709 and n. 1. The Italian military failures were so painful that the German Embassy in Rome on 27 December urged that Germany take the lead in the Mediterranean. See No. 583, pp. 983–87. Hitler declined this suggestion. He felt that he himself could exert much influence by personal discussion with Italian leaders. See vol. XII, No. 17, pp. 26–30; No. 24, pp. 44–45; and No. 35, pp. 62–63.

The concept of parallel war did not long endure. In his enthusiasm to march with Hitler, Mussolini strewed his forces all over the map. During the summer of 1941, when Hitler attacked Russia, Mussolini sent an expeditionary corps of four divisions to help; a year later, the strength of this force had reached the size of an army totaling 217,000 men: the *Eighth Army*, containing three corps and eight divisions.[12] In Croatia, Slovenia, Dalmatia, Albania, Montenegro, Greece, and the Aegean Islands, there were 579,000 troops. In North Africa, by the end of September 1942, the Italians had 147,000 men. After the Allied invasion of North Africa, when the unoccupied zone of Vichy France ceased to exist, an army of some 200,000 men moved into southern France. By January 1943, Italian ground forces were stationed in Russia, Greece, the Balkans, southern France, North Africa, and the Italian homeland. About 1,200,000 of Italy's best trained soldiers and best equipped units were on foreign soil, about 800,000 in Italy.[13]

In the early stage of the war, only a simple expedient was necessary to maintain liaison between the *Comando Supremo* and the OKW. General der Infanterie Enno von Rintelen, German Military Attaché in Italy since 1936, became the OKW representative to the *Comando Supremo*. In addition to reporting to OKH and the German Foreign Office as Military Attaché, Rintelen now had direct communication with OKW as well. Having mastered the Italian language, holding a high appreciation of the admirable qualities of the Italian people, and enjoying a sympathetic understanding and friendship with many Fascist leaders, Rintelen nevertheless estimated the capabilities of the Italian armed forces on a basis strictly professional. He felt that Nazi enthusiasm for Mussolini and fascism seriously distorted and magnified the military power of Italy.[14]

Though Rintelen sufficed during the brief period of Mussolini's parallel war, something more than a single liaison officer was necessary to link the Germans and Italians when Germany moved into the Mediterranean to rescue Italy in November 1940. As the Germans prepared to invade Greece, to dispatch armored forces (later to be known as Generalfeldmarschall Erwin Rommel's German *Africa Corps*, the *Deutsches Afrika Korps*) to North Africa, and to shift some 400 to 500 planes of the German *X Air Corps* (the *X Flieger Korps*) to fields in southern Italy and Sicily, the problem of commanding the combined forces became acute. Hitler solved the problem in a directive of 5 February 1941 when he specified that the German troops in Libya (and if the occasion arose, in Albania as well) would be under the direct tactical command of the Italian theater commander; the *X Air Corps* was to

---

[12] Roatta, *Otto milioni*, pp. 185–93; MS #T-15, an. 6, The Italian Expeditionary Corps in Russia (General der Infanterie Friedrich Schulz et al.), pp. 2–4.

[13] These figures include replacements and troops of the Territorial Defense. See Statistics of 30 September 1942, Italian Collection, item IT 1178.

In the present study the individual folders of the Italian Collection will be identified by the designation appearing on them, or by a description of their contents, followed by the key letters IT and the number. (See Bibliographical Note.)

[14] Enno von Rintelen, *Mussolini als Bundesgenosse: Erinnerungen des deutschen Militaerattachés in Rom, 1936–1943* (Tuebingen: R. Wunderlich, 1951), p. 26; Howe, *Northwest Africa*, p. 9.

remain subordinate to Goering but was to co-operate closely with the Italian authorities.[15] Over those units crossing Italian territory to reach southern Italy, Sicily, and North Africa, over convalescents and men returning from furlough, over service troops and, later, antiaircraft batteries stationed in Italy, Rintelen was to exercise command.

This arrangement lasted until December 1941, when Hitler sent the German *Second Air Force* (*Luftflottenkommando 2*) to Italy. He named the air commander, Feldmarschall Albert Kesselring, Commander in Chief South (*Oberbefehlshaber Sued*).[16] The title Commander in Chief South had little real significance at this time, for Kesselring's command was not much more than an air force headquarters located at Taormina, Sicily, for the units operating from Italian airfields and under Italian operational control.[17]

A gifted, thoroughly trained, and experienced officer, Kesselring had a strong sense of duty as well as considerable personal charm and tact. He found much to admire in Italy and in the Italian people, and he developed a high regard for Mussolini and a firm bond of friendship with Cavallero, then chief of *Comando Supremo*.

In October 1942, when OKW began to be apprehensive over the possibility of an Allied move in the Mediterranean, Hitler gave Kesselring command over all the German armed forces in the Mediterranean, with the exception of the German-Italian panzer army in North Africa. General von Rintelen was made subordinate to Kesselring for all his command functions, but as the immediate OKW representative in Italy, Rintelen retained the right of direct communication with that staff. Kesselring thereby became and remained the only German to hold a unified theater command.[18] He moved his headquarters to Frascati, near Rome, to facilitate close co-operation with *Comando Supremo*. The size of his staff increased not only through the addition of a small operations group but also by the attachment of Italian air force and naval liaison officers.[19]

---

[15] Rintelen's new title was German General at the Headquarters of the Italian Armed Forces (*Deutscher General bei dem Hauptquartier der italienischen Wehrmacht*).
See Howe, *Northwest Africa*, ch. I; Hitler Directive 18, 12 Nov 40, and Hitler Order, 5 Feb 41, both in Office of Naval Intelligence (ONI), *Fuehrer and Other Top-Level Directives of the German Armed Forces, 1939–1941* (hereafter cited as ONI, *Fuehrer Directives, 1939–1941*). This is a selection of translated documents from German military and naval archives, in two volumes; the second volume covers the period 1942–45.

[16] The term Commander in Chief South will be used in this volume to refer to the person holding the title *Oberbefehlshaber Sued*, while the abbreviated form (*OB SUED*) will refer to his headquarters.

[17] Order signed by Keitel, 29 Oct 41, and Hitler Directive 38, 2 Dec 41, both in ONI, *Fuehrer Directives, 1939–1941*. Though the German naval forces in the Mediterranean remained under the OKM, the German admiral attached to *Supermarina* reported to Kesselring.

[18] Vice Admiral Eberhard Weichold, commander of the German naval forces in Italy (which consisted of one destroyer, about fifteen submarines, an E-boat flotilla, about a dozen mine sweepers, and several landing boat flotillas), came under the Commander in Chief South.

[19] Hitler Order, 13 Oct 42, ONI, *Fuehrer Directives, 1942–1945;* MS #D-008, *Beauftragung des Oberbefehlshabers Sued (O.B. Sued) durch "Fuehrerweisung" im September 1942 mit dem Oberbefehl im Mittelmeerraum* (General der Flieger Paul Deichmann).
For a few months Kesselring also controlled the five and a half divisions in Greece and the Balkans. But at the end of the year (1942) Hitler created an army group headquarters under Generalfeldmarschall Wilhelm List, named *List Oberbefehlshaber Suedost*, and removed him from

FIELD MARSHAL KESSELRING AND GENERAL VON RINTELEN, WITH PRINCE DI SAVOIA

Hitler extended Kesselring's command further in January 1943, when he placed him over the two German armies in Tunisia. Kesselring's staff again increased in size.[20]

While Kesselring's increasing authority represented the growing German influence, Mussolini was concluding that an Axis military victory was no longer possible. As early as December 1942, he thought that the Axis ought to make a separate peace with the Soviet Union so that Germany would be free to commit the bulk of its forces against the Anglo-Americans in the Mediterranean. To Goering, who was in Italy at the time, Mussolini said that if the war in the east could not be terminated by agreement with Russia, the Axis forces should withdraw to a shorter line. Because he expected the "Anglo-Saxons" to make their major effort in 1943, Mussolini thought that the Axis should defend Africa, the Balkans, and perhaps even the west with the greatest possible number of divisions. Apparently encouraged by Goering, who suggested that Hitler might approve a new Brest-Litovsk, with compensation to Russia in middle Asia, Mussolini proposed a conference of the dictators.

Because of the critical developments at Stalingrad, Hitler refused to leave his headquarters for a meeting with Mussolini. Because of his ulcers, Mussolini decided against taking the long trip to see Hitler. The Duce therefore entrusted the mission of persuading Hitler to make peace with Stalin to Count Galeazzo Ciano, his son-in-law and Minister of Foreign Affairs.[21]

At Hitler's headquarters, Ciano, who was accompanied by Cavallero, found no inclination to discontinue the war against the Soviet Union. During three days of

---

any subordination to Kesselring. Kesselring, however, retained control over all German aerial warfare in the entire Mediterranean area, with the exception of the southern France-Mediterranean area, until June 1943. See Hitler Directive 47, 28 Dec 42, and Change to Directive 47, 1 Jun 43, ONI, *Fuehrer Directives, 1942–1945.*
[20] Hitler Order, 5 Jan 43, ONI, *Fuehrer Directives, 1942–1945.*

[21] *Goebbels Diaries*, p. 249, entry for 18 Dec 42; Roatta, *Otto milioni*, p. 192; Leonardo Simoni (pseudonym for Michele Lanza), *Berlino, Ambasciata d'Italia 1939–1943* (Rome: Migliaresi, Editore, 1946), pp. 296–97; *Ciano Diaries*, pp. 555–56; Min of Conv, Mussolini and Goering, 6 Dec 42, Ciano Papers (Rose Garden), pp. 713–14, copy in OCMH. The last source is a typewritten German translation of supporting papers referred to in the published Ciano diaries. It consists of 749 pages of documents for the years 1938–43. A German woman, employed as a translator in Italy, retained a copy, which she buried in the garden of a house in Munich. U.S. Army Counter Intelligence Corps investigators discovered the papers at the end of the war.

## THE AXIS ON THE DEFENSIVE

conferences, 18-20 December, the German Fuehrer as usual doing most of the talking, it became clear that Hitler saw no advantage to be gained by terminating the war in the east. Hitler's strategic views were defensive in nature, designed to hold the territories overrun by the Axis armies, and Hitler thought that the Axis could do so. He had the wishful notion that the Russians would bleed to death and make it possible for the Germans to push again to the Don River, which he conceived as the ultimate barrier between Europe and the Bolshevist east. He considered it essential to hold not only a bridgehead in North Africa to protect the central Mediterranean and retain Italy's alliance but also Greece and the Balkans for the bauxite, copper, and oil necessary for the German war machine.[22]

When he returned to Rome on 22 December and reported to Mussolini the discouraging results of his mission, Ciano was not altogether displeased. He believed that if Italy collapsed through Mussolini's failure, the Western Powers would be glad to negotiate with him as Mussolini's successor.[23] Count Ciano also found the occasion to disparage Cavallero, who, he said, had been servile to the Germans at Hitler's headquarters.

Cavallero personified the policy of close integration with Germany, and the Germans regarded him highly. But at the turn of the year Cavallero began to undergo a change of heart. He resented the German accusation that Russian success at Stalingrad was largely the fault of the Italian troops there. He objected to the German proposal that the Germans, in the event of Allied landings, assume command over Italian units in the Balkans. He urged Kesselring to recall Rommel from North Africa because Rommel had embittered the Italian officer corps by his conduct toward the Italians after El'Alamein.[24]

Cavallero's change of heart came too late. Mussolini suddenly dismissed him on 1 February 1943. The day before, he had summoned Generale d'Armata Vittorio Ambrosio to the Palazzo Venezia in Rome and told him that the cycle of Cavallero was closed, the cycle of Ambrosio opening. When Ambrosio expressed surprise and some disinclination

---

[22] The Italian record is found in military subjects discussed in the conversations at German General Headquarters, *Comando Supremo, Rapporti,* 18 and 20 December 1942, IT 107. The German records survive on microfilm only. Members of the German War Documents Project, in the course of assembling the records of the former German Foreign Office, discovered a box containing microfilm copies of memorandums summarizing conversations of Hitler and of Ribbentrop with foreign statesmen, the so-called Loesch Film. Copies of these microfilms, designated by serial and frame numbers, are deposited at the National Archives in Washington, D.C. and in the Public Record Office in London. See *Documents on German Foreign Policy, 1918-1945,* Series D, vol. II (Washington, 1950), pp. viii, 1021, and 1041-42. The memorandums of the conversations of December 1942, all composed by Paul Otto Schmidt, the senior interpreter in the German Foreign Office, are as follows: F-45, Hitler-Ciano conversation, 18 Dec F 20/580-626 and F 7/243-245; RAM-48, Ribbentrop-Ciano conversation, 19 Dec F 20/254-253; F-49, Hitler-Ciano conversation, 19 Dec F 20/252-248; RAM-50, Ribbentrop-Ciano conversation, 19 Dec F 20/247-242; RAM-51, Ribbentrop-Ciano conversation, 19 Dec F 20/241-237;

F-52, Hitler-Ciano conversation, 20 Dec F 20/236-226.

Cf. Ciano Papers, pp. 716-28; Simoni, *Berlino, Ambasciata,* pp. 298-99; MS P-049 (Warlimont), pp. 18-19. See also Hitler Directive 47, 28 Dec 42, ONI, *Fuehrer Directives, 1942-1945.*

[23] Simoni, *Berlino, Ambasciata,* p. 300.

[24] *Ibid.;* Cavallero, *Comando Supremo,* pp. 433-34, 441.

GENERAL AMBROSIO

to inherit Cavallero's legacy, Mussolini declared, "We will divide the responsibility." He then asked Ambrosio for his ideas. Unprepared, Ambrosio nevertheless stated three points: lighten the organization of *Comando Supremo*; bring back to the Italian homeland the greatest possible number of Italian divisions; and stand up to the Germans. To the last point, Mussolini exclaimed, "*Benissimo!*"[25]

Ambrosio thoroughly disliked the Germans.[26] He had a faithful protégé in Generale di Brigata Giuseppe Castellano, who not only hated the Germans violently but was predisposed to political intrigue. Ambrosio met Ciano through Castellano, and together with Generale di Corpo d'Armata Giacomo Carboni, who was also close to Mussolini, these officers hoped that the dependence of Italy on Germany could be brought to an end.[27]

The cordial relationship between *Comando Supremo* and OKW ceased with Ambrosio's appointment, and this change was part of a general shift by Mussolini toward a greater independence with respect to Germany. The Germans regarded Ambrosio as correct, but it was a cold and formal type of correctness. The wartime spirit of comradeship in arms vanished, and Kesselring and Rintelen found Ambrosio to be a stickler who made difficulties. When it appeared to the Germans in Italy that Ambrosio hampered or frustrated the execution of Mussolini's declared intentions, they frequently found it necessary to appeal directly over Ambrosio's head to Mussolini.[28]

Though Ambrosio made but few changes in *Comando Supremo*, retaining the basic structure and powers established by Cavallero,[29] he made strenuous efforts to carry out the second and third points of his program. In February 1943, when Joachim von Ribbentrop, Hitler's

---

[25] Castellano, *Come firmai*, pp. 26-27; MS #P-058, Events in Italy, 1 February-8 September 1943.

[26] Ambrosio had commanded a cavalry squadron in the Libyan war of 1912-13, served as chief of staff of a cavalry division, then of an infantry division in World War I. An army commander at the beginning of World War II, with experience in Yugoslavia in 1941, he was appointed chief of the Army General Staff in January 1942.

[27] Castellano, *Come firmai*, pp. 15, 23-26; *Ciano Diaries*, pp. 558, 572, 576.

[28] MS #C-013, Special Report on the Events in Italy, 25 July-8 September 1943 (Generalfeldmarschall Albert Kesselring), pp. 3-4; Deichmann in MS #T-1a, *Der Feldzug in Italien* April 1943-11 May 1944 (General der Kavallerie Siegfried Westphal *et al.*), ch. I, p. 9; General der Infanterie Enno von Rintelen in MS #T-1a, ch. II, pp. 8-9.

[29] Chart of organization of *Comando Supremo*, IT 101.

GENERAL CARBONI

Foreign Minister, and General der Artillerie Walter Warlimont, Jodl's deputy at OKW, traveled to Rome to plan the suppression of the resistance forces in Yugoslavia, Warlimont was startled to hear Ambrosio state his intention of withdrawing some Italian forces from Croatia. Throughout several conferences Ambrosio stubbornly refused to participate in measures to disarm the Mihailovitch elements. Considering the Axis forces in the Balkans inadequate to crush all the partisans completely, he preferred to use the Chetniks against the Communists. The discussions reached a degree of argument never before heard, and what seemed like obscure Italian political intentions in the Balkans first excited Hitler's suspicions that the Italian generals were plotting "treason" against the Axis.[30]

Italy could ill afford to provoke Germany, for Italy by this time was an economic province of the Reich. With the weakest war potential of all the states classified as great powers, Italy lacked almost all the raw materials required for warfare in the modern industrialized age. Cut off from overseas supplies of coal, scrap iron, cotton, oil, and rubber, Italian heavy industry had too narrow a base to supply the new types of aircraft engines, tanks, and guns necessary to put the Italian armed forces on a par in equipment with the leading armies of the world. The coal and iron for heavy industry and the oil for the ships and planes could come only from Germany or German-controlled areas of Europe. As the Axis shifted to the defensive, Italy faced a contraction of its war production.[31]

Germany, too, was showing serious economic strains by the spring of 1943. After the manpower losses at Stalingrad, Germany began to draw from marginal groups. Although German production increased greatly, the increase did not equal both losses and new requirements. By March 1943 the rubber supply and the production of motor vehicles had become critical and fuel oil had to be carefully allotted.

Submarine warfare remained the only offensive German activity in the spring of 1943. Elsewhere, the Axis was on the defensive. Fully committed in support of the ground forces in the east and to convoy protection in the Mediterranean, even the once mighty Luftwaffe had ceased to be significant as an offensive weapon. But reflecting more clearly the state of affairs was the fact that the Axis no

---

[30] MS #P-049 (Warlimont), p. 21.

[31] Carlo Favagrossa, *Perchè perdemmo la guerra: Mussolini e la produzione bellica* (Milan: Rizzole and Co., 1946), p. 192.

longer had the semblance of a clear strategic aim.[32]

During February and March, 1943, tension grew between the Axis partners as Mussolini pressed for peace with the Soviet Union or withdrawal in the east, Hitler concentrated on destroying Bolshevism, Ambrosio and the OKW wrangled over the Balkans, and the Italian war machine began to sputter for lack of German supplies.[33]

Though the German Government and high command had never entertained a high esteem for the Italian people as allies, they had placed great faith in Mussolini. After March 1943, German trust even in Mussolini began to waver. When Ribbentrop explained Hitler's reason why a renewed offensive in the east was necessary, Mussolini promised to give energetic help, both political and military. Yet Mussolini wrote Hitler on 8 March and again on 26 March to urge a separate peace with the Soviet Union.[34]

Having made up his mind on a given course, Hitler was merely annoyed by advice to the contrary. This was evident early in April when the Duce and the Fuehrer, accompanied by military and diplomatic staffs, met for three days (7–10 April) at the Klessheim Castle near Salzburg, Austria, their first meeting in almost a year. Hitler's fanatical will to concentrate all available power to destroy the Soviet Union determined all aspects of the conference, and the results of the meeting were a bitter disappointment to the Italians. Mussolini was ill during most of the time and was confined to his suite, and though Hitler visited the Duce twice a day, the Italian's illness put him at a decided disadvantage. Germany seemed unwilling to send men or materials to support the Italian homeland threatened by direct attack. In the face of the great superiority of material the Allies enjoyed in the Mediterranean, Hitler spoke in a lofty vein: hopes for future success in submarine warfare; an iron will in the face of all obstacles; and a ruthlessness toward Greek and Yugoslav rebel forces. The only concrete offer came from Reichsfuehrer SS Heinrich Himmler who promised thirty-six heavy German tanks for a special division of Fascist militia to be assigned the task of preserving order in Rome.[35]

The Klessheim Conference did not bring Italy and Germany closer together; it served only to increase the growing friction. Ambrosio, no longer believing that a separate peace could be made in the east, saw hope for Italy only in the possibility that Mussolini would be able to break the alliance with Germany.

---

[32] MS #P-049 (Warlimont), pp. 25–29.

[33] Simoni, *Berlino, Ambasciata,* p. 316.

[34] *Hitler e Mussolini: Lettere e documenti,* (Milan and Rome: Rizzoli Editore, 1946), pp. 141–45, 151–54; *Goebbels Diaries,* p. 286; Simoni, *Berlino, Ambasciata,* pp. 324–28.

[35] Vittorio Ambrosio, *Promemoria sui colloqui di Klessheim,* 14 Apr 43, IT 109. The principal German records are the memorandums composed by interpreter Schmidt and preserved in the Loesch microfilms: RAM-19, Ribbentrop-Bastianini conversation with Mackensen and Alfieri present, 8 Apr 43, F 13/055–090; RAM-20, Ribbentrop-Bastianini conversation, 9 Apr 43, F 4/51–36; RAM-20a, Ribbentrop-Bastianini conversation, 9 Apr 43, F 4/35–23. See also Paolo Monelli, *Roma 1943* (3d ed., Rome: Migliaresi, 1945). p. 76; Leonardo Vitetti, Notes on the Fall of the Fascist Regime, pp. 4–5. This last is a ten-page, typewritten manuscript by a high-ranking official of the Italian Ministry of Foreign Affairs, procured for the authors by the Honorable Harold C. Tittmann, in 1946 assistant to the Honorable Myron C. Taylor, Personal Representative of the President of the United States to His Holiness the Pope.

## The Disintegration of Fascism

The difficulty of breaking the alliance lay in the fact that the Fascist regime was secure only so long as the prospect of victory existed. And victory without the power of Germany was hard to imagine.

As early as the summer of 1942, Mussolini's personal popularity had begun to diminish, and the Fascist party structure to crack. Mussolini was ill during much of the winter, and many Italians hoped and prayed that God might solve the country's problems by removing the Duce. But the Duce remained alive, his capacity for work scarcely impaired in spite of his illness, even though he apparently considered giving up command of the armed forces and restricting his efforts to the political leadership of the state.[36]

Failing at Klessheim to persuade Hitler to end the war in the east so as to make it possible for the Germans to concentrate their forces in the Mediterranean against the Allies and in support of Italy, Mussolini apparently reached the definite conclusion that the Axis had lost the war. He had felt this several months earlier, and he had already taken steps to tighten the reins of power over his increasingly disenchanted people. Soon after dismissing Cavallero from the *Comando Supremo*, Mussolini on 5 February discharged almost all the members of his cabinet and appointed new ones. The most important change was in foreign affairs—Ciano became Ambassador to the Holy See, Mussolini, himself, took the Ministry, and Giuseppe Bastianini, a faithful follower of Mussolini, became Under Secretary. Soon after his return from Klessheim to Rome, Mussolini dismissed Carmine Senise, Chief of Police and Prefect of Rome, and replaced him with a reliable Fascist. On 18 April he made Carlo Scorza, an ambitious thug, secretary of the Fascist party, and Scorza sought to rejuvenate the party by a return to the club and castor oil tactics of the early twenties.[37]

But Mussolini was incapable of checking the decline in Italian morale. Defeatism became widespread. Clandestine political parties became more vigorous. On 12 March, when almost 50,000 working men in northern Italy went on strike ostensibly to demand compensation payments to bombed-out families, leaflets were circulated demanding liberty and peace. Unable to cope with what was the first open labor strike under a totalitarian regime, the Fascist authorities acceded to the demands for compensation, then arrested and executed several of the reputed leaders.[38] On 1 May, despite police prohibitions, labor unions marched in May Day demonstrations.

An obvious solution was to make peace with the Allies, but two factors complicated the situation: reluctance to break the alliance with Germany and, later, disinclination to accept unconditional surrender. Though some of Mussolini's associates urged him to find a way out of

---

[36] Vitetti, Notes on the Fall of the Fascist Regime, pp. 1-2; Benito Mussolini, *Il tempo del bastone e della carota: Storia di un anno, Ottobre 1942-Settembre 1943* (Supplemento del *Corriere della Sera*, No. 190 del 9 Agosto 1944), p. 17; *Memoriale Cavallero*, 27 August 1943, in Francesco Orlando, *Mussolini volle il 25 luglio* (Milan: Edizioni "S.P.E.S.," 1946), pp. 82-83.

[37] Vitetti, Notes on the Fall of the Fascist Regime, pp. 4-5; Monelli, *Roma 1943*, pp. 76, 80.

[38] Elizabeth Wiskemann, *The Rome-Berlin Axis: A History of the Relations Between Hitler and Mussolini* (London, New York, Toronto: Oxford University Press, 1949), p. 295.

COUNT GRANDI

the war, Mussolini was at an impasse. In October 1942, the Honorable Myron C. Taylor, Personal Representative of the President to His Holiness the Pope, informed the Pope that Mr. Roosevelt would not receive any peace overtures made by Mussolini through the Holy See. When Count Dino Grandi, former Italian Ambassador to London, made arrangements in November 1942 to travel to Madrid in order to talk with the British Ambassador, Sir Samuel Hoare, Mussolini at first did nothing to prevent the trip, but finally refused to let Grandi leave the country.[39] In the same month, members of the Italian embassy in Berlin drew up a plan not only to dissolve the alliance with Germany but also to secure a united withdrawal from the war by Italy, Hungary, Rumania, and Bulgaria.[40] In January 1943, after the Italian minister at Bucharest had several frank discussions with Ion Antonescu, the Rumanian Prime Minister, on how Italy might take the lead in a joint peace maneuver, Ciano laid the proposal before Mussolini who listened but declined to take action.[41]

By early 1943, three distinct groups of Italians were trying to find a way out of the war: dissident Fascists; military officers; and underground anti-Fascist parties. The first two had the primary aim of finding a solution to end the war, and their object was to do so with Mussolini if possible, without him or even against him if necessary. The anti-Fascists wanted Mussolini's overthrow and the end of the Fascist system as goals in themselves. With only the most tenuous connections with each other, all looked to the King for initiative.

After Ciano left the cabinet, he became leader of the dissident Fascists. He had frequent contacts with Grandi, Giuseppe Bottai, Roberto Farinacci, and other Fascists who expressed criticism of the Duce's leadership. Though Ciano himself had negotiated the German alliance, he disliked the Germans and disbelieved in the pact. He assumed it was possible to force Mussolini out of office by means of intrigue and yet maintain the Fascist party intact. Grandi, Luigi Federzoni, and others shared Ciano's hope of tossing Mussolini overboard without swamping the Fascist boat. They could then seize the rudder and steer the ship into the port of a separate peace with the Allies. These men suddenly discovered that they were monarchists at heart, and as their contacts with the royal palace increased,

---

[39] "Count Dino Grandi Explains," *Life*, vol. 18, No. 9 (February 26, 1945), p. 80.
[40] Simoni, *Berlino, Ambasciata*, pp. 294–95.

[41] Renato Bova Scoppa, *Colloqui con due dittatori* (Rome: Nicola Rufolo, 1949), pp. 70–72; *Ciano Diaries*, pp. 572–73.

they suggested themselves as successors to Mussolini.[12]

The military party began to take form under Ambrosio, though it remained small. Most officers had neither the time nor the inclination for political activity. Their oath of office was to the King, and their stronger loyalty, in case of conflict between fascism and monarchy, was to him. Seeing no point in war for its own sake, or war by Italy for the sake of Hitler, and believing the war lost as early as February 1943, Ambrosio favored terminating the German alliance. He wanted to cut Italy's losses and save not only the Army but the monarchy as well. By keeping Mussolini clearly informed of the military situation, he hoped that the Head of the Government would draw the proper inference that a political solution of the war was essential. When he went further and suggested openly the suitability of terminating the German alliance, he only stirred Mussolini to vigorous reaction, Mussolini declaring fervently that he would march to the very end with his German ally.[43]

Close to Ambrosio were Generals Castellano and Carboni, both of whom recognized far earlier than Ambrosio that any hope of getting Mussolini to break with Hitler was illusory. Castellano, in particular, rapidly added to his contacts, and he was soon on good terms with Bastianini in the Ministry of Foreign Affairs and with Duke Pietro Acquarone, the King's personal secretary.[44]

COUNT CIANO

By March 1943, Castellano was so deep in intrigue that he drew up a detailed plan for a *coup d'état*. He provided measures to capture Mussolini and those leading Fascists most pro-Duce, and he included steps to be taken against possible Fascist and German reactions. He submitted the plan to Ambrosio who kept it twenty-four hours. But Ambrosio thought the idea premature, and he returned the paper with the suggestion that Castellano limit himself to alerting Army commanders in a general way to the possibility of public disturbances and orienting them on their duties should such situations arise. Not satisfied, Castellano submitted the plan to Ciano, who read it, refused to commit himself, and carefully locked the treasonable paper in his embassy safe at the Holy See.[45]

In May, Ambrosio had some rather candid discussions with Mussolini. He

---

[12] Franco Maugeri, *From the Ashes of Disgrace* (New York: Reynal and Hitchcock, 1948), p. 89; Castellano, *Come firmai*, pp. 40-41.

[43] Castellano, *Come firmai*, pp. 33-34; MS #P-058, Project #46. 1 Feb-8 Sep 43. Question 3.

[44] Vitetti, Notes on the Fall of the Fascist Regime, p. 3; Castellano, *Come firmai*, pp. 36-38.

[45] Castellano, *Come firmai*, pp. 38-40; Vitetti, Notes on the Fall of the Fascist Regime, p. 3.

pointed out the Duce's responsibility for the war and the absurdity to which the concept of a lightning war had been reduced. But he received no favorable response. Losing hope that Mussolini would separate Italy from Germany, he began to make certain that the King received all the important papers on the state of the Italian armed forces and on the over-all military situation. Ambrosio was ready to help overthrow Mussolini if the King gave the word, but without that word, he would not act.[46]

Castellano, meanwhile, had been busy making contacts and lining up men in key positions for his *coup d'état*. He won over Bastianini, and he secured from Renzo Chierici, head of the police, assurances that there would be no interference from that quarter with a political upheaval. When the Duke of Acquarone in mid-June hinted to several dissident Fascists that the King was thinking of replacing Mussolini as Head of Government, the isolation of Mussolini was virtually complete. By the end of June, both dissident Fascists and military party members were waiting only for a signal from the King to turn against the Duce.[47]

As for the underground anti-Fascist parties, they gained a new lease on life during the second half of 1942—Liberals, Christian Democrats, Socialists, Labor Democrats, Communists, and the Party of Action, each of which proposed different remedies for Italy's ills. The most conservative, the Liberals, wished the complete abolition of the Fascist system and the restoration of parliamentary government as it had existed before 1922, while the Party of Action regarded the monarchy and the church as the chief evils of Italy. Ivanoe Bonomi, a former Prime Minister, was influential in drawing the leaders of the underground parties together in a loose coalition. He was concerned in particular with restraining the Party of Action, which he feared might drive the crown to the embrace of the dissident Fascists. In March Bonomi secured agreement on a kind of party truce for the periods of wartime transition and reconstruction. Thus, despite their divergent views on the future needs of Italy, all the underground parties in the spring of 1943 were monarchical in the sense that they, too, looked to the King for action against Mussolini.[48]

Bonomi himself expected little from the King in the way of vigorous action, and he therefore made no approach to the throne until April, when he learned that the British Minister at the Holy See had indicated the British Government's preference for a monarchical solution to Italy's political problem. Since the British Minister, Sir D'Arcy Osborne, had not repulsed the efforts of Ciano and Grandi to see him, Bonomi began to be apprehensive that the Anglo-Americans might be willing to deal not only with the monarchy but even with the dissident Fascists. He therefore made an appeal to the King through an old and retired admiral, Grand Admiral Paolo Thaon di Revel, who had an almost superstitious reverence for the crown. The elderly admiral went to church and prayed before undertaking the audience, but when

---

[46] Castellano, *Come firmai*, pp. 42-43; MS #P-058, Project #46, 1 Feb-8 Sep 43, Question 3.

[47] Castellano, *Come firmai*, pp. 45-46; Vitetti, Notes on the Fall of the Fascist Regime, p. 7.

[48] Ivanoe Bonomi, *Diario di un anno (2 Giugno 1943-10 Giugno 1944)* (Cernusco sul Naviglio: Garzanti, 1947), pp. XXI-XXVIII.

he explained the tragic situation of the country to the King, the monarch revealed nothing of his thoughts. The King's sphinxlike attitude came as quite a shock to Paolo Thaon di Revel's monarchist principles.[49]

More satisfactory was Bonomi's secret meeting on 26 May, two weeks after the end of the Tunisian campaign, with the Duke of Acquarone. The course Bonomi urged was: arrest Mussolini; nominate a ministry headed by a prominent general and staffed by anti-Fascists; and denounce the alliance with Germany. Acquarone did little more than agree to arrange an audience for Bonomi with the King.[50]

King Victor Emmanuel III held the pivotal position in Italy's political situation during the spring of 1943. Having virtually withdrawn from public life during the turbulent war years, a cautious, timid, and secretive person, he disliked making decisions. First urged in November 1942 to dismiss Mussolini, he stated that he would act "when and if he thought it was necessary, and in whatever manner he himself deemed best for the country."[51] Yet the King had begun, it appeared, to be skeptical of Axis victory at least as early as 19 November 1942, for on that date he kept Ciano for an hour and twenty minutes at an audience and requested news of the neutral powers—Spain, Switzerland, and Turkey. Apparently concerned over the scarcity of troops in Italy, he asked Ciano to suggest to Mussolini, without revealing that the suggestion came from the King, that some troops be brought home. Though the monarch repeated rather generic statements of faith in the progress of the war, he asked many questions about Washington and London, and he advised the Foreign Minister to cling to any thread leading in those directions, even if the thread was "as thin as a spider's web."[52]

Throughout the early months of 1943 the King remained impassive. He listened discreetly to all suggestions but said nothing. To Badoglio, who gained an audience at the insistence of his friends that he explain the situation and recommend a change in political leadership, the King listened attentively but revealed nothing of his thoughts.

Bonomi had his day before the King on 2 June 1943. He drew a picture of impending disaster and suggested that the crown had the power, by the Italian constitution, to recall Mussolini. Since the alliance with Germany was a pact between National Socialist and Fascist regimes, Bonomi said, Mussolini's dismissal would give the Italian Government a sound legal basis for denouncing the treaty. The King refused to commit himself.

Six days later, the King remained quiet during an audience with Marcello Soleri, lawyer and politician, and eight days later still, during a meeting with Badoglio, he maintained his silence.[53]

Although it was not apparent to those who sought comfort in the King, Victor Emmanuel III had in actuality come to

---

[49] *Ibid.*, pp. XXVIII–XXIX, XXXVII–XXXVIII; Domenico Bartoli, *Vittorio Emanuele III* (Milan: Arnoldo Mondadori, 1946), p. 229.

[50] Bonomi, *Diario*, pp. XXXVIII–XXXIX.

[51] Maugeri, *Ashes of Disgrace*, p. 96.

[52] *Ciano Diaries*, pp. 545–46.

[53] Bonomi, *Diario*, pp. III–IX; Bartoli, *Vittorio Emanuele III*, pp. 234–37; Pietro Badoglio, *L'Italia nella seconda guerra mondiale: Memorie e documenti* (Milan: Arnoldo Mondadori Editori, 1946), pp. 61–62; Vitetti, Notes on the Fall of the Fascist Regime, pp. 6-7.

a decision. On 15 May 1943 he presented Mussolini with three memorandums, a clear suggestion for the course the King wished the Duce to follow. Based on the military data provided by Ambrosio, the first paper compared the military forces of the Axis and the satellite powers with those of the Allies and the Soviet Union; the second paper listed the Allied military capabilities and contrasted the scanty possibilities of Italian resistance. The third memorandum outlined a course of action:

One ought now to do everything to hold the country united, and not make rhetorical speeches with a purely Fascist basis. It is necessary to maintain close contact with Hungary, Rumania, and Bulgaria, countries that have little love for the Germans. One ought not to neglect making whatever courtesies are possible toward the governing men of England and of America. It is necessary to consider very seriously the possibility of separating the fate of Italy from that of Germany whose internal collapse can come unexpectedly like the collapse of the German Empire in 1918.[54]

Disliking the Germans, fearful of their reaction if he removed Mussolini, the King was also scrupulous in his conduct. He wished to terminate the German alliance, but only with German consent. Admiring, even envying Mussolini's power and cleverness, the Italian monarch saw no one in Italy as well qualified as the Duce to solve the incredibly difficult problem of ending the alliance and withdrawing from the war.[55]

Perhaps the task was insuperable. Mussolini had lost prestige in the eyes of his allies, his military forces, his government associates, his party members, and his people. The Fascist system was nothing more than a hollow shell. Thoroughly war-weary, the Italian people desired only an end to bombings and hardships and sorrow. The military units had lost confidence in themselves, and their commanders were without hope of victory. Defeatists staffed the foreign service, and their reports from Berlin, Budapest, Bucharest, and the neutral capitals insisted that continuing the war would bring only disaster to Italy. A considerable number of Mussolini's personal followers, members of the Fascist Grand Council, began to see the beginning of the end.

In this situation, Mussolini could only grope for a way out. The Allies, however, blocked the way toward a separate peace with their publicly proclaimed demand for unconditional surrender.

### The Allied Threat

Expecting the Allies to invade the European continent, aware of Russian demands on the Allies for a second front, and anticipating therefore that the Allies would try to time their offensive move to coincide with Russian attacks tying down German forces in the east, Axis intelligence agencies shrewdly guessed that build-up and other invasion preparations would occupy the Allies until the end of June or the beginning of July. But where the blow would strike was, of course, the other side of the coin. The likely targets in the Mediterranean were southern France, Sicily, Sardinia, southern Italy, Rhodes, Greece, and the Balkans; some reports mentioned Spain, Turkey, Sweden, the Netherlands, and northern France; and a rumor persisted that

---

[54] The three memorandums are printed in full in Enzo Galbiati, *Il 25 Luglio e la M.V.S.N.* (Milan: Editrice Bernabò, 1950), pp. 180–83.
[55] Bartoli, *Vittorio Emanuele III*, pp. 205–06.

the Allies would invade the Continent by way of Norway.[56]

Among the various Axis headquarters, there was no agreement on the most likely target in the Mediterranean. *Comando Supremo*, in general, inclined toward Sardinia for many reasons—Allied forces could converge there from Gibraltar and North Africa; Sardinia was a necessary preliminary on the way to southern France; Allied air based on Sardinia could range over the entire Italian mainland and also over southern Germany; Sardinia was the gateway to the Po valley; Allied possession of Sardinia would bottle up the Italian Fleet in the Tyrrhenian Sea. Sicily, in contrast, would neither appreciably shorten the air distance to the industrial centers in the Po valley and southern Germany nor increase the threat to central Italy by air or ground forces.

Ambrosio, chief of *Comando Supremo*, saw Sardinia as being important only if the Allies intended to occupy the Italian mainland, and he thought that the Allies would figure a mainland campaign too costly and time-consuming for the results they could expect. He chose Sicily, which did not necessarily presuppose a later invasion of the Italian mainland. Sicily would assure the Allies freedom of sea movements in the Mediterranean, and would prevent the Italian Navy from shifting even its small ships and submarines from the Tyrrhenian Sea to the Ionian and Adriatic Seas.[57]

Mussolini, possibly motivated by wishful thinking, expected the Allies to harass the Italian mainland by air attacks and perhaps try to occupy the major Italian islands for use as bases in future operations. But he did not believe that the Allies would attempt to invade the Italian boot. He thought that the Allies were mainly interested in free passage through the Mediterranean, a condition they would have achieved by securing the North African coast. Though doubting

---

[56] Rpt, *Feindlagebericht Nr. 10/43*, GenStdH, Abt. Fremde Heere West to GenStdH, Op.Abt., 15 May 43, OKH.Op.Abt. (II), *Feindnachrichten England, noch Bd. IV* (H 2/186); Rpt, *Feindlagebericht, OKW/WFSt*, 10 Jun 43, and Rpt, Roenne, Chef, Abt. Fremde Heere West to Chef, GenStdH, 20 Jun 43, both in OKH/Op.Abt., *Feindnachrichten Allgemein vom 6.III.43–13.I.44* (H 22/384); Rpts, *Feindlageberichte Nr. 12 and Nr. 13/43*, GenStdH, Abt. OKH/Op.Abt. (II), *Fremde Heere, Bd. III., 1.III.–15.VII.43* (H 2/182); Estimates of Allied Intentions, IT 106; The Trip of the Commander in Chief, Navy, to Rome and His Subsequent Report to the Fuehrer, 12 May 1943–15 May 1943 (cited hereafter as CinC Navy Visits Italy, 12–15 May 43), pp. 44–68; Office of Naval Intelligence, *Fuehrer Conferences on matters dealing with the German Navy, 1943* (hereafter cited as ONI, *Fuehrer Conferences, 1943*). *Fuehrer Conferences* is a selection of translated documents from German naval archives. The conferences cover the period from 1939 to 1945, and each ONI issue covers one year. Pietro Maravigna, "Lo sbarco Anglo-Americano in Sicilia," *Rivista Militare*, vol. VIII, No. 1 (Rome, January 1952), pp. 7–31 (cited hereafter as Maravigna, *Rivista Militare*, 1952).

[57] Emilio Faldella, *Lo sbarco e la difesa della Sicilia* (Rome: L'Aniene, Editrice 1956), pp. 31, 34; Rpt, *Valutazione d'importanza della Sardegna nel quadro strategico e nel quadro tattico*, 27 Jan 43, IT 1179; Rpt, *Comando Supremo, Prospettive operative per la difesa dell'Italia e della Balcania*, 15 Feb 43 (hereafter cited as Rpt, *Prospettive operative, Comando Supremo*), IT 1181; Min, *Riunione operativa esigenza S.S., Impiego dei mezzi dell' Aeronautica e della Marina*, 28 May 43, item 156, Min of Confs, *Comando Supremo*, IT 26. (The documents in this folder are copies of minutes of conferences held by members of *Comando Supremo*. They are hereafter identified only by date and item number in IT 26.); Rpt, *Studio operativo, Superaereo*, 21 Feb 43, IT 1189; Marc'Antonio Bragadin, *Che ha fatto la Marina?* (1940–1945) (Cernusco sul Naviglio: La Lampada, 1950), pp. 434–35; CinC Navy Visits Italy, 12–15 May 43, ONI. *Fuehrer Conferences, 1943*.

that the Allies would consider it imperative to occupy Sicily or Sardinia, he thought Sicily the more directly threatened. In May 1943, as the Tunisian campaign drew toward its close, Mussolini was saying that the Allies would probably land in France for a direct attack on Germany, or perhaps in the Balkans.[58]

Hitler expected the Allies to land in Greece or the Balkans, and his reasoning was sound. Both areas were more important to the German economy than Italy. The populations were friendly to the Allies. An Allied invasion would supplement Russian pressure, force the dispersal of Axis troops over widely separated areas, and forestall a Russian occupation of the Balkans.[59]

Noting the movement of New Zealand troops back to the Middle East after the capture of Tunis, and inferring that the entire British Eighth Army was to follow, OKW guessed that the Allies were planning to mount an attack against Greece and the Balkans from eastern Mediterranean ports. The Germans gave credence to an Allied intelligence plant, and, as a consequence, OKW in May 1943 looked toward Greece.[60]

Kesselring saw the gravest threat in the western Mediterranean, and in May he was considering such places as Spain, the Balearic Islands, Sardinia, and Sicily. He ruled out southern France, northern Italy, and the Balkans as being too far removed from effective air support, a prerequisite, he figured, in any Allied planning. Guessing in mid-May from air reconnaissance photos of the distribution of Allied divisions and landing craft in North Africa, he chose Sicily first, Sardinia second.[61]

How well prepared were the Axis nations to meet the blow?

*Comando Supremo* had hoped in February 1943 that the Italian Fleet, with the support of air, both German and Italian, would defeat an Allied landing before the ground troops got ashore. But a survey made early in May indicated that the Navy, whose major elements consisted of three battleships, four cruisers, and ten destroyers, did not have enough surface vessels to defeat an invasion fleet. Submarines and small craft could only harass but not deter approaching enemy convoys.

The combined German and Italian air forces in the Mediterranean early in 1943 consisted of some 2,000 planes, one-half of them fighters. By May 1943 the number had dropped more than fifty percent, and of these many were obsoles-

---

[58] MS #P-049 (Warlimont), p. 17; Msg, Mussolini to Hitler, 9 Mar 43, *Oberkommando der Wehrmacht-Wehrmachtfuehrungsstab, Kriegstagebuch* (cited hereafter as *OKW/WFSt, KTB*) *1.-31.III.43*, 14 Mar 43; Min, 6 May 43, item 138, Min of Confs, Comando Supremo, IT 26; CinC Navy Visits Italy, 12-15 May 43, ONI, *Fuehrer Conferences, 1943*; MS #R-115, The Fall of Pantelleria and the Pelagian Islands, 11-13 June 1943, ch. II of Axis Tactical Operations in Sicily, July-August 1943 (Magna E. Bauer).

[59] Deichmann in MS #T-1a (Westphal et al.), ch. I, pp. 7-8; Rpt, *Prospettive operative*, Comando Supremo, IT 1181.

[60] Memo, Gen.St.d.H., Abt. Fremde Heere West, Nr. 874/43, g.K., 9 May 43, and Telg, Fremde Heere West, Nr. 27/43, g.Kdos.Chefs., 12 May 43, both in *OKH/Op.Abt., Allgemein Mittelmeer, Chefs.*, 9.III.-29.XII.43 (H 22/147); CinC Navy Visits Italy, 12-15 May 43, ONI, *Fuehrer Conferences, 1943*; Telg, *OKW/WFSt/ Op.Nr. 661055/43, g.Kdos.Chefs.*, 12 May 43, ONI, *Fuehrer Directives, 1942-1945*, pp. 79-80. (See below, pp. 64-65.)

[61] Min, 4 May 43, item 132, Min of Confs, Comando Supremo, IT 26; MS #T-3, P 1, pt. II, *Mittelmeerkrieg, II. Teil, Tunesien und die gleichzeitigen Kaempfe der Achsenmaechte in Tripolitanien* (Kesselring), pp. 65ff.

## THE AXIS ON THE DEFENSIVE

cent. Hundreds of planes had been destroyed on the ground because of failure to camouflage and disperse them and because antiaircraft defenses proved ineffective.[62]

The Italian ground forces appeared completely unequal to the task of doing more than retarding or delaying an invasion. With Italian strength drained and equipment expended in Russia and North Africa, with very little having been done to improve coastal defenses, with units spread much too thin along the extensive Italian coast line, there was little hope of defensive success. "We may be able to put up an honorable defense against a large-scale landing," a high-ranking Italian officer said, "but we have no chance to repel the enemy."[63]

Italy urgently needed help, not only planes, tanks, and guns, but fuel and ammunition as well. The Germans promised to deliver 166 guns to Italy during the month of March 1943, but German requirements delayed the first shipment until the end of April. The Germans were ready to send planes and crews to the extent that Italy could provide airfields and ground defenses, but, while Ambrosio claimed the capacity of accommodating 2,500 aircraft, Goering considered the airfields unfit for immediate use and the protection offered inadequate.[64]

Italy needed ground troops, too, but Mussolini was reluctant to request them. Concerned chiefly with his tattered prestige, he sought to deny his dependence on Germany by trying to persuade himself that the Allies would not attempt to occupy Italian territory, and at the same time that there would be an upsurge of spirit among Italian units defending the homeland. If the burden of defense fell on German units, Mussolini's dependence on Hitler would become too obvious, and he would lose any freedom for political maneuver.

The Italian Army commander in Sicily, Generale di Corpo d'Armata Comandante Designato d'Armata Mario Roatta, concerned purely with his military problem, advocated the use of German divisions, welcomed German offers of assistance, and provided his superiors with arguments on why German troops should be sought.[65]

Ambrosio adopted a middle position. From a professional point of view, he was aware that German ground forces were indispensable for the defense of Italy, and occasionally he appeared willing to accept them. But Ambrosio was very conscious of representing a break with the tradition of intrusive German ascendancy, and he wished to disentangle *Comando Supremo* from the influence of OKW. To obviate German help, he withdrew the Italian Army from Russia; he tried to recall to Italy some of the divisions occupying France and the Balkans; and he prevented the dispatch to North Africa of an effective unit, the 4th (*Livorno*) *Infantry Division*, which was stationed in Sicily. Unfortunately for Ambrosio, he was endeavoring to re-

---

[62] Rpt, *Prospettive operative*, Comando Supremo, IT 1181; Rpt, *Studio operativo Superaereo*, 21 Feb 43, IT 1189; CinC Navy Visits Italy, 12–15 May 43, ONI, *Fuehrer Conferences, 1943*.

[63] Faldella, *Lo sbarco*, pp. 32–33; quotation from Roatta in Faldella, *Lo sbarco*, p. 33.

[64] Deichmann in MS #T-1a (Westphal et al.), ch. I, pp. 20–22; III, pp. 10–12; Min, 27 Jun 43, Min of Confs, Comando Supremo, IT 3032; MS #T-2, K 1, *Der Kampf um Sizilien: Abschliessende Betrachtung des seinerzeitigen Oberbefehlshabers Sued, Generalfeldmarschall Kesselring*, p. 7.

[65] Rintelen in MS #T-1a (Westphal et al.), ch. II, p. 11; Roatta, *Otto milioni*, p. 261.

assert Italian prestige at a time when the military need for German reinforcement was becoming irresistible. Unable to deny the need, he feared that the presence of German ground troops would make them master of the Italian house. He therefore sought zealously to guard and maintain the established principle of Italian command over the German troops stationed in Italy. But this, he recognized, was ultimately only a device to save face. Unable to take a wholly military view of Italian problems, neither did he envisage a purely military solution of the war, which he regarded as hopelessly lost.[66]

On 4 May 1943, Kesselring met with Mussolini to discuss how to meet the next Allied move after Tunisia. Mussolini said that the Allies might try to land on Italian soil, but he doubted that they would attempt an invasion. Perhaps he was trying to distinguish between a small Dieppe-style landing and a full-scale invasion such as that in North Africa. In any case, after Kesselring presented a lucid analysis of Allied capabilities, Mussolini agreed that Sardinia and Sicily might be threatened. With this admission stated, Kesselring offered the Italians the use of one German division.[67]

Two days later, Rintelen submitted to OKW a comprehensive and devastating report on the combat effectiveness of the Italian armed forces. They "have not up to now fulfilled the missions assigned them in this war," he wrote, "and have actually failed everywhere." The reasons, Rintelen found, were inadequate and insufficient armament and equipment; faulty training of the officers; and a lack of spirit and *élan* among the troops, the latter stemming from a "disbelief in a favorable outcome of the war." Only with German support, he affirmed, could the Italians repel a large-scale invasion of their homeland.[68]

On the same day, 6 May, Kesselring again met with Mussolini. He told the Duce that Hitler had promised to send a division from Germany to Italy and that Hitler had ordered Kesselring to reconstitute into a complete unit those parts of the *Hermann Goering Division* that had not gone to Tunisia because of lack of transportation and that were, therefore, still in Italy. In addition to these two German divisions that would soon be available, Kesselring pointed out, other contingents of various German units still in Italy because they had not been shipped in time to Tunisia could be gathered together and formed into a third division. Though Kesselring insisted that Sardinia and Sicily needed immediate reinforcement, Mussolini preferred to believe that the Allies intended to land in France.[69]

Four days later, on 10 May, Ambrosio accepted the three divisions Kesselring had offered to reinforce the defense of Italy. Ambrosio planned to station one in Sicily, another in Sardinia, and a third on the mainland, stipulating carefully that they would be under his operational command.

---

[66] Rpt, German Military Attaché, Rome, on Cooperation with Italian High Command/Commitment of German Forces in Italy, 14 Jul 43, *OKW, Amtsgruppe Ausland, 30.VI.43–31.VIII.44, Wehrmacht Attaché Italien* (OKW 1029); *OKW/WFSt, KTB, 1.–31.VII.43,* 21 Jul 43, p. 3.

[67] Min, 4 May 43, item 132, Min of Confs, *Comando Supremo,* IT 26.

[68] Rpt, *Beurteilung der derzeitigen Kampfkraft der italienischen Wehrmacht,* OKH, Op. Abt. (II), Afrika–A I Berichte, Bd.3, 16.I.–18.V. 43 (H 22/190).

[69] Min, 6 May 43, item 138, Min of Confs, *Comando Supremo,* IT 26.

## THE AXIS ON THE DEFENSIVE

In a subsequent discussion with Rintelen that same day, Ambrosio reiterated that the German divisions in Italy would be under Italian tactical command, and he declared unnecessary the retention of a German liaison group that had entered Italy with an Italian corps withdrawn from the Russian front. With the fall of Tunis, Ambrosio said, there would be less need for OKW liaison with *Comando Supremo*. Hereafter, he continued, German officers might be in contact with *Superesercito*, which had command in the national territory, but, in any case, he would issue the orders in this regard.[70]

On either the same day or a day later, Hitler offered Mussolini five fully equipped German mobile divisions for the defense of Italy. Mussolini at first was ready to accept, but Ambrosio induced him to reconsider, and on 12 May, Mussolini declined the new German offer.[71] Mussolini's refusal to accept Hitler's offer of five additional German divisions constituted an important turning point in the Italo-German alliance.

Hitler considered two things essential for the defense of Germany: critical materials from the Balkans, in particular bauxite, copper, and chrome; and Italian political stability. Reports from German visitors to Italy had long warned of the possible collapse of fascism.[72] As Hitler's special adviser on the Mediterranean, Field Marshal Erwin Rommel, embittered since his relief in Africa, excited the Fuehrer's suspicions of Italy as an ally.[73] Increasingly apprehensive of Italian defection from the alliance, Hitler was concerned because he was convinced that if Italy withdrew from the war, whether voluntarily or otherwise, he would have to give the Mediterranean front at least temporary priority over the other theaters, even the east. Thus, in February and March 1943, partly as a precaution against Italian defection, partly to bolster Italy, and partly to reinforce the defenses of two of the most threatened areas in the Mediterranean, Hitler had ordered strong German elements placed on Sardinia and Sicily. He also gave high priority to Italy on the weapons being produced in Germany.[74]

In May, speculation in the German camp on Mussolini's intentions, as well as on his strength, was far from favorable. Joseph Goebbels, Minister of Propaganda, noted that "the Duce no longer sticks to a clear line, either in his policies or in his war strategy." Mussolini seemed unable to rely on anyone for help in waging the war or in carrying out his policies. "If it be true," Goebbels remarked, "that the Fuehrer, despite his tremendous powers, has nevertheless been lied to and cheated so often by the generals, how much more must that be the case with Mussolini!" The Duce had become "an old and tired man," and Hitler was "not

---

[70] Min, 10 May 43, item 137, and Min, 10 May 43, item 139, both in Min of Confs, *Comando Supremo*, IT 26.

[71] Rintelen in MS #T-1a (Westphal *et al.*), ch. II, p. 11; Deichmann in MS #T-1a (Westphal *et al.*), ch. I, pp. 24-25; Westphal in MS #T-1a (Westphal *et al.*), ch. IV, p. 6; Westphal, *Heer in Fesseln*, p. 218.

[72] See, for example, Rpt, *Reise nach Rom und Sizilien vom 11.-14.V.43*, signed by Maj. I. G. Freiherr von Tisenhausen, *OKH, Op. Abt. (II), Afrika-A I Berichte, Bd. 3, 16.I.-18.V.43* (H 22/190).

[73] Canadian Historical Section (G.S.), Army Headquarters, Ottawa, Report by Bogislaw von Bonin, Considerations on the Italian Campaign, 1943-1944, copy in OCMH; Deichmann in MS #T-1a (Westphal *et al.*), ch. I, p. 34.

[74] MS #P-049 (Warlimont), p. 17; Deichmann in MS #T-1a (Westphal *et al.*), ch. I, pp. 22-24.

at all convinced that the Italians will stay put when the heaviest strain comes."[75]

On 19 May OKW submitted to Hitler a report on the defense of Italy. The situation, OKW declared, was hardly encouraging. There were no principles established to guide the co-operation of OKW and *Comando Supremo*. Italy demanded command and other prerogatives, yet failed to mobilize completely. Italy could not be defended on the basis of the alliance as then constituted. What were needed were predominant German influence on the command structure and German ground troops as "corset stays" for the Italian units. The three divisions proposed by Kesselring were not sufficient. If Sardinia were lost, the threat to northern Italy would be acute, and the Po valley was the key area for the whole of Italy, for the Balkans, for southern France, and for an Allied air offensive against southern Germany. OKW recommended an immediate build-up of supplies for the defense at least of northern Italy.[76]

A long discussion took place at the Fuehrer's headquarters on 20 May with Keitel, Rommel, Warlimont, and others in attendance. Like many of the conferences when Hitler was in the process of making up his mind, the talk was often desultory. Hitler listened to a description of conditions in Italy, heard how Italian commanders lacked confidence in their abilities, deliberated over the rumor that the German troops in Sicily were not well liked, learned that Italian authorities were doing nothing to check expressions of anti-German sentiment. Many Italians were apparently not to be trusted; some were Anglophiles. Rommel suggested that the Italians might suddenly close the Brenner frontier and cut off the German troops in Sicily and southern Italy. Gossip was reported that in certain circumstances the Italians might turn against the Germans. Hitler remarked that he would not be surprised if the Italian crown, with the support of the Army chiefs, tried to overthrow Mussolini and the Fascist party. At the end of the meeting, Hitler told Keitel that it would be well, in the event of Italian treachery, for Rommel to have authority to handle the situation.[77]

Two days later OKW issued Plan *ALARICH*, a course of action to be taken if fascism collapsed or Italy defected. Essentially, the plan provided for a German occupation of northern Italy, with evacuation by German troops of the rest of the Italian boot.

Initially, six or seven mobile divisions were to be withdrawn from the Eastern Front when necessary to carry out the occupation. In command of the occupation operation, Rommel expected an eventual force of thirteen or fourteen divisions. But when no Allied attack materialized and when the internal affairs of Italy seemed to quiet down, Hitler decided to launch an offensive in the east. As a consequence, the only divisions remaining to execute Plan *ALARICH* were a total

---

[75] Entry of 10 May 1943 from *The Goebbels Diaries*, by Louis P. Lochner. Copyright 1948 by The Fireside Press, Inc. Reprinted by permission of Doubleday & Company, Inc.

[76] Memo, OKH, *Vortragsnotiz*, 19 May 43, *Westl. Mittelmeer Chefs.* (H 22/290).

[77] Minutes of Conference 5 Between Hitler and Sonderfuehrer von Neurath, 20 May 1943, part of the collection known as Minutes of Conferences Between Hitler and Members of the German Armed Forces High Command, December 1942–March 1945 (cited hereafter as Min of Hitler Confs).

of eight that could be withdrawn from the command of *OB WEST* in France.[78]

While Hitler, the OKW, and Rommel made their secret preparations, Kesselring continued to co-operate with the Italians on the defense of Italy, and Mussolini and the *Comando Supremo* gradually diminished their opposition to additional ground reinforcement. After Kesselring visited Sicily in May 1943 and discussed matters thoroughly with the Italian generals, Rintelen on 22 May obtained from the Italians firm agreement to employ four German divisions—a panzer grenadier division (to be known later as the *15th*) to be reconstituted in Sicily by 1 June and trained by 15 June; another panzer grenadier division (eventually designated the *90th*) to be expanded from a brigade stationed in Sardinia; a panzer division (the *Hermann Goering*) to be reconstituted on the mainland; and another panzer division (the *16th*) to arrive after being reconstituted in France. The Italians also agreed to permit General der Panzertruppen Hans Valentin Hube and his staff of the *XIV Panzer Corps* to come to Italy to prepare the German divisions for combat.[79]

Still more German troops for Italy were in the offing. Ambrosio, despite his wish to sever the German alliance, was becoming increasingly concerned by the Allied threat. And Kesselring, whose views were diametrically opposed to those of Rommel, believed that if the Italians co-operated, the Germans could defend the whole of Italy. As long as Mussolini remained in power, Hitler was willing to support him. And as the Italians demonstrated, even though reluctantly, their intention to react positively to the next Allied move, OKW made no plans to withdraw to a shorter line on the Italian mainland. Despite Rommel's suspicions of Italian trickery, Plan *ALARICH* receded into the background, a vague expedient to be executed in the unlikely event of political change in Italy.

Mussolini was altogether uncomfortable. Resenting German domination of the war effort, anxious to save his Fascist regime, ambitious to restore Italy's status and prestige, fearful of Allied capabilities and intentions, he was looking for a way out. But as hurtful as the acknowledgment of German superiority was, more painful was the acceptance of unconditional surrender. If he could, with German help, repulse an Allied invasion, if he could gain even a small moment of triumph, the conditions might be propitious for approaching the Western nations for a negotiated peace.

Italy was in a predicament. Fascist Italy, which Mussolini had advertised as a great power, was in the tragic and ridiculous position of being unable either to make war or to make peace. Exactly how ridiculous was to become apparent in June 1943 when the Allies made their next offensive move in the Mediterranean.

---

[78] For information on Plan *ALARICH* see: Msg, *OKW/WFSt* to Rommel, *No. 661138/43, G.Kdos.Chefs.*, 22 May 43; Msg, *OKW/WFSt* to *OB WEST* and others, *No. 661127/43, G.Kdos. Chefs.*, 24 May 43; Rpt, *WFSt-Op. H. Tarnwort "ALARICH,"* 27 May 43; Msg, *OB WEST* to *GenStdH, Op.Abt.II*, 31 May 43; Msg, *OKW/ WFSt-Op. (H)* to *OB WEST*, 25 Jun 43; all in *Westl. Mittelmeer Chefs.* (H 22/290).

[79] Min, 17 May 43, item 148, Min, 18 May 43, item 150, Min, 22 May 43, item 152, all in Min of Confs, *Comando Supremo*, IT 26; see also Roatta, *Otto milioni*, pp. 242–43; Giacomo Zanussi, *Guerra e catastrofe d'Italia, giugno 1943–maggio 1945* (Rome: Casa Editrice Libraria Corso, 1946), vol. I, pp. 287–313; MS #T-3, P 1 (Kesselring), pt. II, pp. 67–70.

# CHAPTER III

# Preparations and Preliminaries

*The Beginnings*

In directing General Eisenhower to execute an amphibious operation to seize Sicily, the Combined Chiefs of Staff at Casablanca had in mind securing Allied sea lanes through the Mediterranean, trying to knock Italy out of the war, and diverting German strength from the Russian front. Whereas almost any objective in the Mediterranean might have contributed equally well to the last of these aims, the very location of Sicily made the island a particularly likely target for contributing to the other two. For Sicily lies only ninety miles across the Sicilian channel from the tip of Africa at Cape Bon and a scant two miles across the Strait of Messina off the southwestern tip of the Italian peninsula.

The Greeks had a word for Sicily— Trinacria, the three-cornered, a great triangle encompassing an area of approximately 10,000 square miles, roughly the size of the state of Vermont. (*Map I*) The northern side measures some 180 miles; the southwestern side is almost as long, approximately 170 miles; the eastern edge, running in a general north-south direction, is considerably shorter, about 125 miles.

Of strategic importance since the earliest history of migrations and wars in the Mediterranean, a steppingstone for Romans, Carthaginians, and Moors, Sicily in the modern age of air power had assumed new significance. When Mussolini was building up the Italian Fleet, he made no provisions for aircraft carriers because he felt that Italy already had them in the existence of the southern extremity of the Italian peninsula, Sardinia, and, above all, Sicily. Sicily and its airfields had forced Britain to abandon the direct Mediterranean route for maritime traffic with the Near and Middle East and had compelled the Admiralty to maintain two fleets in the Mediterranean, one based on Gibraltar, the other on Alexandria and Port Said. Sicily, together with the small island of Pantelleria, which lies between the western tip of Sicily and Cape Bon, had given the Axis a domination of the air over the central Mediterranean that might have been complete had not the British held on to Malta, some 55 miles off the southeastern tip of Sicily.

Scalloped with wide, sweeping bights separated by capes, the coast of Sicily has numerous beaches of sand and shingle. They range in length from less than a hundred yards to several miles. A narrow coastal plain backs the beaches in the blunt northwestern corner of the island, then widens somewhat midway along the southwestern coast opposite the Gulf of Gela and maintains this width on either side of the sharp southeastern corner, the Pachino peninsula. Less than halfway up the east coast near the port city of Catania the plain widens into the only sizable stretch of flat land in Sicily, the plain of Catania. All the island's airfields were located on the coastal plains, none more than fifteen miles inland.[1] From Catania northward on the east coast and all along the north coast, steep slopes and precipitous cliffs face the sea. In the northeastern triangle stand the highest and most rugged mountains of the island whose surface is almost all mountainous, the Caronie Mountains with peaks from 4,500 to 5,400 feet, and massive Mount Etna itself, 10,000 feet high and twenty miles in diameter at its base.

Throughout the island the more important and better roads were close to the coast, including those riding a narrow shelf between beach and mountain in the north and northeast. In the interior the roads were poorly surfaced and narrow, with sharp curves and steep grades. The roads were particularly difficult for military traffic in the towns and small cities, for most of the settlements were established in classical or medieval times, and they were built on hilltops for the sake of defense, with steep, winding approaches and narrow streets designed not for trucks and tanks but for pedestrians, chariots, and mule carts. The bulk of the island's dense population of some four million was located in the towns and cities.

The major ports were Messina near the northeastern tip, Catania and Syracuse on the eastern side, and Palermo near the western end, each with a daily capacity of more than 1,000 tons. Messina, the largest port, was closest to the mainland. There, ferry service across the strait to Calabria connected the Sicilian railroads with the continental system. Messina was clearly the most strategic objective on the island, for, as the link with the mainland, its capture by an invading force would seal off the island's defenders and deny them reinforcement or resupply. Catania, with a port capacity somewhat less than Messina and Palermo, was scarcely less important by virtue of its location and its relative proximity to the Italian mainland.

The problem of attacking Sicily had been blocked out in a general way in London and submitted to the CCS at the Casablanca Conference.[2] The ground forces to be committed, the planners predicted, would have to be in sufficient strength to attain a decisive superiority over an Axis force estimated to have a maximum potential of eight divisions. If Axis strength did not reach this figure by the time of the invasion, the rate of build-up was calculated at one German or one and a half Italian divisions per week by the Messina ferry

---

[1] The listing of airfields and seaplane bases on Sicily is contained in S.S.O. 17/3 (Final), par. 11, and mentions nineteen known airfields and landing grounds in Sicily (Salmon Files, 5-G-3, item 5). Likewise the same figure of nineteen known airfields, later raised to thirty at the time of the Allied attack, is mentioned in The Conquest of Sicily, 10 July 1943-17 August 1943, Despatch by His Excellency Field Marshal the Viscount Alexander of Tunis (cited hereafter as Alexander Despatch), p. 2, in NARS. The figure of thirty at the time of the Allied attack is not borne out by enemy accounts and is probably achieved by counting landing strips. Cf. Samuel Eliot Morison, "History of United States Naval Operations in World War II," vol. IX, *Sicily—Salerno—Anzio, January 1943-June 1944* (Boston: Little, Brown and Company, 1954), p. 12n.

For information on the Sicilian ports see Alexander Despatch, p. 65, and S.S.O. 17/3 (Final), par. 10.

[2] Br JP (43) 7 (Final), an. I, 10 Jan 43, 0100/4/59. I.

service alone. On the other hand, Messina was vulnerable to air attack and might be eliminated or severely crippled before the invasion. Of the eight Axis divisions likely to be defending Sicily, the planners estimated, four could be concentrated against any one Allied landing within two or three days. The Allied forces, it appeared, would have to total at least ten divisions, and if separate landings were made, each would have to be strong enough to defeat a force of four enemy divisions.

The heavy fortifications known to exist along the strait ruled out a direct blow against Messina. Similar defenses excluded direct assaults against the naval bases of Syracuse, Augusta, and Palermo. Admiral Horatio Nelson's adage, "A ship's a fool to fight a fort," was as relevant for battleships and modern harbor defenses as it was in the days of wooden vessels and stone forts. Because the technique of bringing supplies across the assault beaches was still only theoretical, the Allies would have to secure ports at once. They would have to come ashore along the relatively unfortified stretches of coast line close to one or more major ports.

Another reason militating against a direct assault on Messina was its distance from fighter aircraft bases on Malta and in North Africa. The range of the planes would preclude adequate fighter protection of an amphibious landing. The Catania area, within the extreme range of fighter aircraft, was also more attractive because of the assault beaches and a nearby group of airfields, but the port could be expected to handle initially the needs of only four divisions and later, after expansion of the port facilities, only six, four less than the ten needed for invasion. Palermo was adequate to supply ten divisions, but a landing near Palermo alone would leave the enemy in possession of the two other major ports—Messina and Catania—and a majority of the airfields. Also, it would be difficult, perhaps impossible, to land at Palermo alone forces superior to those that the Axis might quickly concentrate.

The London planners thus suggested two simultaneous assaults in the general areas of Palermo and Catania. Landings there would deny the Axis two of the island's major ports and most of the airfields; would block the major routes to Messina; and would reduce the enemy's ability to concentrate against a single landing.

The disadvantages of the Palermo-Catania scheme derived primarily from the great resources required. The two areas would not be mutually supporting. Each attacking force would have to be in sufficient strength to avoid defeat in detail. The forces and shipping required would be greatly increased over those for a single, concentrated attack. And unless the Italian Fleet were driven back into the Adriatic before the assaults, two naval covering forces would be required. Nevertheless, the planners concluded that a single assault would be feasible only if the Axis forces in Sicily numbered distinctly less than eight divisions, and only if enemy ability to make rapid reinforcements within the island and from the mainland were drastically reduced. If these conditions prevailed, a single assault could be considered in the Catania area.[3]

The CCS directive of 23 January ordering General Eisenhower to invade

---

[3] *Ibid.*

Sicily also established the chain of command and determined the organization for planning. General Eisenhower as Supreme Commander had the ultimate responsibility. General Alexander, named Deputy Commander in Chief, was charged "with the detailed planning and preparation and with the execution of the actual operation when launched," in effect, the ground command. Admiral Cunningham was to command the naval forces; Air Chief Marshal Tedder the air forces. Contemplating the use of two task forces, one American, the other British, the Combined Chiefs directed General Eisenhower to recommend the officers to be appointed to the subordinate command positions. Because the Tunisian campaign was still under way and attracted the major energies of AFHQ, the CCS also directed Eisenhower, in consultation with Alexander, to set up a special operational and administrative staff, separate from AFHQ, to plan the invasion.[4]

To command the British task force in the invasion, Eisenhower settled quickly on Gen. Sir Bernard L. Montgomery, the experienced Eighth Army commander. To lead the American force, he gave serious consideration to General Clark, who commanded the Fifth U.S. Army in French Morocco and who had demonstrated great diplomatic skill. But because Clark and his army, organized only in early January 1943, were charged with keeping French Morocco under control and with being ready to invade Spanish Morocco should Spain become less than neutral, Eisenhower turned instead to Maj. Gen. George S. Patton, Jr. Having commanded the Western Task Force in

GENERALS MONTGOMERY AND PATTON *in Sicily, July 1943.*

the North African invasion, having gained considerable combat experience in North Africa, and soon to be promoted to lieutenant general, Patton was, moreover, free for a new assignment. As commander of the U.S. I Armored Corps, not actively engaged in Tunisia, Patton had a staff already available to plan the American role in the Sicily invasion.[5]

CCS approval of Eisenhower's nominations set the scene for the contrasting operations of two of the most highly individualistic ground commanders of World War II. Patton was of the "rough and ready" school, Montgomery the "tidy" type. These differences in temperament, technique, and personality, to become markedly apparent in northwest Europe

---

[4] CCS 171/2/D, 23 Jan 43, Directive to CinC, Casablanca Conf Book, pp. 127-28.

[5] AFHQ NAF 143, 11 Feb 43, and AFHQ CofS Mtg 1, 25 Feb 43, both in 0100/12C/101; AFHQ, HUSKY, Min of Mtg, 10 Feb 43, 0100/4/59, I.

in 1944, were not pronounced during the early days of planning for Sicily; but before the campaign was over, the differences would be more than noticeable.[6]

In conformity with the CCS instructions to set up a separate headquarters to plan the invasion of Sicily, General Eisenhower in late January 1943 established in Algiers the nucleus of what became known as Force 141—from the number of the room in the St. George's Hotel where the originally assigned officers first met. The headquarters eventually moved into the École Normale in La Bouzaréa. Without administrative responsibilities, the staff remained a part of the AFHQ G-3 Section until the end of the Tunisian campaign, when, on 15 May, it became an independent operational headquarters. American officers assigned to Force 141 came for the most part from the United States, though some were transferred from the Fifth Army headquarters and others from the I Armored Corps. British personnel came largely from the United Kingdom and the Middle East. At the end of the Tunisian campaign, Alexander's 18 Army Group headquarters was deactivated and merged into Force 141; and on D-Day of the Sicily invasion the whole organization became the 15 Army Group headquarters, commanded by Alexander and with a staff of American and British officers who had served together and could make a combined headquarters work.

As deputy chief of staff and senior American representative in Force 141, General Eisenhower initially appointed Maj. Gen. Clarence R. Huebner, who soon found himself in a situation of friction. In this period of the war, in February 1943, General Alexander had a rather low estimate of the combat effectiveness of American troops. Though he considered the material, human and otherwise, magnificent, he deemed the American troops inexperienced and of little value in combat. Even at the end of the Tunisian campaign, Alexander would still consider them below the standard of the British fighting man. Apparently resenting this attitude, Huebner felt impelled to become the protector of American interests. Not until Brig. Gen. Lyman L. Lemnitzer succeeded Huebner in July 1943 would American relations with Alexander show marked improvement.[7]

Force 141 had difficult problems to solve. Lacking a G-2 Section, the force had to co-ordinate intelligence matters with AFHQ. Commanders who had been selected for roles in the invasion were actively engaged in Tunisia (Patton commanded the U.S. II Corps during most of March and April 1943) or scattered on three continents. Units were coming from the United States, the United Kingdom, and the Middle East. Because all the key personnel involved in

---

[6] Among the many characterizations of Patton are, for example, Omar N. Bradley, *A Soldier's Story* (New York: Henry Holt and Company, 1951), p. 159; Eisenhower, *Crusade in Europe*, pp. 40-41, 82, 176, 225; Maj W. G. Bell and Martin Blumenson, "Patton the Soldier," *Ordnance*, XLIII, No. 232 (January-February 1959), pp. 589-90. One of the best appraisals of Montgomery is found in Major General Sir Francis de Guingand, *Operation Victory* (New York: Charles Scribner's Sons, 1947), pp. 165-93.

[7] Intervs, Dr. Sidney T. Mathews with Field Marshal Alexander, 10-15 Jan 49, at Government House, Ottawa, Canada, pt. I, North Africa and Sicily, par. 22. The typescript of the interviews was submitted to Alexander and his corrections are inserted in ink. (All interviews cited in this volume are in OCMH, unless otherwise noted.)

the ground, sea, and air planning could not be gathered in one place, co-ordination of some aspects of the operation would still be somewhat lacking even on D-day.[8]

Designating Patton's I Armored Corps to head the American forces led to some confusion in command relationships, for another corps headquarters was also scheduled to take part in the operation. To clarify command channels and also to match the British organization, the I Armored Corps (Reinforced), known as Force 343 during the planning phase, would become the Seventh U.S. Army headquarters on D-day of the invasion.[9]

The major elements under Seventh Army control were to consist of one corps headquarters and six divisions—four infantry (one to be the follow-up force), one armored, and one airborne. Because of the desire to employ experienced units, the II Corps headquarters replaced the VI Corps, which had been originally assigned, and the 1st Infantry Division replaced the 36th Infantry Division.[10]

The British force, known as Force 545, as well as the Twelfth Army during the planning period, was somewhat larger. Under Eighth Army there would be two corps headquarters, the 13th and the 30th (a third, the 10th, was held in Tripoli), six infantry divisions, one armored division, one airborne division, a tank brigade, and an infantry brigade.[11]

---

[8] History of Allied Force Headquarters and Headquarters NATOUSA, December 1942–December 1943, pt. II, sec. 1, pp. 137–40 (copy in OCMH); Msg, Force 141 to AFHQ, 12 Feb 43, 0100/4/67, II; AFHQ JPS P/47 (Final), 26 Jan 43, Planning for HUSKY, and AFHQ Memo, 4 Feb 43, Formation of New Units, both in 0100/21/1207; Min of Mtg, Hotel St. George, 15 Apr 43, to discuss the Revised War Establishment and T/O of Hq Force 141, 0100/12C/854, with copy in 0100/4/59, I; AFHQ, Min of CofS Mtg 16, 19 Apr 43; Mtg 18, 26 Apr 43; Mtg 21, 10 May 43; and Mtg 23, 17 May 43, all in 0100/12C/101; Msg, 18 Army Gp to AFHQ, 0920, 13 May 43, 0100/21/1473. T/O for U.S. element of Hq Force 141 is contained in OPD 320.2 Security, sec. II, case 53; the allotment of grades is in same file, case 47.

[9] Ltr, AFHQ, AG 322.12/384 A–M, to CG I Armd Corps, 5 Apr 43, sub: Redesignation of Hq I Armd Corps and Activation of Force 141, job 10A, reel 80F; AFHQ Out Msg 3972 to AGWAR, 2 Mar 43, OPD Exec 3, item 13; Memo, Hull for Marshall, 13 May 43, sub: Br Twelfth Army, OPD Exec 3, item 1c; AFHQ In Msg SD/55602 from MidEast, 26 May 43, AFHQ CofS Cable Log; AFHQ Min of Exec Planning Mtg 39, 4 Jun 43, 0100/12A/146, I; AFHQ Out Msg 2003, 6 Apr 43, to AGWAR, OPD Exec 3, item 11; FREEDOM Out Msg 5008, 1 Apr 43, to NATOUSA, OPD Exec 3, item 10; NATOUSA Out Msg 332 to AGWAR, 30 Mar 43, and AFHQ Out Msg 9069 to AGWAR, 25 Mar 43, both in OPD Exec 3, item 13; AFHQ Min of Exec Planning Mtg 42, 11 Jun 43, 0100/12A/146, I; AFHQ, Min of CofS Mtg 22, 13 May 43; Mtg 24, 20 May 43; Mtg 27, 31 May 43; and Mtg 30, 10 Jun 43, all in 0100/12C/101. See also Matloff, *Strategic Planning for Coalition Warfare, 1943–1944*, pp. 148–49.

[10] The VI Corps and 36th Division went under Fifth Army control. See AFHQ NAF 185, 23 Mar 43, ABC 381 HUSKY (1943), sec. 1A; AFHQ Out Msg 7645 to AGWAR, 19 Mar 43, OPD Exec 3, item 13; AFHQ Min of Exec Planning Mtg 19, 19 Apr 43, 0100/12A/146, II; Ltr, Force 141 to Maj. Gen. Geoffrey Keyes, 16 Apr 43, Seventh Army G–3 File; AFHQ, Min of CofS Mtg 18, 28 Apr 43, and Mtg 21, 10 May 43, both in 0100/12C/101; AFHQ Out Msg 1828 to 18 Army Gp, 11 May 43, and AFHQ Out Msg 2384 to Fifth Army, 17 May 43, both in NARS; Report of Operations of the United States Seventh Army in the Sicilian Campaign, 10 July–17 August 1943 (hereafter cited as Seventh Army Rpt of Opns), pp. B–1–B–3.

[11] Twelfth Army Opns Order 1, 31 May 43, 0100/12A/141; app. A. to S.S.O. 17/3 (Final), 21 May 43, 0100/12A/182; Field Marshal Sir Bernard L. Montgomery, *Eighth Army: El Alamein to the River Sangro* (Germany: Printing and Stationery Services, Army of the Rhine, 1946) (hereafter cited as Montgomery, *Eighth Army*), pp. 89–90.

## The Plan

Detailed planning started on 12 February when Force 141 distributed copies of the basic design formulated by the London planners before the Casablanca Conference and accepted by the CCS.[12] Since General Alexander and his staff had not had an opportunity to study the plan in detail, Alexander accepted it as preliminary and tentative, recognizing the need of some modification.[13]

This plan sought to secure adequate port facilities and sufficient airfields by means of two simultaneous assaults: one in the west, the other in the southeast. Subsequent landings closer to the principal objectives were to follow at Palermo and Catania. Ten divisions were to be ashore in a week.

Though this plan in some respects looked like an intended double envelopment of the enemy forces in Sicily, it was in reality focused less on enemy troops than on the ports of Palermo and Catania. A provision for the immediate seizure of all the important airfields would add to the dispersal of the assault forces because the airfields were widely scattered throughout the island. The great disadvantage, as already mentioned, was the fact that the two task forces would not be mutually supporting. Thus, the enemy might concentrate against either one and roll it back into the sea. Though General Alexander considered landing both task forces together in a concentrated assault against the southeastern corner, he rejected the idea temporarily because his staff believed that the port facilities that could be seized in a single assault (Catania, Syracuse, and Augusta) would be inadequate to support the total Allied forces required for the operation.[14]

The commander of the British invasion force, General Montgomery, found the CCS concept objectionable on another ground. His Eighth Army was to land in a great arc around the southeastern tip of Sicily, with part coming ashore on the southwestern side near the ports of Gela and Licata, the remainder on the eastern face. Those forces landing on the eastern side were more important because they were oriented toward the ports of Syracuse and Augusta as immediate objectives. Yet the CCS had designated only about a third of the initial British assault force—one division plus a brigade—to make these landings. This seemed hardly enough, and in mid-March Montgomery emphatically indicated that he could not accept the plan as presented.

To Montgomery the plan was valid only against weak Italian opposition. Against German troops, or against Italian troops backed by Germans, the plan seemed to be of little value. Montgomery wanted another division in his main assault on the eastern face of Sicily, and to get it he recommended elimination of the landings in the Gela-Licata area. Not only would this make his main landings stronger, but his army would be united, an important point in Montgomery's concept of any tactical operation. Though he realized that his substitute

---

[12] Force 141 Planning Inst 1, 12 Feb 43, printed in Alexander Despatch, pp. 30–31.

[13] AFHQ JPS P/53 (Final), 2 Feb 43, Preliminary Directive to Commanders of Ground, Naval, and Air Forces, 0100/12A/103. I; AFHQ Preliminary Directive to CinC's of Naval, Ground, and Air Forces, 2 Feb 43, 0403/10/300; AFHQ Out Msg 4063 to MidEast and Malta, ABC 381 HUSKY (1943), sec. 1A.

[14] Alexander Despatch, p. 5.

plan did not provide for the seizure of some airfields, it seemed to him that even if he took the airfields, he would be unable to hold them with the two divisions allotted for that task.[15]

Air force and naval commanders immediately raised a hue and cry. Air Chief Marshal Tedder pointed out that failure to land in the Gela-Licata area and to occupy the group of airfields there would not only "gravely affect the whole air situation in the Southeast corner of Sicily" but would also "seriously increase the risk of loss of the big ships involved in certain of these assaults." To Tedder, this was intolerable, even when he made allowance for the weakening of the enemy air strength which Tedder was "determined to achieve before the assault takes place." To the Allied air commander, air superiority was as vital as securing the ports, and the only sure way to weaken air opposition critically was to capture the enemy's airfields.[16]

Admiral Cunningham agreed with Tedder. He preferred attacking with widely dispersed forces instead of concentrating against what Cunningham considered the most strongly defended part of the island. Furthermore, Montgomery's plan would involve a large number of ships lying offshore with protection against air attack severely lessened by failure to take the airfields in the Gela-Licata area.[17]

While General Alexander recognized as valid the points raised by the air and naval commanders, he nevertheless accepted Montgomery's modification "from a purely military point of view."[18] He agreed to transfer the British forces from the Gela-Licata landings to strengthen those on the east coast. But to satisfy the air and naval requirements, Alexander reached into the U.S. task force and plucked the U.S. 3d Infantry Division for use in the British sector under Montgomery's command. The 3d Divison, scheduled for a D-day landing far up the southwestern coast near the western end of the island, was to sideslip southeastward to make the Gela-Licata landings. To compensate in some degree for this weakening of the American assault, he proposed that the American landings be delayed several days until the British were ashore and thus, presumably, had attracted the bulk of the opposition.[19]

General Patton objected to the loss of the 3d Division. The Montgomery plan assumed, Patton felt, that enemy airfields in the American sector would be so neutralized prior to the invasion that adequate air support for the main American landings would be assured. But since the same thesis when applied to the Gela-Licata airfields had been acceptable neither to the air forces and Navy, nor "presumably" to Montgomery and Alexander, it was "no less unacceptable" to Patton when applied to the Palermo airfields. For under the Montgomery plan, the American assault on Palermo could be made only if the British were highly

---

[15] Opn HUSKY: Comdrs Mtgs, 0410/2/297; AFHQ, Min of CofS Mtg 7, 18 Mar 43, 0100/12C/101; Alexander Despatch, p. 6; De Guingand, *Operation Victory*, pp. 249–50.

[16] Ltr, Tedder to Alexander, 18 Mar 43, 0100/4/66, II; Opn HUSKY: Comdrs Mtgs, 0410/2/297.

[17] Alexander Despatch, p. 6; Andrew B. Cunningham, *A Sailor's Odyssey: The Autobiography of Admiral of the Fleet Viscount Cunningham of Hyndhope* (London, New York: Hutchinson and Co., 1951), p. 535.

[18] AFHQ, Min of CofS Mtg 7, 18 Mar 43, 0100/12C/101.

[19] AFHQ NAF 182, 20 Mar 43, ABC 381 HUSKY (1943), sec. 1A; Alexander Despatch, p. 6.

successful, that is, if the enemy defenders cracked completely. Furthermore, withdrawal of a division from the U.S. troop list would not only weaken the American assault force but also would deprive the Americans of close air support from the airfields the 3d Division was to have taken. If the British were stopped after getting the bulk of their divisions ashore, would all the forces be withdrawn from Sicily? Or would Patton continue trying to carry out an operation predicated on prior British success? Under Montgomery's plan, Patton believed, the Americans were provided with inadequate forces.[20]

Despite Patton's protest, General Eisenhower approved the new plan because of "the obvious fact that initial success in the southeast is vital to the whole project." Even though the change made the later U.S. landings more difficult because air support expected from Montgomery's area would not equal that which the original plan had contemplated, as Eisenhower admitted, "the decision must stand, under the existing circumstances."[21] At the same time, Eisenhower began to seek another division he could assign to Montgomery in order to move the U.S. division back to its original landing area. The problem was less that of finding additional troops than of finding the shipping necessary to transport an additional division to Sicily.[22]

When the British eventually provided another division and the necessary shipping for Montgomery's assault, Alexander on 6 April returned the U.S. 3d Division to Patton. But he still retained the features of staggered landings. The 3d Division was to assault on D plus 2 rather than on D-day as originally planned, and the other American landings in the Palermo area were moved back to D plus 5, by which time the 3d Division would have secured the airfields in its zone, thereby affording air support for the Palermo landings.[23]

None of the ground force commanders selected for the Sicily operation could, in this early period, devote much attention to planning. Alexander was busy with ground operations in Tunisia. Patton had been shifted on 7 March to temporary command of the U.S. II Corps, also in Tunisia. Montgomery's attention was devoted to the immediate task of commanding the British Eighth Army. It was, as Montgomery subsequently put it, a period of "absentee landlordism."[24] The planning staffs of Forces 343 and 545 largely functioned without benefit of the views of those on whom the responsibility for successful execution of the plan would fall.

For all their inability to devote full attention to the Sicilian planning, few of the commanders involved were satisfied

---

[20] Ltr, Hq Force 343 to CinC Allied Forces, 23 Mar 43, sub: Outline Plan for Opn HUSKY, 0100/12C/645, IV.

[21] AFHQ NAF 182 and 185, 20 and 23 Mar 43, ABC 381 HUSKY (1943), sec. 1A; Ltr, Eisenhower to Alexander, 23 Mar 43, 0100/4/66, II; Ltr, AFHQ to Force 343, 26 Mar 43, sub: Outline Plan for Opn HUSKY, 0100/12C/645, IV.

[22] Memo, JSP for U.S. JCS, 25 Mar 43, and CCS 161/5, 26 Mar 43, both in ABC 381 HUSKY (1943), sec. 2; Memo, COS for CCS, COS (W) 546, 25 Mar 43, ABC 381 HUSKY (1943), sec.

1B; GHQ MEF, Min of Mtg, 28 Mar 43, 9th Mtg, 0100/4/59, I; AFHQ, Min of CofS Mtg 8, 22 Mar 43, and Mtg 9, 25 Mar 43, 0100/12C/101.

[23] Min of AFHQ Exec Planning Mtg 14, 7 Apr 43; Mtg 15, 9 Apr 43; and Mtg 16, 12 Apr 43, all in 0100/12A/146, II. Map in ABC 381 HUSKY (1943), sec. 2, shows the approved plan. Also, see Alexander Despatch, p. 7.

[24] Rpt of 21 Army Gp Mission on Opn HUSKY, 15 Aug 43, 21 Army GP/89/Opns; Montgomery, *Eighth Army*, p. 86.

# PREPARATIONS AND PRELIMINARIES

with Alexander's latest solution. Still concerned over what he considered too dispersed landings, Montgomery sent his own chief of staff, Maj. Gen. Francis de Guingand, to Cairo to serve at Force 545 headquarters as his deputy and chief of staff. Arriving in Cairo on 17 April, de Guingand for the next several days carefully studied the 6 April outline plan, and discussed it with Lt. Gen. Miles C. Dempsey, commander of the British 13 Corps, earmarked to participate in the operation. De Guingand's analysis of the new plan agreed with that of his chief— a much greater concentration would be required if the Allies were to overcome resistance on a scale similar to that encountered in North Africa.[25]

His reasoning having been confirmed, Montgomery himself flew to Cairo on 23 April for additional study and consultation. Though Montgomery appreciated the need to seize ports and airfields, he considered the plan to be based on an underestimate of enemy capabilities. "To spread four divisions, with a relatively slow build-up of forces behind them, between the Gulf of Catania and the Gulf of Gela," he wrote later, "obviously implied negligible resistance to our assault and a decision by the enemy not to send reinforcements from Italy to oppose us." On 24 April he made known his objection in a message to Alexander. "Planning so far has been based on the assumption that the opposition will be slight and that Sicily will be captured rather easily," he wired. "Never was there a greater error. The Germans and also the Italians are fighting desperately now in Tunisia and will do so in Italy."[26]

What Montgomery wanted was to confine the British landings within a much more restricted area in order to give his force more strength in the assault. He urged that his landings be restricted to the Gulf of Noto (south of Syracuse) and the two sides of the Pachino peninsula. Since this area was within range of fighter planes based on Malta, the landings would have adequate air cover. From a beachhead in the Gulf of Noto, the port of Syracuse might be captured rapidly, and operations could then be extended northward to secure Augusta and Catania. Most important of all, his whole force would be concentrated.

Montgomery's proposed plan received no enthusiastic reception in Algiers. Alexander again faced conflicting army and air-naval demands. Tedder and Cunningham still pointed to additional airfields (at Ponte Olivo, near Gela, and Comiso) which they wanted included in the beachhead. Montgomery countered by asking for two more assault divisions. Only with additional strength, he said, could he extend the beachhead as far as Gela.[27]

Though Alexander called a new conference for 27 April in Algiers to iron out the differences, it had to be postponed two days when Montgomery's representative, de Guingand, suffered injuries in an aircraft crash en route to the conference. Lt. Gen. Oliver Leese, com-

---

[25] De Guingand, *Operation Victory*, pp. 269, 272–74.

[26] Montgomery, *Eighth Army*, pp. 86–87; De Guingand, *Operation Victory*, p. 278; Alexander Despatch, p. 7.

[27] Montgomery, *Eighth Army*, pp. 87–88; De Guingand, *Operation Victory*, p. 280.

GENERAL DEMPSEY

mander of the British 30 Corps, took his place.[28]

The conference at Algiers of 29 April was less than conclusive. After ably presenting Montgomery's arguments, Leese introduced a new concept. He proposed that the basic design of the two-pronged attack be abandoned and that both the United States and the British forces assault the southeastern corner, the British along the Gulf of Noto and the Americans close by on both sides of the Pachino peninsula. Admiral Cunningham at once demurred, citing his conviction that amphibious landings should be dispersed, not concentrated, and that the enemy airfields had to be taken at the earliest possible moment in order to protect the shipping which would be lying off the beaches, less than thirty miles away. Air Chief Marshal Tedder objected even more vigorously. He pointed out that the new plan would leave thirteen airfields in enemy hands, far more than could be neutralized by air action alone. Tedder declared he would oppose the whole operation unless the plan included prompt seizure of the principal Sicilian airfields.

The deadlock was now complete. The contradictory demands of army, navy, and air could not be reconciled on the plan proposed either by Alexander or by Montgomery.[29]

To break the deadlock, General Eisenhower called another conference in Algiers on 2 May. Though Alexander was unable to attend because of bad flying weather, Montgomery appeared in person to state his views. On the following day, Eisenhower accepted the new Montgomery proposal. The invasion of Sicily, the first large-scale amphibious assault to be made by the Allies against a coast line expected to be staunchly defended, was to be a concentrated thrust limited to the southeastern part of the island.[30]

Alexander's plan of 3 May, issued as an order later that month, embodied Montgomery's strategic conception.[31] The independent American assault on the

---

[28] Alexander Despatch, p. 8; De Guingand, *Operation Victory*, p. 281.

[29] Alexander Despatch, p. 8.

[30] Min of AFHQ Exec Planning Mtg 26, 5 May 43; Mtg 27, 7 May 43; and Mtg 28, 10 May 43, all in 0100/12A/146, II; AFHQ NAF 215, 5 May 43, 0403/10/321; CCS 161/6, 10 May 43, ABC 381 HUSKY (1943), sec. 3; Ltr, AFHQ to Force 141, 8 May 43, sub: Directives to Task Force Comdrs, 0100/12C/331, II; Memo, Force 141 to Patton, 141/F/G(P), 3 May 43, sub: Change in Plan for HUSKY, Seventh Army G-3 File.

[31] Force 141 Opn Inst 2, 21 May 43, printed in Alexander Despatch, pp. 74-83.

western corner of Sicily was discarded. The whole weight of the U.S. force was shifted to the southeastern corner with landings to be made along the Gulf of Gela from Licata eastward to the Pachino peninsula. The whole weight of the British force was concentrated on the coastal sector from the Pachino peninsula almost to Syracuse. The new plan did not embody such a radical bunching of assaults as General Leese had proposed on 29 April because the American sector was considerably extended to the northwest.

Moving the entire assault to the southeastern corner of Sicily in effect rejected the CCS concept of the necessity to take major ports and airfields quickly. For the Americans, it meant no major port at all—they would have to rely for their supplies on maintenance over the beaches for an indefinite period of time. The exclusion as immediate objectives of both the cluster of airfields in the southwest and the complex in the Catania-Gerbini area disturbed air officers, as well as Admiral Cunningham, who continued to have misgivings on what he considered the sacrifice of the tactical advantage of dispersion.

Whatever the merits of dispersion versus concentration, there was no gainsaying the loss of airfields. And this led to a new Allied focus on the island of Pantelleria.

*Other Factors*

One of the major questions that concerned the planners was whether the Axis would reinforce the island defenders beyond Allied expectations. According to Allied estimates the Axis garrison consisted of three major elements: Italian coastal divisions, Italian field divisions,

GENERAL LEESE

and German units. All were under the Italian *Sixth Army* headquarters at Enna which controlled two corps and four Italian field divisions. The *XII Corps* commanded the *28th (Aosta)* and the *26th (Assietta) Infantry Divisions* in the northwest corner of the island. The *XVI Corps* controlled the *4th (Livorno)* and the *54th (Napoli) Infantry Divisions*, in position to counter a landing on both sides of the Pachino peninsula in the southeast. Five or six coastal divisions added to this strength.[32]

---

[32] Hq Force 343, FO 1, 20 Jun 43, an. II, Seventh Army Rpt of Opns, p. d-7ff; Alexander Despatch, pp. 15-16.

For some time, Allied intelligence officers mistakenly believed that the *103d (Piacenza) Infantry Division* was south of Catania. The mistake, as Alexander stated, "was discovered before it could have any untoward effect."

How well would the Italian units fight? A few bold spirits among Allied planners predicted that the Italians would be a pushover. Their arms and equipment were well below the standards of German, British, and American divisions. The *Sixth Army* had no combat experience. Sicilians made up a high proportion of all units. "Ersatz stuff, all of it," one American officer said. "Stick them in the belly and sawdust will run out." [33]

But no one really knew. Fighting on home soil, they might have higher morale than in North Africa. To be safe, the Allies assumed that the Italians on Sicily would resist strenuously.[34]

Allied intelligence discovered two German divisions in support of the Italians. Though definite data on the German order of battle in Sicily was hard to come by, the information was accurate. Not until the approach of D-day, however, did a relatively clear picture emerge. Of the two German divisions identified in Sicily, the *15th Panzer Grenadier* and the *Hermann Goering*, the latter was somewhat puzzling, for it had been destroyed in Tunisia. Apparently, then, it had been reconstituted. The *15th Panzer Grenadier Division* was divided into three battle groups, one in the extreme western part of the island, the second near the center (together with division headquarters), the third near Catania. Shortly before D-day, division headquarters and the center battle group moved to the west.

The *Hermann Goering Division* was also divided, but into only two battle groups, one in the Catania area, with supervision over the panzer grenadier battle group already there, the other poised for action in the southeast and capable of operating against the Gela and Comiso airfields. The distribution of forces indicated that the enemy anticipated landings on the southwestern corner, along the Gulf of Gela, near Catania, and along the Gulf of Noto. The Germans had not reinforced Sicily to the extent possible, a failure the Allies correctly attributed to their cover plan.[35]

The efforts of the Allies to disguise their intentions were based in the main on a central cover plan requested by Force 141 and developed in London by British intelligence. One part of this plan, known as Operation MINCEMEAT, was designed to convince the enemy high command that the objectives of the impending Allied offensive in the Mediterranean were Sardinia and the Peloponnesus rather than Sicily. The plan itself was simple but highly imaginative. With painstaking care a counterfeit letter from "Archie Nye" of the British War Office in London was drawn up and addressed to General Alexander. Indicating that a feint against Sicily would be a deception maneuver to screen an invasion of Sardinia, the letter suggested that Gen. Sir Henry Maitland Wilson, the British commander in chief in the Middle East, veil his thrust against the Greek mainland by simulating action against the Dodecanese islands.

To get this letter into Axis hands, British intelligence obtained with great difficulty the body of a service man who had been a victim of pneumonia. Endowed with the fictitious personality of Major Martin of the Royal Marines, the corpse, whose lungs and general condition would

---

[33] Quotations from *A Soldier's Story*, by Omar N. Bradley, p. 114. Copyright 1951 by Holt, Rinehart and Winston, Inc. Reprinted by permission of Holt, Rinehart and Winston, Inc.

[34] Msg 8707, AFHQ to TROOPERS, 7 Jun 43, job 24, reel 118D.

[35] Alexander Despatch, pp. 15–17.

# PREPARATIONS AND PRELIMINARIES

indicate death by drowning, was carried in a sealed container by a British submarine to the coastal waters of Spain. With a courier's briefcase realistically chained to the wrist, the body was cast adrift at a predesignated spot where tide and current would carry it to shore.

Three days after the submarine accomplished its mission, London received a telegram from the British Naval Attaché in Madrid to the effect that the counterfeit body of Major Martin, "the man who never was," had been picked up by friends of the Axis, who believed him to be an official messenger drowned after an aerial mishap. Subsequent scrutiny of the contents of the brief case, after the body had been duly transferred to British authorities in neutral Spain, indicated that Archie Nye's letter had been opened, then refolded and replaced.

The information reached the Germans who accepted it as authentic. On 12 May the OKW directed that measures to be taken in Sardinia and the Peloponnesus were to have priority over any others.[36]

The other part of the HUSKY cover plan, Plan BARCLAY, sought to inspire the Axis to give priority to maintaining and reinforcing its sizable forces in southern France and in the Balkans.[37] If these areas appeared subject to imminent attack, the Germans would be loath to weaken them in favor of reinforcing Sicily.

By the end of June, German intelligence could not yet decide the ultimate purpose of bogus shifts of Allied troops along the North African coast and other signs of impending invasion. Corsica seemed in no immediate danger, but whether the Allies would attack the Balkans, Sicily, Sardinia, or any combination of targets was far from clear.[38]

Not all the Axis commanders were deceived. To some the signs were unmistakable. Increased Allied air attacks, increased naval activity, and the concentration of ground forces near North African ports of embarkation argued for the contention that Sicily was next.

While Allied feints were in process, some Allied planners began to wonder whether an earlier invasion of Sicily might be advantageous. If the Axis forces on Sicily were actually as confused and unprepared as they seemed, would it not be better to strike at the island just as soon as the Allies destroyed the Axis armies in North Africa? The prospect particularly attracted planners in Washington. Several times during April and May they raised the question of the feasibility of what would be in effect an *ad hoc* HUSKY.[39] In North Africa, too, AFHQ

---

[36] Memo, Gen.St.d.H., Abt. Fremde Heere West, Nr. 874/43, g.K., 9 May 43, and Telg, Fremde Heere West, Nr. 27/43, g.Kdos. Chefs., 12 May 43, both in OKH/Op.Abt., Allgemein Mittelmeer, Chefs., 9.III.–29.XII.43 (H 22/147); Telg, OKW/WFSt/Op. Nr. 661055/43, g. Kdos. Chefs., 12 May 43, ONI, *Fuehrer Directives, 1942–1945*, pp. 79–80; Ewen Montagu, *The Man Who Never Was* (Philadelphia: J. B. Lippincott Company, 1954); Cf. *Goebbels Diaries*, p. 394.

[37] Force 141, Intelligence Opns Prior to 10 Jul. Salmon Files, 5–G–1–1b; Plan BARCLAY, 0100/4/308; Progress Rpt on Plan BARCLAY, folder 3, job III, NWD, Record Group 13, NARS.

[38] SKL/1. Abt., KTB, Teil A. 1.–30.VI.43, 13 and 14 Jun 43 (see Bibliographical Note); Rpt, Beurteilung der Lage auf den Inseln Sizilien, Sardinien und Korsika, Der Oberbefehlshaber Sued, Fuehrungsabteilung to GenStdH/Op. Abt. (II), 30 Jun 43, OKH/Op. Abt., Westl. Mittelmeer, Chefs., 19.V.43–11.VII.44 (H 22/290) (cited hereafter as Westl. Mittelmeer. Chefs. (H 22/290).

[39] Msg, FORTUNE 116, 117, 118, to AFHQ, 18 Apr 43, and Msg, OPD 164 to AFHQ, 30 Apr 43, both in OPD Exec 3, item 10; Memo, Strategy Sec Strategy and Planning Gp OPD to Gen Marshall, 12 Apr 43; Msg, OPD 3465 to AFHQ, 18 Apr 43; and Memo, U.S. JSP for U.S. CofS, 19 Apr 43, all in OPD 381 Security, sec. 1B.

planners were working on a plan for a surprise landing in Sicily in conjunction with an amphibious assault—Operation VULCAN—against the remaining Axis forces still holding out on Cape Bon.[40]

To General Eisenhower and his principal subordinate commanders, however, an *ad hoc* HUSKY seemed impractical and almost impossible. As Eisenhower informed the Combined Chiefs in April, AFHQ was finding it difficult enough to meet the requirements of a formal invasion in the time required. To prepare alternate plans would undoubtedly cause a delay.[41]

In response, General Marshall suggested that "your planners and mine may be too conservative in their analyses." The element of suprise contained in a modified HUSKY, Marshall continued, and the lack of time afforded the enemy to strengthen his forces in Sicily lent tremendous advantages to an early HUSKY and "may justify your accepting calculated risks." Planners were notoriously orthodox, Marshall added. They lacked the boldness and daring "which won great victories for Nelson and Grant and Lee." Eisenhower's conclusion, he noted, might "suggest a lack of adaptability."[42]

General Eisenhower was quick to reply. AFHQ planners were continually searching, he said, for ways to exploit success. Quite obviously, stronger invasion forces would be necessary after the Axis had had two months to prepare Sicily's defenses. "I am willing," he wrote, "to take the risk of capturing important Southeastern airfields with no greater strength than that necessary to hang on to a bridgehead while all of the later strength is brought along to exploit the initial success." But AFHQ was having enough trouble getting the ground, naval, and air commanders to agree on the landing sites; securing their agreement on an earlier operation would be almost impossible.[43]

Making his final decision on 10 May, Eisenhower concluded there would be no impromptu invasion to try to exploit the confusion among the Axis forces incident to their final defeat in North Africa. He so informed the Combined Chiefs on the following day. "We have not sufficient landing craft at the moment," he wrote, "to carry a total of more than one division and, of this, assault landing craft for one regimental combat team only. I consider an attack with less than two divisions . . . too great a risk. . . ." The prospect of having more landing ships and craft later in the year made a thoroughly planned operation infinitely more desirable.[44]

Hardly had this matter been settled when a new CCS directive arrived. It embodied the decision reached at the TRIDENT Conference: to continue Mediterranean operations after Sicily with the purpose of eliminating Italy from the war and containing the maximum number of German forces. While Mr. Churchill was in Algiers immediately after

---

[40] AFHQ JPS P/75, 4 May 43, job 10A, reel 138E; AFHQ JPS P/64 (Final), 2 Apr 43, job 10A, reel 13M.

[41] Msgs 7728 and 7729, AFHQ to AGWAR, 28 Apr 43, OPD Exec 3, item 11.

[42] Msg, FORTUNE 164 to AFHQ, 30 Apr 43, OPD Exec 3, item 10.

[43] Msg, AFHQ Out 9271 to AGWAR, 4 May 43, Smith Papers.

[44] AFHQ, Rcd of Mtg Held by CinC AF, 10 May 43, 0100/4/59, I; AFHQ JPS P/75 (Third Draft), 10 May 43, job 10A, reel 138E; Msg, AFHQ Out W-305 to AGWAR, 11 May 43, Diary Office CinC, Book VI, p. A-373; see also Memo for Personal Rcd, 1 Jul 43, Diary Office CinC, Book VII, p. A-515.

TRIDENT, AFHQ continued its planning of future operations in the Mediterranean. Despite Churchill's efforts to badger General Eisenhower and his staff into a direct attack on the Italian mainland, AFHQ studied several alternative courses: attacks against Sardinia and Corsica, followed by an invasion of the Tyrrhenian coast, and attacks against the toe and sole of the Italian boot. The chief tangible result of Churchill's visit was his definite offer to make some eight British divisions then in the Middle East available to AFHQ.

General Rooks, the AFHQ G-3, on 3 June outlined the general scheme of AFHQ's alternative operations. It differed from earlier plans drawn in May only in its elimination of MUSKET (an amphibious attack against Taranto) as a possibility. BUTTRESS, an assault on the toe near Reggio, and GOBLET, an assault near Crotone, were the operations proposed. Provided that conditions were auspicious, the two assaults would be closely correlated and the objective would be, not the mere occupation of the Calabrian peninsula, but the seizure of Calabrian ports and airfields to enable Allied forces to march overland and gain control of port facilities adequate to maintain a larger force in southern Italy. An advance up the west coast to Naples or a drive to Taranto and the southern Adriatic ports in the heel were alternatives.[45]

Invasions of Sardinia and Corsica were considered to be easier. The Allies would need a separate headquarters to plan and execute the operation, though follow-up forces might be drawn from Sicily. The U.S. Fifth Army, under General Clark, appeared to be the logical headquarters for the task, which might be launched by 1 October. It was also decided that the Fifth Army would be directly under AFHQ's command.

On 10 June, therefore, General Eisenhower directed General Clark to prepare plans for seizing Sardinia, a task Fifth Army completed by the end of the month. Eisenhower also asked General Giraud, French commander in North Africa, to name a commander and a staff to plan an assault on Corsica as a purely French operation.

The plans for seizing Sardinia and Corsica at this time were alternative courses to be followed in case AFHQ judged an attack on the Italian mainland too risky. This denoted a change in AFHQ strategy. Before the Casablanca Conference, General Eisenhower would have preferred Sardinia over Sicily if, at that time, the ultimate objective had been fixed as the invasion and occupation of the Italian mainland. In early May, likewise, Eisenhower endorsed Rooks' strategic concept that the next operations after Sicily should be the occupation of Sardinia and Corsica. Once the Allies controlled the airfields on those islands, they would be able to mount amphibious attacks against southern France or against any point along the western coast of Italy. But since the CCS after the TRIDENT Conference had defined AFHQ's mission as eliminating Italy from the war, the occupation of Sardinia and Corsica and intensified aerial bombing attacks hardly seemed likely in June to be sufficient to force the Italian Government out of the war. The considered opinion of AFHQ's intelligence agencies was that Italy would collapse only after the Allies had invaded

---

[45] AFHQ JPS P/87 (Final), 3 Jun 43, job 54A, reel 88 Special.

the mainland and were marching on Naples and Rome.

By the last week of June, AFHQ had delegated the detailed planning of mainland operations to 15 Army Group (still using the code name Force 141), while the Fifth Army worked on the invasion of Sardinia. By then, BUTTRESS, the invasion of the toe, had been assigned to the British 10 Corps, and GOBLET, the invasion of the sole, to the British 5 Corps. No time schedule for these operations could be forecast, but their sequence seemed evident. BUTTRESS would have to wait one month after Sicily, and GOBLET one month after BUTTRESS. Thus, if the Sicilian Campaign ended 1 August, BUTTRESS might be launched 1 September, GOBLET the following month. If no mainland operations were undertaken, the assault on Sardinia might be launched, Eisenhower believed, by 1 October.[46]

These cautious plans for attack on the Italian mainland inspired little enthusiam at AFHQ. BUTTRESS and GOBLET promised only a toe hold on the Calabrian peninsula. They offered small hope of striking a blow to Italy capable of eliminating it from the war; they did not even guarantee an area suitable as a base for future large-scale operations. What the Allies needed was a strike at Rome. But such a step demanded the prior seizure of ports. And this in turn led to preoccupation with Naples. Various proposals for overland approaches ran into the problem of the intervening terrain— the ground in southern Italy favored the defense. Until there were more definite indications of a weakening of Italian morale, Allied commanders fitted all the schemes for gaining adequate ports on the mainland into a cautious framework— capturing the toe of Italy first. The Allies were aware, however, that success in Sicily might open new and exciting courses of action.[47]

---

[46] JIC Algiers, Estimates on Italian Morale, 29 Jun 43, job 10A, reel 17C; Br JP (43) 218 (Final), an. II, 21 Jun 43, Mediterranean Strategy, job 10A, reel 21C; an. I, 21 Jun 43, to Br JP (43) 218 (Final), sub: Note by C.G.S., MidEast; HF/M/2, Mtg to Discuss Future Opns in Mediterranean, 14 Jun 43, job 10A, reel 18C; COS (43) 134th Mtg, 23 Jun 43, item 2, job 10A, reel 21C; Notes of Mtg at Hq Force 141 on 24 Jun 43 To Discuss the Mounting of Opns BUTTRESS and GOBLET, job 26A, reel 225B; AFHQ JPS P/92 (Final), 26 Jun 43, sub: Memo G-3 AFHQ for CofS AFHQ, Post-HUSKY Opns, job 10C, reel 138E; Msg, AFHQ NAF 250 to CCS, 29 Jun 43, printed in Alexander, Allied Armies in Italy, vol. I, an. II to app. B, pp. 60–63; Min of AFHQ Exec Planning Mtg 2, 7 Jul 43, job 61C, reel 138C.

[47] See further discussion below in section one of Chapter XIV, Sardinia Versus the Mainland.

## CHAPTER IV

# The Axis Situation

### Pantelleria

A small island about eight miles long, five miles wide, Pantelleria is rugged, with sheer cliffs rising out of the sea. The few small areas of level ground were intensively cultivated except around the airfield, which could handle eighty single-engine fighter aircraft. About 120 miles southwest of Palermo, Pantelleria is about the same distance as Malta from Catania.

Since late 1940, the British had wanted to reduce Pantelleria in order to remove the air threat which it posed. But by the time the British could devote some attention and effort to the problem, the German Air Force had moved into Sicily, making the risks of assaulting Pantelleria too great. British plans lay dormant until the end of 1942, when they began to receive consideration.[1] Still, seizing Pantelleria would not be easy, for by the spring of 1943 the island was a seemingly impregnable fortress garrisoned by about 12,000 troops, with underground aircraft hangars hewn from solid rock impervious to bombardment.

AFHQ began to look hard at Pantelleria in early February 1943, when General Marshall informed General Eisenhower that the U.S. Navy could not provide eight auxiliary aircraft carriers requested for air cover of the American assault on Sicily. Marshall suggested instead that Eisenhower seize Pantelleria for its airfield, from which Allied fighters could support the Sicily operation.[2]

Though Eisenhower at first was not impressed, he set his staff to prepare a plan to reduce Pantelleria, but only "if the capture became necessary."[3] The conclusion of the planners was unfavorable. Pantelleria posed difficult problems even if unlimited resources were available. With preparations for Sicily limiting available resources sharply, Pantelleria seemed altogether too tough. Pantelleria could be taken only at the expense of postponing the Sicilian assault, and planners felt that the importance of Pantelleria to the success of HUSKY was too small to justify delay.[4]

So the matter rested until May, when the invasion plan moved the entire Allied assault to the southeastern corner of Sicily. General Eisenhower again con-

---

[1] Winston S. Churchill, "The Second World War," vol. III, *The Grand Alliance* (Boston: Houghton Mifflin Co., 1950), pp. 56–59.

[2] Msg. AGWAR Out 2152, 12 Feb 43, and Msg. AFHQ Out 1413, 17 Feb 43, both in 0100/21/1079; Ltr, King to Marshall, 11 Feb 43, sub: Opn HUSKY—Employment of ACV's (auxiliary aircraft carriers), WDCSA HUSKY.

[3] Msg, AFHQ Out 1409 to AGWAR, 17 Feb 43, OPD Cable File.

[4] AFHQ JPS P/58 (Third Draft), 30 Mar 43; Memos, AFHQ G-3 for AFHQ CofS, sub: Capture of Pantelleria, 4 May 43, and Interrelationships of Certain Opns, 9 May 43, all in 0100/12C/311, II.

sidered seizing Pantelleria. He admitted that there were disadvantages in such an operation: possible heavy losses in men, ships, and landing craft, which could be ill afforded on the eve of the Sicilian invasion; the fact that a successful defense at Pantelleria would put heart into the Sicilian defenders at a time when "we sought to break it;" and the fact that the operation would point rather obviously to the next Allied move in the Mediterranean. Yet Eisenhower now saw great advantages in having the island: better air cover for the American landings; removal of a serious Axis threat to Allied air and naval operations during the Sicilian invasion; the use of Pantelleria as a navigational aid for Allied aircraft and for bases for air-sea rescue launches; denial of Pantelleria as a refueling base for enemy E-boats and submarines; and elimination of enemy radio direction finder and shipwatching stations to insure a better possibility of achieving tactical surprise for the Sicilian invasion.[5]

Intelligence reports were promising. Only five Italian infantry battalions, for the most part untested in battle, defended Pantelleria, and they were supported mainly by antiaircraft batteries manned by militia troops. The only evidence of the state of their morale was "the poor display of the antiaircraft gunners when our air forces raided on 8 May."[6]

On 10 May, perhaps still stung by General Marshall's rebuke on his "lack of adaptability," Eisenhower decided to seize Pantelleria, but without expending heavily in men or matériel. To obviate a full-scale assault, Eisenhower thought of making the operation "a sort of laboratory to determine the effect of concentrated heavy bombing on a defended coastline." He wished the Allied air forces "to concentrate everything" in blasting the island so that the damage to the garrison, its equipment and morale, would be "so serious as to make the landing a rather simple affair." Constant artillery pounding on the defenders of Corregidor in 1942 seemed to have had that effect and Eisenhower wanted "to see whether the air can do the same thing."[7]

The British 1st Infantry Division, supported by appropriate naval forces, was to follow the bombardment and seize and occupy the island. The smaller nearby Pelagian Islands—Lampedusa, Linosa, and Lampione—were also to come under attack.[8]

All three services established a headquarters at Sousse and went to work. Increasingly heavy air bombardments and a naval shoot soon reduced Pantel-

---

[5] Msg, AFHQ Out W-2460 to AGWAR, 11 Jun 43, 0100/21/1079; Col. Joseph I. Greene, "Operation CORKSCREW: Tough Decision," *Infantry Journal*, vol. LIX, No. 5 (November, 1946), pp. 20-21.

[6] Eisenhower's Pantelleria Dispatch, copy in OCMH: app. XL to the Zuckerman Rpt, 0100/11/966 and 0100/21/1081, II. Professor S. Zuckerman was the scientific adviser to NAAF with the official title of Chief, Operations Analysis Unit, A-3.

[7] Ltr, Eisenhower to Marshall, 13 May 43, Diary Office CinC, Book VI, pp. A-400-A-402; Memo for Personal Rcd, 1 Jul 43, Diary Office CinC, Book VI, pp. A-515-A-519; AFHQ, Rcd of Mtg Held by CinC AF, 10 May 43, 0100/12C/331, II; Eisenhower, *Crusade in Europe*, p. 165.

[8] Ltr, MAC to NAAF, 14 May 43, sub: Opn CORKSCREW, 0403/11/968; Msg, AFHQ Out W-2460 to AGWAR, 11 Jun 43, 0100/21/1079; Ltr, AFHQ to Br 1st Inf Div, 14 May 43, sub: Opn CORKSCREW, 0100/12C/523, I; AFHQ JPS P/81 (Final), 15 May 43, sub: Action Against Lampedusa, job 10A, reel 138E; Memo, AFHQ DCofS for AFHQ G-3, 19 May 43, sub: Opn Against Lampedusa, 0100/12C/331. I.

PANTELLERIA UNDER ATTACK, *"a hurricane of fire and smoke."*

leria to shambles. Enemy casualties were few in number, but damage to housing, roads, and communications was severe. By 1 June the port was in ruins, the town practically destroyed, and the electric plant knocked out. Shortages in water, ammunition, and supplies, plus the almost incessant explosions, began to have serious effects on morale. During the first ten days of June, more than 3,500 planes dropped almost 5,000 tons of bombs.[9]

On the morning of 8 June, members of the Italian garrison brought to the island commander some surrender leaflets dropped by the aircraft. As *Supermarina* proudly reported the incident to *Comando Supremo*, Pantelleria had not replied to the Allied ultimatum, Pantelleria would resist to the utmost.[10]

Again on 10 June the Italians refused to accept surrender. The single radio station working assured Rome that "despite everything Pantelleria will continue to resist." Successive telegrams, as many as twenty that night, told of Pantelleria's crumbling endurance, but none mentioned surrender.[11]

---

[9] Craven and Cate, eds., *Europe: TORCH to POINTBLANK*, pp. 425–26.

[10] *Notiziari operativi Supermarina*, IT A 1175; *Informazioni dei vari servizi relativi alle Forze Aeree, Servizio Informazioni Militari (SIM)* Rpts. IT 1423. See also Enzo Girone, *L'isola disperata (Pantelleria) 1942–1943* (Milan: Edizioni Ariminum, 1946).

[11] MS #R-135, Report on Visit to Rome During January 1959 (Bauer), pp. 24–25; see also MS #R-115 (Bauer).

On the morning of 11 June, the Allied invasion fleet carrying the British 1st Division halted about eight miles off the harbor entrance of the port of Pantelleria. The ground troops loaded into assault craft. The weather was good, the sea calm. Only a few low-hanging clouds flecked the sky. Pantelleria itself was cloaked in the haze and dust raised by air bombardment earlier that morning.

The Italian island commander had followed his usual custom of holding a staff conference that morning, even though Allied planes were plunging the island into a "hurricane of fire and smoke." Heavy smoke and dust clouds blocked a view of the ocean, and the island commander was unaware of the Allied fleet offshore. Discussion at the staff meeting soon showed everyone in agreement—the situation had become untenable because of lack of water, communications, ammunition, and also because of the danger of disease. Furthermore, no Axis planes remained on Pantelleria; help from outside could not be expected; and the 24,000 people on the island had about reached the end of their endurance. Since the commander had wired *Supermarina* several hours earlier that "the situation is desperate, all possibilities of effective resistance have been exhausted," he ordered his air commander to display a white cross on the field. Because it would take almost two hours for the order to reach all the posts, the commander set the time for the cessation of hostilities at 1100. Shortly after he made his decision, the clouds opened and he saw the Allied ships.[12]

At about that time the landing craft started their final run to the beaches.

There was a strange stillness, the only noise being the pounding of the assault craft, the drone of fighters orbiting overhead. Cruisers started to fire at shore battery positions around 1100, and thirty minutes later escorting destroyers added their fires. No reply came from the island. At 1135, U.S. Flying Fortresses bombarded the island in "the most perfect precision bombing of unimaginable intensity." At 1145, the assault echelon commander released his craft. By noon British troops were ashore. Shortly afterwards white flags appeared on many of the buildings.[13]

Lampedusa had also refused the Allied surrender offer, the island commander notifying Rome that "bombardments are continuing without interruption, both from the air and from the sea. Air Support required urgently." Instead of help, only words of intended cheer arrived: "We are convinced that you will inflict the greatest possible damage on the enemy. Long live Italy." Disappointed, resentful, feeling that they had done their duty, the members of the garrison, after being ordered to do so by the island commander, raised white flags in surrender.[14] Linosa fell the next day, 13 June. The Allies found Lampione unoccupied.

Allied intelligence had overestimated the will to resist of the defending garri-

---

[12] MS #R-135 (Bauer), pp. 19-21.

[13] Rpt of SNOL, Force 2, 13 Jun 43, Encl 2 to Rpt, CinC Med Station, 0100/21/1080, I; Rpt, Lt Comdr G. A. Martelli (Br), Diary Office CinC, Book VI, pp. A-495–A-498; AFHQ G-2 Weekly Intel Sum 42 and AFHQ Special Communique, 11 Jun 43, job 10A, reel 138E.

[14] Review of Sebi Caltabiano, *Missione a Lampedusa* (Catania: Edizione Camene), *Rivista Militare*, vol. XI (Rome, 1955), p. 1364; MS #R-115 (Bauer), pp. 47-50. See also Rpt, 15th Cruiser Squadron, Encl 5 to Rpt, CinC Med Station; Rpt, LCI(L) 161, 22 Jun 43, Encl 6 to Rpt, CinC Med Station.

sons. Despite Fascist propaganda, Pantelleria and the Pelagian Islands were hollow shells manned largely by over-age and inexperienced individuals, many of whom had their homes on the isles. When the Allies attacked, quite a few succumbed to the temptation of looking after their families instead of remaining at their posts. But against the power of the Western Allies, there was probably little they could have done with their inadequate and obsolete equipment.

On 20 June British aircraft began to operate from the field at Lampedusa, and six days later a group of U.S. P-40 fighters was based at Pantelleria.

Eisenhower's laboratory experiment had been eminently successful. Pantelleria and the Pelagian Islands gave the Allies a safer channel for shipping in the central Mediterranean and, more important, valuable airfields closer to Sicily and the Italian mainland.

### Growing German Strength

Allied seizure of Pantelleria furnished no sure indication to Axis intelligence of the future course of Allied operations in the Mediterranean. Whether the attack on the outlying Italian islands was preliminary to an attack on Sicily or whether it served a plan of greater scope was not clear.[15]

What was more than clear was the speed with which Pantelleria and the other islands had fallen. The rapid collapse showed that the Axis had definitely lost the initiative, for the Axis Powers could do little more than await invasion elsewhere, prepare to counterattack, and hope to repel the landings. Naval forces could react with only light surface craft and submarine activity against Allied shipping. Air forces were reduced to purely defensive efforts. Moreover, Pantelleria seemed to prove to Mussolini that air bombardment, like artillery, conquered ground and allowed the infantry to occupy it. Considering the fact that the Allies were blessed with a superiority of artillery and other equipment, the inference was evident.[16]

To the Italians, the loss of Pantelleria was depressing. If this was the start of the battle for Sicily, Sardinia, or the Italian mainland, it was a poor beginning. As the Italian people awakened increasingly to the realization that they had lost the war, defeatism spread.[17]

To the Germans, loss of the islands meant not only a military defeat and a blow to Axis morale, it served also as an indication of the performance they could expect in the future from their Italian allies. The Germans could not understand why the outlying islands had not been sufficiently stocked with the supplies of war. It was difficult for them to comprehend why the Italians, fighting on their own soil, had offered so little resistance. Did the speedy fall of Pantelleria foreshadow the course of future operations in the Mediterranean?[18]

If the capitulation of Pantelleria made the Germans feel that they could expect no resurgence of Italian morale in defense of the homeland, it made *Comando*

---

[15] *Promemoria, Comando Supremo*, 15 Jun 43, *SIM* Rpts. IT 1423; MS #R-115 (Bauer), p. 53.

[16] Speech by Mussolini, 12 Jun 43, summarized in OSS Rpt A-63366, undated, OCMH.

[17] See Zanussi, *Guerra e catastrofe*, II, 13.

[18] Rpt, *8.Armee, 8.VII.1943: Bereitschaft wegen Einnahme von Pantelleria*, IT 53/2; SKL/1.Abt., KTB, Teil A. 1.-30.VI.43, 12 Jun 43, referring to a report received from the Italians dated 11 June 1943.

*Supremo* much more willing to accept German help in the form of divisions to defend Italian soil.[19]

Just before the fall of Pantelleria, Ambrosio, increasingly worried over defending Italy, had reluctantly concluded that two robust and highly mobile German divisions were necessary for the defense of Sicily. But if the *Hermann Goering Division* moved to Sicily, southern Italy would be exposed, for the *16th Panzer Division* could not act as mobile reserve against landings on both east and west coasts.[20] Ambrosio discussed these problems with Kesselring and Rintelen on 1 June. And when Kesselring forced the issue by asking, "Do you request me to inquire with the OKW to see if there is another division in addition to the 16th Panzer Division?" Ambrosio admitted that that was what he meant.[21] The Italians were now willing to accept five German divisions, the number Hitler had originally offered to Mussolini.

Believing that the Germans could defend Italy if the Italians co-operated, having great faith and confidence in Mussolini though suspicious of the Italian military command, Kesselring asked Ambrosio whether the Italians needed more antiaircraft protection for the arterial railway lines and the power dams. Ambrosio did not commit himself at once, but a month later a formal, written request reached Kesselring. The Italians asked for antiaircraft guns and also for German crews. These would not arrive in Italy until August; by then they would be too late.[22]

Meanwhile, Kesselring returned to Rome on 8 June after visiting Hitler's headquarters. Hitler had told him that he was willing to send more planes, tanks, reconnaissance units, self-propelled guns, and troops to Italy. All the Italians had to do, Hitler said, was to have the Duce and *Comando Supremo* ask for them.[23]

But Ambrosio was in a quandary. If Mussolini was really going to break with the Germans, the fewer German troops in Italy the better. If, on the other hand, Italy was to oppose an Allied attack, more German troops were necessary.

More were available, as Kesselring pointed out to Ambrosio on 11 June, the day that Pantelleria surrendered. But when Kesselring said that both General Hube, the *XIV Panzer Corps* commander, and the Italian commander in Sicily thought that additional German troops were needed, Ambrosio professed to be unconvinced. He wondered whether the *16th Panzer Division* might be sent to Sardinia, the *Hermann Goering Division* held in southern Italy. Kesselring objected on two counts: Sardinia was inappropriate terrain for employing an armored division—the *16th Panzer Division* should therefore stay on the

---

[19] Deichmann in MS #T-1a (Westphal *et al.*), ch. I, p. 33; Rintelen in MS #T-1a (Westphal *et al.*), ch. II, p. 15.

[20] The *Hermann Goering Division* was officially named the *Hermann Goering Panzer Fallschirmjaeger Division*, and was a unit of the German Luftwaffe. The new men were drawn largely from the Luftwaffe, and thus the division acquired the name of a paratroop division.

[21] Min, 1 Jun 43, item 158, Min of Confs, *Comando Supremo*, IT 26.

[22] MS #T-2, K 1 (Kesselring), pp. 5–6; Min, 1 Jun 43, item 158, Min of Confs, *Comando Supremo*, IT 26; Ltr, Comando Supremo (Generale di Corpo d'Armata Carlo Rossi) to the Commander in Chief South (Kesselring), 1 Jul 43, No. *14450/Op.*, sub: *Difesa controaerea delle communicazioni ferroviarie Italia-Germania*, an. 6, folder IV, IT 3029.

[23] Min, 8 Jun 43, item 165, Min of Confs, *Comando Supremo*, IT 26.

mainland; and one mobile German division was insufficient as a reserve in Sicily because two areas of attack were likely, in the west and in the southeast. Kesselring urged that Ambrosio, if he planned to request additional German forces, make his requests promptly so that OKW would have adequate time to prepare the divisions and move them. Ambrosio replied with some irritation that he was not prepared to make a formal request, though he said he would submit a complete statement of Italy's requirements within a few days.[24]

The fall of Pantelleria and the Pelagian Islands, which prompted Hitler to order both Sardinia and Sicily reinforced, caused Ambrosio to change his mind. When Ambrosio met again with Kesselring on 12 June, he was in a completely different mood. He acknowledged the validity of not moving the *16th Panzer Division* to Sardinia, though he wanted to be sure that there were adequate guns and tanks on the island. Upon learning that the Germans intended to send additional strength to Sardinia, Ambrosio agreed to keep the *16th Panzer Division* on the mainland. Kesselring then announced that the Germans had another motorized division—the *3d Panzer Grenadier*—available and, if requested, it could be promptly moved to southern Italy, making possible the transfer of the *Hermann Goering Division* to Sicily. Ambrosio agreed to this proposal and to another by Kesselring that the reconnaissance battalion of the *Hermann Goering Division* proceed to Sicily at once. He also agreed that the *3d Panzer Grenadier Division* might move into Italy immediately. Kesselring then said that if the Italians wished, the Fuehrer could send a fourth division for the defense of the Italian soil, making a total of six German divisions in Italy. Ambrosio replied that he would have to study the distribution of divisions carefully, and would give a formal answer in a few days.[25]

A few days later professional advice from field commanders overcame Ambrosio's reluctance to admit additional German troops to Italy. After a very pessimistic report by the Italian commander in Sicily on 14 June, *Comando Supremo* three days later requested OKW to send to Italy two additional armored or motorized divisions. OKW complied by selecting the *29th Panzer Grenadier* and the *26th Panzer Divisions*, units that in mid-May had been earmarked for the occupation of northern Italy under Plan *ALARICH*.[26]

By the end of June 1943, five German divisions, in whole or in part, were in Italy; two more divisions were about to enter the country; the *XIV Panzer Corps* headquarters was already in Italy; and agreement had been reached for the arrival of another corps headquarters (the *LXXVI Panzer Corps*). Italy was beginning to resemble an occupied territory.

### The Defenses of Sicily

Recognizing the impossibility of constructing and manning effective fortifica-

---

[24] Min, 11 Jun 43, item 166, Min of Confs, *Comando Supremo*, IT 26.

[25] Min. 12 Jun 43, item 167, Min of Confs, *Comando Supremo*, IT 26.

[26] Rpt, Generale d'Armata Alfredo Guzzoni to S.M.R.E., *Comando Supremo: Situazione difensiva della Sicilia*, IT 3027; *OKW/WFSt, KTB 1.-31.VII.43*, 21 Jul 43, pp. 3-4; Rintelen in MS #T-1a (Westphal et al.), ch. II, p. 12; Rpt, German Military Attaché, Rome, on Co-operation With Italian High Command/Commitment of German Forces in Italy, 14 Jul 43, *OKW/Amtsgruppe Ausland, 30.VI.43-31.VIII.44. Wehrmacht Attaché Italien* (OKW 1029).

tions along the entire extensive Italian coast line, *Comando Supremo* had originally decided to concentrate the defenses on the major islands, plus part of the southern mainland. During the winter of 1942-43, the Italians began to give precedence to the defenses of Sardinia, the most likely Allied target. Around March 1943, they started to make special efforts to brace Sicily.[27]

German coastal defense advisers, who had supervised the construction of the Atlantic Wall on the Channel coast, arrived in Italy in the spring of 1943, and one group went to Sicily to make recommendations for its defense. Though Italian fortification experts, some of whom had visited the Atlantic Wall, were impressed and anxious to duplicate it, the Italians lacked the resources to build and man such a fortified belt. Despite strenuous efforts to improve and extend the few existing fortifications on the coast of Sicily, the Italians made little progress.[28]

The Italian *Sixth Army* had been stationed on Sicily since the autumn of 1941. Generale di Corpo d'Armata Comandante Designato d'Armata Mario Roatta, former chief of staff of the Italian Army, took command in February 1943 and assumed responsibility for part of Calabria as well as for Sicily. Roatta controlled almost a dozen divisions under two corps headquarters, an air reconnaissance force, and, through liaison, certain German units. With only partial control over the territorial antiaircraft defenses manned by the Fascist Militia (headquartered at Palermo), Roatta had no control over ground militia, naval, and air forces on Sicily. He had no direction of the units under the civilian prefects of the provinces. To co-ordinate his dispositions with the plans of various independent headquarters, Roatta had to rely on liaison. In all, the Italian command authority was divided among seven military and nine civilian agencies. Except for the naval bases and a few ports, the island in early 1943 was not on a wartime basis.[29]

Shortly after assuming command, Roatta obtained a degree of unified command by having *Comando Supremo* give his *Sixth Army* headquarters the additional title of *Armed Forces Command, Sicily*.[30] Roatta then became responsible for the tactical commitment of the Italian Army, Navy, Air, and militia elements, plus the German ground troops in Sicily and in southern Calabria. Through a high commissioner for civilian affairs, Roatta also assumed control of the civilian administration of the nine provincial prefects. The relatively small German air and naval elements remained under autonomous German control.[31]

Roatta next requested troops and weapons to bring his ground forces up to wartime strength. He wanted manpower and materials so he could construct

---

[27] Roatta, *Otto milioni*, pp. 222-24; Faldella, *Lo sbarco*, pp. 34, 41.

[28] Deichmann in MS #T-1a (Westphal et al.), ch. I, p. 24; Mario Caracciolo di Feroleto, "*E poi?*": *La tragedia dell'esercito italiano*, (Rome: Casa editrice libraria Corso 1946), pp. 94-95; cf. Memoirs of General Caracciolo di Feroleto, Commanding General of the Italian *Fifth Army*. EAP-21-a-14/32.

[29] Rpt, *Difesa della Sicilia*, 9 Mar 43, IT 3024; Deichmann in MS #T-1a (Westphal et al.), ch. I, p. 14.

[30] The designations *Armed Forces Command, Sicily* and *Sixth Army* are used interchangeably in this volume.

[31] Cir, *Unità di comando in Sicilia e in Sardegna*, No. 9880, in a separate folder entitled *Costituzione Comando FF.AA.della Sardegna*, part of IT 830; Zanussi, *Guerra e catastrofe*, I, 301.

GENERAL ROATTA

GENERAL GUZZONI

additional fortifications, improve communications, make possible the evacuation of the civilian population from battle areas, and stockpile supplies and food. But the men and materials he received were far below the amounts he considered minimum requirements.

Roatta nevertheless set soldiers and civilians to work to enlarge and improve the defenses on the beaches and at vital points on the main highways. He also began to construct a belt of fortifications and obstacles twelve to fifteen miles behind the beaches in order to contain Allied forces that might get ashore. He assigned each military unit a specific coastal sector for defense.[32]

After serving as commander for three months, Roatta issued a proclamation that the population interpreted as a slight to Sicilian patriotism.[33] This, added to changes recently made in the Italian high command, prompted *Comando Supremo* to appoint Roatta chief of the Army General Staff (*Superesercito*) and to nominate Generale d'Armata Alfredo Guzzoni in his place.

Guzzoni's appointment was somewhat surprising, for he was sixty-six years old and had been in retirement for two years. Furthermore, he had never been to Sicily, nor had he ever displayed interest in the island and its military problems. Guzzoni's chief of staff, Col. Emilio

---

[32] Dante Ugo Leonardi, *Luglio 1943 in Sicilia* (Modena: Società tipografica modenese editrice in Modena, 1947), p. 55; Zanussi, *Guerra e catastrofe*, vol. I, pp. 303-04.

[33] The proclamation and the consequences are discussed in detail by Roatta, *Otto milioni*, pp. 251-53. See also Zanussi, *Guerra e catastrofe*, I, 312-13.

Faldella, a young and capable officer, appeared a good choice, but he, too, was a stranger to Sicily. Nor had Faldella, contrary to the usual Italian practice of keeping a commander and his chief of staff together, ever served with Guzzoni.[34]

The Italian command structure was not rigid but rather relied on co-operation and co-ordination among commanders. An officer's ability to engage in teamwork was therefore important. Similarly, unit organization was flexible. Commanders formed small groups of varied composition to meet various situations, without formal reassignment or reorganization, designating them by location, the name of the commander, or by letters of the alphabet. When the need disappeared, the task force was informally dissolved and its elements returned to the original units.[35] These features were particularly significant in Sicily where an army headquarters had become responsible for employing a diversity of forces, Italian and German. Despite his unified command, Guzzoni exercised real control in great part only through liaison and mere recommendations.

The co-ordination of German and Italian units on Sicily varied, with the result that the German elements were partially under German and partially under Italian control. In due course, parallel channels of communication and command developed, one from Guzzoni to *Comando Supremo* and Mussolini, the other from the individual German headquarters on the island to *OB SUED*. Liaison between Kesselring and Ambrosio, chief of *Comando Supremo*, re-established co-ordination at that level.

Part of this setup was the outgrowth of the organization established during the North African campaign. Hitler's predilection for dual control channels, mutual distrust between Italians and Germans after their defeat in Tunisia, and the need for flexibility brought about considerable vagueness, not to say confusion, in the command organization of the Axis partners.

At the close of the North African campaign, when an Allied attack on Italy appeared in the offing, Kesselring was the main connecting link between Hitler and OKW on one hand and Mussolini and *Comando Supremo* on the other. Kesselring had controlled the German armed forces in Italy and the central Mediterranean through German representatives in Italy who also maintained liaison with *Comando Supremo*. Now, for better liaison, Kesselring established within *Comando Supremo* a mixed staff of Germans and Italians headed by his own chief of staff, General der Artillerie Siegfried Westphal.[36]

In mid-June, when Kesselring relinquished his air command to Feldmarschall Wolfram Freiherr von Richthofen but

---

[34] Zanussi, *Guerra e catastrofe*, I, 313–14. Faldella was subsequently promoted to brigadier general.

[35] Army Map Service, U.S. Army, *Handbook on the Italian Army* (Provisional Copy) (Washington, 1943).

[36] Kesselring was also the commander of the German *Second Air Force* until replaced in June 1943 by Field Marshal von Richthofen, who assumed command over all German air forces on the Italian mainland, Sicily, Sardinia, and Corsica, and certain training units in France. He was also responsible for the Luftwaffe ground units, most of the German antiaircraft units in Italy, Luftwaffe signal units, and all air force administrative matters. See Deichmann in MS #T-1a (Westphal et al.), ch. III, pp. 3–4, 34; British Air Ministry Pamphlet No. 248, *The Rise and Fall of the German Air Force (1933 to 1945)* (London, 1948).

# THE AXIS SITUATION

retained his prerogatives as Commander in Chief South, he emerged as the strongest German officer in Italy. As theater commander, unifying in his person control of all the German armed forces in Italy, Kesselring was Hitler's representative on all questions concerning the conduct of the war in the central and western Mediterranean areas. Guzzoni found Kesselring a typical German officer who had a determined though courteous and conciliatory manner and who promised effective co-operation. Two of Kesselring's major problems were trying to reconcile the sometimes conflicting demands of German commanders and Italian prerogatives and trying to combat Italian pessimism on defending Sicily.

Guzzoni, like his predecessor, saw little strength in the Sicilian defenses. The coastal battalions, he reported to *Comando Supremo*, were composed of men of older age groups, often badly commanded, and in some instances covering defensive sectors up to twenty-five miles in length. Guzzoni, lacking antinaval guns and deficient in all other types of artillery, had but one antitank gun for each five miles of coast line. As against a daily need of 8,000 tons of supplies to meet civilian and military requirements, he was receiving 1,500 to 2,000 tons. The morale of the civilian population was very low because of Allied air bombardments and the restricted food supply—the rationing system had broken down, and black-market operations were widespread. The people wanted only an end to the war. If resolutely committed, Guzzoni estimated, his forces might hold back the initial Allied landings but could not check successive attacks. Reiterating Roatta's earlier demands for more artillery and tanks, he urged in addition the immediate transfer of the *Hermann Goering Division* to Sicily.[37]

Except at the naval bases, no continuous system of coastal defenses existed. Obstacles, mine fields on and off shore, antitank ditches, and concrete fortifications appeared only at widely separated points. Many fortifications lacked garrisons or weapons, many were poorly camouflaged and lacked troop shelters. In the interior, only a few roadblocks were ready, and most of these were inadequate. On the highway from Licata to Campobello, for a distance of more than twelve miles, for example, the entire antitank defense consisted of one 47-mm. gun. The inland blocking line consisted of a beautiful colored pencil mark on a map.[38]

The three naval bases on Sicily were equipped with antinaval and antiaircraft artillery, and their seaward defenses were effectively organized. Their weaknesses were the undependable militia who manned many of the guns, the age of the guns, and their small caliber and short range. The bases had little defense against landward attack.[39]

Though the naval commanders remained in control of technical, administrative, and training matters, Guzzoni was responsible for the defense of their bases. In the event of a ground attack, he was to send army reinforcements. Because of the importance of liaison to the command channels, the poor condition of signal communications caused serious

---

[37] Rpt, Guzzoni to S.M.R.E., *Comando Supremo: Situazione difensiva della Sicilia*, 14 Jun 43, IT 3027.

[38] Faldella, *Lo sbarco*, pp. 46–48, 62; Maravigna, *Rivista Militare*, 1952, pp. 13–14.

[39] Maravigna, *Rivista Militare*, 1952, p. 14.

GENERAL RODT    FIELD MARSHAL VON RICHTHOFEN    GENERAL CONRATH

apprehension among all the commanders concerned.[40]

Expecting the Allies to try to seize airfields quickly, the Italians started work to surround the airfields with obstacles and strongpoints manned by infantry supported by artillery. They mined all landing strips to render them useless in the event of loss.[41]

The heart of Sicily's defenses consisted of forces under the two corps commanded by the *Sixth Army:* six coastal divisions, two coastal brigades, one coastal regiment, and four mobile divisions. In addition, two mobile German divisions were in Sicily by the end of June.

The Italian units, numbering some 200,000 men (including the airfield defense troops), generally had a poor combat effectiveness. The coastal units especially had antiquated or deficient armament and virtually no transportation, they were badly commanded in many cases, and their indigenous personnel, as much as 75 percent in some units, reflected the low morale of the Sicilian population. Tactical groups created from division elements and from corps reserves were deployed relatively close to the beaches to support the coastal units, and these had some mobile elements.

The special groups organized to defend the airfields consisted usually of one infantry and one artillery battalion per airfield, but they were soon augmented by mobile elements—light tanks, self-propelled guns, armored cars, motorized infantry and artillery, and various engineer units—and they served as a mobile reserve for general defensive operations.

The four Italian mobile divisions, the best of the Italian combat forces on the island, were none too good. The *Aosta* and *Napoli Divisions,* largely composed of Sicilians, were poorly trained. The *Assietta Division* was somewhat better. But all three operated under reduced

[40] Marc'Antonio Bragadin, *The Italian Navy in World War II* (Annapolis, Md.: United States Naval Institute, 1957), ch. XIII.

[41] Faldella, *Lo sbarco,* pp. 50–53 and an. 2, p. 421; Roatta, *Otto Milioni,* p. 218.

GENERAL VON SENGER  COLONEL BAADE  GENERAL HUBE

Tables of Organization, and their artillery and other equipment were for the most part antiquated. Only the *Livorno Division* was at full strength and had organic transportation. In all four divisions, artillery ammunition was generally in short supply or nonexistent, signal communications varied from poor to inadequate.[42]

The two German divisions made quite a contrast. The *Division Sizilien*, redesignated the *15th Panzer Grenadier Division* on 29 June and commanded by Generalmajor Eberhard Rodt, was ready for commitment. It had supplies for twenty days of operations. Though not completely mobile, the division could move relatively quickly with its organic equipment.[43] The *Hermann Goering Division*, under the command of Generalmajor (later, General der Fallschirmtruppen) Paul Conrath, moved from southern Italy into Sicily during June. It was somewhat deficient in infantry, but was also well trained and equipped, although the process of combined training did not effectively begin until the arrival of the division on Sicily. Airborne elements and other German units in southern and central Italy, if necessary, could also be employed in the defense of Sicily.[44]

Though operational command of German units—totaling some 30,000 men—

---

[42] Rpt, Guzzoni to *S.M.R.E., Comando Supremo: Situazione difensiva della Sicilia*, IT 3027; Faldella, *Lo sbarco*, pp. 50–53, 58–60; Maravigna, *Rivista Militare*, 1952, pp. 13–14; Comando Supremo, *Situazione operativa logistica al 1° luglio 1943*, IT 17; MS #R-117, The Mission of General Guzzoni, ch. IV of Axis Tactical Operations in Sicily, July–August 1943 (Bauer); MS #R-135 (Bauer), pp. 10–13, 18.

[43] MS #C-077, *Studie ueber den Feldzug in Sizilien bei der 15.Pz.Gren.Div., Mai–August 1943* (Generalleutnant Eberhard Rodt); Unit Record Card, *OKH/Org Abt., Karteiblatt, 15.Pz.Gren.Div.* (H 1/540).

[44] MS #T-2, *Der Kampf um Sizilien* (General der Panzertruppen Walter Fries et al.); the detailed order of battle for the Italian and German units on Sicily can be found in MS #R-125, Order of Battle, 1 July 1943, ch. V of Axis Tactical Operations in Sicily, July–August 1943 (Bauer).

remained in Italian hands, Hitler and the OKW sometimes sent instructions directly to local commanders, who frequently communicated directly with the OKW. The Italians soon came to accept the view that obtaining German co-operation was preferable to a strict imposition of Italian authority.[45]

The *XIV Panzer Corps* headquarters, located in southern Italy, functioned under *OB SUED* to administer and supply the German units in Sicily. The Italians could hardly object to this, and the Germans had a headquarters ready to take over active operations should such a course of action become necessary or desirable. General Hube had commanded the corps in Russia and had received high praise for his performance.[46]

Late in June 1943, the Germans introduced another officer into the command picture, Generalleutnant Fridolin von Senger und Etterlin, who became liaison officer with the *Sixth Army* headquarters and responsible for co-ordinating the employment of German troops committed on the island.

The Italian battle fleet, stationed at La Spezia and far removed from Sicily, was seriously reduced in strength, lacked radar and aircraft carriers. It could be effective against an Allied armada only with adequate air protection, which was not available. Furthermore, it needed twenty-four hours to reach the waters off Sicily. For these reasons and because of apprehension that the first major battle of the surface fleet might well be its last, *Comando Supremo* decided late in May to commit the naval forces in the defense of Sicily only if an extraordinarily good opportunity presented itself and if sufficient fuel oil was on hand to support the operation. *Comando Supremo* also directed the small naval craft stationed in Sicilian and Sardinian waters to remain in defense of their home stations rather than join forces in the event one or the other island came under attack.

The most important German vessels consisted of a landing craft flotilla at Messina. Plans to supplement the few German submarines in the Mediterranean had to be abandoned because the passage through the Strait of Gibraltar had become increasingly difficult.[47]

The better to organize their services of supply across the Messina Strait, the Germans in May unified a number of Army, Navy, and Air Force transportation installations into a single headquarters. Eventually known as *Commandant Messina Strait* under Col. Ernst Guenther Baade, it was responsible for ferry service, depots, and antiaircraft defenses, controlling in the latter function some seventy antiaircraft batteries on the Italian mainland and on Sicily to guard the strait.[48]

---

[45] Deichmann in MS #T-1a (Westphal et al.), ch. I, pp. 24–25; Faldella, *Lo sbarco*, p. 65; Rintelen in MS #T-1a (Westphal et al.), ch. II, p. 12; *OKW/WFSt, KTB, 1.–31.VII.43*, 1 Jul 43.

[46] Deichmann in MS #T-1a (Westphal et al.), ch. I, p. 27; *XIV Panzer Korps, Ia, Taetigkeitsbericht mit Anlagen, 29.III.–19.V.43* (33394/3), 17 May 43; Unit Record Card, *OKH/Org Abt., Karteiblatt, XIV Panzer Korps* (H 1/540).

[47] CinC Navy Visits Italy, 12–15 May 43 and Rpt on the War Situation by the German Staff, *Supermarina*, 2 Apr 43, both in ONI, *Fuehrer Conferences, 1943*; *SKL/1. Abt., KTB, 1.–30.VI. 43*, 9–10 Jun 43.

[48] Details on the organization and execution of the ferrying service are contained in the Translation of the Report on the Evacuation of Sicily (August 1943) by Vice-Admiral Friedrich von Ruge (1946), with enclosures (cited hereafter as Ruge Rpt), folder X-111, OCMH, and in *Kommandant Messina Strasse, KTB, 25.VII.–25.VIII. 43 und Anlagen* (35746/1–3) (cited hereafter as Baade Diary).

# THE AXIS SITUATION

The Italian Air Force was in a hopeless situation because of obsolete and inferior aircraft. After the fall of Tunisia, Allied air attacks on Sicilian airfields became so intense that toward the end of May the Axis withdrew its bombers to the mainland. Italo-German co-ordination of air matters was poor, the German fighter units taking over the protection of Sicily from their own fields as though the Italians were not even present. But in a series of twenty-one air battles from the latter half of May through the early days of July, the Germans sustained heavy losses. Goering, who recognized what was happening but not the cause, brought heavy pressure to bear on the German *Second Air Force,* calling for incessant commitment of long-range bombers and fighters. But the German aircraft were not able to match the speed and armament of Allied planes. Goering added insult to injury by sending a special message to the fighter pilots of the *Second Air Force:*

Together with the fighter pilots in France, Norway, and Russia, I can only regard you with contempt. I want an immediate improvement and expect that all pilots will show an improvement in fighting spirit. If this improvement is not forthcoming, flying personnel from the commander down must expect to be remanded to the ranks and transferred to the Eastern front to serve on the ground.[49]

Though Generaloberst Hans Jeschonnek, chief of staff of the OKL, visited Kesselring and learned that decisive numerical and technical inferiority of German aircraft to those of the Allies was at the bottom of German air failure, Goering stubbornly refused to admit that the responsibility was his own.

Because of air and naval weakness, the whole burden of the defense of Sicily fell on the Axis ground forces. Misunderstandings and misinterpretations among Italian and German commanders further aggravated the situation.[50]

Despite inadequate forces, matériel, and fortifications to defend the entire coast, the Italians felt impelled to fight at the water's edge. Small tactical reserves were to stand ready close behind the coastal defense forces, and mobile reserves in centrally located positions farther to the rear were to be available to counterattack as soon as the point of the main Allied attack became apparent. Because the Italians considered their coastal units incapable of repelling a landing, the commitment of these units to stubborn defense meant their sacrifice. Since reserves were few, the commanders hoped to increase their effectiveness by holding them together and ready to move to any one of a number of widely separated points. The great drawback in this concept was the lack of sufficient mobility on the part of most units. The German units, with far greater mobility, could form the only effective reserve. Appreciating this, Kesselring, late in May, instructed German commanders to counterattack as soon as they knew the location of the main Allied attacks without waiting for orders from Guzzoni's headquarters.[51]

---

[49] Deichmann in MS #T-1a (Westphal *et al.*), ch. III, pp. 9, 13, 14-15, 20-23, 29-30; Min, 28 May 43, item 156, Min of Confs, *Comando Supremo,* IT 26; Note, *Comando Supremo* to OKW, 20 Jun 43, sub: *Problema aereo del Mediterraneo, Giugno 1943,* IT 3029, folder IV, an. 2; *Operazioni in Sicilia dal 9 al 19 luglio, Narrativa, Allegati* (cited hereafter as IT 99 a), an. 2.

[50] CinC Navy Visits Italy, 12-15 May 43, ONI. *Fuehrer Conferences, 1943.*

[51] MS #T-3, P 1 (Kesselring) pt. II, pp. 73-75; MS #T-2, K 1 (Kesselring), pp. 12-13; Faldella, *Lo sbarco,* pp. 65-67, 82-86.

Guzzoni's headquarters was near Enna, fairly close to the center of the island. The Italian *XVI Corps* under Generale di Corpo d'Armata Carlo Rossi was to defend the eastern half of the island; the Italian *XII Corps,* first under Generale di Corpo d'Armata Mario Arisio, later under Generale di Corpo d'Armata Francesco Zingales, was assigned the western half of the island. By the latter part of May the coastal units were in their assigned sectors, and the *Sixth Army* had attached the Italian mobile divisions to both corps for commitment in their respective areas—*Aosta* and *Assietta* under *XII Corps* in southwest Sicily, *Napoli* near Catania, and *Livorno* near Gela under *XVI Corps*. In the *Sixth Army* reserve and reinforced by a self-propelled Italian regiment of artillery, the *15th Panzer Grenadier Division* split its forces into three regimental teams—*Group Ens* in the southwest; *Group Fullriede* in the southeast; and *Group Koerner* in the Enna area as an unassigned reserve.[52]

General Rodt, the *15th Panzer Grenadier Division* commander, represented by his chief of staff, discussed with Guzzoni the possibility of holding the mobile reserves closer to the coast. He proposed moving two of his regimental groups quite close to Gela and Catania, the third to the west but keeping it ready for immediate transfer to the east if necessary. Assuming that the Italian coastal divisions would barely delay the attackers, and estimating that the Allies would land in several different places before moving inland in pincer movements, Rodt wanted to counterattack immediately and eliminate each landing in turn. He asked Guzzoni to attach to his division the mobile groups organized to defend the airfields. Convinced that the airfields would be immediately threatened, Guzzoni refused.

Admitting that the southeastern corner of Sicily was vulnerable and that the *Napoli Division* lacked sufficient mobility to move in time to any area under attack, Guzzoni, contrary to the German view, doubted that the Allies would space their landings in such a way as to permit counterattacking forces to execute successive operations. He nevertheless issued a revised plan on 9 June. The *Aosta* and *Assietta Divisions* under the *XII Corps* and the *Napoli Division* under the *XVI Corps* were to remain in their previously assigned areas. But because General Guzzoni was very conscious of the German determination to attack immediately, he feared that the German units, representing his only truly mobile reserves, would escape his grasp. Deeming it wise to have some Italian troops firmly in hand, he transferred the *Livorno Division* to army reserve and moved it closer to his *Sixth Army* headquarters. The German elements remained generally in place. But additional units arriving in Sicily formed a fourth reserve force as *Group Neapel* in the center.[53]

---

[52] Faldella, *Lo sbarco,* pp. 62–63; Rintelen in MS #T-1a (Westphal *et al.*), ch. II, p. 10; see Overlay, app. B.: Deployment as Planned by Mid-May 1943, MS #R-126, Deployment, ch. VI of Axis Tactical Operations in Sicily, July–August 1943 (Bauer).

[53] Faldella, *Lo sbarco,* p. 69; MS #C–077 (Rodt); see Overlay, app. C: Planned Deployment of Reserves, 9 June 1943, MS #R-126 (Bauer).

The identity and composition of *Group Neapel* is unclear. It may have included the *215th Tank Battalion* (German general headquarters troops), attached later to the *15th Panzer Grenadier Division;* it may also have included the reconnaissance battalion of the *Hermann Goering Division.* The deployment of German troops on Sicily as it appeared on a German map dated 12 June 1943, but not otherwise identified, is shown as an overlay in Appendix D, MS #R-126 (Bauer).

LOOKING SOUTH FROM THE HEIGHTS OF ENNA, site of General Guzzoni's 6th Army Headquarters.

Transfer of the *Hermann Goering Division* to Sicily as the second German division created a new problem. The German commanders in Sicily wished to use the *15th Panzer Grenadier Division* in the eastern half of the island where they saw the greatest Allied threat and where the division was well acquainted with the terrain—where, in fact, the division had executed a map maneuver based on a simulated Allied landing in the Gela area. They therefore wanted the *Hermann Goering Division*, which was not so far advanced in combined training as the *15th*, committed as a whole in the western part of the island, where the threat seemed not so great.[54]

Guzzoni, convinced that the main Allied attack would hit the eastern coast near the southeastern corner, wanted to hold both German divisions together as a mobile reserve in the eastern part of Sicily. He envisioned the *Livorno* and *Napoli Divisions* fighting delaying actions until the two German divisions could mount a counterattack and strike.

Kesselring reiterated the German view that an invader was weakest when he left his assault boats and waded ashore. He therefore wanted the reserves very close to the coast because he believed that the Axis forces were too weak to eliminate beachheads once they were well established, and because he was concerned that Allied air might retard daylight movements of the reserves on the narrow, winding, Sicilian roads. Furthermore, reserves stationed inland would literally have to come down the mountains in daylight and would thus present good targets for Allied naval gunfire. Reserves stationed close to the coast would be spared long and difficult approach marches and casualties from Allied air attacks.[55]

The decision reached was to commit the German divisions as much as possible as complete units, one in the east, the other in the west. The *Hermann Goering Division* was to assemble in the southeastern area in *Sixth Army* reserve but was to be available for use by the *XVI Corps* with Guzzoni's permission. *Group Koerner* of the *15th Panzer Grenadier Division*, located near Catania, was to be attached to the *Hermann Goering Division*. *Group Ens* of the *15th* was to remain in the west under direct army control. *Group Fullriede*, integrating *Group Neapel* into its organization, would be in the center near Caltanissetta.

Guzzoni then had as the *Sixth Army* reserve the augmented *Group Fullriede* and the *Livorno Division*. This fully motorized reserve near Caltanissetta would be ready for commitment toward Catania, sixty miles to the east; Gela, thirty miles to the southeast; Licata, thirty miles to the south; and Agrigento, thirty miles to the southwest.

When the *Hermann Goering Division* established its headquarters at Caltagirone, twenty miles northeast of Gela, it assembled about two-thirds of its units in the area. The other third combined with *Group Koerner* of the *15th Panzer Grenadier Division* to form *Group Schmalz* and went into position near Catania. The *15th Panzer Grenadier Division* headquarters and *Group Fullriede* moved into the western part of Sicily.

Kesselring, though expecting the main Allied landings to take place on the eastern or southern coasts, was still pre-

---

[54] MS #C-077 (Rodt); MS #C-095, *Der Kampf um Sizilien* (General der Panzertruppen Fridolin von Senger und Etterlin), pp. 7-10.

[55] MS #T-2 K 1 (Kesselring), pp. 11-14; MS #C-095 (Senger), p. 7.

# THE AXIS SITUATION

occupied with a possible secondary attack in the west. He proposed transferring *Group Fullriede* to the western sector, leaving *Group Neapel* in the Caltanissetta area. He also proposed moving the German units closer to the coast than the Italians contemplated, and he suggested concentrating them in the south central part of the island.

Guzzoni agreed. On 26 June Kesselring summarized his concept of repelling an invasion: the battle was to be fought at the coast line by coastal units supported by local reserves under division and corps control; mobile reserves—the four Italian mobile divisions—relatively close to the coast in small groups, were to be ready to pounce as soon as the Allies set foot on shore; finally, the German divisions were to clean up.[56]

At the end of June, then, the *Aosta* and *Assietta Divisions* and the bulk of the *15th Panzer Grenadier Division* were in the west; the *Napoli, Livorno, Hermann Goering Divisions,* and one-third of the *15th Panzer Grenadier Division* were in the south and east. (*See Map I.*)

Expecting the Allies to land in several quite separate places, the Axis commanders planned to counterattack the landings immediately, wipe them out one after another, and prevent the establishment of a continuous front. When Guzzoni committed his mobile reserves, he hoped to do so at that "fleeting moment" when the main invasion sites were evident but the individual beachheads were not yet fully merged.

The axis commanders believed they had several more weeks to complete their final preparations, for they expected the Allies to attack about the middle of July.[57]

---

[56] MS #T-2 K 1 (Kesselring), pp. 10-14; MS #C-095 (Senger), pp. 5-10; MS #C-077 (Rodt), pp. 9-10; Schmalz in MS #T-2 (Fries et al.), p. 72; see Overlay, app. E: Plan for Deployment of Reserves on 26 June 1943, in Effect 9 July 1943, in MS #R-126 (Bauer).

[57] Faldella, *Lo sbarco,* pp. 65-66, 86; MS #T-2 (Fries et al.), pp. 6-7 *Aosta Division,* though under *XII Corps,* could be moved only after securing army approval.

CHAPTER V

# Final Allied Preparations

*Missions and Forces*

The Allied concept of making a concentrated assault on the southeastern corner of Sicily did not mean that all the troops would land bunched together. It meant instead that more than seven divisions, preceded by airborne operations involving parts of two airborne divisions, would come ashore simultaneously along a front of one hundred miles. Both frontage and initial assault forces would be larger than those of the Normandy invasion a year later. In fact, the invasion of Sicily, the first crack at Europe's "soft underbelly," was to be at once the largest and most dispersed amphibious assault of World War II.

Though the Combined Chiefs of Staff had hoped that the invasion could go in June, the length of the Tunisian campaign, which ended 13 May, and the difficulties of preparing the Sicilian operation made it impractical before July. Important in the choice of date and invasion hour were the conflicting requirements of the naval forces, which would convey the ground forces to Sicily, and of the airborne troops, which were to drop onto the island to disrupt the enemy rear and thereby assist the amphibious elements ashore. Specifically, moonlight, necessary for airborne operations, was unfavorable for naval operations.

Allied planners had assumed from the outset that an airborne attack was essential for a successful assault on Sicily. Yet as plans were developed, Washington planners began to feel that it was absurd to threaten the success of the naval effort by requiring the Allied naval convoys to approach the hostile shore in broad moonlight simply to accommodate an airdrop of relatively small proportions. To them, it seemed that Eisenhower was "jeopardizing the entire operation because of the desire to use paratroops." Since current doctrine favored beach assaults during the hours of darkness, the planners noted, could not the airborne troops be dropped at dusk the evening before D-day to enable the naval convoys to approach during the night and the amphibious troops to hit the shore just before daylight?[1]

General Eisenhower thought not. Supported by Admiral Cunningham and Air Chief Marshal Tedder, and also by his airborne adviser, Maj. Gen. F. A. M. Browning, the Allied commander in chief stated that moonlight was necessary so that troop-carrying aircraft could find the proper drop zones. Thus, moonlight was not a requirement imposed by the airborne troops; it was "mandatory for the air force." Though Cunningham realized the disadvantages of such an action, he believed that heavy air attack would diminish the threat of enemy air

[1] Msg, OPD 138 to AFHQ, 23 Apr 43, OPD Exec 3, item 10.

action against the naval forces and also that moonlight would enhance Allied defense against enemy surface ships and submarines. In the Sicilian region, Eisenhower concluded, a second quarter moon provided the necessary light and darkness. This occurred between the 10th and 14th of July.

Having secured the agreement of the planners in Washington, Eisenhower designated H-hour as 0245, D-day as 10 July, for the beach assaults. The airborne drops would occur around midnight, some two and a half hours earlier.[2]

Under Admiral Cunningham's operational command, the Western Naval Task Force, commanded by Vice Adm. Henry K. Hewitt and numbering more than 1,700 ships, craft, and boats, was to carry the American troops to Sicily; the Eastern Naval Task Force under Vice Adm. Sir Bertram H. Ramsey was to transport the British troops. Though enemy air attack was the major naval concern, Cunningham assigned six battleships to cover the convoys against the potential threat of surface attack by the Italian Fleet.[3]

Under General Alexander's 15th Army Group headquarters, Montgomery's Eighth Army was to land on the beaches fronting the Gulf of Noto, just south of Syracuse, and on both sides of the southeastern point of Sicily; Patton's Seventh Army was to come ashore on seventy miles of beach along the Gulf of Gela. (*Map II*) Both the southwestern cluster of airfields and the Catania-Gerbini complex remained excluded as immediate objectives, and the hope was that the major port of Syracuse would be occupied soon after the landings. If operations developed quickly out of the initial beachhead, Augusta and Catania would soon add their facilities to Allied port capacity.

Though the British thus expected to have three major ports quickly, the Americans, served only by the minor ports of Licata and Gela, would have to depend on beach maintenance. Alexander justified this logistical risk for two reasons: the probability of good weather in July, and the availability of a newly developed two-and-a-half-ton amphibious truck called the Dukw, which could ferry men and matériel directly to beach dumps. Furthermore, after the British captured and opened the port of Syracuse, they agreed, after the fourteenth day of the campaign, to dispatch 1,000 tons of supplies daily to the Seventh Army. But whether this, plus beach maintenance, would be enough remained to be seen.[4]

Before the landings, Alexander made no specific plans to develop the land campaign growing out of the initial beachhead. He preferred to get the two armies firmly ashore before launching out. But he counted on the British Eighth Army to make the main effort, and he expected Montgomery to drive quickly through Catania to the Strait of Messina.[5] He

---

[2] AFHQ, Min of CofS Mtg 6, 15 Mar 43, 0100/12A/145; AFHQ NAF 182, 20 Mar 43, and AFHQ NAF 186, 23 Mar, in ABC 381 HUSKY (1943), sec. 1A; AFHQ NAF 188, 25 Mar 43, OPD Exec 3, item 13; AFHQ NAF 199, 5 Apr 43, and Msg, AFHQ Out 6666 to AGWAR, 24 Apr 43, both in OPD Exec 3, item 11.

[3] Eisenhower Sicilian Dispatch, p. 81. See also Morison, *Sicily–Salerno–Anzio*, pp. 27–29.

[4] Alexander Despatch, pp. 9–10; Force 343 Outline Plan, 18 May 43.

[5] Lt. Col. G. W. L. Nicholson, "Official History of the Canadian Army in the Second World War," vol. II, *The Canadians in Italy 1943–1945* (Ottawa: Edmond Cloutier, Queen's Printer and Controller of Stationery, 1956), pp. 86–87; De Guingand, *Operation Victory*, p. 285; Eisenhower, *Crusade in Europe*, p. 178; Churchill, *Hinge of Fate*, p. 827.

GELA BEACH, *designated landing area for Patton's Seventh Army troops.*

# FINAL ALLIED PREPARATIONS

was aware of possible resentment in the American Seventh Army over the fact that the Americans would only protect the British flank and rear while Montgomery drove for the main strategic objective in Sicily. Patton's army would be the shield in Alexander's left hand; Montgomery's army the sword in his right.

As Alexander expected, some resentment did arise, for Admiral Cunningham reported that the Americans were "very sore about it." Maintenance, too, was bound to be "a tricky problem" for the Americans, for whether they could bring 3,000 tons ashore daily for six weeks over the beaches and through the small ports was highly questionable. Yet Patton, Cunningham learned, had taken "the attitude that he has been ordered to land there and he will do it."[6] Though some of Patton's associates urged him to protest, he refused. An order was an order, and he would do his "goddamndest to carry it out."[7] He apparently convinced Alexander of his good faith and firm intention to do the best he could.[8]

As finally drawn up, the plan provided for the employment of thirteen divisions and one brigade. The British Eighth Army was to land four divisions and one brigade, most of them on the Gulf of Noto beaches, the 1st Canadian Division on one beach around the southeastern corner of the island. Their objectives were the port of Syracuse and a nearby airfield. The British 1st Airlanding Brigade was to precede the main British amphibious landings and seize the bridge called Ponte Grande over the Anapo River just south of Syracuse. The American Seventh Army was to land three divisions on beaches oriented on the ports of Licata and Gela and several airfields nearby. A reinforced regimental combat team from the 82d Airborne Division was to drop several hours ahead of the main American landings to secure important high ground a few miles inland from Gela.[9]

The British Eighth Army planned to make five simultaneous predawn landings, preceded by the air-landing operation just south of Syracuse. The 13 Corps (General Dempsey) on the right was to come ashore on the northern beaches of the Gulf of Noto, the 5th Division near Cassibile, the 50th Division near Avola. Troops of the 1st Airborne Division were to land south of Syracuse on the corps north flank, and together with Commando units landing just south of Syracuse, were to assist the 5th Division to take the port. With a beachhead and Syracuse secured, the 13 Corps was to advance to the north to take Augusta and Catania.

The 30 Corps (General Leese) was to make its amphibious landings on both sides of the Pachino peninsula, the southeastern corner of Sicily. The 231st Infantry Brigade was to protect the right flank and gain contact with the adjacent 13 Corps in the Noto area; the 51st Division was to take the town of Pachino. On the left, the 1st Canadian Division, with two Royal Marine Commando units attached, was to capture the Pachino airfield and make contact with the American Seventh Army at Ragusa. After a secure beachhead was established, Montgomery planned to have the 51st Division

---

[6] Cunningham, *A Sailor's Odyssey*, p. 538.
[7] Quoted in Morison, *Sicily—Salerno—Anzio*, p. 20n.
[8] Alexander Despatch, p. 10.

[9] AFHQ FAN 121, 12 May 43, 0100/4A/29; AFHQ, Min of CofS Mtg 22, 13 May 43, 0100/12C/101.

relieve the 50th Division at Avola to enable the latter unit to move north toward Messina with the 13 Corps.[10]

The British airborne troops, unlike the Americans who would parachute into Sicily, planned to come in by glider. They were to seize two objectives: the Ponte Grande over the Anapo River on Highway 115, and the western part of Syracuse itself. Montgomery hoped that the glider troops would assist the advance of his ground troops into the city and quicken the opening of the port of Syracuse, essential to Eighth Army's logistical plans. The U.S. 51st Troop Carrier Wing, which had worked with the British airborne troops since April 1943, was to furnish a majority of the gliders and the tow planes.

Again, unlike the Americans, who preferred not to schedule follow-up airborne operations, the British scheduled two, one against Augusta, and one in the Catania area. But until the invasion actually started, no one could say with certainty which, or if indeed either, of these operations would be needed.[11]

The problem of mounting, assembling, and supplying the various units in the Eighth Army was rather more difficult than the one faced by the Seventh Army, primarily because of the dispersed locations of the units. The 5th and 50th Divisions and the 231st Infantry Brigade were to be mounted in the Middle East.

The 1st Canadian Division was to come from the United Kingdom; the 51st Division was to be mounted in Tunisia and partly staged in Malta. The 78th Division and a Canadian tank brigade, follow-up units, were to be mounted in the Sfax-Sousse area of North Africa.[12]

In the American invasion, perhaps the most dramatic role was assigned to the paratroopers of the 82d Airborne Division, the newest member of the invasion team, a unit which had yet to celebrate its first birthday.

Delivering ground combat troops to a battlefield by air was not a new idea in 1943, nor was Sicily the first place which saw the use of this dramatic method of warfare. But Sicily was to be the scene of the first Allied employment of a large number of airborne combat troops, delivered by parachute and glider, to support larger bodies of combat troops engaged in conventional ground warfare. Sicily also marked the first test of the airborne division concept, which had not been accepted by the U.S. Army until 1942.[13]

---

[10] Twelfth Army Opns Order 1, 31 May 43, 0100/12A/141. See also Nicholson, *The Canadians in Italy*, pp. 62-63; Montgomery, *Eighth Army*, pp. 89, 94-95.

[11] Br 1st AB Div Plan, job 61C, reel 124A; NAAFTCC Rpt of Opns, 31 Jul 43, 0403/11/949; John C. Warren, *Airborne Missions in the Mediterranean, 1942-1945*, USAF Historical Study 74 (Air University, Maxwell Air Force Base, Ala. 1955) (hereafter cited as Warren, USAF Hist Study 74) pp. 21-29, 42.

[12] Eisenhower Sicily Dispatch; Bradley, *A Soldier's Story*, p. 124; Montgomery, *Eighth Army*, p. 90.

[13] Generally, the authors will not differentiate between parachute and air-landed operations, but will use the term airborne for methods of aerial delivery of troops and supplies into a combat zone. For details in the growth of the airborne division concept see: Robert R. Palmer, Bell I. Wiley, and William R. Keast, *The Procurement and Training of Ground Combat Troops* (Washington, 1948), pp. 433-54, and Kent R. Greenfield, Robert R. Palmer, and Bell I. Wiley, *The Organization of Ground Combat Troops* (Washington, 1947), pp. 96-98, both volumes in UNITED STATES ARMY IN WORLD WAR II; John T. Ellis, Jr., *The Airborne Command and Center*, AGF Study 25, 1946; John A. Huston, Airborne Operations, MS in OCMH; William H. Peifer, *Supply by Sky*, QMC Historical Studies, Series II, No. 2, pp. 7-71.

# FINAL ALLIED PREPARATIONS

Commanded by Maj. Gen. Matthew B. Ridgway, the 82d Airborne Division had been activated in August 1942. It had had a difficult training period. Shortages of transport aircraft, gliders, and parachutes hampered the program, and as late as March 1943 inspection revealed an "insufficient training in the field" and a need for "maneuver experience" before the division could be certified "fully prepared for combat duty." [14] Organizational changes immediately before the scheduled departure of the division for the Mediterranean theater disrupted what little training time remained. With only about one-third the amount of training normally accorded the infantry divisions, the 82d sailed for North Africa. It arrived early in May, two months before the projected invasion of Sicily.

Training continued "in a fiery furnace," according to Ridgway, "where the hot wind carried a fine dust that clogged the nostrils, burned the eyes, and cut into the throat like an abrasive." [15] Pilots of the Northwest African Air Forces Troop Carrier Command (NAAFTCC), activated on 21 March 1943, worked with both the 82d Airborne and the British 1st Airborne Divisions, but a lack of unity of command between the airborne and the air units precluded full co-ordination. Although an American air force officer was attached to the 82d Airborne Division and an airborne liaison officer was attached to the 52d Troop Carrier Wing (the specific NAAFTCC component scheduled to support the American airborne operations), the efforts of a few liaison officers could not overcome the deficiencies of a system which split command in a single operation.[16]

GENERALS BRADLEY AND ALLEN

Arriving in North Africa in April 1943, the 52d Troop Carrier Wing was considered fully qualified in dropping parachutists and towing gliders, but only on daylight missions. Accordingly, the troop carrier units concentrated on night formation and navigational flying, using both normal navigation lights and, later, as proficiency increased, small and lavender-colored resin lights, which would be the only aids available during the Sicily operation. But no real effort was made by the wing to check the location of pinpoint drop zones at night. A night joint training program with airborne troops and carriers fared poorly.

---

[14] Huston, Airborne Operations, ch. III, p. 8; see also General Matthew B. Ridgway, *Soldier: The Memoirs of Matthew B. Ridgway* (New York: Harper and Brothers, 1956), pp. 59–60.

[15] Ridgway, *Soldier*, p. 65.

[16] Lt. Col. C. Billingslea, Report of Airborne Operations, HUSKY and BIGOT, 15 August 1943 (cited hereafter as Billingslea Rpt), 0100/21/1071, I.

GENERAL MIDDLETON    GENERAL RIDGWAY    GENERAL TRUSCOTT

General Ridgway selected the 505th Parachute Infantry Regimental Combat Team, commanded by Col. James M. Gavin, reinforced by the 3d Battalion, 504th Parachute Infantry, to make the initial drop. With no specific assignment, the remaining airborne units worked on several plans covering various contingencies that might lead to their commitment.

Unlike the airborne troops, the American ground units scheduled to make the invasion were for the most part combat-experienced. Despite its new title, to become effective on D-day, the Seventh Army headquarters was essentially that of the I Armored Corps. The headquarters planned the Sicilian operation first at Casablanca, then at Oran, later at Rabat, and finally at Mostaganem. The chief planner was Maj. Gen. Geoffrey Keyes, deputy commander. Patton, himself, participated only in the resolution of major problems.[17]

The subordinate ground units most concerned with the detailed planning of the operation were those eventually allocated to the Seventh Army: the II Corps headquarters; the 1st, 3d, and 45th Infantry Divisions; the 2d Armored Division; the 82d Airborne Division; and a portion of the 9th Infantry Division, the bulk of the latter cast in the role of a follow-up unit to be committed only with General Alexander's approval.

Scheduled to control a sizable portion of the assaulting echelon, the II Corps had played an important role in the North African campaign, first under Maj. Gen. Lloyd Fredendall, then under General Patton, and finally under Maj. Gen. Omar N. Bradley. A West Point graduate in the class of 1915 and the first of that class to receive a star, General Bradley had commanded in turn two infantry divisions in the United States before coming to North Africa in early 1943 to act as General Eisenhower's personal representative in the field. On 16 April, Bradley had assumed command of the II Corps and had demonstrated a competence that marked him for higher command.

The 3d Infantry Division had participated in the North African invasion and

---

[17] Seventh Army Rpt of Opns, pp. A-2-- A-6; Bradley, *A Soldier's Story*, p. 112.

GENERAL EDDY      GENERAL GAFFEY      COLONEL DARBY, *leader of Force X. (Photograph taken in 1944.)*

in part of the ensuing campaign. Its commander, Maj. Gen. Lucian K. Truscott, Jr., had served as head of the American mission to the British Combined Operations Headquarters, where he had conceived the idea of creating American Ranger battalions patterned after the British Commandos. An observer in the ill-starred Dieppe raid of August 1942, he had helped plan the North African invasion, and had commanded the American landings at Port-Lyautey in Morocco. Truscott assumed command of the 3d Division on 8 March 1943.

The 1st Infantry Division, the oldest division in the American Army, had participated in the North African invasion and had seized Oran after some of the bitterest fighting of the campaign. The division had then served throughout the remainder of the North African campaign, often under trying circumstances. Maj. Gen. Terry de la Mesa Allen had assumed command shortly before the division had shipped overseas.

The 45th Infantry Division was an Oklahoma National Guard unit that had been federalized in 1940. Alerted in January 1943 for an amphibious operation in the Mediterranean theater, the division was probably one of the best trained divisions in the American Army when it sailed from the United States in June 1943. Its commander, Maj. Gen. Troy H. Middleton, had been the youngest regimental commander in the American Army in France during World War I. He had retired in 1937, but had returned to active duty in early 1942 and soon assumed command of the division.

The 2d Armored Division, which was to provide supporting armor to the assault forces as well as to constitute a floating reserve, was a comparatively new unit on the rolls of the American Army, although its tank strength could be traced back through the 66th Infantry (light tanks)—the nation's only tank regiment in 1940—to the American Tank Corps of World War I days. Three invasion teams had been drawn from the division to provide armored support in the American landings in North Africa but had taken no part in the later Tunisian fighting. In early 1943 the division provided some two thousand replacements and numerous wheeled and tracked vehicles to the 1st Armored Division. Maj. Gen. Hugh J. Gaffey, who as Patton's chief of staff in the II Corps had gained considerable experience during the Tunisian campaign, assumed command of the 2d Armored Division on 5 May 1943. Gaffey had been one of the pioneers of the American armored effort in the early days of World War II.

The follow-up 9th Division, which had participated in the invasion of North Africa and had fought in the Tunisian campaign, notably at Hill 609, was under Maj. Gen. Manton S. Eddy, who had been in command since mid-1942. Its 39th Infantry Regiment and division artillery were alerted for commitment in Sicily any time after D-day.

In addition to the major ground units, the Seventh Army included a number of units designed for specialized functions. Of primary importance to the assault phase were three Ranger battalions, the 1st, 3d, and 4th. The latter two had been newly activated in North Africa. The 1st Rangers, led by Lt. Col. William O. Darby, had earned an enviable combat reputation in the Tunisian fighting.

Another special unit was a motorized chemical battalion equipped with the 4.2-inch mortar, an extremely accurate, rifled-bore, muzzle-loading weapon. Four of these battalions were assigned to the Seventh Army, one to each infantry division. Each consisted of forty officers and over five hundred men, equipped with forty-eight of the big mortars, a Chemical Corps weapon designed originally for firing smoke and gas shells, although quite capable of firing high explosive and white phosphorus rounds. There was little opportunity for combined training and for instructing infantry commanders and their staffs on the capabilities and limitations of the mortar. This was doubly unfortunate because the 4.2-inch mortar was, in effect, a new weapon and few infantry personnel in North Africa had had any previous experience with it.

To give the Free French, who were re-equipping their Army units in North Africa with United States assistance, at least token representation in the Sicilian invasion, General Eisenhower accepted a battalion-size unit, the 4th Moroccan Tabor of Goums, to operate with the American forces. Numbering almost 900 men, the tabor had French officers and noncommissioned officers, Berber goumiers in the ranks, 117 horses, and 126 mules. Attached to the 3d Division, the goums were scheduled to come ashore on the fifth day of the invasion.[18]

*Seventh Army Plans*

The troops of the Seventh Army were to land on the beaches of the Gulf of Gela west of a boundary line running from the coast near Pozzallo inland through Ragusa to Vizzini, these towns and the road connecting them being assigned to the British. Patton was to seize the airfields of Licata, Ponte Olivo, Biscari, and Comiso. He was to capture

---

[18] W. C. Baxter, "Goums Marocains," *Cavalry Journal*, LIII, No. 2 (March–April 1944), pp. 62–64; for U.S. assistance to the French, see Marcel Vigneras, *Rearming the French*, UNITED STATES ARMY IN WORLD WAR II (Washington, 1957).

and put into operation the ports at Licata and Gela. He was then to be ready for future operations as directed.

As Patton analyzed the terrain, he saw a dome-shaped plateau facing his landing areas as the important piece of ground— a high saddle springing from the Caronie Mountains in the north and extending southeast from Enna to Piazza Armerina and onto the peak of the plateau at Monte Lauro. Hardly less important was the Salso River on the left.

These terrain features indicated roughly an outline of the beachhead that the army would have to secure. The obvious strongpoint on which to base the beachhead on the west was a secondary ridge east of the Salso River, which would provide a further obstacle to enemy intrusion. Elsewhere the high ground at Piazza Armerina would delineate the beachhead. Possession of this terrain would deprive the enemy of ground overlooking the assault beaches and give the Seventh Army protection for building up its strength preliminary to a push inland. But this beachhead would not give the army two of its important and assigned objectives, the port and airfield at Licata.

To get these, Patton extended the beachhead line on the west to a high ridge fourteen miles northwest of Licata. But the key to the entire problem remained the high ground at Piazza Armerina, which was not only commanding terrain but also carried the main road (Highway 117) leading from Enna to Gela and Syracuse. The enemy would most certainly utilize this road in shifting his forces from the western and central portions of the island to oppose the Allied landings. To get to this high ground quickly became the basic motive of Seventh Army planning.

The seventy miles of beach assigned the Seventh Army from Licata on the west to Pozzallo on the east comprised the crescent shore line of the Gulf of Gela. Though only a few of the beaches had good exits, almost all had some access to inland trails and roads. Except for the small ports of Licata and Gela and the tiny fishing village of Scoglitti, the coast was open, with sandy beaches and occasional rocky outcroppings. The beaches appeared ideal for amphibious landings, but in reality they were not. Gradients were too gentle for many of the assault landing craft. False beaches, shifting sand bars covered by sufficient water to float smaller landing craft but not enough for the larger craft carrying vehicles and heavy equipment, fronted much of the shore line.

The shallow plains behind the assault beaches extended inland only a few miles before merging with the foothills of the dome-shaped plateau. The main rivers flowing from the high ground—the Salso, the Gela, and the Acate—presented problems for cross-country movement.

The length of assault frontage and the compartmenting of terrain created by the rivers strongly influenced General Patton in organizing the army for the invasion. He assigned the II Corps the bulk of the assault units and a large section of the front. He kept the 3d Division, reinforced heavily with combat and service support units, directly under his control. The II Corps was to make the main effort and seize the key terrain features in the Piazza Armerina area; the 3d Division was to attack in the Licata area and anchor the beachhead on the west by seizing the ridge line west of the Salso River. An army reserve was to comprise four principal elements: (1) the 2d Armored Division, minus Combat Command A but reinforced by the 18th Infantry Regimental Combat Team (RCT) of the 1st Division, which was to sail with the assault forces prepared to land in support of any assault; (2) the remainder of the 82d Airborne Division, which was to be on call any time after H-hour; (3) the 39th Infantry RCT of the 9th Infantry Division, plus the 9th Division's artillery, which was to be ready to move from North Africa at any time after D-day; and (4) the remainder of the 9th Division.[19]

Patton's scheme of maneuver called for simultaneous landings in the Licata-Gela-Scoglitti areas in order to capture the airfields, the air landing ground at Farello, just east of Gela, and the ports of Licata and Gela by darkness of D plus 2. For control, Patton designated two phase lines. The first, called the Yellow Line, marked a secure initial beachhead and included the initial objectives—a line through Palma di Montechiaro, Campobello, Mazzarino, Caltagirone, and Grammichele, roughly twenty miles inland. The second, denoted the Blue Line, through Campobello, Piazza Armerina, and Grammichele, included the high ground overlooking the lateral roads in the army sector.

To General Bradley's II Corps went three principal missions. Under the cover of darkness on D-day, the assault units—the 1st and 45th Infantry Divisions—were to land at Gela and near Scoglitti, and capture the Ponte Olivo airfield by daylight on D plus 1. After pressing inland and seizing the Comiso airfield by daylight on D plus 2 and the Biscari airfield by darkness of that day, the corps was to extend its beachhead to the Yellow Line, from Mazzarino on the west to Vizzini on the east, and gain contact with the British Eighth Army at Ragusa.

Truscott's reinforced 3d Division also had three principal missions. It was to land in the Licata area on D-day and capture the port and airfield there by nightfall. After extending its beachhead to the Yellow Line (from Palma di Montechiaro on the west up to and through Campobello toward Mazzarino) to protect the army's beachhead from enemy interference from the west and northwest, the division was to gain and maintain contact with the II Corps on the right.[20]

Expecting Truscott's 3d Division to capture the port and airfield at Licata by nightfall of the first day and the high ground around Naro soon after, and anticipating that Bradley's II Corps would have the three airfields in its zone by the end of the third day, General Patton hoped to have his initial objectives in three days. Then he wanted the beachhead expanded to the final phase line, named Blue. To bolster the II Corps landing in the Gela area, he directed that a parachute task force in reinforced regimental strength be dropped in front of the 1st Division to secure the high ground overlooking the 1st Division's assault beaches.

Commanding the left invasion forces, Truscott, with CCA of the 2d Armored Division and the tabor of goums attached to his 3d Division, had about 45,000

---

[19] Seventh Army Rpt of Opns, p. a-8.

[20] Force 343 Outline Plan, 18 May 43, Seventh Army Rpt of Opns, p. d-2; Map, Final Allied Plan (HUSKY), Seventh Army Rpt of Opns, p. a-5; Hq Force 343 FO 1, 20 Jun 43, Seventh Army Rpt of Opns, pp. d-7—d-8; the detailed order of battle of the Seventh Army may be found in Seventh Army Rpt of Opns, pp. d-9—d-12.

# FINAL ALLIED PREPARATIONS

men. About half were to land on D-day on a front of more than twelve miles. His objective, Licata, a city of about 30,000 people, a minor port, rail, and road center, nestled against a mound that rises about 500 feet above the Licata plain, flat terrain rimmed, five miles away, by the foothills of the dome-shaped plateau. In the middle of the plain, three miles northwest of the city and adjacent to the highway running north to Caltanissetta and Enna, was the Licata airfield.

The Seventh Army designated four assault beaches as suitable for the 3d Division—two west of Licata, two east of the town. Because beach data was far from complete, Truscott appealed personally to Maj. Gen. James Doolittle, who commanded the Northwest African Strategic Air Force (NASAF), for serial photos of the landing sites, which Doolittle supplied.[21]

Early capture of Campobello and Palma di Montechiaro, both on Patton's Yellow Line and both controlling avenues of approach from the northwest, were Truscott's essential objectives for protecting the army's left flank. But the Salso River, bisecting his zone, could be crossed only by road and railway bridges at Licata. The beaches west of Licata were poor, those east of the city good. Assuming that the enemy would destroy the bridges across the Salso, should Truscott commit his entire force to the eastern beaches and risk its temporary confinement within the narrow limits of the river, hill, and sea? Or should he land in strength on both sides of the river and risk isolation of the western landings in view of the necessity for seizing Campobello and Palma di Montechiaro? Even though it would be difficult to reinforce from the sea over the beaches west of Licata, Truscott chose to land on both sides of the river.

Truscott wished to land all his infantry as rapidly as possible, with some tanks in close support, and seize four key points in the foothills dominating the Licata plain. With a beachhead formed and secured, he would then strike immediately for Campobello and Palma di Montechiaro, using if necessary CCA of the 2d Armored Division, his floating reserve.

The right invasion force, Bradley's II Corps, was to bite off more than fifty of the seventy miles of army front, though in actuality the landings would occur on somewhat separated fronts totaling fifteen miles. The 1st Division was to land on the left, the 45th Division on the right.

The 1st Division's zone extended from a point midway between Gela and Licata eastward to the Acate River. Gela, about twenty miles east of Licata, was an overgrown fishing village with 32,000 inhabitants. It had a pier jutting 900 feet into the water from near the center of the town to serve small ships. Behind the town was the treeless plain of Gela, used for growing grain. The Gela River reached the sea a mile or so east of the town. Three miles east of Gela and adjacent to the coastal highway was the Gela-Farello landing ground. Six miles east of Gela, the Acate (or Dirillo) River emptied into the sea.

General Allen, controlling two regiments of the 1st Division, two Ranger battalions, and supporting units, was assigned six beaches with a total frontage of five miles. He split his troops into

---

[21] Lucian K. Truscott, *Command Missions* (New York: E. P. Dutton and Co., Inc., 1954), pp. 200–201.

three attack groups. The Rangers were to take the city of Gela; one of the infantry regiments was to assist the Rangers, if necessary, or was to take high ground overlooking the Ponte Olivo airfield from the west; the other regiment was to move to the northeast toward the hilltop town of Niscemi, thirteen miles northeast of Gela, make contact with paratroopers dropped inland, and advance against the Ponte Olivo airfield from the east.

Between the Acate River and the Seventh Army boundary on the right, a distance of fifteen miles, lay the zone of the 45th Division, a smooth arc of coast line virtually devoid of indentation. Two rocks jutting above the water signaled the entrance to two coves that served the fishing village of Scoglitti. Behind the shore was a broad, relatively open plain sloping gradually to the foothills of the mountainous terrain and to inland towns on relatively high ground. About ten miles inland, Biscari and its airfield (three miles to the north of the town) and Comiso and its airfield (three miles north of the town), were the main objectives of General Middleton's division. Between the relatively uninhabited coast line and the coastal highway, which sheers away from the coast after leaving Gela, there were no good roads. One regiment coming ashore just east of the mouth of the Acate River was to drive north to Biscari to take the town and airfield and seize the crossing of the coastal highway over the Acate River—Ponte Dirillo. Another regiment was to seize Scoglitti, then capture the town of Vittoria, seven miles inland, and be prepared to help take the Comiso airfield. The third regiment was to drive on the Comiso airfield, protect the II Corps right flank, and gain contact with the Canadians at Ragusa.[22]

The assault forces and the floating reserve were paired off with the naval task forces which comprised the component parts of Admiral Hewitt's Western Naval Task Force. The 3d Division was to be transported on a shore-to-shore basis by Naval Task Force 86 under the command of Rear Adm. Richard L. Conolly. Two light cruisers and eight destroyers were to perform escort and gunfire support duties for this task force. The 1st Division and the army's floating reserve were to be carried by Rear Adm. John L. Hall's Naval Task Force 81 on both a ship-to-shore and shore-to-shore basis, escorted and supported by two light cruisers and thirteen destroyers. The 45th Division was paired off with Rear Adm. Alan G. Kirk's Naval Task Force 85 on a wholly ship-to-shore operation. One light cruiser and sixteen destroyers were allotted to this force for supporting duties. There was to be no naval counterpart to the II Corps headquarters, nor did General Bradley have a naval opposite number. The II Corps commander and a few key members of his staff were allotted space aboard Admiral Kirk's flagship, while the remainder of the corps' staff was distributed among five LST's of the same force.[23]

---

[22] For details of the divisions' plans see: 3d Inf Div FO 5, 26 Jun 43; II Corps FO 8, 15 Jun 43; 1st Inf Div FO 26, 20 Jun 43; AGF Rpt 217, sub: Rpt on Opn HUSKY, 1943.

[23] Action Report, Western Naval Task Force, The Sicilian Campaign, Operation HUSKY, July-August 1943 (cited hereafter as WNTF Action Rpt), pp. 25–26; Bradley, *A Soldier's Story*, p. 119; Morison, *Sicily—Salerno—Anzio*, pp. 27–33; Interv, Maj. A. N. Garland and Mr. Martin Blumenson with Lt. Gen. Troy H. Middleton (Ret.), 16 Jun 59, at Louisiana State University.

A total of 601 ships and 1,124 ship-borne landing craft were assigned to WNTF. This figure includes 32 Liberty ships and 92 LCM's carried

# FINAL ALLIED PREPARATIONS

The airborne mission, designed primarily to assist the 1st Division landing, was the seizure of the high ground (Piano Lupo) in the Gela area for the purpose of blocking enemy approach from the north and east. The troops were also to cover the Ponte Olivo airfield by fire and facilitate its capture by the seaborne infantry. Under Seventh Army control until they made contact with the ground forces, the parachute troops were then to come under the II Corps. General Bradley planned to attach the 3d Battalion, 504th Parachute Infantry, to the 1st Division to assist the latter unit in taking Niscemi, while the remainder of the parachute combat team assembled near Gela as 1st Division reserve.

The drop zone for the major parachute elements—Piano Lupo—was a hill mass which dominated a road intersection seven miles northeast of Gela. There the roads from Caltagirone (via Niscemi) and Vittoria met, providing excellent approaches for an enemy force arriving to contest the 1st Division's landings. Drop zones for lesser elements were chosen for similar reasons—troops dropped in these areas were to knock out roadblocks and obstruct the highway approaches to the beaches. One party of forty-two men was to drop from three planes in the early minutes of 10 July to demolish or hold the vital Dirillo bridge across the Acate River.

Attachments of engineers, signal troops, medical personnel, and naval gunfire and air support parties reinforced Colonel Gavin's combat team. Though the planners hoped for early contact with the seaborne forces, they planned at least one aerial resupply mission.

The 52d Troop Carrier Wing planned to employ 227 aircraft, all C-47's, organized into five groups to transport the paratroopers. They were to fly at just above sea level in closed V of V formations of nine craft, rising during their final approaches to 600 feet and widening their formations. All were to arrive over the drop zones between 2330, 9 July, and 0006, 10 July. After discharging their loads, they were to execute a wide 180-degree turn and fly back to their home bases in North Africa.

Though the initial route proposed for the troop carriers was a relatively short and straight flight over Pantelleria, the planners eventually chose a route over Malta in order to keep the planes away from the naval convoys and their antiaircraft guns. The final route accepted had three sharp turns over water during dim moonlight, "a complicated dog-leg course requiring over three hours flight each way." [24]

The pilots were to identify their drop zones from aerial photographs carried in their cockpits. There were to be no markers on the drop zones; no pathfinder teams. But this seemed satisfactory, for on a previous night reconnaissance, Colonel Gavin found that "all check points and terrain showed up clearly in the moonlight, exactly as we had memorized them from photographs." [25]

A problem of great concern to General Ridgway, the 82d Airborne Division's commander, was adequate night fighter protection for the troop carriers, which

---

on those Liberty ships which arrived off the beaches between D plus 1 and D plus 8. WNTF Action Rpt, p. 96.

[24] Harry L. Coles, Participation of the Ninth and Twelfth Air Forces in the Sicilian Campaign. USAF Historical Study 37 (Air University, Maxwell Air Force Base, Ala., 1945), p. 80.

[25] James M. Gavin, *Airborne Warfare* (Washington: Infantry Journal Press, 1947), p. 5. See also Warren, USAF Hist Study 74, p. 28.

were vulnerable to attack. No one could guarantee that the Allied air forces would have complete air mastery by the time of the invasion. Though Ridgway requested fighter protection, and though General Patton and the troop carrier commander supported him, the NATAF disapproved the request on the basis that other missions were of greater importance to the operation as a whole. As a result the paratroopers and the troop carrier crewmen would have to bank on achieving tactical surprise or possibly on the unwillingness of enemy air to make a fight of it.[26]

Though tactical planning was not particularly troublesome, logistics posed its problems. Planners provided the 45th Infantry Division with twenty-one days maintenance plus ten units of fire in the assault and first follow-up convoy of D plus 4. Seven additional days maintenance, plus one and one-sixth units of fire, would be carried on the second follow-up convoy on D plus 8.[27] The 1st Division, furnished with enough supplies for the airborne elements committed in its zone, was to carry on its assault convoy seven days maintenance plus two and one-third units of fire, while its D plus 4 follow-up was to bring in an additional seven days of maintenance plus one and one-sixth units of fire. Fourteen days maintenance, plus two and one-third units of fire, were provided on the D plus 8 convoy. The 3d Division generally followed the same plan: seven days maintenance plus one and one-sixth units of fire on the assault convoy; seven days maintenance and one and one-sixth units of fire on the first follow-up convoy; but only seven days maintenance and one and one-sixth units of fire on the D plus 8 convoy.

There was also to be a floating supply reserve. In Oran, Algiers, and Bizerte, twenty days maintenance and four units of fire were to be loaded in seven cargo ships and held on call to unload over the beaches any time after D plus 14. In addition, the logistical planners established on the ground in the Bizerte area a reserve of supplies of three and one-half units of fire, 25 percent combat vehicles, 10 percent general purpose vehicles, and 10 percent weapons, plus fifteen days maintenance for 140,000 men, to be available on call for movement to Sicily.

An emergency stockpile of supplies, established in the Kairouan area of central Tunisia for the 82d Airborne Division and available for shipment on call from army, consisted of seven days maintenance and two and one-third units of fire for one infantry regimental combat team reinforced by three antiaircraft battalions and one tank battalion.

The division commanders were responsible for their own supply from ships and landing craft over the beaches, or through any of the captured ports, until the Seventh Army could assume the logistic function. This responsibility in-

---

[26] For details of the airborne planning, see: II Corps FO 8, 15 Jun 43; 82d AB Div FO 1, 23 Jun 43; 505th RCT (Reinf) FO 1, 28 Jun 43; 1st Inf Div FO 26, 20 Jun 43; 82d AB Div 2d rev. an. 2 to FO 1, 8 Jul 43; Ltr, U.S. Naval Forces, NWA Waters, to CinC U.S. Fleet, 24 Jul 43, sub: Naval Gunfire Liaison Offs Operating With AB Troops, with Incl, Rpt from Ensign Seibert; History of 3d USAF Air Support Communications Squadron, 10 January 1944, Sq–A–Sup–Com–3–Hi, Air University, Maxwell Air Field Base, Ala., p. 16; Billingslea Rpt; NAAFTCC Rpt.

[27] The units of fire used in the Sicilian operation are shown in Annex 3, FO 1, Headquarters Force 343, 15 June 1943, Seventh Army Report of Operations, p. d–44. A unit of fire represents a specific number of rounds of ammunition per weapon, which varies with the type and caliber of weapons.

# FINAL ALLIED PREPARATIONS

cluded maintaining all the beaches in the division areas. To carry out this function, each assault division received an engineer shore regiment or an engineer combat regiment. When the army took over the supply mission, the 1st Engineer Special Brigade (a permanent headquarters) was to assume command of all division beach groups and become responsible for the execution of all supply plans emanating from army, including the operation of captured ports. The II Corps would have no administrative functions other than those pertaining to corps troops unless an emergency arose.[28]

The most crucial aspect of all army logistical planning remained the balancing of army requirements with the available naval shipping capacity. The limitations on the number of landing craft assigned to the division task forces caused logistical planners many sleepless nights. Artillery wanted its guns ashore as quickly as possible and did not particularly care if the weapons displaced necessary service units. Engineers wanted more bridging equipment and did not hesitate to argue for the displacement of certain artillery units. General Bradley, whose headquarters was responsible for the preparations of two of the three assault forces, was in the middle of the dispute. Bradley fought, pleaded, cajoled, and ordered his supply people to come up with a workable plan. But the separate arms and services were difficult to handle, "each contending," Bradley said, "that if its particular allotment were cut, the whole invasion might fail." [29]

Truscott's supply people faced much the same problem. Since the 3d Division would be almost three times the size of a normal infantry division and expected to be responsible for its own supply and maintenance for a long time, Truscott found it necessary to establish an administrative organization much larger than that normally found in a division, one that was comparable to an army-size unit.[30]

The assault against Sicily represented an enormous improvement in specialized craft and in the technique of amphibious operations over the North African landings of 1942. Several new devices were to be used on a large scale for the first time. A whole new series of landing craft and ships were to play a prominent part. The most important of these were the LST (landing ship, tank), the LCT (landing craft, tank), the LCI (landing craft, infantry), and the LCVP (landing craft, vehicle or personnel). Their function was to come aground on the shore and disgorge men and matériel rapidly. Yet they were so new that no one could be sure of certain aspects of their performance. For example, the LCI had never been beached successfully in water shallow enough for infantry to wade ashore; many naval officers thought that the troops would first have to disembark into canvas or rubber boats. No one knew precisely how many men could be loaded into an LST or LCT with both comfort during the voyage and

---

[28] Seventh Army Rpt of Opns, pp. E-1—E-4; I-10; I-16—I-21.

[29] Bradley, *A Soldier's Story*, p. 117.

[30] Truscott, *Command Missions*, p. 204. The variety of organizations scheduled for the operation was in no way an aid to the logisticians. The II Corps alone contained 151 different types of units "ranging from infantry regiments to engineer well-drilling sections, balloon batteries, MP prisoner-escort companies, auxiliary surgical groups, graves registration companies, and naval shore battalions." Bradley, *A Soldier's Story*, pp. 117-18.

PONTON CAUSEWAY *extending from an LST to shore was first used in invasion of Sicily.*

adequate egress ashore. There was also the Dukw, an ingenious vehicle able to swim and roll, and on this vehicle rested much of the hope of supplying the Seventh Army adequately over the beaches. Basically an amphibious 2½-ton truck capable of carrying twenty-five troops and their equipment, or five thousand pounds of general cargo, or twelve loaded litters, the Dukw, with its six-cylinder engine and propeller, could make a speed of five and a half knots in the water in a moderate sea, and race fifty miles per hour on land on its six wheels.[31]

The various new craft, products of American and British imagination and industrial skill, in large measure provided the answer to the chief problem of amphibious warfare—the rapid transfer of

[31] For descriptions of landing craft see ONI 226, Allied Landing Craft and Ships; Samuel Eliot Morison, "History of United States Naval Operations in World War II," vol. II, *Operations in North African Waters, October 1942-June 1943* (Boston: Little, Brown and Company, 1947), pp. 266-71; ASF Manual M409, 14 Dec 43, sub: Logistical Planning and Reference Data.

For their development see: James Phinney Baxter 3d, *Scientists Against Time* (Boston: Little, Brown and Company, 1946), pp. 69-77; Matloff and Snell, *Strategic Planning for Coalition Warfare, 1941-1942*, pp. 192-94; George E. Mowry, *Landing Craft and the WPB (Historical Report on War Administration: WPB Special Study 11)*, rev. ed., Washington, 1946). For a description of the large troop-carrying transports see Roland W. Charles, *Troopships of World War II* (Army Transportation Association, Washington, 1947).

For the development of the Dukw see: Constance McLaughlin Green, Harry C. Thomson, and Peter C. Roots, *The Ordnance Department: Planning Munitions for War* (Washington, 1955), pp. 227n, 227-28, and Chester Wardlow, *The Transportation Corps: Movements, Training, and Supply* (Washington, 1956), pp. 442-91, both volumes in the UNITED STATES ARMY IN WORLD WAR II.

men and matériel to the far shore. But the Sicilian beaches presented a peculiar problem. Between the false beaches and the true beaches were depressions, or runnels. To overcome this hazard, the Navy devised two methods of transferring vehicles and other cargo from the large landing craft across the runnels to the shore line. The first was the ponton causeway, several of which were constructed at Bizerte and Arzew under the direction of Admiral Conolly. A number of ponton units were clamped securely together to form a causeway or portable bridge either to be towed to Sicily or carried there on the sides of LST's.

The second method married an LCT to an LST. Cut out, hinged sections of selected LCT's permitted these modified craft to be joined to the bow of an LST, at right angles to the larger vessel. The vehicles, or other cargo, on the LST could then be moved across the lowered bow ramp of the LST onto the LCT. From the first LCT, the vehicle or cargo could then be transferred to a second LCT, bow to bow, and the second LCT could transport the load to shore.[32]

## Naval and Air Plans

The peculiar difficulty in planning HUSKY was that the operation did not fall specifically into either a ship-to-shore or a shore-to-shore operation. In the first place, it could not be called shore-to-shore since the 45th Division was tactically loaded in the United States before the final tactical plan was firm. On the other hand, many of the vessels allotted to the army units were the types specifically designed for shore-to-shore operations, a situation which posed untold problems since this technique of amphibious warfare had been given little study in the United States and there was little official American literature on the subject.

As late as the middle of May the naval staff was planning to employ equipment whose capabilities and limitations were virtually unknown.[33] Nor was there a sufficient number of any category of craft for component forces within the Army to be similarly equipped. The 45th Division, coming directly from the United States, was loaded on the pre-TORCH principle of "Trans-Divs" (Transport Divisions), consisting of combat-loaded AP and AK ships.[34] The 1st Division, executing a shore-to-shore operation, had for the most part ship-to-shore ships and craft with the bulk of its vehicles loaded into AK or other types of cargo ships. The 3d Division alone had an adequate number of shore-to-shore craft entirely suitable for its task.

There could be no argument with the suballotment of the available shipping: Patton did not have enough of any one kind to go around. He chose to concentrate in a single sector—that of the 3d Division—the means to put ashore rapidly a powerful armored force which in the initial phases could have a material effect on the whole of the subsequent campaign. When deciding on the allotment of landing craft to the divisions, Patton felt that one of the most vital, if least spectacular, of the assigned tasks was the protection of the left flank of the Allied

---

[32] Morison, *Sicily—Salerno—Anzio*, p. 31.

[33] COHQ Bull Y/1, sub: Notes on Planning and Assault Phases of the Sicilian Campaign, October 1943, 8-7.0010/43.

[34] The term AP is used to denote a troop transport vessel; the term APA to denote an attack transport. The AK designation refers to a cargo ship; the term AKA to an attack cargo ship.

landings against counterattacks from the strong German formations known to be in the western part of the island. The rapid disgorgement of armor onto the 3d Division beaches would greatly assist in meeting any such threat.

Whether it was vital to soften the beach defenses by naval gunfire before the landings was a question on which the Army and Navy took opposite views. Not optimistic about the effect of naval gunfire on fixed beach defenses, Army planners were concerned with the safety of paratroopers dropped ashore before the landings; they were also interested in achieving tactical surprise. The Navy planners argued that it was impossible to expect to achieve surprise because of the heavy preparatory air bombardments, the dropping of paratroopers several hours before the beach assault, and the approach of huge convoys in bright moonlight.

The Army prevailed. There was to be no preparatory naval fire. Yet the Army wished the warships to be ready to furnish fire support after the troops were ashore. To this end, fire control parties from each artillery battalion received some training in observing and controlling naval gunfire on ground targets; arrangements were made for air observation and control of naval fires; and a naval gunfire liaison officer was assigned to each infantry division staff.

In the event that the enemy discovered the invasion forces offshore and began to take effective measures to prevent the landings, the Navy was to be ready to take shore targets under fire. The planners prepared a system of prearranged fires, Army planners selecting certain targets for the Navy, others for the Air Forces.[35]

Unlike the naval planners who co-operated closely with Army planners, the Air Forces refused to co-ordinate its planning with either Army or Navy. Part of this was due to the influence of the British concept, which held that the air service was independent of and co-equal with the other services—a concept different from the American point of view, which saw the air arm as having a support function as well as a more or less independent mission. But the Air Forces adopted as its primary mission the neutralization of Axis air power, and until that objective was accomplished to the satisfaction of air commanders, little could be done to secure ground support. The Air Forces' position was that air strength should not be parceled out to individual landings or sectors, but should instead be kept united under a single command to insure the greatest possible flexibility. Thus, air power could be massed where it was needed and not kept immobilized where not needed. Because the enemy air forces remained the overriding target, and since enemy aircraft comprised "a fluid target not easily pinpointed in advance," the air plan gave ground and naval commanders no concrete information on the amount and type of air support they could expect on D-day.[36]

The air plan issued late in June was described by one American general as a "most masterful piece of uninformed prevarication, totally unrelated to the Naval and Military Joint Plan." [37] D-day

---

[35] Seventh Army Rpt of Opns, pp. A-10–A-12; WNTF Action Rpt, pp. 86-87.

[36] Quote is from Craven and Cate, eds., *Europe: TORCH to POINTBLANK*, p. 445; see also Sir John Slessor, *The Central Blue* (New York: Frederick A. Praeger, 1957), pp. 417-27.

[37] Quote is from COHQ Bull Y/1. The air plan may be found in 0407/488, Rpt of Opns

# FINAL ALLIED PREPARATIONS

bombardment targets were not disclosed, except those diversionary bombardments in support of the airborne drops.[38] Ground and naval commanders had no idea of the degree of protection they could expect, and when the assault troops set sail for Sicily, their commanders had not the faintest idea of when, where, under what circumstances, and in what numbers they would see their own aircraft.

The U.S. XII Air Support Command (Maj. Gen. Edwin House) had the mission of providing air support for the Seventh Army. The command comprised seventeen squadrons of aircraft: six of fighter-bombers, ten of day fighters, and one reconnaissance squadron. The command also included signal construction and signal operation units for maintaining and operating an extensive communications network plus a signal aircraft warning battalion which could provide radar coverage over the battle area and ground control for the aircraft. Of the allotted aircraft, however, only the reconnaissance squadron operated under the direct control of the XII Air Support Command; all fighter-bomber and day fighter aircraft were placed under the operational control of the RAF's Malta Command and under NATAF itself, operating through XII Air Support Command's rear headquarters in Tunisia.[39]

The most support that would be furnished the Seventh Army during the initial phases of the Sicilian Campaign consisted of a maximum of eighteen tactical reconnaissance missions per day, each mission lasting some thirty minutes.

Despite ground dissatisfaction with air plans, the Allied air forces actually performed their preinvasion roles effectively. Furnishing all the fighter and fighter-bomber support and much of the light and medium bomber support, the NATAF moved three Spitfire wings from North Africa to Malta in June to bring the air strength on that island to twenty fighter squadrons. An American P-40 fighter group moved to Pantelleria, also in June, to cover the assault landings at Gela and Licata. American aviation engineers in the remarkably short time of twenty days constructed a new airfield on the island of Gozo, near Malta, to base another American fighter group. By the end of June, Allied planes based on the three islands totaled 670 first-line aircraft.

On the Cape Bon peninsula of North Africa, twelve newly constructed, or improved, Axis airfields went to the XII Air Support Command and to the Tactical Bomber Force. The British Desert Air Force, based in the Tripoli area and employing fighter-bombers entirely, was

---

by Northwest African Tactical Air Force in the Capture of Sicily.

[38] Ltr, NAAF to NASAF, 4 Jul 43, sub: Radio Counter-Measures, and HUSKY Outline Plan for Attack on Enemy Radar, 21 Jun 43, both in 0403/11/947; see also Ltr, NAAF to multiple addressees, 7 Jul 43, sub: Diversionary Air Opns, same file; Coles, USAF Hist Study 37, p. 87; Warren, USAF Hist Study 74, pp. 25-26.

[39] See files 0407/430, sub: Co-operation With Force 343, and 0407/418, sub: Operational Planning—XII ASC, for details of working out the air support plan. Several air officers tried to secure close co-ordination with the ground forces, Col. Lawrence Hickey in particular. Working with General Patton on air problems, Hickey became *persona non grata* with air force commanders and was prevented from receiving a command as the result of the personal intervention of Air Marshal Cunningham, who felt that the "Hickey-Patton relationship [was] a weakness." See correspondence in 0407/418. See also Ltr, No. 1 Planning Staff, Force 545 (Air), 2 Jun 43, to Deputy Air CinC on Matter of Air Support for Seventh Army, 0403/10/251.

ready to support ground operations in Sicily and prepared to move to Malta as soon as planes there shifted to newly captured airfields on Sicily.

The NASAF started its Sicilian operation by first attacking the southwestern group of Sicilian airfields, then shifted during the final week before the invasion to the eastern fields. Enemy air opposition proved surprisingly light.

*The Final Days*

The general plan for the forces approaching Sicily from the west, which included the entire American assault and a goodly portion of the British assault force, was an accretive process in which the layers were added in consideration of the mounting areas, the relative speeds of the vessels, the mutual protection of the convoys, and to the end of providing maximum traveling comfort for the troops.

First to sail, the 45th Division re-embarked on the afternoon of 4 July at Oran on the same ships that had brought the division from the United States only a short time before. The 1st Division, less a few units staging through Tunis, boarded transports in the Algiers harbor on the following afternoon. Still later, the 3d Division departed Bizerte, CCA of the 2d Armored Division, Oran. General Patton, accompanied by General Ridgway, sailed on Admiral Hewitt's flagship, the *Monrovia*. The subordinate ground commanders sailed with the naval commanders who headed the smaller task forces carrying the three major elements of the Seventh Army invasion force: Generals Bradley and Middleton with Admiral Kirk on the *Ancon;* General Allen with Admiral Hall on the *Samuel Chase;* General Truscott and Admiral Conolly aboard the *Biscayne*.

The Mediterranean was relatively calm until the morning of 9 July when wind and sea began to rise. From a velocity of ten miles per hour, a westward wind increased to a maximum of almost forty miles in early afternoon. Discomfort and seasickness increased, especially among the troops crowded into the LCI's.

As the invasion fleet turned to the north in the late afternoon of 9 July for the final approach, the ships began taking the wind and seas broadside. This slowed the landing craft to the point where it was difficult to maintain the speed required to keep up with the convoy. Some of the LCT formations began to straggle. Other vessels, including control ships, lost their places in column. As LST's and LCI's rolled heavily, cargoes shifted, and courses and speeds had to be changed. All the convoys were about an hour late in arriving at their assigned areas offshore, and many of the vessels were not on proper station.

The gale also had its effect on Generals Eisenhower and Alexander who had gone to Malta to await reports on the invasion. As increasing tension developed over the weather, the question arose whether the operation ought to be postponed twenty-four hours. Once made, the decision could not be revoked, for the naval forces needed at least four hours to transmit the information to all concerned. After conferring with Admiral Cunningham's meteorological experts, Eisenhower decided against postponement.

After dinner, hoping to catch a glimpse of some of the troop carrier aircraft towing the gliders filled with men of the British 1st Airborne Division, Eisenhower scanned the skies. He saw a few planes.

LANDING CRAFT MASSED IN BIZERTE HARBOR FOR THE INVASION OF SICILY. *3d Division troops marching aboard, 6 July 1943.*

He rubbed his ever-present seven lucky coins and offered up a silent prayer for the safety and success of all the troops under his command. Returning to the governor's palace, he sent a wire to General Marshall to inform him that the invasion would take place as scheduled. Then he returned to Cunningham's underground headquarters to await first news of the invasion.[40]

---

[40] Eisenhower, *Crusade in Europe*, pp. 171–172; Butcher, *My Three Years With Eisenhower*, pp. 347–52; *Stars and Stripes*, London ed., 12 July 1943, p. 1.

On Sicily, meanwhile, General Guzzoni's intelligence had reported early in July that 90 percent of available Allied troops, 60 percent of the air forces, and 96 percent of the landing craft were concentrated in the central-western Mediterranean and directly threatening Sicily. As the weather during the first ten days of July seemed particularly propitious for an amphibious landing, information from Italian and German intelligence sources repeatedly warned of the Allied danger to Sicily and Sardinia, with emphasis on Sicily. Though the Germans were not entirely convinced, the Italians began to feel certain that the Allies would make a massive effort including, in all probability, the use of parachute troops.[41]

When news came to the *Sixth Army* headquarters at Enna on 4 July that an Allied convoy of twenty-five merchant vessels with naval escorts had been observed in North African waters, Guzzoni issued an estimate of the situation that stressed the lessened threat to Sardinia, the increased danger to Sicily, particularly the eastern part, and also to Calabria. Noting the "substantial number" of Allied fighter planes on Malta, the movements of heavy Allied warships, and increased Allied air bombardments, Guzzoni alerted his forces to the possibility of an Allied invasion during the period up to 10 July—when the moon would be invisible. The Germans still inclined toward the opinion that the Allies would launch simultaneous attacks against Sardinia, Sicily, and Greece, though not in the immediate future, but Guzzoni thought an attack "against Sicily could come even today. We must be extremely alert."[42]

Noting on 5 July an increase in Allied hospital ships from two to sixteen, the Italians took this to mean an operation was imminent. By nightfall, Italian reconnaissance pilots observed a convoy traveling under an umbrella of barrage balloons. With the location of the British Eighth Army confirmed on the same day, Guzzoni in his evening bulletin concluded that that army would operate against Sicily. To him this was "a very serious and decisive indication. The danger of an imminent attack is increasing."[43]

Italian military commanders in Rome by then held a similar opinion.[44] So much on edge were staffs in Rome that many officers interpreted *Supermarina* reports on numerous fires near Marsala on 7 July as indications of Allied landings. Late that same day, German reconnaissance pilots reported the presence of a large Allied convoy four miles off Licata. The report turned out to be false, but in the meantime an alert had sent coastal defenders hurriedly to their posts.[45]

By 8 July Guzzoni had ordered the ports of Licata, Porto Empedocle, and Sciacca on the southern shore prepared for demolition. *Comando Supremo* ordered Trapani and Marsala rendered useless by dumping earth and rock into the harbors; when this proved impractical, the Italians demolished the docks in the hope of interfering with Allied landings. When Luftwaffe headquarters on the morning of 9 July reported seventy to ninety landing craft and transports traveling at high speed not far from Pantelleria, Guzzoni concluded that an invasion on the southeastern corner of Sicily, from Gela to Catania, was not far off.[46]

At 1810, 9 July, Guzzoni received another message reporting the approach of additional convoys. Late in the evening and during the night, information kept coming in to *Sixth Army* headquarters of several Allied convoys of varying size off the southeastern corner of the island. Meanwhile, Guzzoni, at about

---

[41] Italian intelligence report quoted in Faldella, *Lo sbarco*, pp. 100–101.

[42] *Ibid.*, p. 101.

[43] *Ibid.*, pp. 101–102.

[44] Telecon, Roatta and Guzzoni, 1245, 7 Jul 43, mentioned in Faldella, *Lo sbarco*, p. 102.

[45] Faldella, *Lo sbarco*, p. 102; II/Pz. Rgt. H.G., *KTB Nr. 1, 9.XI.42–15.IX.43*. Typewritten copy of the war diary of the *2d Battalion* of the *Panzer Regiment* of the *Hermann Goering Division*, in OCMH folder X-878.

[46] Faldella, *Lo sbarco*, p. 102.

# FINAL ALLIED PREPARATIONS

1900, issued the order for a preliminary alert; three hours later, he ordered a full alert.[47]

When Hitler learned of the approaching Allied fleet on 9 July, he ordered the German *1st Parachute Division* to be alerted for immediate transfer, by air if necessary, from France to Sicily, a movement that could be made in five days.[48]

That evening Allied air forces bombed Caltanissetta (headquarters of the *Livorno Division*), Syracuse, Palazzolo Acreide (headquarters of the *Napoli Division*), and Catania, where serious damage was caused to the various Italian command installations. Naval gunfire was reported to have struck Syracuse, Catania, Taormina, Trapani, and Augusta.[49]

At nightfall on 9 July the waters off Sicily seemed deserted. Yet despite the windy weather and rough sea, the coastal defenders were aware of the presence of a huge fleet of vessels somewhere in the darkness. Filled with American and British soldiers, the ships were moving toward the island. The Italian and German island defenders could do little except await the resumption of Allied air bombardments that would signal the start of the invasion.

---

[47] IT 99a, 9 and 10 Jul 43; *OKW/WFSt, KTB, 1.-31.VII.43*, 9 and 10 Jul 43 (time of first alert reported by *OB SUED* as 1840); MS #T-2 (Fries et al.), p. 10; Faldella, *Lo sbarco*, p. 105 (time of first alert reported as 1930); Maravigna, *Rivista Militare*, 1952, p. 17.

[48] *OKW/WFSt, KTB, 1.-31.VII.43*, 9 Jul 43.

[49] Faldella, *Lo sbarco*, p. 105; IT 99a, 10 Jul 43.

PART TWO

OPERATIONS AND NEGOTIATIONS

# CHAPTER VI

# The Assault

*The Airborne Operations*

At various airfields in North Africa during the afternoon of 9 July, British and American airborne troops, under a glaring sun, made the final preparations for the operation scheduled to initiate the invasion of Sicily.[1] While crews ran checks on the transport aircraft, the soldiers loaded gliders, rolled and placed equipment bundles in para-racks, made last-minute inspections, and received final briefings. Heavily laden with individual equipment and arms, with white bands pinned to their sleeves for identification, the troops clambered into the planes and gliders that would take them to Sicily.

The British airborne operation got under way first as 109 American C-47's and 35 British Albermarles of the U.S. 51st Troop Carrier Wing at 1842 began rising into the evening skies, towing 144 Waco and Horsa gliders. Two hours later, 222 C-47's of the U.S. 52d Troop Carrier Wing filled with American paratroopers of the 505th Parachute Infantry Regimental Combat Team and the attached 3d Battalion, 504th Parachute Infantry, were airborne.

The British contingent made rendezvous over the Kuriate Islands and headed for Malta, the force already diminished by seven planes and gliders that had failed to clear the North African coast. Though the sun was setting as the planes neared Malta, the signal beacon on the island was plainly visible to all but a few aircraft at the end of the column. The gale that was shaking up the seaborne troops began to affect the air columns. In the face of high winds, formations loosened as pilots fought to keep on course. Some squadrons were blown well to the east of the prescribed route, others in the rear overran forward squadrons. Despite the troubles, 90 percent of the air-

---

[1] Major sources for the British and American airborne operations are: Warren, USAF Hist Study 74 (an excellent account of the part played by the troop carrier units); 82d Airborne Division in Sicily and Italy (a mimeographed historical study prepared by the division's historical officer and found in the division's files, probably the best single account of the 82d Airborne Division's part in the Sicily Campaign); 505th Para Inf Regt AAR; NAAFTCC Rpt of Opns, 0402/11/949; 82d AB Div G-3 Jnl, 4 Jul-21 Aug 43; Rpt, Maj. Gen. F. A. M. Browning, 99-66.2; Gavin, *Airborne Warfare*; Ridgway, *Soldier*; Maj. Edwin M. Sayre, The Operations of Company A, 505th Parachute Infantry (82d Airborne Division), Airborne Landings in Sicily, 9-24 July 1943 (Fort Benning Ga., 1947); Maj. Robert M. Piper, The Operations of the 505th Parachute Infantry Regimental Combat Team (82d Airborne Division) in the Airborne Landings on Sicily, 9-11 July 1943 (Sicilian Campaign) (Fort Benning, Ga., 1949); *By Air to Battle, the Official Account of the British Airborne Divisions* (London: Great Britain Air Ministry, His Majesty's Stationery Office, 1945), pp. 56-60; Robert Devore, "Paratroops Behind Enemy Lines," *Collier's*, vol. 112, No. 12 (September 18, 1943), pp. 18-19, 54-55; Lt. Col. William T. Ryder, "Action on Biazza Ridge," *Saturday Evening Post*, vol. 216, No. 26 (December 22, 1943), pp. 14, 49-54.

PARATROOPERS, IDENTIFIED BY WHITE ARM BANDS, *preparing to emplane for Sicily.*

GLIDER CASUALTY

# THE ASSAULT

craft made landfall at Cape Passero, the check point at the southeastern tip of Sicily, though formations by then were badly mixed. Two pilots who had lost their way over the sea had turned back to North Africa. Two others returned after sighting Sicily because they could not orient themselves to the ground. A fifth plane had accidentally released its glider over the water; a sixth glider had broken loose from its aircraft—both gliders dropped into the sea.

The lead aircraft turned north, then northeast from Cape Passero, seeking the glider release point off the east coast of Sicily south of Syracuse. The designated zigzag course threw more pilots off course, and confusion set in. Some pilots released their gliders prematurely, others headed back to North Africa. Exactly how many gliders were turned loose in the proper area is impossible to say— perhaps about 115 carrying more than 1,200 men. Of these, only 54 gliders landed in Sicily, 12 on or near the correct landing zones. The others dropped into the sea. The result: a small band of less than 100 British airborne troops was making its way toward the objective, the Ponte Grande south of Syracuse, about the time the British Eighth Army was making its amphibious landings.

As for the Americans who had departed North Africa as the sun was setting, the pilots found that the quarter moon gave little light. Dim night formation lights, salt spray from the tossing sea hitting the windshields, high winds estimated at thirty miles an hour, and, more important, insufficient practice in night flying in the unfamiliar V of V's pattern, broke up the aerial columns. Groups began to loosen, and planes began to straggle. Those in the rear found it particularly difficult to remain on course. Losing direction, missing check points, the pilots approached Sicily from all points of the compass. Several planes had a few tense moments as they passed over the naval convoys then nearing the coast—but the naval gunners held their fire. Because they were lost, two pilots returned to North Africa with their human cargoes. A third crashed into the sea.

Even those few pilots who had followed the planned route could not yet congratulate themselves, for haze, dust, and fires— all caused by the preinvasion air attacks— obscured the final check points, the mouth of the Acate River and the Biviere Pond. What formations remained broke apart. Antiaircraft fire from Gela, Ponte Olivo, and Niscemi added to the difficulties of orientation. The greatest problem was getting the paratroopers to ground, not so much on correct drop zones as to get them out of the doors over ground of any sort. The result: the 3,400 paratroopers who jumped found themselves scattered all over southeastern Sicily—33 sticks landing in the Eighth Army area; 53 in the 1st Division zone around Gela; 127 inland from the 45th Division beaches between Vittoria and Caltagirone. Only the 2d Battalion, 505th Parachute Infantry (Maj. Mark Alexander), hit ground relatively intact; and even this unit was twenty-five miles from its designated drop zone.[2]

Except for eight planes of the second serial which put most of Company I,

---

[2] 505th RCT Drop Zones, 10 Jul 43 (an overlay and table prepared by Capt. John Norton, 10 Aug 43), in Gen. James M. Gavin's Papers; Msg 4597, NAAFTCC to AFHQ, 10 Jul 43, 0100/21/1099, IV. Eight aircraft were shot down by enemy antiaircraft fire after releasing their paratroopers. Warren, USAF Hist Study 74, pp. 33–34.

THE PONTE DIRILLO CROSSING SITE, *seized by paratroopers on D-day.*

505th Parachute Infantry, on the correct drop zone just south of the road junction objective; except for eighty-five men of Company G of the 505th who landed about three miles away; and except for the headquarters and two platoons of Company A and part of the 1st Battalion command group, which landed near their scheduled drop zones just north of the road junction, the airborne force was dispersed to the four winds.

The planes carrying the headquarters serial, which included Colonel Gavin, the airborne troop commander, were far off course, having missed the check point at Linosa, the check point at Malta, and even the southeastern coast of Sicily. The lead pilot eventually made landfall on the east coast near Syracuse, oriented himself, and turned across the southeast corner of the island to get back on course. Assuming that the turn signaled the correct drop zone, the pilots of the last three planes—carrying the demolition section designated to take care of the Ponte Dirillo over the Acate River southeast of Gela—released their paratroopers. The other pilots, about twelve of them, dropped their loads in a widely dispersed pattern due south of Vittoria about three miles inland on the 45th Division's right flank.

Coming to earth in one of these sticks, Gavin found himself in a strange land. He was not even sure he was in Sicily. He heard firing apparently everywhere, but none of it very close. Within a few minutes he gathered together about fifteen men. They captured an Italian soldier who was alone, but they could get no information from him. Gavin then led his small group north toward the sound of fire he believed caused by paratroopers fighting for possession of the road junction objective.

The fire actually marked an attack by about forty paratroopers under 1st Lt. H. H. Swingler, the 505th's headquarters company commander, who was leading an attack to overcome a pillbox-defended crossroads along the highway leading south from Vittoria. Other sounds of battle came from Alexander's 2d Battalion, which was reducing Italian coastal positions near Santa Croce Camerina. Near Vittoria, scattered units of the 3d Battalion, 505th Parachute Infantry, had coalesced and were also engaged in combat. The eighty-five men from Company G, under Capt. James McGinity, had seized Ponte Dirillo. Elsewhere, bands of paratroopers were roaming through the rear areas of the coastal defense units, cutting enemy communications lines, ambushing small parties, and creating confusion among enemy commanders as to exactly where the main airborne landing had taken place.[3]

But less than 200 men were on the important high ground of Piano Lupo, near the important road junction, hardly the strength anticipated by those who had planned and prepared and were now executing the invasion of Sicily.

## The Seaborne Operations

General Guzzoni, the *Sixth Army* commander, received word of the airborne landings not long after midnight. Certain that the Allied invasion had begun, he issued a proclamation exhorting soldiers and civilians to repel the invaders. At the same time he ordered the Gela pier destroyed. Phoning the *XII Corps* in the western part of Sicily and the *XVI Corps* in the east at 0145, 10 July, he alerted them to expect landings on the southeastern coast and in the Gela-Agrigento area.[4]

An hour later, the initial waves of the 15 Army Group assault divisions began to come ashore. Near Avola in the Gulf of Noto, on both sides of the Pachino peninsula, near Scoglitti, Gela, and Licata, small British and American landing craft ground ashore and started to disgorge Allied soldiers. Hard on their heels came the larger LCT's and LST's with supporting artillery and armor. Offshore stood Allied war vessels ready to pound Italian coastal defense positions into submission.

Overhead, Allied fighter aircraft from Malta, Gozo, and the recently captured Pantelleria, covered the landings. Concerned lest the enemy make his maximum air effort against Allied shipping and the assault beaches early on D-day and disorganize the operation at the outset,

---

[3] See review comments of Lt. Col. Charles W. Kouns (former commander of the 3d Battalion, 504th Parachute Infantry) for an example of individual initiative and resourcefulness. OCMH.

[4] Faldella, *Lo sbarco*, pp. 111, 120–21.

Allied air planners had spread their available aircraft over as many of the assault beaches as possible while maintaining a complete fighter wing in reserve. As the ground troops went ashore, fighter aircraft patrolled in one-squadron strength over all the landing areas to ward off hostile air attacks, a commitment that was decreased later in the day.[5] In addition, at daylight, formations composed of either twelve A–36 or twelve P–38 fighter-bombers were dispatched every thirty minutes throughout the day to disrupt potential counterattacks by hitting the main routes leading to the assault beaches.[6] Because of the heavy commitment of Allied aircraft to these and other missions, no direct or close support was available to the ground troops this day.[7]

The seaborne landings of the British Eighth Army were uniformly successful. Everywhere the first assault waves achieved tactical surprise and Italian coastal defense units offered only feeble resistance.[8] Some fire from coastal batteries and field artillery positions inland did strike the beaches but it was quickly silenced by supporting naval gunfire and the rapid movement of assault troops inland.

In Enna, General Guzzoni received a phone call from the commander of the *Naval Base Messina* at 0400. The German radio station at Syracuse, the naval commander said, had announced that Allied troops had landed by glider near the eastern coast and that fighting had started at the Syracuse seaplane base. In response, Guzzoni instructed the *XVI Corps* commander to rush ground troops to the apparently endangered *Naval Base Augusta–Syracuse*. This, plus the previous information from German reconnaissance aircraft that Allied fleets were close to the southern coast as well, brought home to Guzzoni the fact that the Allies would land simultaneously in many different places. Realizing his forces would be unable to counter all of the landings, he committed his available reserves to those areas he considered most dangerous to the over-all defense of the island: Syracuse, Gela, and Licata. Of these three, Guzzoni considered Syracuse on the east coast the most serious. But he also apparently felt that the presence there of both *Group Schmalz* and the *Napoli Division*, plus the supposedly strong defenses of the naval base itself, would be sufficient to stabilize the situation and prevent an Allied breakthrough into the Catania plain. Thus, he or-

---

[5] Patrols in one-squadron strength flew continuously over two beaches throughout the daylight hours on 10 July. The same sized patrols also flew over all landing beaches from 1030 to 1230, from 1600 to 1730, and for the last one and a half hours of daylight. See 0407/386, sub: Preliminary Rpt on HUSKY Opns by Malta-Based Aircraft, 9–17 Jul 43; see also NATAF Rpt of Opns, 0407/488; NASAF Opns Rpt, 12 Jul 43, II Corps file 202-20.1; Craven and Cate, eds., *Europe: TORCH to POINTBLANK*, pp. 449–52; Coles, USAF Hist Study 37, pp. 99–106.

[6] The A–36 was a modified P–51 fighter aircraft, a single-engine, low-wing monoplane. The P–38 was a twin-engine, single-seat fighter, the first U.S. fighter aircraft which could be compared favorably with the British Spitfire or the German ME–109. As a fighter-bomber, it could carry a bomb load of 2,000 pounds in external wing racks. See Wesley Frank Craven and James Lea Cate, eds., "The Army Air Forces in World War II," vol. VI, *Men and Planes* (Chicago: The University of Chicago Press, 1955), pp. 198–99; 214–15.

[7] Or for that matter, with but one exception, for the next several days. The terms direct and close support used in this volume are terms defined in TM 20-205, 18 January 1944.

[8] The account of the British landings is based on: Alexander Despatch, pp. 12–13; Montgomery, *Eighth Army*, pp. 94–95; De Guingand, *Operation Victory*, pp. 284–85; Nicholson, *The Canadians in Italy*, pp. 20, 62–63; Morison, *Sicily—Salerno—Anzio*, pp. 148–61.

USS BOISE BOMBARDING COASTAL DEFENSES *in Gela landing area.*

dered the bulk of the *Hermann Goering Division* to strike the Allied landings near Gela.[9]

In front of the easternmost British landing the small band of British airborne troops, eight officers and sixty-five men, seized Ponte Grande. By 0800, the 5th Division held Cassibile, on the coastal highway, and by the middle of the afternoon successfully consolidated its beachhead and started north to join with the air-landed troops at the bridge site. (*Map 1*)

But by 1500, the small band of British soldiers at Ponte Grande found themselves in difficult straits. After battling with Italian soldiers, marines, and sailors sent against them from the *Naval Base Augusta–Syracuse*, only fifteen men remained unwounded. At 1530, these men were overrun. Only eight managed to make their way southward to meet the advancing 5th Division, a column of which, supported by artillery and tanks,

---

[9] Faldella, *Lo sbarco*, pp. 118–23; *OKH, Op. Abt., Meldungen des Ob. Sued, 1.–31.VII.43* and *1.–31.VIII.43* (H 22/137 and 138) (cited hereafter as *OB SUED, Meldungen*), 10 Jul 43.

MAP 1

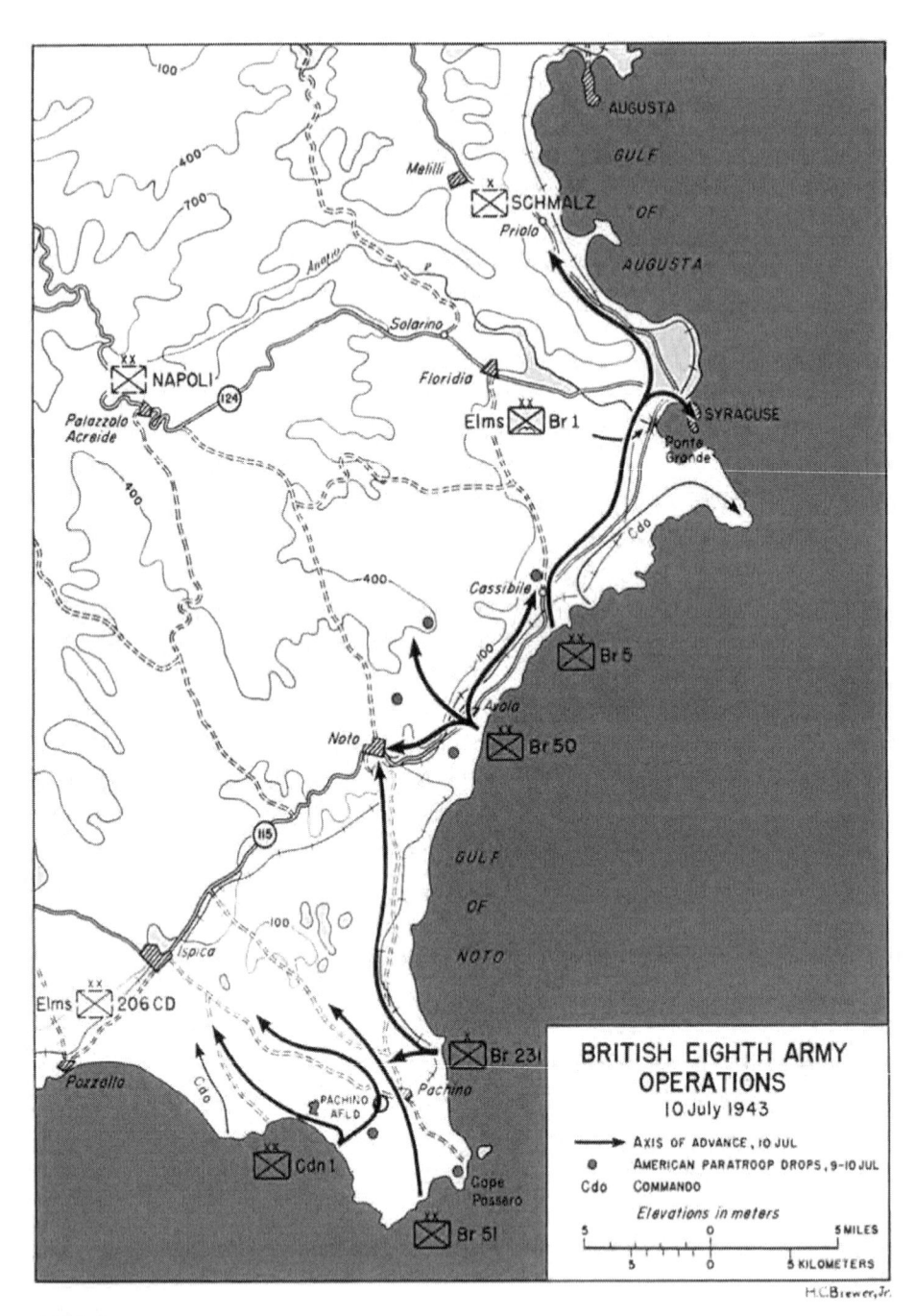

# THE ASSAULT

recaptured the bridge intact. As Italian opposition disintegrated, the British column continued unopposed into Syracuse. Scarcely pausing, British troops continued northward along the coastal highway on the way to Augusta. But early in the evening at Priolo, midway between Syracuse and Augusta, *Group Schmalz*, which had rushed down from Catania to counter the British landings, halted the 13 Corps advance.

According to Axis defense plans *Group Schmalz*, in conjunction with the *Napoli Division*, was supposed to counterattack any Allied landing on the east coast. But on 10 July, Col. Wilhelm Schmalz had been unable to contact the Italian unit and had proceeded alone toward Syracuse. Unknown to the German commander, the *Napoli Division* had tried to counterattack, but some units had been turned back by British forces near Solarino, while other units were lost trying to stem British advances in the Pachino area.[10]

By the end of D-day the British 30 Corps had secured the whole of the Pachino peninsula as far as Highway 115, which crossed the base between Ispica and Noto. The 1st Canadian Division, the British 51st Highland Infantry Division, and the 231st Independent Infantry Brigade had gone ashore against only feeble resistance and had pushed on in good fashion.

Unloadings over the British beaches progressed slowly but steadily during the day, despite small-scale enemy air attacks that proved annoying but caused relatively little damage. By the end of the day, the Eighth Army had secured a beachhead line extending from north of Syracuse on the east coast, west to Floridia, thence southward roughly paralleling Highway 115.

The Seventh Army had a more difficult time. The gale and high seas had delayed the three naval task forces and after fighting their way to the landing craft release points in the Gulf of Gela, they were somewhat disorganized. Yet only one was seriously behind schedule, that carrying the 45th Division. Those landings were postponed an hour.

Admiral Conolly's Naval Task Force 86 brought the 3d Division to the Seventh Army's westernmost assault area in four attack groups, one group for each of the landing beaches on both sides of Licata.[11] Conolly's flagship, the *Biscayne*, dropped anchor in the transport area at 0135. The winds had made it difficult for the LST's, LCI's, and LCT's of his task force to maintain proper speed and formation, so that Conolly, around midnight, when it had seemed virtually impossible to meet H-hour, had ordered his vessels to go all out to make the deadline. Since he had not heard from his units, all of which had been instructed to break radio silence only to report an emergency, Conolly assumed that all his units were in position and ready to disembark the troops of the 3d Division.

At 0135, 10 July, Admiral Conolly's assumption that all units were in posi-

---

[10] Generalleutnant Wilhelm Schmalz in MS #T-2 (Fries *et al.*); Faldella, *Lo sbarco*, pp. 130–32, 143–44; IT 4432.

[11] The account of the 3d Division landings is based on: COHQ Bull Y/1, Oct. 43; Joss Force Planning File, Sicilian Campaign, vol. I (Operations); 3d Inf Div in Sicilian Campaign AAR, 10–18 Jul 43; WNTF Action Rpt; Rpt of Arty Opns, Joss Force; Truscott, *Command Missions*, pp. 192–212; ONI, The Sicilian Campaign, pp. 73–95; Morison, *Sicily—Salerno—Anzio*, pp. 71–86; Interv, Howard McGaw Smyth with Maj Gen William W. Eagles (former asst div comdr 3d Inf Div), 17 Jan 51.

LICATA AND BEACH AREAS TO THE EAST *toward Gela. Note Licata's cliffs in left foreground.*

# THE ASSAULT

tion was not altogether correct. Particularly in the west, the landing ships and craft carrying the 7th RCT had had considerable difficulty making headway in the heaving Mediterranean. All were late in reaching the transport area, but no one had reported that fact to Admiral Conolly.

By using all four of his assigned beaches, General Truscott had adopted two axes of advance for his assault units—actually axes that formed the outer and inner claws of a deep pincer movement against Licata. The left outer claw consisted of the 7th Infantry Regimental Combat Team (Col. Harry B. Sherman) landing over Red Beach. The left inner claw, consisting of a special force (the 3d Ranger Battalion; the 2d Battalion, 15th Infantry; a company of 4.2-inch mortars; a battery of 105-mm. howitzers; and a platoon of 75-mm. howitzers) under the command of the 15th Infantry's executive officer, Lt. Col. Brookner W. Brady, was to land over the two Green Beaches. As the right inner claw of the pincer, and the counterpart of the special force, the remainder of the 15th Infantry, led by Col. Charles R. Johnson, was to land over Yellow Beach. Meanwhile, the right outer claw, the 30th Infantry Regimental Combat Team (Col. Arthur R. Rogers), was to assault across Blue Beach. Each assault was to move in columns of battalions. Combat Command A, under Brig. Gen. Maurice Rose of the 2d Armored Division, constituted the 3d Division's floating reserve, prepared to land in support of any of the assaulting units or for commitment against Campobello to the north, Agrigento to the west, or Gela to the east.

The division's assault plan, involving two distinct pincer movements one inside the other, was somewhat complicated. Its execution was aided by the intensive training program undertaken after the end of the North African campaign; by General Truscott's extensive knowledge of amphibious and combined operations learned in England and in North Africa; and by the extremely close and pleasant working relations which existed between the division and Admiral Conolly's naval task force. The assault was further facilitated by the weakness of the enemy's defenses in the Licata area, probably the weakest of all the Seventh Army's assault areas. Only one Italian coastal division, backed by a few scattered Italian mobile units, stood initially in the 3d Division's path. Two Italian mobile divisions—*Assietta* and *Aosta*—and two-thirds of the German *15th Panzer Grenadier Division*, the only effective fighting forces in the *XII Corps* sector, were well off to the west near Palermo.

Fully exposed to the westerly wind that was churning up the surf, the LST's carrying the 7th Infantry had great difficulty hoisting out and launching the LCVP's that would take the assault waves to Red Beach. When one davit gave way and dumped a boatload of men into the water, nine men were lost. Nevertheless, around 0200 the small craft were loaded with troops and in the water, and soon afterwards they were heading for the rendezvous area. The LCVP's had trouble locating the control vessels, which had been serving as escort ships during the voyage across the Mediterranean and which had not been able to take their proper places. Shortly after 0300, already fifteen minutes beyond the time scheduled for touchdown on the beach, the attack group commander ordered the LCVP's in to shore. He was fearful

THE RIGHT FLANK BEACH AT LICATA, *10 July 1943*.

that the LCI's, scheduled to land at 0330, would use their superior speed to overtake the LCVP's and he was unable to contact the LCI flotilla commander.

As it was, the first wave, Lt. Col. Roy E. Moore's 1st Battalion, did not touch down until 0430. The delay was imposed partly by the late start, partly by the longer run to the beach than was originally contemplated because of the faulty disposition of the LST's in the transport area. The latter error also helped cause the LCVP's to land at the far right end of the beach rather than at the center as planned. The small craft met no fire on the way in, and only light and ineffective artillery fire on the beach after the landings were made.

Red Beach lay in a shallow cove, the seaward approach clear of rocks and shoals. Only 8 to 20 feet deep, 2,800 yards long, the beach at its widest part was backed by cliffs, many reaching a height of 60 feet. Exits were poor: a small stream bed near the center, three paths over the cliff at the left end. Lying in the Italian *207th Coastal Division's* zone (as were all the division's landing areas), Red Beach was probably the most heavily fortified of all. Artillery pieces dominated the exits and most of the beach; numerous machine gun posi-

# THE ASSAULT

HIGHWAY 115, *the coastal road, shown running west to Licata in the distance.*

tions near the center and western end provided the defenders with ample firepower to contest an assault landing; an extensive defensive position along some 350 yards of the bluff line contained three coast artillery pieces and another ten machine gun emplacements, all connected by a series of trenches; and the San Nicola Rock at the right end and the Gaffi Tower off the left end gave the defenders excellent observation posts and positions from which to place enfilading fire.

Once ashore, the 1st Battalion promptly set to work. While one company turned to the west and began clearing out beach defenses, a second swept the center of the landing area and set up a covering position on three low hills just inland from the beach. The third company wheeled to the east and occupied San Nicola Rock and Point San Nicola, completing both tasks an hour and a half after landing. (*Map III*)

The six LCI's bearing Maj. Everett W. Duvall's 2d Battalion, 7th Infantry, had assembled just east of the LST anchorage, more than two miles farther offshore than planned. Unaware of this, the flotilla started for shore at 0240, exactly on the schedule planned for the second wave. At this moment the 1st Battalion's LST's were completing their launching of the LCVP's. Because the 1st Battalion's landing craft had veered to the right, the

LCI's carrying the 2d Battalion saw no signs of small boat activity as they passed the LST's. Assuming that the assault had not yet started, the flotilla commander turned his craft back to the LST anchorage to find out whether H-hour had been postponed.

After ascertaining that no delay was in order, the flotilla commander again turned his craft shoreward. He sighted a control vessel herding a number of LCVP's toward shore. Recognizing thereby that the assault wave was behind schedule, he halted his own craft, planning to wait twenty-five minutes to give the 1st Battalion time to clear the beach. At 0415, as the sky began to get light, he started the final run to shore. There was no evidence of the 1st Battalion's LCVP's. The LCI's sailed straight toward the center of Red Beach, the troops of the 2d Battalion little realizing that they constituted an initial assault wave.

The LCI's were about 450 yards from the beach in a wide, shallow V-formation just opening into a line abreast formation when enemy artillery batteries opened a heavy fire directed chiefly at the left half of the line. The LCI's increased their speed temporarily, then 150 yards from shore slowed down quickly, dropped stern anchors, and beached at 0440 in the face of heavy small arms fire on the beach. The LCI's on the right side of the line escaped the heaviest fire because the Italian gunners could not depress their gun tubes enough to take these craft under fire.

Five of the LCI's beached successfully. One stuck on the false bar off the shore line, tried three times without success to ride over the bar, landed a few troops in rubber boats, and finally transferred the remainder of its troops to an LCI bringing in the third wave. The heavy surf added to the difficulties of the five craft that did manage to ride over the false beach. One lost both ramps soon after they were lowered and was able to land its troops only after salvaging the port ramp.

Almost constant enemy fire harassed the boats. Soldiers in some instances became casualties before they reached the ramps, others were hit while disembarking. The LCI on the left flank drew the heaviest fire, a flanking fire from both left and right. The Italians shot away her controls and communications as she beached, and though able to lower both ramps, the LCI started to broach almost immediately and had to cut the ramps away. She swung completely around until her stern rested on the shore. Disdaining normal disembarkation procedures, the troops scrambled over her stern and dropped to the beach. By 0500, the bulk of the 2d Battalion was ashore. Two companies swarmed inland and seized Monte Marotta (some four and a half miles inland west of the north-south Highway 123), while the third turned northeast after landing, cut the railroad, and established a roadblock at Station San Oliva where the railroad crossed Highway 123 some three and a half miles northwest of Licata. By 1000, after by-passing most of the enemy resistance along the beach, the 2d Battalion was on its objectives and successfully drove off a dispirited counterattack launched against Station San Oliva by an Italian coastal battalion, a *XII Corps* reserve unit.

While the five 2d Battalion LCI's were trying to retract from the beach, six LCI's carrying Lt. Col. John A. Heintges' 3d Battalion came in, along with three LCI's transporting part of the engineer beach group. With some overlapping of the 2d

Battalion's LCI's, the 3d Battalion touched down at 0500 on the left end of Red Beach and received the same heavy fire from the shore defenders which was peppering the leftmost LCI of the 2d Battalion group. In fact, it was not until the LCIs' guns went into action to provide covering fires that the 3d Battalion troops were landed.

The section of beach where the 3d Battalion landed—near Gaffi Tower—had not been cleared either by the 1st or 2d Battalion. Nevertheless, despite wire entanglements along the side of the bluff and despite heavy Italian rifle and machine gun fire from positions along the top of the bluff, the battalion pushed aggressively inland and cleared the immediate beach area. One company, after capturing nineteen Italians along the cliff, pushed westward and inland, took the tower, and occupied the high ground just south of the railroad and coastal highway. The other two companies occupied the hill mass north of the highway. An eight-man demolition section pushed on to the west through a defile and blew the railroad crossing over the Palma River, some two miles in front of the battalion's hill positions.

The LCI bearing Colonel Sherman and his staff came ashore near the center of the beach as dawn was breaking. Tangling with another LCI on its way to assist the broached LCI of the first wave, the boat lost both ramps after only fifteen men had disembarked. The LCI commander tried to discharge the rest of his troops by rigging wooden ladders and rope lines over the side of the boat. But the weight of individual equipment hampered the men, and they floundered in the water, helpless against the fire coming from shore. The craft commander stopped the unloading by this method, deliberately broached the LCI, and sent the RCT command group over the sides. The RCT headquarters opened ashore at 0615, just inland from the beach on top of the cliff.

Naval gunfire might have helped the small craft to the beach, but the two fire support destroyers assigned to Red Beach —the *Swanson* and the *Roe*—had collided near Porto Empedocle at 0255 and were concerned with their own troubles. However, help was arriving. At 0520, with enemy fire still falling on the beach, twenty-one LCT's carrying the RCT's supporting armor and artillery approached through the heavy seas. Fearful for the safety of the LCT's landing under enemy fire, the commander of the Red Beach naval force ordered the craft to halt until the fire could be silenced. But four of the LCT's, either ignoring the order or failing to receive it, kept on going and beached at 0630. The four carried the 10th Field Artillery Battalion. Unloading quickly, utilizing the full-tracked mobility of its M7's, the artillery unit established firing positions 500 to 1,000 yards inland and began firing in support of the infantry units.[12]

At about the same time, the destroyer

---

[12] Before embarking them in North Africa, General Truscott had his organic artillery battalions exchange their towed 105-mm. howitzers for the full-tracked M7's of the 5th Armored Field Artillery Group, a swap to last during the assault phase only. Once ashore, the units exchanged pieces again.

The M7 (called the Priest because of its pulpit-like machine gun platform) had a 105-mm. howitzer mounted on the medium M3 tank. The tank was modified for this purpose by having its turret removed and its armor reduced. See Green, Thomson, and Roots, *The Ordnance Department: Planning Munitions for War*, pp. 314–15.

SHORE-TO-SHORE LCT *at Licata Beach.*

ARMY DONKEYS *wading ashore at Licata.*

# THE ASSAULT

*Buck*, which had been serving as escort for the LCT convoy, was sent in by Admiral Conolly to take over the Red Beach fire support role.[13] The cruiser *Brooklyn*, which had been firing in support of the Green Beach landings, also moved over on Conolly's orders and opened fire on Italian artillery positions which had been firing on Red Beach.[14] By 0715, Italian fire had slackened appreciably. Seven minutes later, Conolly ordered the remaining LCT's to beach regardless of cost. Two additional destroyers moved over to assist the *Buck* in laying a smoke screen on the beaches to cover the LCT landings. Concealed by the smoke and covered by the *Brooklyn's* six-inch guns, the LCT's touched down without incident. By 0900 the supporting tanks and the 7th Infantry's Cannon Company were ashore, followed soon after by the remainder of the engineer beach group and two batteries of antiaircraft artillery.

The 7th RCT's assigned objectives were secured by 1030 and its establishment of a defensive line on the arc of hills bordering the western side of the Licata plain assured the protection of the beachhead's left flank. Heavy equipment and supplies were pouring ashore and being moved inland over the soft sand.

A mile to the east of Red Beach and three miles west of Licata, Green Beach, flanked by rocks, had the most dangerous approach. Divided into two distinct parts by the Mollarella Rock (82 feet high), which was joined to the island by a low, sandy isthmus, the western part (350 yards wide and almost 20 yards deep) was rockbound except for a short stretch of about 150 yards, the eastern part (400 yards wide, 40 yards deep) lay within a snug cove with a mouth 200 yards across. The eastern beach opened into a stream bed and to a number of tracks providing good vehicular and personnel exits to Highway 115, about a mile and a half inland. The west beach also possessed exits, but its limited size would restrict its use to personnel traffic. Both appeared to be obstructed by barbed wire entanglements. Gun positions on Mollarella Rock dominated the west beach. Immediately back of a stretch of vineyards on the sector of land forming the beach, a defensive position containing at least four machine gun positions and a trench and wire system had been located.

The special force, spearheaded by the 3d Ranger Battalion, touched down at 0257, just twelve minutes behind schedule. Moving smartly, three Ranger companies cleared the beaches and Mollarella Rock and established a defensive line on the high ground at the left end of Green West, while the other three companies cleared the way inland to the western edge of Monte Sole. Lt. Col. William H. Billings' 2d Battalion, 15th Infantry, went in over Green West at 0342, reorganized, passed through the Rangers at Monte Sole as planned, and thrust toward Licata, the left inner claw of the planned pincer movement. Clearing enemy hill positions as they moved eastward, the men of the 3d Battalion by 0730 had possession of Castel San Angelo, but a strong naval

---

[13] The *Buck* carried a main armament of four 5-inch 38-caliber guns. Information on the armament of the various gunfire support ships has been taken from Navy Department, Chief of Naval Operations, Naval History Division, *Dictionary of American Naval Fighting Ships*, vol. I (Washington, 1959).

[14] The *Brooklyn* carried a main armament of fifteen 6-inch 47-caliber guns, a secondary battery of eight 5-inch 25-caliber guns.

BRINGING UP SUPPLIES *by cart at Licata Beach.*

ITALIAN RAILWAY BATTERY ON LICATA MOLE *destroyed by American naval bombardment on D-day.*

# THE ASSAULT

bombardment of Licata in support of the Yellow Beach landings prevented the battalion from pushing immediately into the city.

Yellow and Blue Beaches east of Licata were much better for assault landings. Beginning not quite two miles east of the mouth of the Salso River and running almost due east for a mile and a half, Yellow Beach was of soft sand, about 60 yards deep at the western end, narrowing gradually to 15 yards at the eastern end. Licata on the left and the cliffs of Punta delle due Rocche on the right would serve as general guides in the approach. Many good paths and cart tracks ran from the beach across a cultivated strip to Highway 115, here only some 400 yards inland. One-half mile to the east lay Blue Beach, which consisted generally of firm sand with occasional rocky outcrops. Not quite a mile wide, Blue Beach deepened from 15 yards on the left to 60 yards on the right. Low sand dunes backed up the right half of the beach; a low, steep bank, the left half. Exits for personnel and vehicles were easy and plentiful, and Highway 115 ran everywhere within 500 yards of the beach.

Naval bombardment was the American answer to the only real Italian interference with the Yellow Beach landings. The opposition consisted primarily of an Italian railway battery on the Licata mole, an armored train mounting four 76-mm. guns. When the naval fire finally lifted, the train had been destroyed and other Italian resistance silenced. Soldiers from both Green and Yellow Beaches swarmed into Licata, while a battalion which had swung north from Yellow Beach to the bend in the Salso River moved south into the city shortly after.

At Blue Beach, farthest to the right, the Italian defenders put up a somewhat bigger show of resistance, though not so strong as that offered at Red Beach. With the 30th RCT forming the right outer claw of the pincer, the naval task force had been delayed in reaching its transport area. The LST's leading the convoy moved into position and began anchoring at 0115. But the anchorage later proved to be well south of the correct position, thus forcing the LCVP's carrying the assault battalion to make a much longer run to the beaches than planned. Despite this, the first LCVP's grounded just two hours after the LST's had begun anchoring and only a half-hour behind schedule. The first wave met some rifle and machine gun fire from pillboxes on the beach, and some artillery fire from guns on Poggio Lungo, high ground off to the right. Like its counterpart on the far left, the 7th RCT, the 30th RCT before noon occupied its three primary objectives: three hill masses bordering the eastern side of the Licata plain.

Shortly after daybreak Admiral Conolly took the *Biscayne* close in to shore so that both he and General Truscott could see the beaches. What they saw was encouraging, and reports from two light aircraft that had taken off from an improvised runway on an LST confirmed their impressions.[15] The infantry troops were on their objectives or about to take them. The airfield and city of Licata

---

[15] Piloted by 1st Lts. Oliver P. Board and Julian W. Cummings, the Piper L-4 grasshoppers took off from a flight deck (approximately 216 feet long, 12 feet wide) built along the center and over the top deck of the LST. The pilots flew over the beaches for more than two hours and reported enemy positions and the locations of friendly units. On occasion, they directed landing craft to proper beaches. See Rpt of Arty Opns, Joss Force; 41st FA Bn AAR; 10th FA Bn AAR; WNTF Action Rpt, p. 97.

ENEMY DEFENSE POSITIONS ALONG COAST ROAD *east of Licata.*

# THE ASSAULT

were in hand. Artillery and armor were moving into position to support further advances. One counterattack had been beaten back. The beaches were well organized, men and equipment coming ashore without difficulty. The Seventh Army's left flank seemed well anchored. In the process, the 3d Division, its commander ashore by midmorning, had suffered fewer than 100 casualties.

Ten miles southeast of the 3d Division's Blue Beach, and extending twenty miles to the southeast, General Bradley's II Corps was landing to secure three primary objectives lying at varying distances inland from the assault beaches: the airfields at Ponte Olivo, Biscari, and Comiso. Ponte Olivo, along with the city of Gela, was the responsibility of the left task force, the 1st Division; the others belonged to the 45th Division.

East of the mouth of the Gela River, high sand dunes with scrubby vegetation lay back of the coast. Three miles east of the city and adjacent to and on the inland side of the coastal highway (Highway 115) was the Gela-Farello landing ground, an intermediate division objective. Farther to the east, relatively high ground (400 feet at Piano Lupo, one of the paratroopers' objectives) flanked the right side of the Gela plain and separated the Gela River drainage basin from that of the Acate River, which empties into the gulf six miles east of Gela. The Acate River, which swings to the northeast at Ponte Dirillo, and its tributary, the Terrana Creek, marked the boundary between the division task forces of the II Corps.[16]

From Gela, the railroad paralleled the coast to Ponte Dirillo, but the highway, while initially following the coast line, swung inland some five miles east of Gela as it wound around Piano Lupo. From the height of Piano Lupo, a good secondary road branched off northward to Niscemi, following high ground on the eastern edge of the Gela plain. From this point, known to the paratroop task force as Road Junction Y, the coast road took a sharp turn to the southeast to cross the Acate River at Ponte Dirillo.

Another good road, Highway 117, led directly inland from Gela, paralleling the western bank of the Gela River for five and a half miles. A vivid line bisecting the treeless plain, the highway crossed to the east side of the river at Ponte Olivo to a triple road intersection. There, while Highway 117 continued on its northeasterly course, a secondary road swung almost due east to Niscemi, another ran northwest to Mazzarino. In the right angle formed by Highway 117 and the secondary road to Niscemi lay the Ponte Olivo airfield.[17]

In contrast with the 3d Division's assault plan of landing initially only one battalion from each assault force, the 1st Division plan committed two assault battalions from each regimental task force

---

[16] The Acate is sometimes called the Dirillo River. The Acate River from Ponte Dirillo northeastward lay in the zone of the 45th Division.

[17] Chief sources for the 1st Division landings are: 1st Inf Div FO 26, 20 Jun 43; 1st Inf Div G-3 Opns Rpts, 10-14 Jul 43; AAR's of units involved; Lucas Diary, pt. I, pp. 28-31, OCMH; ONI, Sicilian Campaign, pp. 49-58; Morison, *Sicily—Salerno—Anzio*, pp. 93-100; CO NTF 81 Action Rpt, 6-1.2610.43; Interv, Smyth with Lt Col Bryce F. Denno (former ExO 2d Bn, 16th Inf) and Maj. Melvin J. Groves (former CO Co E, 16th Inf), 24 Oct 50, with an addendum dated 27 Oct 50 by Maj Groves; James J. Altieri, *Darby's Rangers* (Durham, N.C.: The Seeman Printery, Inc., 1945); Bradley, *A Soldier's Story;* Maj. James B. Lyle, The Operations of Companies A and B, 1st Ranger Battalion, at Gela, Sicily, 10-11 July 1943 (Fort Benning, Ga., 1947).

simultaneously, the third battalion remaining in reserve.

To capture Gela, General Allen, the 1st Division commander, created what he called Force X, a special grouping of Rangers and combat engineers.[18] Under Colonel Darby (commander of the 1st Ranger Battalion), the force was to land directly on the beach fronting Gela, one portion on each side of the pier. While the special force worked on the city, the division would make its main effort east of the Gela River, where the division's two remaining combat teams were to land over four sections of the three-mile-long beach extending southeast from the river. For want of natural boundaries, the four sections were given color designations arbitrarily marking off one section from the other.

The two left sections of the beach—Yellow and Blue—were assigned to Col. John W. Bowen's 26th RCT. While one battalion forced a crossing over the Gela River to aid Force X to subdue Gela, the remainder of the 26th RCT was to bypass the city on the right, cut Highway 117, and occupy high ground two miles to the north. There the RCT would be ready to attack Gela from the landward side if the city still held out, or move farther inland to take other high ground overlooking Ponte Olivo from the west.

Over the other two sections, Red 2 and Green 2, the 16th RCT under Col. George A. Taylor was to come ashore. After reducing the beach defenses, the regiment was to cross the railroad, bypass the long, swampy Biviere Pond on the force's right, cut the coastal highway, and move along the highway to Piano Lupo to join Colonel Gavin's paratroopers. From there, the 16th RCT was to drive on Niscemi.

Although the Italian *XVIII Coastal Brigade* (thinly stretched from west of Gela to below Scoglitti) caused no serious concern, the *Livorno Division,* concentrated to the northwest near Caltanissetta, and the bulk of the *Hermann Goering Division,* assembled to the northeast near Caltagirone, presented serious problems. Two fairly strong Italian mobile airfield defense groups at Niscemi and at Caltagirone were also in position to strike.

Short one combat team—the 18th RCT was a part of the Seventh Army's floating reserve; shy supporting armor, for only ten medium tanks were in direct support of the entire 1st Division; with no division reserve (the parachute task force was to form the division reserve after link-up)—the 1st Division faced the strongest grouping of enemy forces in Sicily.

In three long columns, with transports in the center and LST's and LCI's on the flanks, Admiral Hall's Naval Task Force 81 brought the 1st Division to the Gela area in the center of the Seventh Army zone. The eleven transports reached their proper stations at 0045, 10 July. Thirty minutes later, eleven of the fourteen LST's were in position (the other three turned up later in the 45th Division's zone). The twenty LCI's came up just a few minutes later. Shortly before midnight the wind had dropped, and as the transports and landing ships and craft anchored offshore, the sea leveled off into a broad swell. Behind Gela the entire coastal area, it seemed, was aglow as the result of fires started by the preinvasion aerial bombardments and because the few paratroopers at Piano Lupo had

---

[18] The 1st and 4th Ranger Bns; the 1st Bn, 39th Engr Combat Regt; three companies of the 83d Chem Bn (4.2-inch mortars); and the 1st Bn, 531st Engr Shore Regt.

ROAD JUNCTION Y, *the road to Niscemi at its junction with coastal Highway 115, seen from the Piano Lupo area.*

lighted a huge bonfire. The beach contours appeared plainly in silhouette.

While the two Ranger battalions on the left were sailing toward shore, a great flash and loud explosion signaled the destruction of the Gela pier in accordance with Guzzoni's instructions. An enemy searchlight fixed its beam on the boats, but the destroyer *Shubrick*, designated to render gunfire support if the enemy detected the invasion, immediately opened fire and knocked the light out after five quick salvos. Three salvos destroyed a second light.[19] By this time, Italian coastal units were at their guns, and mortar and coastal artillery fire began to fall around the landing craft. The *Shubrick* and soon afterwards the cruiser *Savannah* returned a steady stream of naval gunfire.[20] Five hundred yards offshore, the Rangers came under machine gun fire, and some Rangers answered, as best they could, with rockets from their bazookas.[21] As the enemy fire continued, the Rangers touched down at 0335, fifty minutes late, followed shortly by the 39th Engineers.

Incurring a few casualties from mines on the beaches, losing an entire platoon from one company to enemy rifle and

---

[19] The *Shubrick* carried a main battery of four 5-inch 38-caliber guns.

[20] The *Savannah* had a main battery of fifteen 6-inch 47-caliber guns and a secondary battery of eight 5-inch 25-caliber guns.

[21] A rocket launcher, 2.36 inches in diameter, merely a tube open at both ends that fired an electrically triggered, shaped-charge rocket. See Green, Thomson, and Roots, *The Ordnance Department: Planning Munitions for War*, pp. 328–29.

ITALIAN PRISONERS TAKEN AT GELA *on D-day.*

machine gun fire, the Rangers finally cleared the beach defenses and by dawn pushed up the face of the Gela mound into the city. Two companies under Capt. James B. Lyle wheeled to the west and captured an Italian coastal battery of three 77-mm. guns on the western edge of the mound. None of the guns had been fired, although an ample supply of ammunition lay in the battery position. Though the Italians had removed the gun sights and elevating mechanisms, the weapons could still be fired. Captain Lyle decided to turn the guns around, face them inland, and use them, if necessary, against any enemy force moving against his positions. As the two Ranger companies prepared hasty defensive positions straddling Highway 115, Lyle manned the Italian artillery pieces with Rangers who had a working knowledge of this particular weapon. He also set up an observation post in a two-story building from which he could adjust the fire of the captured guns.

In the meantime, the remainder of the special force had worked its way through the city and had established a defensive

# THE ASSAULT

perimeter around the northern and eastern outskirts. By 0800, the entire city had been cleared of resistance, two hundred Italians taken prisoner, and a strong line formed facing inland. The three companies of 4.2-inch mortars were ashore and ready to fire. Portions of the town were still burning, and clouds of billowing smoke poured into the sky.

To the southeast, the 26th RCT was coming on strong to link up with the special force. Having met little resistance at the beaches, the 1st Battalion (Maj. Walter H. Grant) by 0900 was nearing Gela, while the other two battalions were across the highway, past the Gela-Farello landing ground, moving slowly inland to cut Highway 117 north of Gela.

The 16th RCT had slightly more trouble. Enemy searchlights picked up the assault waves on their way in, but no opposition came from the beach defenders until the troops started to disembark, just two minutes after the scheduled H-hour. From several pillboxes on the beach and from a few scattered Italian riflemen, light and largely ineffective fire fell upon the leading American infantrymen, then petered out. Yet vigorous enemy machine gun fire from apparently bypassed positions struck the second wave. Even after these positions were eliminated, the Italians continued to be active, firing mortars and artillery against the third and fourth waves, which landed after 0300. Not until 0400 when supporting naval guns opened up—from the cruiser *Boise* and the destroyer *Jeffers*—did the enemy fire begin to diminish.[22]

Holding one battalion in reserve, Colonel Taylor sent two battalions of his 16th Infantry toward Piano Lupo in order to link up with Colonel Gavin's parachute force. The leading battalions made contact with Company I, 505th Parachute Infantry, which had been holding the southern portion of Piano Lupo since early morning, but they were unable to locate the sizable numbers of paratroopers they expected.

Thus, by 0900 on 10 July, the 1st Division, with much less difficulty than anticipated, was well on its way to securing the first day's objectives: Gela, the Gela-Farello landing ground, and Niscemi. Unfortunately, General Allen was unaware that the important high ground in front of the 16th Infantry was not in the firm possession of the paratroopers.

On the far right of the Seventh Army's assault area, Admiral Kirk's naval task force brought the 45th Division to offshore positions in the face of a fairly rough sea and heavy swell. The landings in that area had been postponed one hour, but the pitch and roll of the ships, straggling, and confusion dispersed and disorganized the assault waves.[23]

The 45th Division would land southeast of the Acate River, along a coast line extending fifteen miles in a smooth arc almost devoid of indentation. The stretch of sandy, gentle beach was broken only by a few patches of rocky shore or

---

[22] The *Boise* carried fifteen 6-inch 47-caliber guns and eight 5-inch 25-caliber guns; the *Jeffers*, four 5-inch 38-caliber guns.

[23] See as major sources: AGF Rpt 217, Rpt on Opn HUSKY, 1943; AAR's of the units involved; 45th Inf Div Arty AAR, 4 Jul–16 Aug 43; Observation and Comments on the Sicilian Campaign, 345-11.5; II Corps G-3 Jnl; Interv, Garland with Middleton, 16 Jun 59; Rpt of Opn HUSKY, Comdr Transports, Amphibious Force, U.S. Atlantic Fleet, 17 Jul 43, 6-1.1707/43; Rpt, Trans Div 5, 17 Jul 43, 6-1.1409/43; ONI, Sicilian Campaign, pp. 28–36; Interv, Smyth with Brig Gen Charles M. Ankcorn (Ret.) (former CO 157th Inf), 20 Mar 51; Morison, *Sicily—Salerno—Anzio*, pp. 126–37, 143.

The Coast Line *west from Scoglitti.*

# THE ASSAULT

low stone cliffs. The only harbor was the tiny fishing village of Scoglitti, where two rocks jutting above the water marked the entrance to two coves forming a haven for fishing boats. The passage was only some fifty yards wide, with a rocky bottom at a depth of eight feet. A mile southeast of Scoglitti lay the low headland of Point Camerina, a rocky bank about fifty feet high faced by five small patches of underwater rocks. At Point Branco Grande, two miles down the coast, and at Point Braccetto, a little farther along, submerged rocks fronted low cliffs.

Inland was a broad, relatively open plain sloping gradually to the foothills of the mountain core of southern Sicily, which held the cities and larger towns.[24] Highway 115 proceeded eastward beyond the Acate River, swinging gradually inland and upward, following a southeasterly course cutting across the center of the 45th Division's zone through Vittoria (36,000) and Comiso (23,000) to Ragusa (48,000 people), the Seventh Army's eastern boundary and co-ordinating point with the British Eighth Army. Seven miles north of Biscari was the Biscari airfield; three miles north of Comiso was the airfield of that name.

Avenues of approach from the assault beaches to the airfields were limited and poor. Between the relatively uninhabited stretch of coast line and the highway there were no good roads. A fourth class road connected Scoglitti with Vittoria; a scarcely better road led from the eastern beaches through the little town of Santa Croce Camerina to Comiso. An unpaved road followed the east bank of the Acate River from the western beaches as far as Ponte Dirillo, while a secondary road connected Highway 115 and Biscari with the junction near Ponte Dirillo.

To insure the capture of Scoglitti (which could be used as a minor port); to narrow the gap between the 45th Division and the 1st Division on the left; and to put the assaulting units on as direct a route as possible to the Biscari and Comiso airfields, General Middleton selected two sets of beaches for his landing, one on each side of Scoglitti, with a total frontage of some 25,000 yards.

Three beaches northwest of Scoglitti—Red, Green, and Yellow—nicknamed Wood's Hole by the naval force, actually constituted an extension of the 16th RCT's beaches and were similar in terrain. Lying in an uninterrupted line for almost four miles, the beach area was of soft sand which rose gradually for half a mile to an uninterrupted belt of forty- to eighty-foot sand dunes. Pillboxes were scattered along the beaches, the dune line, and the highway. A few coastal artillery batteries dotted the area.

Two regiments would land there. On the left, Col. Forrest E. Cookson's 180th RCT would come ashore with two battalions abreast, the left battalion to seize Ponte Dirillo (also a paratrooper objective), the right battalion to take Biscari. On the right, Col. Robert B. Hutchins' 179th RCT would send its left battalion to seize Vittoria, then the Comiso airfield, the right battalion to capture Scoglitti.

On the division right, Col. Charles M. Ankcorn's 157th RCT was to land over two beaches southeast of Scoglitti. Included in an area nicknamed Bailey's Beach, pressed between Point Branco Grande and Point Braccetto, these beaches were quite different from those to the west. Rock formations and sand dunes came almost to the water's edge, and

---

[24] Vittoria, 880 feet; Comiso, 803 feet; Biscari, 660 feet; Ragusa, 1,680 feet.

rocky ledges jutted into the surf. The beaches, Green 2 and Yellow 2, were small, ten to twenty yards deep, less than a half-mile wide. Neither was suitable for bringing vehicles ashore.

Landing nine miles southeast of the other combat teams and fifteen miles northwest of the 1st Canadian Division, the 157th RCT constituted an almost independent task force. Yet Ankcorn had to get to Comiso as quickly as possible to join with the 179th RCT for a co-ordinated attack on the airfield. Colonel Ankcorn therefore planned to land a battalion on each of his beaches, the one on the right to move due east to capture Santa Croce Camerina, the left battalion to bypass the town to the north for a direct thrust to Comiso. The RCT's major effort would follow the left battalion's axis of advance. All of the 45th Division's supporting armor, a medium tank battalion, was attached to the 157th.

Enemy forces in the division's zone were few and scattered, mainly troops from the *XVIII Coastal Brigade*, right flank units of the *206th Coastal Division* (where the 157th RCT would be landing), and a mobile airfield defense group at Biscari. The *Hermann Goering Division* might be expected to strike at part of the division's beachhead, but disposed as it was in the Caltagirone area, it posed a more serious threat to the 1st Division's landings. If the 179th and 157th RCT's moved fast enough, they would have little to fear from enemy attempts to interfere with their juncture at Comiso.

An unexpected benefit came from the dispersed paratroopers who landed in large numbers in the division's zone. At the very time the 45th Division started ashore, Captain McGinity's Company G, 505th Parachute Infantry, was making its way toward Ponte Dirillo; Major Alexander's 2d Battalion, 505th Parachute Infantry, was reorganizing preparatory to moving on Santa Croce Camerina; Lieutenant Swingler's forty paratroopers were reducing an Italian strongpoint along the Santa Croce Camerina–Vittoria road; and elements of the 3d Battalion, 505th, were creating confusion and havoc in the rear areas of the *XVIII Coastal Brigade* from the Acate River east to Vittoria.

In a few cases, postponing the division's landings led to some additional difficulties, particularly in the 180th RCT, the westernmost landing force. The transport *Calvert's* crew did a splendid job of getting the landing craft loaded with Lt. Col. William H. Schaefer's 1st Battalion and into the water. Thirty of the thirty-four boats of the first four waves were circling in the small craft rendezvous area by 0200 and, under guidance of a control vessel, started for shore shortly thereafter. But the *Calvert* had performed too well. Her small boat waves were far ahead of the others. Just before 0300, as word of the H-hour postponement reached the *Calvert*, her commander had no choice but to recall the four assault waves to the rendezvous area. When the control vessel arrived back near the transport, the assault waves were in a bedraggled condition: some of the small craft had straggled, others had lost the wave formations and had headed off in various directions. When the control vessel received new orders to take the assault waves in to the beach to meet the new H-hour, she obediently turned to execute the order. The result of this movement back and forth in unfamiliar waters and in complete darkness was that the 1st Battalion, 180th Infantry, landed late and badly scattered. What could be collected of the first wave eventually touched down on Red Beach at 0445, almost three hours after its start. Parts of the other three waves arrived at brief intervals thereafter.

In contrast, the transport *Neville*, carrying Lt. Col. Clarence B. Cochran's 2d Battalion, had a most difficult time launching her small craft. It took almost four hours to load most of the first four assault waves. At 0337, about three-fourths of the total number of landing craft started in to shore even as the ship's crew still struggled to get the remaining landing craft loaded and launched. But like the 1st Battalion's waves, the 2d Battalion's first assault waves scattered on the way in, and only five boats of the first wave touched down on Red Beach at 0434, eleven minutes before the first wave from the *Calvert*. Only three boats from the second wave found the beach, three minutes later. Seven boats from the third wave touched down at 0438, and eight boats from the fourth wave made it at 0500. Fortunately for both of Colonel Cookson's assault battalions, Italian opposition at the shore line was negligible. Though Italian machine guns fired briefly at the *Neville's* decimated second wave, no one was hit.

The rest of both assault waves were scattered from Red Beach 2 in the 16th RCT's sector all the way down the coast to Scoglitti. Colonel Cookson and part of his RCT staff landed on the 1st Division beach. Instead of a compact landing along twelve hundred yards of coast just east of the Acate River, the 180th RCT was scattered along almost twelve miles of shore line.

Of the 2d Battalion, only Company F landed relatively intact. With this unit, plus a few men from Company E, Colonel Cochran started inland after first clearing out some pillboxes. Following the secondary road parallel to the Acate River, Cochran's small force was at Ponte Dirillo by dawn, there to find and join McGinity's paratroopers. With Cochran in command, the combined American force put a guard on the bridge and then established and consolidated its position on the high ground just to the north to block the coastal Highway 115.

Meanwhile, Colonel Schaefer had gathered what he could find of his 1st Battalion. Just before daylight, he began moving inland across the dune area to the highway. There he paused to reorganize before marching on Biscari.

The landing craft that could retract from the beaches returned to the transport *Funston* to get the 3d Battalion, 180th Infantry (Lt. Col. R. W. Nolan), ashore. The first wave was ready to go at 0700 and the commander of the wave's control vessel, who had been with the *Calvert's* waves on the earlier landings, started the wave shoreward. But soon after leaving the rendezvous area, the wave commander noticed that landing craft from other transports were crossing his front and heading toward shore on a northwesterly course. Mistakenly concluding that Red Beach had been shifted, he changed course and followed the other craft. The *Funston's* first wave grounded on the 16th RCT's Red Beach 2, west of the Acate River, as did the second and fourth waves. For some strange reason, the third wave landed on the correct Red Beach at 0800. The 3d Battalion troops which landed in the 1st Division's sector, almost 300 men from all units of the battalion, banded together under three officers and started the three-mile trek to the correct beach area. The group crossed the Acate River about 0900, met the battalion's executive officer who had landed with the third wave, and moved into an assembly area just inland from the beach, there, in II Corps reserve, to await further orders.

On the other two Wood's Hole beaches, the landings proceeded more smoothly. The first waves of the 179th RCT touched down either right on time or just a few minutes late against no enemy opposition. The only resistance occurred after daylight, when fire flared briefly from an Italian pillbox against the fifth wave.

Lt. Col. Earl A. Taylor's 3d Battalion on the left quickly secured the dune line. After a speedy reorganization, the battalion moved inland, reached Highway 115, and as day broke turned toward Vittoria. Sixty paratroopers of the 3d Battalion, 505th Parachute Infantry, and three howitzers from Battery C, 456th Parachute Field Artillery Battalion, joined Taylor's battalion, taking places in the line of march.

Lt. Col. Edward F. Stephenson's 1st Battalion had turned southeast immediately after landing to work toward Scoglitti. One company remained on the beach to clear enemy installations, while the others pushed along the dune line to Point Zafaglione, which dominated Scoglitti from the north and which proved to be well fortified against a seaward approach. Attacked from the landward side, the Italian garrison of seventy artillerymen quickly surrendered.

At Bailey's Beach the landings of the 157th RCT proceeded smoothly, although a few landing craft grounded on the rocky ledges thrusting out into the surf.

From the transport *Jefferson*, Lt. Col. Irving O. Schaefer's 2d Battalion started toward shore at 0303. Battling wind and sea, grazed by what appeared to be friendly fires from supporting warships, the control vessel veered off course and at 0355 finally touched down, not on Green 2, but on the southern end of Yellow 2 close to Point Braccetto. A few scattered rifle shots greeted the first Americans ashore but caused no casualties. A machine gun crew surrendered without firing a shot. There was little will here to contest the invasion.

The *Jefferson's* second wave veered off even farther to the right. About fifty yards offshore, the boat crews finally woke to the fact that they were heading straight for the rocks at Point Braccetto and into a ten- to twelve-foot surf. Too late to change course, the first two landing craft went broadside into the rocks and capsized. Twenty-seven men drowned, weighed down by their equipment and pounded against the submerged rocks. The other landing craft managed to get to the point without capsizing, and their passengers with some difficulty crawled ashore.[25]

Six of the seven landing craft from the third wave followed close behind. In vain did the men already on the rocks try to wave off the approaching boats. Only two of the six incoming craft grounded on sand. Four hit the rocky area along the north side of Point Braccetto, and though able to unload their troops and cargo, were unable to retract. The seventh boat, far off course from the begin-

---

[25] Three more men would have drowned had it not been for Sgt. Jesse E. East, Jr., Company F, 157th Infantry, who, after scrambling ashore, tossed off his equipment and dove back into the surf three times to save fellow soldiers. He tried a fourth time, but, apparently tired from his previous efforts, failed, and drowned with the man he was trying to save. See correspondence in the possession of Mr. Sherrod East, Chief Archivist, World War II Branch, National Archives and Record Service.

# THE ASSAULT

LANDING HEAVY EQUIPMENT *over the causeway at Scoglitti.*

ning, landed most of Company G north of Scoglitti on the 179th RCT's beaches.

The first wave from the transport *Carroll,* carrying Colonel Ankcorn, his RCT staff, and Lt. Col. Preston J. C. Murphy's 1st Battalion, touched down an hour after the *Jefferson's* first wave, a delay caused by the loading and lowering of the assault craft. All six of the *Carroll's* waves landed within the next hour on the correct beach—Yellow 2. No assault troops landed on Green 2.

Despite the lateness of its landing, the 1st Battalion was the first to leave the immediate beach area. The 2d Battalion, disorganized by its troubles with the rocks, spent some time in reorganizing and worked mainly on clearing enemy installations along the shore line. Nevertheless, by 0900 both battalions were pushing inland toward Santa Croce Camerina and Comiso. Though enemy resistance around Point Braccetto and Point Branco Grande had been eliminated, the sandy hinterland behind the beaches made it all but impossible to move the RCT's vehicles inland to follow the assault battalions. Eventually, after much effort, a third beach—Blue 2, south of Point Braccetto—was opened, and the original beaches closed.

Across the entire Seventh Army front by 0900, 10 July, infantry battalions were pushing inland. The assault had been accomplished with a minimum of casualties against only minor enemy resistance. Supporting armor and artillery were coming ashore; mountains of supplies began appearing on many of the beaches; and commanders at all echelons were urging their troops to keep up the momentum of the initial assault.

# CHAPTER VII

# The First Day

## *The Axis Reaction*

The Axis was unable to react effectively against the initial Seventh Army landings. At 0430, 10 July, the first enemy planes appeared over the Allied shipping massed in front of the assault beaches. The destroyer *Maddox* took a direct hit and sank within two minutes, just before 0500, and a mine sweeper went down at 0615. Enemy fighters shot down several planes that were spotting targets for the cruisers' guns, and occasionally enemy bombs fell in the transport area. The air raids interfered but little with the landings.[1]

Axis commanders were already trying that morning to stem the American advances. To counter the Gela landings and back up the weak *XVIII Coastal Brigade*, General Guzzoni attached to the *XVI Corps* the two Italian mobile airfield defense groups intended for the defense of the Ponte Olivo and Biscari airfields, the *Livorno Division*, and the *Hermann Goering Division* (minus *Group Schmalz*). He wished these forces to counterattack before the Americans could consolidate a beachhead. At the same time, despite his continued apprehension over an Allied landing in the western part of the island, Guzzoni ordered the *15th Panzer Grenadier Division*, the larger part of which had just completed its transfer to the west, to retrace its steps and return to the Canicattì–Caltanissetta–San Cataldo area in the center of the island.[2]

With these new units, the *XVI Corps* intended to launch a co-ordinated attack against the Gela landings, the *Hermann Goering Division* and the two Italian mobile groups to strike from the northeast, the *Livorno Division* from the northwest. But since telephone communications, poor to begin with, had been almost totally severed by the scattered groups of American paratroopers and by Allied bombing raids during the night, many of the units failed to receive the corps order. They proceeded to act on their own initiative according to the established defensive

---

[1] The spotting aircraft were SOC's (Seagull scout observation float planes), Curtiss single radial engine biplanes with large single floats and two-man crews: pilot and radioman. The aircraft were used primarily for spotting gunfire and for scouting purposes and had a top speed of 126 miles per hour. Each U.S. cruiser had two catapults and carried four SOC's.

[2] IT 99a; Faldella, *Lo sbarco*, p. 123; MS # C-077 (Rodt); MS #T-2, K 1 (Kesselring); MS #C-095 (Senger), *KTB* entry for 1425, 10 Jul 43. This manuscript contains certain entries from the war diary of the German liaison staff with the *Armed Forces Command, Sicily;* the war diary itself is not available. These war diary excerpts will be cited as follows: *KTB* entry, hour, and date.

Parts of the *15th Panzer Grenadier Division* (an infantry regiment, plus artillery and other units) were operating under Schmalz's control on the east coast; other smaller elements had not yet made the move to the west. Basically the two major units involved in moving back to the east were *Group Ens* and *Group Fullriede*.

doctrine for the island.[3] The broad-fronted, massive, co-ordinated push visualized against the Gela beaches would turn out to be a series of un-co-ordinated, independent thrusts by small Axis units at varying times and at various places along the center of the American front.

General Conrath, the *Hermann Goering Division* commander, had learned of the American landings early that morning, not from the *Sixth Army* headquarters but from messages relayed to him from Kesselring's headquarters in Italy and from his own reconnaissance patrols, several of which clashed with American paratroopers near Niscemi. Later, word from Colonel Schmalz reporting his commitment of troops against the British landings convinced Conrath that the time had come to carry out the predetermined defense plan. He decided to counterattack at Gela.[4]

The German division was not altogether unprepared. General Conrath had alerted his units at 2200 the previous night, instructing them to stand by for definite word on the expected Allied assaults. Because his communications with both *Sixth Army* and *XVI Corps* had gone out early on 10 July, and because he wished someone in authority to know of his counterattack plan, Conrath phoned General von Senger, the German liaison officer with the *Sixth Army*, outlined his plan, and told him he was jumping off without delay.[5] He was not aware of the *XVI Corps'* plan for a co-ordinated attack. Nor did he know that his division was attached to the corps for the attack.

The bulk of the *Hermann Goering Division* was assembled in and around Caltagirone. Conrath had organized the division forces into two reinforced regiments, assembled as task forces.[6] One, heavy in infantry, consisted of a two-battalion infantry regiment mounted on trucks, an armored artillery battalion, and an attached Tiger tank company of seventeen Mark VI tanks.[7] The other task force, heavy in tanks, had a two-battalion tank regiment (about ninety Mark III and Mark IV tanks), two armored artillery battalions, and the bulk of the armored

---

[3] Faldella, *Lo sbarco*, pp. 118-19.
[4] MS #C-087 a, *Division Hermann Goering* in Sicily 1943 (Bergengruen); MS #C-087 c, *Division Hermann Goering* in Sicily 1943, Commentary (Conrath); MS #C-087 d, *Hermann Goering Division* Questionnaire, 11-12 July 1943 (Generalmajor Hellmuth Reinhardt and Col. Helmut Bergengruen); Bergengruen in MS #T-2 (Fries *et al.*).

[5] It seems odd that Conrath could contact Senger, but not General Guzzoni or the *XVI Corps*. He presumably used a separate German telephone net.
[6] Called *Kampfgruppe*, a term loosely assigned to improvised combat units of various sizes, usually named after the commander.
See MS #R-137, ch. VIII, The Counterthrust on the First Day, 10 July 1943, Axis Tactical Operations in Sicily (Bauer), pp. 4-6. For a complete order of battle of the *Hermann Goering Division*, see MS #R-125 (Bauer), pp. 46-49; for its tank strength, see pp. 50-51.
[7] The colloquial name, Tiger, was not applied officially to this tank until 1944. This was a heavy tank, 60 tons, with a 5-man crew, an 88-mm. gun as main armament, and carried the thickest armor ever to be fitted on a German tank up to this time. The vehicle was 21 feet long, 12 feet wide, and could do 15 miles per hour on roads, 5 miles per hour cross-country.
The Tiger tank company, part of the *215th Tank Battalion, 15th Panzer Grenadier Division*, had been left behind when that division moved to the west, only the forty-six Mark III and Mark IV tanks of the battalion having gone along. The Tiger tank company was attached to the *Hermann Goering Division* either just before or at the beginning of the operations.

# THE FIRST DAY

reconnaissance and engineer battalions, which functioned as infantry.[8]

General Conrath planned to commit his task forces in a two-pronged attack toward the beaches east of Gela. The troops were to move on three secondary roads to assembly points south of Biscari and Niscemi. With the infantry-heavy force on the Biscari side, both were then to jump off in a concentric attack on the beaches. Conrath hoped to begin his attack before 0900, 10 July, for a later hour would put the sun in his men's eyes and make it easier for the Americans to locate his units. Besides, the earlier he could attack, the better his chances for success.

Both German task forces were on the move shortly after 0400. *(See Map III.)* Although the roads had been previously reconnoitered and found to be passable, if mediocre, the approach march to the assembly areas turned out to be much slower than Conrath had anticipated. Allied armed reconnaissance air strikes against the columns and clashes with scattered groups of American paratroopers caused some confusion and delay. Accompanying his tank regiment, Conrath had to work hard more than once to prevent panic among his inexperienced troops and admittedly not very capable junior commanders. The task forces soon lost contact with each other, and 0900 came and went with both groups still struggling toward their assembly areas.[9]

Meanwhile, the Italian *Mobile Group E* under *XVI Corps* orders had started its movement south from Niscemi. Organized into two columns, one moving along the secondary road leading to Piano Lupo and Highway 115, the other turning west toward Ponte Olivo to pick up Highway 117 for a drive south on Gela, the group had no contact with the *Hermann Goering Division*. But it was aware of a corps order to the *Livorno Division* to commit a battalion in an attack on Gela from the northwest. Moving by truck, this battalion approached a jump-off point near Gela for an attack in conjunction with the mobile group.

At 0900, 10 July, therefore, three Axis forces were moving against the center of Seventh Army's front. In the path of these forces lay the special force in Gela, the 26th RCT moving around Gela toward Highway 117, the 16th RCT advancing toward Piano Lupo, and the badly disorganized 180th RCT immediately east of the Acate River, with one of its battalions preparing to push from Highway 115 to Biscari. Elsewhere, there seemed to be no contest. On the right, only a few static Italian defensive positions remained. On the left, the *XII Corps* was trying to scrape together enough units

---

[8] The Mark III was a medium (24½-ton) tank, carried a 5-man crew, and was armed with a long-barreled 50-mm. or short-barreled 75-mm. gun. It was 17½ feet long, almost 10 feet wide, could do 22 miles per hour on roads, and about half that speed cross-country. The Mark IV medium (26 tons) tank also carried a 5-man crew, but was armed with the long-barreled, high-velocity (3,200 feet per second) 75-mm. gun. It was 19 feet long, about 9½ feet wide, and had roughly the same speed characteristics as the Mark III.

For an excellent description of the development of German armor, see Garrett Underhill, "Introduction to German Armor," Part I, *Armored Cavalry Journal*, vol. 58, No. 4 (July-August 1949), pp. 3-9, and Part II, *Armored Cavalry Journal*, vol. 58, No. 5 (September-October 1949), pp. 42-47.

[9] Italian coastal defense troops fleeing inland from Gela and Scoglitti with confusing and alarming reports of speedy American advances did little to help.

## The Battle

At Casa del Priolo, halfway between Piano Lupo and Niscemi, where less than 100 men of the 1st Battalion, 505th Parachute Infantry, had, under Lt. Col. Arthur Gorham, reduced a strongpoint and set up a blocking position, an American soldier saw a column of Italian tanks and infantry heading his way. Alerted, the paratroopers allowed the point of the column, three small vehicles, to enter their lines before opening fire, killing or capturing the occupants. The sound of firing halted the main body.

After thirty minutes of hesitation, about two infantry companies shook themselves out into an extended formation and began moving toward the Americans, who waited until the Italians were 200 yards away. Then they opened a withering fire not only of rifles but of the numerous machine guns they had captured when they had taken the strongpoint. Their first fusillade pinned down the enemy troops except for a few in the rear who managed to get back to the main column.

Several minutes later, the Italians moved a mobile artillery piece into firing position on a hill just out of range of any weapon the paratroopers possessed. As the gun opened fire, a previously dispatched paratrooper patrol returned and reported to Colonel Gorham that there appeared to be no strong enemy force at the battalion's original objective. This was the road junction on Piano Lupo, where only a few Italians armed with machine guns held a dug-in position surrounded by barbed wire.

Unable to counter the artillery fire, Gorham decided to make for Piano Lupo. The move would have several advantages: it would put him on his objective and closer to the 16th RCT, which he was supposed to contact; it would probably facilitate contact with other paratroopers. Even though naval gunfire began to come in on the Italian column, Gorham had no way of controlling or directing the fire. Leaving one squad to cover the withdrawal, he started the paratroopers south, staying well east of the Niscemi–Piano Lupo road to escape the effects of the naval fire. It was then close to 0930.[10]

The naval gunfire had come in response to a call from observers with the 16th RCT's leading battalions, which were moving toward Piano Lupo. Because the RCT's direct support artillery unit, the 7th Field Artillery Battalion, was not yet in firing position, the destroyer *Jeffers* answered the call with nineteen salvos from her 5-inch guns.[11] A few of the Italian tanks were hit, but the majority were unscathed.[12] No Italian infantry ventured

---

[10] There is a brief account of this action in the 505th Parachute Infantry Regiment AAR, 9–11 July 1943, and in 82d Airborne Division in Sicily and Italy, pp. 10–11. A complete account is contained in the Sayre narrative, The Operations of Company A, 505th Parachute Infantry. The material presented by General Gavin in *Airborne Warfare*, pp. 6–8, is drawn from Sayre's account.

[11] The 7th Field Artillery Battalion managed to get its personnel ashore early on D-day, but its howitzers were aboard the LST's which veered off into the 45th Division's zone. Two batteries were unloaded during the course of 10 July east of the Acate River and were moved up the beach (northwestward) and across the river by late afternoon.

[12] The cruiser *Boise*, at the request from the pilot of one of her scout planes, had previously fired two minutes of rapid fire with 6-inch guns at the same target. Apparently the *Boise*'s skipper was not aware of the nature of the target, for as he said later: "Had we only known what

PIANO LUPO, LOOKING DOWN THE NISCEMI ROAD *to the high ground south of the crossroads*

past the Piano Lupo road junction, for they preferred to take cover from the relatively flat trajectory naval fire in previously prepared defensive positions. Masked on the south by high ground that caused most of the naval fire to overshoot the junction, the Italian infantrymen reached and occupied their positions just a few minutes ahead of Gorham's paratroopers.

The Italian tanks that passed through the fire, about twenty, continued past the road junction and turned on Highway 115 toward Gela.[13] They proceeded downhill only a short way. The two forward battalions of the 16th RCT, though armed only with standard infantry weapons,

---

we were shooting at, we would have cut loose with the whole fifteen-gun battery." (Morison, *Sicily—Salerno—Anzio,* p. 103.)

The scout planes, continually harassed by enemy fighter planes, had to take continual evasive action as long as they were in the air and had little opportunity to keep any target in sight long enough to accurately adjust fires.

[13] The 16th RCT reported twenty tanks in this attack. (1st Inf Div G-3 Jnl, entry 17, 10 Jul 43.) The exact number of tanks in this group is not known. One report indicates *Mobile Group E* had nearly fifty tanks when it started its movement on 10 July (Morison, *Sicily—Salerno—Anzio,* p. 103). Another report (MS # R-125 (Bauer)) indicates that the Italian unit had one company (twelve to fourteen) of Renault 35 tanks; possibly sixteen 3-ton tanks; and possibly some Fiat "3,000" tanks. The Renault tanks, captured from the French in 1940, weighed two tons and were armed with 37-mm. guns. From reports contained in other American sources, the number of Italian tanks appears to have been between thirty and forty total in both Italian groups.

knocked out two of the tanks, thoroughly disrupted the Italian thrust, and halted the column. Without infantry support, its artillery under heavy counterbattery fire from American warships, the Italian tankers broke off the fight and retired north into the foothills bordering the Gela plain on the east.[14]

The threat dispersed, the 16th RCT resumed its movement to the Piano Lupo road junction. But Gorham's paratroopers, approaching from the opposite direction, arrived first. After reducing one Italian strongpoint, the paratroopers made contact with scouts from the 16th RCT at 1100.[15] The 1st Battalion, 16th Infantry (Lt. Col. Charles L. Denholm), then cleaned out several remaining Italian positions around the road junction, a task facilitated by a captured map, while the 2d Battalion (Lt. Col. Joseph Crawford) and the paratroopers moved across the road and occupied high ground to the northwest.

Meanwhile the heterogeneous Ranger-engineer force in Gela had observed a column of thirteen Italian tanks escorted by infantry moving south along Highway 117 toward the city—the right arm of *Mobile Group E's* two-pronged attack. Another column, the *Livorno Division's* battalion of infantry, could also be seen moving toward Gela along the Butera road. While the destroyer *Shubrick* started firing at the tank-infantry column on Highway 117, the Ranger-manned Italian 77-mm. guns opened up on the *Livorno* battalion.

The first *Shubrick* salvos halted the Italians in some confusion. But the tankers recovered a measure of composure; they resumed their movement, though fewer now, for several tanks were burning in the fields along the highway. Without further loss, nine or ten tanks dashed down the highway and into the city. But the same thing happened here that had happened on the Niscemi–Piano Lupo road—Italian infantrymen did not follow the tanks. And so, in the city, the Rangers and the engineers began a deadly game of hide and seek with the Italian tanks, dodging in and out of buildings, throwing hand grenades and firing rocket launchers. Colonel Darby jumped in a jeep, dashed down to the beach, commandeered a 37-mm. antitank gun, returned with it to the city and knocked out a tank. Another burned as Rangers and engineers teamed up, first to stop it and then to destroy it. After twenty minutes of this kind of fighting, the Italians started back out of the city hotly pursued by American fire. The Italian crews suffered heavily. Almost every survivor carried with him some kind of wound.[16]

As for the *Livorno Division's* battalion —in almost formal, parade ground formation, the Italian infantrymen advanced against the western side of Gela. The two Ranger companies firing their captured Italian artillery pieces took heavy toll among the closely bunched enemy soldiers. Rifles, machine guns, and mortars joined in as the range closed. Not an

---

[14] 16th Inf Regt AAR, Jun–Jul 43; ONI, Sicilian Campaign, pp. 60–61; Morison, *Sicily—Salerno—Anzio,* p. 103.

[15] In a letter received by OCMH 26 December 1950, Brig. Gen. George A. Taylor (Ret.), former commander of the 16th RCT, noted: "Any report that any unit of the 82d Division captured anything and turned it over to me is without foundation." But the 16th Infantry's report of action shows that paratroopers were on Piano Lupo by the time the leading elements of the RCT arrived. This is also shown in the 82d Airborne Division's records.

[16] Faldella, *Lo sbarco,* p. 117.

# THE FIRST DAY

AMERICAN TROOPS IN GELA ON D PLUS 1.

enemy soldier reached the city. Leaving behind numerous dead and wounded, the remnants of the Italian battalion fled.[17]

The Italian thrust against Gela stopped, the 26th Combat Team moved from the Gela-Farello landing ground into Gela and made contact with Darby's force by noon. Two battalions swept past the city on the east, cut Highway 117, and took high ground two miles to the north.

With the city firmly in American hands, Colonel Bowen, the 26th RCT commander, began to think of seizing the terrain overlooking Ponte Olivo airfield from the west. Yet he was not anxious to start until he had adequate field artillery and armor support. As of noon, Bowen had neither. Nor was the situation along the Piano Lupo–Niscemi axis clear.

South of Niscemi, the right column of Conrath's two-pronged counterattack, the

---

[17] 1st Ranger Bn AAR, 10–14 Jul 43; 4th Ranger AAR, 10–12 Jul 43; 39th Engr Combat Regt AAR, 10 Jul–18 Aug 43; Morison, *Sicily—Salerno—Anzio*, pp. 103–04; Lyle, Operations of Companies A and B, 1st Ranger Bn, p. 16; Altieri, *Darby's Rangers*, p. 50; Faldella, *Lo sbarco*, pp. 119, 120, 123.

tank-heavy force, closed into its assembly area. The infantry-heavy force closed in the Biscari area. With all in readiness at 1400, five hours late, Conrath sent his *Hermann Goering Division* into its attack.

The tank regiment struck the 2d Battalion, 16th Infantry, which had prepared defensive positions on ground overlooking the road junction at the coastal highway and had sent patrols almost to Casa del Priolo.

Colonel Crawford's 2d Battalion, along with Colonel Gorham's paratroopers, bore the initial brunt of the German tank thrust, and soon Colonel Denholm's 1st Battalion was drawn into the fight. Calls for naval gunfire soon had shells dropping on the Niscemi road, but the German tanks, accompanied by reconnaissance and engineer troops in an infantry mission, rolled slowly past Casa del Priolo. Not far from Casa del Priolo the tanks slowed, sputtered, and eventually stopped. The tankers could not go on because they had nothing to cope with the five- and six-inch naval shells that came whistling in from the sea. Also, American small arms fire had knocked out the accompanying foot soldiers and had thrown the lead tanks into confusion. Then, too, no support developed from the infantry-heavy column on the left.[18]

Conrath ordered the tank attack renewed at 1500. But even Conrath's inspiring and hard-driving presence was not enough to furnish impetus. The attack failed to get rolling. Still uncertain about the location and the fate of the infantry-heavy task force, which was supposed to have crossed the Acate River and attacked Piano Lupo from the southeast, Conrath called off his offensive action. "The tanks are trying to withdraw," the 16th Infantry reported around 1700. And at 1845, "Tanks are withdrawing, it seems we are too much for them."[19]

Conrath's infantry force had jumped off at 1400, had promptly lost communications with division headquarters, and had run into the 1st Battalion, 180th Infantry, which, together with some paratroopers picked up along the way, was moving toward Biscari. Their attack blunted by the relatively small American force supported by one battery of the 171st Field Artillery Battalion, the Germans came to a halt by 1530. Though the terraced terrain was well suited for infantry operations, dense groves of olive trees interfered with the movement of the heavy Tiger tanks that were part of the column. Moreover, some of the Tigers, among the first produced, had defective steering mechanisms, and those that dropped out blocked the others. Inexperience among junior officers and some of the troop units, failure to get the Tiger tanks forward, and American tenacity on the ground stopped the German attempt.

Regaining communications later that afternoon, Conrath relieved the task force commander. After much prodding from Conrath and under a new commander, the infantry-heavy force regrouped and jumped off again. This time the German attack was better co-ordinated. The Tiger tanks led off, followed closely by foot soldiers. Breaking through the thin American lines, the Germans overran the positions of the 1st Battalion, 180th In-

---

[18] None of the 16th RCT's AT guns (37-mm. in the battalions, 57-mm. in the regimental AT platoon) were up at this time. The guns did not arrive until later that night and early the following morning.

[19] 1st Inf Div G-3 Jnl, entries 21 and 23, 10 Jul 43.

# THE FIRST DAY

fantry, and took prisoner the battalion commander, Colonel Schaefer, and most of the surviving troops. The remnants of the battalion streamed south toward the coastal Highway 115.[20]

The way seemed open for German exploitation that would endanger the 1st Division beaches, when the 3d Battalion, 180th Infantry, suddenly appeared. Released from corps reserve to counter the German attack, this American force took defensive positions and held fast. Imminent American disaster was averted as the Germans unexpectedly panicked. German soldiers broke and ran in wild disorder, their officers finally stopping the rout just short of Biscari. The Americans were content to remain along a line paralleling the south side of Highway 115.[21]

Some confused fighting among combat patrols lasted until well after dark. Though strong enemy forces ringed the Gela plain and the Acate River valley, though commanders were concerned about the arrival of supporting tanks and artillery and the extent of their frontages, the troops in the center of the American beachhead had earned the right to a brief pause.

On the army left, General Truscott sent the 15th RCT, his center unit, seven miles up Highway 123 toward Campobello, holding the others ready to counter Axis thrusts. Reconnaissance pilots had picked up the movement of the *15th Panzer Grenadier Division*, which was returning from the western part of Sicily, and Truscott was preparing to meet the threat. Landing the 3d Division's floating reserve, General Rose's CCA, would help, and the armored command began coming ashore over the beaches east of Licata and through Licata itself. Truscott planned to send the armor to Naro, a small town fifteen miles northwest of Licata, between Palma di Montechiaro on the south and Campobello on the east. With troops at Naro and Campobello, Truscott would block an important avenue of approach to the division's beachhead from the northwest.

On the army right, General Middleton kept pushing his easternmost regiments, the 179th and 157th. By nightfall they were seven miles inland. In contrast with the 180th Infantry's rough experience in the Acate River valley, the 179th Infantry had Colonel Taylor's 3d Battalion, and some paratroopers who had joined, at the outskirts of Vittoria before 1600. A few men entered the city, but small arms fire drove them out. Unwilling to unleash his supporting artillery until city authorities had a chance to surrender, Colonel Taylor spent much time trying to persuade a civilian to go into the city to bring out the mayor or some other

---

[20] Maj. Gen. Stanhope B. Mason, former chief of staff of the 1st Infantry Division, a close, personal friend of Colonel Schaefer's, later had the pleasure of seeing the former 45th Division battalion commander released by American troops from the U.S. V Corps in Germany in 1945. See comments of Maj. Gen. Stanhope B. Mason on MS.

[21] 180th Inf Regt AAR, 10 Jul 43; AGF Rpt 217; 171st FA Bn AAR; 45th Inf Div Arty AAR; MS #C-087 a (Bergengruen).

The wartime German record states simply that the attack mounted by the *Hermann Goering Division* against the Allied forces advancing from the Gela beaches to the area west of Caltagirone did not bear results. See *OB SUED, Meldungen*, No. 0114, 0340, 11 Jul 43, and *Daily Sitrep West*, 10 Jul 43, in *OKH, Tagesmeldungen WEST*. It was apparently the early evening advance of the German force that was used in ONI, Sicilian Campaign, page 47, to indicate withdrawal of the 180th RCT to the beaches at 2150, 10 July 1943. No doubt part of the 1st Battalion did go all the way back to the beaches, but there is no indication that any part of the 3d Battalion did the same.

municipal official. The civilian refused. Infantry attack preceded by artillery bombardment appeared the only solution.

Unknown to Taylor, negotiations for Vittoria's surrender were already taking place. Three of the ubiquitous paratroopers had been in the city since early morning, having been captured by the Italians shortly after dropping to ground. Two by this time were roaring drunk. The third, 1st Lt. William J. Harris (Headquarters Company, 3d Battalion, 505th Parachute Infantry), was trying to persuade the Italian commander to capitulate. The approach of Taylor's battalion strengthened Harris' arguments considerably. At 1640, as American artillery units prepared to open fire, the Italians agreed to surrender. Beckoned by the hurried display of white flags, the infantrymen outside the city marched in unopposed.

Farther to the right, where Americans were moving on the Comiso airfield, Santa Croce Camerina was taken in the early afternoon as the result of an unplanned pincer movement. Colonel Murphy's 1st Battalion, 157th Infantry, and Major Alexander's 2d Battalion, 505th Parachute Infantry, neither of which apparently knew of the other's presence, attacked the town about the same time. The Italian garrison, concerned with Murphy's approach from the west and totally unprepared for the paratrooper attack on the east, conceded defeat.

While Alexander's paratroopers moved off to the north and west in search of a higher parachute headquarters, Murphy outposted the town and sent a partially motorized company thirteen miles northeast to Ragusa, the 1st Canadian Division objective. With only negligible opposition, the two motorized platoons entered Ragusa at 1800. No Canadians and only a few Italian soldiers were in the city. Since they were unwilling to chance an ambush during the night, the American platoons withdrew to the western outskirts, where the remainder of the company joined them shortly before midnight.

Sliding past Santa Croce Camerina on the west, the other two battalions of the 157th Infantry overran a strongpoint at Donnafugata. A four-truck motorized patrol to high ground northeast of Comiso secured an assembly area for the leading battalion. And from that point, Hill 643, the battalion the next day would support by fire the attack planned to seize the airfield.[22]

*The Beaches*

By nightfall of D-day, 10 July, the Seventh Army was firmly established on Sicily. Only in the center was there cause for any immediate concern, and this stemmed from the failure of the airborne drop. The absence of paratroopers on Piano Lupo deprived the 1st Division of a reserve, put the 16th Infantry at a disadvantage, and increased the threat of enemy counterattack. The paratroopers had created confusion in enemy rear areas, but they had not seriously interfered with the movement of German and Italian units against the invasion.

---

[22] 179th Inf Regt AAR; an account of the Sicilian Campaign (22 pages) written by Brig. Gen. Raymond S. McLain, then Commanding General, 45th Infantry Division Artillery, probably in late July or early August 1943, copy in OCMH; 45th Inf Div Arty AAR; AGF Rpt 217; 157th Inf Regt AAR; Interv, Smyth with Ankcorn, 20 Mar 51; 158th FA Bn AAR; 160th FA Bn AAR; 45th Inf Div G-3 Jnl, entries 9-10 Jul 43.

THE FIRST DAY                                                                                   157

The cause of failure lay with the troop carriers. As late as 20 June, three weeks before the invasion, observers had considered the 52d Troop Carrier Wing deficient in night formation flying, night navigation, and drop zone location during darkness. The wing had had only two practice missions at night under simulated combat conditions. One of these had scattered the 505th Parachute Infantry all along the flight route. Further training was impossible after 20 June because of the need to start moving troops and planes to the advanced take-off airfields.[23]

On the evening of 9 July, serious doubts had existed in some quarters on the ability of the troop carrier units to deliver the paratroopers to the correct drop zones; at least one commander felt that the Troop Carrier Command was far too optimistic about the proficiency of the aircraft crews.[24] Late in July 1943, General Ridgway was unequivocal in stating that the operation "demonstrated beyond any doubt that the Air Force . . . cannot at present put parachute units, even as large as a battalion, within effective attack distance of a chosen drop zone at night." [25]

German commanders tended to minimize the effect of the American airborne operation. Col. Hellmut Bergengruen, a staff officer with the *Hermann Goering Division,* judged that the airdrops "were made in rear of the Italian coastal divisions, but in front of the German units and did not interfere with the conduct of the battle." He conceded only the possibility that the parachute landings might have helped cause panic among some Italian units.[26] Generalmajor Walter Fries, the *29th Panzer Grenadier Division* commander, was less impressed. "Since they landed in front of the Germans," he wrote later, "even if they were in rear of the Italian troops, there was little prospect of their being able to intervene decisively." [27] Kesselring took a different tack. Admitting that the paratroopers "effected an extraordinary delay in the movement of our own troops and caused large losses," he was more inclined to place blame on the leadership of General Conrath and other officers of the *Hermann Goering Division.* The command, he said, "was not fortunate." Because the "march groups" were "incorrectly composed," the paratroopers delayed the division. "It is incorrect armor tactics," Kesselring continued, "for the tank units to march separate from the armored infantry as occurred here. With proper composition of the march groups the armored infantry riflemen would quickly have cleared out the snipers." [28]

---

[23] Warren, USAF Hist Study 74, pp. 28, 37.
[24] *Ibid.,* p. 28.
[25] Ltr, Ridgway to AFHQ, 26 Jul 43, sub: Analysis of Methods of Employment of 82d AB Div, in Seventh Army 373 file labeled Parachute Air Support, KCRC.

[26] Bergengruen in MS #T-2 (Fries *et al.*), Answer to Question 14 re *Feldzug Gruppe Sizilien,* p. 60.
[27] See Fries in MS #T-2 (Fries *et al.*), p. 12.
[28] MS #T-2 K 1 (Kesselring), pp. 20–21; Quotation from copy of a draft, initialed "Z," 16 Jul 43, *OB SUEDWEST, Abt. Ic, 18.VI.43-23.II.44* (*Heeresgruppe "C,"* 75138/28). A summary of the analysis is given in *OKW/WFSt, KTB, 1.-31.VIII.43,* 13 July 1943. This analysis of the first direct German experience against a large-scale amphibious attack was immediately transmitted by OKW to the headquarters in the other OKW theaters of war and areas under its command.

Very probably this analysis was the basis for the statement of Generaloberst Kurt Student in October 1945 that "It is my opinion that if it had not been for the Allied airborne forces blocking the *Hermann Goering Armored Division* from reaching the beachhead, that division would have driven the initial seaborne forces back into

General Patton's solution to the vacuum created by the unsuccessful airborne drop was to get his floating reserve ashore. In the early afternoon, as the threat of the Axis counterattack developed in the center, Patton directed General Gaffey to land his 2d Armored Division (less CCA but augmented by the 18th RCT) in the 1st Division's zone, to assemble just inland, and to prepare for commitment as later ordered. A second, reinforcing airborne drop, considered for that evening and shelved in view of the need for armor ashore, was tentatively scheduled for the following night.

Throughout the morning the armored division's headquarters aboard the transport *Orizaba* had been intercepting messages from the 1st Division to the Seventh Army, messages that urged the immediate landing of artillery and armor to support the assault units. By noon, not one piece of artillery, nor any of the ten tanks attached to the 1st Division had gotten ashore.[29]

For better information on possible plans for his commitment, Gaffey boarded the *Monrovia*, the naval force flagship which also carried Patton and his army headquarters. Just before 1400, Gaffey received the order to land. He was to go ashore over the 1st Division's Yellow and Blue Beaches, the beaches nearest Gela.

Returning to the *Orizaba*, General Gaffey sent ashore his chief of staff, Col. Redding L. Perry, to reconnoiter the assigned beaches and to make the necessary arrangements with the 1st Division for assembly areas, routes, and guides.

On shore, Perry discovered a picture quite different from that visualized on the *Monrovia*. General Allen, the 1st Division commander, expressed concern about getting armor ashore. Brig. Gen. Theodore Roosevelt, the assistant division commander who had visited all the division beaches, brought word that Yellow and Blue were heavily mined—both had been closed. He strongly recommended bringing in the 2d Armored Division across Red Beach 2.

Apprised of Roosevelt's recommendation upon Perry's return, Gaffey approved the change to Red 2, even though it entailed some delay in amending the previous orders.

About 1700, the command echelon of Col. I. D. White's CCB landed on Red Beach 2. After contacting General Allen and reconnoitering several possible assembly areas, White settled on a site near the Gela-Farello landing ground which was being vacated by the rearmost units of the 26th Infantry.

The first unit scheduled to land was the 18th RCT. When General Gaffey learned that the LCI's carrying the unit had remained in a cruising formation during the day instead of shifting to the planned landing formation, he nevertheless ordered debarkation from the cruising

---

the sea." (Quoted in Gavin, *Airborne Warfare*, p. 16.) General Student was in France at the time of the Sicilian invasion, but as commander of the XI Parachute Corps he probably received the analysis.

[29] The landing of the Seventh Army's floating reserve is covered in: 2d Armored Division in the Sicilian Campaign, a research report prepared at Fort Knox, 1949–50 (cited hereafter as 2d Armd Div in Sicilian Campaign), p. 20; 2d Armd Div AAR, 22 Apr–25 Jul 43; WNTF Action Rpt, p. 25; Comments of Col Redding L. Perry on MS; Morison, *Sicily—Salerno—Anzio*, p. 108; 18th Inf Regt AAR, Jul 43; Lt Col F. M. Muller, "2d Armored Division Combat Loading, Part Two, Sicily," *Armored Cavalry Journal*, vol. 56 (September–October 1947), pp. 9–13; CCB, 2d Armd Div AAR, Jul 43; Interv, Smyth with Lt Col Russel G. Spinney (former CO Co F, 18th Inf Regt), 31 Oct 50.

# THE FIRST DAY

formation, counting on subsequent reorganization on shore. Because the beach was unsuitable for LCI's, the beachmaster was expected to provide LCVP's to discharge the men from the LCI's and take them ashore. But apparently because of a failure in communications between the landing craft and the beachmaster, LCVP's were not available, so the LCI's approached as near to shore as possible and the infantrymen waded the rest of the way through the high surf. One officer and two enlisted men were drowned. Considerable equipment was lost. But the first wave was ashore by 2130; the entire regiment was on the ground soon after midnight.

Col. George A. Smith moved his regiment into an orchard near the landing ground. The dismounted riflemen of the 1st Battalion, 41st Armored Infantry Regiment, landed soon afterwards and took positions nearby. Two platoons of Company I, 67th Armored Regiment, came ashore at 0200, 11 July, and the ten medium tanks immediately stalled in the soft sand. High surf and beach congestion prevented the landing of additional armored vehicles.

By morning of 11 July, the chief result of Patton's decision to land the army's floating reserve was that four additional infantry battalions equipped with hand-carried weapons only were ashore. The ten medium tanks were still having considerable trouble getting off the beach. Difficult beach conditions had not only interfered with landing the reserve, they had impeded all the other landings.

The delay in the arrival of the 1st Division's supporting artillery and armor could be traced to enemy artillery fire, particularly in support of the various counterattacks, to enemy air raids against Allied shipping lying off the Gela beaches, and to the poor beaches themselves. Enemy air strikes had begun two hours after the invasion. After daylight, enemy batteries inland, from Ponte Olivo to Niscemi, had started pounding the beaches. By 0900, such heavy fire came in that Yellow Beach (26th Infantry) was closed. Shipping was diverted eastward to Blue Beach. Enemy artillery fire soon forced this beach to be closed, too, and boat traffic was again diverted eastward, this time to Red Beach 2. Soon after 1000, enemy shelling became so accurate that this beach had to be closed for twenty minutes. Only one beach, Green 2, was then available to receive landing craft. Though Red 2 was reopened at 1030, enemy artillery fire and intermittent enemy air attacks throughout the day greatly delayed unloadings and did considerable damage to landing craft and beach supply. Even after the enemy artillery fire slackened, both Yellow and Blue Beaches remained closed because numerous uncleared mine fields lay in the dune area just back from the shore.[30]

The closing and shifting of beaches created serious problems, particularly in getting the 1st Division's heavy equipment ashore. General Allen's calls for armor and artillery support during the morning were so pressing that Admiral Hall finally ordered in those LST's carrying the heavy equipment even though there were few places to accommodate the large landing ships. Furthermore, because of the assumption that the Gela pier would be captured intact and put to immediate use, Hall's naval task force had only three ponton causeways. One, unfortunately, was carried by one of the three LST's

---

[30] ONI, Sicilian Campaign, p. 59.

that had beached by mistake in the Scoglitti area.

One causeway was finally rigged on Red Beach 2. By 1030 one LST was fully unloaded and a second was moving in to start. As other LST's began rigging the second causeway on Green 2 late in the afternoon, an enemy aircraft coming in low dropped a bomb directly on one of the landing ships. Loaded with elements of the 33d Field Artillery Battalion and an antiaircraft artillery battalion, the LST blew up with a horrendous roar, scattering fragments of trucks, guns, and exploding ammunition in all directions. All of the vehicles of Battery A, 33d Field Artillery, and of one section of the antiaircraft battalion were lost. Fortunately, the howitzers were already ashore, having been landed by Dukws. But what was more serious was the fact that fragments from the exploding LST knocked out the ponton causeway in operation on Red Beach 2.

By 1800, only three LST's had been unloaded over the Gela beaches. Only one field artillery battalion and four separate field artillery batteries were ashore. These were the 33d Field Artillery Battalion (minus two howitzers lost when Dukws overturned on the way to shore); two batteries of the 7th Field Artillery Battalion (the howitzers were landed in the 45th Division zone, the personnel in the 1st Division's area); and two batteries of the 5th Field Artillery Battalion (delayed in landing until late afternoon when the LST carrying the batteries made landfall off Licata and had to traverse almost the entire length of both the 3d Division and 1st Division beaches). Available all together were eighteen 105-mm. howitzers and eight 155-mm. howitzers. As for the 16th RCT's Cannon and Antitank Companies, they were unloaded in the 45th Division's zone, and were still east of the Acate River.

With Red Beach 2 receiving everything coming ashore, it became so congested with landing craft and supplies that many of the small craft had to turn away without unloading. Beach parties were completely swamped with work even before the 18th RCT started ashore. And General Allen continued to call for more artillery and armor.[31]

Across the Acate River, the 45th Division beach situation was little better, although more supporting units did move ashore during the day. Except for the 171st Field Artillery Battalion, the 180th RCT's direct support battalion, the division artillery landed in good fashion.[32] The medium tank battalion came ashore in the 157th RCT's sector during the late afternoon.

---

[31] For a full discussion of the 1st Division's beach situation see: ONI, Sicilian Campaign, pp. 65–66; Morison, *Sicily—Salerno—Anzio*, pp. 105–09; 1st Inf Div Arty AAR, 9 May–9 Aug 43; 5th FA Bn AAR, Jun–Dec 43; 33d FA Bn AAR, Jun–Dec 43; 7th FA Bn AAR, Sicilian Campaign, 10 May–31 Aug 43; Comments of Col Leonard G. Robinson (former executive officer of the 5th Field Artillery Battalion) on MS; WNTF Action Rpt, pt. II, Narrative of Events, entries timed 2215 and 2350, 10 Jul 43.

[32] In the 171st Field Artillery Battalion, Battery A was badly scattered in landing: some of its vehicles landed on the proper beach, but the howitzers unloaded on the 1st Division's Red Beach 2 and other battery impedimenta on the 179th RCT's beaches nearer Scoglitti. The battery was not ready to fire until 2000, and then with only three pieces. The fourth howitzer arrived near midnight. Battery B was also scattered on landing but got itself together quickly and was ready to fire at 1230. It moved to a new position at 1530 and fired its first mission fifteen minutes later in support of the 1st Battalion, 180th Infantry. Because of the shortage of landing craft, Battery C remained afloat until 11 July.

# THE FIRST DAY

But, in general, the 45th Division beaches presented a most deplorable picture throughout D-day. Backed by soft sand dunes and with few usable exits, the five assault beaches were cluttered with masses of stranded landing craft and milling groups of men and vehicles soon after the initial landing. Many landing craft were hung up on offshore sand bars, unable to retract. Others broached on the beaches, the sea breaking completely over some, eddying into others over lowered ramps. Scattered and disorganized shore parties were still not functioning properly as late as 0800. In the meantime, landing craft waited on the beaches for three to four hours to be unloaded. Because the efforts of the naval salvage parties to get stranded craft off the beaches were largely unsuccessful, a diminishing number were available to unload the supplies still on board the transports. An inshore movement of the transports just after 0600 helped a little, but the ever-growing shortage of landing craft soon vitiated even this slight improvement.

Because they were simply unsuitable, all the southern beaches except Blue 2 were closed at 1050, and even though Blue 2 was no prize, it had a good exit. North of Scoglitti, Red and Green Beach traffic used the exit road from Yellow Beach, where the sandy area behind the beaches was smaller in size.

Concerned by the beach conditions and the serious loss of landing craft, Admiral Kirk sent one of his transport division commanders ashore in the middle of the morning to see what could be done to alleviate the situation. The report was pessimistic: between 150 and 200 stranded landing craft on the beaches; insufficient naval salvage parties; not enough beach exits; poor boat handling; poorer shore party work. Except for trying to get some of the stranded craft off the beaches and back into operation, there was little that could be done.

In the early afternoon, after the division shore party command post and a reinforced engineer shore company moved into Scoglitti and reconnoitered the area around the village, Admiral Kirk and General Middleton were told it was advisable to close the three northern assault beaches at noon the next day and to open six new beaches—three above Scoglitti, two at Scoglitti itself, and one just below the village. Both commanders approved the recommendation, but improvement was still almost two days away.[33]

Only in the 3d Division sector was the beach situation satisfactory. Red and Green beaches west of Licata were closed very early and all further unloadings were made over the two beaches east of the city and in the port itself.[34] Enemy air attacks spilling over from the 1st Division beachhead were a nuisance, but none caused more than superficial damage to the mounting accumulation of supplies at the dumps.[35]

---

[33] AGF Rpt 217; Morison, *Sicily—Salerno—Anzio*, pp. 138–41. On 13 July, another set of beaches was opened above Scoglitti, and another beach was added to the one below Scoglitti.

Morison (page 140) states that a survey as of noon, 11 July, revealed that only 66 of the original 175 LCVP's and LCM's in this naval task force were still usable. The 18 transports left almost 200 LCVP's on the beaches, many of which were subsequently salvaged.

[34] Most of the 3d Division's LST's were unloaded in Licata harbor.

[35] On 10 July 1943, over the Gela beaches, 20,655 men, 1,027 vehicles, and 2,000 long tons of supplies were put ashore. Over the Licata beaches and through Licata harbor, 18,464 men, 3,310 vehicles, and 4,714 long tons of supplies were landed. (See Seventh Army Rpt of Opns, pp. E-15—E-16.) Figures for the 45th Divi-

Despite formidable obstacles the invasion thus far appeared eminently successful. The next test would be whether the Allies could stand up to the inevitable Axis attempts to push them back into the sea.

sion are lumped together for the three-day period 10–12 July 1943.

# CHAPTER VIII

# The Axis Threat

On the evening of 10 July, Guzzoni had a far from clear understanding of the situation.[1] Reports indicated that British and Canadian forces had established beachheads along the eastern coast between Syracuse and the Pachino peninsula. But because signal communications with the naval base had failed completely that day, General Guzzoni dismissed reports of British proximity to Syracuse as exaggerations. Not until 0300, 11 July, did he learn from General von Senger that Syracuse had fallen and that Augusta had been evacuated briefly by Axis forces.[2] Until then, though he was aware that only isolated pockets of Italian troops still resisted near Noto and south of Modica, he counted on *Group Schmalz* and the *Napoli Division* to destroy the British and Canadian beachheads. General Guzzoni also knew that American troops had been located in Vittoria and near Comiso, apparently moving inland from a well-established beachhead near Scoglitti. The failure of the counterattacks against the Gela beaches disappointed him.[3]

About 2000, 10 July, Guzzoni ordered the *XVI Corps* to commit both *Group Schmalz* and the *Napoli Division* in a determined attempt to knock out the British beachhead south of Syracuse. He instructed the *Hermann Goering Division* and the *Livorno Division* to launch a co-ordinated attack against the American beachhead at Gela. He directed the reinforced *207th Coastal Division* to strike the American beachhead at Licata.

At his headquarters near Rome, Field Marshal Kesselring, who lacked communications with Guzzoni and who had been receiving information from Luftwaffe headquarters in Catania and Taormina, was unaware of Guzzoni's intention to counterattack on 11 July. Learning of the fall of Syracuse (and promptly notifying *Comando Supremo*), Kesselring concluded that this, plus the earlier breakdown of the Italian coastal defenses, meant the Italian units were putting up little resistance. There seemed little likelihood of a more determined stand in the future. Convinced that only the German units were effective, Kesselring sent a message through Luftwaffe channels to the *Hermann Goering Division* and ordered it to counterattack toward Gela on the morning of 11 July. If pressed home with great vigor and before the Americans could land the bulk of their artillery and armor the attack, he believed, would be successful.[4]

---

[1] *OKH, Meldungen, Dtsch. Gen.b.H.Qu.d.Ital. Wehrmacht, 1.VII–8.IX.43* (cited hereafter as *OKH, German General with Comando Supremo*) (H 22/144), 10 Jul 43.
[2] Faldella, *Lo sbarco*, p. 157; IT 99a.
[3] IT 99a; *OB SUED, Meldungen; Heeresgruppe C, OB SUED, Ic, 18.V.43–30.IX.43*, 10 Jul 43.

[4] *OB SUED, Meldungen*, 0350, 11 Jul 43.

Conrath, the *Hermann Goering Division* commander, who had received a call from the *XVI Corps* commander, went to the corps headquarters at Piazza Armerina. He learned for the first time of his attachment to the corps and together with Generale di Divisione Domenico Chirieleison, the *Livorno Division* commander, also in attendance, he received word of Guzzoni's plan for a co-ordinated attack against Gela. According to the plan, the attack, starting at 0600, would have the German division converging on Gela from the northeast in three columns, the Italian division converging on Gela from the northwest, also in three columns.[5]

Upon returning to his command post, Conrath received Kesselring's order. But this posed no complication. He reorganized his division into three attack groups: two tank-heavy forces west of the Acate River, one infantry-heavy force east of the river. One tank battalion was to move from the Ponte Olivo airfield south along Highway 117, then east across the Gela plain, and meet with the other tank battalion at Piano Lupo. Several tanks of the Ponte Olivo force were to make a feint north of Gela to deceive the Americans into believing that the city of Gela was the main objective. Instead, the main effort was to be made by the other tank column south along the Niscemi–Piano Lupo road to occupy Hills 132 and 123 (the southern edge of Piano Lupo). Joined by the tank battalion coming across the Gela plain from the west, the tanks were to strike south for the sparsely wooded area between the Biviere Pond and the Gulf of Gela. The infantry-heavy force, meanwhile, was to cross the Acate River at Ponte Dirillo and join the tank forces on Piano Lupo. From the sparsely wooded area near the shore line, the entire force was then to roll up the 1st Division's beachhead from east to west, while the *Livorno Division,* coming in from the west, was to overrun Gela and roll up the 1st Division's beachhead from the west.[6]

Northwest of Gela, General Chirieleison ordered one column to strike at Gela from the north, a second to advance astride the Gela-Butera road and strike Gela from the northwest, the third, while guarding the division right flank against American forces near Licata, to move southeast from Butera Station to Gela. The remnants of the Italian *Mobile Group E* were to support the first column.

While the division commanders were completing their attack preparations, Guzzoni, at his headquarters in Enna, finally learned of the fall of Syracuse. The Syracuse-Augusta area, previously considered the strongest defensive sector in all of Sicily, had turned suddenly into a major danger area. If the British advanced quickly from Syracuse into the Catania plain and from there to Messina, they would bottle up all the Axis forces on Sicily.

Since all his reserves were too far away or already committed, Guzzoni modified his previous orders to the *XVI Corps*. Early on 11 July, he had instructed the corps to execute its counterattack as planned. But now, as soon as the *Hermann Goering Division* attack showed signs of success, the division was to wheel eastward, not to the west, and advance on Vittoria, Comiso, and Palazzolo Acre-

---

[5] Faldella, *Lo sbarco,* pp. 144–46.

[6] MS #R-138, The Counterattack on the Second Day, 11 July 1943, ch. IX of Axis Tactical Operations in Sicily, July-August 1943 (Bauer), pp. 1–3.

# THE AXIS THREAT

ide in succession. With the entire German division then reunited, a strong blow could be mounted against the British. At the same time, the move would knock out the 45th Division's beachhead around Scoglitti. The *Livorno Division,* after taking Gela, was to wheel westward and destroy the American beachhead at Licata. The *15th Panzer Grenadier Division,* returning from the west, would assist the *Livorno Division* against Licata.[7]

Before the Axis divisions could launch their attacks, the 1st Division acted. In keeping with General Allen's confidence in the skillful use of night attacks, the 26th Infantry on the left and the 16th Infantry on the right jumped off at midnight, 10 July, toward the division's major objectives, the Ponte Olivo airfield and Niscemi.

Lt. Col. John T. Corley's 3d Battalion, 26th Infantry, moved up Highway 117 toward Monte della Guardia (Hill 300), the commanding terrain west of the highway overlooking the airfield. But within thirty minutes, heavy enemy fire from the front and flanks brought the battalion to a halt.[8]

On the Niscemi–Piano Lupo road, Colonel Denholm's 1st Battalion, 16th Infantry, advanced north toward Casa del Priolo, while Company G of Colonel Crawford's 2d Battalion paralleled this movement on the west side of the road. Though the 1st Battalion reached Casa del Priolo without difficulty and began digging in, Company G spotted German tanks to its left front and returned to its original position near Piano Lupo. Dismayed at the return of his company and fearing the German tanks would pounce on the unprotected left flank of the 1st Battalion, Crawford ordered Companies E and F to move out and dig in on the little orchard-covered ridge at Abbio Priolo, about a thousand yards north and west of Casa del Priolo. Accompanied by Colonel Gorham's paratroopers, these companies reached the ridge at 0530.[9]

In Gela, the Rangers and engineers continued to improve their defenses. Across the Acate River, in the path of the infantry-heavy German task force, the 180th Infantry remained in a disheartening situation. Though the 1st and 3d Battalions had thrown back the German counterattack on the previous evening, the regiment still had no contact with the 1st Division on the left and with the 179th Infantry on the right. In addition, the regimental commander probably had no more than a faint notion of the location of his front. Whether he knew that most of the 1st Battalion had been captured by the Germans is not clear. Communications with Colonel Cochrane's 2d Battalion were tenuous at best, and often lost, and the regimental headquarters had no knowledge of the whereabouts of portions of Companies E, G, and H, which, in actuality, held a strongpoint astride Highway 115 near Ponte Dirillo and occupied the high ground just north of the bridge. The one bright spot in the 180th Infantry zone was that the bulk of the 171st Field Artillery Battalion was prepared to fire in support.[10]

Unable to make contact with the *Livorno Division,* but assuming that the Italian division would launch its attack, General Conrath at 0615, 11 July, sent

---
[7] Faldella, *Lo sbarco,* p. 158.
[8] 26th Inf Regt S-1 Jnl, 11 Jul 43.
[9] Interv, Smyth with Denno and Groves, 24 Oct 50; Sayre, Operations of Company A, 505th Parachute Infantry, p. 15; 16th Inf Regt AAR, 11 Jul 43.
[10] 180th Inf Regt AAR; 171st FA Bn AAR; AGF Rpt 217.

PARATROOPERS MOVING IN ON THE RIDGE AT ABBIO PRIOLO

the three task forces of the *Hermann Goering Division* forward. (*Map IV*) At the same time, one Italian task force, the one nearest Highway 117, jumped off, but on its own initiative, apparently after seeing the German tank battalion start south from Ponte Olivo airfield. To help support the converging attacks on Gela, German and Italian aircraft struck the beaches and the naval vessels lying offshore.

The 3d Battalion, 26th Infantry, which had been advancing up the east side of Highway 117, bore the brunt of the German attack. Company K was driven to the south and west toward Gela, but the remainder of the battalion held firm. The Italian column passed the 26th Infantry, bumped into Company K, which was trying to get back to Gela, and headed directly for the city. Colonel Darby's force in Gela laid down heavy fire on the approaching enemy. The 33d Field Artillery Battalion began pounding away at both columns. The two batteries from the 5th Field Artillery Battalion joined in. The 26th Infantry's Cannon Company and the 4.2-inch mortars in Gela also opened fire. The combination of fires stopped the Italians.

The German tanks then swung east across the Gela plain to join the force descending the Niscemi–Piano Lupo road. There, the situation had quickly dissolved into a series of scattered infantry-tank actions. First to feel the weight of the German attack was the 2d Battalion, 16th Infantry, at Abbio Priolo, where the

AMERICAN SHIPS UNDER AIR ATTACK *off Gela on 11 July.*

infantrymen and paratroopers had little time to complete more than hasty foxholes and weapons emplacements. German tanks, a conglomeration of Mark III's and IV's, appeared, flanking the 2d Battalion from the west. The tanks rushed in, shooting their machine guns and cannon at almost point-blank range. With only a few bazookas plus their regular weapons, the infantrymen and the paratroopers fought back. Aided by fires from eight howitzers of the 7th Field Artillery Battalion and part of the regiment's antitank company, which had finally managed to get across the Acate River that very morning, the battalion held.[11] As yet, there was no naval gunfire support. Nor were there aircraft available to fly direct or close support missions.[12]

[11] The 7th Field Artillery Battalion fired a total of 561 rounds in ten missions during the day.

[12] Morison, in *Sicily—Salerno—Anzio* (page 110), suggests that the shore fire control parties probably did not call for fires because smoke obscured the targets. It seems more likely, however, since the 7th Field Artillery Battalion was firing—indicating the battalion had observation —that the field artillerymen either felt they could handle this counterattack without additional help, or the very nearness of the enemy troops and the rough nature of the terrain made it too dangerous to call in naval fires at this time.

Six requests for direct air support were made on 10 July—five by the 1st Division, one by Seventh Army. None of these missions were flown. On 11 July, the 1st Division requested five more direct air support missions; one was flown, in the late afternoon. See Seventh Army File, G-3 Opns, sub: Air Support, KCRC.

Personally directing the attack on the Niscemi–Piano Lupo road, General Conrath regrouped his forces and again sent them rushing at the American positions. This time, the tanks rolled directly down and tried to circle both flanks. The swinging German movement to the right brought the 1st Battalion at Casa del Priolo into the fight. As German tanks swept past the embattled Americans and joined with other German tanks at the eastern edge of the Gela plain, the Americans pulled slowly back to Piano Lupo under cover of supporting fires, both artillery and naval. By 1100, the Americans were back where they had started from around midnight.

East of the Acate river, the German infantry-heavy task force drove down from Biscari to Highway 115, where Company F, 180th Infantry, defending Ponte Dirillo, delayed it a short while. But the company could not hold, and retired to the beaches. North of the bridge, Colonel Cochran, with the remainder of the 2d Battalion, 180th Infantry (less than 200 men), and the small group of paratroopers, lost all contact with regimental headquarters. Fortunately, he made contact with the 171st Field Artillery Battalion, and through the battalion with naval vessels. The artillery and the destroyer *Beatty* both gave heroic support.[13]

At that very moment, about 0900, as the German force pushed past the highway toward the mouth of the river, a group of American paratroopers led by Colonel Gavin appeared from the east and struck the enemy column.

Colonel Gavin had halted about noon on D-day to await darkness before continuing westward with his small party of paratroopers. As yet, he had made no contact with any American force. As the sun began to set on 10 July, Gavin and his men set forth. At 0230, 11 July, five miles southeast of Vittoria, the paratroopers finally made their first contact with an American unit, Company I, 179th Infantry. For the first time since landing in Sicily, Colonel Gavin knew his exact location. Entering Vittoria about 0500, and collecting the paratroopers and three airborne howitzers that had assisted in the capture of the city the previous afternoon, Gavin then turned west on Highway 115. Five miles west of the city, Gavin met 180 men of the 3d Battalion, 505th Parachute Infantry, led by Maj. Edward C. Krause. Krause had halted here the previous evening after he, too, had failed to make contact with other American forces.

Instructing Krause to organize the now sizable paratrooper force into march formation and to follow, Colonel Gavin and his S–3, Maj. Benjamin H. Vandervoort, continued westward along the highway. After covering another two miles, Gavin came upon a group of forty men from Company L, 180th Infantry, and twenty paratroop engineers. They told Gavin that the Germans were astride the highway farther to the west, but they could provide no details on strength or dispositions.

Wanting to see the German force for himself, and apparently not knowing the location of the 180th Infantry, Gavin took the paratroop engineers and began walking along the highway toward Biscari Station. A German officer and a soldier

---

[13] The *Beatty*, from 0730 to 1030, fired a total of 799 five-inch rounds on this one German column. Three other destroyers also fired on this column during the course of the day: the *Laub* (751 rounds); the *Cowie* (200 rounds); and the *Tillman* (46 rounds). See Morison, *Sicily—Salerno—Anzio*, p. 113. See also Infantry Combat, pt. Five: Sicily, (Fort Benning, 1943), p. 1 (copy in OCMH); 171st FA Bn AAR, 11 Jul 43.

on a motorcycle suddenly came around a bend in the road and were captured. Though the two made no effort to resist, they refused to give information. With enemy troops close by, Gavin sent Vandervoort back to hurry along the force of 250 paratroopers under Major Krause. Vandervoort was then to continue on to the 45th Division command post near Vittoria to let General Middleton know Gavin's location.

Gavin took his engineers toward Casa Biazzo, a group of five buildings on high ground sloping gently westward and overlooking the Acate River. Across what the paratroopers would call Biazzo Ridge ran the road to Biscari.

A few hundred yards short of the buildings, Gavin's little group came under small arms fire. Gavin pushed his men forward to the crest of the ridge where they drove a small detachment of Germans down the far slope. As they prepared to follow, enemy fire increased. Gavin ordered his men to dig in and hold until the arrival of Krause's force.

The appearance of Gavin's small unit drew German attention from Piano Lupo and the Gela beaches, where the entire 1st Division front was aflame. The bulk of the *Livorno Division* had by this time joined the *Hermann Goering Division* attack. General Conrath's two tank battalions were once again united, and though he still contended with the 16th Infantry on Piano Lupo, he decided to send the bulk of his armored force across the Gela plain to the beaches. General Chirieleison, the *Livorno Division* commander, was also pushing for a concentrated attack that would surge over the American positions. He had already lost one hour waiting for contact with the German unit. He did have one column engaging the

COLONEL GAVIN *in Biazzo Ridge area on the morning of 11 July.*

Americans in Gela. Now he sent a second from Butera toward the city.

With most of the Rangers and engineers heavily engaged against the Italian thrust down Highway 117, only two Ranger companies on the west side of Gela stood in the way of Chirieleison's second column. "You will fight with the troops and supporting weapons you have at this time," Colonel Darby told them. "The units in the eastern sector are all engaged in stopping a tank attack." [14]

When the Italian column came within range, the two Ranger companies opened fire with their captured Italian artillery pieces, and with their supporting platoon of 4.2-inch mortars. The Italian movement slowed. General Patton appeared at the Ranger command post in this sector, a two-story building, and watched the

[14] Lyle, Operations of Companies A and B, 1st Ranger Battalion, p. 17.

Italian attack. As he turned to leave, he called out to Captain Lyle, who commanded the Rangers there, "Kill every one of the goddam bastards."[15]

Lyle called on the cruiser *Savannah* to help, and before long almost 500 devastating rounds of 6-inch shells struck the Italian column. Through the dust and smoke, Italians could be seen staggering as if dazed. Casualties were heavy. The attack stalled. Moving out to finish the task, the Ranger companies captured almost 400 enemy troops. "There were human bodies hanging from the trees," Lyle noted, "and some blown to bits."[16] As it turned out, a large proportion of the officers and more than 50 percent of the Italian soldiers were killed or wounded.

North of Gela, artillery and naval fire, small arms, machine gun, and mortar fires reduced the *Livorno* column to company size, and these troops were barely holding on to positions they had quickly dug. The third Italian column, in about battalion size, starting to move from Butera Station to Gela, ran into a combat patrol which had been dispatched by the 3d Division to make contact with the Gela force. The company-size patrol inflicted heavy casualties on the Italians, who pulled back to their original position.

The battering received during this attack on Gela finished the *Livorno Division* as an effective combat unit.[17]

East of Gela, as General Conrath sent the major part of both his tank battalions toward the beaches, the Gela plain became a raging inferno of exploding shells, smoke, and fire. The lead tanks reached the highway west of Santa Spina, two thousand yards from the water. As they raked supply dumps and landing craft with fire, the division headquarters reported victory: "pressure by the *Hermann Goering Division* [has] forced the enemy to re-embark temporarily."[18] At *Sixth Army* headquarters, General Guzzoni was elated. After discussion with General von Senger, he instructed *XVI Corps* to put the revised plan into action—wheel the German division that afternoon to the east toward Vittoria and continue movement during the night to Palazzolo Acreide and the Syracuse sector.[19]

But the German tanks never reached the 1st Division beaches. Nor was there any thought of American re-embarkation.[20] The 32d Field Artillery Battalion, coming ashore in Dukws moved directly into firing positions along the edge of the sand dunes and opened direct fire on the mass of German armor to its front. The 16th Infantry Cannon Company, having

---

[15] *Ibid.*, p. 18.
[16] *Ibid.*
[17] MS #R-138 (Bauer), pp. 13-20.
[18] *OKH, Tagesmeldungen West, 1.V.-31.VIII. 43, Teil II* (cited hereafter as *OKH, Tagesmeldungen West*), 11 Jul 43; MS #C-095 (Senger), *KTB* entry 0110, 12 Jul 43, for the day before; *OB SUED, Meldungen*, TWX No. 0134, 0940, 12 Jul 43; *OKW/WFSt, KTB, 1.-31.VII. 43*, 12 Jul 43.
[19] Faldella, *Lo sbarco*, p. 158.
[20] There is no evidence in the official records of any order to re-embark personnel or equipment from any beaches. The WNTF Action Report, page 56, indicates that the engineer shore parties were called inland to establish a temporary defensive line, "and the withdrawal seaward by boats of other beach personnel." Morison (*Sicily—Salerno—Anzio*, page 116) states "neither they [the Navy's advanced base group] nor anyone else were given orders to re-embark, as the enemy reported." General Faldella, the *Sixth Army* chief of staff, reported (*Lo sbarco*, page 148) an intercepted Seventh Army radio message that ordered the U.S. 1st Division to prepare for re-embarkation. Faldella repeated this to Mrs. Magna Bauer in Rome during an interview in January 1959, asking repeatedly whether the original message appeared in the records. The intercept was probably misinterpreted.

AFTER THE TANK BATTLE, *wrecked German tanks dot Gela Plain at Highway 115.*

just been ferried across the Acate River, rushed up to the dune line, took positions, and opened fire. Four of the ten medium tanks of Colonel White's CCB finally got off the soft beach, and, under White's direction, opened fire from the eastern edge of the plain. The 18th Infantry and the 41st Armored Infantry near the Gela-Farello landing ground prepared to add their fires. Engineer shore parties stopped unloading and established a firing line along the dunes. Naval gunfire, for a change, was silent—the opposing forces were too close together for the naval guns to be used.

Under the fearful pounding, the German attack came to a halt. Milling around in confusion, the lead tanks were unable to cross the coastal highway. The German tanks pulled back, slowly at first and then increasing their speed as naval guns opened fire and chased them. Sixteen German tanks lay burning on the Gela plain.

On Piano Lupo, the 1st and 2d Battalions, 16th Infantry, had managed to hold the road junction, even though six German tanks had broken into their lines. The single remaining 37-mm. antitank gun in the 2d Battalion disabled one. A lucky round from a 60-mm. mortar dropped down the open hatch of another. A bazooka round badly damaged a third. Colonel Gorham, the paratroop commander, put a fourth out of commission with bazooka fire. The other two retired.

With almost one-third of his tank strength destroyed or disabled, General Conrath called off the attack shortly after 1400. Though fighting east of the river continued until late that evening, the tank units withdrew to the foothills south of Niscemi.[21]

---

[21] It is difficult to state exactly how many tanks the *Hermann Goering Division* lost in this counterattack. The division had 90 Mark III and IV tanks on 9 July. Attached were the 17 Tiger tanks from the *215th Tank Battalion*. The division reported 54 tanks operational on 11 July, and 45 on 14 July. Since none of the division's tanks were attached to *Group Schmalz*, all tank

At Enna, General Guzzoni again changed his plans. The fierce American resistance at Gela, the known arrival of additional Allied units, and the continued pressure of the 45th Division in the Vittoria-Comiso area indicated the difficulty of getting the *Hermann Goering Division* to the east coast by way of Vittoria and Palazzolo Acreide. In addition, a further American advance inland from Comiso might bypass the *Hermann Goering Division* and cut it off entirely from the east coast. Thus, during the afternoon of 11 July, Guzzoni ordered the *XVI Corps* to suspend all offensive action in the Gela area, to withdraw the *Hermann Goering Division* to Caltagirone for movement on the following day to Vizzini and commitment against the British, and to consolidate the *Livorno Division* along a line from Mazzarino to Caltagirone to cover the German withdrawal.[22]

Before Guzzoni's instructions reached Conrath, General von Senger visited the *Hermann Goering Division*. Though disappointed because the tanks had not broken through to the beaches, Senger considered the situation favorable for turning the division eastward toward Vittoria and Comiso. This would cut off from the beaches those units of the 45th Division that had pushed well inland. Feeling that the 1st Division, which had borne the brunt of Axis counterattacks for two days, was in no position seriously to contest this movement, he ordered Conrath to the east.

Conrath was in agreement with Senger's estimate. Still expecting his tanks to reach the beaches, he was sure his infantry-heavy task force could wheel to the east from Biscari to strike at Vittoria. Unfortunately for Conrath, his infantry-heavy force had been so manhandled by Gavin's men on Biazzo Ridge that it was hardly in any condition to initiate any offensive action.

About 1000, a good many of the paratroopers, coming from Vittoria under Major Krause, had joined Colonel Gavin on Biazzo Ridge. Gavin directed this force to advance westward along Highway 115, seize Ponte Dirillo, and open a route to the 1st Division's zone. Augmented by random troops of the 180th Infantry rounded up by Gavin, the paratroopers got going. After a mile of slow progress against increasing German resistance, the attack halted when four Tiger tanks, supported by infantrymen, came into view and began pressing the paratroopers back. Though American soldiers crawled forward singly with bazookas, they could not get close enough to register a kill. Fortunately, two of the three airborne howitzers came in behind Biazzo Ridge, went into position, and opened fire.

The fight continued until well after noon. As American casualties increased to the danger point, artillerymen manhandled one of the little howitzers to the top of the ridge just in time to engage

---

losses during the period 10–14 July 1943 occurred in the battle for Gela and in the subsequent withdrawal, with a majority of these lost on 11 July. Thus, the German tank loss is estimated as being a minimum of 26, and a maximum of 45. In addition, 10 of the 17 Tiger tanks were also lost. See Mins of Conf 13 Between Hitler, Buhle, Jodl and Others, 25 Jul 43, in Min of Hitler Confs. See also *OB SUED, Meldungen, 1.–31.VII.43*, Telg No. 0940, 12 Jul 43, and Telg No. 0618, 1940, 14 Jul 43; MS #T-2 (Fries *et al.*); MS #C-087 a and d (Bergengruen); Faldella, *Lo sbarco*, p. 425; MS #C-077 (Rodt); Rpt, Maj Gierga to *Generalinspekteur der Panzertruppen*, 28 Aug 43, in *XIV Panzer Corps, KTB Nr. 5, Anlagenheft I, 8.–30.IX.43* (No. 48702/8).

[22] Faldella, *Lo sbarco*, p. 158; MS #C-095 (Senger), *KTB* entry 1315, 11 Jul 43.

# THE AXIS THREAT

in a point-blank duel with a Tiger tank. In the face of heavy small arms fire and several near misses from the tank gun, the paratrooper crew got off several quick rounds, one of which knocked out the tank. Two half-tracks towing 57-mm. antitank guns arrived from the 179th Infantry, went into firing positions, and engaged the other three Tiger tanks. Around 1500, the Germans had had enough.

The antitank guns had arrived in response to Colonel Gavin's request, through another staff officer dispatched to the 45th Division command post for assistance, especially for antitank guns, artillery liaison parties, and tanks. General Middleton had been quick to react. Shortly after the antitank guns rolled up, a naval gunfire support party and a liaison party from the 189th Field Artillery Battalion reached Colonel Gavin's headquarters. Within a very few minutes, the field artillery battalion signaled rounds on the way and the Navy joined in blasting the German troops along the Acate River. Still later in the afternoon, eleven tanks from the 753d Medium Tank Battalion arrived. At the same time, Gavin received word that Lieutenant Swingler, commander of the 505th's Headquarters Company, was on the way with an additional one hundred paratroopers. With this growing strength, Gavin decided to switch to the offensive.

On trucks furnished by the 45th Division, Lieutenant Swingler and his men arrived shortly after 2000. Forty-five minutes later, after a tremendous artillery concentration, the paratroopers launched their second attack. Every available man was committed, including a few from the Navy who had enrolled in the unit during the day. Not long afterwards, the German force was scattered, most of the troops making their way north toward Biscari, a few crossing at Ponte Dirillo to rejoin the main body of the division, a smaller number remaining near the bridge in blocking positions. With the advent of darkness, Gavin called off the attack before his troops reached the river. Pulling his men back, he organized a strong defensive line along the ridge.

The paratrooper stand on Biazzo Ridge prompted General Conrath to change his plans. Learning of the heavy losses being sustained by his infantry-heavy force, he decided, apparently on his own initiative, to break off contact with the Americans near Gela. Ignoring General von Senger's instructions to wheel eastward, he decided to withdraw to Caltagirone in compliance with Guzzoni's orders. But instead of retiring at once to Caltagirone, Conrath planned to pull his *Hermann Goering Division* back in stages. He would reach Caltagirone during the night of 13 July, a day later than Guzzoni wished.[23]

Though bitter patrol clashes continued in the hills near Piano Lupo during the night, and though the 16th Infantry reported an enemy infantry and tank build-up, the 1st Division beachhead was no longer in any serious danger. General

---

[23] For a complete discussion of Conrath's decision, see MS #R-138 (Bauer), pp. 7-9, and MS #R-164 b, General Remarks to Individual Chapters and Suggested Corrections, Comments on Chapter XIX (Bauer). Though General Conrath, it seems certain, ordered a withdrawal to start during the night of 11 July, this information apparently did not reach all of his units. Interrogation of a German prisoner by 2d Armored Division personnel on 12 July disclosed that the prisoner's unit was ordered to attack Gela, which was reported clear as a result of the tank attack on 11 July. See 1st Inf Div G-2 Jnl, 10-14 Jul 43.

Allen had established physical contact with the 3d Division on his left. Almost all of the floating reserve was ashore. The Navy stood by to render gunfire support. More supplies and equipment were arriving.[24]

Despite the fact that the 1st Division had taken quite a battering on 11 July, in particular the 16th Infantry, and despite the fact that enemy air raids had caused some damage, notably the destruction of a Liberty ship filled with ammunition, General Patton was ashore urging General Allen to get on with the business of taking Ponte Olivo and Niscemi, objectives which, according to the Seventh Army's plan, should have been taken that day.[25]

---

[24] By nightfall, 11 July, all tanks of the 3d Battalion, 67th Armored Regiment; eight light tanks from the 82d Reconnaissance Battalion; all of Company E, 67th Armored Regiment; and the bulk of the 78th Armored Field Artillery Battalion were ashore. All this, of course, was in addition to the foot elements put ashore during the night of 10 July.

Colonel Perry, then Chief of Staff, 2d Armored Division, disagrees with one report (Morison, *Sicily—Salerno—Anzio,* page 111) that the desperate need for more armor ashore was not fully appreciated. Colonel Perry states (see his comments on the MS) that the need for armor was appreciated by the 2d Armored Division, but that due to the lack of causeways and the slowness of unloading tanks from LST's to LCT's and then to shore, tanks could not be gotten ashore quickly. Colonel Perry further states that on 11 July there was no causeway operating on any 1st Division beach until late in the afternoon. The only U.S. tanks to see action on 11 July were four of the ten medium tanks that were unloaded early in the morning.

[25] See Combat Operations of the 1st Infantry Division During World War II (a 43-page mimeographed document prepared by General Allen), p. 36. According to General Allen's report, General Patton was very much "wrought up" because the 1st Division had not as yet taken Ponte Olivo airfield.

CHAPTER IX

# Airborne Reinforcement

Early on the morning of 11 July, in order to bolster the Gela forces, General Patton ordered the 504th Combat Team to drop into the 1st Division's beachhead that evening.[1] At 1900, about the time that Colonel Gavin on Biazzo Ridge was issuing his second attack order of the day, Col. Reuben H. Tucker's 504th began taking off from the airfields in Tunisia—the 1st and 2d Battalions, 504th Parachute Infantry; the 376th Parachute Field Artillery Battalion; and Company C, 307th Airborne Engineer Battalion—in all a few more than 2,000 men.[2]

One hundred and forty-four aircraft from the U.S. 52d Troop Carrier Wing in the aerial column flew a basic nine-ship V of V's formation stepped down to make it easier to see the silhouette of the lead aircraft against the sky. The air over the Mediterranean Sea was quiet and calm. A quarter moon offered some illumination. Many pilots, who remembered the earlier flight, were confident that this mission would not suffer from the vagaries of the weather. Knowledge that they would be flying a course over friendly territory made them feel secure. They looked forward to a relatively quiet and peaceful night—a milk run.

The course had been worked out in planning sessions attended by General Ridgway (the 82d's commander); Maj. Gen. Joseph M. Swing (American airborne adviser at Allied Forces Headquarters); British General Browning (the AFHQ airborne adviser); and representatives from Air Chief Marshal Tedder's Mediterranean air command and Admiral Cunningham's Mediterranean naval command. Concerned because the airborne troops might be fired on by friendly naval vessels off the Seventh Army assault beaches, Ridgway had tried repeatedly to get assurances that the Navy would clear an aerial corridor to the island. He had even gone to General Browning with a strong request for assurances that the Navy would not fire on any reinforcing missions. Since it had already been planned that any reinforcing mission would be flown over the same route used by the 505th Combat Team, General Ridgway was most anxious lest his follow-

---

[1] General Ridgway dispatched the order at 0839, 11 July. The order was received in North Africa at 1100, and acknowledged fifteen minutes later. See 82d AB Div G-3 Jnl, entry 42, 11 Jul 43: "Mackall tonight wear White Pajamas." See also, Warren, USAF Hist Study 74, p. 39.

[2] The NAAFTCC Report (page 85) states that 2,008 troops were carried on the mission; Brig. Gen. Paul L. Williams (commander of TCC) states in his report that 2,304 troops participated. There is no airborne report available that gives the number of men carried, but, according to the strengths of the units at the time, it appears that the TCC report is more nearly accurate. Undoubtedly, General Williams based his figure on an average load of sixteen men per aircraft; the TCC report indicates an average load of slightly less than fourteen men per aircraft.

up units draw fire from the large number of naval vessels which would be off the beaches. General Browning could offer no such assurances.

On 22 June, General Ridgway had presented his views to a joint conference presided over by General Eisenhower. The naval representatives in attendance refused to provide a definite corridor for any airborne mission flown after D-day in the Seventh Army sector. Ridgway had then written to General Keyes, the Seventh Army deputy commander, and recommended that, unless a clear aerial corridor into Sicily could be provided, no subsequent airborne troop movement be made after D-day.

As a result of energetic action by Generals Keyes and Swing, General Ridgway and the Troop Carrier Command received assurance from the Navy on 7 July that if a follow-up air transport movement followed certain designated routes and made its last leg overland, the withholding of friendly naval fire could be guaranteed. Accordingly, the 504th's route was carefully plotted to hit the island at Sampieri, thirty miles east of Gela and at the extreme eastern end of the Seventh Army zone. Once over land, the troop-carrying aircraft were to turn to the northwest and fly toward the Gela-Farello landing ground—over friendly lines all the way—along a corridor two miles wide and at an altitude of 1,000 feet.[3] Earlier AFHQ radio instructions and Seventh Army warnings were supplemented at 0845 on 11 July when General Patton sent a top priority message to his principal subordinate commanders. He directed them to notify their units, especially the antiaircraft battalions, that parachutists would drop on the Gela-Farello landing field about 2330 that night.[4]

General Ridgway, on Sicily, visited six crews of antiaircraft artillerymen near the 1st Division command post during the afternoon of 11 July to make sure that the warning had been sent down the chain of command. Five crews had received the warning; the sixth had not. When he brought this to the attention of an officer from the 103d Coast Artillery Antiaircraft Battalion he learned that a conference of all officers from the antiaircraft units in the vicinity was being held later that afternoon. The officer assured Ridgway that he, personally, would see to it that the subject of the airborne mission was discussed.[5]

Following the prescribed course, the air column rounded the corner at Malta in good shape and headed for Sicily with all formations intact. A few aircraft encountered some light antiaircraft fire from Allied shipping north of Malta, but no damage was done and the column continued serenely on its way. Inside the planes, some paratroopers closed their eyes and dozed; others craned their necks to look down at the sea.

---

[3] Warren, USAF Hist Study 74, p. 37; Ltr prepared by Ridgway, 2 Aug 43, sub: Reported Loss of Transport Planes and Personnel Due to Friendly Fire, in Ridgway Personal File, 1942–1943, item 42; Admiral of the Fleet Sir Andrew B. Cunningham, *Despatch, The Invasion of Sicily*, a Supplement to the London *Gazette*, April 25, 1950, p. 2081; Notes on the Routing of Troop Carrier Aircraft, 24 Jul 43, 99-66.2, sub: AFHQ Rpt of Allied Force Airborne Board in Connection With the Invasion of Sicily.

[4] Annex A, Ridgway Ltr, 2 Aug 43; Warren, USAF Hist Study 74, p. 37; 82d AB Div in Sicily and Italy, p. 19n; 82d AB Div G-3 Jnl, entries 43 and 44B, 11 Jul 43; Bradley, *A Soldier's Story*, pp. 132–33; Seventh Army G-3 Opns File, sub: Air Support. This last contains copies of the various messages dealing with the warnings issued to various commands.

[5] Ridgway Ltr, 2 Aug 43.

Off the Seventh Army beaches, though, all had not been serene on 11 July. Dawn of the 11th had brought with it a heavy aerial attack. At 0635, twelve Italian planes had swept down over the transport area off Gela, forcing the ships to weigh anchor and disperse. Two transports received near misses. One, the *Barnett*, was badly damaged by a near miss which blew a hole through her side. Enemy air attacks against the beaches and shipping continued throughout the day.[6] At 1400, four planes strafed the Gela beaches while a high level enemy bomber dropped five bombs in the anchorage area. In the Scoglitti area, four bombs fell about 700 yards off the port bow of the *Ancon* at 1430. At 1540, around thirty Junker 88's attacked the Gela area, harmlessly bracketing the cruiser *Boise* with bombs but striking the Liberty ship *Robert Rowan* (one of seven arriving in the first follow-up convoy). Loaded with ammunition, the *Rowan* took an enemy bomb in her Number Two hold, caught fire, exploded, and sank in shallow water. Her bow exposed, with smoke pouring from the hulk, she provided a perfect beacon for later waves of enemy bombers.

Around 2150 came a massive strike. Near Gela, the *Boise* and all the destroyers except one were closely straddled. Many ships were damaged by near misses. Bomb fragments hurt another Liberty ship. Again the transports weighed anchor and dispersed. The sky over Gela became a confused jumble of friendly and enemy aircraft flying among the puffs of smoke of ground and naval antiaircraft fire. The melee lasted about an hour. Just before the planes carrying paratroopers of the 504th crossed the coast line, the enemy bombers withdrew. The antiaircraft fire died down. Into this calm flew the 504th.

The leading flight flew peacefully to the Gela-Farello landing ground. At 2240, five minutes ahead of the scheduled drop time, the first paratroopers jumped over the drop zone. The second flight was in sight of Biviere Pond, the final check point, when the calm was rudely shattered by a lone machine gun. Within the space of minutes, it seemed as though every Allied antiaircraft gun in the beachhead and offshore was blasting planes out of the sky. The slow-flying, majestic columns of aircraft were like sitting ducks. As one company commander (Capt. Willard E. Harrison) remembered later: ". . . guns along the coast as far as we could see . . . opened fire and the naval craft lying offshore . . . began firing."[7] Only the few planeloads of paratroopers who had jumped several minutes ahead of schedule floated safely to the correct drop zone.

The first flights of the second serial were just turning into the overland aerial corridor when the firing started. Squadrons broke apart, tried to re-form, then scattered again. Eight pilots gave up and returned to North Africa still carrying their paratroopers. Those pilots who managed to get over Sicily dropped paratroopers where they could. Troops dropped prematurely, some dropped in the sea. A few planes turned to the east and

---

[6] The Axis air forces committed 198 Italian and 283 German planes against the various Allied beachheads on 11 July. By far the largest number of enemy air missions was flown against the Seventh Army beaches. *OKH, Tagesmeldungen West;* IT 99a, an. 2.

[7] 82d AB Div in Sicily and Italy, p. 7.

THE ROBERT ROWAN *exploding off the coast at Gela, 11 July.*

released their loads in the British zone. Six aircraft received hits as paratroopers were struggling to get out of the door. Many pilots, after dropping their paratroopers, tried to escape the gantlet of fire that extended the length of the beachhead corridor by turning immediately out to sea, flying as low as possible, and taking evasive action against the deadly hail of fire rising from the ships.[8]

Control over Army and Navy antiaircraft gunners vanished. One aircraft passed low over the bow of the *Susan B. Anthony* (off Scoglitti) and close by the *Procyon.* Not identifying the C-47 as friendly, both ships opened fire. The plane crashed in flames just off the stern of the cruiser *Philadelphia.* Seconds later, fire from all the nearby ships blasted another C-47 out of the sky.[9]

At his command post in Scoglitti, General Bradley, the II Corps commander,

---

[8] A few of the pilots reported they were under fire for as much as thirty miles after leaving Sicily.

[9] CO Transport Div 5 Action Rpt, p. 6.

## AIRBORNE REINFORCEMENT

watched in helpless fury as the antiaircraft fire from both ground and naval batteries cut the troop carrier formations to pieces. At the Gela-Farello landing ground, waiting to receive the paratroopers, General Ridgway was thunderstruck at the events around and above him. At his command post just north of Gela, Colonel Bowen, the 26th Infantry commander, felt stunned by the terrific volume of naval fire.

In the lead aircraft of the third serial, which broke apart even before reaching Sicily, Colonel Tucker was dumbfounded. His aircraft, well off course, flew through the smoke pouring up from the still-smoldering *Robert Rowan*, came out on the Gela side, and went in low over the 1st Division beaches. Heavy fire raked the aircraft. The pilot could not find the drop zone. By this time, the plane was alone. The wingmen were gone, the rest of the serial completely scattered. Going forward, Colonel Tucker instructed the pilot to turn west until he could locate some identifiable geographical feature. Licata eventually came into view. The pilot turned and flew back toward Gela. Though the fire was still heavy, Colonel Tucker and his men jumped over the landing ground. On the ground, Tucker stopped the crews of five nearby tanks from firing on the aircraft with their .50-caliber machine guns.[10]

Other paratroopers and aircrew members were not so fortunate. Some paratroopers were killed in the planes before they had a chance to get out. Other paratroopers were hit in their chutes while descending. A few were even shot on the ground after they landed. It seems that each succeeding serial received heavier fire than those preceding it. The last, carrying the 376th Parachute Field Artillery Battalion, received the heaviest fire and suffered the greatest losses. Flight Officer J. G. Paccassi (the 61st Group) lost sight of his element leader after the turn to the northwest had been made and he went on alone to the drop zone, encountering heavy antiaircraft fire all the way. Paccassi's plane was hit just as the paratroopers went out the door and he quickly turned and headed out for sea, flying almost at surface level. Just off the coast, the plane was hit again, the rudder shot away, then both engines failed. As naval vessels still fired, Paccassi crash-landed into the sea. The destroyer *Beatty* fired on the downed aircraft for five seconds with 20-mm. guns before realizing that the plane was American, then dispatched a small boat to pick up the survivors.[11]

Two survivors from an aircraft of the 314th Group picked up by the destroyer *Cowie* stated that their element of three planes passed over the drop zone, but received such intense fire that the pilots considered the dropping of paratroopers suicidal. Their plane turned back to the coast and followed it south at an altitude of 500 feet before being hit. As the plane filled with smoke and flame, the pilot ordered everybody out just before the plane crashed.[12] The destroyer *Jeffers* picked up seven survivors from an air-

---

[10] Interv, Garland with Brig Gen Reuben H. Tucker III, Washington, 24 Sep 59; Interv, Garland with Maj Gen John W. Bowen, Washington, 4 Nov 59; Bradley, *A Soldier's Story*, p. 133; Ridgway, *Soldier*, p. 71.

[11] Statement of Flight Officer J. G. Paccassi (F/O, AC, T-185665) on board USS *Beatty*. The statement is attached to Report of Action of the *Beatty*, dated 15 July 1943, DD640/A16, ser. 001, part of NTF 85's report of action.

[12] Rpt, USS *Cowie*, 15 Jul 43, DD632/A16-3, ser. 09.

AIRBORNE REINFORCEMENTS *in a C-47 heading for Sicily on 11 July.*

craft of the 316th Group which had crash-landed nearby—the entire five-man crew, plus Maj. C. C. Bowman from 82d Airborne Division headquarters, who had been flying as an observer, and one paratrooper who had refused to jump.[13]

Capt. Adam A. Komosa, who commanded the 504th's Headquarters Company, later recalled:

It was a most uncomfortable feeling knowing that our own troops were throwing everything they had at us. Planes dropped out of formation and crashed into the sea. Others, like clumsy whales, wheeled and attempted to get beyond the flak which rose in fountains of fire, lighting the stricken faces of men as they stared through the windows.[14]

---

[13] Rpt, USS *Jeffers*, 15 Jul 43, DD621/A16, ser. 025. Morison (in *Sicily—Salerno—Anzio* page 121, note 51) points out that this ship did not fire on the troop-carrying aircraft because its gun crews had been intensively trained in plane recognition. If so, this was one of the few ships that did not fire.

[14] Capt. Adam A. Komosa, Airborne Operation, 504th Parachute Regimental Combat Team, Sicily, 9 July–19 August 1943: Personal Experiences of a Regimental Headquarters Company Commander (Fort Benning, Ga., 1947), p. 13.

# AIRBORNE REINFORCEMENT

Chaplain Delbert A. Kuehl made a bruising landing against a stone wall somewhere in the 45th Division sector, well southeast of Gela. Almost immediately after landing, the chaplain and a few men with him were taken under fire by American troops. Confidently, Chaplain Kuehl shouted the password. The reply was heavier fire. While he tried in vain to identify himself as an American, the firing continued. Then, as several of the paratroopers fired into the air, the chaplain maneuvered around the flank, crawled through a vineyard, and closed in on the American position from the rear. He crept up to one soldier who was blasting away at the paratroopers, tapped him on the shoulder, and asked him what he was doing. The firing soon stopped. It appears that not every American unit had the same sign and countersign.[15]

Of the 144 planes that had departed Tunisia, 23 never returned, 37 were badly damaged.[16] The loss ratio in aircraft was a high 16 percent. Brig. Gen. Charles L. Keerans, Jr., the assistant division commander, had been aboard one of the planes that did not return.[17]

Of the six aircraft shot down before the paratroopers had a chance to jump, one carried 5 officers and 15 enlisted men from the 504th's Headquarters and Headquarters Company; another carried '3 officers and 15 men from the 2d Battalion's Headquarters and Headquarters Company; and the remaining four carried 1 officer and 32 men from Battery C, 376th Parachute Field Artillery Battalion. Of these 9 officers and 62 men, a few miraculously survived. Lt. Col. L. G. Freeman the 504th's executive officer, 2 other officers, and 12 men (11 of them wounded), crawled from the wreckage of their downed plane. 1st Lt. M. C. Shelly, from the 2d Battalion's Headquarters Company, standing at the door of the aircraft when it crashed, was thrown clear. All the other occupants were killed. One of the Battery C planes was shot down at sea, carrying with it all the occupants. From the other three aircraft, 5 men saved themselves by using their reserve chutes— 2 managed to get out of one plane after it had been hit twice and was afire, 3 men were blown clear when antiaircraft fire demolished their planes.

A total of twelve officers and ninety-two men were aboard the eight planes which returned to North Africa without dropping: two planes with personnel from the 504th's Headquarters Company; one plane, Company F, 504th; two planes, Battery C and two planes Battery D, 376th Parachute Field Artillery Battallion; and one plane, Headquarters Battery, Division Artillery. Four dead and six wounded paratroopers were taken from the planes that returned.

A final computation would show that

---

[15] Komosa, Airborne Operation, 504th Parachute RCT, p. 16. Also see the Ridgway letter of 2 August which brings out the firing on paratroopers by American troops. Both the 171st and 158th Field Artillery Battalions (45th Division) reported skirmishes with paratroopers during the night of 11 July. The 171st Field Artillery Battalion's report states that "since no news of the American Paratroopers had reached this Hq, they were assumed to be hostile and the Bn was deployed for all around defense." During the period of confusion which existed after the drop of the 504th, one artilleryman was killed by his own men when "mistaken for an enemy paratrooper."

[16] General Tucker stated that the aircraft in which he flew to Sicily did return to North Africa; the crew later reported over 1,000 holes in the craft.

[17] Warren, USAF Hist Study 74, p. 40; 82d AB Div in Sicily and Italy, p. 8.

the 504th Combat Team suffered a total of 229 casualties on the night of 11 July 1943: 81 dead, 132 wounded, and 16 missing.[18]

In less than an hour, the 504th Combat Team had become a completely disorganized unit. The first few sticks landed on and around the drop zone, and the bulk of the parachutists carried by the lead group managed to drop fairly near the Gela-Farello landing ground. For the most part, the other groups dispersed before they reached the drop zone, and a large number of the aircraft dropped paratroopers between Vittoria and the Acate River in the 45th Division's sector. The 504th's dispersal was as great as that of the 505th, with paratroopers landing on Sicily from Gela on the west to the east coast. Colonel Tucker himself did not locate General Ridgway until 0715 the next morning. At that time, of his 2,000-man force, Tucker counted as present for duty the equivalent of one rifle company and one battery of airborne howitzers. By late afternoon, the effective troops of the 504th numbered only 37 officers and 518 men.[19]

General Eisenhower quickly demanded a full report of the disaster. On 13 July, Brig. Gen. Paul L. Williams, commanding the Troop Carrier Command, submitted his report to Lt. Gen. Carl Spaatz, the NAAF commander. Williams stated that the heavy ground and naval antiaircraft fire directed against the troop-carrying aircraft showed a definite lack of coordination between air, naval, and ground forces, or a definite breakdown in the communication systems used to disseminate the instructions of higher headquarters to lower echelons. General Williams would not say which opened fire first—the Navy or the Army—but stated simply that his troop carriers were fired on by both ground and naval antiaircraft batteries.

Endorsing General Williams' report, Spaatz added that the greatest mistake, in his opinion, was the failure to place definite restrictions on all antiaircraft units during the time period when the aerial column approached Sicily as well as during the period when the parachutists dropped. Air Marshal Tedder agreed with Spaatz and Williams, but went even further. He considered the airborne mission to have been operationally unsound because it had required aircraft to fly over thirty-five miles of active battle front. "Even if it was physically possible for all the troops and ships to be duly warned, which is doubtful," Tedder said, "any fire opened either by mistake or against any enemy aircraft would almost certainly be supported by all troops within in range—AA firing at night is infectious and control almost impossible."[20]

Admiral Cunningham, quick to defend the naval gunners, felt that the lack of antiaircraft discipline was only partially responsible for the tragic occurrence. At night, he pointed out, "no question of A.A. undiscipline can arise. All ships fire at once at any aeroplane particularly low flying ones which approach them." Noth-

---

[18] Rpt, Ridgway to TAG, 19 May 44, sub: Casualties, Sicilian Campaign, CT 504, Ridgway Personal File, item 32; 82d AB Div in Sicily and Italy, pp. 8, 19. On 24 July, 52d Troop Carrier Wing casualties were reported as 7 dead, 30 wounded, and 53 missing.

[19] 82d AB Div G-3 Jnl, entries 51A and 58A, 12 Jul 43; 82d AB Div in Sicily and Italy, p. 13.

[20] File 99–66.2, sub: AFHQ Rpt of Allied Force Airborne Board in Connection With the Invasion of Sicily. See also 0100/4/78, sub: Airborne Operations in HUSKY; 0100/21/1072, sub: Airborne Employment, Operation and Movement of Troops, vol. 2, 23–30 Jul 43; and 0100/12A/71, III, sub: Airborne Forces.

SCATTERED PARATROOP REINFORCEMENTS *moving through Vittoria the morning of 13 July.*

ing less than that could be acceptable to the Navy, otherwise merchant vessels and naval combat ships would incur severe losses and strong damage. The major cause of the tragedy, Cunningham felt, was either bad routing or bad navigation on the part of the aircraft crews.[21]

[21] Admiral of the Fleet Sir Andrew B. Cunningham, *Despatch, The Invasion of Sicily,* a Supplement to the London *Gazette,* April 25, 1950, p. 2081; Msg, Cunningham to Eisenhower, 23 Jul 43, sub: Airborne Troops—Enquiry, 99-66.2.

Admiral Cunningham carefully left unsaid why the naval fire was not stopped sooner, or why the ships' crews failed to recognize the C-47 aircraft, particularly when they were flying at such a low altitude and were flashing recognition signals (amber belly lights) continuously.

The exact cause of the catastrophe could not be pinpointed. A board of officers appointed by AFHQ to investigate the circumstances uttered only generalities. Despite agreement that advance warning had been given to naval vessels and ground antiaircraft batteries, some individuals and units hotly denied ever receiving such a warning order. Other units and individuals claimed that enemy bombers returned and mixed with the friendly aerial column. Still others reported that the antiaircraft fire came from enemy guns. To the last charge, it was true that at least one plane was brought down by enemy machine gun fire near Comiso. But returning pilots and paratroopers alike noted that the heaviest fire came not from the right—the direction of the front—but from Allied guns to the left of the overland aerial corridor. As one pilot said: "Evidently the safest place for us tonight while over Sicily would have been over enemy territory."[22]

General Ridgway probably expressed it best of all:

The responsibility for loss of life and material resulting from this operation is so divided, so difficult to fix with impartial justice, and so questionable of ultimate value to the service because of the acrimonious debates which would follow efforts to hold responsible persons or services to account, that disciplinary action is of doubtful wisdom.

Deplorable as is the loss of life which occurred, I believe that the lessons now learned could have been driven home in no other way, and that these lessons provide a sound basis for the belief that recurrences can be avoided.

The losses are part of the inevitable price of war in human life.[23]

---

[22] Warren, USAF Hist Study 74, p. 41.

[23] Ridgway Ltr, 2 Aug 43.

CHAPTER X

# The Beachhead Secure

*Straightening Out the Sag*

Gradually, around midnight of 11 July, the antiaircraft fire died down. The tragic show was over. As groups of 504th paratroopers made their way toward Gela, their advance sometimes marked by fire fights with other Americans, a relative stillness stole over the front. It was the lull before the next phase of operations, aimed at moving the Seventh Army to the Yellow Line, which would signify that the beachhead was secure.

Though the 1st Division fought primarily a defensive battle on 11 July, it would go over to the offensive the following day. Late on the afternoon of 11 July, after his troops broke the *Hermann Goering Division* counterattack and drove the Italians from Gela, General Allen announced his intention in blunt words: "Sock the hell out of those damned Heinies," he ordered, "before they can get set to hit us again."[1]

The first task was to straighten out the sag in the 1st Division front, and in the very early hours of 12 July, three American columns departed their defensive positions fronting Gela and set out to do just this. (*Map V*) A composite force under Colonel Darby captured Monte Lapa and Monte Zai on the Gela-Butera road by daylight to cover the 26th Infantry advance up Highway 117.[2] The 26th Infantry, reinforced by Lt. Col. Ben Sternberg's 2d Battalion, 18th Infantry, drove toward Monte della Guardia and the Ponte Olivo airfield. Quickly clearing a small Italian roadblock just north of Gela, the troops pushed on to Castle Hill (Il Castelluccio), an eminence topped by the ruins of a medieval tower. There they came under fire from an artillery battalion of the *Livorno Division,* and at dawn the three forward battalions were somewhat scrambled in the ditches and ravines below the hill.

Daylight facilitated reorganization and permitted observed artillery fire on the Italian lines and artillery positions. After the 33d Field Artillery Battalion pounded the rocky eminence with telling effect, and the cruiser *Boise* lobbed in 255 rounds, the 2d Battalion, 26th Infantry, surged forward, gained the crest and the tower, and rounded up the remnants of a *Livorno Division* rifle battalion. While the 1st Battalion, 26th Infantry, swung left and took Monte della Guardia, the 2d

---

[1] Maj. Gen. Terry Allen, Situation and Operations Report of the First Infantry Division, 8 August 1942–7 August 1943 (a 22-page mimeographed report prepared for the Society of the First Division), p. 12.

[2] Darby's command consisted of the 1st and 4th Ranger Battalions; the 1st Battalion, 41st Armored Infantry Regiment (minus Company A); the 1st Battalion, 39th Engineer Combat Regiment; Company A, 83d Chemical Weapons Battalion; and a platoon of medium tanks.

PONTE OLIVO AIRFIELD, *secured on 12 July.*

Battalion of the 18th Infantry dashed forward to take Ponte Olivo airfield. By 1000, the combat team's objectives were secure. A large portion of the sagging center had been moved forward five miles.

The third American column, the 16th Infantry, had harder fighting as it advanced astride the Piano Lupo–Niscemi road to secure the division's eastern flank and to protect the 26th Infantry's right during the advance to the Ponte Olivo airfield. The 16th Infantry struck the bulk of the *Hermann Goering Division,* reinforced by those Tiger tanks that had withdrawn across the Acate River after the fight at Biazzo Ridge. Though Conrath had decided to withdraw, the German forward units had had no opportunity to begin their retirement. Early morning patrols had reported the disquieting news of the Germans' presence, but Colonel Taylor ordered the advance as planned.

Colonel Crawford's 2d Battalion, with Colonel Gorham's paratroopers leading the way, moved out from positions west of Piano Lupo, crossed the road, and advanced up the east side of the road toward Casa del Priolo. Without opposition, the battalion reached the ridge line just south and east of the Casa and quickly occupied the trenches and emplacements earlier dug by the Germans. On reverse slopes to their left, the Americans could hear German troops digging in.

Soon after first light, about 0530, heavy German fire struck the 2d Battalion from the north and northwest. West of the road, between the forward battalion elements and a single rifle company left near Piano Lupo, the Americans saw Germans threatening to cut off the route to the rear. When Colonel Crawford and Capt. Bryce F. Denno, the executive officer, left their command post to visit the front-line units, Crawford took a couple of machine gun bullets in the neck and shoulder. Denno carried the battalion commander back to the command post and saw to his evacuation.

Three hours later, the remaining company came up from Piano Lupo bringing with it an M7 105-mm. howitzer and a half-track 75-mm. howitzer. About the same time, the German infantrymen across the road pulled back to the north. With the German threat removed, the 1st Battalion moved up in echelon to the right rear of the 2d Battalion and faced east toward the Acate River valley.

Near 1000, southeast of Piano Lupo, Lt. Col. Robert H. York's 1st Battalion, 18th Infantry, supported by a platoon of medium tanks, had to fight off a column of three German tanks moving northwest along Highway 115. This American force had gone into position shortly after midnight as part of the army reserve, with the mission of screening between the two forward combat teams of the 1st Division and protecting the division's east flank. Artillery fire from the 7th Field Artillery Battalion, plus fires from the five medium tanks, destroyed two of the three German tanks. The third withdrew out of range. Half an hour later, American artillery fire broke up another German tank reconnaissance effort in the same area. One tank burned, the others withdrew.

Thirty minutes later, six Mark VI tanks, supported by armored cars, half-tracks, and two platoons of infantry, moved down the Acate River valley and turned westward against the 16th Infantry positions near Casa del Priolo, while artillery fire from Niscemi gave support.

In the 2d Battalion area, Denno moved his two howitzers into position to fire on the approaching enemy armor. Hardly had the 75-mm. piece got out of defilade when it was hit and destroyed by an enemy artillery round. The 105-mm. howitzer managed to get off five rounds before it was knocked out by tank fire. Colonel Gorham, trying to repeat his bazooka work of the previous day, was killed by a direct hit from an enemy tank.

Despite the threat, the 16th Infantry was in good shape. The regimental Cannon and Antitank Companies were up and in position, armored support was nearby, and the 7th Field Artillery Battalion was giving excellent fire support. The 5th and 32d Field Artillery Battalions were taken off reinforcing missions elsewhere to lend their weight.[3] Two platoons of medium tanks arrived near the 1st Battalion and added their fire power—though they lost four of their own tanks, they got three Tigers.

By noon the German threat had petered out, but by this time the forward infantry battalions were badly battered. Colonel Denholm, the 1st Battalion commander, had been shot and evacuated. The rifle companies were at less than half strength. The 2d Battalion was left with perhaps 200 men, including the few surviving paratroopers.

Despite the ragged strength of his elements, Captain Denno moved his troops forward and occupied Casa del Priolo with ease. Colonel Taylor urged further movement, but Denno was reluctant— his companies were tired and understrength, his flanks were open, the enemy appeared strong between the Casa and Niscemi. Denno prevailed on the regimental commander to hold what had been gained. Increased German artillery fire, growing in intensity just before dark and continuing until midnight, seemed to indicate a possible attack. In reality the *Hermann Goering Division* was covering its withdrawal. The Piano Lupo road junction remained under heavy interdictory fire throughout the night. But no more German soldiers or tanks molested Casa del Priolo.[4]

The 16th Infantry had not taken its objective, Niscemi, and a sag remained in the center of the Seventh Army front. But enemy resistance, despite the heavy artillery fire, was lessening, and on the following morning, 13 July, as the *Hermann Goering Division* continued to pull back toward Caltagirone, the Americans entered Niscemi unopposed.

The 16th Infantry, particularly the 1st and 2d Battalions, had had by far the severest fighting thus far in the invasion. These two battalions had been largely responsible for blunting the *Hermann Goering Division*'s counterattacks. Each battalion had lost its commander. And each subsequently would receive a citation for its outstanding performance. Casualty figures alone indicated the sev-

---

[3] The 7th Field Artillery Battalion fired 15 missions, 914 rounds during the day. The 32d Field Artillery Battalion fired 7 missions, 304 rounds. The 5th Field Artillery Battalion fired 6 missions, 583 rounds.

[4] 1st Inf Div G-3 Jnl, 11-12 Jul 43; 1st Inf Div G-3 Diary, 11-12 Jul 43; II Corps Rpt of Opns, p. 5; AAR's 16th Inf Regt; CCB; 18th Inf Regt; 5th FA Bn; 7th FA Bn; 32d FA Bn, and 2d Armd Div; 2d Armd Div in Sicilian Campaign, pp. 28-31; *Danger Forward: The Story of the First Division in World War II* (Washington, 1947), pp. 107-10; Lt. John W. Baumgartner et al., *The 16th Infantry, 1798-1946* (Bamberg, Germany: Sebaldus Verlag, 1946), pp. 11-13; *History of the 67th Armored Regiment* (Brunswick, Germany: Georg Westermann, 1945), pp. 235-40; Morison, *Sicily—Salerno—Anzio*, p. 113; Interv, Smyth with Denno and Groves, 24 Oct 50; Sayre, Operations of Company A, 505th Parachute Infantry, pp. 17-18.

erity of the fighting between Piano Lupo and Casa del Priolo on the 11th and 12th of July. During these two days the 1st Battalion lost 36 dead, 73 wounded, and 9 missing, the 2d Battalion lost 56 dead, 133 wounded, and 57 missing.[5]

But if the sag had not been eliminated by nightfall 12 July, the bulge represented no serious threat to the 1st Division. Rather, American units on the flanks were threatening to outflank the German salient.

*On to the Yellow Line*

On the Seventh Army right, the town of Comiso fell without opposition to the 157th Infantry early on 11 July. The regiment then looked to the west for the arrival of the 179th Infantry, which was to comprise the left arm of the division's deep pincer movement against the Comiso airfield. Stopped at times by enemy artillery fire, slowed occasionally by long-range machine gun fire, the 179th Infantry in the early afternoon was ready to attack the airfield in conjunction with the 157th. Co-ordination between the two direct support artillery battalions was quickly established, and the artillery radio net was used from then on to regulate the moves of the infantry units.

Soon after 1600, as artillery fires lifted, two battalions of the 179th Infantry moved into the airfield proper from the west, driving the defenders into a battalion of the 157th Infantry coming in from the southeast. Within twenty minutes, the field was in American possession, along with 125 enemy planes (20 in operating condition), 200,000 gallons of aviation gasoline, and 500 bombs. One German plane escaped.[6]

Turning over the job of clearing the airfield to supporting engineers, the infantry continued inland, the 179th Infantry going due north along the secondary road leading to the Acate River, the 157th Infantry turning due east, and then north toward Chiaramonte Gulfi.

Disregarding the boundary line between the Seventh U.S. and British Eighth Armies, a rifle company entered Ragusa, captured the mayor and chief of police, and seized the city's switchboard intact. The rest of the day, in addition to policing the city, the Americans amused themselves by answering phone calls from anxious Italian garrisons that wanted to know what was going on near the beaches. As night fell on 11 July, the company had still not made contact with the Canadians.

The 180th Infantry, which had been having some trouble, finally untracked itself and on 12 July began advancing. Having been allowed a day's breathing spell by the paratrooper action at Biazzo Ridge, the regimental commander was able to reorganize his units and now moved through Colonel Gavin's lines. That evening, by 2000, Biscari was secured.

The movement to Biscari was heartening, for the performance of the regiment had hitherto been less than impressive. General Middleton considered relieving the commander, and went so far as to request General Bradley for a replacement. Bradley asked General Patton for

---

[5] WDGO 60, 29 Jul 44.

[6] II Corps Rpt of Opns, pp. 5–6; 157th Inf Regt S–1 Jnl, 11 Jul 43 (which reports approximately 150 planes captured or destroyed on Comiso airfield in one entry; over 200, in serviceable condition, in another entry); 179th Inf Regt S–1 Jnl, 11 Jul 43; McLain MS, Sicily Campaign, pp. 8–9.

Lt. Col. William O. Darby, the 1st Ranger Battalion commander. Though Patton offered the young Ranger commander the 180th Infantry and an immediate promotion, Darby turned down the offer. He preferred to stay with his unit. With no other qualified replacement immediately available, Middleton made no change, except to send the assistant division commander to that headquarters to exercise close supervision.[7]

The 179th Infantry, which had met only minor Italian resistance on 11 July, next day encountered stiffer opposition north of Comiso as it began to meet increasing numbers of Germans. This resulted from General Conrath's response to urgent messages from General Guzzoni directing him to make an immediate withdrawal to the east coast. Pulling some of his units out of line in the Gela area, Conrath sent them to the northeast, his intention to occupy first a line along Highway 124 from Caltagirone east to Vizzini. The sudden thrust by the 1st Division prevented him from denuding his defenses until the American advance from Gela was stopped. The 180th Infantry push posed another problem, for if the regiment crossed the Acate River north of Biscari it would threaten to cut the German withdrawal route. Thus, small German units, primarily interested in securing the routes of withdrawal to Highway 124, moved northeast and across the routes of advance of the 179th Infantry.

Just before noon, part of the *Hermann Goering Division* armored reconnaissance battalion jumped the forward units of the 179th Infantry. Not until late in the afternoon did the regiment stabilize the situation. Further advance toward Highway 124, the Seventh Army's Yellow Line, it seemed, would be hotly contested.

In contrast, the 157th reached Chiaramonte Gulfi, fourteen road miles northeast of Comiso, without incident. Here for the first time since landing, Colonel Ankcorn was able to pull his scattered battalions together. At Ragusa, where the rifle company was waiting for Canadian troops to show up before rejoining the regiment, a misdirected shelling from a British artillery unit preceded the arrival of 1st Canadian Division elements.[8]

The contact followed good gains on the part of the British 30 Corps on the Seventh Army right. The corps had reached the Pozzallo-Ispica-Rosolini line at the end of 11 July, and next day, while the British 51st Division advanced and took Palazzolo Acreide, the 1st Canadian Division cleared Modica, entered Ragusa, and moved ten miles beyond to Giarratana. The 30 Corps advance, paralleling the 45th Division inland movement, threatened to interpose a strong Allied

---

[7] McLain MS, Sicily Campaign, pp. 11-14; 45th Inf Div G-3 Jnl, entries 45 and 53, 12 Jul 43; 753d Med Tk Bn AAR, 12 Jul 43; George S. Patton, Jr., *War As I Knew It*, annotated by Col. Paul D. Harkins (Boston: Houghton Mifflin Co., 1947), p. 58; Bradley, *A Soldier's Story*, pp. 139-40; OPD 201 Wedemeyer, A. C., Security, case 5; 180th Inf Regt AAR, p. 6; II Corps Rpt of Opns, p. 6.

[8] 157th Inf Regt S-1 Jnl, 12 Jul 43; 45th Inf Div G-3 Jnl entries 39, 40, 41, 43, 47, 62, 64, 66, 12 Jul 43; Nicholson, *The Canadians in Italy*, p. 81; *History of the 157th Infantry Regiment (Rifle)*, by the regimental society (Baton Rouge, La.: Army and Navy Publishing Co., 1946), p. 24; Rpt, 45th Inf Div in Sicilian Opn (mimeographed), p. 4, with maps 2B, 2C, 2D; 179th Inf Regt S-1 Jnl, 12 Jul 43; 160th FA Bn AAR, 12 Jul 43; 45th Inf Div Arty Jnl, entries 57 and 70, 12 Jul 43; 753d Med Tk Bn, 12 Jul 43; *OB SUED, Meldungen*, 13 Jul 43, First Report; MS #C-095 (Senger).

force between the *Hermann Goering Division* and those Axis forces opposing the British 13 Corps north of Syracuse. If the British 30 Corps moved into the gap between these two Axis forces—a gap of eighteen miles from Vizzini to Lentini—it would prevent the *Hermann Goering Division* from joining the defenders blocking the road to Catania and, ultimately, Messina.

Progress in the British 13 Corps zone was slower. The stubborn resistance of *Group Schmalz* prevented the 5th Division from advancing north from Syracuse on 11 July. Despite his defensive success, Schmalz was concerned, for his *Kampfgruppe* could not hold indefinitely against the stronger British forces. If the British broke into the Catania plain, they would block the bulk of the Axis forces from access to Messina and would, themselves, have an unobstructed passage to this key Sicilian city. Because no units backed *Group Schmalz* on the east coast, because he needed reinforcement from the main body of the *Hermann Goering Division,* Schmalz decided to fight a delaying action along the coastal highway (Highway 114) in the hope of preventing an Allied breakthrough. During the night of 11 July, Colonel Schmalz withdrew to a defensive line centered on Lentini.

The withdrawal uncovered the port of Augusta, and on 12 July British troops entered the city. But advance north to the Catania plain was impossible, for *Group Schmalz* held firm.

Schmalz's situation remained serious. He did not have enough troops to hold for long at Lentini. Nor did he have sufficient troops to close the gap to the west between him and the bulk of the *Hermann Goering Division,* which had just started to move northeast from Niscemi.[9] The British 50th Division, paralleling the British 5th Division's advance, headed directly toward the gap, having moved from its landing areas at Avola through Cassibile, Floridia, and Sortino.

On the west flank of the Seventh Army, the 3d Division, heavily supplemented by armored and reconnaissance units, highly mobile and readily employable in the terrain ahead, had gained an ideal position from which to exploit inland to Highway 124. Such an advance would cut the *Sixth Army* in two at Enna, the important hilltop town almost in the geographical center of Sicily.

General Guzzoni was concerned by the deep penetration of the 3d Division toward Campobello, fourteen miles north of Licata, for continued advance would cut off the Axis forces in the western part of the island and would threaten the *Hermann Goering Division's* right flank. To counter this movement Guzzoni gathered together what forces he could.

During the night of 10 July, Colonel Venturi, who commanded the Italian *177th Bersaglieri Regiment,* had arrived with one of his battalions at Favarotta, where a makeshift force of Italian artillerymen and motorcyclists had managed to halt 3d Division progress along Highway 123. Taking over the Italian units then on the ground, Venturi created a provisional tactical group—*Group Venturi*—and ordered a counterattack the next morning to recapture Licata.

West of Licata, along Highway 115, the Italian *207th Coastal Division* organized a tactical group near the Naro River bridge with the mission of advanc-

---

[9] Nicholson, *The Canadians in Italy*, pp. 81–84; Schmalz in MS #T-2 (Fries et al.), pp. 74–75; *OB SUED, Meldungen,* 12 Jul 43, Third and Fourth Reports.

ing east toward Licata. Other Italian units arriving during the night and going into defensive positions at Agrigento and Canicattì were alerted to the possibility that at least one might move through Naro to Palma di Montechiaro in order to assist the attack on Licata from the west.[10]

Meanwhile, the *15th Panzer Grenadier Division* was hurriedly retracing its steps to the central part of the island. Like other Italian and German units, the German division had received no specific orders on 10 July on its probable future operations. But from fleeing Italian coastal units, General Rodt was able to learn that the original *Sixth Army* plan to throw the Allies back into the sea was not having great success. He therefore decided to try to stop the several American columns moving inland on the roads emanating from Licata. The result of this decision was to embroil elements of the division during the transfer from west to east in numerous small actions, generally in battalion strength.

Arriving at his new command post south of Pietraperzia (some twenty miles northeast of Campobello) about 0400, 11 July, Rodt learned more about the invasion. From additional reports he concluded that the Americans who had landed in Gela were advancing north toward Piazza Armerina, while those American forces which had landed in Licata planned to drive on through Campobello to Canicattì.

Feeling that he could not block both major thrusts, he decided to strike the closer one, the advance of the 3d Division from Licata. Sending the bulk of *Group Ens* (the reinforced *104th Panzer Grenadier Regiment*) to screen against the thrust from Gela and to protect his east flank, he planned to move one battalion from Pietraperzia through Riesi in a flanking movement from the east against the American column moving toward Canicattì. This attack would relieve pressure on both the *Livorno* and *207th Coastal Divisions*. The reinforced reconnaissance battalion of the division, known as *Group Neapel*, was to block the main roads north and east from Canicattì and delay the Americans as long as possible. *Group Fullriede* (the reinforced *129th Panzer Grenadier Regiment*) would deploy along a line from Canicattì through Delia to Sommatino to halt advances inland along the roads leading from Licata, Palma di Montechiaro, and Agrigento to Caltanissetta. His main hope was to disrupt the 3d Division advance by dealing it a damaging blow on its deep eastern flank by means of the battalion attack from Riesi.[11]

General Truscott, meanwhile, had called his senior commanders together on the evening of 10 July and issued his orders for the next day's operation. The 7th Infantry was to thrust westward to take Palma di Montechiaro and the high ground just beyond; the 15th Infantry was to continue north along Highway 123 to seize Campobello; General Rose's CCA, operating between these two combat teams, was to seize Naro, then assemble on the high ground to the north and east

---

[10] Faldella, *Lo sbarco*, p. 152, and corrections made available to Mrs. Bauer by Faldella.

[11] MS #C-077 (Rodt) and sketch; MS #C-095 (Senger); *OB SUED, Meldungen*, 12 Jul 43.

The commitment of the reconnaissance battalion from the *15th Panzer Grenadier Division* is controversial. It seems that part of the battalion was also deployed between Palermo and Canicattì at major road intersections. It is difficult to reconstruct the actions of this unit from the scanty Axis reports available.

TANK-MOUNTED CCA MEN *push through Palma en route to Naro.*

and prepare for further action. The 30th Infantry, guarding the division's exposed right flank, was to send one battalion cross-country to seize Riesi, there blocking an important avenue of approach into the division's eastern flank.

The 3d Battalion, 7th Infantry (Lt. Col. John A. Heintges), led the advance on Palma di Montechiaro early on 11 July. Crossing the Palma River bridge without incident, the battalion encountered heavy fire from Italian troops who occupied strong positions along a line of low hills just south of the town. Deploying his troops, building up a base of fire, and using supporting weapons to excellent advantage, Heintges pushed slowly ahead and drove the Italians into the town itself. As the battalion prepared to push into Palma around 1100, numerous white flags appeared on buildings in the town. Colonel Heintges dispatched a small patrol to accept the surrender. Unfortunately, civilians, not soldiers, had displayed the white flags, and the small American patrol came under fire. Two men were killed, another two were wounded. Enraged, Heintges gathered together ten men and personally led them across an open field to a building which seemed to house the heaviest fire. They reached the building safely, planted demolitions on the lower floor, withdrew a short distance, and set off the explosives. The blast signaled start of the attack, and the battalion swept into town behind its commander. The Palma defenders had been reinforced by a task force that had moved down from the Naro River, and heavy fighting erupted up and down the main street. For two hours the battle raged from house to house. Around 1300, having had enough, the surviving Italians began pulling out westward along Highway 115. Quickly reorganizing his battalion, Heintges followed in close pursuit, rapidly cleared the hills on the south side of the highway, and dug in there to await the rest of the combat team.[12]

To Heintges' right, General Rose's CCA had begun to move against Naro.[13] With a reconnaissance company forming a screen and the 3d Battalion, 41st Armored Infantry, reinforced by a company of medium tanks as the advance guard, the combat command proceeded slowly along the narrow, secondary roads and trails northwest of Licata. The terrain was difficult, the roads were poor, but the only opposition came from snipers, scattered long-range machine gun fire, and a strafing attack by two German aircraft. For the first time in a procedure that would become standard, the armored infantrymen mounted the tanks and rode the last few miles.

Just outside Naro, a civilian volunteered the information that the town was unoccupied and the population friendly. Unwilling to take any chances on this rather nebulous bit of information, Col. Sidney R. Hinds, the 41st Armored Infantry commander, placed the civilian and his small son on the hood of his half-track and led the column into town while small tank-infantry teams cleared the flanks and secured the exits. The civilian was right. By mid-morning of 11 July, CCA was in possession of Naro.

Continuing toward Canicattì, six miles north, a company of tanks was briefly delayed by an attack delivered by friendly P-38 aircraft, which, fortunately, caused no damage to men or equipment. Two miles northeast of Naro, on the approaches to a pass between two hills, the company ran into stiff resistance. An Italian infantry battalion had moved up from Agrigento that morning, and despite repeated Allied air attacks, had reached the pass minutes before the American tanks arrived. Halting and deploying, the tankers called for infantry support. The battalion of armored infantrymen under Lt. Col. Marshall L. Crawley, Jr., came forward, and an attack at 1600 made slow progress against hard-fighting Italians. With the approach of darkness, the Italians withdrew. By nightfall, the

---

[12] 7th Inf Regt Unit Jnl, 11 Jul 43; 3d Inf Div in Sicilian Campaign AAR, p. 11; 7th Inf Regt AAR, p. 3; overlay showing dispositions of 7th Infantry troops, 1100, 11 Jul 43, 3d Inf Div G-3 Jnl File, 11 Jul 43; 7th Inf Regt S-3 Opns Rpt 2, 11 Jul 43; 10th FA Bn in Sicily Campaign AAR, 11 Jul 43; Nathan W. White, *From Fedala to Berchtesgaden: A History of the 7th U.S. Infantry in World War II* (Germany, 1947), pp. 26–27.

[13] On 11 July, CCA consisted of the 66th Armored Regiment; the 41st Armored Infantry Regiment, minus the 1st Battalion; the 14th Armored Field Artillery Battalion; the 62d Armored Field Artillery Battalion (which, at this time, had only one battery ashore); reconnaissance, engineer, and service units. The remainder of the 62d Armored Field Artillery Battalion closed at 1600, 11 July 1943.

Americans were in possession of the pass and were four miles short of Canicattì.[14]

The mistaken strafing by friendly planes turned out to be a harbinger of things to come for CCA. During the week of 11 July, CCA was to lose fourteen vehicles and seventy-five men from such attacks. The friendly pilots, who were briefed to be alert for the *15th Panzer Grenadier Division,* mistook the CCA armored vehicles for enemy vehicles despite the rather prominent display of yellow smoke—the agreed signal for the identification of friendly vehicles. One pilot, 1st Lt. R. F. Hood (86th Fighter-Bomber Group), shot down over Naro by CCA's antiaircraft fire, said that he had seen the yellow smoke but had not been informed of its meaning. Later, the 15th Army Group changed the method of recognition from smoke to pennants, and this apparently solved the problem.[15]

The 15th RCT, meanwhile, was advancing north along Highway 123 from Favarotta to Campobello.

Under Colonel Johnson's plan of attack, the 3d Battalion moved directly up the highway to capture the high ground west of Campobello, while the 1st Battalion made a wide, ninety-degree envelopment of the enemy left flank, using for its approach a series of north-south draws, well defiladed from Campobello and the highway. With the 2d Battalion in reserve and the 39th Field Artillery Battalion and a battery of the 9th Field Artillery Battalion in support, the attack started at 0445.

Because the 1st Battalion, east of the highway, was delayed almost an hour in assembling, the 3d Battalion moved out cautiously. At Station Favarotta the leading elements ran into *Group Venturi,* which was moving down the highway to attack Licata. For four hours, Americans and Italians battled for the commanding terrain around Favarotta, American artillery units firing with devastating effect on Italian artillery pieces and armored vehicles emplaced near the small town.[16] The end came after a rifle company worked its way around the right of the Italian line on the west side of the highway. Under fire from four or five enemy machine guns on the western edge of Favarotta, the company called for support. Because these particular enemy positions were defiladed from the artillery, Colonel Johnson ordered his available elements of the 15th Infantry Cannon Company, a platoon of three half-tracks mounting 75-mm. howitzers, to come forward. To do so, the half-tracks had to move along a stretch of road that had several hairpin turns.

The hairpin area was no place for half-tracks to leave the road, and besides, the enemy had several artillery pieces registered on the treacherous curves. The first half-track stuck its nose out from behind a hill and into the open and three enemy salvos checkerboarded the road. The half-track quickly reversed and got back to shelter. Another try five minutes later brought the same result. The platoon commander decided to dash down

---

[14] 41st Armd Inf Regt AAR, 11 Jul 43; 66th Armd Regt AAR, 11 Jul 43; overlay of opns, CCA, 10–18 Jul 43, in 602-CC (A)-3.6; disposition of troops, CCA, overlay as of 1900, 11 Jul 43, 3d Inf Div G–3 Jnl File, 11 Jul 43; 2d Armd Div in Sicilian Campaign, pp. 36–38; CCA S–3 Jnl, 11 Jul 43; Faldella, *Lo sbarco,* pp. 152–55, 179.

[15] 3d Inf Div G–3 Jnl, entries 10 and 12, 12 Jul 43; CCA S–3 Jnl, entries 13 and 15, 12 Jul 43; 2d Armd Div in Sicilian Campaign, p. 39.

[16] The 39th Field Artillery Battalion fired 1,484 rounds in the day's actions; the battery of the 9th Field Artillery Battalion, 86 rounds.

the road on a dead run. First withdrawing farther into defilade in order to get a running start, he burst out from behind the hill at thirty miles an hour. The others followed at fifty-yard intervals. The enemy laid down at least four salvos, and the bursts seemed to be within inches of the half-tracks, but the half-tracks kept going and managed to stay on the road. Through the hairpin area safely, they dashed into position to give support.

With this added fire, the 3d Battalion overwhelmed the roadblock. Having lost three artillery pieces and more than half its automatic weapons, and with the infantry battalion seriously reduced in strength, *Group Venturi* withdrew to Campobello.

In the meantime, the 1st Battalion, advancing almost without resistance on its wide enveloping movement, reached high ground east of Campobello at 1300, just as the 3d Battalion, following *Group Venturi* from Favarotta, gained high ground west of the town. Though Campobello seemed ripe for a squeeze play, it was harder than it appeared.

That morning, the *XII Corps* had ordered Generale di Brigata Ottorino Schreiber, commander of the *207th Coastal Division*, to go from his headquarters at Agrigento to Canicattì and assume command of a counterattack aimed at retaking Licata. Schreiber was to take over all the Italian and German forces already at Canicattì and those who would arrive during the day. Col. Augusto de Laurentiis, commander of the military zone of *Port Defense "N"* at Palermo, assumed command of the coastal division.

At Canicattì around 1130, Schreiber planned to attack south along Highway 123 with *Group Venturi*, already engaged, and *Group Neapel*, dispatched by Rodt. Schreiber immediately sent *Group Neapel* to Campobello to reinforce *Group Venturi*, both to be supported by Italian artillery at Casa San Silvestro, two miles south of Canicattì.

General Schreiber's counterattack, scheduled to jump off at 1330, never started. *Group Venturi* had been mauled too severely to think of offensive action, *Group Neapel* became involved in defending Campobello, and American artillery fire and the threat to his right flank posed by the advance of CCA into Naro prompted General Schreiber to withdraw to Casa San Silvestro. *Group Neapel* remained at Campobello temporarily to cover the withdrawal.[17]

At 1500, behind a thunderous concentration laid down by the 39th Field Artillery Battalion, the 1st and 3d Battalions of the 15th Infantry advanced on Campobello. The attack progressed slowly but steadily until just short of town where concentrated German fire forced a halt. Another artillery preparation and the squeeze of the two American battalions hurried the Germans out of town. At 1600 the 3d Battalion entered Campobello.[18]

---

[17] Faldella, *Lo sbarco*, pp. 153–55.

[18] 15th Inf Regt AAR, 11 Jul 43; 15th Inf Regt Jnl, 11 Jul 43; overlay showing routes traveled and positions occupied by 15th Infantry troops, 11 Jul 43, 303-70.4; 66th Armd Regt AAR, 11 Jul 43; 3d Inf Div in Sicilian Campaign AAR, p. 11; 39th FA Bn AAR, 11 Jul 43; 9th FA Bn AAR, 11 Jul 43; Donald G. Taggart, ed., *History of the Third Infantry Division in World War II* (Washington, 1947), pp. 56–57.

In the final push on Campobello, 1st Lt. Robert Craig, Company L, 15th Infantry, singlehandedly knocked out two enemy machine gun positions, killing eight Germans and wounding three others before he, himself, was killed. Lieutenant Craig was posthumously awarded the Medal of Honor.

That day also, the 3d Battalion, 30th Infantry, marched over fourteen miles of rugged mountains, overcoming scattered enemy resistance, and occupied Riesi. After making physical contact with the 1st Division on its right, the 3d Division at nightfall on 11 July—a day ahead of time—was in possession of its invasion objectives. With the Yellow Line now extended to Palma di Montechiaro, Naro, and Campobello, the division front formed a broad semicircle from Palma on the west to Poggio Lungo on the east.

Now that he had carried out the order to gain the Yellow Line so as to protect the army group left flank, General Truscott had no further mission. Nor had General Patton been instructed on how to develop the situation beyond the Yellow Line. General Alexander had been less than explicit in his instructions—the Seventh Army was "to prevent enemy reserves moving eastwards against the left flank of Eighth Army."[19]

Unwilling to sit still, Truscott ordered General Rose to reconnoiter toward Canicattì during the evening of 11 July as the prelude to a possible attack the next day. Since Caltanissetta and Enna appeared to be logical objectives, Truscott decided to seize Canicattì as a necessary preliminary first step.[20]

At Casa San Silvestro, General Schreiber's hasty development of new defensive positions was interrupted at 1800 when an Allied bombing attack on Canicattì severely damaged the town and railroad station and produced heavy casualties in the Italian infantry battalion that had retired from Favarotta earlier that day.

Not long afterwards, Schreiber received word from the *XII Corps*. He was to counterattack the next morning with several new units being sent to him—an infantry battalion from the *Assietta Division*, an infantry battalion and an antitank gun company from the *Aosta Division*, and two Italian artillery battalions. Apprehensive over the developments in the Licata sector, Guzzoni apparently hoped that Schreiber's counterattack on 12 July would not only delay further American advances inland but would also block the major avenues of approach into central Sicily.[21]

At 2000, 11 July, Col. Fritz Fullriede reported in to General Schreiber as the commander of all German troops in the area and placed himself and his units under the Italian general's tactical leadership.[22] Fullriede reported American tanks had driven through to points west of Canicattì, thus threatening to cut off German and Italian units south of that town. Fullriede told General Schreiber that he had assembled the bulk of his German force north of Canicattì, leaving detachments at Sommatino and Delia, small towns to the east of Canicattì, to cover his flanks. He urged the Italian commander to do the same with the Italian units. Fullriede also stated that he had received instructions from *Sixth Army* headquarters to switch to the defensive in the Canicattì area and to await the arrival of additional German units.

What then of Schreiber's counterattack? Several telephone calls to *XII Corps* and to *Sixth Army* cleared up the confusion. Guzzoni had changed his mind. On 12

---

[19] 15th AG Opns Inst 1, 19 May 43; Truscott, *Command Missions*, pp. 214–15.

[20] COHQ Bull Y/1, Oct 43, p. 26; Truscott, *Command Missions*, p. 215.

[21] Faldella, *Lo sbarco*, p. 155.

[22] *Ibid.*; IT 99a, Sitrep, 2000, 11 Jul 43. There is no confirmation of this in German sources.

CANICATTÌ BEING SHELLED *by CCA supporting armored field artillery.*

July, Schreiber was to limit his actions to local thrusts only, those that would not seriously deplete manpower and material. In view of his amended orders, General Schreiber decided to withdraw his units during the night to positions north of Canicattì and behind *Group Fullriede's* lines. American patrols hung on tenaciously to the withdrawing Italians; one Italian artillery battery, unable to fall back quickly enough, blew up its 105-mm. guns and surrendered.[23]

The leading elements of *Group Ens* were by then arriving at Pietraperzia. Col. Karl Ens was slightly wounded when Allied aircraft bombed General Rodt's headquarters, but he continued in command of his battle group. He ordered one battalion to a position just south of Pietraperzia, its counterattack through Riesi called off because the 3d Division occupied the town; a second battalion to Barrafranca; and the third to Piazza Armerina, to gain contact with the *Her-mann Goering Division* which was known to be somewhere off to the east.[24] The *Herman Goering Division* was in the precarious position of operating with a gap in its center. Between its left flank and the *15th Panzer Grenadier* right was another gap, this one covered by the *Livorno Division.* But the combat efficiency of the *Livorno Division* was near zero. If the Italians could not, as seemed likely, prevent the Allies from breaking through to Highway 124, the Germans would suffer disastrous consequences.

General Keyes, the Seventh Army deputy commander, visited General Truscott on the morning of 12 July. Though Keyes had no information on further missions for the division, he agreed with Truscott that Canicattì should be seized as a prelude to further advances into central Sicily. At Canicattì Highway 123 from Licata met Highway 122 from Agrigento, the latter continuing north to

---

[23] Faldella, *Lo sbarco,* pp. 155–56.

[24] MS #C–077 (Rodt) and sketch; MS # C–095 (Senger); *OB SUED, Meldungen,* 12 Jul 43.

## THE BEACHHEAD SECURE

Caltanissetta. Except for the mountain pass at Naro, the secondary road northeast to Canicattì was a valley thoroughfare practicable for mechanized forces. The road went through the pass (occupied by CCA late on 11 July) and emerged on a plain in front of Canicattì. East from Canicattì a good secondary road ran to Delia, Sommatino, and Riesi, the base of the secondary road net in the upper part of the Licata-Agrigento-Canicattì triangle. Quite certain that General Patton would approve, Keyes told Truscott to go ahead and take Canicattì.[25]

Truscott immediately telephoned General Rose to get CCA moving on Canicattì.[26] At the same time, he ordered the 30th Infantry to move to Naro, leaving its 3d Battalion in Riesi. He notified the 15th Infantry to move forward on the right of the armored command to seize Delia and Sommatino and then swing to the west to aid the armor in taking Canicattì. The 7th Infantry was to guard the division left flank. After taking Canicattì, General Truscott planned to place CCA in division reserve as a mobile force for exploitation north or west.[27]

Preceded by a five-minute preparation from the two supporting armored field artillery battalions, CCA jumped off at 1330, 12 July, through the pass and down the road toward the southern outskirts of Canicattì. A tank-infantry team (with infantry on the tanks) leading the advance was still some distance from the town when observers saw a white flag flying over one of the buildings. Colonel Hinds and another officer jumped into a jeep and drove toward town to accept the surrender. Hardly had Hinds started forward when enemy artillery fire from high ground north of Canicattì began to pattern the road. At that moment, Hinds noted that the white flag was actually a Red Cross flag on top of a hospital. By then white sheets, towels, and other signs of surrender began to appear. Taking no more chances, Hinds deployed his force on both sides of the road and called in the supporting artillery.

The 14th and 62d Armored Field Artillery Battalions obliged. For thirty minutes the two artillery units methodically worked over the town from end to end, shifting their fires periodically to batter the German positions in the hills north of town.[28] As the last artillery rounds were being fired, a company of tanks roared down the road and into town. There was no opposition. Canicattì was secured at 1500.

Scarcely pausing, the company of tanks drove out the northern exit from town and ran into Colonel Fullriede's main battle position. After expending all its ammunition and losing one tank, the company pulled back to town to await reinforcements. A tank-infantry team swung to the right and secured the eastern edge of a ridge line a mile north of town. Though the Germans fought stubbornly, they were driven off the ridge line by 2000. By darkness, CCA had Canicattì, but *Group Fullriede* held the bulk of the hill mass northwest of the town.

The enemy was in poor shape, however. American counterbattery fire had destroyed most of the supporting Italian artillery. The German battalion holding

---

[25] Truscott, *Command Missions*, p. 215.
[26] CCA S-3 Jnl, entry 19, 12 Jul 43.
[27] 3d Inf Div FO 7, 12 Jul 43.

[28] The 14th Armored Field Artillery Battalion fired a total of 1,862 rounds during the day, most of them at this time. The 62d Armored Field Artillery Battalion fired a total of 627 rounds.

the ridge line had been severely mauled. Other small German detachments east of Canicattì—on the road to Delia and Sommatino—suffered heavy losses from American tank-infantry teams that overran their positions. Deeming his forces too small to hold longer, Colonel Fullriede, with General Schreiber's approval, pulled back that evening to a new line along the railroad running from Serradifalco to San Cataldo.[29]

The 15th Infantry had contributed to Fullriede's decision. It moved smartly and by dark of 12 July had both Delia and Sommatino, although the former would not be entirely secure until the following morning. Here, the 3d Battalion, 15th Infantry, had quite a stiff fight with part of the *Group Ens* battalion which had gone into position earlier in the day. With the entire important secondary east-west road from Canicattì east to Riesi in 3d Division hands, General Truscott again faced the problem of what to do. The 7th Infantry was patrolling vigorously westward toward Agrigento; the 30th Infantry closed in Naro and prepared to relieve CCA at Canicattì; the 15th Infantry, with the 3d Battalion, 30th Infantry, at Riesi, lay along the secondary road running east from Canicattì. Truscott could go either west against Agrigento or north toward Enna. Canicattì had been taken with General Keyes' approval, but to go any further would require, Truscott thought, a nod from General Patton himself. To go ahead and take Caltanissetta and Enna, Truscott would need at least one more regimental combat team to guard his lengthy western flank. His front was almost fifty miles long, and both flanks were open. Though patrols had traversed with relative ease the area between Riesi and Butera, the area was far from secure. Less than two miles east of Riesi lay a strong enemy roadblock, and no one knew for certain how many other such positions were in the general area. Until the 1st Division on the right moved up from Ponte Olivo, Truscott would have to classify the area as uncertain, though not particularly dangerous. Truscott would also need a stronger reserve, stronger than the 3d Ranger Battalion, which for two days had been the only uncommitted unit.

General Keyes, who had spent the day with General Truscott observing the capture of Canicattì, phoned General Patton that evening. He reported the successful attack and stated that the situation was favorable for a prompt operation against either Agrigento or Caltanissetta. But, concluded General Keyes, "Neither will be instituted tomorrow without your instruction." [30]

General Patton could give no instruction because he had none from General Alexander. And the 15th Army Group commander was primarily concerned with protecting the British Eighth Army left flank. With continued reports from pilots on sizable enemy movements from west to east, Alexander remained apprehensive over the possibility of a massive enemy

---

[29] 41st Armd Inf Regt AAR, 12 Jul 43; 66th Armd Regt AAR, 12 Jul 43; overlay of opns, CCA, 10–18 Jul 43; CCA S–3 Jnl, 12 Jul 43; 14th Armd FA Bn AAR, 12 Jul 43; 62d Armd FA Bn AAR, 12 Jul 43; Faldella, *Lo sbarco*, pp. 179–80; OB SUED, *Meldungen*, 13 Jul 43, Third Report and Fourth Report; 14 Jul 43, Third Report.

[30] Seventh Army G–3 Jnl, entry 13, 13 Jul 43.

# THE BEACHHEAD SECURE

counterattack.[31] And thus he was not anxious to move the 3d Division, which provided a solid block on the army group left.

Still, Keyes was loath to leave the 3d Division completely sedentary. Before leaving Truscott's headquarters, he verbally approved a reconnaissance in force in battalion strength toward Agrigento. At the same time, the division was to gain the heights northwest of Canicattì and eliminate the troublesome enemy roadblock southeast of Riesi. Beyond this, Keyes would not go, though on the following afternoon, apparently after consulting with General Patton, Keyes restated his approval in writing.[32]

These small movements were to develop in a surprising fashion. They would help General Alexander make up his mind on how to use the Seventh Army in Sicily.

---

[31] General Alexander feared that the road complex in central Sicily would be used by the Germans to launch an attack against the Eighth Army. Until the day the Seventh Army captured Palermo, Alexander continued to be worried about this possibility. Alexander Despatch, pp. 12, 24; 15th AGp Radios J47, 13 Jul 47; 184, 16 Jul 43; and 0165, 18 Jul 43, all quoted in Seventh Army Rpt of Opns. These are indicative of Alexander's concern for Eighth Army's left flank. See also, Interv, Smyth with Lt Gen Lucian K. Truscott (Ret.) and Maj Gen William W. Eagles, 19 Apr 51.

[32] Seventh Army G-3 Jnl, entry 36, 14 Jul 43 (memo dated 13 July but filed one day later).

CHAPTER XI

# Continuing the Campaign: The Decisions

## Sixth Army and OB SUED

At *Sixth Army* headquarters in Enna, it was clear by the morning of 12 July that the period of counterattacks against the various Allied beachheads had ended. Until further decisions were made at higher levels in Rome and Berlin on whether or not to reinforce the island's defenders, *Sixth Army* had no choice but to go over to the defensive.[1]

Lacking the manpower to erect a solid line around the Allied beachheads, General Guzzoni planned to shorten his front to a line across the northeastern corner of Sicily—from the east coast south of the Catania plain to Santo Stefano di Camastra on the north coast. He planned to withdraw slowly the forces in contact with the British and Americans to the eastern end of this line—from Catania to Nicosia—while the forces in the west moved to the sector of the line running between Nicosia and the north coast. Seeing this as a final defense line, Guzzoni planned to pull the units back first to intermediate defensive positions, along a line from Priolo on the east coast, through Melilli, Vizzini, Caltagirone, Canicattì, to Agrigento on the southwestern coast.

After temporarily delaying the Allied advance from the southeastern corner of the island, Guzzoni would fight a delaying action while falling back to the Catania—Santo Stefano line. But if this line was breached, Guzzoni intended to establish a third defensive line—a final battle line that was to be held at all costs. Guzzoni did not immediately determine the location of this third line, except that he wanted it anchored on the east coast south of the Catania plain.[2]

Guzzoni realized that the success of this withdrawal maneuver depended on preventing an Allied breakthrough at the eastern hinge: Catania. This was the critical spot. This was the reasoning behind the order of 11 July that had directed the bulk of the *Hermann Goering Division* to disengage and move northeast, first to the new intermediate defensive line, then to the southern edge of the Catania plain. The *Livorno Division* was also to fall back to this new line, screening the area between the *Hermann Goering Division* on the east and the *15th Panzer Grenadier Division* on the west. For the Italian division, this meant a withdrawal of fifteen miles, from Mazzarino (where contact with the German *Group Ens* was to be made) east to San Michele di Ganzeria (on Highway 124 northwest of Caltagirone), where contact with the *Her-*

---

[1] Faldella, *Lo sbarco*, p. 163. Maravigna, *Rivista Militare*, 1952, p. 21, and Maravigna, "La conquista della Sicilia (Luglio - Agosto 1943)," *Rivista Militare*, vol. VIII, No. 7 (Rome, July 1952), pp. 793-812.

[2] Faldella, *Lo sbarco*, pp. 163, 185-87, 304-06.

*mann Goering Division* was to be made. With part of the *15th Panzer Grenadier Division* even then nearing Mazzarino, Guzzoni hoped the *Livorno Division* would be strong enough to block any American penetration into the important network of roads near Enna. But his entire plan relied on transferring the bulk of the *Hermann Goering Division* quickly to the northeast.[3]

While Guzzoni was making his tactical arrangements, higher headquarters in Italy and Germany were following the campaign closely. In Germany OKW, after Pantelleria, had modified its views that the Allies were preparing a twin invasion of Sardinia and Greece. But as late as 9 July, OKW still considered that the Allies were preparing an invasion of Greece, with the first step being the occupation of Sicily, Sardinia, and Corsica. OKW had considered that an Allied landing in Calabria might take place in conjunction with the landing in Sicily, but that a subsequent Allied landing on the Italian mainland was far less probable than the use of Sicily (or Sicily and Calabria) as a springboard for a jump to the Peloponnesus.

On the basis of this appreciation, OKW on 9 July had directed Kesselring to move the German *29th Panzer Grenadier Division* to the area north of Cosenza (ninety miles north-northeast of Reggio di Calabria); to shift the German *26th Panzer Division* to an area east of Salerno; and to retain the German *16th Panzer Division* near Bari, on the Adriatic Sea. Under the *XIV Panzer Corps*, the German units were to co-operate with the Italian *Seventh Army* in opposing an Allied landing in southern Italy. With one jaundiced eye directed at Mussolini's unstable control of Italy, OKW retained the German *3d Panzer Grenadier Division* and *LXXVI Corps* headquarters north of Rome. On Hitler's order, OKW alerted the German *1st Parachute Division*, stationed near Avignon in southern France, for possible air movement to Sicily.[4]

The first reports of the fighting in Sicily did not give Hitler or the OKW a clear picture of the situation. Kesselring reported during the evening of 10 July that he had issued orders to General von Senger directing the bulk of the *Hermann Goering Division* to destroy the American forces advancing toward Caltagirone and *Group Schmalz* to counterattack immediately and recapture Syracuse.[5]

With a better grasp of the situation on 11 July, Hitler decided to reinforce the German units in Sicily. Specifically, Kesselring was to transport the *1st Parachute Division* by air to Sicily; transfer the *29th Panzer Grenadier Division* to that island; and, upon commitment of the latter division, shift the headquarters of the *XIV Panzer Corps* to Sicily in order to give unified direction to all the German units there.[6]

Kesselring, too, by 11 July, had a much better appreciation of the strength which the Americans and British had landed on the 10th, and he also realized that his plan to throw the invading Allied forces back into the sea had failed. He believed that he had an accurate view of the developments on the island

---

[3] *Ibid.*, pp. 159–60, 187–88; IT 99a, 12 Jul 43; *OKH, Tagesmeldungen West*, rpt for 12 Jul 43; MS #R–140, Withdrawal, First Phase, 12–16 July 1943, ch. XI of Axis Tactical Operations in Sicily, July–August 1943 (Bauer), pp. 1–10.

[4] *OKW/WFSt, KTB, 1.–31.VII.43,* 9 Jul 43.
[5] *OB SUED, Meldungen,* 10 Jul 43.
[6] *OKW/WFSt, KTB, 1.–31.VII.43,* 11 Jul 43.

from reports furnished him by the German *Second Air Force*. He attributed the failure of the Axis counterattacks chiefly to what he considered was Guzzoni's delay in ordering the *15th Panzer Grenadier Division* back to the central part of the island and to General Conrath's slowness in counterattacking at Gela early on the morning of 10 July.[7]

Kesselring flew to Sicily on 12 July to see the situation at firsthand. At *Sixth Army* headquarters, Guzzoni and Senger were pessimistic about repelling the Allied invasion, and Kesselring had to agree. Resuming the offensive would have to await the arrival of reinforcements. Guzzoni doubted that he could hold all of Sicily. His main concern was no longer defending the entire island, but holding eastern Sicily until help arrived. Then a new counteroffensive could be started. He felt that his immediate tasks were to prevent any Allied breakthroughs into the interior of the island, and to consolidate all Axis forces then on Sicily in one strong battle position forward of Mount Etna.

Kesselring shared Guzzoni's doubts on the ultimate outcome of the battle of Sicily. But he also felt that the Allies had not yet gained a free hand on the island. Strong and immediate countermeasures might delay the Allies indefinitely.

The prospective arrival of the *1st Parachute* and *29th Panzer Grenadier Divisions* brought mixed feelings to Guzzoni and Senger. Both feared that the additional troops would accentuate an already serious strain on transportation and supply lines. Moreover, Senger privately opposed the introduction of more German forces into Sicily because he was convinced that the best course of action was an immediate evacuation from the island.

Accompanied by Senger, Kesselring flew to the Catania airfield, where he met with Colonel Schmalz. Pleased with the steady and sure leadership demonstrated by Schmalz, Kesselring assured Schmalz that reinforcements were on the way. The *3d Regiment, 1st Parachute Division,* was en route and would be placed immediately at Schmalz's disposal.

Like Guzzoni, Kesselring believed that the Axis might, at best, establish a tenable position across the northeastern neck of the island. But even this, Kesselring believed, required a strong directing headquarters such as the *XIV Panzer Corps,* reinforcement by at least one additional German division, and great improvement in the system of tactical communications.

About 1800, while Kesselring waited to take off for Frascati, the three infantry battalions of the *3d Regiment, 1st Parachute Division,* flew in under fighter plane escort and dropped near the Catania airfield. The successful execution of this operation convinced Kesselring that more paratroopers could be brought safely to Sicily by air.[8]

As Kesselring departed the Catania airfield, the three paratrooper rifle battalions loaded on trucks and moved into line to reinforce *Group Schmalz,* two battalions

---

[7] MS #T-2 K 1 (Kesselring), pp. 19–21. Kesselring was wrong in his assumption that Guzzoni was slow in ordering the *15th Panzer Grenadier Division* to retrace its steps. Guzzoni had issued this order on 10 July, a quick decision considering the limited amount of information available as to Allied intentions.

[8] MS #T-2 K 1 (Kesselring); MS #C-095 (Senger); *OKW/WFSt, KTB, 1.–31.VII.43,* 13 Jul 43; Msg., Mil Attaché Rome to *Gen StdH., Att. Abt.,* 13 Jul 43, *OKW/Amtsgruppe Ausland, 30.VI.43–31.VIII.44, Wehrmachtsattaché Italien* (OKW 1029).

south of Lentini, between the coastal highway and the coast line, the third battalion to Francofonte, a crucial point for the link-up with the main body of the *Hermann Goering Division.*

General Conrath had executed only minor withdrawals during the night of 11 July when General Guzzoni ordered him early on 12 July to hurry his withdrawal to the Caltagirone-Vizzini-Palazzolo Acreide area. Still, Conrath did not appear in any rush to conform. While the *Hermann Goering Division* fought near Niscemi and Biscari, Guzzoni repeated his order—Conrath was to disengage from the Gela sector and move back as quickly as possible to Highway 124. General von Senger confirmed and amplified this order in two radio messages dispatched before noon, directing Conrath to make contact at Palazzolo Acreide with the *Napoli Division* and *Group Schmalz,* while the *Livorno Division* covered his western flank.

Planning to wait until nightfall to pull his major units out of line, Conrath started his reconnaissance battalion back during the afternoon. After encountering the 179th Infantry north of Comiso, the battalion reached Vizzini during the late afternoon of 12 July. There it was reinforced by an infantry replacement battalion.[9]

At 2140, 12 July, General von Senger dispatched another radiogram to Conrath instructing him to speed up his withdrawal to the Caltagirone line (Highway 124). The division's slow movement was causing apprehension at *Sixth Army* headquarters, for the division was needed not only to strengthen the eastern wing but also to stop the American and British thrusts northward from Comiso and Ragusa. Just before midnight, *Sixth Army* ordered General Conrath to attack from Vizzini toward Palazzolo Acreide the following day. But by the morning of 13 July, the division was still south of Caltagirone, along a line running from Vizzini on the east almost to Highway 117 on the west.[10]

To top off an extremely trying day for *Sixth Army,* the headquarters at Enna received a heavy Allied bombing attack late in the evening, making a transfer to Passo Pisciaro, east of Randazzo, imperative. The transfer was completed late the next day.[11]

*The Allied Problem: How to Continue*

Even as the Axis commanders sought ways and means of slowing up the Allied advances, General Patton, late on the afternoon of 12 July, moved his headquarters ashore. He opened the first Seventh Army command post on Sicily at the eastern edge of Gela "in a very handsome mansion, abandoned in a hurry by the prominent owner, a doctor and fascist apparently, who lived there . . . in a spot which was apparently a Roman villa or something."[12] Optimism pervaded the army headquarters. Despite the *Hermann Goering Division*'s resistance to the 16th Infantry's advance on Niscemi, and German opposition along part of

---

[9] See OB SUED, Meldungen, 13 Jul 43, First Report; MS #C-095 (Senger); MS #R-138 (Bauer), p. 11; MS #R-140 (Bauer), pp. 24-25. Conrath's reconnaissance battalion was reinforced by elements of an infantry regiment, probably the *382d;* this regiment had been on Sicily for some time, had been attached to the *15th Panzer Grenadier Division* until 1 July, and subsequently, while stationed at Regalbuto, to the *Hermann Goering Division.*

[10] MS #R-140 (Bauer), pp. 30-31.
[11] Faldella, *Lo sbarco,* p. 191; MS #C-095 (Senger).
[12] Lucas Diary, pt. I, pp. 58-59.

the 45th Division's front, General Patton and General Bradley were aware of the indications of Axis withdrawal from the 1st Division's front. Reports from both the 16th and 26th RCT's during the night were cheering. The 45th Division seemed to be encountering no more than delaying forces in its push to the Yellow Line. And General Keyes returned from the 3d Division's area with a very satisfactory report. All in all, General Patton was happy with the performance of the Seventh Army units. A number of distinguished visitors that day had been most complimentary. Admiral Lord Louis Mountbatten, the chief of the Combined Operations Headquarters, was greatly impressed by the operation in the II Corps zone. General Eisenhower, though pleased with the extent of the beachhead, was unhappy with what he considered General Patton's failure to get news of the Seventh Army's operations back to AFHQ promptly. "Ike . . . stepped on him hard." [13]

Determined to keep the Seventh Army moving aggressively, General Patton directed the II Corps to continue its movement inland to seize its portion of the Yellow Line—from Mazzarino on the west to Grammichele on the east. He approved Keyes' instructions to the 3d Division for a reconnaissance toward Agrigento, the seizure of Canicattì, and the reduction of the roadblock southeast of Riesi. Without General Alexander's approval, General Patton felt that he could not tell Truscott to exploit toward Caltanissetta and Enna, or toward Agrigento and the western part of the island.[14]

General Bradley's two divisions moved quickly on 13 July. (*Map VI*) The 1st Division, with the 18th RCT returning to its control, entered Niscemi at 1000, advanced six miles north of Ponte Olivo airfield to seize two important hill masses astride Highway 117, and sent a third column seven miles northwest of Ponte Olivo to seize two other hill masses astride the Ponte Olivo–Mazzarino road. These advances were opposed only by long-range sniper and artillery fire.

The 45th Division, in contrast, met with an unexpected complication. Late in the evening of 12 July, General Middleton sent word to his combat team commanders to continue driving toward Highway 124, the Yellow Line, by leapfrogging battalions forward and maintaining constant watchfulness to the flanks. On the left the 180th RCT was to cross the Acate River, secure the Biscari airfield, then push north toward Caltagirone. In the center, the 179th RCT was to push to Highway 124 in the vicinity of Grammichele. On the right, the 157th RCT was to drive northeast to Monterosso Almo, then swing northwest to take Licodia Eubea, almost on the highway. Because the 157th would be operating in part across the army boundary and in the British zone, Middleton warned Colonel Ankcorn to maintain careful liaison with the 1st Canadian Division on his right.

Unknown to General Middleton, as well as to Generals Patton and Bradley, General Montgomery, the Eighth Army commander, had decided that Highway 124

---

[13] *Ibid.* pt. I, p. 64; OPD 201 Wedemeyer, A. C., Security, case 5; Butcher, *My Three Years With Eisenhower*, p. 360. Cf. Morrison, *Sicily—Salerno—Anzio*, p. 123 and 123n.
Lucas states, "I didn't hear what he [Eisenhower] said but he must have given Patton hell because Georgie was much upset."

[14] Seventh Army Directive, 13 Jul 43, Seventh Army Rpt of Opns, p. D-6.

west of Vizzini (the Seventh Army's Yellow Line) belonged to him. Though the original invasion plan reserved the highway to the Americans, Montgomery halted the 1st Canadian Division at the small town of Giarratana and directed General Leese to use the rest of his 30 Corps in a drive on Caltagirone, Enna, and Leonforte. While the 30 Corps thus moved directly across the Seventh Army front, the 13 Corps was to continue to try to break through into the Catania plain. The Eighth Army would then advance on Messina on two widely separated axes: one up the coastal road on the east, the other into the interior through Enna, Leonforte, on to Nicosia, Troina, and Randazzo, in a swing around the western side of Mount Etna. The 13 Corps was to make the Eighth Army's main effort. A second airborne drop was to seize the Primosole bridge over the Simeto River and a Commando landing was to capture the Lentini bridge. The operation was to start on the evening of 13 July. Without General Alexander's approval, Montgomery ordered his units to start the operation.[15]

General Montgomery's new plan gave to the British Eighth Army the use of all the roads leading to Messina. There were only four roads on the entire island leading toward the important port city, and of the four, only two went all the way. The first was the east coast highway, on which Montgomery had his 13 Corps. The other through road was the north coast highway. Two roads to Messina were inland routes that ran toward Messina from Enna. The southernmost of these ran along the rim of Mount Etna; the other, some fifteen miles south of the north coast road, passed through Nicosia and Troina. Both the inner roads converged at Randazzo, on the Messina side of Mount Etna, where one road headed for the east coast road, and the other ran toward Messina. Montgomery's specified axis of advance for the 30 Corps, if carried through to the north coast, would give that corps the possession of the fourth one. The assignment of these roads would effectively restrict the Seventh Army's activities to the southwestern part of the island.

In keeping with the Eighth Army directive, General Leese, commander of the 30 Corps, directed the British 23d Armored Brigade to seize Vizzini during daylight of 13 July, Caltagirone during the evening of the same day. The British 51st Highland Infantry Division was to follow the armored brigade to secure Vizzini, and drive on the town of Scordia to protect the corps' north flank. The 1st Canadian Division was to remain near Giarratana.[16]

Thus, when daylight came on 13 July, American and British units were heading toward the same objectives. Pushing out

---

[15] General Montgomery knew of Seventh Army's plan to take Highway 124, since this was part of the original plan for the invasion of the island. But apparently General Montgomery felt that American operations should be restricted to the Caltanissetta-Canicattì-Agrigento area, while the Eighth Army made the main effort against Messina (Montgomery, *Eighth Army*, page 99). The fact that Montgomery had not yet secured Alexander's approval to his new plan is indicated in a message which the 30 Corps commander sent to the 1st Canadian Division on 13 July: "45 U.S. Div now on general line Chiaramonte–Biscari. Information received they intend to send one brigade Vizzini, two brigades Caltagirone tomorrow 14 July. Army Comd rapidly attempting to direct them more to west to avoid clash with you, but in case NOT retire from accordingly. Warn all concerned." Quoted in Nicholson, *The Canadians in Italy*, p. 87n.

[16] Nicholson, *The Canadians in Italy*, p. 88.

of Biscari in difficult terrain, along a single, narrow, secondary road effectively blocked by the Germans, facing strong delaying forces of the *Hermann Goering Division,* the 180th RCT did not get across the Acate River until late in the afternoon and then pushed only a little way farther on before being stopped again at the narrow Ficuzza River. Though the Ficuzza was no more than a small stream, both banks were precipitous, and the Germans had destroyed the bridge and blocked the narrow road which wound down to the crossing site.[17]

On the 179th RCT front, the regiment quickly abandoned the leapfrogging procedure and advanced on a wide front, battalions abreast. Detachments from the *Hermann Goering Division* fought stubborn rear guard actions while withdrawing toward Highway 124. Often the leading battalions were delayed by a few German troops supported by one or two armored vehicles left on critical terrain features. To dislodge even these small units, the battalions either had to deploy or wait for the flank security elements to catch up and flush out the Germans. In one or two cases, the Germans, from positions on especially good terrain features, counterattacked sharply before withdrawing to the next hill. The supporting American tanks proved of little use in the rugged terrain, but the 160th Field Artillery Battalion, a platoon of 4.2-inch mortars, and a platoon of self-propelled howitzers from the regimental Cannon Company performed yeoman service in aiding the infantry's advance. By late afternoon, the 3d Battalion, 179th

---
[17] Infantry Combat, pt. V: Sicily, pp. 1, 3–4; 180th Inf Regt AAR, 13 Jul 43; McLain MS. Sicily Campaign, pp. 14–15; 45th Inf Div G-3 Jnl, entries 13, 22, 30, 44, 57, 13 Jul 43.

Infantry, entered the small village of Granieri, about five miles south of Highway 124. By this time, too, the advance on a wide front had been discarded in favor of a column formation. Because civilians indicated that the Germans had a large armored force (an estimated 500 men and 35 tanks) deployed in an olive grove about three miles north of Granieri, the 3d Battalion commander pushed his men to gain the high ground just north of the village. It took a night attack to accomplish this, but by 2300 the 3d Battalion was in position on the hill mass astride the narrow dirt road it had been following all day. The remainder of the combat team closed in near the village.

On the right Monterosso Almo fell to the 1st Battalion, 157th Infantry, at noon. A further advance by the battalion of almost three miles toward Vizzini was registered before increasing German resistance called a halt to the day's activities. Licodia Eubea fell late in the afternoon to the 3d Battalion, 157th Infantry, but not before the battalion lost twenty men killed and forty wounded. Across its front, the 157th RCT stood less than three miles from the Yellow Line.

Just before the news of the seizure of Licodia Eubea reached the combat team's command post at Monterosso Almo, Colonel Ankcorn received an inkling of the Eighth Army's new plan of action. Shortly after 1700, the leading elements of the 51st Highland Division began to arrive at Monterosso Almo. Surprised, Ankcorn learned that the Highlanders were on their way to take Vizzini. The 23d Armored Brigade, advancing northeastward from Palazzolo Acreide, had run head on into the *Hermann Goering Division* (going the opposite way) and had been stopped by fierce resistance from

# CONTINUING THE CAMPAIGN: THE DECISIONS

Germans and Italians (the remnants of the *Napoli Division*) east of Vizzini. The Highlanders had been committed to the south of Vizzini to clear the town for the armored brigade. Colonel Ankcorn had been told of the armored brigade's move on Vizzini, but since he had neither seen nor heard anything from that column, he had continued his attack on Vizzini. Now it appeared to Colonel Ankcorn that the British were to take Vizzini after which the Eighth Army would swing northward along the army boundary. But as far as the 157th Combat Team commander was concerned, the rest of the highway was in the Seventh Army's area and that part of the highway west of Vizzini was still his objective. Nevertheless, he radioed General Middleton news of the latest British movements.[18]

The news from the 157th Combat Team's front near Vizzini must have created some confusion at Seventh Army's command post late in the afternoon of 13 July. General Alexander had visited General Patton that very morning. Patton asked for approval to take Agrigento and Porto Empedocle, the ports which he felt would be needed to continue the logistical support of Seventh Army. The army group commander did not disapprove the request, but he did not want the Seventh Army to get entangled in a fight which might interfere with its primary mission: the protection of the Eighth Army's left flank. Accordingly, he told General Patton that the Seventh Army could take Agrigento and Porto Empedocle provided this could be done by reconnaissance troops and provided the operation did not cost too much in manpower or material. Nothing was said about any change in the boundary between the Seventh and Eighth Armies. Nothing was said about the assignment of Highway 124 to the British.[19]

Just before midnight, any confusion that may have existed was cleared up when General Alexander radioed the following directive to the Seventh Army:

Operations for the immediate future will be Eighth Army to advance on two axes, one to capture the port of Catania and the group of airfields there and the other to secure the network of road communications within the area Leonforte-Enna. Seventh Army will conform by pivoting on Palma di Montechiaro–Canicattì–Caltanissetta —gaining touch with Eighth Army at road junction HOW 1979 [the junction of Highways 117 and 122 southwest of Enna]. Boundary between Seventh and Eighth Armies, road Vizzini–Caltagirone–Piazza Armerina–Road Junction HOW 1979–Enna, all inclusive to Eighth Army. Liaison will be carefully arranged between Seventh and Eighth Armies for this operation.[20]

The directive came as a surprise and a distinct disappointment to the Seventh Army staff, for the order gave the Americans a passive role in the campaign.

---

[18] 157th Inf Regt AAR 13 Jul 43; 157th Inf Regt S-1 Jnl, 13 Jul 43; 158th FA Bn AAR, 13 Jul 43; Nicholson, *The Canadians in Italy*, pp. 85, 88; Montgomery, *Eighth Army*, pp. 99, 101.

[19] Lucas Diary, pt. I, p. 64; Truscott, *Command Missions*, p. 218. Seventh Army's directive of 13 July, which was issued shortly before noon on 13 July, and which must have been seen by General Alexander, indicates that nothing was said about any change in the boundary between the two Allied armies. It also indicates that General Montgomery must have approached General Alexander with his new proposal after the latter returned from visiting the Seventh Army, and that the approval to Montgomery's new plan was given at the same time.

[20] Seventh Army Rpt of Opns, p. D-6; Alexander Despatch, app. C-1, p. 84; Seventh Army G-3 Jnl, entry 4, 14 Jul 43. The message was received at 2316, 13 July, and posted in the journal at 0145, 14 July 1943.

Patton's staff had expected to advance to the general line Agrigento-Canicattì-Caltanissetta and the II Corps to advance inland along Highway 124. The Americans had expected to make the swing around the western side of Mount Etna toward Messina, while the British Eighth Army massed its power for a drive around the eastern side.

But General Patton did not dispute the order. On the morning of 14 July he called General Bradley to Seventh Army headquarters and explained the new directive. It entailed sideslipping the 45th Division to the west; giving up Highway 124; and shifting the II Corps advance from north to west.

General Bradley was keenly disappointed. "This will raise hell with us," he exclaimed. "I had counted heavily on that road. Now if we've got to shift over, it'll slow up our entire advance." The II Corps commander asked whether he could use Highway 124 at least to move the 45th Division to the left of the 1st Division in order to maintain the momentum of his advance. The answer was, "Sorry, Brad, but the changeover takes place immediately. Monty wants the road right away."

After reading General Alexander's directive, Bradley returned it gloomily to Patton. He knew that the Germans were falling back toward the northeast. He felt certain that the Axis commanders were pulling back hoping to reassemble their forces across the narrow neck of the Messina peninsula. The delay encountered in pulling the 45th Division out of line and moving it around the rear of the 1st Division to a new position on the left of General Allen's unit would take considerable pressure off the *Hermann Goering Division* and perhaps enable the Germans to recover their balance. To General Bradley, it appeared that General Montgomery planned to take Messina alone, while the Seventh Army confined its efforts to the western half of the island.[21]

Although there had been no prepared plan by 15th Army Group for the maneuver of the two armies after the seizure of the initial assault objectives, the assault plan itself contained by implication the general scheme which General Alexander hoped to follow. While the Eighth Army thrust forward into Catania and then into Messina, the Seventh Army was to protect the flank and rear of the main striking force because General Alexander was convinced that the Eighth Army was better qualified for the main task than the Seventh Army.[22] On 13 July, when General Alexander issued his directive to General Patton, he felt it necessary to restrain the impetuous American commander, to keep the Seventh Army doing its primary job, and not to endanger the operation by movements which might expose the Eighth Army to strong Axis counterattacks. Events were going according to plan: the Eighth Army had secured a firm beachhead and was moving on Catania with seeming

---

[21] Bradley, *A Soldier's Story,* pp. 135–36.

[22] Intervs, Mathews with Alexander, 10–15 Jan 49, p. 12.

The views which Alexander entertained of the capabilities of American troops were by no means unique but were widespread among British officers and officials. See Bradley, *A Soldier's Story,* pp. 58–59, 67–68.

Alexander's skeptical attitude regarding the quality of American troops persisted long after the Sicilian Campaign; in fact, it persisted to the period when the situation had changed radically, when American troops in Italy had to bear the brunt of the fighting because of the exhaustion of British divisions. See Interv, Smyth and Mathews with Marshall, 25 Jul 49, at the Pentagon, p. 20.

good speed. The inexperienced American divisions could best be nursed along with limited assignments which would gradually build up their fighting morale and experience.

In addition to his confidence in the Eighth Army and his distrust of American troops, General Alexander was most concerned about the network of roads which converged in the center of Sicily like the spokes of a huge wheel—in the rough quadrangle bounded by Caltanissetta–San Caterina–Enna–Valguarnera Caropepe. As long as this network of roads remained in enemy hands, General Alexander feared that the Axis might use the area to launch a mighty counterattack against General Montgomery's left flank. It was this concern that led Alexander to make sure that his armies held a solid front—meaning that the Eighth Army would be firmly established on a line from Catania to Enna—before pushing the campaign any further.

Seventh Army, General Alexander felt, should cover the Eighth Army's left flank until the latter had secured the firm line. Once that line had been secured, the exploitation phase of the operation could begin. It would then be safe to thrust out. General Alexander feared that if the Seventh Army pushed out prematurely all over the western half of the island, the enemy might drive in on Eighth Army's left flank. This could cause the Allied armies on Sicily a serious reverse, if not a disaster. Alexander wanted no defeat. He wanted to be certain that the Eighth Army was in a secure position before he let "Georgie" go and exploit.[23]

*Comando Supremo and OKW*

After telephoning a report of the situation in Sicily to General Jodl, Field Marshal Kesselring saw Mussolini on 13 July. Kesselring's account of developments on the island shocked Mussolini.

News of the apparently successful counterattacks on 10 July had raised Italian hopes and prompted joyful celebrations in Rome. Disappointment was therefore greater when, less than two days later, the scanty war bulletins spoke of "containment" instead of "elimination" of the Allied beachheads. Even in those military circles where no one had seriously expected the coastal defense units to put up much more than token opposition, the resistance appeared disappointingly brief. The two mobile divisions, the *Livorno* and *Napoli*, had shown some good fighting qualities, but as soon as they had come into range of the Allied naval guns, they had halted their attacks and retired. The collapse of the naval base at Augusta and Syracuse was beyond comprehension.[24] For Mussolini, news of the fall of the naval base was the more depressing because it reached him through German channels and on the heels of the first favorable reports from Gela.[25]

The unfavorable developments on Sicily increased the already serious friction between the Italian and German high com-

---

[23] Intervs, Mathews with Alexander, 10–15 Jan 49, pp. 11, 15–16.

[24] MS #R-139, High Command Decisions, 12 July–15 August 1943, ch. X of Axis Tactical Operations in Sicily (Bauer), p. 4.

[25] *OKW/WFSt, KTB, 1.–31.VII.43*, 13 Jul 43. General von Rintelen, the German Military Attaché, brought Mussolini a copy of the message received in OKW on 12 July 1943. See Benito Mussolini, *The Fall of Mussolini, His Own Story*, translated by Frances Frenaye (New York: Farrar Straus, 1948), pp. 37–38.

mands. Discussions soon went beyond the defense of the island and entered the far-reaching problems connected with the Italo-German partnership in the war effort.

Examining the situation at the end of 12 July, *Comando Supremo* determined that the coastal defenses had indeed collapsed and that Axis inferiority in naval and aerial strength had made it relatively easy for the Allies to land additional troops faster and in greater numbers than the Axis countries could hope to match. Since the counterattacks had failed, the only effective defense now appeared to be to wage unrelenting warfare on the Allied sea lanes. But in order to do this, it was imperative to increase the Axis air forces committed to the defense of Sicily. Since Italy had no reserve of planes, Mussolini asked Hitler for help. In an appeal to the Fuehrer, the Duce pointed out that German planes were needed immediately, but only for a short time. Once the crisis in Sicily had been overcome, the aircraft would again be available for other commitments. If Germany really came to Italy's aid and German planes arrived promptly, Mussolini saw some hope for the defense of Sicily. Otherwise, "if we do not throw out the invaders right now, it will be too late." [26]

On 14 July, Mussolini continued to find the situation on Sicily to be disquieting but not irretrievable. Before he would make any further decisions, the Duce wanted to know from *Comando Supremo* exactly what had happened, what the remaining potential was, and how that potential could be increased.[27]

But if Mussolini saw a possibility of saving the situation in Sicily—provided the Germans sent planes and reinforcements—*Comando Supremo* was ready to toss in the sponge. Ambrosio, on 14 July, notified Mussolini that the fate of Sicily had been sealed, and he urged the Duce to consider ending the war to spare Italy further waste and destruction.[28]

In Germany, Hitler's spontaneous reaction upon learning of the Allied invasion had been to send help in the form of the *1st Parachute Division*. But the news immediately after of the failure of the coastal defense troops and the collapse of the *Naval Base Augusta-Syracuse* called for a review of the situation.

Kesselring's telephone report to General Jodl on 13 July described the situation on the island as critical. Because of Allied strength, the failure of the Italian coastal units, and the lack of mobility of the German units, Kesselring said there was no chance to mount another concerted counterattack against the Allied beachheads. The best that could be hoped for was to fight for time. This in itself, Kesselring believed, would be an accomplishment of great importance in view of the detrimental effect the loss of Sicily would have on Italian determination to continue the war. In Kesselring's opinion, all was not yet lost. He proposed to move the remainder of the Ger-

---

[26] Msg 1017/S to *Comando Supremo*, 12 Jul 43, IT 99a, an. 15; Msg 51505, Ambrosio to Generale di Corpo d'Armata Efisio Marras, Italian Military Attaché to the Berlin Embassy, 12 Jul 43, IT 99a, an. 16; Msg, *Comando Supremo* to Kesselring, 12 Jul 43, IT 99a, an. 17; Translation of Msg, Mussolini to Hitler, sent through OKW, in folder *OKL, von Rhoden Collection*, 4576/5; *OKW/WFSt, KTB, 1.-31.VII.43*, 12 and 13 Jul 43 (quotation in entry 13 Jul 43, referring to 12 Jul 43); MS #C-093, OKW Activities, 1 July-30 September 1943 (Warlimont).

[27] Msg, Mussolini to Chief of *Comando Supremo*, 14 Jul 43, in Faldella, *Lo sbarco*, an. 6; Mussolini, *The Fall of Mussolini*, pp. 35–37.

[28] See page 241, note 7.

man parachute division and all of the *29th Panzer Grenadier Division* to Sicily; to reinforce the Luftwaffe; and to increase the number of submarines and small motor boats operating against Allied convoys.[29]

Aware of the danger inherent in fighting a two-front war, Hitler had known for months—at least since the defeats at Stalingrad and in North Africa—that he would have to weaken the Eastern Front if he wanted to strengthen the German position in the Mediterranean. The German offensive to retake Kursk on the Eastern Front—Operation *ZITADELLE*—had started on 5 July, only five days before the Allied invasion of Sicily. But in view of the changed military situation in the Mediterranean, and because of Hitler's wish to have politically reliable troops in Italy, he decided to call off *ZITADELLE* on 13 July. This measure gave Hitler the troops for Italy, including in particular an SS Panzer corps on whose political attitude he could rely.

Although predominantly preoccupied with the events in Russia, Hitler saw the possible loss of Sicily principally in the light of a threat to the Balkans. Moreover, the probable loss of air bases on Sicily would decrease the radius of Axis air activity and increase that of the Allies, thus bringing Allied air power closer to the northern Italian industrial cities as well as to the German homeland.

If the Germans intended to hold on to the Italian mainland as a bulwark against an assault on the Balkan peninsula, or on Germany itself, they could do so only with Italian co-operation. The German high command knew full well that the Italians were tired of the war. Long before, Hitler had planned *ALARICH* to keep the Italians from going over to the Allies. But the invasion of Sicily by strong British and American armies renewed German fears of a possible overthrow of Mussolini and the withdrawal of Italy from the war.

General Jodl felt that Sicily could not be held for any great length of time. He decided that the moment had come to prepare for the defense of the Italian mainland and of the German homeland. He also felt that no German forces should be sent south of the line of the northern Apennines for fear that they would be cut off in the event of a military or political upheaval in Italy. But Kesselring's recommendation to continue the defense of Sicily coincided with Hitler's doctrine of holding whatever territory German soldiers occupied, and Kesselring's recommendation helped override Jodl's objections. Hitler decided to aid his Italian ally. He was prepared to take radical action in case of a political change in Italy, but as long as Mussolini remained in power, Hitler was willing to give him all possible support.

Hitler acknowledged that the German forces on Sicily were, alone, not strong enough to throw the Allies back into the sea, the more so since another Allied landing on the western coast had to be anticipated. He therefore redefined the task of the German troops on the island as "to delay the enemy advance as much as possible and to bring it to a halt in front of the Aetna along a defense line running approximately from San Stefano via Adrano to Catania." In other words, only eastern Sicily was to be held, western Sicily was to be abandoned. Hitler also confirmed the insertion of the *XIV Panzer Corps* under General Hube into the chain of command on the island—without,

---

[29] *OKW/WFSt, KTB. I.-31.VII. 43*, 13 and 14 Jul 43.

however, rescinding his previous orders that the Italians were to hold all tactical commands—and he ordered the rest of the *1st Parachute Division* moved to Sicily. At the same time, the *29th Panzer Grenadier Division* was to move to Reggio di Calabria to await possible transfer to Sicily. The final decision on its transfer across the Strait of Messina would depend on the amount of supplies within the German position on Sicily and on the maintenance of safe traffic across the Strait of Messina. The German *Second Air Force* was to receive three bomber groups (including one night bomber group) as reinforcements. One additional bomber group and a torpedo plane squadron were to be added at a later date. Hitler also ordered eight 210-mm. guns sent to the Strait of Messina, and demanded the addition of German personnel to the crews of the Italian coastal batteries, a measure to which Ambrosio agreed.

Hitler then issued special instructions to the *XIV Panzer Corps*, with the understanding that the instructions were to be kept secret from the Italians and that knowledge of the instructions was to be confined to a restricted group of German officers. Working closely with General von Senger and the German liaison staff then at *Sixth Army*, General Hube was quietly to exclude the Italian command echelons from any further German planning; assume complete direction of operations in the Sicilian bridgehead; and extend his command to the remaining Italian units on the island.

General Jodl, most anxious to save German manpower for the future defense of the Italian and German homelands, enlarged on Hitler's secret instructions. Jodl directed Hube to conduct operations on Sicily with the basic idea of saving as much of the German forces as possible. This, too, was to be kept secret from the Italians.[30]

Kesselring may not have known of Hitler's and Jodl's secret orders to Hube when he informed Ambrosio and Roatta on 14 July that the existing line on Sicily could not be held with the then available Axis forces. After a general withdrawal all along the line, however, the northeastern part of Sicily could be defended on a line between Santo Stefano and Catania. This was in agreement with Guzzoni's views. Kesselring also announced General Hube's transfer to Sicily to assume command of the German forces, and he received assurances from Ambrosio that *Comando Supremo* had issued sharp orders for the restoration of discipline in the Italian Army.[31]

On the next day, 15 July, Mussolini, Ambrosio, Kesselring, and Rintelen met in a conference in Rome. The discussions satisfied no one. Mussolini wanted the proposed defensive line extended farther west to include all of the Madonie Mountains. Ambrosio pressed for the immediate transfer of the *29th Panzer Grenadier Division* to Sicily and for the movement of the *3d Panzer Grenadier Division* into Calabria to protect the toe of Italy. Kesselring had the unpleasant task of explaining that the *29th Panzer Grenadier*

---

[30] MS #T–2 K 1 (Kesselring); MS #T–2 (Fries et al.), p. 22; *OKW/WFSt, KTB. 1.–31.VII.43,* 13–15 Jul 43; quotation and text of Hitler's directive for further warfare in Sicily, 13 Jul 43, in ONI, *Fuehrer Directives, 1942–1945;* German text in Msg, Keitel to *OB SUED,* 13 Jul 43, in folder *OKH, Op Abt, Westliches Mittelmeer, Chefs., 19.V.43–11.VII.44; SKL/1.Abt. KTB, Teil A., 1.–31.VII.43,* 14 Jul 43; Erich von Manstein, *Verlorene Siege* (Bonn: Athenaeum-Verlag, 1955), pp. 501–04.

[31] OKW/WFSt, KTB, 1.–31.VII.43, 15 Jul 43.

*Division* could not be shifted into Sicily until its requisite supplies were assured. Meanwhile, everything should be done to protect the traffic over the Strait of Messina. Ambrosio, holding to his views, urged that since Calabria represented a most delicate zone, the *3d Panzer Grenadier Division* should be moved immediately to that area. Here Kesselring was at a loss. The Fuehrer insisted on holding that particular division near Lake Bolsena to protect the area of Livorno (Leghorn), Kesselring declared, but why Hitler had fears for Leghorn, Kesselring did not know. This concluded the conference.[32] Although no specific decisions had been made, it was evident that at least some of the Axis leaders intended to defend Sicily as long as possible.

On the same day, Kesselring talked with Roatta, the chief of *Superesercito*, about the best place to defend Italy: in Sicily or on the northern Apennines line. Kesselring convinced Roatta that holding a bridgehead on Sicily was imperative for both military and political reasons. The two men then decided to establish a defensive front "around the Etna" from which the Axis forces on Sicily would first offer stubborn resistance and then resume the offensive. Since General Hube was scheduled to arrive in Sicily on this day to take over command of the German troops, Kesselring assured Roatta that in all circumstances the tactical command over the German forces on the island would remain in General Guzzoni's hands. General von Senger was to retain only his function as liaison officer with *Sixth Army*. Kesselring also suggested that Italian units be intermingled with the German divisions, but Roatta deferred a decision on this point. The two generals estimated that the addition of the two German divisions and Hube's corps headquarters would make it possible to hold a front on Sicily, at least until mid-August.[33]

Thus, by 15 July, Kesselring and Guzzoni seemed united in believing that at least a part of Sicily could be held. Kesselring wanted always to fight, as long as there was a chance. Guzzoni wanted to do his duty, but he fully realized that his only effective troops on Sicily were German, and that he would have to depend on full German support to hold even the northeastern corner of the island.

At the higher echelons of Axis military command, this unity of feeling was not so apparent. Ambrosio felt that the war was lost, and he wanted to save the Italian armed forces and to separate Italy from Germany. Jodl did not want to risk having the German forces in Sicily cut off, or to send good money after bad. Mussolini appeared undecided. He wanted to end the war but he needed a tactical success to achieve the proper time for making a peace move. Hitler did not want to withdraw, and he was willing to support Mussolini if the Italians would fight.

On Sicily itself after Kesselring's departure Guzzoni found little good in the situation. *Group Schmalz* was barely holding on to its Lentini positions; the delay in the withdrawal of the bulk of the *Hermann Goering Division* prevented the blocking of the Allied advances toward Francofonte and Vizzini, and made it doubtful that the formation could be moved east fast enough to defend at the

---

[32] Min of Mtg between Mussolini, Kesselring, and others, in Rome, 15 Jul 43, IT 3037. See Faldella, *Lo Sbarco*, p. 191.

[33] Rpt, Confs, Kesselring-Roatta, *OB SUEDWEST, Abt. Ic, 18.VI.43–23.II.44* (*Heeresgruppe C, 75138-28*).

southern edge of the Catania plain. There was, consequently, no assurance against an Allied advance into the Catania plain. Guzzoni did not know when he could expect the *29th Panzer Grenadier Division*. The Italian units had suffered heavy casualties and were exhausted. Italian morale was at a low ebb. The Allies seemed to be exerting their strongest pressure on both wings of the invasion front while, at the same time, maintaining dangerous pressure in the center.

General Guzzoni still expected to form and hold a main defensive line with its eastern hinge south of the Catania plain. Again, on 13 July, he urged the *Hermann Goering Division* to move to the Catania area with the greatest possible speed. Guzzoni also picked this time to define his main battle position farther to the rear, the position which would be held at all costs and from which the Axis forces could return to the initiative. He proposed the line running from Acireale (north of Catania)–Adrano–Cesarò–San Fratello, and he notified *Superesercito* to this effect, adding that he planned to start the withdrawal of the units immediately, delaying as much as possible.[34] *Superesercito* reluctantly consented to Guzzoni's proposal but qualified its approval by stating that such a movement to the rear was authorized only if it should prove impossible to prevent an Allied breakthrough into the Catania plain and only if the new eastern wing would be strong enough to permit Axis units in central and western Sicily to move to eastern Sicily in time.[35]

Just a short time later, though, *Comando Supremo* overrode the army command's approval. The Italian high command insisted that the positions then occupied by *Sixth Army* be held at all costs. Specifically, the Catania plain and the airfields at Catania and Gerbini were to remain in Axis hands. The telephone message transmitting these instructions closed with the remark that "very numerous" German planes were on their way to Sicily.[36]

Because the British 13 Corps was regrouping preparatory to making its major effort that same evening, *Group Schmalz* had little difficulty in holding its positions just south of Lentini on 13 July. Colonel Schmalz received further reinforcements in the form of other units from the *1st Parachute Division*: a parachute machine gun battalion; an airborne engineer battalion; and four batteries of airborne artillery. In addition, two separate German infantry battalions which had crossed into Sicily on the 11th were also attached to his command.[37]

In the late afternoon of 13 July, Colonel Schmalz was able to get through a telephone call to General Conrath. After some discussion, the German commanders agreed that both groups would fall back to a position along the northern rim of the Catania plain, there to make contact on the morning of 15 July. The whole of the *Hermann Goering Division* would then be united and would form its main line of resistance along the line Leonforte-Catenanuova-Gerbini-Catania. For the remainder of 13 and 14 July, Colonel

---

[34] IT 99a, 13 Jul 43; Faldella, *Lo sbarco*, pp. 170, 190–201.

[35] IT 99a, an. 20 and entry, 13 Jul 43 (no time given, but apparently late at night, 13 Jul 43).

[36] IT 99a, an. 21, 13 Jul 43.

[37] Schmalz in MS #T-2 (Fries *et al.*), pp. 77–79 and sketch III; OKH, *Tagesmeldungen West*, 14 and 15 Jul 43; maps, *Sizilien*, (1:200,000), *WFSt Op. (H)*, 11, 12, and 13 Jul 43.

Schmalz would have to hold where he was.[38]

By late evening of 13 July, the *Hermann Goering Division* completed its withdrawal to the Caltagirone-Vizzini line, although it kept strong elements south of that line to blunt the various American thrusts inland from Niscemi, Biscari, and Comiso. The Italian *Livorno Division* also withdrew further into the interior to establish a new line between the two German divisions and to prevent a possible American breakthrough at Piazza Armerina.

In the *15th Panzer Grenadier Division* area, the German units had little trouble holding their new line on 13 July. Only minor actions took place between American patrols and the German and Italian units. *Group Fullriede*, still under General Schreiber's control, extended its front eastward toward Caltanissetta. *Group Ens* remained along a line running from Piazza Armerina to Pietraperzia. Sometime during the late evening of 12 July, General Rodt, the division commander, received word from *Sixth Army* to prepare to withdraw to the new line of resistance south of Mount Etna. The division was to fight delaying actions back to a new line which extended from Agira-Leonforte-Nicosia-Gangi, and at the same time establish contact with the *Hermann Goering Division* across the remnants of the *Livorno Division*. Accordingly, General Rodt moved his division headquarters to Grottacalda (two and a half miles southwest of Valguarnera) and started to transfer the division's service elements to the new line.[39]

The Axis defenses were giving way, but they were not crumbling. The Allies had yet to conquer Sicily.

---

[38] Schmalz in MS #T-2 (Fries *et al.*), p. 79.

[39] MS #R-140, p. 35, n. 52; Faldella, *Lo sbarco*, pp. 170, 179-80, 189-90; *OB SUED, Meldugen*, 13 Jul 43, Third Report; 13 Jul 43, Fourth Report. The date of the order to Rodt's division is not clear. General Rodt, in MS #C-077, says 12 July; Senger, in MS #C-095, says 15 July; Faldella says 0800, 15 July 1943. Map, *Sizilien* (1:200,000), *WFSt OP. (H)*, 15 July 1943, indicates that the withdrawal was either planned or under way. It appears logical that the date listed by Rodt is the correct date, since this would tie in with Guzzoni's plan to withdraw to a shorter defensive line south of Mount Etna.

CHAPTER XII

# Seventh Army Changes Directions

*The Eighth Army Attempt To Break Through*

General Montgomery's major effort to break through into Catania got under way on the evening of 13 July when Commando units landed and seized the Lentini bridge soon after dark. Though the commandos removed the demolition charges from the bridge, the Germans soon drove off the British raiders.

The airborne operation (code named FUSTIAN) on the same evening to seize the Primosole bridge (seven miles south of Catania) over the Simeto River and establish a bridgehead on the river's north bank suffered double bad luck. In the first place, the American and British troop carrier pilots ran into heavy antiaircraft fire from Allied ships massed along the southeastern shores of Sicily. A route supposedly cleared proved to be replete with ships, and the aircraft began to receive fire from the time they rounded Malta. Off Cape Passero, the real trouble started—more than one-half of the aircraft reported receiving fire from friendly naval vessels. Though only two troop carriers were hit and downed, nine turned back after injuries to pilots or damage to planes. Those aircraft that flew on soon ran into what seemed to be a solid wall of antiaircraft fire thrown up by the enemy along the coast line. A large number of the pilots lost formation and circled up and down the coast trying to find a way through the fire into the four drop zones. Ten more aircraft turned back, each with a full load of British paratroopers. Eighty-seven pilots managed to thread their way through the fire, but only 39 of these dropped their paratroopers within a mile of the drop zones. All but four of the remainder managed to get their sticks within ten miles of the Primosole bridge; the other four sticks landed on the slopes of Mount Etna, about twenty miles away. Of the 1,900 men of the British 1st Parachute Brigade who jumped into Sicily on the evening of 13 July, only about two hundred men with three antitank guns reached the bridge. Though they seized it and removed the demolition charges, they comprised a dangerously small contingent for holding the bridge until the ground forces arrived.

The second piece of bad luck was that the main drop came in almost on top of the machine gun battalion of the German *1st Parachute Division*. The German paratroopers themselves had jumped just north of the river only a few hours earlier, and they reacted in a savage manner. Yet the little band of British paratroopers managed to hold on to the bridge all day long. At nightfall, the paratroopers withdrew to a ridge on the south bank of the river, where they could cover the bridge with fire and prevent the Germans from damaging it.[1]

General Montgomery's main assault was executed by the 50th Division and a brigade of tanks against the *Group Schmalz* Lentini positions. On the afternoon of 14 July, some of the British tanks worked their way between the German positions along Highway 114 and the two German parachute battalions east of the highway, thereby threatening to isolate the paratroopers from the rest of the German battle group. Colonel Schmalz, who had been apprehensive all along of being outflanked and cut off from withdrawal, decided to leave the Lentini positions and fall back faster than he had anticipated. Leaving small delaying forces behind, he pulled back in two steps, first, eight miles to the north behind the Gornalunga River, then, early on 15 July, three miles farther north behind the Simeto River. (*See Map VI.*)

In the wake of the German withdrawal, the British 50th Division moved forward readily and joined the British paratroopers at the southern end of the Primosole bridge. A thrust north of the river on 15 July netted nothing. Additional German reinforcements rushed forward to strengthen the Simeto line, and Colonel Schmalz finally made contact with the bulk of the *Hermann Goering Division*. On 16 July, a heavier British attack regained the bridge that the Germans had been unable to destroy and pushed a shallow bridgehead across the river, extending it by the 17th to a depth of 3,000 yards. Another attack by the 50th Division during the night of 17 July made little headway. The British had failed to break Schmalz's Catania defenses. The Germans were in strong positions, and after the 17th they felt certain they could block the east coast road.[2]

*The II Corps Front*

The bulk of the *Hermann Goering Division*, retiring to the northeast to gain contact with Colonel Schmalz's battle group, had not had an easy time making it back to the Simeto River line. Successful on 13 July in holding General Guzzoni's intermediate defensive line along Highway 124, the division began to run into trouble on the 14th. The Germans had to contend not only with American attacks against the entire front from Caltagirone on the west to Vizzini on the east, they also had to face the British 30 Corps attacking along the axis of the highway toward Vizzini.

Opposite the eastern flank of the German division, Colonel Ankcorn, the 157th

---

[1] Warren, USAF Hist Study 74, pp. 47–54; *By Air to Battle*, pp. 60–64; Montgomery, *Eighth Army*, p. 100. See also 99–66.2, sub: AFHQ Report of Allied Forces Airborne Board in Connection With the Invasion of Sicily; 0100/4/78, sub: Airborne Operations in HUSKY; 0100/21/1072, sub: Airborne Employment, Operation, and Movement of Troops, vol. 2; NAAFTCC Rpt of Opns; Alexander Despatch, p. 23. Cf. B. H. Liddell Hart, *The Other Side of the Hill*, rev. ed. (London: Cassell, 1951), p. 355; *OB SUED, Meldungen*, 14–16 Jul 43 (implicit testimony of the toughness of the British paratroopers); Schmalz in MS #T-2 (Fries *et al.*), pages 11–12 criticizes the operation as incorrect use of paratroopers. FUSTIAN started with 145 aircraft, 126 carrying paratroopers, 19 towing gliders. There were 1,856 paratroopers and 77 glider-borne artillerymen starting out on the mission.

[2] *OB SUED, Meldungen*, 15 Jul 43, Second Report; Schmalz in MS #T-2 (Fries *et al.*), p. sub: Airborne Operations in HUSKY; 0100/21/ George Aris, *The Fifth British Division, 1939–1945* (London: The Fifth Division Benevolent Fund, 1959), pp. 123–25.

RCT commander, found himself on the evening of 13 July in a rather uncomfortable position: his forces were between the British on the south and east and the Germans to the north. By this time, through British liaison officers, Colonel Ankcorn knew that the British 30 Corps was intent on taking Vizzini. Ankcorn had no objection. He pulled one battalion away from Vizzini and sent it to occupy the high ground northeast of Licodia Eubea. He assembled the rest of his combat team in the same general area.

On the morning of the 14th, Colonel Ankcorn again made contact with the British south of Vizzini. Despite a two-pronged advance, the 30 Corps was having some trouble securing Vizzini. An attack during the night by the British 51st Division had been thrown back, as had another by the armored brigade in the early morning. Together with British officers, Colonel Ankcorn surveyed the situation at Vizzini and agreed to furnish what support he could to the British 51st Highlanders in a renewed attempt to wrest that town from the Germans' grasp. Returning to his command post at Monterosso Almo, Colonel Ankcorn reached up to an abandoned Italian railway car, tore off an old shipping ticket, and across the back of the ticket scrawled a note to Colonel Murphy, the 1st Battalion commander: "Murphy, go help the British." [3]

From positions northeast of Licodia, Murphy's 1st Battalion struck at Vizzini at noon in conjunction with the renewed British attempt from the south and east.

The added weight of the American battalion, ably supported by the 158th Field Artillery Battalion, was not enough. As on the day before, the Germans, fighting to hold their withdrawal route open, threw back every Allied thrust.

Staunch opposition also developed from the *Hermann Goering* elements west of Vizzini. Early in the morning, a strong German tank-infantry force struck the leading battalion of the 179th RCT. Close-in fighting raged throughout the morning, additional infantry and artillery units finally turning the tide. Resuming its advance, the 179th reached a point just two miles south of Grammichele by nightfall.[4]

On the favorable side, the sag that had existed on the left of the II Corps zone straightened out nicely on 14 July after Darby's Ranger force took Butera. A typical Sicilian town with feudal antecedents, Butera lies on high, almost inaccessible ground, an objective to intrigue the military imagination. Flouting an old tradition that previous conquerors of Sicily had always bypassed the town, the Rangers occupied Butera after a swift night approach and a dash into the center of town past startled Italian defenders.[5]

On the right side of the sag, the 180th RCT finally secured Biscari airfield, despite several strong German counterat-

---

[3] *The Fighting Forty-Fifth*, compiled and edited by the Historical Board (Baton Rouge, La.: Army and Navy Publishing Co., 1946), p. 23; *History of the 157th Infantry Regiment*, p. 25; 45th Inf Div G-3 Jnl, entries 34, 42, 43, 51, 14 Jul 43.

[4] Maj. Ellsworth Cundiff, The Operations of the 3d Battalion, 179th Infantry, 13–14 July 1943, South of Grammichele, Sicily: Personal Experience of a Regimental S-2 (Fort Benning, Ga., 1948); Infantry Combat, pt. V: Sicily, pp. 8–14; 179th Inf Regt AAR, 14 Jul 43; 179th Inf Regt S-3 Jnl, 14 Jul 43; 45th Inf Div G-3 Jnl, 14 Jul 43; 753d Med Tk Bn AAR, 14 Jul 43.

[5] 1st Ranger Bn AAR, 14 Jul 43; Remarks by Col Darby to Col R. F. McEldowney, 12 Oct 43, in Rpt, AGF Bd NATO, 8 Nov 43, sub: Remarks Regarding Ranger Force, 4-1.67/43.

BUTERA, taken by Darby's Rangers to straighten the sag in the center of the II Corps Line, 14 July.

tacks which came after two infantry battalions gained the field by surprise. The German counterattacks persisted throughout most of the day, but were all turned back. Toward evening, the Germans began pulling back to the north and the 180th set out in pursuit. Its leading battalion finally caught up with the Germans early the next morning at the very outskirts of Caltagirone.[6]

In the center, that is, in the vicinity of Niscemi in the 1st Division's sector, the line also pushed forward, not because of any action by the 16th RCT but because of the general withdrawal of the German forces to the northeast. Though the town of Niscemi remained a hot spot during the morning, by early afternoon the rate of enemy firing decreased and 16th Infantry patrols moved almost into Caltagirone before meeting German resistance. The 16th Infantry did not follow up this advantage; the advance of friendly units to the east and west made the move unnecessary.

While inclined to keep the 16th RCT in position, General Allen was in no way disposed to let the retiring enemy get away without some action. Early on 14 July— a few hours after the Rangers jumped Butera—the 26th RCT moved toward Mazzarino, its Yellow Line objective. The 26th met little opposition—the *Livorno Division's* few remaining battalions had withdrawn the previous evening—and before noon consolidated on high ground north and west of Mazzarino. With the 26th RCT pushed out this far, General Allen ordered the 18th RCT straight north toward Bivio Gigliotto—the juncture point of Highways 117 and 124— to secure the 26th's right flank. By late afternoon, the 18th RCT came to rest on two high hills, some two miles south of the road junction.[7]

By early morning of 15 July, then, both the 1st and 45th Divisions stood at or near the Seventh Army's Yellow Line across the entire II Corps front. But in the higher echelons of American command, the impact of General Alexander's directive of 13 July to Seventh Army began to be felt. At II Corps headquarters just before 0900, 14 July, General Bradley received from Seventh Army a general outline of the army group's order. Accordingly, before going to the army headquarters to receive the specifics, General Bradley notified the 45th Division to halt its forward units at least two miles south of Highway 124: that road was now in the British zone and had been turned over to General Montgomery. General Bradley later visited the 1st Division and left the same instructions.[8] Still later, American artillery units were instructed not to fire within an area extending from one mile south of the highway north to and past the highway, this to prevent the artillery from firing on British troops.[9]

The initial effect of these orders was slight. Only the 157th RCT had by then come within two miles of Highway 124. General Bradley's instructions stopped the 179th and 180th RCT's from entering Grammichele and Caltagirone, although the 2d Battalion, 180th Infantry, had quite a tussle with the Germans in the southern outskirts of Caltagirone early on the morning of 15 July. Since the 26th

---
[6] 180th Inf Regt AAR, 14–15 Jul 43; Infantry Combat, pt. V: Sicily, pp. 4–8, 14–16; 753d Med Tk Bn AAR, 14 Jul 43.

[7] AAR's of 16th, 18th, and 26th Inf Regts; S–1 Jnls of the same units; 1st Inf Div G–3 Jnl, 14 Jul 43.
[8] 45th Inf Div G–3 Jnl, entries 28 and 29, 14 Jul 43; 1st Inf Div G–3 Jnl, entry 37, 14 Jul 43.
[9] 45th Inf Div Arty Jnl, entry 19, 14 Jul 43.

RCT stood on its Yellow Line objective at Mazzarino, it was in no way bothered by the change of plans. On the other hand, the new instructions would have affected at least one American unit on 15 July had not the 1st Division commander, General Allen, chosen to persist in his advance. The 18th RCT, striking for Bivio Gigliotto, had just a little way to go before reaching the highway. General Allen declined, apparently with General Bradley's tacit approval, to halt the 18th RCT two miles south of the highway. On the morning of 15 July, the 18th RCT continued its advance and after mauling a battalion from the *Livorno Division* in a cork tree grove just south of the road junction (taking 200 prisoners and 11 artillery pieces in the process) sent patrols into Bivio Gigliotto. Only there did General Allen halt the combat team.[10]

The American thrusts caused General Conrath to become increasingly worried about his situation. News in the late afternoon of 14 July of *Group Schmalz's* withdrawal from the Lentini positions along the east coast highway deepened his concern, for this move left the *Hermann Goering Division's* left flank open. Conrath therefore decided to take the bulk of his division back in one movement, not pausing to defend until after he reached the Simeto River line. When Conrath notified the *XVI Corps* of his decision, the corps chief of staff, with *Sixth Army's* approval, went to General Conrath's headquarters near Caltagirone and begged the German commander to hold the Vizzini-Caltagirone line through 15 July so that the Axis troops holding the remainder of the front would have time to withdraw. Conrath agreed.[11] But later in the day, General von Senger, urged by Kesselring to strengthen the endangered eastern wing by weakening the center, ordered the *Hermann Goering Division* to move immediately to the Catania area.[12]

With General Conrath's verbal agreement, *Sixth Army* formally ordered the German division to stay in the Vizzini-Caltagirone line until nightfall on 15 July. During that night, the division was to move back to the Gornalunga-Raddusa line, starting its movement with its eastern wing. The *Livorno Division* was also to withdraw at the same time, adjusting its movements to those of the German division.[13]

Not long afterwards, General Conrath reported to *XVI Corps* that Allied pressure made it impossible for him to hold his positions along Highway 124. *Sixth Army* then authorized General Conrath to start his withdrawal.

In the confusion of the previous contradictory orders, beset by the British and the Americans, apprehensive of his eastern flank, unable to contact the *15th Panzer Grenadier Division* to the west, Conrath ordered his units to withdraw immediately. In executing this withdrawal, elements of the division in Vizzini and Caltagirone lost several tanks and suffered light casualties during the morning of 15 July. The bulk of the division moved to the rear in good order and took up positions (along with *Group Schmalz*) on a line from the mouth of the Simeto River along the Dittaino River to Castel

---

[10] 18th Inf Regt AAR, 15 Jul 43; 1st Inf Div G-3 Jnl, 15 Jul 43. There is no indication of disapproval of General Allen's actions in the records.

[11] MS #R-140 (Bauer), pp. 36-37.
[12] MS #C-095 (Senger), *KTB* entry, 2330, 14 Jul 43.
[13] Faldella, *Lo sbarco*, pp. 174-75.

Judica and Raddusa, with outposts further south. On its right, a wide gap separated these troops from the *15th Panzer Grenadier Division*, which stuck far out to the south.[14]

The tenacious defense put up by the Germans in Vizzini caused another change in plans for the the British 30 Corps. Although the armored brigade and the 51st Division entered Vizzini early on 15 July, the two British units had been severely strained in the process. Aware of this even before the town fell, General Leese, the corps commander, ordered the 1st Canadian Division to pass through the 51st Division and press on to Enna.

At 0600, 15 July, one Canadian brigade moved west along Highway 124 toward Grammichele. Unfortunately, the 45th Division's artillery was silenced by the previous day's order and could provide no assistance. The 157th and 179th RCT's could only watch helplessly as the Germans, then pulling out to the northeast, massed a small rear guard to block the Canadian approach.[15] At 0900, as the Canadian advance guard neared Grammichele, which was situated on a high ridge well above the surrounding countryside, it was halted by German tank and antitank guns firing at almost pointblank range. Not until noon were the Canadians able to clear the road center.

Pushing on to the west, but delayed by mines along the road, the Canadians entered an undefended Caltagirone by midnight. General Montgomery, his major effort on the east coast stalled at the Simeto River, then ordered the 30 Corps to push on "with all speed to Valguarnera-Enna-Leonforte." [16]

*Agrigento*

General Patton paid his first visit to the 3d Division shortly after noon on 14 July and told General Truscott something of his future plans. With his eyes set on Palermo, Patton said he would need Porto Empedocle to support such a drive. But because of the limitations imposed by General Alexander, Patton declared, the Seventh Army could not attack the port in strength for fear of becoming involved in a costly battle which might expose the Eighth Army's left flank to an Axis counterattack.

General Truscott, who with army approval had already conducted one small-scale reconnaissance effort against Agrigento and Porto Empedocle on the 13th, felt that the 3d Division could take both towns without too much trouble. All he needed was General Patton's approval. The Seventh Army commander agreed to another reconnaissance in force, this time in greater strength than the one battalion used previously. But Patton specified that the move was to be made on Truscott's own responsibility. For General Truscott, there was much to gain and little to lose. If he could take Agrigento and Porto Empedocle, everybody would be happy. If he failed, he nevertheless would have gained valuable information on the status of the enemy's defenses.[17]

Porto Empedocle serves Agrigento in somewhat the same fashion as Piraeus

---

[14] Faldella, *Lo sbarco*, p. 175; *II/Pz. Regt. H.G., KTB Nr. 1, 9.XI.42–15.IX.43*, copy in folder OCMH X-878.

[15] 45th Inf Div Arty AAR, pp. 3-4.

[16] Quoted in Nicholson, *The Canadians in Italy*, p. 92.

[17] Truscott, *Command Missions*, pp. 218–19; Patton, *War As I Knew It*, p. 380; Lucas Diary, pt. I, p. 71.

AGRIGENTO AND THE SURROUNDING HIGH GROUND

serves Athens. A town of 14,000 people, Porto Empedocle had a town mole, almost completely surrounded by two breakwaters jutting from a narrow shelf of land slightly above sea level. On the eastern and western sides of town, abrupt cliffs rose in some places two hundred feet or so above the level of the shelf, and parts of the residential area faced the sea on these heights. In the center of town, a deep ravine cut through the cliffs to the lower shelf, sharply dividing the upper part of town into eastern and western halves. The daily capacity of the port was 800 tons, approximately the same as that of Licata.

Agrigento, a city of some 34,000 inhabitants, was perched on a hilltop about three miles from the coast. Seventeen miles west of Palma di Montechiaro and twenty-two miles southwest of Canicattì, Agrigento was the most important road center along the southwestern coast of Sicily. Highway 115 connected Agrigento with Licata and Gela. Highway 122 linked it to Caltanissetta, Canicattì, and Favara.

For the Seventh Army, Agrigento represented the gateway to western Sicily. From there, Highway 115 continued northwestward along the coast to Marsala and Trapani; Highway 118 zigzagged northward over the mountains through Raffadali, Prizzi, and Corleone to the north coast and Palermo. Veering at first northeastward, a second-class road also led to the north coast by way of the inland towns of Conistini and Lercara Friddi. The seizure of Agrigento thus was essential for a drive on Palermo, while Porto Empedocle would give Seventh Army a port twenty-five miles closer to its front.

General Patton's preoccupation with Palermo amounted to an obsession. Porto Empedocle was a logical objective in terms of augmenting the minor capacities of Gela and Licata. But with Porto Empedocle in hand, why Palermo, too? Perhaps he thought of a rapid, dramatic thrust to draw public attention to the capabilities of U.S. armor. Perhaps it was the only objective that could compensate partially for having been relegated the mission of acting as Alexander's shield. "Palermo," General Truscott would write after the war, "drew Patton like a lode star." [18]

The 1st Battalion, 7th Infantry, which had conducted the reconnaissance toward Agrigento on 13 July, had reported considerable enemy artillery defending Agrigento along the eastern perimeter. There appeared to be at least twelve direct fire, high-velocity weapons and one or more battalions of field artillery positioned against an approach along Highway 115. Too, the enemy appeared dug in east of Agrigento along the Naro River. Although General Truscott estimated the enemy's infantry strength at no more than one coastal regiment—a fairly accurate appraisal—he ruled out a frontal assault because of the strength of the enemy ar-

---

[18] Truscott, *Command Missions*, p. 222. Truscott remarks elsewhere: "It was perfectly clear to me why General Patton was obsessed with Palermo, it had been made so by all planning connected with the Sicilian operation from the first. . . . The reasons had also been made clear in many discussions with both General Patton and General Keyes. . . . General Patton made no secret of the fact that he was not only desirous of emulating Rommel's reputation as a leader of armor, he wanted to exceed it. General Patton was also anxious for the U.S. armor to achieve some notice. . . . The capture of Palermo by an armored sweep through western Sicily appeared to suit this purpose. . . ." Comments of Lt. Gen. Lucian K. Truscott, Jr. (Ret.) on MS.

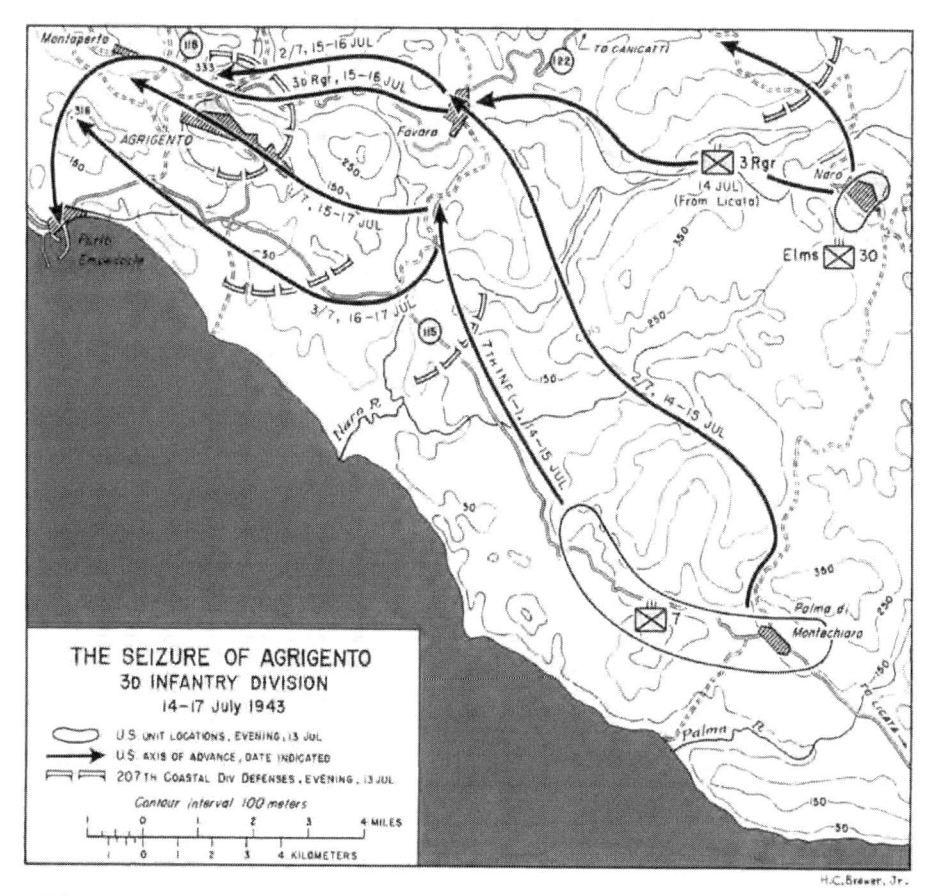

MAP 2. THE SEIZURE OF AGRIGENTO, 3D INFANTRY DIVISION, 14–17 July 1943

tillery. He determined instead on a flanking movement to strike at Agrigento from the northeast by way of Favara on Highway 122. To do the job, General Truscott selected the 7th Infantry Regiment, the 10th Field Artillery Battalion, and one battalion from the 77th Field Artillery Regiment.[19]

The route to Favara had already been checked by a company of the 7th Infantry that had worked its way cross-country during the night of 13 July, entered Favara early the next morning, and stayed there. Basing his decision on the information sent back by this company, General Truscott directed Colonel Sherman, the 7th Infantry commander, to move two battalions in the company's path, one to go all the way into Favara, the other to advance on the north side of Highway 115 to high ground before the Naro River. (*Map 2*) The 3d Ranger Battalion, which was in division reserve, was to move to Favara, then reconnoiter to the west of Agrigento.

[19] 3d Inf Div FO 8, 14 Jul 43; Truscott, *Command Missions*, p. 219.

Until the ground troops could get within striking distance of both towns, the enemy was to be allowed no rest. The Navy agreed to furnish the maximum possible gunfire support. Since 12 July, the cruisers *Birmingham* and *Brooklyn* had been firing missions against Agrigento and Porto Empedocle. On 14 July, the *Birmingham* concentrated on Italian shore batteries, and as the foot troops moved out to the new areas that night, the British monitor, H.M.S. *Abercrombie,* joined the *Birmingham*. The next day, the guns of the *Philadelphia* added their fires.[20]

Before daylight on 15 July, the two infantry battalions occupied their objectives without difficulty. Now General Truscott attached the Ranger battalion to the 7th Infantry and ordered a continuation of the reconnaissance effort against Agrigento. That night the 3d Ranger Battalion was to move from Favara to the little town of Montaperto, situated on commanding ground northwest of Agrigento. The 2d Battalion, 7th Infantry, at Favara was to move on Agrigento to take Hill 333, which commanded the northern approaches into Agrigento. These two moves would block the northern and western exits from Agrigento. Then the 1st Battalion, 7th Infantry, along Highway 115 was to push straight to the west, cross the Naro River, and drive on Agrigento. Only one change was made in this plan: after taking Montaperto, the 3d Ranger Battalion was to swing south over Hill 316 to take Porto Empedocle.

As night fell on 15 July, the Rangers moved out from Favara. Though they came under scattered artillery fire, they suffered no casualties. A half hour after midnight, 16 July, the Rangers ran into an Italian roadblock just east of the junction of Highways 122 and 118. While scouts uncovered the Italian position, Maj. Herman W. Dammer, the Ranger battalion commander, deployed his men and sent them in. Within an hour the action was over; one hundred and sixty-five Italians surrendered.

At daylight, 16 July, Major Dammer started his men westward cross-country toward Montaperto. The Rangers had crossed Highway 118 and were on high ground some two hundred yards west of it when an enemy column composed of ten motorcycles and two truckloads of troops came unsuspectingly down the highway toward Agrigento. Deploying along the high ground, the Rangers permitted the enemy force—all Italians—to come fully abreast before opening fire. The first shots threw the enemy column into complete confusion. Many Italians were killed; forty were added to the bag of prisoners.

Without further incident, the Rangers moved into Montaperto. From the hilltop, they had a commanding view of the valley below where four batteries of Italian artillery were emplaced. Major Dammer quickly set up his 60-mm. mortars and opened fire. Individual Rangers joined in with their small arms. Though a few Italians escaped toward the south, most came up the hill with hands held high.

Meanwhile, the two battalions of riflemen from the 7th Infantry were execut-

---

[20] Rpt, Lt (jg) H. C. Manning, USN, to 3d Inf Div, 23 Jul 43, sub: Naval Gunfire Support for the JOSS Attack Force During HUSKY Opn, in 3d Inf Div file, Special Material; Rpt, 3d Inf Div Arty to CG 3d Inf Div, 25 Aug 43, sub: Rpt of Naval Gunfire Support Joss Force, same file; 10th FA Bn AAR, 14 and 15 Jul 43; ONI, Sicilian Campaign, pp. 98-99; Morison, *Sicily—Salerno—Anzio,* pp. 174-75.

THE VERSATILE DUKW *bringing in supplies to Seventh Infantry troops in Port Empedocle.*

ing their roles in what was euphemistically called a reconnaissance in force. The 2d Battalion, advancing westward along Highway 122 from Favara, gained two hills about a thousand yards east of its objective by 0900. Little resistance was encountered, but loss of contact with the Rangers and spotty communications with combat team headquarters prompted Major Duvall, the battalion commander, to hold his attack until he could further develop the situation to his front and flanks. The 1st Battalion, along Highway 115, was having a hard fight trying to get into Agrigento. After dark on 15 July, Colonel Moore, the battalion commander, sent his men across the Naro River and onto three barren hills which fronted the city. His companies soon found themselves hotly engaged with Italian infantrymen representing parts of two infantry battalions. By early afternoon of 16 July the 1st Battalion was still unable to move forward.

In the early afternoon, General Truscott ordered the 3d Battalion, which had been in reserve, to move south of Highway 115 to assist the 1st Battalion. Just after 1400, Colonel Heintges led his 3d Battalion down to the highway. Quickly, the battalion finished off one of the Italian forces opposing the 1st Battalion. Together the two battalions started for Agrigento, as Italian resistance slowly crumbled. In Agrigento, Colonel de Laurentiis, commander of the defense forces, was undergoing some trying moments. His command post had been the object of heavy Allied naval and ground bombardments during the day. By early afternoon of 16 July all of the Italian artillery batteries had been silenced. Fires had broken out in many places. The town was completely enveloped. The Americans were nearing the town. Finally, after the 1st Battalion had broken into the city proper, Colonel de Laurentiis, his staff, and his troops surrendered to Colonel Moore. By this time, too, Porto Empedocle had fallen to the Rangers.[21]

*Army Directive of 15 July 1943*

The 7th Infantry's thrust against Agrigento and Porto Empedocle was only one of a number of events growing out of General Alexander's directive of 13 July, which turned the Seventh Army's axis of advance from the north to the west. On 15 July, even as the 7th Infantry's reconnaissance in force gathered momentum, General Patton outlined his plan and issued his instructions for executing the army group's order. Apparently still anticipating a drive on Palermo, he rearranged his forces in the belief that he could win sanction for a thrust to the north coast. While recognizing the initial line of advance as spelled out by General Alexander to be a line from Caltanissetta to Palma (a line already outstripped by the 3d Division), General Patton extended the army boundary past Enna (where General Alexander's army boundary stopped) to the north coast just west of Santo Stefano di Camastra. Within this new zone, he disposed his forces under two corps headquarters, the existing II Corps and a newly created Provisional Corps. To each of the corps, General Patton assigned roughly one-half of the new zone of operations.

The right sector, running from just east of Serradifalco to Mussomeli, Lercara Friddi, Marineo, and Palermo, went to General Bradley's II Corps. The newly organized Provisional Corps, under the command of General Keyes, the Seventh Army deputy commander, took over the left sector. To the new corps went the 3d Infantry Division, minus CCA and other supporting units; the 82d Airborne Division; units from the 9th Infantry Division; and artillery units which had been supporting the 3d Division. The 3d Division was to continue on its mission of taking Agrigento and Porto Empedocle and of securing Highway 122 in its sector before passing to Provisional Corps control. The 2d Armored Division was to form the army reserve.

Once the II Corps had shifted the 45th Division from the east to the west of the 1st Division, the divisions were to drive

---

[21] 7th Inf Regt S-3 Rpts, 14-17 Jul 43; 7th Inf Regt S-3 Jnl, 14-17 Jul 43; 3d Inf Div G-3 Jnl, 14-17 Jul 43; 10th FA Bn, 77th FA Regt, 3d Inf Div Arty, and 3d Ranger Bn AAR's; Truscott, *Command Missions*, pp. 217-21; Morison, *Sicily—Salerno—Anzio*, pp. 174-76; Lt Col Roy E. Moore, A Reconnaissance in Force at Agrigento, Sicily, 12-16 July 1943 (Command and General Staff College, Fort Leavenworth, Kansas, 1947); Maj Edward B. Kitchens, Operations of the 3d Ranger Infantry Battalion in the Landings at Licata and Subsequent Attack on Porto Empedocle, 10-17 July 1943 (Fort Benning, Ga.: 1950); MS #R-141, Withdrawal, Second Phase (12-21 July 1943), ch. XI of Axis Tactical Operations in Sicily (Bauer), pp. 1-10.

In an action west of Agrigento, 1st Lt. David C. Waybur, 3d Reconnaissance Troop, 3d Infantry Division, earned the Medal of Honor when, though seriously wounded, he stood in the middle of a road and opened fire with a submachine gun on a column of Italian tanks. Waybur knocked out the leading tank and brought the others to a halt. See 3d Recon Troop AAR, 16 Jul 43.

to the northwest to secure Caltanissetta and a stretch of Highway 122 by nightfall on 19 July. Expecting the 3d Division to secure the line Serradifalco-Agrigento by dark on 17 July (which was an extension forward of the army group's contemplated line), General Patton directed the 82d Airborne Division, plus the 9th Division's units then on the island, to relieve the 3d Division along Highway 115 by dark on 19 July as a first step in continuing the drive to the west. The 2d Armored Division was to be prepared to exploit any offensive operation toward the north coast, operating principally in the Provisional Corps zone.[22]

Thus, General Patton apparently hoped that by the end of 19 July the situation on the island would have developed sufficiently to enable the Seventh Army to start on a thrust to the north coast. As indicated by the extension of the army boundary past Enna, General Patton was not thinking at this time of Messina as a Seventh Army objective. Seventh Army, of course, could not launch out to the west until General Alexander gave approval. But General Patton fully intended to be ready to go as soon as General Montgomery had firmly established the Eighth Army on a line from Catania to Enna.

General Bradley, with the problem of pulling his front apart and putting it together again, started the 45th Division to a new assembly area near Riesi on 16 July. Thus, the 1st Division became the right guide for the Seventh Army, responsible for maintaining contact with the British on the right. Since the east boundary of the "Enna loop" belonged to the British, the 1st Division's axis of advance was along an axis to the west of that boundary, cutting the middle of the loop roughly parallel to the Salso River.

The 26th RCT, on 15 July, held the old Yellow Line positions on the hills in and around Mazzarino and was astride a secondary north-south road that paralleled Highway 117 and joined Highway 122 about midway between Enna and Caltanissetta. The latter road was the division objective and the 26th RCT had a direct line of advance to it. Because of the rough terrain ahead, General Allen ordered the combat team to advance on 16 July by leapfrogging battalions. Barrafranca was the first intermediate objective. The 16th RCT shuttled over from Niscemi, while the 18th RCT, after making contact with the 1st Canadian Division along Highway 117, began moving south to follow the division's main axis of advance.

On the first day of the advance, the 26th RCT quickly developed a pitched battle with *Group Ens* at a point just forward of Barrafranca. Because the retiring Germans had not destroyed the bridge north of Mazzarino, the 1st Battalion, 26th Infantry, had no trouble crossing. The mile and a half stretch before the road entered the plain in front of the first intermediate objective was also traversed without incident. But from this point on, German reaction to the advance became heavy.

From the approach taken by the 1st Battalion, the town of Barrafranca gave the impression of being "over behind" rather than "up on top" the high ground. Pocketed in a hill plateau, the town was shielded by lower hill masses west of the Mazzarino road. At the town's left front, a stream made a corridor from

---

[22] Seventh Army Directive, 15 Jul 43, in Seventh Army Rpt of Opns, p. D-7, and map to accompany directive, p. D-8.

the Mazzarino road to a traverse road at the rear, and below this narrow valley a line of lesser hills screened the town from a larger plain. Barrafranca was well suited for defense. The Germans, expert in such matters, had dug in well, and controlled all approaches and most of the plain where tanks could be employed. The Germans sat in positions of their own choosing, looking down the throat of the American advance.

On reaching the plain in front of Barrafranca, the 1st Battalion swung to the left of the road and took position on Hill 432, close to the road. The 2d Battalion bypassed to the left of the 1st Battalion and moved on Hill 504. Here, the 2d Battalion came under heavy fire from positions west of the town and was driven back. Meanwhile, the 3d Battalion entered the low line of hills to the right of the road, fronting the plain. From these low hills, covered by Hills 432 and 504 on the left, the 3d Battalion was to debouch onto the plain and advance on Barrafranca in a frontal attack. But even as the 2d Battalion fought to get Hill 504, the Germans sent a column of tanks down into the plain toward the 3d Battalion. American light tanks (the 70th Light Tank Battalion) from positions on the rim of Hill 432 opened fire on the German tanks, but their guns were not heavy enough to be effective and a number of the light tanks lost out in the ensuing encounter.

Though three supporting artillery battalions opened a steady fire on the approaching German armor, the advance was not halted. Unable to counter the tanks from its exposed positions on the low hills, the 3d Battalion pulled back across the road to Hill 432 where it tied in with the 1st Battalion and where the remaining light tanks continued their efforts to slow down the enemy armor. The 3d Battalion's withdrawal also permitted the supporting artillery battalions to turn the plain into a killing zone. Concentration after concentration patterned the plain. Slowly the enemy drew back to Barrafranca; eight German tanks lay smoldering in the fields.

In the afternoon, the reorganized 1st and 3d Battalions again made for Barrafranca. Their advance was unopposed; the Germans had gone. Immediately, the 16th RCT moved up to keep the pressure on the withdrawing enemy. That night the 16th passed through Barrafranca, leapfrogged the 26th RCT, and pushed on to Pietraperzia. Though they met some resistance, the advance detachments occupied the high ground northeast of the town. Late on 17 July, the 16th forced a crossing over the Salso River and reached Highway 122.[23]

The 1st Division's advance from Mazzarino was closely paralleled by that of the 45th Division. Faced with the extremely difficult task of moving his combat teams from the far east of the Seventh Army sector facing north to the center of the Seventh Army sector facing west, General Middleton, the 45th Division commander, at daylight on 16 July began to move his units, pulling them from right to left away from Highway 124.[24] The 157th RCT was the first to move; its front had been the first uncovered by

---

[23] 16th, 18th, and 26th Inf Regt AAR's; 1st Inf Div G-3 Jnl; 753d Med Tk Bn AAR; 70th Lt Tk Bn AAR; 33d FA Bn AAR; 1st Inf Div Arty AAR.

[24] As General Middleton points out, the move had to be made through the rear areas of the 1st Division and over a limited road net. See comments by Lt Gen Troy H. Middleton (Ret.) on MS.

the 1st Canadian Division thrust along Highway 124. On trucks borrowed from other units throughout the II Corps zone, the combat team was forced to retrace its steps south to Highway 115, through Gela, and then northwest toward its new sector. At midnight, 16 July, after a ride of almost ninety miles, the 157th RCT reached Mazzarino. Close behind came the 753d Medium Tank Battalion and two battalions of division artillery.

Four hours later, at 0400, 17 July, the 157th jumped off in the attack. It passed through Pietraperzia, already cleared by the 1st Division, and went up to the Salso River where a demolished bridge stopped its advance. By nightfall crossing sites had been reconnoitered, and at 0100 on 18 July the 157th RCT crossed with Caltanissetta as the first objective and, if opposition proved weak, Santa Caterina (another ten miles away) the final objective.

The attack met no serious opposition. By 1600, Caltanissetta was secured and three hours later Santa Caterina fell. Practically the only opposition came when patrols pushing out from Santa Caterina along Highway 121 ran into a strong, Italian-defended roadblock which had been established the day before at Portella di Recattivo, one of several bottlenecks on the highway. There was no town here, but the road at this point had narrow curves and a steep incline. Moreover, it was close to one of the rare side roads which ran through the barren, hilly area to Highway 120, and thus was an important point for the enemy to hold.[25]

The rest of the 45th Division, following the same difficult route traversed by the 157th RCT, closed in the Caltanissetta area on 18 July. From all appearances, and though it was now held up at Portella di Reccativo, the 157th had scored a clean breakthrough of the enemy's defensive line and little or no resistance appeared to confront the division farther to the west. In contrast to the 1st Division, which confronted the Enna loop and an apparently strong enemy force, the 45th Division appeared ready for a dash on Palermo.[26]

The Germans had indeed fallen back. General Rodt, commander of the *15th Panzer Grenadier Division*, had received orders from General Guzzoni to withdraw northeastward and to take up a defensive line running from Agira to Leonforte and on to Nicosia and Gangi to block an American advance from the west into the Catania area. As an additional measure, Guzzoni ordered *Group Schreiber* (minus *Group Fullriede*, which returned to Rodt's control) to pull back from Serradifalco to Alimena and Portella di Reccativo to hold the roads open for the passage of the German division. By evening of 17 July, *Group Schreiber* was in position and fighting off the 157th RCT thrust from Santa Caterina.

General Rodt had started his rearward movement during the evening of 16 July. *Group Ens* drew back from Barrafranca, passed Valguarnera, and by daylight, 17 July, was in positions in the hills northeast and northwest of that town, opposing the advance of the 1st Canadian Division. *Group Fullriede* by that same morning had fallen back to a westward-

---

[25] 157th Inf Regt AAR, 18 Jul 43; MS #R-141 (Bauer), pp. 30–33. The designation "Portella" which appears frequently on Sicilian maps —literally translated "narrow passage"—indicates a particularly difficult spot in the road net.

[26] 157th, 179th, and 180th Inf Regt AAR's; 45th Inf Div G-3 Jnl; 45th Inf Div Arty AAR; II Corps Rpt of Opns.

SIGNAL CORPS LINEMEN *setting up wire installations in Caltanissetta, 18 July.*

facing salient running from the southwest to the northwest of Enna in line with the Imera River. From these positions, the German unit could maintain fire on the 1st Division advancing across the base of the Enna loop.[27]

---

[27] Nicholson, *The Canadians in Italy*, pp. 93–95; Faldella, *Lo sbarco*, pp. 192–95, 201–04; MS #C-095 (Senger); IT 99a, 16 Jul 43; MS #C-077 (Rodt); *OB SUED, Meldungen*, 16 Jul 43, Second Report, and 17 Jul 43, First Report; Rpt, Liaison Staff at *Sixth Army* to OKH, 17 Jul 43, *OB SUED, Meldungen*.

## Discord and Harmony

Even as General Patton prepared to thrust to Palermo, General Alexander became increasingly worried about the problems of clearing the Messina peninsula—the "long, mountainous, isosceles triangle with the great mass of Etna filling its base."[28] The German withdrawal from the west to a strong defensive line across the base of the peninsula was becoming apparent, and General Alexander was

---

[28] Alexander Despatch, p. 12.

anxious for the British Eighth Army to strike hard around both sides of Mount Etna before the Germans could get set.[29]

With this hope in mind, the army group commander on 16 July issued a new directive. In reality, this was nothing more than a modification of his 13 July order, slight at best, made to conform with what appeared to be a quick Eighth Army sweep around the western slopes of Mount Etna and the failure of the British 13 Corps to break through to Catania on the east coast. General Alexander for the first time spelled out his plan to exploit from the "firm line"—a term he used to refer to positioning Eighth Army along a line from Catania in the east to Enna in the west.

General Montgomery was to drive into the Messina peninsula along three main axes: along the east coast road through Catania; to Adrano on Highway 121 in order to cut the enemy's lateral communications; and from Nicosia around the western slopes of Mount Etna. If the 30 Corps could reach the north coast and cut the island in two, General Montgomery would no longer have to fear an attack against his left flank and could concentrate on getting to Messina.

The major task of the Seventh Army, its only task, was to protect the Eighth Army's rear. General Patton was to do this by securing the Enna loop area, which would cut important roads, and by advancing to the north coast on the British left. Apparently ignorant of General Truscott's reconnaissance in force, by then substantially completed, General Alexander authorized the seizure of Agrigento and Porto Empedocle. As for Palermo, or even the lesser course of moving beyond Agrigento, Alexander said nothing. For Patton and Bradley, the outlook seemed dim. Montgomery was to get the first prize, Messina; the Americans were to be denied even the consolation prize, Palermo.[30]

Having accepted General Alexander's earlier directive without audible comment, Patton was "mad as a wet hen" when he got the new directive. What rankled was not the assignment of Messina to the British (and with it assignment of three of the four main roads leading to Messina) but what he considered a slight to the U.S. Army: the passive mission of guarding Montgomery's rear. The directive also knocked out Patton's hope of gobbling up Palermo.

After conferring with General Keyes, Maj. Gen. John P. Lucas, Brig. Gen. Albert C. Wedemeyer, and Brig. Gen. Hobart R. Gay, Patton decided to protest his assigned mission, and he did so by presenting an alternate plan whereby the Seventh Army would make an enveloping attack on Palermo through Castelvetrano (sixty-eight miles west of Agrigento) and Corleone (fifty-eight miles northwest of Agrigento). Impinging in no way on Montgomery's operations, the plan led the Americans westward toward the only objective of consequence after Messina, Palermo.

---

[29] Ibid.; Intervs, Mathews with Alexander, 10–15 Jan 43, pp. 11, 15.

[30] Seventh Army Rpt of Opns, p. D–9; Alexander Despatch, p. 12; Nicholson, *The Canadians in Italy*, pp. 88, 92; Truscott, *Command Missions*, p. 221; Bradley, *A Soldier's Story*, p. 140; Seventh Army G–3 Jnl, entry 1, 17 Jul 43. The directive was received in Seventh Army's headquarters at 2355, 16 July 1943.

Montgomery (*Eighth Army*, page 102) states that Alexander decided on this course of action on 15 July.

Meeting with Alexander in La Marsa, Tunisia, on 17 July, Patton argued his case. Since the enemy had been knocked back, he declared, aggressive action was not only imperative but the only way to give Montgomery complete protection of his left flank and rear. An American drive to Palermo would split the enemy forces irreparably. Alexander reluctantly agreed and gave his consent to Patton's proposal.

At the same time, General Lucas was meeting with Maj. Gen. Lowell Rooks, the AFHQ G-3, General Eisenhower being absent from Algiers on that day. Not until General Eisenhower returned on the 20th could Lucas unburden his soul. By then his resentment over seeming British determination to keep the Americans in a secondary role had been erased by news that Alexander had accepted Patton's plan. In any case, Lucas thought the situation was rapidly becoming dangerous and that something should be done about it. General Eisenhower stated that he had never encountered a case where the British had deliberately tried to put something over on the Americans. In the circumstances, Eisenhower continued, Alexander should not be blamed for being cautious. But, said Eisenhower, Patton should be made to realize that "he must stand up to Alexander" or else Eisenhower would relieve Patton from his command.[31]

Whereas there was widespread indignation among American officers regarding the original scheme of maneuver, British officers apparently were hardly aware of this feeling. Patton was the only American officer to raise the point about pushing out to the west, and until he went to Alexander the army group commander did not know how strongly the Americans felt about carrying out only a passive role. When confronted with this sentiment, Alexander realized that he probably could not restrain Patton indefinitely from pushing out; if he waited too long Patton would probably say, "To hell with this," and push out anyway. With the situation then developing and with the enemy withdrawing into the Messina peninsula, Alexander was now willing to go along with Patton's plan, albeit reluctantly.[32]

Somewhat paradoxically, even as the element of disunity emerged between the British and Americans, the politically enforced co-operation between Germans and Italians on Sicily was going through a period of relative calm. Two command changes in the German structure might have led to friction, but both took place smoothly.

The first was the arrival on 15 July of General Hube, *XIV Panzer Corps* commander, who was to take charge of all the German forces on the island. On the same day, Kesselring gave Colonel Baade increased responsibility for protecting the Messina Strait.[33]

---

[31] Lucas Diary, pt. I, pp. 82–83; Patton, *War As I Knew It,* p. 380; Bradley, *A Soldier's Story,* pp. 140, 144; Butcher, *My Three Years with Eisenhower,* p. 368; OPD 201 Wedemeyer, A. C., 201 Security, case 5; Seventh Army Rpt of Opns, p. D-10 (a true copy of the map showing Patton's proposed plan).

[32] Intervs, Mathews with Alexander, 10–15 Jan 43, pp. 15–16.

[33] *OKW/WFSt, KTB, 1.–31.VII.43,* 15 Jul 43; *ibid.,* 14 Jul 43. For organization of the German ferrying service, see MS #R-146, Facts, Figures, and Thoughts, ch. XVII of Axis Tactical Operations in Sicily, July–August 1943 (Bauer), pp. 27–38. See also Capt. S. W. Roskill, "History of the Second World War, United Kingdom Military Series," *The War at Sea, 1939–1945,* vol. III, pt. I, 1 June 1943–31 May 1944 (London: Her Majesty's Stationery Office, 1960), pp. 143–46.

After establishing his command post in the eastern portion of the island, Hube reported to General Guzzoni on 16 July and was briefed on Guzzoni's plans for the Italian *XVI Corps* to organize the Etna line as a final defensive line behind temporary positions toward which the Axis forces were then moving. When the two German divisions reached the forward defenses, Hube was to supplant General von Senger but remain under Guzzoni's tactical control.[34]

Kesselring, too, visited Guzzoni's *Sixth Army* headquarters that day. He found no fault with Guzzoni's plans, both for deploying the troops in Sicily and for holding the Etna line. The two divisions in Hube's corps, the *Hermann Goering* and the *15th Panzer Grenadier*, were to be held in reserve for counteroffensive operations provided they were not needed to man the line itself, though Kesselring agreed to let the latter relieve the *Livorno Division* in the line so that the Italian unit could have needed rest and rehabilitation. Kesselring promised to try to reinforce the troops on Sicily by dispatching units from the Italian mainland, and Guzzoni promised to capture the initiative as soon as possible. As a result of conversations during two days, Kesselring and Guzzoni, though aware that the Allies might resort to additional amphibious operations, agreed that they would not evacuate the island of Sicily.[35]

To forestall command difficulties, Guzzoni entrusted Hube's *XIV Panzer Corps* with the eastern sector of the front. He gave the Italian *XII Corps* responsibility for the western half. He placed the Italian *XVI Corps* in reserve and in command of the northeastern portion of Sicily, where it was to receive and process units expected from the mainland, in particular the *29th Panzer Grenadier Division*.[36]

Another problem Guzzoni tried to deal with was the Italian ferry service across the Strait of Messina. Though the Germans operated an independent ferry service with utmost regularity and started to move the *29th Panzer Grenadier Division* to Sicily (as authorized by Hitler on 19 July), the Italian movements were on the verge of breakdown. From all over Italy came Sicilians, including military personnel on leave, who converged on Reggio di Calabria, demanding transportation to the island on the pretext of defending their homeland. Many who reached the island disappeared at once, presumably having rushed off to join their families. Other Italian troops in Sicily used all their ingenuity to move in the other direction. In an attempt to tighten the water service, Guzzoni urged the *Naval Base Messina* commander to enforce rigid discipline and regulate traffic across the strait in the strictest conformance with military necessity.[37]

Meanwhile, during the evening of 16

---

[34] Faldella, *Lo sbarco*, pp. 202–03, 220–21; Min, *Riunione a Palazzo Venezia del 15.7.1943*, IT 3037; IT 99a, an. 31, and map, 15 Jul 43; MS #C-095 (Senger); see *OB SUED, Meldungen* for the dates in question. A description of the over-all situation as seen in OKW is contained in *OKW/WFSt, KTB, 1.-31.VII.43*, 15 Jul 43.

[35] *Comando Supremo*, Liaison Staff with *OB SUED*, 18 Jul 43, sub: Notes on Conversation With Kesselring, 16, 17 Jul 43, IT 99a, an. 42; Telg, *Armed Forces Command, Sicily to Comando Supremo*, 0020, 18 Jul 43, IT 99a, an. 43.

[36] IT 99a, an. 51, signed Guzzoni. Effective 2400, 18 July 1943, Hube assumed tactical command over the *Hermann Goering*, the *15th Panzer Grenadier*, and the *Livorno Divisions*.

[37] Faldella, *Lo sbarco*, pp. 203–04; IT 99a.

July, Guzzoni learned of the fall of Agrigento. The way was now open to the Americans to advance and cut off all the remainder of the *XII Corps*. The last moment had obviously come to move these forces to the east. Early on the following morning, Guzzoni ordered the *XII Corps* to begin withdrawing immediately to a defensive line running from Nicosia west along Highway 120 to Cerda. Two coastal divisions were to be left in place to ward off any Allied amphibious attack.

The *XII Corps* thus had to execute a difficult tactical maneuver. The major units—the *Assietta* and *Aosta Divisions*—mobile in name only, had to make flanking movements from the west to east across the spearheads of the American columns advancing toward Palermo and the north coast. To defend Palermo, Guzzoni ordered Generale di Divisione Giovanni Marciani, commander of the *208th Coastal Division*, to take charge of all coastal units in and around Palermo and to keep the Palermo-Cerda portion of Highway 113 open. All told, the Italians had almost 60,000 men in the western portion of Sicily, including the units at the Palermo and Marsala naval bases.[38]

The aura of accord between Italians and Germans in the face of adversity as demonstrated on Sicily failed to extend back to the Continent. Here, rifts in Italo-German unity widened to great proportions.

---
[38] Faldella, *Lo sbarco*, pp. 204–06.

# CHAPTER XIII

# The Drive to the Climax

*The Feltre Conference*

In the early summer of 1943 Benito Mussolini's hopes and plans were all based on a successful resistance to an Allied invasion of the Italian homeland. Though convinced that the Axis had lost the war, he was caught in the dilemma between Hitler's insistence on continuing the war and the Allied demand for unconditional surrender. The only solution seemed to be Victor Emmanuel's, for the King had, in May, given Mussolini three memorandums suggesting a separation from Germany as a means of terminating the war.[1] Mussolini's halfhearted efforts to convince Hitler of the need for peace had failed. Perhaps the Western Allies might relent in their demand for absolute defeat. Mussolini had therefore asked the King to give him three more months to prepare for a peace move.[2]

The Under Secretary of Foreign Affairs, Bastianini, on 15 June had presented the Duce with a memorandum suggesting the close collaboration of Italy with the Danubian countries as the path to a political solution of the war. On 1 July, when Mussolini met with Ion Antonescu, and listened to the Rumanian premier speak long and openly in advocating a joint approach to the Western Powers, he apparently agreed except with respect to the timing. What he needed, he said, was a better bargaining position, an improved military situation, a time when the Italian Army would have repulsed the then impending invasion of Sicily or Sardinia. Sometime later that month, though neither his political nor his military situation had ameliorated, he orally requested his ambassador at Madrid, the Marchese Giacomo Paulucci di Calboli, to sound out the Western Powers on a compromise peace.[3]

The King, with great confidence in Mussolini's political skill, gave no encouragement to those who since February had suggested the dismissal or arrest of the Duce in order to save Italy from total defeat. The King considered Mussolini much better qualified to achieve a compromise peace than any of his possible successors.

The entire Fascist propaganda system in early July turned to the theme of an impassioned defense of the homeland by the Italian armed forces and people. However indifferently the Italian soldier had previously fought in overseas theaters, Mussolini fully expected an improvement

---
[1] See above, pp. 43–44.
[2] MS #P-058, 1 Feb–8 Sep 43, Question 3.
[3] Bova Scoppa, *Colloqui con due dittatori*, pp. 112–15; Gheorghe Barbul, *Mémorial Antonesco: le III<sup>e</sup> Homme de l'Axe* (Paris: Éditions de la Couronne, 1950), vol. I, p. 98; Cf. Andreas Hillgruber, *Hitler, König Carol und Marschall Antonescu: Die deutsch-rumänischen Beziehungen 1938–1944* (Wiesbaden: Franz Steiner Verlag, 1954), p. 171.

in fighting morale when the war reached Italian soil. He himself definitely proclaimed that the invaders would be hurled back at the shore line.[4]

Always a journalist and therefore tending to regard the published account of an event as of equivalent importance to the action itself, Mussolini helped delude the Italian people with optimistic initial bulletins on the campaign in Sicily. The third bulletin, which on 12 July conceded the Allied occupation of the coast line from Licata to Augusta, pricked the bubble of popular enthusiasm and faith.[5] With Allied success a rude jolt not only for the Italian people but for the Duce himself, who had believed his own propaganda, Mussolini had sent his impassioned plea to Germany for rescue.

To Hitler and the OKW the complete failure of the defense of Sicily appeared to be due essentially to the collapse of the Italian armed forces—the refusal of the Italian units to fight. Colonel Schmalz had submitted through channels a critical report on the conduct of Contrammiraglio Priamo Leonardi at Augusta, accusing Leonardi of blowing up his guns and throwing his ammunition into the sea before the Allies arrived. Forwarding this report to Mussolini, OKW seemed to request Leonardi's punishment. In a personal reply to Mussolini's message for help, Hitler declared that he shared the view of the seriousness of the developments in Sicily, promised additional planes, but sharply criticized the faulty Italian ground organization for its failure to provide for protective dispersal of planes on the ground: "In the last three weeks alone in Sicily and southern Italy," he wrote, "there have been more than 320 fighter planes destroyed on the ground as a result of enemy aerial attack, a majority of which could have been employed against the enemy." [6]

Mussolini swallowed the bitter cup and on the same day that he received Hitler's message, 13 July, he assured Field Marshal Kesselring that the *XIV Panzer Corps* might be committed in Sicily.

The *Comando Supremo,* much closer to the visible manifestations of Anglo-American power than the OKW, now concluded that continuation of the war was without military justification. In a memorandum presented to Mussolini on 14 July, Ambrosio stated:

The fate of Sicily must be considered sealed within a more or less brief period.

The essential reasons for the rapid collapse are: the absolute lack of naval opposition and the weak aerial opposition during the approach to the coast, the debarkation, the penetration of the adversary and during our counter offensive reactions; the inadequacy of the armament and of the distribution of our coastal divisions; the scarcity and lack of strength of our defensive works; the slight efficiency (armament and mobility) of Italian reserve divisions.

It is useless to search for the causes of this state of affairs: they are the result of three years of war begun with scanty means and during which the few resources have been burned up in Africa, in Russia, in the Balkans.

The memorandum continued by stating that the Allies would be able to invade the Italian peninsula at will, unless the main weight of the Axis effort were shifted to the Mediterranean. A second

---

[4] Rintelen, *Bundesgenosse,* pp. 199, 206–07; Badoglio, *Memorie e documenti,* pp. 63–64; Westphal, *Heer in Fesseln,* p. 215.
[5] Mussolini, *Storia di un anno,* p. 11.

[6] Translation of Msg, Mussolini to Hitler, sent through OKW, in folder *OKL, von Rhoden Collection, 4576/5;* Msg, Hitler to Mussolini (Italian translation), 13 Jul 43, IT 3029, folder V, an. 1.

front would be opened up with the invasion of Italy, and as long as the Russian campaign continued there was no hope of Axis victory unless the constitution of such a second land front could be prevented. If not, "it pertained to the highest political authorities to consider if it be not appropriate to spare the country further fighting and defeats, and to anticipate the end of the struggle, given that the final result will undoubtedly be worse within one or a few years." What the *Comando Supremo* hoped for was that a meeting of the Duce and the Fuehrer could be arranged for a real showdown.[7]

Hitler's immediate military advisers in OKW also hoped for a showdown, for they were disgusted with the feeble Italian resistance in Sicily, with the ineptitude of Mussolini's government, and with the perpetual bickerings of *Comando Supremo*. On 14 July the OKW revised and brought up to date plans *ALARICH* (occupation of northern Italy by Rommel's *Army Group B*) and *KONSTANTIN* (reinforcement of German troops in the Balkans and Greece).[8]

On 15 July, Jodl had reached the conclusion that Sicily could probably not be held. He advocated evacuating the troops from the island. Together with Rommel, he prepared a memorandum suggesting that Hitler make certain demands of Mussolini: for full unity of command in the Mediterranean theater under the Duce; for this supreme command over both German and Italian ground forces to be entrusted to a German commander in chief, most likely Rommel; for the key positions in *Comando Supremo* to be filled with officers whom the Germans considered competent and trustworthy; and for a unified command of the air forces under Feldmarschall Wolfram Freiherr von Richthofen.[9]

Meeting on 17 July with Doenitz, Keitel, Jodl, Rommel (who was present only during part of the conference), and others, Hitler admitted that Sicily could not be held. The units were to be denied no supplies, but ultimately they would have to withdraw. For the moment, until the issues with Italy were clarified, the *29th Panzer Grenadier Division* was not to be moved to Sicily. If Italy collapsed politically, the Germans would execute *ALARICH* and take over the positions formerly held by Italian units. In this case, the Germans would have to withdraw to a shorter line in Italy, for "without the Italian army we cannot hold the entire Italian peninsula." If there was no political collapse in Italy, the Germans could defend the entire Italian peninsula, but only with Mussolini's full support. Jodl accordingly urged Hitler to present Mussolini with his memorandum of 15 July as an ultimatum. Or, Hitler had to convince the Duce of the need to take radical measures to improve Italian morale. The Italian Army was demoralized, Hitler declared, and only the most severe measures, like those taken by the French in 1917 or by Stalin in 1941, could save it. As for the com-

---

[7] *Comando Supremo, Appunto per il Duce, Prospettive operative nell' eventualità di perdita della Sicilia,* 14 Jul 43, IT 112 (another copy in IT 3029, folder VI). The concluding paragraph of the memorandum is printed in Francesco Rossi, *Come arrivammo all' armistizio* (Cernusco sul Naviglio: Garzanti, 1946), p. 41.

[8] *OKW/WFSt, KTB, 1.-31.VII.43,* 14 Jul 43.

[9] *OKW/WFSt, KTB, 1.-31.VII.43,* 15 Jul 43; MS #C-093 (Warlimont), pp. 27-29. Some inkling of this German plan reached the Italian Government. See Simoni, *Berlino, Ambasciata,* pp. 359-60; Dino Alfieri, *Due dittatori di fronte* (Milan: Rizzoli, 1948), p. 306.

petent Italian officers available, Rommel mentioned Roatta. Though the Germans considered him abler than the others, they did not trust him and thought him devoid of character. Hans Georg von Mackensen, Ambassador to Italy, suggested—and Hitler decided to say nothing about it to Mussolini—that Rommel become the German commander in chief in Italy. Still hoping that the Fuehrer would present an ultimatum to Mussolini and secure unified command under a German general, Jodl urged the value of a political revolution in Italy that would eliminate the monarchy and retain Mussolini in full power.[10]

On 18 July Mussolini adopted the view of the *Comando Supremo* and sent Hitler a long telegram. He refuted the charge that the Italian units had failed to fight; he criticized the delay in the dispatch of German reinforcements. The final paragraphs, which followed closely the *Comando Supremo*'s memorandum of 14 July, were ominous:

In Italy the enemy has opened up the second front on which the enormous offensive possibilities of England and America will be concentrated, not only to conquer Italy but also to open up the Balkan route precisely at the moment in which Germany is heavily committed on the Russian front.

The sacrifice of my country cannot have as its principal purpose that of delaying a direct attack on Germany.

Germany is stronger economically and militarily than Italy. My country, which entered the war three years earlier than was foreseen and after it already had engaged in two wars, has step by step exhausted itself, burning up its resources in Africa, Russia, and the Balkans.

I believe, Fuehrer, that the time has come for us to examine the situation together attentively, in order to draw from it the consequences conforming to our common interests and to those of each of our countries.[11]

It was not, then, that the faithful Duce's work was being sabotaged by his incompetent collaborators as Hitler had hitherto preferred to believe: Mussolini himself was weakening. The Fuehrer immediately forgot his fears of being poisoned and discarded the scruples which had restrained him since the spring from visiting Italy. In the greatest haste arrangements were made for a new meeting of the two dictators at Feltre in northern Italy. Hitler's whole purpose was to put Mussolini back on the rails. For this reason he discarded the tentative plans for an ultimatum demanding German command in the Italian theater. In his own peculiar fashion Hitler again prepared to treat Mussolini with deference, to reinfuse him with faith in ultimate Axis victory, to concentrate his criticisms on the work of Mussolini's subordinates, and at the same time to offer whatever was possible in the way of German reinforcements.[12]

Mussolini was accompanied to Feltre by Ambrosio and Bastianini. Ambassador Dino Alfieri flew down from Berlin. The Italian delegation was not briefed in advance: neither the military men nor the diplomats had any knowledge of the purpose of the meeting. The military men,

---

[10] Min of Conf of CinC with Fuehrer at Hq Wolfsschanze, 17 Jul 43, ONI, *Fuehrer Conferences, 1943;* Field Marshal Erwin Rommel, Private KTB, 9 May 1943–6 September 1943, entries for 17 and 18 July, copy in OCMH (X-743).

[11] Telg, Mussolini to Hitler, 18 Jul 43, IT 3029. Rossi, in *Come arrivammo,* page 42, prints the final sentences of this telegram, states that it was drafted in the *Comando Supremo* and presented to Mussolini on 18 July, but doubts that it was sent. It is filed in a folder marked *Scambio messagi fra Fuehrer e Duce,* and the folder heading describes it as *telescritto allegato 2,* which would indicate that it was sent.

[12] MS #C-093 (Warlimont), pp. 32–33.

however, had shown Mussolini the complete military weakness of Italy, and had prepared him for a frank declaration to Hitler that Italy could not continue the war.

The plenary session consisted of one item: a harangue by Hitler which lasted a couple of hours and left everyone but himself worn out. Hitler made it quite clear that the faulty Italian ground organization was responsible for plane losses in Sicily and southern Italy.

"If, as had happened," he declared, "some 300 or 400 machines out of 500 or 600 were destroyed on the ground, that meant that the organization was bad." The Fuehrer said it was "absolutely intolerable that in Sicily, through unskillful and unsoldierly conduct of the ground personnel, on one day 27 machines should have been destroyed on the ground and on another day 25."

Turning to the question of Sicily, Hitler said that "he was of two minds on this subject. If it were possible to insure the supply line, Sicily should be defended and at a certain point the defense should be transformed into an attack." He advised that Reichsmarshall Goering was prepared to concentrate a large number of flak batteries at Messina. It would be far better, Hitler urged, to fight the decisive battle in Sicily rather than in Italy. If such a decision were made, "Germany would send superior troops down there. Such a decision required great capacity in the way of leadership. What was now done in Sicily could not be recalled. Many German units must be despatched down there in order first to establish a defensive front and, following that, a front suitable for an attack." Italy, in such a case, should send additional divisions. Germany, Hitler said, did not have 2,000 planes available but would send two special bomber groups.[13]

During the course of Hitler's speech reports were brought in to Mussolini that the Americans were bombing Rome. Following a few questions by the Italian representatives the session ended. Hitler and Mussolini then had lunch together, apart from the rest.

Ambrosio was perplexed and disillusioned. After the luncheon he, Bastianini, and Alfieri saw Mussolini and bitterly reproached him for his silence. They urged that it was his duty to save Italy from the situation into which he had plunged it, and that he should take the opportunity which still remained for direct contact with Hitler and explain the true situation. Mussolini, a sick man, listened impassively—made some dry remarks—but failed to pluck up his courage.[14]

Ambrosio had two discussions with Keitel during the course of the Feltre Conference. During the automobile trip from the Treviso airfield to the Villa Gaggia at Feltre the conversation was a brief bit of fencing, Ambrosio revealing what was in his mind and Keitel what was in Hitler's. Keitel asked for infor-

---

[13] "Memorandum of Conversation Between the Fuehrer and the Duce in North Italy on July 19, 1943," (translation from the German) U.S. Department of State *Bulletin*, XV, No. 349 (6 October 1946) 607–14, 639; *Breve sintesi questioni militari trattate al convegno di Feltre 19 luglio 1943*, IT 3031, II; *Relazione sopra le dichiarazioni del Fuehrer in occasione del suo incontro col Duce nell' Italia settentrionale il 19/7/1943*, IT 3029. With some artful deletions of Hitler's sharpest specific criticisms, this document is printed by Rossi, in *Come arrivammo*, pages 324–35.

[14] MS #P-058, 1 Feb–8 Sep 43, Question 1; Alfieri, *Due dittatori*, pp. 314–16. See also: Castellano, *Come firmai*, pp. 55–56; Badoglio, *Memorie e documenti*, pp. 64–65; Simoni, *Berlino, Ambasciata*, pp. 367–68.

mation regarding Sicily and Ambrosio asked how things were going on the Russian front. The German replied in substance that they were wearing the Russians down. "This," said Ambrosio, "is not an active program but the renunciation of the initiative in operations. In substance the Axis is besieged, it is closed in a ring; it is necessary to get out. What prospects have you for doing this?" The question was eluded and the subject switched back to the Mediterranean.[15]

On the return trip Keitel again rode with Ambrosio, and, at Hitler's orders, the discussion was confined to those matters which Hitler had mentioned in his speech. If Italy would contribute two additional divisions, preferably Alpine divisions, then Germany, said Keitel, was prepared to send two additional divisions to reinforce Sicily and southern Italy. It was up to Italy to decide whether or not Sicily would be defended to the limit. Keitel declared that the two additional German divisions would be sent immediately once the Italian High Command made the decision to fight to the limit in Sicily. There were three essential points on which the OKW would insist:

(1) From the tactical point of view, the increase of the forces so as to permit the forming of a strong line and withdrawal of the mobile forces (*15th Panzer Grenadier Division* and *Hermann Goering Division*) to a secondary line;

(2) From the operational point of view, the assurance of supplies and the creation of a strong defense in Calabria and Puglia;

(3) From the organizational point of view, firmness and rigor in arrangements giving maximum liberty to the military authorities of southern Italy for organizing and strengthening the defense—aviation fields, railroads, roads, depots, etc.

Keitel reiterated the demand for a formal pledge by Italy to fight to the limit in Sicily and to accept the three points. Ambrosio promised to examine the possibility of sending two additional Italian divisions to Calabria. But as to the three points, which concerned the civil power, the decision would be placed before Mussolini.[16]

## Planning the Western Sweep

This friction on the Axis side obviously could not be so quickly nor so happily resolved as the relatively minor discord in the Allied camp. Having returned during the evening of 17 July from his visit to General Alexander's headquarters in North Africa, General Patton the next day issued his directive spelling out Palermo as the Seventh Army objective. General Bradley's II Corps (the 1st and 45th Divisions) was assigned a dual mission. First of all, using the 1st Division, the corps was to gain control of the western half of the Enna loop (the eastern half of the loop and Enna belonged to the Eighth Army). Thereupon, the 1st Division was to strike for the north coast along the axis Alimena-Petralia-Cefalù, thus paralleling the advance of the British 30 Corps, which was expected to reach the north coast by using the axis

---

[15] *Comando Supremo*, 20 July 1943, *Convegno di Feltre (19 luglio 1943): Sintesi primo colloquio Ecc. Ambrosio Mar. Keitel*, IT 3029, folder VII, an. 3. Rossi, in *Come arrivammo*, pages 335-36 prints a portion of this document, but his whole document, (pages 335-38) is incomplete and is a fusion of the record of two separate discussions.

[16] *Comando Supremo*, 20 July 1943, *Convegno di Feltre*, IT 3029, folder VII, an. 4; OKW/WFSt, KTB, I.VII.-31.VII.43, 19 Jul 43; Cf. Rossi, *Come arrivammo*, pp. 336-38.

# THE DRIVE TO THE CLIMAX

of Highway 117 through Enna–Nicosia–Santo Stefano di Camastra.

Meanwhile, the 45th Division was to advance to the northwest toward Palermo, using Highway 121 as its main axis of advance. Once the division reached the north coast road, it was to wheel to the west and, if necessary, strike at Palermo. II Corps' eastern boundary, and the army's as well, was a line running due north from Enna to the north coast just west of Santo Stefano di Camastra. The corps' western boundary, and the boundary with the Provisional Corps, ran from Serradifalco (entered by the 3d Division on 18 July) northwestward to Palermo, paralleling Highway 121.

On the II Corps left, the Provisional Corps was assigned the zone from Highway 121 (exclusive) on the east to the sea on the west and north. With the 82d Airborne and 3d Infantry Divisions, General Keyes was to advance on Palermo from the south and southwest. The 2d Armored Division was to remain in army reserve, follow the Provisional Corps advance, and be prepared to exploit a breakthrough or to extend the envelopment of Palermo to the west.

General Patton designated three phase lines for control purposes, but he specified that the units were not to stop unless ordered to do so. He expected to coordinate the final assault on Palermo himself, and he planned to use the 2d Armored Division for the final thrust into the city.[17]

Though the mountains in western Sicily are not high or rugged, they are not easy to cross. A network of secondary roads, spaced at intervals of about twenty miles, are good near the coast but become progressively poorer inland. Following the intermediate slopes and ridges rather than the valleys because of winter floods, the roads are easily blocked by demolition work. The towns, located on hilltops or on the upper slopes of the mountains, are difficult to approach, for the access roads are usually steep. The Platani and Belice Rivers, though insignificant as water courses during the dry summer season, run through valleys which offer excellent sites for interrupting road traffic. The Salso River, a potential barrier, had already been crossed by the 1st and 45th Divisions. The mountainous terrain and the poor road network would constitute the main obstacles to a rapid advance.

Seventh Army intelligence officers painted a picture of fluidity on 19 July, noting the difficulty of locating the enemy front. They deemed the Italian units capable of only limited defensive action, but the Germans might be dangerous, even though they seemed to have withdrawn from the entire Seventh Army front in favor of final defensive positions protecting Messina.[18]

Four hours after Patton ordered the advance to Palermo, Seventh Army received General Alexander's written confirmation of approval. But instead of giving Patton *carte blanche*, Alexander imposed certain restrictions, conditions which he had not indicated to Patton during the conference the preceding day. Now Alexander said go ahead, and exploit, but first, capture Petralia; then send detachments to the

---

[17] Seventh Army Directive, 18 Jul 43, in Seventh Army Rpt of Opns, p. D-11, with accompanying opns map on p. D-12; Truscott, *Command Missions*, p. 222; Harry H. Semmes, *Portrait of Patton* (New York: Appleton-Century-Crofts, Inc., 1955), p. 162.

[18] Seventh Army Periodic Rpt 9, 19 Jul 43; G-2, G-3 Jnl, Prov Corps, 16-21 Jul 43.

north coast from Petralia, cutting the island in two at Campofelice, eleven miles west of Cefalù; and, finally, establish the Seventh Army along a line running from Campofelice on the north coast, through Petralia, Santa Caterina, Caltanissetta, to Agrigento on the south coast—a long, curving line established across the width of Sicily that would provide protection to Eighth Army's rear as it swung around Mount Etna. Only then, after establishing this line, was the Seventh Army to advance and mop up the western end of the island. Alexander was willing to let Patton exploit, but only on his terms, and not on the terms laid down in the 17 July conference.[19]

General Gay, the Seventh Army's chief of staff, apparently kept Alexander's order from reaching the army commander. Instead, Gay used only the first portion of the message as an order to General Bradley to modify II Corps' instructions: the 1st Division was to advance through Petralia to the north coast, coming out now at Campofelice instead of at Cefalù. Gay ignored the rest of the message.[20]

General Bradley was disappointed at the role assigned to II Corps. He had wanted all along to join with the Eighth Army in a drive against Messina. Indeed, the II Corps commander completely misinterpreted the motives behind Patton's visit to Alexander's headquarters on the 17th. Bradley thought that Patton was going to propose using the Seventh Army against Messina. Thus, Gay's message to II Corps on 19 July meant to General Bradley that the worst had come: Seventh Army would be confined to the western half of the island where "there was little to be gained" and where "there was no glory in the capture of hills, docile peasants, and spiritless soldiers." General Bradley sided with an officer from General Patton's staff who noted that after the Seventh Army reached the north coast "we can sit comfortably on our prats while Monty finishes the goddam war."[21]

But II Corps was encountering problems of its own in the loop area south and west of Enna. The corps mission had called for the securing of Caltanissetta and Highway 122 by dark on 19 July. The first objective had been taken care of. To secure the highway within II Corps' zone, which would also secure

---

[19] Seventh Army G-3 Jnl, entry 66, 18 Jul 43, TOO 1820, is a copy of Seventh Army's 18 July directive; entry 74, same file and date, TOR 2220, is Alexander's directive.

[20] Seventh Army G-3 Jnl, entry 85, 18 Jul 43, TOO 2256, is a message to II Corps; II Corps G-3 Jnl, entry 43, 19 Jul 43, TOR 0401, is the message received in II Corps headquarters. According to Semmes (*Portrait of Patton*, page 168), Gay saw to it that the message (after taking out the portion he planned to use) was a long time in being decoded and then, saying the original message had been garbled, asked 15th Army Group for a repeat. By the time this process was completed, the Seventh Army was on the outskirts of Palermo.

There is no verification in Seventh Army's G-3 Journal for this statement. But if Gay did hold up the message, he almost certainly would also have seen to it that no entry would be made in the journal where Patton would probably have picked it up. Semmes further states that Patton did not know of Gay's action until days afterward. Be that as it may, the Seventh Army did not delay the start of the advance, moved without the southern half of the loop area being established, and reached Palermo before cutting the island in two. Semmes' story, apparently based on an interview with General Gay, gains strong credence from the course of these operations.

[21] Bradley, *A Soldier's Story*, pp. 140, 144.

CALTANISSETTA, SOUTHWEST CORNER OF THE ENNA LOOP

the American portion of the loop, General Bradley decided that, while the 45th Division was taking Santa Caterina, the 1st Division would move as far as Santa Caterina, turn eastward on Highway 121, and take the small town of Villarosa, seven miles northwest of Enna. With elements of the two divisions along this road, Highway 122 would be secure from an enemy attack from the north. The Canadians on the right, then nearing Enna, would secure the highway from the east.

Accordingly, the 18th RCT moved to Santa Caterina on the evening of 18 July, and next morning, the 19th, started eastward toward Villarosa. Though some German resistance slowed the 18th RCT at the stream crossing some three miles west of Villarosa, by noon the combat team had forced a crossing and was on high grand overlooking the approaches to the town.

By this time, however, the new Seventh Army directive had arrived. This called for a change in the 1st Division's mission, from one of securing the loop area to one of pushing on to the north coast. Before General Bradley could draw up his own plans to carry out the army's directive, word came from the 1st Division that the British 30 Corps, which had finally cleared Piazza Armerina on the morning of the 17th but then had been delayed by strong German resistance farther along Highway 117, had also received new orders: the 30 Corps was now to bypass Enna to the east and advance instead on Leonforte and Assoro. The 1st Canadian Division, which had been leading the corps advance, was now to swing its axis of advance to the north. This was in keeping with a new Eighth Army plan which called for a renewed push on Messina. On the night of 17 July, the British 50th Division had tried once again to break through into Catania; again, a breakthrough had not been made. General Montgomery then decided to shift the weight of his advance to the 13 Corps left flank. He brought the British 5th Division up on the left of the 50th Division and directed an attack toward Misterbianco. But here, too, the Germans offered stubborn resistance, and the 5th Division could do little more than draw even with the 50th Division's bridgehead north of the Simeto River.

It soon became apparent to General Montgomery that the Eighth Army was not strong enough to encircle Mount Etna on both sides. Accordingly, he got General Alexander's permission to bring in his reserve, the British 78th Infantry Division, from North Africa. This would enable the Eighth Army to shift the main axis of its advance from the east coast highway to the western side of Mount Etna. If sufficient pressure could be brought to bear there, Montgomery felt, the Germans would have to withdraw from their Catania positions. Until the 78th Division arrived, the 13 Corps, on the east, was to confine itself to patrol activity to keep the Germans pinned down at Catania. The 30 Corps was to continue pushing the 1st Canadian Division around Mount Etna, not on the route originally planned, that through Nicosia and Randazzo, but instead, to the northeast. Before reaching Enna, the division was to take the secondary road leading from Highway 117 to Leonforte, and push along Highway 121 toward Agira and Regalbuto. General Montgomery planned to commit the 78th Division in the 30 Corps zone, but he could not do so before 1 August. On that date, Montgomery hoped to start

## THE DRIVE TO THE CLIMAX

the final offensive to throw the Axis forces out of Sicily.[22]

General Bradley, whose II Corps had been tied in tightly with the 30 Corps since 11 July, felt that the change in British plans endangered his right flank too much to be ignored. Unwilling to take any chances on the Germans using this entree from Enna into his rear areas, Bradley dashed off a note to General Leese and told him of his intention to take Enna: "I have just learned you have sideslipped Enna leaving my flank exposed. Accordingly, we are proceeding to take Enna at once even though it is in your sector. I assume we have the right to use any of your roads for this attack." Leese, who had assumed that his staff had notified the Americans of the bypassing of Enna and the shift in the Canadian axis of advance, replied immediately. Bradley, he said, was to use whatever roads he needed to take the town.[23]

With this settled, Bradley then told General Allen to send the 18th RCT into Villarosa and then against Enna from the west, while the 16th RCT advanced to the north from its Salso River crossings to strike Enna from the south. Until such time as the Enna situation was clarified, General Bradley was going to send the 1st Division neither to Petralia nor to the north coast.[24]

The 45th Division, on the other hand, was not involved in the Enna crisis. To General Middleton's Thunderbirds, then, fell the task of cutting the island in two. By the afternoon of 18 July, the 45th Division was ready to go for the north coast. The 180th RCT began moving up to pass through the 157th RCT. Once this had been accomplished, and the Italian roadblock at Portella di Reccativo cleared, the 180th was to continue pushing just as hard as it could along Highway 121. The north coast was eighty miles away; it would take aggressive and hard-hitting leadership to get the 45th Division to the sea.

Elsewhere, the Provisional Corps, without a worrisome problem like that faced by General Bradley's II Corps, regrouped its newly assigned forces for the thrust at Palermo. Drawing a boundary that extended from Agrigento northwestward between Highway 115 on the south and Highway 118 on the north, General Keyes disposed the 82d Airborne Division, reinforced by the 39th RCT (from the 9th Division), on the left and the 3d Infantry Division on the right. Both divisions were to advance by phase lines; both were to advance within their zones and were not to halt at the phase lines unless ordered to do so by corps headquarters; and both were to get to the north coast and to Palermo as rapidly as possible.

By the late afternoon of 18 July, the Provisional Corps was ready to go for Palermo. In a meeting held during the early evening, General Keyes passed the word: the attack would begin at 0500 the following morning, 19 July.[25]

---

[22] Alexander Despatch, pp. 25-26; Nicholson, *The Canadians in Italy*, pp. 95-102; Montgomery, *Eighth Army*, pp. 104-06; Aris, *The Fifth British Division*, pp. 123-29.

[23] Bradley, *A Soldier's Story*, p. 143; II Corps G-3 Jnl, entry 61, 19 Jul 43; II Corps G-3 Jnl, entry 90, 20 Jul 43 (a letter from Bradley to Patton outlining what had happened at Enna and giving Bradley's strong feelings toward having his right flank left open); II Corps G-3 Jnl, entry 96, 20 Jul 43 (Bradley's letter to Leese).

[24] II Corps Rpt of Opns, pp. 9-10; II Corps G-3 Jnl, entry 80, 19 Jul 43 (a copy of Bradley's verbal orders to Allen).

[25] Prov Corps FO 1, 18 Jul 43; Prov Corps Rpt of Opns, p. 3; Truscott, *Command Missions*, p. 224; Ridgway, *Soldier*, p. 73; 82d AB Div FO 2, 18 Jul 43; Ketterson, 82d AB Div in Sicily and Italy, p. 14.

GENERAL RIDGWAY AND STAFF *at the edge of Ribera near the 2d Armored Division assembly area.*

### The Pounce on Palermo

Jumping off on 19 July for Palermo, more than a hundred miles away, the Provisional Corps would strike through rough, mountainous country for the first fifty miles, then through forty miles of undulating interior plateau terrain, and finally through rugged highlands blocking Palermo on the west and south. (*Map VII*)

The advance turned out to be little more than a road march. Swarms of planes struck at targets of opportunity. Naval vessels standing by to render gunfire support were, as it turned out, not needed. On this same day, Hitler and Mussolini were meeting at Feltre; on this day, too, more than 500 U.S. heavy bombers struck in the first large-scale Allied bombing attack on Rome.

The initial advance forecast the shape of things to come. Paratroopers of Colonel Tucker's 504th Parachute Infantry swept through the 39th Infantry two hours ahead of schedule, and six hours later had crossed the Platani River, seventeen miles from their starting point. A demolished bridge had threatened to hold up the advance, but quick engineer work produced a vehicular bypass, and the movement continued with hardly a stop. Reconnaissance troops screening the advance brushed aside the few opposing

MORTAR SQUAD PREPARING TO ATTACK SANTO STEFANO *in the drive on Palermo, 20 July.*

Italians. A few rounds of cannon fire, a few rounds of small arms fire, the deployment of a squad or two of infantry, were usually enough to convince the Italians they had no chance of success.

The most serious resistance occurred in early afternoon, when an Italian antitank gun concealed in a pillbox across the Verdura River fired on the lead American vehicle—a 75-mm. gun mounted on a half-track. Backing off, the half-track slid into a fairly deep ditch. Fortunately, when the vehicle came to rest, its gun pointed directly at the pillbox. The gunner opened fire at once. As the reconnaissance troops deployed along the river bank, and as the supporting weapons—machine guns, mortars, and several 37-mm. guns—began to fire, seventy Italian soldiers came out of their positions with their hands held high.

By nightfall, when General Keyes halted the advance, the paratroopers had gained twenty-five miles.

The second day's advance was the same—scattered Italian garrisons offering little resistance, occasional mine fields, and surrendering enemy troops. By the end of the day, the Americans were in possession of Sciacca and its abandoned airfield and had moved another twenty miles toward Palermo.

Convinced that the lack of resistance offered an opportunity for armored ex-

THE 2D ARMORED DIVISION ROLLS INTO PALERMO *and an enthusiastic welcome. Note white surrender flags.*

ploitation, Keyes decided to commit General Gaffey's 2d Armored Division. With General Patton's approval, Keyes ordered Gaffey to assemble his division, which stretched over an area of more than twenty-five miles between Ribera and Agrigento. While the armor assembled, Keyes formed Task Force X, composed of the two Ranger Battalions (reinforced by artillery and the 39th Infantry, which had landed just three days before), and put it under Colonel Darby for another push to the west. The task force was to secure the Belice River line astride Highway 115, and then push on through Castelvetrano to establish a line covering the flank of the armored division as it moved into an assembly area along the Belice River line.

At the same time, Keyes turned Ridgway's 82d Airborne Division north to cover the armored division's assembly along the Belice River line on the east. From this assembly area, the 2d Armored Division was to thrust to the northeast to take Palermo.

Wasting little time assembling the units to make up Task Force X, Darby moved out from Menfi on the morning of 21 July. Because the Italians had demolished both the highway and railroad bridges across the Belice River and because the river was a hundred feet wide and four feet deep, engineer support was needed to get the task force vehicles across. Pending the arrival of engineers, Darby directed one of the Ranger battalions to ford the

# THE DRIVE TO THE CLIMAX

GENERAL KEYES AND ITALIAN GENERAL MOLINERO *enter Palermo together following surrender of the city.*

river to establish a bridgehead. Pillboxes and field fortifications on the far side might have been used to obstruct the crossing, but the Italians had abandoned them. By the time the battalion had a secure bridgehead, Rose's CCA of the 2d Armored Division had arrived. His engineers lost little time constructing a bridge.

While waiting for the bridge, a reconnaissance platoon of Darby's force managed to snake several light tanks and jeeps across the river. After removing a mine field along the highway, the platoon raced to Castelvetrano where four hundred Italians surrendered without a fight.

After a bridge was in, Darby sent his regiment of infantry, the 39th under Lt. Col. John J. Toffey, Jr., in pursuit of the reconnaissance platoon, which was by then rushing toward Alcamo, thirty-five miles to the northeast and only twenty-seven miles from Palermo. At Alcamo 800 Italians surrendered and a large stock of gasoline was discovered.

Moving like wildfire through the Task Force X zone of advance, Rangers and infantry collected almost 4,000 Italian prisoners that day. The time was obviously ripe for a swift thrust and Rose moved his units across the river and prepared for what Patton would later characterize—despite the paucity of opposition—as "a classic example of the use of tanks."[26]

[26] Semmes, *Portrait of Patton*, p. 163.

Meanwhile, Truscott's 3d Division, after marching to the Belice River in three days of grueling effort, was also ready to drive on Palermo. The division's advance, like that of the units following the coastal road, had been marked for the most part by only spotty enemy resistance. By this time, too, the 45th Division, which had been driving for Palermo, had been diverted farther to the east, and its plan now was to come out on the north coast near Termini Imerese, thirty miles east of Palermo.

As events developed, there was to be no concentrated, powerful assault on Palermo. Both the 3d Division and the 2d Armored Division by the evening of 22 July were in position to launch such an assault. But the city's defenders and the civilian population had had quite enough of the war and were willing to give up without a fight. In fact, one delegation of civilians arrived at the 7th Infantry's command post in the early afternoon of the 22d and offered to surrender the city to Brig. Gen. William W. Eagles, the 3d Division's assistant commander. The offer was declined; General Eagles had instructions from General Truscott that General Keyes was to accept the surrender of the city.

General Marciani, commander of the Italian defense forces, fell prisoner to the 82d Reconnaissance Battalion, and the final act of the drama devolved on Generale di Brigata Giuseppe Molinero, the commander of *Port Defense "N,"* Palermo. Late in the afternoon, one of CCA's patrols returned with General Molinero; the patrol had pushed into the city without encountering any opposition. Molinero offered to surrender the city to General Keyes. Together with the Italian general, Generals Keyes and Gaffey entered Palermo. At the royal palace, shortly after 1900, 22 July, the American officers formally accepted Palermo's surrender. With this, General Patton, trying to get up to the armored division's leading elements, sent word to occupy the city. At 2000, from the east and from the west, the two American divisions marched into the largest city on the island. General Patton, with Colonel Perry, the 2d Armored Division's chief of staff, serving as guide, threaded his way into Palermo an hour later. Palermo was his.[27]

*Denouement*

After the capture of Palermo, only the now isolated ports of western Sicily remained to be mopped up. Early on 23 July, Keyes instructed General Ridgway to shift the 82d Airborne Division from the Belice River line, move behind the 2d Armored Division, and seize Trapani and the extreme western tip of the island. Colonel White's CCB, 2d Armored Division, was to take care of the port cities along the north coast east of that line, a move accomplished the same day. To assist in the mopping-up operations, General Ridgway was given Colonel Darby's

---

[27] For details of the pounce on Palermo see: Prov Corps Rpt of Opns; Ketterson, 82d AB Div in Sicily and Italy; 39th Inf Regt AAR; Col. Paul A. Disney, Operations of the 82d Armored Reconnaissance Battalion in the Sicilian Campaign (Fort Leavenworth, Kansas, 1947), file X-2253.53; 7th, 15th, and 30th Inf Regt AAR's; 1st, 3d, and 4th Ranger Bn AAR's; 3d Inf Div in Sicilian Campaign, 19-23 Jul 43; 82d AB Div, 2d Armd Div, 3d Inf Div, 45th Inf Div, II Corps, and Seventh Army G-3 Jnls; Truscott, *Command Missions*, pp. 222-27; Patton, *War As I Knew It*, pp. 61-62; Semmes, *Portrait of Patton*, pp. 163, 165; Comments of Maj Gen William W. Eagles on MS; Comments of Gen Truscott on MS.

Task Force X. Accordingly, the airborne division commander directed Darby to Marsala (twenty-seven miles west of Castelvetrano); Colonel Gavin and the 505th Parachute Infantry to Trapani (nineteen miles north of Marsala); and Colonel Tucker's 504th Parachute Infantry to Castellammare (forty miles north of Castelvetrano).

At noon on 23 July, Colonel Darby moved the 39th RCT west along Highway 115 toward Marsala. By late afternoon the RCT was halted by a demolished bridge over the Marsala River and as engineers moved forward to construct a bypass, enemy artillery began shelling the crossing site. Colonel Toffey, the RCT commander, thereupon decided to halt his advance for the night. Early the following morning, 24 July, Toffey sent two battalions across the river under covering fire laid down by the 26th Field Artillery Battalion and quickly overran the city.

Meanwhile, on the 23d, Colonel Gavin had started his 505th Parachute Infantry moving by truck toward his objective—Trapani. Without opposition, the column rolled through Santa Ninfa and Salemi, then to Highway 113, where it turned and started west for Trapani. The motor march proved to be a pleasant parade; all along the route west of Santa Ninfa the local population exuberantly welcomed the paratroopers, showering the Americans with fruit, bread, and chocolate—the fruit obviously home-grown, the chocolate obviously pilfered from abandoned Italian military stores.

The mood suddenly changed at 1600 just before the column reached the eastern outskirts of Trapani. Here, the lead vehicles ran into a defended roadblock and mine fields, and as the advance guard detrucked and deployed to return the small arms fire, the Italians, from positions on the hills southwest and north of the city, laid down a concentration of artillery fire on the road.

For the next two or three hours the Italians kept up a steady drumfire of largely ineffective shelling. While the paratroopers moved against the roadblock, the 376th Parachute Field Artillery and the 34th Field Artillery Battalions rolled onto position and began answering the Italian fire. This fire, coupled with the clearing of the roadblock and the envelopment of the positions in the hills, persuaded Contrammiraglio Giuseppe Manfredi, commander of the Trapani naval district, to give up the fight, the city, and his sword and field glasses. Even as Gavin's men entered Trapani, the trucks which had transported the unit this far turned and headed back to shuttle the 504th Parachute Infantry to its objective on the north coast. By noon, 24 July, the 504th was in Alcamo; by 1730, in Castellammare.[28]

The Provisional Corps' combat operations in Sicily ended on this happy note. At a cost of 272 casualties (57 killed, 170 wounded, 45 missing), the corps captured 53,000 of the enemy (mostly Italians), and killed or wounded another 2,900. In addition, a grab bag filled with 189 guns of 75-mm. caliber or larger, 359 vehicles, and 41 tanks was collected. For the rest of its existence, until 20 August, the Provisional Corps would concentrate on garrisoning and administering western Sicily. For the 2d Armored Division and the 82d Airborne

---

[28] Prov Corps Rpt of Opns, p. 8; Ketterson, 82d AB Div in Sicily and Italy, pp. 16–17; 39th Inf Regt AAR; Ridgway, *Soldier*, pp. 74–75.

Division, the fighting in Sicily was over, and under Provisional Corps control, they settled down to occupation duties.

Palermo, the objective of this drive to the west, would now become the center of the Seventh Army's logistical operations. The preparation of the port and of the city for this function became a matter of great urgency. Though the opening of the port would not signal an end to supply operations across the assault beaches (now over a hundred miles away), it would mark a gradual reduction in the amount of supplies unloaded in the southeastern part of the island.[29]

By 19 July, the 1st Engineer Special Brigade had taken over the operation of the beaches and ports and was operating the supply services in the south directly under Seventh Army control. New supply points had been opened as the army advanced inland, with the main axis of supply running to the north and northwest. But the capture of Palermo placed in the army's hands for the first time a deepwater port capable of handling ships bringing stores and supplies directly from the United States. On 24 July, the 540th Engineer Shore Regiment and the 20th Engineer Combat Regiment moved into Palermo to open the port. A great amount of work had to be done in cleaning up the harbor area and the piers, opening road exits, and bridging over wrecked vessels so as to secure more berthing space. On 28 July the first supply ships—six coasters (two of which unloaded at Termini Imerese) from North Africa—entered the harbor. By this time, the engineers could operate the port at only some 30 percent of its full capacity because of the still uncleared wreckage of forty-four enemy vessels that had been sunk alongside of moles and in the channel.[30]

On 27 July, the Seventh Army directed that the main axis of supply be transferred as quickly as possible from the southeastern beaches to Palermo, a move made even more necessary by the turn of the fighting forces to the east. But until the port could be placed in better operating condition and until the stocks of supplies already gathered in the south had been reduced, the 1st Engineer Special Brigade was to remain responsible for supply to the north in the direction of Caltanissetta and to the northwest toward Alessandria and Sciacca. The troops moving to the east were thus to be supplied from two directions: from Licata and Porto Empedocle in the south, from Palermo in the west.[31]

By this time, too, the railroad lines on the island could be counted on to carry a heavy share of the supply burden. The entire 727th Railway Operating Battalion had arrived in Sicily by the end of July and had rapidly restored rail service in southern and central Sicily. The line east along the north coast from Palermo was usable as far as Termini Imerese at

---

[29] Scoglitti was closed on 17 July and Porto Empedocle opened the following day; Gela was closed on 7 August except for tankers—by this time, pipelines extended from the Gela pier to Comiso and Biscari airfields; Licata was kept open during the entire campaign. For details on the unloading of men and supplies in Sicily, see Seventh Army Rpt of Opns, pp. E-15—E-16.

[30] Palermo's operating capacity was raised to 60 percent by 29 August. During the period from 28 July to 31 August, the port received forty-eight ships, excluding craft. During this same period, 120,706 dead-weight tons of supplies were discharged at the port. See Seventh Army Rpt of Opns, p. E-15; Joseph Bykofsky and Harold Larson, *The Transportation Corps: Operations Overseas* (Washington, 1957), p. 198.

[31] Seventh Army Rpt of Opns, p. E-15.

# THE DRIVE TO THE CLIMAX

the seacoast end of Highway 120. The line from Termini to the Enna loop area at Caltanissetta was put into operating condition, as was the lower section running from Licata to Caltanissetta. The first train moved eastward from Palermo on 29 July, and with Italian help, the line was opened along the north coast as far as Cefalù.[32]

With the build-up of supplies through Palermo, General Patton could now turn his full attention to getting the Seventh Army moving to the east on Messina. The use of the Seventh Army in a drive on Messina had finally been ordered by General Alexander.

But elsewhere, in Italy and in North Africa, events of great importance, though not directly influencing the operations on Sicily, were taking place, events that would have a profound effect on the future course of the war.

---

[32] Bykofsky and Larson, *The Transportation Corps: Operations Overseas*, p. 200.

# CHAPTER XIV

# The Climax

*Sardinia Versus the Mainland*

The successful invasion of Sicily clarified strategic problems and enabled the Allies to turn from debate to decision. The Combined Chiefs of Staff at the TRIDENT Conference in May had directed General Eisenhower to knock Italy out of the war and contain the maximum number of German forces, but they had not told him how. Preparing to launch operations beyond the Sicilian Campaign, AFHQ had developed several outline plans: BUTTRESS, invasion of the Italian toe by the British 10 Corps; GOBLET, a thrust at the ball of the Italian foot by the British 5 Corps; BRIMSTONE, invasion of Sardinia; and FIREBRAND, invasion of Corsica. But a firm decision on the specific course of action to be taken was still lacking.[1]

The four plans, Eisenhower had explained to Churchill during the Algiers meetings in June, pointed to two broad alternative courses. If the Axis resisted vigorously in Sicily, thereby forecasting high Italian morale and a bitter and protracted struggle for the Allies, then BRIMSTONE and FIREBRAND, insular operations, were preferable. Otherwise, operations on the Italian mainland were more promising. Despite Churchill's articulate enthusiasm for the latter course, Eisenhower had made no commitment. He awaited the factual evidence to be furnished in Sicily.

Meanwhile, the Americans and British continued to argue over strategy. The Americans remained intent on guaranteeing a cross-Channel attack in 1944 and also advocated operations in Burma. The British were still intrigued by Mediterranean opportunities. The crux of the argument hinged on resources.

Conscious of theater requirements after Sicily, no matter what operations were launched, General Eisenhower on 29 June asked the Combined Chiefs whether two American convoys could be diverted to his command. He requested a total of 13 combat loaders (9 for personnel, 4 for cargo) for retention in the theater. He recommended retaining 15 American destroyers in the area. He forecast his need for 930 military government officers in case of rapid Italian collapse. He again sought assurance that 40 ships per month were to be allocated

---

[1] Memo, G-3 AFHQ for AFHQ CofS, 1 Jun 43, sub: Opns After HUSKY, 0100/12C/534,II; AFHQ Directive to Comdrs of Naval, Ground, and Air Forces, 5 Jun 43, 0100/12C/534,II.

For details of planning the invasion of Italy prior to the evolvement of AVALANCHE, see Martin Blumenson, Salerno to Cassino, a volume in preparation for the series UNITED STATES ARMY IN WORLD WAR II. See also Matloff, *Strategic Planning for Coalition Warfare, 1934–1944*, pp. 152–61, 245–46.

# THE CLIMAX

to meet civilian supply requirements in Italy.[2]

The Combined Chiefs made no immediate commitment, for they too were awaiting the initial results of the Sicily invasion. Not until 15 July—five days after the invasion—did the Combined Staff Planners draft a proposed reply to Eisenhower's requests, and they favored granting Eisenhower's wishes. Still, the divergence of American and British views prevented acceptance. The U.S. planners called attention to requirements elsewhere in the world. The British planners saw "the potential results" in the Mediterranean "so great" as to make unthinkable denying Eisenhower the resources he wished.[3]

Discussing their planners' recommendations on 16 July, the CCS decided to defer action on Eisenhower's requests for resources, even though the news from Sicily was good. At Admiral Leahy's suggestion, the Combined Chiefs agreed to accept Eisenhower's strategic concept (as embodied in AFHQ's four outline plans,) but only "for planning purposes," and at General Marshall's suggestion, they informed Eisenhower of their interest in a direct landing at Naples in place of an invasion of Sardinia, "if the indications regarding Italian resistance should make the risks involved worthwhile."[4]

Indications of crumbling Italian resistance continued to encourage the Allies. With increasing frequency, reports from Sicily made clear the advanced state of disintegration in the Italian Army. In contrast, German units were displaying "their traditional determination and skill," probably stimulated, AFHQ guessed, by the "poor performance of their Allies."[5]

Looking to the Italian mainland, AFHQ believed that the Germans would reinforce the Italians and prepare for a strong defense of the Italian heel because of its proximity to the Balkans. In contrast, AFHQ planners underestimated the importance of the toe, Calabria, to the Axis. The planners felt that the terrain was not suitable for employing large forces, supply routes were vulnerable to Allied air attack, the Germans would find air support of their ground troops almost impossible, and their forces in that area would be continually threatened by the possibility of successive Allied seaborne outflanking movements. AFHQ estimated that the Germans would elect to defend Italy south of Naples but would place only small forces in Calabria.[6]

Disintegrating Italian morale, the expectation of finding small enemy forces in Calabria, and the relatively light losses in landing craft during the invasion of Sicily prompted AFHQ to become somewhat bolder in its strategic thinking. Allied success achieved in Sicily as early as the first three days of operations gave rise to the hope that the British Eighth Army would sweep rapidly up the east coast to Messina, making unnecessary the commitment of the British 78th and 46th Infantry Divisions as planned. AFHQ

---

[2] Telg, Eisenhower to CCS, NAF 250, 29 Jun 43, printed in Alexander, *Allied Armies in Italy*, vol. I, pp. 60–63.

[3] CCS 268/2, Post-HUSKY Opns North African Theater, Rpt by Combined Staff Planners, 15 Jul 43.

[4] Min, 192d Mtg CCS, 16 Jul 43, Supplementary Min, item 6.

[5] AFHQ G–2 Weekly Intel Sum 46, 12 Jul 43, and AFHQ G–2 Weekly Intel Sum 47, 20 Jul 43, both in job 9, reel 23A. See also Telg 1783, AFHQ G–2 to TROOPERS, and 5110 to AGWAR, 17 Jul 43, job 24, reel 118D.

[6] JIC (A) 13/43, JIC Algiers Estimate of German Intentions in the South of Italy, 12 Jul 43, job 26, reel 73, Special.

decided to employ these divisions to gain lodgment in Calabria, and approved a plan called BAYTOWN, which was, in effect, an *ad hoc* BUTTRESS. This projected an assault on the tip of Calabria, in the Reggio area, five days after the capture of Messina, by a brigade of the British 13 Corps assisted by paratroopers and commandos. The 78th and 46th Divisions were then, soon afterward, to make an assault landing on the shore of the Gulf of Gioia.[7]

But the tenacious defense conducted by the Germans around Catania blocked the British sweep toward Messina, and in conformity with original plans the 78th Division was committed in Sicily. The formal BUTTRESS and GOBLET, plans to be executed by the British 10 and 5 Corps remained valid.[8]

In addition, AFHQ began seriously to consider alternative plans leading to a rapid build-up of forces in the Naples area—MUSTANG, a rapid overland drive from Calabria, and GANGWAY, a seaborne landing to reinforce those troops that had seized Naples after an overland advance. More important was Eisenhower's directive to General Clark, the U.S. Fifth Army commander, on 16 July: if the Allies landed in the toe, Clark and his army were to be ready not only to invade Sardinia but also "to support Italian mainland operations through Naples."[9]

On 17 July, after meeting with his chief subordinates, Tedder, Alexander, and Cunningham, General Eisenhower came to a major decision. He canceled the invasion of Sardinia in favor of operations on the Italian mainland, the best area for "achieving our object of forcing Italy out of the war and containing the maximum German forces." Though the situation had not sufficiently crystallized to permit informing the CCS precisely how the mainland was to be attacked or even the dates on which operations might be undertaken, the commanders discussed, as suggested by the Combined Chiefs, the possibility of a direct amphibious assault on Naples. This appeared impractical for two reasons: Naples lay beyond the limit of effective land-based fighter support, and too few landing craft would be available for such an assault in addition to BUTTRESS and GOBLET. MUSKET, on the other hand, a plan to invade the heel near Taranto, now appeared feasible even though it had earlier been rejected. The unexpectedly light losses of landing craft in Sicily would compensate for the difficulty of furnishing air protection over the Taranto assault area. Eisenhower therefore instructed Clark to plan MUSKET as an alternative to GANGWAY, which was oriented on Naples.[10]

---

[7] Min of Third Weekly Exec Planning Sec, 14 Jul 43, item 22, job 61C, reel 183C: Alexander, *Allied Armies in Italy*, vol. I, p. 10; Eisenhower, Italian Dispatch, p. 8.

[8] Eisenhower, Italian Dispatch, p. 10; Memo. AFHQ for multiple addressees, 25 Jun 43, sub: Chain of Command for, and Channels of Communication for Mounting, Opns BRIMSTONE, BUTTRESS and GOBLET, 0100/12C/534,II; Ltr, MIDEAST to AFHQ, 15 Jul 43, sub: BUTTRESS and GOBLET Order of Battle, same file.

[9] Directive, CofS AFHQ to CG Fifth Army, sub: Opns on Italian Mainland, 16 Jul 43, Fifth Army Rcds, KCRC, Opn GANGWAY, cabinet 196, drawer 4.

[10] Rcd of Mtg at La Marsa, 1430, 17 Jul 43, job 26A, reel 225B; Telg, Eisenhower to CCS, NAF 265, 18 Jul 43, Salmon Files, 5–B–1 (NAF, 1 Jun 43–31 Dec 43); Directive, Maj. Gen. J. F. M. Whiteley, DCofS AFHQ, to CG Fifth Army, sub: Opns on Italian Mainland, 22 Jul 43, printed in Alexander, *Allied Armies in Italy*, vol. I, pp. 66–67. The outline plan for Operation MUSKET (AFHQ P/96 Final, 24 Jul 43) is found in job 10A, reel 13C.

The crucial aspect of this project was the great distance of the Bay of Naples from the airfields which the Allies would be able to use—those in Sicily and those in Calabria to be seized in the initial attack on the mainland. Auxiliary aircraft carriers were not feasible for reinforcing land-based fighters because they could not launch modern fighters. In contrast, the Axis air forces, able to use airfields around Naples and Taranto, would have an extreme advantage. The P-39's (Airacobras) and P-40's (Kittyhawks) had short ranges. The P-38's (Lightnings) and A-36's (Mustangs) had the required range but lacked other desired characteristics. Spitfires, the best of the available fighters, if equipped with auxiliary ninety-gallon gasoline tanks, could reach the target areas but would not be able to operate over Naples for long. Only one aircraft carrier was operating in the Mediterranean, and this could not furnish enough planes to adequately support an amphibious operation.[11]

Despite the problem of air cover, enthusiasm grew in Washington and London for a direct attack against the Naples area, with the American and British Chiefs united and drawn toward this bold course by the manifest weakness of Italian resistance. But the argument over the allotment of resources continued. The British wished to pour into an invasion of the Italian mainland everything that could be made available, the better to guarantee success. The Americans, while recognizing the opportunity for aggressive action, insisted on holding to the previous over-all decisions limiting Mediterranean resources so as to make possible operations in northwest Europe and the China-Burma-India Theater.[12]

Reports on disintegrating Italian morale continued to come in. In Greece and the Balkans at least five instances came to Allied attention of Italian commanders who indirectly approached British representatives attached to the patriot forces in Greece and in Yugoslavia. Italian war-weariness and a desire to come to terms seemed quite obvious from such overtures as well as from negotiations which some Italian officers were conducting with Mihailovitch, the Yugoslav Partisan leader. The Germans, appreciating clearly the danger of defection, had begun to occupy vital areas formerly held exclusively by Italians, thereby hoping to stiffen such areas, particularly those vulnerable to invasion. As the Allies continued in their conquest of Sicily and as the collapse of Italy seemed to draw ever nearer, the Allies believed that the Italian troops in the Balkans would remain passive except to defend against guerrilla attack; the Germans, in contrast, would remain staunch.[13]

With the benefit of such intelligence, the CCS came to partial agreement. On 20 July they approved General Eisenhower's decision to invade the Italian

---

[11] Notes on the Air Implications of an Assault on Italian Mainland—Naples Area, 25 Jul 43, printed in Alexander, *Allied Armies in Italy*, vol. I, pp. 68–71. See also Craven and Cate, eds., vol. II, *Europe: TORCH to POINTBLANK*, pp. 489–91.

[12] CCS 268/3, sub: Post-HUSKY Opns North African Theater, Memo by the Representatives of British Chiefs of Staff, 19 Jul 43, ABC 384 Post-HUSKY (14 May 43), Sec. 3; Matloff, *Strategic Planning for Coalition Warfare, 1943–1944*, pp. 158–60; Bryant, *The Turn of The Tide*, pp. 549–51.

[13] Telg, MIDEAST to TROOPERS, repeated to FREEDOM, sub: Enemy Morale in the Balkans, 1/83652, 19 Jul 43, job 24, reel 188D. Cf. Butcher, *My Three Years With Eisenhower*, p. 274 (entry for 2 Aug 43).

mainland, and then instructed him to extend his amphibious operations "northwards as shore-based fighter cover can be made effective." [14]

The British, however, were not satisfied. On the next day, 21 July, the British Chiefs wired their representatives in Washington that the "Italian will to continue the war may be within measurable distance of collapse." They urged immediate bold action, specifically an amphibious attack against Naples. A day later the British Chiefs went further. They provided a plan, code-named AVALANCHE, for such an invasion and suggested the last week of August as a favorable, if fleeting, moment. The prospect of success, they admitted, depended largely on the adequacy of air cover, and they proposed allotting Eisenhower four escort carriers and one large British carrier, plus about forty cargo vessels over and above the TRIDENT allocations. Until General Eisenhower indicated his requirements for an attack in the Naples area, the British Chiefs urged that orders be issued to stop the movement of forces away from the Mediterranean theater.[15]

The Americans did not consider additional resources necessary. AFHQ already had, they believed, sufficient means to take Naples, and, if not, "reasonable hazards could be accepted." They therefore proposed that the CCS instruct Eisenhower to prepare a plan, as a matter of urgency, for such an invasion, but using only the resources already made available for operations beyond Sicily. This meant an assault in the strength of about four divisions, as compared with the seven mounted for Sicily.[16]

The British were "most disappointed." The Sicilian Campaign, it seemed to them, was even stronger proof that Italy could be eliminated from the war. This, they believed, would increase the chances not only for a successful but a decisive cross-Channel attack into northwest Europe. Italian defeat the British regarded as the best if not the essential preliminary to the earliest possible defeat of Germany. And AVALANCHE, if feasible, was the best and quickest way to knock Italy out of the war.[17]

By this time AFHQ had made a formal study of the possibility of landing in the Naples area. General Rooks, the AFHQ G–3, on 24 July suggested the beaches fronting the Gulf of Salerno as the most suitable for an initial assault. He proposed that Clark's Fifth Army start planning the operation as an alternative to MUSKET, a landing near Taranto. He thought an assault force of about four divisions would be enough, if provision was made for rapid follow-up and buildup. He felt that the Allies should make their main effort and strike their first blow in Calabria, by means of BUTTRESS and GOBLET. If as the result of these operations the Allies held the toe of Italy by the beginning of October, they could go ahead

---

[14] CCS 268/4, 20 Jul 43, sub: Post-HUSKY Opns North African Theater, Rpt by Combined Staff Planners, 20 Jul 43; Min, 97th Mtg JCS, 20 Jul 43, item 12; Telg, CCS to Eisenhower, FAN 169, 20 Jul 43, Salmon Files, 5–B–1.

[15] CCS 268/6, 21 Jul 43, sub: Post-HUSKY Opns North African Theater, Memo by Representatives of British Chiefs of Staff; CCS 268/7, 22 Jul 43, sub: Post-HUSKY Opns North African Theater, Msg From British Chiefs of Staff.

[16] Min, 103d Mtg CCS, 23 Jul 43, Supplement, item 7.

[17] CCS 268/8, sub: Post-HUSKY Opns North African Theater, Memo by Representatives of British Chiefs of Staff, 24 Jul 43.

# THE CLIMAX

and launch an invasion in the Naples area at Salerno.[18]

AFHQ's conservative and deliberate approach to an invasion of the Italian mainland changed radically because of a revolutionary event which occurred on the next day.

### The Overthrow of Mussolini

Soon after the Italian delegation returned from the Feltre conference to Rome on 20 July, Mussolini told Ambrosio that he had decided to write a letter to Hitler to request termination of the alliance. Because Mussolini's abject behavior at Feltre had dispelled Ambrosio's last illusions that the Duce might break away from Germany, Ambrosio made a sharp rejoinder. The opportunity of the spoken word, Ambrosio said, had been lost at Feltre. Declaring that he could no longer collaborate in a policy that jeopardized the fate of Italy, Ambrosio offered Mussolini his resignation. Mussolini refused to accept it and dismissed the chief of *Comando Supremo* from the room.[19]

At this time, arrangements began to take definite form in *Comando Supremo* for a *coup d'état* against the Duce as the essential step for getting Italy out of the war. Yet in a curiously inconsistent policy, Ambrosio made arrangements with OKW to reinforce the troops in Sicily. Either on 21 or 22 July, the decision was made to fight the campaign in Sicily to the limit. Formal assurance was made to OKW and the request forwarded for two additional German divisions. *Comando Supremo* promised to do all within its power to this end and Ambrosio asked that German coastal and antiaircraft artillery be shipped to the Messina Strait area immediately, and that the *29th Panzer Grenadier Division* be transferred from Calabria to Sicily.[20]

The Germans replied on 22 July. The *29th Panzer Grenadier Division* would immediately be sent to Sicily.[21] Two days later, Ambrosio conferred with Kesselring on getting more German divisions. Kesselring named the *305th* and *76th Infantry Divisions* as available. Both were in France but ready for transportation to Italy. Roatta had already discussed their commitment with Kesselring; he planned to place one in Calabria, the other in Puglia.[22] Thus, while some Italians intrigued to get rid of Mussolini and the German alliance, others—in some instances the same ones—were permitting the Germans to tighten their military grip on Italy.

At the beginning of July 1943 there were still three distinct groups in Italy who were actively working and plotting for Mussolini's overthrow: dissident Fascists; the anti-Fascist opposition; and the military conspiracy. The dissident Fas-

---

[18] AFHQ P/98 (Final), 24 Jul 43, sub: Appreciation of an Amphibious Assault Against the Naples Area, job 10A, reel 13C.

[19] MS #P-058, Project 46, 1 Feb–8 Sep 43, Question 4; Castellano, *Come firmai*, pp. 56–57; Badoglio, *Memorie e documenti*, p. 65.

[20] Ltr, Ambrosio to Rintelen, *Comando Supremo*, Prot. N. 15112, 22 Jul 43, IT 3029, folder IV, an. 4bis. There is another copy in *Operazioni in Sicilia dal 20 al 31 luglio 1943*, Narrativa, Allegati, It 99b, an. 67 (hereafter referred to as IT 99b). See also *OKW/WFSt, KTB, 1.–31.VII.43*, 23 Jul 43.

[21] Ltr, Lt. Col. Jandl (on behalf of Rintelen), Ia No. 0641/43, Rome, 22 Jul 43, *Comando Supremo, Protezione vie comunicazione del Brennero, 1943*, IT 102.

[22] Min, *Colloquio a Palazzo Vidoni, Roma, 24 luglio 1943*, IT 3037.

MARSHAL BADOGLIO

cists were led by Count Ciano and Dino Grandi. They were in touch with the Duke of Acquarone (the King's private secretary) and, through him, with the King. Their hope was to supplant Mussolini but to retain the Fascist system. The underground anti-Fascist parties were held together by Ivanoe Bonomi. Their minimum program was a complete overthrow of the Fascist system and an immediate return to the pre-Fascist, parliamentary system of government. General Castellano and the small group associated with him in *Comando Supremo* were, like the others, in frequent contact with Acquarone and waited only for the King to give the word. For this group, the questions of institutional changes were altogether secondary to the problem of terminating the war, but they wished the command of Italy's armed forces restored to the King in accordance with the *Statuto*.

All three groups thought alike with respect to the German alliance. Dino Grandi wished an immediate break of the alliance following Mussolini's dismissal, and a simultaneous approach to Great Britain for a separate peace. Bonomi advocated overtures to the Allies as soon as the new government was formed. Castellano's whole purpose in plotting against Mussolini was to permit Italy to make a quick and direct approach to the Western Powers to end the war.

Among the small groups who had access to the Royal Palace, it was known that the King was considering a change in the head of the government, but he had not yet definitely made up his mind. On 5 July he mentioned to his aide de camp, Generale di Divisione Paolo Puntoni, that Ambrosio was making preparations for the removal of Mussolini which would be followed by a military dictatorship headed by either Maresciallo d' Italia Enrico Caviglia or Marshal Badoglio. The King was not happy about either choice: he did not trust Badoglio's character; he thought that Caviglia in power would mean a revival of freemasonry and rapprochement with the Anglo-Americans. Victor Emmanuel did not want to overthrow fascism at one stroke: he wished for gradual changes only. He recognized that Badoglio had a certain following among the masses which would be useful if Mussolini were dismissed. The King remarked to Puntoni that Ambrosio was undertaking too much and was having too many contacts outside military circles.[23]

---

[23] Paolo Puntoni, *Parla Vittorio Emanuele III* (Milan: Aldo Palazzi editore, 1958), pp. 136-37 (entry for 5 Jul 43).

Alessandro Casati, an intimate of Bonomi, spoke with Acquarone on 12 July and learned that the King's private secretary was a gradualist, opposed to approaching the Allies at the same time that Mussolini was removed from power. Hoping to get Badoglio to change Acquarone's position, Casati and Bonomi had a long conversation with the marshal on 14 July. Badoglio agreed that denunciation of the alliance with Germany should immediately follow the formation of a new government. He agreed that the new government would need the support of all the anti-Fascist parties— Liberal, Christian Democrat, Socialist, Communist, Actionist, and Democracy of Labor. He agreed with Bonomi that the proper solution was a politico-military cabinet that would eliminate fascism and break with Germany. He agreed to become the head of the prospective government and to name the military members of the cabinet while Bonomi selected the civil members and served as vice president. But he objected to Bonomi's desire for Della Torretta as Foreign Minister, insisting instead on Raffaele Guariglia, Ambassador to Turkey. Bonomi acceded on this point after some heated argument.[24]

At an audience with the King on 15 July, Badoglio presented a proposal for a new government under himself and the inclusion of Bonomi and other politicians in the cabinet. The King seemed to be decidedly averse to the proposal. He said he did not want any politicans. The men whom Badoglio proposed were all old, the King said, and they would simply give the appearance of a return to the pre-Fascist system. Unwilling to admit that he was even thinking of moving against Mussolini, Victor Emmanuel remarked that prearranged coups had little chance of success, particularly in Italy where people were not accustomed to keeping secrets. He terminated the audience without coming to a decision.

Two days later, when Badoglio discussed with Bonomi and Casati the royal reception of his idea, he was only lukewarm on the feasibility of forming a government based on party support. Either the King would accept the Badoglio-Bonomi proposal, said the marshal, or else he, Badoglio, would withdraw the suggestion, thereby letting everyone resume his liberty of action. Sometime during the next few days, he sent personal and unofficial representatives to Switzerland to inform the British Government that he desired to make contact with the Western Allies.[25]

On 18 July, Acquarone let it be known that the King was preparing to act against Mussolini but that he wanted the new cabinet to consist of nonpolitical civil servants. Bonomi was greatly alarmed. The mere dismissal of Mussolini would leave the problem of the war and the German alliance unsolved. Calling on Badoglio on 20 July, Casati and Bonomi learned that Badoglio had been won over to the course of gradualism favored by Acquarone and the King. To warn the sovereign that gradualism would not solve the pressing problems of breaking the alliance and getting out of the war, Bonomi and Casati on 22 July submitted a memorandum to Acquarone. The memorandum was prescient though without effect. It pointed out that Germany would have no doubt of Italy's real intentions once Mus-

[24] Bonomi, *Diario*, pp. 19–21.

[25] *Ibid.*, pp. 22–24; Badoglio, *Memorie e documenti*, pp. 63, 70–71; Puntoni, *Vittorio Emanuele III*, p. 139.

solini was eliminated from power; that a gradualist policy would give Germany time to prepare for action against a new Italian Government; that a cabinet of civil servants devoid of political tendencies would be viewed as an enemy by Fascists, yet would find no support in the anti-Fascist circles; that the Anglo-American coalition would not be favorably disposed to such a cabinet because it would lack men of guaranteed anti-Fascist reputations; that in choosing politicians representing the people the King would follow custom, but in appointing civil servants he would draw upon himself the responsibility for the policies of that cabinet.[26]

Badoglio had several conversations with Ambrosio, who brought him up to date on the military situation and who carefully explained that Italy's position toward Germany excluded a unilateral Italian declaration of withdrawal from the war because Italy had insufficient forces to back up an immediate breach of the alliance. Badoglio cautioned Ambrosio to do nothing without the express approval of the King. But in one of their discussions attended by Acquarone, they agreed that two things were necessary for the good of the country: to arrest Mussolini and half a dozen leading Fascist officials; and to use the Regular Army to neutralize the force of the Fascist militia. Acquarone carefully reported this discussion to the King.[27]

On 20 July, under the impact of Mussolini's failure at Feltre and of the American bombing of Rome, the King made up his mind to act. He told Puntoni: "It is necessary at all costs to make a change. The thing is not easy, however, for two reasons: first, our disastrous military situation, and second, the presence of the Germans in Italy." Two days later Victor Emmanuel apparently tried to induce Mussolini to offer his resignation. There was a long discussion between the Duce and the King who subsequently told Puntoni:

I tried to make the Duce understand that now it is only his person, the target of enemy propaganda and the focal point of public opinion, which impedes an internal revival and which prevents a clear definition of our military situation. He did not understand and he did not wish to understand. It was as if I had spoken to the wind.[28]

Through Acquarone, the sovereign informed General Castellano that he had made up his mind to appoint Badoglio as Mussolini's successor. All preparations for the change in regime would have to be completed within six or seven days. Acquarone said that Mussolini had an audience scheduled with the King for 26 July, and Castellano made plans to have the Duce arrested shortly after that event.[29]

Another critical step was to protect the new government against a reaction by the Fascist militia. *Comando Supremo* therefore moved the *10th (Piave) Motorized Infantry Division* and the *135th (Ariete) Armored Division* to the Rome area, both to constitute a special corps under General Carboni. An intimate of Count

---

[26] Bonomi, *Diario*, pp. 26–28.
[27] Badoglio, *Memorie e documenti*, pp. 62–63, 71, 76; Castellano, *Come firmai*, pp. 51–52; MS #P-058, Project 46, 1 Feb–8 Sep 43, Question 6. Castellano (*Come firmai*, page 49) states that at this time the German reaction appeared less of a danger than that of the Fascists.

[28] Puntoni, *Vittorio Emanuele III*, pp. 140–41. See also Castellano, *Come firmai*, p. 57; Vitetti, Notes on the Fall of the Fascist Regime, p. 10; Bonomi, *Diario*, p. 25.
[29] Castellano, *Come firmai*, pp. 57–60.

Ciano and at the same time of Castellano, Carboni was ambitious. Though he had at times been a difficult subordinate, he was strongly anti-German and pro-Ally.[30] No measures were planned in advance against a possible German reaction. The King intended neither to create an immediate rupture in the Axis alliance nor to make an immediate approach to the Western Powers.

As for Badoglio, in deciding to accept the high office, he acted with a soldierly sense of duty toward his sovereign. Whatever course the King wished to follow, Badoglio made clear that he, Badoglio, would execute. If the King commanded continuance of the war in alliance with Germany, Badoglio would loyally carry out that policy. If the King directed an approach to the Allies, Badoglio would undertake that course. The responsibility, Badoglio also made clear, would remain with the King.[31]

Victor Emmanuel was not happy to have the responsibility placed on his royal person, and he almost regretted the imminent change. Things were much easier with Mussolini, he thought, who was very clever and who took responsibility upon himself. The appointment of Badoglio meant, not a return to pre-Fascist constitutional procedures, but a return to absolute monarchy. While Mussolini as *Capo del Governo* claimed for that office all the power he could grasp, Badoglio deliberately restricted himself to the role of the King's executive secretary.[32]

Curiously enough, Mussolini himself helped set the stage for his overthrow. Early in July, Carlo Scorza, the new Fascist party secretary, had planned a series of mass meetings in the principal cities of Italy and invited leading Fascists to exhort the people to determined resistance. Largely at Dino Grandi's instigation, quite a few party officials refused the invitation. Several of these men saw Mussolini on 16 July, expressed their dissatisfaction with the situation, and proposed convening the Grand Council of Fascism, which had not met for more than three years. Surprisingly enough, five days later, on 21 July, after returning from the Feltre conference, Mussolini called the Fascist Grand Council to a meeting on 24 July.[33]

Aware of the King's intention to oust Mussolini, Grandi skillfully lined up a majority of the council members against the Duce. He drew up a resolution calling for the King to resume command of the armed forces. Some members signed it in the belief that it would merely force Mussolini to relinquish the military power he had exercised since the beginning of the war. Grandi and others hoped that a majority vote favoring his resolution would be taken as a lack of confidence in Mussolini's leadership and would induce the King to replace Mussolini by a trium-

---

[30] Roatta, *Otto milioni*, pp. 262–63; Rossi, *Come arrivammo*, p. 204. For unfavorable comments on Carboni as a general officer, see *Generale Comandante di Corpo d'Armata Carboni, Giacomo*, IT 972; for his early friendship with Ciano and Castellano, see Castellano, *Come firmai*, pp. 22ff.

[31] See the penetrating comments in Telg, Col. Helfferich, Rome, *Chef. Amt Ausland Abwehr*, 22 or 23 Jul 43, *OKW/Amtsgruppe Ausland, 19.IV.–1.XI.43* (OKW/1000.2).

[32] For Badoglio's constitutional position, see Howard McGaw Smyth, "Italy: From Fascism to the Republic," *The Western Political Quarterly*, vol. I, No. 3 (September 1948), pp. 205–22.

[33] Vitetti, Notes on the Fall of the Fascist Regime, pp. 8–9; Mussolini, *Storia di un anno*, p. 14; Ltr, Dino Grandi, 23 Jun 44, Incl 3 to Dispatch 835, 9 Aug 44, from the American Embassy, Lisbon, U.S. Dept of State Files; George Kent, "The Last Days of Dictator Benito Mussolini," *Reader's Digest* (October 1944), p. 13.

virate: Grandi, Ciano, and Federzoni (president of the Royal Academy).[34]

The Grand Council of 28 members met at 1700, Saturday, 24 July. The debate on Grandi's resolution lasted almost nine hours. Around 0300, 25 July, Mussolini acceded to Grandi's demand for a vote. Of the 28 members, many of whom had remained silent during the course of the debate, 19 voted with Grandi against Mussolini.[35]

Neither Mussolini nor Grandi immediately realized what had happened. The Grand Council meeting was but a sideshow designed to furnish an appropriate occasion, a constitutional crisis, for dismissing the Head of Government. When Mussolini saw the King after the fateful poll, he told the monarch that the Grand Council vote did not require his resignation. The King would not listen. Coldly he told Mussolini that he had to resign—Marshal Badoglio would take his place. On leaving the palace, Mussolini was unable to find his car. Accepting the help of a *carabinieri* officer, he was escorted into an ambulance and whisked away. Not until later did he realize that he was under arrest.[36]

Grandi hung around all day waiting to be called to an appointment in the new cabinet. Like Bonomi, he believed in making immediate contact with the Allies, and to this end he sought permission to leave for Spain at once. Grandi wished to talk to the British Ambassador at Madrid, Sir Samuel Hoare, whom Grandi had known when he was Mussolini's Ambassador to London. But Grandi had already played the part deftly assigned to him by Acquarone, and Grandi cooled his heels in Rome. Not until several weeks passed did the new government permit Grandi to go to Madrid, but without instructions, credentials, or power.[37] As it turned out, Grandi's trip proved to be of value, but as a red herring, for the Germans, who were hot on Grandi's trail, failed to pick up the scent of the official mission dispatched to make contact with the Allies.

The meeting of the Fascist Grand Council on 24 July gave the Roman public a sense of the political crisis. When news of Mussolini's dismissal raced through the city on 25 July, people embraced each other in joy, danced in the streets, and paraded in gratitude to the King. Mobs attacked Fascist party offices. Fascist symbols were torn down.

With one stroke the House of Savoy had removed the great incubus that had brought Italy into the war on the losing side, and everyone expected the new government to bring about an immediate peace. Never was a people's faith in royalty destined to be more bitterly disappointed.

No one paid much attention to the Germans, who disappeared from public view.[38]

*Allied Reaction*

The overthrow of Mussolini took the Allies by surprise. At the TRIDENT Conference the Americans had argued that

---

[34] "Count Dino Grandi Explains," *Life*, vol. 18, No. 9 (February 26, 1945), pp. 81–82; Badoglio, *Memorie e documenti*, pp. 73–74, 82.

[35] Mussolini, *Storia di un anno*, pp. 16–18; Bonomi, *Diario*, pp. 30–32.

[36] Mussolini, *Storia di un anno*, pp. 19–20; Monelli, *Roma 1943*, pp. 188–94; Puntoni, *Vittorio Emanuele III*, pp. 143–45.

[37] Ltr, Dino Grandi, 20 Feb 44, Incl 2 to Dispatch 835, 9 Aug 44, from the American Embassy, Lisbon, U.S. Dept of State Files.

[38] Monelli, *Roma 1943*, pp. 156–57; Bonomi, *Diario*, p. 36.

# THE CLIMAX

the Allies might bring about the collapse of Italy without invading the Italian mainland. The conquest of Sicily and intensified aerial bombardment of the mainland, they believed, might be enough. The British felt that only an invasion of the Italian mainland would guarantee Italian surrender, and this course of action had become the basic Allied concept—continuing ground force operations beyond Sicily in order to knock Italy out of the war.

The U.S. Department of State had as yet scarcely discussed the peace terms to be imposed upon a vanquished Italy. On 26 July, if it had been necessary, the Allies would have found it impossible to state their basic terms for peace—aside from unconditional surrender.

The Allies even lacked a set of armistice terms for an Italy offering to surrender. They had discussed this matter but without reaching agreement. The British had proposed a long and detailed list of conditions to be imposed upon a defeated Italy. The Americans had not concurred because the British list did not mean total surrender. They had instead proposed a series of diplomatic instruments to obtain unconditional surrender and allow the extension of Allied military government over the whole of Italian territory. Differences in ultimate objectives effectively hindered Anglo-American agreement. The Americans had no qualms about putting the House of Savoy into protective custody and undertaking the political reconstruction of the country. To the British, the prospect of another dynasty going into discard was too painful to contemplate. Transatlantic discussions were continuing without definite conclusions when the developments on the Tiber made a decision vital.

Contradictory crosscurrents further complicated the discussions. The troublesome Italian Fleet had aroused British passion for revenge, and Churchill's and Eden's bitter experiences with Mussolini made them endorse a complete Italian surrender. American feeling against Mussolini had never reached a boiling point; the U.S. Government had no wish to gain territory at Italian expense, and a significant element in the American electorate was of Italian descent or origin and could not be ignored. These factors exerted a moderating influence on U.S. policy.

The Combined Chiefs of Staff held a special meeting on 26 July, the day after Mussolini's overthrow; greatly elated by the news, they reached a decision of some import. Though the Americans refused to alter their stand on resources for an attack on Naples, they did not object when the British added one heavy and four escort carriers to the Mediterranean resources. The CCS agreed to expedite the elimination of Italy from the war by authorizing Eisenhower to launch AVALANCHE at the earliest possible date and with the resources available to him.[39]

In Tunis, also heartened by word of Mussolini's downfall, Eisenhower was meeting with his principal subordinates to review the new situation. They decided that promising conditions called for a bolder course of action. Upon receipt of the CCS directive authorizing an invasion in the Naples area, Eisenhower ordered Clark to draw detailed plans for executing AVALANCHE. He also instructed Clark to prepare one division to sail directly into Naples and seize the port in conjunc-

[39] Min, Special CCS Mtg, 26 Jul 43; Telg, CCS to Eisenhower, FAN 175, 26 Jul 43, CCS Cable Log.

tion with an airborne operation. Sensing the prospects of securing a speedy capitulation of the Italian Government, Eisenhower looked forward to occupying rapidly key points on the Italian mainland with Italian consent.[40]

By this time, Allied intelligence reports of Italian morale in the battle for Sicily were caustic. One stated:

For the most part the Italian field formations have not shown a standard of morale and battle determination very much higher than that of the coastal units whose performance was so lamentably low. . . . Sheer war weariness and a feeling of the hopelessness of Italy's position have, however, obviously been more potent influences and these have moreover permeated the field army to a considerable degree, with the result that a sense of inferiority and futility has destroyed its zest and spirit.[41]

To exploit the new political situation and Italian war weariness, General Eisenhower decided to pull all the stops on the organ of psychological warfare. If he could, by offering a simple set of armistice terms, eliminate Italy as a belligerent, the Allies would be able to use Italian territory in the war against Germany.

Therefore, Eisenhower asked CCS approval of a radio message he proposed to broadcast constantly to the Italian people. He wished to commend the Italians and the Royal House for ridding themselves of Mussolini; to assure them that they could have peace on honorable conditions; to promise Italy the advantages of the Atlantic Charter and the Four Freedoms and also a voice in the final negotiations for world peace; to suggest that if the King remained at war with the Allies much longer, British and American odium concentrated on Mussolini would be transferred to the monarch, thereby making an honorable surrender difficult. The radio broadcasts, Eisenhower proposed, should urge the King to make immediate contact with the Allied commander in chief.[42]

General Eisenhower also drafted a set of armistice terms:

1. Immediate cessation of all hostile activity by the Italian armed forces with disarmament as dictated by the C-in-C, and a guarantee by the Italian Government that German forces now on the Italian mainland will immediately comply with all provisions of this document.

2. All prisoners or internees of the United Nations to be immediately turned over to the C-in-C, and none of these may, from the beginning of these negotiations, be evacuated to Germany.

3. Immediate transfer of the Italian fleet to such points as may be designated by the C-in-C Med., with details of disarmament and conduct to be prescribed by him.

4. Immediate evacuation from all Italian territory of the German Air Force.

5. Immediate beginning of the evacuation of German land forces from the Italian mainland on phase lines to be so prescribed by the Allied C-in-C that the evacuation from all Italy will be complete within one month. German forces in Sicily are not affected by this armistice and will either surrender unconditionally or will be destroyed.

6. Immediate surrender of Corsica and of all Italian territory, both islands and mainland, to the Allies, for such use as opera-

---

[40] Telg, Eisenhower to CCS, NAF 300, 27 Jul 43, Salmon Files, 5-B-1; Directive, DCofS AFHQ to CG Fifth Army, sub: Opns on the Italian Mainland, 27 Jul 43, Personal Papers of Col Robert J. Wood, file Outline Plan, Operation AVALANCHE; Min of Exec Planning Mtg 5, 27 Jul 43, job 61C, reel 183C.

[41] AFHQ G-2 Weekly Intel Sum 48, 27 Jul 43, job 9, reel 23A.

[42] Telg, Eisenhower to CCS, NAF 266, 26 Jul 43, OPD TS Cable, IN, 1 Jul–31 Jul 43. Cf. Butcher, *My Three Years With Eisenhower*, p. 371.

# THE CLIMAX

tional bases and other purposes as the Allies may see fit.

7. Immediate acknowledgment of the overriding authority of the Allied Commander-in-Chief to establish military government and with the unquestioned right to effect, through such agencies as he may set up, any changes in personnel that may seem to him desirable.

8. Immediate guarantee of the free use by the Allies of all airfields and naval ports in Italian territory, regardless of the rate of evacuation of the Italian territory by the German forces. These ports and fields to be protected by Italian armed forces until the function is taken over by the Allies.

9. Immediate withdrawal of Italian armed forces from all participation in the current war from whatever areas in which they may now be engaged.

10. Guarantee by the Italian Government that if necessary it will employ all its available armed forces to insure prompt and exact compliance with all the provisions of this armistice.[43]

General Eisenhower proposed that this set of terms serve as the basis for a CCS directive, and that it also be broadcast to Italy. Knowledge of the terms and the assurances therein of honorable conditions of peace, he believed, would make the Italian population force the government to sue for an armistice. He did not envisage the active co-operation of Italian troops in the war beyond the enforcement of German withdrawal from Italian soil, for he believed that "they would deem it completely dishonorable to attempt to turn definitely against their former allies and compel the surrender of German formations now in the mainland of Italy."[44] His terms were an attempt to meet an Italian request for armistice before an Allied invasion of the mainland, and he made no mention of unconditional surrender.[45]

Neither did President Roosevelt urge the unconditional surrender formula when he heard the news of Mussolini's downfall. Cabling Churchill immediately, he suggested that if the Italian Government made overtures for peace, the Allies ought to come as close to unconditional surrender as possible and then follow that capitulation with good treatment of the Italian people. Roosevelt thought it essential to gain the use of all Italian territory, the transportation system and airfields as well, for the further prosecution of the war against the Germans in the Balkans and elsewhere in Europe. He wished provision made for the surrender of Mussolini, "the head devil," and his chief associates, and he asked the Prime Minister for his views on the new situation.[46]

As Minister of Defence and with the approval of his War Cabinet, Mr. Churchill sent the President his proposals on how to deal with a defeated Italy. Considering it very likely that the dissolution of the Fascist system would soon follow Mussolini's overthrow, Churchill expected the King and Badoglio to try to arrange a separate armistice with the Allies. In this case, he urged that every possible advantage be sought from the surrender

---

[43] Telg, Eisenhower to CCS, NAF 302, 27 Jul 43, Capitulation of Italy, p. 14 (a bound file of copies of telegrams and other documents relating to the Italian surrender, assembled for Maj. Gen. Walter B. Smith, Chief of Staff, AFHQ).

[44] Ibid.

[45] Butcher, *My Three Years With Eisenhower*, p. 372 (entry for 27 Jul 43).

[46] Telg 324, President to Prime Minister, 25 Jul 43, OPD 300.6 Security (OCS Papers); Winston S. Churchill, "The Second World War," vol. V, *Closing the Ring* (Boston: Houghton Mifflin Company, 1951), p. 55.

to expedite the destruction of Hitler and Nazi Germany.[47]

The text of Churchill's proposals reached AFHQ soon after Eisenhower had dispatched his draft of terms to the CCS. Both sets of terms were closely similar. Both required the use of all Italian territory; insisted on control of the Italian Fleet; stipulated the return of prisoners of war to prevent their transfer to Germany; demanded the withdrawal of the Italian armed forces from further participation in the war against the Allies; and assumed that the Italians on Italian soil would be able to enforce German compliance with the terms of surrender.

There were some differences. Using phraseology originally suggested by Roosevelt, Churchill called for the surrender of Mussolini and the leading Fascists as war criminals. Churchill thought of gaining the active aid of Italy's armed forces against the Germans. If the Italian Fleet and Army came under Allied control by the armistice, the Prime Minister apparently would have been willing to acquiesce in the retention of sovereignty by the Italian Government (the monarchy) on the mainland. Eisenhower, in contrast, wished not only the power to establish military government but also an overriding authority over the Italian Government with power to appoint and dismiss officials.

Eisenhower on 27 July explained to the CCS why he preferred his own conditions to Churchill's. He wished to have a simple set of terms that could be broadcast directly to the Italian people. Hope for an honorable peace among the population, he thought, would make it impossible for any government in Italy to remain in power if it declined to make peace. But he did not wish to ask Italy to turn against the Germans, for he doubted the existence of much "fury" among the Italian people. Requiring active aid against the Germans would be offering the Italians merely a change of sides, whereas the great desire of the Italian people, he felt, was to be finished with the war.[48]

Eisenhower's program of psychological warfare, designed to bring the Badoglio regime to prompt capitulation, came under close scrutiny and eventual change by the heads of the British and American Governments. On the same afternoon, 27 July, that Eisenhower renewed his recommendation for a simple set of terms, the Prime Minister, in the House of Commons, was making the first official public declaration in response to Mussolini's downfall. Churchill said:

We should let the Italians, to use a homely phrase, stew in their own juice for a bit, and hot up the fire to the utmost in order to accelerate the process, until we obtain from their Government, or whoever possesses the necessary authority, all our indispensable requirements for carrying on the war against our prime and capital foe, which is not Italy but Germany. It is the interest of Italy, and also the interest of the Allies, that the unconditional surrender of Italy be brought about wholesale and not piecemeal.[49]

---

[47] Telg 383, Prime Minister to President, 26 Jul 43, ABC 381 Italy-Arm-Surr (5-9-43), Sec 1-A; a copy of this telegram, No. 4116, which was forwarded by General Devers (in England) to Eisenhower was received at AFHQ at 0850, 27 July 1943, Capitulation of Italy, p. 9; Churchill (*Closing the Ring*, pages 56-58) prints the whole message.

[48] Telg 4894, Eisenhower to Devers for Prime Minister, 27 Jul 43, Capitulation of Italy, p. 17.

[49] *Onwards to Victory: War Speeches by the Right Hon. Winston S. Churchill*, compiled by Charles Eade (Boston: Little, Brown and Company, 1944), pp. 186-87.

As he explained to Eisenhower privately, Churchill saw "obvious dangers in trying to state armistice terms in an attractive, popular form to the enemy nation." It was far better, he said, for all to be "cut and dried and that their Government should know our full demands and their maximum expectations."[50] On the following day, 28 July, President Roosevelt in a public address reiterated the strong stand to be taken with Italy. He said:

Our terms for Italy are still the same as our terms to Germany and Japan—'Unconditional Surrender.' We will have no truck with Fascism in any way, shape, or manner. We will permit no vestige of Fascism to remain.[51]

The arguments seemed to be a luxury in view of the immediate prospect of getting Italy to surrender, and General Marshall explained the difficulty involved. The British Government, he telegraphed Eisenhower, had the attitude that a surrender involved political and economic conditions as well as military stipulations. The British therefore viewed Eisenhower's authority as limited to purely local surrenders. And the President agreed that the Allied commander should not fix general terms without the approval of both governments.[52]

Eisenhower replied by asking for a directive from both governments empowering him to state general terms. There might be, he wrote, a fleeting opportunity to gain all objectives. Most important, he felt, was the prospect of obtaining Italian co-operation in seizing vital ports and airfields. But he had to be able to speak precisely and authoritatively to the commander in chief of the Italian forces. If economic and political matters could be settled later, he might by the use of military terms alone be able to bring the campaign in the Mediterranean to a rapid conclusion, thus saving resources for operations elsewhere.[53]

At the same time, he sent a message to Mr. Churchill, explaining his request for a directive on a slightly different ground. Because he was conducting the war in the Mediterranean in accord with the CCS instruction to force Italy out of the war, he felt it his duty to take quick and full advantage of every opportunity.[54]

Meanwhile, the British Foreign Office on 27 July had informed the U.S. State Department that the British considered the King of Italy or Badoglio acceptable for the purpose of effecting surrender. What continued to be a problem was whether the surrendering authority should be permitted to continue in office.[55]

The Combined Civil Affairs Committee took up the surrender matter on 29 July, but was unable to reach a decision or to make any positive recommendations. The British representative urged that the earlier proposal, the lengthy draft of detailed conditions known as the Long Terms, be approved by both governments so that General Eisenhower could present civil as well as military terms. The Americans

---

[50] Churchill, *Closing the Ring*, pp. 60–61.

[51] *United States and Italy 1936–1946: Documentary Record*, U.S. Department of State Publication 2669, European Series 17 (Washington, 1946), p. 45.

[52] Telg 3600, Marshall to Eisenhower, 28 Jul 43, Capitulation of Italy, p. 30.

[53] Telg W-6024, Eisenhower to Marshall, 29 Jul 43, Capitulation of Italy, pp. 48–49.

[54] Telg 5499, Eisenhower to Devers for Prime Minister, 29 Jul 43, Capitulation of Italy, pp. 46–47.

[55] Copy of Msg from Br Foreign Office to U.S. State Dept, 27 Jul 43, OPD Files, Prime-President, Exec 10, item 63.

objected, as they had previously, on the ground that the Long Terms did not provide for unconditional surrender.[56]

On the same day, the British Defense Committee cabled its views to the CCAC. Unconditional surrender, the British believed, had political and economic, as well as military, connotations. The armistice terms should therefore be comprehensive and inclusive. They recommended that General Eisenhower be authorized to accept a general surrender, but urged that the Long Terms be used as the surrender instrument. Considering it rather unlikely for the Italians to approach General Eisenhower directly, they anticipated as more probable an Italian bid for peace through the Vatican or some neutral state. The proposal to secure an initial surrender on the basis of military terms, this to be followed by agreement to economic and political terms, struck the British as faulty. What if the Italian Government refused to sign at the second stage? Precise terms were needed, and civil as well as military conditions would have to be included. And toward that end, the British planned in the near future to submit to the U.S. Government a comprehensive draft of terms in the expectation that the two Allied governments would reach agreement in plenty of time for AFHQ to conduct the actual negotiations.[57]

At this juncture President Roosevelt, though concurring in the British view that the precise armistice terms should not be broadcast, urged that General Eisenhower's recommended draft of surrender articles be accepted.[58] He seemed mainly impressed by Eisenhower's argument that great military gains would accrue at little cost if a simple set of terms of surrender could be used to secure the rapid elimination of Italy from the war. Thus, although he had publicly proclaimed his adherence to unconditional surrender, and although he had left the American members of the CCAC with the impression that he was standing by that formula, he did not mention the phrase in his correspondence with Churchill. Furthermore, he recognized that insisting on having Mussolini turned over as a war criminal might prejudice the primary objective of getting Italy quickly out of the war, and he did not recommend a modification of Eisenhower's draft on this point.[59]

As Mr. Roosevelt explained to the press, he did not care with whom he dealt in Italy so long as that person—King, prime minister, or a mayor—was not a member of the Fascist government; so long as he could get the Italian troops to lay down their arms; and so long as he could prevent anarchy. At the same time, the President warned neutral nations against sheltering Axis war criminals.[60]

Meanwhile, the British and American Governments had approved an emas-

---

[56] Min, 3d Mtg CCAC, 29 Jul 43, ABC 381 Italy-Arm-Surr (5-9-43), Sec 1-A, item 6.

[57] Telg 4995, Foreign Minister Eden to Viscount Halifax (repeated to British Resident Minister, Algiers), 29 Jul 43; Telg 387, Churchill to Roosevelt, 29 Jul 43, both in OPD Misc Exec 2, item 5; Telg 4157, Churchill to Eisenhower, 29 Jul 43, Capitulation of Italy, pp. 43-44; Cf. Churchill, Closing the Ring, pp. 60-61.

[58] The President stipulated one slight change dealing with the withdrawal of the German forces on the Italian mainland. Telg 330, Roosevelt to Churchill, 29 Jul 43, ABC 381 Italy-Arm-Surr (5-9-43), Sec 1-A.

[59] Telg, Roosevelt to Churchill, 30 Jul 43, OPD Misc Exec 2, item 5.

[60] Harold Calendar in the New York Times, July 31, 1943, p. 1. Cf. Churchill, Closing the Ring, p. 64.

culated version of Eisenhower's draft message to be broadcast to the Italian people. References to the Atlantic Charter and to peace conditions were dropped. The return to Italy of Italian prisoners captured in Tunisia and Sicily was promised if all Allied prisoners held by the Italians were repatriated. On 29 July, therefore, AFHQ began to transmit the following broadcast to Italy:

We commend the Italian people and the House of Savoy on ridding themselves of Mussolini, the man who involved them in war as the tool of Hitler, and brought them to the verge of disaster. The greatest obstacle which divided the Italian people from the United Nations has been removed by the Italians themselves. The only remaining obstacle on the road to peace is the German aggressor who is still on Italian soil. You want peace. You can have peace immediately, and peace under the honorable conditions which our governments have already offered you. We are coming to you as liberators. Your part is to cease immediately any assistance to the German military forces in your country. If you do this, we will rid you of the Germans and deliver you from the horrors of war. As you have already seen in Sicily, our occupation will be mild and beneficent. Your men will return to their normal life, and to their productive avocations and, provided all British and Allied prisoners now in your hands are restored safely to us, and not taken away to Germany, the hundreds of thousands of Italian prisoners captured by us in Tunisia and Sicily, will return to the countless Italian homes who long for them. The ancient liberties and traditions of your country will be restored.[61]

The day this broadcast hit Italy, 29 July, Hitler was directing the new divisions for Rommel's *Army Group B* to make their way across the borders into Italy through use of force if necessary. Roatta, chief of the Italian Army, was drafting instructions to commanders in northern Italy to mine the railways against German incursion. Guariglia, the new Foreign Minister, had just returned to Rome where rumors were current of an impending German descent upon the capital in force. In Sicily, where the U.S. Seventh and British Eighth Armies were pressing forward vigorously all along the line, Italian resistance had virtually collapsed. Throughout Italy the population expected Badoglio to bring about an end to the war. Though the Badoglio government banned Eisenhower's broadcast from publication, the message in mimeographed form quickly appeared on the streets of the principal cities, where it became the chief topic of discussion in street cars and cafes. According to one competent observer, the Allied broadcast was the straw that broke the camel's back.[62]

As Churchill and Roosevelt clearly wished, the psychological warfare beamed to Italy from the Allied headquarters in Algiers was sharply differentiated from the problem of agreeing on suitable articles of capitulation. There was a difficult problem regarding armistice terms, General Marshall telegraphed General

---

[61] The revision and clearance with the Joint Chiefs of Staff of the broadcast to Italy can be traced in: Telg 327, Roosevelt to Churchill, 27 Jul 43, and Telg 384, Churchill to Roosevelt, 28 Jul 43, as repeated in Telg 4135, Churchill to Eisenhower, 28 Jul 43; Telg 3611, Marshall to Eisenhower, 28 Jul 43; Telg 4399, Eisenhower to Churchill, 29 Jul 43, all in Capitulation of Italy, pp. 20-21, 31, 46. The Italian text as received in Italy is printed in: *Ministero degli Affari Esteri, Il contributo italiano nella guerra contro la Germania* (Rome: Istituto Poligrafico Dello Stato, 1946), p. 1. See also Telg 324, Roosevelt to Churchill, 25 Jul 43, and Telg Roosevelt to Eisenhower, 28 Jul 43, both in OPD 300.6 Security (OCS Papers).

[62] Associated Press dispatch from Berne, Switzerland, July 30, 1943, New York *Times*, July 30, 1943, p. 3; Rossi, *Come arrivammo*, p. 72.

Eisenhower on the 28th, because the attitude of the British Government was that political and economic conditions were involved as well as strictly military stipulations. Meeting on 30 July, the British War Cabinet agreed to accept Eisenhower's draft conditions for Italian capitulation, subject to several amendments. The British wished to omit all references to German forces and to add a stipulation that the Italians must do their best to deny to the Germans facilities useful to the Allies. They proposed to augment Eisenhower's power by enabling him to order the Italian Government to take such administrative or other action as he might require—this in addition to his authority to establish military government. They wanted greater clarity in spelling out the power to prescribe demobilization, disarmament, and demilitarization. They wanted provision made for the surrender of Italian war criminals, and for the disposition of Italian merchant shipping. With these changes, the cabinet was willing to authorize Eisenhower's terms as an emergency arrangement—if the Italians suddenly sued for peace and if military developments required immediate acceptance. If it turned out that the Allies had time to negotiate through diplomatic channels, the British desired the Americans to give careful consideration to the formal set of articles—the Long Terms—proposed earlier by the British.[63]

On the following day, the last day of July, the President and Prime Minister approved the short military terms. Nothing was to be said about war criminals, for Roosevelt believed that problem might better be taken up later. Churchill suggested two changes of wording for the sake of precision; emphasized his government's agreement to the short terms only to meet an emergency situation; and revealed that London found puzzling Washington's lack of reference to the original British terms, a comprehensive and more carefully worded version of the armistice terms.[64]

On the same day Churchill suggested to Foreign Secretary Anthony Eden that concluding an armistice with Italy in two stages—initially the short military terms, later the signature of the long terms—might be a sound procedure. Even in the event of a diplomatic approach, Churchill felt, the military conditions might serve very well, for the short terms would be more easily understood by an Italian envoy. The British Foreign Office was not particularly receptive to Churchill's thought. Eden preferred unconditional surrender.[65]

General Eisenhower now had, by the end of July, a draft of armistice terms ready for presentation to Badoglio if the latter should seek to get out of the war, as he was expected to do. But it was still not clear between London and Washington what should happen to the Italian Government after acceptance of the short terms. President Roosevelt studied the British draft of comprehensive terms, but

---

[63] Telg 3600, Marshall to Eisenhower, 28 Jul 43, Capitulation of Italy, p. 30; Telg, Churchill to Roosevelt, No. 389, 30 Jul 43, ABC 381 Italy-Arm-Surr (5-9-43), sec. 1-A, repeated to Eisenhower through Devers, Msg 4180, Capitulation of Italy, pp. 51–52 (copy also found in OPD 300.6 Security (OCS Papers).

[64] Telg, Roosevelt to Churchill, 31 Jul 43, ABC 381 Italy-Arm-Surr (5-9-43), sec. 1-A, (copy to Eisenhower in Telg 3824, Marshall to Eisenhower, 31 Jul 43, Capitulation of Italy, pp. 59–60); Telg, Churchill to Roosevelt, as given in Telg 4222, Devers to Eisenhower, 31 Jul 43, Capitulation of Italy, pp. 66–67.

[65] Churchill, *Closing the Ring*, pp. 64–65.

he did not wish to use it. He wired this view to Churchill: that in the future he preferred to let Eisenhower act to meet situations as they might arise. A copy of this message was given to the American Joint Chiefs and to the British Joint Staff Mission for their guidance. At the same time, in deference to Churchill's inquiries, President Roosevelt directed the Joint Chiefs to re-examine the British draft of the Long Terms.[66]

On 3 August, the Joint Chiefs again studied the Long Terms, the British proposal which had first been considered in the Combined Chiefs of Staff meeting of 16 June. The Joint Chiefs submitted four objections to the British proposal: there was no statement or reference to unconditional surrender; it referred to the "Supreme Command of the United Nations," a position which did not exist; the document did not deal with German troops in Italy; and it provided for implementation by a Control Commission under the authority of the United Nations, rather than by Eisenhower under the authority of the United States and British Governments through the Combined Chiefs of Staff. The Joint Chiefs expressed agreement with President Roosevelt's view that Eisenhower be permitted to act to meet situations as they arose, using the terms already furnished him as he saw fit. They conceded that the British proposal, with appropriate amendments to meet U.S. objections, might serve a useful purpose for later phases of the Italian situation, since it did embrace in a single document many well-considered military, political, and economic conditions to be imposed on Italy.[67]

The British Government now reintroduced its draft of the Long Terms, with changes of wording to meet the American objections, particularly in regard to unconditional surrender.[68] At its fourth meeting, the Combined Civil Affairs Committee again considered terms for Italian surrender. The British members presented the British War Cabinet's point of view: a comprehensive and all-inclusive statement of terms would be necessary in addition to the terms which General Eisenhower already possessed and they submitted the revised and amended British draft of the Long Terms for this purpose. The committee agreed that additional terms dealing with political and economic matters would be necessary at a later date. The American members pointed out that the short terms did not include any saving clause empowering General Eisenhower to impose the political as well as military conditions. The committee then recommended the inclusion of such a saving clause. No other decision was made.[69]

On 6 August, the Combined Chiefs accepted the committee's suggestion for a saving clause, and instructed General Eisenhower that if he employed the draft

---

[66] Memorandum for General Marshall, Admiral King, and General Arnold, 2 Aug 43, sub: Surrender Terms, OPD Exec 2, item 5, tab 25 (copy in OPD 300.6 Security (OCS Papers).

[67] JCS Memo for President, 3 Aug 43, sub: Draft Instrument of Surrender of Italy, ABC 381 Italy-Arm-Surr (5-9-43), sec. 1-A.

[68] Memo for rcd, Surrender Terms for Italy, n.d., Document A, n.d., ABC 381 Italy-Arm-Surr (5-9-43), sec. 1-A. Document A is the revised version of CCS 258 with Article 30 filled out, and with the formula for unconditional surrender incorporated in the preamble. The Civil Affairs Division of the War Department and the Strategy and Policy Group of OPD made the suggestions for the rewording.

[69] Min, 4th Mtg CCAC, 5 Aug 43, ABC 381 Italy-Arm-Surr (5-9-43), sec. 1-A.

terms which he already had, he should make it clear that they were purely military and that other conditions, political, economic, and financial, would follow.[70]

Mussolini's downfall, therefore, marked no turning point in Allied strategy. It merely hastened the decision to invade the Italian mainland, but it in no sense brought about the decision itself. At American insistence, operations in the Mediterranean beyond Sicily were to be limited—subordinate to the main effort to be launched later in northwest Europe. With his resources consequently curtailed, General Eisenhower was to find that the success or failure in the campaign after Sicily would depend not on the power marshalled in support of the invasion but rather on negotiations to eliminate Italy as a belligerent. The blow at the Italian mainland, originally conceived as a means of forcing the Italians to surrender, was to become contingent on first eliminating Italy from the war as the result of military diplomacy.

### Rome: Open City

During the last few days of July, while working out the terms of military diplomacy to induce Italy to quit the war, while broadcasting to the Italian people a program of psychological warfare, and while expecting word from the Badoglio government on the prospect of peace, General Eisenhower had suspended heavy air raids on Italian cities. The lull coincidentally served another purpose. The Mediterranean Allied air forces had been operating at close to full capacity for a long time, and air commanders wished to give their crews a rest.[71]

On the first day of August, after conferring with Tedder, Eisenhower decided to resume air bombardments, particularly in the Naples area and on the railroad marshaling yards around Rome. Before doing so, he broadcast his intention a day earlier. Another Algiers radio broadcast on 2 August warned the Italian people of dire consequences if the Badoglio government made no move to end the war.[72]

The Allied air forces then bombed the Italian mainland. U.S. Flying Fortresses attacked Naples twice, night-flying British Wellingtons raided Naples three times during the first week of August. An operation planned against the Rome marshaling yards for 3 August was canceled at the last minute because AFHQ received word from the Combined Chiefs that the Italian Government had requested a statement of conditions necessary to recognize Rome as an open city.[73]

The Italian attempt to gain for Rome the status of an open city was the first diplomatic approach received by the Allies. The initiative apparently had come from the Holy See, for on 31 July the Vatican received in response to its

---

[70] Min, 105th Mtg CCS, 6 Aug 43, Supplementary, item 9; Telg 4363, Marshall to Eisenhower.

[71] Telg W-6503, Eisenhower to Marshall, 4 Aug 43, and Telg 4115, Marshall to Eisenhower, 3 Aug 43, both in Smith Papers, box 4. See also Butcher, *My Three Years With Eisenhower*, pp. 382–83.

[72] Butcher, *My Three Years With Eisenhower*, p. 375; Telgs W-6406 and W-6509, Eisenhower to Marshall, 3 and 4 Aug 43, and British Resident Minister in Algiers to Churchill, 4 Aug 43, Smith Papers, box 4; New York *Times*, August 3, 1943, p. 1.

[73] Coles, USAAF Hist Study 37, pp. 163–64; Telgs W-6406 and W-6509, Eisenhower to Marshall, 3 and 4 Aug 43, and Telg W-6516/7711, AFHQ to AGWAR, 4 Aug 43, all in OPD Exec 2, item 6; see also, Butcher, *My Three Years With Eisenhower*, pp. 378–79.

# THE CLIMAX

request, a written statement from the Italian Government that the decision had been made to declare Rome an open city. Transmitting this information, the Apostolic Delegate in Washington informed Sumner Welles, Under Secretary of State, on 2 August that the Papal Secretary of State wished to ascertain what conditions the Allies deemed necessary for regarding the Italian capital in this light. The State Department informed the British Government and General Marshall, and the latter advised Eisenhower, suggesting that air bombardment of Rome be halted for the moment. It was then that General Eisenhower canceled the bombardment planned for 3 August. Next day Eisenhower learned that he was free to attack airfields near Rome being used by Italians and Germans, but bad flying weather around the Italian capital caused him to cancel the mission.[74]

The War Department, meanwhile, on 2 August had submitted to the President and to the State Department a list of seven conditions considered essential for recognizing Rome as an open city. Churchill and his War Cabinet vigorously opposed such recognition. Apprehensive lest such a move be taken by the Allied public as an abandonment of the principle of unconditional surrender and as a willingness to make a patched-up peace with the Badoglio regime, Churchill also suspected that the Italian Government might be taking the first step toward trying to secure recognition of all of Italy as a neutral area so that the government could withdraw painlessly from the war. Believing that Allied troops would be in Rome within a few months, Churchill saw the city's communication and airfield systems as a requirement for further advance up the Italian peninsula.[75]

Though agreeing with the Prime Minister's objections, the JCS recommended that the President avoid making a direct denial to the Holy See's request. In accordance with the suggestion, Mr. Sumner Welles on 5 August told the Apostolic Delegate that the matter was receiving the fullest consideration by the highest American authorities. He concluded: "I am instructed by the President to state that, in accordance with the accepted principles of international law and of pertinent international agreements, there is nothing to prevent the Italian Government from undertaking unilaterally to declare Rome an open city." [76]

The first diplomatic move made by Italy toward the Allies, tentative and tangential though it was, thus received an *ad hoc* reception that was rather cold. Without further communication, the Ital-

---

[74] Ltr 492/42, Archbishop Cicognani to Sumner Welles, 2 Aug 43, OPD Exec 2, item 6; Memo, Col Hammond for President, White 22, 2 Aug 43, OPD Exec 2, item 5; Memo, Sumner Welles for Marshall, 2 Aug 43, inclosing request from Apostolic Delegate; Memo, Marshall for Handy, 2 Aug 43, sub: Rome an Open City; Telg, Marshall to Eisenhower, FAN 181, 2 Aug 43; Memo, Col Hammond for President, White 25, 2 Aug 43; Memo, Col Hammond for Marshall, 3 Aug 43, all found in OPD 300.6 Security (OCS Papers).

[75] Msg 403, Churchill to Roosevelt, 4 Aug 43, OPD Exec 2, item 6; Telg 401, Churchill to Roosevelt, 3 Aug 43, and Telg 402, Churchill to Roosevelt, 4 Aug 43, OPD 300.6 Security (OCS Papers). There were some reports of this plan in the press. See Associated Press dispatch of July 31, 1943, Berne, Switzerland, in New York *Times,* August 1, 1943, and article by Edwin L. James, p. E–3.

[76] Memo, JCS for President, 5 Aug 43, and for General Hull, 19 Aug 43, both in OPD Exec 2, item 6; Telgs, Eisenhower to Marshall and Marshall to Eisenhower, Smith Papers, box 4.

ian Government on 14 August formally declared Rome an open city.

At first the CCS instructed Eisenhower to make no further air attacks against the Italian capital until its status could be clarified. But on the following day, 15 August, the CCS decided that the Allies should not commit themselves on the matter, and they thereby left Eisenhower free to bomb such military objectives in the Rome area as he judged necessary.[77]

---

[77] CCS 306, 14 Aug 43, Rome an Open City; Min, 108th Mtg CCS, 15 Aug 43, item 2; Telg, CCS to Eisenhower, FAN 191, 14 Aug 43, and Telg, CCS to Eisenhower, FAN 194, 15 Aug 43, OPD Exec 2, item 6; Telg 5309 Marshall to Eisenhower, 14 Aug 43, and Telg 1682, AFHQ to KKAD, Quebec, 15 Aug 43, both in Smith Papers, box 4.

# CHAPTER XV

# Dissolution of the Rome-Berlin Axis

## Badoglio's First Moves

About 1700, 25 July, the Italian monarch summoned Marshal Badoglio, informed him of his appointment as Head of Government, and handed him the list of his cabinet members—civil servants without party connection or support—that the sovereign and the Duke of Acquarone had selected. As Head of Government, Badoglio was to be responsible for civil functions only. Victor Emmanuel III resumed the supreme command of the Italian armed forces, a power that Mussolini had exercised since 11 June 1940. Ambrosio was to continue as chief of *Comando Supremo,* Roatta as chief of the Army General Staff, *Superesercito.*

Badoglio accepted the situation and the conditions, including two proclamations already drafted, which the marshal issued over his own signature and communicated through the press and radio. The first announced Badoglio's appointment and assured Italy and the world that "The war continues." The second proclamation warned the Italian people, the Fascist organization, and other political parties against agitating the government with precipitate demands for wholesale political changes or for peace.[1] The first was a clear, official announcement of the continued vitality of the treaty of alliance with Germany.[2]

Though the Badoglio government dissolved the Fascist party and began to incorporate the Fascist militia gradually into the Regular Army, the government was non-Fascist rather than anti-Fascist. The change of regime seemed to mark the first step toward a restoration of constitutional government, but the actual basis of Badoglio's powers was in the Fascist constitutional laws. The King had been careful to maintain his role as a constitutional monarch, accepting Mussolini's resignation and appointing Badoglio his successor as *Capo del Governo,* with all the powers of that office created by the Fascist laws of 1925 and 1926. But Badoglio refused to take any action without the explicit authorization of the King. In actuality, Italy reverted to absolute monarchy. At Badoglio's insistence, whatever civil power he exercised was to be construed as a direct emanation of the King's will. Whatever military commands and directives Ambrosio issued were in accordance with the King's direct wishes.

Relieved of the Fascist burden, the country seethed with political excitement

---

[1] Badoglio, *Memorie e documenti,* p. 71. Badoglio learned later that Vittorio Emanuele Orlando, Italian Premier during World War I, had assisted in drafting the proclamations.

[2] *Il Processo Carboni-Roatta: L'Armistizio e la difesa di Roma nella sentenza del Tribunale Militare (Estratto della "Rivista Penale," Maggio–Giugno 1949)* (Rome: Società Editrice Temi), p. 9 (cited hereafter as *Il Processo Carboni-Roatta*).

and with the expectation of immediate peace. To check the unrest, Roatta transferred control of four divisions from himself to the Minister of War, Generale di Brigata in Riserva Antonio Sorice, who moved two from the interior of Italy to Turin and two from France to Milan. Eventually, Sorice controlled five divisions, all to be used for maintaining public order and therefore not available for defense against attack by either the Allies or the Germans.[3]

While awaiting the return to Italy of Raffaele Guariglia, Ambassador to Turkey, who was to become Minister of Foreign Affairs, Badoglio took charge of foreign policy. In accordance with the King's wishes, the immediate aim was to avoid conflict with the Germans. Badoglio wished to end the war, jointly with the Germans if possible. At the least, he was to try to secure German consent to a dissolution of the Pact of Steel.[4]

At the *carabinieri* barracks where he spent his first night in captivity after his forced resignation, Mussolini received a note from Badoglio. The measures taken toward him, Badoglio explained, were in the interest of his personal safety, for a plot had been discovered against his life. Mussolini replied, thanking Badoglio for his consideration. He would make no difficulties, he added, but would, rather, co-operate to the fullest extent. Expressing satisfaction over the decision to continue the war, he wished Badoglio well in his task of serving the King, "whose loyal servant I remain."[5]

Immediately after the Feltre conference, Hitler and the OKW had felt reassured over the situation in Italy. The Italian High Command had promised to commit four additional Italian divisions in the south: one in Sicily, two in Puglia, and one in Calabria. On 22 July, Hitler had released the *29th Panzer Grenadier Division* for employment on Sicily. That same day, Ambrosio had accepted the conditions laid down by Keitel at Feltre and had formally requested two additional German divisions. Field Marshal Rommel, who had been designated to command *Army Group B* in the *ALARICH* plan, was on 21 July removed from this assignment and sent to Salonika to take command of German troops in Greece. The warning orders for operations *ALARICH* and *KONSTANTIN* were suspended.[6] On 23 July, Hitler issued orders in accordance with Ambrosio's request alerting the *305th* and *76th Infantry Divisions* for movement from France to southern Italy. Hitler entertained no suspicion whatsoever that his friend Mussolini might secretly be searching for contact with the Western Powers. General von Rintelen did report, however, that *Comando Supremo* had little confidence that Sicily could be held and, on 24 July, he indicated that tension in Italy had increased rather than diminished as a result of the Feltre conference.[7]

News of the political change in Italy

---

[3] *Comando Supremo, I Reparto, Operazioni: Regio Esercito—Quadro di battaglia alla data del 1 luglio 1943; Quadro di battaglia alla data del 1 agosto 1943*, IT 10 a-h; Roatta, *Otto milioni*, pp. 263–64; Rossi, *Come arrivammo*, pp. 94, 174–75, 404; Zanussi, *Guerra e catastrofe*, II, 54.

[4] MS #P-058, Project 46, 1 Feb–8 Sep 43, Question 11; Rossi, *Come arrivammo*, p. 199; Roatta, *Otto milioni*, p. 291; Badoglio, *Memorie e documenti*, pp. 84–85; Rintelen, *Mussolini als Bundesgenosse*, p. 224.

[5] Badoglio, *Memorie e documenti*, p. 72; Mussolini, *Storia di un anno*, p. 20.

[6] *OKW/WFSt, KTB, 1.–31.VII.43*, 25 Jul 43; Rommel, Private KTB, entry 22 Jul 43.

[7] MS #C-093 (Warlimont), pp. 40–41.

came as a surprise to the Germans. The first reports to reach Berlin on 25 July were not alarming. They indicated merely that the Fascist old guard had brought about the convocation of the Grand Council to urge the Duce to take more energetic measures against defeatism. Not until the next day did the Germans learn that Ciano and Grandi had led a revolt, that Mussolini had resigned, and that the King had appointed Badoglio in his place.[8]

Hitler could not believe that Mussolini had resigned voluntarily. He was sure that force had been used, and he felt that the convocation of the Grand Council had been a show carefully prepared by the King and Badoglio. He feared that these two, who in his opinion had been sabotaging the war all along, might already have done away with his friend.

Hitler's first impulse was to strike with lightning speed—seize Rome with the *3d Panzer Grenadier Division* (located near Lake Bolsena 35 miles north of the city), and the *2d Parachute Division* (to be air-transported from France to the Rome area); kidnap the King, the Heir Apparent, Badoglio, and the cabinet ministers; and discover and liberate Mussolini as the only means of rejuvenating the Fascist party. So extreme was Hitler's anger and apprehension that he thought even of seizing the Vatican and the Pope. Goebbels and Ribbentrop, after lengthy argument, persuaded Hitler to drop this extreme measure.[9]

The main issue was whether to act at once in Italy with the forces available or to make more careful preparations that involved delay. Hitler favored immediate action, even if improvised, in order to capture the Badoglio government before it could consolidate its power. A quick, bold stroke, he believed, would restore the prestige of Fascism.

Rommel and others advocated caution. They feared that German moves would invite the Allies to establish themselves on the Italian mainland and that a blow against the King would turn the Italian officer corps against the Germans. Since Rommel concurred in the general belief that Mussolini's overthrow had been carefully prepared, and since he believed that the new government had already approached the Allies with an offer of peace, Rommel thought it best to retire from Sicily, Sardinia, and southern Italy, but to hold northern Italy. He recommended that Kesselring withdraw his forces and consolidate with Rommel's forces in the north, where all would come under Rommel's command.[10]

The first German orders prompted by Mussolini's overthrow were issued on the night of 26 July. The general framework and outline of Plan *ALARICH* were at hand but the German reaction to the new situation in Italy had a large measure of improvisation. Field Marshal von Rundstedt, *OB WEST*, was ordered to move two divisions toward the Italian border: the *305th Infantry Division* toward Nice, and the *44th Infantry Division* toward the Brenner Pass. He was to carry out two operations which had formed integral parts of the *ALARICH* plan: *KOPENHAGEN*, the seizure of

---

[8] *Goebbels Diaries*, p. 403, entry 25 Jul 43. Ambassador von Mackensen's early reports did not reveal the full extent of the crisis, and he was bitterly criticized by Ribbentrop, Minister of Foreign Affairs. See MS #C-013 (Kesselring), p. 5.

[9] *Goebbels Diaries*, pp. 407–09.

[10] Min of Confs 14, 15, and 16, 25 and 26 Jul 43, in Min of Hitler Confs.

the Mount Cenis pass; and *SIEGFRIED*, the occupation of the southern coast of France in the area of the Italian *Fourth Army*. Field Marshal Rommel was recalled from Salonika to command *Army Group B*, with headquarters in Munich. Meanwhile, Ambassador von Mackensen, Field Marshal Kesselring, and General von Rintelen were instructed to learn all they could regarding the intentions of the new government.[11]

Plans against Italy began to develop at once in three main stages. First, *Army Group B* was to occupy north Italy. Behind the two initial divisions dispatched toward Italy, Rundstedt was to move up four more divisions from France. The *II SS Panzer Corps*, comprising two SS panzer divisions, was to be withdrawn from the Eastern Front to become part of Rommel's new command. Second, Generaloberst Kurt Student was to fly to Rome, take operational control of the *3d Panzer Grenadier* and *2d Parachute Divisions*, seize the capital and the leading political personalities, and liberate Mussolini. Capt. Otto Skorzeny, personally selected by Hitler, was to have the special mission of locating and liberating the Duce. Because earlier *ALARICH* planning had designated Student to occupy the Alpine passes with his *XI Flieger Korps* (*1st* and *2d Parachute Divisions*), OKW assigned this task to General der Gebirgstruppen Valentin Feurstein, who was to use troops stationed at the Mountain Training School in Mittenwald, fifteen miles north of Innsbruck. Third, as soon as all was in readiness for the stroke planned against the Italian Government, Rommel was to take command of all German forces in north Italy. Kesselring was then to withdraw the German troops from the Italian islands and from south Italy and consolidate his forces with Rommel's command in the north. At that time, Kesselring's command in Italy would come to an end.

In connection with the third step, Hitler's headquarters dispatched a naval officer to Frascati to explain Kesselring's role in the plan. Kesselring was to halt all movements of additional troops to Sicily; prepare to evacuate all air units from Sicily, Sardinia, and Corsica, destroying, if necessary, their heavy equipment; concentrate in assembly areas the *16th* and *26th Panzer Divisions* and that part of the *29th Panzer Grenadier Division* still on the Italian mainland, suspending thereby further movements to the south; alert the *3d Panzer Grenadier* and *2d Parachute Divisions* (the latter upon its arrival near Rome) to their mission; be ready to take over all the antiaircraft defenses in Italy, repossessing the flak material furnished Italian units; and send transport aircraft to France to carry the *2d Parachute Division* to Italy.[12]

Kesselring took a different view of the situation from that of OKW. Optimistic by temperament and inclined to trust those with whom he worked, he had called on Badoglio on 26 July, accompanied by the German Ambassador, Mackensen. Badoglio assured the Germans that he had known nothing of the movement against Mussolini until he was summoned by the King to take office. He had insisted, Badoglio continued, on maintaining the alliance with Germany as a condition of taking office, and his proclamation made clear that the war would continue. When

---

[11] *OKW/WFSt, KTB, 1.VII–31.VII.43*, 26 Jul 43; Rommel, Private KTB, entries for 25–28 Jul 43.

[12] *OKW/WFSt, KTB, 1.–31.VII.43*, 26 Jul 43.

the Germans expressed some curiosity as to Mussolini's fate, Badoglio showed Mussolini's letter as proof not only of his personal safety but also of his intention to do nothing to oppose the new regime. When Kesselring turned the conversation to military matters and said it was necessary to overcome the sense of fatigue among Italian troops and to eliminate certain impediments to the military effort raised by the civil administration, Badoglio declared he would do everything he could to improve the co-operation of Italian civil officials. Problems of morale, however, concerned the military, and Badoglio urged Kesselring to take up the problem directly with Ambrosio, chief of *Comando Supremo*.

Kesselring and Rintelen called on Ambrosio, who assured them that the political change had no effect on military operations. Like Badoglio, Ambrosio emphasized Italy's determination to continue in the war on the side of her ally. As to improving Italian troop morale, Ambrosio observed that this was not an easy matter, it would take time. Kesselring reminded Ambrosio that Hitler at Feltre had promised to send all the reinforcements Germany could spare, and he urged measures to restore the sense of comradeship between Italian and German troops.[13]

Badoglio's and Ambrosio's declarations conformed with the King's basic policy—to avoid a unilateral breach of the alliance by Italy, and to take no action that would bring Italians into conflict with Germans. These assurances were not altogether dishonest. Kesselring, on his side, appreciated the Italian participation in the war. He respected Ambrosio and Roatta. Accepting the Italian statements in good faith, he bent his efforts toward maintaining the alliance.[14]

Though Goebbels cynically wrote that "Kesselring fell for a well-staged show," Kesselring felt that more was to be gained by exploiting the current willingness of the Italian Government to co-operate than by precipitating a crisis that might lead to collapse and chaos. After receiving the instructions brought personally by the naval officer, Kesselring reported to OKW his belief that the Fascist party had lost out because of its own weakness and lack of leadership and that no support could be expected from it. He thought that the measures planned by Student and Skorzeny could be executed, but not without care and consequent delay. Action against the Italian forces guarding Rome would completely alienate, he felt, all who still bore some good will toward Germany. Furthermore, an armed struggle in the Rome area would disrupt all traffic to the south, halt the movement of supplies and reinforcements, and expose the German forces in Sicily and southern Italy to the danger of being cut off. In the interest of these troops at least, he urged, the Germans should exploit the willingness of the Italian Government to receive additional German units. In contrast with Rommel's estimate, Kesselring believed that he could, if reinforced, defend all of Italy and the Balkans, and he recommended this course of action to Hitler.[15]

---

[13] Rintelen, *Mussolini als Bundesgenosse*, pp. 224–25; *OKW/WFSt, KTB, 1.–31.VII.43*, 26 Jul 43; Min, *Colloquio a Palazzo Vidoni, Roma, 26 luglio 1943*, IT 3037.

[14] Westphal, *Heer in Fesseln*, p. 224; MS #T–2, K 1 (Kesselring), pp. 6–7; Eugenio Dollmann, *Roma Nazista* (Milan: Longanesi & Co., 1949), p. 138.

[15] *OKW/WFSt, KTB, 1.–31.VII.43*, 27 Jul 43; MS #C–013 (Kesselring), p. 13.

Kesselring's representations had an effect. On 28 July, OKW suspended Student's mission, ordering him instead merely to be ready to seize the Italian Government and liberate Mussolini.[16] Student and Skorzeny were by then at Frascati, and the first lift of the *2d Parachute Division* arrived that day at Pratica di Mare, an airfield not far from Frascati. Roatta was curious about the sudden arrival of German paratroopers, but he accepted with seeming good grace Kesselring's explanation—they were reinforcements for the *1st Parachute Division* in Sicily. While the Germans thus set the stage for Hitler's coup—kidnapping the Italian Government—Skorzeny threw himself wholeheartedly into the mission of finding Mussolini. Dazzled by the honor of having been summoned to Hitler's headquarters, Skorzeny had fallen under Hitler's spell. Mussolini, the Fuehrer had said, was the last of the Romans and his only true friend. He would go to any length to save him from being turned over to the Allies. Skorzeny vowed to be worthy of Hitler's trust.[17]

Meanwhile, on 27 July, Badoglio formulated his plan for a joint peace effort and presented it to the King, who authorized it as official policy. Badoglio then sent a telegram to Hitler proposing a meeting on Italian soil between the King and the Fuehrer. His purpose was to explain candidly the need for a joint peace before the Axis bargaining power was diluted by divergent diplomatic courses.[18]

Because Alfieri, the Italian Ambassador at Berlin, had come to Rome to attend the meeting of the Grand Council, where he had voted against Mussolini, and had not returned to his post, the Italian Military Attaché at Berlin, Generale di Corpo d'Armata Efisio Marras, received instructions to fly to the Fuehrer's headquarters to reinforce the request for a conference. Without knowledge of Badoglio's intentions, Marras did not know whether Badoglio was trying to secure a joint Italo-German peace move, though the idea was not excluded. According to his instructions, Marras was to establish contact with Hitler on behalf of the new Italian Government, read a copy of Mussolini's letter indicating his continuing loyalty to the King, propose a meeting of the heads of state, and indicate the Italian desire to withdraw the Italian *Fourth Army* from southern France to Italy.[19]

The same day that Marras was getting ready to visit Hitler, 29 July, Kesselring was in conference with the Fuehrer. There Kesselring reinforced his argument in favor of maintaining correct relations with the Badoglio government—at least until the Germans could introduce additional German divisions into Italy peaceably.

On the surface at least, Hitler accepted Kesselring's program. He instructed Kesselring to direct all his dealings with *Comando Supremo* toward securing the movement of the maximum number of German troops into northern Italy. Ac-

---

[16] *OKW/WFSt, KTB, 1.–31.VII.43*, 28 Jul 43.

[17] Otto Skorzeny, *Geheimkommando Skorzeny* (Hamburg: Hansa Verlag Josef Toth, 1950), pp. 100–101. For additional material on Skorzeny see Extract From Revised Notes 1 on The German Intelligence Services, VFZ/34, copy 23, 6 Dec 44, Source M.I.-6, AFHQ reel 365F, and Hq U.S. Forces European Theater, Interrogation Center, Consolidated Intelligence Report (CIR) 4, 23 Jul 45, sub: The German Sabotage Service, unprocessed files, NARS.

[18] Badoglio, *Memorie e documenti*, pp. 84–85.

[19] Simoni, *Berlino, Ambasciata*, pp. 377–78; Interv, Smyth with Marras, 20 Dec 48.

tually, however, Hitler was using Kesselring, Rintelen, and Mackensen—the "Italophiles" as they were called in OKW—to allay Italian suspicions and to keep Badoglio in the alliance while OKW made ready to take drastic action.[20]

Though all reports from Kesselring and Mackensen, and from Admiral Wilhelm Canaris, intelligence chief, as well, gave credence to the solemn declarations of loyalty to the Axis by the King, Badoglio, Ambrosio, and Roatta, the reports made little impression on Hitler. He was certain that the Italian Government was planning "treason." A transatlantic conversation between President Roosevelt and Mr. Churchill intercepted by Germany on 29 July confirmed Hitler's suspicions that negotiations between Italy and the Allies were under way, even though the conversation indicated no more than an expectation of receiving Italian overtures.[21]

Hitler received Marras at his headquarters on the morning of 30 July. Marras felt that Hitler suspected him of being Badoglio's "torpedo" with the job of rubbing out the Fuehrer. For while Marras delivered Badoglio's message, he was conscious that Jodl, Generalmajor Rudolf Schmundt, and Ambassador Walter Hewel were facing him from three different points in the room, each with his hand on a revolver in his pocket. Marras remained rigid, not even venturing to make a move for his handkerchief. Hitler, who appeared calm, criticized the sudden Italian political change in the midst of war, and asked why a military attaché should be drawn into a political matter. Accepting Badoglio's declaration that the war would continue, Hitler saw no immediate need for a conference with the King or Badoglio, particularly because of the recent meeting with Mussolini at Feltre. Hitler suggested rather that the ministers of foreign affairs and the chiefs of staff might examine the situation from the standpoint of continuing the war. He made no direct reply to the proposed withdrawal of the Italian Army from southern France. He admitted that it might be useful at a later date for him to confer with the King and Badoglio, in which case the Heir Apparent—Prince Humbert—ought also to be present.[22]

Marras submitted his report to Badoglio on 1 August, and on the same day a telegram arrived from Hitler proposing a conference of foreign ministers and chiefs of staff at Tarvis, just across the border from Italy, on the 5th or 6th of August. Badoglio accepted Hitler's proposal.[23]

Hitler refused to confer on Italian soil or to leave Germany because he feared an attempt on his life. He proposed, instead, the meeting of second echelon officials in order to avoid a discussion of what Badoglio and others considered the fundamental issue: whether or not to make peace with the Allies. Badoglio, hoping for a frank talk with Hitler in the near future, declined to initiate any approach to the Western Allies until the Germans had clearly revealed their intentions.

By then, 1 August, OKW had a completely formulated plan, code-named *ACHSE*, to meet the possibility of an

---

[20] *OKW/WFSt, KTB, 1.-31.VII.43*, 29 Jul 43; MS #C-093 (Warlimont), p. 79; MS #C-013 (Kesselring), p. 12.

[21] *OKW/WFSt, KTB, 1.-31.VII.43*, 29 Jul 43. MS #C-093 (Warlimont), page 84, mistakenly gives credence to this alleged proof.

[22] Simoni, *Berlino, Ambasciata*, pp. 379-86; Interv, Smyth with Marras, 20 Dec 48.

[23] Badoglio, *Memorie e documenti*, p. 96; Simoni, *Berlino, Ambasciata*, p. 387.

Italian double cross. Like *ALARICH*, drawn up in the latter part of May in anticipation of political change in Italy, *ACHSE* was based on the premise of Italian defection. Upon receipt of the code word, German units in Italy were to take over the country by force.[24]

Events occurring on the Italian frontier during the last days of July seemed to indicate that the *ACHSE* button might be pushed at any moment.

*Friction Along the Alps*

In accordance with OKW instructions issued during the night of 26 July, Rundstedt started to move the *305th Infantry Division* from the interior of France toward Nice and the *44th Infantry Division* toward the Brenner Pass. At the border, transportation was to be arranged with Italian authorities on the assumption that the divisions were destined for southern Italy in accordance with agreements concluded with *Comando Supremo*. When on 27 July the leading elements of the *305th Infantry Division* reached Nice, which was in the area controlled by the Italian *Fourth Army*, they learned that *Comando Supremo* objected to further movement into Italy because of a shortage of railway transportation. *Comando Supremo* refused to provide transportation on the following day, and on 29 July the Italians informed OKW that the *305th Infantry Division* would have to wait at least several days before transportation could be made available to move it to southern Italy.[25]

*Comando Supremo* at least had a good excuse and perhaps a legitimate reason. Roatta, who as chief of *Superesercito* had operational control over all the ground forces, German and Italian, in Italy (except those Italian troops moved to the large cities to restrain civil disturbances), conferred with Kesselring on 28 July and reaffirmed that he wanted two more German divisions in the defense of southern Italy. But he explained that railway traffic was particularly congested because of the dispatch of an Italian division northward to check civilian unrest in Milan, Turin, and Bologna. German movements had to be halted temporarily, Roatta said, otherwise situations might occur wherein German troops would find Italian forces unexpectedly blocking their way. Roatta hoped to overcome the traffic problem by prohibiting all civilian travel, and proposed that half the train space be allocated for Italian movements, half for German. Kesselring seemed placated.[26]

On 29 July, Mussolini's birthday, while a rumor swept Rome that the Germans were preparing to seize the Italian capital, while Ambassador von Mackensen brought greetings to Mussolini with inquiries as to his whereabouts, and while Kesselring carried a handsome set of the works of Nietzsche as a present from Hitler to Mussolini and asked to deliver it personally, the Italian Ministry of War received three alarming telegrams from Generale di Corpo d'Armata Alessandro Gloria, commander of the *XXXV Corps*

---

[24] English translation of two telegrams, *OKW/WFSt, Nrs. 661747* and *661747/43 g.k.chefs.*, both dated 1 Aug 43 and signed by Keitel, in ONI, *Fuehrer Directives, 1942–1945* pp. 87–88; *OKW/WFSt, KTB, 1.–31.VII.43*, 1 Aug 43; MS #C–093 (Warlimont), pp. 87–90.

[25] *OKW/WFSt, KTB, 1.–31.VII.43*, 27, 28, and 29 Jul 43.
[26] *Ibid.*, 28 Jul 43.

at Bolzano, forty miles south of the Brenner Pass. Gloria reported German troops assembling in the German Tyrol and at least one group moving on foot toward the Brenner Pass.[27]

While the Italians politely frustrated Mackensen's and Kesselring's attempts to discover Mussolini's whereabouts, *Comando Supremo* prepared to resist the Germans on two fronts—to ward off a surprise attack against Rome and to oppose the incursion of unwanted German reinforcements into Italian territory. Summoning Roatta, Ambrosio informed him that providing for the defense of Rome against a possible German *coup d'état* had priority over protecting the coast against the threat of Allied landings. He also told Roatta to oppose the movement of German units across the frontier, except those specifically requested or permitted by *Comando Supremo*.

For the first mission, Roatta constituted a command called the *Army Corps of Rome* (the *12th (Sassari) Infantry Division*, elements of the *21st (Granatieri) Infantry Division*, police forces, African police troops, and depot units) under Generale di Corpo d'Armata Alberto Barbieri to provide for the internal security of the city and to reinforce General Carboni, who a week earlier had been placed in command of the *Motorized Corps* (the *Piave Division*, the *Ariete Armored Division*, the remainder of the *Granatieri Division*, and the *131st (Centauro) Division*) in the outer defenses of the city. To augment the defenses of Rome still further, Roatta had the *XVII Corps* move the *103d (Piacenza) Motorized Division* to positions just south of the capital, leaving only two coastal divisions to guard the nearby shore area.[28]

For the second mission, Roatta on 30 July sent officer couriers to the *Fourth Army* in southern France, to the *Second Army* in Slovenia-Croatia-Dalmatia, and to the *XXXV Corps* in Bolzano, warning them to be ready to oppose by force unauthorized German incursions and directing them to place demolition charges along the railway lines to impede frontier crossings.[29]

The *26th Panzer Division*, whose entry into Italy had been authorized earlier by the *Comando Supremo*, was not affected by these orders. About half of that division was already in southern Italy in accordance with the joint plans of *Comando Supremo* and OKW for the defense of the Italian peninsula. The remaining parts of the division crossed the Brenner Pass without incident during the late afternoon and early evening of 30 July. These troops reported evidence of demolition charges planted by Italian troops and the impression that the Italian forces in the frontier area had been reinforced.[30]

---

[27] Rpt, Admiral Canaris, *Chef Ausland Abwehr, OKW/WFSt, KTB, 1.-31.VII.43*, 31 Jul 43; Simoni, *Berlino, Ambasciata*, pp. 376–377, 386; Bonomi, *Diario*, pp. 46–48; Telgs, *Comandante XXXV Corpo d'Armata Nos. 414, 454, 472/OP.*, to *Ministero Guerra Gabinetto*, 29 Jul 43, IT 102.

[28] *Comando Supremo, Operazioni, Regio Esercito: Quadro di battaglia alla data del 1 agosto 1943*, IT 10 a–h; Roatta, *Otto milioni*, pp. 274, 294, 297–99; Zanussi, *Guerra e catastrofe*, II, 58; Rossi, *Come arrivammo*, p. 204; MS #P-058, Project 46, 1 Feb–8 Sep 43, Question 7.

[29] Zanussi, *Guerra e catastrofe*, II, 56; Rossi, *Come arrivammo*, pp. 204–05; Roatta, *Otto milioni*, pp. 274–75. *Comando Supremo* informed OKW that Italian forces had been ordered to react vigorously to whatever violation or threat. See *Comando Supremo, Appunto per il Ministero Affari Esteri*, 5 Aug. 43, IT 3030. Cf. Rommel, Private KTB, entry 29 Jul 43.

[30] *OKW/WFSt, KTB, 1.-31.VII.43*, 30 Jul 43.

Hitler was outraged by this seeming manifestation of Italian perfidy. He directed the divisions moving to Italy to carry out their orders even if bloodshed resulted. Specifically, he wanted an assault group of the *60th Panzer Grenadier Division* to move to the head of the *305th Infantry Division* column in the Nice area and to fight its way, if necessary, across the border into Italy. But since the movement of the assault group to Nice required two days, the Nice area remained quiet.[31]

The test came, instead, in the Brenner area. OKW instructed Kesselring to notify *Comando Supremo* that divisions authorized and scheduled to enter Italy—such as the *26th Panzer Division*—were still crossing the border; and that to avoid aggravating the railway congestion still further, the motorized elements of these divisions were planning to move by road. But Kesselring was not to tell Ambrosio that the *305th Infantry* and the *44th Infantry Divisions,* units not authorized to enter, had also been instructed to make a road march into Italy, an instruction passed along to these divisions the same day. Without awaiting the result of Kesselring's discussions with the Italians, OKW directed *OB WEST* to begin moving the other divisions assigned to the *Army Group B* from France toward Italy.[32]

Shortly before midnight, 30 July, General Gloria, the *XXXV Corps* commander at Bolzano, received a message from General Feurstein who commanded the German Mittenwald Training School near Innsbruck. Feurstein said he was coming to Gloria's headquarters the following morning to co-ordinate the arrival of certain troops. In accordance with the OKW–*Comando Supremo* agreement, Feurstein stated, German elements were reinforcing Italian garrisons along the Brenner railway line. Before replying, Gloria telephoned Rome for instructions.[33]

Ambrosio made the decision early the next day. He directed Roatta "to make certain that there enter into Italy only those elements authorized, that is, the remaining parts of the *26th Panzer Division* and 30 antiaircraft batteries, and their 100–200 trucks." [34]

When the leading elements of the German *44th Infantry Division* reached the Brenner frontier on 31 July, Gloria refused to let them pass. Feurstein appeared at Gloria's headquarters at 1000 and the two commanders conferred about an hour. Feurstein made two points. The *44th Infantry Division,* he said, was to march from the Brenner Pass to Bolzano in three days on the basis of OKW–*Comando Supremo* agreements. Because the British were expected to bomb the Brenner railway line heavily in the near future, German antiaircraft batteries were to reinforce the protection of the pass. After a formal and polite discussion, Feurstein returned to Innsbruck, and Gloria reported a summary of the conversation to his immediate superior command, the *Eighth Army,* and to the Ministry of War in Rome. The report arrived in Roatta's operations section before noon, and from there was transmitted to Ambrosio.[35]

---

[31] *Ibid.,* 31 Jul 43.
[32] *Ibid.,* 30 Jul 43; MS #C-093 (Warlimont), p. 85.
[33] *Ministero della Guerra-Gabinetto, Notizie pervenute dal Comando d'Armata Bolzano nella notte dal 30 al 31 luglio 1943,* IT 102.
[34] *Telg 15403, Comando Supremo to Superesercito,* 31 Jul 43, IT 102.
[35] *Telg, Comando XXXV Corpo d'Armata, No. 577 Op. to Ministero della Guerra-Gabinetto,* 31 Jul 43, *Comando XXXV Corpo d'Armata,* IT 120.

Ambrosio that afternoon addressed a sharp note to Rintelen. He pointed out that the *44th Infantry Division* was scheduled to move to southern Italy, not to guard the railway lines in the north. He made it plain that the congested railroads would make it impossible to move the *44th* and *305th Infantry Divisions* for at least ten days. He requested Rintelen to wait until rail transportation was clear before moving the German divisions into Italy.[36]

Kesselring called on Badoglio later that afternoon to clarify the situation. When Badoglio explained that military questions were outside his competence, Kesselring went to Ambrosio. He urged that the common war aims of the Axis Powers ought to make it possible for the two German divisions to be permitted to continue their movements. Ambrosio refused, but after a lively exchange he agreed to meet again with Kesselring the next morning. Rintelen then requested OKW to suspend the movements of the two divisions pending the outcome of the Kesselring-Ambrosio conference.[37]

Rintelen was deeply distressed by the growing Italo-German conflict. He knew beyond all doubt that Badoglio considered the war lost, and he found himself in sympathy with this point of view and with Badoglio's policy of seeking to end the war in conjunction with the Germans. Not only the Italians, Rintelen was well aware, but also certain high-ranking German officers and politicians recognized that the Axis had lost the war. Before the Feltre conference some of them had secretly voiced the hope that Mussolini would take the bull by the horns, that as Hitler's equal he would bring up the subject which they, Hitler's subordinates, dared not suggest—a compromise peace as the only way to save Europe from communism. Now they wished, and Rintelen with them, that Badoglio would speak the words to Hitler that Mussolini had not ventured to utter.

Disturbed by Hitler's suspicions that Badoglio was already trying to make peace with the Allies, Rintelen urged Kesselring to resign his command rather than execute orders to occupy Italy. Plans *ALARICH* and *ACHSE* not only involved a flagrant breach of faith but also constituted a danger for the German troops in the country. How could the war continue? For certainly the execution of the plans to occupy Italy would throw the Italians into the Allied camp. Speaking by telephone with Keitel on 31 July, Rintelen requested an appointment to report personally to the Fuehrer his views on the Italian situation. Keitel agreed.[38]

Next day, while Rintelen prepared to fly to East Prussia to see Hitler, a further crisis occurred in Italo-German relations. Momentarily expecting Hitler to give the code word *ACHSE,* OKW instructed Feurstein to continue to march the *44th Infantry Division* through the Brenner Pass into Italy.[39]

In Rome, Kesselring met with Ambrosio at 0930. Following OKW instructions, Kesselring made an impassioned plea that the *44th Infantry Division* be allowed to proceed, a unit being sent, he emphasized, in accordance with Am-

---

[36] Msg, *Comando Supremo,* No. *15416/Op* to Rintelen, 31 Jul 43, IT 102.
[37] *OKW/WFSt, KTB, 1.-31.VII.43,* 31 Jul 43.
[38] Rintelen, *Mussolini als Bundesgenosse,* pp. 195, 224; Simoni, *Berlino, Ambasciata,* pp. 314-15, 326, 341; Raffaele Guariglia, *Ricordi 1922-1946* (Naples: Edizioni Scientifiche Italiane, 1950), pp. 548-49.
[39] MS #C-093 (Warlimont), pp. 87-88.

brosio's promise of 22 July to defend Sicily to the utmost and in accordance with Ambrosio's request of that same day for two additional German divisions for duty in southern Italy. Ambrosio turned a deaf ear. He insisted that the German division would have to wait at the frontier until railway transportation became available.[40]

Soon after the conference, Generale di Corpo d'Armata Giuseppe De Stefanis, Roatta's deputy, telephoned Gloria at Bolzano. Gloria was to advise Feurstein to consult with OKW on the result of the conference at Rome. Gloria was to oppose the movement of the *44th Infantry Division* into Italy, and he was to tell Feurstein that an outbreak of armed strife would be Feurstein's responsibility. Gloria telephoned this information to Feurstein.[41]

Feurstein called back at 1550. He said that he had received word from OKW at 1100. OKW indicated that an agreement had been reached in Rome to allow the entry of the *44th Infantry Division*. Twenty minutes later Feurstein called again. He reiterated the information that Rome had agreed to permit the German division to march. If Gloria opposed its movement, Feurstein said, the responsibility for initiating armed conflict would fall on the Italians.[42]

Though the Italians were actually in the process of changing their minds, OKW's information was probably premature. The main factor modifying Ambrosio's blunt stand was Badoglio, who was in frequent contact throughout the day with the *Comando Supremo* chief.

Badoglio insisted that Ambrosio avoid any action that would bring about an Italo-German battle. He needed time, Badoglio said, to carry out his basic policy: make the Germans realize Italy's plight and the need for a common effort to terminate the war.[43]

Having learned of Rintelen's intention to see the Fuehrer, Badoglio asked Rintelen, as an old friend, to call on him before leaving Rome. Rintelen did so, at 1600, and Badoglio explained his position. Fascism, Badoglio said, had fallen of its own weight. As an old soldier he had obeyed the call of the King. Now he wanted to meet with Hitler, who had rebuffed him. "I have given my pledge to continue the war and I stand by my word as a soldier," Badoglio declared. "But for this I need the trust of my ally; it will go bad for both of us if we do not cooperate." Pointing out the serious military situation, the preponderance of Allied resources, particularly in the air, which the bombings of Hamburg and Rome had made quite clear, Badoglio said that the Germans and Italians had to "work together to bring the war to an honorable conclusion." Would Rintelen, Badoglio asked, communicate this to Hitler?[44]

Rintelen readily accepted the mission entrusted to him by Badoglio. Immediately after this conversation, Rintelen went home and wrote down a summary

---

[40] *OKW/WFSt, KTB, 1.-31.VIII.43,* 1 Aug 43.

[41] Tel Conv, 1400, 1 Aug 43, IT 120.

[42] Tel Conv, 1550, 1 Aug 43, IT 120.

[43] MS #P-058, Project 46, 1 Feb-8 Sep 43, Questions 8 and 11; Cf. Badoglio, *Memorie e documenti,* p. 96.

[44] Rintelen, *Mussolini als Bundesgenosse,* pp. 227-32. Rintelen dispatched a telegram outlining Badoglio's views, a copy (Telg 3706 of 1 Aug 43) of which is in *Westl. Mittelmeer, Chefs.* (H 22/290). pp. 91-93. The text as printed by Rintelen does not exactly agree with this copy which is the copy received from the German Foreign Office.

of the discussion. He then consulted with Ernst von Weizsaecker, German Ambassador to the Holy See. Although both men could not completely exclude the possibility that Badoglio was acting merely to win time, they agreed that Badoglio's wish to restore mutual confidence was probably genuine.[45]

By then, Badoglio had probably informed Ambrosio of his conversation with Rintelen, for at 1810, 1 August, Roatta's operations chief, Generale di Brigata Umberto Utili, telephoned new instructions to General Gloria. Gloria was to permit the head of the *44th Infantry Division* column to march to the nearest railway station and there await trains for further movement into Italy. Some train space would be provided on the following morning. But the division was not to march beyond Bolzano. The elements of the *26th Panzer Division*, however, could proceed by road if they wished in order to rejoin the remainder of the division already in Italy. Less than three hours later, Gloria was conferring with Feurstein's representative and making arrangements for the continued movement of the *44th Infantry Division* into Italy by rail.[46]

Thus it was that *Army Group B* made its initial penetration with Italian consent. It was seduction, not rape.[47]

As quickly as Hitler was successful in this test case, and while Badoglio was still hoping that Rintelen's mission would bear fruit, Hitler directed Field Marshal Kesselring to announce that two panzer divisions would follow along the Brenner line, and that another infantry division would follow the *305th Infantry Division* by way of Nice. To keep the passage clear for the other troops, the *44th Infantry Division* held the sector of the railway line from Brennero to Bolzano. By 2 August the infiltration of *Army Group B* into northern Italy was in full swing, and the first lifts of the *2d Parachute Division* had arrived near Rome, a movement substantially completed after four days. Kesselring's explanation to Roatta now was that the division was needed in that area because of the possibility of an Allied parachute attack.[48]

A day later, 3 August, OKW transmitted through Kesselring a formal note to explain its haste in reinforcing the troops in Italy. The Germans had feared, OKW said, that the political change in Italy might encourage the Allies to use an estimated thirteen to fifteen available divisions in a landing on the Ligurian or north Adriatic coast. OKW therefore thought it prudent to provide for the

---

[45] Rintelen, *Mussolini als Bundesgenosse*, p. 233.

[46] Tel Conv, 1810, 1 Aug 43, and Tel Conv. 2230, 1 Aug 43, both in IT 120; Rommel, Private KTB, entry 1 Aug 43.

[47] Telg *No. 636/Op, XXXV Corps* to Ministry of War, Rome, 1 Aug 43, IT 102. Italian memoirs after the war all state that the descent of German reinforcements over the frontiers began on 26 July 1943 and without warning. See Badoglio, *Memorie e documenti*, p. 85; Roatta, *Otto milioni*, p. 272; Rossi, *Come arrivammo*, p. 88; Zanussi, *Guerra e catastrofe*, II, 47; Castellano, *Come firmai*, p. 73; and Guariglia, *Ricordi*, p. 576. The date 26 July appears first to have been fixed for subsequent writers in the article: Lt. Col. Mario Torsiello, "L'aggressione germanica all'Italia nella sua fase preliminare (26 luglio–7 settembre 1943)," *Rivista Militare*, I, vol. 4 (Rome, July, 1945). It is solemnly stated as a matter of court record in *Il Processo Carboni-Roatta*, p. 14. Actually, the only German troops entering Italy between 26 July and 1 August were parts of the *26th Panzer Division* (the bulk of which was already in Italy) and parts of the *2d Parachute Division* (which came by air).

[48] *OKW/WFSt, KTB, 1.–31.VIII.43*, 1 and 2 Aug 43; Rommel, Private KTB, entry 1 Aug 43.

security of all forces by moving divisions first into the north, then into the south. The *305th Infantry* and *76th Infantry*, under *LXXXVII Corps*, were to protect the Ligurian coast. The *94th Infantry*, moving through the Mount Cenis pass, as well as the *1st SS Panzer Division Leibstandarte Adolf Hitler*, the *2d SS Panzer Division "Das Reich,"* and the *65th Infantry* were also to enter north Italy. OKW added that it was considering sending one or two additional armored divisions to Italy to form a reserve. It planned to reinforce the Mediterranean French coast defenses with the *715th Infantry* and *60th Panzer Grenadier Division,* plus two unspecified infantry divisions. All the details of co-ordination, OKW proposed, were to be settled at the conference scheduled for 6 August at Tarvis.[49]

Though the Germans had not mentioned the *94th Infantry* and *65th Infantry* before, the Italians accepted the note without demur. They bent their efforts toward effecting such a distribution of the German divisions as to make for the least threat to Rome and to the principal northern bases of the fleet—La Spezia and Pola—and for the most appropriate dispositions to resist an Allied invasion of southern Italy. The crisis having passed, Ambrosio and Roatta faced the Germans with seeming good grace. Italo-German discussions on 3 August were friendly. Ambrosio agreed to provide transportation in the Brenner area. Roatta urged that German reinforcements be sent to the south as quickly as possible. Roatta also complained that some German troops behaved as though they believed that the Italians sympathized with the Allies, an attitude he found insulting to Italian honor. "Italy," he declared, "is not thinking of changing course."[50]

So far as Roatta knew, he had made an honest declaration. What he did not know was that attempts had already been initiated to make contact with the Allies.[51]

On the same day, Rintelen was personally delivering Badoglio's message to Hitler, with Keitel and Jodl in attendance. After listening to Rintelen explain Badoglio's position, Hitler exploded. "This is the biggest impudence in history. Does the man imagine that I will believe him?"

"I have the impression," Rintelen replied, "that he is honorably working for the establishment of trust."

Hitler brushed this aside, remarking that the Anglo-Americans had probably repulsed Badoglio's effort to make peace and that Badoglio was therefore again seeking German support. After a brief discussion of the conference scheduled in a few days at Tarvis, Hitler dismissed Rintelen without a reply for Badoglio.[52]

Later that day Rintelen received some sympathy from General der Infanterie Kurt Zeitzler, an old friend in the headquarters and Chief of Staff of the German Army. Zeitzler knew that Hitler's

---

[49] *OKW/WFSt, KTB, 1.-31.VIII.43,* 3 Aug 43; *Colloquio Generale Rossi–Generale Westphal,* 1230, 3 Aug 43, *Comando Supremo, Colloqui 1943,* IT 104.

[50] *OKW/WFSt, KTB, 1.-31.VIII.43,* 3 and 4 Aug 43.

[51] See Guariglia, *Ricordi,* p. 619. n. 1.

[52] Rintelen, *Mussolini als Bundesgenosse,* pp. 233-34. A briefer statement by Rintelen is to be found in MS #T-1a (Westphal et al.), Chapter II, page 23, where the interview with Hitler is dated the second rather than the third of August. *OKH/Attaché Abt., KTB 1.III.43-31.V. 44* (H27/56) contains the entry that Rintelen met with the Fuehrer on the Italian problem on 3 August 1943. Practically the same entry can be found in *OKH/Attaché Abt., Taetigkeitsberichte zum KTB,* Feb. 43-15 Jun 44 (H27/58).

alleged proof of Badoglio's negotiations with the Western Powers was not true. Rintelen also spoke with Keitel and Jodl and told them that fascism was dead, that Mussolini was a sick man, and that it was necessary to support the Badoglio government as a bulwark against communism. When Jodl mentioned this view to Hitler the next day, he was roundly cursed and abused. Rintelen, Hitler said, was a traitor.

Rintelen had already returned to Rome, where he went directly to Kesselring's headquarters at Frascati. Richthofen, the air commander, was somewhat surprised to see him; he had been doubtful that Hitler would allow Rintelen out of Germany.[53]

Badoglio felt that his hand had again been refused. His initial steps to bring about a joint peace move or to secure German understanding of the Italian situation had ended in failure. Badoglio nevertheless continued to hope that he might yet obtain German consent to a dissolution of the alliance and thereby exclude any action that might bring on Italo-German conflict.[54]

The Italians, however, continued to work with the Germans to maintain the defense of Sicily and to prepare to oppose an invasion of the Italian mainland. At the same time they watched closely for a hostile German act against Rome and sought to make contact with the Allies. They were increasingly worried by the stranglehold the Germans had on Italy. The locations of the new German divisions offered no protection to the south, where an Allied threat was real and acute. Rather, the Germans were in position to seize the Italian naval bases, to occupy the north, and to grab Rome.[55]

*The Italian Course is Changed*

About the same time that the crisis of 29 July–1 August was being overcome by the decision of the Italian Government and High Command to accept unwanted German reinforcements, the assumption of the Ministry of Foreign Affairs by Raffaele Guariglia gave a new impulse and a new direction to Italian foreign policy.

Brought from his post as Ambassador to Turkey, Guariglia was uninformed on the true state of affairs in Italy and as a result had indulged in some daydreams and wishful thinking. He fancied that Mussolini, out of love for Italy, had recognized that he himself was the greatest obstacle in the way of an approach to the Allies, and had therefore made the sacrifice of removing himself from power in order to save Italy from total disaster. Perhaps, Guariglia thought, a secret understanding with both Germany and the Allies had preceded Mussolini's resignation. Assuming that the first step of the

---

[53] Rintelen, *Mussolini als Bundesgenosse*, pp. 234–36.

[54] On 24 August, Badoglio told Bonomi: "If the Germans would attack, the situation would have a solution. We cannot, by an act of our own will, separate ourselves from Germany to whom we are bound by a pact of alliance, but if attacked we shall resist and we will be able to turn for aid to our enemies of yesterday." (Bonomi, *Diario*, p. 82).

As late as 3 September the German Naval Attaché in Rome reported: "In higher circles the opinion prevails that ever since he assumed office, Badoglio has been trying to bring the war to as favorable a conclusion as possible, but only with Germany's consent, for Badoglio takes Italy's honor as an Axis partner very seriously." ONI, translation *German Naval Staff: Operations Division War Diary*, pt. A, vol. 49 (September 1943), p. 37.

[55] Roatta gave a very clear and prophetic analysis in his memorandum, S.M.R.E., Ufficio di Capo di Stato Maggiore, N. 26/CSM di Prot., 4 Aug 43, IT 104; Cf. Roatta, *Otto milioni*, p. 284.

Badoglio government would naturally be an approach to the Allies, he interpreted Badoglio's proclamation of continuing the war merely as a method of gaining time. Before leaving Istanbul, Guariglia asked the Turkish Minister of Foreign Affairs to convey to the Allied representatives in Turkey Guariglia's personal conviction that Italy had to change course as quickly as possible. Though he could make no commitment, he asked that the Allies have faith in Italy's intentions and understanding of her plight. As an indication of their faith and understanding, he felt, the Allies should cease bombing Italian cities.[56]

After arriving in Rome late in the afternoon of 29 July, Guariglia took over his office, and then met with Badoglio. He agreed with Badoglio to limit knowledge of any negotiations for peace to the smallest circle of officials—the matter should not be discussed even in the Council of Ministers. But at this point he was rudely awakened from the dreams he had conjured up in Istanbul, for he found his position in the new Italian Government enormously prejudiced by certain stark facts: the war continued; there was no contact with the Allies. He learned also that his position had been prejudiced by Badoglio's proposals to Germany through General Marras, and Badoglio's acceptance of Hitler's counterproposal of a meeting of foreign ministers, scheduled for 6 August.

Scarcely had Guariglia taken his oath of office on 30 July when General Castellano presented himself and tendered a memorandum from Ambrosio, chief of *Comando Supremo*. Identifying Castellano as an intimate colleague who had played a certain role in the developments leading to Mussolini's dismissal, Ambrosio's note said that it was absolutely necessary for Italy to conclude an armistice with the Allies and that therefore immediate contact had to be made with the Western Powers.[57]

Guariglia tried to do so that very evening. In the greatest secrecy he visited the Papal Secretary of State and asked him to request the British Minister to the Holy See, Sir D'Arcy Q. Osborne, to transmit a message to the British Government. Unfortunately, the British diplomatic code at the Holy See had been broken and was known to the Italians and the Germans. This ruled out that channel of communication. At about the same time, Franco Babuzzio Rizzo, a subordinate of Guariglia's, was meeting with Harold Tittmann, assistant to Myron C. Taylor, Personal Representative of the President to His Holiness, the Pope. Rizzo wanted to get a message to the American Government. But the American office within the Vatican walls had no safe and speedy communication channel either. Though the American office could forward dispatches through Switzerland or Portugal in safety, this was a slow process.[58]

On the following day, 31 July, the crown council met at the Quirinal Palace. Guariglia vigorously advocated an immediate approach to the Allies for the purpose of concluding a separate armistice. He stated that he had already taken steps

---

[56] Guariglia, *Ricordi*, pp. 553–54, 559–61.

[57] *Ibid.*, pp. 582–85, 609. See MS #P-058, Project 46, Question 9 and *Il Processo Carboni-Roatta*, pp. 18–19.

[58] Badoglio, *Memorie e documenti*, p. 96; Guariglia, *Ricordi*, pp. 586–87; Ltr, Osborne to Maj Gen Orlando Ward, OCMH, 6 Jul 50; Ltr and Incls, Tittmann to Ward, OCMH, 19 Jul 50. The British minister received a new and safe cypher later that summer.

in that direction by speaking to the Turkish Foreign Minister and by approaching the Allied representatives to the Holy See. As he understood the situation, the decision to approach the Western Powers had already been made by the King some days ago. The crown council formally decided to separate Italy from the alliance with Germany and to seek an armistice with the Allies.[59]

Guariglia implemented this decision by securing approval from the King and Badoglio to send an emissary to Portugal. He chose the Marchese Blasco Lanza D'Ajeta, Counselor of the Italian Embassy at the Holy See, who through Ciano had been kept informed of the movement to overthrow Mussolini. D'Ajeta spoke English, and was the godson of the wife of Sumner Welles, the American Under Secretary of State. Furthermore, he was of intermediate rank and his transfer from the Holy See would excite no German suspicions. Accordingly, the Foreign Office nominated D'Ajeta Counselor of the Italian Legation at Lisbon. Guariglia had D'Ajeta take along a large suitcase full of Foreign Office documents to keep them from falling into German hands. The gossip of polite circles in Rome promptly had it that D'Ajeta's mission was to save the Countess Ciano's jewels.[60]

D'Ajeta received his instructions on 1 and 2 August from Guariglia, Castellano taking part in the second session. Sir D'Arcy Osborne provided a letter introducing D'Ajeta to his cousin, Sir Ronald Hugh Campbell, British Ambassador at Lisbon. D'Ajeta was to make a full and candid explanation of the situation of the Italian Government, and point out that it was threatened internally by the Communists and by German occupation. He was to explain that the government wished to break with Germany, but that to do this the government needed help for its armed forces. He was to make it clear that he had no power to negotiate, but he was to suggest the desirability of military and political agreement by the Allies and the Italians in order to enable Italy to break with the Germans or turn against them. As a demonstration of faith, he was to inform the Allies of the German order of battle in Italy. Castellano carefully drilled D'Ajeta on the name, strength, and location of each German unit in Italy and of those expected to enter the country, and D'Ajeta committed this information to memory.[61]

D'Ajeta flew to Lisbon on 3 August, and presented himself at once to Renato Prunas, the Italian Minister. He sent his note of introduction to Sir Ronald, and the British Ambassador requested and received from his own government authorization to receive the Italian emissary. The conference took place the following day.

A trained diplomat, D'Ajeta carefully carried out his instructions. After giving a candid and detailed exposition of the Italian situation, he urged the ambassador to inform the British and American Governments that Italy was most anxious to escape the German yoke and to withdraw from the conflict. He pleaded for understanding in London and Washington of Italy's tragic situation: Italy, he said,

---

[59] Guariglia, *Ricordi*, pp. 585–86, 619n; *Il Processo Carboni-Roatta*, p. 19.

[60] Guariglia, *Ricordi*, p. 587. Castellano (*Come firmai*, page 72) records that he knew of the D'Ajeta mission but remains silent on whether he had any part in instigating the appointment. In any event, Castellano did not know the full scope of D'Ajeta's instructions.

[61] Guariglia, *Ricordi*, pp. 587–88.

was on the eve of a German military occupation. Besides the German divisions already in Italy, two more had begun to arrive from France on 2 August, bound for Turin, and about 200,000 German troops assembled around Innsbruck were occupying the Brenner Pass installations. Because Rome was in danger of immediate German seizure—an armored SS division with the most modern Tiger tanks was moving toward the capital—the King and the government had plans to escape to the island of Maddalena, off the coast of Sardinia. Some 300,000 Italian workmen were virtual hostages in Germany. After three years of warfare, Italy was on the verge of economic exhaustion. Italy, D'Ajeta continued, wished to negotiate. Hungary and Rumania would probably follow suit.

D'Ajeta then gave the exact locations of the German divisions as of 2 August. He explained that Italian troops had been moved to protect Rome, thereby leaving the coast of central Italy practically undefended. To maintain its independence, the Italian Government was resolved to defend the capital against German attack, even though the only good division in the area was the reconstituted armored *Ariete Division,* which had only enough ammunition to furnish a total of eighty-eight shells for each of its guns.

Emphasizing his lack of authority to negotiate, D'Ajeta urged that his disclosure of the German order of battle be the starting point for synchronizing Italian help with the Allied political and military plans. He requested a cessation of propaganda attacks against the King and Badoglio, a halting of bombings against Italian cities. He asked that Britain and America not misinterpret the impending Italo-German conference at Tarvis.

Ambassador Campbell listened attentively, asked several questions. D'Ajeta warned that the German armed forces were numerous and powerful. Reports of serious cleavage between the Nazi party and the military command, he said, were to be discounted. Campbell explained that he had no instructions except to listen. His personal opinion was that the Allies had already determined their military plans and had clearly announced their political views in the unconditional surrender formula.[62]

The Italian Government waited for an official reply to D'Ajeta's overture. None came.

Meanwhile, on the day that D'Ajeta had left Rome for Lisbon, Guariglia and Badoglio decided to send another emissary to make contact with the British Government. They directed Alberto Berio, former Counselor of the Embassy at Ankara, to fly immediately to Tangier, there to replace Badoglio's son as Consul General. Berio's real mission was to inform the British Consul that Italy was willing to negotiate.

On the morning of 3 August, the day that D'Ajeta reached Lisbon, Guariglia gave Berio his detailed instructions. Berio was to make known the fact that because the Italian Government was a prisoner of the Germans, it would be useless and damaging to the Allied cause to demand of Italy an immediate and public capitulation. The Allied armies should attack the Balkans in order to draw German troops away from Italy, thereby making it possible for the Italians to join the Allies in clearing the Italian peninsula of German forces. Finally, the Allied press

[62] Guariglia, *Ricordi,* pp. 589–99; Telg, Churchill to Roosevelt, 5 Aug 43, OPD Exec 9, item II, No. 55.

campaign against the Badoglio government ought to continue in order to deceive the Germans.

When Badoglio briefed Berio later that day, he added the point that the Allies would find it to their interest to aid the Italian Government maintain itself against the internal threat of communism. In this connection, the Allies should cease bombing Italian cities. The Marshal's son, Mario, who was present, made an additional suggestion: the Allies should land in Italy as soon and as far north as possible.[63]

In Tangier on 5 August, Berio at once made contact with Mr. Watkinson, temporarily in charge of the British Consulate. After carrying out his instructions, Berio wired Rome of his action and, like D'Ajeta in Lisbon, waited for an Allied reply.[64]

---

[63] Alberto Berio, *Missione segreta (Tangeri: Agosto 1943)* (Milan: Enrico Dall'Oglio, 1947), pp. 34-42.

[64] *Ibid.*, pp. 54-70. D'Ajeta later presented his own account of the mission in his defense at epuration proceedings. See *Consiglio di Stato: Sezione speciale per l'epurazione, Memoria a svolgimento del ricorso del Consigliere di Legazione Blasco Lanza d'Ajeta contro la decisione della Commissione per l'epurazione del personale dipendente dal Ministero degli Affari Esteri* (Rome: Tipografia Ferraiolo, 1946), pp. 79-81, 84-87; and *Documenti prodotti a corredo della memorai del Consigliere di Legazione Blasco Lanza d'Ajeta* (Rome: Tipografia Ferraiolo, 1946), pp. 17-35.

CHAPTER XVI

# The Drive to the East

*Developing an East Front*

Little affected by the bubbling, boiling political pots in Washington, London, North Africa, Italy, and Germany, little concerned with AFHQ's plans for the invasion of the Italian mainland, General Alexander's American, British, Canadian, and French soldiers continued their fight to clear Sicily. The arena of battle had shifted from the lowlands of the southeast corner to the mountainous Messina peninsula.

The Provisional Corps' spectacular advance to Palermo completely overshadowed General Bradley's II Corps maneuvers which, like those to the south, had also kicked off on 19 July. (*See Map VII.*) Enna, perched high on a mountain, dominated by the ruins of a large feudal castle, fell without a struggle, its importance to the Germans nullified by the advance of the 1st Canadian Division on Leonforte (which fell on 23 July) and the breakthrough by the 45th Division toward the north coast.

Matching the rapid advance of the Provisional Corps to Palermo, General Middleton's 45th Division started its move for Palermo on the evening of 19 July. With the 180th RCT spearheading the advance northwest along Highway 121, the Americans overcame the Italian roadblock at Portella di Reccativo and made a nineteen-mile advance on the 20th.

By the morning of 22 July, the 180th RCT was in the small town of Villafrati, only twenty-two miles from Palermo, and had patrols probing the outskirts of that port city. But the change in boundary, which gave the Provisional Corps the use of Highway 121, diverted the division's main effort from Palermo to the north coast town of Termini Imerese, thirty-one miles east of Palermo. Accordingly, General Middleton sent his remaining two combat teams, the 179th and 157th, swinging north from Highway 121. At 0900 on 23 July, the 157th RCT reached the north coast road—Highway 113—at Station Cerda, five miles east of Termini Imerese. There the regiment turned left and right and cleared a stretch of the highway. Termini fell without a struggle, but a battalion moving eastward met *Group Ulich*, part of the newly arrived *29th Panzer Grenadier Division*, just west of Campofelice. Though the battalion, aided by a company of tanks, managed to clear Campofelice, heavy enemy artillery and small arms fire coming from the ridge line across the Roccella River brought the Americans to a halt.[1]

---

[1] 157th, 179th, 180th Inf Regt AAR's; 753d Med Tk Bn AAR; 45th Inf Div Arty AAR; 45th Inf Div G-3 Jnl, 21-23 Jul 43; *OB SUED, Meldungen,* 23 Jul 43; Faldella, *Lo sbarco,* pp. 234-37; MS #D-095 *29th Panzer Grenadier Division,* 30 July 1943 (Generalmajor Max Ulich); MS #C-077 (Rodt).

# THE DRIVE TO THE EAST

On the 45th Division right, the 1st Division advanced from Enna in a far less spectacular, less rapid fashion because of greater opposition. *Group Fullriede's* withdrawal from its westward facing salient southwest of the city during the evening of 19 July had not gone unnoticed, and General Allen sent the 26th Combat Team in pursuit. By then, the German battle group had passed through an Italian roadblock at Alimena and was sideslipping into a new east-west defensive line along Highway 120 from Gangi to Sperlinga. Facing south, these troops, according to the expectation of General Rodt, the *15th Panzer Grenadier Division* commander, would prevent an American sweep around his division's right flank. Although a small gap was still open in the center of his line, his left flank was secure, for *Group Ens* had withdrawn slowly from Canadian pressure east of Enna and had finally made contact with the *Hermann Goering Division's* right flank near Regalbuto.

For the first time since the invasion, the two major German fighting units on the island had made physical contact. The gap which had existed in the center of the Axis front since 10 July was closed.[2]

Shortly before midnight on 20 July, the 2d Battalion, 26th Infantry, led off the 1st Division's advance on its new axis, the secondary road which wound through rough, mountainous terrain almost due north from Enna to Petralia. Pushed on by its aggressive commander, Lt. Col. Darrell M. Daniel, the 2d Battalion moved into Alimena at 0500 the following morning. There, the Italian *Group Schreiber* made its final appearance. Sadly reduced by ten days of fighting and the loss of units at Portella di Reccativo, the Italian unit collected the remnants of an infantry battalion and a cavalry squadron north of Alimena to counterattack the 26th Infantry's battalion. But American light tanks, which had been supporting Daniel's battalion, spotted the concentration and, roaring down the road from Alimena, blasted into the Italian formation with all guns blazing. This dashing attack proved too much for the sorely tried Italians. Leaving most of their equipment behind, the Italians scattered into the surrounding hills and were seen no more. A few other Italians, hiding in the buildings of Alimena, proved more difficult to handle, and it was not until late afternoon that Colonel Daniel could report that the last of the enemy soldiers had been flushed out of basements and other hiding places.

The light tanks pushing on along the road to Petralia soon ran into direct enemy artillery fire covering a blown bridge just south of Bompietro, halfway to Petralia. The Germans, fearful that the 1st Division would move east from Alimena cross-country through the hills to Nicosia and into the gap which existed between the two battle groups, had deployed a provisional group at this point the previous afternoon to plug the hole.

It took until noon the next day, 22 July, before supporting 1st Division engineers could repair the bridge. Then, after a concentration by three artillery battalions, the 1st and 3d Battalions, 26th Infantry, attacked across the small stream. *Group Fullriede's* outposts put up stiff resistance—"the enemy resisted stubbornly, and, for the second time in Sicily, showed

---

[2] *OB SUED, Meldungen,* 19-21 Jul 43; Map, Sizilien (1:200,000), *WFSt Op (H), Stand,* 18 Jul 43; Faldella, *Lo sbarco,* pp. 201, 210-12, 221-22; Nicholson, *The Canadians in Italy,* p. 100; 1st Inf Div FO 28, 20 Jul 43.

SOUTHERN APPROACH TO ENNA

artillery strength."[3] It was this German artillery, and the difficult terrain, that slowed the advance. The tanks were road-bound. The infantrymen were pinned down until the tanks could move forward to knock out at least some of the opposing guns. It was not until 1900 that the tanks managed to get through Bompietro with the 3d Battalion, 26th Infantry, hard on their heels.

With Bompietro taken, General Allen leapfrogged the 18th Combat Team to continue the push on Petralia, and to open a hole through which the 16th Combat Team, still at Enna, could move to the north coast.[4] For this was still the mission of the 1st Division, even though it had been temporarily diverted by the need to clear up the Enna area. With Enna in hand, the division could move to the north coast at Cefalù, paralleling the British 30 Corps advance. Near midnight, 22 July, the 1st and 2d Bat-

[3] 33d FA Bn AAR. The 1st Division Artillery fired a total of 1,146 rounds on 22 July in the various attacks on Bompietro.

[4] Change 1, 1st Inf Div FO 28, 21 Jul 43.

# THE DRIVE TO THE EAST

LEONFORTE

talions, 18th Infantry, dismounted from trucks at Bompietro, and moved through the 26th Infantry on the road to Petralia. Just before 0900, 23 July, after a stiff fight along the southern slopes of the high ground overlooking Petralia, the 2d Battalion, 18th Infantry, together with two companies from the 1st Battalion, entered the town. Immediately, Colonel Smith, the combat team commander, started his battalions east along Highway 120 toward Gangi to block the secondary road which leads northward toward Cefalù, the route the 16th RCT was to follow to the north coast. This was done by late afternoon.[5]

But Petralia proved to be as far to the north as the 1st Division would go on its drive. The division would not be given a chance to reach the Tyrrhenian Sea as had the 45th Division farther west, for the Seventh Army axis of advance was changed again, this time to the east.

On 20 July, General Alexander had

---

[5] 18th and 26th Inf Regt AAR's; 1st Inf Div Arty AAR; 1st Inf Div G-3 Jnl; IT 99b, entry and an. 71 (map); Map, *Sizilien* (1:200,000), *WFST Op (H)*, *Stand* 22 Jul 43.

issued new instructions to General Patton. Upon reaching the coast north of Petralia, Seventh Army would send strong reconnaissance patrols eastward along the two main east-west highways left uncovered by the Eighth Army's shift of its western axis of advance. These were the north coast road and Highway 120 through Sperlinga, Nicosia, and Troina. Thus, General Alexander changed the boundary between the two Allied armies. From its previous location running due north paralleling Highway 117, the new boundary ran due east between Highway 120 and the road serving as the British 30 Corps axis of advance. If possible, General Alexander continued, the Seventh Army was to follow up these reconnaissance forces in strength. Apparently, then, General Alexander intended to make Palermo the Seventh Army main base of supply, and to bring at least a part of the Seventh Army on line with the Eighth Army. General Montgomery concurred in the need for Seventh Army assistance.

Except for the assignment of the two northern roads to the Seventh Army, General Alexander's 20 July directive amounted to little more than a modification of his 18 July directive. It did not indicate his intention of throwing the Seventh Army full tilt against the Axis forces in the Messina peninsula. General Montgomery's attempt to break through the enemy lines on the east coast was still in process, though getting nowhere, when Alexander published his new order. The Army group commander apparently still hoped that Montgomery's push would be successful. The directive did nothing to the U.S. II Corps plans, except to add two more roads to worry about. General Bradley's mission of going to the coast "north of Petralia" remained; the directive merely moved the point at which the north coast was to be reached from Campofelice east to Cefalù.[6]

Montgomery's decision on 21 July to bring over the British 78th Division from North Africa to reinforce a new push around the western slopes of Mount Etna, his calling off of attacks by the British 13 Corps at the Catania plain, and his previous shifting of the British 30 Corps main axis of advance from Highway 120 farther south to Highway 121, indicated to General Alexander that the Eighth Army alone was not strong enough to drive the Germans from the Messina peninsula.

Just two days later, on 23 July, and after the capture of Palermo, General Alexander abandoned his scheme for a cautious, exploratory probing by the Seventh Army. Patton was now to employ his maximum strength along the two roads Alexander had given the Americans on 20 July. General Alexander had finally decided to place the Seventh Army on equal footing with the Eighth in order to finish off the remaining Axis forces. In other words, Messina was no longer solely an Eighth Army objective; Messina was now up for grabs.[7] (*Map 3*)

---

[6] Seventh Army Rpt of Opns, p. D-11; Alexander Despatch, app. C-4, p. 85. Exactly when General Alexander reached his decision to turn the Seventh Army eastward is not certain. He appears to have informed General Eisenhower on 19 July of the decision to turn part of Patton's forces to the east. This could have well been done at Eisenhower's insistence that the Seventh Army play a larger role in the campaign. See Ltr, Eisenhower to Marshall, 21 Jul 43, Diary Office CinC, Book VII, pp. A-599—A-600. Nicholson, *The Canadians in Italy*, p. 118. Montgomery's new view was a distinct change from the view held by him in early June.

[7] Seventh Army Rpt of Opns, p. D-13; Alexander Despatch, app. C-5, p. 86; Intervs, Mathews with Alexander, p. 16; Nicholson, *The Canadians in Italy*, p. 119.

# THE DRIVE TO THE EAST

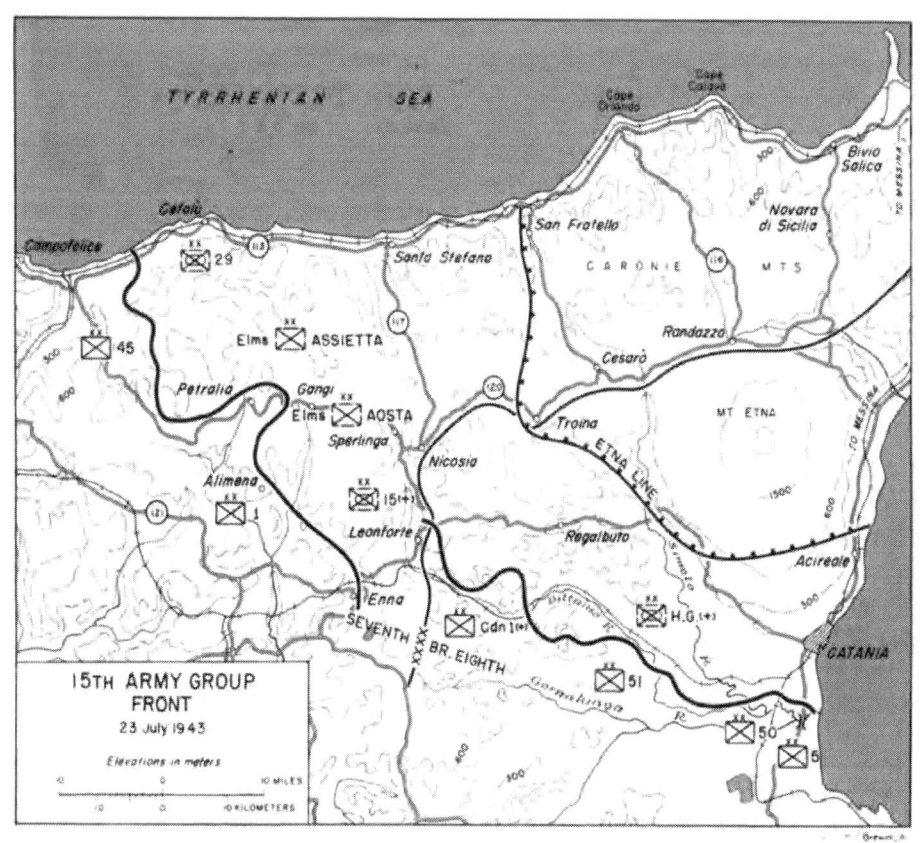

*MAP 3*

Stopping the 1st Division drive for Cefalù at Petralia, and pivoting on the division, General Bradley began shifting the II Corps axis of advance to the east. General Patton had said that "the British have the bear by the tail in the Messina Peninsula and we may have to go in and help."[8] He therefore bolstered II Corps, to which he assigned the entire Seventh Army front. He stripped the Provisional Corps of the French 4th Tabor of Goums (which had performed well with the 3d Division since its landing in Sicily on 14 July); the 9th Division's 39th Infantry and its attached 34th Field Artillery Battalion; and other artillery units—and sent them scurrying eastward.[9] General Patton also called for the remainder of General Eddy's 9th Infantry Division to come over from North Africa because the 2d Armored Division would be less useful in the mountainous terrain of northeastern Sicily and because both the 45th Infantry and 82d Airborne Divisions would shortly have to be relieved to prepare for the invasion of Italy. General Eddy, a Regular Army officer since 1916, had led the

---

[8] Semmes, *Portrait of Patton*, p. 162.

[9] Seventh Army Rpt of Opns, p. b–12; Bradley, *A Soldier's Story*, p. 146.

9th Division throughout the North African campaign, and would bring a tried fighting outfit to the Seventh Army for the final phases of the Sicilian operation.[10]

The news of Mussolini's overthrow did not evoke much enthusiasm among the members of the Seventh Army's front-line units. The soldiers did not believe it had really happened, and the news, if true, appeared to have little effect on reducing the scale of enemy resistance. If anything, the enemy seemed to be fighting more fiercely than ever to hold his mountain strongholds.[11]

*Axis Reactions*

Outwardly, with the fall of Mussolini, nothing had changed in Italy's military policy or in the conduct of operations on Sicily. In reality, a profound change had taken place. The change did not stem from Rome, where Marshal Badoglio's proclamations announced the continued vitality of the German alliance. Rather, the change stemmed from Hitler's headquarters in far-off East Prussia.

Here, on 25 July, news of Mussolini's dismissal led the angry Fuehrer, among other things, to take drastic steps to save his embattled forces on the island. He excitedly told Jodl to evacuate all German personnel immediately from Sicily—take out the men, leave all the heavy equipment behind; move troops into northern Italy; occupy the mountain passes on the northern border; maintain firm control of the Italians; occupy Rome; capture the King, Badoglio, the Crown Prince, and other high-ranking officials; let the Germans take over the Italian Government; and find Mussolini and liberate him.

Relieved when he remembered that only part of the *1st Parachute Division* had crossed into Sicily, he insisted that all the troops had to be taken out. What happened to their matériel did not matter in the least. "Everything will have to be done so fast," Hitler said, "that the entire movement will be completed in two days—perhaps only one." Warned by Jodl that no more than 17,000 men could be ferried over in one day under normal conditions, Hitler burst out with: "Well, they'll have to crowd together. Do you remember how it was at Dunkerque? Is it not ridiculous to think that our Navy cannot ferry these men over such a small piece of water in two—nay in one day—provided the matériel stays behind?"

In closing the discussion, Hitler reminded Jodl of an important point. "Of course," he said, "we will have to continue the game as if we believed in their [the Italians] claim that they want to continue [fighting]." To which Jodl agreed: "Yes, we will have to do that." From then on, the Germans would mask their activities behind a cloak of secrecy.[12]

---

[10] Seventh Army G-3 Jnl, 22-24 Jul 43; Seventh Army G-3 Rpts, 14, 16, and 17 Jul 43.

It was probably just as well that the 2d Armored Division did not have to be used in the later stages of the campaign. On the division's arrival at Palermo, 151 miles from its starting point at Agrigento, about 75 percent of the tanks had completely ruined their tracks. The rubber track blocks, made of a synthetic material supposedly good for 300 miles and new when the division departed North Africa, simply had not held up under the pounding they had to take on the dash west. See Rpt by Gen Gaffey on Opns of the 2d Armd Div in Sicily, 5 Aug 43, in file 602-0.3.

[11] See Richard Tregaskis, *Invasion Diary* (New York: Random House, 1944), pages 28-29 for how the news was received by the 1st Division. Truscott, *Command Missions*, does not even mention the occurrence.

[12] Min of Conf 14, Second Meeting Between Hitler, Keitel, Jodl, and Others, 25 Jul 43, in Min of Hitler Confs. Compare also Min 13, 15, and 17 of 25 and 26 Jul 43.

# THE DRIVE TO THE EAST

That night, General Jodl sent a teletype ordering Kesselring to evacuate Sicily. Since Jodl did not dare to entrust detailed instructions to conventional means of communication, he dispatched a personal representative to Rome to brief Kesselring on his role in Plan *ACHSE*.[13]

More detailed information and the repeated Italian declarations of continued cobelligerence mollified Hitler. He changed his mind on immediately evacuating the German troops from Sicily. The final evacuation would be delayed as long as possible.[14]

In Sicily, General Guzzoni was certain that the Allies would not invade the Italian mainland until after Sicily had first been subdued. Thus, the *Sixth Army* commander saw his mission as postponing the Allied conquest of the island as long as possible. If he received substantial reinforcements, he might even return to the offensive.[15]

But by then the command relationships in Sicily had changed. General Hube had committed elements of the *29th Panzer Grenadier Division* along the north coast on 22 July, when he had nominally had tactical control of only the eastern half of the front. The commitment deployed German troops all along the front, from the eastern to the northern coast of Sicily. Since the Italian troops had lost almost all their combat effectiveness, the German troops had become the mainstay of the defense of the Messina peninsula.

On that same day, Hube had informed Guzzoni that he wanted tactical control of all the ground forces on the entire front. Guzzoni refused for two reasons. First, this arrangement would deal a severe blow to Italian prestige. Second, Guzzoni realized that Hube had developed a different concept of defense—one that he, Guzzoni, could not approve.[16] Whereas Guzzoni still hoped eventually to regain the initiative, he suspected, and rightly, that Hube had no intention of ever mounting a major counterattack—even though the situation had become somewhat stable by 21 July with the British advance on Catania stopped. The shift of the British main effort from Catania to Regalbuto and Leonforte and the highway system west of Mount Etna indicated a dispersal of effort. Withdrawal of the Axis forces from the invasion front and from western Sicily to the northeastern corner had been generally completed, except for some *15th Panzer Grenadier Division* outposts in the northern sector. British attempts to break through would therefore meet solid opposition. Thus far, the American forces, still some distance west of the main defense line, constituted no immediate threat.

Guzzoni considered it feasible to defend northeastern Sicily on what the Italians and Germans commonly designated as the main line of resistance, a line from south of Catania to Santo Stefano di Camastra. He expected to hold this line long enough to gain enough time to build up the Etna line—from Acireale to San Fratello. In order to save those troops still west of

---

[13] *OKW/WFSt, KTB, 1.-31.VII.43*, 25, 26, and 28 Jul 43; *SKL/1. Abt, KTB, Teil A. 1.-31.VII.43*, 26 Jul 43.

[14] Bonin in MS #T-2 (Fries *et al.*).

[15] Faldella, *Lo sbarco*, pp. 218, 236, 305.

[16] *Superesercito* supported Guzzoni and confirmed on 23 July that the tactical command on Sicily would remain divided between the Italians and Germans. Later the same day, the Italian Army headquarters clarified the issue by stating that it would not tolerate Hube's assumption of tactical command over all the fighting forces. IT 99b, an. 73; Faldella, *Lo sbarco*, pp. 233-34.

the main line of resistance Guzzoni on 21 July ordered both the *XIV Panzer Corps* and the Italian *XII Corps* to withdraw any outposts in the northern sector. He considered the troops on Sicily and those earmarked to arrive in the near future adequate not only to hold the line but also to form a reserve for a counterattack to regain the initiative, if only temporarily. What he needed was to keep together as a unit the newly arriving *29th Panzer Grenadier Division*, rather than dissipate its strength by commitment in driblets.

But Hube refused to withdraw the northern outposts. He even committed a part of the new German formation on the northern coast. Quoting Hitler's well-known doctrine of holding every foot of ground, Hube disclosed that no German commander would withdraw except under overwhelming pressure. These actions put an end to any intentions Guzzoni had to return to the offensive, even before it became painfully evident that Italian reinforcements were not going to be sent to Sicily. And although Guzzoni was still nominally in command of all tactical operations on Sicily, the preponderance of German over Italian combat troops on the island prompted him to bow to Hube's decisions.[17]

On the other hand, General Hube's actions were dictated by sound tactical reasons. He wished to give those German troops escaping from Palermo a chance to reach the Messina triangle. He also wanted to prevent the American Seventh Army from getting around the right flank of the *15th Panzer Grenadier Division* and rolling up the entire Axis line. In accordance with the mission given him when he was sent to Sicily, Hube's intentions were to execute an orderly withdrawal from the island, to include local counterthrusts but no major counterattack operations. The purpose of the entire operation was to gain time and to save German manpower for the expected future battles on the Italian mainland.

The Seventh Army's arrival on the north coast on 22 July completely changed the situation. Except for remnants of Italian divisions, nothing stood in the way of an American drive on Messina via the north coast road. Experience had shown that Italian coastal units could not be depended on. The *15th Panzer Grenadier* could not further stretch itself to cover the north coast road. Up to this time, the eastern and central sectors of the front had swallowed up all Axis reinforcements arriving on the island. To prevent an American breakthrough on the north, then, was the reason Hube had committed the *29th Panzer Grenadier Division*.[18]

Convinced that a dual or vague command organization was detrimental to the future conduct of operations, Guzzoni settled for a compromise. In a conference on 25 July, he and Hube agreed, subject to the approval of their respective higher headquarters, that Guzzoni would nominally retain the over-all tactical command but with the tacit understanding that Hube would henceforth conduct the defense of the land front.[19]

The political upheaval in Rome having prevented an immediate reply to Guzzoni's

---

[17] Faldella, *Lo sbarco*, pp. 218, 221–24, 234–38, 305–06. The difference of opinion between Guzzoni and Hube is not corroborated in German sources.

[18] *OB SUED, Meldungen*, 23 Jul 43; MS # D-095, *29th Panzer Grenadier Division*, 30 Jul 43 (Ulich); MS #C-077 (Rodt).

[19] IT 99b, an. 83; Faldella, *Lo sbarco*, pp. 237–38.

# THE DRIVE TO THE EAST

and Hube's joint proposal, Hube took over the actual conduct of ground operations on Sicily. He continued to discuss plans and decisions with Guzzoni and the *Sixth Army* staff directly or through the German liaison officer, General von Senger. And he tried to create the impression that the Germans on Sicily intended to fight to the bitter end. Guzzoni saw through the deception, but he was realistic enough to accept the situation. Though Guzzoni remonstrated with Hube against some of the latter's decisions, he accepted German pre-eminence.

## Nicosia

Hube's assumption of real command and his employment of German divisions brought to an end the rapid advances of the Seventh Army. Oriented eastward, the II Corps would face difficult terrain and a most tenacious foe, highly skilled in the conduct of defensive operations.

The II Corps was to advance toward Messina along two separate axes: Highway 113 along the north coast, and Highway 120 through Nicosia, Troina, Cesarò, and Randazzo. Between the two major axes of advance, and parallel to them, ran the Caronie Mountain chain, the highest mountains on the island except Mount Etna. Extremely rugged, not flattening out to any appreciable degree until just west of Messina, the mountain chain had practically no road net save the four roads that crossed it in a general north-south direction.

The north coast axis of advance—Highway 113—skirted the rim of what resembled a washboard, created by numerous short streams flowing down from the mountain crests at frequent intervals to empty into the sea. The streams themselves were obstacles to advance, but high, steep ridges separating the streams were even more formidable and created positions of great natural strength. In addition, those ridges over which the four transverse roads ran also provided significant defensive lines. The coastal highway itself followed a narrow level belt between the ridge ends and the beaches. At some places where the ridge ends came flush to the Tyrrhenian Sea, the road lay bracketed into the cliff directly above the surf. In one instance—at Cape Calavà (east of Cape Orlando)—the road swung past the point through a short tunnel. The coastal railroad from Palermo to Messina also followed the beach line, usually running between the highway and the sea, crossing the streams on iron bridges, tunneling frequently through the ridges. Though exposed to attack from the sea, the coastal highway offered defenders a series of good positions.

The other axis of advance—Highway 120—passed along the southern slopes of the Caronie Mountains. The road was narrow and crooked, with steep grades and sharp turns. In many places, heavy vehicles had to stop and back up in order to negotiate a turn. Like the coastal region, the mountainous area would provide a determined enemy with numerous ideal defensive positions. But unlike the north coast road, which lay exposed to seaborne assault, the mountains dominated Highway 120 on both sides.

The highland divide between the axes of advance would also contribute a special feature to the campaign in the Messina peninsula. Because the divide contained some of the most rugged and inaccessible terrain in Sicily, and because its slopes dominated the two major east-west arteries, the mountain chain would separate the

CARONIA VALLEY, *typical of the rugged terrain in the Caronie Mountains.*

GANGI, *with Mount Etna in the distant background.*

American forces advancing along the roads except at lateral roads, thereby precluding mutual support. Supply problems would be greatly magnified. The II Corps advance toward Messina would proceed over two distinct battlegrounds.

In order to establish a solid front before pushing on to the east, General Bradley first brought the 45th Division on line with the 1st Division while keeping the momentum of the latter's attack. The 45th Division had come out on the north coast near Termini Imerese, and though it immediately turned toward the east, its front line was fifteen miles behind the 1st Division at Petralia. Until the 45th Division came up with the 1st Division, the II Corps would exert unequal pressure and enable the Germans to shift forces from one highway to the other to counter the two distinct American thrusts. The 91st Reconnaissance Squadron filled the gap between the 1st Division and the British 30 Corps on the right, but because General Bradley was again concerned about the Enna situation, he held the 16th RCT in corps reserve to counter a sudden Axis movement against his right flank. (*Map 4*)

General Allen brought forward the

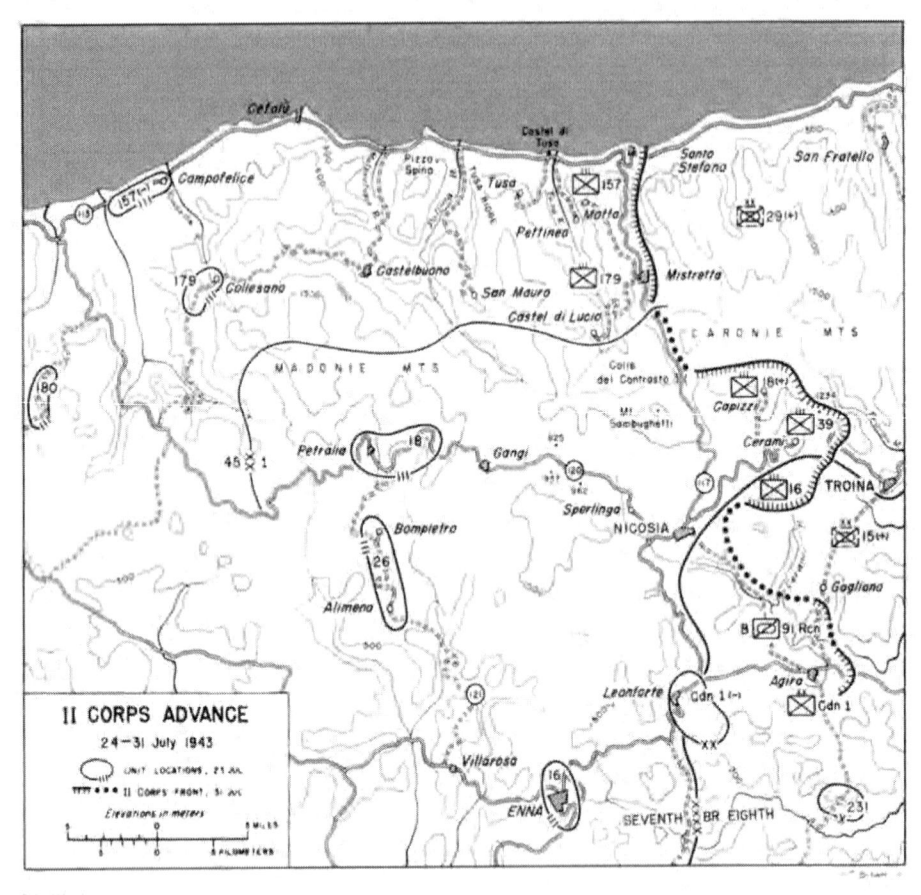

MAP 4

26th RCT and passed it through the 18th RCT east of Petralia on the morning of 24 July to take Gangi and the high ground beyond, then Sperlinga, just three miles from Nicosia.[20]

---

[20] 1st Inf Div G-3 Jnl 43, entry 94; for General Bradley's worries about the east flank, see 1st Inf Div G-3 Jnl, 23 Jul 43, entries 23, 28, 30, 50, 66, and 67.

The maintenance of contact with the British Eighth Army units had posed a problem for the 1st Division ever since the initial change was made in the Seventh Army axis of advance on 14 July. It was always necessary for the 1st Division to divert a portion of its strength—sometimes as much as a battalion—to maintain that

To cover this movement, the 18th Combat Team, late in the afternoon of 23 July, dispatched a company of infantry to the high ground southeast of Gangi. But before the company reached its objective, the regimental reconnaissance platoon moved into Gangi and found the

---

contact and to protect the division's right flank against any unexpected enemy movement into its rear areas. It was not until late in the campaign that this problem subsided; in fact, it was not until the fall of Randazzo. See comments of Maj Gen Ray W. Porter, Jr., on MS.

# THE DRIVE TO THE EAST

town clear of Germans. *Group Fullriede* had pulled its outposts back toward the main defensive line extending in an arc forward of Nicosia.

The 26th Infantry, after clearing the Bompietro road junction, pushed toward Gangi, straddling Highway 120 with a two-battalion front. Against light and intermittent artillery fire, the 1st Battalion moved north of the road toward Hills 825 (Monte Cannella) and 937 (Monte Caolina), while the 3d Battalion headed for Hill 937 south of the road. When the 1st Battalion commander, Major Grant, reported Hill 825 nothing more than a big, barren slab of rock, impracticable to occupy, which the battalion could cover from high ground then held farther to the west, the combat team commander, Colonel Bowen, agreed that it was not necessary to take it. Though the 2d Battalion commander, Colonel Daniel, made a similar report on Hill 937, Colonel Bowen directed him to secure the objective because Bowen wanted to push the 3d Battalion around to the right and then cross-country directly into Nicosia, eight miles away. Daniel complied, and sent Company G to occupy the hill, one platoon of which reached the crest near midnight.

Daybreak of 25 July brought heavy enemy artillery fire across the entire 26th Infantry's front. General Rodt had reinforced *Group Fullriede* during the night with troops that had just returned from the eastern sector. With this added strength, Colonel Fullriede sent a battalion of infantry to retake Hill 937. The American platoon outposting the crest, its leader a casualty, withdrew and rejoined the rest of the company at the western base of the hill. Disturbed by the failure to hold Hill 937 without a fight, Colonel Bowen ordered the 2d Battalion to "work hard on it—get it back." [21] As Generals Allen and Roosevelt began pressing Bowen to retake the hill, Bowen, in order to relieve some of the pressure on the 2d Battalion, directed the 1st Battalion, north of the road, to move forward and occupy Hill 825, even though Major Grant felt "there is no place to put anyone if we did have it." [22] Bowen also directed the 3d Battalion to swing around the right of Hill 937 and pinch the Germans between the other two battalions.

Regaining the hill in the early afternoon, two companies of the 2d Battalion began a short-range, murderous fire fight with the Germans, who withdrew just off the crest down the eastern slope. German and Italian artillery fire raked the hilltop, but the two American companies stood firm. By this time, Brig. Gen. Clift Andrus, the 1st Division's artillery commander, had six artillery battalions plus two 155-mm. gun batteries firing in support of the 26th.[23] As the 3d Battalion came almost in line with the hill and turned toward the highway to take Hill 962 (Monte Barnagiano) in rear of the Germans on Hill 937, the Germans pulled away from this enveloping threat, and just before midnight, the 3d Battalion pushed onto Hill 962.

The enemy was far from finished. Instead of hitting with a counterattack, then pulling out when American counterpressure became strong, the German reaction to the capture of Hill 962 was as strong

---

[21] 26th Inf Regt S-1 Jnl, entry timed 0952, 25 Jul 43.

[22] 26th Inf Regt S-1 Jnl, entries timed 1017, 1105, 1116, and 1404, 25 Jul 43.

[23] The artillery in support of the 26th Infantry fired almost 2,000 rounds during the day. The 33d Field Artillery Battalion, in direct support, alone fired 687 rounds, while the 7th Field Artillery Battalion, reinforcing the 33d, fired 620 rounds.

as against the loss of Hill 937. When Colonel Bowen, on 26 July, sent the 1st Battalion to Hills 921 and 825, eight hundred yards farther east, the Germans knocked the assault elements back to their starting line. South of the road, the Germans threw the 3d Battalion off Hill 962, to start a seesaw battle, with Germans and Americans in alternate possession of the crest. Hill 962 soon became a no man's land, with Germans on the eastern slopes, Americans on the western, and artillery controlling the top. Not until evening did the 3d Battalion, with support from a battalion of the 16th Infantry, finally gain full possession of Hill 962.

General Bradley had released two battalions of the 16th Infantry from corps reserve that morning to enable General Allen to make a double envelopment of Nicosia. With the 26th Infantry apparently stopped on Highway 120 and the Germans showing no signs of giving up their positions around Sperlinga and Nicosia, General Allen that afternoon sent the two battalions of the 16th Infantry south of the highway and around Hill 962 toward Sperlinga. The 18th Infantry, north of the highway, was to swing past the 26th Infantry, take high ground north of Sperlinga and cut Highway 117, the lateral road through Nicosia, then move south to assist the 16th in clearing Nicosia and Sperlinga. The 91st Reconnaissance Squadron was to continue roving in the gap between the two armies, the 4th Tabor of Goums was to work on the left of the 18th Infantry. In explaining his attack plan, General Allen said, "Had we kept up just a frontal attack, it would have meant just a bloody nose for us at every hill." [24]

[24] Tregaskis. *Invasion Diary*, p. 52; 1st Inf Div FO 29, 26 Jul 43.

The envelopment started at 1600, 26 July, as the 26th Infantry fought off renewed German counterattacks; the approach of darkness prevented more than a slight advance. Next day, 27 July, the 16th RCT south of the road was stopped cold in its drive on Sperlinga and Nicosia. North of the highway, while one battalion of the 18th Infantry cleared the two hills that had given the 26th Infantry so much trouble, another battalion, aided by the Goumiers, swung farther north to the approaches to Monte Sambughetti, a towering hill mass 4,500 feet high. An infantry company pushing up the hill took 300 Italian prisoners, and battalion patrols moved farther to the east and cut Highway 117.

Trying to jar the Germans loose from their positions forward of Sperlinga and Nicosia, General Allen ordered thirty-two light tanks from the 70th Tank Battalion, plus a platoon of tanks from the 753d Medium Tank Battalion, to sweep south to the highway in front of Hill 825, coming out near Hill 962. The light tanks deployed at 2030 that evening and, covered by the mediums, roared down to the highway, where they "sprayed for miles around for at least ten or fifteen minutes before receiving artillery fire" and withdrawing. The sweep cost three light tanks and six casualties, but it gained one German antitank gun and bolstered the morale of the American infantrymen on the surrounding hills. By then, the German forces on the Nicosia front had decided to withdraw.

The German withdrawal during the night of 27 July opened the way to the 1st Division. By 0830, 28 July, the 3d Battalion, 16th Infantry, had patrols in Sperlinga, and two hours later in Nicosia. Some sniping was encountered as well as resistance from dug-in emplacements on a few high, rocky points in the north end of town. Before the day was over, the 16th Infantry had captured seven hundred Italians and a few Germans who failed to escape from Nicosia.

For General Guzzoni, the loss of Nicosia was a frustrating development. He had intended to hold Nicosia, which he considered one of the key positions on his main line of resistance. He thought that Hube had the same idea. But during the afternoon of 27 July, Guzzoni had learned from the *XII Corps* headquarters that Colonel Fullriede had received orders to withdraw.

General Guzzoni's immediate inquiries produced the information that Hube was beginning the withdrawal to the Etna line. Though the *Sixth Army* commander did not know it, Hube's chief of staff on 26 July had attended a meeting at Kesselring's headquarters and had returned the same day to Sicily with verbal authorization to start consolidating the German forces on the island for immediate evacuation. Hitler's reaction to Mussolini's dismissal was taking effect. Early on 27 July, therefore, Hube had instructed Rodt to reconnoiter suitable defensive positions just forward of the Etna line for the withdrawal of *Group Fullriede* that night.

At Guzzoni's request late in the afternoon of 27 July, Hube promised to amend his orders to *Group Fullriede*. The German battle group would stop its withdrawal and would organize a new line running along the Nicosia-Agira road, thus closing the gap which had existed between Rodt's two battle groups. Guzzoni then promised that the remnants of the *Aosta Division* would hold the 3,000-foot-high mountain pass (Colle del Contrasto) on Highway 117 about halfway between Nicosia and Mistretta. By consolidating the *15th Panzer Grenadier Division* and holding the pass, the Axis could stop an American thrust north along Highway 117 and thus protect the interior flanks of the *29th Panzer Grenadier* and *Assietta Division* deployed along the north coast. Guzzoni was also worried that an American breakthrough at the pass would unhinge from the north coast the entire main line of resistance, a move that would seriously endanger all of the Axis units to the south.

Apparently neither Rodt nor Fullriede received word of Hube's promise to delay *Group Fullriede's* withdrawal from Nicosia, for without informing the *Aosta Division,* Fullriede began withdrawing his battle group that night to the new positions he and General Rodt had previously reconnoitered: six miles east of Nicosia extending from Gagliano (just north of Agira), through Serradifalco and Cerami (both on Highway 120), to Capizzi (some three miles north of Cerami). The *Aosta Division* hastily joined the German withdrawal. The result was that some units became lost in the mountainous terrain while others, apparently not receiving the withdrawal order, stayed to fend off the American thrust on Nicosia the following day. At the important mountain pass on Highway 117, a battalion of the *Aosta Division* pulled back to join the general rearward movement, and, as a consequence, opened the north coast road to American advance.[25]

---

[25] IT 99b, 27 Jul 43; Faldella, *Lo sbarco*, pp. 231–32, 239–40, 242–43; *OKW/WFSt, KTB, 1.–31.VII.43*, 26 Jul 43; *OB SUED, Meldungen*, 27 Jul 43; *OKH Tagesmeldungen West*, 28 Jul 43.

COAST ROAD PATROL *passing the bombed-out Castelbuono railroad station, 24 July.*

*Along the North Coast*

Despite mine fields and blown bridges, the 45th Division had advanced rapidly during the night of 23 July and the following day. The newly committed *Group Ulich* of the *29th Panzer Grenadier Division* was not strong enough to contest seriously the American advance. By blowing the bridge over the Malpertugio River, five miles east of Cefalù, and by liberally planting mines in the river bed, *Group Ulich* brought the 157th Infantry to a temporary halt. The 179th Infantry, which had been following a secondary road six miles inland, reached the town of Castelbuono, eight miles north of Petralia.

This brought the 45th Division on line with the 1st Division.

When General Bradley directed General Middleton to keep the pressure on along the north coast road, Middleton sent the 180th Infantry through the 157th on the evening of 24 July. The 180th Infantry crossed the Malpertugio River during the night, and under almost constant artillery, mortar, and machine gun fire, on the following day uncovered a new German line on the high ground just forward of the Pollina River, where the Germans occupied an extremely strong, natural defensive position hinged on the 3,000-foot-high Pizzo Spina. The coastal highway skirts the base of almost vertical cliffs lead-

# THE DRIVE TO THE EAST

ing to the crest of the heights. With their main battle position on the west side of the river, the Germans did not demolish the highway bridge, but deployed their infantrymen and supporting weapons on the ground controlling the coastal highway.

The first American task was seizure of Pizzo Spina, and Colonel Cochrane, the 2d Battalion commander, hoping to nutcracker the Germans, sent Company F to occupy a defended blockhouse at a bend in the highway just under the enemy guns on Pizzo Spina, and Company E inland up a ravine to come in on the left of the German line.

While Company E made its tortuous way through the ravine toward the southern slopes of Pizzo Spina, Company F, under heavy German artillery and small arms fire, took, but soon gave up, the blockhouse and withdrew.

Cochrane immediately sent in Company G, which, with the reorganized Company F, tried a frontal attack against the German positions. Scaling the almost vertical cliffs, with friendly artillery bursting fifty to seventy yards ahead of the skirmish line, using rifle fire, rifle grenades, and 60-mm. mortars to aid their advance, the two companies climbed from sea level to almost 3,000 feet in less than a thousand yards. But it was slow going. The advance brought down damaging barrages from enemy artillery and heavy weapons, and German infantrymen rolled hand grenades down the slopes. The supporting 4.2-inch mortars, from positions 500 yards behind the line of departure, blanketed observed and suspected targets, and with white phosphorus shells neutralized some enemy positions high among the crags.

Just as the advance seemed about to stop, Company E bounded in on the German left and overran that end of the enemy line, gaining positions near the pinnacle of Pizzo Spina. Able to enfilade the rest of the German line, the company drove the Germans down the eastern slopes. Company F moved up to the pinnacle, while Company G dropped off the slopes to occupy the blockhouse position on the highway.

*Group Ulich* was not yet ready to give up its Pollina River line. Shortly after the Americans occupied Pizzo Spina, the Germans launched the first of three counterattacks against the mountain pinnacle. German direct artillery fire from across the river at ranges of less than 3,000 yards was precise in searching out American positions. But observation posts on Pizzo Spina enabled American artillery observers to bring down heavy fire on the counterattacking forces. Along the coastal highway, a platoon of 4.2-inch mortars stopped one German thrust by laying down a 100-round, thirty-minute, mixed white phosphorus and high explosive concentration. Though some small units gave way slightly, and though the line close to the shore surged back and forth for a depth of three hundred yards, the Americans held. After one last try just before darkness, the Germans pulled back across the river, with American artillery fire so heavy and accurate that the Germans could not demolish the bridge.[26]

The 180th Infantry could not seize the opportunity to pursue. Fourteen unidentified naval vessels, four of which were believed to be cruisers, were sighted off

---

[26] Infantry Combat, Part Five: Sicily, pp. 19-24; OKH, *Tagesmeldungen West*, 25 Jul 43; IT 99b, an. 81. The 171st Field Artillery Battalion fired 1,100 rounds in support of the 180th Infantry; the 189th Field Artillery Battalion, reinforcing, fired 500 rounds.

Campofelice, between Cefalù and Termini Imerese. Fearing that these were Axis ships, General Bradley halted the 45th Division advance and instructed General Middleton to prepare to defend the coast line against a possible Axis amphibious landing. The 180th Infantry consequently faced toward the sea near Pizzo Spina, while the 157th Infantry, with tanks from the 753d Medium Tank Battalion, deployed along the beaches in the rear. Not until early the next afternoon, 26 July, did a division artillery liaison plane identify the vessels as American destroyers and mine sweepers.[27]

Oddly enough, General Hube feared that these vessels were part of an Allied amphibious force moving to a landing in the rear of the Santo Stefano line, the northern hinge of the main line of resistance. He, therefore, alerted Axis units all the way to Calabria to be ready to repel a landing.[28]

*Group Ulich,* meanwhile, had moved to a new line closer to Santo Stefano di Camastra, a line which ran from Castel di Tusa (on the coast) south through Pettineo to Castel di Lucio, the northern half resting behind the Tusa River. Late in the afternoon of 26 July, the 2d Battalion, 180th Infantry, reached the Tusa River, halted in the face of heavy German small arms and artillery fire, and found the Germans in a strong, natural defensive position on a very steep hill forming the eastern slope of the Tusa River valley. Here, too, the Germans had not demolished the highway bridge.

While the 2d Battalion made a show of crossing the river near the bridge, the 3d Battalion, 180th Infantry, swung inland to outflank the German position. At 2030, the battalion seized a high hill overlooking the village of Tusa, two miles inland from the coast, west of the Tusa River and at the end of a fishhook road. Across the river, on a high ridge at another road end, lay the village of Pettineo. Since the Tusa and Pettineo ridges formed the key to a successful Tusa River crossing, the 3d Battalion's mission was to get up on the Pettineo ridge, from where it could then drive north and strike the main German position near the coast on the flank and in the rear.

Early on the morning of 27 July, the 3d Battalion made its move. Tusa fell at 0600; there was little opposition. But nine hours later, the 3d Battalion had managed to progress only a few hundred yards more, up to the curve of the fishhook road overlooking the river. Cognizant of the threat that this movement presented to his main battle position, Col. Max Ulich had a reinforced infantry battalion well dug in on the Pettineo ridge to block the 3d Battalion.

The inability of the 3d Battalion to get across the Tusa River and outflank the main German line threw the entire weight of the attack on the 1st Battalion, 180th Infantry, which tried to cross the river near the coast. One company managed to get across the bridge just after noon, but artillery fire had so damaged the bridge structure that it collapsed shortly there-

---

[27] II Corps G-3 Jnl, entries 95 and 96, 25 Jul 43; II Corps G-3 Jnl, entries 110 and 133, 26 Jul 43; 45th Inf Div G-3 Jnl, entries 40, 41, and 43, 26 Jul 43; ONI, Sicilian Campaign, pp. 101-02.

[28] Msg, *OB SUED* to *LXXVI Panzer Corps,* in *LXXVI Panzer Corps, KTB, Anlagen, 10. VII.–30.VIII.43* (CRS 43005/2). This message was probably the cause for a German air strike against the American ships on the next day, a strike which caused considerable damage to one of the destroyers. See ONI, Sicilian Campaign, p. 102.

# THE DRIVE TO THE EAST

after. This, coupled with heavy enemy fire, prevented the battalion from reinforcing the one company on the east bank of the river. Though it managed to hold on to a precarious position for the rest of the afternoon, just after dark the battalion commander pulled the company back to the west side of the river.

It was on the same evening, thirty miles inland, that the Germans had given up Nicosia. Though Guzzoni might disagree with Hube on some matters, he was in basic agreement with the German commander that the Axis front as it was then constituted could not long be held with the forces available on the island. The eastern third of the front, manned by the reinforced *Hermann Goering Division*, appeared to be relatively strong and could be expected to hold. But the pressure being exerted by the Americans and the Canadians against the northern and central sectors seemed to demand a consolidation of the Axis forces on the shorter front of the Etna line. The German withdrawal from Nicosia was the beginning of this consolidation. On the next day, 28 July, as the 1st Division entered Nicosia, *Group Ens* gave up Agira to the 1st Canadian Division and pulled back toward Gagliano to join forces with *Group Fullriede*. The *Hermann Goering Division* extended its eastern flank to block a further Canadian advance, while the entire *15th Panzer Grenadier Division* prepared to block a push eastward by the 1st Division. Thus, on 28 July, the central sector of the Axis front had consolidated near the Etna line. To cover this pullback, and to delay the Americans on the north coast as long as possible, General Hube ordered the *29th Panzer Grenadier Division* to hold forward of Santo Stefano di Camastra at least through the night of 30 July before moving back on line with the *15th Panzer Grenadier Division*.

In the meantime, plans for a combined Anglo-American August offensive had solidified. On 25 July, General Alexander had met with his two army commanders at Cassibile, the new 15th Army Group command post south of Syracuse. Here, the plan for the expulsion of the Axis forces from the Messina peninsula was agreed on and placed in effect. The Seventh Army was to continue eastward along the two axes previously assigned in "a sustained relentless drive until the enemy is decisively defeated."[29] General Bradley's II Corps would continue to control the ground operations along both axes.[30]

The Eighth Army was to make its major effort on the left with the British 78th Division thrusting to the north along the Catenanuova-Centuripe-Adrano axis and the 1st Canadian Division driving to the east along Highway 121 through Regalbuto. On the Eighth Army's right, the 13 Corps was to feint an attack toward Catania to deceive the Germans into thinking this was the main British effort. After the fall of Adrano, which General Montgomery estimated to be the key to the main Axis Etna positions, he expected the Germans to pull out of Catania. Then the 13 Corps would exploit to Messina around the eastern side of Mount Etna.[31]

General Bradley, in accordance with the new directive to push on to the east—although his push had never really stopped—decided to relieve the 45th Di-

---

[29] Seventh Army Rpt of Opns, p. b–15.
[30] Seventh Army Directive, 31 Jul 43, Seventh Army Rpt of Opns, p. D–13.
[31] Nicholson, *The Canadians in Italy*, p. 139; Montgomery, *Eighth Army*, p. 106; Butcher, *My Three Years With Eisenhower*, p. 373.

vision with the 3d Division on 31 July and to pass the 9th Division through the 1st Division. But assembling the bulk of the 9th Division would take time, and Bradley directed General Allen to keep the 1st Division moving toward Cerami and Troina until the 9th Division could effect relief.[32]

The American and British foot soldiers would have plenty of help in this final push to evict the Axis forces from Sicily. The Allied air forces roamed almost at will through the skies above the battlefield. Almost no hostile aircraft rose to contest Allied air superiority. By the time Palermo fell, no Axis aircraft were operating from Sicilian airfields; all had been withdrawn to the Italian mainland or destroyed. With the enemy's air out of the way, the attention of the Allied air commands could turn to rendering direct and close support to the foot soldiers.

The Seventh Army's advance on Palermo had been so swift that it had been unnecessary to call in many close support air missions, with the result that most tactical sorties had been flown well ahead of the advancing units in strafing and bombing attacks against targets of opportunity and the road networks leading to the active front. *Group Ulich* had suffered heavily from just such attacks, losing fifty vehicles and a complete artillery battery while on the way to oppose the 45th Division's advance along the north coast road.[33]

By this time, too, Allied fighters, fighter-bombers, and light bombers operated from captured airfields on Sicily—at Licata, Ponte Olivo, Comiso, and others. Both the U.S. 31st and 33d Fighter Wings flew under XII ASC control. By 30 July, all units of the U.S. 64th Fighter Wing had moved to Sicily. Ample air support would be available to support the final drive.[34]

Naval support was also available, if not in the quantity that had been available on 10 July. On 27 July, when Palermo was first opened to Allied shipping, Admiral Hewitt created Naval Task Force 88, consisting of the last few remaining American warships in Sicilian waters. Under the command of Rear Adm. Lyal A. Davidson, NTF 88 became "General Patton's Navy"—set up to support the Seventh Army's operations along the north coast.[35] To carry out this mission, Admiral Davidson was initially assigned 2 cruisers, 14 destroyers, 14 MTB's, 19 landing craft (2 LST's, 10 LCI(L)'s, 7 LCT's), and a number of small escort craft.[36] On the east coast, Admiral Cunningham had warships available to support the Eighth Army operations, and was prepared to furnish a number of landing craft to lift British ground units around the stubborn German Catania defense line. Rear Adm. R. R. McGrigor, the senior British naval officer in Sicily, had completed all preparations necessary to launch an amphibious end run.[37]

Even as the 3d Division began its move forward to effect the relief of the 45th Division on the north coast road, General Middleton on the morning of 28 July leapfrogged regiments, ordering the 157th Infantry forward to take up the fight. Colonel Ankcorn's leading battalions failed

---

[32] II Corps FO 11, 31 Jul 43.
[33] MS #D-095 (Ulich).
[34] Craven and Cate, eds., *Europe: TORCH to POINTBLANK*, pp. 462–66; Coles, USAF Hist Study 37, pp. 122–28; 0403/9/3, sub: NAAF Daily Opns Summary, Jun–Jul 43; Seventh Army G-3 Opns File, sub: Air Support.
[35] Morison, *Sicily—Salerno—Anzio*, p. 191.
[36] WNTF Rpt of Opns, p. 72.
[37] Roskill, vol. III, pt. I, pp. 142–43.

THE DRIVE TO THE EAST

to get off to a fast start, for a blown section of the coastal road west of the Pollina River delayed their arrival at the Tusa River until late in the afternoon. Eventually, at 1745, the 1st Battalion, 157th Infantry, relieved the 180th Infantry Battalion at the river. Immediately, Colonel Murphy, the battalion commander, sent Company B across the river to the left of the demolished bridge and along the flat coastal strip. Though it suffered some casualties from mines and from enemy artillery fire, Company B started working up the slopes of the Tusa ridge—Hill 335—across the top of which the *3d Battalion, 15th Panzer Grenadier Regiment* had dug in. In the meantime, Company C crossed the river to the right of the demolished bridge and started up the forward slopes of the hill, finally reaching a terrace just under the steep crest where heavy small arms and mortar fire forced a halt. Company A, put in on the right of Company C, could make no more progress. As night came, both companies clung precariously to their terrace perch. But by this time, Company B had succeeded in reaching the top of the ridge overlooking the sea. The company was low on ammunition, but it formed a line near the edge of a clearing, and, though harassed throughout the night by sniper fire and hand grenades, it held.

While the 1st Battalion developed the Tusa ridge positions, the 2d Battalion, 157th Infantry, had swung inland, passed through the 3d Battalion, 180th Infantry, at Tusa, and crossed the river into Pettineo by darkness of 23 July. In contrast to the tough resistance encountered by the 180th Infantry the previous day, the only opposition to the advance on the 28th came in the form of a small counterattack launched by a portion of the *2d Battalion, 15th Panzer Grenadier Regiment*. Thereafter, the Germans pulled back to the high ground along the Motta d'Affermo-Mistretta road. The same day, to the south, the 18th RCT began sending patrols north on Highway 117 toward Mistretta, thereby threatening the *29th Panzer Grenadier Division's* open left flank.

On the morning of 29 July, the 2d Battalion pushed out toward Motta, driving for two hills south of town. This day, though, the enemy refused to relinquish ground, and the battalion's attempt to flank the German line to the north was of no avail. To add weight to the turning movement, Colonel Ankcorn, the 157th Infantry Combat Team commander, committed the 3d Battalion, which crossed the Tusa River behind the 1st Battalion, moved south toward Pettineo, then turned inland to drive directly on Motta. Covered by a three-battalion artillery concentration (almost 1,500 rounds) which forced the two forward companies from the 1st Battalion to cling to their terrace walls while shells exploded almost in their faces, the 3d Battalion moved slowly toward Motta. The advance was still uphill, for Motta itself was some 900 feet higher than the Tusa ridge line and represented the key terrain before Santo Stefano, the 45th Division's objective. This ground the 45th Division would remember as "Bloody Ridge." By 1900, somewhat disorganized, the two 157th Infantry battalions halted for the night short of Motta.

The *29th Panzer Grenadier Division* was still not ready to give up this line before 30 July. Though General Fries had lost the Tusa River line and faced the threat of an envelopment of Santo Stefano from the south—Mistretta (ten miles to the south) was entered by Ameri-

DEMOLISHED BRIDGE ALONG HIGHWAY 117 *between Santo Stefano and Mistretta slows down 45th Division troops.*

can troops on 29 July—he ordered Colonel Ulich to mount a counterattack on the morning of 30 July to retake the Tusa ridge to slow the American advance toward Santo Stefano from the west. General Fries was confident that the rough nature of the terrain between Mistretta and Santo Stefano, coupled with the ease with which Highway 117 could be blocked at almost any point, precluded any rapid American advance from the south. The most serious threat to Santo Stefano remained the 45th Division; this was the unit that had to be halted if Santo Stefano was to hold out another twenty-four hours. To make the counterattack, General Fries attached to *Group Ulich* a battalion from the *71st Panzer Grenadier Regiment* and two battalions from the division's artillery.

At 0430, 30 July, without preparatory artillery fires, the German attack jumped off from just north of Motta. Initially, it achieved full surprise and gained some ground, but at heavy cost. The 1st and 3d Battalions, 157th Infantry, recovered their composure quickly and dug in to hold. Alert to its supporting role, the 45th Division artillery began firing soon after the attack developed. From the south, the 2d Battalion poured heavy fire on the German flank. By noon, the impetus of the German attack slowed considerably. After taking a fifteen-minute, three-battalion artillery concentration shortly after 1300, the Germans stopped.

# THE DRIVE TO THE EAST

That night, the 157th Infantry resumed its advance. Motta fell without a fight. Leaving one reinforced battalion to hold Santo Stefano as long as possible, General Fries moved his division eastward. The town fell the next morning.[38]

For the 45th Division, Santo Stefano marked the end of active combat operations in Sicily, although the 157th Infantry would take part in an operation near Messina late in the campaign.

For a short time, at least, the division could enjoy a respite from the bloody business of war.

In its first twenty-one days of combat in World War II, the 45th Division had earned an enviable reputation. It had marched and fought from Scoglitti to the north coast, suffered 1,156 casualties, and taken 10,977 prisoners.

As the 3d Division moved into line on the north coast, the 1st Division, on the II Corps southern axis, Highway 120, began what was to be its hardest and bloodiest battle of the Sicilian Campaign—Troina.

---

[38] 157th Inf Regt Rpt of Opns; Infantry Combat, Part Five: Sicily, pp. 24–30; MS #D–095 (Ulich); *OKH, Tagesmeldungen West*, 29 Jul 43.

## CHAPTER XVII

# The Battle of Troina

The 1st Division's pursuit of the *15th Panzer Grenadier Division* from Nicosia came to an end on 29 July, when heavy rain and stubborn rear guard resistance stopped the 16th RCT about four miles east of the former Axis stronghold. That afternoon the forward troops of the 16th Infantry dug in on three hills which commanded the highway about three miles short of Cerami. Beyond Cerami, eight more miles of road would have to be taken before the 1st Division could enter Troina.

Meanwhile, General Rodt's *15th Panzer Grenadier Division* had completed its preparations to move back toward the Etna line, which, in the northern sector extended from Sant'Agata to San Fratello and Cesarò, first occupying an intermediate defense line hinged on Troina. Along this forward line, General Rodt disposed *Group Fullriede* in Troina and along the high ground north of the town, *Group Ens* in the terrain to the south.[1] Rodt's division, united for the first time during the campaign, maintained a loose contact with the *Hermann Goering Division* on its left near Regalbuto, and on the right with the *29th Panzer Grenadier Division*, also pulling back along the north coast toward the Etna line. The *Aosta Division*, holding a vague sector between the *15th* and *29th Panzer Grenadier Divisions*, placed its four artillery battalions under German control just east of Troina.[2]

As early as 22 July, American intelligence officers were describing the Etna line with accuracy.[3] But they guessed that the Germans were building up another, more highly organized, final defensive line from which they could launch a vigorous counterattack as well as screen a possible withdrawal to the Italian mainland.[4]

In this the Americans guessed wrong. General Hube had no concept of a final defensive line. Rather, he saw in the northeast sector of the island ground on which he could establish a succession of strongpoints—as opposed to a line of defenses—almost, but not quite, as though lateral means of communication did not exist. The fact that the terrain denied freedom of maneuver was something Hube could use to his advantage. If small garrisons proved effective, they could stay as long as they were not endangered by the fall of a flanking stronghold. And when the garrisons were in imminent danger of falling or of being encircled, they would have at their rear a good road along which

---
[1] 1st Inf Div Consolidated Preliminary Interrogation Rpt, 2 Aug 43; 1st Inf Div G-2 Periodic Rpt 27, 7 Aug 43; *OB SUED, Meldungen*, 0750, 30 Jul 43.

[2] Faldella, *Lo sbarco*, p. 244 and Table 12.

[3] Seventh Army G-2 Periodic Rpt 14, 22 Jul 43, in Seventh Army Rpt of Opns, p. C-35; see also Seventh Army G-2 Est of Enemy Sit 5, 23 Jul 43, in Seventh Army Rpt of Opns, p. C-17.

[4] Seventh Army G-2 Periodic Rpts 18 and 19, 27 and 28 Jul 43.

they could withdraw. At the same time, most of the defending forces would be well away from the front lines.

It was the failure to appreciate the priority which the Germans gave to their withdrawal movement that caused the Americans most of their trouble at Troina. This failure was spotlighted by the unremitting search for a final defensive line in the Seventh Army's zone. All information pointed to heavy troop and matériel movements passing through, and not stopping at, Troina. Air reconnaissance also discovered a large bivouac area near Cesarò, and when direct observation from Nicosia and Cerami showed how lightly Troina was held, the guesses about where the Germans would hold focused farther and farther eastward. On 28 July, the II Corps G-2 believed the Germans would continue their rear guard actions and make a final stand either along a line located on high ground some five miles east of Troina, or along a line between Cesarò and Randazzo. The reason: "The successful defense of Catania and the Catania Plain have raised German morale and hopes to the point where they are willing to gamble two or three more divisions to hold a Sicilian bridgehead."[5]

On 30 July, the II Corps G-2 said: "Indications from observed bivouac areas north of Cesarò and the general withdrawal of the enemy east of Cesarò following the day's fighting are that the enemy is falling back to that area."[6]

The II Corps and the 1st Division intelligence estimates also emphasized the poor condition and small size of the enemy force holding Troina. Relying chiefly on prisoner of war and civilian testimony, the 1st Division G-2 (Lt. Col. Ray W. Porter, Jr.) reported at 1215, 29 July, "Germans very tired, little ammo, many casualties, morale low."[7] And two days later, he said: "Offering slight resistance to our advancing force, the enemy fought a delaying action while the bulk of the force withdrew toward Cesarò. The delaying forces consisted of small groups of infantry with mortars and machine guns and were supported by artillery."[8] That same evening, 31 July, the II Corps announced: "Indications are Troina lightly held."[9]

The terrain facing the II Corps forces on Highway 120 was difficult. Half a dozen ridge systems running generally north and south compartmentalize the terrain between Nicosia and Randazzo, and each series of hills commands the highway. Any of several might have served to anchor a defensive line forward of the Etna positions but the Troina ridge in particular possessed several choice features: avenues of communication in the vicinity of the town were so few and the hill systems so arranged that half a dozen fortified hills could completely control not only Highway 120 but also any endeavor to flank these positions—any attempt to envelop the town would require a very wide encirclement; gun positions in the town not only looked down on the highway, they could also pour effective fire on Cerami (from which an attack had to be launched) and especially on a wide curve which the highway made as it left Cerami; the cup-shaped valley between Cerami and Troina was exceptionally barren and devoid of cover; and, above all, since the Germans had shown from the beginning of the campaign

---

[5] II Corps G-2 Est 9, 28 Jul 43.
[6] II Corps G-2 Periodic Rpt 18, 30 Jul 43.
[7] 1st Inf Div G-2 Jnl, 29 Jul 43.
[8] 1st Inf Div G-2 Periodic Rpt 20, 31 Jul 43.
[9] II Corps G-2 Jnl, 31 Jul 43.

TROINA RIDGE FROM THE HIGH GROUND NEAR CERAMI. *Mount Etna is in the background.*

LOOKING WEST FROM THE TOWN OF TROINA

that the one line they insisted on holding was the line stretching along the southern base of Mount Etna, Troina was the best place along Highway 120 that would serve as the continuation of the line from Etna to the north coast. Nicosia and even Cerami were not only comparatively easy to outflank, but were also too far from the towns holding out against the Eighth Army—first Agira and Regalbuto, but above all Adrano and Catania. To give up these towns (except on a definite timetable) would mean that the greater part of the German garrison in Sicily would be trapped in the Etna area, the limited communications and stone walls of which had been a major factor in the entire delaying action. Again, to let Troina go and try to use Cesarò (which had nearly the same bundle of things to recommend it) would bring the Allies entirely too close to the southern portion of the Etna line. Cesarò had to be given up after, not before, Adrano, to allow the German center to evacuate along two roads to Messina instead of only one. In other words, the loss of Troina would mean that the entire Etna line would become a dangerous liability.

The terrain canalized the 1st Division's advance, and Troina was an effective blocking point. The road itself came under interdiction possibilities at Cerami. Just south of Cerami, a high hill (Hill

1030), and just beyond that the Cerami River, afforded cover for an assembly area, and a stream-bed approach to the southeast of Troina—the so-called Gagliano salient. These features in the approaches to Troina weakened somewhat the all around defense capabilities.

Unlike most other towns in Sicily, Cerami has wide streets. Through traffic would not be a great problem, and a few blown houses would not become an effective barrier. But as the highway comes in from the southwest, crosses the south end of town, then turns north, the exposed road emerges into point-blank range for any artillery in or south of Troina. Beyond Cerami, the highway bears east for a mile and a half before making a reverse loop which is a pocket. Sheltered from artillery positions on Monte Acuto by Hill 1234 on the north and from Troina by Hills 1140 and 1061 on the east, the road pocket around a small valley head was in complete defilade; high-angle fire alone could reach it. But the mountain streams that run through the pocket make steep gulches, and two blown bridges in the loop would add considerably to the 1st Division's engineering problems.

Beyond the face of Hill 1030, Troina looks down the throat of any force approaching from the west. Two and a half miles of the road were completely dominated by positions in Troina and on the north extension of the Troina ridge.

Besides controlling the highway, positions in Troina also covered the hill noses west of the town. Any approach to Troina by troops north of the road must come down these noses, and artillery fire from across the small valley between them and Troina could literally slap an advance in the face. The major hill noses are those of Hills 1061 and 1035, which could be fired upon also from Monte Acuto. The south and southwest faces of Hill 1061 were defiladed from fire from Monte Acuto; but Hill 1035 (Monte Basilio), an extension of the Acuto ridge, was vulnerable to enfilade on both faces. Thus, an advance on Troina in the terrain north of the highway would be caught between two fires.

The Monte Acuto position, almost a mile high, marked one of the strong features of the German line. It dominated the lower ridges and ridge noses toward Troina. It covered the valley and the entire Troina front; the highway for some distance west of Troina, and east of the town as far as the Troina River crossing; the front of the positions south of Troina along the Gagliano road; and its own approaches: west from Capizzi, and southwest around the flank of Hill 1254 towards Cerami. Only from the north, where the ground ascended to Monte Pelato, was the Monte Acuto position vulnerable, but only if the defenders could not hold the higher points.

Troina proper, a town of 12,000 people, was itself a natural strongpoint, built on a bluff ridge, high and dominating. The highway did not go through the town; rather, it ran along the town's front, then turned left and crossed the ridge through a sort of pass. This had several significant implications. First, Troina was not in itself a roadblock, but its high fortified position enabled it to control not only Highway 120, but also the road southeast to Adrano and a secondary road running southwest to Gagliano. Second, the highway swung around behind the ridge and was defiladed for some distance northeast toward Cesarò. This would make use of the highway possible even under attack from the west, and make it available for a withdrawal from Troina should the situation become untenable. These advantages did not obtain against positions on the Troina ridge at Monte Basilio (Hill 1035) which, if taken, would threaten to cut off any forces in Troina from withdrawal to the east.

Troina's streets were narrow with right angle turns. The main street made such a turn on the northeast face of a cliff. At the top of the town, two spires of a Norman church overlooked a small public square. At the cliff front a round feudal tower provided an ideal observation post. The streets, buildings, and massive stone houses made good holding places for infantry. Once beaten down from the front, the infantry could always crawl out the back way and down the road to Cesarò.

The Troina ridge extended northeast beyond the town, covered the Cesarò road, and afforded excellent artillery emplacements. Shielding the town on the west was another ridge system, with key strongpoints both north and south of the highway, and there would occur some of the bitterest fighting in the battle for Troina, particularly at three key points: Hill 1061, north of the highway; Hills 1006 and 1034, south of the road. Below Hill 1034 the same ridge turned to the east, so that south of Troina the town's defenses were at right angles to the positions north and west of the town. The south face held the key strongpoints of Hill 851, Monte Bianco, and Monte San Gregorio. Farther south lay the Gagliano salient: Gagliano, Monte Pellegrino, and Monte Salici, the latter two lying on high ground extending east across the Troina River. Gagliano was accessible by road from the south; it had few natural defenses and was too far from Troina to be held by a large force. An attacker could make use of the lower half of the Gagliano-Troina road to help gain flanking approaches to the other two hills in the salient and to the key points on the ridge line south of Troina. A powerful strike here could crack the salient and turn up both flanks, or else force a rapid withdrawal from the Pellegrino positions north to the ridge. This would pose a serious threat to the left flank of the Troina positions, and like Monte Basilio north of the town, the occupation of Monte Pellegrino would put the attackers in position seriously to threaten the highway east of Troina, the only good route of withdrawal.

Throughout the Troina area, the ground was rugged. Hill slopes rose abruptly, forming canyons rather than valleys, and usually separated by rocky streams only a few feet wide. The Americans would find these streams sown with mines. Soldiers would have to scramble over surfaces that would tax the agility of a mountain goat. They would find objectives as difficult to recognize as to reach, for the hills looked much alike, and a distinguishing feature noted from one angle would tend to disappear when viewed from a different angle. The Troina area was a demolition engineer's dream. The smallest ravine was a deep gulch, and a destroyed road would require a bypass down a long descent. The terrain favored the first comer, especially the defender, and the Germans proved to be most adept in selecting and employing the terrain for defense.

1st Division patrols, from both the 16th and 18th RCT's, on 30 July had already probed the approaches to Cerami. Noting some artillery and much activity in the town, they made no attempt to enter it. A 39th Infantry attack was scheduled for the following day. This

4TH TABOR OF GOUMS *moving north of Highway 120 toward Capizzi, 30 July.*

unit, now under Col. H. A. Flint, had been attached to the 1st Division pending the arrival of the remainder of the 9th Division.

North of Highway 120 the 4th Tabor of Goums, attached to the 18th Infantry, moved toward Capizzi on 30 July without incident until late in the day. Then small arms and mortar fire stopped the goums. Not until daylight, 31 July, and only after a heavy volume of covering artillery fire were the Goumiers able to enter Capizzi. An advance that afternoon of a mile and a half northeast of Capizzi to Hill 1321 (Monte Scimone) stirred up only minor resistance. The Italian troops from the *Aosta Division* were falling back and in the process, though unknown to the Americans or Goumiers, were strengthening the right flank of the German defenses at Troina.[10]

South of the highway similar incidents occurred. A troop from the 91st Reconnaissance Squadron occupied Monte Femmina Morta (less than 1500 yards west of the German ridge positions—Hills 1006 and 1034—west of Troina) on 30 July and gained contact with 16th Infantry patrols. Another troop of the reconnaissance squadron, furnishing right flank protection for the division, made

---

[10] Capt Verlet, CO 4th Tabor, Rpt of Opns, 31 Aug 43, KCRC X-15667; IT 99b; *Operazioni in Sicilia dal 1 al 17 agosto 1943, Narrativa, Allegati,* IT 99c (cited hereafter as IT 99c); Faldella, *Lo sbarco,* pp. 249-51.

# THE BATTLE OF TROINA

contact with the Canadians in Agira, then moved northeast along the unimproved road toward Gagliano. Late in the afternoon, a huge crater just short of the village halted further progress. The enemy was nowhere in evidence.

Not until the following morning, 31 July, when the reconnaissance troop tried to repair the crater south of Gagliano did a detachment of the *15th Panzer Grenadier Division* put in an appearance and contest the road. And not until the next day, 1 August, after heavy supporting fires were laid on the enemy, did the reconnaissance troop enter Gagliano.[11]

Meanwhile, Colonel Flint's 39th Infantry on 30 July had passed through units of both the 16th and 18th Regiments immediately north and south of the highway and by evening was prepared to jump off at dawn to take Cerami, then continue to Troina. Both objectives seemed ready to fall, for prisoners' statements that day underscored the weakness of Troina's defenders. Air reconnaissance confirmed this impression, for pilots could find little evidence of strong defenses around the town. Only light traffic passed between Troina and Randazzo. Troina seemed to be just another place with a skeleton garrison to fight a brief delaying action before pulling out, even though one report indicated that "they seem to be right in there."[12] Consequently, General Allen late on the evening of 30 July planned to reinforce the 39th Infantry's attack by committing the 26th Infantry through the 16th south of the highway at darkness on 31 July for a direct thrust to Troina by daylight of 1 August.[13] This, Allen hoped, would coincide with the 39th Infantry's advance eastward from Cerami toward the northern edge of Troina.

In support of the attack, General Andrus, the 1st Division's artillery commander, deployed an impressive array of supporting fires. Controlling the eight organic battalions of the 1st and 9th Divisions, plus almost the same number of artillery battalions attached from the II Corps, General Andrus had at his disposal 165 artillery pieces.[14]

This massive artillery support actually did not appear to be needed, for when Flint's 39th Infantry jumped off toward Cerami at dawn on 31 July the troops met no opposition except that offered by the rough terrain north of the highway. By 0900 that morning a battalion was in Cerami.

Though Allen had contemplated moving Bowen's 26th Infantry through the 16th Infantry for a direct thrust to Troina, Flint's easy success made committment of the 26th seem unnecessary. Allen therefore instructed Flint to continue alone, his mission to capture Troina and the high ground east of Troina astride Highway 120.[15]

Optimism was the order of the day when Generals Bradley and Allen visited Flint's command post early in the afternoon. They passed along a report from civilians who said the town contained only a few troops, some antitank guns, an antiaircraft battery, and one heavy gun.

---

[11] 91st Rcn Squad AAR. Sgt. Gerry H. Kisters, who knocked out two German machine gun positions though five times wounded, was later awarded the Medal of Honor.

[12] 1st Inf Div G-2 Periodic Rpt 19, 30 Jul 43; 1st Inf Div G-3 Jnl, entry 69, 30 Jul 43.

[13] 1st Inf Div G-3 Jnl, entry 84, 30 Jul 43.
[14] 1st Inf Div Arty AAR.
[15] 1st Inf Div G-3 Jnl, entries 12, 14, and 24, 31 Jul 43; 39th Inf Regt Jnl, entries 23 and 41, 31 Jul 43.

FORWARD OBSERVATION POST *near Cerami.*   *Artillery fire is being directed on Troina, in the distance.*

ARTILLERY IN POSITION NEAR CERAMI.   *The 155-mm. rifle is firing on Troina.*

They informed Flint that they had no specific deadline for his capture of Troina. They also suggested he use a trail along an aqueduct for his approach to the town while artillery worked over the reverse slopes of the hills shielding Troina.[16]

Despite this optimism Flint's troops were already running into trouble. German mortar and artillery fire denied the Americans a direct approach to Troina. Covered by heavy concentrations of supporting artillery, the regiment advanced only with difficulty. By the end of the day one battalion had reached Monte Timponivoli (Hill 1209), about halfway to the objective north of the highway, and two hills south of the road on line with Monte Femmina Morta.

Yet American optimism persisted. German prisoners emphasized "There is a pull-out now. Troina has a couple of guns in it."[17] General Allen still felt the 39th Infantry could take Troina alone, but he again turned to the idea of bringing up the 26th Infantry if it became necessary in the next few days.[18]

For Flint's second day of attack on Troina, 1 August, the Tabor of Goums, released from attachment to the 18th Infantry and placed under division control, was to cover the 39th's left flank by moving eastward toward Monte Acuto, then southeast to Monte Basilio, and eventually past Troina and the highway east of town. Flint's scheme of maneuver envisioned Lt. Col. Van H. Bond's 3d Battalion making the main effort by following the general line of the highway to seize high ground adjacent to and north of the town. The other two battalions were to be echeloned to the rear on both flanks, the one on the right operating as far as two miles south of the highway.

Though the plan for the ground assault seemed to promise success, the artillery was unable to give the expected support because all the battalions could not be brought far enough forward in time for the attack. The road was in poor shape and clogged with traffic. The Luftwaffe (making one of its rare appearances) had strafed and bombed artillery positions and caused some confusion if not casualties. And German artillery was interdicting the routes of displacement.[19]

Despite the absence of what was considered adequate artillery support, Flint decided to go ahead. Perhaps he had little choice in the matter. The remainder of the 9th Division was scheduled to unload in Palermo on 1 August and General Allen felt a moral obligation to capture Troina before turning over "a tight sector" to General Eddy.[20] In any event, almost everybody expected Troina to fall easily.

When Colonel Bond's 3d Battalion, 39th Infantry, jumped off at 0500, 1 August, the regiment was already halfway from Cerami to Troina: a scant four miles from the objective. Advancing southeast from Monte Timponivoli (Hill 1209)

---

[16] 39th Inf Regt Jnl, entries 43 and 44, 31 Jul 43.
[17] 1st Inf Div G-3 Jnl, entry 45, 31 Jul 43.
[18] Ibid., entry 36, 31 Jul 43.

[19] 39th Inf Regt Scheme of Maneuver, 1 Aug 43; Verlet Rpt of Opns, 4th Tabor; 1st Infantry Division G-3 Journal, entry 54, 31 July 1943 states: "Tell 39th we can't give them all artillery they ask for." See also 39th Inf Regt Jnl, entries 47 and 57, 31 Jul 43.
On 31 July, for example, it took the 7th Field Artillery Battalion three hours to complete a seven and a half mile move to new positions southwest of Cerami. See 7th FA Bn AAR, 31 Jul 43.
[20] 1st Inf Div G-3 Jnl, entry 27, 2 August 43; see also Allen, 1st Inf Div Sit and Opns Rpt, 8 Aug 42–7 Aug 43, p. 19.

39TH INFANTRY HALF-TRACK *squeezing through a narrow street in Cerami.*

north of Highway 120, Bond hoped to move as rapidly as the terrain permitted. He would have to cross a series of abrupt hills that paralleled the highway, but these constituted no ridge line in the real sense of the term. The 3d Battalion, though, would be advancing along hill noses west of Troina, noses covered by fire from Troina as well as from Monte Acuto. Colonel Bond was to be disappointed. His battalion immediately encountered mortar and small arms fire, and beyond one thousand yards from Monte Timponivoli the battalion could not advance. Artillery fire against suspected enemy positions having no effect on the intensity of the German reaction, Bond in midmorning pulled back to his line of departure. (*Map 5*)

The withdrawal was fortunate. As a result, Bond was ready to meet and repel a relatively small German counterattack down the aqueduct trail from the north. With effective artillery support, Bond's 3d Battalion turned back the threat before noon. Yet continued mortar and machine gun fire from German positions east and north of Monte Timponivoli was in sufficient volume to negate hopes for any advance at all toward Troina.

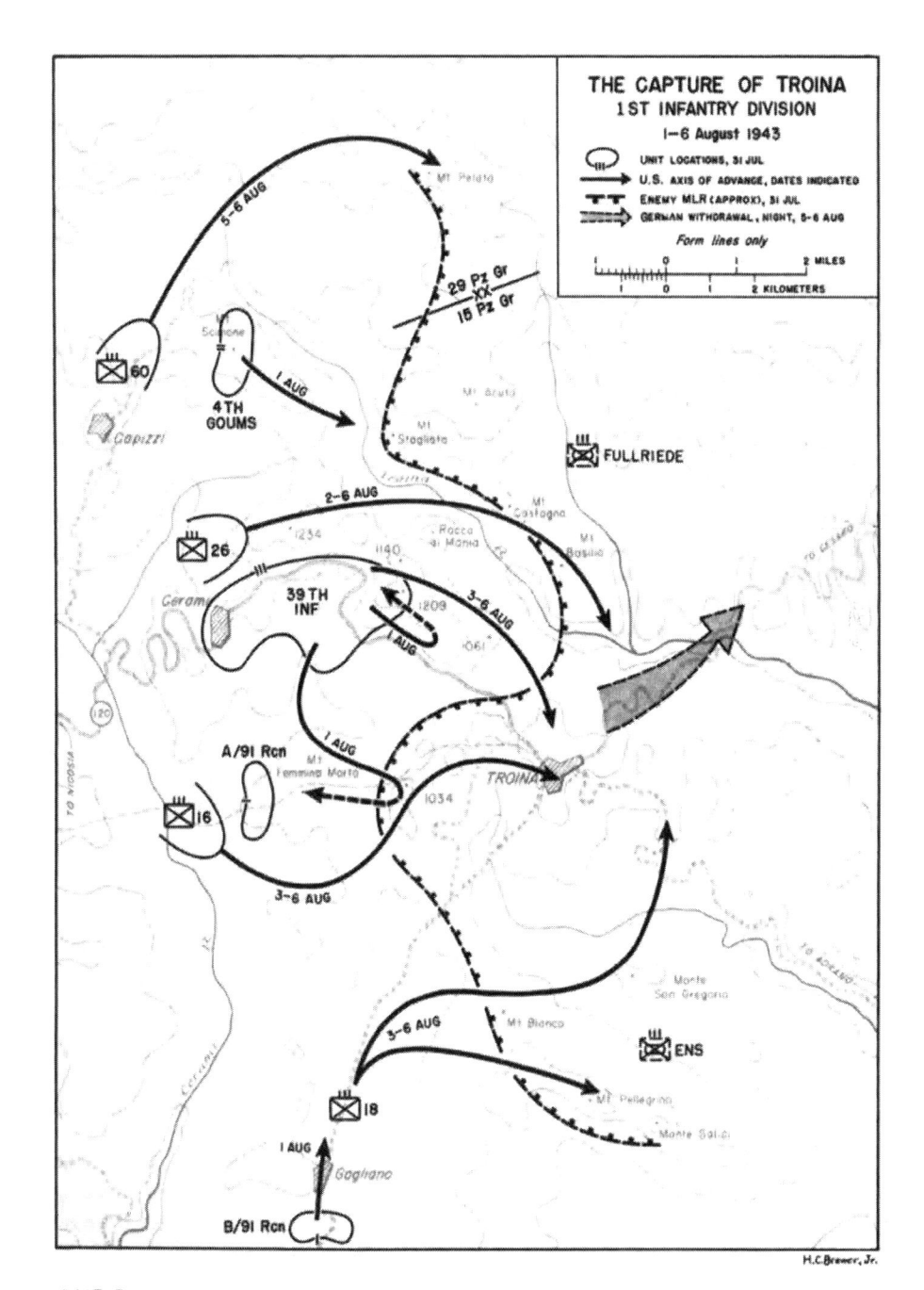

MAP 5

Pessimism might have been warranted had not *Group Ens'* defenses south of the highway proved porous indeed compared to the defense put up thus far by *Group Fullriede* north of the road. Maj. Philip C. Tinley's 1st Battalion, 39th Infantry, had its leading company three miles ahead of its line of departure and ensconced on Hill 1034, a key spot on the important ridge position west of Troina, about the time that Bond was repelling the counterattack to the north. Because the company had met no opposition, Tinley reinforced it early in the afternoon with another rifle company. As the lead company dug in on Hill 1034, the company coming up behind rounded up thirty prisoners and entered the perimeter. Either the 1st Battalion had moved too rapidly or *Group Ens* did not yet have its defenses well organized. In any event, Colonel Ens began to prepare to retake the high ground, less than a mile west of Troina, and dislodge the Americans, who had a clear view not only of the streets of Troina but of artillery positions farther to the east.

The contrasting fortunes of the battalions north and south of Highway 120 gave General Allen no sure guidance on whether or not to commit the 26th Infantry to reinforce the 39th Infantry's attack. He first decided to act on the side of prudence and in midmorning ordered Colonel Bowen to pass his 26th Infantry around Flint's forces, to the north of the highway, instead of on the south side as originally planned. Operating north of the 39th Infantry positions, Colonel Bowen was to cut the highway about two miles beyond Troina by striking eastward, first to Monte Basilio, and then to a hill mass commanding the road. Now, too, the 16th Infantry was also to join the fight. Allen directed Colonel Taylor to attack on the 39th Infantry right, striking out from Monte Femmina Morta toward the south side of Troina and then on to Hill 1056, south of the highway and about a mile east of the town. By gaining Hill 1056, the 16th Infantry would cut the road leading from Troina to Adrano, one of the two exit roads from Troina available to the Germans. In effect, Allen was applying the same tactics used at Sperlinga and Nicosia the week before: a double envelopment of a strong, natural defensive position. General Andrus promised full support for the attack, scheduled to go off at 0500 on 2 August.[21]

Later, however as word of Tinley's encouraging progress south of the highway came into division headquarters, Allen began to reconsider. After Flint insisted that his 39th Infantry could do the job alone, Allen definitely made up his mind to let Flint have another try at Troina. Adding support to this decision was a conversation Allen had with General Bradley. The II Corps commander expected the 9th Division to relieve the 1st, not on 4 August as originally anticipated but a day or two later. Since the 39th Infantry seemed to be moving, Bradley agreed that there was no reason for concern over the possibility that the arrival of Eddy's troops might interfere with Allen's attack—Troina would surely be taken in ample time to allow the 1st Division to retire to Nicosia and cede the field of battle to the 9th.[22]

But an hour later, near 1400, Allen again changed his mind. Now, though Flint's regiment was to continue making the division's main effort against Troina,

---
[21] 1st Inf Div G-3, Jnl, entry 18, 1 Aug 43.
[22] *Ibid.*, entries 31 and 32, 1 Aug 43.

the 26th Infantry was to come up on Flint's left to go for the hill mass which commanded the highway east of Troina. Taylor's 16th Infantry was not to be used on Flint's right, for it appeared that Tinley's 1st Battalion, 39th Infantry, would be able to take the objective earlier contemplated for Taylor.

As for Bowen, since Allen did not specify the strength Bowen was to employ, the 26th Infantry commander proposed to use two battalions on Flint's left, as Allen had suggested earlier in the morning. The 1st Division G-3, Lt. Col. Frederick W. Gibb, thought one battalion would be enough, since the Tabor of Goums would be operating on Bowen's left. Bowen finally decided to jump off in a column of battalions. To satisfy his request for all possible artillery assistance, General Allen gave him four batteries of 155-mm. guns (Long Toms), four battalions of light artillery, and one medium battalion for direct support.[23] Despite this help, Colonel Bowen was still worried over the scale of German resistance around Troina: "I think there is a hell of a lot of stuff there up near our objective," he said, "and down south also." All the information at Bowen's disposal pointed toward "a very strong defense," and he questioned whether "we have strength enough to do the job." Later, when the 2d Battalion, 26th Infantry, was moving toward its line of departure, Bowen thought it was "moving right into the teeth of the enemy and not around him."[24]

The 4th Tabor of Goums would have been in agreement with Colonel Bowen's estimate, for the Goumiers that day, trying to push from Monte Scimone to Monte Acuto, had advanced only a mile to the Troina River before being stopped by showers of mortar and artillery fire. Efforts to advance during the night and on the following day, 2 August, met with no success.[25]

Meanwhile, Flint, on the afternoon of 1 August and with General Allen's permission, had been trying to take Troina alone. He ordered the 2d and 3d Battalions to launch a co-ordinated attack to the high ground north of Troina. But the push turned out to be a gentle shove that got nowhere. Enemy shelling was the obstacle. Adding to Flint's problems was a counterattack at nightfall directed by *Group En*s against Tinley's 1st Battalion on Hill 1034, just west of Troina. The Germans "thumped hell out of A and C Companies." Strong German artillery and mortar fire accompanied the thrust by some two hundred men, which scattered the American companies badly. Hoping to use his reserve company positions—more than a mile to the rear—as a rallying point, Tinley asked permission to withdraw. Flint grudgingly assented. By midnight, Tinley had the battalion well in hand, though Company A had only two platoons left, Company C slightly less. The entire battalion numbered about 300 men, and the Germans were less than 2,000 yards from the 1st Battalion's positions. Ens had gained his objective, the important ridge line strongpoint at Hill 1034, but instead of exploiting this success, he set his troops to digging in along the ridge to block further

---

[23] 1st Inf Div G-3 Jnl, entries 37, 38, 40, 45, and 58, 1 Aug 43; 26th Inf Regt S-1 Jnl, entries timed 1446, 1504, 1516, and 1532, 1 Aug 43.

[24] 26th Inf Regt S-1 Jnl, entries timed 2115 and 2340, 1 Aug 43.

[25] Verlet Rpt of Opns, 4th Tabor.

American attempts against Troina he expected from the west and south.[26]

The third day of the action against Troina on 2 August again proved fruitless. The Goumiers on the division's left could not cross the Troina River and remained in place throughout the day. Flint's 39th Infantry was able to do no more, every attempt to advance meeting scorching enemy fires. Only in the terrain between the Goumiers and the 39th Infantry, where the 26th Infantry entered the battle, did the 1st Division achieve any success, and this gain, a result of cautious advance, was only tentative in nature.

Jumping off at 0500 that morning in a column of battalions, the 26th Infantry moved eastward slowly, hampered by the lack of success of the units on its flanks as well as by unsatisfactory communication with them. The leading battalion met little ground opposition, and though they received increasingly heavy enemy artillery fire as well as occasional small arms fire, the forward elements pushed ahead more than a half a mile to Rocca di Mania. With the regiment's flanks already exposed, further advance seemed not only risky but pointless. Bowen halted his troops and awaited the following day and the execution of a stronger attack which General Allen was even then planning and preparing.

By this time, Allen was finally convinced that he had to make a large-scale and coordinated effort to smash the Troina defenses. His new plan involved employing additional forces in a frontal assault which he hoped would develop in its later stages into a double envelopment.[27] He attached a battalion of the 18th Infantry to the 16th on the division's right for an attack from Gagliano to Monte Bianco, about two miles south of Troina, a key strongpoint on the German ridge defense line. The organic infantry battalions of the 16th Infantry were to take the town and cut the road to Adrano. The 39th Infantry was to seize Monte San Silvestro, two miles northwest of Troina and then go into division reserve. The 26th Infantry was to continue its encircling movement of Troina, swinging past the 39th Infantry to take Monte Basilio and then moving southeast to cut the highway behind Troina.

Though the main attack was scheduled to start at 0300, 3 August, the 2d Battalion, 16th Infantry, moved out shortly after midnight, leading the regiment in its swing to the south toward the southern corner of the German ridge positions, where the ridge line swings in its arc to the east. The 3d Battalion followed. By dawn, the leading elements of the battalions were halfway up the slopes of the ridge, ready for the final assault. But as daylight came, German small arms and machine gun fire interfered. The men were pinned to the ground. Several attempts to get the assault moving failed, and by noon it was evident that the 16th Infantry could not move.

Having reached that conclusion shortly before noon, General Allen ordered the battalion of the 18th Infantry attached to the 16th to push beyond its originally assigned objective and take high ground a half mile south of Troina. The 1st Battalion, 16th Infantry, was to assist.

---

[26] 39th Inf Regt Jnl, entries 51 and 53, 1 Aug 43, and entry 1, 2 Aug 43; 26th Inf Regt S-1 Jnl, entries timed 0020, 0625, and 0847, 2 Aug 43; 1st Inf Div G-3 Jnl, entries 73, 75, 76, and 79, 1 Aug 43.

[27] 1st Inf Div FO 30, 2 Aug 43.

# THE BATTLE OF TROINA

The battalion from the 18th Infantry had been advancing from Gagliano without opposition, though hindered by terrain. General Allen wanted the battalion to speed up its movement, for the two battalions of the 16th Infantry, pinned down on the ridge slope, appeared to be in a precarious position. What Allen wanted to do was divert German attention from the main body of the regiment.[28]

Before the battalions coming up from the south could start a real push, *Group Ens* mounted a counterattack around noon, using infantry and tanks in an attempt to throw the advance troops of the 16th Infantry off the slopes of the ridge. Responding to a request from Colonel Taylor, General Andrus put the fire of six battalions of artillery along the high ground. This, plus dogged fighting by the infantry, prevented the men from being overrun.

Although stalled in this counterattack, Colonel Ens kept exerting pressure throughout the afternoon. The strongest effort occurred around 1500, when two hundred men came into such close contact with the American troops that artillery support could not be used. By the end of the day, Companies E and F, 16th Infantry, seemed to have little more than one platoon each remaining, with the others missing. Though the 3d Battalion, 16th Infantry, was in better shape, it was in no condition to resume the attack.[29]

Nor could the two battalions on the south make much progress in driving toward Troina from Gagliano. German raids on both flanks and effective fire stopped the push about halfway to Troina.[30]

Still hoping to keep the attack going on his right (south) flank, General Allen ordered one of the two battalions to make a wider swing to the east and attempt to outflank Troina completely. But a few minutes later, the assistant division commander, General Roosevelt, arrived in the area, took one look at the terrain to the east, and advised Allen against the move. The terrain, much of it sheer rock, and the condition of the units—badly scattered in the process of getting this far—seemed to rule out success.[31]

Conditions north of the highway were hardly better. A battalion of the 26th Infantry reached its initial objective, Monte Basilio, with surprising ease, about the same time that a battalion of the 39th Infantry had, with the same facility, reached Monte San Silvestro. Yet soon after the leading troops of both regiments reached these hill masses, enemy artillery began to pound them. Observing that the fire was coming from reverse slope positions to the north and east, positions difficult to reach with artillery, Bowen called for an air strike. Some half a dozen Spitfires responded about 1100 and bombed and strafed the north slopes of Monte Castagna and Monte Acuto. The enemy shelling lessened as a result.[32]

About the time that Bowen was getting his air strike, Flint called for another. He had learned that a road, not shown on available maps, ran generally east and northeast from Capizzi for some fifteen miles to link Monte Acuto, Monte Pelato,

---

[28] 1st Inf Div Adv G-3 Jnl, entries 9, 10, and 11, 3 Aug 43.

[29] 1st Inf Div Adv G-3 Jnl, entry 45, 3 Aug 43; 1st Inf Div Arty Jnl, entry 99, 3 Aug 43.

[30] 1st Inf Div Adv G-3 Jnl, entry 41, 3 Aug 43.

[31] *Ibid.*, entries 48 and 49, 3 Aug. 43.

[32] 1st Inf Div Rear G-3 Jnl, entry 43, 3 Aug 43; 26th Inf Regt S-1 Jnl, entry timed 1125, 3 Aug 43.

and Monte Camolato. Guessing that the Germans had concentrated their artillery along this road, Flint requested help from the air. Unfortunately, part of Bowen's forward units and the Goumiers were so close to the road that division headquarters disapproved the request.[33]

Part of the caution at division headquarters developed after the Spitfires which had responded to Bowen's call inadvertently strafed the Goumiers, though no serious harm had been done. The Goumiers were still immobilized at the Troina River under the shadow of Monte Acuto, still trying to get across the river and up on the high ground, still incurring heavy casualties in the process.

Communication with the 4th Tabor was rarely as good as with American subordinate units, and for seven hours that day the division headquarters had no word from the Moroccans and consequently no clear knowledge of their location. This did not prevent three artillery battalions from delivering counterbattery fire most of the afternoon against reported enemy guns a hundred yards from where the Goumiers had last reported their positions.

After dark, Capt. Guido Verlet was able to pull his Tabor of Goums back from the Troina River and out of enemy fire. Shortly thereafter Verlet himself was in Capizzi to plead for a half-hour artillery concentration on enemy positions two hundred yards east of where the 4th Tabor had spent the day. This, he was sure, would enable the Goumiers finally to take Monte Acuto.[34] Dubious, the artillery refused; friendly troops were too close, and their locations not altogether clear.

Meanwhile, a battalion of the 26th Infantry had moved east early that morning with the purpose of coming abreast of the other two battalions of the regiment near Monte Basilio. The battalion became lost, wandered in the hills, and finally came to rest on Monte Stagliata, some two miles west of the other regimental elements on Rocca di Mania and Monte Castagna.

This lost battalion could have been of use on Monte Basilio, which was struck in the early afternoon of 3 August, first by a heavy barrage of artillery fire, and then by *Group Fullriede* infantrymen. Stubborn defensive fires from the American riflemen and machine gunners, supported by effective artillery concentrations, repulsed the German effort to retake this key terrain feature. But Monte Basilio, vulnerable to enfilade fire on both faces, continued to take a pounding from Monte Acuto and from the Troina area.

Although successful in its defensive stand, the battalion on Monte Basilio was in no condition to resume the 26th Infantry's attack to cut the highway east of Troina. During a lull that afternoon, when General Allen suggested that the 39th Infantry might move its leading battalion forward about 800 yards to Monte di Celso, Flint agreed. "There is nobody there now," Flint said. "We can take it over if you want."[35] Yet when a company started to move toward the high ground shortly before dark, artillery and mortar fire heralded an infantry counterattack that scattered and disorganized the American unit and drove

---

[33] 1st Inf Div Rear G–3 Jnl, entries 38 and 47, 3 Aug 43; also see II Corps Rpt of Opns, p. 14.

[34] Verlet Rpt of Opns, 4th Tabor; 1st Inf Div Rear G–3 Jnl, entries 46, 47, and 79, 3 Aug 43.

[35] 1st Inf Div Adv G–3 Jnl, entry 52, 3 Aug 43.

## THE BATTLE OF TROINA

the riflemen back to the regimental positions.

Actually, the Germans had telegraphed their intention, but the division headquarters had been asleep at the switch. About an hour and a half earlier, the 26th Infantry had become aware of German infiltration—troops "walking up the stream bed"—on its right flank. Colonel Bowen had reported this to division headquarters, but the Division's G-3 had apparently failed to pass the information on to Flint.[36]

Despite its failure to take Troina by the fourth day of the attack, the division had made some important gains. The 16th and 39th Regiments, though temporarily disorganized by counterattacks, retained positions seriously threatening the town. And Bowen's 26th Infantry on Monte Basilio could call interdictory fire on Highway 120 beyond Troina, thereby disrupting German communications.

During the evening of 3 August, General Allen ordered renewal of the attack by the units already committed and with added strength from the south against the Gagliano salient. Instructing Colonel Smith to bring forward a second battalion of his 18th Infantry, General Allen gave Smith responsibility for a zone on the extreme right flank. Smith was to control not only two of his own organic battalions, but also the 1st Battalion, 16th Infantry, already in the area. By these means, Allen hoped to execute what would be in effect a pincers movement by the two regiments on the flanks: the 18th Infantry on the south, the 26th Infantry in the north, while the two regiments in the center, the 16th and 39th, exerted frontal pressure against the town.[37]

General Allen would have been even more hopeful of success had he known what effect the fighting of the past two days had had on the *15th Panzer Grenadier Division*. The German division had incurred heavy losses, at least 1,600 men. Furthermore, the *XIV Panzer Corps* had given General Rodt the last of its reserve units during the night of 3 August.[38]

General Hube, the *XIV Panzer Corps* commander, was not only watching the situation closely at Troina, he was also concerned with the sector immediately to the south where the Canadians were advancing along Highway 121. Early 30 July, following a heavy artillery preparation, Canadian troops had struck hard in a move to jump the Dittaino River, clear Catenanuova, and present the newly arrived British 78th Division with a bridgehead for the attack toward Regalbuto on the left, Centuripe on the right. As both Canadian and British troops converged against Regalbuto and Centuripe, the former fell on the evening of 2 August, the latter the following morning. The two main outposts in the German defense of Adrano thus lay in Allied hands.[39]

If the British pressed beyond Regalbuto and cut the Troina-Adrano road, as Hube was sure they would, the German corps commander had to face the danger that the Canadians might turn north and cut Highway 120 east of Troina. In that

[36] 26th Inf Regt S-1 Jnl, entry timed 1725, 3 Aug 43; see also 39th Inf Regt Unit Jnl, entry 30, 3 Aug 43.

[37] 1st Inf Div Adv G-3 Jnl, entry 55, Outline Plan, 3, 4 Aug 43, 3 Aug 43.

[38] MS #R-144, The Loss of the Etna, ch. XV of Axis Tactical Operations in Sicily, July-August 1943 (Bauer), pp. 22-23; see also 1st Inf Div G-2 Periodic Rpt 27 (app. A), 7 Aug 43.

[39] Nicholson, *The Canadians in Italy*, pp. 139-57.

case, withdrawal of Rodt's division would be imperative.[40] But as long as Rodt's troops retained their escape route to the east, there was no reason to give up the defenses at Troina that had proved so effective. Although the Allies were seriously threatening the Etna line by 4 August they had not yet cracked it. Hube's timetable for evacuating Sicily (although formal evacuation had not yet been ordered) hinged on holding the Etna line as long as possible, and this Hube was determined to do. As a result, Rodt's units dug in still more firmly around Troina for what they expected might be a last-ditch stand.[41]

The Germans were surprisingly successful during the morning of 4 August, the fifth day of the battle for Troina. North of Highway 120, *Group Fullriede* was particularly aggressive in its defense. Counterattacks by infiltrating parties kept the Americans off balance and inflicted heavy casualties. South of the highway, *Group Ens*, perhaps not quite so aggressive in launching counterattacks, remained firm in its defensive positions. By noon, it was evident that the 1st Division needed more assistance to get the attack moving.

Help appeared from the skies. General Bradley had successfully solicited two large-scale air attacks, one scheduled around noon, the other at 1700, each by thirty-six P-51 planes. In addition, General Allen had obtained the promise of eight P-51's to bomb and strafe Monte Acuto at 1445.[42]

The planes turned out to be A-36's (modified P-51's), but this made little difference. Throughout a good part of the afternoon, as artillery added its weight, American aircraft plastered Troina and the surrounding hills, though Monte Acuto escaped—the pilots failed to identify that target. Reactions from the ground units were uniformly enthusiastic: "Air and artillery bombardment lovely." "The enemy is completely unnerved." "Have captured a few Germans and they are jittery, and they seem to be attempting to give themselves up." "It took a lot of pressure off our troops."[43]

Though all four of General Allen's regiments moved rapidly during the afternoon of 4 August to take advantage of the demoralization of German troops, the benefit proved to be only temporary. The American units could register only slight gains before meeting fire and counterattacks. One battalion of the 18th Infantry managed to dislodge the Germans from the base of Monte Pellegrino (a key strongpoint in the Gagliano salient positions) before setting up its own perimeter for the night; but try as it might, the battalion could not dislodge the Germans from the rest of the hill. North of Highway 120, two battalions from the 39th Infantry moved quickly down the slopes of Monte San Silvestro and against

---

[40] *OB SUED, Meldungen*, 0740, 5 Aug 43.
[41] MS #R-144 (Bauer), pp. 24-26.
[42] 1st Inf Div Adv G-3 Jnl, entries 15, 16, 28, and 29, 4 Aug 43. The aircraft were dispatched from the 27th and 86th Fighter-Bomber Groups. See Attack Order 22, 3d Air Defense Wing, 4 Aug 43.

[43] 1st Inf Div Adv G-3 Jnl, entries 41, 45, 46, and 47, 4 Aug 43. The Canadians at Regalbuto were not happy with the air strikes. American planes had flown over Regalbuto the day before and dropped several bombs. And on 4 August two flights discharged their loads on the Canadians. When American aircraft bombed Regalbuto again on the following day, General Leese, the British 30 Corps commander, asked General Bradley to call a halt. The bombings of Canadian troops at Regalbuto came to an end. II Corps G-3 Jnl, entry 278, 6 Aug 43; see also Bradley, *A Soldier's Story*, p. 152.

some ineffectual fire reached Monte San Mercurio, about a mile northwest of Troina. The 26th Infantry finally cleared Rocca di Mania, more than two miles northwest of Troina, but when the men on Monte Basilio tried to move eastward, they ran into *Group Fullriede*'s last reserve, but a force strong enough to make the Americans retire to their mountain position.

The best gain had been made in the south, where part of the 18th Infantry was getting into position to roll up the Gagliano salient and thrust an attack home against the southern approaches to Troina. This development seemed promising, all the more so since the Canadians, pressing on beyond Regalbuto, had that same day crossed the Troina River and taken firm possession of a stretch of the Troina-Adrano road.

By this time, the remainder of Eddy's 9th Division was coming into the Nicosia area preparatory to relieving the 1st Division. General Bradley had instructed General Eddy to replace Allen's forces east of Troina so that the 9th Division could continue along the axis of Highway 120 to break the next German defensive line, expected to be uncovered in the Cesarò area. Eager to enter the fray, yet denied maneuver room in the Troina area, Eddy, with his sights fixed on Cesarò, planned to commit Col. Frederick J. DeRohan's 60th Infantry on the 1st Division left. With the Tabor of Goums attached, DeRohan was to make a difficult cross-country advance generally eastward from Capizzi, across Monte Pelato and Camolato; he was to debouch from the hills on the north-south Sant' Agata–Cesarò road and be ready to attack Cesarò. By that time, Eddy hoped, the 1st Division would have cleaned up Troina so that he could commit Col. George W. Smythe's 47th Infantry along Highway 120 for a direct advance on Cesarò. There the 47th Infantry could assist DeRohan's enveloping attack from the north.

What Eddy envisioned was making a wide bypass of Troina on the north and striking quickly toward the next enemy defensive line. As an added dividend, DeRohan's movement, starting before the Germans had given up Troina, might prompt the Germans to loosen their hold on Troina in order to escape a trap at Cesarò. On the assumption that Allen would have Troina by nightfall on 5 August (at the end of the sixth day of attack) and that the relief could be completed that night, General Bradley directed Eddy to start moving the 60th Infantry eastward from Capizzi on the morning of 5 August. This would permit the 60th to work its way toward Cesarò while the 1st Division and the attached 39th Infantry completed the reduction of Troina.[44]

As the 60th Infantry, with the Goumiers attached, started its cross-country strike toward Cesarò on 5 August, the 1st Division resumed its attack against Troina. On the left, Bowen's 26th Infantry was unable to move forward because of rifle fire and artillery shelling. Twice Bowen asked for air support—once against Monte Acuto, the second time against "some guns which we cannot spot from the ground . . . . Make it urgent."[45] But the missions scheduled could not get off the ground because of fog at the airfields.[46]

The 26th Infantry, without gaining

---

[44] 9th Inf Div AAR.
[45] 1st Inf Div Adv G-3 Jnl, entries 37 and 43, 5 Aug 43.
[46] *Ibid.*, entry 39, 5 Aug 43.

ground, sustained serious casualties. In the afternoon, after an estimated sixty Germans attacked Monte Basilio, only seventeen men from Company I could be located. The fighting had been hot and heavy. Pvt. James W. Reese, for example, had performed with exceptional heroism. Moving his mortar squad to a more effective position, he had maintained a steady fire on the attacking Germans. When they finally located his squad and placed fire against the mortar position, Reese sent his crew to the rear, picked up his weapon and three rounds of ammunition (all that was left), moved to a new position, and knocked out a German machine gun. Then picking up a rifle, Reese fought until killed by a heavy concentration of German fire.[47]

By late afternoon the 26th Infantry was in bad shape. The 2d and 3d Battalions, on Monte Basilio for almost three days, had been virtually cut off from supplies for much of the time and were running low on food and ammunition. Two aerial resupply missions, one by artillery observation planes on 5 August and one the following day by XII Air Support Command aircraft, failed to bring sufficient relief.[48]

In contrast with the 26th Infantry, Flint's 39th Infantry made a solid gain. During the preceding night, two battalions worked their way east from Monte di Celso and Monte San Mercurio. Reaching a point about a mile due north of Troina, they turned southeast to cut the highway. When daylight came, the Germans spotted the movement. Accurate machine guns, small arms, and mortar fire in heavy volume stopped the American advance and sent the men of one rifle company back in disorganization. Using two tanks as roving artillery, the Germans pounded away at Flint's troops. At noon, Colonel Flint ordered his men to desist from further eastward advance. It would be enough, he instructed, if they dug in where they were and did no more than threaten the eastward exit from Troina.

Late in the afternoon, eighteen A-36's in two groups bombed east and west of Troina. Flint, thinking this was the start of another air-artillery show (although he had not been informed that one was coming off), queried Colonel Gibb on this matter. Gibb laconically answered: "Bombing unscheduled." The division had no plans to exploit the unexpected appearance of the American fighter-bombers. The 39th remained buttoned up.[49]

Similarly, Taylor's 16th Infantry spent the day trying to advance against the two key points on the ridge system west of Troina—Hills 1034 and 1006—but made no headway because it had to devote its major effort to warding off German counterattacks and digging in for cover against accurate German fire.

South of Troina, where Smith's 18th Infantry tried to seize the dominating hills of the Gagliano salient as well as the two hills—Bianco and San Gregorio—closer to Troina, the Americans were no more successful. Heavy German fire, small counterattacks, and mine fields reduced American units in strength and prevented them from seizing the commanding ground. Rifle companies numbering

---

[47] *Ibid.*, entry 51, 5 Aug 43. Reese was posthumously awarded the Medal of Honor.

[48] 26th Inf Regt S-1 Jnl, entries timed 1622, 5 Aug 43, and 1310, 6 Aug 43.

[49] 1st Inf Div Adv G-3 Jnl, entries 15, 22, 23, 45, and 54, 5 Aug 43; 39th Inf Regt Unit Jnl, entries 6, 8, 13, 15, 21, 26, 33, 36, and 39, 5 Aug 43.

# THE BATTLE OF TROINA 345

sixty-five men became common. At the end of the day, *Group Ens* still held the vital heights.

Despite his defensive success on 5 August, General Rodt knew that he could not hold out in Troina much longer. With his units badly depleted and his men near exhaustion, he had already requested—though it was disapproved—Hube's permission to withdraw some 5,000 yards to a new defensive line. Rodt's greatest concern was the threat that American units north of Troina, particularly the 26th Infantry on Monte Basilio, were exerting against Highway 120 east of the town. Sensitive to the necessity of preventing the Americans from cutting his single escape route out of Troina, Rodt had made his strongest effort north of the highway where his troops had manhandled Bowen's and Flint's regiments. Though he felt he had the situation under control at Troina, Rodt had nothing substantial with which to contest the wider envelopment that DeRohan's 60th Infantry represented. Also, he was concerned with maintaining contact on his left flank with the *Hermann Goering Division*, which was slowly being pushed back up against Mount Etna by the British 30 Corps. Only a slight penetration as yet existed on his left flank, but the absence of German reserves on the island made Rodt doubtful that the Germans could long contain the British threat.

Because of the tense situation along the entire front late on 5 August—the greatly reduced combat efficiency of the *15th Panzer Grenadier Division*, the over-all lack of German reserves, the danger of an Allied breakthrough of the Etna line in the Cesarò area, the possibility of Allied seaborne landings in his rear—Hube followed Rodt's suggestion and decided to withdraw to a shorter line. This line, which Hube designated as the shorter bridgehead line (Guzzoni called it the Tortorici line), extended from Giarre on the east coast over Mount Etna to Randazzo, Poggio del Moro, and on to the north coast at Cape Orlando. Ordering his divisions to make a fighting withdrawal on successive phase lines, Hube hoped to gain a week in pulling back to the new line. If he could have his troops in this new position by the morning of 12 August, he would be more than satisfied.[50]

Guzzoni, still nominally in command of the Axis forces on Sicily (though he had surrendered most of his prerogatives on 25 July), protested Hube's decision to start withdrawing from the Etna line on 5 August. Guzzoni thought the movement premature, particularly since the *29th Panzer Grenadier Division* still held firmly in the northern sector near San Fratello. But over Guzzoni's protests, Hube started to withdraw his forces in the eastern and central sectors of the front during the night of 5 August. In fact, on the east coast, the *Hermann Goering Division* began withdrawing from Catania during the evening of 4 August, leaving only a rear guard to contest British entry the following morning. The

---

[50] *OB SUED, Meldungen,* 0815, 6 Aug 43; MS #R-144 (Bauer), pp. 26-29. There seems to be an error in the *OB SUED* entry which designates the highway from Troina to Nicosia instead of from Troina to Cesarò. The description of the new line varies greatly in different sources. It was merely a line drawn across the map, and was in no way reconnoitered or fortified. Its eastern hinge is shown anywhere from 2,000 yards north of Acireale to just south of Giarre; its northern hinge from 6,000 yards east of Sant'Agata to Cape Orlando, and as far west as Station Zappulla, with the Zappulla River in between. In this narrative, the general description Giarre-Mount Etna-Cape Orlando will be used.

GENERALS HUEBNER AND ALLEN, 8 August.

29th Panzer Grenadier Division was to hold until forced to withdraw by pressure.

At the conference with Guzzoni on 5 August, the Germans urged the *Sixth Army* commander to transfer his headquarters to the Italian mainland. Suspecting that the Germans requested this because they wanted a completely free hand in Sicily, Guzzoni asked whether the Germans intended to withdraw even beyond the Messina Strait. Though the Germans emphatically denied this, Guzzoni remained on Sicily five more days. Not until *Comando Supremo* charged him with the defense of a part of Calabria did Guzzoni evacuate his headquarters to the mainland.[51]

At Troina, with permission at last to withdraw, Rodt started to pull out his troops late in the evening of 5 August. Leaving behind rear guards to delay the Americans, he moved his forces east along Highway 120 to Cesarò. By nightfall of 6 August, Rodt's men occupied a defensive line just west of Cesarò, and most of his heavy equipment was already on its way to Messina for evacuation from Sicily.[52]

The *15th Panzer Grenadier Division* did not slip away from Troina without detection. American patrols late on 5 August reported Monte Acuto abandoned, German fires slackening, and even some positions no longer held. One patrol managed to reach the crest of Monte Pellegrino, earlier firmly defended, without opposition.

Despite the signs of German withdrawal, General Allen had had enough experience at Troina to be wary. He made elaborate preparations for the renewal of the attack on 6 August, the seventh day of his effort to take the town. Planners outlined harassing and preparatory fire missions in great detail. Staff members requested at least seventy-two A–36's to bomb the last half-mile of the highway east of Troina and to strafe the road as far east as Randazzo. Yet Allen withheld the hour of the attack until noon, presumably on the basis that if the Germans were going, it was better to let them go. For the subordinate units, the missions remained much the same as they had been for the past two days. A fifteen-minute artillery concentration was to precede the attack.[53]

All this proved unnecessary. By dawn of 6 August it was clear that the Germans were gone. Soon after 0800, 16th In-

---

[51] Faldella, *Lo sbarco*, pp. 259–62, 269–70.

[52] *OB SUED, Meldungen*, 0735, 7 Aug 43 and 0030, 9 Aug 43.

[53] 1st Inf Div Adv G–3 Jnl, entries 55, 56, 57, 58, and 59, 5 Aug 43.

# THE BATTLE OF TROINA

fantry patrols were in Troina and meeting only sporadic rifle fire that was easily silenced.

Troina itself was in ruins. Only several hundred inhabitants remained to welcome the Americans, most of the others having fled to the hills. One hundred and fifty dead—civilians as well as German and Italian soldiers—lay in the highway, in the streets, in demolished houses, in the round feudal tower that had been used as a German observation post. Plaster dust and the stench of death filled the air. Rubble completely blocked one street. The water mains were broken. The main street, where it made the right-angle turn on the northeast face of the cliff, was completely blown away. A 200-pound aerial bomb lay unexploded in the center of the church.

That afternoon, General Allen relinquished his zone to General Eddy, and the 47th Infantry passed around Troina on its way to Cesarò.

General Allen also relinquished command of the 1st Division. He and the assistant division commander, General Roosevelt, turned the division over to Maj. Gen. Clarence R. Huebner and Col. Willard G. Wyman. General Allen would return to the United States to take command of another division, the 104th Infantry Division, which he would lead with distinction in northwest Europe; General Roosevelt, after serving as Fifth Army liaison officer to the commander of the French Expeditionary Forces in Italy, would earn a Medal of Honor during the Normandy invasion of 1944 as assistant division commander of the 4th Infantry Division.[54]

The end of the battle for Troina may well have seemed to the 1st Division commander and his assistant like a most unsatisfactory time to turn over the command of "The Big Red One" to General Huebner. For it had taken the 1st Division, reinforced with an additional regiment, a solid week to reduce defenses that had originally seemed easy enough to crack with a single regiment. In the process, the division was depleted in strength, reduced to weariness. Perhaps some of this depletion, some of this weariness, could have been avoided had the intelligence estimates of the last few days in July not been so inaccurate. Perhaps more could have been avoided had General Allen, after the failure of the 39th Infantry to take Troina on 1 August, committed more of the division's strength, instead of waiting for two more days to do so. Evaluation of the division's performance in the fighting at Troina might also involve an answer to the question: did the expected relief by Eddy's incoming 9th Division contribute to the initial optimism and a possible desire to spare the troops?

---

[54] See AFHQ Msgs, 28 and 29 Jul 43, in Smith Papers, box 4; Butcher, *My Three Years With Eisenhower*, p. 376; Bradley, *A Soldier's Story*, p. 156.

CHAPTER XVIII

# Breaking the San Fratello Line

On the same day (31 July) that Colonel Flint's 39th Infantry opened the battle for Troina, Truscott's 3d Infantry Division arrived at Santo Stefano di Camastra to take the place of the 45th Division on the II Corps northern axis of advance.

Like Allen, Truscott faced difficult terrain and a stubborn enemy. From Licata to Palermo, the 3d Division had operated generally in terrain where it had space for maneuver, sufficient roads and trails to accommodate supporting artillery and supply trains, and alternative routes forward. Now all this changed. Highway 113, the coastal route, is a good, hard-surfaced road, capable of carrying two-way military traffic. As Sicilian roads go, it is not crooked. But it has numerous curves, ideal places for roadblocks. On the inland side of the highway there are few lateral roads except the four that cross the mountains—usually they dead-end in the mountainous interior at typical Sicilian ridge-end towns, medieval in origin, and built on sites chosen because they were almost inaccessible. Thus, General Truscott had a choice of making his main effort either along the highway or across the northern slopes of the Caronie Mountains to outflank German coastal defensive lines. Either way, the defenders possessed the advantage: they could deny use of the highway by fire, by demolitions, and by liberal use of mines; they could delay inland movement by plotting defense positions along the several well-defined ridge lines which lie behind deep-cut mountain streams. Faced with this choice, Truscott decided that the 3d Division would make its major effort through the mountains while units along the road would keep constant pressure on the enemy. To supply and to communicate with the units operating in the mountains, Truscott organized a Provisional Pack Train (mules) and a Provisional Mounted Troop (horses) under the command of Maj. Robert W. Crandall, a former cavalryman who had served under Truscott before the war. Some of the animals had been brought with the division from North Africa; the others had been acquired during the preceding three weeks of campaigning.[1] Some had already seen action with the 179th Infantry the week before during that regiment's advance to Mistretta.[2]

Despite the similarities of terrain and enemy, General Truscott had one trump card not available to General Allen. This was the possibility of amphibious landings—seaborne end runs. The enemy

---
[1] Truscott, *Command Missions*, p. 230. Before reaching Messina the 3d Division would use more than 400 mules and over 100 horses.

[2] See Comments of Col. Robert B. Hutchins (Ret.) (former Commanding Officer, 179th Infantry) on MS. The 179th at first had considerable trouble with the Sicilian animals, but after some experimentation found the correct way of handling them.

PROVISIONAL PACK TRAIN *and mounted troops organized for 3d Division supply and communication in the Caronie Mountains.*

along the north coast, almost no matter where he chose to make a stand, was vulnerable to this type of operation. As early as 30 July, Generals Patton and Bradley had taken note of this valuable military asset. In fact, they had considered an amphibious operation to assist the 45th Division in cracking the enemy's Santo Stefano position, but enemy withdrawal had canceled this plan. By 2 August, General Patton had definitely decided to utilize his "Navy"—Rear Adm. Lyal A. Davidson's Task Force 88—to assist the 3d Division's advance. But Davidson had sufficient landing craft to lift one reinforced infantry battalion, no more. Accordingly, the Seventh Army selected four tentative landing places, each behind a predicted enemy defense line, where a battalion-size amphibious end run might be executed. At General Bradley's request, General Patton agreed to let the II Corps commander time any such operation so that an early link-up between the relatively small amphibious force and the main body of the 3d Division would be assured. Bradley apparently felt that the Seventh Army commander might be hasty and rash in deciding missions to be executed, and he wanted the II Corps, in co-ordination with Truscott, to exercise full control over the forces involved.[3]

---

[3] Seventh Army Ltr of Instr to CG II Corps, sub: Special Opns, 2 Aug 43, in Seventh Army Rpt of Opns, p. D-15; see also Bradley, *A Soldier's Story*, p. 157, and Truscott, *Command Missions*, p. 231.

The four possible landing areas selected by the Seventh Army were: just east of Sant'Agata; west of Brolo; near Patti; and at Barcellona. Each of these areas was behind an anticipated German defense line. See map to accompany 2 Aug Ltr of Instr, in Seventh Army Rpt of Opns, p. D-16.

Enemy Field of Fire Over Furiano River Crossing Site *from San Fratello Ridge.*

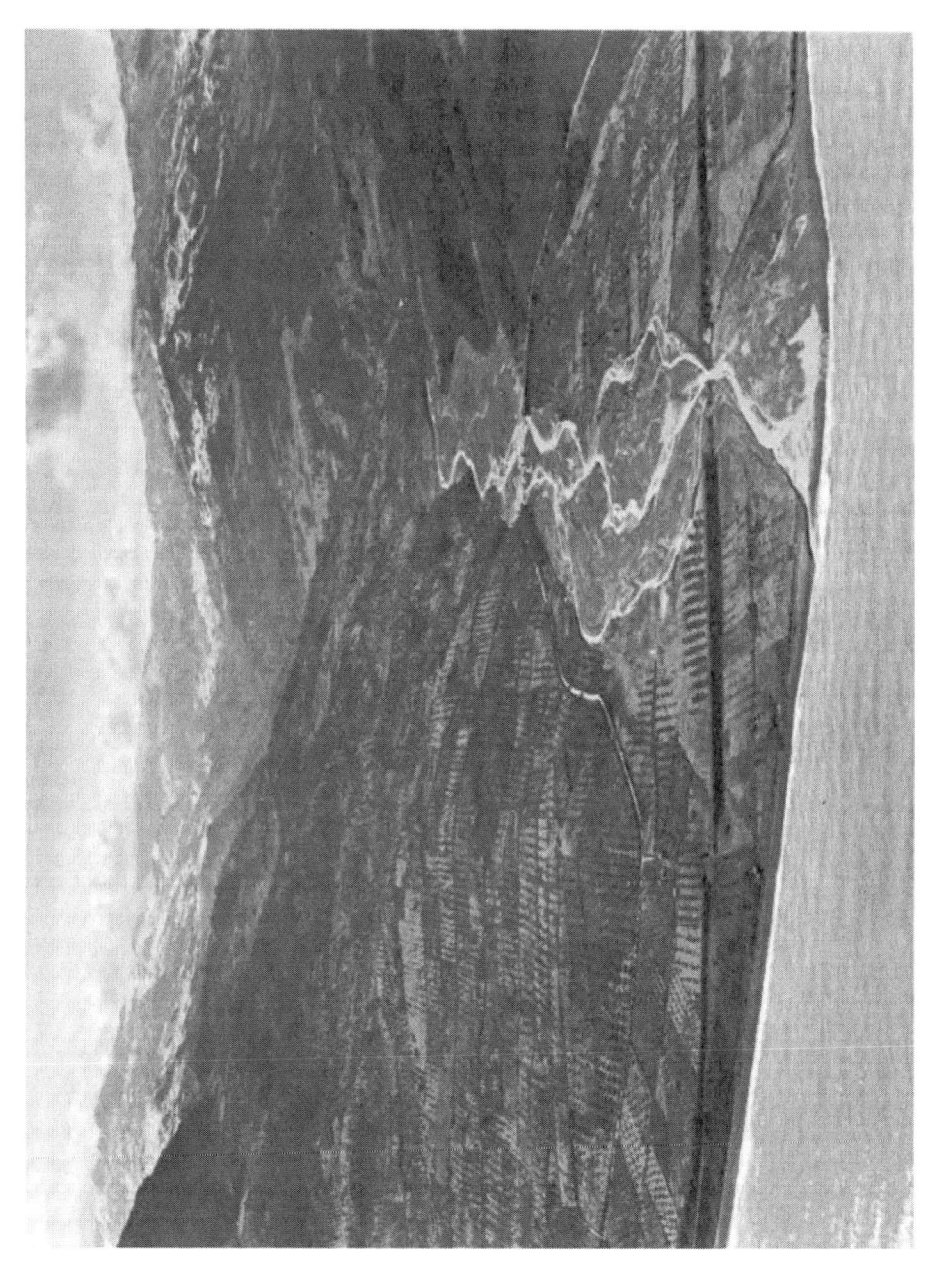

LOOKING SOUTH OVER THE FURIANO RIVER VALLEY from the mouth of the Furiano River, San Fratello Ridge rising at the left. Railroad crossing can be seen in foreground, with highway crossing slightly above.

For the first amphibious operations General Truscott selected Lt. Col. Lyle A. Bernard's 2d Battalion, 30th Infantry (which had been one of the assault battalions on 10 July), reinforced by Batteries A and B, 58th Armored Field Artillery Battalion, a platoon of medium tanks, and a platoon of combat engineers. The first mission of the task force was to plan a landing near the small town of Sant'Agata east of the Furiano River. Immediately beyond the Furiano River (fifteen miles east of Santo Stefano) lay the San Fratello ridge. If the Germans were going to fight anywhere on the north coast, Truscott judged that this would be the place.

The switch of American divisions gave General Fries' *29th Panzer Grenadier Division* ample time to retire along and near the coast to the Etna line, which ran roughly along the San Fratello–Cesarò road. The withdrawal was hampered, however, by heavy American artillery and naval gunfire and by repeated Allied air strikes. Naval gunfire bothered Fries' units most, as Admiral Davidson's warships busied themselves with numerous fire support missions along the coast from Santo Stefano eastward to Cape Orlando. To delay the 3d Division's advance to the new line, Fries deployed strong rear guards, units which included Italian troops.

By morning of 3 August, Fries' outpost line had been driven in. The 15th Infantry, with the 2d Battalion under Maj. Frank J. Kobes, Jr., operating on the road, and the 3d Battalion under Lt. Col. Ashton Manhart paralleling the advance on the slopes of the mountains, hit the Furiano River during the afternoon. Here, the 2d Battalion came under heavy fire, found the river bank and all likely crossing sites heavily mined, and halted.

Though Colonel Johnson, the regimental commander, sent his Ammunition and Pioneer Platoon and the Antitank Company's mine platoon forward to clear lanes, heavy fire from across the river put a stop to these efforts. It was obvious that a bridgehead would have to be established before the mines could be cleared. In preparation for seizing such a bridgehead the next morning, Johnson moved the 1st Battalion (Lt. Col. Leslie A. Prichard) up on line with, and inland from the 2d Battalion. Farther inland some three miles, the 3d Battalion had also arrived at the river, some two miles west of the town of San Fratello, after a slow and grueling march across deep gorges and over mountain trails so precipitous that several of the mules carrying rations and ammunition had lost their footing and tumbled to their deaths hundreds of feet below.[4]

At San Fratello, Fries had terrain scarcely less formidable than Rodt had at Troina, where, on this same day, the *15th Panzer Grenadier Division* was throwing back every 1st Division thrust. Near its mouth the Furiano River is wider than most Sicilian rivers. Completely dominated by the ridge beyond, the river bed provided the Germans with a wide field of fire, as well as an ideal setting for liberal use of mines. The San Fratello ridge across the river has a seaward face about a mile and a half long, rising from a point six hundred yards from the beach and reaching a climax in the stony plug of Monte San Fratello, a rugged, flat-topped mountain some 2,200 feet high. The ridge then descends into a saddle to the town of San Fratello, a thousand yards farther south, before rising again into the Caronie Mountains. The road leading

[4] Taggart, ed., *History of the Third Infantry Division*, p. 65.

southward to Cesarò, one of the four transverse roads across the mountains between Santo Stefano and Messina, twists and turns up the northeast angle of the ridge, and about halfway up turns west directly across the end of the ridge. It continues on this course for about a mile then turns south around the west face of Monte San Fratello against a sheer rock cliff, hairpins up the ridge crest, and then passes through the town. It is about eight miles by road from the coast to the town; it is another sixteen miles to Cesarò.

Along the entire face of the San Fratello ridge, pillboxes, trenches and gun emplacements made things tough for the 3d Division. Particularly strong was a pillbox area near San Fratello, a strongpoint that extended along the road and up the mountainside against the cliff. Connected by trenches, these pillboxes blocked the approaches on the road from any direction and completely covered the Furiano River below. South of San Fratello, the ridge rises up as distinct as a camel's back and is covered with large boulders and rock fences. Not far west of the town—where Manhart's 3d Battalion ended its march on 3 August in a state of exhaustion—the Nicoletta River comes into the Furiano River from a southwesterly direction. Between the two rivers, the Nicoletta ridge runs north and south along the approaches to the Furiano River. This high piece of ground, almost indispensable to an attacker before he could jump the Furiano River, was enfiladed from the north by Monte San Fratello, from the south by higher ground along the Cesarò road.

Just west of the Furiano River, Highway 113 passed southward around a prominent spur, about one-third the height of Monte San Fratello, and crossed the river on a high stone-arched bridge, now blown from end to end. From the bridge north to the sea, a distance of about a mile, the river bed widened out. From the high ground east of the river the defenders could observe the narrow coastal plain as far west as Caronia. This advantage the Germans put to good account, and in the days ahead accurate enemy artillery fire played havoc with any movement eastward along the highway. Inland, a flanking movement might be covered from the enemy's view, but the roughness of the terrain would make progress slow and co-ordination difficult. This was by far the toughest enemy position the 3d Division had as yet encountered in Sicily. Like Middleton's men on Bloody Ridge, Truscott's regiments were to learn to stay "with the damn fight till it's over."[5]

At 0600 on 4 August, after spending the night in developing the enemy's defenses along the river, the 1st and 2d Battalions, 15th Infantry, jumped off in the attack. A scheduled thirty-minute artillery barrage failed to come off because the supporting artillery battalions had displaced forward only during the night and had had no chance to register. On the left, Kobes' 2d Battalion tried first to cross the river to the left of the demolished highway bridge, between the bridge and the sea. Within forty minutes the battalion was stopped cold by heavy enemy fire pouring down from the ridge, and by the dense mine fields in the river bed. For almost four hours the battalion tried to get across the open area. Every attempt failed. Even naval gunfire support and the smoking of Monte San Fratello did little to help.

---

[5] Infantry Combat, Part Five: Sicily, p. 30.

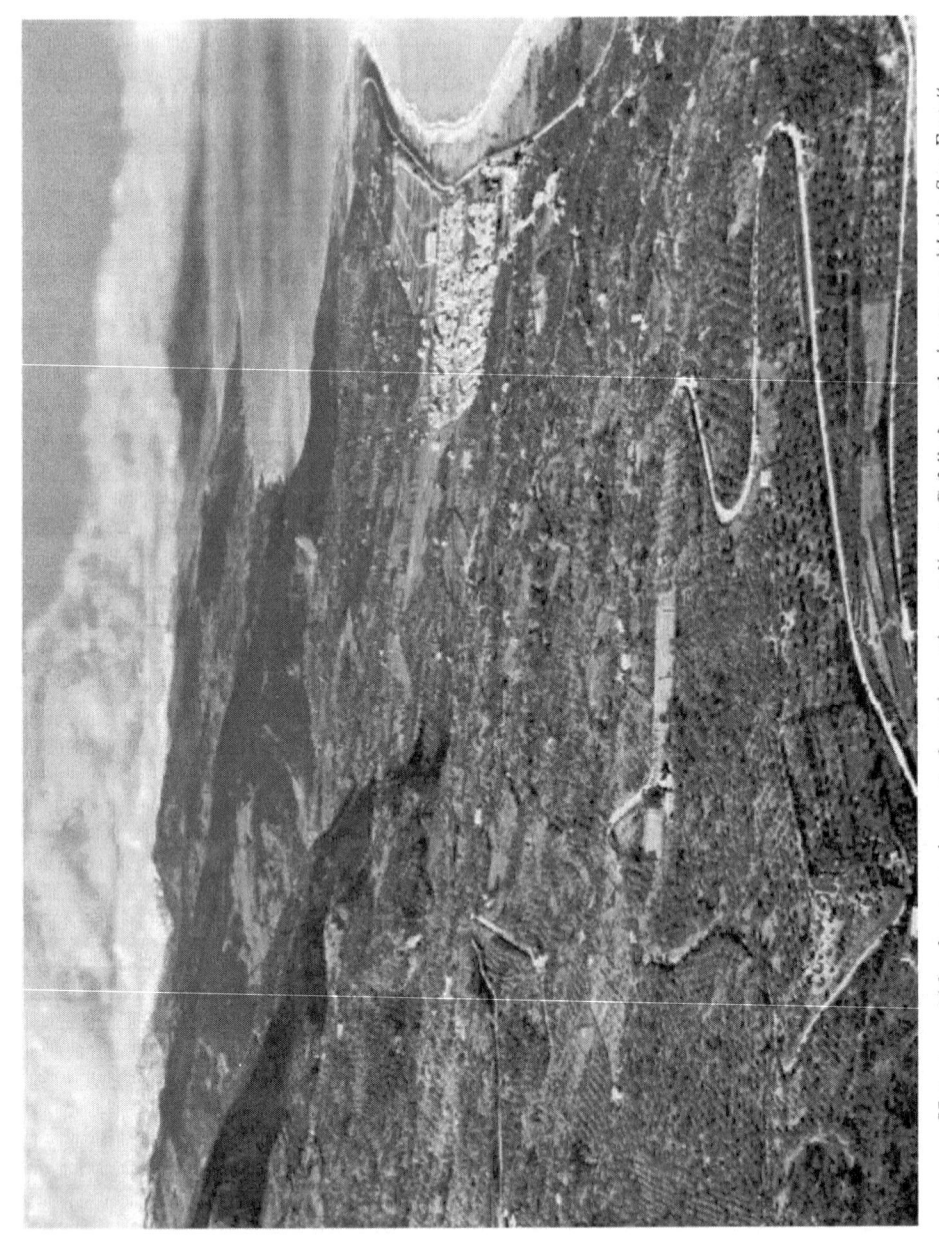

HIGHWAY 113, shown running west along the north coast line to Cefalù from the juncture with the San Fratello–Cesarò road at lower left.

Looking North Over the San Fratello-Cesarò Road. *Cesarò (left center) and Highway 120 are at the southern terminus of the San Fratello road.*

SAN FRATELLO RIDGE *from the highway.* *The town of San Fratello is at upper right.*

In the middle of the afternoon, Kobes changed the direction of his attack, lunged to the right of the bridge site, and sent two companies to attack Hill 171, just across the river and an apparent German strongpoint. All went well on the near bank. But when the two companies came into the open river bed, the Germans met them with a withering hail of machine gun and mortar fire. A few men of the forward platoons managed to get across the river to huddle under the steep river bank. At dark, Kobes called them back. Prichard's 1st Battalion suffered much the same fate; it too had been unable to get across the river.

It had been a costly day for the 15th Infantry—103 casualties, no ground taken. But this action showed General Truscott that the San Fratello ridge was not to be taken by a frontal attack executed by only two infantry battalions, no matter how much fire support those battalions were given.

The next day (5 August) turned out to be more a day of preparation than of progress. Truscott decided to shift the division's main effort to the right, through the mountains, to strike at the San Fratello ridge from the south and roll the defenders into the sea. Truscott ordered Colonel Rogers to take the two remaining battalions of his 30th Infantry to the area then occupied by the 3d Battalion, 15th Infantry, west of San Fratello, to attack the next day with all three battalions to take the town and cut the road to Cesarò. At the same time, the two 15th Infantry battalions near the coast were again to storm the west slope of Monte San Fratello.[6]

Across the river, however, General Fries was already taking steps to evacuate the San Fratello ridge. The withdrawal of the *15th Panzer Grenadier Division* from Troina during the night had uncovered Fries' left flank. Farther south the British 78th Division was nearing Adrano, the key to the center of the Axis front, while on the east coast, the British 50th Division had entered Catania. The entire central and eastern sectors of the front were pulling back slowly in accordance with General Hube's decision to form a shorter defensive line nearer Messina. Though American units on the south had not yet reached the Cesarò road, General Fries feared that they would do so shortly, thus making an envelopment of his San Fratello positions possible. Too, ever since the commitment of his division on the north coast, Fries had been worried about the possibility of an Allied attack from the sea behind his main lines of resistance. He had tried to provide some safeguard against such an attack, but he could never spare more than one battalion for this purpose. It was a lengthy coast line with numerous suitable landing places, and Fries knew he could not guard them all. He had instructed all service troops and other units committed on or near the coast to guard against a surprise Allied landing, but even this measure afforded little real security; it only provided a watch at the most dangerous points.

Because of the lack of adequate roads through the mountains, Fries' units south of San Fratello, as well as some of those in Rodt's sector, had to use the Cesarò–San Fratello road to reach the coastal highway to withdraw to the east. Realizing this, Fries kept one reinforced battalion in the Monte San Fratello positions to hold until all troops and vehicles to

---

[6] 3d Inf Div FO #20, 5 Aug 43.

the south had passed around the mountain on their way to the east. He also deployed a reinforced Italian regiment from the *Assietta Division* to hold the ridge line south of the town. The remainder of the two divisions, less the artillery which stayed in position to cover the withdrawal, began moving eastward during the night.[7]

General Truscott had not fully appreciated the difficulty of the mountainous terrain over which the 30th Infantry would be operating. What was supposed to be a co-ordinated attack on the morning of 6 August turned into a series of un-co-ordinated battalion-size thrusts.

At the highway bridge, following a half-hour artillery and smoke preparation, both Prichard's 1st Battalion and Kobes' 2d Battalion, 15th Infantry, jumped off at 0600. The belts of German fire proved to be so effective that progress was limited to only a few yards. Prichard's battalion on the right managed to get across the river and to within a thousand yards of the Cesarò road. But this cost heavy casualties and by 1400 the battalion was barely hanging on. On the left, Kobes' battalion met much the same fate trying to take Hill 171. Company G, followed by Company F, crossed the river and went 600 yards up the slopes of the hill before the Germans began firing automatic weapons, following this up with deadly accurate mortar fire. If the small arms fire lacked the intensity of previous days, the German mortar fire proved to be as effective as before. Company G stalled.

A flanking maneuver by Company F offered more promise. Swinging around the stalled Company G, passing along the river bank for a short distance, Company F turned right and advanced up a draw toward a German outpost line. Though eventually spotted, the troops were close enough to leap into the German positions before heavy fire could be brought to bear. But even this success was not sufficient to drive the Germans from the crest of the hill. While reorganizing in a small grove of trees preparatory to going for the top, Company F was hit by a small counterattack supported by mortar fire. The last two company officers were hit, and though the company, under its noncommissioned officers, beat off the German threat, it could not get moving again.

Kobes, feeling that his two companies could not gain the hill, sent word for them to hold until nightfall, then to pull back across the river. Despite strong German combat patrols that ranged the slopes of the hill that night, Companies F and G, after several fire fights, recrossed the Furiano where the 2d Battalion, 7th Infantry, had moved up to cover their withdrawal. Just a little earlier, the 1st Battalion had also recrossed the river. At a cost of thirty dead and seventy wounded, the 15th Infantry had failed to gain any ground.

While this action was taking place near the highway bridge, Colonel Rogers' attempt to roll up the German flank also bogged down. It had taken Colonel Rogers' two battalions until 2200 on 5 August to get even as far as a forward assembly area, well to the west of the Nicoletta River. Colonel Manhart's 3d Battalion, 15th Infantry—attached to Colonel Rogers for this operation—had crossed the Nicoletta River earlier that evening and had gained a foothold on the Nicoletta ridge overlooking the Furiano River, a good position from which to start

---

[7] MS #R-144 (Bauer), pp. 49-53.

an assault on San Fratello at the prescribed time the following morning. Having gained this position, Manhart sent guides back to lead Colonel Rogers' two 30th Infantry battalions to the ridge.

When the guides arrived, Lt. Col. Fred W. Sladen, Jr.'s 1st Battalion and Lt. Col. Edgar C. Doleman's 3d Battalion prepared to move forward. The early morning hours turned out to be nightmarish for both battalions. Leaving their assembly area at 0200, the battalions moved slowly through murky darkness preceded by Manhart's guides. Unfortunately, the guides had trouble picking their way through the woods and down the rocky ridges, and the 3d Battalion, leading the way, soon became badly strung out. Not until 0530 did the head of Doleman's battalion arrive at Manhart's positions on the Nicoletta ridge; it took another hour and a half (until 0700) for the rest of the battalion to come in. Sladen's 1st Battalion had even tougher going. Its guides lost their way, and the battalion wasted thirty minutes backtracking to the correct trail. After several more delays caused by the rough terrain and by the need to wait for the mule train to catch up, the head of the 1st Battalion finally arrived on the west slopes of the Nicoletta ridge—south of the other two battalions—at 0630. But not until 0900 did Sladen have all of his men together.

In the meantime, Manhart's battalion had jumped off at 0730. Despite heavy enemy fire, it reached and crossed the Furiano River, and began working its way up Hill 673, the key to the enemy's ridge positions on the south. It got only part way up the southern slopes of the hill before being stopped by enemy fire. As soon as Manhart's battalion cleared the ridge, Doleman began to move, echeloned to the right rear. But Doleman's battalion was delayed an hour when one company strayed off course and was punished severely by enfilading fire along the Nicoletta ridge. At 0900, Doleman's battalion finally crossed the Nicoletta ridge and went down the eastern slopes toward the river. Below the crest the going was easier. A crossing was made and Doleman came up on line with the 15th Infantry battalion. Here it too was stopped by enemy fire. Though Manhart finally managed to get one platoon to the crest of the hill later in the afternoon, it was promptly forced back by the Italian and German defenders. At midnight, the two battalions still lay along the lower slopes of Hill 673.

Sladen's 1st Battalion, 30th Infantry—the farthest to the right of the three battalions—was out of touch with the other two American units for most of the day and had little idea of what was happening on its left. At 0930, Sladen finally was able to send his men up and across the Nicoletta ridge, two companies leading, two companies behind. But as with Doleman's one company, enfilading fire from Monte San Fratello and from positions south of the Nicoletta ridge played havoc with the companies. For almost an hour the battalion suffered under a rain of heavy explosives. Both leading companies became badly disorganized. Finally, one of the companies, plus about half of the other one—the rest of the unit had gone astray while moving through thick brush—reached the Furiano River. The depleted company never did get across because of heavy artillery fire and it remained for the rest of the day in a draw at the bottom of the ridge. The other company did get across the river at 1530, got to within six hundred yards of the crest of the ridge, but could progress no further. Since the company's effort was isolated, Sladen called the men back.

Several hours before this, General Truscott, after touring the area in which the 30th Infantry was operating and realizing just how difficult the terrain was, decided to outflank the San Fratello line by sea: to land Colonel Bernard's small task force behind the enemy's line in conjunction with a renewal of the division's attack the next morning.[8] Just after noon, Truscott ordered Bernard's force to an embarkation point a mile west of Santo Stefano. Unfortunately, the Luftwaffe picked this particular time to interfere with Truscott's operations. Even as Bernard marched his infantrymen, artillerymen, and engineers toward Santo Stefano, four German aircraft swooped out of the sky over Santo Stefano's beaches, bombing and strafing the loading area. Although two of the attackers were shot down by antiaircraft fire, one LST was badly damaged. Because this was a key landing vessel, General Truscott postponed the amphibious end run for twenty-four hours while the Navy brought up another LST from Palermo.[9]

With the amphibious end run postponed for at least a day, General Truscott turned again to the job of keeping the pressure on the San Fratello defenders, hoping that the limited successes gained on the far right might be exploited. He sent General Eagles, the assistant division commander, to supervise the 30th Infantry's operations on that flank, and he ordered Colonel Sherman's 7th Infantry into position along the Furiano River near the coast to exploit any successes the 30th Infantry might gain.[10]

Both Manhart's 3d Battalion, 15th Infantry, and Doleman's 3d Battalion, 30th Infantry, launched another attack on Hill 673 early in the morning of 7 August. This time, Doleman's battalion made the main effort. Again there was difficulty in maintaining contact, and again units became disorganized.

Using one platoon from Company I in the lead—the rest of the company had disappeared during the previous day's fighting—and pushing Company K after it, Doleman started his attack at 0530. Almost immediately the infantrymen received heavy fire. As daylight broke, Doleman could see that the face of the hill on which his two companies were trying to move forward was subject to enfilading fire from the south. This fire, combined with the defenses on the hill itself, made an advance to the top seem most unlikely. Doleman accordingly called off these two companies, started them back down the hill, and dispatched his last unit, Company L, to work up the hill farther to the west. But during the withdrawal, the two forward units became even more scattered, so that by the time they returned to their starting position, Doleman could count—in addition to Company L—only one platoon from Company K, one squad from Company I, and two platoons from Company M. Company L attacked up the west slopes of Hill 673 only a short distance before being halted by heavy enemy fire pouring

---

[8] 3d Inf Div FO #21, 6 Aug 43.

[9] 2d Bn, 30th Inf (while atchd to 3d Inf Div) AAR, p. 1; WNTF Action Rpt, p. 76; 30th Inf Regt AAR; ONI, Sicilian Campaign, pp. 106–07; Morison, *Sicily—Salerno—Anzio*, p. 198n; Truscott, *Command Missions*, p. 234.

[10] 3d Inf Div FO #23, 6 Aug 43.

down from the summit. Doleman left the company on the slopes while he tried to reorganize his battalion for another attack.

Late in the afternoon, the two battalion commanders, Colonel Rogers, and General Eagles worked out a new plan for a co-ordinated attack on Hill 673. Manhart agreed to turn over to Doleman his Company K and a mortar platoon, and to send his other two companies in on Doleman's left when the attack went off. Doleman was to make the main effort, this time just before total darkness set in.

At 1930, the battalions jumped off, with Company L, 30th Infantry, leading the way. Despite heavy enemy fire, the rifle companies moved slowly up the slopes, maintaining contact with each other, fighting a truly co-ordinated battle. The line that had held for so long began giving way and finally cracked. Just before midnight, Company L, 30th Infantry, gained the crest of the hill, closely followed by the rifle companies of the 15th Infantry. Once on top, the Americans began digging in, as Doleman and Manhart pushed up their supporting heavy weapons companies to provide close fire support.

This proved fortunate because the Italians and Germans, under a withering forty-five minute artillery barrage, moved back against the two depleted American battalions on Hill 673. For almost two hours, a savage, close-in, sometimes hand-to-hand battle raged across the top of the hill. Manhart and Doleman committed everything they had in the effort to hold on, even distributing machine gun ammunition to the riflemen to keep them firing. Grenades, bayonets, even rocks, played a part in the struggle. Finally, at 0200 on 8 August, the enemy pulled away from the hill, going north toward the coast.[11]

To the south of Hill 673, an area from which enemy fire had plagued Doleman and Manhart all day, Sladen's 1st Battalion, 30th Infantry, had tried hard to cover the other units by going for the high ground to knock out the enemy guns. The battalion's attempt was unsuccessful, as the men from the other two units could testify. It took Sladen's rifle companies until the middle of the afternoon to get organized, and even then Sladen could not find all of his small units. Except for a platoon from Company C that managed to get a short way beyond the river and annoy the Italians along the ridge—taking a beating for its pains—and for another patrol that eventually contacted the units on Hill 673, the 1st Battalion, 30th Infantry, did little to assist in reducing the San Fratello positions.

By this time, however, Colonel Bernard's small task force was nearing the beaches east of Sant'Agata. At noon, 7 August, General Truscott, with General Bradley's approval, had decided to launch the once-postponed end run early on the morning of 8 August. Sherman's 7th Infantry was to penetrate the enemy's defenses on the coast to effect the link-up, which Truscott hoped would take place before noon.[12]

At 1700, then, Bernard's force again moved from its bivouac area to the beaches west of Santo Stefano. Another LST had arrived from Palermo. But again the Luftwaffe almost knocked out the operation. Just before the ground troops be-

---

[11] War Department General Order 15, 5 February 1946, awarded the Distinguished Unit Citation to the 3d Battalion, 15th Infantry, for the period 3–8 August 1943.
[12] 3d Inf Div FO #24, 7 Aug 43.

362                    SICILY AND THE SURRENDER OF ITALY

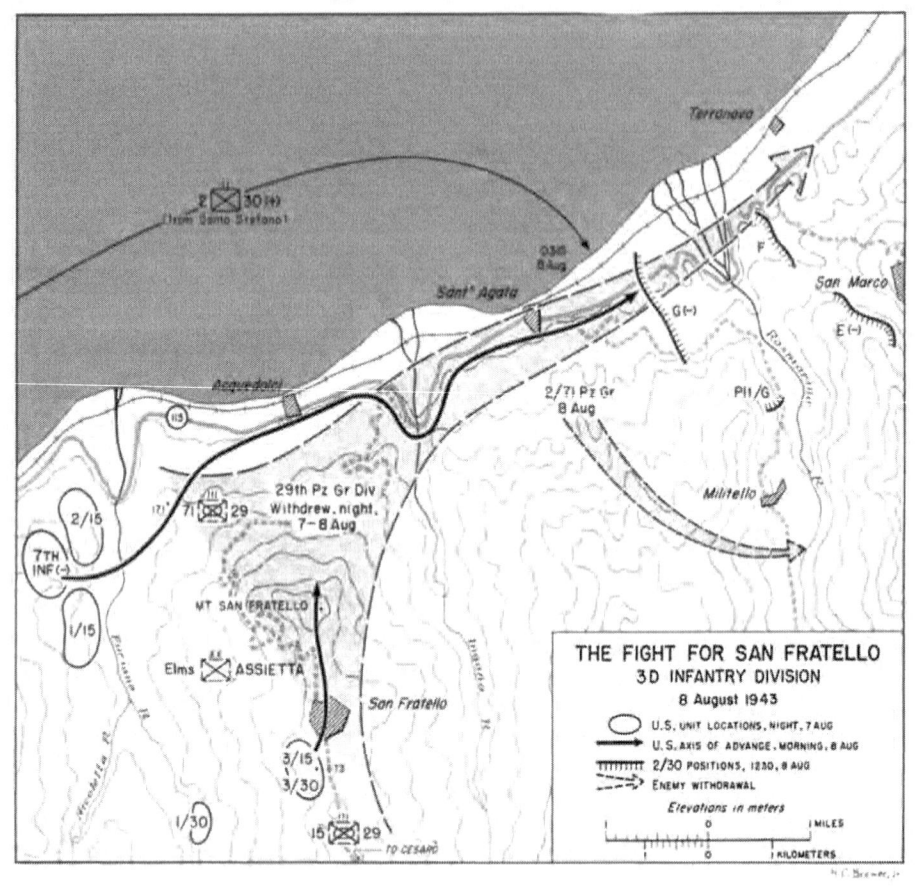

*MAP 6*

gan loading, German aircraft dropped out of the clouds in a bombing and strafing attack aimed at the beached landing craft. This time the Luftwaffe did not succeed. Though an LST and an escort vessel were damaged, hurried repairs made the LST sufficiently seaworthy to go on with the operation. At 1940, the ten landing craft pulled away from the beaches as Admiral Davidson's two cruisers and six destroyers moved in to provide cover.

At the San Fratello line, despite shelling from Davidson's warships during the day, General Fries' rear guards had begun pulling out of their positions, covered by the defenses on Hill 673. That evening, one of the warships laid a barrage on the highway bridge across the Rosmarino River, some two and a half miles east of Sant'-Agata, and set off demolitions which the Germans had placed to blow the bridge after passage of the last group of defenders from the San Fratello ridge. Since the river bed had already been heavily mined, the withdrawal of the rear guard units had

## BREAKING THE SAN FRATELLO LINE

to be halted until engineers could clear a route. (*Map 6*)

By 0300, German engineers completed the bypass across the river. The *2d Battalion, 71st Panzer Grenadier Regiment*, plus part of the *Assietta Division*'s *29th Infantry Regiment* (most of this regiment was left along the San Fratello ridge to delay American follow-up movements) started across the bypass. At this very moment, Bernard's infantrymen came across the beaches.

According to General Truscott's concept of Bernard's operation, the amphibious force was to land near Terranova (east of the Rosmarino River), attack inland to seize Monte Barbuzzo (about a mile to the southwest), cut the coastal highway, and trap the defenders holding the San Fratello ridge. At 0150, 8 August, the small naval force hove to off the coast, its presence undetected. Companies F and G, 30th Infantry (the first wave) and one tank platoon and an engineer platoon (the second wave) immediately began loading into LCVP's from the two LST's. At 0230, the two waves started their final run in from about six thousand yards out. The LST's and the one LCI (which carried Company E) followed to about 1,500 yards offshore, where the LST's launched sixteen Dukws loaded with Bernard's headquarters personnel and Company H.

At 0315, Companies F and G touched down and started inland toward the high ground less than a mile away. The other waves followed at fifteen-minute intervals, with all troops and vehicles unloaded by 0415.

Surprise was complete, but reaction was swift from the German battalions spread from the Rosmarino River all the way back to San Fratello. Company G on the right drew the first German fire just after crossing the railroad, some two hundred yards inland. A short while later, Company F jumped a small group of Germans drowsily awakening from a sound sleep. By 0430 the beach was secured, and the lead companies began moving inland for what they thought was Monte Barbuzzo. But Colonel Bernard now realized that his force had not landed where it was supposed to land. Rather than being east of the Rosmarino River near Terranova, he had been put ashore west of the river, nearer Sant'Agata, and he began to change his plans. Since his force could not get to Monte Barbuzzo before the 7th Infantry jumped off to link up, Bernard determined to occupy high ground on both sides of the river. This would give him good defensive terrain and would also provide cover for the oncoming 7th Infantry.

At just about this time, however, the Germans launched their first counterattack. Part of the German battalion had already crossed to the east side of the river, but the elements in and near Sant'Agata, delayed by the demolished bridge, now found themselves between the 7th Infantry—which had jumped off at 0600—and Bernard's task force. Fighting in two directions, the Germans sent a small infantry detachment supported by two Italian Renault and two German Mark IV tanks to open a route to the east along the coastal highway.

It was a short-lived effort. Bernard's armored field artillery batteries and the platoon of medium tanks took the German counterattack under fire and quickly destroyed both Italian and one of the German tanks. At this, the Germans pulled back into Sant'Agata. The American artillery pieces and the tanks moved

SANT'AGATA FROM THE SEAWARD SIDE OF SAN FRATELLO RIDGE. *The view follows Highway 113 along the coast past Sant'Agata (middle distance) to Cape d'Orlando (top center). The town of Acquedolci is at extreme left.*

into position in a lemon grove north of the highway. From here they could cover the coastal road east and west.

Meanwhile Company G, having finished off the small pocket of German resistance which had been opposing its advance, moved up to the highway. One platoon established a roadblock covering the eastern exits from Sant'Agata, another took up security positions around the artillery and tanks, while the remainder of the company established a block on the secondary road which winds inland to Militello. At the same time, Company F fanned out toward the Rosmarino River, crossed it without difficulty, and secured the high ground on the east bank blocking the highway and the trail which leads inland to San Marco d'Alunzio. Both of Company H's machine gun platoons went into position to cover Company F's right flank.

Hardly had these dispositions been completed when the Germans, trying to find an inland route around Bernard's coastal positions, struck at Company F. One German group with two motorcycles, a vehicle loaded with cans of gasoline, and two troop carriers filled with soldiers, moved down the trail from San Marco. At the same time, another small column came down the coastal highway from the east. With Company H's machine guns sending out steady streams of flanking fire at both German columns, Company F held fast. The German gasoline vehicle was hit and burned; all other German vehicles were put out of action. Again the armored artillerymen came into action. This combination of American fires proved too much. As the German column on the coast road pulled back toward Terranova, a few Germans from the San Marco column managed to get past Company F's roadblock and to escape to the east.

Bernard's third rifle company, Company E, met problems of a different nature. Late in receiving Bernard's change of plans, the company had moved inland from the beaches toward what the company commander mistook for Monte Barbuzzo. But in the rough terrain, the company broke in half. Two of the rifle platoons stayed with the company commander; the other rifle platoon and most of the weapons platoon went off to the south, still moving inland toward what the rifle platoon leader thought was his objective. The company commander then learned of Bernard's change of plans and he took his two rifle platoons to a position on Company F's right flank and helped that company fend off the German counterattacks. The rest of the company, which did not learn of the change in plans, continued up the river bed and finally turned east, well inland from the rest of the battalion. The men entered San Marco at 1130, passed through, and climbed up to a high ridge about a mile northeast of the town. This the platoon leader took to be Monte Barbuzzo, and dug in to hold on until the rest of the battalion arrived.

At San Fratello, meanwhile, the thinning out of the German and Italian defenders made the task of clearing the ridge a relatively easy one for the 7th Infantry. By 1130, the 2d Battalion, 7th Infantry, was in Sant'Agata after overcoming the remnants of the small force that had previously tried to break out of Bernard's trap. What was left of the *2d Battalion, 71st Panzer Grenadier Regiment*, moved inland to circle past the American block east of town. At 1230, 7th Infantry patrols made contact with Bernard's Company G east of Sant'Agata. By this time,

PLASMA BEING ADMINISTERED *to a wounded soldier in a first-aid station in Sant'Agata.*

too, Colonel Rogers' 30th Infantry, with Manhart's battalion still attached, was in San Fratello and on Monte San Fratello. This day, the Italians did not seriously contest the American advance. Either because they knew they were being left behind by the Germans, or because they had fought themselves out, the *Assietta* men surrendered in droves, almost a thousand to Doleman's battalion alone.

For Bernard's Companies E, F, and H, the fighting was not over, for they lay in the line of German withdrawal to the east. Concentrating on the hill mass in and near San Marco, the Germans, usually in small parties, pushed continuously at the three American companies, and at the two American platoons northeast of San Marco. Sometimes small enemy counterattacks came down the coastal highway from the east, in an evident attempt to co-ordinate attacks with withdrawals inland. Eventually, except for about one company and a few vehicles, the German battalion succeeded in making good its escape.

Truscott's first amphibious end run, while achieving surprise, had failed to cut off the German *29th Panzer Grenadier Division*. Most of that division had already retired by the time Bernard's force landed. At best, the end run deprived the Germans of the use of the Rosmarino River as a defensive phase line. It prob-

SAN MARCO D'ALUNZIO, *with the mouth of the Rosmarino River at left center and with railroad bridge just visible.*

ably did encourage the Germans to give up the San Fratello ridge a few hours earlier than they had intended. Even a landing on the correct beaches east of the Rosmarino River would have done little better.[13]

Late in the afternoon of 8 August, the 7th Infantry closed up to the Rosmarino River. That evening it resumed the advance along the north coast road.

---

[13] See 7th, 15th, and 30th Inf Regt AAR's; Opns Rpt, 2d Bn, 30th Inf Regt (while atchd to 3d Inf Div) AAR; Truscott, *Command Missions*, p. 234; Rupert Prohme, *History of the 30th Infantry Regiment in World War II* (Washington: Infantry Journal Press, 1947), pp. 61–64; Taggart, ed., *History of the Third Infantry Division*, pp. 66–67; Morison, *Sicily—Salerno—Anzio*, pp. 198–99; *Heeresgruppe C, OB SUED, Ic,* 18.V.43–30.IX.43, 8 Aug 43; *OKH, Tagesmeldungen West*, 8 and 9 Aug 43.

# CHAPTER XIX

# Evacuation

### The Tarvis Conference

While the Italian emissaries, D'Ajeta and Berio, were sounding out the Allies in Lisbon and Tangiers, *Comando Supremo* was continuing its wary co-operation with the Germans on the basis that its primary mission was to defend Italy against the Allies, the secondary one to guard against a German coup. Ambrosio and Castellano knew of the diplomatic missions to the Allies; Roatta, the Army chief of staff, knew nothing of this.

German strategic planning at this time was quite fluid. On 5 August OKW canceled its plan drawn up for the rapid seizure of Rome and of the members of the Italian Government. By this time the Italians had assembled such forces around the capital as to make its capture appear more formidable than before. Furthermore, Skorzeny, busy with a variety of false leads provided by the Italian counterespionage service, had been unable to locate Mussolini.

Kesselring had helped induce OKW to postpone its program of seizing Rome with the argument that he would, in that event, be forced to withdraw all his units from Sicily and southern Italy. Believing that the Italian Government showed a genuine will to co-operate, and hoping that personnel losses could be restored and sufficient munitions supplied, he was sure that the Axis could hold Sicily for a relatively long period and thereby tie down eleven or twelve Allied divisions.

The weakness of Kesselring's position lay in Calabria and southern Italy, where he had only alarm units (in the Naples-Salerno area) and the *16th Panzer Division* (dispersed over the interior). Because he could not guard Puglia and the west coast at the same time, Kesselring asked for reinforcement so that he might have at least one division for each of the three critical areas: Calabria, Puglia, and Naples-Salerno.

Jodl, chief of the OKW operations section, the *Wehrmachtfuehrungsstab,* held the opposite view. He argued that the Allies in Sicily were tying down German divisions. He feared that if the Allies were to land in force in Calabria, they would bag the entire *XIV Panzer Corps* in Sicily and be able to advance at will to the northern Apennines. Jodl wanted an immediate withdrawal from Sicily and southern Italy.

Hitler refused to send reinforcements to southern Italy, but he could not make up his mind to withdraw from Sicily. Intent on finding and liberating Mussolini, he believed that the rescue would be such a shock to the "English" as to deter them from any further large-scale landings. Student's and Skorzeny's search for Mussolini therefore continued. And until they found Mussolini, the German commanders in Italy were to observe the appearance of

# EVACUATION

good faith toward the Badoglio government.[1]

Just before the Tarvis conference scheduled for 6 August, the Germans considered asking for a greater share in the command of the Axis armed forces in the Mediterranean area. To this end they wanted a liaison staff attached directly to *Comando Supremo* or to the Army General Staff (*Superesercito*), a staff that would represent Kesselring's views on the use of forces in central and southern Italy. They also wanted a German Army headquarters to exercise command over all the German and Italian ground forces in northern Italy under the supreme command of the King. They thought of bringing up for discussion the matter of possible withdrawal from Sicily. But on the day before the conference, they decided not to mention the change of command or a withdrawal.

The conference itself between German and Italian foreign ministers and chiefs of staff was marked by solemn statements by each group which it did not mean, and which the other group knew it did not mean. Despite Badoglio's intention, the conferees explored the means of continuing the war rather than the possibilities of achieving peace. The Italians, intent on keeping up the appearance of being a faithful ally and on maintaining the notion that German troops in Italy were under operational control of *Comando Supremo*, pressed for agreement on the movement of German reinforcements to the south and away from the capital and from the naval bases of La Spezia and Pola (where the bulk of the Italian Fleet was stationed). The Italians also hoped to reach agreement on withdrawing to the homeland the Italian divisions in southern France and the Balkans. Fundamentally, the Italians were stalling for time until they received word of the Allied reply to the overtures of D'Ajeta and Berio.

Ribbentrop, Keitel, Guariglia, and Ambrosio met on the morning of 6 August. Guariglia declared the change of government in Italy to be purely an internal matter; Italy held to Badoglio's declaration that the war was to continue. Ambrosio complained that Germany appeared to place little faith in Italy's word; he was astonished at the numerous German divisions coming, in part, unannounced. Though southern Italy was threatened, Ambrosio said, the Germans were concentrating near Rome and in the north, creating the suspicion that the Germans had other intentions than the defense of Italy. Keitel said that questioning German good faith was quite unacceptable, and he expressed indignation that the Italians were not thankful for generous German aid. Ribbentrop asked directly whether Guariglia had had any conversation with the English or Americans. Guariglia replied in the negative, admitting, however, that he had spoken with the Turkish Foreign Minister. Ambrosio reaffirmed the intention of the Italians to march with all their strength by the side of the Germans.

At the afternoon session, attended by Keitel, Rintelen, Warlimont, Ambrosio, Marras, and Rossi, Ambrosio suggested that Italian assurances regarding German divisions in transit to Italy were not final. Keitel insisted that the north would first have to be fully protected before German reinforcements could move to the south. Ambrosio stated his intention of withdraw-

---
[1] *OKW/WFSt, KTB, 1.-31.VIII.43,* 5 Aug 43; situation appreciation by *OB SUED* of 4 Aug 43 and comments by *Chef WFSt,* in MS #C-093 (Warlimont), pp. 102-03.

AXIS SECOND ECHELON LEADERS *meet in Tarvis, 6 August 1943. From left: General Keitel, German Foreign Minister Ribbentrop, Interpreter Paul Schmidt, Italian Foreign Minister Raffaele Guariglia, General Ambrosio.*

ing the Italian *Fourth Army* from France and three divisions from the Balkans, and he expressed the hope that the Germans would provide for the protection of the areas vacated by the Italians. Keitel replied by saying a decision on this matter was beyond his authority, but he agreed to present the Italian proposal to Hitler. He recommended that the movement of German reinforcements to southern Italy, on which the Italians placed such emphasis, receive priority over the withdrawal of Italian troops from occupied territories.

Except for an understanding that the German units in Sicily and southern Italy were to be brought to full strength and adequately supplied, no real agreement was reached at Tarvis. Pious declarations of alliance were exchanged. The Germans believed, or professed to believe, that the conferees were in accord that protection not only of the Brenner Pass but of all the Alpine passes into Italy had become a joint responsibility. The Italians understood that joint protection by ground forces applied to the Brenner Pass alone, the other passes remaining under Italian competence except for antiaircraft batteries.[2]

The fundamental question of the command and distribution of forces was in no way resolved. The Italians, maintaining the sham that all German forces in Italy were under the *Comando Supremo*'s operational control, complained that the German troops in the north behaved as though they were in an occupied country. When Ambrosio asked whether Kesselring commanded the new troops entering Italy from the north, Warlimont replied: "Up to now, yes. However, it will be necessary to establish a command over the German divisions in North Italy. Notification will be given at an appropriate time." Until the traffic crisis was overcome or dissipated, the Germans insisted on keeping their new forces concentrated in the north. The Italians had no chance to expound a plan of joint defense that would have left not a single German division in the Po valley.[3]

The conference had opened in an atmosphere of gravest mutual suspicion. It closed in the same spirit. Ribbentrop brought up the matter of a future meeting of Hitler with the King and Badoglio on German soil and suggested that the Heir Apparent also attend. Guariglia did not press the subject because he feared that the King might be seized and held in custody or as a hostage. He had, in any case, already started on another course.[4]

Leonardo Vitetti complained that the trip to Tarvis was like Columbus' first voyage: he did not know where he was going and when he came back he did not know where he had been or what he had done.[5]

### The Italian Dilemma

With the Tarvis conference providing formal Italian concurrence for reinforcing the north, German troops continued to move into north Italy, General Gloria reporting on 7 August that approximately 30,000 troops had crossed the Brenner Pass by that date.[6] OKW's policy in this respect, representing an uneasy day by day compromise between its own views and *OB SUED's* wishes, exploited the willingness of *Comando Supremo* to receive reinforcements. Although Hitler remained convinced that Italy was planning treason, although plans and preparations for seizing Italy were constantly reviewed and kept up to date, there existed a wide divergency in strategies to be followed in case of Italian betrayal or of Allied attack in southern Italy.

Skeptical and pessimistic of German success, Rommel was disappointed in the number of forces actually assigned to his *Army Group B* (for the most part infan-

---

[2] See the contrasting minutes in *OKW/WFSt, KTB, 1.-31.VIII.43,* 6 August 1943, and *Colloquio del giorno 6 agosto ore 1530,* pages 12–13, IT 3030. The minutes of the three sessions at Tarvis are printed, but not in full, in *Hitler e Mussolini: Lettere e documenti,* pages 190–209.

[3] See map, *Comando Supremo, Ufficio Operazioni Esercito, Scacchiere occidentale, Progetto dislocazione grandi unità italiane e germaniche per la difesa d'Italia,* IT 3030.

[4] Guariglia, *Ricordi,* pp. 628–29.

[5] Simoni, *Berlino, Ambasciata,* pp. 392–98 (Vitetti statement, p. 392). See also: Guariglia, *Ricordi,* pp. 613–30; Rintelen, *Mussolini als Bundesgenosse,* pp. 236–39; MS #C-093 (Warlimont), pp. 104–10; Rossi, *Come arrivammo,* pp. 95–98; Badoglio, *Memorie e documenti,* p. 98; Zanussi, *Guerra e catastrofe,* vol. II, pp. 59–60; Castellano, *Come firmai,* pp. 74–77.

[6] Telg, *Comando XXXV Corpo d'Armata No. 970/OP to Ministero della Guerra,* 7 Aug 43, IT 102.

try divisions). They were so meager in comparison with the panzer army originally planned in June that he estimated he could defend northern Italy against Allied invasion only with Italian cooperation. To oppose an invasion without Italian support or while fighting the Italians would be, he felt, an impossible task. Unaware of how thoroughly the Italian officers hated him—he doubted, for example, that an announcement of his command would cause much reaction among the Italians—he wished to move his headquarters from Munich to northern Italy, hoping in that way to gain the cooperation and good will of the Italian generals.[7]

Kesselring, who no doubt had little relish for the prospect of merging his command into Rommel's, continued to take an optimistic view. He and Rintelen, in agreement on the matter, made great efforts to prevent the harsh and suspicious attitude of OKW from completely alienating the Italians.[8]

The full scope of German intentions—to compel the Italian Government to continue the war whether it wished or not, to seize the Italian Fleet and capital, and to convert the Italian peninsula into a battlefield for the defense of Germany—was abundantly clear after the Tarvis conference. The German occupation of Italy, which had been Ambrosio's greatest fear since May, was rapidly becoming an accomplished fact. Though the Italian Government had formally accepted unwanted German reinforcements, and though the unwelcome guests were already in the house, Comando Supremo did not wish them to have the keys to all the rooms. Ambrosio therefore ordered certain troop movements to counteract the German strangle hold. He strengthened the forces guarding Rome and alerted them to take increased precautions against German moves. He had the *105th* (*Rovigo*) *Infantry Division* and the *6th* (*Alpi Graje*) *Alpine Division* moved from Turin, where they had been maintaining public order, to La Spezia, the main base of the Italian Fleet, from which the Germans were to be excluded.[9]

In the Brenner Pass area, General Gloria's *XXXV Corps* had had only the *2d* (*Tridentina*) *Alpine Division*, a unit in the process of reconstitution after return from the Russian front. The *4th* (*Cuneense*) *Alpine Division*, which also shared bitter memories of German behavior in the retreat from Stalingrad, had been moved to Cosenza (in Calabria) in July. Now, however, Ambrosio ordered that division moved northward up the whole length of the Italian peninsula to become part of Gloria's corps.[10]

On 8 August, in accordance with instructions, Gloria sent a note to General Feurstein. He stated that Roatta, the Army chief of staff, had directed the two Alpine divisions to take over the protection of the Brenner Pass in order to free the German *44th Infantry Division* for further movement southward. German antiaircraft batteries were to remain, but under Gloria's command. Feurstein re-

---

[7] *OKW/WFSt, KTB, 1.–31.VIII.43,* 7 Aug 43.

[8] Westphal, *Heer in Fesseln,* p. 224; Rintelen in MS #T-1a (Westphal et al.), ch. II, pp. 22–23; Rintelen, *Mussolini als Bundesgenosse,* p. 239; General der Panzertruppen Heinrich von Vietinghoff gen. Scheel in MS #T-1a (Westphal et al.), ch. VI, p. 8.

[9] Rossi, *Come arrivammo,* p. 97; Zanussi, *Guerra e catastrofe,* vol. II, p. 57.

[10] *Comando Supremo, Operazioni Regio Esercito Quadro di battaglia alla data del 1 agosto 1943,* IT 10 a-h; Ambrosio's order of 2 Aug 43, *Comando Supremo, No. 15492/Op.,* IT 102.

# EVACUATION

plied firmly that the *44th Infantry Division* would stay where it was and be wholly responsible for protecting the Brenner-Bolzano sector. Professing great indignation over the northward movement of Italian troops while German divisions were not only moving south to defend Italy against Allied invasion but also carrying the main burden of the campaign in Sicily, Kesselring submitted a formal note of protest to Ambrosio. He demanded the withdrawal of all the Italian troops that had moved into the Trentino after 5 August. Otherwise, he threatened, responsibility for the consequences would fall upon the Italian Government.[11]

Confirming all the points in the Tarvis agreement, Ambrosio nevertheless refused to suspend the movement of the *Cuneense Alpine Division* into the South Tyrol. It was to complete its mountain training, he said, before commitment against the Allies. An uneasy compromise resulted, as German and Italian troops continued to share the protection of the Brenner area.[12]

A new misunderstanding in the South Tyrol occurred on 9 August, when Feurstein notified Gloria of new troop movements and requested the plans and keys of installations suitable for accommodating the German units. Informed by Gloria and interpreting the request as a demand for the plans and keys of all the Italian fortifications in the Reschen and Sillian Passes, Roatta energetically protested to Kesselring the presumptious German behavior. Kesselring notified OKW, which agreed to confirm all troop movements with *Comando Supremo* through Kesselring, in accordance with the Tarvis conference. Yet OKW directed *Army Group B* to prepare to occupy the Tarvis Pass, the northeastern gateway into Italy from Ljubljana and from Villach-Klagenfurt.[13]

By this time, *Comando Supremo* had developed schizophrenic tendencies under the contradictory pressures of opposing the Allies in the south and the Germans in the north. In accordance with Ambrosio's order, Castellano on 9 August traveled to Monterotondo, just outside Rome, whither the Army staff was moving in anticipation of the proclamation of Rome's open city status, and directed Roatta to make certain troop dispositions in view of a probable conflict with the Germans. Roatta objected. The orders implied a change in policy, and Roatta did not wish to act unless the order for the change came from the King and Badoglio. Calling on Ambrosio that evening, Roatta urged him to take the matter to the King. At an audience with Victor Emmanuel III on 10 August, Ambrosio secured the King's approval of the proposed troop movements and informed Roatta, who issued a written directive to his subordinate commanders.

The directive confirmed and elaborated the verbal orders Roatta had issued at the end of July. Italian forces were to react positively against German violence, safeguard command posts and assembly areas against German surprise attack, reinforce the protection of hydroelectric plants and other important installations, observe closely and report all German troop movements and all supporting actions by Fascists, plan and prepare for action against

---

[11] Memo of the German General at Headquarters of the Italian Armed Forces, No. 0717/43, 8 Aug 43, IT 102.

[12] *OKW/WFSt, KTB, 1.-31.VIII.43*, 7-8 Aug 43; Min, 8 Aug 43, item 193, Min of Confs, *Comando Supremo*, IT 26.

[13] *OKW/WFSt, KTB, 1.-31.VIII.43*, 8-9 Aug 43; Cf. Roatta, *Otto milioni*, p. 273.

such vital German installations as motor parks, munition depots, and airfields. Unless the Germans took the initiative and resorted to force, Italian units were to execute these plans only upon order from Roatta's headquarters. Like previous instructions of this nature issued by Roatta, these orders were defensive in nature. There was no anticipation of possible co-operation with the Allies against the Germans. Roatta still knew nothing of the missions of D'Ajeta and Berio.[14]

*The Decision to Evacuate Sicily*

The Tarvis conference had not settled on a future course of action to be followed by the Axis armies in Sicily, for Sicily had been discussed only incidentally. Wanting to avoid a repetition of the Tunisian disaster and fearing that Hitler would delay a decision until too late, Kesselring took it upon himself to solve the problem.

Kesselring had received the OKW order of 26 July to prepare for an eventual evacuation of the island. To prevent leakage of German plans to the Italians as directed by OKW, Kesselring had called a conference on 27 July to brief the German commanders on the planned conduct of future operations on the island. "If the Italians should leave the alliance with Germany," Kesselring said, "the *XIV Panzer Corps* will immediately disengage from the enemy and evacuate all troops from Sicily. Preparations for the evacuation will start right away in co-ordination between *XIV* and *LXXVI Panzer Corps* and other headquarters involved." Col. Bogislaw von Bonin, chief of staff of *XIV Panzer Corps,* who attended the meeting, informed General Hube when he returned the same day to Sicily. Hube directed Colonel Baade, the commandant of the Strait of Messina, and the German sea transport commander, Fregattenkapitaen Gustav von Liebenstein, to start preparations for the evacuation. Hube also authorized the withdrawal of the ground forces from Nicosia that evening and informed General Guzzoni the next day that German forces would no longer execute a stubborn defense of Sicily.[15]

On 2 August Kesselring approved the detailed evacuation plan submitted to him by Colonel von Bonin, asking only to be notified before Hube implemented the plan. The next day he informed OKW that the evacuation plan was ready and that the transfer of troops and matériel to the Italian mainland could be made in five nights.

The fall of San Fratello on 8 August coincided with several other notable events on Sicily. On that day, the 9th Division entered Cesarò; the British 78th Division seized Bronte; and the British 13 Corps on the east coast was eight miles beyond Catania striving to break the *Hermann*

---
[14] Roatta, *Otto milioni,* pp. 275, 287, 289–91; Rossi, *Come arrivammo,* pp. 200–201, 205; Zanussi, *Guerra e catastrofe,* II, pp. 56–57; MS #P-058, Project 46, 1 Feb–8 Sep 43, Question 7.

[15] Since most of the German orders were given verbally during this period, only scanty documentary evidence is available. A reconstruction of the transmittal of the order from *OKW/WFSt* to Hube on 27 July is based on: Instructions from *OKW/WFSt* on the future conduct of operations in Italy reached *OB SUED* on 26 and 27 July 1943, as proven by two mentions—with hardly any details—in *OB SUED, Meldungen,* 0725, 26 July 1943 and 2025, 27 July 1943; arrival of TWX with instructions from *OKW/ WFSt* early in the morning of 26 July 1943, Rintelen, *Mussolini als Bundesgenosse;* Kesselring's conference on 27 July 1943 and his directive, *LXXVI Panzer Corps, Anlagen, 10.VII.–30. VIII.43;* Bonin's presence at the conference, *OB SUED, Meldungen,* 2025, 27 July 1943; *LXXVI Panzer Corps, KTB, 22.VI.43–2.II.44,* and *Anlagen,* 8 August and 10 August for 8 August 1943.

# EVACUATION

*Goering Division's* hold on Highway 114.

On that day, too, General von Senger visited Kesselring and reported the seriousness of the situation on Sicily. Kesselring then ordered Hube to go ahead with the evacuation. He did not directly inform Hitler or ask his approval. He depended on his chief of staff, General Westphal, to set matters straight with *Comando Supremo*.[16] When OKW on 9 August learned of Kesselring's order, Hitler accepted the decision as a *fait accompli*. General Warlimont, Jodl's deputy chief, recalled after the war that the decision to evacuate Sicily was one of the instances where Jodl "in his calm way . . . succeeded in guiding Hitler to undesirable but necessary decisions . . . ."[17]

The decision could not be kept from General Guzzoni and his staff. Guzzoni accordingly examined the possibility of continuing to defend Sicily with Italian forces alone. He concluded that such a course of action was not feasible. The Italian forces on the island might delay the Allied occupation of all of Sicily by a few days, but only at the price of human sacrifice and loss of equipment out of proportion to any advantages that might be gained. He informed *Comando Supremo* of his views, and on 9 August *Comando Supremo* ordered Guzzoni to take over the defense of part of Calabria and to start evacuating Italian forces from Sicily.[18]

With Kesselring finally giving the word to evacuate, Hube instructed Baade and the three German division commanders to prepare for final transfer of troops and equipment to Messina and across the Strait to the Italian mainland.[19] Late on the afternoon of 10 August, Hube issued the formal order for evacuation, designating the night of 11 August as the first of five nights for ferrying troops across the strait in Operation LEHRGANG.

By this time, Baade had practically completed his preparations for receiving and transporting the troops and equipment from the front-line divisions. Within the large, oval-shaped area of his command—including the northeast tip of Sicily and an area directly across the Strait of Messina in Calabria—Baade exercised command not only over all German Army troops, but over the German antiaircraft installations and their personnel, even though the latter were administratively part of the German *Second Air Fleet*.

To counter Allied air and naval supremacy, Baade had under his control about five hundred guns, a majority of them dual-purpose weapons.[20] In addi-

---

[16] *Colloquio Generale Westphal–Generale Rossi del giorno 9 agosto 1943, ore 1200,* IT 104; *SKL/1.Abt, KTB, Teil A, 1.–31.VIII.43,* 16 Aug 43; Min of Confs in Rome, 1943, IT 26; Min, 8 Aug 43 Item 193, Min of Confs, *Comando Supremo,* IT 26; MS #T-1a (Westphal et al.).

[17] *SKL/1.Abt, KTB, Teil A, 1.–31.VIII.43,* 15 and 16 Aug 43 and one entry 20 Aug 43 referring to 9 Aug 43; Warlimont in OI–II R/22, Hq U.S. Forces European Theater, Mil Intel Center, German General Staff Series; Bonin in MS #T-2 (Fries et al.); Westphal's comments on the evacuation order as quoted by Fries in MS #T-2 (Fries et al.), p. 28; *OKW/WFSt, KTB, 1.–31.VIII.43,* 9 Aug 43.

[18] Faldella, *Lo sbarco,* pp. 269; IT 99c, an. 121.

[19] Baade Diary; *LXXVI Panzer Corps, KTB* and *Anlagen,* 8 and 10 Aug for 8 Aug 43.

[20] It is difficult to determine just how many guns Baade controlled during the evacuation period. A report dated 14 August (Baade Diary, pages 119–20) shows 333 antiaircraft guns on hand that day. These were in addition to the coast defense guns, which were not dual-purpose weapons. Other reports (an undated map, probably late July, in Baade Diary; a map dated 18 July 1943, part of collection *Sizilien* (1:200,000), *WFSt Op (H)*) shows even more guns as being present. See also Roskill, *The War at Sea,* vol. III, pt. I, pp. 145–46.

tion, just before the evacuation started, the *15th Panzer Grenadier Division* relinquished to Baade the two most powerful batteries on Sicily (170-mm. guns with an effective range of over ten miles) for commitment as part of the coastal defenses on both sides of Villa San Giovanni (just across the strait from Messina).[21]

Thus, what many Allied officers had regarded as one of the most heavily defended areas in Europe during 1942 and early 1943 had perhaps become *the* most heavily defended. One Allied officer was later to call the antiaircraft fire at Messina "the heaviest ever encountered in the Mediterranean—heavier than 'flak alley' between Bizerte and Tunis—greater than the inner artillery of London." [22] The single weakness in Baade's antiaircraft defense system was the limited range of his guns. A large number would not be able to reach high-flying Allied bombers, aircraft like the B-17, the B-24, and the British Wellington. This was one reason why Baade had taken over the *15th Panzer Grenadier Division*'s large weapons. If the Allied air forces attacked the strait using fighter, fighter-bomber, light and medium bomber aircraft, then the antiaircraft fire would be most effective. If the Allied air forces sent mainly high-flying heavy bombers, Baade's defenses would prove woefully inadequate. In the latter case the German infantrymen on Sicily would have to depend on the German *Second Air Fleet* to cover the withdrawal. But this was a task that the German air force in Italy could not possibly hope to perform, for the air force was decimated by the previous fighting, frustrated by Italian officials who demanded conformity with impossible regulations, and left with less than three hundred operational aircraft of all types.

In addition to controlling the defenses of the Messina Strait area, Baade also co-ordinated the German naval ferrying service, although this function remained the direct responsibility of Captain Liebenstein, the Sea Transport Commander, Messina Strait. Liebenstein had command of three naval flotillas, an engineer landing battalion, two or three engineer fortification battalions, and two port maintenance companies. The flotillas had, by the end of July, 33 naval ferry barges (somewhat similar to American LCT's), 12 *Siebel* ferries (10-ton, flat-bottomed, multipurpose supply and troop carriers), 2 naval gun lighters, 11 large engineer landing craft capable of transporting 2 trucks, and 76 motorboats designed to transport personnel only.[23]

At Hube's request, four of six ferrying routes developed by Liebenstein during the course of the campaign (with each route having several landing places on both coasts) were set aside to evacuate German troops, all starting from points north of Messina. A fifth route, south of Messina, was designated a spare route, to be used only in emergency. Routes 1 and 2, near the northeastern tip of the island, were reserved for the *15th* and *29th Panzer Grenadier Divisions;* Route 3, two miles north of Messina, was to be used by *XIV Panzer Corps* headquarters and headquarters troops; Route 4, a mile north of Messina, was set aside for the *Hermann Goering Division* and attached elements of the *1st Parachute Division*. Other German units were to adjust their movements

---

[21] Baade Diary; Bonin in MS #T-2 (Fries et al.); MS #C-077 (Rodt).
[22] Quoted in Tregaskis, *Invasion Diary*, p. 70.

[23] For additional details, see MS #R-146 (Bauer), pp. 34-35; see also Roskill, *The War at Sea*, vol. III, pt. I, pp. 144-45.

SMOKE PALL COVERS PORTIONS OF MESSINA *after bombing attack by B-17's.*

to those of the divisions and were to be evacuated on a space-available basis. Personnel were to cross the strait only during the hours of darkness; weapons and miscellaneous equipment were to be evacuated during both the day and the night and in line with a priority of antitank weapons first, then artillery pieces, then self-propelled weapons of all kinds, and, finally, trucks and motor vehicles. All matériel that could not be evacuated was to be destroyed.[24]

On 10 August, the day Hube announced the formal evacuation order, the German ferrying service was ready to transport about 8,000 men each night, with ferry barges, *Siebel* ferries, and engineer landing craft ready to go into action at each of the four designated ferrying sites. All that remained was for General Hube to get the right number of men to the proper embarkation points at the right time in order to make full use of the available shipping without creating bottlenecks.

All troops at the front or in the rear areas had, by 10 August, received orders to move toward the ferrying routes. Generalleutnant Richard Heidrich, commander of the *1st Parachute Division*,

---

[24] *LXXVI Panzer Corps, KTB* and *Anlagen*, 10 Aug 43.

drew the assignment of organizing the reception of the troops in Calabria. The Tortorici, or shorter, bridgehead line was to be held until 12 August, when Hube planned to begin moving the entire front back in three big strides, delaying at phase lines across the northeastern tip of the island. To prevent overcrowding on the north coast highway, Hube picked the *15th Panzer Grenadier Division* to start moving through Randazzo toward ferry Routes 1 and 2 on 10 August so that its transfer to the Italian mainland could be completed by 15 August. The *29th Panzer Grenadier Division* was to follow along the north coast. At the same time, the *Hermann Goering Division,* withdrawing around both sides of Mount Etna, was to fall back toward Route 4. Hube planned that each of the three major displacements to the rear would be made at night, and only on dates that he would specify. Upon arrival at each of the phase lines, the divisions would release up to two-thirds of the troops then on line and start them moving toward the embarkation points. Since each line was shorter than the preceding one, Hube felt this procedure was feasible and that it assured a steady stream of men to and across the strait.[25]

For the Italians, who had started a limited evacuation on 3 August, official word to evacuate the island came from *Comando Supremo* on the 9th, when General Guzzoni was ordered to help defend Calabria. On the following day, after giving Hube command authority over all Italian and German units still in Sicily, Guzzoni and his *Sixth Army* headquarters moved across the strait.[26] Like the Germans, the Italians organized four ferrying routes, two starting from Messina itself, the other two from points north of the city. Operating independently of the German service, the Italian ferrying service consisted of one train ferry (capable of lifting 3,000 men at a time), two small steamboats, and four navy-manned motor rafts. Since the Italian vessels were not capable of lifting heavy equipment, General Hube offered to take over some of it, if space should become available on the German craft.

### Allied Reaction

Allied commanders and Allied intelligence agencies seemed quite aware of the Axis intention to evacuate Sicily, although they refused to hazard a guess as to when this evacuation might begin. General Alexander, himself, as early as 3 August, felt that the Germans would start back across the strait at almost any time and he requested Admiral Cunningham and Air Chief Marshal Tedder to co-ordinate the Allied forces' naval and air efforts to prevent an enemy evacuation from the island.[27] On 5 August, the Seventh Army G-2 announced that "in all probability evacuation is taking place. The entire operation from the enemy viewpoint, therefore, is to delay advance against time."[28] Two days later the same officer again indicated evacuation of German troops as the most likely enemy course of action, a report issued daily thereafter.[29] From a British intelligence

---

[25] MS #C-077 (Rodt); MS #T-2 (Fries *et al.*); Baade Diary.

[26] Faldella, *Lo sbarco,* pp. 269-70, 308; IT 99c, an. 112 and 121.

[27] Nicholson, *The Canadians in Italy,* p. 172; Roskill, *The War at Sea,* vol. III, pt. I, p. 146; Morison, *Sicily—Salerno—Anzio,* pp. 212-13.

[28] Seventh Army G-2 Periodic Rpt 27, 5 Aug 43.

[29] Seventh Army G-2 Periodic Rpt 29, 7 Aug 43.

# EVACUATION

office on Sicily came the following statement on 9 August: "From now on it seems to be a question of who can walk back the fastest. The Germans are definitely getting out everything they can." [30]

While it appears that Allied commanders knew of the impending enemy evacuation, if not the exact date when the evacuation would start, it also appears that these same commanders had no over-all plan for thwarting such an operation. To General Alexander's query of 3 August requesting a co-ordination of the Allied air and naval efforts to prevent an enemy evacuation from Sicily, Admiral Cunningham replied that he was aware of the possibility of the enemy forces leaving Sicily, that he had small craft operating at night in the strait, but that he could not employ larger warships in the strait area until the air forces knocked out the enemy's strong coastal batteries. Cunningham promised that the activities of the small craft would be "intensified," and that once the air forces knocked out the coastal batteries he would send "surface forces to operate further in the straits." [31]

Air Chief Marshal Tedder agreed with Cunningham's proposal to knock out the coastal batteries, as well as with another proposal of Cunningham's to permit Allied air forces to operate without "let or hindrance" over the whole of the Messina Strait area, and he notified his American subordinate, General Spaatz (commander of the NAAF), to put the air forces to work immediately. Thus, Spaatz' two major combat air forces—NATAF and NASAF—were committed to blocking Hube's evacuation. An order issued on 2 August which had prohibited the use of General Doolittle's NASAF heavy bombers against the strait was rescinded, with the provision that the heavies would not be used during the day except at Doolittle's discretion, and then only on a request from Air Vice Marshal Sir Arthur Coningham (NATAF's commander) with a twelve-hour notice. General Doolittle's command was suffering from combat fatigue and it had been found necessary to decrease the frequency of NASAF's operations during the last week in July in order to give the combat air crews more rest. Too, NASAF had many targets on the Italian mainland: airfields, lines of communications, marshaling yards, and rail and road bridges that had to be destroyed before the Allied invasion of the Italian mainland. Coningham felt that his NATAF could handle any enemy evacuation that might take place during daylight hours, provided NASAF could handle the night hours. Thus, from 5 to 9 August, although British medium Wellington bombers struck nightly at the beaches north of Messina, American B-17 heavy bombers flew only three daylight missions against Messina. Despite this round-the-clock aerial bombardment, Air Vice Marshal Coningham felt that unless the Navy could provide a "positive physical barrier" at night across the strait NAAF could not prevent an enemy evacuation from Sicily.[32]

Unfortunately, Admiral Cunningham, after giving "the matter very careful thought," concluded that regardless of the method used by the Allies, "sea or air," there was no "effective method" of stopping an enemy evacuation. Admiral Hewitt, the American naval commander,

---

[30] Quoted in Tregaskis, *Invasion Diary*, p. 70.
[31] Roskill, *The War at Sea*, vol. III, pt. I, p. 146.

[32] Roskill, *The War at Sea*, vol. III, pt. I, pp. 147-48; Craven and Cate, eds., vol. II, *Europe: TORCH to POINTBLANK*, p. 472.

agreed. Admiral McGrigor's small "Inshore Squadron," originally created to work with the British Eighth Army, was left on its own to do what it could to establish the "positive physical barrier" in the strait; no larger warships were ordered to help out.[33]

From the point of view of the ground fighters, only two possibilities existed for getting sizable numbers of Allied ground forces into Messina before the enemy could evacuate: additional amphibious landings of the type conducted by the Seventh Army at San Fratello, and airborne drops designed to sever the last few remaining routes of enemy withdrawal to Messina. Both the Seventh and Eighth Armies, on 8 August, were still some distance from Messina—seventy-five and fifty-two miles, respectively—with little possibility of moving any faster than they had during the preceding eight or nine days unless they sailed around or flew over the enemy's defensive lines.

General Patton, pleased with the results of the II Corps first seaborne end run, kept Bernard's small task force intact, intending to use it again to expedite the Seventh Army advance along the north coast road. If such landings in the future could be made deeper in the enemy rear than at San Fratello, they might be able to cut off sizable numbers of German soldiers; they might even cut off the entire *29th Panzer Grenadier Division*. Patton also wanted to use an airborne drop to further speed up the Seventh Army advance, and he directed preparations aimed at using a parachute battalion, the 509th, to drop behind the German lines either in conjunction with an amphibious landing or alone to cut off more German units.

As of 8 August, General Montgomery still had indicated no desire to use any of Admiral McGrigor's Inshore Squadron to speed the Eighth Army's advance up the east coast, although McGrigor was ready and willing to undertake such an operation. In fact, McGrigor twice before had embarked a large Commando force (one had actually sailed) to land it behind the Germans' Catania defense line to cut the vital east coast highway. Both times Montgomery had canceled the operation. Four small British airborne missions designed to harass enemy communications and supply areas in northeastern Sicily had been tried; all had failed. Montgomery gave no hint of a desire to employ larger numbers of airborne troops to aid his army's advance.[34] The Eighth Army commander apparently preferred to slog his way slowly around the Mount Etna massif, using much the same plan he had developed four days after the invasion.[35]

With the Allied naval forces practically out of the picture, with the Allied ground forces miles away from Messina, the entire burden of stopping Hube's evacuation initially fell on the Allied air forces, who were not quite ready to assume the task. Instead of calling on Doolittle's NASAF to help out after 9 August, Air Vice Marshal Coningham relied almost exclusively on his NATAF to stop the evacuation. From 9 August on, the NATAF pilots tried desperately to halt the flow of traffic across the strait, but they found it difficult

---

[33] Morison, *Sicily—Salerno—Anzio*, pp. 213, 216; Roskill, *The War at Sea*, vol. III, pt. I, pp. 147, 149–50.

[34] These were the four so-called CHESTNUT missions, three consisting of two planes, the last of one aircraft.

[35] Roskill, *The War at Sea*, vol. III, pt. I, pp. 142–43; Morison, *Sicily—Salerno—Anzio*, pp. 206–07; Montgomery, *Eighth Army*, pp. 110–11.

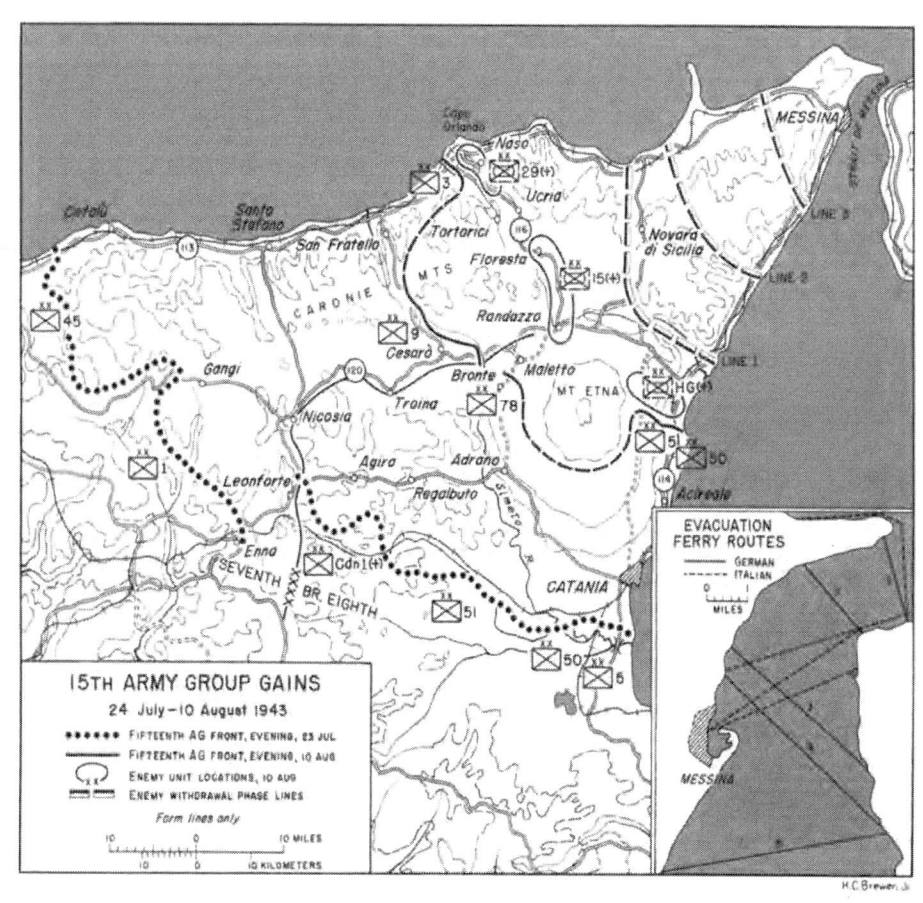

MAP 7

to penetrate Baade's antiaircraft defenses. "My squadron lost two out of twelve planes yesterday," said one American flyer. "And I lost two wing tips," reported another. "And I lost my tail wheel," said a third. "They put up a hell of a lot of flak," stated a fourth.[36] But on the same day (11 August) that Hube started his evacuation, Coningham reported that should "withdrawal develop on a big scale . . . we can handle it with our own resources and naval assistance."

He recommended that Doolittle's heavy bombers be released from their commitment to bomb Messina by day, if requested, but asked that the British Wellington bombers keep up their night strikes.[37]

Despite Coningham's optimistic appraisal of the situation, it appeared that unless the ground troops could hurry their forward movement and exert sizable pressure on Hube's retiring divisions, it was unlikely that Allied air alone, with only

---
[36] Tregaskis, *Invasion Diary*, p. 71.

[37] Roskill. *The War at Sea*, vol. III, pt. I, p. 149.

limited naval support, could do much to stop Hube from getting most of his men and equipment off the island.

### The Evacuation Begins

The three German divisions reached the Tortorici line by 10 August, pressed by the American and British forces only on the extreme eastern and northern wings. (*Map 7*) Still holding positions west of the northern hinge of that line, the *29th Panzer Grenadier Division* tried to delay the 3d Division's advance forward of the Tortorici line for as long as possible, giving way only to extreme pressure and completing its withdrawal by 12 August. Here again, General Fries' division would occupy strong natural defensive positions, ideally suited to fighting a delaying action. Here again, the coastal anchor of the line had the same washboard ridges as the San Fratello line, and the Zappulla River crossings corresponded with those of the Furiano. Highway 116, running south across the Caronie Mountains from Cape Orlando through Naso and Ucria to Randazzo (on Highway 120), runs over high and mountainous terrain like the San Fratello–Cesarò road. Roughly halfway between Cape Orlando and Randazzo, commanding terrain offered the Germans positions from which to cover the southern terminus of the northern portion of the Tortorici line.

On 9 August, the *71st Panzer Grenadier Regiment* still occupied a salient extending westward of the Zappulla River. The regiment was under orders to hold until forced to withdraw. The *15th Panzer Grenadier Regiment* deployed west of Highway 116, south of Naso. Most of the *29th Panzer Grenadier Division*'s artillery battalions were in positions near the coast. The Italian elements, reduced to a handful of *Assietta Division* infantrymen and a few artillery pieces, were intermingled among the German units.

South of the mountain chain, the remnants of the *15th Panzer Grenadier Division* slipped into place along Highway 116 between Floresta and Randazzo. This was the division Hube had earmarked as the first to be evacuated from Sicily. Forward of this main battle line, General Rodt deployed strong rear guards astride Highway 120 to delay a quick American follow-up from Cesarò. He also resorted to extensive use of mines and demolitions, taking full advantage of the rough terrain, narrow road, numerous bridges, and difficult bypasses to aid the defense.

From the German viewpoint, if the evacuation was to succeed, the advance of the Allied ground forces had to be slowed considerably. In particular, Rodt had to hold Randazzo—now threatened by both the 9th U.S. Division and the British 78th Division—until both his own and those elements from the *Hermann Goering Division* north of Mount Etna could withdraw through the only exit now available in the central sector of the Axis front. Randazzo was a prime target for the Allied air forces—at least for those air units not committed to the Messina Strait area. A quick movement by the two Allied divisions into and through Randazzo would not only cut off portions of two German divisions, it would endanger the German units on both the northern and eastern coasts.

Colonel Smythe's 47th Infantry, committed to taking Randazzo, retained positions around Cesarò during the night of 8 August, despite Smythe's repeated urgings to his battalion commanders to move on to the high ground which overlooked

RANDAZZO from the southern approach. Highway 116 is barely visible winding down from the mountains (beyond the steeple at left center).

DESTROYED BRIDGE ALONG HIGHWAY 116 *just north of Randazzo. Slope of Mount Etna can be seen in background.*

the Simeto River, about one-third of the way to Randazzo. Since the advance was to continue the following morning, Smythe wanted to be in position to jump across the river quickly. General Eddy, also concerned with getting to Randazzo as fast as possible, brought all but one battalion of DeRohan's 60th Infantry out of the mountains to follow Smythe's advance. This, Eddy felt, would strengthen the division's main effort; for the time being, he was content to give up the mountain-scaling strategy to which the 60th Infantry had been committed since 6 August.

Colonel Smythe's worries were justified when, after jumping off at 0600, 9 August, his battalions just barely got to the Simeto River's west bank where they were halted by heavy enemy fire. A try that night also failed to get them across the river. Although the regiment managed to clear the west bank of the river for some distance on 10 August and make contact with the British 78th Division off to the south, it could not cross the river. General Eddy thereupon sent the 60th Infantry back into the mountains to outflank Randazzo from the north, and brought up Flint's 39th Infantry (now almost fully recovered from the Troina battle) to resume the advance along Highway 120.

At 0645, 11 August, the 39th Infantry crossed the Simeto River without incident, continued to the east for another several miles, but at the Maletto road junction ran into an area where the ground was practically interdicted by German mines. Moving for the most part north of the highway, the 39th Infantry at midnight had two battalions just west of a long ridge about three miles west of Randazzo. Despite the almost total lack of opposition—there was only some artillery and small arms fire along the highway during the day—the 39th Infantry had covered only three and a half miles, obvious testimony to the effectiveness of the German mines.

Coupled with an equally slow advance by the British 78th Division, the ground movement was doing little to halt German evacuation. Not only was the *15th Panzer Grenadier Division* still holding the Randazzo escape route open, but General Rodt was even depleting his front-line units in accordance with Hube's withdrawal plan. Not all was going according to plan, however, for Rodt's units found it increasingly difficult to pass through the Randazzo area because Allied air had destroyed two important highway bridges while other aircraft worked over the entire area almost incessantly. Randazzo itself quickly became one of the most heavily bombed targets in Sicily.[38] German troops began calling the highway through Randazzo the "death road." Despite these difficulties, German casualties were kept comparatively low by strict traffic discipline and by the fact that the German troops, through necessity, had long since learned how to take care of themselves during Allied air attacks.[39]

Early on 12 August the 39th Infantry resumed its advance on Randazzo. On its right, and almost abreast of Flint's front lines, the British 78th Division attacked for Maletto. The British unit took its objective; Flint did not take his. General Rodt required only a few more hours of delay at Randazzo, and he picked out

---

[38] During the first thirteen days of August, Randazzo was hit by a total of 425 medium bomber, 249 light bomber, and 72 fighter-bomber sorties. See Craven and Cate, eds., vol. II, *Europe: TORCH to POINTBLANK*, p. 470.

[39] MS #R-145, The Evacuation of Sicily, ch. XVI of Axis Tactical Operations in Sicily, July-August 1943 (Bauer), p. 22.

THE AMERICANS AND THE BRITISH MEET AT RANDAZZO, *13 August.* From the left: Col George A. Smith, Col. H. A. Flint, Maj. Gen. Vyvyan Evelegh, and Brig. Gen. E. E. Cass.

the 39th Infantry as the Allied unit representing the most serious threat to the town. Accordingly, heavy fire was laid on the approaching Americans.

In the meantime, DeRohan's 60th Infantry tried to make its presence felt. But the distance the regiment had to travel and the mountainous country through which it had to move precluded its having any real effect on the situation along the highway. The 2d Battalion, 60th Infantry, finally managed to make its way into Floresta (on the road north of Randazzo) early on 13 August, but the advance fell hours short of catching any of Rodt's troops. During the evening of 12 August, Rodt had pulled his units out of Randazzo and Floresta, one group going back through Novara di Sicilia, the others north to and along Highway 113, preceding the *29th Panzer Grenadier Division.*

The closing scene of the Randazzo operation came early on 13 August. American patrols probed cautiously into the shattered town, followed by an infantry battalion. Just a short time later, the British 78th Division arrived on the scene. Like Troina, the capture of Randazzo was anticlimactic. Rodt had been able to make good his escape by excellent use of the terrain, liberal use of mines and demolitions, and by the almost complete absence of any Allied ground threat to his escape routes.[40]

The advances registered by the U.S. 9th and British 78th Divisions, while slow, were faster than those made by units of the British Eighth Army on the eastern side of Mount Etna. Montgomery, still ignoring Admiral McGrigor's Inshore Squadron as a possible means of speeding up his advance, even went so far as to try a two-division attack across the southern slopes of Mount Etna. The push was slow and costly and gained little ground. With every advantage of terrain, General Conrath, using the *Hermann Goering Division,* fought an almost leisurely withdrawal battle, fending off the British with a part of his force, sending the remainder to Messina to cross the strait.

---

[40] See 39th, 47th, and 60th Inf Regt AAR's, 5–13 Aug 43; 9th Inf Div AAR.

CHAPTER XX

# Brolo

Only along the north coast was the German withdrawal at any time seriously threatened. For that matter, the entire German northern and central sectors almost fell prey to another American amphibious end run, an operation that for a short time altered Hube's carefully conceived timetable for the evacuation of Sicily.[1]

After relieving Colonel Bernard's battalion at the Rosmarino River on 8 August, Colonel Sherman's 7th Infantry had pushed on east along Highway 113 against steadily stiffening German resistance. By the evening of 10 August, after being knocked back once, the 7th Infantry gained a foothold across the Zappulla River just south of the highway crossing. The opposing *71st Panzer Grenadier Regiment* pulled back up the slopes of the Naso ridge roughly in line with Cape Orlando. It had been unable to delay the 3d Division advance until 12 August, as originally contemplated.

The new German defensive line looked as formidable as that at San Fratello, but Patton, Bradley, and Truscott were not disposed to pick at this line. Even as the 7th Infantry fought to cross the Zappulla River, Truscott sent Johnson's 15th Infantry inland to cross the river south of Sherman in order to gain the ridge below Naso and roll up the German line. This was to be the division's main effort. General Patton, however, had another idea on how he could more quickly reduce the Naso ridge position.

Wanting desperately to get to Messina ahead of the Eighth Army and "trying to win a horse race to the last big town," [2] Patton called General Bradley to his command post on 10 August and ordered an amphibious end run for the next morning. The maneuver was to be similar to the

---

[1] The account of the battle at Brolo and along the Naso ridge line, unless otherwise noted, is based on the reports of operations and journals of the units involved; Truscott, *Command Missions*, pp. 234-40; Morison, *Sicily—Salerno—Anzio*, pp. 203-05; Rpt, USS *Philadelphia* to CinC U.S. Fleet, 22 Aug 43, sub: Opns From 10 to 18 Aug 43, in 6-1.1008/43; Maj. James L. Packman, The Operations of the 2d Battalion (Reinforced), 30th Infantry Regiment in the Amphibious Attack on Brolo, 11-12 August 1943 (Fort Benning, Georgia, 1950); MS #R-144 (Bauer), pp. 60-63; Taggart, ed., *History of the Third Infantry Division*, pp. 68-71; Prohme, *History of the 30th Infantry Regiment*, pp. 65-70; White, *From Fedala to Berchtesgaden*, pp. 34-37; Bradley, *A Soldier's Story*, pp. 158-59. See also, comments of Truscott and Bernard on this MS.

The account of the Brolo landing from the enemy side is based principally on Fries in MS #T-2 (Fries *et al.*), supplemented and corrected by entries in OKH, *Tagesmeldungen West*; OB SUED, *Meldungen*; IT 99c; Faldella, *Lo sbarco*; and German and Italian maps for the days in question.

The units participating in the amphibious landings as part of Bernard's task force were later awarded the Distinguished Unit Citation (WD GO 44, 30 May 44). Bernard was awarded the Silver Star.

[2] Semmes, *Portrait of Patton*, p. 167.

one executed three days before. Patton had wanted to launch the operation on the morning of the 10th in conjunction with the 15th Infantry's turning movement, but a Luftwaffe attack the evening before had sunk one of the LST's earmarked to lift the task force. This setback, together with the 7th Infantry's trouble at the Zappulla, induced the Seventh Army commander to call off the operation for twenty-four hours.[3] Now Patton was in no mood for another postponement, and he left no doubt in Bradley's mind of this fact.

Patton was not the only American who was keen on beating Montgomery into Messina. Of late, several unfortunate remarks had allegedly been made by the British Broadcasting Corporation (the BBC)—the going on the Seventh Army front had been so easy that the troops were eating grapes and swimming while the Eighth Army was fighting hard against strong German opposition. Because the BBC was the principal radio service heard by all the troops in Sicily, Americans were quite upset by the disparaging comments. Many an American, like Patton, wanted to get to Messina ahead of the British in order to give the lie to these remarks.[4] Besides, the Seventh Army's capture of Palermo, its rapid and successful dash across western Sicily, and its entire conduct thus far in the campaign had whetted American appetites for the greater prize: to beat the proud and vaunted Eighth Army to Messina. The success of the Seventh Army had, for the first time, enabled Americans in the Mediterranean theater to hold their heads high among British and other Allied soldiers, who had been somewhat doubtful of the American soldier's ability after Kasserine.

General Truscott, initially at least, agreed with the plan. He apparently felt that the flanking 15th Infantry could occupy the Naso ridge on the evening of 10 August. This would put the 15th in position to link up quickly with the amphibious task force.

But the 15th Infantry did not get to the Naso ridge on the 10th. Although one battalion progressed as far as the little town of Mirto, overlooking the river, enemy fire from across the way forced a halt and delayed the arrival of the other two battalions. Not until 2100 did the last of the battalions close in the new area. In addition, the lack of roads prevented artillery units from displacing forward to support a further advance. These factors, and the rough terrain, prevented any move by the 15th Infantry across the Zappulla River that evening.

With things not working out as he had planned, Truscott wanted to postpone Bernard's landing for another twenty-four hours. When the Bernard task force had been established, General Keyes had assured Truscott that the force would be entirely under Truscott's command and that he would have the responsibility for the timing of any operation involving the force. A delay, Truscott believed, would permit both the 7th and 15th Infantry Regiments to get into better positions from which to move forward to effect a quick link-up with the seaborne forces. As the situation on the evening of 10 August appeared to him, Truscott doubted that the two regiments could get through the Naso ridge positions fast

---

[3] Seventh Army G-3 Jnl, entries 83, 8 Aug 43 and 68, 10 Aug 43. The LST sunk was the same one that had previously been damaged, but had nevertheless participated in the San Fratello landing.

[4] Butcher, *My Three Years With Eisenhower*, pp. 384, 388.

PILLBOX OVERLOOKING HIGHWAY 113, *east of the Zappulla River crossing.*

enough to save Bernard's small force from the expected German reaction.

When General Keyes arrived at the 3d Division's command post that evening to see how the planning was coming along, Truscott informed the deputy commander of his desire to postpone the end run. Knowing full well Patton's intense feeling, Keyes replied that he doubted whether the army commander would agree to any postponement. Furthermore, Keyes said, Patton had arranged for a large number of correspondents to accompany Bernard's force, and Patton would not relish having to tell the writers that the end run had again been delayed. Patton wanted no unfavorable publicity for the Seventh Army.

Nevertheless, Truscott picked up the telephone and called General Bradley. He explained the situation to the II Corps commander and his desire to postpone the landing. Bradley agreed, and tried to get Patton to agree. But his plea fell on deaf ears. Patton insisted that the landing proceed as scheduled. Shortly thereafter, Keyes called Patton and stated that Truscott did not want to carry out the landing. Truscott, called to the telephone, tried to explain his reasons for wanting to delay, but Patton was in no mood to listen. "Dammit," Patton said, "The operation will go on." In the face of this bald statement, what could Truscott do? He issued orders to Bernard to load his force for the landing.

*Link-up.* This was what worried Truscott. How to effect a quick link-up be-

CAPE ORLANDO *(extreme left center) with Naso ridge rising inland. The railway can be detected running along the coast line. Route 113 hugs the base of Naso ridge.*

came the major problem at the 3d Division's command post the evening of 10 August. At the time Patton brusquely concluded his telephone conversation with Truscott, no 3d Division battalion was within ten miles of Bernard's objective—Monte Cipolla, a steep hill about midway between the Naso and Brolo Rivers which dominated the coastal highway and the ground to the east and west.[5] The coastal highway constituted the *29th Panzer Grenadier Division*'s main escape route to the east, and Truscott knew that German reaction to Bernard's landing would be swift and heavy. Accordingly, the 3d Division commander committed every element in the division, including the recently attached 3d Ranger Battalion, to break through the Naso ridge line defenses. From left to right he deployed the remainder of the 30th Infantry, then the Rangers, then the 7th Infantry, and, finally, the 15th Infantry.

Even as General Truscott prepared his link-up plan, the bulk of the *29th Panzer Grenadier Division* continued to hold its portion of the Tortorici line. Farther to the south, the *15th Panzer Grenadier Di-*

---

[5] On the 1:50,000 map this hill is shown as Monte Criole; on the 1:100,000 map, as Monte Cipolla. In the unit After Action Reports, the term Monte Creole is used. For the purposes of this narrative, the designation as shown on the 1:100,000 map is used.

BROLO BEACH, *from the east, showing the nose of Monte Cipolla.*

*vision* was holding the 9th Division at bay along the Simeto River, although it was then in the process of pulling back into Randazzo.

Immediately in the rear of General Fries' main line of resistance along the Naso ridge, a fairly strong German force was stationed in and east of the town of Brolo maintaining guard along the north coast against the kind of landing the Americans had made at San Fratello. Under Col. Fritz Polack, it consisted of the *29th Artillery Regiment,* containing the regimental headquarters; the headquarters of the regiment's antiaircraft artillery battalion with two 20-mm. four-barreled antiaircraft guns; and parts of the *1st Battalion, 71st Panzer Grenadier Regiment.* Polack had located his headquarters on the northeastern slopes of Monte Cipolla; the bulk of his troops stretched eastward along the coast from Brolo.

At 1800, 10 August, Colonel Bernard's troops completed loading near Caronia and put to sea—one LST, two LCI's, and six LCT's covered by the *Philadelphia* and six destroyers. At 0100 the next morning (11 August) the small task force arrived some three thousand yards off the landing beach, and the troops quickly loaded in LCVP's and Dukws for the final run-in. Thus far, Colonel Polack's beach defenders showed no sign of having discovered the amphibious force.

The terrain in the landing area was dominated by Monte Cipolla, the base of which lies some 450 yards inland from the beach, the top of which—divided into two small knobs—reaches an altitude of some 750 feet. The slopes are precipitous, and the northeast nose—on which Polack's headquarters was located—constituted the only usable approach to the knob nearest the beach. The terrain inland from the beach rises in terraces to the base of the hill. The terraces themselves are stone-faced, and many other stone fences and drainage ditches crisscross the area. Covered with lemon trees, this area was soon to be called "the flats." Parallel to the beach and only a hundred yards inland, a thirteen-foot railroad embankment, through which ran several small underpasses, extended east and west bisecting the flats, while the coastal highway, another three hundred yards inland, skirted the base of Monte Cipolla.

Colonel Bernard's plan for the operation was fairly simple. He planned to land Company E and the naval beach marking party at 0230 in the first wave. The rifle company was to destroy any beach defenses, clear the lemon grove between the railroad embankment and the highway, and block the entrances to the beach from the east and west. Fifteen minutes later, the tank platoon and the platoon of combat engineers were to land: the tanks, to reinforce Company E, the engineers, after assisting the tanks ashore, to make ready to receive the two self-propelled artillery batteries scheduled to land in the fourth wave. In the third wave, due to land at 0300, Bernard put his headquarters and the other three lettered companies of the infantry battalion. Companies F and G were to make their way up Monte Cipolla, with Company F to occupy the knob nearest the coast. After landing, Company H was to send one section of machine guns to each of the rifle companies and a section of 81-mm. mortars to each of the two companies on the hill. Finally, at 0315, the two field artillery batteries, the naval gunfire liaison officer, and fifteen mules (the battalion's ammunition train) were to land. The artillery batteries were to go into

ENEMY VIEW *of landing area at Brolo, from the northeast nose of Monte Cipolla.*

position in the lemon grove in the flats with Battery B firing to the west, Battery A to the east. Once established on their objectives, the units were to dig in, block any German attempt to withdraw to the east from the Naso ridge, and defend until relieved by the main portion of the 3d Division.

The final run-in to the beaches started at 0210. At 0243, thirteen minutes late, the first wave touched down. (*Map 8*) Company E streamed from its five LCVP's and splashed ashore against no opposition. Quickly cutting passages through a double-apron barbed wire fence twenty yards inland, the rifle company crossed the railroad embankment and paused briefly to reorganize. Pushing on, the company soon cleared the lemon grove, capturing ten Germans in the process without having to fire a shot. As one rifle platoon and the weapons platoon swung to the right to block the Naso River crossing, the remainder of the company turned to the left to block the railroad and highway bridges across the Brolo River.

The second wave landed almost on the heels of the first. Although the tanks moved quickly up to the railroad embankment, intending to go through the several underpasses to support Company E, the passageways proved too small. As the tank platoon leader dismounted to search for a way around the obstacle, an Engineer officer appeared and offered his services in seeking a way either around or over the embankment His offer accepted, the Engineer officer rushed off one way, to the east, while the tank platoon leader headed in the other direction.

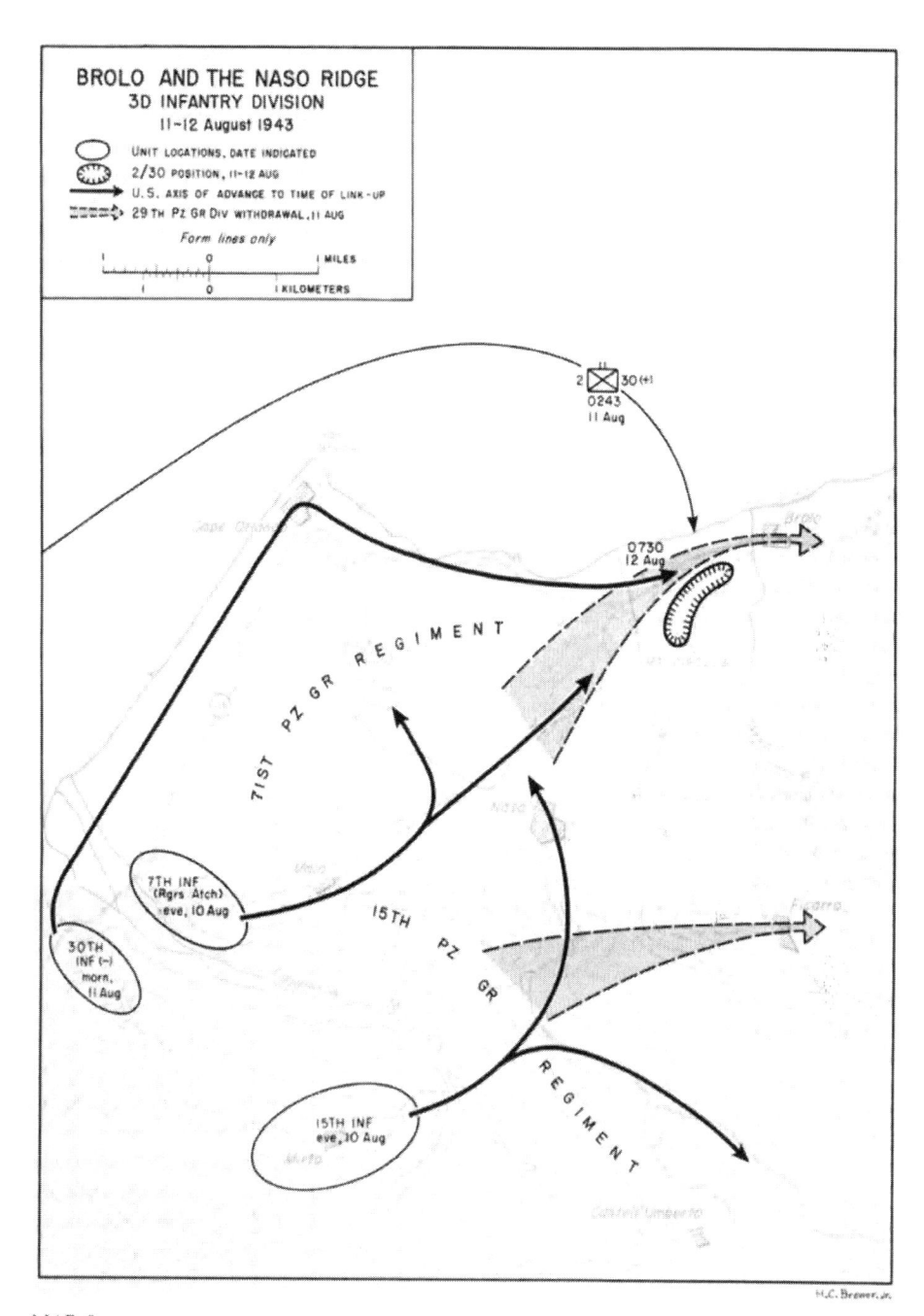

MAP 8

Right on schedule, part of the third wave—Companies F and G in LCT's—landed, followed in another fifteen minutes by sixteen Dukws carrying the rest of the wave: Bernard, his headquarters, and Company H, which promptly dispatched its sections to support the rifle companies. The Dukws continued inland following the two rifle companies until they, too, had to halt because of the railroad embankment. At 0330, the fourth and last wave touched down; by 0400, Bernard's entire force was ashore without loss. By this time, Company E was in its blocking positions.

Companies F and G reached the highway without incident at 0345. At the railroad, the Engineer officer returned to the tanks and reported that he had found a way around the thirteen-foot high embankment, via the Brolo River bed. The tank officer had not yet returned, so the Engineer officer offered to guide the two artillery batteries into position. His offer was accepted and the artillery pieces started to move slowly toward the east. The tank commander returned about this time and said that he, too, had located a bypass route, via the Naso River bed, and he started his tanks moving toward that exit.

Even as the tanks and artillery pieces began moving out, half of Companies F and G crossed the highway and began ascending Monte Cipolla by its northeast nose, close to the junction of Highway 113 and the secondary road which wound inland to the small mountain town of Ficarra. Thus far, not a shot had been fired. Colonel Polack's coast defense units showed no signs of having discovered the landing.

A German motorcycle, apparently heading for Naso, suddenly came roaring down the highway. Freezing in place, the Americans allowed the motorcycle to pass. They then continued crossing the highway and ascending Monte Cipolla's slopes. The element of surprise still might have been maintained had not a German half-track approached from the west. Seeing troops on the road, the driver halted his vehicle. As he rose from his seat to see whose troops these were, some twenty anxious American riflemen opened fire. The driver slumped back in his seat, dead. Seconds later, a small sedan with two occupants pulled up behind the half-track. A German officer stepped out to see what had happened. A well-placed bazooka round exploded the car, killing the officer and wounding the driver.

The noise of the rifle fire and the exploding of the bazooka round woke all Germans in the neighborhood, including Colonel Polack and his headquarters troops on Monte Cipolla. Gathering fifteen men around him, Polack opened fire on the leading elements of Companies F and G. Machine guns in Brolo began to fire seaward, while other machine guns and the 20-mm. guns located on high ground east of Brolo opened up on the landing beach. By the light of flares, Polack's men delivered accurate machine gun fire that cut down several of the Americans. But the rest pushed on, grabbing at long shoots of grass and small bushes to pull themselves up the steep slope.

Seeing that his headquarters personnel could not stop the Americans, Polack gathered up the unit's classified documents (including Hube's evacuation order of 10 August) and made his way down the far slopes of the hill into Brolo. Here, from a nearby switchboard, he called General Fries and informed the division comman-

DIGGING IN A MACHINE GUN POSITION *on Monte Cipolla, 11 August.*

der of the situation. For the first time, Fries knew that the bulk of his division was in danger of being cut off. He ordered Polack to attack the American beachhead as soon as possible, using the elements of the *1st Battalion, 71st Panzer Grenadier Regiment*, the antiaircraft unit, and a few German tanks located east of Brolo.

Companies F and G managed to reach the top of Monte Cipolla at 0530; within thirty minutes both companies were dug in. Down on the flats, however, the artillery and tanks were having a difficult time trying to get into position to support the rifle companies. Three of the tanks bellied trying to cross ditches on the beach side of the railroad; the last two were damaged trying to knock down stone fences. Though the tanks could be used as fixed guns, their inability to maneuver made them practically useless in the action that was soon to follow. The artillery batteries were more fortunate, and though they had difficulty traversing ditches and terraces, they managed to get around the embankment and into firing positions before daylight in the lemon grove north of the highway.

With the coming of daylight, Polack's men in Brolo turned their guns from the beaches and began sweeping the eastern slopes of Monte Cipolla. Bernard's men soon found it hazardous to make the long climb down to the beach, and those on the beach found it equally hazardous to climb up. Some fifteen men—mainly communications personnel and ammunition bearers—were killed during the course of the early morning trying to work on the slopes of the hill. The battalion's mule train carrying badly needed ammunition from the Dukws up to the machine guns and mortars on top of the hill lost all but two of its fifteen animals to the German fire. From this time on, ammunition resupply was hazardous, spotty, and largely unsuccessful.

Trying to aid Bernard's men, the *Philadelphia* had opened fire shortly after 0530 at prearranged targets in the area, and then shifted her fires under the shore party's direction to Polack's units massing to strike back at the seaborne force. To the west, General Fries had ordered the *6th Company, 15th Panzer Grenadier Regiment* (then deployed in a reserve position near Naso), to attack the American beachhead from the east. He also ordered a smaller German force at Ficarra to attack the Americans he now knew to be on Monte Cipolla.

The first German ground reaction noted by Bernard's companies came at 0700 when the Germans from Ficarra sent two reconnaissance vehicles down the secondary road to probe the American lines. Company G allowed the two vehicles to come close, opened rapid fire, set the vehicles on fire, and scattered the occupants. Shortly thereafter, the main German force of thirty men began working their way down the Brolo River bed. Again Company G allowed the Germans to come close before opening fire. Dropping in mortar concentrations and opening up with the heavy machine guns, Company G proceeded to decimate the German force. The survivors beat a hasty retreat up the river bed, dragging their wounded with them.

For almost an hour the situation remained fairly quiet. Then, the *6th Company*—about one hundred strong—made its effort down the Naso River bed, marching boldly forward. Engaged by Company H's machine guns, the Germans stopped and began deploying. But before they could get into an extended formation, Company H's mortars opened fire, and round after round dropped in on the German company. Trapped between the high banks of the river, the Germans broke and ran. The Americans estimated they killed and wounded at least seventy of the attacking force. This thrust proved to be the last German attack from the south, and this sector remained fairly quiet until after darkness fell.

General Fries, nevertheless, continued his efforts to knock Bernard's men off their lofty perch. Placing heavy fire on all points on the hilltop and on the slopes of the hill, the German commander at 0900 started a truck-borne infantry column—another of his reserve units—eastward from Cape Orlando toward the Naso River. Fries was deliberately weakening his Naso ridge positions in attempts to open a way to the east. He had to regain control of the coastal highway if he expected to get the bulk of his division out of the American trap.

The *Philadelphia* spotted the German column and opened fire, knocking out several vehicles and forcing the rest to leave the highway. Continued firing scattered the German infantrymen. Thirty minutes later, an artillery forward observer on Monte Cipolla spotted two German tanks with some infantry on the highway, also moving toward the Naso River. Bringing Battery A in on the target, the forward observer forced the tanks to leave the road well before they could reach the river, and the German infantrymen to seek shelter north of the highway.

By this time, Bernard's 81-mm. mortars, because of the mule train's failure to get up the hill, were low on ammunition and could fire only harassing missions in support of the artillery batteries. Bernard's firepower was reduced even further when, at 1025, the *Philadelphia* and her covering destroyers set a course for Palermo. Having attended to all the prearranged targets and having received no more requests for fire after the shoot on the truck convoy, Admiral Davidson figured that his task had been accomplished and that the two field artillery batteries could handle any further German threat. Thus far, only four enemy aircraft—Italian torpedo-bombers—had made any sort of threatening gesture toward the American warships, but Davidson felt that the longer he lay off Brolo the greater the danger that enemy air would strike at his ships. Since he was assured of Allied air cover only until 1200, Davidson thought it wise to have the protection of the shore-based Allied antiaircraft guns at Palermo.

To the west and across the Naso ridge, the units of the 3d Division which General Truscott had so carefully lined up the preceding evening had started their attacks to break Fries' hold and link up with Bernard's force. In his command post on the eastern edge of Terranova, Truscott anxiously awaited the outcome of the drive. Having committed everything he had to the effort, there was nothing more he could do but wait. Leaving nothing to chance, Truscott had dispatched a liaison officer, Capt. Walter K. Millar, with a powerful jeep-mounted radio, to go along with Bernard's force. Through this radio, Truscott hoped to keep track of the situation at Monte Cipolla. Throughout the early morning, starting at 0600, Millar's messages were most reassuring, and General Truscott began to feel better even though the progress of his other units up the Naso ridge was slow in the face of extensive German mine fields and of light to heavy German fire.

The German division was in a bad way. By noon, Fries had pulled the bulk of the *15th Panzer Grenadier Regiment* back behind the Naso River. Near the coast, the *71st Panzer Grenadier Regiment* was caught between the 7th Infantry on the west and Bernard's battalion on the east. Whereas the *15th Panzer Grenadier Regiment* had a relatively free and protected route to the rear from the Naso ridge—by moving cross-country through Ficarra to San Angelo di Brolo (on the first defensive phase line as laid down by General Hube)—the northern German regiment had only the coastal highway for withdrawal. Fries ordered the regiment to fight to open a way to the east by falling back off the Naso ridge, first behind the Naso River, then behind the Brolo River, and then to Piramo, the northern hinge of Hube's first phase line.

With these orders Lt. Col. Walter Krueger, commanding the *71st*, began assembling what troops he could spare to try to force a passage along the highway. Krueger also turned one of his attached field artillery battalions around and began firing to the east.

Colonel Polack continued his efforts to

LT. COL. LYLE A. BERNARD AND HIS RADIOMAN *in the command post atop Monte Cipolla.*

assemble his scattered units for an attack against the American beachhead. By 1100, Polack managed to get together two infantry companies mounted on personnel carriers plus several tanks, brought them into Brolo, and began probing toward Company E along the Brolo River.

Polack's assembling of troops did not go unnoticed on Monte Cipolla. Company H's mortars began firing slowly on the town. Battery B joined in, but, because of the short range, encountered some difficulty in placing effective fire on the town. Polack sent snipers and machine guns into the buildings overlooking the river to keep up a steady fire on the single American rifle platoon guarding the highway bridge. At 1140, seriously worried by this new German threat, Bernard began relaying messages by radio through Company E to Captain Millar requesting an air strike and naval gunfire on Brolo. Twenty minutes later, Bernard asked for long-range artillery support: the 3d Division had some attached 155-mm. guns (Long Toms) that could reach Brolo, although the town was at the extreme range of these guns.

Bernard's first message caused a stir at Truscott's command post in Terranova.

The 3d Division commander did not know that Admiral Davidson had withdrawn the warships and he could not understand why Bernard was asking for naval support. Thinking that Bernard's shore fire control party's radio had gone bad, he got several of his staff officers to telephone urgent messages to Seventh Army for naval and air support. These requests had just gone out when Bernard's second message came in. Truscott ordered the 155-mm. guns—though firing at the maximum range—to open fire on Brolo. At the same time, he renewed the requests for naval and air help. Word on the naval support was slow to arrive, but Seventh Army stated that the XII Air Support Command had promised an air mission, although it could not give a specific time when the mission would be flown or the number of planes to participate. General Truscott was really worried now—his forward units were still moving slowly up the Naso ridge, but they were still some hours away from a linkup. He knew Bernard's force was too small to beat off a serious German counterattack.

Actually, help was already on the way. Just as Admiral Davidson's warships were about to enter Palermo harbor, the Admiral received word from TF 88's liaison officer at the Seventh Army of Truscott's urgent request for gunfire support. Turning the cruiser back to the east, taking two destroyers along to cover, Davidson sped back along the coast, and shortly after 1400 began firing on Polack's troops in and around Brolo. By this time, Bernard was adjusting the 155-mm. guns on Brolo. And just as the *Philadelphia* opened fire, the air strike materialized in the form of twelve A-36's that dropped bombs on Brolo and on the area just east of the town. Thirty minutes later, twelve more A-36's zoomed in over the area and strafed the German assemblage.

The combination of American fires proved too much. Polack's men scattered, trying to avoid the rain of American shells. Three German tanks remained in Brolo, however, huddled near the stone buildings, and escaped damage. Unfortunately, at just this moment, the shore fire control party's radio link with the *Philadelphia* stopped functioning. Not wanting to fire on targets without shore control, and since friendly air seemed to have the situation well in hand, Admiral Davidson at 1505 withdrew his warships a second time and turned again for Palermo.

Now a new threat to Bernard's beachhead appeared. On the west side of the Naso River, Colonel Krueger had managed to get together a battalion of infantry for an attack across the river. The rest of his regiment he left in position to delay any American attack from Naso or Cape Orlando. At about the same time, General Truscott left his command post to visit his forward regiments; he wanted personally to urge them on with all possible speed. Truscott, because of the German mines and demolished roads, could reach only the 30th Infantry which was then trying to cross the coastal flats into Cape Orlando. From Colonel Rogers' command post, Truscott called Colonel Sherman and told the 7th Infantry commander to forget the town of Naso and push forward as quickly as possible on Rogers' right.

The 1st and 3d Battalions, 30th Infantry, began crossing the Zappulla River at 1420 under a smoke screen laid down by supporting chemical mortars. The 1st Battalion soon ran into terrain that was heavily mined and booby-trapped, and moved only slowly through the coastal flats toward Cape Orlando. The 3d Battalion also was slowed by much the same type of obstacle, but it managed to keep pace with the 1st Battalion. The 7th Infantry renewed its attack at 1500 straight up the west slopes of the Naso ridge, but its advance, too, slowed in the face of extensive mined areas. Along the ridge, Colonel Krueger's remaining defenders strengthened the mined areas with sporadic artillery fire, frequent periods of heavy small arms fire, and with just enough infantry action to keep the American units from rushing quickly forward.

Within the beachhead, the situation worsened by the minute. After the withdrawal of the American warships, and the ending of the air strike, the three German tanks that had taken shelter in Brolo, supported by a few infantrymen, started toward the eastern end of the highway bridge. The one American platoon guarding the bridge crossing managed to drive off the German foot soldiers, whereupon, the tanks halted just at the river's edge and opened fire on this annoying group of Americans. At the same time, Polack's 20-mm. guns (undamaged by either the naval or air strikes) resumed heavy firing on the flats and on Monte Cipolla's slopes. From the west, Krueger's field artillery battery joined in. On Monte Cipolla, Bernard rushed off another message to General Truscott: "Repeat air and navy immediately . . . Situation still critical."

Again, Admiral Davidson was flashed the word that his guns were needed at Brolo; again, the XII Air Support Command promised another air strike, again without mentioning numbers of planes or time of mission.

Before either Davidson's warships or Allied planes could come to Bernard's aid, the three German tanks crossed the Brolo River. The platoon of American infantrymen scattered, most moving toward the beach to join with the other platoon at the railroad bridge. As the tanks waddled slowly down the highway, Battery B tried to engage them with direct fire, but a high wall near the bridge not only limited observation but also prevented the howitzers from opening fire. German infantrymen, who crossed behind the tanks, turned to engage the Americans near the railroad bridge. The tanks continued moving slowly along the road, seemingly intent on going through the American beachhead. Battery B tried to displace to positions from which it could fire on the tanks, but the Germans spotted this movement. In the ensuing fire fight, the tanks knocked out two of the American guns and two ammunition half-tracks. The exploding ammunition drove the Battery B crews from their other two guns, although one crew returned to its vehicle and moved it onto the highway, just around a bend in the road. No sooner had it gone into position than the lead German tank rounded the bend. The American artillery crew fired first, and missed. Then the tank fired, and also missed. The second rounds from both vehicles, fired almost simultaneously, struck home. Both the tank and the self-propelled gun started to burn furiously.

From Monte Cipolla, Company F, overlooking the fight below, sent a shower of rifle fire on the other two German tanks without much effect. Company H's mortars and machine guns remained silent, hoarding their few remaining rounds for a last-ditch stand.

On the right, Battery A had finally managed to maneuver its guns into position to fire on the last two German tanks. The battery set one on fire, whereupon the last turned and trundled slowly back to the east. Before recrossing the river into Brolo, the tank paused for a brief moment to destroy the unmanned but still serviceable Battery B howitzer. The German infantrymen followed the tank back across the river.

Worried about Company E, Bernard started Company F down Monte Cipolla to take over the Brolo River defenses, telling Company F's commander to send what he could find of Company E to the Naso River to defend from that direction. One platoon of Company E was still in position there, and Bernard hoped that by consolidating the remnants of Company E into one group, he could use it to hold on to the highway crossing. Because of continued German fire, Company F's progress down the hill was slow, and it was almost 1600 before the company debouched on to the flats and moved to the river line.

Unfortunately, Company F's arrival in the flats coincided with the promised air strike. Seven A-36's swept in low over Monte Cipolla at just about 1600. Apparently not fully oriented to the ground, the pilots dropped two bombs on Bernard's command post, killing and wounding nineteen men, and the rest on Battery A's howitzers. Though Company F was unscathed, when the smoke cleared the infantrymen discovered that the four remaining artillery pieces had been destroyed. With nothing left to support the two companies in the flats, Bernard ordered everybody up onto Monte Cipolla. Bernard figured the time had come to make his last-ditch stand.

The *Philadelphia* arrived back on the scene just as Bernard finished ordering everybody up out of the low ground. Seeing the vessels, an officer from the shore fire control party commandeered a Dukw to take him out to the cruiser to get supporting fires. Through some misunderstanding, three of the other Dukws (all loaded with ammunition) followed. An artillery officer took a fifth Dukw to recall the three carrying ammunition. Thus, practically all of the task force's remaining ammunition supply headed out to sea. The Dukws managed to make the cross-water run successfully. After taking the men aboard, the cruiser began firing on Cape Orlando, Brolo, and the highway east of Brolo. Admiral Davidson did not want to bring the fires in any closer to Monte Cipolla.[6]

After about fifteen minutes of naval fire, just before 1700, eight German aircraft struck the three American warships. In a brisk thirty-minute fight which featured violent evasive actions by the ships, near misses from German bombs, and the appearance of friendly aircraft, only one German plane managed to make its escape. The cruiser claimed five of those shot down. Again, Admiral Davidson decided to withdraw his warships. He was still devoid of communications with Bernard's force; his ships were still prey for enemy air attacks. He could see nothing that he could do to ease Bernard's situation. Again, the warships set a course for Palermo, this time going all the way.

Company F, with men from the engineer platoon and the artillery batteries, got back up on Monte Cipolla before complete darkness set in. Bernard expended the last of his mortar ammunition in a concen-

---

[6] In all, the *Philadelphia* expended 1,062 six-inch rounds during the day.

tration on a suspected German assembly area across the Naso River. This he followed with rifle and machine gun fire on the bridge to cover Company E's disengagement. The latter unit, still badly disorganized, began dribbling in to Bernard's command post a short time later. Some of the company never made it to the hill, but dug in on the flats for the night, fighting as best they could with rifles and hand grenades against the retiring German columns. Bernard passed the word for the units on Monte Cipolla to break into small groups and move back toward the 3d Division's lines as soon after daybreak as possible.

By 1900, the *71st Panzer Grenadier Regiment* was in control of the highway and a narrow stretch of land on each side. Glad to have opened an escape route, it paid little attention to Company E's survivors still in the flats. At 2200, Colonel Krueger began withdrawing his units to the east, taking with him his vehicles. Krueger made no attempt against Monte Cipolla.

At his command post in Terranova, General Truscott was becoming increasingly worried about Bernard's small force. Captain Millar, before ascending Monte Cipolla, had sent one last message just before 1900 to General Truscott and then destroyed his radio set. Only part of the message (which asked again for naval support) got through; General Truscott felt that the small American force had been overrun before the complete message could be dispatched: he could see "the final German assault swarming over our gallant comrades." To add to his worries, both the 7th and 30th Infantry Regiments reported they had lost contact with their leading battalions; the units had outrun their communications with the regimental command posts.

Unknown to General Truscott, both regiments by 2200 had gained the Naso ridge and were even then starting down the eastern slopes to link up with Bernard's force. By this time, the bulk of Colonel Krueger's regiment had made good its escape to the east, past the trap which had been so neatly set but which could not be held.

The 1st Battalion, 30th Infantry, crossed the Naso River and entered the flats. Men from Company E leaped from their hiding places to greet the relieving force. Patrols were immediately dispatched to Monte Cipolla to locate Colonel Bernard, who, hearing the sounds of firing which marked the approach of the bulk of the division, rescinded his previous instructions for the men to make their way to the east after daybreak. At 0730, 12 August, Bernard made contact with a 1st Battalion patrol. His force—minus 177 men killed, wounded, and missing—came down off the hill.

The 3d Battalion, 30th Infantry, moved through to take up the pursuit of the *29th Panzer Grenadier Division,* which had been forced to give up its portion of the Tortorici line twenty-four hours ahead of time. For a short while, this withdrawal had posed a threat to General Rodt's evacuation of Randazzo. But the *29th* was able to slip into position in front of Patti, where Rodt's escape route from Randazzo came out to the north coast. Here, aided by the terrain, Fries was not only able to gain back the day he had lost, but to hold open Rodt's escape route as well.

Except for forcing General Fries to give up the Naso ridge a day ahead of time, no mean feat considering the natural defensive strength of the position, Bernard's landing accomplished little. But the operation had come close to trapping a large part of the *29th Panzer Grenadier Division,* and had come even closer to rolling up the whole northern sector of Hube's defensive line. It was only because Bernard's force was too small, and because continuous air and naval support was not available, that Hube's entire northern flank was not rolled up and cut off from Messina. If a stronger force had been landed—at least an RCT—and if continuous naval and air support had been provided, General Fries could hardly have cleared a way out of the trap along the coastal highway.

Operations against the rear of the German defensive line undoubtedly would have eased the way for the bulk of the 3d Division, and would have made for a quicker link-up. Pressure from front and rear might have so hampered Fries' regiments that probably few if any of the Germans could have made their way to the east. With Fries' division out of the way, advance east along Highway 113 might have been virtually unopposed. In conjunction with American advances from Randazzo, General Truscott might have effectively severed General Rodt's withdrawal routes to Messina. This, in turn, might have led to a rapid dash into Messina where at least a part of the *Hermann Goering Division* could have been prevented from making good its escape.

As it turned out, the *29th Panzer Grenadier Division,* which suffered about the same number of casualties as the 3d Division, made good its get-away. It managed to withdraw most of its heavy equipment to Hube's first phase line just east of Piraino—three miles from Brolo— thus holding open Rodt's escape route to the north coast. If the German division's morale was damaged by this second American amphibious end run—and it must have been—its physical capability for fighting more delaying actions was only slightly weakened.

CHAPTER XXI

# The End of the Campaign

## The Race to Messina

Wasting little time in congratulations, General Truscott urged his men on after General Fries' back-pedaling German division. Tired from their exertions at the Naso ridge, the men of the 3d Division wearily resumed their eastward trek. The preceding five-day battle had been slow, costly, and difficult. The 7th Infantry reported losses of fifteen officers and four hundred men killed, wounded, and missing, a figure approximated by each of the other infantry regiments.

South of the mountains, General Bradley, the II Corps commander, brought the 1st Division back into line. Eddy's 9th Division drew the secondary road leading from Floresta northeastward through Montalbano to Furnari. Huebner's 1st Division was to pass through the British 78th Division east of Randazzo, then turn north to Bivio Salica.[1] If they were able to move fast enough, Bradley believed, the divisions just might catch the German division up north and squeeze it against the 3d Division. (*Map VIII*)

During the evening of 12 August, German units all across the front withdrew to Hube's previously designated first phase line. This line was to be held at least until nightfall on 13 August, whereupon the units were to withdraw again to the east, nearer Messina. Thus, on the north coast, by the morning of 13 August, the *29th Panzer Grenadier Division* as it pulled back some fifteen miles lost contact with the 3d Division. Before moving into the new line east of Falcone (twenty-eight miles east of Cape Orlando)—a line which extended south almost to Novara di Sicilia—German engineers effectively blocked the coastal highway by partially demolishing the highway tunnel at Cape Calavà and, just to the east, by blowing a 150-foot section of the road, bracketed 300 feet high on a cliff, into the sea. It was a masterful demolition job; overcoming it was to become a landmark of American engineer support in Sicily.

Yet even this stratagem would not save the *29th Panzer Grenadier Division*, General Patton felt, if a new plan reached fruition. On the same day (12 August) that Truscott executed the link-up with Bernard's amphibious force near Brolo, Patton had set his staff to preparing still another dash around the Germans' right flank. With the Navy's promise to supply more landing craft, and with General Alexander's permission to use the 2d Battalion, 509th Parachute Infantry, Patton planned a full-scale operation well behind the German defenders. Late on 12 August, Patton's staff came forth with the plan, calling for a landing any time between 14 and 18 August in the Bivio Salica–Barcellona area. The Seventh Army

---
[1] II Corps FO 12, 12 Aug 43.

The Objective, Messina

30TH INFANTRY TROOPS MOVING AROUND THE CAPE CALAVÀ CLIFF *where the roadbed had been blown out by the Germans.*

would retain control of the participating units until such time as those units actually landed.[2]

This attempt to cut off the *29th Panzer Grenadier Division,* and possibly other German units, was to be much more ambitious than either of the earlier amphibious efforts. Patton hoped to cut Highway 113 as well as the secondary road along which the 1st Division would be advancing. The battalion of paratroopers was to drop at 2000, D minus 1, near Barcellona to prevent German forces from moving to the west to relieve the encircled German units, and to seize and hold the highway bridge just west of Barcellona until the seaborne force landed. Colonel Ankcorn's 157th RCT (from the 45th Division), reinforced by a company of medium tanks and a company of 4.2-inch mortars, was to land near Bivio Salica, join with the paratroopers, then attack westward to link up with the 3d Division.

As the Seventh Army staff completed the details for the new end run, the three American divisions then on line kicked off to clear the Messina peninsula. On the north coast, the 15th and 30th Infantry Regiments crossed the Brolo River, the 30th toward Cape Calavà, the 15th cross-country toward Patti. Neither advance was seriously contested.

The 15th Infantry had a more difficult task, for its route led through the mountainous interior over difficult terrain. Yet, the 15th reached Patti long before the 30th, entering the town at 1530. Along the highway, the 30th Infantry had come to an abrupt halt upon reaching the partially demolished tunnel and blown out road section at Cape Calavà. Pausing just long enough to start his foot troops inland around the obstacle and across the neck of the cape, Colonel Rogers loaded two Dukws (which had been in a follow-up motor column for just such a purpose as this) with water, signal equipment, and a few communications personnel and chugged around the cape, rejoining the foot elements east of that point.

The 10th Engineer Battalion moved up to restore the highway for vehicular traffic. By hanging "a bridge in the sky" the engineers were able to permit a jeep—carrying General Truscott—to cross the wooden structure eighteen hours after starting work. Six hours later, after a

---

[2] Seventh Army Directive, 12 Aug 43, in Seventh Army Rpt of Opns, p. D-15; see also, Seventh Army G-3 Jnl, entries 3, 20, 28, and 39, 12 Aug 43.

THE BRIDGE THAT WAS "HUNG IN THE SKY" BY THE 10TH ENGINEER BATTALION

bit of shoring here and there, heavier vehicles began to cross.[3]

By 0300 the following morning, 14 August, the 3d Battalion, 15th Infantry, after a night's march, entered Oliveri. The *29th Panzer Grenadier Division* had again pulled back to the east. It was now on General Hube's second phase line, with the northern hinge resting on the coast town of Furnari. The *15th Panzer Grenadier Division* was well on its way toward completing its transfer to the Italian mainland. Parts of the other German divisions were also moving toward the embarkation points. In fact, by nightfall on 14 August, only one reinforced infantry battalion held the *29th Panzer Grenadier Division's* front. This battalion was to hold the second phase line until dark on 15 August.[4]

At Messina, the German ferrying service had swung into full operation with the arrival of the first troops from the front on the night of 11 August. During this first night, Captain von Liebenstein's craft ran at full capacity until 2045, when the pace slowed and then stopped, partly because

---

[3] Ernie Pyle, *Brave Men* (New York: Henry Holt and Co., 1944), pages 65-73, gives a vivid account of the construction of this bridge. See also Truscott, *Command Missions*, pp. 241-42.

As General Truscott points out in his comments on this MS, it was just as well the Germans did not destroy the tunnel at the same time they were blowing the section of road. "The race to Messina would have ended right there," says Truscott.

[4] MS #R-145 (Bauer), pp. 25-27.

British Wellingtons bombed the strait, partly because troops were slow in reaching the ferrying sites. Despite renewed attacks by Allied bombers, the evacuation resumed during the early morning of 12 August after additional troops from the *15th Panzer Grenadier Division* arrived. On the second night of Hube's evacuation efforts, the night of 12 August, telephone communications between Messina and the mainland failed, and some confusion resulted in getting the naval craft and the ground troops together on the Messina side. Ferrying craft stood by at one of the landing places for three hours, only to leave shortly before the troops finally arrived.

Ferrying did not get under way again until 0200, 13 August. Strong Allied air attacks, persisting until 0500, made it impossible to use the ferries at the narrow part of the strait. But, then, contrary to the original plan of crossing troops only at night, Liebenstein ordered the ferrying continued throughout the 13th. By evening of 13 August, a total of 15,000 men, 1,300 vehicles, 21 tanks, and 22 assault guns had completed the crossing.[5]

While Liebenstein's fleet of small craft lifted German troops and matériel across the strait, the Italian ferrying service operated as best it could with its somewhat limited equipment. The train ferry caught fire on 12 August and was out of commission for forty-eight hours. Motor rafts saved the situation and transported 20,000 men at the rate of 1,000 a trip. In an attempt to relieve the situation, the Italians loaded one of the other inoperable train ferries with heavy artillery, planning to tow it across to the mainland. But after all that work, the Italians could not find a towboat. Eventually, they scuttled the craft to keep the artillery pieces from falling into Allied hands.

The Italians now accepted Hube's previous offer to transport their remaining heavy equipment in German craft. But at the same time, to keep the equipment from falling to the Allies, Hube issued additional instructions to all German units to take charge of any Italian matériel that could not be moved by the Italians. Thus, many pieces of Italian equipment were saved but, at the same time, lost to the Italians, for on the mainland the Germans simply appropriated them for their own divisions. In fact, after completing its evacuation on the evening of 14 August, the *15th Panzer Grenadier Division* found that it had more and better wheeled equipment than at the beginning of the campaign, for the simple reason that the troops had acquired Italian motor vehicles of all kinds before leaving Sicily.[6] Instances were also reported of German commanders who retained Italian personnel, put the men into German uniforms, and refused to let them return to their own units.[7]

Despite these difficulties, the evacuation of Italian personnel from Sicily was virtually completed by 16 August. Generale di Brigata Ettore Monacci, commander of Italian army troops at the *Naval Base Messina*, was the last to leave Messina after setting mines to blow up the port's installations. All told, the Italians evacuated between 70,000 and 75,000 men; from 227 to 500 vehicles; between 75 and 100 artillery pieces; and 12 mules.[8]

---

[5] *Ibid.*, pp. 40-42.

[6] MS #C-077 (Rodt).

[7] Correspondence to and from *Comando Quinta Armata, Stato Maggiore, Situazione, militari reduci dalla Sicilia*, IT 792.

[8] IT 99c, 14 Aug 43; Faldella, *Lo sbarco*, p. 276; Mario Puddù, *Tra due invasioni, campagna d'Italia, 1943-1945* (Rome: A. Nardini, 1952).

The German ferrying service continued operations on the evening of 13 August —the third night—even though British Wellington bombers were again out in force. While these bombing attacks time and again forced cessation of the ferrying service across the neck of the strait, at the wider parts the service proceeded pretty much according to schedule. Concluding that these continued heavy bombing attacks made it almost impossible to conduct any sort of satisfactory ferry service in the narrow part of the strait at night, Liebenstein ordered daylight ferrying service only in this zone, though round-the-clock transfers would continue in the wider parts of the strait. Until the end of the operation, most of the remaining German troops on Sicily were ferried to the Italian mainland during daylight hours. Though the frequent Allied air attacks caused some damage to the embarkation points, the damage was light and quickly repaired, particularly because no heavy bombers appeared over the strait during the day. And thanks to Baade's massed guns, Allied NATAF flyers operating during daylight hours encountered great difficulty in aiming accurately enough to cause any serious damage to either ships or landing points.[9]

Though quite unknown to the Axis, both German and Italian ferrying services were being aided, inadvertently to be sure, by the actions of certain commanders in the Allied hierarchy of command.

Almost since the beginning of the Sicilian operation, General Montgomery had had ample opportunities to launch amphibious end runs around the German defenses in the Catania plain area. Rather than make use of "the priceless asset of sea power, and flexibility of maneuver," Montgomery chose instead to slug his way forward up the difficult east coast road, first with one division, then with two, and then again with one.[10] Montgomery steadfastly refused to launch any amphibious end runs.

Furthermore, there was the failure on the part of the Allied air commanders to assess correctly Hube's evacuation plan: they believed almost to the end that the Axis forces would cross the strait only during the hours of darkness, and that NATAF alone could handle any daylight evacuation attempts. Almost one-half of the available Allied air power—the 869 aircraft that belonged to NASAF—was used in only a limited way to stop the evacuation.[11] True, British Wellington bombers, flying an average of eighty-five sorties each night against Messina, did force Liebenstein to shift from night crossings to day crossings. But except for three daylight U.S. B-17 attacks on Messina, up to 8 August there were no other calls on the NASAF heavies to bomb Messina, the evacuation beaches, the embarkation

---

[9] MS #R-145 (Bauer), pp. 46-47. Craven and Cate (*Europe: TORCH to POINTBLANK*, page 473) list Allied air force claims as follows: 23 ferrying craft destroyed; direct hits on 43 more; near misses on 204. On the other hand, the Axis forces listed their losses as follows: 8 Italian and 7 German craft sunk (only 1 of which was lost in action); 5 Italian and 1 German craft damaged. See also, Roskill, *The War at Sea*, vol. III, pt. I, p. 150; Morison, *Sicily—Salerno—Anzio*, p. 215.

[10] Quotation from Cunningham Despatch, par. 40.

[11] In August 1943, NASAF had 181 U.S. heavy bombers, 130 British and 278 U.S. medium bombers, and 280 fighters and fighter-bombers. NATAF had 112 U.S. medium bombers. 94 British and 43 U.S. light bombers, and 344 British and 377 U.S. fighters and fighter-bombers. See chart in Roskill, *The War at Sea*, vol. III, pt. I, p. 148.

points, and Baade's gun emplacements, until it was too late. In fact, on 11 August, the NATAF commander had even released the heavy bombers from any commitment in the Messina Strait area. On 13 August, when the Germans shifted to daylight crossings, "the land battle [on Sicily] was going so well" that NASAF scheduled a huge raid on the Littorio airfield and Lorenzo marshaling yards near Rome, committing 106 B-17's, 102 B-26's, 66 B-25's, and 135 P-38's to this mission.[12]

Despite numerous signs of Axis withdrawal and evacuation, it was not until 14 August that General Alexander felt the German evacuation had really begun. He radioed this belief to Air Chief Marshal Tedder, but NASAF was committed too deeply to striking at mainland targets to be turned loose against Messina. It did release some medium and light bombers, as well as fighters and fighter-bombers, to assist the NATAF in a round-the-clock pounding of Messina, the strait, and the Italian toe.

The NATAF had undoubtedly tried hard to disrupt Hube's schedule, but the pilots found it almost impossible to penetrate the antiaircraft defenses. "The immense concentration of flak on both sides of the Narrows makes it impossible to go down and really search for targets thoroughly with fighter bombers," reported the Desert Air Force (the U.S. XII Air Support Command's counterpart). "It also greatly restricts the use of light bombers. The Hun knows very well that if we really put up a lot of bomber formations into his main flak concentration, we should have the whole lot unserviceable in no time."[13] Without the support of the U.S. B-17's during the daylight hours, and with Admiral Cunningham's refusal to commit any large warships in the strait area to form a "positive physical barrier," the NATAF pilots faced an almost impossible task.

Thus it was that Hube's evacuation proceeded fairly close to schedule. By 14 August it was too late to catch any sizable number of enemy ground troops forward of Messina. General Patton, however, continued with his plans for launching another amphibious end run.

During the evening of 13 August, the *Hermann Goering Division* gave up Taormina (twenty-nine miles from Messina) and fell back to Hube's second phase line, anchored at the small town of Santa Teresa. Here, twenty miles south of Messina, the German division had orders to hold through the evening of 15 August. Leaving a strong rear guard at Santa Teresa, General Conrath started the rest of his division back to the ferrying sites.

The British 50th Division followed slowly, impeded by efficient German demolition and mine work. The British 78th Division swung around Mount Etna, cleared Highway 120 between Randazzo and Linguaglossa, five miles from the east coast highway. But contact was not regained with the *Hermann Goering Division* until late on 15 August, by which time even the German rear guards had started to pull back to Hube's third phase line just short of Messina.

In the center of the Allied front, both the U.S. 1st and 9th Divisions encountered little trouble in closing out their roles in the Sicilian Campaign. Leaving

---

[12] Quotation and figures from Craven and Cate, eds., *Europe: TORCH to POINTBLANK*, p. 474.

[13] Ltr, Desert Air Force to NATAF, 15 Aug 43, in 0407/0/490.

# THE END OF THE CAMPAIGN

Floresta early on 14 August, DeRohan's 60th Infantry pushed northeast along the secondary road leading to the north coast, and that same afternoon his patrols made contact with the 3d Division at Furnari. On the same day, the 18th Infantry (1st Division) passed through Randazzo, through the British 78th Division, and turned north on the secondary road leading through Novara di Sicilia. This movement soon turned largely on how fast the division's engineers could remove mine fields and construct bypasses. The 18th Infantry moved slowly along the road—there was no enemy opposition—and across the ridges to Novara di Sicilia. Just after noon, General Bradley telephoned General Huebner the information that Truscott's units had already passed Bivio Salica and had, therefore, pinched out the 1st Division. There was little point in going any farther, although 18th Infantry patrols did link up with the 3d Division later in the day.

On the north coast road, the 3d Division pushed on, nearing the very place where General Patton planned to pull off his combined amphibious-airborne operation—Barcellona. At 0930, 15 August, the 7th Infantry, which leapfrogged the 15th Infantry, punched into Barcellona. Continuing its drive to the east, brushing aside a series of roadblocks defended by a few German machine gunners and mortar men, the regiment pushed all the way to the point where the coastal highway swings inland across the northeastern tip of the island to Messina. At daylight, 16 August, the 7th Infantry was ready to turn for Messina, only twelve miles away.

At Messina, the German evacuation proceeded unimpeded. Hube, confident that his troops could fend off the advancing Allied armies and determined to get as much equipment as possible off the island, had decided on 14 August to extend the evacuation by one night. In order not to upset the announced timetable, he ordered the additional night inserted between the previously ordered third and fourth nights. Thus, the evening of 14 August became known simply as the additional night, while 15 August was still designated as the fourth night, and 16 August as the fifth.[14]

When both German divisions reported contact regained with the Allied armies on 15 August, Hube completed arrangements to transfer the last elements of the divisions still on Sicily to the Italian mainland during the evening of 16 August. The *Hermann Goering* and *15th Panzer Grenadier Divisions* were, after arrival in Calabria, to march to the north. The *1st Parachute Division,* the *29th Panzer Grenadier Division,* and Colonel Baade's headquarters were to remain in Calabria attached to the *LXXVI Panzer Corps.*[15]

Even as the 7th Infantry neared the turn in the road leading to Messina on 15 August, General Patton was calling General Bradley to inform the II Corps commander that the 157th RCT was to land on the morning of 16 August, not at Bivio Salica as originally planned but at Spadafora, ten miles farther to the east. The airborne battalion was not going to participate, Patton said, since the 3d Division had already passed Barcellona. General Patton apparently felt that, even if the amphibious landing caught no Germans, it would put additional troops on shore to

---

[14] It was probably due to this device that some German commanders later claimed to have completed the evacuation in five nights. Hube's order of 14 August 43 in Baade Diary, 1900, 15 Aug 43, p. 107.

[15] Baade Diary, p. 109.

help speed Truscott's advance into Messina. The thought of taking Messina, of beating the Eighth Army to this prime objective of the entire campaign, may well have appealed even more strongly to the Seventh Army commander than the spectacular dash across western Sicily.

Not pleased with Patton's idea of using the 157th RCT at this late stage of the campaign in what he considered a useless operation, knowing that the 7th Infantry was encountering only light rear guard resistance and could outrun any amphibious force, Bradley protested the operation. Determined to go ahead despite General Bradley's statement that "we'll be waiting for your troops when they come ashore," [16] Patton sent his deputy, General Keyes, to Truscott's command post to co-ordinate the details.

Like Bradley, Truscott was astonished when Keyes outlined the Seventh Army plan. The 7th Infantry was even then approaching Spadafora and undoubtedly would be past that town by the time the 157th RCT started landing. Fearing that the amphibious landing taking place in the middle of the 7th Infantry's column might lead to confusion and possibly some internecine fighting, Truscott bitterly remonstrated with the Seventh Army deputy commander. But, as before the Brolo landing, Keyes was reluctant to cancel the amphibious end run, knowing full well that General Patton counted on the favorable publicity such a spectacular operation would bring to the Seventh Army. Finally, after Truscott stated flatly that he would halt the 7th Infantry and withdraw it west of Spadafora in order to prevent any conflict with Colonel Ankcorn's units, Keyes relented. Though the operation would still take place, it would be staged at Bivio Salico on the originally assigned beaches. Truscott reluctantly agreed, although he preferred to see the landing canceled.[17]

On the same day, 15 August, General Montgomery had finally decided that the Eighth Army, too, would launch an amphibious operation. Early on 16 August, tanks from the British 4th Armored Brigade and a Commando unit were to land at Cape d'Ali, cut off what Germans they could, and speed the Eighth Army's advance into Messina. Almost four hundred British troops were to be involved, and they too had a strong desire to beat the Americans into Messina.[18]

The same evening, the *Hermann Goering Division* rear guards began moving out of Santa Teresa, heading for Hube's third phase line, anchored at Scaletta, three miles beyond Cape d'Ali.[19]

Despite the increase in Allied air attacks on 15 and 16 August, the evacuation of German troops and matériel had continued without serious interruption. General Hube and General Fries, commander of the *29th Panzer Grenadier Division*, crossed to Calabria at 0530 on the 16th. Before leaving, General Fries deployed his now less than 200-man rear guard in two widely separated positions: half at Acqualadrone to block the road around the northeastern tip of Sicily; the others at the Casazza crossroads, four miles

---

[16] Bradley, *A Soldier's Story*, p. 162.

[17] Truscott, *Command Missions*, pp. 242–43; ONI, Sicilian Campaign, p. 110.

[18] Tregaskis, *Invasion Diary*, pp. 74, 86; Montgomery, *Eighth Army*, p. 111; Nicholson, *The Canadians in Italy*, p. 171.

[19] *OB SUED, Meldungen*, 0250, 17 Aug 43. This, and the ensuing British landing are reported belatedly on 17 August, but dated 15 August. It is confirmed on the German map for 15 August 1943.

GENERALS EISENHOWER AND MONTGOMERY OBSERVING THE EFFECT OF AMERICAN ARTILLERY SHELLING *on the Italian mainland. Commander Harry C. Butcher is behind General Montgomery.*

west of Messina. These two positions protected the ferrying sites.

In the Seventh Army sector, Bradley's and Truscott's prediction of the day before held true when, early on the morning of 16 August, the 1st Battalion, 7th Infantry passed through Spadafora. By early afternoon, the 7th was on the highway to Messina.

Colonel Ankcorn's 157th Infantry, meanwhile, had splashed ashore near Bivio Salica just after midnight, 16 August. Except for the loss of eleven men in a landing craft accident, the landing was uneventful. That afternoon, Truscott ordered Ankcorn to send one battalion to follow the 7th Infantry and assist in the capture of Messina; the remainder of Ankcorn's command was to stay at Bivio Salica.

By the time the 157th Infantry battalion caught up with the 7th Infantry, the latter unit had already cleared the German rear guards at the Casazza crossroads and controlled the ridge line overlooking Messina. The 30th Infantry had swung past the 7th along the road around the northeastern tip of the island. It was nearing Messina from the north. By this time, too, Truscott had a battery of 155-mm.

howitzers (Battery B, 9th Field Artillery Battalion) firing across the strait onto the Italian mainland. Just after dark, after driving off a small patrol from Company I, 7th Infantry, which was probing toward Messina, the last German rear guards along both roads pulled back to the outskirts of Messina on the edge of the last ferrying site that was still operating.

On the east coast highway, Montgomery's landing caught the tag end of the *Hermann Goering Division*'s withdrawing rear guard unit, which halted and stopped the British column just north of Scaletta. Not until dark on 16 August, as the Germans again started back for Messina, did the British column move forward, finally passing through Tremestieri, two miles south of Messina, at daylight 17 August. Here again the British column halted, this time because of a demolished bridge over a deep ravine. By now it was broad daylight—about 0815—and the Commando leader, a lieutenant colonel and distant relative of the British Prime Minister, decided to bypass the obstacle in a jeep and start for Messina. He was determined to get to the city before the Americans.[20]

The British officer might have spared himself a bouncing, jostling ride. The evening before, a reinforced platoon from Company L, 7th Infantry, under the command of 1st Lt. Ralph J. Yates, had pushed into the city proper. Early next morning, patrols from the other 7th Infantry battalions plus a platoon from the 1st Battalion, 157th Infantry, entered Messina. Except for occasional rifle fire, they met no resistance.

The last of the German defenders had crossed to the Italian mainland just about two hours earlier. In Calabria, General Hube reported at 0635, 17 August, "Operation *LEHRGANG* completed." The last Axis troops to leave Sicily were eight men of an Italian patrol picked up by a German assault boat about an hour later.[21]

On the ridge line overlooking the city, General Truscott received Messina's civil dignitaries at 0700, and one hour later, Col. Michele Tomasello, who offered to make the formal military surrender. However, because he had been told by General Keyes to wait for General Patton before entering Messina, Truscott sent General Eagles, his assistant division commander, into the city with Tomasello to prepare for the surrender of the city after Patton arrived, to supervise the activities of the various American units then roving about the port city, and "to see that the British did not capture the city from us after we had taken it." [22]

General Patton came onto the ridge at 1000, asked "What in hell are you all standing around for?," took his place in a car at the head of a motor cavalcade, and roared down into the city, accompanied all the way by enemy artillery fire from the Italian mainland.

---

[20] For an account of the British operation, see Tregaskis, *Invasion Diary*, pp. 74–89.

[21] Faldella, *Lo sbarco*, p. 275; *OB SUED, Meldungen*, 2000, 17 Aug 43. The Germans evacuated from Sicily 39,569 men, of which number 4,444 were wounded; 9,605 vehicles; 94 guns; 47 tanks; 1,100 tons of ammunition; 970 tons of fuel; and 15,700 tons of miscellaneous equipment and supplies. See Translation of Report on the Evacuation of Sicily (August 1943) by Vice Admiral Friedrich von Ruge (1946), and an. A, in folder X-111, OCMH; Baade Diary. For details of the last two days' fighting by the 3d Division, see AAR's of the units involved, including that of the 157th Infantry Regiment (which claims the honor of having the first American troops in Messina); II Corps Rpt of Opns; 3d Inf Div G-3 Jnl; II Corps G-3 Jnl.

[22] Comments of Eagles on MS.

# THE END OF THE CAMPAIGN

At the southern edge of Messina, the British armored column had finally caught up with the Commando officer, who had, by this time, made contact with General Eagles and learned that the Americans had beaten him to the prize. Continuing through the southern outskirts and into the center of Messina, the British column clanked its slow way forward, arriving in a large park just after General Patton had accepted the city's surrender. The senior British officer walked over to General Patton, shook hands, and said: "It was a jolly good race. I congratulate you." [23]

The Sicilian Campaign was over. The Western Allies had reached the southern gateway to the European continent.

## Conclusions

The Allied invasion of Sicily and subsequent reduction of the island accomplished the objectives laid down by the Combined Chiefs of Staff at Casablanca in January 1943: to make more secure the Allied lines of communication in the Mediterranean; to divert as much German strength as possible from the Russian front during the critical summer period; and to intensify pressure on Italy. More, the invasion of Sicily on 10 July and the attendant heavy bombing raids on key Italian cities and installations led directly to the overthrow of Mussolini and of the Fascist regime, Italy's first step toward leaving the war. Allied armies had taken from the Axis Powers the Sicilian bridge to the European mainland, and had placed on one end of that bridge a force which constituted a serious threat to all Axis-held portions of the European continent. All this had been accomplished at a cost of less than 20,000 men—7,402 in the Seventh Army, 11,843 in the British Eighth Army. Measured against Axis losses of 12,000 German dead and captured and 147,000 Italian dead, wounded, and captured, the Allied losses were slight.[24]

From the American point of view, the Seventh Army—the first United States field army to fight as a unit in World War II—had done more than well. Landing on exposed beaches, its airborne mission an almost complete failure, initially facing the bulk of the German defenders, hit by strong Axis counterattacks within hours after landing, the men of the Seventh Army had clawed their way inland. Within seventy-two hours after the initial seaborne landings, the army had established a firm and secure beachhead. Stopped by General Alexander from continuing on to Messina, the Seventh Army refused to relinquish all thought of offensive action and punched its way across the western tip of the island and into Palermo. Allowed to turn to the east, alternately bucking and plunging, it traveled the mountainous roads on and near the north coast to enter Messina just a few hours before the Eighth Army.

There were many noteworthy accomplishments in the thirty-eight days of fighting. Chief among these was the performance of the American fighting man. What he may have lacked in North Africa, if indeed he lacked anything but experience, he more than made up for in Sicily. On this Italian island, the American infantryman was a first-class fighter, in top physical condition, aggressive, al-

---

[23] Tregaskis, *Invasion Diary*, p. 89; Comments of Truscott on MS; Comments of Eagles on MS.

[24] The Seventh Army had a peak strength on Sicily of 217,000 men; the Eighth Army, a peak strength of 250,000 men. See Morison, *Sicily—Salerno—Anzio*, p. 223n.

ways pushing ahead. The tenacious defense by the 1st Division at Gela; the aggressive, hard-moving actions by the 157th and 179th Combat Teams at Comiso, Scoglitti, and Vittoria; the 3d Division's capture of Agrigento; the 505th Parachute Infantry at Biazza Ridge; the sweep across western Sicily, where daily thirty- and forty-mile foot marches were common; the fighting at Bloody Ridge and San Fratello; Troina; Randazzo; Brolo; all stand in testimony to this man's fighting ability.

Scarcely less notable were the accomplishments of the supporting arms. All of these played key parts in keeping the infantrymen moving forward. From the first day of the campaign, the field artillery battalions, divisional and nondivisional, provided tremendous support, and their actions in Sicily were marked by a high degree of success. Events clearly demonstrated that well-trained artillery units could maintain effective and continuous fire support despite the difficulties imposed by mountainous terrain, scarcity of good position areas, limited and congested roads, and, at times, a rapid rate of advance. Probably the most important lesson learned by the artillerymen was the necessity for vigorous and aggressive employment requiring continued rapid displacements in order to maintain fire support in a fast-moving situation. At no time did the artillery fail to deliver requested fires, although there were times when the infantrymen complained that they were not receiving enough. While the island's road net did not permit all of the artillery units to stay near the front lines at all times, their fires were massed when real resistance was encountered. As many as nine battalions of artillery were placed on a single important target; four and five battalions frequently were used on a single target. By the end of the campaign, in II Corps alone, over 120,000 rounds of 105-mm. howitzer, 34,000 rounds of 155-mm. howitzer, and 6,000 rounds of 155-mm. gun ammunition had been expended.

Vital, too, was the information gained on the value and versatility of the artillery observation aircraft. These small aircraft —grasshoppers, puddle-jumpers—proved most effective in carrying out fire missions and, in addition, served in a variety of important secondary roles despite the difficulties posed by scarce and restricted airfields.

The rugged, mountainous country and the difficult and limited road net precluded any mass action by the one armored division which participated in the campaign. Thus, the major role of the tanks took the form of rapid pursuit action and, where necessary, of assistance to the infantry in small units. The confined areas and narrow valleys flanked by high mountains provided little space for large-scale armored operations. The main operation of the 2d Armored Division as a whole was the rapid and successful dash for Palermo which involved a pursuit action from Agrigento to the latter city in only three days.

The administrative and technical services also provided outstanding support to the infantrymen. Engineer support rendered throughout the Seventh Army's various zones of action bordered on the spectacular. After operating the assault beaches, Engineer units pushed inland to repair airfields, roads, and bridges, and sometimes to act as infantrymen. Despite extensive road demolitions (the Axis forces on Sicily demolished 130 highway bridges and cratered roads in 40 places), mines, and enemy opposition, the Engineer

# THE END OF THE CAMPAIGN

units managed to maintain the Seventh Army's limited road net in a most satisfactory manner and contributed largely to the successful ground operations. Military police of the Seventh Army, too, operating with a limited number of units, contributed to the successful ground operations by relieving the combat units of the staggering total of 122,204 prisoners of war, of whom almost 75,000 were evacuated to North Africa, while another 34,000 were granted island paroles. The almost 9,000 Seventh Army Signal Corps troops rehabilitated 4,916 miles of telephone wire; laid almost 1,800 miles of spiral-four cable; and handled over 8,000 radio messages. The Seventh Army Medical Corps personnel, usually the unsung heroes of any campaign, processed 20,734 hospital admissions of U.S. personnel and established two field and six evacuation hospitals. Of the total admissions, 7,714 were for wounds or injuries; the other 13,320 were for diseases, with malaria and diarrhea accounting for two-thirds of these. Roughly half of the hospital cases were evacuated to North Africa, an equal number each by air and water.

Outstanding, too, was the close cooperation between the ground forces and the supporting naval units. Even with the mistakes made at some of the assault beaches—notably in the 180th Infantry's sector—the amphibious phase of the operation was an almost unqualified success. Certainly no complaints could be raised by the ground forces about the naval gunfire support so lavishly rendered during the first forty-eight hours.[25] Naval gunfire support on both the 10th and 11th of July played a key role in throwing back the strong Axis counterattacks near Gela, and in paving the way for a resumption of the inland movement the following day.

Throughout the campaign, American naval elements continued to furnish support for the Seventh Army divisions, and not only in the form of naval gunfire support. On the north coast in particular, in addition to the three amphibious end runs, the Navy furnished landing craft to ferry troops, supplies, and artillery pieces around badly damaged sections of the coastal highway to facilitate the ground advance. And while some complaint might be registered over the lack of continuous naval gunfire support at Brolo, this would have to be weighed against the performance of the naval gunners at Gela, Niscemi, Biscari, Scoglitti, Agrigento, and San Fratello.

None of this should be construed to mean that HUSKY was a perfect military campaign, that there were no flaws in the planning and execution of the operation.

In analyzing the Sicilian Campaign, one might naturally question why the original plan was ever changed: why the Allied armies were bunched on the southeastern coast instead of landing at widely separated points and then converging on Messina. The final plan was based on anticipation of strenuous Italian resistance. The whole approach toward Sicily was cautious and conservative. Emphasis was on ensuring success and on the avoidance of calculated risk or gamble for high stakes at little cost. The plan was also designed to avoid the possibility of enemy ground force superiority at any point. If any sub-

---

[25] The U.S. cruisers which participated in HUSKY fired a total of 7,537 six-inch rounds rendering close support on the southern beaches, and another 5,651 six-inch rounds on the north coast. The twenty-four U.S. destroyers fired a total of 6,912 five-inch rounds on both coasts. See Morison, *Sicily—Salerno—Anzio*, p. 222n.

task force landing were to fail or miscarry through enemy interference, the adjacent landings would guarantee numerical superiority over the defenders.

The final HUSKY plan was for a power drive, a frontal assault along a single sector of the coast. At no time during the course of planning of the Sicilian invasion did the Allied commanders aim to achieve an envelopment of the defending forces— to launch the initial attacks behind the flanks of the enemy. Even the two-pronged attack envisaged in the initial plan was designed to gain port facilities, not to get between the enemy and Messina. In the final plan, the two Allied armies were to land abreast and to advance together. This was to minimize the danger of having the enemy concentrate against one task force at a time. The risks in the plan were strictly in the matter of supply and mainly affected the Seventh Army.

Sound, cautious, conservative, the final plan was well designed to achieve the occupation of Sicily, the objective set by the Combined Chiefs. At the same time, Alexander's idea of first consolidating a firm base on the southeast corner offered little scope for maneuver with the object of destroying the enemy garrison.

In essence, the plan as finally designed was Montgomery's. No one except Montgomery was particularly happy with it. The strategic conception inherent in the plan was both disadvantageous to and disparaging of the American force. Although the original two-pronged attack was based solely on logistical considerations, it implied a twofold advance on Messina. Each army, having gained its port, would advance by its own route to Messina, the hinge of Sicily. The defending forces were expected either to concentrate against one attacking force, leaving the route of advance open to the other, or to withdraw quickly to the northeastern corner of the island where the two Allied armies would converge. The final plan changed all this, and embodied an altogether different conception. There would be but one thrust against Messina—the drive through Catania along the east coast highway by the Eighth Army. The Seventh Army would protect the flank and rear of Montgomery's forces. Only reluctantly and under pressure did General Alexander finally consent to release the Seventh Army from a subordinate and purely supporting mission.

The numerous changes in the HUSKY plan during the February–May period came about as a direct result of the command structure which had been specifically spelled out by the Combined Chiefs of Staff at Casablanca. For the second time—the first had been in North Africa— an Allied military operation was to be conducted under the control of a triumvirate of commanders, rather than under the direction of one. General Alexander (Eisenhower's deputy) was made responsible for the ground operations; Air Chief Marshal Tedder for air operations; Admiral Cunningham for naval activities. General Eisenhower was to act as a sort of chairman of the board, to enter into the final decision-making process only when the board members presented him with unsolved problems. If the three board members agreed on policy, there was little that Eisenhower could do to change the policy unless he was willing to dispense with the board members' services. Eisenhower was raised involuntarily far above the operational level; only indirectly could he influence the course of operations once that course had been agreed on by his committee of three.

The committee system of command

would have been more palatable if the headquarters had not been physically separated—if the committee members had established and maintained a joint headquarters at a single location. But with the invasion of Sicily, Alexander established his headquarters on the island; Tedder's headquarters remained in North Africa, near Tunis; Cunningham's naval headquarters was at Malta; and General Eisenhower's staff remained in Algiers. While the separation had little effect on the conduct of the campaign during the month of July, although it appears logical to assume that a joint headquarters might have prodded General Montgomery into doing more on the east coast in the way of amphibious end runs, one result of maintaining such widely separated headquarters became painfully evident during the last ten days of the operation, when the Axis forces began evacuating the island. A joint plan was not drawn up to prevent an enemy evacuation from the island. Each of the three services operated independently of the others, doing what it thought best to prevent the evacuation. Since the issue was not presented to the chairman of the board (General Eisenhower), the issue remained unsolved, and the Germans and Italians completed one of the most successful evacuations ever executed from a beleaguered shore.

Furthermore, there was the question of air support: whether or not Allied air plans were meshed sufficiently with ground and naval plans. Simply put, the Allied air forces in the Mediterranean refused to work out detailed plans in co-operation with the army and navy. This was particularly true in the case of the Seventh Army—to a much lesser degree in the Eighth Army, where Montgomery's relations with the British Desert Air Force were somewhat different from Patton's relations with the U.S. XII Air Support Command. The official air force historians explain the airman's views:

It should be noted that the air plan dealt for the most part with broad policies and that it had not been integrated in detail with the ground and naval plans. This was deliberate, and the result of sound strategical and tactical considerations emphasized by experience in the Tunisian and Western Desert campaigns. There would be no parceling out of air strength to individual landings or sectors. Instead, it would be kept united under an over-all command in order to insure in its employment the greatest possible flexibility. It would be thrown in full force where it was needed, and not kept immobilized where it was not needed. Too, the chief immediate task of the air arm was to neutralize the enemy air force, a fluid target not easily pinpointed in advance.[26]

Primarily concerned with other matters —neutralizing enemy air, strategic targets, armed reconnaissances, cover over the beaches—the Allied air commanders devoted little thought and attention to providing close air support to the ground forces during the campaign. During the first critical forty-eight hours, no close air support missions were flown in support of the Seventh Army, and no close support missions were handled by the air support parties with the II Corps and with the assault divisions until 13 July. Even then the cumbersome system of requesting missions, with attendant delays in transmission and in identifying targets, proved almost unmanageable. It resulted in the scrapping of many requested and approved missions, and sometimes worked out in disastrous ways for friendly forces.

As regards the execution of the plan,

---

[26]Craven and Cate, eds., *Europe: TORCH to POINTBLANK*, p. 445; see also, Slessor, *The Central Blue*, pp. 417-27.

questions might well be raised as to the conduct of the ground phases of the campaign. The ground assault started auspiciously on 10 July with the greatest amphibious attack ever undertaken by any armed force. Within seventy-two hours after the initial seaborne landings, the two Allied armies advancing abreast had practically secured their designated objectives. On the east coast, the Eighth Army entered Augusta on the morning of 12 July. Thus far, its advance had not been seriously contested. The bulk of the defending forces, particularly the German contingent, was off to the west, one portion counterattacking the Seventh Army near Gela and Biscari, the other part hurriedly moving eastward to block any further American advances inland from Licata. Catania was almost in sight. The only force of any consequence opposing Eighth Army's two assault corps was the German *Group Schmalz,* and this force was almost certainly not strong enough to stop an aggressive thrust north from Augusta. The Seventh Army, for its part and after the initial Axis counterattacks at Gela, had pushed on strongly, so strongly that its left task force—the reinforced 3d Division—had run out of objectives and was poised to strike inland at the key communications center of Enna. Highway 124, the important east-west highway, was almost in Seventh Army's grasp. Several huge gaps had been created in the Axis line, gaps that were being held halfheartedly by remnants of the *Livorno* and *Napoli Divisions.*

It was at this very point on the evening of 12 July, when the Allied armies were in the best position of the entire campaign for finishing off the Axis defenders quickly and pushing on through to Messina, that General Alexander, for some unknown reason, permitted General Montgomery to change the Eighth Army's plans. Instead of moving along a single major axis of advance, throwing his army's entire weight against the German defenders at Catania, Montgomery split his assault corps into a two-pronged effort, one prong continuing along the east coast highway, the other prong swinging to the west across Seventh Army's front around Mount Etna. At the same time, Alexander changed the Seventh Army axis of advance from the north to the west and again relegated Patton's force to the passive role of guarding Montgomery's flank and rear. For all practical purposes, Seventh Army could have stayed on the beaches; its brilliant assault achievements were completely nullified by the new British plan.

Why Alexander permitted this to happen has never been satisfactorily explained. Seventh Army was moving ahead nicely; it almost had Highway 124; the German and Italian forces in front of it had been practically dissolved or withdrawn. The German forces from the west, not really strong enough to contest an advance all along the line, were still scrambling to the east in a desperate effort to close the tremendous gap in the center of the Axis line. No enemy force of any size opposed either the 1st or 45th Divisions. General Bradley, the II Corps commander, was ready and willing to take Highway 124 and Enna, thus encircling the German defenders facing Eighth Army. In North Africa, the remainder of the 82d Airborne and 2d Armored Divisions lay ready to sail for Sicily to reinforce the American effort. But apparently it was Alexander's distrust of the American fighting man that permitted him to accept Montgomery's plan of a two-pronged British advance, of dividing Eighth Army in the face of the

## THE END OF THE CAMPAIGN

enemy. Or it may be that General Eisenhower's opinion of Alexander—"At times it seems that he alters his own plans and ideas merely to meet an objection or a suggestion of a subordinate, so as to avoid direct command methods"—was correct.[27]

Alexander's permission given to Montgomery to launch Eighth Army on its ill-fated two-pronged offensive constituted the turning point in the Sicilian Campaign. From this date on the course of the campaign could not have proceeded much differently. The Axis forces, suddenly relieved of the tremendous American pressure along most of their front, were now given enough time to prepare strong defensive positions in the mountainous interior, and the rest of the campaign turned into little more—except for Patton's spectacular dash into Palermo, almost a publicity agent's stunt—than digging the enemy out of strongpoints and knocking him off mountain tops. It was not until 23 July, when General Alexander finally turned Seventh Army toward Messina, that even these tactics paid off.

Questions, too, might be raised about the tragic confusion which marked the four major Allied airborne operations. The scattering of the American paratroopers and British glidermen on the evening of D minus 1, followed by the shooting down of large numbers of friendly aircraft on the evenings of 11 and 13 July 1943, almost brought American airborne efforts in World War II to an end. Much disillusionment set in following the disastrous airborne operations, and many responsible officers became convinced that the basic structure of the airborne division was unsound.

Sicily was an especially bitter disappointment for men who had put great faith in airborne operations. General Swing, American airborne adviser at AFHQ, attributed the unsatisfactory results to five principal causes: insufficient planning in co-ordinating routes with all forces several weeks earlier; the inability of troop carrier formations to follow the routes given, partly because of poorly trained pilots, and partly because of the complicated routes; the rigid requirement that naval forces fire at all aircraft at night coming within range, regardless of their efforts to identify themselves; the unfortunate circumstance wherein an enemy bombing raid coincided with the arrival of the airborne force; and the failure of some ground commanders to warn the men manning antiaircraft weapons of the expected arrival of the troop carrier formations.[28]

General Browning, British airborne expert and the AFHQ airborne adviser, was sharp in his criticism of the aerial navigation:

In spite of the clear weather, suitable moon, the existence of Malta as a check point only 70 miles from Sicily and the latter's very obvious and easily recognizable coast line, the navigation by the troop carrier aircrews was bad.

The troops comprising both British and American Airborne Divisions are of a very high quality and their training takes time and is expensive. They are given important tasks which may acutely affect the operations as a whole. It is essential both from the operational and moral point of view that energetic steps be taken to improve greatly on the aircrews' performance up to date.

---

[27] Memo for personal file, 11 Jun 43, Diary Office CinC, Book VI, pp. A-472—A-474.

[28] Memo, Swing, 16 Jul 43, sub: Comments on Night Opns, 82d AB Div, Night of D plus 1 to D plus 2. Photostat incl with Ltr, Swing to Ward, 5 May 50.

Intensive training in low flying navigation by night, especially over coast lines, must be organized and carried on continuously. This must form part of the aircrews' training before they reach a theater of war and the standard set must be very high.[29]

General Ridgway, commander of the 82d Airborne Division, stated weeks later that "both the 82d Airborne Division and the North African Air Force Troop Carrier Command are today at airborne training levels below combat requirements." He emphasized that airborne and troop carrier units were "unprepared to conduct with reasonable chances of success night operations either glider or parachute, employing forces the size of Regimental Combat Teams."[30]

A report on the Sicilian airborne operations by the Fifth Army Airborne Training Center was more blunt:

> The (82d) Division was in superb physical condition, well qualified in the use of infantry arms, in combined ground operations, and in individual jumping. It was extremely deficient in its air operations. The (52d) Troop Carrier Wing did not cooperate well. Training was, in general, inadequate. Combat efficiency for night glider operations was practically zero. The combined force of (82d) Airborne Division and troop carrier units was extremely deficient.[31]

Allied airborne operations did live up to some expectations, but they might have been far more vital in the conquest of Sicily had the airborne troops been dropped, not between the reserves and the beach defenses, but en masse on the central plateau, where they could have assembled with little interference and then struck aggressively at the enemy's rear.[32]

In some respects Allied airborne operations in Sicily bear certain similarities to the German airborne invasion of Crete. In each case the attacker considered the operation a disappointment, while the defender considered the operation a more or less spectacular success. Each operation was something of a turning point in the airborne effort of both sides. For the Germans, Crete was the end of major airborne operations. For the Allies, Sicily was only the beginning of airborne operations on an even larger scale.

After Sicily, however, it was not certain that airborne divisions were here to stay. The reaction of the Army Ground Forces in the United States was that the airborne program had been overemphasized. They could see no immediate requirement for the airborne strength which had been assembled, and were willing to abandon the idea of special airborne divisions. AGF suggested that the airborne divisions then in being be reorganized as light divisions. Parachute units would be removed and the light divisions would be given a variety of special training. Whenever an airborne operation was contemplated, then the light division could be trained, preferably in the theater, for that specific operation. Parachute units would be organized into separate battalions, after the fashion of the armored infantry battalions,

---

[29] Browning Rpt, 24 Jul 43, Incl 6 with AFHQ Proceedings of Board of Officers.

[30] Ltr, Ridgway to OPD, 6 Nov 43, in AFTCC 353 (AB Training), quoted in AAF, 1 Troop Carrier Command, The Operational Training Program, pp. 296–97.

[31] Brief of Rpt of AB Opn, HUSKY, 17 Sep 43, Incl with OPD Memo 319.1 (15 Aug 43) for CofS U.S. Army, 20 Sep 43; quoted in AGF Study 25, p. 47; also see extracts of Billingslea Rpt, in AB Overseas Rpts, ATTNG, AB Br.

[32] As suggested by General Swing in a letter to General Ward, 5 May 1950.

# THE END OF THE CAMPAIGN

and would then be grouped as necessary for training and tactical employment.[33]

At the same time, writing from North Africa, General Eisenhower also suggested a reorganization:

> I do not believe in the airborne division. I believe that airborne troops should be reorganized in self-contained units, comprising infantry, artillery, and special services, all of about the strength of a regimental combat team. Even if one had all the air transport he could possibly use the fact is at any given time and in any given spot only a reasonable number of air transports can be operated because of technical difficulties. To employ at any time and place a whole division would require a dropping over such an extended area that I seriously doubt that a division commander could regain control and operate the scattered forces as one unit. In any event, if these troops were organized in smaller, self-contained units, a senior commander, with a small staff and radio communications, could always be dropped in the area to insure necessary coordination.[34]

Opposing this trend was General Swing, who had served as an airborne adviser in Allied Forces Headquarters and who was now at the Airborne Command in the United States. He protested that these views were based upon a campaign marked by certain adverse conditions which were remediable. He pointed to the Markham valley operation in New Guinea (September 1943) as an example of what could be done with proper training and planning. His conclusion was that airborne divisions were sound and that the successful employment of those divisions required careful and exact planning and co-ordination with the major ground effort. In this connection, General Swing recommended, as he had done earlier, that an airborne staff section be established in each theater to assist the theater commander in taking full advantage of the capabilities of airborne units.[35]

In a later study of the subject, the American and British Combined Staff Planners saw nothing in combat experience, either British or American, which indicated that the division was not the proper organization for airborne troops. Taking cognizance of the expressed views of Eisenhower, Swing, and others, the planners recommended that no changes be made in that structure until further experience indicated the need for a change.[36] This recommendation was accepted by both Americans and British. It had been a near thing for the airborne effort. For with the loss of the division structure and a reversion to battalion size units only, the airborne units would have been no more effective than if they had retained the same mission originally contemplated for them in the days before the war—the seizure of an airhead for the benefit of air-transported infantry units.

## Patton

The campaign had done more from an American viewpoint than deal the enemy a serious blow and prove the abilities of the American soldier. The campaign also had produced an American field commander, who, on the one hand, by his

---

[33] Memo, CG AGF for CofS U.S. Army, 22 Sep 43, sub: Rpt of Board on AB Opns, file 353/17 (AB).

[34] Ltr, Eisenhower to Marshall, 20 Sep 43, Misc Exec File, bk. 12, case 80; extracts in CPS 91/1, 19 Oct 43, ABC 322 (23 Sep 43).

[35] Ltr, Swing to CG AGF, 4 Oct 43, sub: Overseas Rpts on AB Opns, AGF AB Misc 1942-1945/15, ATTNG, Air 2d AB Brigade.

[36] App. A, CPS 91/1, 19 Oct 43, ABC 322 (23 Sep 43).

verve, élan, and professional ability, had captured the fancy of his troops and the American public, and on the other hand, because of some of his actions, had incurred severe, even hostile, criticism from his superiors, his troops, and the public.

This commander was General Patton. Having first emerged as a colorful, capable leader in North Africa, Patton in the Sicilian Campaign had developed as the American answer to Montgomery. Part of Patton's distinction was sheer histrionics—the characteristic riding breeches and the pearl-handled pistols that set him apart, gave him a trademark. Of a piece with this was the fervor with which he pursued a relatively empty but nonetheless spectacular objective like Palermo.

But, as even his severest critics would admit, Patton had done a masterful job. He had created a battle-worthy field army and shaped it in his own image—tenacious, bold, aggressive, resourceful, an army imbued with Patton's own passion for beating the British to Messina. Yet in the process, under the pressure of the same consuming drive which brought achievement, Patton had proven himself cold, uncompromising, and even cruel in dealing with any subordinate who seemed to be remiss or who might hinder him in attaining his goals.

If the subordinate was a division commander, like General Allen, who felt the lash of Patton's tongue on the beaches near Gela, or like General Truscott, who questioned what he considered too much haste in the end run at Brolo and drew for his protests stinging rebuke, there would be no widespread repercussions. But when these hard, personal methods, exaggerated by moments of rage, reached down to private soldiers in a war-swollen army, closely, even jealously watched by the people at home, the situation could be different.

Two incidents involving hospitalized privates came close to damaging the morale of the Seventh Army and even closer to knocking Patton from the military pedestal to which the Sicilian Campaign had elevated him. These two incidents did not affect the actual conduct or outcome of the campaign, but, like the debacle of the airborne reinforcement, their scandalous nature and the attendant publicity have made them an integral part of the story of the campaign, sometimes to the point of eclipsing the achievements of the Seventh Army in Sicily and of Patton himself. These were the two so-called "slapping incidents" involving General Patton and two soldiers whom he suspected of malingering.[37]

The first of the incidents took place on 3 August in the receiving tent of the 15th Evacuation Hospital (Lt. Col. Charles N. Wasten), then in the 1st Division's area near Nicosia, during one of Patton's periodic visits to medical installations supporting Seventh Army. Patton, in company with General Lucas, entered the receiving tent escorted by Colonel Wasten and other medical officers assigned to the hospital, spoke to various patients, and especially commended the wounded men. Then he came upon a private from Company L, 26th Infantry, who had just re-

---

[37] Information on the slapping incidents has been drawn from the official reports of the incidents, actions taken by General Eisenhower, and Patton's actions found in Diary Office CinC, Book IX, pp. A–915—A–922; papers and telegrams in reference to the incidents in Smith Papers, box 5; Eisenhower, *Crusade in Europe*, pp. 179–83; Bradley, *A Soldier's Story*, pp. 160–62; Butcher, *My Three Years With Eisenhower*, pp. 393, 403, 450; Semmes, *Portrait of Patton*, pp. 165–66, 168–72; Lucas Diary, pp. 111, 113–15, 141–43.

# THE END OF THE CAMPAIGN

cently arrived in the hospital area with a preliminary diagnosis made at the clearing station of "psychoneuroses anxiety state—moderate severe."[38] Approaching, Patton asked the soldier what the matter was. The man replied: "I guess I can't take it." Patton immediately flew into a rage, cursed him, slapped the private soldier across the face with his gloves, and finally grabbed him and threw him out of the tent.[39] In General Lucas's words: "We stopped at an Evacuation Hospital before reaching Nicosia to visit the wounded boys and try to cheer them up. Brave, hurt, bewildered boys. All but one, that is, because he said he was nervous and couldn't take it. Anyone who knows him can realize what that would do to George. The weak sister was really nervous when he got through."[40]

Patton concluded the inspection of the hospital's facilities, toured the front lines, and returned to his headquarters where he had the following memorandum prepared and distributed to his senior commanders:

It has come to my attention that a very small number of soldiers are going to the hospital on the pretext that they are nervously incapable of combat. Such men are cowards, and bring discredit on the Army and disgrace to their comrades who [sic] they heartlessly leave to endure the danger of a battle which they themselves use the hospital as a means of escaping.

You will take measures to see that such cases are not sent to the hospital, but are dealt with in their units.

Those who are not willing to fight will be tried by Court-Martial for cowardice in the face of the enemy.[41]

Apparently, this particular incident caused no serious repercussions on the island or at Allied Force Headquarters in North Africa. Nor did General Lucas mention the incident to General Eisenhower on his return to North Africa on 6 August. Patton, himself, was not overly concerned with the incident, and in his diary noted: "I gave him the devil, slapped his face with my gloves and kicked him out of the hospital. . . . One sometimes slaps a baby to bring it to."[42]

The soldier, in the meantime, had been picked up by a hospital corpsman after being thrown out of the receiving tent and had been taken to a ward tent where he was found to be running a high fever and where he gave a history of chronic diarrhea. Two days later, the final diagnosis in his case was made: chronic dysentery and malaria, and on 9 August the man was evacuated to North Africa.[43]

Just the day after the ailing soldier was sent off the island, General Patton dropped in unexpectedly at the 93d Evacuation Hospital (Col. D. E. Currier)

---

[38] Rpt, Lt Col Perrin H. Long to Surgeon, NATOUSA, 16 Aug 43, sub: Mistreatment of Patients in Receiving Tents of the 15th and 93d Evacuation Hospitals, Diary Office CinC, Book IX, pp. A-915–A-916.

[39] Long Rpt, 16 Aug 43, Diary Office CinC, Book IX, pp. A-915–A-916; Semmes, *Portrait of Patton*, pp. 165–66; Cf. Lucas Diary, pp. 114–15.

[40] Lucas Diary, p. 111. After the war, General Lucas wrote that he could see nothing serious about the incident at the time. "There are always a certain number of such weaklings in any Army," he noted in his diary, "and I suppose the modern doctor is correct in classifying them as ill and treating them as such. However, the man with malaria doesn't pass his condition on to his comrades as rapidly as does the man with cold feet nor does malaria have the lethal effect that the latter has." Lucas Diary, pp. 113–14.

[41] Seventh Army Memo to Corps, Div, and Separate Brigade CO's, 5 Aug 43, 107-10.2, NARS.

[42] Semmes, *Portrait of Patton*, pp. 165–66.

[43] Long Rpt, 16 Aug 43, Diary Office CinC, Book IX, pp. A-915—A-916; AFHQ Out Msg W-6291 to AGWAR, 27 Nov 43, Smith Papers, box 5.

where he was met by Maj. Charles B. Etter, the hospital's receiving officer, and taken to the receiving tent, where fifteen patients had just arrived from the front. Patton started down the line of cots, asking each man where he had been hurt and how, and commending each. The fourth man Patton reached was a soldier from Battery C, 17th Field Artillery Regiment, who had been previously diagnosed at a clearing station as suffering from a severe case of shell shock. He was huddled on his bunk and shivering. Patton stopped in front of the bed and, as was his way, asked the soldier what the trouble was. The man replied, "It's my nerves," and began to sob. Patton, instantly furious, roared, "What did you say?" The man again replied, "It's my nerves," and continued, "I can hear the shells come over, but I can't hear them burst."

Patton turned impatiently to Major Etter and asked, "What's this man talking about? What's wrong with him, if anything?" Etter reached for the soldier's chart but before the doctor could answer Patton's questions, Patton began to rave and rant: "Your nerves, Hell, you are just a goddamned coward, you yellow son of a bitch." At this point, Colonel Currier and two other medical officers entered the receiving tent in time to hear Patton yell at the man, "You're a disgrace to the Army and you're going right back to the front to fight, although that's too good for you. You ought to be lined up against a wall and shot. In fact, I ought to shoot you myself right now, goddam you!" With this, Patton reached for his pistol, pulled it from its holster, and waved it in the soldier's face. Then, as the man sat quivering on his cot, Patton struck him sharply across the face with his free hand and continued to shout imprecations. Spotting Colonel Currier, Patton shouted, "I want you to get that man out of here right away. I won't have these other brave boys seeing such a bastard babied."

Reholstering his pistol, Patton started to leave the tent, but turned suddenly and saw that the soldier was openly crying. Rushing back to him, Patton again hit the man, this time with such force that the helmet liner he had been wearing was knocked off and rolled outside the tent. This was enough for Colonel Currier, who placed himself between Patton and the soldier. Patton turned and strode out of the tent. As he left the hospital, Patton said to Colonel Currier, "I meant what I said about getting that coward out of here. I won't have those cowardly bastards hanging around our hospitals. We'll probably have to shoot them sometime anyway, or we'll raise a breed of morons."[44]

General Patton left the hospital area, still fuming "about the cowardice of people who claimed they were suffering from psychoneuroses" and exclaiming that "they should not be allowed in the same hospital with the brave wounded men," and went forward to General Bradley's headquarters where he casually mentioned what had just happened.[45] So casual was Patton about the incident that General Bradley tended to disregard the whole matter.[46] For the soldier, the preliminary diagnosis made of his case was later fully

---

[44] The account of this episode has been reconstructed from Long Report, 16 Aug 43, Diary Office CinC, Book IX, pp. A-915—A-916; Report by Demaree Bess (Associate Editor, *Saturday Evening Post*) submitted to General Eisenhower on 19 Aug 43; Eisenhower, *Crusade in Europe*, p. 180; Bradley, *A Soldier's Story*, pp. 160-61.

[45] Eisenhower, *Crusade in Europe*, p. 180.

[46] Bradley, *A Soldier's Story*, p. 160.

# THE END OF THE CAMPAIGN

confirmed by the 93d Evacuation Hospital's psychiatrist.[47]

Two days later, on 12 August, Bradley had cause to remember Patton's casual mention of the incident. Colonel Currier had submitted a report through the II Corps surgeon on the incident at his hospital, and Gen. William B. Kean, Bradley's chief of staff, rushed it into the II Corps commander's trailer. No one else at II Corps headquarters had seen the communication, which was a full report of the occurrence. Bradley instructed Kean to lock the report in a safe and to do nothing more about the matter.[48] Other than going directly to Eisenhower with the report, which would mean jumping channels, there was little else General Bradley could do. He was still under Patton's command, and forwarding the report to Seventh Army headquarters probably would have accomplished nothing. This was General Eisenhower's problem and General Bradley apparently did not want to be a party to accusing the Seventh Army commander of any wrongdoing.

By this time, however, the incident was common knowledge all over the island. An account of it had been carried back orally to Allied Force Headquarters press camp by three reputable newsmen who had been covering the fighting on Sicily. One of the correspondents stated that there were at least 50,000 American soldiers on Sicily who would shoot Patton if they had the chance; a second felt the Seventh Army commander had gone temporarily insane. Just a few days later, another correspondent brought in a detailed written report of what had happened at Colonel Currier's hospital. Thus far, none of the correspondents had filed a story on either of the slapping episodes. They realized the seriousness of the incidents, and the impact such a story would have on the public in the United States; they were willing to hush the story at their end for the sake of the American effort.[49]

General Eisenhower had already acted in the matter. On 16 August the Supreme Allied Commander had in his hands a detailed report of the two incidents prepared by NATOUSA's surgeon's office. General Eisenhower was shocked by the report, but determined to give Patton a chance to explain. On the following day, 17 August, Eisenhower wrote a personal letter to his senior American subordinate, a letter which offered Patton a chance to deny the allegations made against him, but which also included a strong rebuke if all, or any part of, the allegations proved correct.

Though General Eisenhower planned no formal investigation, in the letter to Patton, delivered personally by a general officer, he indicated his feelings. "I am well aware of the necessity for hardness and toughness on the battlefield," Eisenhower wrote. "I clearly understand that firm and drastic measures are at times necessary in order to secure desired objectives. But this does not excuse brutality, abuse of the sick, nor exhibition of uncontrollable temper in front of subordinates." While Eisenhower felt that Patton's "personal services" as commander of Seventh Army had been of immense value to the Allied cause during the Sicilian fighting, he stated bluntly that "if there is

---
[47] Bess Rpt, Diary Office CinC, Book IX, pp. A-917--A-919.
[48] Bradley, A Soldier's Story, p. 160.

[49] AFHQ Out Msg W-6291 to AGWAR, 27 Nov 43, Smith Papers, box 5; AFHQ Out Msg W-6017 to AGWAR, 24 Nov 43, same file; Butcher, My Three Years With Eisenhower, pp. 393, 403.

a very considerable element of truth in the allegations accompanying this letter, I must so seriously question your good judgment and your self-discipline as to raise serious doubts in my mind as to your future usefulness." The Allied commander then stated that if any of the allegations were true, Patton was to make amends, "apology or otherwise," to the individuals concerned, and stated baldly that "conduct such as described in the accompanying report will not be tolerated in this theater no matter who the offender may be." [50]

At the same time, General Eisenhower ordered General Lucas to Sicily to talk to Patton, and sent the theater inspector general to the island to see what effect Patton's conduct had had on Seventh Army. Lucas arrived in Palermo on 21 August and spoke in a "kindly but very firm" tone to the Seventh Army commander. By this time, Patton had received Eisenhower's letter, and Lucas found him "chastened" and agreeable to "everything I suggested including never doing such things again." [51] Lucas knew of General Eisenhower's strong feelings about Patton's actions and realized Patton was in serious danger of being relieved. As far as the inspector general was concerned, he felt that no great harm had been done to Seventh Army by Patton's conduct.[52]

Patton, apparently not fully realizing the seriousness of his actions at the evacuation hospitals—"evidently I acted precipitately and on insufficient knowledge"—felt that "my motive was correct because one cannot permit skulking to exist." [53] He regretted what had happened more because of making "Ike mad when it is my earnest desire to please him." [54] But he set about making amends before answering General Eisenhower's letter. He talked to the two soldiers, explained his motives, and apologized for his actions. "In each case I stated I should like to shake hands with them, and in each case they accepted my offer." [55] Then, acting on General Lucas' suggestions, Patton talked to the medical personnel who were present when the incidents occurred and expressed his regrets for "my impulsive actions." And, finally, he addressed all Seventh Army divisions and expressed his regret "for any occasions when I may have harshly criticized individuals." [56]

On 29 August, Patton sent his reply to General Eisenhower, assuring the senior American commander in the theater that he had had no intention of "being either harsh or cruel in my treatment of the two soldiers in question. My sole purpose was to try and restore in them a just appreciation of their obligation as men and as soldiers." Continuing, Patton recalled a World War I incident when a close friend lost his nerve "in an exactly analogous manner." After suffering years of mental anguish, Patton wrote, his friend had committed suicide. "Both my friend and the medical men with whom I discussed his case assured me that had he been roundly checked at the time of his first misbehavior, he would have been restored to a normal state." It was recalling this incident, Patton stated, that caused him to "inaptly" try "the remedies sug-

---

[50] Ltr, Eisenhower to Patton, 17 Aug 43, Diary Office CinC, Book IX, pp. A-916—A-917.

[51] Lucas Diary, p. 142.

[52] AFHQ Out Msg W-6017 to AGWAR, 24 Nov 43, Smith Papers, box 5.

[53] Semmes, *Portrait of Patton*, p. 169.

[54] *Ibid.*

[55] Ltr, Patton to Eisenhower, 29 Aug 43, Diary Office CinC, Book IX, p. A-920.

[56] *Ibid.* See also Semmes, *Portrait of Patton*, p. 170.

# THE END OF THE CAMPAIGN

gested," and, "after each incident I stated to officers with me that I felt I had probably saved an immortal soul."[57]

Patton's admission of the allegations contained in the 16 August report placed General Eisenhower in a most difficult position: were the incidents sufficiently damaging to Patton and to his standing in Seventh Army to relieve him? Eisenhower could rationalize the incidents, although he admitted that Patton's behavior was undeniably brutal. He knew that Patton was impulsive and was, when the incidents occurred, in a "highly emotional state."[58] Eisenhower wanted Patton "saved for service in the great battles still facing us in Europe."[59] He did not want to get rid of the general "who had commanded an army in one of our country's most successful operations and who is the best ground gainer developed so far by the Allies."[60] Weighing one set of facts against the other, General Eisenhower concluded that Patton was too valuable a man to lose, and he determined to keep him in command of Seventh Army.[61]

He then called in the group of reporters who had brought the story over from Sicily, explained what actions had been taken, and his reasons for keeping Patton in command of Seventh Army. The correspondents were satisfied and voluntarily declined to file stories back to the States. As far as AFHQ was concerned, the matter was closed.[62]

Although much was later said about the Patton incidents when a reporter, fresh from the United States, got wind of the story and released it over the radio in November 1943, Eisenhower did not waver in his decision to back General Patton. Writing then, Eisenhower said simply, "I still feel my decision sound," and refused to rescind it.[63] But the incidents did convince General Eisenhower that the horizon of Patton's command role was limited. In a later message to General Marshall, Eisenhower stated emphatically: "In no event will I ever advance Patton beyond Army command . . . ."[64]

---

[57] Ltr, Patton to Eisenhower, 29 Aug 43, Diary Office CinC, Book IX, p. A-920.

[58] Eisenhower, *Crusade in Europe*, p. 181.

[59] *Ibid.*

[60] Butcher, *My Three Years With Eisenhower*, p. 393.

[61] Eisenhower, *Crusade in Europe*, p. 181; AFHQ Out Msg W-6017 to AGWAR, 24 Nov 43, Smith Papers, box 5.

[62] Eisenhower, *Crusade in Europe*, p. 182; Butcher, *My Three Years With Eisenhower*, p. 403.

[63] AFHQ Out Msg W-6017 to AGWAR, 24 Nov 43, Smith Papers, box 5; see also Eisenhower, *Crusade in Europe*, p. 182; Butcher, *My Three Years With Eisenhower*, p. 450; AFHQ Out Msg W-6291 to AGWAR, 27 Nov 43, Smith Papers, box 5; Bradley, *A Soldier's Story*, p. 161.

[64] Msg, Eisenhower to Marshall, 29 Dec 43, Diary Office CinC, Book IX, p. A-973.

PART THREE

THE SURRENDER

CHAPTER XXII

# The QUADRANT Conference and the Quebec Memorandum

Even as the military operations on Sicily neared an end, President Roosevelt and Prime Minister Churchill, together with their chief military and political advisers, in August 1943 met in conference at Quebec. Code-named QUADRANT, this meeting was the focal point in the formulation of Allied strategy for the second half of 1943. Marking a new stage in the Anglo-American strategic argument toward delimiting Mediterranean operations and solidifying the cross-Channel plan, the conference incidentally and accidentally provided the final conditions for Italian surrender, determined the methods of applying the terms, and gave final approval to an invasion of the Italian mainland.

*Strategic Issues at Quebec*

Toward the end of July, the Joint War Plans Committee of the U.S. Joint Chiefs of Staff had suggested that the decisive action against the Axis had already taken place in the successful Russian counteroffensive against the Germans, together with the Anglo-American superiority established in the air and on the sea. Since Germany, the committee said, was no longer capable of defeating the Soviet armies, the assumption that Anglo-American power had to be directed primarily to relieve the pressure on Russia was no longer valid. Hence, the argument ran, the cross-Channel attack could not inflict the decisive defeat on Germany; it could only, in conjunction with continued Russian advances, deliver the final blow. The members also suggested that an inflexible adherence to the cross-Channel concept was incorrect; that the decision to remove seven battle-tested divisions from the Mediterranean was unsound. Robbing the Mediterranean offensive of momentum might nullify the attempt to knock Italy out of the war or to exploit Italian collapse into an invasion of southern France. Furthermore, the committee believed that the Allies had not given due consideration to the possibility that Germany might defend Italy with strong forces.[1]

The return of seven divisions from the Mediterranean to the United Kingdom by 1 November was the crucial agreement through which General Marshall had sought to make it possible to direct the weight of Anglo-American power into the cross-Channel blow, thereby limiting the Mediterranean offensive to a subordinate role. Although some men who served

[1] JPS 231, Operations in the European-Mediterranean Area, 1943-1944, Rpt by the Joint War Plans Committee, 26 Jul 43, CofS 381 File.

him had doubts, Marshall believed that the decisive defeat of Germany could be inflicted on the classic battlegrounds of northern France and nowhere else.

Among the British planners who served Churchill, some were quite sympathetic with Marshall's strategic view. Yet the British Chiefs of Staff had a genuine conviction that the elimination of Italy from the war was a prerequisite for a successful cross-Channel attack, and that everything possible should be done to make sure that the attack against Italy would knock it out of the war.

Despite the qualifications and shadings around the edges of agreement, an acute conflict of views prevailed between Churchill and Marshall. The latter held resolutely to the concept that the British Isles constituted the only base in which to gather sufficient power for a decisive blow against the heartland of Germany. He had no hope for decisive results by an offensive into the Balkans, with or without Turkish support. He considered attempts to reach the German heart by way of the Italian peninsula, the Postumia-Ljubljana gap, or the Danube valley to be logistically and strategically unsound. He did not believe it possible to inflict a decisive defeat on the German armies by landing in Italy and pursuing them up the ridges of the Italian peninsula and over the Alps, whether toward Austria or toward France. He wanted a main effort in the cross-Channel attack, a simultaneous diversionary amphibious landing in southern France, and the continued employment of limited holding forces in the Mediterranean. This Marshall believed to be the best way to achieve decisive defeat of Germany in the west.

Despite the TRIDENT agreements, there were indications that Mr. Churchill and his advisers shrank from the plan to strike the main blow across the Channel in 1944. At the Algiers conference in late May, immediately after TRIDENT, General Brooke had privately told General Eisenhower that he would be glad to reconsider the cross-Channel project, even to the extent of eliminating it from Allied strategy, for he feared that a ground conflict in a large theater would be disadvantageous for the Allies and might result in tremendous losses.[2] Churchill at a later date frankly told General Wedemeyer that if he had been able to persuade the Combined Chiefs of Staff the Allies would have gone through Turkey and the Balkans from the south and into Norway on the north, thus surrounding the enemy and further dispersing his forces.[3]

The British Chiefs of Staff immediately after TRIDENT fully recognized the priority of operations in the western Mediterranean directed by AFHQ over those projected by the British Middle East Command: ACCOLADE (seizure of the Dodecanese) and HARDIHOOD (aid to Turkey to induce it to enter the war). They instructed General Wilson, the Middle East commander, to make some of his resources available to General Eisenhower.[4] Despite the American JCS veto against employing American ground forces east of Sicily, British strategists kept the Aegean-Balkan area in mind as a potential route toward the Danube once Italy was knocked out of the war.

During July the British representatives

---

[2] Eisenhower, *Crusade in Europe*, p. 167. Cf. Bryant, *Turn of the Tide*, pp. 520-21.

[3] Ltr, Wedemeyer to Handy, 13 Apr 44, OPD Misc Exec File, case 611, book 18.

[4] Br JP (43) 218 (Final), 21 Jun 43, Rpt by Br JPS, sub: Mediterranean Strategy, and CCS (43) 134th Mtg, 23 Jun 43, both in job 10A, reel 21C.

in Washington, on orders from London, kept pressing the CCS to allot resources to General Eisenhower beyond those allocated at TRIDENT. The JCS, however, continued to insist that Eisenhower's invasion of the Italian mainland could be made without additional resources.

When the Secretary of War, Henry L. Stimson, visited England in July, he became alarmed by what he heard from Churchill and Eden. Mr. Stimson suggested that political reasons made it necessary to press for a cross-Channel attack. Though Mr. Churchill seemed to understand—he "confined his position to favoring a march on Rome with its prestige and the possibility of knocking Italy out of the war"—Eden contended for carrying the war into the Balkans and Greece. Both American and British officers working on plans for the cross-Channel attack gave Stimson an impression that the great threat to the plan came from the danger of becoming too deeply involved in the Mediterranean. When Marshall suggested on 16 July that AFHQ study the possibility of an amphibious attack in the Naples area, Churchill interpreted it as an indication that Marshall was shifting from his basic position. A transatlantic phone call quickly reassured Stimson that he knew Marshall's mind better than Churchill did. Yet the check received by the British Eighth Army before Catania led Churchill to speak of a cross-Channel attack as producing a Channel full of corpses.[5]

The vision of occupying the Italian capital captivated Churchill's mind, and Rome was the minimum territorial objective in Italy acceptable to him. Still, he told Stimson that if by good luck the Allies gained the complete capitulation of Italy, he would favor going as far as the northern boundary. Stimson received the impression that Churchill was looking "constantly and vigorously for an easy way of ending the war without a trans-Channel assault." At Algiers, however, Stimson was relieved to find Eisenhower in agreement with Marshall's basic idea—the attack on Italy was to be for a limited objective, one not impairing or substituting for the cross-Channel attack, but rather one that would aid and facilitate it. At AFHQ, Mr. Stimson gained the impression that the Foggia airfields were considered the main objective of the campaign.[6]

Upon returning to Washington Mr. Stimson on 4 August sent a recommendation to the President. "The main thing therefore to keep constantly in mind," he wrote, "is that the Italian effort must be strictly confined to the objective of securing bases for an air attack and there must be no further diversions of the forces or matériel which will interfere with the coincident mounting of the ROUNDHAMMER [cross-Channel] project."[7]

On 9 August, General Marshall called on the President in order to ascertain the President's views and the American position to be presented at the impending Quebec Conference. Roosevelt stated that in a choice between cross-Channel invasion and the invasion of the Italian mainland he would insist on the former. But he felt that more could be done for

---

[5] Henry L. Stimson and McGeorge Bundy, *On Active Service in Peace and War* (New York: Harper & Brothers, 1947, 1948), pp. 429–32; Butcher, *My Three Years With Eisenhower*, p. 373; Bryant, *Turn of the Tide*, pp. 551–53, 572–74.

[6] Stimson and Bundy, *On Active Service*, pp. 432–34; Eisenhower, *Crusade in Europe*, p. 160.
[7] Stimson and Bundy, *On Active Service*, p. 434.

the latter than had been proposed. The seven battle-tested divisions should be moved to England, but perhaps an equal number of divisions could go from the United States directly to Italy. He stated that he would resist an operation into the Balkans or any expedition that might involve a heavy loss of ships and landing craft without the possibility of achieving decisive results. He thought that the Allies should secure a position in Italy just north of Rome and occupy Sardinia and Corsica, thus setting up a serious threat to southern France.[8]

The following day Secretary of War Stimson called on the President. He presented a memorandum making a plea for holding to the American strategic concept. As a result of talks, personal contacts, and conversations during his recent overseas trip, Stimson said, he had reached the conclusion that there was no rational hope for a successful cross-Channel attack under a British commander. He urged that the American Government take the leadership, insist on a cross-Channel attack, and guarantee its execution by securing the appointment of General Marshall as its commander. After reading the memorandum, Mr. Roosevelt stated that he himself had reached the same conclusions.[9]

During the few remaining days before the conference opened, American policy makers, after thorough discussion, formulated their views. The President told the Joint Chiefs that he favored setting up a great force in Britain as soon as possible. Having more American soldiers than British for the cross-Channel operation, he said, would make the appointment of an American commander easier to secure. As for the Mediterranean, the President stated that he wished to invade Italy for the purpose of establishing bases; he would go no farther north than Rome.[10]

The American position to be presented at Quebec, therefore, reaffirmed the strategy agreed upon in May—because "conditions have not changed as to justify on sound military grounds the renunciation of the TRIDENT concept." The Americans did not wish to jeopardize a sound over-all strategy "simply to exploit local successes in a generally accepted secondary theater, the Mediterranean, where logistical and terrain difficulties preclude decisive and final operations designed to reach the heart of Germany." The essence of American strategy was the cross-Channel attack, carefully synchronized with the combined bomber offensive. The Mediterranean, strictly delimited to a subordinate area, was to be exploited with only those resources already available. Three phases of operations in Italy were forecast: eliminating Italy as a belligerent and establishing air bases at least as far north as the Rome area; seizing Sardinia and Corsica; and maintaining pressure on German forces and creating conditions favorable for entry into southern France.[11]

The American and British Chiefs of Staff opened the argument on 15 August, the second day of the conference—the day Seventh Army entered Messina. The British expressed complete agreement

---

[8] Memo, Marshall for Handy, 9 Aug 43, CofS 381 File.

[9] Stimson and Bundy, *On Active Service*, pp. 436-38.

[10] *Ibid.*, 436-39; Matloff, *Strategic Planning for Coalition Warfare, 1943-1944*, pp. 214-16.

[11] CCS 303, 9 Aug 43, sub: Strategic Concept for the Defeat of the Axis in Europe: Memorandum by the U.S. Joint Chiefs of Staff, QUADRANT Conf Book, pp. 72-77; Telg 4751, Marshall to Eisenhower, 11 Aug 43, Smith Papers, box 4.

with the Americans in principle, but they challenged the phrases used by the Joint Chiefs to guarantee the principles. The British Chiefs, according to General Brooke, were in entire agreement that OVERLORD should constitute the major offensive for 1944 and that Italian operations should be planned against that background. But they saw operations in Italy as creating a situation favorable and even necessary for a successful cross-Channel attack—by holding down German reserves and by bombing German fighter plane factories from Italian airfields. Therefore, Brooke said, giving overriding priority to the cross-Channel attack over any Mediterranean operation was too binding, for sufficient forces had to be used in Italy to make the cross-Channel attack possible. Suggesting that the Allies could achieve far greater success in bombing the fighter plane factories in Germany from Po valley airfields than from those in central Italy, Brooke proposed that the Allies consider the line of the Apennines as merely the first phase line of their advance, a preliminary for seizing the north Italian plain.

At this point Admiral King bluntly remarked that, as he understood it, "The British Chiefs of Staff had serious doubts as to the possibility of OVERLORD." The British protested that they were thinking only of conditions required for a successful cross-Channel attack. General Marshall then put his finger on the central issue. "The essence of the problem," he said, "was whether or not the required conditions for a successful OVERLORD could only be made possible by an increase of strength in the Mediterranean." He agreed that the Allies should seize as much of Italy as possible if resistance was weak, for it would be better if the Allies rather than the Germans held the northern airfields. Yet he thought that almost as much could be achieved by securing the Florence area. On the other hand, unless the Allies decided to remove the seven divisions from the Mediterranean, and unless the Allies gave overriding priority to OVERLORD, the cross-Channel operation, he believed, would become only a subsidiary operation. The operation would then be "doomed and our whole strategic concept would have to be recast." [12]

So frank an exchange of views followed that the Combined Chiefs preferred not to keep a formal record of the discussion.[13] Not until 17 August did the American Chiefs secure written agreement that largely fulfilled their demand for a guarantee of OVERLORD. They did not quite get "overriding priority" for the cross-Channel operation, but they obtained assurance that the Mediterranean theater would be subordinate and that the stage would be set for only limited operations. Ground operations in the Balkans were ruled out, and the purpose of an attack against southern France was defined as: "to establish a lodgment in the Toulon-Marseilles area and exploit northward in order to create a diversion in connection with OVERLORD." [14]

The Allies thus stipulated OVERLORD as the main effort for 1944. But despite the cogency of his arguments, General Marshall did not obtain a formula for the Mediterranean which would serve to ward off his most acute fear: the drawing off of resources into a secondary theater. This was partly due to the general expectation that Italy would promptly surren-

---

[12] Min, 108th Mtg CCS, 15 Aug 43.
[13] Bryant, *Turn of the Tide*, p. 579.
[14] CCS 303/3, 17 Aug 43, sub: Strategic Concept for the Defeat of the Axis in Europe, QUADRANT Conf Book, pp. 87–88.

der and that, in consequence, the Germans would withdraw to a line somewhere north of Rome. QUADRANT set the Rome area as the minimum Allied territorial objective in Italy and called for "unremitting pressure" against the German forces in "Northern Italy." But in case the Germans did not withdraw to the line of the northern Apennines, in case the Italian capital did not fall before the momentum of the Allied attack, what then? For the sake of conquering central Italy, how much in men and matériel would the Mediterranean theater be permitted to absorb at the expense of the cross-Channel build-up? In the over-all strategy of the war, how much was the occupation of the Italian capital and the use of its airfields worth to the Allies once Italy was eliminated from the war? QUADRANT did not answer these questions because the problem was not set in those terms. Churchill was fascinated by Rome and the prospect of its capture. Marshall was profoundly skeptical of the Italian theater and considered it the greatest threat to the build-up in England required for the main blow.

The QUADRANT Conference devoted but little attention to specific plans for invading the Italian mainland. The Combined Chiefs had delegated the formulation of precise operations to AFHQ, and at the meeting held on the last day of the conference, 24 August, Generals Whiteley and Rooks presented in outline the plans for BAYTOWN (a crossing of the Strait of Messina), and AVALANCHE (an assault in the Naples area). The CCS merely noted the exposition of General Eisenhower's plans and gave their approval.[15]

[15] Min, 116th Mtg CCS, item 3; Telg, Roosevelt and Churchill to Stalin, 25 Aug 43, OPD 300.6 Security (OCS Papers).

*The Mission of General Castellano*

In Rome, General Castellano, who hated the Germans for their ill-concealed contempt for Italian officers and soldiers, watched with growing alarm the increasing German occupation of northern Italy. One of the chief conspirators against Mussolini and predisposed to political activity, he saw a means for saving Italy and the House of Savoy only in shifting sides in the war, a feat which that House had often performed with dexterity in the 17th and 18th centuries when it ruled Piedmont only. Disappointed in the outcome of Mussolini's overthrow and regarding Badoglio as a fool for not recognizing Italy's obvious course, Castellano flung himself with ardor into the task of making contact with the Allies.[16]

Castellano was not alone in searching for a way to avert the intolerable situation into which Italy was drifting because of the lack of firm direction by the King and Badoglio. Many individuals on lower levels of authority were formulating and advocating courses of action for the government. Generale di Brigata Umberto Utili and Generale Addetto al Capo di Stato Maggiore Giacomo Zanussi of Roatta's headquarters, for example, urged an immediate break with the Germans independent of agreement with the Allies, for they believed that the resulting Italo-German conflict would draw the Allies into Italy on the Italian side. Though less attractive after 1 August, this course

[16] To borrow a phrase from Churchill, Castellano's tragedy was in trying "to carry out a major and cardinal operation of war from a subordinate position," and, as Churchill warns, "Men are ill-advised to try such ventures." Winston S. Churchill, "The Second World War," vol. II, *Their Finest Hour* (Boston: Houghton Mifflin Company, 1949), p. 15.

of action was suggested even after the Tarvis conference.[17]

In contrast to this point of view, Ambrosio, Francesco Rossi, his deputy chief of staff, and Castellano, felt that the Italians had to oppose the Germans, but only after reaching agreement for military cooperation with the Allies.[18] Guariglia, the Foreign Minister, wished military and political agreements with the Allies, but he wanted the negotiations to be conducted by diplomatists. He preferred not to conclude an armistice with the Allies until they had landed on the mainland and could occupy and defend Rome.

Ambrosio pushed for action, but, having great respect for Badoglio, he would go no further than the marshal wished. Badoglio would take no step except on the explicit word of the King. The King, however, refused to take any step that would lead to a break with the Germans.[19]

In this situation Castellano acted. After conversations with Roatta, Utili, and Zanussi on 9 August, Castellano urged Ambrosio to see the King on the problem of reaching agreement with the Allies. Italy, Castellano felt, should not surrender, but go over to the Allied side. An Italian emissary, he thought, should be sent immediately to make contact with the Allies. The emissary should have documentary instructions and credentials authorizing him to make agreements for military collaboration. After reaching agreement, the Italians would turn against the Germans.

At an audience granted to Ambrosio on 10 August, the King assented to Ambrosio's proposal for sending a representative to the Allies, but the monarch declined to furnish any credentials or written instructions. Guariglia, when consulted by Ambrosio, was not enthusiastic over an additional emissary; he preferred to await the outcome of the missions of D'Ajeta and Berio, and he declined to send a member of the Ministry of Foreign Affairs to accompany another emissary. Thus far, the Italian military men did not know the full scope of the D'Ajeta and Berio missions. It was Badoglio who decided that a military man should be sent, and Castellano was chosen.

Ambrosio alone instructed Castellano. Castellano was to negotiate only with Allied military representatives. He was to furnish them military information. He was to agree with them on a common plan of action against the Germans. Though he received no written instuctions, he secured from Acquarone a letter of introduction by Sir D'Arcy Osborne to Sir Samuel Hoare, the British Ambassador at Madrid. Guariglia at first declined to issue an individual passport for Castellano, arranging instead for Castellano to travel on a collective passport being provided several diplomatic officials bound for Portugal, but Castellano finally obtained a passport for himself made out with the fictitious name "Raimondi."

Before departing from Rome on 12 August, Castellano saw Guariglia, who urged the greatest caution, warning that discovery of Castellano's mission would mean death to the members of the government. Guariglia reminded Castellano that the government was practically a prisoner of the Germans and quite unable to separate from them unless the Allies made it possible. Because Rome was in

---

[17] Castellano, *Come firmai*, p. 78; Zanussi, *Guerra e catastrofe*, vol. II, pp. 49–51.

[18] Rossi, *Come arrivammo*, pp. 113–18, 121; Castellano, *Come firmai*, p. 78.

[19] MS #P-058, Project 46, 1 Feb–8 Sep 43, Question 11.

great danger, Castellano should urge the Allies to land on the mainland north of the capital.[20]

On that day, General Eisenhower's AFHQ diary noted that "what had appeared to be a quick collapse of Italy had disappeared into uncertainty . . . ."[21] And on the following day, Allied bombers operating from North Africa and England attacked Milan, Turin, Genoa, and Rome as a reminder to Badoglio that the Allies were in earnest in demanding unconditional surrender.

The Italians scarcely knew where the greater threat lay. The Allied armies were making steady progress in Sicily, and Allied planes were bombing Italian cities at will. In northern Italy, the Germans were rapidly consolidating their control. The *2d Parachute Division* completed its move to areas just north and south of Rome; elements of the *26th Panzer Division* had reinforced the *3d Panzer Grenadier Division* near Lake Bolsena; these plus the headquarters troops of *OB SUED* at Frascati constituted an immediate threat to Rome. The movement of the units under *Army Group B* into northern Italy was approximately half completed, and even though Rommel's headquarters was still at Munich, the *44th Infantry Division* controlled the Italian side of the Brenner Pass, the *Brigade Doehla* held the entrances to the auxiliary passes leading to Bolzano. Along the Brenner route, the *SS Panzer Division Leibstandarte Adolf Hitler* had moved to the Parma area, the *65th Infantry Division* had moved by the same route southwest of Parma, the *24th Panzer Division*, destined for Modena, was moving into Italy by way of the Tarvis Pass, and the *71st Infantry Division* was to follow and occupy the eastern passes into Italy over the Julian Alps. The *305th Infantry Division,* in the Nice area since 1 August, was ready to follow the *76th Infantry Division,* which had moved to the Genoese coast. The *94th Infantry Division,* not yet in Italy, was awaiting transportation at the entrance to the Mount Cenis pass and was poised to gain control of the Modane-Bardonecchia sector of the Turin-Lyons railway. Not a single German division had moved south of Rome in this period, and the German intention seemed clear—to seize the Italian capital; to grab the Italian Fleet; to pull German forces out of the south and defend a line in the northern Apennines.[22]

In the meantime, the Allies were tackling the proposals of D'Ajeta and Berio. Right after his conversation with D'Ajeta on 4 August, Ambassador Campbell in Lisbon had telegraphed to London the substance of D'Ajeta's remarks. From Downing Street the report was forwarded to Churchill, who was on the point of sailing for Canada. Though Churchill had been anxious upon Mussolini's downfall to gain maximum advantage from the political change and to turn the "fury" of the Italian people against the German "invader," his reaction to the D'Ajeta mission was chilly. He relayed Campbell's report to President Roosevelt without recommendation, commenting only: "D'Ajeta never from start to finish made any mention of peace terms and his whole story, as you will have observed, was no more than a plea that we

---

[20] Castellano, *Come firmai,* pp. 80–84; Guariglia, *Ricordi,* pp. 640–47.
[21] Butcher, *My Three Years With Eisenhower,* p. 386.
[22] Data on German divisions in Italy from *OKW/WFSt, KTB, 1.–31.VIII.43,* 6–13 Aug 43.

should save Italy from the Germans as well as from herself, and do it as quickly as possible."[23]

Several days later, when the report of the Berio feeler reached London, Churchill was on the high seas and Eden was at the Foreign Office. After noting that Berio's proposal was an offer to negotiate on terms, Eden suggested that the Allies take the single course of action in consonance with the Anglo-American public declarations:

Should we not then reply that, as is well known, we insist on unconditional surrender, and the Badoglio Government must as a first step notify us that Italy surrenders unconditionally? Subsequently, at a later stage, if the Badoglio Government were to do this, we should then inform them of the terms on which we should be prepared to cease hostilities against Italy.[24]

Though Churchill wrote a note to himself: "Don't miss the bus," he radioed the Foreign Secretary: "We agree with the course you have taken." When Churchill arrived in Canada on 9 August, he sketched out somewhat more fully an appropriate reply. "Badoglio must state," the Prime Minister wrote, "that he is prepared to place himself unreservedly in the hands of the Allied Governments who have already made it plain that they desire Italy to have a respectable place in the new Europe." Yet, as Churchill warned Eden, and himself as well, "Merely harping on 'unconditional surrender,' with no prospect of mercy held out even as an act of grace, may well lead to no surrender at all."[25]

Eden then drafted the full text of a reply to be given to Berio in Tangier, a draft first forwarded on 12 August to President Roosevelt, who approved the concept and the precise language. On the following day, the day after Castellano departed Rome, Berio received word that the Allies were unwilling to negotiate:

Badoglio must understand that we cannot negotiate, but require unconditional surrender, which means that Italian Government should place themselves in hands of Allied Governments, who will then state their terms. These will provide for an honourable capitulation.[26]

Several days earlier, on 8 August, Mr. Harold Tittmann, assistant to the President's Personal Representative to the Pope, sent a message through Lisbon that reached the Allied leaders in Quebec on 15 August. Tittmann reiterated the Badoglio government's desire to make immediate peace with the Allies, made plain its inability to do so because of the German threat to seize control of the Italian Government and to occupy the entire country. He stated that Badoglio was forced to play for time in the hope that the Allies would come to Italy's assistance by intensifying air warfare against the Germans and by landing in the northern part of the peninsula. Hitler, the Italians insisted, was seeking a suitable pretext to occupy Italy.[27]

Tittmann sent another message by way of Berne on 12 August, a statement that reached the Allied leaders on 18 August. He repeated that the Badoglio government's chief concern remained the Nazi threat of occupation, that the Nazis were looking for an excuse to carry out their

---

[23] Churchill, *Closing the Ring*, p. 100; Telg 55, Churchill to Roosevelt, 5 Aug 43, OPD Exec 9, Book 11.
[24] Churchill, *Closing the Ring*, p. 101.
[25] *Ibid.*

[26] *Ibid.*, pp. 102-03.
[27] Telg 58, Handy to QUADRANT, KKAD, 15 Aug 43, OPD Exec 2, item 5, tab 32.

threat, and that if the Italians tried to surrender to the Allies, the Germans would undoubtedly take over the country within two hours after learning of the effort.[28]

To Badoglio's earliest efforts to persuade the Allies that he was not free, that he could not unconditionally do anything because of the German noose around the Italian capital, the Anglo-American leaders gave little, if any, attention—no more, in fact, than to the question of exactly how Badoglio was to surrender unconditionally. The capabilities of the Allied navies and air forces notwithstanding, the Allies could not occupy Rome or any part of Italy until Allied ground troops were on the Italian mainland. No Allied force was in a position to accept a surrender and exploit its advantages.

General Eisenhower saw the close connection between strategy and policy, but Churchill and Roosevelt seemed to ignore it. The first Italian-Allied exchanges resembled two persons talking to each other in their sleep, each the victim of his own hallucination. In the nightmare of the German occupation, Italy gasped, "Help, I am not free." After a long pause, the Allies replied, "Say Uncle." Part of the Allied reaction came from Churchill's suspicion—"Badoglio admits he is going to double-cross someone"—and Churchill was not at all willing to be the victim.[29]

Yet there was something decidedly intelligible in what D'Ajeta had said at Lisbon on 4 August. He had faithfully regurgitated before Ambassador Campbell the German order of battle in Italy which he had spent hours memorizing. This information would have been helpful to the Allied military leaders, for AFHQ was then toying with plans based on the hope of an unopposed landing in the Naples area. Unfortunately, Allied diplomatic channels were distinctly different and quite separate from strategic and military channels. Although General Marshall had been careful to keep AFHQ fully informed of the negotiations to establish Rome as an open city, General Eisenhower learned nothing of the D'Ajeta and Berio missions.[30]

Leaving Rome by train on 12 August, Castellano intended to present himself to the Allies as a representative not of a conquered country bowing to the inevitable and asking aid to surrender, but of a country that still had sufficient force to disown a detested ally and energy enough to fight for redemption. The essential point he wished to make was that Italy asked for help to enable it to join the battle on the side of the United Nations.[31]

Traveling as Signor Raimondi of the Italian Ministry of Exchange and Currency and in company with a party of officials, Castellano arrived in Madrid at noon, 15 August. While the party was visiting the Prado Museum, Castellano took Consul Franco Montanari aside and revealed his identity. Swearing Montanari to secrecy and asking him to serve as his interpreter, Castellano took him to the British Embassy. Montanari was not altogether surprised. Before his departure from Rome, Guariglia had briefed him on Castellano's mission.[32]

Castellano presented his letter of in-

---

[28] Telg 5012, Minister Harrison at Berne to State Dept, forwarded to Gen Deane at Quebec as Telg 3465, OPD Exec 2, item 5, tab 36.

[29] Churchill, *Closing the Ring,* p. 102.

[30] The Capitulation of Italy has no reference to these missions. General Smith told Howard Smyth on 13 May 1947 that he, Smith, had no knowledge of any Italian overtures prior to Castellano's mission.

[31] Castellano, *Come firmai,* pp. 86–87.

[32] Guariglia, *Ricordi,* p. 646; Castellano, *Come firmai,* pp. 88–90.

troduction, and Sir Samuel Hoare received him. Explaining his position as chief of Ambrosio's military office, Castellano said that his mission was official and that he had complete backing from Marshal Badoglio. Italy, he declared, was exhausted, the ground forces were poorly armed, aviation was weak, and German troops were streaming into the country. Until the Allies landed on the Italian mainland, Castellano said, the government was powerless to act. But if and when the Allies invaded the mainland, Italy was prepared to join them in fighting the Germans. If the Allies were willing to accept Italian help, Castellano was prepared to give detailed information on German dispositions and strength. The Italians were ready to co-operate with Mihailovitch in the Balkans, to repudiate the independence of Croatia, and to reach agreement with Yugoslavia over Dalmatia. Attempts had been made to bring Italian troops home, all units had been withdrawn from the Russian front, and German units had taken over the duty of garrisoning Greece, particularly at Salonika. Because of the rapid build-up of German forces in Italy, Badoglio wished to take immediate action. Thirteen German divisions were already in Italy, and more were arriving. The Germans, Castellano said, planned to defend the Genoa-Ravenna line.

The greatest danger Italy faced, according to Castellano, was the prospect that the Germans would seize control of the country. The Germans had threatened to bomb Italian cities and use gas if the Badoglio government did not continue in the war. Hating the Germans, the Italian people would support a military alignment with the Allies. Mussolini and the Fascists were discredited. Though the Fascist militia had been disarmed, it was bitterly hostile to the Italian Regular Army. If Badoglio could not reach agreement with the Allies, he feared that the Germans might re-establish Mussolini in power and bring back the militia. If the Germans caught Castellano, they would kill him. Hence the need for secrecy, and the necessity for Castellano to proceed under his false name to Lisbon on the ostensible mission of meeting the SS *Cabo de Bueno Esperanza*, which was bringing home the Italian Ambassador to Chile. Castellano had to return to Rome with the Ambassador's party some time after the 20th of August.

Sir Samuel asked what the Italians would do with respect to the Allied demand for unconditional surrender. Castellano declared: "We are not in a position to make any terms. We will accept unconditional surrender provided we can join the Allies in fighting the Germans." Stating that his mission was—as he firmly believed it to be—to make the first official proposal by Italy to the Allies, Castellano again expressed his willingness to give information concerning both the Germans and Italians to the British military attaché if the British Ambassador gave an immediate reply to his proposal. If they could reach agreement, Castellano said, the Italian Army could do much to cut the German supply lines.

Ambassador Hoare expressed no opinion, for he was without instructions, but he promised to forward at once Castellano's offer to the British Government. In addition, he gave Castellano a letter of introduction to Sir Ronald Hugh Campbell, the British Ambassador at Lisbon.[33]

[33] Telgs 1404 and 1406, Hoare to Foreign Office, 15 Aug 43, as repeated in Telg 4488, Devers to Eisenhower, 17 Aug 43, in Capitula-

After leaving the British Embassy, Castellano went to a hotel to make notes of his conversation. It occurred to him that perhaps he had not been sufficiently explicit in requesting to meet Allied military leaders. Nor had he definitely referred to the Americans, whom he wished to meet as well as the British. He returned to the Embassy and asked Hoare whether General Eisenhower might send a senior staff officer to Lisbon to take part in the discussions. That evening, Castellano departed from Madrid in company with Montanari and the others of the party.

Sir Samuel made haste to wire his government a full account of his meeting with Castellano. His opinion, based solely on the interview, was that the Italian Government was prepared to accept unconditional surrender if the Allies landed on the Italian mainland, and if the Italian Army could join in the fight against the Germans. "Without these two conditions," he telegraphed, "the Italian Government will not have sufficient courage or justification to make a complete volte-face and will drift impotently into chaos." He recommended that serious attention be given to Castellano's proposal, if for no other reason than to obtain intelligence of German intentions and dispositions.[34]

## The Quebec Memorandum

When Foreign Secretary Eden forwarded Hoare's telegrams to Churchill at Quebec, he informed the Prime Minister that he had instructed Ambassador Campbell in Lisbon to hold Castellano there, to listen to what he had to say, but for Campbell to make no reply until he received instructions. Castellano's offer of Italian co-operation Eden found tempting, but he advised Churchill against accepting the proposal on the ground that it might cause the Allies political difficulties.[35]

In Canada, Churchill, in a wire to President Roosevelt at Hyde Park on 16 August, outlined a reply to the Italian general. Churchill's draft made no mention of the short terms or of any other terms. Nor did it state a demand by the Allies for unconditional surrender. This was implied in the phraseology of Churchill's initial paragraph, which, at the same time, excluded any joint Italo-Allied planning of operations prior to Italy's breaking with Germany. Churchill said that the Allies could make no bargain on the prospect of Italy's changing sides in the war. Rather, "by taking action against the common enemy, the Italian Government,

---

tion of Italy, pp. 76–77, 79–80; Castellano, *Come firmai*, pp. 91–95; Sir Samuel John Gurney Hoare, Viscount Templewood, *Ambassador on Special Mission* (London: Collins, 1946), pp. 212–16.

The Ambassador's memoirs must be used with caution. Though he denies his intent to do so, the Ambassador criticizes Allied leadership for "the slow motion with which the picture was unfolded which gave the Germans time for sending strong reinforcements to Italy." Nor is his account as closely based on letters and daily notes as stated in the preface (page 7). The text is colored by retrospection.

The content of Castellano's account agrees quite closely with the contemporary telegrams of Hoare, except for a slight discrepancy in chronology. Hoare states that the offer of an armistice was made to him on 13 August, a Sunday (pages 212, 216), but the telegrams indicate that he received the two Italians on the morning of 15 August; Castellano states they were not received until the afternoon of 15 August sometime after 1400.

[34] Telg 1405, Hoare to Foreign Office, 15 Aug 43, as repeated in Telg 4488, Devers to Eisenhower, 17 Aug 43, Capitulation of Italy, p. 79. Castellano, *Come firmai*, pp. 96–98.

[35] Telg 4488, Devers to Eisenhower, 17 Aug 43, sub: Repeat of Telegrams Sent to QUADRANT (Nos. 231, 232, 233, 234), in Capitulation of Italy, pp. 76–81.

Army, and people could without any bargain facilitate a more friendly relationship with the United Nations." Recognizing Badoglio's predicament—Kesselring's forces surrounding Rome and Allied forces ready to invade Italy—Churchill proposed that Castellano be told: "The Italian Government should . . . resist the Germans to the best of their ability as soon as possible, pending arrival of Anglo-American armies." Until the Allies arrived, the Italian Government might cut German communications in southern Italy, safeguard Allied prisoners, sail the fleet to Allied ports, provide intelligence information, aid the invasion forces to disembark, and co-operate with guerrilla forces in the Balkans.[36]

On the following day, 17 August, as President Roosevelt and Mr. Eden were arriving in Quebec, the CCS produced what became known as the Quebec Memorandum: "Suggested Action on Italian Peace Feelers." Shaping the memorandum were several factors: the unconditional surrender formula, Churchill's message to Roosevelt, the approved text of the short terms, the still unapproved text of the long terms, and an imperfect realization of the military difficulties in mounting and executing Operation AVALANCHE, the projected invasion of the Italian mainland near Naples.

The CCS in the Quebec Memorandum suggested that Eisenhower send two staff officers, one American, the other British, to Lisbon at once to meet Castellano. They were to tell Castellano that: the Allies would accept the unconditional surrender of Italy on the conditions of the short terms, which were to be handed to the Italian emissary; political, economic, and financial terms were to be communicated to the Italian Government later; though the Allies visualized no "active resistance" on the part of Italy in fighting the Germans, they expected Italy to hamper German operations, and in return the Allies promised to restrict bombing to targets affecting the German forces alone; hostilities were to cease at a time to be determined by General Eisenhower; the Italian Government was to proclaim the armistice at once and from that time "to collaborate with the Allies and to resist the Germans"; it was to send Navy, merchant shipping, and aircraft to Allied territory. Until the hour of the armistice, the Italians were to institute general passive resistance and minor sabotage against the Germans, safeguard Allied prisoners of war, prevent Italian ships and aircraft from falling into German hands, prevent the Germans from taking over Italian coast defenses, and arrange to march Italian units in the Balkans to coastal areas for evacuation by the Allies. If the Italians complied, Eisenhower was to have authority to soften the armistice terms proportionately with the scale of the assistance the Italians rendered to the Allies. Eisenhower was also to arrange for a secure channel of communication between him and the Italian Government.[37]

This precise course of action laid down by the CCS gave General Eisenhower

---

[36] Churchill, *Closing the Ring*, pp. 103–04.

[37] CCS 311, 17 Aug 43, sub: Italian Peace Feelers, QUADRANT Conf Book, pp. 141–44; See Telg, CCS to Eisenhower, FAN 196, 18 Aug 43, Capitulation of Italy, pp. 90–92. Churchill prints an incomplete text in *Closing the Ring*, pp. 105–06. Most of the memorandum is printed in translation by Castellano, *Come firmai*, pp. 109–12. The full title of the Quebec Memorandum is: "Aide-Memoire to accompany conditions of Armistice, presented by General Eisenhower to the Italian C-in-C." See File 10,000/136/584; Bryant, *Turn of the Tide*, pp. 580–82.

authority to bring about the surrender of Italy, but no power to negotiate. He was not to reveal his military plans to Badoglio's representative. He was to announce the armistice a few hours before the execution of AVALANCHE, the principal invasion of the Italian mainland, which he had decided on 16 August, two days before receiving the Quebec Memorandum, to launch on the shores of the Gulf of Salerno. He could offer the Badoglio government but scant inducement to surrender: a general assurance that the Allies would modify the terms of surrender in the future if Italy surrendered completely on the eve of the Allied invasion, and if Italian forces gave positive aid to that invasion. But he could provide no answer to Badoglio's vital questions: were the Allies able, willing, and planning to occupy the seat of his government? Or would surrender to the Allies signal the German occupation of Rome and the immediate establishment of a neo-Fascist Quisling regime in Italy?

During the months following the TRIDENT Conference, the Italian surrender and the invasion of the Italian mainland had become curiously reversed. TRIDENT had directed Eisenhower "to knock Italy out of the war," and the assault of the mainland was conceived as the most appropriate means of doing so. With the collapse of fascism, the basic design of Allied plans for invading the Italian mainland—BUTTRESS, BARRACUDA, BAYTOWN, AVALANCHE—changed. The plans envisaged not knocking Italy out of the war but getting Allied troops onto the mainland to exert pressure on the Germans. What then dominated Allied thinking was the idea that Italy, as a consequence of Mussolini's downfall, would surrender. Capitulation was not expected to result from the assault on the mainland; rather, the surrender was to precede and facilitate the invasion.

## Approval of the Long Terms

The QUADRANT Conference settled an additional problem, that of the long terms of armistice for Italy. The British members of the CCAC had continued to urge the necessity for political and economic terms in addition to the military clauses, and General Eisenhower on 6 August had been informed that if he used the short terms he was to make clear that other conditions were to be imposed later. But it was not clear to the CCAC members what the additional conditions would be. Would there be a list of purely economic and political terms to supplement the short terms? Or would there be a single comprehensive instrument to supersede the short terms? Hoping that the QUADRANT conferees would answer these questions, the committee on 12 August began to prepare for both courses. The members made some changes in the British draft and, at American insistence, the unconditional surrender formula reappeared.[38]

When Mr. Eden raised the issue at Quebec with Cordell Hull, the Secretary of State consulted with the President and learned that Mr. Roosevelt had not changed his mind. Roosevelt was satisfied to have Eisenhower use the short terms to obtain Italian surrender, with the understanding that political conditions would be imposed later. Mr. Hull therefore told Eden that he had neither recommendations nor objections to make on the long terms. So far as nonmilitary

---

[38] Min, 6th Mtg CCAC, 12 Aug 43, and Special Mtg, 21 Aug 43, ABC 381 Italy-Arm-Surr (5-9-43), sec. 1-A.

matters were concerned, the Department of State concurred with the latest draft of the text.

Churchill and Eden then sought President Roosevelt's approval. Mr. Roosevelt must have given them some sort of assurance of concurrence, for on 23 August the British Foreign Office informed the Department of State that the Prime Minister and the President had reached agreement and that the British were instructing their Ambassador in Lisbon to use the long terms in place of the short terms in any future dealings with Italian emissaries. Because the Foreign Office was not fully certain of the President's concurrence, however, the British asked the State Department to clear the matter with the President and have the combined Chiefs direct Eisenhower to use the long terms—the "Comprehensive Instrument," as it was called—in place of the short terms—the military terms. Declining to take initiative in a matter outside its province, the Department of State indicated that it would be more appropriate for the Foreign Office to take up the matter with the British Chiefs of Staff.

The President gave his final and formal concurrence on 26 August, when he directed the JCS to instruct Eisenhower to substitute the long terms for the short terms in any subsequent dealings with Badoglio's representatives. Eden on the same day instructed the Ambassador at Lisbon—Campbell—to use the long terms in any negotiations with Italian emissaries. On the following day the CCS wired the text of the long terms to Eisenhower and instructed him that this document, including the military terms, was to be used in any future negotiations.[39]

[39] Memo, Mr. James Clement Dunn for the U.S. Secy of State, 1 Sep 43, sub: Conditions

General Eisenhower thus received several difficult assignments as a result of the QUADRANT Conference. With limited forces and resources (particularly in landing craft), he was to invade the Italian mainland in two places—across the Strait of Messina and on the shores of the Gulf of Salerno. From the latter landing, he was to sweep rapidly to Rome, 140 miles to the north. Without revealing his hand, he was to bluff Badoglio into surrender to make possible the Allied invasion. In accordance with instructions to use the long terms—an extraordinary complication because negotiations with Badoglio were already under way on the basis of the short terms and the Quebec Memorandum—Eisenhower was to insist on unconditional surrender. By this time, AFHQ intelligence, too, had obtained a clearer picture of German strength in Italy. The estimates of enemy capabilities on which the AVALANCHE plan for a landing at Salerno had been based were radically wrong. German strength had been grossly underestimated.

When the British Resident Minister at Algiers, Mr. Harold Macmillan, learned of the long terms, he protested against their immediate use. "I am told," he wired his superiors, "that military difficulties involved in operation of AVALANCHE are so great that we cannot exaggerate the value of an armistice concluded and announced

for the Italian Surrender, OPD Exec 2, item 5; Extract from Min, 7th Mtg CCAC, 26 Aug 43, ABC 381 Italy-Arm-Surr (5-9-43), sec. 1-A; Telg 5718, 26 Aug 43, Foreign Office to Sir Ronald Campbell at Lisbon, OPD Exec 2, item 5, tab 50 (the context of which indicates the long terms had already been received at Lisbon); Memo, Deane for JCS, 27 Aug 43, ABC 381 Italy-Arm-Surr (5-9-43), sec. 1-A; Telg, CCS to Eisenhower, FAN 203, 27 Aug 43, Capitulation of Italy, p. 137.

in accordance with timing suggested by the President and the Prime Minister."[40]

But the die had been cast. General Eisenhower had no alternative but to carry out his sometimes conflicting, always difficult, dual assignment—one a military mission, the other a diplomatic matter.

---

[40] Telg 1537, Resident Minister Algiers to Washington and Quebec, 26 Aug 43, as forwarded in Telg 5717 (MS), Campbell, Lisbon, to Foreign Office, OPD Exec 2, item 5, tab 50.

# CHAPTER XXIII

# The Surrender Preliminaries

## *The Zanussi Mission*

After Castellano's departure for Madrid and Lisbon, Ambrosio continued to co-operate warily with the Germans; until Castellano brought back word that the Allies were willing to support open rupture with the Germans, the Italians could do little else.

Roatta, Army chief of staff who was responsible for defending Italy against Allied attack, still did not know of Castellano's mission. His recognition since May that Italian forces alone were not equal to the task of opposing an Allied invasion prompted him to keep calling for German reinforcements, ground as well as air. But the German troops in Italy were poorly distributed for defense against the Allies. Anxious to defend the entire peninsula and believing the most threatened area to be southern Italy, particularly the Naples-Salerno area, Roatta pointed out to the Germans that loss of southern Italy would open the Balkans to Allied operations. He proposed that the Germans group their divisions into mobile reserves deployed at several key points throughout Italy to meet various Allied capabilities. A heavy concentration of German units in northern Italy would then be unnecessary, Roatta urged, unless, of course, the Germans intended to abandon southern and central Italy at the very outset.[1]

Because the Germans and Italians at the Tarvis conference had not agreed on a common plan for the defense of Italy, on the command problem posed by German forces in Italy, and on the return of the Italian *Fourth Army* from France, Roatta proposed a new conference for purely military matters. The German Government accepted on the condition that the meeting be held at Bologna, the area where the *II SS Panzer Corps* was stationed.[2]

Roatta's strategic views were not essentially different from those of Kesselring, who still believed that the Italians showed a genuine will to co-operate. Kesselring also discerned, by the middle of August, a slight but definite improvement in the morale of the Italian troops. Intent on defending the whole of Italy and believing the task feasible, he reported that it would be difficult for the Germans quickly to seize Rome and the Italian Government. The *26th Panzer Division*'s vehicles, essential to render fully mobile the German forces around Rome (*3d Panzer Grenadier* and *2d Parachute Divisions*), had not yet arrived. More important, Italian forces were present around Rome in considerable strength. If Italo-German conflict started in the Rome area, the German

---

[1] Situation appreciation by Roatta of 11 Aug 43, as forwarded by Rintelen, *OKW/WFSt, KTB, 1.–31.VIII.43*, 13 Aug 43. Cf. Roatta, *Otto milioni*, p. 261.

[2] *OKW/WFSt, KTB, 1.–31.VIII.43*, 12 Aug 43; Simoni, *Berlino, Ambasciata*, pp. 399–400.

forces in Sicily and southern Italy would be cut off. Kesselring therefore urged a postponement of the seizure operation (*Operation SCHWARZ*) until the Germans had incontrovertible proof of Italian negotiations with the Allies. Continued co-operation with the Italians, he felt, would gain the Germans enough time to move in sufficient reinforcements to hold the entire peninsula, thus preventing the Allies from seizing southern Italy, the springboard to the Balkans.

The weakness of Kesselring's position lay in his lack of troops in southern Italy. He had only a few battalions of the *1st Parachute Division* and certain security units in the Naples-Salerno area. The *16th Panzer Division* alone could not hold both Puglia (the heel) and Calabria (the toe). Pleading for reinforcements to enable him to station a full division in each of the most threatened areas in the south— the heel, the toe, and Naples-Salerno—he, like Roatta, regarded the heavy concentration of German troops in northern Italy as wasteful.[3]

Jodl and Rommel, in contrast, saw the main danger not in Allied power but in Italian treason. Since southern Italy needed stronger forces, and since the movement of forces from the north would merely aggravate the supply problem, Jodl recommended an immediate withdrawal from Sicily (this was already under way). With the *XIV* and *LXXVI Panzer Corps* concentrated on the mainland, the time would be ripe for grabbing Rome. Then Kesselring's forces would fall back northward and be absorbed by Rommel's *Army Group B*.[4]

The decision was left for Hitler. Hitler continued to insist on the liberation of Mussolini, though General Student and Captain Skorzeny were still unable to locate him. Hitler refused to permit reinforcement of south Italy, and he instructed Kesselring to keep the *3d Panzer Grenadier* and *2d Parachute Divisions* near Rome, to move the *16th Panzer Division* from the Taranto area to the Gulf of Salerno area. This left the heel unguarded, and Hitler asked Kesselring to use his influence with the Italians to induce them to assume the defense of Puglia, even though the Italians since July had sent no forces to southern Italy. Hitler refused to evacuate Sicily at once because arrangements for defending the Balkans were not yet complete. He wanted the Allies tied down in Sicily (although by this date a large part of the *XIV Panzer Corps* had already been ferried over to the mainland) as long as traffic could cross the strait. Eventually, the movement of the *XIV Panzer Corps* from Sicily to the mainland could provide a force to help defend against an Allied invasion of southern Italy.[5]

The military conference at Bologna on 15 August was as inconclusive and unsatisfactory for both Italy and Germany as was the earlier conference at Tarvis. Diplomatic representatives, as well as Keitel and Ambrosio, were absent. Jodl represented OKW and attended in company with Rommel. The presence of Kesselring and Rintelen tended only slightly to soften the brusqueness of the German attitude. Roatta, Rossi (deputy chief of *Comando*

---

[3] Kesselring's estimate of the situation, 12 Aug 43, in *OKH/Op. Abt.,Westl. Mittelmeer, Chefs., 19.V.43–II.VII.44* (H 22/290).

[4] Addendum by Jodl to Kesselring's situation estimate; see also, *OKW/WFSt, KTB, 1.–31.VIII.43*, 13 Aug 43.

[5] *OKW/WFSt, KTB, 1.–31.VIII.43*, 13 and 14 Aug 43.

# THE SURRENDER PRELIMINARIES

*Supremo*), and Zanussi (of Roatta's office) represented Italy.

When Roatta stated the need to withdraw the *Fourth Army* from France to Italy to help defend the Italian homeland, Jodl asked the direction of an anticipated attack—the Brenner frontier or southern Italy? Roatta refused to answer the question on the ground that it was tendentious, but he agreed to leave two coastal divisions and a corps headquarters in southern France. Acrimonious discussion took place on the northward movement of Italian divisions into the Brenner area. When Rommel was presented as commander of all German forces north of the Apennines, Roatta said that he had not been informed that the German troops in northern Italy were to remain there. Who would be Rommel's superior? Roatta asked. The Germans then agreed to recognize Ambrosio's supreme command on condition that the Italians recognize the German command over the forces of both nations in the Balkans and Greece. Both parties then professed to agree, but in bad faith, to reduce their forces along the Brenner frontier. As for Roatta's proposal that an additional German division be sent to Sardinia, Jodl replied that none could be spared. Jodl made no objection to moving an Italian corps from Thessaly to Albania, and three divisions from the Balkans to southern Italy.[6]

When the Italian representatives returned to Rome on 16 August, the King summoned Badoglio, Ambrosio, and Roatta to a special council at the Quirinal Palace and asked about the outcome of the conference. Roatta described the cold, suspicious, almost hostile attitude of the Germans. He ascribed their use of a detachment of SS troops as a guard during the meeting to their fear of an Italian ambush. Badoglio stated that it would be necessary to act toward the Germans with the greatest prudence for a few days more, in view of the negotiations initiated with the Allies. Otherwise, the Germans would descend upon Rome in force and seize the Italian Government. Roatta thus learned of Castellano's mission. The King reaffirmed the fundamental lines of the Badoglio government, stipulated at the time of its formation: personnel limited to military men and technicians, excluding politicians; and the prevention by force if necessary of political agitation and organization to avoid "the absurdity of judging and condemning by implication the work of the King."[7]

A few days afterward, Ambrosio suggested to Badoglio the advisability, in view of Castellano's mission, of issuing written instructions to the top commanders to inform them of Castellano's mission and to outline the course the armed forces were to pursue in case of an armistice. Badoglio disapproved. He wished to keep the secret of negotiations with the Allies limited to the smallest possible circle. He told Ambrosio, "We must not give Germany the least possibility of discovering our intentions."[8]

Roatta, because he had not been informed of Castellano's mission before he

---

[6] *OKW/WFSt, KTB, 1.–31.VIII.43*, 15 Aug 43; Rossi, *Come arrivammo*, pp. 385–401; Rintelen, *Mussolini als Bundesgenosse*, pp. 242–45; Rommel, Private KTB, 9 May–Sep 43, entry for 15 Aug and appended rpt.

[7] Mussolini, *Storia di un anno*, p. 25; Zanussi, *Guerra e catastrofe*, II, 77; Roatta, *Otto milioni*, p. 294; Monelli, *Roma 1943*, pp. 298–99.

[8] Monelli, *Roma 1943*, p. 299; MS #P-058, Project 46, 1 Feb–8 Sep 43, Question 11.

met with the Germans at Bologna, had been something of a dupe—a mere tool for negotiating with the Germans while Ambrosio himself was making contact with the Allies. Roatta could not object to the new course of the government, but he questioned whether Castellano was the most appropriate choice as emissary. In any event, Roatta wished to learn more about what was going on.[9]

Roatta found an ally in General Carboni, commander of the *Motorized Corps* protecting Rome and known for his pro-Allied sympathies. Appointed by Ambrosio director of Military Intelligence Service on 18 August in the hope that Carboni would be able to disentangle the close connection between Italian and German intelligence offices, Carboni quickly picked up the news of Castellano's departure. Though Roatta may have had some doubts as to Castellano's suitability for the mission, Carboni had none. He hated Castellano, whom he blamed, along with the Duke of Acquarone, for Carboni's having been passed over for an appointment in Badoglio's cabinet. Believing that Castellano was inadequate for the task and untrustworthy besides, Carboni urged that a more reliable envoy be sent to control Castellano and to prevent that ambitious Sicilian from trying to grab all the glory in representing Italy "in dealings with" the Allied powers. Carboni appealed to Badoglio, Acquarone, Ambrosio, and Roatta. But all apparently wished to await Castellano's report. After more than a week passed without word, they began to fear that the Germans had discovered Castellano. Roatta then took the lead in urging that a second dove of peace be released from the ark, with the same mission as the first.[10]

A suitable man was at hand. With no clearly defined functions in Roatta's office, General Zanussi could be spared. His absence would be no more noticeable to the Germans than Castellano's. Like Castellano, Zanussi thoroughly believed in changing sides. He had written several memorandums for his colleagues and superiors, indicating that a switch to the Allied side was the only sensible course after the overthrow of Mussolini.

Ambrosio probably wanted to keep the dispatch of a second emissary secret from Badoglio, but in the end he decided to let the Marshal know. Badoglio approved, as he had earlier assented to Castellano's mission. But because Guariglia, Minister of Foreign Affairs, would probably object to what he might consider another military usurpation of a diplomatic function, the Foreign Office was not approached for a passport.[11] As credentials, Carboni suggested that Zanussi take with him a British prisoner of war. Lt. Gen. Sir Adrian Carton de Wiart was selected. He was a good choice, for he was well known and easily recognized—he had lost an eye and an arm in the service of his country. If the Germans discovered him in Zanussi's company, it would be obvious that the mission concerned merely the exchange of prisoners. Lt. Galvano Lanza di Trabia, Carboni's aide, was to go along as the interpreter.[12]

[10] Giacomo Carboni, *L'armistizio e la difesa di Roma: Verità e menzogne* (Rome: Donatello de Luigi, 1945), pp. 18, 23-24; Zanussi, *Guerra e catastrofe*, II, 82; Roatta, *Otto milioni*, pp. 294-95.
[11] Guariglia, *Ricordi*, p. 671.
[12] *Happy Odyssey: The Memoirs of Lieutenant General Sir Adrian Carton de Wiart* (London: Cape Publishers, 1950), pp. 225-29; Zanussi, *Guerra e catastrofe*, II, 83-85; Roatta, *Otto milioni*, pp. 295-96.

[9] Zanussi, *Guerra e catastrofe*, II, 75.

## THE SURRENDER PRELIMINARIES

On 22 August, two days before Zanussi departed from Rome, Ambassador Prunas in Lisbon informed Guariglia that Castellano had made contact with the Allies and would soon report. Expecting Castellano's quick return, Guariglia saw no reason to inform Badoglio or Ambrosio. Because Ambrosio and Badoglio had kept the Zanussi mission secret from Guariglia, they did not know that Castellano had already carried out his mission by the time Zanussi had left.

Like Castellano, Zanussi carried no written orders. Ambrosio briefed him, but his instructions were broad and vague. If Castellano had disappeared, Zanussi was to take his place. If Castellano were still in Lisbon, Zanussi was to support him in his quest to concert plans with the Allies for a war against the Germans.

Zanussi informed Roatta of Ambrosio's instructions. Carboni passed along some advice—first, Ambassador Prunas could be trusted, and second, it was important to urge the Allies not to fight their way up the Italian peninsula but to land in force north of Rome.[13]

### Castellano at Lisbon

General Castellano had arrived in Lisbon at 2200, 16 August. On the next day he called on Sir Ronald Hugh Campbell, the British Ambassador. Campbell told Castellano he would inform him of developments just as soon as he, Campbell, received instructions to negotiate. A day later Campbell learned that Osborne, British Minister to the Holy See, had verified to the Foreign Office the letter of introduction he had prepared for Castellano. Sir D'Arcy had also obtained a signed statement from Badoglio to the effect that Castellano was authorized to speak for the Marshal.[14]

On the same day, 18 August, Maj. Gen. Walter B. Smith, the AFHQ chief of staff, and Brigadier Kenneth W. D. Strong, the AFHQ G–2—appointed by General Eisenhower to meet with Castellano—were flying to Gibraltar in civilian clothes and without titles. From there they went to Lisbon, where they arrived on the morning of 19 August. That evening, at 2200, Smith and Strong, accompanied by Mr. George F. Kennan, U.S. Chargé d'Affaires, met Castellano and Montanari at the British Embassy.[15]

After an introduction by the British Ambassador, General Smith opened the discussion by stating that on the assump-

---

[13] Zanussi, *Guerra e catastrofe*, II, 87.

[14] Castellano, *Come firmai*, p. 98; copy of Telg, Foreign Office to Lisbon, 18 Aug 43, Capitulation of Italy, p. 89.

[15] The conference is described in: Minutes of a conference held at the residence of the British Ambassador at Lisbon on August 18, 1943 at 10 P.M., Capitulation of Italy, pp. 85–88. These are condensed minutes, not a verbatim record. They were telegraphed to Washington and London in Telg, NAF 334, 21 Aug 43, Capitulation of Italy, pp. 112–17. The second part of the conference, which concerned purely military matters, is summarized in Telg, Eisenhower to Marshall, NAF 335, 21 Aug 43, Capitulation of Italy, pp. 126–27.

At the end of the conference, Castellano was handed a copy of the minutes and asked to check them for accuracy; it appears in translation in his *Come firmai* as Appendix 1, pages 211–15 (his résumé of the military discussions is in pages 215–18); in addition, he gives his account of the conference which in some points supplements the minutes (pages 102–09).

The copy of the minutes in Capitulation of Italy (pages 85–88) and NAF 334 dates the conference 18 August, which is incorrect. Smith and Strong arrived in Lisbon only on the morning of 19 August. The correct date is the 19th, as given by Castellano, and by Churchill in a speech to the House of Commons on 21 September 1943.

SECRET EMISSARIES TO LISBON *(left to right)* Brigadier Kenneth W. D. Strong, Generale di Brigata Giuseppe Castellano, General Smith, and Consul Franco Montanari, an official from the Italian Foreign Office.

tion that the Italian armed forces were ready to surrender, he was authorized to communicate the terms on which General Eisenhower was prepared to agree to a cessation of hostilities. The terms, Smith said, constituted a military armistice only and had to be accepted unconditionally.

Somewhat surprised by this abrupt statement, Castellano said he had come to discuss how Italy could arrange to join the United Nations in expelling the Germans from Italy.

Smith replied that he was prepared only to discuss the terms of Italy's surrender. The status of the Italian Government and Army operations against the Germans were, he declared, matters of high governmental policy to be decided by the heads of the United States and British Governments. But the Allies were ready to assist and support any Italian who obstructed the German military effort. General Smith then read the armistice conditions point by point, the short terms that had been furnished General Eisenhower on 6 August.[16]

---

[16] See Appendix C for the text of the short terms. Clause 3 now read: "All prisoners or internees of the United Nations to be immediately turned over to the Allied Commander-in-Chief, and none of these may *now or at any time be evacuated to Germany.*" On instruction from President Roosevelt and Prime Minister Churchill the words indicated by italics were substituted for the original phrase, "from the beginning of

To permit careful translation of the documents and an opportunity for study, the British and Americans withdrew from the room, leaving Castellano and Montanari alone.

When the group reassembled, Castellano stated that he had no power to accept the armistice but that he wanted an explanation of certain terms for his government's information. With regard to prisoners and internees, practical limitations might hinder the extent to which the Italians could prevent the movement of such personnel to Germany, though the Italians would make every effort to comply with this condition. General Smith replied that the United Nations understood the problem, but expected the Italian authorities to do their best.

When Castellano requested clarification of the clause on Italian ships and aircraft, Smith explained that this meant surrender of the fleet and of the planes, their future disposition to be decided by General Eisenhower. Castellano mentioned the lack of fuel that might prevent some warships and planes from complying. The authorities, Smith said, had to make every effort to provide sufficient fuel.

As for Allied use of Italian airfields and ports, Castellano pointed out that most of the airfields were already in German hands; those remaining under Italian control were small and scattered.

As for withdrawing Italian armed forces to Italy and moving units stationed inland in the Balkans, this might prove an impossible task. Smith assured Castellano that the Allies did not expect the impossible; certain Italian divisions, however, were near enough to the coast to permit their removal to Italy by Allied ships.

Castellano inquired about the meaning of setting up an Allied military government and also about the decision to give General Eisenhower an overriding authority over the Italian Government—would the Italian Government retain sovereignty? Smith reiterated that his instructions referred only to the terms of a military armistice. He was not empowered to discuss questions relating to the future government of Italy. He said that the Allies would establish military government over parts of Italian territory, and he observed that this was being exercised in Sicily in a fair and humane manner.

Castellano cited the danger to the person of the King. Accepting the terms might prompt the Germans to hold the King as a hostage and even to threaten his life. It was suggested that the King might leave Italy on an Italian naval vessel. Castellano was assured that the King would be treated with all due personal consideration.

The discussion then returned to the essential point in Castellano's proposal: the manner and extent of Italian military collaboration with the Allies against Germany. The Allied representatives reiterated that the clauses of the armistice were a military capitulation, not an agreement for Italy's participation in the war on the Allied side. Immediately thereafter, however, Smith read to Castellano a paragraph based on the Quebec Memorandum:

The extent to which these terms of armistice would be modified in favor of Italy would depend on how far the Italian Government and people did in fact aid the United Nations against Germany during the remainder of the war, but that wherever

---

the negotiations," in order to avoid any possible inference that they were "negotiating" with the Badoglio government. (Telg, USFOR to AFHQ, repeated to Lisbon, No. 4522, 19 Aug 42.)

Italian Forces or Italians fight the Germans, destroy German property or hamper German movements they will be given all possible support by the forces of the United Nations.

He then asked Castellano to weigh carefully the significance of the paragraph and explained that the Allied terms had been drawn up by General Eisenhower and approved by the Allied governments without considering the possibility of active Italian participation in the war against Germany. As President Roosevelt and Prime Minister Churchill had declared at Quebec, with Stalin's approval, the conditions enforced would be modified to Italy's advantage in proportion to the sum total of Italy's participation in the war. Without using the unconditional surrender phrase, without modifying the impression demanded by the predominant Allied powers, Smith skillfully used the Quebec telegram as an inducement to secure Italian capitulation.[17]

Castellano returned to the point he had emphasized to Hoare in Madrid: the Italian Government, without effective aid from the Anglo-Americans, was unable to turn against the Germans. If Italy accepted and put into effect the armistice terms, the Germans would counter with immediate reprisals. Italy was an occupied country, and Italians were alarmed by the degree of control already exercised by the Germans. Nor was Castellano exaggerating, he said, in order to try to convince the Allies to accept his proposal to co-ordinate military plans. Though the Luftwaffe was relatively weak, it could wreak great damage on Italy. The strength of the German Army was impressive. The war, Castellano believed, would continue for some time because the Germans had not used up their reserves in their recent Russian operations. Castellano hated the Germans because of their abominable behavior toward Italian troops in Russia. Each time Kesselring visited Ambrosio, it was an occasion for a row. Despite the fact that the Italian secret services worked closely with German intelligence, and despite the fact that many pro-German officers were in the Italian Army, including Roatta, Castellano believed that Badoglio was quite capable of directing policy as the situation required.

When Castellano again cited the German threat to use gas, the Allied representatives pointed out the folly of such an act because the Allies would themselves counter with gas. In any event, the effect of a few days' vindictive action by the Germans would be far less serious for Italy than a long war of attrition.

Stating that he now fully understood both the terms of the armistice and the supplementary information derived from the Quebec telegram, Castellano added that he was not authorized to accept the terms but would submit them to his government. He said that it would be useful for the Italian Government to know when or where the Allies planned to invade the mainland because German countermeasures would probably make it necessary for at least part of the government to leave Rome simultaneously with the armistice announcement. It was in the Allied interest, he believed, to prevent capture of that government which, he again insisted, wanted to reach an understanding. General Smith replied that Castellano, as a soldier, would understand why it was impossible to reveal Allied plans in detail. Castellano therefore repeated that he

---

[17] Ambassador Campbell, a professional diplomatist, was much impressed with the skill displayed by General Smith as a negotiator. See Interv, Smyth with Mr. George F. Kennan, 2 Jan 47.

# THE SURRENDER PRELIMINARIES

would limit his function to that of acting as bearer of the Allied terms to his government.

They then discussed arrangements for a direct channel of communication, and it was proposed that if Badoglio should accept the terms, General Eisenhower would announce the armistice five or six hours before the main Allied landing on the Italian mainland. Castellano objected vigorously. Such short notice, he declared, would not allow his government enough time to prepare for the landing. He asked for longer notice, preferably two weeks. Smith thought a longer advance notice might be possible, and he assured Castellano that he would present the Italian views to General Eisenhower. But Smith maintained the point that public announcement of the armistice would have to precede the principal Allied landing by a few hours only.

All agreed that the Italian Government was to signify its acceptance of the armistice by a radio message. If it proved impossible for the Italians to do so directly, the government was to send a message to the British Minister at the Holy See as follows: "*Il Governo italiano protesta contro il ritardo nella comunicazione delle liste complete die nomi dei prigionieri catturati in Sicilia.*" (The Italian Government protests against the delay in the communication of the complete list of names of Italian prisoners captured in Sicily.)

The Italian Government was to communicate its acceptance by 28 August. If no reply came by 30 August, the Allies would assume that the terms had been refused. Acceptance of the armistice terms meant also acceptance of the method of announcement as then determined—a radio announcement by General Eisenhower with five or six hours preliminary warning to Italy. For a secret channel of communication with AFHQ, Castellano was to receive a portable radio, a code, and instructions on their use. All communications from the Italian Government to AFHQ were to be in the Italian language. In case of acceptance, Castellano was to meet again with General Eisenhower's representatives in Sicily, and the precise hour of the meeting and the course of Castellano's flight to Sicily was stipulated: from Rome at 0700, 31 August, to reach Termini Imerese shortly before 0900.

After copies of the armistice terms and of the AFHQ memorandum based on the CCS directive were furnished to Castellano, Ambassador Campbell and Mr. Kennan withdrew and the discussion turned to purely military matters. Brigadier Strong began to question Castellano on German troop dispositions, first in general, then in detail. Castellano offered only general information until he observed Strong's map, which had accurate information on it. Castellano then gave detailed unit locations, hoping thus, as he stated later, to show his good faith. Strong asked no questions about Italian units, but Castellano noted that the AFHQ map showed them quite as correctly as the maps of the Operations Section of *Comando Supremo*.

Castellano estimated the total German military strength in Italy as 400,000 men. More troops could come from France. The Germans intended to defend on a line from Genoa to Ravenna and to fall back, if necessary, to the Po. They also planned to hold Sardinia and Corsica.

Castellano painted a pitiful picture of the Italian armed forces. The fleet had enough oil for only one action. The air force was very short of matériel, though the fighter elements were quite good. All airfields except a few small ones were under German control. The Italian Army was short of gasoline, entirely dependent on the Germans for fuel, very short of antitank guns, antitank ammunition, and even of such items as boots. If Italy detached itself from the German alliance, the nation would require supplies of wheat and coal from the Allies.

The Italian general urged the Leghorn area as the best place for an Allied landing. German lines of communication were extremely vulnerable, particularly along the Brenner route, and Castellano recommended attacking the Brenner Pass. The Italians planned to withdraw their troops from Corsica, he explained, but not from Sardinia. At the Bologna conference of 15 August, Roatta had discussed plans for defending Italy with Rommel and Jodl, but, of course, Castellano was ignorant of the results.

Though a number of German commanders wished to get rid of Hitler, loyalty to the Fuehrer was so widespread throughout the armed forces, Castellano believed, that overthrow appeared unlikely. The Gestapo was an important factor in preventing the collapse of German morale.

In conclusion, Castellano mentioned his part in Mussolini's downfall—how Grandi had been induced to take the lead in the Fascist Grand Council only to be doublecrossed when Badoglio was named Mussolini's successor. On the whole, Castellano made a favorable impression. He seemed earnest and sincere, and he had an intense hatred of the Germans. Yet the Allied representatives wondered why he had neither credentials nor formal written instructions from Badoglio. Nor was Allied confidence in the new Italian regime enhanced by Castellano's disquisitions on honor, peculiar accompaniment to his description of the double-cross of Grandi and the idea of turning against Germany and jumping into the Allied camp.[18]

The conference lasted all night, breaking up at 0700, 20 August, nine hours after it had started. Smith shook hands with Castellano and expressed the hope that their meeting would prove to be the beginning of a new collaboration between their countries. Smith and Strong then flew back to Algiers and AFHQ. Castellano and Montanari remained in Lisbon to await the arrival of the Italian Ambassador to Chile, whose ship was several days late.

After reflecting on the conference, Castellano realized that the situation was far different from that imagined in Rome at the time of his departure. He and Ambrosio had believed that Italy was still in a position to bargain. Actually, it was too late. They had thought that the British and Americans would be receptive to the proposal that Italy switch sides. Allied suspicion and distrust came as a sobering shock. Castellano had, however, been able to avoid the humiliating phrase, "unconditional surrender." And the Quebec telegram offered assurance that the terms of capitulation would be modified in Italy's favor if the government and people rendered effective aid to the Allies. Castellano believed that the Allied invasion of the Italian mainland would be short and successful because of Allied air su-

---

[18] See Telg, AFHQ to CCS, NAF 336, 22 Aug 43, Capitulation of Italy, pp. 126–27; Interv, Smyth with Ambassador Walter B. Smith, 13 May 47, and with Brigadier Kenneth D. Strong, 29 Oct 47.

periority. He had great faith in Anglo-American generosity.

On the following morning, 21 August, Castellano presented himself at the Italian legation in Lisbon, where D'Ajeta was astonished to see him. D'Ajeta took him immediately to Prunas, the Italian Minister, who could not conceal his disappointment that such important negotiations had taken place without his knowledge and participation. Prunas on 22 August sent two cables to Guariglia and informed him that Castellano had made contact with the Allies and would soon report. The British Embassy delivered to Montanari the radio and code for future communications. On Ambassador Campbell's advice, Castellano, who had been thinking of returning to Rome by plane, took his place among the party of officials who left Lisbon by train on 23 August. The Italian Ambassador to Chile carried Castellano's papers across French territory, restored them at the Italian frontier. Reaching Rome on the morning of 27 August, Castellano made haste to report to his superiors.[19]

## Zanussi's Negotiations in Lisbon and Algiers

Three days earlier, the second Italian emissary, General Zanussi, together with General de Wiart, had arrived in Madrid. More fortunate than Castellano, Zanussi traveled by plane. The next morning, 25 August, he was in Lisbon. He promptly got in touch with Prunas, who was not overjoyed to see him. Prunas cautioned Zanussi to be on his guard, not only against German spies, but also against some members of the Italian legation.

Though Zanussi learned that Castellano has been successful in meeting members of General Eisenhower's staff, and was even then on his way back to Rome, he asked to see the British Ambassador. Sir Ronald replied through an intermediary, since he saw no reason why he should meet another Italian general. The Allied terms were already in Castellano's hands. Still, he asked Zanussi to remain in Lisbon until he, the Ambassador, was certain that there was no message for him. General Carton de Wiart, the British "prisoner-of-war," offered to return to Rome with Zanussi since it began to appear that Zanussi had come on a futile mission.[20]

At Quebec on 26 August, Churchill and Roosevelt had at last agreed on the long terms for Italy. The Foreign Office therefore instructed Campbell to present the comprehensive document to Zanussi and to explain that it embodied both the short terms, already in Castellano's possession, and the political and economic terms that Castellano had been told to expect. He was also to suggest that Zanussi fly back to Rome immediately with the text of the long terms.[21]

Accordingly, on the morning of 27 August, Campbell met Zanussi and gave him the long terms. Zanussi immediately noticed the absence of reference to Italian military co-operation with the Allies, and asked why no mention of this had been made. Campbell read the Quebec telegram to him; this at least left the door open for eventual Italo-Allied co-operation.

---

[19] Castellano, *Come firmai,* pp. 116–25.

[20] Zanussi, *Guerra e catastrofe,* II, 91–94; Telg 1721, 26 Aug 43, Campbell to Foreign Office, and Telg 1723, Campbell to Foreign Office, 26 Aug 43, both in OPD Exec 2, item 5, tab 50; Carton de Wiart, *Happy Odyssey,* p. 230.

[21] Telg 1352, Deputy Prime Minister to Campbell, 26 Aug 43. OPD Exec 2, item 5, tab 50. See also, pp. 448–50.

Zanussi and his interpreter retired to their hotel to study the comprehensive conditions of capitulation.[22]

The British Government had acted with extraordinary speed in getting the text of the long terms into Zanussi's hands. So fast had the government acted that Ambassador Campbell at Lisbon had the comprehensive document before AFHQ received it. When Eisenhower's headquarters later that day received the document, Allied commanders became thoroughly alarmed. The main invasion of the Italian mainland, planned for the Salerno area, was less than two weeks away. It was a risky operation, particularly because the rate of German reinforcement was seriously changing the estimates on which the landing plan had been based. The success of the operation, it seemed, was becoming increasingly dependent on getting the Italian Government to surrender beforehand. Not only did Italian opposition have to be eliminated before the landing, but Italian assistance during the critical period of getting troops ashore now appeared necessary. Even Eisenhower had doubts that Castellano would be able to persuade the Italian monarch and high command to accept surrender on the conditions of the short terms; now the CCS had insisted on introducing the long terms with the harsh initial statement of unconditional surrender and had ordered their use in all additional negotiations with Badoglio.

General Eisenhower therefore appealed to the Joint Chiefs for some leeway. The President relented, and Eisenhower received authorization to proceed with the surrender negotiations on the basis of the short military terms. After getting the Italians to accept and sign this document, Eisenhower could submit the comprehensive paper to the Italian Government.[23]

Anxiety still persisted at AFHQ, however. The Allied commanders hoped to receive some sort of message from Castellano re-establishing contact with the Italian Government. Presumably Zanussi was a representative of Roatta, who was believed to have strong pro-German tendencies. Castellano had told Smith and Strong at Lisbon that Roatta had not been taken into the confidence of the Badoglio government, though Castellano had added that he presumed Roatta, as a soldier, would loyally follow the government if it shifted to the Allied side. Zanussi had no credentials whatsoever, whereas Castellano at least had brought a letter of introduction from Osborne. Did the two emissaries represent two distinct factions within the Italian Government, one in close co-operation with the Germans? Or was the Zanussi mission bona fide, and were Roatta and Ambrosio working semi-independently toward the same end?[24]

What General Smith feared most was that Zanussi would make immediate use of the diplomatic channels of the Lisbon Embassy to inform Roatta of the long terms and thereby nullify Castellano's negotiations. Smith therefore made arrangements to get Zanussi out of the hands of the diplomatists and into military hands

---

[22] Telg, 27 Aug 43, British Embassy at Lisbon to Foreign Office, OPD Exec 2, item 5, tab 53; Zanussi, *Guerra e catastrofe*, II, 91-94.

[23] Telg, CCS to Eisenhower, FAN 203, 27 Aug 43, with text of long terms; Telg, Eisenhower to CCS, NAF 342, 28 Aug 43; and Telg 6398, AGWAR to Eisenhower, 29 Aug 43, all in Capitulation of Italy, pp. 137, 160-64.

[24] Telg, Eisenhower to CCS, NAF 342, 28 Aug 43, and Telg, Eisenhower to Lt Gen Sir Noel Mason-MacFarlane, 28 Aug 43, both in Capitulation of Italy, pp. 160-64.

before Zanussi could do any damage. While Carton de Wiart was kept out of sight and later returned to London, Zanussi was invited to visit the Allied camp. Zanussi accepted. Relieved of his copy of the long terms, and flown first to Gibraltar under the assumed name of Pierre Henri Lamartine, Zanussi, accompanied by his interpreter, departed Gibraltar in the early afternoon of 28 August; to his surprise he found himself that evening at Algiers.[25]

Castellano later asserted that General Eisenhower at first planned to admit the Italian armed forces to full collaboration with the Allies and that Eisenhower was about to explain his plans in full when Zanussi's intervention rendered AFHQ suspicious, thereby inhibiting the Allies from divulging their plans to Castellano. Castellano also believed that AFHQ contemplated shooting Zanussi as a spy. But this was mere speculation; at no time did Eisenhower and Smith consider revealing Allied plans to Castellano, and they had no thought of shooting Zanussi. General Smith was prepared to hold Zanussi in case he turned out to be, under questioning, something other than a genuine emissary.[26]

During several conferences with General Smith, Brigadier Strong, and Mr. Robert D. Murphy, General Eisenhower's U.S. political adviser, Zanussi gave considerable information about the German forces in Italy, information that checked quite well against that obtained from other sources. He did not, however, divulge the Italian order of battle, though he convinced the Allied officers that he was genuine and sincere in his efforts to arrange the armistice. As "Chief of Staff of Roatta," he was in a position to know the military situation, and he seemed as thoroughly persuaded as Castellano of the necessity for Italy to make an arrangement with the Allies. Like Castellano, Zanussi labored under the incubus of the German threat to overthrow the Badoglio government and occupy Italy.

Zanussi saw five possible developments, each of which made it essential to act in concert with the Allies: (1) if Germany took the initiative and attacked the Badoglio government, it would be in the interest of the Allies and the Italians to join forces and prevent the return of fascism or the advent of communism in Italy; (2) though the Italians did not favor an Allied attack on Germany through the Italian mainland, a campaign requiring an estimated fifteen to twenty divisions, the Italians wanted their armed forces to have a specific role in any such campaign; (3) if the Allies directed their attack into the Balkans, the Italians wished to co-operate; (4) if the Allies avoided the Italian mainland and occupied Sardinia and Corsica, they should make no request for direct Italian assistance, for in that case the Germans would immediately occupy Italy; (5) if the Allies bypassed Italy and attacked the Germans on the Continent beyond Italy's borders, the Germans might withdraw some divisions from Italy, which would make it possible for Italy to fight the Germans unaided.

Zanussi's exposition indicated careful consideration of Italy's plight and the conclusion that Italy had no way out except by joining forces with the Allies. He made no objection to the specific clauses of the

---

[25] Carton de Wiart, *Happy Odyssey*, p. 231; Interv with Smith, 13 May 47; Telg 6990, AFHQ to Gibraltar, 28 Aug 43, and Telg 25227, Gibraltar to Lisbon, repeated to AFHQ, 28 Aug 43, both in Capitulation of Italy, pp. 156-57. Cf. Zanussi, *Guerra e catastrofe*, II, 90-99.

[26] Castellano, *Come firmai*, pp. 174-75; Interv with Smith, 13 May 47.

terms—military, political, or economic—demanded by the Allies, but he was certain that Badoglio would object strenuously to the formula of unconditional surrender as stated in the preamble and in the initial article of the long terms. Could not the Allies secure everything they wished, he asked, without imposing this unneccesary indignity, which might even result in a refusal of the armistice by the Badoglio government?[27]

Zanussi painted a gloomy picture of the Italian political situation—the government was dominated by old men who were tainted by long association with the Fascist regime and who were incapable of vigorous action. He compared Badoglio to Marshal Henri Pétain, and asked how long the Germans would allow Italy any freedom whatsoever. Badoglio's slowness, he said, had given the Germans time to occupy the country. At any moment the Germans might decide to oust Badoglio and set up a Quisling government under Farinacci. The only hope, according to Zanussi, was in the younger Army officers, all of whom, he declared, were fed up with the Germans and would welcome collaboration with the Allies. He insisted that the Italians would defend Rome at all costs if the Germans tried to seize control, and he cited the movement of five or six Italian divisions into positions from which they could protect the capital. Although these troops had no written orders, Mussolini's overthrow told them what was expected of them.

Assertions that Rome would be defended were not altogether consistent with Zanussi's expressions of fear for the safety of the members of the government. He and his friends, he said, "for months have given much study and thought to these eventualities [and] have considered the means necessary to effect the escape from German control of the Government and King." These old men, he said, were rather helpless in their expectation of being rescued by the Allies, and Zanussi felt that some scheme to rescue them ought to be planned. If the Allied landing on the mainland would not be able, in conjunction with the Italian Army, to protect Rome, the King and government leaders might escape on a naval vessel from La Spezia to Sardinia. There, he said, "the four Italian divisions could easily overcome the German division present, especially if the Allies could provide a little support." Zanussi regarded Ambrosio as the only man who could possibly replace Badoglio, though he admitted that the chief of *Comando Supremo* lacked the marshal's prestige.

The Italian Government, Zanussi explained, was not only obsessed by fears for its own immediate safety but greatly alarmed that the German High Command, realizing that the war had been lost, might throw Germany into the arms of the Soviet Union. In this case, Italy, in the Anglo-American camp, would face a Russo-German combination at its front door with Britain and America far away. Zanussi stated his opinion that the House of Savoy had to be preserved to avert chaos in Italy; the dynasty, he said, had been a stabilizing influence for six centuries.[28]

As a result of these conversations with Zanussi, General Eisenhower decided to permit Zanussi's interpreter, Lt. Galvano

---

[27] Telg, AFHQ to CCS, NAF 344, 30 Aug 43, Capitulation of Italy, pp. 166–71; Zanussi, *Guerra e catastrofe*, II, 101–08.

[28] Telgs W-8750 and W-8751, FREEDOM to AGWAR, 30 Aug 43, Capitulation of Italy, pp. 179–84.

Lanza, to return to Italy with a message from Zanussi to Ambrosio—a letter urging the Italian Government to accept immediately the military terms of the armistice; indicating that the clauses of the long terms were relatively unimportant as compared to the main issue of how much practical assistance Italy would give the Allies against Germany; and recommending that the Italian Government trust the good faith of the Allies and send Castellano to Sicily in accordance with the agreement reached in Lisbon.

On 29 August Lanza was to take the letter to Sicily, and there he was to be transferred to an Italian plane for the remainder of the journey to Rome. The text of the long terms, which Zanussi had received in Lisbon, was not entrusted to Lanza, for AFHQ, besides having no official confirmation of Zanussi's mission, did not wish to run the risk of having the document fall into German hands. Zanussi, therefore, retained his copy of the long terms, which had been returned to him.

In reporting his action, General Eisenhower urged the American and British Governments to delay communicating the text of the long terms to the other United Nations governments. He expressed astonishment at the thought of a public armistice ceremony in the Compiègne tradition when negotiations were still not only tenuous and delicate but also being conducted with emissaries who had come at great risk to themselves and to the members of the Italian Government.[29]

As increasing information on the buildup of German forces in Italy came to AFHQ's attention, it became increasingly necessary, it seemed to Eisenhower, to have the Italian surrender as a condition essential for the success of AVALANCHE, the projected invasion of Italy at Salerno. The co-operation of Italian forces, even though those forces had little fighting power, could well prove the difference between defeat and success and could possibly assure a rapid advance up the Italian mainland.

## Thoughts in Rome

In Rome, meanwhile, Castellano had returned on the morning of 27 August, just three days after Zanussi's departure. Finding Ambrosio temporarily gone from the capital, Castellano spoke briefly with Ambrosio's deputy, General Rossi, and arranged to see Marshal Badoglio. Guariglia and Rossi were also present to hear Castellano report on the Lisbon meeting.

When Castellano explained that the Allies insisted on announcing the armistice at their own discretion in order to have it coincide with their main landing on Italy, Guariglia was much upset. Declaring that Castellano had not been authorized to state Italy's intention to attack the German forces—a statement Castellano countered by saying that he had received no precise instructions—Guariglia advocated a different approach. Since it appeared that the Allies intended to invade the Italian mainland, the government should wait until after the landing had been made and the Allies were within striking distance of Rome. At that time, when the Allies were in position to rescue the Italian Government, and only then should the Italian Government request an armistice. Badoglio listened to all that was said, but said nothing himself. At the end of the meeting, Badoglio took Castellano's documents of the Lisbon con-

---

[29] Telg W-8726, AFHQ to AGWAR, 30 Aug 43, Capitulation of Italy, pp. 175-76.

ference and consigned them to Guariglia.[30]

Later that day Castellano managed to get in touch with Ambrosio by telephone. Ambrosio promised to return to Rome on the next day. At *Comando Supremo*, Castellano learned that Zanussi had been sent to Portugal to make contact with the Allies. This development disturbed him because he feared it would complicate the negotiations. Furthermore, he was not reassured by the lack of frankness on the part of those who had sent Zanussi— Roatta denied his knowledge of the affair, as did Carboni.

Ambrosio, on the morning of 28 August, was in Rome as promised, and he listened to Castellano's account. Ambrosio then took Castellano and Carboni to Badoglio's office, where he found Guariglia. The Minister of Foreign Affairs again declared that Castellano had had no authorization to offer Italian military collaboration, and he protested once more against agreeing to announce the armistice at the time of the Allied invasion. In any case, Guariglia considered the negotiations to be essentially political. On that basis, he argued, his ministry alone should conduct diplomatic negotiations. Ambrosio and Carboni advocated continuing the negotiations through Castellano. No decision was reached.

A few hours later Guariglia prepared a memorandum as a counterproposal to the Allies. While not objecting to any of the Allied terms, Guariglia's memorandum stressed the fact that Italy was unable alone to separate from the Germans. Consequently, it was essential that the Allies land before the armistice and in sufficient force to guarantee the safety of the Italian Government against German reaction.

When Ambrosio and Castellano studied Guariglia's proposal, Castellano, though agreeing with Guariglia's analysis, said that he had already explained the situation and the Italian position to the Allied generals at Lisbon. The decision, therefore, rested with the Italian Government.

Ambrosio and Castellano saw Badoglio again on 29 August. Badoglio said that he would have to consult with the King before reaching a decision. Badoglio, Ambrosio, and Guariglia then arranged for an audience. When they arrived at the Quirinal Palace, they met Acquarone, who asked Ambrosio for a detailed account of Castellano's mission and for a copy of the Allied terms. Acquarone took these to the King.

Acquarone returned to tell the three who waited that before the King gave the final word, Badoglio, as Head of Government, should reach a decision and suggest a definite course of action. The three men discussed the matter but had reached no decision when the King received them for a brief audience.

Immediately after seeing the King, Ambrosio called Castellano and asked how a reply could be sent to the Allies, a reply which would not refuse the armistice and at the same time not accept the conditions stipulated at Lisbon. The King and his advisers did not, apparently, object to the terms of the armistice, but they feared that if they surrendered without knowing where, when, and in what strength the Allies would land, they would expose themselves to capture by the Germans—particularly if the Allies were not planning to land in strength near Rome.

Castellano replied that the Allies demanded a yes or no answer. The message

---

[30] Castellano, *Come firmai*, pp. 125-26; Badoglio, *Memorie e documenti*, p. 101; Guariglia, *Ricordi*, pp. 663-65.

could be sent through Osborne (in the Vatican) or by means of the radio he had brought from Lisbon.

After speaking briefly with Guariglia and Ambrosio once more, Badoglio departed, leaving to the others the decision on how to arrange the details of the message.

After further discussion with Guariglia, Ambrosio called Castellano again. Admitting that the Allies in Lisbon had clarified all points, Ambrosio nevertheless felt it essential to secure an agreement that the proclamation of the armistice would be made only after the Allies had landed in force. He directed Castellano to encode and transmit a message to the Allies to embody this request.

Castellano did not dispatch the message. For at that moment Carboni came in with news that he had word from Zanussi, believed to be in Lisbon (though in actuality Zanussi was in Algiers). Zanussi said he had documents of the greatest importance and requested that a plane be sent to the Boccadifalco airfield near Palermo, Sicily, in order to bring those documents to Rome. Though it was not clear how Zanussi in Lisbon could have gotten papers to Sicily, Castellano dispatched a plane as requested, then informed the King and Badoglio of his action.[31]

The plane dispatched by Castellano reached Palermo safely, picked up Lanza, and returned to Rome the same day, 29 August. But Lanza carried only two letters, one to Ambrosio recommending acceptance of the armistice conditions as explained to Castellano, the other to Carboni urging him to support those who were trying to arrange an armistice. Since Zanussi had not wired the text of the long terms from Lisbon, Badoglio and his advisers remained in ignorance of it.[32]

Summoning Ambrosio, Guariglia, and Castellano to him on the morning of 30 August, Badoglio gave Castellano a revised version of the Guariglia memorandum as his written instructions. Castellano was to make contact with the Allies again and present the following points. If Italy had still enjoyed liberty of political and military action, the government would have requested an armistice immediately and accepted the conditions offered. But Italy was not able to do this at once because the Italian military forces in contact with the German forces inside and outside Italy were inferior to these forces. Unable to withstand a collision with the Germans, the Italian forces would be crushed in a very brief time. The whole country, but Rome above all, would be exposed to German reprisal. Since the Germans intended, at whatever cost, to fight in Italy, Italy was bound to become a second Poland. Consequently, Italy was able to request an armistice only when, because of landings by the Allies with sufficient forces and at appropriate places, the conditions were changed, or when the Allies were in a position to change the military situation in Europe.

Marshall Badoglio canceled the penultimate paragraph of the memorandum. In its stead he wrote out with pencil on a piece of paper which he gave to Castellano

---

[31] Castellano, *Come firmai*, pp. 126–30; Guariglia, *Ricordi*, pp. 672–74. Castellano's is the only account in detail. There is no mention of particulars by Badoglio (*Memorie e documenti*, page 101), and by Rossi (*Come arrivammo*, pages 126–27). Carboni's account (*L'armistizio e la difesa di Roma*, pages 24–25) is quite fantastic and in glaring contradiction to all the other evidence. It is testimony only of Carboni's violent hatred of Castellano.

[32] Castellano, *Come firmai*, p. 130; Zanussi, *Guerra e catastrofe*, II, 110.

the following points as guidelines for his discussion with the Allied generals:

"1. Report the memorandum.

2. In order not to be overwhelmed before the English [sic] are able to make their action felt, we cannot declare our acceptance of the armistice except after landings have taken place of at least 15 divisions, with the greater part of them between Civitavecchia and La Spezia.

3. We will be able to place at their disposition the following airfields . . .

4. The fleet goes to Maddalena; learn the approximate period in order that preparations may be made.

5. Protection of the Vatican.

6. The king, the heir apparent, the queen, the government and the diplomatic corps remain at Rome.

7. The question of prisoners."

Badoglio instructed Castellano to indicate the airfields still in Italian hands and on which Allied planes might land. Castellano was to explain that the German authorities had asked repeatedly about the status of Allied prisoners, and that the Italian Government had put off the Germans with various excuses. But German insistence made further delay difficult, if not impossible.

Happy at last to have a piece of paper and precise instructions, Castellano made haste to confirm, by means of his secret radio, his appointment with the Allied generals.[33]

---

[33] Castellano, *Come firmai*, pp. 130–32. Cf. Badoglio, *Memorie e documenti*, p. 101; Guariglia, *Ricordi*, p. 675.

# CHAPTER XXIV

# The Italian Decision

## ACHSE

What of Italian-German relations? After the Bologna conference of 15 August, the relations between the Axis partners continued to be as unsatisfactory as before. The only agreements reached had been to build German units in southern Italy up to strength and to reduce the forces of both nations in the Brenner area. From the German point of view, no satisfactory solution to the problem of command had been made, and no suitable agreement reached on the distribution of forces to defend against Allied invasion. The Germans remained suspicious of Italy's intentions.[1]

The Italian declaration of Rome as an open city the day before seemed to be related in some fashion to peace moves, and of course boded no good for the Germans. OKW realized that the Allies would recognize the status of Rome as an open city only if all movements of troops and war materials through the city ceased. Because traffic to southern Italy could not bypass the capital, however, the Germans had no way of supplying their forces in southern Italy except through Rome.[2]

German anxiety lessened somewhat two days after the Bologna conference because on 17 August the evacuation of Sicily was completed. With some 40,000 German troops, plus their weapons and vehicles, withdrawn from Sicily to southern Italy, the Germans no longer had to suffer the fear that had beset them ever since the overthrow of Mussolini—that an Allied landing in Calabria would cut off the *XIV Panzer Corps* in Sicily. After the units that had fought on the island had had some rest and enough time to make up deficiencies in matériel, the six divisions south of Rome would be a strong bulwark against an Allied invasion in the south. On that same day, 17 August, Rommel and his *Army Group B* took command of all the German formations in northern Italy; Rommel moved his headquarters from Munich to Garda, not far from the Brenner-Verona railway.[3]

Hitler and OKW, for their part, had no plans to defend Italy south of Rome. They did not consider the task feasible without Italian aid, and Hitler still felt intuitively certain of the eventual capitulation of the Badoglio government to the Allies. Accordingly, all *Army Group B* unit commanders were warned to be ready to act against the Italians should the political situation change. The *71st Infantry Division* was to occupy the city of Ljubljana and the Ljubljana-Tarvis pass.

---

[1] *OKW/WFSt, KTB, 1.-31.VIII.43*, 15 Aug 43; MS #C-093 (Warlimont), p. 128.
[2] *OKW/WFSt, KTB, 1.-31.VIII.43*, 15 and 21 Aug 43.

[3] *OKW/WFSt, KTB, 1.-31.VIII.43*, 16 and 18 Aug 43; Vietinghoff in MS #T-1a (Westphal et al.), ch. VI, pp. 11-12.

German forces were to defend permanently the Pisa-Arezzo-Ancona line along the southern slopes of the northern Apennines.[4]

A new headquarters, the *Tenth Army*, would be activated in southern Italy to control the *XIV* and *LXXVI Panzer Corps*, and General der Panzertruppen Heinrich von Vietinghoff genannt Scheel was nominated commanding general on 8 August. As Hitler explained to Vietinghoff on 17 August, when the latter had been summoned to the Fuehrer's headquarters, "I have clear proof that Badoglio is already negotiating an armistice with the Allies." It was possible, Hitler said, that Italian officers were not informed. Hitler believed that the Allies would soon invade the Italian mainland with large forces. The first mission of the *Tenth Army* after activation, therefore, would be to withdraw the German divisions in southern Italy as rapidly as possible to the area southeast of Rome. Vietinghoff was to be careful not to give the Italians any excuse for getting out of the war, and he was therefore not to withdraw prematurely. During the withdrawal toward Rome, Vietinghoff was to operate under Kesselring's *OB SUED*. After the withdrawal to central Italy and the elimination of Kesselring's command, *Tenth Army* was to come under Rommel's *Army Group B*.[5]

As for Kesselring, the signal for the start of a German withdrawal from south Italy would be the seizure of Rome. This Kesselring was to achieve with the *3d Panzer Grenadier* and *2d Parachute Divisions*. But if Skorzeny located and liberated Mussolini, Kesselring was to act independently of Allied action: he would seize Rome, restore Mussolini to power, re-establish fascism, and induce loyal Fascist elements to co-operate with the Germans in defending northern Italy.[6]

About this same time, 17 August, Skorzeny learned that Mussolini, guarded by about 150 *carabinieri*, was being held on the Sardinian island of Maddalena. While he was preparing to raid Maddalena and liberate Mussolini, Skorzeny suddenly received orders from OKW to execute a parachute drop on a small island near Elba. There, OKW had been informed, Mussolini was being held. But the Italian secret service had planted this information, and Mussolini was, in reality, at Maddalena. Only after a personal appeal to the Fuehrer did Skorzeny get OKW's order revoked. This, however, delayed Skorzeny's preparations, and when his plans for the Maddalena raid were completed ten days later, on 27 August, he learned that Mussolini had again been moved.[7]

Kesselring, inclined to believe the repeated declarations of loyalty to the alliance made by Badoglio, Ambrosio, and others, continued to view the problem of defending Italy differently from either Hitler, Rommel, or Jodl. Though he recognized the low combat effectiveness of the Italian units, he wished to gain as much as possible from Italian co-opera-

---

[4] *OKW/WFSt, KTB, 1.-31.VIII.43*, 16 Aug 43.

[5] Vietinghoff in MS #T-1a (Westphal et al.), ch. VI, pp. 6-7; MS #D-117, *Beurteilung der Lage durch die hoechsten Dienststellen im August 1943. Einsatz des AOK 10.* (Vietinghoff), p. 4.

[6] Lutz Koch, *Erwin Rommel: Die Wandlung eines grossen Soldaten* (Stuttgart: Walter Gebauer, 1950), pp. 152-53. Some rumors of this German plan reached the Italian Embassy in Berlin. See Simoni, *Berlino, Ambasciata*, p. 403, entry for 22 Aug 43.

[7] MS #D-318, The Rescue of Mussolini (SS Oberstleutnant Otto Skorzeny and SS Major Karl Radl), pp. 48-134. Cf. Mussolini, *Storia di un anno*, pp. 22-23.

tion. Along with Rintelen, he feared that Hitler's and Rommel's tactless and suspicious attitude might drive the Italians into needless overt hostility.[8]

Despite Kesselring's Italophile views, OKW activated Vietinghoff's *Tenth Army* headquarters on 22 August. Viewing the Naples-Salerno area as the one most immediately threatened, OKW gave Vietinghoff three missions: to concentrate as quickly as possible in the Naples-Salerno area a strong group of three mobile divisions, plus all units lacking organic transportation; to protect the Foggia airfields with part of the *1st Parachute Division;* and to oppose strongly any Allied landing in the Naples-Salerno area, but to institute only a delaying action against an invasion of Calabria south of the Castrovillari neck.[9]

The day after *Tenth Army* activation, Vietinghoff made a formal call on General Arisio, commander of the Italian *Seventh Army* stationed in southern Italy. The two agreed that the six German divisions in southern Italy were to be under Vietinghoff's command and not under Arisio's, as before. Arisio also agreed that his Italian units would form the first line of defense along the coast, leaving the more mobile German divisions to constitute a reserve for counterattack purposes. In the event of an Allied landing, and in conformity with German principles, the stronger force would assume command of all the troops within the sector where the reserve force was committed. The two generals also agreed on maintaining close liaison and co-operation.[10]

To OKW Sardinia also seemed endangered, but the threat of an Italian capitulation to the Allies inhibited the Germans from sending additional troops to reinforce the *90th Panzer Grenadier Division* and the six fortress battalions on the island. Considering a protracted defense impossible, the Germans prepared to evacuate Sardinia by way of Corsica and Elba. But the troops were not to be evacuated unless the Italians failed to co-operate or unless developments on the Italian mainland, for example an Allied invasion of the coast near Rome, threatened to cut off the Germans.[11]

Kesselring, by contrast, believed Sardinia in greater danger than the Naples-Salerno area. Flying to Hitler's headquarters on 22 August, he urged that additional forces be moved to Sardinia, for the troops withdrawn from Sicily, he reasoned, gave the Naples-Salerno area sufficient protection. In effect, Kesselring was supporting a request by *Comando Supremo* for an additional German division for Sardinia. OKW refused. Instead, OKW instructed Kesselring to propose to Ambrosio that Sardinia be guarded exclusively by Italian troops so that German troops could take full responsibility for Corsica. The *Tenth Army*, OKW emphasized, was to make its main stand in the Naples-Salerno area, even if this meant giving up Puglia, the Italian heel.[12]

---

[8] *OKW/WFSt, KTB, 1.-31.VIII.43*, 19 and 21 Aug 43; Rintelen, *Mussolini als Bundesgenosse*, pp. 246-47; MS #C-013 (Kesselring), p. 20.

[9] Telg, *OKW/WFSt/Op.* No. 661966/43 G. K. Chefs to *OB SUED* and others, 18 Aug 43, *Westl. Mittelmeer Chefs.* (H 22/290).

[10] MS #D-117 (Vietinghoff), pp. 9-10.

[11] *OKW/WFSt, KTB, 1.-31.VIII.43*, 18 Aug 43.

[12] Estimate of the Situation by *OB SUED*, 18 Aug 43, *OKW/WFSt, KTB, 1.-31.VIII.43*, 19 Aug 43; *OKW/WFSt, KTB, 1.-31.VIII.43*, 22 and 23 Aug 43.

A day after Kesselring's visit to Hitler, the Badoglio government sent a strong note of protest to Germany. Reports from the Italian Embassy in Berlin and from other sources indicated that certain Nazis were working closely with Fascists to overthrow Badoglio and re-establish a Fascist government in Rome. On the following day, 24 August, the Italian Government arrested several former Fascist leaders, including General Ugo Cavallero, who had been Ambrosio's predecessor at *Comando Supremo*. Perhaps this action averted an incipient Fascist revolt. Whether it did or not, it had the effect of causing Hitler to postpone his projected stroke against Rome.[13]

By this time, though, another Italo-German crisis was in the making. The forces of Rommel's *Army Group B* were carrying out their movement into northern Italy, a movement that Rommel planned to complete by the end of the month. But despite the peaceful German occupation of northern Italy, relations between the two governments and the two armed services worsened when friction developed during the relief of the Italian *Fourth Army* in France, a relief that began on 23 August: the Germans objected to the movement of the *7th* (*Lupi di Toscana*) *Infantry Division* to Nice, and they insisted that Italian naval vessels evacuate Toulon.[14]

Then on 24 August, after guerrilla bands attacked a *24th Panzer Division* supply train near Lubliana, OKW instructed Rintelen to protest to *Comando Supremo* and to indicate to the Italians that the Germans would have to reinforce the troops protecting the Tarvis-Feistritz-Ljubljana passes. Before *Comando Supremo* could reply, the German *71st Infantry Division* on 26 August began to move to Tarvis and toward the passes of the Julian Alps, the only ones still held and controlled exclusively by the Italians. At first threatening to use force to resist German violation of the Tarvis agreement, *Comando Supremo* in the end consented to the German move, just as Ambrosio had earlier acquiesced in the German occupation of the Brenner Pass, the Riviera, and the Mount Cenis pass.[15]

Meanwhile, the question of who was to exercise command over Italian and German forces had again arisen to trouble both nations. On 20 August, OKW had made an elaborate proposal for all theaters fronting on the Mediterranean: southern France, Italy, and the Balkans. OKW proposed Italian supreme command in Italy, German supreme command in southern France and in the Balkans, with each having the power to direct the organization of defense and the conduct of battle in case of Allied invasion. The distribution of the forces of both nations in all three areas was to be regulated from time to time by OKW and *Comando Supremo*. In Italy, *Army Group B* and *OB SUED* were to be under the immediate command of the King, who would issue his directives through *Comando Supremo*. The Italian *Fourth* and *Eighth Armies* in northern Italy were to be attached to *Army Group B*. Four days later, on 24 August, Ambrosio accepted the proposal as it related to France—Italian units remaining in southern France were to be under the command of Generalfeldmarschall Gerd von Rundstedt as Com-

---

[13] Simoni, *Berlino, Ambasciata*, p. 403; Guariglia, *Ricordi*, p. 651; Bonomi, *Diario*, pp. 80–82.
[14] *OKW/WFSt, KTB, 1.–31.VIII.43*, 22–24 Aug 43.
[15] *OKW/WFSt, KTB, 1.–31.VIII.43*, 24–26 Aug 43; Simoni, *Berlino, Ambasciata*, p. 405.

## THE ITALIAN DECISION

mander in Chief West. Ambrosio made considerable concessions in the Balkans. But in Italy, Ambrosio rejected the German proposal and suggested, rather, as he had before, a radical regrouping of German forces. For the time being there would be no change in the command structure of the two military forces in Italy.[16]

By the end of the month, the Germans had received increasing indications both of an impending Allied invasion and of the imminent Italian desertion. Which threat was the greater was difficult for the Germans to determine.

As aerial reconnaissance reports revealed extensive Allied troop loadings in North African ports, Kesselring's original estimate that Sardinia was the area most immediately threatened by invasion changed; these preparations were much larger than an attack on Sardinia alone required. But the distribution of Allied shipping in North Africa and Sicily, plus the pattern of Allied bombing, still seemed to indicate several possibilities—Sardinia and Corsica; an attack on the southwest coast of Italy followed by a drive to cut off Calabria and to reach Naples; or an invasion of Puglia. Should the Italians abandon the alliance, the coastal region near Rome was not out of the realm of possibility, and this prospect was not pleasing. The German force near the Italian capital—two reinforced divisions—was considered sufficient to eliminate the Italian forces guarding Rome but hardly adequate to resist an Allied invasion aided by Italian co-operation.[17]

Though an Allied invasion was an ever-present danger, the Germans began to regard the prospect of Italian treachery as the graver threat. Kesselring, while not unmindful of the possibility that he could be wrong, continued to accept in good faith repeated Italian assurances.[18] But Hitler had no such illusions. When he received from Kesselring and Rintelen favorable reports on Italian co-operation, he conjectured that Badoglio had approached the Allies, found their terms too severe, and swung back momentarily to the Axis. Convinced that the reporting of his "Italophiles" at Rome was not accurate, he sent General der Infanterie Rudolf Toussaint on 1 September to relieve Rintelen as military attaché, and Rudolf Rahn to replace Ambassador von Mackensen.[19]

Two days before, on 30 August, OKW made what turned out to be its final revision of Operation *ACHSE*, the plan to seize control of Italy. German units were to disarm Italian soldiers, except those who remained loyal. Italian troops who wished to fight on the German side were to be permitted to come over to the Wehrmacht; those who wished to go home were to be allowed to do so. *OB SUED* was to withdraw German units from southern Italy to the Rome area, then conduct further operations in accordance with instructions from *Army Group B*. The latter headquarters was to reinforce the troops at all the passes leading into Italy, occupy Genoa, La Spezia, Leghorn, Trieste, Fiume, and Pola, and pacify northern Italy

---

[16] *OKW/WFSt, KTB, 1.-31.VIII.43*, 20 and 25 Aug 43.

[17] Situation appreciation by *OB SUED*, 28 Aug 43, *OKW/WFSt, KTB, 1.-31.VIII.43*, 29 Aug 43; See also *OKW/WFSt, KTB, 1.-31. VIII.43*, 26 Aug 43.

[18] See the account of Badoglio's discussion with Rintelen on 29 Aug 43, *OKW/WFSt, KTB, 1.-31.VIII.43*, 29 Aug 43; MS #C-013 (Kesselring), pp. 26-27.

[19] Rintelen, *Mussolini als Bundesgenosse*, pp. 249-55; *OKW/WFSt, KTB, 1.-31.VIII.43*, 4 Sep 43.

through the instrumentality of a revived Fascist organization. The German Navy was to take over the tasks formerly performed by the Italian Fleet, and the German Luftwaffe was to do the same for the Italian Air Force; both were to cooperate to prevent Italian warships from going over to the Allies.[20] By the beginning of September 1943, the Germans were ready to meet the twin perils of Italian capitulation and Allied invasion.

## The Parleys at Cassibile

Even as the Germans were taking steps to counteract a possible Italian defection from the Pact of Steel, General Castellano and his interpreter, Montanari, reached the Termini Imerese airfield near Palermo a little before 0900, 31 August. Brigadier Strong met them, and an American plane took the party to the 15th Army Group headquarters at Cassibile.

Earlier that morning, General Smith, Mr. Murphy, and Mr. Macmillan had flown from Algiers to Cassibile with General Zanussi, who again had the text of the long terms of armistice which he had originally received from the British Ambassador at Lisbon.

The Italian generals met at Cassibile, and their meeting was not altogether cordial. Resenting what he considered Zanussi's intrusion into the negotiations, Castellano asked why Zanussi had gone to Lisbon. The reason, Zanussi replied, was the lack of a report from Castellano. Castellano then asked why Zanussi had requested a special plane for Lieutenant Lanza, who had not brought any important documents to Rome. The Allies, Zanussi explained, had taken the text of the long terms from him at Algiers, and had just now returned it. Zanussi seems to have briefly mentioned these additional conditions of armistice, but Castellano did not ask to see the document and Zanussi did not offer it. Castellano remained ignorant of the long terms.[21]

At Cassibile, Castellano, Zanussi, and Montanari conferred with Generals Alexander and Smith, Brigadier Strong, Commodore Royer Dick (Admiral Cunningham's chief of staff), Maj. Gen. John K. Cannon (NATAF's deputy commander), and a British army captain named Deann who served as interpreter. General Smith presided and opened the discussion by asking Castellano whether he had full power to sign the military terms of the armistice. Castellano replied in the negative, added that he had precise instructions, and read the memorandum furnished by his government: If the Italian Government were free, it would accept and announce the armistice as demanded by the Allies. Because the Italian Government was not free but under German control (as the result of the considerable increase of German forces in Italy since the Lisbon meeting), Italy could not accept the condition that the armistice be announced before the main Allied landings. The Italian Government had to be certain that Allied landings were in sufficient strength to guarantee the security of Rome, where the King and the government intended to remain, before it would hazard the announcement of an armistice. Because of the inferiority of their equipment, the Italians could not face the Germans alone. If they did, they would be quickly eliminated. Having eliminated the Italian military forces, the Germans could turn

---

[20] *OKW/WFSt, KTB, 1.–31.VIII.43,* 29 Aug 43.

[21] Castellano, *Come firmai,* pp. 133–34; Zanussi, *Guerra e catastrofe,* II, 116–17.

their undivided attention to the Allied invaders. Therefore, the Italian Government insisted that the Allies make their main landings north of Rome and in the force of at least fifteen divisions.

General Smith bluntly declared the Italian proposal unacceptable. The Italian Government had two alternatives: it could accept the conditions or refuse the armistice. He explained that General Eisenhower had had great difficulty securing authorization from the Allied governments to undertake any discussions with the Italians, and these were restricted to military matters only. The Quebec Memorandum offered Italy an opening, Smith said, and General Eisenhower had full power to modify the conditions in accordance with the degree of support rendered by Italy in the war. If the Italian Government refused the offer of an armistice, with its proclamation on the day of the Allied landing—as had been planned by General Eisenhower with the approval of the British and American Governments—then General Eisenhower would have no power to treat with Italian military leaders or to conclude an armistice in the future. In this case, negotiations would have to be turned over to the Allied diplomats, who would necessarily impose much harsher conditions.

Smith was striking at Castellano's essential program of military collaboration with the Allies by which the dynasty and the government might maintain themselves and save something from the disastrous wreck into which the Fascist regime had plunged Italy. Ruling out military discussions in the future meant the inability of Italy to participate in the war, the exclusion of any mitigation of terms in proportion to Italian aid. General Smith clearly implied that unless the Italian Government at once accepted all of General Eisenhower's conditions, Italy's role during the rest of the war would be passive, and her ultimate fate at the peace table would be determined purely on the basis of Allied wishes. As for the fifteen divisions that Badoglio regarded as essential, Smith said that if the Allies were in a position to land such a force, they would not be offering an armistice. The Allies intended to invade the Italian peninsula with or without Italian aid, and the Italians themselves would have to decide whether the struggle would be long and devastating or relatively brief.

Perceiving that the Allies planned to commit a total of fifteen divisions in Italy rather than to invade with that many, Castellano tried to secure a modification of the Allied plan to announce the armistice at the time of the main Allied landing. Castellano and Zanussi both tried repeatedly to gain some indication of the place and approximate time of the principal Allied debarkation, but General Smith refused to divulge any information.

Castellano then declared that he could say nothing further. He would have to refer the decision to his government, because he was obliged to follow his instructions strictly. He raised the question of whether the Italian Fleet might go to Maddalena, off Sardinia, rather than to an Allied port in order to soften the blow of its loss to the Italian people. Again Smith refused to modify the terms.

Still trying to learn when and where the Allies would invade the Italian mainland, Castellano asked how the Allies planned to protect the Vatican City, and when they hoped to reach Rome. To no avail. And when he made the threat that the Italian Fleet would not remain idle as it had during the Sicilian Campaign, but would attack Allied convoys, Smith replied with stronger threats: whatever the German strength or the Italian attitude, the Allies would drive the Germans out of Italy regardless of any suffering on the part of the Italian people. Nothing could prevent Italy from becoming a battlefield, but the Italian Government might shorten the duration of the battle by accepting completely the Allied conditions.

The Italian generals faced a cruel dilemma. Italy's refusal to accept the military armistice terms, with the possibility that later military collaboration might favorably modify the terms, opened the way to an overthrow of the dynasty and the disappearance of the regime. And yet, even more immediate was the threat that the Germans would occupy Rome and seize the government unless the Allies landed close to the capital. The course of the discussion revealed to General Smith and the others that Badoglio and his emissaries feared the Germans more than the Allies. At Lisbon, Castellano had given full information on German troop dispositions in Italy; at Cassibile, he refused to do so.

The conference terminated on an inconclusive note, though Smith had the impression that the Italian Government would not pluck up its courage to sign and announce the armistice unless the Allies gave assurances of strong landings in the Rome area as a means of protecting the government against the Germans.

While adamant during the conference, General Smith was nevertheless courteous. He invited the Italian representatives to lunch, where, after an initial embarrassing silence, discussion was resumed. Smith repeated that if Italy lost this opportunity, its situation in the future would be much more difficult. Castellano reiterated his government's contention that it would accept the armistice, no matter how harsh the terms, if the proclamation were postponed. The Italian Government, he said, would gladly provide military cooperation, but Italy could not do this unless the Allies offered guarantees to make it possible. Now almost certain that the Allies intended to land south of Rome, Castellano remarked that Italian forces alone could not save the capital, the nerve center of the country. He urged the Allies, in their own interest, to furnish help: if Rome fell to the Germans, he warned, a costly battle would be necessary to regain the city.

When Smith mentioned the Italian divisions disposed around Rome as being able to resist a German attack, Castellano countered that their weapons were so inferior to those of the Germans that only an Allied landing near Rome in addition to the main landing could save the capital. Smith then asked Castellano to make a specific request, bearing in mind that the Allies could not change their general plan of operations because of the long and minute preparations required for an amphibious landing. In response, Castellano requested one armored division to debark at Ostia, the old port of Rome at the mouth of the Tiber River, and one airborne division to drop nearby.

After lunch, General Smith conferred with Generals Eisenhower (in Africa) and Alexander and with AFHQ staff officers, while Messrs. Murphy and Macmillan conversed with Castellano and Zanussi. The Allied political advisers urged the Italians to act immediately on what was the last chance of the Badoglio government to salvage something from the war. Otherwise, they said, the Allies would refuse to deal with the King and the Badoglio government and would bomb relentlessly the major cities, including Rome. It was like preaching to the converted. The government of Rome remained more afraid of the immediate German threat than of the danger posed by the Allies. According to Castellano and Zanussi, the problem was to induce the cautious, fearful men in Rome to take the initiative against the Germans. Much as they yearned to be rid of the Germans, they feared that the Allies were not strong enough, even with Italian help, to take over and protect a large part of the country against the considerable German forces stationed there.

The German strength in Italy, which made the Badoglio government hesitate to accept an armistice, was precisely the factor that made the surrender of Italy essential to the Allies. General Eisenhower felt that the German forces in Italy had become so powerful as to change materially the estimates on which AVALANCHE had originally been based. The reserves concentrated in north Italy constituted a mobile threat, and though Allied air could delay their movement, it could not impose a paralysis on enemy traffic. The success of AVALANCHE, Eisenhower believed, might very likely turn upon gaining such a degree of Italian aid as would materially retard the movement of German reserves toward the battlefield. Eisenhower had no thought of abandoning AVALANCHE, but he needed every possible ounce of support from the Italians.

General Alexander, on whom would fall the immediate responsibility for the first large-scale invasion of the European mainland, was even more concerned than General Eisenhower. The Germans had nineteen divisions, he estimated, the Italians sixteen. AVALANCHE projected an initial Allied landing of three to five divisions, and a build-up over two weeks to a maximum of eight divisions. If the Italian units, fighting on their home soil, supported the Germans, the Allies might face a disaster of the first magnitude, a failure that would have catastrophic repercussions in England and in the United States. Literally everything had to be done, he told Mr. Murphy, to persuade the Italians to help the Allied forces during the landing and immediately afterwards.

In their anxiety to induce the Italian Government to surrender and provide military assistance, the Allies agreed to Castellano's request for protective forces at Rome. They decided to send the U.S. 82d Airborne Division to Rome at the time of the main invasion. Two plans for using the 82d in AVALANCHE had not been approved—one, a plan to seize the inland communication centers of Nocera and Sarno to block the movement of German reserves (neither place was suitable for drop zones); the other, named GIANT I, to air-land and drop the division along the Volturno River to secure the north flank of the Allied beachhead (canceled because of the difficulty of supplying the airborne troops so far from the ground forces). The division was therefore available, and a new plan, GIANT II, was drawn up for a drop near Rome.

Designed to induce the Italians to surrender, a prerequisite on which the entire invasion of the Italian mainland seemed to depend, the projected airborne operation offered certain military advantages. In conjunction with the Italian divisions assembled around Rome, the Allies would thereby gain control of the Italian capital and cut off reinforcements and supplies from the German units south of Rome. The psychological effect of a quick stroke against the city might be so stimulating as to cause the Italians to turn against the Germans. Caught by surprise, the Germans might pull out of south and central Italy at once. This was the basis of the decision made by General Eisenhower, in discussion with Generals Alexander and Smith on 31 August, to accede to Castellano's request for protecting the government at Rome.

When Smith returned to the tent occupied by the Italian emissaries, Murphy and Macmillan departed, and the discussions continued on a military basis. Smith told the Italian generals that it would be very difficult to get an armored division to Rome but quite possible to obtain an airborne division—if the Italians could provide certain airfields. Castellano saw no difficulty in making airfields available, but he thought armored units necessary to give the whole operation what he termed consistency. If an entire armored division could not be committed near Rome at once, at least some antitank guns at the mouth of the Tiber were indispensable. Smith assured Castellano that he would study the feasibility of the project; perhaps an entire armored division could be landed at a somewhat later date.

The conference then came to an end, and both parties summarized the results: (1) The Italian Government might accept or refuse the conditions of armistice, but if it accepted it must accede to the method indicated by the Allies for the official declaration. (2) The Allies were to make a subsidiary landing on the mainland, and against this operation the Italian troops could not avoid offering resistance. (3) Soon afterwards, the Allies would make their main landings south of Rome, bringing the total forces employed in both landings to at least the fifteen divisions regarded as essential by Badoglio; at the same time, the Allies would land an airborne division near Rome and one hundred antitank guns at the mouth of the Tiber. (4) The Italian Government was to make known its acceptance of the armistice by radio within twenty-four hours of 2 September; if it refused, no communication was to be made.[22]

After leaving Cassibile at 1600 in an American plane, Castellano, Zanussi, and Montanari transferred to the Italian plane at Termini Imerese and arrived in Rome around 1900. During their flight, the two generals talked over the problem. Sharing Castellano's conviction that the Italian Government could follow but one course—accept the armistice on the military conditions—Zanussi had supported Castellano at Cassibile. There was, however, little cordiality between the two men, because Castellano saw Zanussi as a rival. When Zanussi tried to explain the long terms, Castellano, believing them to be no different from those contained in the papers he had received at Lisbon, refused to listen. Zanussi did not insist and Castellano still remained ignorant of the long terms. When Zanussi expressed his fear that Castellano might not be able to persuade Badoglio to accept the armistice, he offered to support Castellano's argu-

---

[22] Telg, Eisenhower to CCS, NAF 346, 1 Sep 43, Capitulation of Italy, pp. 198–202; Castellano, *Come firmai*, pp. 135–44, and the minutes of the conference which he prints as Appendix 2, pp. 219–22; Zanussi, *Guerra e catastrofe*, II, 117–20; Ltr, Murphy to President Roosevelt, 8 Sep 43, OPD Files, Italy; Interv with Ambassador Smith, 13 May 47; Interv with Strong, 29 Oct 47; Interv, Smyth with Maj Gen Lowell W. Rooks, 28 Sep 48; Gavin, *Airborne Warfare*, pp. 19–24; 82d AB Div in Sicily and Italy, pp. 41–45; Warren, USAF Historical Study 74, pp. 56–57. The minutes printed in Castellano are authentic (see interview with Strong).

ments. Castellano was not particularly receptive. And when Zanussi offered to try to get Carboni to feel more favorably disposed toward Castellano, the latter was surprised. He had had no previous intimation that Carboni bore him any hostility.[23]

Both generals realized that the Allies had made but slight concessions regarding Badoglio's requests for a landing of fifteen divisions north of Rome and for an announcement of the armistice after the landing. It was quite apparent that the Allies had completed their plans, that they would not land north of Rome or even in that latitude. Where and when the Allies would invade the Italian mainland were questions which had not been answered. Zanussi thought the Allies might come ashore in the Formia-Gaeta sector some forty-five miles northwest of Naples, and Castellano appeared to share his opinion. The memorandum the Allies had given to Castellano indicated only the possibility that the main attack would come within two weeks.[24]

Castellano had not quite carried out his instructions to get the Allies to land in strength north of Rome. The Allies, it was clear, planned a subsidiary landing far to the south and a main landing closer to the capital, but still not within immediate striking distance. The Allies, General Smith had said, would land "as far north as possible, within the possibility of protection by fighter planes."[25] The total of all the forces employed by the Allies would approximate fifteen divisions. The decision the Badoglio government had to make could be only in these terms.

The Allies indicated not the slightest willingness to modify the plans they had formulated before Castellano had first contacted them, and they declined to make their invasion of Italy primarily an attempt to rescue the Italian Government.

As for the long terms, the Allies expected the Italian Government to be fully informed of them, for Zanussi had received them in Lisbon and carried a copy with him back to Rome. But Zanussi, who was Roatta's subordinate, was to give his copy of the terms to Roatta on 1 September with the suggestion that the paper be passed to Ambrosio. Whether Roatta did so or not, Castellano continued uninformed of the comprehensive surrender conditions, and for the moment Badoglio too was to remain in ignorance of them.[26]

*The Decision at Rome*

Back in Rome on the evening of 31 August, Castellano hastened to *Comando Supremo* where he found Ambrosio and reported the results of the Cassibile discussions. Since Badoglio had retired for the night, Ambrosio made an appointment to see him the next morning.

Accompanied by Ambrosio, Guariglia, Acquarone, and Carboni, Castellano on 1 September presented his copy of the minutes of the Cassibile conference to Badoglio and gave a detailed account of what had been said. He admitted frankly that he had been unable to obtain what the Italian Government desired—postponement of the armistice until after the main Allied landings. The Allies, he stated, would not modify their plan to invade southern Italy. The Allied leaders,

---

[23] Castellano, *Come firmai*, pp. 145-46; Zanussi, *Guerra e catastrofe*, II, 123-24.
[24] Zanussi, *Guerra e catastrofe*, II, 119, 124.
[25] Castellano, *Come firmai*, p. 222.

[26] Zanussi, *Guerra e catastrofe*, II, 124; Castellano, *Come firmai*, 160; Badoglio, *Memorie e documenti*, pp. 102, 132.

he explained, considered the Italian units around Rome strong enough to defend the city. Only after he had made clear the absolute inferiority of the Italian troops in comparison with the nearby German troops had he obtained the promise of an American airborne division, one hundred pieces of artillery, and the subsequent commitment of an armored division. Sending these troops, Castellano said, would automatically entail the support of Allied aviation. Badoglio listened in silence until Castellano finished. Then he asked Ambrosio's opinion. Ambrosio said he saw no course open other than to accept the proffered conditions.

At this point, Carboni spoke out in decided opposition. It was he, Carboni, who commanded the *Motorized Corps* of four divisions. It was he who would have to defend Rome against the Germans. He believed that the Anglo-American assurances were not to be trusted. They were oral promises rather than a written agreement. Furthermore, he said, his troops could not withstand a German attack because they lacked gasoline and ammunition.

Carboni's remarks came as a disagreeable surprise to Castellano, for Carboni had favored Castellano's mission to Cassibile, and he had not earlier mentioned his lack of ammunition and gasoline. But Zanussi had spoken to Carboni on the preceding evening and apparently had told him something of the discussions at Cassibile. Learning that he would have the unenviable task of defending Rome against the Germans with very little Allied assistance, Carboni had become depressed.

Guariglia, for his part, said there was nothing to do but accept the armistice. The Italian Government was committed, he believed, because so much of Castellano's negotiations had been placed on paper, a fact which the Allies might use to precipitate an Italo-German conflict. Apparently uncertain, Acquarone said nothing. Badoglio expressed no opinion. He would, he said, refer the problem to the King.[27]

That afternoon Badoglio saw the King. The Italian monarch consented to the armistice. Badoglio informed Ambrosio, who notified AFHQ by a telegram: "The reply is affirmative repeat affirmative. In consequence, known person will arrive tomorrow two September hour and place established. Please confirm." AFHQ received this message shortly before 2300, 1 September.[28]

Though this act had the appearance of a decision, Badoglio in reality had not made up his mind. He still hesitated, still hoped that the Allies would rescue him. Unwilling to make any move against the Germans, he made no suggestion to any subordinate to start planning for eventual co-operation with the Allies. Perhaps he was upset by the replacement that very day of the German Ambassador and of the military attaché, whom Badoglio could hardly expect to be so Italophile as the men, Badoglio's good friends, they replaced.

---

[27] The records of this meeting consist merely of the autobiographical accounts composed much later by some of the participants: Badoglio, *Memorie e documenti*, p. 102 (brief and inexact); Carboni, *L'armistizio e la difesa di Roma*, p. 26 (brief and suspect); Castellano, *Come firmai*, pp. 146-49 (a full account but prejudiced in his own behalf); Guariglia, *Ricordi*, pp. 677-78. See also Zanussi, *Guerra e catastrofe*, II, 133-34, and *Il Processo Carboni-Roatta*, p. 25.

[28] Telg, Eisenhower to CCS, NAF 348, 1 Sep 43, Capitulation of Italy, p. 205; Castellano, *Come firmai*, p. 149; Badoglio, *Memorie e documenti*, p. 102.

Ambrosio also remained passive. He issued no orders, gave no word to his subordinates of the newly projected orientation of the government.

For both Badoglio and Ambrosio, it was one thing to tell the Allies that the armistice was accepted; it was quite another to take steps to meet the consequences of the decision. Perhaps more could not have been expected. To decide to capitulate, even half-heartedly and after much soul-searching, was in itself a traumatic experience that robbed them, at least temporarily, of further initiative.

It remained for Roatta to act. Without instructions from higher authority, he issued *Memoria 44*, an outline order prepared ten days earlier in anticipation of a German seizure of Rome and an attempted restoration of Fascist control. Italian troops, in the event of open German hostility, were to protect railways, command posts, and centers of communication, be ready to interrupt German traffic, seize German headquarters and depots, and sabotage German communications. Upon Roatta's order or in case the Germans initiated hostile actions, the Italian forces on Sardinia and Corsica were to expel the Germans; the *Seventh Army* in southern Italy was to hold Taranto and Brindisi; the *Fifth Army* was to protect the fleet at La Spezia and at the same time attack the German *3d Panzer Grenadier Division*; the *Eighth Army* in the South Tyrol and Venezia Giulia was to attack the German *44th Infantry Division*; the *Fourth Army* in Piedmont and Liguria was to cut the passes leading from France; and the *Second Army* in the northeast was to attack the German *71st Infantry Division*.

Between 2 and 5 September, officer couriers carried the order to the generals who commanded the forces under Roatta. Each recipient, after reading the warning order, was to burn it in the presence of the courier except for the last page, which was to be signed as a receipt.[29]

Roatta's was the only action taken by the Italian Government—and this at the third level of command—as a consequence of the decision to accept the armistice. Ironically, Roatta had been considered somewhat pro-German in sentiment.

The King, intent on playing the role of a constitutional monarch, took no further action once he had sanctioned Badoglio's proposed course. Those immediately below him, Badoglio and Ambrosio, were timid, cautious, and undecided. Only at the third level and below were men to be found with a real appreciation of Italy's predicament and some determination to seek a solution. It was the paralysis of will at the top which doomed Italy.

---

[29] Zanussi, *Guerra e catastrofe*, II, 142–44; Rossi, *Come arrivammo*, pp. 207–10; Roatta, *Otto milioni*, pp. 287–88; Antonio Basso, *L'Armistizio del settembre 1943 in Sardegna* (Naples: Rispoli, 1947), p. 33.

# CHAPTER XXV

# The Armistice

### *The Signature*

When General Castellano, accompanied by Montanari as his interpreter, by Maj. Luigi Marchesi, an aide, and by Major Vassallo, the pilot of his plane, returned to Cassibile on the morning of 2 September, he found himself in a fog of misunderstanding. The Allies had wanted him to return to Sicily for a formal signing of the armistice terms. Castellano understood that the Italian Government had already formally accepted the armistice by means of the radio message Ambrosio had sent on the previous day. Castellano thought he had returned to Cassibile to arrange for Italo-Allied co-operation, specifically for the airdrop near Rome.[1]

General Smith disabused Castellano of this idea when the two met. Smith asked him at once whether he had full power to sign the surrender document. The reason for the blunt request was the growing Allied concern over the risks of invading the Italian peninsula. Montgomery's Eighth Army was scheduled to execute Operation BAYTOWN on the following day—to cross the Strait of Messina from Sicily to Calabria in a subsidiary Allied landing. Though reasonably confident of success in this operation, the Allies had become increasingly concerned over the inherent hazards of Operation AVALANCHE, the main invasion that Clark's Fifth Army was scheduled to make on 9 September on the beaches of Salerno. This amphibious assault posed many difficulties: the convoys transporting the ground troops from North Africa to the landing beaches would be vulnerable to German air and Italian sea power; the landing beaches were at the extreme range of Allied fighter aircraft; and the three initial assault divisions could not be reinforced quickly enough and in sufficient strength to meet the German and Italian troops on even equal terms. For these reasons, the Allies needed the help that the Italian surrender promised—neutralization of the Italian Fleet and the aid of Italian ground troops in diverting or at least interfering with the movements of German units to the landing sites. Because of the obvious indecision and fright among the members of the Italian Government, the Allies wished to make certain that the Italians would stick to their agreement to capitulate. The Allies wanted no misstep, no faltering at the last minute to jeopardize the already risky plans of their first re-entry into the European mainland.

To Smith's question, Castellano answered that he did not have full power to sign the armistice terms.

Despite the summer heat in Sicily, the temperature dropped suddenly. The Allied officers departed. For several hours, the Italians were completely ignored.

---

[1] Castellano, *Come firmai,* pp. 152ff.

# THE ARMISTICE

They found that spending the day alone in their tent in the midst of an Allied headquarters was not without its embarrassing aspect.

Late that afternoon, General Smith returned to ask Castellano whether he wished to radio Rome for permission to sign the surrender document. Castellano agreed to do so. Smith also suggested that the Italian Government authenticate Castellano's authority to sign by means of a message to Osborne, the British Ambassador at the Vatican.

That evening General Smith received a message from *Comando Supremo* indicating Italian acceptance of an airborne operation near Rome and suggesting the use of three specific airfields. But no word came in answer to Castellano's request.

Again at 0400, 3 September, when the Eighth Army was crossing the Strait of Messina to invade Calabria, Castellano repeated his request. Would the government authorize him to sign the armistice?

In Rome that same morning, Badoglio summoned the chiefs of staff of the three military services. "His Majesty," Badoglio announced, "has decided to negotiate for an armistice." He then ordered each service chief to make appropriate dispositions of his forces, but he declined to put the order in writing because he feared that too many persons would learn of the decision.[2]

Sometime later Badoglio decided to authorize Castellano to sign the armistice terms. As a result, the Allies at Cassibile received a radiogram about 1400, 3 September. "Present telegram is sent from Head Italian Government to Supreme Commander Allied Force." The affirmative reply dispatched two days earlier, Badoglio wired, had contained "implicit acceptance [of the] armistice conditions."[3]

Implicit acceptance was not enough. The Allies wanted to be absolutely sure. And around 1700 Castellano finally received explicit authority to sign. "General Castellano," Badoglio wired, "is authorized by the Italian Government to sign the acceptance of the conditions of armistice."[4]

By then it was clear that Operation BAYTOWN was a success. The British Eighth Army had landed on the toe of Italy with the 13 Corps on a 3-brigade front, and had seized Reggio di Calabria and a nearby airfield. Virtually no resistance, Italian or German, had materialized.[5]

On that day, too, 3 September, the new German Ambassador to Italy, Rudolf Rahn, presented his credentials to Badoglio. Rahn took the occasion to bring up the matter of reorganizing the chain of command in the Italian theater so that the Germans would be in control of active operations. Declaring that he welcomed

---

[2] Basic sources are: Castellano, *Come firmai*, pp. 161ff; Rossi *Come arrivammo*, pp. 210ff; Badoglio, *Memorie e documenti*, pp. 112ff; Guariglia, *Ricordi*, pp. 681ff. See also Monelli, *Roma 1943*, p. 304.

[3] Telg, AFHQ Adv to AFHQ, No. 121, 3 Sep 43, Capitulation of Italy, p. 252, relayed by AFHQ to CCS, NAF 354, same file, p. 257.

According to Guariglia (*Ricordi*, pages 681–82), Badoglio decided to authorize Castellano to sign the armistice terms at the meeting with the chiefs of staff of the Italian armed forces.

[4] Telg 121, AFHQ Adv to AFHQ, 3 Sep 43, cited n. 3; See also Armistice Meetings, Fairfield Camp, Sicily, Sep 43, in AFHQ 0100/4/330. A copy of the armistice document is found in 10,000/136/584.

[5] For a detailed account of the landing, see Montgomery, *Eighth Army*, pp. 123–24; Nicholson, *The Canadians in Italy*, pp. 202–06; and Blumenson, Salerno to Cassino.

Rahn's proposal, Badoglio said that he could not intervene directly in military matters. He promised, however, to arrange an audience with the King and a meeting with Ambrosio for the following day.[6]

At Cassibile, at 1715, 3 September, General Castellano signed the text of the short terms on behalf of Badoglio, Head of the Italian Government. General Smith signed for General Eisenhower, who had flown over from North Africa to witness the ceremony.[7]

As General Eisenhower explained to the CCS, the signing of the short terms was absolutely necessary before specific plans could be made with Italian representatives to secure the maximum possible aid from the Italians, and to obtain the co-operation of the *Motorized Corps* for the 82d Airborne Division's projected operation near Rome. Formal signature of the long terms, he added, would take place later and be timed to fit Allied operational plans.[8]

After the signature of the armistice agreement, the Italians withdrew to their tent. Castellano sent a message to Rome to report his action, whereupon General Alexander appeared and invited him to dinner.[9]

Somewhat later, General Smith handed Castellano a copy of the long terms entitled "Instrument of Surrender of Italy." He attached a brief note to explain that the document

Contains the political, financial, and economic conditions which will be imposed by the United Nations in accordance with paragraph 12 of the Armistice terms. The military conditions of the Armistice are contained in the document which we have just signed. The attached paper is identical with the one handed to General Zanussi by H. M. Ambassador in Lisbon.[10]

Having managed to avoid use of the humiliating unconditional surrender phrase in all his negotiations, and having been responsible for initiating a joint Italo-Allied operation to defend Rome, Castellano was painfully surprised to read the initial clause of the comprehensive terms: "The Italian Land, Sea and Air Forces wherever located, hereby surrender unconditionally."

When Castellano protested, Smith said that Zanussi had received the document in Lisbon; the Italian Government certainly knew the conditions of the long terms. Castellano was not so sure. He doubted that his government would accept the additional clauses. When Smith reminded him of the modifying force of the Quebec Memorandum, Castellano said that it contained only general promises, that his government had no recourse if the Allies did not convey their promises in writing. Thereupon General Smith sat down and made the promise in writing. "The additional clauses," he wrote for Badoglio's benefit, "have only a relative value insofar as Italy collaborates in the war against the Germans."[11]

---

[6] Badoglio, *Memorie e documenti*, pp. 110–11, gives an untruthful account of this meeting. See Rahn's Report, Telg 4370, 3 Sep 43, German Foreign Office Documents, U.S. Department of State, Serial 131/ frames 71960–62, NARS.

[7] Castellano, *Come firmai*, pp. 156–57; Armistice Meetings, Fairfield Camp, Sicily, Sep 43, 0100/4/330; Butcher, *My Three Years With Eisenhower*, pp. 405–06; Diary Office CinC, Book VIII, p. A–720.

[8] Telg 121, AFHQ Adv to AFHQ, 3 Sep 43, Capitulation of Italy, p. 252, relayed by AFHQ to CCS, NAF 354, 3 Sep 43, Capitulation of Italy, p. 257.

[9] Castellano, *Come firmai*, pp. 157–58.

[10] Capitulation of Italy, p. 224.

[11] Castellano, *Come firmai*, pp. 160–61; Interv with Ambassador Smith, 13 May 47.

## THE ARMISTICE

At 2030 that evening, Castellano met again with Allied officers to discuss what the Italian Government should do now that it had concluded the armistice agreement. General Alexander presided, Generals Smith, Rooks, and Cannon, Brig. Gen. Patrick W. Timberlake (A–3, Mediterranean Air Command), Brigadier Strong, and General Lemnitzer (Deputy Chief of Staff, 15th Army Group) took part. After the meeting, Castellano received an *aide-mémoire* enumerating the general actions the Italian Government would take before the announcement of the armistice. Commodore Dick handed Castellano a memorandum containing instructions for the movement of Italian warships and merchant shipping to ports under Allied control.[12]

### Planning GIANT II

The Allies also consulted Castellano on the plans even then being readied for the airborne drop near Rome. Before the signing of the armistice, while Castellano was waiting explicit permission to sign, the Allies had begun to plan the airborne operation. At 1430, 3 September, Castellano had met with several Allied officers to explore possible alternatives. Presiding at the meeting, Rooks, the AFHQ G–3, stated that the airborne division had the mission of co-operating with Italian units in the defense of Rome. Castellano then outlined how he thought the Germans might act against the airborne landing.

[12] Capitulation of Italy, pp. 221–23. The copy in AFHQ microfilm records, reel R–62–I, item Giant Two, indicates that copy 1 of the *aide-mémoire* was given to Castellano. See also copy 2, 3 Sep 43, in AFHQ 0100/4/330, with change to par. 5, dated 6 Sep 43, sent to Rome via the secret radio channel.

The *3d Panzer Grenadier Division*, located between Viterbo and Lake Bolsena, could advance on Rome by three parallel roads and would probably make the main effort. Two Italian units stood in its way, the *Piave Division*, immediately north of the city, and the *Ariete Division*, some fifteen miles beyond. The commanders of these divisions, Castellano ventured, could defend just south of Lakes Bracciano and Martignano. The *Sassari Division*, stationed in Rome, could reinforce them. South of Rome, the *Centauro Division* could block the *2d Parachute Division's* approach to the capital.

The Italians did not lack men, Castellano explained. They lacked firepower. The *Ariete Division*, for example, had no antitank guns at all and could hold the Germans back for perhaps twenty-four hours, no more.

General Ridgway, commander of the 82d Airborne Division, who had suddenly been called to the conference, said that he had 57-mm. antitank guns able to penetrate Mark IV and VI tanks at ranges up to 500 yards, and still heavier weapons possibly might be landed. Furthermore, the proposed seaborne expedition to the mouth of the Tiber River could bring even more arms.

But Ridgway and the others were more concerned with protecting the airfields where the landings were to take place, and assuring that no Italian antiaircraft battery would fire on the incoming planes. Could Castellano give assurance that Italian antiaircraft batteries would not fire on the Allied planes?

Castellano gave several specific guarantees. The Italians would secure the fields. Antiaircraft defenses would not open fire. A route north of the Tiber River would pass over minimum antiaircraft defenses.

It was pointed out, and agreed to by Castellano, that sufficient time would have to be allowed to enable a specific order to get down to every gun. Castellano also promised that Italian officers of high rank would meet the commander of the airborne division on a field to be decided upon by the Allies. Navigational aids would be furnished. The airfields would be illuminated; the outlines of the fields in orange-red lights, the outlines of the runways and any obstacles within five hundred yards of the fields by means of red lights. Castellano also promised that the Italians would provide motor transportation for concentrating the airborne troops and their supplies. Finally, he gave assurances that all available intelligence regarding both German and Italian units in the Rome area would be furnished the Allies before the operation.

Castellano suggested six available airfields, none occupied by the Germans.[13] He produced maps showing the location of German and Italian troops near Rome. He suggested troop landings at Centocelle and Littoria airfields, heavy equipment at Guidonia airfield. He recommended the Littoria airfield, just north of the city, as the point of concentration. Also, to reach these fields, which together formed a triangle with its base along the eastern outskirts of the Italian capital and its apex at Guidonia, the planes should fly in from the west-northwest.

During the meeting, certain other matters were briefly mentioned. General Rooks noted that consideration was being given to running two or three ships up the Tiber River with ammunition and supplies, and Commodore Royer Dick asked if the swing bridges could be opened. Castellano stated that the bridge at Fiumicino could be kept open, and that this would permit ships to go as far as the Magliano airfield where supplies could be landed along the banks. The Tiber River was thirty feet deep as far as the Littoria airfield, Castellano said, but the area south of the river was occupied by German troops armed with antiaircraft batteries. This was Castellano's reason for recommending that the approach of the planes should be about eight miles north of the river. General Taylor, the 82d Airborne Division's artillery commander, felt that such a route would be more difficult to find at night than one directly up the river, and urged that the German troops south of the river be mopped up by the Italians as an initial move in the operation. Rooks then asked if a small planning staff from the airborne division could be sent to Rome in advance to complete the details of the operation; Castellano agreed, and offered to take two or three American officers with him on his return to Rome on the following day.

After some discussion on the availability of 100-octane gasoline for such Allied fighter aircraft as might be flown into the Rome area, General Ridgway said that he had enough information on which to draft his outline plan. The meeting adjourned.[14]

---

[13] These were Littoria (Urbe), in the northern suburbs; Centocelle, southeast of the city; The Race Course, opposite Littoria; Magliana, on the river west of Rome; Guidonia, fifteen miles northeast of Rome; and Ciampino, southeast of the city (not to be thought of since it was in the midst of German troops).

[14] Min of Mtg held at Cassibile on Friday, 3 Sep 43, to discuss a certain projected airborne operation, reel R-62-I, item Giant Two; Giant Two Outline Plan, 3 Sep 43, copy 5, reel R-62-I; Giant Two Outline Plan, copy 3, 3 Sep 43, typewritten copy with ink insertions and corrections, 82d AB Div G-3 Jnl, 1-15 Sep 43; Gavin, *Airborne Warfare*, pp. 24-27; Ridgway.

The Tiber River at Fiumicino

As General Ridgway worked with a small planning group on an outline plan for GIANT II, he grew increasingly concerned over the possibility that the Italian authorities might not be able to silence a sufficient number of the guns in Rome's belt of antiaircraft defenses. Should too few be silenced, the unescorted C-47's would be fat targets as they came in low to drop paratroopers or to land supplies. General Ridgway remembered how Allied fighters on 18 April had intercepted and shot down seventy-three Junker 52's flying supplies into Tunisia, and recalled painfully the unfortunate experience during the invasion of Sicily when friendly fire had shot down twenty-three allied transport aircraft. He also felt that he could not rely on the Italians for other acts of cooperation in the degree "considered essential to success." [15]

Late that night Castellano was called in for additional consultation. The Italian general was now less certain than he had been during the afternoon session, and under the pressure of questioning he admitted the enormous difficulty of silencing every gun in Rome's antiaircraft defenses. Instead of following the instructions of his government and suggesting, as he had earlier, the Guidonia, Littoria, and Centocelle airfields, he admitted that the latter two fields lay in the midst of extensive flak batteries. He now proposed that initial drops be made at the Furbara and Cerveteri airfields, slightly to the north of Rome and on the coast. Located outside the city's antiaircraft defenses, they were completely in Italian hands. The *Lupi di Toscana Division,* coming from southern France and scheduled to concentrate on 8 September between these two airfields, could provide additional ground security.

The airborne planners worked all night, and on the morning of 4 September they had an outline plan. Initial forces were to land on the Cerveteri and Furbara fields, followed during the next night by parachute drops on the Guidonia, Littoria, and Centocelle fields. The division was then to assemble in the western outskirts of Rome, not at Littoria. The plan carefully defined Italian responsibilities. The Italians were to secure and protect the five airfields. They alone, without German help, were to man all the antiaircraft defenses around those fields. The flak batteries were to have explicit orders against taking any aircraft under fire during the nights of the operation. Italian troops were to block avenues of approach open to the Germans, furnish local protection of the airfields and drop zones, and guarantee unmolested passage of naval craft up the Tiber River to Rome. The Italians were to have a horizontal searchlight beam pointing due west at Furbara airfield, and two Rome radio stations were to broadcast throughout the night as navigational aids. The Italians were to out-

---

*Soldier,* pp. 80-83; Warren, USAF Hist Study 74, pp. 57-58; Craven and Cate, eds., *Europe: TORCH to POINTBLANK,* pp. 519-20; 82d AB Div in Sicily and Italy, pp. 45-49; copy 2 of Giant Two Outline Plan may be found in 0100/12A/173; see also Hq NAAF, A-5/4363, sub: Amendment 1 to Opn AVALANCHE—Outline Plan of Troop Carrier Opns (A-5/P.501) (Final), 0100/12A/173 and Addendum to A-5/P.501 (Final), same file; Operation Giant, in 0403/4/1029; Directive, AFHQ to multiple adressees, sub: Operation Giant Two, 4 Sep 43, 0100/4/330; Ltr, Rpt by Maj Patrick D. Mulcahy, AFHQ Obsv, AFHQ, AG 370-1 (Airborne) GCT-AGM, 22 Sep 43, sub: Airborne Activities in the AVALANCHE Opn, to Air CinC, Med, 0403/10/296.

[15] Rpt, Ridgway to Eisenhower, 25 Oct 43, sub: Lessons of Airborne Operations in Italy, contained in USAAF, A Report of TCC Activities Including the Italian Invasion, 1 Aug-30 Sep 43, II, 120; Ridgway, *Soldier,* pp. 80-81; Warren, USAF Hist Study 74, p. 58.

# THE ARMISTICE

line the perimeter of each field with amber lights, the airfield runways with white lights; to remove or silence all antiaircraft guns in a 10-mile-wide corridor astride the Tiber and along a shorter, secondary, and more direct route from the sea to the Cerveteri and Furbara fields; to have a senior staff officer of the *Motorized Corps* meet General Ridgway at Furbara airfield and a senior staff officer at each airfield to receive the American troops; and to furnish one interpreter guide to each company.[16]

Castellano later claimed, incorrectly, that he had obtained an agreement for the American division to "be placed at the orders of General Carboni."[17] The 82d Airborne Division was rather to "secure the city of Rome and adjacent airfields and prevent their occupation by German forces," accomplishing this "in cooperation with Italian forces." As General Taylor described the relationship:

> The airborne troops upon arrival will co-operate with the Italians in the defense of Rome and comply with the recommendations of the Italian High Command without relinquishing their liberty of action or undertaking any operation or making any disposition considered unsound.[18]

The outline plan, a copy of which Castellano received, also stipulated the amount of logistical aid the Italians were to provide: 23,000 rations, 355 trucks, 12 ambulances, 120 tons of gasoline and oil, 12 switchboards, 150 field telephones, 100 picks, 200 shovels, 5,000 wire pickets, and 150 miles of barbed wire. A labor pool of 500 men was to be provided by the second day. The Americans would bring in rations for two days, gasoline for one day, medical supplies for the initial period, and ammunition for the entire operation.

Convinced by this time that any airborne drop in the Rome area would be a tragic mistake, General Ridgway protested strongly to Generals Smith and Alexander. Ridgway's opposition led the Allies to send two American officers to Rome to confer with the leaders of the Italian forces around the capital about the final details of Italo-American co-operation. The real purpose of their mission was to assess the feasibility of the airborne operation.

### Second Thoughts in Rome

After working with the Allied officers on the GIANT II outline plan, Castellano was informed that General Eisenhower wanted to have an Italian military mission attached to AFHQ, a mission composed of ground, air, and naval representatives headed by Castellano himself. Castellano radioed a request to Rome for authority to constitute such a mission, and canceled his plans to return to Rome. Other arrangements would be made for getting the two Allied officers to Rome.

During the early afternoon of 4 September, Smith visited Castellano once more. Castellano raised the question of when the Allied landing would take place and when the armistice was to be announced. Replying through the interpreter, Smith said: "I understand very well the great anxiety you have to know these dates, but unfortunately I can tell you nothing; it is a military secret which I must keep." Then, in a lower voice, "I can say only that the landing will take place within two weeks."[19] Smith then departed and that afternoon returned to Algiers.

---

[16] Giant Two Outline Plan.

[17] Castellano, *Come firmai*, pp. 167–68.

[18] Giant Two Outline Plan; Program for Giant II, 6 Sep 43, signed by Gen Taylor, 82d AB Div G-3 Jnl, 1–15 Sep 43.

[19] Castellano, *Come firmai*, p. 71; Interv with Ambassador Smith, 13 May 47.

During the afternoon Castellano saw several other Allied officers on the problems of co-ordinating various aspects of the armistice announcement. The Allies would notify the Italian Government what day the announcement was to be made by the secret radio link already established with Rome, and, as an alternate channel, by the British Broadcasting Corporation (BBC). The BBC would signal the day by broadcasting two special programs between the hours of 1000 and 1200, British time: a half hour of Verdi's music and a two-minute discourse, during the British overseas program, on the theme of Nazi activities in Argentina.[20]

Castellano then prepared his reports to his government, reports to be flown to Rome on the following day, 5 September. While Montanari translated the documents from English to Italian, Castellano wrote a letter to Ambrosio. "Despite every possible effort to succeed," he stated, "I have not been able to get any information on the precise locality of the landing. Regarding the date I can say nothing precise; but from confidential information I presume that the landing will take place between the 10th and 15th of September, possibly the 12th." [21]

Castellano had reached the conclusion from Smith's spoken statement. If the main Allied invasion was to be launched within one week, Castellano reasoned, Smith would not have spoken of two weeks. Therefore, he deduced that at least one week would elapse between the initial landing in south Italy—BAYTOWN into the tip of Calabria, launched on 3 September—and the main descent on the mainland. Since Smith had talked to him on 4 September, the main attack could not, according to this line of reasoning, be expected before the 11th. It could take place any time during the second week—10 to 15 September.[22]

Castellano's aide and pilot flew his letter and documents, including the GIANT II outline plan, to Rome early on 5 September. The aide delivered the papers to Ambrosio, who read them and turned them over to Badoglio. Castellano's date of 12 September for the Allied landing and the armistice announcement was only a guess, but Ambrosio accepted Castellano's estimate as definite, and he told Badoglio so. As a result, all the Italian military and political leaders involved in the armistice expected the main Allied landing no earlier than 12 September, possibly later.[23]

General Eisenhower and AFHQ staff officers expected the Italians to make vigorous efforts to insure the success of the invasion—or at least of the airborne drop. But Badoglio, Ambrosio, Rossi, and Roatta remained doubtful of their ability to give real help, possibly because they felt that Badoglio had pledged the government to a course of action—the surrender of all of Italy to the Allies—that was beyond its power. The Italian Government and High Command therefore continued to be more interested in being rescued than in helping fight the Germans. While Castellano supported active co-operation with the Allies, the leaders in Rome remained,

---

[20] Memo by Brig Gen Robert A. McClure, 5 Sep 43, Capitulation of Italy, p. 271.

[21] This is the text of the critical paragraph of the letter as given by Castellano (*Come firmai*, page 172). The original letter has not been revealed and there is some doubt about the exact wording. See *Il Processo Carboni-Roatta*, p. 28.

[22] Castellano, *Come firmai*, p. 173.

[23] Badoglio, *Memorie e documenti*, pp. 102–03; Rossi, *Come arrivammo*, pp. 133-35; MS # P-058, Project #46, 1 Feb–8 Sep 43, Question 20. According to the above sources Maj. Luigi Marchesi in delivering Castellano's letter gave oral confirmation of 12 September.

# THE ARMISTICE

in contrast, passive. Castellano had represented the Italian Army as hating the Germans and willing to turn on them. In this way, an American officer later remarked, he "sold the Allies a bill of goods."[24] Badoglio, Ambrosio, Roatta, and Rossi were hardly anxious to fight. Their primary aim was to secure Allied protection of the capital.

On 5 September, Roatta later maintained, he received notice from *Comando Supremo* that the armistice with the Allies was concluded, that the time of the armistice announcement was as yet undetermined but would not occur before 12 September, that in accord with the Italian request the Allies would land a force of six divisions in central Italy and within striking distance of Rome, an unknown number of troops by air, and nine Allied divisions in a subsequent landing perhaps farther to the north. Beyond this, the Italian Government had no details and awaited precise information regarding Allied plans.[25]

Two days earlier, on 3 September, while Badoglio was deciding to authorize Castellano's signature of the armistice terms, Ambrosio had written a memorandum for his deputy chief, Rossi, to outline the instructions he wished issued to *Superaereo*, *Supermarina*, and *Army Group East* (controlling the Italian troops in Greece and in the Balkans). This paper, plus Roatta's *Memoria 44* (drawn on 1 September and in the process of dissemination to the commanders under his control), reached Rossi on 4 September. In compliance with Ambrosio's wish, Rossi drafted several directives. Before they reached final form, Castellano's documents arrived—on 5 September. This held up the instructions for another day. On 6 September, *Comando Supremo* issued *Promemoria 1*, a general directive for each general staff—Army, Navy, and Air Force—that was, in effect, a complementary order to Roatta's *Memoria 44*. Like the earlier Army order, the *Comando Supremo* directive did not refer to co-operation with the Allies. Rather, its chief purpose was to spell out Italian reaction to collective, general German aggression as distinguished from local, irresponsible German acts. Under the illusion that 12 September was the firm date for the Allied invasion and the armistice announcement, *Comando Supremo* intended subsequently to supplement these instructions.[26]

The intermixture of German and Italian headquarters in the Balkans and Greece made it appropriate to issue instructions to *Army Group East* as late as possible. Since Ambrosio thought of 12 September as the target date, he had a draft order (*Promemoria 2*) drawn on 6 September for that headquarters, intending to put it into effect later. The directive instructed the troops in Herzegovina, Montenegro, and Albania to withdraw toward the coast and maintain possession of the ports of Cattaro and Durazzo; the commander in Greece and Crete, before withdrawing his troops to suitable ports for evacuation, was to tell the Germans frankly that the Italians would not fight against them unless

---

[24] Quote is from Interv, Smyth with Maj Gen Lyman L. Lemnitzer, 4 Mar 47.

[25] Roatta is in error (*Otto milioni*, pages 301–02) when he gives the date of reception of this information as 3 September.

[26] Rossi, *Come arrivammo*, pp. 211–15. Curiously enough, Roatta (*Otto milioni*, pages 302–03, 314) later identified this directive as coming from AFHQ. Roatta's Army general staff on the same day issued its *Memoria 45* to supplement the *Comando Supremo* directive.

the Germans resorted to violence. In the Aegean Islands, the Italians were to disarm the Germans to avert open hostilities.[27]

Thus, the only orders actually issued during the three days immediately following the signature of the armistice were essentially defensive. They indicated little intention of pursuing the aggressive action against the Germans that Castellano had described at Cassibile.

The role of the forces defending Rome was not quite so passive. The nucleus of this body of troops had begun to form on 20 July to protect the government against a possible Fascist reaction to Mussolini's imminent overthrow. Since 29 July the troops had been alerted to act against the possibility of a German stroke against the capital. Under the immediate command of Roatta, chief of the Army General Staff, the force consisted of three corps. The *Corpo d'Armata di Roma*, controlling the *Sassari Division, carabinieri*, and service and school troops, was within Rome and had as its task the internal defense of the city against SS agents and other special German troops stationed there. The *XVII Corps* had small detachments of the *220th* and *221st Coastal Divisions* distributed along the coast from Tarquinia to the Volturno River—a distance of 125 miles—and the *Piacenza Division* interspersed among units of the German *2d Parachute Division*. General Carboni's *Motorized Corps* controlled the *Ariete Armored* and *Piave Motorized Divisions* north of Rome, the *Centauro Armored Division* east of the capital, and the *Granatieri Division* south of the city.

As soon as Roatta learned from *Comando Supremo* on 5 September that the armistice had been concluded, he ordered the units regrouped. The *Re* and *Lupi di Toscana Divisions* were scheduled to arrive from the Balkans and from France as a result of the agreement reached on 15 August with the Germans—who believed the divisions were slated for commitment in southern Italy. Instead, the Italians planned to use the divisions, scheduled to arrive in Rome on 8 September, to reinforce the capital's defenses. Roatta intended to have completed by the morning of 12 September the dispositions of these units, plus the deployment of a *Bersaglieri* regiment, scheduled to become available, as well as the final regrouping of the *Motorized Corps*. His faith in this date as the time of the Allied invasion and the armistice announcement was strengthened on 6 September when he received copies of the GIANT II outline plan. According to Generale di Divisione Aerea Renato Sandalli, chief of the Air Force Staff, who also received a copy of the plan and who discussed its implications with Roatta, Italian Air Force preparations to comply with the Allied requirements for the airborne operation would take at least a week. This confirmed Roatta's belief in 12 September as the effective date of the armistice.[28]

---

[27] Rossi, *Come arrivammo*, pp. 215–16. The *Eleventh Army* (in Greece and Crete) chief of staff was summoned to Rome and received the draft order during the evening of 6 September; he returned with it to Athens on the following morning. The chief of staff of *Army Group East* was summoned to Rome on 7 September, received a copy of the directive the next day, but was unable to return to his headquarters at Tirana in Yugoslavia because of bad flying weather. See *Il Processo Carboni-Roatta*, p. 48.

[28] Roatta, *Otto milioni*, pp. 300–305; *Il Processo Carboni-Roatta*, pp. 30–31; Rossi, *Come arrivammo*, p. 135; Badoglio, *Memorie e documenti*, pp. 102–03.

As for the airborne plan itself, Roatta was flabbergasted. It appeared to assign missions to the *Motorized Corps* far beyond its capabilities. Four hundred trucks could be rounded up only by stripping the *Piave* and *Ariete Divisions* of all their vehicles (he did not think of collecting autos, buses, and trucks from the municipality of Rome, an expedient which Castellano had considered quite feasible). Instead of being a plan to defend Rome, it was, Roatta believed, a preliminary step for a future drive north from Rome, with the capital as the base of operations. Though he might have had no objection to this concept, he could not concur in the basic assumption as to the strength of his troops. If his forces were indeed strong enough to carry out all the actions assigned to them in the airborne plan, they would then be strong enough to defend Rome against the Germans without Allied assistance. The plan, therefore, did not project a rescue operation; rather it embodied Castellano's concept of Italian cooperation with the Allies. What was most disappointing to Roatta was the lack of indication that the Allies would land six divisions within striking distance of Rome, a move which, he maintained, *Comando Supremo* had led him to expect.[29]

Something else seemed not quite right. Aerial photographs of the North African ports of Mers el Kebir, Oran, Arzew, and Mostagenem on 4 September and the knowledge that Allied ships were loaded with landing craft indicated an impending amphibious operation. *Comando Supremo* conjectured that the destination of the force might be Corsica. Two days later, Roatta had word of Allied convoys assembling in the open sea north of Palermo. Did this mean that the Allies were about to launch a subsidiary attack independent of and before the armistice announcement expected on 12 September? Or were the Allies getting ready to invade the mainland far south of Rome, or possibly, Sardinia?[30]

In any event, Roatta concluded that the Allies would be in no position to march directly on Rome at once. The Italians themselves would have to defend the capital. From this belief was to come contradictory and ambiguous conduct on the part of the Italian Government for the next two days, behavior that revealed the wide discrepancy between Castellano's views and those of Badoglio, Ambrosio, and Roatta. Part of the trouble was the fact that the King gave no firm indication of his desire to turn actively against the Germans. Thus, Badoglio consistently took a passive attitude. For him, and for Ambrosio and Roatta as well, the armistice, the invasion, and the airborne operation near Rome comprised a multiple plan of rescue, not an opportunity for Italy to pay her passage with the Allies.

The thing that crystallized matters was an estimate of the situation that Roatta presented to Ambrosio during the late afternoon of 6 September. The location of Allied convoys, he averred, made possible only two conclusions as to Allied intentions. Either the Allies were about to make a landing independent of the armistice—like that of the British Eighth Army on the 3d—or they were going to launch their main attack before 12 September, an invasion directed against south Italy or

---

[29] Roatta, *Otto milioni*, pp. 305–06.

[30] *Ibid.*, p. 306; Rossi (*Come arrivammo,* pages 144–46) contradicts Roatta on this point. See also *Comando Supremo, I Reparto, Ufficio del capo reparto*, No. 2087/I, 6 Sep 43. IT 4563, and Zanussi *Guerra e catastrofe*, II, 168.

Sardinia. In either case, there was little prospect of immediate help from Italian forces in the capital. Therefore, the plan for joint action with the Allied airborne division had to be adjusted to reflect the real capabilities of the Italian forces. Convinced that otherwise a fiasco would result, Ambrosio agreed to the necessity for modifying the GIANT II plan.[31] Fortunately for the Italians, a way to get in touch with the Allies was at hand.

In response to General Eisenhower's request that the Italians send a military mission to AFHQ, a request forwarded by Castellano on 4 September, the Italian High Command had selected eleven officers headed by Col. Paolo Decarli of the Military Intelligence Service. These officers were to leave Rome that evening, 6 September. Two hours before their departure several of these officers received instructions at *Comando Supremo* for modifying the Allied plans. There were three relatively minor proposals—a change in the text of Badoglio's contemplated armistice announcement; a request that the Italian Fleet be permitted to sail to Sardinia rather than to Malta; and a request that maximum air support be sent to the Rome airfields immediately after the armistice announcement. But a fourth point was major—the Italians wanted the airborne operation to be executed two days after the main landing rather than at the same time.[32]

Carboni later asserted that he gave one member of the mission, Maj. Alberto Briatore, a memorandum completely repudiating the armistice and the airborne operation, and he accused Castellano of deliberately preventing Briatore from delivering it to the Allies.[33] But Carboni's memorandum was a fabrication.[34] The Italians did not renounce their obligations in this fashion.

That night, at 2200, 6 September, after instructing the members of the military mission, Ambrosio left Rome by train for Turin. His purpose in going, he explained later, was to pick up his diary and other compromising documents.[35] In his absence, Rossi was in charge of *Comando Supremo,* but Rossi felt that he could make no basic decision without the concurrence of his chief. During this time, for two days, Carboni, Roatta, and Rossi, with the full support and co-operation of Badoglio, repudiated Castellano's commitments with respect to GIANT II and contrived to create a situation that struck the Allies as having every appearance of a double cross.

Why Ambrosio chose this moment for a trip to Turin is not clear. Perhaps he was thoroughly convinced that 12 September was to be the effective armistice date. Perhaps he did not altogether comprehend

---

[31] Rossi, *Come arrivammo,* pp. 140–41; Roatta, *Otto milioni,* pp. 306–07; Zanussi, *Guerra e catastrofe,* II, 171.

[32] Castellano, *Come firmai,* p. 181.

[33] Carboni, *L'armistizio e la difesa di Roma,* pp. 27, 59–60, 108–09.

[34] Briatore on 20 January 1945 testified that he had never seen such a document. Ambrosio, Roatta, and Rossi denied that the document printed by Carboni was ever composed in the *Comando Supremo* headquarters. Carboni's text was artful, for its concepts resembled somewhat a memorandum drafted by Roatta late on 6 September after the departure of the military mission. Cf. note 37. See the excellent critical examination of the Carboni fabrication by the *Ufficio Storico, Stato Maggiore dell'Esercito, Ministero della Difesa, Allegato al f.n. 1780/St.,* 12 Mar 48, Incl in Ltr, Maj James A. Gray, Assistant Military Attaché, to Director of Intelligence, GSUSA 16 Jun 48, OCMH files. See also Roatta, *Otto milioni,* p. 315, and *Il Processo Carboni-Roatta,* pp. 33–34.

[35] MS #P-058, Project #46, 1 Feb–8 Sep 43, Question 22.

Roatta's alarm. Perhaps—though rather improbably, for he and Castellano were close associates—he had even misunderstood Castellano's point of view.[36]

After Ambrosio's departure, Roatta talked with Carboni, who not only commanded the *Motorized Corps* but also directed the Military Intelligence Service. Carboni confirmed Roatta's low opinion of the strength of the Italian troops around Rome. The *Motorized Corps*, Carboni said, without reinforcements and more time for preparations, could not put up protracted resistance against the Germans, nor could it provide effective protection for the American airborne landings.

Embodying these objections to GIANT II in a memorandum, Roatta emphasized the danger in announcing the armistice before 12 September at the earliest. He also stressed the necessity of having the main Allied landing take place in accord with Italian expectations: the invasion would have to be made within striking distance of Rome.[37]

As director of the Military Intelligence Service, Carboni transmitted a copy of Roatta's memorandum to Badoglio early on 7 September. Later that morning, Carboni spoke with Rossi. He told Rossi that he had conferred with Badoglio and had explained that his *Motorized Corps* had ammunition for only twenty minutes of fire, the *Ariete Armored Division* had fuel for about one hundred miles of movement. Alarmed, Rossi sought Roatta for confirmation. He learned from Roatta of Roatta's discussion with Carboni the night before, and Roatta explained that the *Lupi di Toscana* and *Re Divisions* were necessary for the defense of Rome but would not now be available until 12 September, rather than 8 September as earlier expected. Rossi thereupon became convinced that it was essential for the armistice to become effective on 15 September if possible, in any case not before the 12th. Like Roatta, Rossi concluded that Castellano had not accurately presented to the Allies the true situation in Rome. At noon, Roatta and Rossi sent a message by the special radio. *Comando Supremo*, they radioed Castellano, would soon send a "communication of fundamental importance."[38]

Not long afterward Rossi learned that the American officers who were coming to Rome to make the final arrangements for the airborne operation were due to arrive in the city that same evening. Ambrosio had already arranged for their trip to Rome, but he had not known their ranks or exact mission. When Rossi found out that one was a general officer, he telephoned Ambrosio urging him to return from Turin to Rome by plane at once. Ambrosio, however, did not return until 1000, 8 September.[39]

Meanwhile, on the previous evening, 6 September, AFHQ had sent two messages to Rome via the secret radio. The first read:

Please maintain continuous watch every day for most important message which will be sent between 0900 hours and 1000 hours, GMT on or after 7 September repeat seven September. It will be necessary for you to reply immediately when you receive this important message that it has been received and understood.[40]

---

[36] *Il Processo Carboni-Roatta*, pp. 30–31.

[37] Roatta, *Otto milioni*, p. 307; Rossi, *Come arrivammo*, pp. 140–41; Zanussi, *Guerra e catastrofe*, II, 171.

[38] Rossi, *Come arrivammo*, pp. 141–42; *Il Processo Carboni-Roatta*, pp. 32–33.

[39] Rossi, *Come arrivammo*, p. 144.

[40] Msgs 34 and 35, "Drizzle" to "Monkey," Capitulation of Italy, pp. 281–82.

The second:

In addition to all other arrangements for the Great (G) day the Italian broadcast transmitted by BBC will give two short talks on German Nazi activity in Argentina between 11:30 hours Greenwich time and 12:45 hours. This broadcast will indicate the Great (G) day. Telegram number 36. There will not be any special program of music as requested. Please acknowledge receipt.[41]

In response to requests for acknowledgement, the Italians replied; the messages acknowledging Italian receipt came in to AFHQ shortly after noon, 7 September.[42]

The Allied messages were a clear indication of the imminent approach of the invasion day and of the time for the surrender announcement. Obviously, both events were scheduled to occur soon after 7 September. Certainly, Carboni must have known because the secret radio given to Castellano at Lisbon was located in the Military Intelligence Service, which Carboni headed. Yet Carboni failed to make the information known to Badoglio, Ambrosio, Roatta, or Rossi.[43]

Thus, when two American officers appeared in Rome on the evening of 7 September, Ambrosio, chief of *Comando Supremo,* was absent on a personal errand in Turin, Roatta and Rossi were attempting to make fundamental changes in the arrangements concluded by Castellano, and Carboni was playing a dishonest game with both the Allies and his own superiors.

---

[41] Msg 36, "Drizzle" to "Monkey," Capitulation of Italy, p. 283.

[42] Capitulation of Italy, p. 300.

[43] *Il Processo Carboni-Roatta,* p. 37.

# CHAPTER XXVI

# The Renunciation

While the Italians toyed with capitulation and became entangled in its meshes, the Germans took further precautions against possible defection. Ambassador Rahn's meetings with Badoglio and Ambrosio on 4 September, the day after Castellano had signed the armistice agreement, produced no mitigation of German suspicion. On the contrary, OKW on 5 September instructed Kesselring to keep his German units well in hand and ready for any emergency. Rommel's *Army Group B*, which had the mission of eliminating the Italian military forces in northern Italy and occupying that part of the country, was ready to act. Contrary to Allied belief, the divisions under Rommel's control were not intended to reinforce Kesselring's troops in the south—on 6 September OKW specifically directed Rommel to remain north of the northern line of the Apennines.[1]

By 7 September, although the Germans still had no positive proof, indications of Italian obstructionism had become clear enough to make Hitler absolutely certain of eventual Italian "treason." He therefore prepared to send an ultimatum to Badoglio, and he ordered Jodl to draw up a draft of the military portion of the paper. In compliance, Jodl listed five of Italy's basic military policies that seemed fundamentally anti-German in purpose: (1) the concentration of Italian troops in northern Italy, particularly in the Alpine area; (2) the seizure by these troops of the commanding ground in the frontier zone; (3) the placement of demolition charges under bridges and other installations near the frontier; (4) the expressions of hostility toward Germany among the Italian troops, so widespread as to be inexplicable unless a central direction was assumed; and (5) the failure to reinforce south Italy even though troops were available in the north and around Rome. Jodl then listed eighteen specific measures he considered it necessary for *Comando Supremo* to take to remove the anti-German character of these policies. It was Hitler's intention to serve the ultimatum on Badoglio on 9 September.[2] Had Hitler done so, he would have left Badoglio no choice but to make a clear decision—for a break with Germany, or for complete co-operation. Acceptance of the ultimatum would have made Badoglio the gauleiter of Italy. Refusal would probably have signaled the start of German action to take over the Italian Government and the country.

But the ultimatum was never delivered. Hitler's intended date of delivery turned out to be the same day on which the Allies landed on the Salerno beaches.

---

[1] *OKW/WFSt, KTB, 1.-31.IX.43,* 5 and 6 Sep 43.

[2] *OKW/WFSt, KTB, 1.-31.IX.43,* 7 Sep 43; MS #C-093 (Warlimont), pp. 164–68.

## "Innocuous"

Proceeding systematically with their plans, the Allies had dispatched from North Africa on 3 September, the date when the Eighth Army crossed the Strait of Messina, the first of fifteen convoys which would leave Tripoli, Bizerte, and Oran. These convoys, carrying assault troops of the U.S. Fifth Army, were to take part in Operation AVALANCHE, the main invasion of the Italian peninsula.[3] Elsewhere, other Allied headquarters worked on the planned airborne operation at Rome.

From the moment that General Ridgway had been summoned to Cassibile on 2 September to take part in the Italo-American planning, sudden change and frantic haste characterized 82d Airborne Division plans and preparations. Already in the final stages of preparing to participate in AVALANCHE and execute GIANT I—securing the north flank of the Allied beachhead at Salerno—the division now faced a completely new assignment.

Those units of the division which had fought in Sicily had, soon after the campaign ended, been shuttled by air back to the Kairouan area in Tunisia. Fully reunited there the division engaged in some sketchy training. Troops scheduled to make an amphibious assault as part of the division's role in AVALANCHE boarded landing craft on 3 September and were ready to sail. On this date GIANT I was canceled, and the entire division received word to prepare to move by air to Sicily.

Having completed the GIANT II plan as the result of the all-night session at Cassibile, General Ridgway on 4 September flew to Bizerte to brief his subordinate commanders and also to try to speed the division's move to Sicily. The division staff and representatives of the Troop Carrier Command worked most of the night of 4 September and developed detailed plans for shifting the division back to Sicily. On 5 and 6 September the division returned by air.[4]

Ready on 5 September, the final plan for the airborne operation near Rome projected a combined drop and air landing of the entire division in successive lifts.[5] On the first night, Colonel Tucker's 504th Parachute Infantry Regiment (minus the 3d Battalion); Company C, 307th Airborne Engineer Battalion; Battery B, 80th Airborne Antiaircraft Battalion (with 57-mm. antitank guns); and signal, reconnaissance, and medical units were to land on the Cerveteri and Furbara airfields and push to Rome. On the second night, Colonel Gavin's 505th Parachute Infantry RCT would drop on the Guidonia, Littoria, and Centocelle airfields.

On the same day, 5 September, with everything in a rush and while the division was preparing to move back to Sicily, a radio message from AFHQ modified the plan. Now, in addition to landing on the airfields near Rome, the division would also send a small seaborne expedition to land at the mouth of the Tiber River: an artillery battalion (the

---

[3] A detailed account of the Salerno invasion may be found in Blumenson, Salerno to Anzio.

[4] 82d AB Div in Sicily and Italy, pp. 41–47; Rpt of TCC Activities Including the Italian Invasion, vol. II; Ltr, Ridgway to Eisenhower, 25 Oct 43, in above rpt, p. 120; Gavin, Airborne Warfare, pp. 19–24; Msg 640, AFHQ to Br X Corps, 5 Sep 43, 0100/4/4,I.

[5] 82d AB Div FO 5, 5 Sep 43, 82d AB Div G–3 Jnl, 1–15 Sep 43; Msg A.284, MAC to AHQ Malta, 7 Sep 43; Msg A.281, MAC to NATAF, 7 Sep 43; and Msg 318, NATAF to MAC, 6 Sep 43, all in 0403/4/1029. See also Tregaskis, Invasion Diary, pp. 99–100.

319th Glider Field Artillery Battalion was chosen); three antiaircraft batteries (of the 80th Airborne Antiaircraft Battalion); an infantry company (of the 504th Parachute Infantry); and three platoons of the 813th Tank Destroyer Battalion (attached for the operation). General Ridgway chose Lt. Col. William H. Bertsch Jr., to command this force.

Leaving Col. Harry L. Lewis, commander of the 325th Glider Infantry Regiment, to supervise the dispatch of the seaborne expedition, Ridgway flew to Sicily to supervise the final arrangements for the airborne operation. Barely in time, Lewis diverted the artillery battalion and antiaircraft batteries from the air movement to Sicily, and after some searching located the tank destroyers, stationed about forty miles from Bizerte, and started them moving to the dock area.

After much negotiating by telephone on 6 September, Colonel Lewis secured the promise of two LCI's, two LCT's, and perhaps some additional British vessels (whereabouts uncertain) for the seaborne force. When the British ships did arrive, confusion developed over their availability. To meet this emergency, the Bizerte harbor commander provided several extra bottoms. Loading began on 7 September, and the men crowded aboard, though no one knew when the armada of three LCI's and one LST—the eventual composition of the task force—would sail. Having organized and loaded the seaborne force, Lewis flew to Sicily with the last remaining elements of the division, leaving Colonel Bertsch in charge of the seaborne troops then afloat in Bizerte harbor.[6]

In Sicily, the 504th and 505th Parachute Infantry Regiments were getting ready to head for Rome. Takeoff time was scheduled for 1830, 8 September, an hour selected to coincide with General Eisenhower's announcement of the Italian surrender. According to the Allied timetable, Badoglio was to make his announcement of the armistice to the Italian people shortly thereafter. On the following morning, at 0330, 9 September, the amphibious assault troops of Operation AVALANCHE would hit the Salerno beaches. At the same time, the airborne troops were to be in the process of securing Rome against the Germans.

To be absolutely certain of Italian cooperation at Rome and to work out the final details of the arrival of the American airborne troops, General Eisenhower had selected two American officers to make the perilous trip to the Italian capital: General Taylor, the 82d Airborne Division's artillery commander, and Col. William T. Gardiner of the Troop Carrier Command. At a briefing conducted at 15th Army Group headquarters, the Allied leaders decided that unless word to the contrary came from Taylor and Gardiner, the airborne operation would go as scheduled. Taylor could recommend changes as well as cancellation, all messages to be made in code by means of the radio given to Castellano and currently operating in Carboni's Military Intelligence Service in Rome. If Taylor was not satisfied with the Italian arrangements, if he judged that the airborne operation should be canceled, and if the Italian authorities refused to transmit that message, Taylor was

---

[6] Ridgway Ltr cited above, n. 4; 82d AB Div in Sicily and Italy, pp. 47–48; Msg 975, AFHQ to 82d AB Div, 5 Sep 43; Msg 1086, AFHQ to Fifth U.S. Army, 6 Sep 43; and Telg 1750, AFHQ to CinC, Med, 7 Sep 43, all in 0100/4/4.I.

to radio to AFHQ a single word—"innocuous."[7]

General Taylor and Colonel Gardiner left Palermo at 0200, 7 September, in a British PT boat and made rendezvous off Ustica Island with an Italian corvette. Escorted to a beach near Gaeta, the Americans came ashore. They entered a sedan belonging to the Italian Navy and transferred to a Red Cross ambulance on the outskirts of Gaeta. With their uniforms intentionally splattered with water to give the appearance of aviators shot down and rescued from the sea, they rode toward Rome without incident, though they passed several German patrols along the Appian Way. Just at nightfall, they entered the city.[8]

Taken to the Palazzo Caprara, opposite the War Office, the Americans found accommodations ready for them. Three officers met them: Col. Giorgio Salvi, chief of staff of Carboni's *Motorized Corps;* Lanza, who had accompanied Castellano to Lisbon as interpreter and who had become Carboni's aide; and Marchesi, who had accompanied Castellano to Cassibile.

Confronted with a surprisingly elaborate meal, the Americans dined with some impatience. Their hosts had not arranged to transact any business that evening, and it was only after becoming insistent that the Americans were able to get someone of high rank to come to see them.[9]

The Americans asked to see Carboni and Rossi. Only Carboni arrived at 2130. He proceeded to give his views of the military situation: the Germans had been building up their forces in Italy since Mussolini's overthrow; they had increased their forces around Rome by 12,000 paratroopers equipped with heavy weapons, including 100 artillery pieces, mainly 88-mm. in caliber; they had raised the effective strength of the *3d Panzer Grenadier Division* to 24,000 men with 150 heavy and 50 light tanks. In contrast, the Germans had ceased supplying the Italians with gasoline and munitions; the result was that his *Motorized Corps,* virtually immobile, had enough ammunition for only a few hours of combat.

As Carboni estimated the situation:

If the Italians declare an armistice, the Germans will occupy Rome, and the Italians can do little to prevent it. The simultaneous arrival of U.S. airborne troops would only provoke the Germans to more drastic action. Furthermore, the Italians would be unable to secure the airfields, cover the assembly and provide the desired logistical aid to the airborne troops. If it must be assumed that an Allied seaborne landing is impossible north of Rome, then the only hope of saving the Capital is to avoid overt acts against the Germans and await the effect of the Allied attacks in the South. He declared that he knew that the Allied landings would be at Salerno, which was too far away to aid directly in the defense of Rome. He stated that General Roatta shared his views.[10]

---

[7] Program for GIANT II, 6 Sep 43, 82d AB Div G-3 Jnl, 1-15 Sep 43; Msgs 822 and 823, AFHQ to 15th AGp, 5 Sep 43, 0100/4/4.I.

[8] Maugeri, *From the Ashes of Disgrace,* pp. 170-77; 82d AB Div in Sicily and Italy, p. 56, which quotes in full Taylor's report on his mission to Rome, a report also in 0100/4/330 and in 0100/12A/65,II.

[9] See David Brown, "The Inside Story of Italy's Surrender," *Saturday Evening Post* (September 16, 1944), p. 65; Richard Thruelson and Elliott Arnold, "Secret Mission to Rome," *Harper's Magazine* (October, 1944), p. 466.

[10] As quoted in Taylor Rpt. Carboni's account (*L'armistizio e la difesa di Roma,* pages 28-29) is highly fictitious. His statement that Taylor revealed the imminent invasion at Salerno is not true. Nor did Taylor charge Castellano with misrepresenting the situation to the Allies at Cassibile. See also, Tregaskis, *Invasion Diary,* pp. 102-08, quoting an interview with Gardiner.

To the Americans, there was nothing new in the facts reported by Carboni. Castellano had explained fully at Lisbon and again at Cassibile. What was new was Carboni's realization—and if Carboni was to be believed, Roatta's too—that the main Allied landing would not be near Rome. What was disturbing was Carboni's "alarming pessimism certain to affect his conduct of operations in connection with GIANT TWO." Bypassing Rossi, the Americans asked to see Badoglio at once.[11]

Rossi, as a matter of fact, was on his way to meet with Taylor and Gardiner. Carboni had telephoned to tell him that Taylor had informed him that the armistice announcement was to be made the next day, 8 September. Rossi said he would be right over and started immediately for the Caprara Palace. Upon his arrival, Carboni met him in an anteroom. "Everything has been fixed up," Carboni said. "We are now going to Badoglio to submit the telegram of postponement to him." Rossi wished to accompany Carboni and the Americans, but Carboni dissuaded him, saying, "No, it is not necessary; everything is already arranged."[12]

Carboni escorted the Americans to Badoglio's villa. As the result of an air raid a few minutes earlier, around midnight, the household was awake. Badoglio received Carboni at once. The Americans waited in an antechamber. After about fifteen minutes, Badoglio admitted them and greeted them cordially.

Taylor and Badoglio spoke French, their conversation being supplemented by English and Italian translated by Lanza. Badoglio repeated the figures of German troop strength exactly as Carboni had stated them earlier and advanced the same proposals: the armistice would have to be postponed, the airborne operation canceled.

To Taylor and Gardiner, it seemed that Carboni had used the fifteen minutes during which he had been alone with Badoglio in order to bring the marshal around to his point of view—wait until they rescue us. Badoglio's bland disregard of the terms signed by his accredited representative, Castellano, and his unwillingness to oppose the Germans were extremely disconcerting to the Americans.

When Taylor asked Badoglio whether he realized how deeply his government was committed as the result of the agreements already signed, Badoglio replied that the situation had changed—Castellano had not known all the facts. Italian troops could not possibly defend Rome. The only effect of an immediate announcement of the armistice would be a German occupation of the capital and the establishment of a neo-Fascist regime.

Taylor then asked whether the Italians feared a German occupation more than the possibility of full-scale Allied bombardment. With considerable emotion, Badoglio replied that he hoped the Allies would attack the Germans, that they would bomb the northern rail centers rather than the Italians, who were friends of the Allies and who were only awaiting the appropriate moment to join them.

When Taylor asked Badoglio how he expected the Allied leaders to react to his changed attitude, Badoglio made repeated professions of sympathy for the Allies and expressed the hope that Taylor would explain the situation and the new Italian point of view to General Eisenhower.

Taylor refused to do this. But he

---

[11] Taylor Rpt, pars. 2 and 4.
[12] *Il Processo Carboni-Roatta*, p. 35; Rossi, *Come arrivammo*, pp. 151–52.

added that if the Allied command instructed him to do so, he would serve as a messenger for whatever communication Badoglio might wish to send. What Taylor was angling for was a definite statement for Allied headquarters, over Badoglio's own signature, of the Italian viewpoint and intention.

Badoglio thereupon wrote a message to General Eisenhower—a message canceling his earlier commitments. Written around 0100, 8 September, less than twenty-four hours before Eisenhower intended to publicize the armistice agreement, the message read:

> Due to changes in the situation brought about by the disposition and strength of the German forces in the Rome area, it is no longer possible to accept an immediate armistice as this could provoke the occupation of the Capital and the violent assumption of the government by the Germans. Operation Giant Two is no longer possible because of lack of forces to guarantee the airfields. General Taylor is available to return to Sicily to present the view of the government and await orders. Badoglio.[13]

At the same time, Taylor wrote a message of his own:

> In view of the statement of Marshal Badoglio as to inability to declare armistice and to guarantee fields GIANT TWO is impossible. Reasons given for change are irreplaceable lack of gasoline and munitions and new German dispositions. Badoglio requests Taylor return to present government views. Taylor and Gardiner awaiting instructions. Acknowledge. Taylor.[14]

Imploring the Americans to trust him, Badoglio swore that there was no trickery in the change and spoke at some length of his honor as a soldier and officer. It was perhaps 0200, 8 September, when Taylor and Gardiner returned to the Palazzo Caprara and turned over both messages to Carboni for encoding and transmission.

To make certain that the Allied command understood the situation in Rome, Taylor sent a third message at 0820, a "summary of situation as stated by Italian authorities," including the Italian request for a cancellation of the airborne operation.[15]

Not long afterwards Taylor learned that AFHQ had acknowledged receipt of Badoglio's message. But he was concerned about his message recommending cancellation of GIANT II. Encoding long messages required, in some cases, three hours, decoding somewhat less. In order to be certain of stopping the airborne operation, scheduled to start at 1830 that afternoon, Taylor, at 1135, sent the message, "Situation innocuous."[16]

Meanwhile, Badoglio had telephoned Roatta early that morning to ask whether he agreed with Carboni's point of view. Roatta was cautious—he did not know what Carboni had said. On reaching Badoglio's house, Roatta learned what had taken place during the night. He then suggested that a proper course of action would be to send a high-ranking officer to explain matters fully to General Eisenhower and to point out what help the Allies would have to give in view of the situation in Rome. Badoglio agreed.[17]

---

[13] Taylor Rpt, Incl 1. There are slight variations in the English translation made at AFHQ, where the message was received at 0535 and decoded at 0810. See *Capitulation of Italy*, pp. 333–35.

[14] Taylor Rpt, Incl 2.

[15] *Ibid.*, Incl 3.

[16] *Ibid.*, par. 8.

[17] *Il Processo Carboni-Roatta*, p. 36; Roatta, *Otto milioni*, p. 311; Zanussi, *Guerra e catastrofe*, II, 177.

After driving to *Comando Supremo* headquarters, Roatta informed Rossi of his meeting with Badoglio and prepared a memorandum of instructions for whoever would be selected to meet with General Eisenhower.

Rossi then went to the railroad station at 1000 to meet Ambrosio, who was returning from Turin. Rossi informed him of the latest developments—Allied convoys were headed for Salerno, the armistice announcement was scheduled for that afternoon, and Badoglio was planning to send a high-ranking officer to Allied headquarters to request basic changes in the Allied plans.[18]

Shortly before noon the Italians took this request to the American officers and asked them to take along a representative on their return flight. As General Taylor later reported:

> The Italians showed great concern over the possible reaction of the Allied Chiefs to their reversal of position on the armistice. The American officers reinforced their apprehension by emphasizing the gravity of the situation in which the Badoglio government found itself. The Italians repeatedly urged the American officers to return and plead their case whereas the latter declined to be anything other than messengers.[19]

Finally, however, the Americans agreed to have a senior Italian officer accompany them to AFHQ. Roatta was first proposed and then immediately withdrawn, for he was considered indispensable in dealing with the Germans. He had an engagement with Kesselring's chief of staff, Westphal, an appointment which he felt he could not cancel without arousing German suspicion. Rossi was then selected to go to Algiers. At 1140, therefore, Taylor sent another message to AFHQ: "In case Taylor is ordered to return to Sicily, authorities at Rome desire to send with him the Deputy Chief of the Supreme General Staff, General Rossi, to clarify issues. Is this visit authorized?"[20]

Thus, Rossi's mission, which had been inadvertently forecast a day earlier by the message to Castellano announcing a "communication of fundamental importance," was not in bad faith. Indeed, Rossi acted entirely with the best of intentions. On the other hand, all members of the Italian High Command were naïve in wishfully thinking that the Allies would, or could, alter their plans radically at the last minute. What they wanted was a delay in announcing the armistice until they were certain that the Allies would occupy Rome. And they had a basis in their belief that Eisenhower was not altogether certain of proclaiming the surrender on 8 September, for certain cues were lacking. Initial arrangements with Castellano had included a special BBC program of Verdi's music as indicating the date of the announcement, a BBC discussion of Nazi activities in the Argentine as further indication, and finally a special message via the secret radio to give the Italians several hours specific warning.

In reality, AFHQ on 6 September had canceled the program of Verdi's music. The Italians had acknowledged receipt of this information, but Carboni had apparently failed to disseminate it.[21] As for the second cue, General Rooks, the AFHQ G-3, had on 6 September requested the BBC to discuss or refer to Nazi activities

---

[18] *Il Processo Carboni-Roatta*, pp. 36–37; Rossi, *Come arrivammo*, pp. 156–57.

[19] Taylor Rpt, par. 9.

[20] *Ibid.*, Incl 5; Capitulation of Italy, p. 336; Zanussi, *Guerra e catastrofe*, II, 177.

[21] Capitulation of Italy, p. 283.

in Argentina during its broadcast of 1130 or 1230 on 8 September.[22] Yet for some unknown reason, London failed to make the broadcast.[23] Finally, Rooks on 6 September also directed that the warning order be sent to Rome via the secret radio.[24] But this too, apparently, was not sent, perhaps because by then General Eisenhower was in direct communication with Marshal Badoglio.[25]

Consequently, when Rossi left Rome in the late afternoon of 8 September in company with Taylor and Gardiner, he had the vivid impression that none of the signals warning of the date of the armistice announcement had been issued. AFHQ, he reasoned, must be holding up the proclamation pending his arrival there. And did he not have General Eisenhower's permission to make the trip?[26]

Actually, he did not. Taylor's message asking whether Rossi might accompany the Americans on their return had not yet reached AFHQ when Taylor received, at 1500, AFHQ's message ordering the American officers to return to North Africa. Despite the lack of authorization for Rossi's visit, Taylor and Gardiner decided to take Rossi—and an interpreter, a Lieutenant Tagliavia—with them on their own responsibility. Though a message from AFHQ later reached Rome granting Rossi permission to come, the party had already departed from the capital.[27]

Rossi therefore assumed that his mission had Eisenhower's approval. The basic misunderstanding lay in the fact that the radiogram ordering Taylor and Gardiner to return was a portion of a message Eisenhower sent to Badoglio, a message encoded and sent in four parts. Had the complete message been revealed at once, Rossi would have known in advance the complete futility of his errand. Without such knowledge, he had the impression that he still had time to explain the situation to the Allied commander. And when the complete text of Eisenhower's message became available in Rome, Carboni, more than likely, withheld the vital information from his superiors and associates.[28]

Meanwhile, after canceling an interview with Ambrosio scheduled for 1830, Taylor and Gardiner rode the Red Cross ambulance to the Centocelle airfield. Hoping that their messages recommending cancellation of GIANT II had reached AFHQ in time to stop the paratroopers,

---

[22] Telg, AFHQ to CCS, NAF 358, 6 Sep 43, Capitulation of Italy, p. 294, with copy in 0100/4/4.I.

[23] In response to a request by Smyth, Mr. Ellis Porter, Foreign Broadcast Information Service, received this reply from Mr. Orin W. Kaye, Jr., Chief, London Bureau, FBIS: "Have now obtained from BBC copies of both 11:30–11:45 GMT and 12:30–12:45 GMT Italian show of 8 September 1943. Neither repeat neither—any reference to Argentina or Nazi activity therein." In reply to further requests by Smyth, additional replies were received on 1 November and 1 December 1948. The second reply reported: "Word had now been received from the Librarian of the Foreign Office that a complete search had been made through the file of broadcasts to Italy and no trace has been found of a broadcast referring to Nazi activities in the Argentine." The documents are in OCMH files. See also *Il Processo Carboni-Roatta*, p. 37.

[24] Capitulation of Italy, p. 320; Interv, Smyth with Rooks, 28 Sep 48.

[25] The message ordered by Rooks does not appear in the "Monkey-Drizzle" code-named series of messages in Capitulation of Italy.

[26] Rossi, *Come arrivammo*, p. 157.

[27] Taylor Rpt, par. 10; Capitulation of Italy, p. 337.

[28] *Il Processo Carboni-Roatta*, p. 38; Rossi, *Come arrivammo*, p. 158. General Eisenhower's message is given in full in Capitulation of Italy, page 341; with one slight variation, it appears in Diary Office CinC, Book VIII, page A-737.

they, together with Rossi and Tagliavia, boarded a trimotored Savoia-Marchetti bomber. The plane took off at 1705. Several hours later it landed near Bizerte. The American and Italian officers were then driven to AFHQ to report to the Allied commander in chief.[29]

## The Announcement

On the Allied side, two days before Taylor's party arrived in Bizerte, intimations of the turmoil in Rome were completely lacking. The Allies informed Castellano on 6 September that arrangements were proceeding smoothly. The Italian military mission was to leave from Rome that evening. The Allies were working hard to complete the preparations for GIANT II.[30]

On that day General Eisenhower informed the CCS that he had made the final adjustments in his planning to take maximum advantage of the Italian surrender. The British Eighth Army was moving through the toe of Italy. The U.S. Fifth Army was on its way to the Salerno beaches—without the help of an airborne operation but with an increase in seaborne lift, secured by diverting some landing craft from the British assault across the Strait of Messina. The 82d Airborne Division was preparing to assist the Italian Government in preventing the Germans from occupying Rome, the Italians having promised to protect the airfields selected for the airborne operation. Surrender of the Italian Fleet would make it possible to think of releasing some Allied cruisers and destroyers from Mediterranean duty. The Italians had offered to open the ports of Taranto and Brindisi in the heel of Italy, and Eisenhower planned to move the British 1st Airborne Division by warship to Taranto as soon as the Italian Navy was under Allied control.[31]

Optimism seemed in order. On 7 September, the secret radio in Rome acknowledged receipt of the stand-by warning order sent the day before. The Allies informed the Italians that two propaganda officers would accompany the first American troops into Rome in order to help the Minister of Information announce the change of sides to the Italian people.[32]

That afternoon the Allies brought Castellano from Cassibile (where he had remained since signing the armistice on 3 September) to Tunis. From here Castellano made a hurried flight to Bizerte where one designated member of the military mission, a Captain Giuriati of the Italian Navy, had refused to give information to British naval officers on the grounds that he had received no instructions. After informing Giuriati that the armistice had been signed and that he could in conscience give the information requested, Castellano flew back to Tunis.

The other members of the military mission had in the meantime arrived in Tunis. Although most of them were without instructions, some even being unaware of the signing of the armistice, a few members brought new instructions for Castellano: the text of Badoglio's proposed armistice announcement for Eisenhower's approval; also requests that the

---

[29] Taylor Rpt, par. 10.
[30] Castellano, *Come firmai*, p. 179.
[31] Telg, AFHQ to CCS, NAF 359, 6 Sep 43, Capitulation of Italy, pp. 291–92.
[32] Msg 13, "Monkey" to "Drizzle," received 1304, 7 Sep 43, and Msg 38, "Drizzle" to "Monkey," 7 Sep 43, both in Capitulation of Italy, pp. 299–300.

Italian Fleet sail to Sardinia rather than to Allied ports, that the airborne operation at Rome be executed two days after the main Allied invasion, and that Castellano make sure of maximum Allied air support immediately after the armistice announcement.[33]

Castellano took up these points with General Eisenhower that evening. The Allied commander made a change in the wording of the last paragraph of Badoglio's proclamation to encourage Italian military opposition to the Germans. He permitted no changes in the program as agreed upon by the armistice—the Italian Fleet was to follow instructions and not sail to Sardinia, the airborne operation would be launched simultaneously with the armistice announcement rather than two days after the invasion of the Italian mainland. He assured Castellano that all possible air support would be furnished operations in Italy.

Though the encoding process, which required several hours, was started promptly, these instructions were not transmitted to Rome until after midnight.[34]

Not long after the final portion of the instructions had gone from AFHQ, at 0530, 8 September, AFHQ received the message from Badoglio that Taylor had transmitted after midnight. Decoding the message took until after 0800. By that time, General Eisenhower had departed Algiers for a visit to the AFHQ advance command post at Bizerte.

When the contents of Badoglio's message, which renounced the armistice, became known in Algiers, the AFHQ staff was thrown off balance. The staff forwarded Badoglio's message to Eisenhower, and at the same time sent a message to the CCS asking whether or not to proceed with the armistice announcement and stating its own belief that the airborne operation would have to be canceled. Perhaps Ambrosio, whom Castellano and Zanussi had mentioned as the only possible successor to Badoglio, might be induced to depart from Rome, announce the armistice from another city, possibly Palermo, and carry out the provisions of the agreement. In any case, they urged, the Badoglio government itself deserved no consideration because Badoglio was retracting a signed document completed in good faith by his authorized representative.[35]

Already nettled by the action of his staff in referring the problem to the Combined Chiefs, Eisenhower was positively enraged by Badoglio's conduct. He immediately drafted a strong reply.[36]

As for Castellano, it appeared to him that Badoglio had scuttled the success he had so patiently achieved. Around 1100, Strong called on him and showed him a copy of Badoglio's message. Shocked,

---

[33] Castellano, *Come firmai*, p. 181.

[34] Msg 40 (TOR 0039, dispatched 0455), "Drizzle" to "Monkey"; Msg 41 (TOR 0015, dispatched 0445); Msg 42 (TOR 0101, dispatched 0430), 8 Sep 43, all in Capitulation of Italy, pp. 330–32. Cf. Castellano, *Come firmai*, p. 182.

[35] Telg. AFHQ to CCS, NAF 365, 8 Sep 43, Capitulation of Italy, p. 347. The plan for Ambrosio as alternate for Badoglio is mentioned in: Min of Confs with Castellano at Cassibile, 3 Sep 43, Capitulation of Italy, p. 245; Telg 129, Rooks to Gen Sugden, 4 Sep 43, Capitulation of Italy, pp. 261–62; Memo by McClure, 5 Sep 43, Capitulation of Italy, p. 272; Telg, AFHQ to CCS, NAF 356, 5 Sep 43, Capitulation of Italy, pp. 279–80.

General Eisenhower, General Rooks, Brigadier Strong, and Captain Royer Dick remember only that such a plan was discussed. See Intervs. Smyth with Eisenhower, 16 Feb 49; with Rooks, 28 Sep 48; with Strong, 29 Oct 47; and Ltr, Dick to Smyth, 5 Nov 48; MS #P–058; Project #46, 1 Feb–8 Sep 43, Question 21.

[36] Eisenhower, *Crusade in Europe*, p. 186; Intervs, Smyth with Eisenhower, 16 Feb 49, and with Lemnitzer, 4 Mar 47.

# THE RENUNCIATION

Castellano prepared a message urging Badoglio to adhere to the original agreed-upon course of action. He then accompanied Strong to Bizerte.

After being made to wait for half an hour in a courtyard where he was completely ignored, Castellano was ushered into a room. At a table sat Eisenhower, flanked by Alexander and Admiral Cunningham and an impressive array of other high-ranking Allied officers. Castellano saluted. No one returned it. He had the feeling he was facing a court-martial.

Eisenhower motioned Castellano to be seated. Then he read Badoglio's message. Finally, the Allied commander made a statement. If Badoglio did not announce the armistice that evening as agreed, he declared, the inference would be inescapable—the Italian Government and Castellano himself had played an ugly role in the armistice negotiations.

At these words, Castellano rose to reply. Neither he nor his government, he said, was guilty of bad faith. Something extraordinary must have developed in Rome. He begged General Eisenhower to reserve judgment until Badoglio should reply to Castellano's message asking adherence to the armistice provisions.

General Eisenhower knew the content of Castellano's message, he said, but he himself was sending a reply to Badoglio. He then read to Castellano his own message, which was in the process of being encoded for transmission:

Part 1. I intend to broadcast the existence of the armistice at the hour originally planned. If you or any part of your armed forces fail to cooperate as previously agreed I will publish to the world the full record of this affair.

Part 2. I do not accept your message of this morning postponing the armistice. Your accredited representative has signed an agreement with me and the sole hope of Italy is bound up in your adherence to that agreement. On your earnest representation the airborne operations are temporarily suspended.

Part 3. You have sufficient troops near Rome to secure the temporary safety of the city but I require full information on which to plan earliest the airborne operations. Send General Taylor to Bizerte at once by aeroplane. Notify in advance time of arrival and route of aircraft.

Part 4. Plans have been made on the assumption that you were acting in good faith and we have been prepared to carry out future operations on that basis. Failure now on your part to carry out the full obligations to the signed agreement will have the most serious consequences for your country. No future action of yours could then restore any confidence whatever in your good faith and consequently the dissolution of your government and nation would ensue.[37]

General Eisenhower then dismissed Castellano, who returned to Tunis to spend the rest of the day in the greatest anxiety.

General Eisenhower informed the CCS of his course of action.[38] He had no reason to be concerned with the action of his staff in informing the Combined Chiefs of Badoglio's broken promise. Exchanges between London and Washington showed the Prime Minister and the President in full agreement. The CCS urged Eisenhower to make whatever public announcement would most facilitate military

---

[37] Castellano, *Come firmai*, pp. 183–85; Text from Capitulation of Italy, p. 341, where it is listed as No. 45 to "Monkey," 8 Sep 43. In transmission, the text was divided into four parts as indicated. Another copy is in Diary Office CinC. Book VIII, p. A-737. Castellano (*Come firmai*, pages 184–85) correctly gives the Italian text.

[38] Telg W-9443/1972, FREEDOM to AGWAR, 8 Sep 43, Capitulation of Italy, p. 354.

operations, without regard for possible embarrassment to the Italian Government.[39]

Whatever else might be necessary, the airborne operation had to be canceled. AFHQ sent a message to the division headquarters in Sicily, but because this would take so much time for encoding, transmission, decoding, and delivery, a quicker method of getting word to the paratroopers was necessary. General Lemnitzer therefore flew from Bizerte to Sicily. His pilot, excellent at night flying, became confused in daylight. His take-off was shaky, his navigation worse. Not until Mount Etna loomed up was the pilot able to identify his location. He changed his course and flew toward the division command post, near Licata, but by then it was very close to the scheduled hour for the start of the operation.[40]

At various airfields in Sicily during the afternoon of 8 September, paratroopers had begun to load into about 150 aircraft. At Licata, where the headquarters of the division and of the Troop Carrier Command were located, General Ridgway waited near a radio. Eisenhower was planning to broadcast his armistice announcement at 1830, Badoglio was to make his announcement immediately afterwards. The latter was to signal the start of Operation GIANT II.

From Bizerte harbor, Colonel Bertsch's small seaborne force had put out to sea that morning under sealed orders delivered to the flotilla commander. Though Bertsch suspected that he was bound for the Rome area, he in fact knew only that his destination was point "FF" on an unknown map (in actuality, a beach at the mouth of the Tiber River). If no one met him at "FF," he was to move on to "GG" (a point halfway between the mouth of the river and Rome).[41]

At AFHQ there was nothing else to do but wait until the time of the surrender broadcast announcements. At 1830, precisely on schedule, though no word had come from Badoglio in reply to Eisenhower's message, the Allied commander broadcast the news of the armistice from Radio Algiers:

This is General Dwight D. Eisenhower, Commander-in-Chief of the Allied forces. The Italian Government has surrendered its armed forces unconditionally. As Allied Commander-in-Chief, I have granted a military armistice, the terms of which have been approved by the Governments of the United Kingdom, the United States, and the Union of Soviet Socialist Republics. Thus I am acting in the interests of the United Nations.

The Italian Government has bound itself by these terms without reservation. The armistice was signed by my representative and the representative of Marshal Badoglio and it becomes effective this instant. Hostilities between the armed forces of the United Nations and those of Italy terminate at once.

All Italians who now act to help eject the German aggressor from Italian soil will have the assistance and support of the United Nations.

Radio Algiers then broadcast a survey of the negotiations to explain how the armistice had been reached. But no announcement came from Badoglio over Radio Rome. After waiting ten minutes, Eisenhower authorized Radio Algiers to broadcast in English the text of Badoglio's proclamation:

---

[39] Telg 7196, Marshall to Eisenhower or Smith, 8 Sep 43, Capitulation of Italy, p. 352.

[40] Interv with Lemnitzer, 4 Mar 47; See also Tregaskis, *Invasion Diary*, pp. 101–102, and Morison, *Sicily—Salerno—Anzio*, pp. 239–42.

[41] 82d AB Div in Sicily and Italy, p. 48; See also Telg A.277, MAC to AHQ Malta, 6 Sep 43, 0403/4/1029.

The Italian Government, recognizing the impossibility of continuing the unequal struggle against the overwhelming power of the enemy, with the object of avoiding further and more grievous harm to the nation, has requested an armistice from General Eisenhower, Commander-in-Chief of the Anglo-American Allied Force. This request has been granted. The Italian forces will, therefore, cease all acts of hostility against the Anglo-American forces wherever they may be met. They will, however, oppose attacks from any other quarter.[42]

At Licata, Sicily, this broadcast signaled the start of GIANT II. Fortunately, only minutes earlier Lemnitzer's pilot had brought his plane to ground. Sixty-two planes carrying paratroopers were already circling into formation to prepare to go to Rome when word of the cancellation came through. About the same time, the telegram sent earlier by AFHQ reached the division headquarters. As for Bertsch's seaborne task force, news of the cancellation reached the flotilla in time to divert the force to the Gulf of Salerno and to a rendezvous with the AVALANCHE convoys.[43]

The atmosphere was tense in Algiers, where General Eisenhower and his staff waited for Badoglio's voice over Radio Rome. Had the Germans already seized the Italian Government to prevent Badoglio from broadcasting? Could Ambrosio escape from the capital and make the announcement elsewhere?

The questions were disturbing because the AVALANCHE convoys were fast approaching the Gulf of Salerno. When the ground troops landed on the following morning of 9 September, would they find Italian and German units embroiled in conflict? Or would they find them joined together in overwhelming numbers ready to oppose the amphibious landing? Unless the voice of Badoglio came over the air, the Allies would not know until the moment the assault troops went ashore.

---

[42] Foreign Broadcast Intelligence Service, Federal Communications Commission, *Daily Report Foreign Radio Broadcasts*, Wednesday, September 8, 1943.

[43] Interv with Lemnitzer, 4 Mar 47; 82d AB Div in Sicily and Italy, p. 48; Telg A.288, MAC to CinC Med, 8 Sep 43, 0403/4/1029; 82d AB Div G-3 Jnl, 1–15 Sep 43.

## CHAPTER XXVII

# The Surrender

### Badoglio's Announcement

On the afternoon of 8 September, General Roatta, the Army chief, drove from Rome to Monterotondo, his headquarters just outside the city. He found a message from Kesselring. Because air observation indicated an imminent Allied landing near Naples, Kesselring asked permission, in accord with protocol, to move the *3d Panzer Grenadier Division* southward to meet the invasion.[1]

Suspecting that the request disguised a desire to move the division closer to the capital, Roatta stalled. It would be well, he replied, to defer the movement until the following morning in order to avoid any incident between the German troops and the *Ariete* and *Piave Divisions* north of Rome. When Rintelen telephoned and renewed Kesselring's request, Roatta yielded, though he limited the German movement to advance elements and, during darkness, to a certain line north of the capital.

Later that afternoon Kesselring's chief of staff, Westphal, telephoned to confirm his appointment with Roatta for early that evening. Roatta said he would be waiting.

At 1800, Roatta received a telephone message from Ambrosio, who urgently requested Roatta's presence at a conference with the King. Assuming that the conference would explore the methods of persuading General Eisenhower to postpone the armistice announcement, and hopeful of its success, Roatta felt it expedient to remain on good terms with the Germans a little while longer. He decided to stay in his office to meet with Westphal and sent his deputy, Generale di Corpo d'Armata Giuseppe De Stefanis, to attend the conference with the King.

Actually, the meeting with the King was prompted by Eisenhower's message to Badoglio insisting that Badoglio keep his word and announce the armistice in accord with his agreement. The message had thrown the Italian Government and High Command into panic. Until the message arrived, at approximately 1730, 8 September, an hour before the scheduled announcement, the Italians had assumed that the climactic moment would be postponed, an assumption based on the fact that Taylor and Gardiner had agreed to take Rossi to North Africa. To them, this had meant that AFHQ was willing to enter into new discussion of joint Italo-Allied plans. Certainly, therefore, it appeared that General Eisenhower would take no decisive action until he heard Rossi's "communication of fundamental importance." And Roatta would have a few more days to complete his preparations for the defense of Rome.

Eisenhower's telegram had destroyed

---
[1] Roatta, *Otto milioni*, p. 318.

these illusions. The opening sentence alone left no room for misunderstanding: "If you or any part of your armed forces fail to co-operate as previously agreed I will publish to the world full record of this affair." This was precisely what Guariglia, the Foreign Minister, had feared when he learned that Castellano had put into writing Italy's willingness to surrender. Worst of all, Eisenhower had the power to frustrate any attempt to patch things up with the Germans.[2]

Upon receiving the full text of the telegram, Badoglio summoned those most intimately involved in the armistice negotiations to assist him in presenting the problem to the sovereign. Attending the conference in the Quirinal Palace at 1815, 8 September, fifteen minutes before Eisenhower's broadcast, were: the King; Acquarone, Minister of the Royal Household; Badoglio, Head of Government; Guariglia, Foreign Minister; Ambrosio, chief of *Comando Supremo;* Carboni, in his capacity as chief of military intelligence; Ammiraglio di Squadra Raffaele de Courten, Minister and Chief of Staff, Navy; Sandalli, Minister and Chief of Staff, Air Force; Sorice, Minister of War; De Stefanis, deputy chief of the Army General Staff and representing Roatta; Puntoni, senior aide-de-camp to the King; and, at Ambrosio's insistence, Major Marchesi, who was asked to attend because of his familiarity with the negotiations Castellano had conducted in Sicily, at which Marchesi had been present.

Ambrosio opened the meeting with a short exposition of the military situation. The Allied armistice date, he said, had caught the Italians with their Army plans not quite complete.

---
[2] Guariglia, *Ricordi,* p. 669.

Sorice, who knew little of the previous negotiations, and Carboni, who had followed the negotiations with great care, both agreed that the Allies had broken faith with the Italian Government by moving up the date of the announcement. Because of their brusque demand, Sorice and Carboni believed that the Allies deserved no consideration. Both urged rejection of the armistice, particularly since the German reprisals would be terrible. Carboni proposed that the King disavow Castellano's negotiations, if necessary dismiss Badoglio, and thereby indicate that the pledges given in Badoglio's name had not been authorized. Sorice thought this a good idea.

In the discussion that followed, some generals appeared blind to every aspect of the situation except the impossibility of having the Italian armed forces face the Germans alone. Eisenhower's telegram, they maintained, was nothing but a trap to compromise them with the Nazis.

Though not asked to speak, Major Marchesi felt that his presence at the signing of the armistice justified his comments. He rose and presented to the senior generals and statesmen a grim picture of the consequences in store for the Royal Government if it failed to keep its pledge. He explained the import of General Eisenhower's threat: if the Allies published the surrender documents, the government would have no chance of continuing the alliance with Germany.

After Marchesi's remarks, Guariglia, seated at the King's left, rose to speak. He had not approved the way in which the military negotiations had been conducted, he declared, but at this stage it would be absurd to disavow them. Disavowal would leave Italy in the position of facing simultaneously the hostility of both the Anglo-Americans and the Germans. Ambrosio expressed agreement with this view.

Thirty minutes had gone by when word arrived of a Reuters dispatch from London announcing the armistice. Carboni promptly proposed that the government issue an immediate denial. But a few minutes later, when the news came that Eisenhower himself was broadcasting a detailed statement of the armistice, the councilors' spirits sank to the nadir. Support for Carboni's proposal to disavow everything vanished.

In Monterotondo, Roatta was conferring with Westphal and the new German Military Attaché, Toussaint, on joint measures to meet the Allied invasion when the German Embassy telephoned. The American Government in Washington, the embassy spokesman revealed, had announced an armistice with Italy. Stunned by the timing of the announcement, Roatta had little difficulty convincing Westphal and Toussaint that he knew nothing of an armistice. He denounced the broadcast from Washington as an Anglo-American trick designed to embroil the Italians and Germans in warfare.[3]

Westphal and Toussaint departed immediately. Roatta decided to move his staff back to the Palazzo Caprara in Rome. Even before the Germans were out of the building, Zanussi alerted other members of the headquarters for the move and began to select papers to be burned. In the Quirinal Palace at the royal conference, Badoglio expressed no conviction,

---

[3] Zanussi, *Guerra e catastrofe*, II, 179–80; Roatta, *Otto milioni*, p. 318; *Il Processo Carboni-Roatta*, pp. 39–41; Albert Kesselring, *Soldat bis zum letzten Tag* (Bonn: Athenaeum-Verlag, 1953), pp. 242–45; Col. Karl Heinrich Graf von Klinckowstroem in MS #T-1a (Westphal et al.), ch. V, p. 9.

even at that late hour, on what course the government ought to follow. He did no more than explain to the King the alternatives which he faced. The sovereign might disavow Badoglio's pledges, declare that Badoglio had contracted them without the King's knowledge, and accept Badoglio's resignation, which he, Badoglio, was ready to offer. Or, the King could accept the conditions on which General Eisenhower insisted, regardless of the consequences.

Both alternatives were staggering. The Allies demanded complete and abject surrender. They refused to believe that the Italian Government was not a free agent. They shared none of their plans. They had avoided giving assurance of their readiness to occupy the country whose surrender they demanded.

What the Italians were not aware of was the politico-military Allied strategy. They did not know that the Allies were assaulting the Italian mainland with limited means, in effect, a holding attack subordinate to a cross-Channel invasion of northwest Europe. Overestimating the strength available to AFHQ for commitment on the Italian peninsula, they did not realize how vital the armistice was to the Allies.

As for what the Italians could expect from Germany, there was only the grim prospect that the Germans would wage war to the bitter end. They expected to fight on the Italian peninsula and use it as the glacis of Fortress Germany. Yet they could not altogether conceal their intention to withdraw to the line of the northern Apennines. In this case, there was a basis at least for a slight hope that Rome might be spared the destruction of combat.

Since Badoglio could not or would not make up his mind on what the government ought to do, the King decided. It was no longer possible, Victor Emmanuel III concluded, to change sides once again. Italy was committed to the armistice.[4]

The decision made, Badoglio hastened to Radio Rome. At 1945, 8 September, an hour late, he read his announcement of the armistice, following exactly the text approved by AFHQ. The broadcasting station recorded the announcement and repeated it at intervals throughout the night.[5]

To the Italian people, Badoglio's armistice announcement came as startling news. His only other public statement had been his declaration on assuming office that the war would continue. The abrupt change itself was a shock, and the announcement gave little explanation—no indication of swift and harsh German reprisals, no suggestion that Germany had become the enemy, no guidance for the future. Badoglio merely acknowledged Italy's defeat, and this had been apparent for some time.[6]

As for the armed forces, the radio broadcast offered no strong and definite instructions for the behavior of the few hundred aircraft, the effective and powerful fleet, the sixty divisions of about 1,700,000 men who, though woefully ill-equipped, still comprised a disciplined force. Without clear directives from a central authority in Rome, the military forces did not know what to do. The vague orders issued before the armistice had reflected Badoglio's indecision. He had not wished, and had not permitted, the armed forces to organize their plans and dispositions for real anti-German action. Hoping to the last to get an Allied guarantee to occupy Rome and protect his government, thereby gaining more time, Badoglio had refused to risk anything that might have brought a showdown with the Germans.

### Flight of the King and High Command

At Monterotondo, as soon as Badoglio's announcement confirmed the news of the armistice, Roatta telephoned *OB SUED* headquarters twice to assure the Germans on his honor as an officer that when he had given his word to Westphal, he had known nothing of the surrender.

Fifteen minutes later, Roatta issued an order to the three Italian corps defending Rome to man the roadblocks around the capital. German troops leaving the city were to be permitted to go; German columns moving toward the capital were to be stopped. All units were to "react energetically against any attempt to penetrate [into Rome] by force or against any hostile actions whatsoever."[7]

The order was defensive in nature. Though reports had come in that two Italian sentinels had been killed by Ger-

---

[4] Chief sources for the Quirinal Palace conference are: Badoglio, *Memorie e documenti*, pp. 105–06; Carboni, *L'armistizio e la difesa di Roma*, pp. 30–31; *Il Processo Carboni-Roatta*, pp. 38–40; Guariglia, *Ricordi*, pp. 704–06; Roatta, *Otto milioni*, p. 312; Zanussi, *Guerra e catastrofe*, II, 179. Puntoni (*Vittorio Emanuele III*, pages 161–62) incorrectly states that Roatta attended the conference.

[5] Badoglio, *Memorie e documenti*, pp. 106–07. *Il Processo Carboni-Roatta*, p. 40; *Daily Report Foreign Radio Broadcasts*, Thursday, September 9, 1943, gives the time of Badoglio's announcement as 1345 Eastern War Time, which was 1945 B time, or Rome time. See also Telg W-9512 AFHQ to AGWAR, 9 Sep 43, 0100/4/4.I, and Telg. AFHQ to CCS. NAF 367, 9 Sep 43, 0100/12A/65.II.

[6] Bonomi, *Diario di un anno*, pp. 93–94; Maugeri, *From the Ashes of Disgrace*, p. 185.

[7] *Il Processo Carboni-Roatta*, p. 58; Zanussi, *Guerra e catastrofe*, II, 185–86.

man troops nearby, Roatta declined to order his forces to attack. He apparently hoped that the Germans would withdraw to the north.

The initial reaction of the staff of the German Embassy to the news of the armistice encouraged this Italian hope. The announcement of the armistice had taken the Germans by surprise. Ambassador Rahn had had an audience with the King shortly before noon, 8 September, and though he attempted to discover some indication of future Italian policy, he had learned nothing. Embassy members burned papers in haste, made frenzied arrangements to evacuate civilians. About 2100, the Chargé d'Affaires requested Italian armed protection, and Rahn took his embassy staff posthaste by special train to the northern border. For the first two hours after the armistice announcement, the German civilians seemed intent on escaping, the German military forces appeared to be trying to withdraw.[8] To expedite the hoped-for exodus, Ambrosio issued instructions around 2200 to let the Germans pass if they presented themselves at the roadblocks peaceably.[9]

The King, his family, and Badoglio had, in the meantime, taken refuge for the night in the Ministry of War, which had a detachment of armed guards. Ambrosio also installed his office there. By 2300, Roatta had transferred the key members of his staff and set up his command post in Rome.[10]

Soon after midnight, in the early minutes of 9 September, Ambrosio issued the first order to the Italian military forces. Because *Promemoria 2*, the order drafted several days earlier for the forces in the Balkans, Greece, and the Aegean Islands, had not reached the various headquarters in Tirana, Athens, and Rhodes, Ambrosio repeated and reaffirmed the provisions of the earlier directive. He made one addition: "Do not in any case take the initiative in hostile acts against the Germans."[11] Though the directive went to Roatta for his guidance, Roatta refused to transmit it to the Army troops under his command because he felt that the final prohibition contained in the addition was in conflict with his own *Memoria 44*, dispatched several days earlier.[12]

Ambrosio's order had not yet gone out when the rosy picture of German reaction to the armistice announcement began to assume dark shadows. Reports coming in to *Comando Supremo* and the Army revealed that German paratroop units along the coast near Rome had surrounded Italian batteries and had begun to attack strongpoints of the *Piacenza Division*. From Milan came a telephone call reporting a German attack and asking for instructions. Though these could have been nothing more than attempts by the Germans to secure their lines of withdrawal to the north, the movement of the *3d Panzer Grenadier Division* against the outposts

---

[8] Rudolf Rahn, *Ruheloses Leben: Aufzeichnungen und Erinnerungen* (Duesseldorf: Diedrichs Verlag, 1949), p. 229; *Il Processo Roatta-Carboni*, p. 59; Rossi, *Come arrivammo*, p. 240; Zanussi, *Guerra e catastrofe*, II, 189; Carboni, *L'armistizio e la difesa di Roma*, pp. 35–36; Guariglia, *Ricordi*, p. 712.

[9] Carboni, in *L'armistizio e la difesa di Roma*, page 36, gives the instruction presented him by Ambrosio to let the Germans pass.

[10] Badoglio, *Memorie e documenti*, pp. 113–14; *Il Processo Carboni-Roatta*, pp. 58–59; Zanussi, *Guerra e catastrofe*, II, 189.

[11] Rossi, *Come arrivammo*, pp. 217–18; *Il Processo Carboni-Roatta*, p. 50.

[12] Roatta, *Otto milioni*, pp. 332–33; *Il Processo Carboni-Roatta*, p. 50.

# THE SURRENDER

of the *Ariete Division* seemed significant—and ominous, clearly not part of a northward withdrawal. Roatta then ordered the three corps in defense of Rome to close all barricades and oppose German moves with force. Not long afterwards, a telephone intercept between the German Foreign Office and the Embassy in Rome gave rise to greater alarm. The *2d Parachute Division*, the message stated, was disarming adjacent Italian units; the *3d Panzer Grenadier Division* was marching south on Rome; and both divisions were confident of success.[13]

Should, then, Roatta put into effect *Memoria 44*, the directive that had alerted each army headquarters in Italy and Sardinia for specified offensive operations? Carboni, De Stefanis, General Utili (Roatta's chief of operations), and Zanussi urged Roatta to issue the order. Roatta declined to take the responsibility since he would be contradicting and disobeying the latest *Comando Supremo* directive, but he put the question to Ambrosio. Ambrosio decided that such a serious decision needed the assent or concurrence of Badoglio. Badoglio could not be found.

The result was that *Memoria 44* was never put into effect.[14] Badoglio's radio announcement, which had failed to launch the armed forces on an anti-German course, remained the determining guide. Having declined to resist the movement of German troops into Italy and having acquiesced in the movement of German troops to key positions, Badoglio now failed to authorize the attempt by Italian ground forces to save themselves and their honor. The only effort toward this end was an order issued by Ambrosio at 0220, 9 September:

The Italian Government has requested an armistice of General Eisenhower, Commander-in-Chief of the Allied Forces. On the basis of the conditions of armistice, beginning today 8 September at 19:45 hours, every act of hostility on our part should cease toward the Anglo-American forces. The Italian Armed Forces should, however, react with maximum decision to offensives which come from any other quarter whatsoever.[15]

This directive too was strictly defensive, its limit precisely set, by inference at least, by the framework of Badoglio's announcement. As for Roatta, he too confined himself to ordering his troops to react against force if hostile German acts were verified.[16]

Increasingly serious reports continued to pour into Rome—a concentric German attack against the capital, a *2d Parachute Division* advance against the *Granatieri Division* south of the city, threats against strongpoints along the Via Ostiense and Via Laurentina, clashes north of Rome between the *Ariete* and *3d Panzer Grenadier Divisions,* a movement in unknown strength north from Frascati, and about 0330, notice from the *XVII Corps* at Velletri that the *15th Panzer Grenadier Division* was marching from the Garigliano River area north along the Via Appia

---

[13] Zanussi, *Guerra e catastrofe,* II, 190–91; *Il Processo Carboni-Roatta,* p. 59.

[14] Zanussi, *Guerra e catastrofe,* II, 190–91. In his postwar testimony, Badoglio affirmed that he was not asked whether to order the execution of *Memoria 44.*

[15] Order No. 11/36463, 9 Sep 43, signed by Ambrosio, receipt acknowledged by countersignature [Generale d'Armata Italo] Gariboldi (commander, *Eighth Army*), IT 2.

[16] Roatta, *Otto milioni,* p. 333; Caracciolo di Feroleto, "*E Poi,*" p. 159. One copy of Roatta's order is found in IT 2 as received at Territorial Defense Headquarters at Treviso, 0430, 9 Sep 43, No. 02/5651.

with its forward point already seventy miles from the capital.[17]

The most dangerous threat was the situation arising from the clash of German paratroopers and the *Granatieri Division* south of Rome. To reinforce the southern defenses, Roatta at 0330 ordered two reserve groups of the *Ariete Division* to move from north of the city to the south, the separate *bersaglieri* regiment to move south as a reserve, and all antiaircraft and field artillery units along the right bank of the Tiber River to come into support of the forces defending along the Via Ostiense.[18]

Having taken these steps, Roatta spoke with Carboni. The latter estimated that a defense of Rome could last no more than twenty-four hours. Shortly thereafter, Roatta received word of German forces southeast of Rome engaged with Italian troops not far from the Via Tiburtina. Thus, the Germans were surrounding the capital, and the Via Tiburtina remained the only exit still open. Of an Allied approach to Rome, there was no sign. The sea south of Naples was filled with Allied ships; north of Naples, the sea was empty.[19]

Shortly before 0400, Roatta reported the situation to Ambrosio. Meeting Badoglio soon afterwards, Roatta, in the presence of Prince Humbert and the King's senior aide, repeated his report.

If the King and the government had any thoughts of escape, he added, they should move quickly. Only the Via Tiburtina remained open, and it too might soon come under fire.

Badoglio reached a decision: the King and the government would leave Rome; the military forces defending the city would withdraw to the eastern outskirts and consolidate on positions near Tivoli.[20]

This was a sudden decision, even though the removal of the King and the government from the German threat had been discussed on earlier occasions. Castellano had mentioned the matter at Lisbon. Badoglio had directed his Minister of the Interior as late as the morning of 8 September to prepare a plan to evacuate the government from Rome; he had canceled the order that afternoon.[21] Similarly, the decision to withdraw the troops defending Rome to the Tivoli area east of the city was made on the spur of the moment. Ambrosio and Roatta had planned to defend Rome if the Allies landed a powerful supporting force within striking distance of the capital. But in the absence of immediate Allied support, Badoglio's decision made sense. It implied only a temporary change. Certainly the Allies would sweep northward quickly and seize the city. Within a week or two, the King and Badoglio would return.

Now more than ever, the Italians depended on the Allies. Hoping to remove any residue of resentment that General Eisenhower might have, Badoglio sent a message about this time to AFHQ to ex-

---

[17] *Il Processo Carboni-Roatta*, pp. 59–60; Zanussi, *Guerra e catastrofe*, II, 192–94.

[18] *Il Processo Carboni-Roatta*, p. 60; Zanussi, *Guerra e catastrofe*, II, 192 (which gives the time of sending the order as between 0200 and 0230). Raffaele Cadorna, in *La riscossa: Dal 25 luglio alla liberazione* (Milan: Rizzoli and Co., 1948), page 37, mentions receipt of the order and the beginning of his movement at 0530.

[19] *Il Processo Carboni-Roatta*, pp. 60–61; Roatta, *Otto milioni*, p. 321; Zanussi, *Guerra e catastrofe*, II, 194–95.

[20] *Il Processo Carboni-Roatta*, p. 61; Roatta, *Otto milioni*, pp. 322–23; Zanussi, *Guerra e catastrofe*, II, 195–96; Badoglio, *Memorie e documenti*, pp. 114–16.

[21] Carmine Senise, *Quando ero Capo della Polizia 1940–1943; Memorie di colui che seppe tutto* (Rome: Ruffolo editore, 1946), p. 244.

plain why he had delayed making his announcement broadcast:

> Missed reception signal agreed wireless and delayed arrival your number 45. He did not consent broadcast proclamation at agreed hour. Proclamation would have occurred as requested even without your pressure being sufficient for us pledge given. Excessive haste has however found our preparations incomplete and caused delay. . . .[22]

Having revealed to Roatta his decision to evacuate Rome, Badoglio now told Ambrosio, then went to see the King. He found Victor Emmanuel III listening to his aide, who was reporting Roatta's appreciation of the situation. The King quickly concurred in Badoglio's decision, and determined to take with him Badoglio, Ambrosio, and the chiefs of the military services.[23]

Some time before 0500, the King, the Queen, Prince Humbert, Badoglio, and four military aides to the sovereign were ready to leave Rome. The King summoned Ambrosio and directed that he, the three chiefs of staff, and the three service ministers depart Rome by way of the Via Tiburtina and plan to meet the King's party later that day at Pescara, on the Adriatic coast. Though Ambrosio protested that he could not leave immediately because he needed time to make final arrangements, the King insisted.

To provide for the civil government of Rome and the country during the absence of the Head of Government, Badoglio left instructions with General Sorice, the Minister of War, to inform the civilian ministers of the King's and Badoglio's departure and to charge the Minister of the Interior, Umberto Ricci, with the task of heading a caretaker, skeleton government. Perhaps the Germans would permit the Italian civil authorities to carry on, for, with the exception of Guariglia, the civilian ministers had no knowledge of the armistice negotiations and no responsibility for them. The departing group comprised those persons who were most directly involved in the surrender and who, therefore, had most to fear from the Germans.

Around 0500, five automobiles carrying the royal party left Rome.[24] Ambrosio returned to his office, notified the Navy and Air Force chiefs, Admiral De Courten and General Sandalli, that they were to leave, and made arrangements for warships and planes to meet the royal party at Pescara. After leaving a message for Generale di Brigata Vittorio Palma to remain in Rome as *Comando Supremo* representative, Ambrosio, shortly after 0600, was ready to depart. Sometime during the night he had given Major Marchesi the diary and other compromising documents he had supposedly gone to Turin to get, and had asked Marchesi to destroy them.[25]

Roatta, after receiving the royal command to leave Rome, though with no destination specified, decided to move his staff to Tivoli to keep in contact with the troops. He went back to his office in the Palazzo Caprara and, about 0515, in the presence of Carboni and Zanussi, he wrote in pencil on a sheet of notebook paper the draft of an order to Carboni—turning over to Carboni command of the forces defending Rome and directing Carboni to

---

[22] Msg 24, "Monkey" to "Drizzle," received 0905, 9 Sep 43, Capitulation of Italy, p. 371; Cf. Castellano, *Come firmai*, p. 187.

[23] *Il Processo Carboni-Roatta*, p. 61; Zanussi, *Guerra e catastrofe*, II, 196.

[24] *Il Processo Carboni-Roatta*, pp. 62–63; Badoglio, *Memorie e documenti*, p. 117.

[25] MS #P–058, Project #46, 1 Feb–8 Sep 43, Question 22.

withdraw those forces to the Tivoli area. Roatta read the order to Carboni and told him to have it typed for his, Roatta's, signature.

After protesting that the order could not be carried out because the troops were already engaged and therefore could not break contact and withdraw, Carboni had a clean copy of Roatta's draft order prepared. When he brought it back for Roatta's signature, he found that the Army chief had gone.[26]

Roatta, it turned out, had hastened to the Ministry of War around 0545 and had discovered Ambrosio ready and anxious to depart. After dashing back to the Caprara palace for a last look, Roatta joined Ambrosio, and the two officers left in the same automobile. Not until they were safely out of Rome did Roatta learn that they were bound for Pescara, there to transfer to a plane or ship that would take them to southern Italy.

Other key figures followed. Zanussi got out in an armored car about the same time. De Stefanis left about 0700, Utili approximately 0815. General Sorice, Minister of War, remained.

Guariglia, the Foreign Minister, remained, too. He was busy all night long, giving instructions to representatives abroad and formally notifying Germany that Italy had concluded an armistice with the Allies. He had received no message whatsoever on the decision of the government to leave Rome.

In Roatta's absence his deputy, De Stefanis, just before his departure, signed the order addressed to Carboni. It was in this fashion that Carboni, commander of the *Motorized Corps*, became the commander of all the forces assembled for the defense of Rome. By now, however, the mission was changed.

Roatta's intention was to concentrate these forces—except for the police and *carabinieri* units, which were to remain in the city to maintain order—in the Tivoli area as a threat to the Germans, who would by then, Roatta expected, have seized Rome. He therefore had ordered Carboni to move his headquarters to Carsoli near Tivoli and had instructed his own staff to set up its command post there.

Carboni, however, had no clear concept of his mission. Assuming that he actually could get those forces engaging the Germans to break contact and withdraw—a difficult maneuver—what was he then supposed to do? The withdrawal would perhaps spare Rome a bombardment by German planes and reprisals on the civil population. Perhaps that alone justified Roatta's order. But why Carsoli, unless the real purpose of the withdrawal and concentration was to protect the Via Tiburtina, the King's escape route?[27]

Carboni's chief of staff, Colonel Salvi, was bitterly critical of Roatta's order. He started to rail against it, but Carboni cut him short. Carboni directed Salvi to prepare orders to the division commanders for the withdrawal to the Tivoli area and asserted that he himself intended to go there immediately as ordered.

After going to the Office of Military Intelligence Service to order certain documents destroyed, Carboni went home and changed into civilian clothes. He returned to the Palazzo Caprara to look once more for Roatta, went a second time

---

[26] *Il Processo Carboni–Roatta*, pp. 63–65; Zanussi, *Guerra e catastrofe*, II, 196–97, 199–200; Roatta, *Otto milioni*, pp. 323, 327; Carboni, *L'armistizio e la difesa di Roma*, p. 37.

[27] *Il Processo Carboni–Roatta*, pp. 63–65; Roatta, *Otto milioni*, pp. 323–29; Zanussi, *Guerra e catastrofe*, II, 197–201.

# THE SURRENDER

to his office in the intelligence bureau, then drove toward Tivoli. His son, who was a captain, and two other junior officers accompanied him. To avoid difficulties from Fascist or German elements along the road, Carboni's automobile bore diplomatic license plates. There were no incidents, and shortly before 0800, the party reached Tivoli.[28]

In Rome, Colonel Salvi, upon Carboni's departure, went to pieces. Though he prepared the detailed orders for the withdrawal to Tivoli, he did not issue them. Suspecting that Carboni was going to Tivoli not to set up a headquarters but to join the King in escape, Salvi tried to get Roatta's order revoked. At 0730 he went to General Utili, who would soon leave the capital, showed Utili Roatta's order, declared that Carboni was dead, and asked who would sign the orders to the division commanders. Utili suggested that Salvi get the senior division commander to do so.

Salvi returned to his office and burst into tears. Embracing a captain who entered, he cried: "We are abandoned by everybody!" With tears streaming down his face, he told the commander of the *Granatieri Division:* "The cowards! They have all escaped and left me alone!" To everyone he saw, he shouted that Carboni had gone off with the King and Badoglio. Though he managed to inform two division commanders by telephone of the withdrawal movement, he appealed to them at the same time to get Roatta's order nullified.

Salvi finally determined to call up the senior division commander, Generale di Divisione Conte Carlo Calvi di Bergolo, the King's son-in-law, who commanded the *Centauro Division.* Carboni, Salvi said, could not be found; would Calvi di Bergolo take responsibility for the defense of Rome? Would Salvi, Calvi di Bergolo countered, put his statement and request in writing? Salvi declined. Calvi di Bergolo then said that he had no authority to assume command of the *Motorized Corps* and that the order for withdrawal must be confirmed.

Only then did Salvi issue, without equivocation, the order to withdraw to Tivoli. But by then, time had elapsed, making the maneuver infinitely more complicated. Furthermore, as the result of his antics, Salvi had disseminated distrust and pessimism in the minds of the troop commanders around Rome.[29]

## Interpretations

In North Africa, no one knew that the Italian Government had fled Rome.

Having flown to North Africa with General Taylor and Colonel Gardiner, Rossi arrived at El Aouina airfield at 1905, 8 September, forty minutes before Badoglio went on the air. The Allies took Rossi to Castellano, who asked him why he had come to AFHQ. To obtain a postponement of the armistice announcement, Rossi explained. Furthermore, he had documents to show why a postponement was necessary. His shock was genuine when he learned that Badoglio had confirmed the surrender.

---

[28] *Il Processo Carboni-Roatta,* pp. 73-75; Carboni, *L'armistizio e la difesa di Roma,* pp. 37-38; Alfredo Sanzi, *Il generale Carboni e la difesa di Roma visti ad occhio nudo* (Turin: Vogliotti editore, 1946), pp. 123-24.

[29] *Il Processo Carboni-Roatta,* pp. 74-75; Carboni, *L'armistizio e la difesa di Roma,* p. 41, n. 9; Sanzi, *Il generale Carboni,* pp. 135-37; Cadorna, *La riscossa,* pp. 37-38.

The Allies then took Rossi and Castellano to Eisenhower. Rossi explained the difficulties of proclaiming the armistice at the same time that the Allies launched their invasion; he explained the advantages, both to the Allies as well as to the Italians, that would have been gained if the armistice announcement had been delayed.[30]

These arguments, and the "documents of fundamental importance," were by now an old story to the Allied commander in chief. From the first meeting with Castellano in Lisbon, the Allies had stipulated in accordance with instructions from the Combined Chiefs of Staff that the announcement of the armistice was to precede the main invasion by a few hours. There had been no subsequent divergence from that condition.

General Eisenhower listened patiently to Rossi despite the irritation he must have felt. When Rossi charged Eisenhower with "anticipating" the date of the armistice announcement because he distrusted the Italians, General Eisenhower, according to Rossi's later recollection, replied: "But we were enemies until two hours ago. How could we have had faith in you?"

At the end of the discussion, Eisenhower sought to establish mutual good faith as the basis for co-operation. "If some mistake has been made," he said, "we ought now to accept the situation as it is." No more than a courteous statement recognizing the lack of complete Italian understanding of Allied plans, the remark was an invitation to look forward. The Italians interpreted the sentence as an admission of error, as conceding that Eisenhower had, in actuality, advanced the date of the announcement.[31]

All the Italians involved in the surrender negotiations believed that the Allies had "agreed to," "suggested," or "indicated" a specific time for the surrender announcement and had then advanced the date. But the Italians displayed a lack of unanimity on the date allegedly given by the Allies. Badoglio expected the time to be the 12th or 15th of September; Roatta the 12th, as did Zanussi; Carboni awaited the 20th or the 25th.[32]

Prime Minister Churchill, speaking in the House of Commons on 21 September 1943, seemed to confirm the Italian belief when he said: "The date, which had originally been the 15th, was, however, in fact brought forward to the 9th—the night of the 8th and 9th."[33] In this remark Mr. Churchill was answering the charge, raised in Parliament and in the British press, that the Allies had been slow in taking advantage of Mussolini's downfall. Precisely what Churchill had in mind was not clear. Perhaps he was referring to the belief at AFHQ during the earliest stages of the AVALANCHE planning that shortages of landing craft appeared to make it necessary to have a longer time interval between BAYTOWN (the Strait of Messina crossing) and the assault landings at Salerno.

Yet the only significant change in the Allied time schedule occurred between the preliminary planning in June and the final

---

[30] Castellano, *Come firmai*, pp. 186–87; Rossi, *Come arrivammo*, pp. 160–61.

[31] Rossi, *Come arrivammo*, p. 161; Castellano, *Come firmai*, p. 187.

[32] Badoglio, *Memorie e documenti*, pp. 103–04, 105, 138; Roatta, *Otto milioni*, pp. 300–301; Zanussi, *Guerra e catastrofe*, II, 164, 166; Carboni, *L'armistizio e la difesa di Roma*, pp. 25–26.

[33] Winston S. Churchill, *Onwards to Victory: War Speeches*, compiled by Charles Eade (Boston: Little, Brown and Company, 1944), p. 259.

# THE SURRENDER

planning started in early August. In June, the earliest date for an invasion of the Italian mainland had appeared to be 1 October. In early August, when it appeared the Sicilian Campaign would be short, an earlier invasion date seemed feasible.

The Allies decided on the timing for the Italian invasion before the Italians had made significant contact with them. On 9 August, AFHQ forecast AVALANCHE for 7 September. On 16 August, three days before the first meeting with Castellano in Lisbon, AFHQ scheduled the Salerno invasion, AVALANCHE, for 9 September. No sudden change in schedule to surprise or take advantage of the Italians was ever made.

# CHAPTER XXVIII

# The Dissolution

*German Reaction*

Like the rest of the Germans in Italy, Field Marshal Kesselring was surprised at the announcement of the armistice. While Hitler and OKW had been basing their calculations on the likelihood of Italian betrayal and were concerned chiefly with Badoglio's suspicious behavior, Kesselring and his *OB SUED* staff had been primarily concerned with the Allies.

Aerial reconnaissance reported on 5 September that Allied landing craft previously assembled between Mers-el-Kebir and Tunis were moving eastward. On 7 September it was known that large numbers of landing craft had moved out of Bizerte and entered the latitude of southern Calabria. Because these flotillas appeared too large for mere tactical landings in support of the British Eighth Army, Kesselring looked for an imminent major invasion of the Italian mainland.

Where the Allied troops would come ashore was the question. The bay of Salerno seemed a likely place, but so did the Rome area—Anzio and Nettuno, possibly even Civitavecchia. Though the Rome area might be too far from their airfields for the Allies to gamble on, and though the Allies had until then displayed a conservative strategic approach, a landing near Rome was within the realm of possibility. So were landings near the northern ports of La Spezia, Genoa, and Leghorn, in Rommel's *Army Group B* area. Nor could Kesselring ignore Puglia, the heel of Italy, for within striking distance in eastern Sicilian harbors were assembled numerous Allied landing craft.

Still, the greatest concern was the possibility that the Allies might land near Rome. The Rome area represented the German waistline—between the hip bulge filled by the six divisions of the *Tenth Army* and the overdeveloped bust containing Rommel's *Army Group B*.[1]

Rommel's forces in the north and Vietinghoff's *Tenth Army* in the south were strong enough to handle the Italian forces and at the same time offer effective opposition to an Allied landing. But in the center, strong Italian units outnumbered Kesselring's relatively small forces. Despite their smaller numbers, the Germans might well be able to handle the Italians alone. But should the Italians join with Allied troops coming ashore near Rome, what chance would the Germans have?

Around noon on 8 September, the Allies delivered a heavy aerial attack against Frascati, where Kesselring's headquarters was located. The bombs wreaked havoc on the town, and several struck in the immediate area of the command post. Kesselring himself was uninjured—when

---

[1] Klinckowstroem in MS #T-1a (Westphal et al.), ch. V, pp. 3-5, 10; Westphal, *Heer in Fesseln*, p. 229.

## THE DISSOLUTION

the last wave of bombers flew away, he crawled out from beneath the wreckage. But communications were disrupted except for one telephone line from General Westphal's bedroom which remained in contact both with OKW and with Kesselring's subordinate commands.[2] The Germans judged correctly that the air attack, obviously meant to interrupt the exercise of command, presaged an Allied landing. After directing certain German units to help rescue civilians and clear wreckage, Kesselring sent Westphal and Toussaint to keep the appointment made earlier with Roatta.

While Westphal and Toussaint were with Roatta, Kesselring received his first intimation of the Italian surrender. Jodl telephoned from OKW headquarters to ask *OB SUED* in Frascati whether the Germans in Italy knew anything about the capitulation. OKW had picked up an English radio broadcast announcing the surrender. One of Kesselring's staff officers, knowing that Westphal and Toussaint were consulting with Roatta, phoned the deputy military attaché and suggested that he put through a call to his chief. This was the telephone call that had come into Roatta's office.

About an hour and a half after Jodl's call, the German Embassy in Rome received Guariglia's formal message from the Ministry of Foreign Affairs: Italy had surrendered to the Allies. The deputy military attaché telephoned the information to *OB SUED*, and Kesselring issued the code word *ACHSE*, the signal to take the offensive against the Italian forces and seize Rome.[3]

Since the armistice announcement implied the close co-operation of Italian and Allied forces, the Germans expected an immediate invasion of the coast near Rome, including an airborne landing. The Germans acted with dispatch. Kesselring's first task was to bring the *3d Panzer Grenadier Division* from the area immediately north of Rome to consolidate with the *2d Parachute Division*, distributed for the most part south of Rome between the Tiber River and the Alban Hills. His major purpose was to seize control of the lines of communication and supply leading to the *Tenth Army* in the south, thereby securing the army's withdrawal route to the north. At the same time, Kesselring sent a detachment of paratroopers to seize Roatta and the Army staff at Monterotondo in a *coup de main*.

Attacking adjacent Italian units immediately, the *3d Panzer Grenadier Division* advanced rapidly along the two highways, the Via Claudia and the Via Cassia, leading from Lake Bracciano into Rome. The *2d Parachute Division* quickly overran some Italian defensive positions south of the city, the *Piacenza Division* making scarcely even a show of resistance. The paratroopers racing to Monterotondo had more trouble. They ran into Italian opposition, and, by the time they seized the Army headquarters the following morning, they found that Roatta and his staff had gone.[4]

---

[2] Jane Scrivener (pseud.), *Inside Rome With the Germans* (New York: The Macmillan Co., 1945), p. 1; Klinckowstroem in MS #T-1a (Westphal et al.), ch. V, p. 8; Kesselring, *Soldat*, pp. 241–42; Westphal, *Heer in Fesseln*, p. 227.

[3] Klinckowstroem in MS #T-1a (Westphal et al.), ch. V, pp. 9–10.

[4] Roatta, *Otto milioni*, p. 321; Zanussi, *Guerra e catastrofe*, II, 200; *Il Processo Carboni-Roatta*, pp. 79–80; Klinckowstroem in MS #T-1a (Westphal et al.), ch. V, pp. 10–11; Kesselring, *Soldat*, p. 255; Carboni, *L'armistizio e la difesa di Roma*, p. 34.

Along with the combat, the Germans conducted a skillful propaganda campaign. Exploiting Italian confusion and lack of central direction, the Germans arranged local truces and appealed to the honor of Italian officers as former comrades for the prevention of bloodshed. They assured the Italian soldiers that the war was over and they might go home if they wished. The latter point of view seemed strangely similar to Badoglio's announcement of the armistice, and many Italians threw away their weapons and disappeared.[5]

Though all proceeded favorably during the early hours of 9 September, German concern over Allied intentions continued until daylight. Only after news of the Allied invasion at Salerno came did the nightmare of an Allied amphibious envelopment vanish. The Allies had then, the Germans sighed in relief, run true to form after all. Their landing on the Italian mainland was a methodical advance beyond Sicily and well within range of Allied air cover—not an employment of their command of the sea and air that would threaten the destruction of the *Tenth Army* in south Italy. The invasion at Salerno was not an operation designed to take advantage of Italian co-operation. Nor was it designed, from the German viewpoint, to exploit fully the surprise and uncertainty arising from the armistice announcement.[6]

## The Battle for Rome

At Tivoli, where Carboni arrived around 0800, 9 September, he found no orders waiting for him as he had expected. Nor could the members of the Army General Staff, who were establishing their headquarters at Tivoli, clarify the situation. General De Stefanis and Generale di Divisione Adamo Mariotti, immediate subordinates of Roatta, passed through Tivoli that morning en route to Pescara, but though they saw Carboni, they did not talk with him. Finding no message from Roatta at the *carabinieri* barracks, Carboni drove eastward along the Via Tiburtina in quest of a mission. At Arsoli, twelve miles beyond Tivoli, he learned that several automobiles containing high-ranking officers had passed through not long before. Deciding to return to Tivoli, Carboni dispatched two junior officers to find Roatta. After driving seven miles to Carsoli, they overtook the Army chief. They reported that Carboni was at Tivoli and that he had sent them to maintain communications between him and Roatta. Roatta listened but gave no orders. Leaving the problem of what to do with the forces around Rome to Carboni, Roatta—and Ambrosio—continued toward Pescara.[7]

On returning to Tivoli around 1300, Carboni took command. His first act was to start the withdrawal to the Tivoli area of the two most reliable mobile divisions, the *Ariete* and the *Piave*. The *Ariete Division* had that morning given the *3d Panzer Grenadier Division* a bloody nose at Manziana (on the Via Claudia) and at Monterosi (on the Via Cassia), when the Germans had tried to rush tank columns through Italian strongpoints which were protected by well-placed road

---

[5] Klinckowstroem in MS #T-1a (Westphal et al.), ch. V, p. 13.

[6] Westphal, *Heer in Fesseln*, p. 230; Klinckowstroem in MS #T-1a (Westphal et al.), ch. V, pp. 11–12.

[7] Carboni, *L'armistizio e la difesa di Roma*, pp. 38–39; *Il Processo Carboni-Roatta*, p. 75.

mines and well-directed artillery fire. The Germans halted, regrouped, brought up infantry, and threatened an attack. During this interval, the *Ariete* and *Piave Divisions* withdrew, replaced in line by the *Re Division*. Unaware of the substitution, the *3d Panzer Grenadier Division* commander maintained his threatening attitude but forebore launching an attack. By the morning of 10 September, the two mobile divisions were in the Tivoli area.[8]

South of Rome the *Granatieri Division*, unlike the *Piacenza Division* which no longer existed, refused two appeals from the *2d Parachute Division* for *pourparlers* to give the Germans the right of passage to the city. Exerting the strongest pressure against strongpoints guarding the Via Ostiense and the Via Laurentina, the paratroopers late in the afternoon knocked out several Italian artillery batteries. The Italians pulled back slightly but maintained a solid front. Carboni telephoned the division commander, Generale di Brigata Gioacchino Solinas, and encouraged him to continue his fight.

Meanwhile, Carboni had been discussing with Calvi di Bergolo, the *Centauro Division* commander, the problem of what to do. Calvi di Bergolo suggested that the Italian forces move eastward along the Via Tiburtina toward the Avezzano River basin and into the Abruzzi Mountains, there to establish a redoubt. Vehicles might be abandoned when they ran out of gasoline, but the units, Calvi di Bergolo recommended, should be maintained intact so far as possible.[9]

Calvi di Bergolo's suggestion did not impress Carboni. What did make an impression were two other developments that afternoon. First, Calvi di Bergolo reported the erratic, disloyal behavior in Rome of Carboni's chief of staff, Salvi. This was discouraging, for the only explanation of such behavior was a disheartening situation in the capital. Carboni asked his Chief of Engineers, Col. Giuseppe Cordero Montezemolo, to serve informally as Salvi's replacement, an arrangement that continued even after Salvi appeared that afternoon at Tivoli. Second, a telephone call came from Generale di Corpo d'Armata Gastone Gambarra, who commanded the *XI Corps* in Fiume. Gambarra asked whether the order to put *Memoria 44* into effect had been issued. At Carboni's direction, Montezemolo did not mention the lack of communication between Carboni's forces and *Comando Supremo* but said that on the basis of Badoglio's proclamation and in consequence of the German attack on Rome, *Memoria 44* should go into effect. The puzzling and discouraging thing about all this was that Gambarra's question indicated that no Italian troops except those under Carboni were actively opposing the Germans.[10]

The Germans, meanwhile, continued their appeals to the Italian divisions to cease fighting their former comrades. These appeals had little effect on the *Granatieri Division*, which fought stubbornly and well.[11] But they did find a receptive audience in the *Centauro Division*, which had thus far taken no part in the fighting. According to the Germans, the initiative for a truce came from the Italians. An Italian lieutenant who had known Westphal in North Africa appeared

---

[8] Cadorna, *La riscossa*, pp. 38–46, 49.
[9] *Il Processo Carboni-Roatta*, p. 83.
[10] Carboni, *L'armistizio e la difesa di Roma*, p. 43.
[11] Klinckowstroem in MS #T-1a (Westphal et al.), ch. V, p. 13.

at Kesselring's headquarters to propose Italian capitulation. Westphal worked out the terms.

According to the Italians, the more plausible account, the initiative came from the Germans. At 1700, 9 September, a German *parlementaire*, Capt. Hans Schacht, presented himself at the *Centauro Division* headquarters at Bagni Acque Albule, about twelve miles east of Rome. Schacht brought an oral appeal from General Student to the Italian division commander, Calvi di Bergolo. Student sent an expression of personal esteem for Calvi di Bergolo, a declaration of faith in the friendly attitude of the *Centauro Division* troops, and a request that Calvi di Bergolo treat his German troops as friends. Whether this constituted a demand for surrender, a request to let the German forces pass unmolested to the north, or an offer of honorable capitulation, was not clear. But Schacht, in any event, declared that "within a few hours the Germans will be unopposed masters of Rome."[12]

In reply, Calvi di Bergolo sent his chief of staff, Lt. Col. Leandro Giaccone, to Kesselring's headquarters to learn exactly what terms the Germans would offer. Whether Calvi di Bergolo was preparing to surrender or whether he was trying merely to gain time is not clear. Whether Carboni knew of and approved Giaccone's mission in advance is not clear either. In any case, when Carboni learned of Giaccone's mission, he, as chief of intelligence, ordered Giaccone closely watched.

Accompanied by a lieutenant as interpreter, Giaccone reached Kesselring's headquarters at 2100, 9 September. With Kesselring, Westphal, and Student, he carried on a protracted discussion of eight points, four formulated by Giaccone, the others stipulated by Kesselring. Giaccone proposed that the Germans continue to recognize the open city status of Rome and evacuate the capital; that one Italian division and the police force remain in the city; that other Italian troops lay down their arms and be sent away on unlimited leave; and that the Italians be permitted to surrender honorably. Kesselring insisted on having German troops occupy the German Embassy, the Rome telephone exchange, and the Rome radio station; the Italian division permitted to serve in Rome was to have no artillery; he wanted the Italian officer designated as commander of the city to render a daily report to Kesselring; Italian soldiers, after their discharge from active duty, were to have the option of taking up military or labor service with the Germans.

At the conclusion of the discussion, Kesselring said that the Italian situation was hopeless. He said he was prepared to blow up the aqueducts and bomb the city if the Italians refused his terms. Giaccone said he thought the conditions were acceptable. He proposed, and Kesselring agreed to, a three-hour truce to start at 0700, 10 September. At the end of the truce, Giaccone promised, the Italian reply would be delivered. At 0130, 10 September, he and his interpreter started back to Tivoli.

Giaccone reported to Calvi di Bergolo, who was quite uncertain what to do. He was disappointed and annoyed because the terms brought from Frascati comprised a surrender—quite different from Schacht's verbal message from Student.

[12] The German view is presented by Klinckowstroem in MS #T-1a (Westphal *et al.*), page 13; the Italian view is in a statement made by Lt. Col. Leandro Giaccone, the *Centauro*'s chief of staff, in *Il Processo Carboni-Roatta*, page 81.

# THE DISSOLUTION

Yet Calvi di Bergolo could not overlook the difficult Italian situation, the unreliability of his own *Centauro* troops, and the impossibility of effectively opposing the Germans.

Calvi di Bergolo sent Giaccone to Carboni. Though Carboni later said he refused the terms (and though Giaccone later said Carboni accepted them), Giaccone at 0530, 10 September, sent his interpreter back to Frascati with a message accepting the German conditions. He, Giaccone, would follow later.

Whatever Carboni's precise words to Giaccone might have been, Carboni had no intention of surrendering. Still hoping for Allied support, from sea or from air, he wished to stall by talking with the Germans, intending to break off the talks at the right time on some pretext. He told Calvi di Bergolo of his aims but the latter would have no part in this scheme.

Giaccone returned to Frascati, reaching Kesselring's headquarters at 0700, 10 September. Carboni, meanwhile, ordered the *Ariete* and *Piave Divisions*, assembling near Tivoli, to attack the *2d Parachute Division* in order to relieve pressure on the *Granatieri Division*. While the divisions prepared to execute the attack that afternoon, Carboni left Tivoli about 0700 and went to Rome with several of his staff officers. He went in response to a telephone call from Sorice, the Minister of War.[13]

On his way to Rome, Carboni noted that all seemed quiet north of the city, but on the south the German paratroopers continued to press closer to the city limits.[14]

Sorice wanted to see Carboni because a peculiar situation had arisen in Rome.

Maresciallo d'Italia Enrico Caviglia, an elderly officer who had been a rival of Badoglio for years, had taken what amounted to *de facto* command of the civil and military forces in the capital and had become what resembled the head of a provisional government.

During the spring of 1943, the King had considered Caviglia as a possible successor to Mussolini, but Caviglia had made no move to further the possibility.[15] He had maintained his contact with the crown but had remained aloof from governmental matters until the summer of 1943, when he became increasingly concerned with what he judged to be Badoglio's mismanagement of affairs. His impatience with Badoglio's leadership had led him to arrange for an audience with the King. Scheduled to see Victor Emmanuel III on the morning of 9 September, Caviglia went to Rome on the 8th. While he was having dinner with friends that evening, he heard a recording of Badoglio's announcement of Italy's surrender. This confirmed his worst suspicions—Caviglia was certain that Badoglio had arranged to escape from Rome. But Caviglia never doubted the King and the high command. With faith that they would remain in Rome to meet the critical situation, Caviglia calmly went to bed.

The next morning, 9 September, Caviglia discovered the greatest confusion in the city. Only the doormen were on duty at the Quirinal Palace—no guards, no *carabinieri*. No responsible official was at the Ministry of War.

Caviglia's mounting concern was heightened when he met Generale di Corpo d'Armata Vittorio Sogno, a corps com-

---

[13] *Il Processo Carboni-Roatta*, pp. 81–90; Cadorna, *La riscossa*, pp. 53–57.
[14] *Il Processo Carboni-Roatta*, p. 77.

[15] Enrico Caviglia, Maresciallo d'Italia, *Diario (Aprile 1925–Marzo 1945)* (Rome: Gherardo Casini editore, 1952), pp. 392–414.

mander stationed in Albania who had come to Rome in civilian clothes to receive orders from *Comando Supremo*. Sogno told Caviglia that he had looked in vain for Barbieri, commander of the *Army Corps of Rome*. Barbieri was not at his office. Carboni, Sogno had learned, had been placed in command of all the forces around Rome, but Carboni had disappeared. Sogno had been at *Comando Supremo* but had found not a single general officer. Roatta's office was empty. And Sogno had heard a rumor that the *carabinieri* and the service school formations had been dissolved. At the Palazzo Caprara, Caviglia ran into Colonel Salvi. His eyes red from weeping, Salvi declared he did not know where his commander, Carboni, had gone. After further efforts to find out what was happening, Caviglia made the painful discovery that the King had fled Rome in company with Badoglio and high-ranking officers. Shocked and depressed, Caviglia went back to the Ministry of War, where he met General Sorice.[16]

Sorice had been having no easy time. Badoglio had instructed him the previous evening, after deciding to leave Rome, to notify the civilian ministers of the government's move. Sorice was to inform the ministers to meet the King and his party at Pescara. But Sorice did not get the civilian members of the cabinet together until the morning of 9 September, when, meeting at the Viminale Palace, with Caviglia present, they were startled by the news of the departure of the King and Badoglio. The first reaction of the Minister of Propaganda, Carlo Galli, was to summon a notary public and make an official record of his complete ignorance of the armistice negotiations. When Sorice advised the Minister of the Interior, Ricci, that Badoglio had invested him with responsibility for the civil government of Rome, Ricci declined the honor.[17]

At this point, Caviglia stepped into the breach. He tried to send a telegram to the King for authorization to assume full powers in Rome during the absence of the Head of Government. But he could not learn precisely where the King was and undertook to act on his own responsibility, deriving his power from his prestige as a marshal of Italy.[18]

Caviglia's first thought was to spare Rome and its population the devastation of battle. To that end, he felt it necessary to pacify the Germans. From Generale di Divisione Umberto di Giorgio, who seemed to have succeeded General Barbieri in command of the internal defenses of Rome, he learned not only that the Italian troops could not stand up to the Germans but also that the available supplies for the civilians were sufficient for only a few days. He made repeated attempts, but in vain, to get in touch with Carboni. He tried to negotiate with the Germans, but the German Embassy staff had gone and Kesselring's headquarters outside the city was hostile. To tranquilize the civil population, Caviglia had the Minister of Propaganda, Galli, issue bulletins over the radio and post billboard notices calling on the people to remain calm and assuring them that negotiations were being carried on with the Germans.[19]

---

[16] Caviglia, *Diario*, pp. 435–40; *Il Processo Carboni-Roatta*, p. 89.

[17] Senise, *Quando ero Capo della Polizia*, p. 249; Maugeri, *From the Ashes of Disgrace*, p. 185; Guariglia, *Ricordi*, pp. 714, 717.

[18] Caviglia, *Diario*, p. 441; *Il Processo Carboni-Roatta*, p. 90.

[19] Caviglia, *Diario*, pp. 439–41.

## THE DISSOLUTION

When the broadcasts and public notices appeared on the morning of 10 September, they undermined whatever spirit remained among the civil population and the troops. Carboni's plan for continued opposition to the Germans thus received a check even before Carboni could move over to the offensive.

When Carboni arrived at Sorice's office in the Ministry of War that morning, he was ushered in immediately to see Caviglia. Out of respect to Caviglia, Sorice took no part in the discussion.[20]

Caviglia had never seen Carboni before, and even though Carboni, now in uniform, made a favorable impression, Caviglia was prepared to dislike him. Caviglia had not thought very much of the military articles Carboni had written for the daily press; Sorice had described him as headstrong and willful. And, finally, Carboni was a product of the Badoglio era of the Italian Army.

Despite these handicaps, Carboni persuaded Caviglia of his competence and of the sincerity of his intentions. He briefed Caviglia on the military situation, explained how he had received from Roatta the order to withdraw his forces to Tivoli for no apparent reason, and indicated that he could not simply leave the troops in Tivoli indefinitely. He had insufficient fuel to move into the Abruzzi Mountains. He was therefore turning the *Ariete* and *Piave Divisions* back to Rome to fight to save the capital from the Germans.

Still without authorization from the King for his assumption of quasi command, Caviglia expressed rather unclearly what Carboni construed as approval of Carboni's intention to continue the fight.

Sorice agreed that Carboni's course of action was correct.[21]

Carboni then set up his command post in a private apartment in Rome—at *Piazza dello Muse* 7—which belonged to an employee of the intelligence bureau. Equipped with two telephones and with good observation of strategic streets, the apartment was well located for Carboni's purpose. There Carboni began to urge civilian resistance against the Germans and to direct the operations of the military units.

Carboni approved General Cadorna's final orders for the *Ariete Division's* attack. He ordered Generale di Divisione Ugo Tabellini, the *Piave Division's* commander, who reported in person, to bring up his troops to support the hard-pressed *Granatieri Division*. He encouraged Generale di Brigata Ottaviano Traniello, the *Re Division* commander. He sent whatever separate units he could locate to reinforce the *Granatieri Division,* and he urged the division commander, General Solinas, to hold out at all costs.

As for getting the civilians to fight in defense of the city, four days earlier, on 6 September, Carboni had secured and set aside 500 rifles, 400 pistols, and 15,000 hand grenades for distribution to the population. Luigi Longo, leader of the Communist party, had taken charge of the distribution, and on 10 September Longo arrived at Carboni's apartment house command post. Carboni urged him to get civilian fighters to support the *Granatieri* troops south of the city. A little later, around noon, Carboni sent Dr.

---

[20] Carboni, *L'armistizio e la difesa di Roma,* p. 44; *Il Processo Carboni-Roatta,* p. 90.

[21] Carboni, *L'armistizio e la difesa di Roma,* p. 44; Caviglia, *Diario,* pp. 443–44; *Il Processo Carboni-Roatta,* p. 90; Sanzi, *Generale Carboni,* p. 224.

Edoardo Stolfi to tell the Committee of National Liberation that it was time to arm the population and to help the troops resist the Germans. The committee declined to take action, though a few individual citizens joined and fought with the military, particularly at Porta San Paolo.

There was nothing in Rome on 10 September even resembling a popular uprising. The Romans were disillusioned, fearful, and tired of war. They had welcomed the armistice with joy. Wanting only peace, they preferred to listen to Caviglia's radio broadcasts and read the billboard announcements that were urging them to be quiet rather than to Carboni who offered only strenuous and dangerous adventure.[22]

Meanwhile, Giaccone and an aide had arrived at Frascati at 0700. Westphal met them. Giaccone stated that the Italian command had accepted the terms formulated the night before. He also complained that the Germans were not properly observing the truce, which was supposed to last for three hours, until 1000. Westphal at once dispatched two staff officers to accompany Giaccone's aide in order to ensure observance of the truce by the German units.

At this point, around 0730, Kesselring appeared. He said that Italian resistance was altogether hopeless because the Allies had confined their invasion to Salerno, thereby leaving the Italian troops near Rome to stand alone. As a result, he presented a new set of terms—drafted by Westphal during the night—considerably more severe. Undeniably, these conditions meant capitulation, nothing less.[23]

Giaccone discussed with Westphal the new terms in detail and with care. At 1000 he departed for Rome, taking with him the surrender document in the German and Italian languages, both already signed by Westphal. Giaccone arrived at the Palazzo Caprara around noon, got the telephone number of Carboni's command post, and phoned Carboni about the outcome of his mission.

Carboni ordered Giaccone to break off negotiations immediately. Replying that the situation was extremely delicate and serious, Giaccone requested an order in writing, or, he added, Carboni could make a direct and personal communication to Kesselring. Responding that the situation was indeed serious and delicate, Carboni declined to assume any responsibility. He recommended that Giaccone refer the problem to Sorice, the Minister of War.[24]

When presented with the problem and after listening to Giaccone's estimate that no other course existed except to agree to Kesselring's terms, Sorice did not feel up to the responsibility of making a decision.

---

[22] Carboni, *L'armistizio e la difesa di Roma*, pp. 44-45; *Il Processo Carboni-Roatta*, pp. 90-92; Sanzi, *Generale Carboni*, pp. 149-50; Scrivener, *Inside Rome With the Germans*, pp. 3-4.

[23] *Il Processo Carboni-Roatta*, pp. 87-88. The authors have followed the recorded testimony as given in the trial of Carboni, Roatta, Ambrosio, *et al.*, in which some, but not all of the relevant facts regarding the surrender were established. German postwar writings are less valid as evidence. Note, however, that both Kesselring and Klinckowstroem assert that General Calvi di Bergolo and Colonel Montezemolo appeared at German headquarters early in the morning of 10 September along with Colonel Giaccone. See Klinckowstroem in MS #T-1a (Westphal *et al.*), ch. V, pp. 13-14; Kesselring, *Soldat*, p. 255. The new set of terms may be found in *Il Processo Carboni-Roatta*, pp. 88-89.

[24] *Il Processo Carboni-Roatta*, pp. 88, 92; Carboni, *L'armistizio e la difesa di Roma*, pp. 46-47. Sanzi (*Generale Carboni*, page 157) states that it was General Calvi di Bergolo who called, not Giaccone.

He suggested that Giaccone lay the matter before Caviglia, the highest ranking military person in Rome. Sorice had that day found out the whereabouts of the King, and he had sent a telegram requesting authority for Caviglia to become the government representative in Rome. But neither Caviglia nor Sorice ever received the King's reply, which was actually sent and which invested Caviglia with full powers "during the temporary absence of the President of the Council who is with the military ministers." [25]

Giaccone, after leaving Sorice, found Caviglia at the house of a friend. Soon after Giaccone's arrival, his commanding officer, General Calvi di Bergolo, appeared in search of Giaccone to learn the results of the second discussion with Kesselring. All three officers discussed the problem of whether to accept the German demands and capitulate. Caviglia said he had no authority to capitulate because he had not heard from the King. But he added that if his assumption of authority had been confirmed, he would decide in favor of accepting the German ultimatum. He did not believe that the military situation permitted further resistance—and this despite his approval of Carboni's decision to resist. Caviglia advised Calvi di Bergolo to send Giaccone back to Frascati to accept the German terms.

The discussion was still under way when other guests were announced—Ivanoe Bonomi, Alessandro Casati, and Meuccio Ruini, politicans who were members of the Committee of National Liberation, and Leopoldo Piccardi, Badoglio's Minister of Industry. Caviglia received them and explained his views. Accepting his estimate of the military situation, for the marshal was an acknowledged military expert, they concurred in the wisdom of Caviglia's decision.[26]

This decided, Calvi di Bergolo and Giaccone shortly after 1400 returned to Sorice at the Ministry of War, where Calvi di Bergolo telephoned Carboni and asked him to come over. Carboni arrived in a matter of minutes.

The four officers argued over whether to accept Kesselring's terms. Sorice and Carboni declared them unacceptable and refused to sign the documents Giaccone had brought. Calvi di Bergolo and Giaccone insisted that they had no alternative but to accept, particularly in view of Kesselring's ultimatum. While the argument continued, machine gun fire sounded nearby. Upon investigation, they learned that German troops had made their way to the Via dell'Impero. Without further ado, Giaccone placed his signature on the documents.[27]

Almost immediately afterwards, Caviglia arrived at the Ministry of War. Carboni was still arguing in favor of resisting the Germans on the basis that the Allied invasion would soon force the Germans to withdraw north of Rome. Caviglia scoffed at the idea—such a belief, he said, was mere propaganda; the landings at Salerno could not free Rome. Only an Allied landing north of the capital, Caviglia said, could liberate Rome and northern Italy from German occupation. Carboni remained adamant. He refused to sign the capitulation papers. Saying that he knew the Germans well, he felt that they

---

[25] Caviglia, *Diario*, p. 441; *Il Processo Carboni-Roatta*, p. 90; Roatta, *Otto milioni*, p. 329; Zanussi, *Guerra e catastrofe*, II, 209.

[26] *Il Processo Carboni-Roatta*, pp. 92–93; Caviglia, *Diario*, pp. 445-46; Bonomi, *Diario di un anno*, pp. 101-03.

[27] *Il Processo Carboni-Roatta*, p. 93; Carboni, *L'armistizio e la difesa di Roma*, p. 47.

would not honor even the harsh terms that they were imposing. Calvi di Bergolo said that he trusted the German officers. He had faith in their honor, and he urged Carboni to speak directly to Kesselring and get his personal assurance.

With some bitterness, Carboni said he would do nothing of the sort. Calvi di Bergolo's *Centauro Division*, he said, had stood by idly while the *Granatieri*, *Ariete*, and *Piave Divisions* had fought and fought with distinction. If Calvi di Bergolo had such faith in the Germans, let him take command of the city and responsibility for the armistice. The others agreed.

Surprised by this turn of events, Calvi di Bergolo after considerable hesitation, acquiesced. Upon Calvi di Bergolo's responsibility then, Giaccone returned to Kesselring's headquarters with the surrender documents bearing his signature opposite that of Westphal. Giaccone reached Frascati at 1630, half an hour beyond the ultimatum's expiration but in time to save Rome from bombardment and the Italian troops from further combat.[28]

Kesselring thus became, after two days, master of Rome. Playing his cards with great skill, he overcame more than five Italian divisions though he himself held only a pair, and in so doing he kept open his line of communications to the *Tenth Army*. By occupying Rome and dispersing the strong Italian forces in the area, he made possible a stubborn defense against the Allies in southern Italy.

In the meantime, the King and his party had reached Pescara on 9 September. That evening the monarch decided to continue the voyage by ship, and shortly after midnight, the party boarded a naval vessel and sailed to the south.[29]

During this time the King and his party were receiving only the vaguest kind of reports from the rest of Italy. Fighting seemed to be going on around Rome, and this caused concern. A message came in asking permission for Caviglia to assume full military and political power in the capital, and this caused puzzlement—what had happened to Carboni and to Ricci?[30] For all the confusion, someone had nevertheless had the foresight to bring the radio and code for communicating with AFHQ. On the evening of 9 September, before the King and his party went aboard the warship, a message went out to the Allies: "We are moving to Taranto."[31]

Around 1430, 10 September, the royal party debarked at Brindisi. There the members of the government stayed, and Brindisi became the new capital of Italy. There was some talk among the generals of sending an officer to Rome by air to discover the extent and results of the fighting. But before an officer could depart, news came that Caviglia had arranged for a cessation of Italo-German hostilities.[32]

## Dissolution of the Italian Armed Forces

At La Spezia the main part of the Italian Fleet had escaped German seizure. Late in the afternoon of 8 September, the battleships *Roma*, *Italia*, and *Vittorio*

---

[28] *Il Processo Carboni-Roatta*, p. 93; Caviglia, *Diario*, pp. 446–47; see also Pietro Pieri, "Roma nella prima decade del settembre 1943," *Nuova Rivista Storica*, vol. XLIV, No. 2 (August 1960), pp. 403–09.

[29] *Il Processo Carboni-Roatta*, p. 64; Badoglio, *Memorie e documenti*, pp. 118–19; Zanussi, *Guerra e catastrofe*, II, 203.

[30] Roatta, *Otto milioni*, p. 329; Zanussi, *Guerra e catastrofe*, II, 209.

[31] Capitulation of Italy, p. 379.

[32] Roatta, *Otto milioni*, p. 330.

# THE DISSOLUTION

*Veneto* had left the harbor, the Germans having been convinced by De Courten that the ships were steaming out to meet and destroy the Allied convoys moving toward Salerno.[33] Joined by cruisers and destroyers from Genoa, the fleet on the morning of 9 September was sailing, in accord with Allied instructions, off the western shore of Corsica. The ships passed south of Corsica to pick up other vessels at Maddalena. That afternoon, German aircraft based on Sardinia attacked the fleet and sank the *Roma* (the commander, Ammiraglio Carlo Bergamini, and most of the crew were lost), and damaged the *Italia*. Ammiraglio Romeo Oliva took command and turned the ships toward North Africa. At 0600, 10 September, this fleet of two battleships, five cruisers, and seven destroyers met the *Warspite*, the *Valiant*, and several destroyers, which escorted the Italian ships to Bizerte. The same afternoon, the battleships *Andrea Doria* and *Caio Duilo*, two cruisers, and a destroyer, on their way from Taranto, reached Malta.[34]

The capitulation of the Italian forces around Rome to the Germans, rather than the surrender of the fleet to the Allies, proved to be the main pattern of Italian action. Paucity of matériel, declining morale, and lack of direction from Rome were the reasons why the half-million troops or more in north Italy and occupied France seemingly vanished into thin air. Four divisions of Rundstedt's *OB WEST*—in a series of police actions rather than military operations—rounded up the Italian *Fourth Army* in southern France and Liguria. Some units of the *5th (Pusteria) Alpine Division* resisted, but only briefly, at the Mount Cenis tunnel. A few soldiers of the *Fourth Army* in France accepted German invitations and volunteered to fight under German command. Some 40,000 Italians were taken prisoner and later sent north to Germany as labor troops.[35]

In the Brenner area, the German *44th Infantry Division*, composed mostly of Austrians, redeemed the South Tyrol with avidity, overrunning General Gloria's *XXXV Corps* headquarters at Bolzano on 9 September, occupying Bologna the same day. The following evening, two thousand railway workers arrived from Germany and took over the major railroad centers in northern Italy.[36]

At La Spezia, German forces disrupted telephone communications, then appealed to the Italian units to disband, the men to go home. The Germans surrounded the Italian *XVI Corps* headquarters (which had been in Sicily), fired several machine guns, then walked into the main building and captured the corps commander and his staff. Enraged by the escape of the Italian warships, the Germans summarily executed several Italian naval captains who had been unable to get their ships out of the port and who had scuttled their vessels.[37]

The German takeover in northern Italy proved much easier than OKW had an-

---

[33] Kesselring, *Soldat*, p. 238; Westphal, *Heer in Fesseln*, pp. 226–27.

[34] Klinckowstroem in MS #T-1a (Westphal et al.), ch. V, p. 21, indicates that the attack was made by the *Support Aviation Wing 4*. In Rome, *Supermarina* seems to have believed that the attack was by Allied planes (Butcher, *My Three Years With Eisenhower*, p. 413). See also Morison, *Sicily—Salerno—Anzio*, pp. 242–43; Basso, *L'Armistizio del Settembre 1943 in Sardegna*, pp. 41, 48; Cunningham, *A Sailor's Odyssey*, pp. 562–63.

[35] See Harrison, *Cross-Channel Attack*, p. 144.
[36] Rossi, *Come arrivammo*, pp. 260–61.
[37] Cunningham, *A Sailor's Odyssey*, p. 573; Rossi, *Come arrivammo*, pp. 258, 261.

ticipated. The initial reports showed such Italian confusion and paralysis as to make Hitler contemptuous and passionately vindictive. As early as 9 September, an order issued by Keitel on the treatment of Italian troops under German jurisdiction reflected Hitler's feelings. Commanders in France, northern Italy, and the Balkans, the order said, could accept Italians who were willing to fight in German units but had to take all others as prisoners of war for forced labor. Skilled workers were to be assigned to the armament industry, the unskilled to help construct a contemplated East Wall. Rommel put the order into immediate effect. His subordinate commanders took Italian troops into custody, disarmed them, and prepared them for transfer to Germany.[38]

In southern Italy, the armistice announcement had taken the Italian *Seventh Army* completely by surprise. Less than six weeks earlier, when Roatta had thought that the government might decide to resist the unwanted German reinforcements, he told the army commander, Generale di Corpo d'Armata Adalberto di Savoia Genova, the Duke of Bergamo, to react energetically in case of German violence. He had repeated the order to General Arisio, who had succeeded to the army command in August—telling Arisio to act against the Germans only if the Germans committed acts of open hostility. Beyond that, there was no warning, no indication—not even the transmittal of *Memoria 44* to Arisio—to suggest that the government was thinking of changing course.

In contrast to the developments in northern Italy and in the Rome area after Mussolini's overthrow, there had been no acute friction between Italian and German forces in the south. The armistice announcement humiliated the Italian generals, who, led by Arisio himself, freely turned vehicles, supplies, and facilities over to the Germans and voluntarily gave German troops the good coastal positions they occupied. Only the *9th (Pasubio) Infantry Division* suffered from German aggression—the division was torn to pieces as the Germans rushed toward Salerno to oppose the Allies. Only one commander suffered, General Gonzaga of the *222d Coastal Division*, who refused German demands that his troops be disarmed and was promptly shot. Only the *209th Coastal Division*, stationed at Bari, remained intact. Except for this latter unit, a few elements of the *58th (Legnano) Infantry Division* (in the Brindisi and Taranto area), a few units of the *152d (Piceno)* and *104th (Mantova) Infantry Divisions* in Puglia, and some unspecified coastal formations—the forces under the *Seventh Army*, three regular divisions and six coastal divisions grouped into four corps—were disarmed, the men permitted to go home.[39]

---

[38] For text of the order, see *Trials of War Criminals before the Nuernberg Military Tribunals under Control Council Law No. 10, Nuernberg, October 1946–April 1949* (Washington, 1950), vol. XI, Doc. NDKW-898, pp. 1078–79. B. H. Liddell Hart, ed., *The Rommel Papers* (London: Collins, 1953), pp. 445–47. See also Caracciolo di Feroleto, "*E Poi?*" pp. 140–55, and Giuseppe Gariboldi-Farina, *Follia delle Folle* (Rome: Staderini, 1945), pp. 194–95.

[39] Vietinghoff in MS #T-1a (Westphal et al.), ch. VI; Rossi, *Come arrivammo*, pp. 257, 277; Col. Gaetano Giannuzzi, *L'Esercito vittima dell'armistizio,* (Turin: P. Castello, 1946), p. 38; *Nazi Conspiracy and Aggression*, Office of United States Chief of Counsel for Prosecution of Axis Criminality (hereafter cited as *Nazi Conspiracy and Aggression*) (Washington, 1946), vol. VII, trans of Doc. L-172, p. 935, shows the *Pasubio Division* as definitely disarmed; Msg 477, Mason-MacFarlane to Whiteley, 15 Sep 43, Capitulation of Italy, pp. 503–04.

# THE DISSOLUTION

In the Balkans, Greece, and the Aegean, the Italian ground forces, numbering more than 600,000 men, were with but few exceptions completely dissolved by 15 September, having offered little aid to the Allies on the Italian mainland and even less resistance to the Germans. On the islands of Sardinia and Corsica, though the Italians outnumbered the Germans by more than four to one, they were unable to exert a positive influence on the war. The Germans evacuated their troops, numbering a division and a half, from Sardinia to the mainland where, a most welcome addition to Kesselring's forces, they participated in the battles south of Rome. A significant part of the Italian *184th (Nembo) Parachute Division* went over to the German side and served actively with the German forces.

The ineptness of the Italian ground troops and the passivity of Badoglio's government during the early and critical days of the Salerno invasion brought serious disappointment to AFHQ. During the afternoon of 10 September, General Eisenhower sent a message to Badoglio in the hope of galvanizing the Italians into action:

The whole future and honor of Italy depend upon the part which her armed forces are now prepared to play. The Germans have definitely and deliberately taken the field against you. They have mutilated your fleet and sunk one of your ships; they have attacked your soldiers and seized your ports. The Germans are now being attacked by land and sea and on an ever increasing scale from the air. Now is the time to strike. If Italy rises now as one man we shall seize every German by the throat. I urge you to issue immediately a clarion call to all patriotic Italians. They have done much locally already but action appears to be uncoordinated and uncertain. They require inspired leadership and, in order to fight, an appeal setting out the situation to your people as it now exists is essential. Your Excellency is the one man that can do this. You can help free your country from the horrors of the battlefield. I urge you to act now; delay will be interpreted by the common enemy as weakness and lack of resolution.[40]

General Eisenhower also recommended that President Roosevelt and Prime Minister Churchill call on the Italian people to oppose fiercely every German in Italy—such opposition, he explained, would greatly assist Allied military operations.[41] Accordingly, on 11 September, Roosevelt and Churchill made public a letter to Marshal Badoglio, calling on him to lead the Italian people against the German invaders. They instructed Eisenhower to convey the message directly to Badoglio.[42]

These efforts to prod the Italian Army into activity were like beating a dead horse. Perhaps the Allies achieved a final wiggle when on 11 September Roatta issued by radio a general order to all army commanders to consider the Germans as enemies.[43] On the same day, Badoglio informed Eisenhower that he had, the day before, ordered all Italian armed forces "to act vigorously against German aggression." For the Allies' edification, he included a final appeal for an Allied landing north of Rome and an airborne drop in the Grossetto area.[44]

[40] Msg 443, sent both over "Drizzle-Monkey" and by naval channels, 10 Sep 43, 1657B time, Capitulation of Italy, pp. 405–07.
[41] Telg W-9635 FREEDOM to AGWAR, 10 Sep 43, Capitulation of Italy, pp. 409–10.
[42] Text of message in U.S. Department of State, *United States and Italy 1936–1946: Documentary Record*, p. 68; Telg 7473, President and Prime Minister to Eisenhower, 11 Sep 43, Capitulation of Italy, p. 414.
[43] Roatta, *Otto milioni*, p. 338; Zanussi, *Guerra e catastrofe*, II, 248.
[44] Radiograms, "Monkey" to "Drizzle," 11 Sep 43, Capitulation of Italy, pp. 428, 434.

By then it was too late. Only a few Italian commands were still functioning actively. Indecision, fear of the Germans, and lack of communication with commanders in the field had doomed the Italian Army. Not only did this inaction facilitate Kesselring's plans and permit him to give his whole attention to the Allied invasion at Salerno, but it also deprived the King and the Badoglio government of resources they might have used to gain a better bargaining position with respect to the Allies.

## Mussolini

Everything seemed to be going Hitler's way except for one thing, the rescue of Mussolini. If Skorzeny, under Student's supervision, could locate Mussolini's prison and kidnap him, Hitler felt that he would have a good chance of restoring fascism in Italy and regaining an ally. Skorzeny had missed getting Mussolini by one day, when the Duce's captors had moved him from the island of Maddalena back to the Italian mainland just before Skorzeny could execute his planned raid.

Shortly thereafter, however, Skorzeny's agents informed him that Mussolini had been moved to the Campo Imperatore on the Gran Sasso, a ski lodge completed shortly before the outbreak of the war and located on the highest peak of the Apennines. No military map carried its location. Not even mountain climbers' charts identified the place. The only information that Skorzeny could get came from a German citizen living in Italy. He had once spent a holiday there, and he had a circular describing the hotel accommodations. This intelligence was hardly adequate for a military operation, so Skorzeny arranged to have a pilot fly him and his intelligence officer over the camp.[45]

On 8 September, while flying over the Gran Sasso in a Heinkel 111 plane, Skorzeny located the Campo Imperatore from the air and noticed a small triangular green area behind the hotel that might serve for an air landing operation. He and his intelligence officer tried to take pictures, but the camera built into the plane froze at 15,000 feet, and it was only with great difficulty that they managed to take some photographs with a hand camera.

This air reconnaissance was responsible for Skorzeny's absence from Frascati during the Allied air bombardment of Kesselring's headquarters. It was fortunate for him that he had left, for his quarters were badly damaged. As a result, he had to go to Rome to have his film developed. In the capital that evening, he pushed his way through joyous crowds of civilians who were celebrating the armistice, made known not long before by Badoglio's announcement.

Before Skorzeny could go ahead with rescue plans, he needed confirmation of Mussolini's presence at the ski lodge on Gran Sasso. He induced a German staff doctor to visit the lodge on the pretext that it might be suitable for use as a convalescent home for soldiers recuperating from malaria. The doctor started out that night and returned the following day. He reported he had been unable to get to the lodge itself. He had reached Aquila, the nearest village, and from there had gone to a funicular station at the base of the mountain. A detachment of Italian soldiers guarded the station. A telephone

---

[45] This account of Mussolini's liberation is based largely on Skorzeny, *Geheimkommando Skorzeny*, pp. 127-59.

# THE DISSOLUTION

call to the lodge disclosed that Italian troops stood guard there, too. Whether Mussolini was at the lodge was uncertain.

On the next day, 10 September, Student and Skorzeny discussed their problem. They felt they had to act quickly, for every hour that went by increased the possibility that the Italians might transfer Mussolini to Allied custody. Though they were not absolutely certain, they decided to act on the chance that Mussolini actually was at the lodge on Gran Sasso.

Because the capitulation of the Italian troops around Rome that day made the 2d *Parachute Division* available for the new mission, Student thought it best to send first a battalion of paratroopers into the valley at night to seize the funicular station. But a ground attack up the side of the mountain was impractical. The troops might sustain heavy losses, the attack would endanger Mussolini's life. A parachute drop in the thin air over the Gran Sasso was also dangerous. Student therefore decided to make a surprise attack on the top of the mountain with a company of glider-borne troops. He ordered twelve gliders flown from southern France to Rome.

Detailed planning for the operation was completed on 11 September. Paratroopers were to seize the cable car station in the valley and make a surprise landing on top of Gran Sasso. H-hour was 0600, 12 September. To help persuade the Italian guards to give up Mussolini without resistance, Skorzeny induced an Italian general to accompany him.[46]

Because the dozen gliders coming from France were late in arriving in the Rome area, Skorzeny postponed the operation for eight hours. The planes towing the gliders took off at 1300, 12 September. Though the paratroopers were well equipped with light arms, Skorzeny counted most on the element of surprise. He rode in the third glider in the hope that the men in the preceding two would have the situation well in hand when he arrived. But the two leading tow planes went off course, and Skorzeny's glider was the first to land. It crash-landed to earth less than fifty yards from the lodge.

Piling out of the glider, Skorzeny and his men rushed to the hotel and scrambled to a second story window. Inside they found Mussolini. The Italian guards offered no resistance. Meanwhile four more gliders landed successfully on the little green area near the lodge.

With Mussolini safely in hand, Skorzeny demanded the surrender of the Italian garrison. The colonel who appeared to be in command asked for time to consider. He withdrew, but he soon returned with a flask of wine and saluted his conquerors. By then, the paratroop battalion in the valley, after a show of force, was in possession of the funicular station.

Skorzeny relayed a message to Student—by telephone to the valley, thence by scout car radio—advising that he had accomplished the first part of his mission. This message reached Student, but subsequent communications were interrupted, and Skorzeny was unable to consult with higher authority on the best way to remove Mussolini from the Gran Sasso.

Wishing to get Mussolini to Hitler's headquarters as fast as he could, Skorzeny got in touch by radio with a small Storch aircraft flying overhead to observe the operation. He wanted the pilot, Captain Gerlach, to land on the mountain. With Italians assisting, the Germans cleared boulders from a short path to create a

---

[46] Identified as General Soleti by Mussolini in *Storia di un anno*, p. 34.

THE "RESCUE" OF MUSSOLINI, *12 September 1943.*

runway. Gerlach brought his small craft down safely. But he was far from pleased at the prospect of taking off from the mountain top with so precious a passenger. Skorzeny's insistence on accompanying Mussolini increased Gerlach's take-off problem by adding to the weight. Skorzeny reasoned that if the little plane failed to get off the ground, he would not be around to explain his failure to an enraged Fuehrer.

After a questioning glance at the little ship, Mussolini climbed into the Storch with Skorzeny and Gerlach. Paratroopers held the wings and tail of the plane as the pilot revved up the engine. Then, with much shaking and bouncing, the plane made its short run, barely cleared the rim of the escarpment, and leveled off only after a breath-taking drop below the mountain top. This was the last of the excitement. Without further incident, the plane proceeded to Pratica di Mare, where three Heinkel 111 aircraft were waiting to transport Mussolini to Germany. They took off at once, and shortly after 1930 that evening, Mussolini and Skorzeny were in Vienna. On the following day they flew to Munich; two days later, on 15 September, they were at

# THE DISSOLUTION

Hitler's headquarters in East Prussia.

Despite his dramatic rescue from the possibility of standing trial before the Allies, Mussolini was but a hollow shell of his former self. Eventually Hitler established him in power to govern that part of Italy under German control. There he served as Hitler's puppet and as the facade of a new government called the Italian Social Republic, which could not conceal the German military power that supported it.

No more than a mere symbol of the final brief revival of fascism, Mussolini, until his death in April 1945 at the hands of anti-Fascist partisans, nevertheless lightened Hitler's problems of holding central and northern Italy. Spared the necessity of establishing a military government for the four-fifths of the Italian peninsula he occupied, Hitler, by rescuing Mussolini, also divided Italian loyalties. The Allies possessed one symbol of leadership in the King; Hitler held the other in Mussolini.

The surrender of Italy achieved by the armistice of Cassibile was not much more than a paper capitulation, for the Allies had neither the Italian capital nor the administrative apparatus of government. What the Allies had was a symbol of sovereignty scarcely one whit more appealing to the Italian people than the discredited Duce.

CHAPTER XXIX

# The Second Capitulation

*Mission to Brindisi*

At Brindisi, the King and his entourage found it difficult even to find accomodations and to organize a mess. Clearly the government was one in name only. Four-fifths of the country was under German control. The Allies on the Salerno beaches seemed perilously close to defeat. Yet the Badoglio government could claim some legitimacy because surrender had brought it Allied recognition as the government of Italy.

Contact with the Allies, therefore, was of critical importance to the King and Badoglio. And fortunately, the royal party had the radio and code originally given to Castellano in Lisbon. This made it possible to communicate with AFHQ. But there were no real facilities at Brindisi for maintaining contact with the rest of the country—Radio Bari was so weak that its emissions scarcely reached Rome.

After receiving from General Eisenhower on 11 September the message from Roosevelt and Churchill urging him to lead the Italian people in a crusade against the Germans, Badoglio asked Eisenhower to send a liaison officer to help maintain close relations.[1] Eisenhower agreed and promptly selected for the post Lt. Gen. Sir Noel Mason-MacFarlane, the Military Governor of Gibraltar. He directed Mr. Murphy and Mr. Macmillan, the American and British political advisers at AFHQ, to accompany Mason-MacFarlane, whose task would be the establishment of official contact with the Badoglio government.[2]

After expressing his pleasure over the choice, Badoglio suggested that Eisenhower and his staff meet with him and his military staff "to discuss further operations in Italy, a theater of war which we [Italians] naturally know perfectly."[3]

The suggestion was not well received. Still grievously disappointed in the performance of the Italian Government from the time of the armistice announcement, Eisenhower was in no mood to confide his plans to members of that government. It seemed hardly logical, now that the Italian Fleet had surrendered and the Army had dissolved into virtual nothingness, for Badoglio to tell Eisenhower how to wage the war and for Eisenhower to listen. What seemed very clear was that "Castellano had been the moving spirit in military armistice," not Badoglio or any member of

---

[1] Msg 38, "Monkey" to "Drizzle," 11 Sep 43, Capitulation of Italy, p. 434; Badoglio, *Memorie e documenti*, pp. 123–24.

[2] Capitulation of Italy, pp. 440–41, also in file 10,000/100/1; Msg 5646, AFHQ to TROOPERS, 17 Sep 43, 0100/4/4,II. See the nine-page typewritten account of the establishment and operations of the Allied Military Mission at Brindisi covering the period 3 September–17 November 1943, 10,000/100/76.

[3] Msg 46, "Monkey" to "Drizzle," 12 Sep 43, Capitulation of Italy, p. 453; Ltr, Whiteley to Mason-MacFarlane, 13 Sep 43, 10,000/100/1.

Badoglio's cabinet. Why had Castellano brought the negotiations to a head? Probably, AFHQ speculated, "chiefly due to his treatment by the Germans who apparently ignored the Italians militarily and told them nothing about operations."[4] But whatever the reason, it was of little import compared to the problem of gaining some benefit from the surrender.

On the day when the Allies at Salerno were closest to defeat, 13 September, General Eisenhower wrote General Marshall to depict how hollow a shell the Allies had inherited as a potential ally:

Internally the Italians were so weak and supine that we got little if any practical help out of them. However, almost on pure bluff, we did get the Italian fleet into Malta and because of the Italian surrender, were able to rush into Taranto and Brindisi where no Germans were present. . . .

The Sardinian and Corsican situations show how helpless and inert the Italians really are. In both those places they had the strength to kick the Germans into the sea. Instead they have apparently done nothing, although here and there they do occupy a port or two.

Badoglio wants to see me and has suggested Sicily as a meeting place. I am telling him he has to come here. He also wants to bring along some of his general staff but I can't make out what his general staff can possibly be directing just now. A few Italian artillery units are supporting the British Airborne Division in Taranto. Aside from that there has been some local battling throughout the peninsula. This has, of course, served to keep the Germans preoccupied, but there has been nothing like the effect produced that was easily within the realm of possibility.[5]

Despite his low expectations, Eisenhower was not giving up in his effort to salvage something practical out of the surrender, and Mason-MacFarlane's mission to Badoglio's government was to be his instrument. Eisenhower defined Mason-MacFarlane's task as the transmission of Eisenhower's instructions to the Italian Government; the collection of intelligence information; and the arrangements "for such coordinated action as the Italian armed forces and people can be induced to take against the Germans." Mason-MacFarlane and his subordinates were to bear in mind "the extreme importance of inculcating in the Italian Government, armed forces and people, the will to resist and hamper in every way the German forces in Italy and the Italian possessions." Mason-MacFarlane received for guidance copies of the short military terms of the armistice and the long comprehensive conditions, but because the Italian Government had not yet officially received the latter, he was not to discuss the contents of the long terms.[6]

On the day that the mission established its first official contact, 15 September, the British Government proposed that the Allies secure Badoglio's signature to the long terms and asked for Eisenhower's views on the proposal. In reply, General Eisen-

---

[4] Telg 441, FAIRFIELD REAR G-2 for Strong, FREEDOM, 10 Sep 43, Capitulation of Italy, p. 412.

[5] Ltr, Eisenhower to Marshall, 13 Sep 43, Diary, Office CinC, Book VIII, pp. A-765—A-767. See also Telg 009, Mason-MacFarlane to Eisenhower, 18 Sep 43, 10,000/100/1.

[6] Instrs for Mil Mission with the Italian Government, 12 Sep 43, Capitulation of Italy, pp. 460-61. General Taylor (82d AB Division) was the senior American representative and apparently handled administration and communications. See Memo, AFHQ for Taylor, 12 Sep 43, sub: Notes for Allied Mil Mission; Organizational Chart for Mission; and Ltr, Taylor to Whiteley, 15 Sep 43, all in 10,000/100/1; see also Telg 584, AFHQ to FATIMA (MacFarlane Mission), 25 Sep 43, and Telg 9907, AFHQ to FATIMA, 26 Sep 43, both in 10,000/100/10; Decisions Made by CinC in Mtgs. Bizerte, 9 Sep-22 Sep 43, 0100/4/168; Notes for Mason-MacFarlane, 15 Sep 43, 10,000/100/76.

hower acknowledged the desirability of obtaining the signature but recommended delay. He also urged strongly the omission of the unconditional surrender formula, for he still had hope of gaining some practical benefits from the capitulation.[7]

For their part, the Italians were also disappointed. The members of the Italian Government had attributed extraordinary military capabilities to the Allies. They had entertained visions of an Allied landing in great strength near Rome. Thus, they felt that the Allies were responsible—at least morally—for the hasty abandonment of the capital. The Allies, they thought, had advanced the timing of the armistice announcement and had come ashore at the wrong place. "They all say we should have landed north instead of south of Naples," Mason-MacFarlane reported. "On this point I tell them they know nothing about it and to shut up."[8]

The impression made by the Italian Government prompted pity rather than confidence. The King appeared

pathetic, very old, and rather gaga; 74 years old; physically infirm, nervous, shaky, but courteous, with a certain modesty and simplicity of character which is attractive. He takes an objective, even humorously disinterested view of mankind and their follies. 'Things are not difficult,' he said, 'only men.' I do not think he would be capable of initiating any policy, except under extreme pressure, e.g. Mussolini's march on Rome

and the Communist threat, which led to his decision of 1920 [sic]; the hopeless state of the Fascist regime which led to his decision of July 25, 1943; the German threat to Rome, which led to his decision on September 9, 1943.

Badoglio seemed

old, benevolent, honest and very friendly. Said all the right things. A loyal servant of his King and country, without ambitions. . . . He is a soldier and clearly without much political sense, believing that he has the popular support at the moment and that it can all be concentrated in a military movement without a political side.

Ambrosio was "intelligent and friendly," though "depressed and lacking in enthusiasm." Roatta was "a good linguist" and "the perfect military attaché" but with questionable loyalty "to any cause that should show remote signs of becoming a lost one." Zanussi's "position in this rather dreary military hierarchy is rather low."[9]

The prospect of getting help from the Italians did not seem bright. All that remained of the Italian Army were: in southern Italy—the *Mantova Division* near Crotone, the *Piceno Division* near Brindisi, part of the *Legnano Division* north of Brindisi, and some coastal formations; in Sardinia—four divisions in a "recuperative" stage; in Cephalonia and the Dodecanese—one division each. The rest of the Italian Army, according to Ambrosio, was "surrounded by the Germans and finished." It could be "written off." Of the divisions in southern Italy, all had "hardly any motor transport left," their armament was "mostly 1918" type, they

---

[7] Telg 4929, Gilmer to Smith, 15 Sep 43, and Telg 478, FAIRFIELD REAR to FREEDOM, 16 Sep 43, both in Capitulation of Italy, pp. 501, 526.

[8] Msg 477, Mason-MacFarlane to Whiteley, 15 Sep 43, Capitulation of Italy, pp. 503-04; see also Ltr, Mason-MacFarlane to Whiteley, 14 Sep 43, and Diary Notes of Mason-MacFarlane Mission, 12-21 Sep 43, both in 10.000/100/1; Diary Notes of Mason-MacFarlane Mission, 22 Sep-4 Oct 43, 10,000/100/2.

[9] Msg 477, Mason-MacFarlane for Whiteley, 15 Sep 43, Capitulation of Italy, pp. 503-04.

had "practically no petrol," very little ammunition, and were "very short of boots." Except for the fleet, "the genuine military help we are likely to get," Mason-MacFarlane estimated, "is going to be practically nil." [10]

As for the political side of the picture, the Brindisi group was hardly worthy of being called a government. It was important only because of its unchallenged claim to legality—"except for the Fascist Republican Party now being organized in Germany by Mussolini and his gang, no other Government has so far claimed authority." [11]

## The Long Terms

While Mason-MacFarlane and the military members of his mission remained at Brindisi, the political advisers—Murphy and Macmillan—returned to report to General Eisenhower. On 18 September, after conferring with these men, Eisenhower informed the Combined Chiefs of Staff of the problem he faced at this juncture of the surrender developments.

The chief question, as Eisenhower saw it, and one that would have significant influence on Allied military operations in Italy, was the status to be accorded the Badoglio government. Determination of the status of Italy would dictate all "executive action" in the military, political, and propaganda spheres. Eisenhower had instructions covering support to be given to Italian units and individuals who resisted the Germans, and to this end he was planning to group three Italian divisions in the Calabria-Taranto area into a corps to be placed under British Eighth Army control for the purpose of defending ports, lines of communications, and vital installations; two or three divisions would become available in Sardinia, and Eisenhower contemplated using them for similar duties; Italian divisions in Corsica were collaborating with French forces landed there and conducting anti-German operations; two Italian cruisers were transporting troops and supplies from North Africa to Corsica "at considerable risk." Yet all this activity, though desirable and even necessary to the Allies, was inconsistent with the terms of the armistice, which called for the Italians to be disarmed and disbanded. Because Eisenhower would soon have to confer directly with Badoglio, he wished to be able to reassure him on a number of matters Badoglio was sure to raise, matters having "a profound effect on our military relations with Italy during the period of active hostilities." Instructions from the CCS, the dictates of military necessity, and his own judgment provided him the answers to most points. But these, Eisenhower found, were "not at all consistent with the provisions of the Long Term Armistice conditions" he was supposed to get Badoglio to sign. Badoglio, he had learned, did not understand the need to sign further terms, for additional conditions were illogical if the Allies expected active Italian co-operation in the war effort against Germany. Finally, drawing up an effective propaganda program to be addressed to the Italian people was impractical "until the government

---

[10] Memo, Mason-MacFarlane for AFHQ, 16 Sep 43; Telg 11, Mason-MacFarlane to AFHQ, 16 Sep 43; and Ltr, Mason-MacFarlane to Eisenhower, 20 Sep 43, all in 10,000/100/1; Msg 5986, AFHQ to USFOR, 17 Sep 43, 0100/4/4.II.

[11] Rpt of Macmillan, 17 Sep 43, Diary Office CinC, Book VIII, pp. A-790—A-796; see also Telg 548, Macmillan to Mason-MacFarlane, 22 Sep 43, 10,000/100/2.

structure and the Italian status are clarified." [12]

His recommendation, Eisenhower continued, was to institute a new Allied policy toward Italy. Could the Allied governments consider giving the Badoglio administration "some form of *de facto* recognition . . . as a co-belligerent or military associate" provided the Italians would strengthen the national character of the administration; restore the former constitution and promise free elections after the war for a constitutional assembly; consider possible eventual abdication of the King in favor of his son or grandson; adhere to whatever military requirements the Allies might decide on; and accept an Allied organization in the nature of an armistice commission, but with a different title, from which the Italian administration could accept guidance and instructions?

What prompted Eisenhower to make such a recommendation was the "hard and risky campaign before us." Italian assistance might spell the difference between complete and only partial success. Since he could defer a meeting with Badoglio for not more than ten days, he wished answers to his questions as soon as possible. And because he realized that his suggestion would "provoke political repercussions" and perhaps "arouse considerable opposition and criticism," he recommended that "the burden be placed upon us, on the ground of military necessity, which I am convinced should be the governing factor." [13]

After another day of reflection, General Eisenhower dispatched another message to the Combined Chiefs. There were, he said, only two alternatives: either to accept and strengthen the legal government of Italy under the King and Badoglio; or to sweep that government aside, set up an Allied military government over an occupied Italy, and accept the heavy personnel and administrative commitment involved in the latter course. He recommended very strongly the first line of action. As a cobelligerent, the legal government would have to declare war on Germany and on the Fascist Republican Government. It would thereby become the natural rallying point for all elements wishing to fight against fascism.[14]

The first major indication of the effect of Eisenhower's recommendation came on 21 September, when Prime Minister Churchill, speaking in the House of Commons, reviewed the war in the Mediterranean and revealed much of the Italian surrender negotiations. Justifying the conduct of the Badoglio government, and noting the threat of civil war arising from Mussolini's escape to Germany, he urged the necessity "in the general interest as well as in that of Italy that all surviving forces of Italian national life should be rallied together around their lawful Government. . . ." [15]

With the assent of his War Cabinet, Churchill on the same day telegraphed President Roosevelt. He recommended that the Allies build up the authority of the Brindisi administration and make it "the broadest-based anti-Fascist coalition

---

[12] Telg, AFHQ to CCS, NAF 409, 18 Sep 43, Capitulation of Italy, pp. 538-42; see also Ltr, Mason-MacFarlane to Eisenhower, 20 Sep 43, 10,000/100/76; Telg 7074, Eisenhower to Mason-MacFarlane, 20 Sep 43, 10,000/100/1; Telg, AFHQ to CCS, NAF 377, 22 Sep 43, 0100/4/3,III; Msg 8636, AFHQ to MIDEAST, 23 Sep 43, 0100/4/4,II.
[13] Telg, AFHQ to CCS, NAF 409, 18 Sep 43.

[14] Telg 502, Eisenhower to Smith, forwarded to CCS, 20 Sep 43, NAF 410, Capitulation of Italy, pp. 544, 548; see also Memo, Whiteley for Mason-MacFarlane, 21 Sep 43, 10,000/100/1.
[15] Churchill, *Onwards to Victory*, p. 267.

# THE SECOND CAPITULATION

Government possible." Rejecting an Allied status for that government, he felt that cobelligerency was sufficient. Yet he did not relinquish his wish for Badoglio to sign the full instrument of surrender.[16]

Churchill informed Stalin of his desires, perhaps as a bid in advance for Stalin's support should Roosevelt be reluctant to have the comprehensive surrender terms imposed. "I am putting these proposals also to President Roosevelt," Churchill wired the Russian, "and I hope that I may count on your approval."[17]

President Roosevelt was, indeed, reluctant. Yet he appreciated Eisenhower's need for a clear and firm directive. On 21 September, therefore, he sent Churchill his views in a message that crossed Churchill's telegram to him. Except with regard to the long terms, the views of the two were similar. With Churchill's concurrence, consequently, Roosevelt on 23 September laid down the basic policy for Eisenhower's guidance in dealing with the Italian Government. Eisenhower was to (1) withhold the long term armistice provisions until a later date; (2) recommend from time to time the relaxing of the military terms to enable the Italians to fight more effectively against the Germans; (3) permit the Italian Government to assume the status of a trusted cobelligerent in the war against Germany if that government declared war on Germany and if it promised to give the people the right to decide the form of government they wished, though not before the Germans were evicted from Italian territory; (4) merge the functions of the Allied military government and of the contemplated armistice control commission into an Allied commission under himself, with the power to give guidance and instructions to the Badoglio government on military, political, and administrative matters; (5) make vigorous use of the Italian armed forces against Germany; and (6) inform the French military authorities of these new instructions to the "extent that you deem advisable."[18]

President Roosevelt also forwarded to Eisenhower the text of Churchill's views. And in response to Eisenhower's suggestions, slight modifications were made in the text of the long terms. Furthermore, invitations previously issued to the other United Nations governments to send representatives to discuss the signature ceremony were not to be renewed.[19]

Upon receipt of the Presidential directive, Eisenhower instructed Mason-MacFarlane to make arrangements for a formal conference between him and Badoglio. The conference, to take place no earlier than 26 September, was to be restricted to the five basic items of the presidential directive. The long terms were not to be discussed. Badoglio was to be informed that additional terms or instructions of a political, financial, and economic nature would be communicated to him from time to time.[20]

---

[16] Churchill, *Closing the Ring*, pp. 189–90.
[17] *Ibid.*, pp. 192–93.
[18] Telg 8432, Presidential Directive, 23 Sep 43, Capitulation of Italy, pp. 560–62; see also Churchill, *Closing the Ring*, pp. 190–91, and Memo, Hammond for Hull and Marshall, 20 Sep 43, OPD 300.6 (OCS Papers).
[19] Revised Proposals for the Signature of the Long Armistice Terms, 21 Sep 43, Capitulation of Italy, pp. 563–64; see also Telg 550, Eisenhower to Mason-MacFarlane, 23 Sep 43, 10,000/100/2.
[20] Telg 565, Smith to Mason-MacFarlane, 24 Sep 43, Capitulation of Italy, p. 583; see also Telg 7134, AFHQ to Mason-MacFarlane, 20 Sep 43; Telg 37, Mason-MacFarlane to AFHQ, 20 Sep 43; and Telg 110, Mason-MacFarlane to Smith, 25 Sep 43, all in 10,000/100/1; Telg 57, Mason-MacFarlane to Eisenhower, 22 Sep 43, 10,000/100/2.

Meanwhile, the naval members of the Mason-MacFarlane mission had worked out the disposition of the Italian Fleet and merchant marine. All ships were to continue to fly the Italian flag. The battleships were to go into a care and maintenance status. Cruisers and small craft, both naval and maritime, were to serve the Allied cause by acting in accord with instructions that Admiral Cunningham would issue to the Italian Ministry of Marine through a liaison officer attached to the Badoglio government.[21]

About this time, Mr. Macmillan sent a personal message to Churchill. He said he thought it might be possible, if the Allies acted promptly, to secure Badoglio's signature to the long terms. With this estimate in hand, and with Stalin's support, the Prime Minister again urged President Roosevelt to agree to Badoglio's signing the comprehensive document. Informed of Churchill's action, Eisenhower instructed Mason-MacFarlane to suggest the 29th of September as the day for his conference with Badoglio. By then, surely, the issue of the long terms would be settled.[22]

President Roosevelt had pretty much had his way in the directive of 23 September, and he had placed a heavy mortgage on the postwar continuance of the Italian monarchy. Although the Prime Minister made no secret of his preference for monarchical government, he had concurred in Roosevelt's directive and had endorsed in the House of Commons the principle of free choice by the Italian people on their form of government at the end of hostilities. It was now the President's turn to defer to Churchill's enthusiasm in favor of the long terms. Late on 25 September, therefore, Roosevelt gave his assent to using the "long set of terms," if Badoglio's signature could be obtained quickly.[23]

The final decision having been made, General Smith, AFHQ's chief of staff, decided to go to Brindisi himself, together with Murphy and Macmillan, and try to insure by careful preliminary discussion the smoothness of the Eisenhower-Badoglio conference. Instructing Mason-MacFarlane to arrange for his reception at Brindisi, Smith intended to have preliminary talks with the Italians in preparation for the formal meeting, scheduled for the 29th.[24]

By this time a rift had developed between the King and Badoglio. Victor Emmanuel III opposed the whole program that AFHQ presented, and the issue came to a head on 26 September, the day before

---

[21] Cunningham, *A Sailor's Odyssey*, pp. 572–73; see Telg, F.O. "Z" to CinC Med, 12 Sep 43, and Telg, F.O.T.A. to CinC Med, 16 Sep 43, both in 10,000/100/1; Memo on Agreement of Employment and Disposition of the Italian Navy and Merchant Marine, No. Med 00380/17D, 23 Sep 43, 10,000/100/76; Telg 066, Mason-MacFarlane to Eisenhower, 23 Sep 43; Telg 061, Mason-MacFarlane to Eisenhower, 22 Sep 43; Telg 560, Eisenhower to Mason-MacFarlane, 24 Sep 43; Telg 583, Smith to Mason-MacFarlane, 25 Sep 43, all in 10,000/100/2.

[22] Memo, Macmillan for Smith, 25 Sep 43, and Telg 583, Smith to Mason-MacFarlane, both in Capitulation of Italy, pp. 585, 590; Msgs, Churchill to Roosevelt, 24 and 25 Sep 43, in Churchill, *Closing the Ring*, p. 194.

[23] Msg, President to Prime Minister, 25 Sep 43, in Churchill, *Closing the Ring*, p. 194; Telg 8611, Roosevelt to Eisenhower, 25 Sep 43, Capitulation of Italy, p. 593; Memo, Hammond to Stimson, 25 Sep 43, OPD 300.6 (OCS Papers).

[24] Telg 583, Smith to Mason-MacFarlane, 25 Sep 43; see also Telg 565, Smith to Mason-MacFarlane, 24 Sep 43, 10,000/100/10; Telg 9780, Smith to Mason-MacFarlane, 26 Sep 43, and Telg 118, Mason-MacFarlane to Smith, 26 Sep 43, both in 10,000/100/2; Telg 120, Mason-MacFarlane to Eisenhower, 26 Sep 43, 10,000/100/76.

# THE SECOND CAPITULATION

General Smith was due to arrive at Brindisi. On that day the King asked to see General Mason-MacFarlane alone.

In conference with Mason-MacFarlane, the King made known his opposition to an immediate declaration of war against Germany. He alone, the King said, could declare war, and then only if a properly constituted government upheld the declaration. The King did not feel he could declare war on Germany until he returned to Rome and constituted a new government. Otherwise, a declaration of war would be unconstitutional. Furthermore, the King was hardly in favor of letting the people decide the form of government they wanted. "It would be most dangerous," the King said, "to leave the choice of post-war government unreservedly in the hands of the Italian people." The King also wanted to know whether the Allies would insist on Badoglio as Prime Minister for the duration of the war. Mason-MacFarlane said he thought so. The King pointed out that it might be very difficult, in that case, to form a representative anti-Fascist government. The sovereign then stated his wish for Italian troops to be among the first when the Allies reached Rome. Mason-MacFarlane suggested that if the King desired to pursue these points, he should instruct Badoglio to raise them during the scheduled conference with Eisenhower.[25]

The King did more than consult with Mason-MacFarlane. Writing in his own name directly to the King of England and to President Roosevelt, Victor Emmanuel III made known his wish for the immediate status of an allied power. President Roosevelt replied that he considered the request premature. Churchill, replying on behalf of his King, stated that there had never been any question of an alliance.[26]

Badoglio's position was quite different from that of the King. Badoglio saw clearly the necessity for Italy to declare war on Germany, not only to regularize the status of Italian soldiers who fell into German hands, but also as a prerequisite for improving Italy's position with the Western Powers. Though Badoglio urged the King to make the declaration of war, the monarch refused. The King feared "that the Germans, who now occupied more than five-sixths of Italy, would certainly be induced to barbarous reprisals against the population." And the King took comfort in the fact that Acquarone stood with him on this issue.[27]

Victor Emmanuel III did not easily grasp the implications of his new role as titular leader of the anti-Fascist effort for which he had been cast by Churchill and Roosevelt. To Badoglio's chagrin, the first royal proclamation from Brindisi made no ackowledgment, implicit or otherwise, that significant changes had occurred—the sovereign issued the proclamation in the name of His Majesty the King of Italy and Albania, Emperor of Ethiopia. At Mason-MacFarlane's insistence, the monarch agreed to refer to

---

[25] Telg 121, Mason-MacFarlane to Eisenhower, 26 Sep 43, Capitulation of Italy, p. 601; Telg 136, Mason-MacFarlane to Eisenhower, 26 Sep 43, 10,000/100/2; Puntoni, *Vittorio Emanuele III*, p. 173.

[26] Badoglio, *Memorie e documenti*, pp. 131–32; Cf. Churchill to Roosevelt, 21 Sep 43, in Churchill, *Closing the Ring*, p. 189. See also Telg, AFHQ to CCS, NAF 379, 23 Sep 43, reel R–67–K; Telg, AFHQ to AGWAR, No. W–993, 26 Sep 43, 0100/4/4,II. Copies of the letters from the President and from King George VI to Victor Emmanuel III found in 10,000/100/2.

[27] Badoglio, *Memorie e documenti*, pp. 133–34.

himself only as the King of Italy. But Victor Emmanuel III insisted stubbornly that he could not surrender his titles without an act of parliament and such an act could not be passed until a constitutional parliament was elected and assembled.[28]

The Allied representatives at Brindisi had scarcely regained their equanimity in the face of this royal gaucherie when the King requested General Eisenhower to forward a message to Dino Grandi, believed to be somewhere in Portugal. Because Guariglia was in Rome, the King wanted Grandi to come to Brindisi to assume the portfolio of Foreign Affairs. According to the King, Grandi was a symbol of anti-Fascism, his presence in the Badoglio government would create a schism in the Fascist Republican ranks. Furthermore, Grandi could produce and develop an active pro-Allied propaganda program among the Italian people.[29]

Meanwhile, General Smith, accompanied by the two AFHQ political advisers, arrived at Brindisi on 27 September with copies of the long terms as most recently revised. Together with General Mason-MacFarlane, they had a lengthy conference with Badoglio that afternoon. Mason-MacFarlane presented two copies of the long terms document to Badoglio, reminding him that they were the additional conditions mentioned in the armistice terms signed at Cassibile. The signature of the long terms, he said, was to be the principal item at the conference with General Eisenhower scheduled for Malta on the 29th. The preamble, as the marshal would note, had been amended. But the Allies required the signature, Mason-MacFarlane explained, for two basic reasons: to satisfy Allied public opinion and to avoid any possibility of later misunderstanding. General Eisenhower had the power to modify the application of the terms as he saw fit, Mason-MacFarlane continued. Already the Allies recognized the course of events had outdated some of the clauses. In any case, the Allies would apply the terms as a whole in the spirit of the declaration made by the President and Prime Minister. Badoglio agreed to discuss the terms with the King that evening and to meet again with the Allied representatives the next morning.

General Smith then took up the other points on the agenda—the coming Malta conference with General Eisenhower, and the program for Italy as outlined by President Roosevelt in his directive of 23 September, which Mason-MacFarlane had discussed with the King the day before. In favor of declaring war on Germany, Badoglio appreciated Smith's arguments; i.e., a declaration of war would give Italian soldiers regular status, and would prepare Allied public opinion for future modifications of the armistice terms. Smith suggested that such modifications might include changes in Allied military government and return of the administration of Sicily to the Badoglio government. The marshal was willing to accept the status of cobelligerency for his country. As for broadening the royal government, Badoglio felt it could be done effectively only

---

[28] Telgs 104, Mason-MacFarlane to Eisenhower, 25 Sept 43; unnumbered, 25 Sep 43; and 124, 26 Sep 43, all in Capitulation of Italy, pp. 586, 594, 603. Cf. Churchill, *Closing the Ring*, p. 195. See also Telg 9525, Eisenhower to Mason-MacFarlane, 25 Sep 43, 10,000/100/1, and Telg 109, Mason-MacFarlane to Eisenhower, 25 Sep 43, 10,000/100/2.

[29] Telg 161, FATIMA to Eisenhower, 28 Sep 43; Capitulation of Italy, p. 647; Summary of Visit by General Taylor to Italian Supreme Command, 28 Sep 43, and Telg 161, Taylor to Eisenhower, 28 Sep 43, both in 10,000/100/2.

# THE SECOND CAPITULATION

after the King returned to Rome. But Badoglio did not want a specific commitment giving the Italian people the right to choose their form of government after the war. He suggested that the Italian leaders pledge only: "It should be understood that free elections will be held after the war." He did not think the King and his government ought to throw open by their own act the question of the monarchy. He doubted that the Italian people were adapted to a republican form of government. The monarchy, in his opinion, was necessary for maintaining the stability and unity of Italy.[30]

The King remained stubborn. Though authorizing Badoglio to sign the long terms, he refused to declare war on Germany, to make a pledge to broaden his government, or to promise to permit the Italian people to choose their own form of government at the end of the war. He repeated his request for Grandi to serve as Foreign Minister.

Nonetheless, his approval for Badoglio to sign the comprehensive surrender document was a significant step. As for Grandi, President Roosevelt had his own ideas of the type of man that Italy needed. On the day that Badoglio was meeting with Eisenhower at Malta, Count Carlo Sforza, a distinguished anti-Fascist politician who had fled Italy years before, got War Department clearance, at the President's instigation, to go to England, thence to North Africa, and General Eisenhower was so notified.[31]

---

[30] Memo by Robert Murphy, Brindisi, 27 Sep 43, Capitulation of Italy, pp. 610–11.

[31] Msg W-9586, AFHQ to AGWAR, 9 Sep 43, 0100/4/4,II; Telg 575, Eisenhower to Mason-MacFarlane, 25 Sep 43, and Telg 155, Mason-MacFarlane to Eisenhower, 28 Sep 43, both in 10,000/100/2; Telg, Marshall to Eisenhower, No. 8935, 30 Sep 43, Reel R-67-K; Memo, John J.

## Malta

The last act of the Italian surrender was anticlimactic. Aboard the British battleship H.M.S. *Nelson*, in Valetta harbor, Malta, around 1100, 29 September, Marshal Badoglio, accompanied by Admiral De Courten, Generals Ambrosio, Sandalli, and Roatta, and four officers of lesser rank, met General Eisenhower. The Allied commander had with him Lord Gort (the Governor of Malta); Admiral Cunningham; Generals Alexander, Smith, Mason-MacFarlane, and Maj. Gen. A. A. Richardson; Air Chief Marshal Tedder and Air Vice Marshal Keith Parks; Messrs. Murphy and Macmillan; and a number of lesser ranking officers. Badoglio and Eisenhower placed their signatures on the long terms.

General Eisenhower then handed Badoglio a letter, which read:

The terms of the armistice to which we have just appended our signatures are supplementary to the short military armistice signed by your representative and mine on the 3rd September, 1943. They are based upon the situation obtaining prior to the cessation of hostilities. Developments since that time have altered considerably the status of Italy, which has become in effect a cooperator with the United Nations.

It is fully recognized by the Governments on whose behalf I am acting that these terms are in some respect superseded by subsequent events and that several of the clauses have become obsolescent or have already been put into execution. We also recognize that it is not at this time in the power of the Italian Government to carry out certain of the terms. Failure to do so

---

McCloy for Admiral Leahy, with draft of cable, 1 Oct 43, OPD 300.6 Sec (OCS Papers); telg, Eisenhower to Mason-MacFarlane, No. 2580, 3 Oct 43, 10,000/100/2; Puntoni, *Vittorio Emanuele III*, p. 174.

ABOARD H.M.S. NELSON, *standing off Malta, 29 September 1943. Officials present at the signing of the long terms surrender document are, from left: Lord Gort, Air Chief Marshal Tedder, Marshal Badoglio, Lt. Gen. Sir Noel Mason-MacFarlane, General Eisenhower, and General Alexander.*

because of existing conditions will not be regarded as a breach of good faith on the part of Italy. However, this document represents the requirements with which the Italian Government can be expected to comply when in a position to do so.

It is to be understood that the terms both of this document and of the short military armistice of the 3rd September may be modified from time to time if military necessity or the extent of cooperation by the Italian Government indicates this as desirable.[32]

Thus, the Italian Government surrendered unconditionally, but in the hope of redemption. The Allies had wanted the conference to serve as the point of departure for charting the new course of cobelligerency. But the conferees did no more than discuss the program outlined in President Roosevelt's directive. The

---

[32] The text is printed in U.S. Department of State, Treaties and Other International Acts, Series 1604, *Armistice with Italy 1943* (Washington, 1947), p. 22.

See further, file 10,000/136/548, sub: Ltrs, Badoglio, Armistice; Telg 151, Mason-MacFarlane to Eisenhower, 28 Sep 43, 10,000/100/2.

The long terms of surrender remained secret until 6 November 1945.

Eisenhower-Badoglio conference was exploratory and reached no agreement. Still underlying the discussion was the frustration imposed by the obduracy of the King.

Badoglio opened the plenary conference with a general statement conveying his own desire to see the formation of a government with a broad, liberal base. But he made no commitment. He stated that the King would determine the new members of the government. Declaring himself to be only a soldier, Badoglio said he could not advise the sovereign with respect to politicians. And to General Eisenhower's question whether the royal government would promptly be given a definitely anti-Fascist character, Badoglio avoided a direct answer. Eisenhower made it clear that the Italian Government would have to take on an anti-Fascist complexion before it could join the Allies in combat. Badoglio replied simply by saying that the King planned to invite the leaders of the political parties to take part in the government.

At the King's direction, Badoglio renewed the request for Dino Grandi as Foreign Minister. Explaining that such an appointment would find no sympathetic response in Allied public opinion, Eisenhower made known the message he had received from Washington—the Americans desired Count Sforza to visit Brindisi in the near future. Badoglio said that the King had a distinct antipathy for Sforza because of Sforza's remarks about the monarch.

Badoglio stated his own desire for a declaration of war against Germany as soon as the Italian Government returned to Rome. He added that until then he personally considered the Italian forces to be in a *de facto* state of war with the Germans in Corsica, Dalmatia, and elsewhere. Eisenhower again urged an immediate declaration of war and said he would turn over to Badoglio the administration of Sicily and other liberated areas if his government took such a step. The marshal would make no commitment. Under Italian law, he said, only the King could declare war.

Toward the end of the conference, venturing the hope that General Eisenhower considered him a complete collaborator, Badoglio asked to be initiated into Allied plans. He requested that Italian troops be permitted to participate in the entry into Rome, an event expected, not only by the Italians but by the Allies as well, to take place in the near future. Eisenhower was evasive on sharing military plans with the Italians, but he promised a token participation of Italian troops in the liberation of the capital if Italy declared war on Germany and co-operated with the Allies.

In conclusion, General Eisenhower expressed his thanks to Badoglio and said he hoped that great good would come from the meeting. In reciprocating, Badoglio referred to the situation prevailing in 1918, when the Italians, he said, gave the decisive blow to the Germans—operating with the Italian Army had been three British divisions and one American regiment, and all had co-operated closely to bring about the German defeat.[33]

---

[33] Robert D. Murphy, Notes of the Conference Aboard H.M.S. *Nelson* in Valetta Harbor, Malta, 11 a.m., September 29, 1943, Capitulation of Italy, pp. 658–59; see also Telg 1647, Phillips to Mason-MacFarlane, 30 Sep 43, and Telg 192, Mason-MacFarlane to Eisenhower, 1 Oct 43, both in 10,000/100/2; Memo, McCloy for Leahy, 30 Sep 43; Telg, AFHQ to CCS, NAF 426, 30 Sep 43; and Telg 9081, Marshall to Eisenhower, 1 Oct 43, all in OPD 300.6 Sec (OCS Papers); Msg, AFHQ to CCS, NAF 431, 30 Sep 43, 0100/4/4.II; Ltr, Badoglio to President Roosevelt, 20 Nov 43, 10,000/136/854.

On that day, 29 September 1943, Allied troops were at the gates of Naples, the Germans were withdrawing to the Volturno River and trying to establish a defensive line across the Italian peninsula. With the Germans retiring northward, with the Allies having established two armies on the Italian mainland (Clark's U.S. Fifth and Montgomery's British Eighth), the prospects for advancing rapidly to Rome appeared to be good. The Allies did not yet realize the extent to which the Germans could use the Italian winter weather, the Italian terrain, and the skill of their own outnumbered troops to deny the Allies, and incidentally the Italians, quick entry into the capital.

Crossing the Strait of Messina had been easy, securing a beachhead at Salerno more difficult. But no one could foresee the bitterness ahead of the fighting at the Volturno and the Sangro Rivers, on the approaches to the Liri valley, along the Rapido and Garigliano Rivers, in the shadow of Cassino, and in the Anzio beachhead. No one could anticipate the expenditure of men and matériel that would be necessary before Rome fell to Allied arms. Least of all the Italians, who on 13 October 1943 finally declared war on Germany.

## Epilogue

What had the Allies gained by the surrender of Italy? A cobelligerent of doubtful value if judged in terms of material military resources—the Army was virtually ineffective; the Air Force was obsolete; only the Navy and merchant marine made substantial contributions to Allied power.

The surrender had eliminated a ground force of tremendous size that, even though ill-equipped and low in morale, had confounded and troubled Allied planners and intelligence experts. Had the Italian Government not surrendered before the Salerno invasion, the Italian units manning the coastal positions along the Salerno beaches, acting in concert with the Germans, perhaps might have increased Allied casualties. Unless, to take the opposite viewpoint, the Germans were relieved by the surrender because they no longer had to bother even to be polite to an ally of dubious worth. Did the Germans, therefore, resist the Allies more effectively without the Italians? Was this perhaps at least part of the reason why the landings at Salerno were more difficult for the Allies than those made on the beaches of Sicily?

What the Allies really achieved by the Italian capitulation was an enormous psychological victory, not only in the eyes of the world, but, more important, for the fighting man. One of the three major enemy powers had fallen to the combined weight of joint Allied arms, and this gave increasing hope that the end of the conflict would not be far distant.

This had been brought about by military diplomacy. Not a new phenomenon, this particular performance showed great ingenuity and unusual perception. A military command and staff had played the role of the diplomatist with considerable skill.

If the Allies were taken in during the negotiations by their belief that the Italian Government was eager to change sides in the war, it was because the Italian representatives—D'Ajeta, Berio, Castellano, and Zanussi—all of them, had misrepresented, perhaps unwittingly, the desires of their government. Though Churchill credited the King and Badoglio with the initiative in Mussolini's downfall and the

# THE SECOND CAPITULATION

subsequent switch to the Allied side, the real motivation was a desire to choose the lesser of two evils—to be crushed by Germany or to be redeemed by the Allies.

"If the Germans would [only] attack [us]," Badoglio had said late in August, "the situation would have a solution." Along with his fear of German armed might was the question of honor. "We cannot, by an act of our own will," Badoglio had said, "separate ourselves from Germany with whom we are bound by a pact of alliance." Only a German attack could relieve Italian pangs of conscience and make it easy to go over to the Allies and "turn for aid to our enemies of yesterday." [34]

As late as 3 September 1943, the day Castellano signed the armistice at Cassibile, the German naval attaché in Rome was reporting to his superiors: "In higher circles the opinion prevails that ever since he assumed office, Badoglio has been trying to bring the war to as favorable a conclusion as possible, but only with Germany's consent, for Badoglio takes Italy's honor as an Axis partner very seriously." [35]

---

[34] Bonomi, *Diario*, p. 82.
[35] ONI, Translation of German Naval Staff Operations Division War Diary, pt. A, vol. 49 (September, 1943), p. 37.

The King, too, felt this way. Despite the fears he expressed of German reprisals on the Italian population, he was also motivated by the desire to be a man of honor. Even after the Germans had destroyed most of the Italian Army, he refused to take the ultimate step of breaking with his former ally. And only as the result of continued Allied pressure, when his government was practically a prisoner of the Allies, did he make his final capitulation and declare war on Germany.

The campaign on Sicily that led to the capitulation of Italy proved several things. Like the invasion of North Africa, the Sicilian landings showed that Axis-held Europe was vulnerable to amphibious and airborne attack. It demonstrated the superiority of Allied weapons and equipment. It illustrated the resourcefulness and skill of the German foot soldier, who, despite numerical and technological inferiority, demonstrated once again the fundamental importance of terrain and its use in a struggle between ground forces. It gave the American field commanders in Europe experience, and particularly with respect to the British ally, a maturity not achieved before. Most of all, the Sicilian Campaign, by making possible the Italian surrender, marked a milestone on the Allied road to victory.

# Appendix A

## Composition of U.S. Forces on D-Day, 10 July 1943

### 3d Division

7th Infantry
    10th Field Artillery Battalion
    Company G, 66th Armored Regiment
    1 battalion, 36th Combat Engineer Regiment

3d Ranger Battalion
2d Battalion, 15th Infantry
Platoon, Cannon Company, 15th Infantry
Company B, 3d Chemical Battalion
Battery B, 39th Field Artillery Battalion
1 battalion, 36th Combat Engineer Regiment

15th Infantry
    1st and 3d Battalions
    Company H, 66th Armored Regiment
    39th Field Artillery Battalion

30th Infantry
    41st Field Artillery Battalion
    Company I, 66th Armored Regiment
    Company C, 3d Chemical Battalion
    1 battalion, 36th Combat Engineer Regiment

*Floating Reserve:* Combat Command A, 2d Armored Division
    66th Armored Regiment (−3d Battalion)
    41st Armored Infantry Regiment (−1st Battalion)
    Company B, 82d Reconnaissance Squadron
    14th Armored Field Artillery Battalion

### 1st Division

FORCE X
    1st Ranger Battalion
    4th Ranger Battalion
    1st Battalion, 39th Combat Engineers
    3 companies, 83d Chemical Battalion
    1 battalion, 531st Engineer Shore Regiment

26th Combat Team
    26th Infantry Regiment
    5th Field Artillery Battalion
    33d Field Artillery Battalion
    6 batteries of antiaircraft artillery
    1 battalion, 531st Engineer Shore Regiment
    1 medium tank platoon, 67th Armored Regiment

16th Combat Team
    16th Infantry Regiment
    7th Field Artillery Battalion
    6 batteries of antiaircraft artillery
    1 battalion, 531st Engineer Shore Regiment
    1 medium tank platoon, 67th Armored Regiment

### 45th Division

180th Infantry
    171st Field Artillery Battalion
    Company C, 2d Chemical Battalion
    2d Battalion, 40th Engineers

179th Infantry
    160th Field Artillery Battalion plus 1 battery self-propelled howitzers
    Companies A and B, 2d Chemical Battalion
    3d Battalion, 40th Engineers

157th Infantry
    158th Field Artillery Battalion plus 1 battery self-propelled howitzers
    753d Medium Tank Battalion
    5 batteries of antiaircraft artillery
    1st Battalion, 40th Engineers

### Seventh Army Floating Reserve

2d Armored Division
    Combat Command B
        67th Armored Regiment (−)
        82d Reconnaissance Squadron (−)
        17th Armored Engineer Battalion
        78th Armored Field Artillery Battalion
        92d Armored Field Artillery Battalion
        1st Battalion, 41st Armored Infantry Regiment

18th Infantry
    32d Field Artillery Battalion
    1 Engineer company

540th Engineers
2 Antiaircraft artillery battalions

# Appendix B

## The Quebec Memorandum

1. General Eisenhower should be instructed to send two Staff Officers, one U.S. and one British, to Lisbon at once to meet General "C."

2. The communication to General "C" should be on the following lines:

   *a.* The unconditional surrender of Italy is accepted on the terms stated in the document handed to him (Armistice Terms for Italy as already agreed. These do not include political, economic, or financial terms which will be communicated later).

   *b.* These terms did not visualize the active assistance of Italy in fighting the Germans. The extent to which the terms will be modified in favor of Italy will depend on how far the Italian Government and people do, in fact, aid the United Nations against Germany during the remainder of the war. The United Nations, however, state without reservation that wherever Italian forces or Italians fight Germans, or destroy German property, or hamper German movement, they will be given all possible support by the forces of the United Nations. Meanwhile bombing will be restricted to targets which immediately affect the movement and operations of German forces.

   *c.* The cessation of hostilities between the United Nations and Italy will take effect from a date and hour to be notified by General Eisenhower. (Note.—General Eisenhower should make this notification a few hours before Allied forces land in Italy in strength.)

   *d.* Italian Government must undertake to proclaim the Armistice immediately it is announced by General Eisenhower, and to order their forces and people from that hour to collaborate with the Allies and to resist the Germans. (Note.—As will be seen from 2 c above, the Italian Government will be given a few hours' notice.)

   *e.* The Italian Government must, at the hour of the Armistice, order that all United Nations' prisoners in danger of capture by the Germans shall be immediately released.

   *f.* The Italian Government must, at the hour of the Armistice, order the Italian Fleet and as much of their merchant shipping as possible to put to sea for Allied ports. As many military aircraft as possible shall fly to Allied bases. Any ships or aircraft in danger of capture by the Germans must be destroyed.

3. Meanwhile there is a good deal that Badoglio can do without the Germans becoming aware of what is afoot. The precise character and extent of his action must be left to his judgment; but the following are the general lines which should be suggested to him:

   (i) General passive resistance throughout the country if this order can be conveyed to local authorities without the Germans knowing.

   (ii) Minor sabotage throughout the country, particularly of communications and airfields used by the Germans.

   (iii) Safeguard of Allied prisoners of war. If German pressure to hand them

# THE QUEBEC MEMORANDUM

over becomes too great, they should be released.

(iv) No Italian warships to be allowed to fall into German hands. Arrangements to be made to insure that all these ships can sail to ports designated by General Eisenhower immediately he gives the order. Italian submarines should not be withdrawn from patrol as this would *let the cat out of the bag*.[1]

(v) No merchant shipping to be allowed to fall into German hands. Merchant shipping in Northern ports should, if possible, be sailed to ports south of the line Venice-Leghorn. In the last resort they should be scuttled. All ships must be ready to sail for ports designated by General Eisenhower.

(vi) Germans must not be allowed to take over Italian coast defenses.

(vii) Make arrangements to be put in force at the proper time for Italian formations in the Balkans to march to the coast, with a view to their being taken off to Italy by United Nations.

4. General Eisenhower's representatives must arrange with General "C" a secure channel of communication between Italian headquarters and General Eisenhower.

(NOTE.—In view of the urgency of the matter, a warning order should be sent to General Eisenhower that instructions as to how he is to deal with peace-feelers are being concerted between the President and the Prime Minister, and that in the meanwhile he should hold two Staff Officers in readiness to proceed to Lisbon immediately on receipt of these instructions to meet General "C," who must leave Lisbon on the night of the 20th at the very latest. He should also make the necessary transportation arrangements with London for entry into Portugal.)[2]

---

[1] Before the message was transmitted to General Eisenhower some purist deleted the italicized words and substituted the clause, "reveal our intentions to the enemy."

[2] CCS 311, sub: Italian Peace Feelers, 17 Aug 43, QUADRANT Conf Book, pp. 141–44. With the one change in phraseology which is noted, the memorandum was sent to Eisenhower as No. 50 (FAN 196), 18 August 1943, Capitulation of Italy, pages 90–92. Churchill prints an incomplete text in *Closing the Ring*, pages 105–06. Most of the memorandum is printed in translation by Castellano, *Come firmai*, pages 110–12. The full title of the Quebec Memorandum is *Aide-Mémoire* To Accompany Conditions of Armistice, presented by General Eisenhower to the Italian Commander in Chief. See 10,000/136/584.

# Appendix C

### Short (Military) Terms in General Eisenhower's Possession on 6 August 1943

1. Immediate cessation of all hostile activity by the Italian armed forces.

2. Italy will use its best endeavors to deny, to the Germans, facilities that might be used against the United Nations.

3. All prisoners or internees of the United Nations to be immediately turned over to the Allied Commander in Chief, and none of them may *from the beginning of the negotiations* be evacuated to Germany.

4. Immediate transfer of the Italian fleet and Italian aircraft to such points as may be designated by the Allied Commander in Chief, with details of disarmament to be prescribed by him.

5. *Agreement that* Italian merchant shipping may be requisitioned by the Allied Commander in Chief to meet the needs of his military-naval program.

6. Immediate surrender of Corsica and of all Italian territory, both islands and mainland, to the Allies, for such use as operational bases and other purposes as the Allies may see fit.

7. Immediate guarantee of the free use by the Allies of all airfields and naval ports in Italian territory, regardless of the rate of evacuation of the Italian territory by the German forces. These ports and fields to be protected by Italian armed forces until this function is taken over by the Allies.

8. Immediate withdrawal to Italy of Italian armed forces from all participation in the current war from whatever areas in which they may now be engaged.

9. Guarantee by the Italian Government that if necessary it will employ all its available armed forces to insure prompt and exact compliance with all the provisions of this armistice.

10. The Commander in Chief of the Allied Forces reserves to himself the right to take any measures which in his opinion may be necessary for the protection of the interests of the Allied Forces for the prosecution of the war, and the Italian Government binds itself to take such administrative or other action as the Commander in Chief may require, and in particular the Commander in Chief will establish Allied Military Government over such parts of Italian territory as he may deem necessary in the military interests of the Allied Nations.

11. The Commander in Chief of the Allied Forces will have a full right to propose measures of disarmament, demobilization, and demilitarization.

12. Other conditions of a political, economic and financial nature with which Italy will be bound to comply will be transmitted at a later date.[1]

---

[1] The italicized phrases were deleted from the short terms prior to their presentation to General Castellano at Lisbon. See Summary of Armistice Terms, Capitulation of Italy, pp. 69–70.

# Appendix D

### Additional Conditions (Long Terms) Signed on 29 September 1943

*Instrument of Surrender of Italy*

Whereas in consequence of an armistice dated the 3rd September, 1943, between the United States and the United Kingdom Governments on the one hand and the Italian Government on the other hand, hostilities were suspended between Italy and the United Nations on certain terms of a military nature;

And whereas in addition to those terms it was also provided in the said Armistice that the Italian Government bound themselves to comply with other conditions of a political, economic and financial nature to be transmitted later;

And whereas it is convenient that the terms of a military nature and the said other conditions of a political, economic and financial nature should without prejudice to the continued validity of the terms of the said Armistice of the 3rd September, 1943, be comprised in a further instrument;

The following, together with the terms of the Armistice of the 3rd September, 1943, are the terms on which the United States and United Kingdom Governments acting on behalf of the United Nations are prepared to suspend hostilities against Italy so long as their military operations against Germany and her Allies are not obstructed and Italy does not assist these Powers in any way and complies with the requirements of these Governments.

These terms have been presented by General Dwight D. Eisenhower, Commander-in-Chief, Allied Forces, duly authorised to that effect;

And have been accepted by Marshal Pietro Badoglio, Head of the Italian Government.

1.—(A) The Italian Land, Sea and Air Forces wherever located, hereby surrender unconditionally.

(B) Italian participation in the war in all Theaters will cease immediately. There will be no opposition to landings, movements or other operations of the Land, Sea and Air Forces of the United Nations. Accordingly, the Italian Supreme Command will order the immediate cessation of hostilities of any kind against the Forces of the United Nations and will direct the Italian Navy, Military and Air Force authorities in all Theaters to issue forthwith the appropriate instructions to those under their Command.

(C) The Italian Supreme Command will further order all Italian Naval, Military and Air Forces or authorities and personnel to refrain immediately from destruction of or damage to any real or personal property, whether public or private.

2. The Italian Supreme Command will give full information concerning the disposition and condition of all Italian Land, Sea and Air Forces, wherever they are situated and of all such forces of Italy's Allies as are situated in Italian or Italian-occupied territory.

3. The Italian Supreme Command will take the necessary measures to secure airfields, port facilities, and all other installations against seizure or attack by any of Italy's Allies. The Italian Supreme Command will take the necessary measures to insure Law and Order, and to use its available armed forces to insure prompt and exact compliance with all the provisions of the present instrument. Subject to such use of Italian troops for the above purposes, as may be sanctioned by the Allied Commander-in-Chief, all other Italian Land, Sea and Air Forces will proceed to and remain in their barracks, camps or ships pending directions from the United Nations as to their future status and disposal. Exceptionally such Naval personnel shall proceed to shore establishments as the United Nations may direct.

4. Italian Land, Sea and Air Forces will within the periods to be laid down by the United Nations withdraw from all areas outside Italian territory notified to the Italian Government by the United Nations and proceed to areas to be specified by the United Nations. Such movement of Italian Land, Sea and Air Forces will be carried out in conditions to be laid down by the United Nations and in accordance with the orders to be issued by them. All Italian officials will similarly leave the areas notified except any who may be permitted to remain by the United Nations. Those permitted to remain will comply with the instructions of the Allied Commander-in-Chief.

5. No requisitioning, seizures or other coercive measures shall be effected by Italian Land, Sea and Air Forces or officials in regard to persons or property in the areas notified under Article 4.

6. The demobilisation of Italian Land, Sea and Air Forces in excess of such establishments as shall be notified will take place as prescribed by the Allied Commander-in-Chief.

7. Italian warships of all descriptions, auxiliaries and transports will be assembled as directed in ports to be specified by the Allied Commander-in-Chief and will be dealt with as prescribed by the Allied Commander-in-Chief. (NOTE.—If at the date of the Armistice the whole of the Italian Fleet has been assembled in Allied ports, this article would run: "Italian warships of all descriptions, auxiliaries and transports will remain until further notice in the ports where they are at present assembled, and will be dealt with as prescribed by the Allied Commander-in-Chief.")

8. Italian aircraft of all kinds will not leave the ground or water or ships, except as directed by the Allied Commander-in-Chief.

9. Without prejudice to the provisions 14, 15 and 28(A) and (D) below, all merchant ships, fishing or other craft of whatever flag, all aircraft and inland transport of whatever nationality in Italian or Italian-occupied territory or waters will, pending verification of their identity and status, be prevented from leaving.

10. The Italian Supreme Command will make available all information about naval, military and air devices, installations and defences, about all transport and inter-communication systems established by Italy or her allies on Italian territory or in the approaches thereto, about minefields or other obstacles to movement by land, sea or air and such other particulars as the United Nations may require in connection with the use of Italian bases, or with the operations, security or welfare of the United Nations Land, Sea or Air Forces. Italian forces and equipment will be made available as required by the United Nations for the removal of the above-mentioned obstacles.

11. The Italian Government will furnish forthwith lists of quantities of all war material showing the locations of the same. Subject to such use as the Allied Commander-in-Chief may make of it, the war material will be placed in store under such control as he may direct. The ultimate disposal of war material will be prescribed by the United Nations.

12. There will be no destruction of nor damage to nor except as authorised or directed by the United Nations any removal of war material, wireless, radio location or meteorological stations, railroad, port or other installations or in general, public or private utilities or property of any kind, wherever situated, and the necessary maintenance and repair will be the responsibility of the Italian authorities.

13. The manufacture, production and construction of war material and its import, export and transit is prohibited, except as directed by the United Nations. The Italian Government will comply with any directions given by the United Nations for the manufacture, production or construction and the import, export or transit of war material.

14.—(A) All Italian merchant shipping and fishing and other craft, wherever they may be, and any constructed or completed during the period of the present instrument will be made available in good repair and in seaworthy condition by the competent Italian authorities at such places and for such purposes and periods as the United Nations may prescribe. Transfer to enemy or neutral flags is prohibited. Crews will remain on board pending

APPENDIX D 561

further instructions regarding their continued employment or dispersal. Any existing options to repurchase or reacquire or to resume control of Italian or former Italian vessels sold or otherwise transferred or chartered during the war will forthwith be exercised and the above provisions will apply to all such vessels and their crews.

(B) All Italian inland transport and all port equipment will be held at the disposal of the United Nations for such purposes as they may direct.

15. United Nations merchant ships, fishing and other craft in Italian hands wherever they may be (including for this purpose those of any country which has broken off diplomatic relations with Italy) whether or not the title has been transferred as the result of prize court proceedings or otherwise, will be surrendered to the United Nations and will be assembled in ports to be specified by the United Nations for disposal as directed by them. The Italian Government will take all such steps as may be required to secure any necessary transfers of title. Any neutral merchant ship, fishing or other craft under Italian operation or control will be assembled in the same manner pending arrangements for their ultimate disposal. Any necessary repairs to any of the above mentioned vessels will be effected by the Italian Government, if required, at their expense. The Italian Government will take the necessary measures to insure that the vessels and their cargo are not damaged.

16. No radio or telecommunication installations or other forms of intercommunication, shore or afloat, under Italian control whether belonging to Italy or any nation other than the United Nations will transmit until directions for the control of these installations have been prescribed by the Allied Commander-in-Chief. The Italian authorities will conform to such measures for control and censorship of press and of other publications, of theatrical and cinematograph performances, of broadcasting, and also of all forms of intercommunication as the Allied Commander-in-Chief may direct. The Allied Commander-in-Chief may, at his discretion, take over radio, cable and other communication stations.

17. The warships, auxiliaries, transports and merchant and other vessels and aircraft in the service of the United Nations will have the right freely to use the territorial waters around and the air over Italian territory.

18. The forces of the United Nations will require to occupy certain parts of Italian territory. The territories or areas concerned will from time to time be notified by the United Nations and all Italian Land, Sea and Air Forces will thereupon withdraw from such territories or areas in accordance with the instructions issued by the Allied Commander-in-Chief. The provisions of this article are without prejudice to those of article 4 above. The Italian Supreme Command will guarantee immediate use and access to the Allies of all airfields and Naval ports in Italy under their control.

19. In the territories or areas referred to in article 18 all Naval, Military and Air installations, power stations, oil refineries, public utility services, all ports and harbors, all transport and all inter-communication installations, facilities and equipment and such other installations or facilities and all such stocks as may be required by the United Nations will be made available in good condition by the competent Italian authorities with the personnel required for working them. The Italian Government will make available such other local resources or services as the United Nations may require.

20. Without prejudice to the provisions of the present instrument the United Nations will exercise all the rights of an occupying power throughout the territories or areas referred to in article 18, the administration of which will be provided for by the issue of proclamations, orders or regulations. Personnel of the Italian administrative, judicial and public services will carry out their functions under the control of the Allied Commander-in-Chief unless otherwise directed.

21. In addition to the rights in respect of occupied Italian territories described in articles 18 to 20—

(A) Members of the Land, Sea or Air Forces and officials of the United Nations will have the right of passage in or over non-occupied Italian territory, and will be afforded all necessary facilities and assistance in performing their functions.

(B) The Italian authorities will make available on non-occupied Italian territory all transport facilities required by the United Nations including free transit for their war material and supplies, and will comply with instructions issued by the Allied Commander-in-Chief regarding the use and control of airfields, ports, shipping, inland transport systems and vehicles, intercommunication systems, power stations and public utility services, oil refineries, stocks and such other fuel and power supplies and means of producing same, as United Nations may specify, together with connected repair and construction facilities.

22. The Italian Government and people will abstain from all action detrimental to the interests of the United Nations and will carry out promptly and efficiently all orders given by the United Nations.

23. The Italian Government will make available such Italian currency as the United Nations may require. The Italian Government will withdraw and redeem in Italian currency within such time limits and on such terms as the United Nations may specify all holdings in Italian territory of currencies issued by the United Nations during military operations or occupation and will hand over the currencies withdrawn free of cost to the United Nations. The Italian Government will take such measures as may be required by the United Nations for the control of banks and business in Italian territory, for the control of foreign exchange and foreign commercial and financial transactions and for the regulation of trade and production and will comply with any instructions issued by the United Nations regarding these and similar matters.

24. There shall be no financial, commercial or other intercourse with or dealings with or for the benefit of countries at war with any of the United Nations or territories occupied by such countries or any other foreign country except under authorisation of the Allied Commander-in-Chief or designated officials.

25.—(A) Relations with countries at war with any of the United Nations, or occupied by any such country, will be broken off. Italian diplomatic, consular and other officials and members of the Italian Land, Sea and Air Forces accredited to or serving on missions with any such country or in any other territory specified by the United Nations will be recalled. Diplomatic and consular officials of such countries will be dealt with as the United Nations may prescribe.

(B) The United Nations reserve the right to require the withdrawal of neutral diplomatic and consular officers from occupied Italian territory and to prescribe and lay down regulations governing the procedure for the methods of communication between the Italian Government and its representatives in neutral countries and regarding communications emanating from or destined for the representatives of neutral countries in Italian territory.

26. Italian subjects will pending further instructions be prevented from leaving Italian territory except as authorised by the Allied Commander-in-Chief and will not in any event take service with any of the countries or in any of the territories referred to in article 25(A) nor will they proceed to any place for the purpose of undertaking work for any such country. Those at present so serving or working will be recalled as directed by the Allied Commander-in-Chief.

27. The Military, Naval and Air personnel and material and the merchant shipping, fishing and other craft and the aircraft, vehicles and other transport equipment of any country against which any of the United Nations is carrying on hostilities or which is occupied by any such country, remain liable to attack or seizure wherever found in or over Italian territory or waters.

28.—(A) The warships, auxiliaries and transports of any such country or occupied country referred to in article 27 in Italian or Italian-occupied ports and waters and the aircraft, vehicles and other transport equipment of such countries in or over Italian or Italian-occupied territory will, pending further instructions, be prevented from leaving.

(B) The Military, Naval and Air personnel and the civilian nationals of any such country or occupied country in Italian or Italian-occupied territory will be prevented from leaving and will be interned pending further instructions.

# APPENDIX D 563

(C) All property in Italian territory belonging to any such country or occupied country or its nationals will be impounded and kept in custody pending further instructions.

(D) The Italian Government will comply with any instructions given by the Allied Commander-in-Chief concerning the internment, custody or subsequent disposal, utilisation or employment of any of the above-mentioned persons, vessels, aircraft, material or property.

29. Benito Mussolini, his Chief Fascist associates and all persons suspected of having committed war crimes or analogous offences whose names appear on lists to be communicated by the United Nations will forthwith be apprehended and surrendered into the hands of the United Nations. Any instructions given by the United Nations for this purpose will be complied with.

30. All Fascist organizations, including all branches of the Fascist Militia (MVSN), the Secret Police (OVRA), all Fascist organisations will in so far as this is not already accomplished be disbanded in accordance with the directions of the Allied Commander-in-Chief. The Italian Government will comply with all such further directions as the United Nations may give for abolition of Fascist institutions, the dismissal and internment of Fascist personnel, the control of Fascist funds, the suppression of Fascist ideology and teaching.

31. All Italian laws involving discrimination on grounds of race, color, creed or political opinions will in so far as this is not already accomplished be rescinded, and persons detained on such grounds will, as directed by the United Nations, be released and relieved from all legal disabilities to which they have been subjected. The Italian Government will comply with all such further directions as the Allied Commander-in-Chief may give for repeal of Fascist legislation and removal of any disabilities or prohibitions resulting therefrom.

32.—(A) Prisoners of war belonging to the forces of or specified by the United Nations and any nationals of the United Nations, including Abyssinian subjects, confined, interned, or otherwise under restraint in Italian or Italian-occupied territory will not be removed and will forthwith be handed over to representatives of the United Nations or otherwise dealt with as the United Nations may direct. Any removal during the period between the presentation and the signature of the present instrument will be regarded as a breach of its terms.

(B) Persons of whatever nationality who have been placed under restriction, detention or sentence (including sentences *in absentia*) on account of their dealings or sympathies with the United Nations will be released under the direction of the United Nations and relieved from all legal disabilities to which they have been subjected.

(C) The Italian Government will take such steps as the United Nations may direct to safeguard the persons of foreign nationals and property of foreign nationals and property of foreign states and nationals.

33.—(A) The Italian Government will comply with such directions as the United Nations may prescribe regarding restitutions, deliveries, services or payments by way of reparation and payment of the costs of occupation during the period of the present instrument.

(B) The Italian Government will give to the Allied Commander-in-Chief such information as may be prescribed regarding the assets, whether inside or outside Italian territory, of the Italian state, the Bank of Italy, any Italian state or semi-state institutions or Fascist organisations or residents in Italian territory and will not dispose or allow the disposal, outside Italian territory of any such assets except with the permission of the United Nations.

34. The Italian Government will carry out during the period of the present instrument such measures of disarmament, demobilisation and demilitarisation as may be prescribed by the Allied Commander-in-Chief.

35. The Italian Government will supply all information and provide all documents required by the United Nations. There shall be no destruction or concealment of archives, records, plans or any other documents or information.

36. The Italian Government will take and enforce such legislative and other measures as may be necessary for the execution of the present instrument. Italian military and

civil authorities will comply with any instructions issued by the Allied Commander-in-Chief for the same purpose.

37. There will be appointed a Control Commission representative of the United Nations charged with regulating and executing this instrument under the orders and general directions of the Allied Commander-in-Chief.

38.—(A) The term "United Nations" in the present instrument includes the Allied Commander-in-Chief, the Control Commission and any other authority which the United Nations may designate.

(B) The term "Allied Commander-in-Chief" in the present instrument includes the Control Commission and such other officers and representatives as the Commander-in-Chief may designate.

39. Reference to Italian Land, Sea and Air Forces in the present instrument shall be deemed to include Fascist Militia and all such other military or para-military units, formations or bodies as the Allied Commander-in-Chief may prescribe.

40. The term "War Material" in the present instrument denotes all material specified in such lists or definitions as may from time to time be issued by the Control Commission.

41. The term "Italian Territory" includes all Italian colonies and dependencies and shall for the purposes of the present instrument (but without prejudice to the question of sovereignty) be deemed to include Albania. Provided, however, that except in such cases and to such extent as the United Nations may direct the provisions of the present instrument shall not apply in or affect the administration of any Italian colony or dependency already occupied by the United Nations or the rights or powers therein possessed or exercised by them.

42. The Italian Government will send a delegation to the Headquarters of the Control Commission to represent Italian interests and to transmit the orders of the Control Commission to the competent Italian authorities.

43. The present instrument shall enter into force at once. It will remain in operation until superseded by any other arrangements or until the voting into force of the peace treaty with Italy.

44. The present instrument may be denounced by the United Nations with immediate effect if Italian obligations thereunder are not fulfilled or, as an alternative, the United Nations may penalise contravention of it by measures appropriate to the circumstances such as the extension of the areas of military occupation or air or other punitive action.

The present instrument is drawn up in English and Italian, the English text being authentic, and in case of any dispute regarding its interpretation, the decision of the Control Commission will prevail.

Signed at Malta on the 29th day of September, 1943.

| BADOGLIO | DWIGHT D. EISENHOWER |
|---|---|
| Marshal Pietro Badoglio, | Dwight D. Eisenhower, |
| Head of the Italian Government. | General, United States Army, |
| | Commander-in-Chief, Allied Force. |

# Bibliographical Note

This volume has been written on the basis of extensive research in the voluminous mass of documentary material held by the World War II Records Division, National Archives and Records Service (NARS), Alexandria, Virginia, supplemented by collections of documents held at the Federal Records Center, GSA, Kansas City, Missouri; the Division of Naval History, Department of the Navy, Washington, D.C.; the Archives Branch, U.S. Air Force Historical Division, Air University, Maxwell Air Force Base, Alabama; and the Office of the Chief of Military History (OCMH), Department of the Army, Washington, D.C. This official material has been further supplemented by the private papers of Generals Eisenhower, Smith, Ridgway, and Gavin; by General Lucas' diary; by interviews with Allied and Axis leaders; by published histories and memoirs; and by detailed comments by persons to whom the manuscript was presented for review.

The Allied Force Headquarters (AFHQ) records constitute the most important single collection of records used in the preparation of this volume. The collection consists of reports, messages, correspondence, planning papers, and other material on all phases of Operation HUSKY and the subsequent campaign in Sicily. According to a 1945 bilateral agreement, most of the original documents in the AFHQ collection were sent to the United Kingdom. Microfilm copies of these documents were made and are located in NARS. The remainder of the original documents came to the United States, and they, too, are located in NARS. The latter group contains the records of the Allied Screening Commission (Italy), the Mediterranean Allied Air Forces Headquarters (except the Target Analysis Files), the Mediterranean Allied Photographic Reconnaissance Wing, the Mediterranean Allied Strategic Air Force, the Mediterranean Allied Tactical Air Force, the Mediterranean Air Transport Service, and the records of Allied Military Government, the Allied Commission (Italy), and other Allied control commissions.

A large number of the microfilm documents in the possession of NARS have been photo-enlarged and arranged in file folders. Both the microfilm and the photo-enlarged documents are organized by job and reel number, as well as by a file classification. Where the authors have cited a document seen on a microfilm reel, the job number and the reel number are given, i.e., job 10C, reel 138E. Where the cited document was seen in a folder of photo-enlarged documents, the catalogue number and the folder number are indicated, i.e., 0100/12A/177. The original documents of the various Allied air commands deposited in NARS are in files prefixed with the catalogue numbers 0401, 0403, 0406, and 0407; of the Allied Control Commission, with the catalogue number 10,000. Use of these records is greatly facilitated by two finding aids: Kenneth W. Munden's *Analytical Guide to the Combined British-American Records of the Mediterranean Theater of Operations in World War II,* prepared in 1948; and a more detailed three-volume *Catalogue of the Combined British-American Records of the Mediterranean Theater of Operations in World War II.* Both of these items are in NARS.

Two collections subsidiary to this larger one are the Smith Papers and the Salmon Files. The Smith Papers, a collection of documents and books belonging to Gen. Walter B. Smith, has been given to the Eisenhower Library, Abilene, Kansas. When last used by the authors, it was split between NARS and the Army War College Library, Carlisle Barracks, Pennsylvania. Of particular importance in this collection is the file designated Capitulation of Italy—a bound file of copies of telegrams and other documents relating to the Italian surrender. A microfilm copy of this file is part of the AFHQ collection. The Salmon Files, stored in OCMH, consist of a body of papers and other materials collected at AFHQ by Col. Dwight E. Salmon.

The records of the Operations Division, War Department General Staff (OPD) are of the utmost importance for determining Allied strategic planning and decisions. These records, described in detail in *Federal Records of World War II,* vol. II, *Military Agencies* (prepared by the General Services Administration, National Archives and Records Service, The National Archives, Washington, 1951) fall into four main categories:

(1) The official central correspondence file (OPD), arranged according to the Army decimal system;

(2) The message center file, arranged chronologically in binders;

(3) The Strategy and Policy Group file, arranged according to the Army decimal system and identified by the letters "ABC" (American-British Conversations); and,

(4) The Executive Office file, an informal collection of papers on policy and planning compiled in the Executive Office of OPD, primarily for the use of the Assistant Chief of Staff, OPD.

The latter two collections were of particular importance to this volume. The ABC file contains an almost complete set of papers issued by the Joint and Combined Chiefs of Staff and their subcommittees. The file also contains the important studies on plans and strategy developed by the Strategy Section of the Strategy and Policy Group. The Executive file contains many documents which cannot be found elsewhere in Department of the Army files. This file was informally arranged after the war and assigned item numbers to permit easier identification. The entire OPD collection of records is in NARS. For additional information on the OPD collection, see the bibliographical note in Maurice Matloff, *Strategic Planning for Coalition Warfare,* UNITED STATES ARMY IN WORLD WAR II (Washington, 1959), p. 557.

The files of the Office of the Chief of Staff were of limited value to this volume. Arranged according to the Army decimal system, the files are not large in comparison with the AFHQ or OPD collections. But they do contain some papers that cannot be located elsewhere in the Department of the Army collection. These files, like those of OPD, are located in NARS.

Interviews and comments on the manuscript of this volume are in OCMH.

Other files and documents which were

of importance for the planning, strategy, and high policy are:

(1) AFHQ Chief of Staff Cable Log, which was brought up to date daily by the secretary of the general staff. It contains typewritten paraphrases of cables addressed to General Eisenhower or sent in his name which his subordinates felt he should see. This log is presently a part of the Smith Papers.

(2) Commander in Chief Allied Force Diary, deposited in Eisenhower Library, Abilene, Kansas. On this diary, see the bibliographical note in Forrest C. Pogue, *The Supreme Command*, UNITED STATES ARMY IN WORLD WAR II (Washington, 1954), pp. 559–60.

(3) NAF–FAN messages. These are the messages between General Eisenhower and the Combined Chiefs of Staff. They may be found in several locations, one of which is the AFHQ files.

(4) The official dispatches of General Eisenhower, General Alexander, and Admiral Cunningham. These dispatches may be found in the AFHQ files, and in other groups of the files mentioned above. In addition, parts of the Alexander and Cunningham dispatches have been published in the London *Gazette*.

The campaign in Sicily has been reconstructed largely from the records of the units involved, supplemented by records in the AFHQ G–3 collection, and from published materials. Unit records include journals, war diaries, after action reports, field orders, situation reports, and, at the higher levels, combined situation and intelligence reports and operations instructions. The records vary from unit to unit, from excellent to poor. They comprise a special collection of combat operations records for World War II in records of The Adjutant General's Office, in NARS.

If one remembers that the Sicilian Campaign was the first serious action for many of the American units involved, the fact that the records for Sicily are not as good as those maintained later in the war is not surprising. In general, the II Corps G–3 Journal and the 1st Division G–3 Journal are the best unit records available. The after action reports of all units are usually skimpy and provide little detailed information. The information in the unit records has been amplified and clarified in the light of the authors' interviews and correspondence with participants.

Details concerning the activities of the British Army have been largely taken from two published accounts: Nicholson, *The Canadians in Italy*, and Montgomery, *The Eighth Army: El Alamein to the River Sangro*. Another valuable source of information on British operations is the collection of AFHQ daily G–3 reports.

For the activities of the Allied air forces, the authors have relied heavily on two studies: USAF Historical Study 37, Participation of the Ninth and Twelfth Air Forces in the Sicilian Campaign, and USAF Historical Study 74, Airborne Missions in the Mediterranean. In addition, the official Air Forces history—Craven and Cate, eds., *Europe:—TORCH to POINTBLANK*—is valuable.

Morison's *Sicily–Salerno–Anzio* has proven indispensable in presenting the activities of the U.S. and British naval forces in Sicilian waters. This published volume has been supplemented by an unpublished ONI pamphlet which covers the same general material.

The account of German and Italian operations has been based principally on four groups of sources: (1) Italian wartime records captured first by the Germans and subsequently by the Allies; (2) German wartime records captured by the Allies; (3) Foreign Military Studies written by former German officers between 1945 and 1954 under the auspices of the Historical Division, Headquarters, United States Army, Europe, 1954; and (4) Italian and German publications.

Groups (1) and (2) are located in NARS, and in the Classified Operational Archives of the Department of the Navy, (referred to in the footnotes as COA/Navy). The Italian records consist of Italian documents captured by the Germans after September 1943 and catalogued by them under the designation *AKTEN-SAMMELSTELLE SUED*. This collection was later captured by the U.S. Army and redesignated as the Italian Collection. The collection is incomplete and not fully catalogued. Its most valuable item for the Sicilian Campaign is IT 99a, b, and c, a narrative written within and upon an order of *Comando Supremo* during the operations in Sicily. The narrative is based on daily reports from the front. Situation maps, copies of messages and orders, and intelligence estimates are included as annexes.

The collection of captured German documents contains three series of particular value. These are the war diary of the *German Armed Forces Operations Staff (OKW/WFSt, KTB)* reporting the developments on all fronts as well as considerations and decisions influencing these developments; the *German Army High Command* daily reports (*OKH, Tagesmeldungen*) giving very brief summaries of operations on all fronts; and the reports of the Commander in Chief, South (*Oberbefehlshaber Sued*) to higher headquarters giving the situation in his area two or three times daily and one intelligence survey per day (*OB SUED Meldungen*). Also contained in (2) are records of the German Navy. They provide insight into the German decisions on the highest level through minutes of conferences in Hitler's headquarters (ONI, *Fuehrer Directives* and ONI, *Fuehrer Conferences*), and also serve to corroborate information garnered from secondary sources.

The manuscript collection mentioned under (3), now in OCMH, provides narrative descriptions of the entire campaign as well as reconstructions of activities down to divisional and lower level. They were written from memory by former German officers who participated in the action, and, generally, give an accurate picture of the events. These manuscripts serve as an excellent supplement to the documentary evidence, although caution must be exercised in regard to dates and to biased views.

Among the published works (4), Gen. Emilio Faldella's *Lo sbarco e la difesa della Sicilia* served as the one, outstanding source covering the entire campaign in Sicily. General Faldella, Sixth Army chief of staff, wrote his book with the full approval of the Italian Army Historical Office. As the chief of that office assured Mrs. Bauer during several lengthy personal interviews in Rome, Faldella's book may be considered authoritative and will probably be fully corroborated in the official Italian Army history now in preparation. Faldella's most recent publication appeared too late to serve this volume; it does not, however, contain information materially changing the narrative.

Personal interviews in Rome by Mrs. Bauer with Generals Guzzoni and Faldella, with the commanding generals of two of the Italian divisions that fought on Sicily, and with the director and members of the Italian Army Historical Office provided valuable supplementary information, while similar interviews with Admiral Pavesi, the commander of Pantelleria, and with Admiral Fioravanzo, the director of the Italian Navy Historical Office were invaluable in reconstructing the events connected with the fall of Pantelleria.

Otherwise published works are listed only in the footnote citations.

# Glossary

| | |
|---|---|
| AAF | Army Air Forces |
| AAR | After action report |
| AB | Airborne |
| Accolade | Seizure of the Dodecanese |
| *ACHSE* | German plan to take over the control of Italy |
| ACV | Auxiliary aircraft carrier or tender |
| Admin | Administrative |
| Adv | Advance |
| AFHQ | Allied Force Headquarters |
| AGF | Army Ground Forces |
| AGp | Army group |
| AGWAR | Adjutant General, War Department |
| AK | Cargo ship |
| *ALARICH* | Occupation of northern Italy by Rommel's *Army Group B* if Italy collapsed politically. |
| AP | Transport ship |
| Arcadia | U.S.-British staff conference at Washington, December 1941–January 1942 |
| Arty | Artillery |
| AT | Antitank (gun) |
| Avalanche | Amphibious assault, Salerno, Italy |
| Barclay | Plan to induce the Axis to give priority to maintaining and reinforcing its forces in southern France and the Balkans |
| Barracuda | Plan for a sea and airborne assault on Naples. Canceled. |
| Baytown | Invasion of the Italian mainland opposite Messina |
| Bd | Board |
| Br | British, branch |
| Brimstone | Plan for capture of Sardinia |
| Buttress | British operation against toe of Italy |
| CAD | Civil Affairs Division |
| CC (A, B, C) | Combat Command (A, B, C) |
| CCAC | Combined Civil Affairs Committee |
| CCS | Combined Chiefs of Staff |
| Cent | Code name for beaches at Scoglitti |
| Chem | Chemical |
| Chestnut | Four airborne missions sent by Montgomery in an effort to aid his army in Sicily with airborne troops |

| | |
|---|---|
| CIC | Counter Intelligence Corps |
| Conf | Conference |
| CORKSCREW | Operation against Pantelleria, Italy, mid-June 1943 |
| COS | British Chiefs of Staff |
| Cositinreps | Combined situation and intelligence reports |
| DCofS | Deputy Chief of Staff |
| DIME | Code name for beaches in Gela area |
| ENTF | Eastern Naval Task Force |
| Exec | Executive |
| FA | Field Artillery |
| FAN | Symbol for messages from Commander in Chief, Allied Expeditionary Force, to the Combined Chiefs of Staff |
| FATIMA | Mason-MacFarlane Mission |
| FBIS | Foreign Broadcast Information Service |
| FIREBRAND | Invasion of Corsica, 1943 |
| FO | Field order |
| G–1 | Personnel section of division or higher staff |
| G–2 | Intelligence section of division or higher staff |
| G–3 | Operations section of division or higher staff |
| G–4 | Logistics and supply section of division or higher staff |
| G–5 | Civil affairs section of division or higher staff |
| GANGWAY | Plan for an unopposed landing in Naples. Canceled. |
| GIANT I | Plan for an air landing and drop along the Volturno River. Canceled. |
| GIANT II | Plan for an airdrop near Rome. Canceled. |
| GMDS | German Military Documents Section, Alexandria |
| GOBLET | Invasion of Italy at Cotrone. Canceled. |
| GSUSA | General Staff, U.S. Army |
| HARDIHOOD | Aid to Turkey to induce her to enter the war |
| HUSKY | Allied invasion of Sicily in July 1943 |
| Instr(s) | Instructions |
| Intel | Intelligence |
| JIC | Joint Intelligence Committee |
| Joss | Code name for beaches in Licata area |
| JP | Joint Planners (British) |
| JPS | Joint Staff Planners (U.S.) |
| JWPC | Joint War Plans Committee |
| *Kampfgruppe* | German combat group of variable size |
| *KONSTANTIN* | Reinforcement of German troops in the Balkans and Greece |
| *KOPENHAGEN* | German plan for seizure of the Mt. Cenis Pass (part of Plan *ACHSE*) |
| LCI | landing craft, infantry |

# GLOSSARY

| | |
|---|---|
| LCI(L) | landing craft, infantry (large) |
| LCM | landing craft, mechanized |
| LCT | landing craft, tank |
| LCVP | landing craft, vehicle and personnel |
| LEHRGANG | Evacuation of German troops from Sicily to the Italian mainland, 11-17 August 1943. |
| LST | Landing ship, tank |
| Ltr | Letter |
| MAC | Mediterranean Air Command |
| Min | Minutes |
| Med | Mediterranean |
| MEF | Middle East Forces (British) |
| MIDEAST | Middle East |
| MINCEMEAT | Cover plan in connection with HUSKY to induce the Germans to believe that Allied objectives were Sardinia and the Peloponnesus |
| MTB | Motor Transport Brigade |
| Mtg | Meeting |
| MUSKET | Projected landing on heel of Italy near Taranto, 1943 |
| MUSTANG | Plan for an overland seizure of Naples after initial landings in Calabria. Canceled. |
| MVSN | Fascist Militia |
| NAAF | Northwest African Air Forces |
| NAAFTCC | Northwest African Air Force Troop Carrier Command |
| NAF | Symbol for messages from the Combined Chiefs of Staff to the Commander in Chief, Allied Expeditionary Force |
| NARS | National Archives and Records Service |
| NASAF | Northwest African Strategic Air Force |
| NATAF | Northwest African Tactical Air Force |
| OB SUED | *Oberbefehlshaber Sued* (Headquarters, Commander in Chief South) |
| OCMH | Office, Chief of Military History |
| OKH | *Oberkommando des Heeres* |
| OKM | *Oberkommando der Kriegsmarine* |
| OKL | *Oberkommando der Luftwaffe* |
| OKW | *Oberkommando der Wehrmacht* (German Armed Forces High Command) |
| OPD | Operations Division |
| Opns | Operations |
| OSS | Office of Strategic Services |

| | |
|---|---|
| OVRA | Italian Secret Police |
| Prov | Provisional |
| Rcd | Record |
| RCT | Regimental combat team |
| Reinf | Reinforced |
| ROUNDHAMMER | A cross-Channel operation, intermediate in size between SLEDGEHAMMER and ROUNDUP |
| ROUNDUP | Various 1941–43 plans for a cross-Channel attack in the final phases of the war |
| S–3 | Operations section, regimental or lower echelon |
| *SIEGFRIED* | German plan for occupying the southern coast of France (part of Plan ACHSE) |
| SIM | Servizio Informazione Militari (Military Intelligence Service) |
| Sitrep | Situation report |
| SLEDGEHAMMER | Plan for a limited-objective attack across the Channel in 1942 designed either to take advantage of a crack in German morale or as a "sacrifice" operation to aid the Russians |
| SNOL | Senior naval officer, landings |
| SOC | "Seagull"; single-engine Navy scout-observation (VSO) land plane or seaplane, biplane |
| *Stato Maggiore Generale (Comando Supremo)* | Italian Armed Forces High Command and General Staff |
| *Stato Maggiore Regia Aeronautica (Superaereo)* | Italian Air Force High Command and General Staff |
| *Stato Maggiore Regio Esercito (Superesercito)* | Italian Army High Command and General Staff |
| *Stato Maggiore Regia Marina (Supermarina)* | Italian Navy High Command and General Staff |
| Sum | Summary |
| Tel | Telephone |
| Telg | Telegram |
| Tk | Tank |
| T/O | Table of Organization |
| TORCH | Allied invasion of North and Northwest Africa, 1942 |
| TRIDENT | International conference in Washington, May 1943 |
| VULCAN | Operation against the Germans holding out on Cape Bon |
| WDCSA | Chief of Staff, U.S. Army |
| WDGO | War Department General Order |
| *WFSt* | *Wehrmachtfuehrungsstab* (German Armed Forces Operations Staff) |
| WNTF | Western Naval Task Force |

# Basic Military Map Symbols*

Symbols within a rectangle indicate a military unit, within a triangle an observation post, and within a circle a supply point.

## Military Units—Identification

| | |
|---|---|
| Antiaircraft Artillery | △ |
| Armored Command | ◯ |
| Army Air Forces | ∞ |
| Artillery, except Antiaircraft and Coast Artillery | • |
| Cavalry, Horse | ╱ |
| Cavalry, Mechanized | ⌀ |
| Chemical Warfare Service | G |
| Coast Artillery | ◇ |
| Engineers | E |
| Infantry | ✕ |
| Medical Corps | ⊞ |
| Ordnance Department | ⌾ |
| Quartermaster Corps | Q |
| Signal Corps | S |
| Tank Destroyer | TD |
| Transportation Corps | ✹ |
| Veterinary Corps | ∨ |

Airborne units are designated by combining a gull wing symbol with the arm or service symbol:

| | |
|---|---|
| Airborne Artillery | ⌣• |
| Airborne Infantry | ✕ |

*For complete listing of symbols in use during the World War II period, see FM 21-30, dated October 1943, from which these are taken.

## Size Symbols

The following symbols placed either in boundary lines or above the rectangle, triangle, or circle inclosing the identifying arm or service symbol indicate the size of military organization:

| | |
|---|---|
| Squad | • |
| Section | • • |
| Platoon | • • • |
| Company, troop, battery, Air Force flight | I |
| Battalion, cavalry squadron, or Air Force squadron | I I |
| Regiment or group; combat team (with abbreviation CT following identifying numeral) | I I I |
| Brigade, Combat Command of Armored Division, or Air Force Wing | X |
| Division or Command of an Air Force | XX |
| Corps or Air Force | XXX |
| Army | XXXX |
| Group of Armies | XXXXX |

### EXAMPLES

The letter or number to the left of the symbol indicates the unit designation; that to the right, the designation of the parent unit to which it belongs. Letters or numbers above or below boundary lines designate the units separated by the lines:

| | |
|---|---|
| Company A, 137th Infantry | A ⊠ 137 |
| 8th Field Artillery Battalion | 8 |
| Combat Command A, 1st Armored Division | A ▭ 1 |
| Observation Post, 23d Infantry | △ 23 |
| Command Post, 5th Infantry Division | ⊠ 5 |
| Boundary between 137th and 138th Infantry | 137 / III / 138 |

## Weapons

| | |
|---|---|
| Machine gun | •→ |
| Gun | ● |
| Gun battery | ⊥⊥⊥ |
| Howitzer or Mortar | ✚ |
| Tank | ◇ |
| Self-propelled gun | ▣ |

# UNITED STATES ARMY IN WORLD WAR II

The following volumes have been published or are in press:

The War Department
*Chief of Staff: Prewar Plans and Preparations*
*Washington Command Post: The Operations Division*
*Strategic Planning for Coalition Warfare: 1941-1942*
*Strategic Planning for Coalition Warfare: 1943-1944*
*Global Logistics and Strategy: 1940-1943*
*Global Logistics and Strategy: 1943-1945*
*The Army and Economic Mobilization*
*The Army and Industrial Manpower*

The Army Ground Forces
*The Organization of Ground Combat Troops*
*The Procurement and Training of Ground Combat Troops*

The Army Service Forces
*The Organization and Role of the Army Service Forces*

The Western Hemisphere
*The Framework of Hemisphere Defense*
*Guarding the United States and Its Outposts*

The War in the Pacific
*The Fall of the Philippines*
*Guadalcanal: The First Offensive*
*Victory in Papua*
*CARTWHEEL: The Reduction of Rabaul*
*Seizure of the Gilberts and Marshalls*
*Campaign in the Marianas*
*The Approach to the Philippines*
*Leyte: The Return to the Philippines*
*Triumph in the Philippines*
*Okinawa: The Last Battle*
*Strategy and Command: The First Two Years*

The Mediterranean Theater of Operations
*Northwest Africa: Seizing the Initiative in the West*
*Sicily and the Surrender of Italy*
*Salerno to Cassino*
*Cassino to the Alps*

The European Theater of Operations
*Cross-Channel Attack*
*Breakout and Pursuit*
*The Lorraine Campaign*
*The Siegfried Line Campaign*
*The Ardennes: Battle of the Bulge*
*The Last Offensive*

    *Logistical Support of the Armies, Volume I*
    *Logistical Support of the Armies, Volume II*
The Middle East Theater
    *The Persian Corridor and Aid to Russia*
The China-Burma-India Theater
    *Stilwell's Mission to China*
    *Stilwell's Command Problems*
    *Time Runs Out in CBI*
The Technical Services
    *The Chemical Warfare Service: Organizing for War*
    *The Chemical Warfare Service: From Laboratory to Field*
    *The Chemical Warfare Service: Chemicals in Combat*
    *The Corps of Engineers: Troops and Equipment*
    *The Corps of Engineers: The War Against Japan*
    *The Corps of Engineers: The War Against Germany*
    *The Corps of Engineers: Military Construction in the United States*
    *The Medical Department: Hospitalization and Evacuation; Zone of Interior*
    *The Medical Department: Medical Service in the Mediterranean and Minor Theaters*
    *The Medical Department: Medical Service in the European Theater of Operations*
    *The Ordnance Department: Planning Munitions for War*
    *The Ordnance Department: Procurement and Supply*
    *The Ordnance Department: On Beachhead and Battlefront*
    *The Quartermaster Corps: Organization, Supply, and Services, Volume I*
    *The Quartermaster Corps: Organization, Supply, and Services, Volume II*
    *The Quartermaster Corps: Operations in the War Against Japan*
    *The Quartermaster Corps: Operations in the War Against Germany*
    *The Signal Corps: The Emergency*
    *The Signal Corps: The Test*
    *The Signal Corps: The Outcome*
    *The Transportation Corps: Responsibilities, Organization, and Operations*
    *The Transportation Corps: Movements, Training, and Supply*
    *The Transportation Corps: Operations Overseas*
Special Studies
    *Chronology: 1941–1945*
    *Military Relations Between the United States and Canada: 1939–1945*
    *Rearming the French*
    *Three Battles: Arnaville, Altuzzo, and Schmidt*
    *The Women's Army Corps*
    *Civil Affairs: Soldiers Become Governors*
    *Buying Aircraft: Materiel Procurement for the Army Air Forces*
    *The Employment of Negro Troops*
    *Manhattan: The U.S. Army and the Atomic Bomb*
Pictorial Record
    *The War Against Germany and Italy: Mediterranean and Adjacent Areas*
    *The War Against Germany: Europe and Adjacent Areas*
    *The War Against Japan*

# Index

A-36's: 120, 120n, 261, 342, 344, 346, 401, 403
Abbio Priolo: 165, 166
Abruzzi Mountains: 525, 529
Acate (Dirillo) River: 97, 99, 100, 101, 117, 118, 135, 135n, 142, 143, 164, 171, 190, 206, 208
Acate River valley: 155, 187
ACCOLADE: 436
*ACHSE,* Plan: 287-88, 291, 307, 473, 523
Acqualadrone: 414
Acquarone, Duke Pietro: 41, 42, 43, 264, 265, 266, 268, 281, 441 454, 466, 479, 480, 511, 547
Adrano: 235, 319, 327, 341, 357
Adriatic ports: 24
Adriatic Sea: 13, 45, 54
Aegean Islands: 12, 17, 32, 492, 514, 534
Aerial bombardment. *See* Air attacks, Allied; Air attacks, Axis.
Aerial navigation, Allied: 423-24
Aerial photographs: 99, 101, 493, 536
Aerial reconnaissance. *See* Air reconnaissance, Allied; Air reconnaissance, Axis.
Aerial resupply missions: 101, 344
AFHQ. *See* Allied Force Headquarters.
Africa. *See* North Africa.
Agira: 233, 319
Agrigento: 86, 125, 192, 194, 200, 202, 209, 224, 226-30, 235, 238, 418, 419
Air attacks, Allied: 23, 72, 110, 136, 197, 205, 240, 269, 296, 298, 299, 342n, 344, 346, 352, 379, 382, 385, 400, 401, 402, 438, 439, 447, 473, 477, 501
  against Frascati: 522-23
  on friendly forces: 195, 403
  on Messina Strait: 410, 411-12
  and Palermo advance: 320
  on Pantelleria: 70-72
  on Rome: 24-25, 250, 278, 279, 292, 442
  and Sicilian invasion: 54, 58-59, 83, 88, 106-07, 111
  in Troina battle: 339, 342
Air attacks, Axis: 89, 159, 174, 177, 318n, 362, 403, 518, 533
Air bases, Allied: 8, 12, 13, 14, 15, 25
Air forces, Allied: 157, 175-76, 177-78, 278, 320, 382. *See also* Air plan, Sicilian invasion.
  and air support failure: 421
  and evacuation of Sicily by Axis: 379, 380-81
Air losses, Allied: 177, 178, 179, 180, 181, 218, 423
Air losses, Axis: 46-47, 189, 189n, 240, 243

Air operations, Allied: 5, 6, 12, 14, 17, 59, 70, 261, 320, 378, 379, 380-81, 420. *See also* Air attacks, Allied; Air support, Allied; Airborne operations, Allied; Airdrops, Allied.
Air patrols, U.S.: 120n
Air plan, Sicilian invasion: 106-07, 421. *See also* Air operations, Allied.
Air power, Allied: 15, 21, 59, 106, 213, 320, 460-61
Air power, Axis: 32, 106. *See also* Air losses, Axis.
Air protection, Allied. *See* Air support, Allied.
Air raids. *See* Air attacks, Allied; Air attacks, Axis.
Air reconnaissance, Allied: 155, 325, 331
Air reconnaissance, Axis: 46, 110, 120, 473, 522, 536
Air support, Allied: 69, 106, 260, 261, 262, 320, 343, 421, 494, 506. *See also* Air attacks, Allied.
  for D-day landings: 119-20
  in Monte Cipolla action: 399, 401, 405
  for Seventh Army: 107, 421
Air Support Command, U.S., XII: 107, 320, 401, 402, 421
Airacobras (P-39's): 261
Airborne drops. *See* Airdrops, Allied.
Airborne operations, Allied. *See also* Air operations, Allied.
  in Italian mainland invasion: 477-78, 482, 483. *See also* GIANT II.
  in Sicilian Campaign: 269-270, 553. *See also* Airdrops, Allied.
    and Allied antiaircraft disaster: 175-84
    British missions: 115, 117, 218, 380
    and corridor to Sicily: 175-76
    D-day: 115, 117-19
    evaluation of: 156-57, 423-25
    FUSTIAN: 218
    tactical planning for: 88-89, 92-94, 101-02, 485-89, 498-99
Airborne operations, German: 204, 424
Airborne Training Center, Fifth Army: 424
Airborne troops, British: 92, 115, 117, 121, 380, 423.
  *See also* British Army units. Division, 1st Airborne.
Airborne units, U.S.: 478, 480, 498-99. *See also* Parachute Infantry units, U.S.; Paratroopers, U.S.
  Division, 82d: 91, 93, 94, 98, 102, 152n, 230,

Airborne units, U. S.—Continued
 Division, 82d—Continued
  231, 245, 249, 252, 305, 422, 424, 477, 505, 508, 509. *See also* Ridgway, Maj. Gen. Matthew B.
  in GIANT II: 489, 498
  importance of, in Sicily: 92
 Battalions
  80th Airborne Antiaircraft: 498, 499
  307th Airborne Engineer Battalion: 498
Aircraft, Allied: 73, 107, 117n, 147n, 175, 411n, 418. *See also* Air losses, Allied; *individual types of planes.*
 attack friendly forces: 195
 attacked by friendly antiaircraft: 175–84, 218, 423
Aircraft, Axis: 83, 166, 177n, 212, 320, 360, 403, 457, 513, 533. *See also* Air losses, Axis.
Aircraft carriers, U.S.: 69, 261
Airdrops, Allied: 207, 218, 380, 535. *See also* Airborne operations, Allied; GIANT II.
 and Allied antiaircraft disaster: 176, 177–78, 179, 182
 planning for: 88–89, 93–94
Airfields: 67, 69, 73, 107
 Italy: 47, 261, 439, 440, 457, 460, 468, 478, 483, 486, 486n, 494, 500, 502, 505, 522
  Centocelle: 486, 488, 498
  Cerveteri: 488, 489, 498
  Foggia: 437, 471
  Furbara: 488, 489
  and GIANT II: 485, 486, 488, 489
  Guidonia: 486, 488, 498
  Littoria: 486, 488, 498
  Magliano: 486
 Sicily: 52, 53, 53n, 54, 58, 59, 60, 61, 62, 63, 64, 66, 80, 83, 84, 89, 91, 96, 98, 107, 108, 135, 261, 320
  Biscari: 96, 98, 100, 141, 147, 206, 220
  Catania: 204, 216
  Comiso: 96, 98, 100, 141, 142, 156, 189, 189n, 320
  Gerbini: 216
  Licata: 99, 320
  Ponte Olivo: 98, 100, 101, 135, 147, 164, 165, 174n, 185, 187, 320
AK's: 105, 105n.
*ALARICH*, Plan: 50–51, 75, 213, 241, 282, 283, 284, 288, 291
Albania: 24, 32, 453, 491
Albermarles, British: 115
Alcamo: 253, 255
Alexander, General Sir Harold R. L. G: 10, 23, 55, 58, 59, 60, 61, 62, 64, 89, 91, 94, 108, 197, 200, 201, 201n, 206, 207, 209n, 222, 224, 231, 234–35, 235n, 248, 257, 304n, 319, 378, 379, 406, 412, 417, 420, 421, 474, 476, 477, 478, 484, 485, 489, 507, 549

Alexander, General—Continued
 directives: 209–10, 230, 234–35, 245–46, 303–04
 and Seventh Army: 209–11, 230, 235–36, 245–46, 304, 422–23
 on U.S. troops: 56, 210n, 211, 422
Alexander, Maj. Mark: 117
Alexandria: 52
Alfieri, Ambassador Dino: 242, 243, 286
Algiers: 56, 102, 108, 421, 437, 463, 509
Algiers Conference: 23–25, 61–62, 436
Alimena: 233, 301
Allen, Maj. Gen. Terry de la Mesa: 95, 99, 108, 136, 139, 158, 159, 165, 173–74, 174n, 185, 222, 223, 231, 249, 302, 311–12, 313, 320, 331, 333, 340, 342, 343, 346, 347, 348, 426
 and Nicosia attack: 314
 and Troina action: 336–37, 338, 339, 341
Allied Force Headquarters (AFHQ): 5, 8, 11, 22n, 55, 56, 66, 67, 68, 176, 183, 206, 258, 259–60, 262, 263, 274, 275, 278, 427, 429, 431, 436, 437, 440, 444, 449, 459, 480, 489, 494, 495, 496, 498, 502, 502n, 503, 504, 505, 508, 510, 512, 513, 516–17, 519, 520, 521, 532, 535, 540, 541, 546. *See also* Eisenhower, General Dwight D.; Planners, Allied, AFHQ.
Alpine passes: 370
Alps: 3, 12, 16, 30
Ambrosio, Generale d'Armata Vittorio: 36n, 38, 44, 45, 51, 78, 281, 282, 285, 287, 289, 293, 294, 296, 368, 451, 452, 458, 460, 462, 470, 471, 482, 484, 490, 491, 493, 494n, 497, 503, 506, 506n, 509, 512, 514, 516, 517, 524, 542, 549
 absence from Rome: 494, 495, 496
 and armistice negotiations: 441, 453, 454, 455, 464, 465, 466, 467, 479, 480, 481, 510, 511, 515
 and Axis command structure: 472–73
 as *Comando Supremo* chief: 35–36
 at Feltre conference: 242, 243, 244
 and German military aid to Italy: 47–49, 74, 74–75
 and German troop movements into Italy: 290, 291, 292, 372, 373
 and Mussolini: 41–42, 212, 214, 215, 240–41, 263, 264
 at Tarvis conference: 370
Ammunition, Italian: 81, 298, 480, 500
Ammunition supply, U.S.: 398, 399, 403, 486
Amphibious operations, Allied: 436, 491, 501
 Italian mainland: 535, 542. *See also* Salerno landings.
  against Naples, planned: 260, 261–63
  Axis speculation concerning: 493–94, 500
  scheduling of: 490
 Sicilian Campaign: 161n, 237, 380, 411, 412, 421, 553

# INDEX

Amphibious operations, Allied—Continued
  Sicilian Campaign—Continued
    air protection for: 119-20, 261, 262
    Axis anticipation of: 45, 64, 84, 86-87
    at Bivio Salica: 406, 407, 413-14, 415
    D-day: 120, 121, 123-46
    improvements and techniques in: 103-05
    in San Fratello action: 348, 349n, 352, 357, 360, 361-63, 366-67
    tactical planning for: 53-54, 58, 59, 60-63, 66, 88-89, 91-92, 96-100, 103-07, 135-36, 406, 408, 413-14
    Task Force Bernard: 388-97, 404-405
Amphibious truck. *See* Dukws.
Amphibious warfare: 104-05. *See also* Amphibious operations.
Anapo River: 91, 92
*Ancon:* 108, 177
Ancona: 470
*Andrea Doria:* 533
Andrus, Brig. Gen. Clift: 313, 331, 336, 339
Ankcorn, Col. Charles M.: 141, 142, 145, 190, 206, 208, 209, 219-20, 321, 415
Antiaircraft, Allied: 102, 131, 175-84, 185, 218, 423, 499
Antiaircraft defense, Axis: 47, 74, 76, 79, 82, 117, 117n, 263, 284, 375-76, 380-81, 412, 485, 486, 488-89
Anti-Fascists, Italian: 40, 42, 263, 264, 265
Antitank companies, U.S.: 160, 167, 188
Antitank defenses, Italian, on Sicily: 79
Antonescu, Ion: 40, 239
Anzio: 522, 552
Apennines: 213, 215, 368, 439, 442, 497, 512
Appian Way: 500
AP's: 105, 105n
Aquila: 536
ARCADIA Conference: 2
Arisio, Generale di Corpo d'Armata Mario: 84, 471, 534
Arezzo: 470
Armed Forces Command, Sicily: 76
Armistice, Italo-Allied: 25, 539. *See also* Surrender of Italy.
  announcement of: 447, 448, 459, 465, 467, 474, 475, 476, 479, 489, 490, 491, 492, 494, 495, 496, 499, 501, 503-04, 505-08, 508-09, 513, 515, 516-17, 519-20, 522, 523, 524
  British-American discussion of: 269, 271-74, 275-78
  Eisenhower's draft: 270-71, 276
  Italian discussion of: 465-68, 479-81
  negotiations: 451-65, 474-79
  orders and directives following: 514-15
  renunciation moves by Italy: 501-02, 506-07, 510-12
  signing. *See under* Long terms; Short terms.

Armistice, Italo-Allied—Continued
  terms. *See* Long terms; Short terms.
Armistice, Italo-German. *See* Capitulation; Truce.
Armistice control commission, Allied, proposed: 544, 545
Armored force, German: 169. *See also* Tanks, German.
Armored support, U.S.: 129, 135, 146, 153, 158, 159, 163, 174n, 418. *See also* Tank units, U.S.; Tanks, U.S.
Armored units, U.S.: 155, 226, 226n, 363, 478, 480. *See also* Combat Commands; Tank units.
  Division, 1st Armored: 96
  Division, 2d Armored: 94, 97-98, 158, 174n, 230, 231, 245, 253, 254, 255, 305, 306n, 418, 422. *See also* Combat Commands.
    characterized: 95-96
    landing of: 157-58
    and Palermo strike: 252
  Regiment, 67th Armored: 159, 174n
Army, U.S.
  and Air Forces: 106
  infantryman's performance: 417-18
Army, Fifth, U.S.: 15, 67, 68, 262, 482, 498, 505, 552
Army, Seventh, U.S.: 89, 92, 101, 102, 108, 135, 176, 185-201, 205, 206, 230-36, 275, 304, 304n, 308, 309, 320, 380, 390, 401, 406, 408, 414, 417n, 422. *See also* Patton, General George S., Jr.
  Agrigento as objective of: 224, 226
  and air support: 107, 421
  and Allied antiaircraft attack disaster: 176-82
  Axis counterattack on. *See* Counterattacks, Axis.
  composition of: 57, 94-96
  and Eighth Army: 89, 91, 206-07, 209-11, 234-36, 388-89, 413-14
  landings of: 123-46, 158-62
  and Palermo advance: 244-54
  performance of: 206, 417-19
  and Messina peninsula drive: 304, 319, 388-89, 417, 420
  tactical plans for: 89, 91, 96-100, 209-10, 245-46, 420
Army Ground Forces: 424. *See also* Ground forces, Allied.
Army Groups, Allied
  15: 56, 89, 119, 195, 210, 319
  18: 56
Arnold, Lt. Gen. Henry H.: 3
Arsoli: 524
Artillery superiority, Allied: 73
Artillery support, Axis: 127, 128, 131, 133, 137, 139, 159, 188, 196, 198, 199, 228, 230, 255, 300, 301-02, 313, 317, 318, 321, 325, 333, 337, 338, 339, 340, 343, 353, 402, 516

Artillery support, U.S.: 129, 135, 146, 153, 158, 159, 160, 163, 167n, 168, 170, 187, 199, 222, 224, 226–27, 230, 232, 302n, 313, 313n, 317, 317n, 321, 322, 330, 337, 339, 346, 348, 352, 353. *See also* Field artillery units.
   evaluated: 418
   at Monte Cipolla: 389, 393–94, 396, 397, 399, 400
   in Troina battle: 331, 333, 334, 340, 342
Arzew: 105, 493
Assault, Allied. *See* Amphibious operations.
Assault plans: 125, 135–36. *See also* Tactical planning, Allied; Tactical planning, Axis.
Assoro: 248
Athens: 514
Atlantic Wall: 76
Augusta: 54, 58, 61, 89, 91, 92, 111, 123, 163, 191, 240. *See also Naval Base Augusta-Syracuse.*
Austrians: 533
AVALANCHE. *See* Naples; Salerno; Salerno landings.
Avola: 92
Axis. *See* Feltre conference; Italo-German alliance; Strategic planning, Axis; Tactical planning, Axis.

B–17's: 376, 379, 411, 412
B–24's: 376
B–25's: 412
B–26's: 412
Baade, Col. Ernst Guenther: 82, 236, 375–76, 381
Badoglio, Mario: 299
Badoglio, Maresciallo d'Italia Pietro: 29, 31n, 268, 271, 273, 276, 281n, 291, 293, 295, 295n, 306, 371, 373, 440, 441, 445, 449, 454, 455, 458, 459, 460, 462, 465–66, 468, 470, 473, 475, 476, 483n, 494, 495, 496, 499, 504, 505, 514, 515n, 519, 520, 522, 524, 525, 528
   and American mission to Rome: 501–02
   and armistice negotiations: 443, 444, 447, 448, 453, 454, 455, 466, 467–68, 483, 484, 506–07, 508, 510, 511, 512–13, 515, 516–17, 543, 546, 548–49
   described by Mason-MacFarlane: 542
   and Eisenhower: 535, 540, 541, 543, 545, 546, 549–51
   and evacuation of Rome: 516, 517, 528
   and Germany: 284–85, 547, 548, 551, 553
   and GIANT II: 502, 503
   government of: 264–65, 266–67, 272, 275, 278, 281, 283, 296–99, 368, 369, 453, 469, 472, 482, 483, 484, 485, 490, 491, 493, 503, 506, 507, 508, 535, 536, 540, 541, 542, 543, 544, 547, 548, 550. *See also* Armistice, Italo-Allied.
   and Hitler: 283, 286, 287, 292, 294–95, 470, 497

Badoglio, Maresciallo d'Italia Pietro—Continued
   ineffectualness of: 464, 512–13, 515, 527
   at Malta conference: 549–51
   and Mussolini: 43, 282
   reassurances to Germans: 284–85
Bagni Acque Albule: 526
Bailey's Beach: 141, 144
Balearic Islands: 46
Balkans: 4, 6, 7, 8, 9, 12, 14, 15, 16, 21, 23, 24, 27, 29, 32, 34, 35, 38, 45, 46, 47, 49, 65, 213, 259, 261, 271, 298, 370, 436, 437, 438, 439, 447, 451, 452, 453, 457, 463, 472, 473, 491, 492, 514, 535
Barbieri, Generale di Corpo d'Armata Alberto: 289, 528
Barcellona: 408, 413
Bardonecchia: 442
BARCLAY, Plan: 65
Bari: 16
*Barnett:* 177
BARRACUDA: 448
Barrafranca: 198, 231–32, 233
Barrage balloons, Allied: 110
Bastianini, Giuseppe: 39, 41, 239, 242, 243
Battleships, Allied: 89
Battleships, Italian. *See* Italian Fleet.
Bauer, Mrs. Magna: 170n
Bay of Naples: 261
BAYTOWN: 260, 440, 448, 482, 483, 490, 520
Bazookas: 137, 137n, 167, 171, 172, 188, 396
Beach parties: 160, 393. *See also* Shore parties.
Beaches, landing. *See also* Beachheads.
   Salerno: 262, 482, 499, 505
   Sicilian: 97, 104–05, 161n, 169, 177, 256. *See also* Blue Beach; Blue Beach 2; Green Beach; Green Beach 2; Red Beach; Red Beach 2; Yellow Beach; Yellow Beach 2.
      closing of: 159, 161
      at Monte Cipolla: 393
      quality of: 99, 141–42, 144–45
Beachheads, Allied: 123, 163, 202, 211. *See also* Beaches, landing.
   in Italy, 552
   Monte Cipolla: 393, 397, 398, 400, 402
   Seventh Army (Sicily): 99, 206
      defined: 96–97
      securing: 185–200
      1st Division: 164, 173
*Beatty:* 168, 168n, 179
Belice River: 245, 252
Bergamini, Ammiraglio Carlo: 533
Bergamo, Duke of. *See* Genova, Generale di Corpo d'Armata Adalberto di Savoia.
Bergengruen, Col. Hellmut: 157
Bergolo, Generale di Divisione Conte Carlo Calvi di: 519, 525, 526, 527, 530n, 531, 532

# INDEX

Berio, Alberto: 298, 368, 369, 374, 441, 443, 444, 552
Bernard, Lt. Col. Lyle A.: 352, 360, 363, 388n, 399, 402, 403–04. *See also* Task Force Bernard.
Bertsch, Lt. Col. William H., Jr.: 499, 508, 509
Bianco: 344
Biazzo Ridge: 169, 172, 173, 175, 189, 418
Billings, Lt. Col. William H.: 131
Biscari: 100, 142, 143, 149, 154, 168, 169, 189, 208, 217, 419
*Biscayne:* 108, 123, 133
Bivicre Pond: 117, 136, 177
Bivio Gigliotto: 222, 223
Bivio Salica: 413, 414, 415
Bizerte: 102, 105, 108, 498, 505, 506, 507, 508, 522, 533
Black-market operations: 79
Bloody Ridge: 321, 353, 418. *See also* Santo Stefano.
Blue Beach: 125, 133, 136, 158, 159
Blue Beach 2: 145–46, 161
Blue Line: 98
Board, 1st Lt. Oliver P.: 133n
*Boise:* 139, 139n, 150n, 177, 185
Bologna: 288, 451, 533
Bologna conference: 452–53
Bolzano: 289, 290, 293, 442, 533
Bomber groups, German: 214, 243
Bombers, Allied: 376
  heavy: 376, 379, 381
  light: 320, 376
  medium: 376
Bombers, British. *See* Wellington bombers.
Bombers, U.S.: 107, 250. *See also* Aircraft, Allied; Air attacks, Allied; B–17's; B–24's; B–25's; B–26's.
Bompietro: 302, 303
Bond, Lt. Col. Van H.: 333, 334
Bonin, Col. Bogislaw von: 374
Bonomi, Ivanoe: 268, 531
  and anti-Fascist parties: 42
  and Mussolini's overthrow: 42, 43, 264, 265
Bottai, Giuseppe: 40
Bowen, Col. John W.: 136, 153, 179, 313, 314, 336, 338, 339, 340, 341, 343
Bowman, Maj. C. C.: 180
Bradley, Lt. Gen. Omar N.: 101, 108, 178–79, 189–90, 206, 231, 235, 304, 305, 311, 314, 316, 318, 323, 331, 336, 342, 343, 349, 361, 388, 389, 390, 406, 415, 422
  career of: 94
  and Enna: 246, 248, 249
  and Highway 124: 210, 222, 223
  and logistical problems: 103
  and Messina drive: 319–20, 413–14
  and Patton slapping incidents: 428, 429

Brady, Lt. Col. Brookner W.: 125
Brenner Pass: 50, 289, 290, 298, 370, 371, 372, 373, 442, 453, 460, 469, 472, 533
Brenner railway line: 290
Brest-Litovsk: 34
Briatore, Maj. Alberto: 494, 494n
Bridgeheads: 253, 341, 352
Bridges: 252, 253, 301, 316, 317, 318–19, 385. *See also* Ponton causeways.
  Dirillo: 101
  Lentini: 207, 218
  Palma River: 193
  Ponte Grande: 91, 92, 117
  Primosole: 207, 218
  Rosmarino River: 362
  swing, over Tiber: 486
BRIMSTONE: 4, 6n, 258. *See also* Sardinia.
  canceled: 260
  debated: 5–6, 7, 8, 10
  plans for: 67, 260
Brindisi: 481, 505, 532
  Allied-Italian discussions at: 545–49
  Mason-MacFarlane mission to: 540–43
British Air Force. *See* Desert Air Force; Royal Air Force.
British Army units:
  Army, Eighth: 46, 57, 60, 92, 98, 110, 117, 141, 197, 200, 201n, 224, 246, 248, 259, 275, 304, 312n, 319, 380, 387, 417, 417n, 421, 422, 437, 482, 483, 505, 522, 543, 552
    and Catania drive: 218–19
    D-day landings of: 120–23
    and Messina drive: 234–35, 304, 319, 388, 389, 414, 416, 420
    and Seventh Army: 89, 91, 206–07, 209–11, 234–36, 388–89, 413–14
    tactical planning for: 58, 89, 91
  Army, Twelfth: 57
  Corps, 5: 68, 258, 260
  Corps, 10: 57, 68, 258, 260
  Corps, 13: 57, 91, 92, 123, 191, 207, 216, 248, 304, 319, 374, 483
  Corps, 30: 57, 91, 123, 190–91, 207, 219, 220, 224, 235, 244–45, 248, 249, 302, 304, 311, 345
  Division, 1st Airborne: 91, 93, 108, 505
  Division, 1st Infantry: 70, 72
  Division, 5th Infantry: 91, 92, 121, 123, 248
  Division, 46th Infantry: 259, 260
  Division, 50th Infantry: 91, 92, 191, 219, 248, 357, 412
  Division, 51st Highland Infantry: 91–92, 123, 190, 207, 208, 209, 220, 224
  Division, 78th Infantry: 92, 248, 259, 260, 304, 319, 341, 357, 374, 382, 385, 386, 387, 406, 412, 413
  Brigades
    1st Airlanding: 91, 218
    4th Armored: 414

British Army units—Continued
  Brigades—Continued
    23d Armored: 207, 208, 224
    231st Independent: 91, 123
British Broadcasting Corporation: 389, 490, 496, 503-04, 504n
British Chiefs of Staff: 2, 19, 436, 449
  at Casablanca: 8-10
  and global war strategy: 6-7
  on Naples attack: 262
  at QUADRANT Conference: 438-40
  at TRIDENT Conference: 20-23
British Defense Committee: 274
British Foreign Office: 273, 276
British Government: 296-99, 445-46, 462. *See also* Churchill, Winston S.
British Joint Planners: 4. *See also* Planners, British.
British Joint Staff Mission: 277
British Middle East Command: 436
British Navy. *See* Naval Task Force, Eastern; Inshore Squadron.
British War Cabinet: 12, 276, 277, 279, 544
Brolo: 396, 400, 401, 403, 418, 419, 426. *See also* Monte Cipolla; Naso ridge.
  Allied assault on: 401
  German defense of: 393, 396-97, 398
  landings. *See* Monte Cipolla, amphibious end run at.
Brolo River: 394, 396, 398, 400, 402, 403, 408
Bronte: 374
Brooke, Field Marshal Sir Alan: 8, 10, 21, 22, 23, 436, 439
*Brooklyn*: 131, 131n
Browning, Maj. Gen. F. A. M.: 88, 175, 176
*Buck*: 131, 131n
Bulgaria: 40, 44
Burma: 258
Butcher, Comdr. Harry C.: 11n
Butera: 169, 170, 220
BUTTRESS: 16, 67, 68, 258, 260, 262, 448

C-47's: 101-02, 115, 178, 183n, 488
*Cabo de Bueno Esperanza*: 445
Cadorna, General: 529
*Caio Duilo*: 533
Cairo, Egypt: 61
Calabria: 53, 67, 68, 76, 110, 203, 214, 215, 244, 259, 260, 261, 262, 263, 282, 368, 375, 378, 413, 414, 416, 452, 469, 471, 473, 522. *See also* BAYTOWN.
Calboli, Marchese Giacomo Paulucci di: 239
Caltagirone: 86, 98, 136, 148, 172, 173, 202, 203, 206, 207, 219, 222, 223, 224
Caltanissetta: 111, 192, 197, 200, 226, 231, 233, 246
*Calvert*: 142, 143
Campbell, Sir Ronald Hugh: 297, 298, 442, 444, 445, 446, 449, 455, 458n, 459, 461, 462

Campo Imperatore: 536
Campobello: 79, 98, 99, 125, 155, 191, 192, 195, 196, 196n, 197
Campofelice: 246, 300, 318
Canadian units: 91, 92, 100, 163, 189, 248, 301, 319, 331, 342n
  Division, 1st: 91, 123, 156, 190, 206, 207, 224, 231, 233, 234, 248, 300, 319
  in Troina action: 341, 343
Canaris, Admiral Wilhelm: 287
Canicattì: 192, 194, 195, 196, 197, 199, 202, 206, 226
Cannon, Maj. Gen. John K.: 474, 485
Cannon companies, U. S.
  15th Infantry: 195
  16th Infantry: 160, 170-71, 188
  26th Infantry: 166
  179th Infantry: 208
Cape Bon: 66, 107
Cape Calavà: 309, 408
Cape d'Alì: 414
Cape Orlando: 345, 352, 401, 402, 403
Cape Passero: 117, 218
Capitulation, Italian: 530-32, 533-34, 539. *See also* Armistice; Surrender.
Capizzi: 315, 330
Caprara. *See* Palazzo Caprara.
*Carabinieri*. *See* Italian Army units, Carabinieri.
Carboni, General di Corpo d'Armata Giacomo: 36, 41, 266-67, 289, 466, 489, 496, 500n, 503, 504, 515, 516, 520, 526
  and American mission to Rome: 500, 501, 502
  and armistice negotiations: 454, 455, 467, 479, 480, 494, 494n, 511, 512
  and capitulation to Germans: 527, 530, 531-32
  and Castellano: 454, 467n, 479
  and Caviglia: 529
  and evacuation of Rome: 517, 518, 519, 524, 525, 527, 528
  and GIANT II: 494, 495
Cargo vessels, Allied: 262
Caronie Mountains: 53, 97, 309, 348, 352
Carriers, British: 262, 269
*Carroll*: 145
Carsoli: 518, 524
Casa Biazzo: 169
Casa del Priolo: 150, 165, 168, 185-89
Casa San Silvestro: 196, 197
Casablanca Conference: 19, 52, 53, 94, 417, 420
  strategic planning at: 1-3, 7-11
  and unconditional surrender formula: 11-12
Casati, Alessandro: 265, 531
Casazza crossroads: 414-15
Cassibile: 121, 319, 482, 483, 484, 498, 505
Cassibile conference: 474-79, 479-80, 492
Cassino: 552
Castel Judica: 223-24
Castel San Angelo: 131

# INDEX

Castelbuono: 316
Castellammare del Golfo: 255
Castellano, Generale di Brigata Giuseppe: 36, 264, 266, 296, 297, 297n, 368, 373, 446n, 451, 455n, 465, 483n, 493, 494, 496, 497, 500n, 501, 503, 504, 511, 516, 519, 520, 552
   and armistice: 465–68, 474, 475, 476, 477, 478, 479, 480, 482, 483, 484, 485, 505–06, 506–07, 540–41
   and Carboni: 454, 467n, 479
   *coup d'etat* plot of: 41, 42
   and Italian mainland invasion: 489, 490
   and military collaboration with Allies: 459–60, 485–86, 488, 489, 490–91, 495
   peace mission of: 440n, 440–42, 444–46, 447, 454, 455–61, 462, 463
   and Zanussi: 455, 462, 463, 474, 478–79
Castelluccio, Il: 185
Castelvetrano: 235, 252, 253
Castle Hill: 185
Casualties, Allied
   British: 417, 552
   U.S.: 135, 137, 144, 146, 159, 172, 181–82, 182n, 188–89, 193–94, 208, 255, 314, 321, 323, 342, 343–44, 357, 358, 398, 403, 404, 406, 415, 417, 419, 552
Casualties, Axis
   German: 71, 200, 223, 255, 341, 347, 385, 398, 417
   Italian: 127, 128, 152, 170, 197, 200, 216, 223, 228, 341, 385, 398, 417
Catania: 54, 58, 61, 63, 64, 86, 89, 91, 92, 111, 191, 202, 209, 210, 211, 214, 215, 218, 223, 233, 235, 248, 260, 307, 308, 319, 357, 380, 420, 422, 437
Catania plain; 53, 164, 191, 207, 216, 304
Cattaro: 491
Causeways. *See* Ponton causeways.
Cavallero, Generale d'Armata Ugo: 29, 30n, 33, 34, 35, 36, 472
Caviglia, Maresciallo d'Italia Enrico: 264, 530, 531, 532
   and capitulation to Germans: 531
   and Carboni: 529
   as head of government: 527–29, 531
Cefalù: 246, 302, 305
Centuripe: 341
Cephalonia: 542
Cerami: 320, 325, 327, 328, 329, 331
Cerami River: 328
Cesarò: 327, 343, 345, 346, 357, 374, 382
Chemical battalions, motorized, U.S.: 96
CHESTNUT missions: 380, 380n
Chetniks: 37
Chiaramonte Gulfi: 190
Chiefs of Staff. *See* British Chiefs of Staff; Combined Chiefs of Staff; Joint Chiefs of Staff, U.S.
Chierici, Renzo: 42

China-Burma-India Theater: 261
Chirieleison, Generale di Divisione Domenico: 164, 169
Christian Democrats: 42
Churchill, Winston S.: 1, 6, 10, 11, 12, 16n, 258, 269, 275, 279, 287, 440, 440n, 535, 540, 547, 552
   at Algiers Conference: 23–24
   on Badoglio government: 544–45
   and Italian armistice: 271–73, 276, 277, 442–43, 444, 446–47, 544, 545, 546
   strategic views of: 4, 23–24, 67, 436, 437
   at TRIDENT Conference: 19–21
Ciano, Count Galeazzo: 34, 35, 36, 39, 40, 41, 42, 43, 264, 267, 268, 283, 297
Ciano Papers: 34n
Civil Affairs Division: 26, 26n
Civil war, Italian, possibilities of: 25, 544
Civilian ministers, Italian: 517, 528
Civilians. *See also* Morale.
   German: 514
   Italian: 505, 528, 536
      and armistice: 271, 272, 513
      Eisenhower's peace broadcast to: 275
      and Rome battle: 528–30
   Sicilian: 77, 193, 194, 208, 254, 255, 331, 333, 347
Civitavecchia: 468, 522
Clark, Lt. Gen. Mark W.: 8, 15, 55, 67, 260, 269
Cochrane, Lt. Col. Clarence B.: 143, 168, 317
Codes, Allied: 504n. *See also* Radio communication, Italo-Allied, secret.
   British diplomatic: 296
   for GIANT II: 499–500, 502
Colle del Contrasto: 315
*Comando Supremo*: 31, 32, 33, 39, 45, 46, 47, 49, 50, 51, 71, 73–74, 75, 76, 77, 78, 82, 110, 163, 212, 214, 216, 242, 242n, 266, 281, 282, 286, 289, 290, 346, 368, 369, 371, 372, 373, 375, 378, 471, 472, 479, 483, 491, 492, 493, 495, 514, 515, 525, 528. *See also* Ambrosio; Generale d'Armata Vittorio; Italian High Command.
   under Ambrosio: 35–36
   growth and importance of: 29–30
   liaison with Germans: 78
   and Mussolini's overthrow: 263
   and *Promemoria I*: 491
   and Sicily's defeat: 240, 241
   and troop movements: 288
Combat commands, U.S.
   A, 2d Armored Division: 98, 99, 108, 125, 192, 194, 196, 199, 200, 253, 254
      attacked by friendly planes: 195
      and Canicattì capture: 199
      composition of: 194n
      Naro captured by: 194
   B, 2d Armored Division: 158, 171, 254

Combat loaders, U.S.: 258
Combined Chiefs of Staff: 1, 10–11, 12, 15, 19, 21, 25, 27, 53, 58, 63, 66, 67, 88, 258, 259, 260, 261–62, 271, 272, 273, 277, 278, 280, 417, 420, 436, 437, 449, 462, 505, 506, 520, 543
   and Italian armistice: 26, 507–08
   and Naples assault planning: 269–70
   organization and membership of: 2, 2n
   at QUADRANT Conference: 439, 440
   and Quebec Memorandum: 447–48
   and resources for Eisenhower: 258–59
   and Sicilian Campaign preparations: 52, 54–56
   at TRIDENT Conference: 19–23
Combined Civil Affairs Committee: 26, 26n, 273, 274, 277, 448
Comiso: 100, 141, 142, 164, 217, 418
Command, Allied: 82, 502
   air: 107, 320
   for Sicilian Campaign: 10–11, 54–55, 56, 420–21
Command, Axis: 307n, 453, 469
   air: 32–33, 241
   chain of: 27–28, 483–84
   German-Italian relationship in: 32–34, 48–49, 50, 78–79, 307, 308–09, 369, 371, 471
   in Sicily: 82, 211–12, 378
   structure, OKW proposal: 472–73
   unification plan: 241–42
Command, German: 27, 33–34, 236, 283, 298, 523. *See also* Command, Axis; Commander in Chief South; *Oberkommando des Heeres; Oberkommando der Kriegsmarine; Oberkommando der Luftwaffe; Oberkommando der Wehrmacht.*
Command, Italian: 29–30, 76, 78, 214, 530. *See also Comando Supremo;* Command, Axis; Italian High Command.
Command, U.S. Air Force. *See* Air Support Command, XII.
*Commandant Messina Strait:* 82
Commander in Chief South: 33, 33n. *See also* Kesselring, Feldmarschall Albert.
Commander in Chief West. *See* Rundstedt, Generalfeldmarschall Gerd von.
Commandos: 91, 207, 218, 260, 380, 416, 417. *See also* Ranger Battalions, U.S.
Committee of National Liberation: 530, 531
Communications, Allied, 175–84. *See also* Codes; Radio communication, Italo-Allied.
Communications, German: 154, 163, 341, 447, 460. *See also* Telephone communications, German.
Communications, Italian. *See* Radio communication, Italo-Allied; Signal communications, Italian; Telephone communications, Italian.
Communications, U.S.: 206, 340. *See also* Radio communication, U.S.
Communist party, Italian: 42
"Comprehensive Instrument." *See* Long terms.

Coningham, Air Vice Marshal Sir Arthur: 379, 380, 381
Conolly, Rear Adm. Richard L.: 100, 105, 108, 123, 125, 131, 133
Conrath, General der Fallschirm-truppen Paul: 81, 148n, 165–66, 168, 169, 170, 171, 172, 173n, 187, 204, 216, 387, 412
   and Axis counterattack in Sicily: 148–49, 153–54, 164, 172, 173
   Kesselring's criticism of: 157
   withdrawals of: 190, 205, 223–24
Convoys, Allied: 88, 106, 108, 110, 476, 482, 493, 498, 503, 509, 533
Convoys, U.S.: 258
Cookson, Col. Forrest E.: 141, 143
Corleone: 235
Corley, Lt. Col. John T.: 165
Corps, U.S.
   Provisional: 230, 245, 249, 250, 255, 300, 305
   I Armored: 56, 57, 94
   II: 56, 57, 60, 99, 100, 103, 103n, 135, 144, 206, 210, 222, 230, 244, 245, 246, 249, 300, 304, 305, 309, 311, 319, 325, 348, 349, 380, 421, 429
      boundaries of: 244, 245
      front: 220, 222
      tactical plans for: 97, 98, 99
   VI: 57
Corregidor: 70
Corsica: 8, 12, 14, 16, 17, 18, 19, 22n, 23, 24, 65, 67, 203, 258, 284, 438, 459, 460, 463, 471, 473, 481, 493, 535, 541, 543, 551. *See also* FIREBRAND.
Cosenza: 372
Counterattacks, Axis: 147–50, 153–54, 163–73, 196, 197–98, 202, 204, 211, 212, 220, 222, 307, 308, 314, 317, 324, 339, 340–41, 342, 344, 363, 366
Counterespionage service, Italian: 368
Courten, De, Ammiraglio di Squadra Raffaele: 511, 517, 533, 549
Cover plans. *See* BARCLAY, Plan; MINCEMEAT.
Craig, 1st Lt. Robert: 196n
Crandall, Maj. Robert W.: 348
Crawford, Lt. Col. Joseph: 152, 165, 187
Crawley, Lt. Col. Marshall L., Jr.: 194
Crete: 9, 12, 424, 491
Croatia: 32, 37, 445
Cross-Channel invasion (OVERLORD): 1, 4, 5, 8, 10, 14, 17, 18, 20, 21, 46, 88, 258, 262, 437, 438, 439, 512
   American position on: 3, 435–36, 437, 438, 439
   British position on: 437, 439
   date set: 22
   and Mediterranean operations, debated: 3, 6, 7, 11, 20–22, 435–36, 439–40
   scale of: 15
   strength for: 8–9

# INDEX

Cross-Channel invasion—Continued
  TRIDENT Conference, discussion of: 20, 21
Crotone: 16, 67
Crown council: 297
Cruisers, Allied: 72, 100, 147n, 320, 419n, 505
Cruisers, Italian. *See* Italian Fleet.
Cummings, 1st Lt. Julian W.: 133n
Cunningham, Admiral Sir Andrew B.: 10–11, 23, 55, 61, 62, 63, 91, 107n, 182–83, 183n, 320, 378, 379, 420, 421, 507, 546, 549
Currier, Col. D. C.: 427, 428, 429
Cyprus: 6

D-day, Sicilian invasion: 57. *See also* Amphibious operations, Sicilian Campaign, scheduling invasion.
D'Ajeta, Marchese Blasco Lanza: 297, 297n, 299n, 368, 370, 374, 441, 442, 444, 461, 552
Dalmatia: 32, 445, 551
Dammer, Maj. Herman W.: 228
Daniel, Lt. Col. Darrell M.: 301, 313
Danube area: 239, 436
Darby, Lt. Col. William O.: 96, 136, 152, 169, 185, 185n, 190, 252, 253, 255
Davidson, Rear Adm. Lyal A.: 320, 349, 352, 399, 401, 402, 403
Deann, Captain: 474
Decarli, Col. Paolo: 494
Defeatism, Italian: 39, 44, 73, 283
Defenses, Axis. *See also* Fortifications, Axis; Sicily, Axis defenses on.
  on Pantelleria: 69–70
  on Sicily: 54, 75–76, 77, 79–80, 83–87, 126–27, 163, 217
Defilades: 195, 196, 328
Delia: 192, 197, 199, 200
Demolition, Axis: 110, 289, 348, 382, 387, 406, 410, 418, 497
Demolition, U.S.: 129
Dempsey, Lt. Gen. Miles C.: 61
Denholm, Lt. Col. Charles L.: 152, 188
Denno, Capt. Bryce F.: 187–88
DeRohan, Col. Frederick J.: 343
Desert Air Force, British: 107–08, 412, 421
Destroyers, Allied: 505
Destroyers, Italian: 533
Destroyers, U.S.: 72, 100, 129, 131, 168n, 177, 258, 318, 320, 393, 419n
Diary of the Office of the Commander in Chief: 11n
Dick, Commodore Royer: 474, 485, 486, 506n
Dieppe raid: 95
Dill, Field Marshal Sir John: 2n, 5, 59, 88, 89
Directives, Allied
  Alexander's: 209–10, 230, 234–35, 245–46, 303–04
  Roosevelt's, on Italy: 545, 548

Directives, Italian. *See Memoria 44;* Orders, Italian; *Promemoria 1; Promemoria 2.*
Dirillo River. *See* Acate River.
Dittaino River: 223, 341
Divisions, Allied: 8–9, 54, 57. *See also* Airborne units, U.S.; Armored units, U.S.; British Army units; Infantry Divisions, U.S.
Divisions, Axis: 53, 54. *See also* German Army units; Italian Army units.
Dodecanese islands: 9, 15–16, 18, 64, 436, 542
Doenitz, Grossadmiral Karl: 27
Doleman, Lt. Col. Edgar C.: 359, 360, 361
Don River: 35
Donnafugata: 156
Doolittle, Maj. Gen. James: 99, 379
Drop zones (Sicily): 88, 93, 101, 117–19, 157, 177, 179, 182, 218
Dukws: 89, 104, 160, 170, 363, 393, 396, 398, 403, 408
Durazzo: 491
Duvall, Maj. Everett W.: 127, 229

E-boats, Axis: 70
Eagles, Brig. Gen. William W.: 254, 360, 361, 416, 417
East, Sgt. Jesse E., Jr.: 144n
Eastern Front, Axis: 213
Ecole Normale: 56
Eddy, Maj. Gen. Manton S.: 96, 305–06, 333, 336, 347, 385
Eden, Anthony: 19, 269, 276, 437, 443, 446, 447, 448, 449
Eisenhower, General Dwight D.: 5, 11n, 15, 17, 22, 25, 52, 54, 55, 56, 60, 62, 66, 67, 68, 88, 94, 96, 108, 176, 182, 206, 206n, 236, 261, 262, 269, 304n, 421, 423, 427, 436, 437, 442, 444, 446, 455, 456, 457, 458, 459, 476, 477, 478, 489, 494, 499, 501, 502, 503, 506n, 509, 515, 516, 547, 548. *See also* Allied Force Headquarters.
  on airborne divisions: 425
  at Algiers Conference: 23, 24
  broadcasts to Italians: 270, 275, 278, 508, 512
  and command structure: 10–11, 420
  and Italian armistice: 270–71, 272, 273, 274, 275–77, 447, 448, 449, 450, 462, 463, 464–65, 475, 484, 504, 505, 506, 507, 508, 510–11, 520, 535, 541–42, 543–44, 545, 546, 549–50
  on Italy's weaknesses: 540–41
  at Malta conference: 549–50, 551
  and Mason-MacFarlane mission: 540, 541
  and Pantelleria question: 69–70
  and Patton slapping incidents: 429, 430, 431
  and strategic planning: 3, 14, 258, 259, 260
El 'Alamein: 1, 35
Elba: 471
Elections, Italian: 544, 546, 549

Elena, Queen of Italy: 517
Enfilade: 317, 328, 353
Enfilading fire: 340, 359, 360
Engineer support, U.S.: 128, 131, 136, 154, 165, 168, 169, 253, 255, 301
  excellence of: 418–19
  in Gela fighting: 152
Engineer units, U.S.: 352, 393, 394, 396, 413. *See also* Shore parties.
  Brigade, 1st Special: 103, 256
  Regiments
    20th Combat: 256
    39th: 137
    540th Shore: 256
  Battalions
    10th: 408
    307th Airborne: 175
Engineers, German: 362–63, 406
England. *See* Great Britain.
English Channel: 6. *See also* Cross-Channel invasion.
Enna: 63, 97, 110, 120, 164, 172, 191, 197, 200, 205, 207, 211, 224, 244, 248, 249, 300, 301, 302, 422
Enna loop: 231, 233, 234, 235, 244, 246, 248
Ens, Col. Karl: 198, 336, 337, 339
Equipment, Allied: 73, 131, 159, 174, 486, 553
Equipment, Axis: 73, 81, 377, 410, 474. *See also* Matériel, Axis.
Escort carriers, Allied: 16, 262, 269
Escort craft, U.S.: 320
Etna line: 315, 319, 324, 327, 342, 352
Etter, Maj. Charles B.: 428
Evacuation of Rome, Italian: 516–19, 527–28
Evacuation of Sicily, Axis: 324, 380, 382, 385, 416n, 452
  Allied failure to stop: 378–79, 409–12, 414, 421. *See also* Monte Cipollo.
  and Italians: 410, 416
  operations for: 375–78, 409–10, 414–15
  plans and debate: 306–07, 368, 369, 374–75
  schedule for: 410, 412, 413, 413n, 416, 469

Faldella, General Emilio: 77–78, 78n, 170n
Farello: 98
Farinacci, Roberto: 40, 464
Fascist Grand Council: 44, 267–68, 283, 286, 460
Fascist Militia: 76, 445
Fascist Party, Italian: 268, 281, 283, 285. *See also* Fascist Grand Council.
Fascist Republican Party: 543, 544, 548
Fascists, Italian: 28, 30, 39, 50, 445
  Badoglio government threatened by: 472
  and Mussolini's overthrow: 42, 263–64
  and surrender movement: 40
Favara: 226, 227
Favarotta: 191, 195

Federzoni, Luigi: 40, 268
Feistritz pass: 472
Feltre conference: 242–44, 263, 282
Ferry barges, German: 376, 377
Ferrying service, German: 82, 82n, 237
  and evacuation of Sicily: 306, 375, 376–77, 378, 409–10, 411
  ferry barges: 376, 377
Ferrying service, Italian: 53–54, 237, 378, 410
Feurstein, General der Gebirgstruppen Valentin: 284, 290, 372, 373
Ficarra: 396, 398
Ficuzza River: 208
Field artillery units, U.S.: 393–94, 399. *See also* Artillery support, U.S.
  Group, 5th Armored: 129n
  Regiment, 77th: 227
  Battalions: 418
    5th: 160, 166, 188, 188n
    7th: 150, 150n, 160, 167, 167n, 187, 188, 188n, 313n, 333n
    9th: 195, 195n, 416
    10th: 129, 227
    14th Armored: 199, 199n
    26th: 255
    32d: 170, 188, 188n
    33d: 160, 166, 185, 313n
    34th: 255, 305
    37th Parachute: 179, 180
    39th: 195, 195n, 196
    58th Armored: 352, 402, 403–04
    62d Armored: 194n, 199, 199n
    78th Armored: 174n
    158th: 181n, 220
    160th: 208
    171st: 154, 160, 160n, 165, 168, 181n, 317n
    189th: 173, 317n
    319th Glider: 499
    376th Parachute: 175, 255
Fighter plane factories, German: 439
Fighter planes, Allied: 102, 107, 110, 119, 261, 320, 376, 479, 482, 486
Fighter planes, Axis: 151n, 240
Fighter-bombers, Allied: 107, 320, 344, 376. *See also* A–36's; P–38's; P–39's; P–40's; P–51's.
Fighter Wings, U.S.
  31st: 320
  33d: 320
  64th: 320
Finland: 27
Fire control parties: 401, 403
FIREBRAND: 258
Fiume: 473
Fiumicino: 486
Flak. *See* Antiaircraft defense, Axis.
Flint, Col. H. A.: 330, 331, 333, 336, 337, 339, 340, 341, 344

# INDEX 589

Floating reserve, U.S.: 99, 100, 125, 136, 155, 158, 159, 174
Florence: 439
Floresta: 386
Flotillas, Allied: 522
Flying fortresses, U.S.: 72, 278
Force 141: 56–57, 58–59, 68
Force 343: 57, 58, 60–61. *See also* Corps, U.S., I Armored.
Force 545 (British task force): 57, 58, 60–61
Force X, U.S.: 136–39
Formia: 479
Fortifications, Axis: 54, 75–76, 79, 126–27, 131, 253. *See also* Defenses, Axis.
France: 27, 45, 46, 47, 48, 51, 492, 545. *See also* Cross-Channel invasion; Southern France; Vichy France.
Francofonte: 205, 215
Frascati: 442, 515, 522
Fredendall, Maj. Gen. Lloyd: 94
Free French: 14. *See also* Goums (4th Moroccan Tabor).
Freeman, Lt. Col. L. G.: 181
French forces: 543. *See also* Free French.
French Morocco: 15, 55
French Northwest Africa: 1, 3–4. *See also* North Africa.
Fries, Generalmajor Walter: 157, 352, 414
 at Monte Cipolla: 396–97, 398, 404, 405
 in San Fratello ridge action: 357–58
 and Tusa ridge counterattack: 321–23
*Fuehrer Conferences:* 45n
Fullriede, Col. Fritz: 197, 199, 200, 313, 315
Funicular station: 536, 537
*Funston:* 143
Furiano River: 352, 353, 358, 359, 360, 382
Furnari: 409, 413
FUSTIAN: 218, 219n


Gaeta: 479, 500
Gaffey, Maj. Gen. Hugh J.: 96, 158, 252, 254
Gaffi Tower: 127, 129
Gagliano: 315, 328, 329, 331, 338, 339, 341, 342, 343, 344
Galli, Carlo: 528
Gambarra, Generale di Corpo d'Armata Gastone: 525
Gangi: 233, 301, 303, 312
GANGWAY: 260
Garda: 469
Gardiner, Col. William T.: 499, 500, 501, 502, 504, 510, 519
Garigliano River: 552
Gas, German threat to use: 458
Gasoline: 253, 480, 486, 500, 502
Gavin, Col. James M.: 94, 101, 118, 136, 173, 175, 255

Gavin, Col. James M.—Continued
 and Axis counterattack: 168–69, 172
 and D-day paratrooper landings: 119
Gay, Brig. Gen. Hobart R.: 235, 246, 246n
Gela: 58, 59, 64, 86, 89, 91, 97, 98, 99, 100, 107, 117, 119, 120, 125, 135, 137, 155, 159, 163, 166, 169, 170, 171, 172, 177, 185, 192, 204, 205, 226, 256n, 418, 419, 422
 Allied assault on: 136–39
 Axis counterattack at: 148–53, 164, 165, 166, 170
Gela-Farello landing ground: 135, 139, 158, 176, 177, 179, 182
Gela River: 97, 99, 135, 136
Genoa: 14, 442, 445, 459, 473, 522
Genova, Generale di Corpo d'Armata Adalberto di Savoia: 534
George VI, King: 547
Gerbini: 63
Gerlach, Captain: 537, 538
German Air Force (Luftwaffe): 37, 69, 74n, 78n, 110, 163, 213, 333, 360, 537, 538, 361–62, 389, 458, 474. *See also* Oberkommando der Luftwaffe.
 *Second:* 33, 78n, 83, 204, 214
 *Second Air Fleet:* 375, 376
 *X Flieger Korps:* 32
 *XI Flieger Korps:* 284
 *Support Aviation Wing 4:* 533n
German alliance. *See* Italo-German alliance.
German Army: 50, 78, 81, 82, 83, 84, 87, 163, 173, 190, 197, 198, 199–200, 241, 243, 245, 259, 261, 285, 288, 290 307, 341, 369, 445, 473, 477, 478, 482, 486, 491–92, 509, 522, 523, 530, 552. *See also* German Army units; Reinforcements, Axis; Reserves, German.
 in Casa del Priolo action: 187–89
 command. *See* Command, Axis; Command, German; *Oberkommando der Wehrmacht.*
 evacuation. *See* Evacuation of Sicily, Axis.
 foot soldier: 553
 glider-borne troops: 537
 ground forces: 47, 48, 369
 and Hitler: 28, 29
 and Italian Army: 30, 32, 36, 47–48, 410, 497, 513–14, 525, 534, 535–36. *See also* Command, Axis.
 Italian equipment and personnel taken over by: 410
 and Italian railway transportation: 288
 in Italy: 213, 282, 287–88, 289, 290–94, 293n, 368, 369, 371–72, 451, 452, 469, 477, 492. *See also* Occupation of Italy, German; Troop movements, German.
 in Sicily: 64, 74, 75, 203, 204, 212–14, 215–16, 217, 237, 242, 243, 244, 263, 308. *See also* Evacuation of Sicily, Axis.
 and Rome battle: 524–25, 528, 531–32

German Army—Continued
  and truce with Italy: 525–26
German Army units
  OB SUED: 33n, 78, 82, 371, 442, 470, 473, 513, 522, 523
  OB WEST: 51, 290, 533
  Army Group B: 241, 275, 282, 284, 290, 293, 371–72, 373, 442, 452, 469, 470, 472, 473, 497, 522
  Army, Tenth: 470, 471, 522, 523, 524, 532
  Corps
    Deutsches Afrika Korps: 32
    II SS Panzer: 284, 451
    XIV Panzer: 51, 75, 82, 203, 204, 213–14, 237, 240, 308, 341, 368, 374, 376, 452, 469, 470
    XVII: 515
    LXXVI Panzer: 75, 203, 374, 413, 452, 470
  Division, Hermann Goering: 48, 51, 74, 74n, 79, 121, 136, 142, 147, 155n, 157n, 163, 166, 169, 198, 205, 208, 210, 215, 217, 219, 220, 237, 244, 301, 319, 324, 345, 374–75, 378, 382, 387, 405, 414, 416
    and Allied advance to Yellow Line: 190, 191
    in counterattack: 154, 164–65, 170, 171–72n, 172, 185, 187, 188
    in evacuation of Sicily: 412
    Kesselring's criticism of: 157
    organization of: 64, 148–49, 164
    stationing of: 64, 75, 81, 86, 87
    withdrawal of: 202–03, 223
  Division, 1st Parachute: 111, 203, 204, 212–13, 214, 216, 218, 286, 306, 376, 413, 452, 471
  Division, 1st SS Panzer Leibstandarte Adolf Hitler: 294, 442
  Division, 2d SS Panzer "Das Reich": 294
  Division, 2d Parachute: 283, 284, 286, 293, 293n, 442, 451, 452, 470, 485, 492, 515, 523, 525, 537
  Division, 3d Panzer Grenadier: 75, 214, 215, 283, 284, 442, 451, 452, 470, 481, 485, 500, 510, 514–15, 523, 524, 525
  Division, 15th Panzer Grenadier (Sizilien): 51, 64, 81, 84, 86, 87, 125, 147, 147n, 150, 155, 165, 192, 195, 202, 203, 204, 204n, 223, 224, 233, 237, 244, 301, 307, 308, 315, 319, 324, 331, 341, 345, 346, 352, 357, 376, 378, 382, 385, 391, 393, 398, 399, 409, 410, 413, 515
  Division, 16th Panzer: 51, 74–75, 203, 284, 368, 452
  Division, 24th Panzer: 442, 472
  Division, 26th Panzer: 75, 203, 284, 293n, 289, 290, 293, 442, 451
  Division, 29th Panzer Grenadier: 75, 203, 204, 213, 214–15, 216, 237, 241, 263, 282, 300,

German Army units—Continued
  Division, 29th Panzer Grenadier—Continued
    307, 308, 315, 319, 321, 323, 324, 345, 346, 366, 376, 378, 380, 382, 386, 409, 413
    in evacuation of Sicily: 405
    at Monte Cipolla: 391, 404, 405
    pursuit of: 406, 408
    at Tortorici line: 382
  Division, 44th Infantry: 283, 288, 290, 291, 292, 293, 372–73, 442, 481, 533
  Division, 60th Panzer Grenadier: 290, 294
  Division, 65th Infantry: 294, 442
  Division, 71st Infantry: 442, 469, 472, 481
  Division, 76th Infantry: 263, 282, 294, 442
  Division, 90th Panzer Grenadier: 51, 471
  Division, 94th Infantry: 294, 442
  Division, 305th Infantry: 263, 282, 283, 288, 290, 291, 293, 294, 442
  Division, 715th Infantry: 294
  Kampfgruppen: 148n
    Ens: 84, 86, 147n, 192, 198, 200, 202, 217, 231, 233, 301, 319, 324, 336, 337, 339, 342, 345
    Fullriede: 84, 86, 87, 147n, 192, 198, 199, 217, 233, 301, 313, 315, 319, 324, 336, 340, 342, 343
    Koerner: 84, 86
    Neapel: 84, 84n, 86, 87, 192
    Schmalz: 86, 120, 123, 147, 148, 163, 171n, 191, 203, 204, 205, 215, 216, 219, 223, 422
    Ulich: 300, 316, 317, 318, 320, 322
  Brigade Doehla: 442
  Regiments
    3d, 1st Parachute Division: 204
    15th Panzer Grenadier: 398, 399
    29th Artillery: 393
    71st Panzer Grenadier: 322, 382, 388, 399, 404
    104th Panzer Grenadier. See German Army units, Kampfgruppen, Ens.
    129th Panzer Grenadier. See German Army units, Kampfgruppen, Fullriede.
  Battalions
    1st, 71st Panzier Grenadier Regiment: 393, 397
    2d, 15th Panzer Grenadier Regiment: 231
    2d, 71st Panzer Grenadier Regiment: 363, 365
    3d, 15th Panzer Grenadier Regiment: 321
    215th Tank: 84n, 148n, 171n
  alarm units: 368
  antiaircraft units: 243, 290, 372, 393, 397, 486
  artillery battalions: 322, 382
  coastal defense units: 393, 396, 398
  divisions: 47, 48, 49, 50, 51, 64, 74, 75, 87, 244, 282, 286, 445, 497
  divisions, mobile: 471

# INDEX

German Army units—Continued
field artillery units: 399, 402
paratroop units: 514. *See also* Paratroopers, German.
patrols: 358, 500
reconnaissance units: 205, 205n
service troops: 357
German Embassy, in Italy: 514, 515, 523, 528
German High Command: 213, 464. *See also* Command, German.
German Navy: 474. *See also* Ferrying service, German.
German War Documents Project: 35n
Germany: 1, 4, 5, 8, 9, 11, 14, 15, 37, 45, 46, 73, 512. *See also* German Army; Hitler.
defeat of, Allied planning for: 2, 3, 6, 17, 21, 23, 262, 435–36. *See also* Cross-Channel invasion.
and Italian armistice announcement: 513, 522
and Italian mainland invasion: 522–24, 552
and Italy. *See* Italo-German alliance; Occupation of Italy, German.
and Russia: 464. *See also* Russo-German campaign.
Gestapo: 460
Giaccone, Lt. Col. Leandro: 530n
and capitulation to Germany: 530, 531, 532
and truce with Germany: 526–27, 530, 531
GIANT I: 477, 498
GIANT II: 490, 492, 498, 504, 506, 508, 509
and Italians: 485–86, 488, 489, 494, 495, 501, 502, 505
planning of: 485–89, 494, 498, 505
purpose of: 477–78
Giarrantana: 190, 207
Gibb, Lt. Col. Frederick W.: 337, 344
Gibraltar: 3, 45, 52, 463
Giorgio, Generale di Divisione Umberto di: 528
Giraud, General Henri Philippe: 14, 67
Giuriati, Captain: 505
Glider troops, British: 92, 423
Gliders, British: 92, 93, 108, 115, 117, 120, 219n
Gliders, German: 537
Gloria, Generale di Corpo d'Armata Alessandro: 288, 290, 292, 293, 371, 372, 373
GOBLET: 16, 67, 68, 258, 260, 262
Goebbels, Joseph: 49, 283, 285
Goering, Reichsmarschall Hermann: 27, 33, 34, 47, 83, 243
Gonzaga, General: 534
Gorham, Lt. Col. Arthur: 150–52, 171, 188
Gort, Lord: 549
Goums (4th Moroccan Tabor): 96, 98, 305, 314, 330, 333, 337, 338, 340, 343
Gozo: 119
Grammichele: 98, 206, 222, 224
Gran Sasso: 536, 537

Grandi, Count Dino: 40, 42, 264, 283, 460
as foreign minister, King proposes: 548, 549, 551
and Mussolini's overthrow: 267–68
peace mission of: 268
Granieri: 208
Grant, Maj. Walter H.: 139, 313
"Grasshoppers": 133n, 418
Great Britain: 2, 3, 5, 6, 7, 12, 22, 92. *See also* British Chiefs of Staff; British Government; Churchill, Winston S.; Planners, British.
Greece: 4, 12, 17, 24, 29, 31, 32, 35, 45, 46, 64, 110, 203, 261, 437, 445, 453, 491, 514, 535
Greek rebels: 38
Green Beach: 125, 131, 141, 144, 161
Green Beach 2: 136, 142, 144, 145, 159, 160
Green West: 125, 131
Grenades. *See* Hand grenades; Rifle grenades.
Grottacalda: 217
Guariglia, Raffaele: 265, 275, 282, 369, 371, 444, 461, 479, 480, 483n, 511, 517, 523, 548
and evacuation of Rome: 518
and peace negotiations with Allies: 295–97, 298, 441, 454, 455, 465, 466, 479, 480
Guerrilla operations
Balkan: 447
Italian: 472
Guingand, de, Maj. Gen. Francis: 61
Gulf of Catania: 61
Gulf of Gela: 52, 61, 63, 64, 89, 96, 123
Gulf of Gioia: 260
Gulf of Noto: 61, 62, 64, 89, 91
Gulf of Salerno: 262, 448, 449, 509
Gun lighters, German: 376
Guns, German: 224, 263, 393, 500
and evacuation of Sicily: 375–76, 375n, 377
20-mm.: 402
170-mm.: 376
210-mm.: 214
Guns, Italian: 75, 133
antiaircraft: 489
antitank: 79, 152, 251, 485
artillery pieces: 81, 126, 138, 150, 152, 169, 223, 382, 410
captured by Americans: 138, 150, 152, 169
Guns, U.S.: *See also* Howitzers.
antiaircraft: 399
antitank: 154n, 171, 173, 478, 485, 498
artillery pieces: 103, 158, 331, 363, 365, 396, 403, 419, 480
75-mm.: 251
155-mm.: 337, 400, 401
Guzzoni, Generale d'Armata Alfredo: 78, 79, 83, 84, 86, 87, 109, 170, 172, 173, 190, 191, 197–98, 202, 203, 204, 204n, 205, 214, 215–16, 219, 233, 237, 238, 307, 319, 345, 346, 374, 375, 378

Guzzoni, Generale d'Armata Alfredo—Continued
and command relationship in Sicily: 77-78, 307-09
and Nicosia loss: 315
and Sicilian invasion: 110-11, 119, 120, 147, 163, 164-65

Half-tracks, German: 396
Half-tracks, U.S.: 173, 195-96, 251, 402
Hall, Rear Adm. John L.: 100, 108, 136, 159
Hamburg: 292
Hand grenades: 317, 321, 404
Handy, Maj. Gen. Thomas T.: 5
HARDIHOOD: 436
Harris, 1st Lt. William J.: 156
Harrison, Capt. Willard E.: 178
Headquarters, Allied: 421, 498. *See also* Allied Force Headquarters.
Heidrich, Generalleutnant Richard: 377-78
Heintges, Lt. Col. John A.: 128, 193, 229
Herzegovina: 491
Hewel, Walter: 287
Hewitt, Vice Adm. Henry K.: 89, 108, 320, 379-80
Hickey, Col. Lawrence: 107n
Highway, coastal. *See* Highway 115.
Highway, east coast. *See* Highway 114.
Highway, north coast. *See* Highway 113.
Highway 113 (north coast): 207, 238, 255, 300, 304, 308, 309, 316, 320, 353, 367, 378, 380, 386, 388, 396, 405, 408, 413
characterized: 348
difficulties of: 309
Highway 114 (east coast): 191, 207, 219, 235, 248, 375, 380, 416
Highway 115 (coastal): 92, 121, 123, 131, 133, 135, 138, 141, 143, 149, 151, 165, 168, 171, 172, 187, 191, 194, 226, 229, 231, 233, 252, 255, 309, 316-17, 391, 398, 399, 405
Highway 116: 309, 382
Highway 117: 97, 135, 139, 149, 152, 153, 165, 169, 185, 206, 222, 231, 245, 248, 309, 314, 315, 321, 322
Highway 118: 226
Highway 120: 233, 238, 301, 303, 304, 309, 313, 314, 323, 328, 341, 343, 345, 346, 382, 385
difficulties of: 309
terrain around: 325
Highway 121: 233, 235, 245, 246, 248, 249, 300, 304, 319, 341
Highway 122: 198, 226, 227, 229, 230, 231, 232, 246, 248
Highway 123: 155, 191, 192, 195, 196, 198
Highway 124: 190, 191, 198, 205, 206-07, 207n, 208, 209, 210, 222, 223, 224, 233, 422. *See also* Yellow Line.
Highways, Italian. *See* Via *entries*.

Hill 123: 164
Hill 132: 164
Hill 171: 357, 358
Hill 300: 165
Hill 316: 228
Hill 333: 228
Hill 335. *See* Tusa ridge.
Hill 432: 232
Hill 504: 232
Hill 643: 156
Hill 673: 359, 360, 361, 362
Hill 825: 313, 314
Hill 851: 329
Hill 921: 314
Hill 937: 313, 314
Hill 962: 313-14
Hill 1006: 329, 330, 344
Hill 1030: 327-28
Hill 1034: 329, 330, 336, 337, 344
Hill 1035. *See* Monte Basilio.
Hill 1056: 336
Hill 1061: 328, 329
Hill 1140: 328
Hill 1209: 333-34
Hill 1234: 328
Hill 1321: 330
Himmler, Reichsfuehrer SS Heinrich: 38
Hinds, Col. Sidney R.: 194, 199
Hitler, Adolf: 3, 28, 31n, 32, 33, 33n, 39, 41, 46, 47, 48, 51, 74, 75, 78, 79, 82, 111, 203, 212, 237, 263, 275, 282, 285, 288, 290, 291, 293, 296, 308, 368, 370, 371, 374, 443, 460, 471, 472, 522, 534
and Badoglio: 283, 286, 287, 292, 294-95, 470, 497
and defense of Italy: 49-50, 452, 469-70
and evacuation of Sicily: 306, 375
at Feltre conference: 242-44
and Italian treachery threat: 37, 49-50, 286-87, 473, 497
and Mussolini: 27, 29, 30, 34, 38, 215, 239, 240, 241, 242, 283, 536, 539
secret orders of: 214
and Sicily: 213, 214, 240, 241, 243
strategic views of: 35, 213
Hoare, Sir Samuel John Gurney: 40, 268, 441, 446, 446n, 458
Holy See. *See* Vatican; Vatican City.
Hood, 1st Lt. R. F.: 195
Hopkins, Harry: 19
Horses: 348, 348n
Hospital ships, Allied: 110
Hospitals, Seventh Army: 419
15th Evacuation: 426
93d Evacuation: 427-28
House of Savoy. *See* Monarchy; Victor Emmanuel III.

# INDEX

Howitzer units, U.S.: 125, 144, 168, 172
Howitzers, U.S.: 150n, 160, 167, 172–173, 402, 403
  75-mm.: 187–88
  105-mm.: 129n, 187, 188
Hube, General der Panzertruppen Hans Valentin: 51, 74, 82, 213, 214, 215, 236, 318, 319, 357, 379, 385, 388
  and command relationship in Sicily: 307–09
  and evacuation of Sicily: 342, 374, 375, 376–77, 378, 381–82, 413, 416
  and Nicosia loss: 315
  phase lines of: 324–25, 345, 378, 406, 409, 412, 414
  in Troina action: 341, 345
Huebner, Maj. Gen. Clarence R.: 56, 347, 413
Hull, Cordell: 448
Humbert, Prince: 283, 287, 306, 371, 468, 516, 517
Hungary: 15, 40, 44, 298
HUSKY, defined: 4

Iberian Peninsula: 3, 17. *See also* Spain.
Infantry Battalions, U.S.
  1st, 7th Infantry: 126, 127, 128, 226, 228, 415
  1st, 15th Infantry: 195, 196, 352, 353, 357, 358
  1st, 16th Infantry: 152, 154, 165, 168, 171, 187, 338, 339, 341
    in Casa del Priolo action: 188–89
    casualties: 189
  1st, 18th Infantry: 187, 302–03
  1st, 26th Infantry: 139, 185, 231–32, 301, 313, 314
  1st, 30th Infantry: 359–60, 361, 401–02, 404
  1st, 39th Infantry: 336, 337
  1st, 41st Armored Infantry: 159
  1st, 157th Infantry: 145, 156, 208, 220, 321, 322, 416
  1st, 179th Infantry: 144
  1st, 180th Infantry: 142–43, 154–55, 155n, 160n, 165, 318
  2d, 7th Infantry: 358, 365
    and Agrigento drive: 228–29
    D-day landing of: 127–28
  2d, 15th Infantry: 125, 131, 195, 352, 353, 357, 358
  2d, 16th Infantry: 152, 154, 165, 166–67, 171, 338
    in Casa del Priolo action: 187–89
    casualties: 189
  2d, 18th Infantry: 185, 187, 302–03
  2d, 26th Infantry: 185, 187, 232, 301, 313, 337, 344
  2d, 30th Infantry: 352
  2d, 60th Infantry: 386
  2d, 157th Infantry: 144, 145, 321, 322
  2d, 180th Infantry: 143, 165, 168, 222, 317, 318

Infantry Battalions, U.S.—Continued
  3d, 7th Infantry: 229
    D-day landing of: 128–29
    in Palma di Montechiaro advance: 193–94
  3d, 15th Infantry: 200, 352, 353, 357, 358–59, 360, 361, 366, 409
    in Favarotta area action: 195, 196
    in San Fratello action: 358
  3d, 16th Infantry: 314, 338, 339
  3d, 26th Infantry: 165, 166, 232, 301, 302, 313, 314, 337, 344
  3d, 30th Infantry: 197, 199, 200, 359, 360, 361, 401, 402, 404
  3d, 39th Infantry: 333, 334
  3d, 41st Armored Infantry: 194
  3d, 157th Infantry: 208, 321, 322
  3d, 179th Infantry: 144, 155–56, 208
  3d, 180th Infantry: 155, 155n, 165, 321
    landings of: 143–44
    in Pettineo ridge action: 318
Infantry Divisions, U.S.
  1st: 57, 94, 98, 100, 101, 108, 117, 135–36, 139, 141, 143, 155, 156, 158, 159, 164, 165, 167n, 169, 170, 170n, 172, 173, 174, 174n, 175, 179, 185, 190, 197, 200, 206, 210, 222, 231, 232, 233, 244, 245, 246, 248, 249, 301, 302, 304, 305, 311, 312n, 314, 316, 319, 320, 323, 324, 325, 327, 329, 330, 331, 336, 338, 340, 343, 352, 406, 408, 412, 417, 418, 422
    command changed: 347
    logistical planning for: 120
    in North Africa campaign: 95
    tactical plans for: 99–100
    in Troina action: 341, 347
  3d: 94–95, 96, 100, 103, 105, 106, 108, 135, 155, 170, 174, 191, 192, 197, 198, 200, 201, 206, 224, 230, 231, 245, 249, 254, 305, 323, 349, 352, 382, 388, 394, 399, 400, 405, 406, 408, 413, 418, 422
    in British task force: 59–60
    Licata assault plan: 123, 125
    logistical planning for: 102
    at Naso ridge: 391
    relieves 45th Division: 319–20, 348
    in San Fratello action: 348, 353
    tactical plans for: 60, 97, 98, 99
  9th: 94, 98, 230, 231, 320, 330, 331, 333, 336, 343, 347, 374, 382, 393, 406
    arrival in Sicily: 305–06
    characterized: 96
  36th: 57
  45th: 94, 99, 105, 108, 117, 119, 123, 136, 142, 165, 172, 173, 206, 210, 222, 224, 230–31, 232, 233, 244, 245, 248, 249, 254, 300, 304, 305, 311, 316, 318, 349, 422
    accomplishments of: 323
    characterized: 95

Infantry Divisions, U.S.—Continued
    landing of: 139
    logistical planning for: 102
    relieved by 3rd Division: 319–20, 348
    and Santo Stefano: 321, 322, 323
    tactical plans for: 98, 100
  104th: 347
Infantry Regiments, U.S.
  7th: 125, 131, 133, 192, 200, 227, 228–29, 230, 360, 361, 365, 367, 388, 389, 391, 399, 402, 404, 406, 413, 414, 415, 416
  15th: 155, 192, 195, 199, 200, 352, 357, 358, 361, 389, 408, 413, 414
  16th: 149, 150, 151, 151n, 152, 154, 154n, 156, 160, 165, 169, 173, 174, 206, 222, 231, 232, 249, 302, 303, 311, 324, 329, 330, 331, 336, 337, 338, 339, 341, 344
    in Casa del Priolo action: 187, 188–89
    D-day objectives of: 136, 139
    in Nicosia action: 314, 315
  18th: 98, 136, 160, 171, 208, 222, 223, 231, 248, 249, 302, 312, 321, 329, 330, 331, 333, 338, 339, 341, 342, 343, 344, 413
    landing of: 158–59
    in Nicosia area action: 314
  26th: 139, 149, 153, 158, 165, 166, 185, 187, 206, 222, 231, 232, 301, 303
    Gela landing: 136
    in Nicosia area action: 311–12, 313, 314
    in Troina action: 331, 333, 336, 337, 338, 339, 340, 341, 343–44, 345
  30th: 125, 133, 193, 199, 200, 357, 358, 359, 360, 363, 365, 366, 401, 408, 415
  39th: 96, 98, 249, 250, 252, 253, 255, 305
    at Randazzo: 385–86
    in Troina action: 329–30, 331, 333, 336, 338, 339, 340, 341, 342–43, 344, 347
  47th: 343, 347, 382, 385
  41st Armored: 159, 171, 194
  60th: 343, 345, 385, 386
  66th: 95
  157th: 142, 155, 156, 189, 190, 206, 208, 222, 224, 233, 249, 300, 316, 318, 320, 321, 323, 408, 415, 418
    in Bivio Salica landing: 415
    D-day landings of: 141, 142
    Mazzarino move: 232–33
    and Messina drive: 413–14
    and Vizzini: 219–20
  179th: 141, 142, 155, 165, 173, 189, 190, 205, 206, 208, 220, 222, 224, 300, 316, 348, 418
    at Comiso: 189
    D-day landings of: 144
  180th: 141, 149, 155, 155n, 160, 168, 172, 189, 190, 206, 208, 220, 222, 249, 300, 316, 317, 320

Infantry Regiments, U.S.—Continued
    and Axis counterattack: 165
    landings of: 142–43
Infiltration, German: 341, 342
"Innocuous" (code word): 500, 502
Innsbruck: 31n
Inshore Squadron, British Navy: 380, 387
Intelligence, Allied: 46, 56, 64, 72–73, 245, 261, 270, 324, 325, 347, 378–79, 449, 541. *See also* MINCEMEAT.
Intelligence, Axis: 45, 46, 65, 73, 109, 447, 454, 458, 486. *See also* Italian Military Intelligence Service.
Internees, Axis: 456n, 457
Invasion targets, Axis speculation on: 45–46, 48, 203. *See also* MINCEMEAT; Strategic planning, Allied.
Ionia Sea: 45
Iraq: 6
Ismay, General Sir Hastings L.: 23
*Italia:* 532, 533
Italian Air Force: 28, 29, 46–47, 83, 459–60, 474, 492, 552
Italian armistice. *See* Armistice, Italo-Allied.
Italian Army: 28, 41, 163, 197, 241–42, 245, 272, 288, 307, 370, 373, 470, 471, 480, 488, 491–92, 501, 509, 515, 522, 523, 524, 540, 545, 547, 553. *See also* Italian Army units.
  command. *See Comando Supremo;* Command, Axis; Command, Italian.
  dissolution of: 524, 534–36
  and evacuation of Sicily: 410
  General Staff: 524
  and German Army: 30, 32, 36, 47–48, 410, 497, 513–14, 525, 534, 535–36. *See also* Command, Axis.
  ground forces: 32, 47, 369, 445, 482, 515, 535, 552
  ground organization: 240, 243
  infantry: 150–51
  and *Memoria 44:* 481, 515
  military collaboration with Allies: 441, 445, 446, 447, 456, 457–58, 464, 465, 466, 473, 475, 476, 477, 482, 484, 485–86, 490–91, 492–95, 505, 535, 541, 542–43, 544, 551. *See also* Military information.
  morale: 239–40, 241, 261, 270, 285, 451, 529, 533, 552
  organization and command of: 29–30
  performance of: 64, 239–40, 259
  and Rome: 464, 516, 517–18, 519, 528, 529–30, 531, 532
  shortages: *See* Shortages, Italian.
  and truce with Germany: 525–26, 531–32
  weakness of: 30, 47, 48, 80–81, 542–43
Italian Army units
  *Army Group East:* 491

Italian Army units—Continued
  Armies
    Second: 289, 481
    Fourth: 286, 288, 289, 370, 451, 453, 472, 481, 533
    Fifth: 481
    Sixth: 63, 64, 76, 80, 82, 83, 84, 86, 110, 148, 191, 192, 202, 205, 214, 216, 223, 237, 309, 346, 378
    Seventh: 481, 534
    Eighth: 32, 290, 481
  Corps: 513
    Corpo d'Armata di Rome: 289, 492
    Motorized: 289, 480, 484, 489, 492, 493, 495, 500, 519
    XI: 525
    XII: 63, 84, 119, 149–50, 196, 197, 237, 238, 308, 315
    XVI: 63, 84, 86, 119, 120, 147, 148, 149, 163, 164, 170, 172, 223, 237, 533
    XVII: 289, 492
    XXXV: 289, 533
  Divisions: 63, 282, 457, 464, 476, 513, 542–43
    Re: 492, 495, 525
    2d (Tridentina) Alpine: 372
    4th (Cuneense) Alpine: 372, 373
    4th (Livorno): 47, 63, 81, 84, 86, 87, 111, 136, 147, 149, 152, 163, 164, 165, 169–70, 185, 192, 198, 202, 203, 205, 211, 217, 222, 223, 237, 242
    5th (Pusteria) Alpine: 533
    6th (Alpi Graje) Alpine: 372
    7th (Lupi di Toscana) Infantry: 472, 488, 492, 495
    9th (Pasubio) Infantry: 534
    10th (Piave) Motorized Infantry: 266, 289, 485, 492, 493, 510, 524, 525, 529, 532
    12th (Sassari): 289, 485, 492
    21st (Granatieri): 289, 492, 515, 516, 525, 529, 532
    26th (Assietta): 63, 80, 84, 87, 125, 197, 238, 358, 366, 382
    28th (Aosta): 63, 80, 84, 86, 87, 87n, 125, 197, 238, 315, 324, 330
    54th (Napoli): 63, 80, 84, 86, 87, 111, 120, 123, 163, 205, 209, 211, 422
    58th (Legnano) Infantry: 534, 542
    103d (Piacenza) Motorized: 63n, 289, 492, 514, 523, 525
    104th (Mantova) Infantry: 534, 542
    105th (Rovigo) Infantry: 372
    131st (Centauro) Armored: 289, 485, 492, 525, 526, 527, 532
    135th (Ariete) Armored: 266, 289, 298, 485, 492, 493, 495, 510, 515, 516, 524, 525, 529, 532

Italian Army units—Continued
  Divisions—Continued
    152d Piceno: 534, 542
    184th (Nembo) Parachute: 535
    206th Coastal: 142
    207th Coastal: 126, 163, 191, 192, 196
    209th Coastal: 534
    220th Coastal: 492
    221st Coastal: 492
    222d Coastal: 534
  Brigade, XVIII Coastal: 136, 142, 147
  Groups
    Mobile Group E: 149, 151n, 152, 164
    Schreiber: 233, 301
    Venturi: 191, 195, 196
  Regiments
    29th Infantry: 363
    177th Bersaglieri: 191, 492, 516
  antiaircraft units: 485, 488, 516
  carabinieri: 492, 518, 527, 528
  coastal units: 80, 83, 84, 87, 120, 125, 137, 138, 141, 149n, 157, 212, 214, 238, 289, 308, 379, 542
    battalions: 79, 128
    divisions: 534. See also Italian Army units, Divisions.
  depot units: 289
  mobile units: 83, 84, 86, 87, 125, 142, 147
  patrols: 416
  police units: 518
  service school troops: 492, 528
Italian Cabinet, Badoglio's: 265, 266, 281
Italian diplomatic corps: 468
Italian Fleet: 17, 45, 46, 52, 54, 89, 269, 272, 369, 372, 442, 459, 468, 474, 475–76, 482, 494, 505, 506, 532, 540, 541, 543
  disposition of: 546
  escape from Germans: 533
  inadequacy of: 82
Italian government. See Badoglio government; Caviglia; Mussolini.
Italian High Command: 77, 462, 494, 503, 510, 527. See also Badoglio, government of; Monarchy.
Italian mainland invasion: 73, 240–41, 278, 295, 379, 435, 437, 438, 439–40, 441–42, 446, 448, 458, 459, 462, 463, 465, 466, 467, 473, 477–78, 498, 522
  airborne operations. See GIANT II.
  and armistice: 474, 475, 476, 482, 491, 492, 499, 508–09, 512
  German preparations for: 469–71, 523–24
  Italian co-operation with. See Italian Army, military collaboration with Allies.
  landings for. See Amphibious operations, Allied, Italian mainland; Salerno landings.

Italian mainland invasion—Continued
  plans and debate: 12, 14, 16, 17, 18–19, 23, 24, 67, 259, 261–63, 269
  scheduling of: 478, 479, 488, 489, 490, 491, 492, 493, 495, 496, 499, 520–21
  strategic planning for: 68, 259–63, 269–70, 440, 449, 512. *See also* BARRACUDA; BAYTOWN; BUTTRESS; GANGWAY; GOBLET; MUSKET.
Italian merchant marine: 546, 552
Italian Military Intelligence Service: 494, 495, 496, 499
Italian military mission: 489, 494, 505–06
Italian Navy: 28, 29, 45, 46, 505, 552. *See also* Italian Fleet.
Italian Riviera: 12
Italian secret service: 470
Italian Social Republic: 539
Italian War Ministry: 29, 288, 290, 514, 518, 527
Italians. *See* Civilians, Italian.
Italo-German alliance (Pact of Steel): 27, 31, 40, 267, 295n, 306
  under Badoglio: 281, 284, 285, 553
  termination question: 38–40, 41, 43, 44, 263, 264, 265, 282, 297, 374, 474

Japan: 1, 2, 4, 5, 11, 16, 21
Jeeps: 253
*Jeffers:* 139, 139n, 179–80, 180n
*Jefferson:* 144, 145
Jeschonnek, Generaloberst Hans: 83
Jodl, Generaloberst Alfred: 27, 37, 211, 212, 287, 294, 295, 306, 307, 368, 453, 460, 470, 523
  defense views of: 213, 214, 215, 452
  and Hitler: 375, 497
  unified command plan of: 241, 242
Johnson, Col. Charles R.: 125, 195, 352
Joint Chiefs of Staff, U.S.: 2, 3, 4, 11, 20, 25, 26, 277, 279, 436, 437, 449, 462. *See also* Joint War Plans Committee.
  at Casablanca: 7–8
  at QUADRANT Conference: 438–39
  and strategic planning: 5, 6, 7–8, 9–10, 18–19, 21–22
Joint Staff Planners: 2n
Joint Strategic Survey Committee: 2n
Joint War Plans Committee: 25, 435
Julian Alps: 442, 472
Junctions. *See* Road junctions.
Junker 52's: 488
Junker 88's: 177

Kairouan: 102
Kaye, Orin W., Jr.: 504n
Kean, Maj. Gen. William B.: 429
Keerans, Brig. Gen. Charles L., Jr.: 181
Keitel, Generalfeldmarschall Wilhelm: 27, 31n, 50, 282, 291, 294, 295, 452, 534

Keitel, Generalfeldmarschall Wilhelm—Continued
  at Feltre conference: 243–44
  at Tarvis conference: 369, 370
Kennan, George F.: 455, 459
Kesselring, Feldmarschall Albert: 33n, 35, 36, 50, 51, 78, 78n, 79, 83, 204n, 211, 223, 236, 240, 263, 283, 287, 288, 289, 290, 291, 293, 307, 368, 369, 371, 372, 373, 374, 458, 497, 530n, 536
  on Allied invasion targets: 46
  and Badoglio government: 284–85, 286
  and capitulation of Italy: 530, 531, 532
  as Commander in Chief South: 33–34
  and counterattack in Sicily: 163
  and evacuation of Sicily: 374–75
  headquarters bombed: 522–23
  on *Hermann Goering Division* failure: 157
  and Italian mainland invasion: 510, 522, 523
  Italian sympathies of: 470–71, 473
  and Italy's defense: 74, 75, 451, 452
  and military aid to Italy: 48, 74–75
  and occupation of Rome: 470, 532
  and Sardinia: 74, 75, 471
  and Sicily: 74–75, 86, 87, 203–04, 212–13, 214–15, 237
  and truce with Italy: 526
Keyes, Maj. Gen. Geoffrey: 94, 176, 198, 199, 200, 201, 206, 226n, 230, 235, 245, 249, 251, 252, 254, 389, 390, 414, 416
King, Admiral Ernest J.: 3, 6, 7, 8, 10, 21
Kirk, Rear Adm. Alan G.: 100, 108, 139, 161
Kisters, Sgt. Gerry H.: 331n
Kittyhawks: 261. *See also* P-40's.
Klessheim conference: 38, 39
Klinckowstroem, Col. Karl Heinrich Graf von: 530n, 533n
Kobes, Maj. Frank J., Jr.: 352, 357, 358
Komosa, Capt. Adam A.: 180
*KONSTANTIN*, Plan: 241, 282
*KOPENHAGEN:* 283–84
Krause, Maj. Edward C.: 168, 169, 172
Krueger, Lt. Col. Walter: 399, 402, 404
Kuehl, Chaplain Delbert A.: 181
Kuriate Islands: 115
Kursk: 213

La Bouzaréa: 56
La Marsa: 236
La Spezia: 82, 294, 369, 464, 468, 473, 481, 522, 532, 533
Labor Democrats: 42
Labor unions, Italian: 39
Lampedusa: 70, 72, 73
Lampione: 70, 72
Landing craft, Allied: 16, 66, 70, 72, 103–04, 143, 144, 159, 160, 161, 259, 260, 320, 362, 406, 419, 449, 493, 505, 520, 522. *See also* LCI's; LCT's; LCVP's; LST's.

# INDEX

Landing craft, German: 376, 377
Landings. *See* Amphibious operations. For *landings of airborne troops, see* Airborne operations: Airdrops.
Lanza, Lt. Galvano: 464–65, 467, 474, 500, 501
Laurentiis, Col. Augusto de: 196, 229–30
LCI's: 103, 108, 123, 126, 127, 128, 129, 136, 158, 159, 320, 363, 393, 499
LCM'S: 100–101n, 161n
LCT's: 103, 105, 108, 119, 123, 129, 131, 320, 393, 396, 499
LCVP's: 103, 125, 126, 127, 128, 133, 159, 161n, 363, 393, 394
Leahy, Admiral William D.: 2n, 7, 21, 259
Leese, Lt. Gen. Oliver: 61–62, 63, 207, 224, 248, 249, 342n
Leghorn (Livorno): 215, 460, 473, 522
*LEHRGANG*. *See* Evacuation of Sicily.
Lemnitzer, Brig. Gen. Lyman L.: 56, 485, 508, 509
Lentini: 191, 216
Leonardi, Contrammiraglio Priamo: 240
Leonforte: 207, 233, 248, 300, 307
Lewis, Col. Harry L.: 499
Liberal Party, Italian: 42
Liberty ships: 100–101n, 174, 177
Libya: 32
Licata: 58, 59, 63, 79, 86, 89, 91, 96, 97, 98, 99, 107, 110, 120, 131, 133, 163, 165, 179, 191, 192, 196, 197, 226, 240, 256, 256n, 422, 508, 509
  as Allied objective: 99
  assault on: 123, 125, 131, 132, 133
Licodia Eubea: 206, 208
Liebenstein, Fregattenkapitaen Gustav von: 374, 376, 409, 410, 411
Light divisions, U.S., proposed: 424
Lightnings: 261. *See also* P–38's.
Linosa: 70, 72, 118
Liri valley: 522
Lisbon. *See* Castellano, peace mission of; Zanussi, peace mission of.
List, Generalfeldmarschall Wilhelm: 33n
*List Oberbefehlshaber Suedost:* 33n
Livorno. *See* Leghorn.
Ljubljana: 373, 469
Ljubljana-Tarvis pass: 469, 472
Loesch Film: 35n
Logistical operations, Allied. *See also* Maintenance, Allied; Shipping, Allied; Supplies, Allied.
  floating supply reserve: 102
  for Sicilian Campaign: 7, 89, 102–03, 420
  Eighth Army: 92
  and GIANT II: 486, 489, 500
  Palermo as center of: 256
  and railroad lines: 256–57
Lombard plain: 14
Long terms: 26, 273–74, 276, 277, 447, 449, 461,

Long terms—Continued
  462, 463, 464, 465, 467, 474, 484, 543, 545, 546, 548, 550n
  modifications in: 545, 548
  QUADRANT agreement on: 448–49
  signing of: 548, 549
  text of: 559–64
Long Toms. *See* Guns, U.S., 155-mm.
Longo, Luigi: 529
LST's: 103, 105, 108, 119, 123, 125, 126, 127, 128, 133, 136, 159, 160, 161n, 320, 360, 361, 362, 363, 389, 389n, 393, 499
Lucas, Maj. Gen. John P.: 206n, 235, 236, 426, 427, 427n, 430
*Luftflottenkommando*. *See* German Air Force, Second.
Luftwaffe. *See* German Air Force.
Lyle, Capt. James B.: 138, 170

Machine guns, Allied: 150, 152, 170, 177, 179, 340, 365, 393, 398, 402, 404
Machine guns, Axis: 126–27, 131, 133, 137–38, 139, 143, 144, 150, 183, 325, 334, 338, 344, 357, 396, 400, 533
Mackensen, Hans Georg von: 242, 283n, 284, 287, 288, 289, 473
Macmillan, Harold: 449, 474, 476, 478, 540, 543, 546, 549
McGinity, Capt. James: 119, 143
McGrigor, Rear Adm. R. R.: 320, 380. *See also* Inshore Squadron, British Navy.
Maddalena: 468, 470, 475, 533
*Maddox:* 147
Madonie Mountains: 214
Madrid: 65, 444
Maintenance, Allied: 91, 102, 102n
Maletto: 385
Malpertugio River: 316
Malta: 52, 54, 61, 92, 107, 108, 110, 115, 118, 119, 421, 494, 533, 541
Malta Command, RAF: 107
Malta conference: 548, 549–51
Manfredi, Contrammiraglio Giuseppe: 255
Manhart, Lt. Col. Ashton: 352, 359, 361
Manziana: 524
Maps, Allied military: 459
Marchesi, Maj. Luigi: 482, 490n, 500, 511, 517
Marciani, Generale di Divisione Giovanni: 238, 254
Mariotti, Generale di Divisione: 524
Marras, Generale di Corpo d'Armata Efisio: 286, 287, 296, 369
Marsala: 110, 255
Marsala naval base: 238
Marsala River: 255
Marshall, General George C.: 3, 14, 21, 69, 70, 109, 259, 273, 275–76, 279, 437, 438, 541

Marshall, General George C.—Continued
  at Algiers Conference: 23, 24
  and Sicilian Campaign: 9–10, 66
  strategic views of: 5, 6, 7, 8, 9–10, 17, 22, 435–36, 437, 439–40
"Martin, Major," and Operation MINCEMEAT: 64–65
Mason, Maj. Gen. Stanhope B.: 155n
Mason-MacFarlane, Lt. Gen. Sir Noel: 540–43, 545, 546, 547, 548
Matériel, Axis: 306, 374, 377. *See also* Equipment, Axis.
Mazzarino: 93, 202, 203, 222, 223, 231, 233
Medal of Honor awards: 196n, 230n, 331n, 347
Medical Corps, U.S.: 419
Medical units, U.S.: 498
Mediterranean operations, Allied: 3, 4–5, 6, 7, 8, 11, 14, 18–19, 20–22, 23, 66–67, 73, 258–59, 262, 278, 435, 436, 438, 439, 440. *See also* Italian mainland invasion.
Mediterranean operations, Axis: 27, 31
Melilli: 202
*Memoria 44:* 481, 491, 514, 515, 515n, 525, 534
*Memoria 45:* 491n
Mers el Kebir: 493
Messina: 82, 164, 191, 207, 207n, 231, 243, 245, 246, 248, 257, 259, 260, 327, 346, 387, 405, 422, 423
  drive for: 210, 234–35, 300–04, 308, 319, 388, 389, 406–17, 420
  and Sicilian invasion plans: 53, 54
Messina peninsula: 210, 234, 408. *See also* Messina, drive for.
Messina Strait: 13, 22, 52, 82, 89, 214, 236, 263, 440, 449, 552. *See also* BAYTOWN.
  Allied bombings of: 409–10, 411–12
  antiaircraft defense of: 376
  and evacuation of Sicily: 378, 379
  traffic regulation across: 237
Middle East: 5, 67, 92
Middleton, Maj. Gen. Troy H.: 95, 108, 141, 155, 161, 169, 173, 206, 209, 232, 232n, 249, 300, 316, 318, 320
Mihailovitch, General Draza: 37, 261, 445
Milan: 288, 442, 514
Military collaboration. *See* Italian Army, military collaboration with Allies.
Military diplomacy: 278, 552. *See also* Armistice, Italo-Allied, negotiations; Rome, American mission to.
Military government for Italy, Allied plans concerning: 19, 26, 258, 272, 276, 457, 544, 545, 548. *See also* Occupation of Italy.
Military information, from Italy to Allies: 445, 459–60, 463, 476, 505. *See also* Order of battle, German.
Military Intelligence Service, Italian. *See* Italian Military Intelligence Service.

Military party, Italian: 41
Military police, U.S.: 419
Millar, Capt. Walter K.: 399, 400, 404
MINCEMEAT: 64–65
Mine fields: 251, 253, 255, 316, 344, 353, 399
Mine sweepers, U.S.: 147, 318
Mines: 137, 158, 159, 224, 316, 321, 329, 348, 352, 362, 382, 385, 387, 401, 402, 410, 524–25
Ministers, Italian: 517, 528
Mirto: 389
Mistretta: 321, 322
Mobile reserves, Axis: 80, 83, 84, 86, 87, 451
Mobilization, U.S.: 5
Modena: 442
Modane: 442
Modica: 190
Molinero, Generale di Brigata Giuseppe: 254
Mollarella Rock: 131
Monacci, Generale di Brigata Ettore: 410
Monarchy, Italian: 19, 25, 40, 41, 42, 50, 242, 269, 272, 281, 440, 464, 475, 476, 546, 549. *See also* Victor Emmanuel III, King.
*Monrovia:* 108, 158
Montanari, Franco: 444, 446, 455, 457, 460, 461, 474, 478, 482
Montaperto: 228–30
Monte Acuto: 328, 333, 334, 339, 340, 342, 343
Monte Barbuzzo: 363, 365
Monte Barnagiano. *See* Hill 962.
Monte Basilio: 329, 333, 336, 338, 339, 340, 343, 344, 345
Monte Bianco: 329, 338
Monte Camolato: 340, 343
Monte Canella. *See* Hill 825.
Monte Caolina. *See* Hill 937.
Monte Castagna: 339, 340
Monte Cipolla, amphibious operation at: 391–405
Monte della Guardia: 185
Monte di Celso: 340
Monte Femmina Morta: 330
Monte Lapa: 185
Monte Pelato: 328, 339, 343
Monte Pellegrino: 329, 342, 346
Monte Salici: 329
Monte Sambughetti: 314
Monte San Fratello: 352, 353, 357, 359, 366
Monte San Gregorio: 329
Monte San Mercurio: 343
Monte San Silvestro: 338, 339, 342
Monte Scimone. *See* Hill 1321.
Monte Sole: 131
Monte Stagliata: 340
Monte Timponivoli. *See* Hill 1209.
Monte Zai: 185
Montenegro: 32, 491
Monterosi: 524
Monterosso Almo: 206, 208, 220
Monterotondo: 373, 510, 512, 513, 523

# INDEX

Montezemolo, Col. Giuseppe Cordero: 525, 530n
Montgomery, Field Marshal Sir Bernard L: 55, 58–60, 61, 62, 89, 91, 92, 206–07, 207n, 209n, 210, 218, 219, 222, 224, 231, 235n, 236, 248, 304, 304n, 319, 380, 387, 389, 411, 414, 416, 420, 421, 422. *See also* British Army units, Army, Eighth.
Moore, Lt. Col. Roy E.: 126, 229, 230
Morale
  Axis: 73
  German: 325, 342, 405, 460
  Italian: 64, 68, 70, 71, 73, 80, 216, 239–40, 241, 259, 261, 270, 285, 451, 529, 533, 552. *See also* Defeatism, Italian.
  U.S.: 314
Moroccans. *See* Goums.
Morocco. *See* French Morocco; Spanish Morocco.
Mortar support, Axis: 137, 139, 321, 325, 330, 334, 337, 344, 357, 358
Mortar support, U.S.: 96, 139, 152, 166, 169, 170, 171, 228, 317, 344, 393, 398, 399, 400, 401, 402, 403–04, 408
Mostaganem: 94, 493
Motor boats, German: 213, 376
Motor rafts, Italian: 378, 410
Motor Transport Brigades (MTB's): 320
Motor transportation, Italian: 486
Motorcycles, German: 396
Motta: 321, 323
Mount Cenis pass: 284, 294, 442, 472
Mount Etna: 53, 207, 210, 218, 235, 246, 248, 304, 307, 319, 345, 378, 387, 422
Mountain Training School, German: 284
Mountains, Sicilian: 245, 309, 348, 352
Mountbatten, Admiral Lord Louis: 206
Mules: 348, 348n, 352, 359, 393, 398, 399
Munich: 442, 469
Munitions, Italian: 500, 502
Murphy, Lt. Col. Preston J. C.: 145, 156, 220, 321
Murphy, Robert D.: 463, 474, 476, 477, 478, 540, 543, 546, 549
MUSKET: 16, 67, 260–61, 262
Mussolini, Benito: 24, 25, 31, 35, 36, 51, 52, 73, 74, 78, 203, 213, 242n, 242–43, 244, 271, 272, 278, 281, 283, 284, 285, 286, 287, 288, 289, 291, 295, 296, 297, 368, 417, 440, 445, 452, 454, 460, 464, 470, 492, 500, 520, 543, 544, 552
  on Allied invasion plans: 45–46, 47, 48
  cabinet changes by: 39
  Goebbels on: 49
  and Hitler: 27, 29, 30, 34, 38, 215, 239, 240, 241, 242, 536, 539
  and Italian Army: 29, 32
  overthrow of: 40–42, 50, 263–64, 266, 267–69, 270, 274, 282, 306
  popularity diminishes: 39, 44

Mussolini, Benito—Continued
  rescue of: 536–39
  and Sicilian Campaign: 211, 212, 214
  and surrender: 34, 39–40, 41, 51, 215, 239
MUSTANG: 260
Mustangs: 261. *See also* A–36's.

Naples: 14, 16, 67, 68, 259, 368, 440, 452, 471, 473, 552
  assault planned: 260, 261–63
  bombing of: 278
Naro: 98, 155, 192, 194, 196, 197, 199, 200
Naro River: 226, 227, 228
Naso ridge: 388, 389, 391, 393, 394, 398, 399, 401, 402, 404, 406. *See also* Monte Cipolla.
Naso River: 394, 396, 398, 403, 404
*Naval Base Augusta-Syracuse:* 120, 121, 211, 212
*Naval Base Messina:* 120, 237
Naval bases, Axis, on Sicily: 79
Naval blockade: 23
Naval bombardment: 133. *See also* Naval gunfire support.
Naval convoys. *See* Convoys, Allied; Convoys, U.S.
Naval fires. *See* Naval gunfire support.
Naval forces, Allied: 88. *See also* Naval operations, Allied; Naval Task Forces.
Naval forces, Axis: 33n, 73, 82
Naval gunfire support, Allied: 106, 111, 120, 129, 131, 137, 139, 150, 150n, 151, 152, 154, 167, 167n, 170, 171, 173, 174, 352, 353, 401, 402, 419n
  excellence of: 419
  friendly planes fired at: 175–76, 178–79, 182–83, 183n, 218
  at Monte Cipolla: 398, 400, 401, 403
Naval operations, Allied: 420. *See also* Amphibious operations, Allied; Naval gunfire support; Naval support; Seaborne operations.
  and evacuation of Sicily by Axis: 378, 379–80
  and Pantelleria assault: 69, 70, 72
  in Sicilian invasion: 59, 88, 89, 100, 103–06, 108, 110–11, 129, 131
Naval salvage parties: 161
Naval support, Allied: 320, 380, 382, 405, 419. *See also* Naval gunfire support.
Naval Task Forces
  Eastern: 89
  Western: 89, 100, 100n
  81 (Hall's): 100, 136, 159
  85 (Kirk's): 100, 139
  86 (Conolly's): 100, 123, 133
  88 (Davidson's): 320, 349, 352, 362, 399, 401, 402, 403
Naval vessels, Allied: 108, 110, 119, 177, 258, 317–18, 485, 486, 488, 516. *See also* Naval gunfire support; Naval operations; *individual names of ships and individual types of ships.*

Naval vessels, Axis: 376, 377, 411n, 457, 472, 474. *See also* German Navy; Italian Fleet; Italian Navy.
Navy, U.S.: 69. *See also* Naval Task Forces.
  and Air Forces: 106
  and Allied antiaircraft catastrophe: 175–76, 182–83
  and Sicilian invasion: 10. *See also* Naval gunfire support; Naval operations.
Nazi party: 30, 298, 472
*Nelson:* 549
Netherlands: 6, 44
Nettuno: 522
*Neville:* 143
New Guinea: 425
Newspaper correspondents: 390, 429, 431
Nice: 288, 290, 442, 472
Nicoletta ridge: 353, 358–60
Nicoletta River: 353, 358
Nicosia: 207, 233, 235, 309–15, 319, 324, 327, 336, 374
Night fighting: 165, 173
Night flying: 93, 101, 117, 157, 175, 177–80, 181, 424
Niscemi: 100, 101, 117, 135, 136, 139, 153, 165, 174, 187, 188, 206, 217, 222, 419
Nocera: 477
Nolan, Lt. Col. P. W.: 143
Normandy invasion. *See* Cross-Channel invasion.
North Africa; 1, 3–4, 5, 6, 8, 10, 14, 29, 32, 33, 34, 35, 45, 46, 47, 48, 54, 61, 64, 65, 66, 92, 93, 94, 95, 96, 107, 177, 213, 256, 257, 419, 421, 422, 473, 482, 498, 519, 553
North African Air Force Troop Carrier Command: 424
Northwest African Air Forces Troop Carrier Command (NAAFTCC): 93, 175n
Northwest African Strategic Air Force (NASAF): 108, 379, 380, 411, 411n, 412
Northwest African Tactical Air Force (NATAF): 102, 107, 379, 380, 411, 411n, 412
Norway: 3, 4, 27, 45, 436
Novara di Sicilia: 386, 413
"Nye, Archie": 64, 65

*Oberbefehlshaber Sued.* *See* Commander in Chief South.
*Oberkommando der Kriegsmarine* (OKM): 27, 33n
*Oberkommando der Luftwaffe* (OKL): 27, 83
*Oberkommando der Wehrmacht* (OKW): 27, 29, 30, 32, 33, 36, 37, 38, 46, 47, 48, 49, 50, 51, 65, 74, 75, 78, 82, 157n, 203, 240, 241, 244, 263, 284, 285, 286, 287, 288, 289, 290, 291, 292, 293, 294, 368, 371, 372, 373, 374, 375, 452, 469, 470, 471, 472, 473, 497, 522, 523, 533–34

*Oberkommando des Heeres* (OKH): 27, 32
Occupation of Italy
  Allied: 12, 17–18, 448. *See also* Military government.
  German: 283–84, 297–98, 372, 448, 464. *See also ACHSE; ALARICH; KONSTANTIN; KOPENHAGEN; SIEGFRIED.*
OKH. *See Oberkommando des Heeres.*
OKL. *See Oberkommando der Luftwaffe.*
OKM. *See Oberkommando der Kriegsmarine.*
OKW. *See Oberkommando der Wehrmacht.*
Oliva, Ammiraglio Romeo: 533
Oliveri: 409
Operations Division (OPD): 3
Oran: 94, 95, 102, 108, 493, 498
Order of battle, German: 297, 298, 444
Order of battle, Italian: 463
Orders, Allied. *See* Directives, Allied.
Orders, German
  for evacuation of Sicily: 374n, 374–75
  Hitler's secret: 214
  on Italian troops: 534
Orders, Italian. *See also* Directives, Italian.
  postarmistice: 514, 515
  Roatta's: 513–14, 517–18, 519, 535. *See also Memoria 44.*
*Orizaba:* 158
Orlando, Vittorio Emanuele: 281n
Osborne, Sir D'Arcy Q.: 42, 296, 297, 441, 455, 462, 483
Ostia: 476
OVERLORD. *See* Cross-Channel invasion.

P–38's: 120, 120n, 194, 261, 412
P–39's: 261
P–40's: 73, 261
P–40 fighter groups: 107
P–51's: 342
Paccassi, Flight Officer J. C.: 179
Pachino peninsula: 52, 61, 62, 63, 91, 123, 163
Pack Train. *See* Provisional Pack Train.
Pact of Steel. *See* Italo-German alliance.
Palazzo Caprara: 500, 502, 512, 517, 518
Palazzolo Acreide: 111, 164–65, 170, 172, 205
Palermo: 53, 54, 58, 60, 76, 196, 201n, 224, 226, 226n, 230, 233, 234, 238, 245, 256, 256n, 300, 304, 320, 399, 401, 403, 417, 418, 423, 506
  drive for: 235–36, 244–54, 246n
  surrender of: 254
Palermo naval base: 238
Palestine: 6
Palma, Generale di Brigata Vittorio: 517
Palma di Montechiaro: 98, 99, 192, 197, 235
Palma River: 129

# INDEX

Pantelleria: 52, 63, 107, 119
  Allied assault on: 69-73
  fall of: 72, 73-74, 75
Parachute Infantry units, U.S.: 424
  Regiment, 504th; 94, 175, 176, 177, 181n, 181-82, 185, 250, 255, 498, 499
  Regiment, 505th: 94, 115, 117, 139, 142, 157, 175, 182, 418, 498, 499
    D-day landings: 117-18, 119
    in Trapani action: 255
  Battalions
    1st, 504th: 175
    1st, 505th: 118, 150
    2d, 504th: 175
    2d, 505th: 117, 119, 142, 156
    2d, 509th: 406
    3d, 504th: 94, 101, 115
    3d, 505th: 119, 142, 144, 168
    376th Field Artillery: 175, 179, 255
    456th Field Artillery: 144
Parachute landings. See Airdrops.
Parachute task force, U.S.: 98, 136
Parachutes: 92, 93
"Parallel war" concept: 30-32
Paratroopers, British: 218-19, 219n, 260. See also British Army units, Division, 1st Airborne.
Paratroopers, German: 204, 218, 500, 514, 516, 523, 525, 527, 537
Paratroopers, U.S.: 92, 93, 101, 102, 106, 110, 136, 139, 154, 155, 165, 167, 185, 187, 423, 508, 509. See also Airborne units; Parachute Infantry units.
  and airdrop failure: 156-57
  and Allied antiaircraft disaster: 175, 176, 177-78, 179, 181, 181n, 192
  Biazzo Ridge stand: 168-69, 172-73
  D-day operations of: 117, 118-19, 142
  in Piano Lupo drive: 150, 152
Parks, Air Vice Marshal Keith: 549
Party of Action, Italian: 42
Passive resistance, Italian: 447
Passo Pisciero: 205
Patrols, U.S.: 155, 156, 170, 187, 193, 198, 217, 233, 254, 304, 321, 329, 330, 346, 347, 365, 386, 404
Patti: 408
Patton, General George S., Jr.: 55, 56, 94, 108, 158, 159, 169-70, 174, 174n, 175, 176, 189, 197, 199, 200, 201, 205, 206, 206n, 209, 231, 245, 246n, 252, 253, 257, 349, 380, 390, 391, 406, 408, 412, 421, 423. See also Army, Seventh, U.S.
  and Agrigento drive: 224
  and Alexander: 210, 211, 235-36, 245-46
  and Messina drive: 304, 305, 388-89, 413, 414
  and Palermo: 224, 226, 226n, 235-36, 244, 254
  performance as commander of Seventh Army: 425-26

Patton, General George S., Jr.—Continued
  rearrangement of forces by: 230-31
  slapping incidents: 426-31
  and tactical planning for Sicilian campaign: 59, 60, 91, 96, 97, 98, 105-06
Pearl Harbor: 2
Pelagian Islands: 70, 73, 75
Peloponnesus: 64, 65, 203
Perry, Col. Redding L.: 158, 174n
Pescara: 517, 518, 524, 528, 532
Pétain, Marshal Henri: 464
Petralia: 245-46, 301, 302, 303, 304, 305, 311
Pettineo: 318, 321
*Philadelphia:* 178, 393, 398, 399, 403, 403n
Photographs. See Aerial photographs.
Piano Lupo: 101, 119, 135, 136, 139, 150, 153, 154, 156, 164, 168, 169, 171
Piazza Armerina: 97, 98, 164, 192, 198, 217, 248
Piccardi, Leopoldo: 531
Pietraperzia: 198, 217, 232, 233
Pillboxes, Italian: 133, 139, 141, 143, 144, 251, 253, 353
Pincer movements, U.S.: 125, 131, 133, 156, 189, 341
Piper L-4's: 133n, 418
Piramo: 399
Pisa: 15, 470
Pizza Spina: 316-17
Planes. See Aircraft, Allied; Aircraft, Axis; and by name and designation.
Planners, Allied. See also Force 141.
  air: 120
  AFHQ: 13, 14, 16, 65-66, 258, 259-60
  CCS: 258-59, 425
  tactical, for Sicilian Campaign: 53, 54, 63, 64, 65-66, 88
Planners, British: 4, 436
  and armistice terms for Italy: 25-26
  strategic: 15-16, 18, 19, 21, 258, 259
Planners, U.S.:
  Army vs. Navy, Sicilian invasion: 106
  for GIANT II: 488-89
  logistical, for Sicilian Campaign: 102
  tactical, for Sicilian Campaign: 88
  strategic: 17-19, 258, 259
Planning. See Assault plans; Strategic planning, Allied; Strategic planning, Axis; Tactical planning, Allied; Tactical planning, Axis.
Plans. See Air plan; Assault plans; Tactical plan.
Platani River: 245, 250
Ploesti oil fields: 14
Po valley: 15, 45, 50, 371, 439
Poggio del Moro: 345
Poggio Lungo: 133, 197
Point Braccetto: 141, 144, 145
Point Branco Grande: 141, 145
Point Camerina: 141
Point San Nicola: 127

Point Zafaglione: 144
Pola: 294, 370, 473
Polack, Col. Fritz: 393, 396, 397, 399–400
Ponte Dirillo: 100, 118, 119, 135, 141, 142, 143, 164, 168, 172, 173
Ponte Grande: 121
Ponte Olivo: 61, 96, 117, 135, 136, 174, 200
Ponton causeways: 105, 159–60, 174n, 408
Pope Pius XII: 40, 283
*Port Defense "N," Palermo:* 196, 254
Port-Lyautey: 95
Port Said: 52
Porta San Paolo: 530
Portal, Air Chief Marshal Sir Charles: 11
Portella di Reccativo: 233, 249, 300, 301
Porter, Ellis: 504n
Porter, Lt. Col. Ray W., Jr.: 325
Porto Empedocle: 110, 209, 224, 226, 228, 230, 235, 256, 256n
Ports
  Adriatic: 24
  Italian: 67, 68, 457
  Sicilian: 53, 54, 58, 63, 89, 96–97, 98, 110
Postumia-Ljubljana gap: 436
Pozzallo: 97
Pratica di Mare: 286
Prichard, Lt. Col. Leslie A.: 352
Priolo: 123, 202
Prisoners of war, Allied: 447, 454, 468. *See also* Casualties, British; Casualties, U.S.
Prisoners of war, Axis: 255, 323, 419, 456n, 457, 468. *See also* Casualties, Axis; Casualties, German; Casualties, Italian; Prisoners of war, German; Prisoners of war, Italian.
Prisoners of war, German: 168–69, 173n, 342, 394. *See also* Casualties, Axis; Casualties, German.
Prisoners of war, Italian: 139, 223, 228, 253, 314. *See also* Casualties, Axis; Casualties, Italian.
  return of, promised: 270, 275
  of Germans: 533, 534
*Procyon:* 178
*Promemoria 1:* 491
*Promemoria 2:* 491, 492n, 514
Propaganda. *See also* Radio broadcasting, Allied; Radio broadcasting, Italian.
  Allied: 298, 543–44
  German: 524
  Italian: 239–40, 548
Propaganda officers, Allied: 505
Provisional Corps. *See under* Corps, U.S.
Provisional Mounted Troop: 348
Provisional Pack Train: 348. *See also* Mules.
Prunas, Renato: 297, 455, 461
Psychological warfare: 272, 275. *See also* Propaganda; Radio broadcasting, Allied; Radio broadcasting, Italian.
"Puddle-jumpers". *See* Piper L–4's.

Puglia: 244, 263, 282, 368, 452, 471, 473, 522, 534
Punta delle due Rocche: 133
Puntoni, Generale di Divisione Paolo: 264, 266, 511

QUADRANT Conference (Quebec)
  Long terms agreed on: 448–49
  and strategic planning: 435–36, 437, 438–40
Quebec Memorandum: 447–48, 457, 475, 484, 556–57
Quebec telegram: 457–58, 460, 461
*Queen Mary:* 19
Quirinal Palace: 511, 512, 527

Rabat: 94
Radar: 82, 107
Raddusa: 224
Radio Algiers: 508–09
Radio Bari: 540
Radio broadcasting, Allied: 278, 508–09. *See also* British Broadcasting Corporation; Eisenhower, broadcasts to Italians.
Radio broadcasting, Italian: 488, 513, 515, 516–17, 528, 529, 530. *See also* Radio Rome.
Radio communication, Italo-Allied, secret: 459, 461, 466–67, 478, 490, 495–96, 503, 504, 505, 532, 535, 540
Radio communication, U.S.: 176, 189, 399, 400, 401, 404, 499–500
Radio Rome: 508, 509, 513
Radio stations, Axis: 71
RAF: 107
Ragusa: 91, 96, 98, 100, 156, 189, 190
Rahn, Rudolf: 473, 483, 497, 514
Railroads
  Italian: 24–25, 288, 291, 293, 412, 533
  Sicilian: 256–57, 309
Railway Operating Battalion, U.S., 727th: 256
"Raimondi, Signor": 441, 444. *See also* Castellano, Generale di Brigata Giuseppe.
Ramsey, Vice Adm. Sir Bertram H.: 89
Randazzo: 207, 345, 346, 378, 393, 404, 418
  and Axis evacuation of Sicily: 382, 385, 386
  bombing of: 385, 385n
Ranger Battalions, U.S.: 95, 100, 165, 220, 252–53
  and Axis counterattack: 169–70
  and Gela assault: 136, 137–39, 152–53
  1st: 96
  3d: 96, 125, 200, 227, 391
    in Green Beach assault: 131–32
    in Montaperto drive: 228
  4th: 96
Rapido River: 552
Ravenna: 15, 445, 459
Reconnaissance, German: 148, 398. *See also* Air reconnaissance, Axis.

# INDEX

Reconnaissance units, U.S.: 107, 192, 194, 201, 224, 228, 229, 230, 235, 250-51, 253, 304, 312-13, 498
    Battalion, 82d: 174n, 254
    Squadron, 91st; 311, 314, 330, 331
Red Beach: 125, 133, 141, 161
    assault on: 125-31, 143
    characterized: 126-27
Red Beach 2: 136, 143, 158, 159, 160
Reese, Pvt. James W.: 344, 344n
Regalbuto: 307, 319, 341, 342n
Reggio di Calabria: 16, 214, 237, 260, 483
Regimental Combat Teams. *See* Infantry Regiments, U. S.
Reinforcements, Axis: 54, 64, 65, 74-75, 203, 204, 212-13, 216, 237, 242, 243, 244, 263, 282, 289, 290-94, 293n, 308, 368, 369, 372, 373, 442, 451, 452, 462, 477, 492, 534
Reporters. *See* Newspaper correspondents.
Reprisals, German: 513
    executions: 533, 534
    threatened: 445, 453, 458, 464, 467, 547
Reschen Pass: 373
Reserves, German: 237, 294, 477. *See also* Mobile reserves, Axis; Reinforcements, Axis.
Reserves, Italian. *See* Mobile reserves, Italian.
Reserves, U. S.: 97-98, 136, 187, 200. *See also* Floating reserve.
Resources, Allied: 3, 5, 6, 7, 8, 25, 258-59, 261, 262, 278, 436, 437, 439, 449
Revel, Grand Admiral Paolo Thaon di: 42, 43
Rhodes: 44, 514
Ribbentrop, Joachim von: 35n, 36-37, 283, 283n, 369, 371
Ricci, Umberto: 517, 528, 532
Richardson, Maj. Gen. A. A.: 549
Richthofen, Feldmarschall Wolfram Freiherr von: 78, 78n, 241, 295
Ridgway, Maj. Gen. Matthew B.: 93, 94, 101-02, 108, 182, 254-55, 498, 508
    on airborne forces: 157, 424
    and Allied antiaircraft disaster: 175-76, 179, 184
    and GIANT II: 485, 486, 488, 489, 498, 499
Riesi: 192, 193, 197, 198, 199, 200
Rifle grenades: 317
Rifle support, Axis: 133, 137-38, 139, 144, 343
Rifle support, U.S.: 150, 152, 317, 340, 402, 404
Rifle units, U.S.: 189, 344-45, 361, 363, 365, 366, 393, 394, 396, 397, 400
Rintelen, General der Infanterie Enno von: 32, 33, 33n, 36, 49, 51, 74, 211n, 282, 284, 285, 287, 291, 292n, 369, 372, 452, 471, 472, 473, 510
    on Italian armed forces: 48
    in Italy: 32, 33
    peace moves of: 291, 292-93, 294-95
Riviera: 472

Rizzo, Franco Babuzzio: 296
Road junctions:
    Bompietro: 313
    highway: 209, 222
    Maletto: 385
    Piano Lupo: 150, 151, 152, 188
    Y: 135
Roadblocks: 79, 101, 185, 196, 200, 201, 206, 228, 233, 249, 255, 300, 301, 348, 365, 513, 514
Roads, Italian. *See* Via entries.
Roads, Sicilian: 53, 100, 101, 135, 141, 149, 195-96, 208, 211, 226, 233n, 245, 249, 301, 318, 336, 339-40, 401, 418-19. *See also* Highway entries.
    Butera: 152
    in Cancicatti area: 198-99, 200
    Cesarò-San Fratello: 352-53, 357
    to Messina: 207
    Niscemi-Piano Lupo: 154, 164, 165, 166, 168
    north coast. *See* Highway 113.
    Ponte Olivo-Mazzarino: 206
    Santa Croce Camerina-Vittoria: 142
Roatta, Generale di Corpo d'Armata Comandante Designato d'Armata Mario: 47, 76, 77, 79, 214, 215, 242, 263, 275, 281, 282, 285, 286, 287, 288, 290, 295, 294, 368, 372, 373, 374, 441, 452, 455, 458, 460, 462, 466, 479, 490, 491, 491n, 494n, 500, 501, 514, 520, 523, 528, 529, 534, 542, 549
    at Bologna conference: 452-53
    and Castellano's mission: 453-54
    and defense of Italy and Rome: 289, 451, 492, 493, 510, 513-14, 515, 516
    and evacuation of Rome: 517, 518, 524
    and German relations: 289, 503, 510, 512, 513-14
    and Italian mainland invasion: 493-94, 495, 496, 502, 503
    orders and directives: 513-14, 515, 517-18, 519, 535. *See also Memoria 44.*
Robert Rowan: 177, 179
Rocca di Mania: 3, 8, 276, 343
Roccella River: 300
Rocket launchers. *See* Bazookas.
Rodt, Generalmajor Eberhard: 81, 84, 192, 196, 198, 217, 233, 301, 313, 315, 324, 341, 342, 345, 346, 352, 382, 385-87, 388, 401, 405
*Roe:* 129
Rogers, Col. Arthur R.: 125, 357, 358, 361, 401, 408
*Roma:* 532-33
Rome: 14, 24, 38, 68, 71, 72, 441, 442, 444, 448, 449, 452, 458, 467, 472, 484, 499, 500, 501, 502, 503, 505, 512, 513, 514, 515
    and airborne operation by Allies. *See* GIANT II.
    American mission to: 499-502, 503-05

Rome—Continued
  battle for, Germans and Italians: 524–32
  bombing of: 24–25, 250, 278, 279, 292, 442
  defense of: 289, 464, 480, 492, 493, 510, 513–14, 516, 524–32. *See also Memoria 44.*
  evacuation of: 516–19, 527–28
  German occupation of: 532
  German threat of seizure of: 283, 284, 285, 288, 289, 298, 368, 372, 442, 451–52, 453, 464, 470, 476, 481, 515–16. *See also ACHSE,* Plan.
  and Italian mainland invasion: 437, 440, 473, 474, 475, 477–78, 522, 531
  liberation of: 551, 552
  as open city: 278–80, 373, 469
Rommel, Generalfeldmarschall Erwin: 4, 32, 35, 49, 50, 51, 226n, 241, 242, 282, 283, 284, 285, 371–72, 442, 452, 453, 460, 469, 472, 497, 522, 534
Rooks, Maj. Gen. Lowell S.: 15, 24, 67, 236, 262, 440, 485, 486, 503, 504, 504n, 506n
Roosevelt, Franklin Delano: 1, 3, 11, 12, 19, 20, 23, 40, 271, 272, 273, 274, 275, 276, 277, 279, 287, 435, 442, 443, 444, 446, 447, 456n, 458, 461, 462, 507, 535, 540, 544, 547, 548, 549, 550
  and Italian armistice: 274, 276–77, 448, 449, 545, 546
  and strategic planning: 4, 7, 437, 438
Roosevelt, Brig. Gen. Theodore: 158, 313, 339, 347
Rose, Brig. Gen. Maurice: 125, 197, 199, 253
Rosmarino River: 363, 365, 366, 367, 388
Rossi, Generale di Corpo d'Armata Carlo: 84, 242n, 369, 441, 452–53, 465, 490, 491, 494, 494n, 495, 496, 500, 501, 505, 510
  and armistice announcement: 503, 504, 519–20
  and GIANT II: 495, 496, 503
ROUNDHAMMER: 437. *See also* Cross-Channel invasion.
ROUNDUP: 3, 5. *See also* Cross-Channel invasion.
*Rowan. See Robert Rowan.*
Royal Air Force, Malta Command: 107
Ruini, Meuccio: 531
Rumania: 8, 12, 40, 44, 298
Rundstedt, Generalfeldmarschall Gerd von: 283, 284, 288, 472–73
Russia. *See* Russo-German campaign; Union of Soviet Socialist Republics.
Russo-German campaign: 22, 23, 32, 35, 45, 46, 241, 244, 417, 435, 445, 458
Sabotage, Italian: 447, 497
St. George's Hotel: 56
Salemi: 255
Salerno: 262–63, 368, 449, 452, 465, 471, 482, 498, 500, 503
Salerno landings: 482, 505, 509, 520, 521, 522, 524, 530, 531, 535, 536, 540, 541, 552. *See also* Italian mainland invasion.

Salonika: 445
Salso River: 97, 99, 232, 233, 245
Salvi, Col. Giorgio: 500, 518, 519, 525, 528
Sampieri: 176
*Samuel Chase:* 108
San Fratello: 349–67, 374, 380, 382, 388, 393, 418, 419
San Gregorio: 344
San Marco d'Alunzio: 365, 366
San Michele di Ganzeria: 202
San Nicola Rock: 127
San Oliva Station: 128
Sandalli, Generale di Divisione Aerea Renato: 492, 511, 517, 549
Sangro River: 552
Santa Caterina: 233, 246, 248
Santa Croce Camerina: 142, 156
Santa Ninfa: 255
Santa Teresa: 412, 414
Sant'Agata: 352, 363, 365
Santo Stefano di Camastra: 214, 307–08, 321–23, 348, 352, 360
Sanzi, Alfredo: 530n
Sardinia: 6, 7, 8, 9, 12, 14, 15, 16, 17, 18, 19, 22n, 23, 24, 45, 46, 48, 49, 50, 51, 52, 67, 73, 74, 109, 110, 203, 239, 258, 259, 283, 284, 438, 453, 459, 460, 463, 464, 471, 473, 481, 493, 494, 506, 515, 535, 541, 542, 543
  defenses of: 75, 76
  invasion plan. *See* BRIMSTONE.
  and MINCEMEAT: 64, 65
Sarno: 477
*Savannah:* 137, 137n, 170
Scaletta: 414
Schacht, Capt. Hans: 526
Schaefer, Lt. Col. Irving O.: 144
Schaefer, Lt. Col. William: 142, 143, 155, 155n
Scheel. *See* Vietinghoff gennant Scheel, General der Panzertruppen Heinrich von.
Schmalz, Col. Wilhelm: 123, 147n, 148, 191, 204, 216, 219, 240
Schmundt, Generalmajor Rudolf: 287
Schreiber, Generale di Brigata Ottorino: 197–98, 200, 217
SCHWARZ, Operation: 452
Sciacca: 251
Scoglitti: 97, 98, 100, 141, 143, 144, 161, 165, 177, 256n, 418, 419
Scordia: 207
Scorza, Count Carlo: 39, 267, 549, 551
Scout planes: 151n
Seaborne operations, Allied: 259, 498–99, 500, 508, 509. *See also* Amphibious operations, Allied.
Second Front, Axis: 240–41, 242
Senger und Etterlin, Generalleutnant Fridolin von: 82, 148, 163, 170, 172, 173, 203, 204, 205, 214, 215, 223, 237, 309, 375

Senise, Carmine: 39
Serradifalco: 233
Sfax: 92
Shelly, 1st Lt. M. C.: 181
Sherman, Col. Harry B.: 125, 129, 227, 401
Ship-to-shore operations: 100, 105
Shipping, Allied: 6, 7, 8, 10, 16, 17, 18, 60, 62, 73, 105, 159, 177, 320, 473, 486
Shipping, Italian: 485
Ships. *See* Naval vessels, Allied; Naval vessels, Axis.
Shore parties, U.S.: 161, 170n, 171, 401, 403. *See also* Beach parties; Naval salvage parties.
Shore-to-shore operations: 100, 105
Short (military) terms: 273, 274, 276, 277, 447, 448, 449, 461, 462, 465, 541, 549, 558
  negotiations over: 455-59. *See also* Cassibile conference.
  QUADRANT discussion of: 448, 449
  signing of: 483, 484, 501
Shortages, German: 37
Shortages, Italian: 37, 81, 298, 457, 459-60, 480, 485, 500, 502, 542-43
Shorter bridgehead line. *See* Tortorici line.
*Shubrick:* 137, 137n, 152
Sicily: 1, 4, 6, 7, 8, 9, 10, 12, 33, 44, 45, 46, 47, 48, 49, 50, 73, 75, 269, 275, 282, 283, 284, 295, 459, 465, 473, 498, 499, 508, 541, 551. *See also* Evacuation of Sicily, Axis.
  Axis defenses on: 66, 75-77, 79-80, 83, 84, 86-87, 126-27, 163
  geographical features: 52-53. *See also* Terrain, of Sicily.
  strategic importance of: 52, 213
*SIEGFRIED:* 284
Signal communications, Italian: 79-80, 163
Signal Corps, U.S.: 419
Signal units, U.S.: 498
Signals, U.S.: 195
Sillian Pass: 373
Simeto River: 207, 218, 219, 223, 224, 385, 393
Skorzeny, Capt. Otto: 284, 285, 286, 368, 452, 470, 536, 537
Sladen, Lt. Col. Fred W., Jr.: 359, 360, 361
SLEDGEHAMMER: 3n
Slovenia: 32
Small arms support, Allied: 154, 170
Small arms support, Axis: 169, 300, 318, 321, 330, 338, 344, 358, 402
Small craft, Italian: 546
Small craft, U.S.: 160, 379
Smith, Col. George A.: 159, 303, 341
Smith, Maj. Gen. Walter B.: 11, 24, 444n, 455n, 485, 546, 547, 549
  and armistice negotiations: 455, 457, 457-58, 458n, 459, 460, 462, 463, 474, 475, 476, 478, 482, 483, 484, 548

Smith, Maj. Gen. Walter B.—Continued
  and Italian mainland invasion: 489, 490
Smoke screens: 131, 401
Smythe, Col. George W.: 343, 382, 385
Snipers: 321, 400
Socialist Party, Italian: 42
SOC's: 147n
Sogno, Generale di Corpo d'Armata Vittorio: 527-28
Soleri, Marcello: 43
Soleti: 537
Solinas, Generale di Brigata Gioacchino: 525, 529
Somervell, Lt. Gen. Brehon B.: 8
Sommatino: 192, 197, 199, 200
Sorice, Generale di Brigata in Riserva Antonio: 282, 511, 517, 518, 527, 528, 529
  and armistice renunciation: 511
  and capitulation to Germans: 530, 531
Sousse: 70
South Tyrol: 373, 533
Southern France: 4, 12, 15, 17, 22, 32, 45, 46, 65, 67, 435, 436, 438, 439, 472. *See also* France.
Soviet Union. *See* Union of Soviet Socialist Republics.
Spaatz, Lt. Gen. Carl: 182, 379
Spadafora: 413, 414, 415
Spain: 5, 8, 43, 45, 46, 55, 65
Spanish Morocco: 55
Sperlinga: 301, 312, 314, 336
Spitfires: 107, 261, 339, 340
SS agents: 492
Stalin, Marshal Joseph: 11, 34, 35, 458, 545, 546
Stalingrad: 1, 34, 37, 213, 372
Stark, Admiral Harold R.: 2n
State Department, U.S.: 19, 26, 269, 273, 279, 449
*Stato Maggiore Generale. See Comando Supremo.*
*Stato Maggiore Regia Aeronautica (Superaereo):* 29, 491
*Stato Maggiore Regia Marina (Supermarina):* 29, 33n, 71, 72, 110, 491, 533n
*Stato Maggio Regio Esercito (Superesercito):* 29-30, 49, 77, 216, 281, 307n, 369
Steamboats, Italian: 378
Stefanis, de, Generale di Corpo d'Armata Giuseppe: 292, 510, 511, 515, 518, 524
Stephenson, Lt. Col. Edward F.: 144
Sternberg, Lt. Col. Ben: 185
Stimson, Henry L: 437, 438
Stolfi, Dr. Edoardo: 529-30
Storch aircraft: 537-38
Strait of Gibraltar: 82
Strait of Messina. *See* Messina Strait.
Strategic planning, Allied: 1-26, 66-67, 258-63, 268-69, 278, 435-40

Strategic planning, Axis: 34–35, 37–38, 213, 368
Strength, Allied: 8–9, 53, 107, 203, 212, 262, 417n, 421, 424, 425, 468, 474, 475, 477, 479, 512
Strength, Axis: 32, 47, 48, 53, 63, 64, 226–27, 238, 301–02, 449, 458, 459, 477, 500, 501, 513, 535
Strikes, Italian labor: 39
Strong, Brigadier Kenneth D.: 455, 455n, 459, 460, 462, 463, 474, 485, 506, 506n, 507
Student, Generaloberst Kurt: 157n, 284, 285, 286, 368, 452, 526, 536, 537
Submarines, Axis: 1, 37, 38, 70, 73, 82, 213
Suez Canal: 1
*Superaereo. See Stato Maggiore Regia Aeronautica.*
*Superesercito. See Stato Maggiore Regio Esercito.*
*Supermarina. See Stato Maggiore Regia Marina.*
Supplies, Allied: 54, 63, 131, 146, 160, 161, 174, 258–59, 311, 348, 352, 420. *See also* Logistical operations.
Supplies, Axis: 37, 47, 77, 79, 82, 445, 452, 469, 477
Supplies, Italian. *See* Shortages, Italian.
Supply ships, Allied: 256
Supply trains: 348
Surprise. *See* Tactical surprise.
Surrender of Italy: 25–26, 39–40, 273, 275, 448, 477, 482, 496, 499, 523, 552. *See also* Armistice, Italo-Allied; Capitulation, Italian; Unconditional surrender, for Italy.
Surrender of Sicily: 25
*Susan B. Anthony:* 178
*Swanson:* 45
Sweden: 45
Swing, Maj. Gen. Joseph M.: 175, 176, 423, 425
Swingler, 1st Lt. H. H.: 119, 173
Switzerland: 43
Syracuse: 53, 54, 58, 61, 89, 91, 92, 97, 111, 120, 123, 163, 164, 203. *See also Naval Base Augusta-Syracuse.*

Tabellini, Generale di Divisione Ugo: 529
Tactical Bomber Force: 107
Tactical planning, Allied (Sicilian Campaign). *See also* Assault plans.
air operations: 59. *See also* Air plan.
airborne operations: 88–89, 92–94, 101–02, 485–89, 498–99
Allied armies' missions: 209–211, 235, 236, 245–46, 319, 420, 422–23
for amphibious operations: 53–54, 58, 59, 60–63, 66, 88–89, 91–92, 96–100, 103–07, 135–36, 406, 408, 413–14
basic plan and modifications: 58–63, 206–07, 209–11, 248–49, 419–20, 422–23
ground operations: 58–59, 60–63, 89–101, 135–36, 141–42, 421–23

Tactical planning, Allied—Continued
for Messina drive: 234–35, 245, 246, 248, 319, 413–14
naval operations: 59, 89, 100, 106
for Nicosia attack: 314
for Palermo drive: 234–36, 244–46
for Troina attack: 333–34, 336–37
Tactical planning, Axis. *See also ALARICH,* Plan; Feltre conference; *KONSTANTIN,* Plan.
to block Allied advance: 192
for counterattacks in Sicily: 147–49, 164–65, 170, 172, 196, 197–98
and dual command: 307–09
for Sicily's defense: 83–87, 120–21, 212–14
withdrawal and defensive lines: 202–03
Tactical surprise: 65–66, 70, 102, 106, 120, 322, 366, 396, 537
Tagliavia, Lieutenant: 504, 505
Tangier: 298
Tank destroyers, U.S.: 499
Tank units, U.S.: 102, 160, 194, 199, 352, 408. *See also* Armored units.
at Monte Cipolla: 393, 394, 396, 397
Corps: 95
Battalions
70th Light: 232, 314
753d Medium: 233, 314, 318
813th Tank Destroyer: 499
Tanks, British: 219
Tanks, German: 75, 164, 165, 166, 167, 168, 223, 232, 344, 399, 401, 500, 524–25
in Brolo action: 402–03
in Casa del Priolo action: 187
in counterattack in Sicily: 154, 166–67, 168, 170, 171, 171n
losses: 171–72n
Mark III: 148, 149n, 167, 171n
Mark IV: 148, 149n, 167, 171n, 363, 485
Mark VI (Tiger): 148, 148n, 154, 171n, 172, 187, 188, 298
Tanks, Italian: 230n
in Gela counterattack: 150, 151n, 151–52
Renault: 151n, 363
Tanks, U.S.: 99, 131, 136, 158, 159, 174n, 179, 188, 197, 199, 208, 253, 306n, 397. *See also* Armored units; Tanks units.
light: 232, 253, 301, 302, 314
M3: 129n
M7: 129, 129n
medium: 194, 314, 363
Taormina: 33, 111, 163, 412
Taranto: 67, 260, 262, 481, 505, 532, 541
Tarvis: 472
Tarvis conference: 287, 294, 298, 369–71, 373, 451, 452, 472
Tarvis pass: 373, 442, 472

# INDEX

Task Force Bernard: 352, 360, 361, 363, 380, 388n, 393–405
Task Force X, U.S.: 252, 254–55
Task forces, Allied: 55–56, 58. *See also* Task Force Bernard; Force 343; Force 545; Naval Task Force *entries*.
Task forces, Italian: 78
Taylor, Lt. Col. Earl A.: 144, 155–56
Taylor, Brig. Gen. George A.: 136, 139, 152n, 187, 188, 336, 339
Taylor, Brig. Gen. Maxwell D.: 486, 489, 499, 500, 500n, 501, 502, 503, 504, 506, 507, 510, 519, 541n
Taylor, Myron C.: 40
Tedder, Air Chief Marshal Sir Arthur: 11, 13, 15, 22n, 24, 55, 59, 61, 62, 88, 182, 278, 378, 379, 420, 549
Telephone communications, German: 410, 515, 523
Telephone communications, Italian: 147, 148, 189, 533
Termini Imerese: 300
Terrain. *See also* Beaches, landing.
    Italian: 259, 552
    of Sicily: 97, 100, 101, 135, 154, 208, 245, 250, 302, 305, 309, 322, 324, 348, 358, 359, 360, 387, 389, 401–02, 408, 553. *See also* Yellow Line.
        of Monte Cipolla area: 393
        of San Fratello area: 352–53
        of Tortorici line: 382
        around Troina: 325–29, 339
Terrana Creek: 135
Terranova: 399, 400
Thessaly: 453
Thunderbirds. *See* Infantry divisions, U.S., 45th.
Tiber River: 485, 486, 488, 498–99, 500, 508, 509, 516
Timberlake, Brig. Gen. Patrick W.: 485
Tinley, Maj. Philip C.: 336, 337
Tirana: 514
Tittmann, Harold: 296, 443
Tivoli: 516, 517, 518, 519, 524, 529
Toffey, Lt. Col. John J., Jr.: 253, 255
Tomasello, Col. Michele: 416
TORCH. *See* North Africa.
Torpedo-bombers, Italian: 399
Torpedo plane squadron: 214
Torretta, Della: 265
Tortorici (shorter bridgehead) line: 345, 345n, 378, 382, 391, 404
Toulon: 472
Toussaint, General der Infanterie Rudolf: 473, 512, 523
Trabia, Lt. Galvano Lanza di: 454
Train ferry, Italian: 378, 410
Traniello, Generale di Brigata Ottaviano: 529
"Trans-Divs": 105

Transportation. *See* Ferrying service, German; Ferrying service, Italian; Railroads.
Transports, air, Allied: 115
Transports, U.S.: 161, 177
Trapani: 110, 111, 254, 255
Treasury Department, U.S.: 26
Tremestieri: 416
TRIDENT Conference: 6, 19–23, 24, 66, 258, 268–69, 436, 437, 438, 448
Trieste: 473
Tripoli: 4, 57, 107, 498
Troina: 207, 320, 323, 352, 418
    battle of: 331–47
    defense of, U.S. estimates: 325, 328, 331, 333, 337
    terrain characteristics: 325–29, 339
Troina River: 337, 338, 340, 343
Troop Carrier Command: 157, 176, 182, 498, 508
Troop Carrier Groups
    314th: 179
    316th: 180
Troop Carrier Wings, U.S.
    51st: 92, 115
    52d: 93, 101, 115, 157, 175, 182n, 424
Troop carriers, Allied: 101–02, 108. *See also* C-47's.
    attacked by friendly antiaircraft: 175, 176, 177–80, 181–84, 218
    failure of: 157, 423, 424
Troop movements, German: 372–73, 442, 472, 492, 510, 514–15. *See also* Evacuation of Sicily; German Army, in Italy; German Army, in Sicily.
Troop movements, Italian: 373. *See also* Evacuation of Sicily; Withdrawal, Italian to Tivoli.
Troop transports. *See* Transports.
Troops, Allied. *See also* Army, U.S., *entries;* British Army units; Corps, U.S.; Infantry *entries;* Divisions, Allied; Task force *entries*.
    airborne: 10
    in North Africa: 9
Troops, Axis. *See* German Army; German Army units; Italian Army; Italian Army units.
Troops, British: 72, 89. *See also* British Army units; Glider troops, British.
Troops, U.S.: 56, 89, 210n, 211, 422. *See also* Army, Seventh, U.S.; Corps, U.S.; Infantry *entries*.
Truce, Italo-German: 525–27, 530. *See also* Capitulation, Italian.
Trucks, German: 290
Truscott, Maj. Gen. Lucian K., Jr.: 98, 99, 103, 108, 125, 129n, 133, 155, 192, 197, 198, 199, 200, 206, 226n, 227, 229, 235, 254, 357, 358, 361, 363, 366, 388, 389, 402, 405, 406, 408, 415, 416, 426

Truscott, Maj. Gen. Lucian K., Jr.—Continued
    and Agrigento drive: 224, 226-27
    career of: 95
    and Messina drive: 414
    and Monte Cipolla: 389-91, 399, 401, 404
    and Naso ridge link-up: 389, 390
    and San Fratello action: 348, 349, 352, 357, 358, 360
Tucker, Col. Reuben H.: 175, 179, 182
Tunis: 46, 49, 269, 505
Tunisia: 5, 8, 9, 34, 48, 56, 60, 61, 64, 92, 107, 175, 275, 488, 498
Tunisian Campaign: 8, 10, 20, 46, 55, 88, 374
Turin: 288, 442, 494, 517
Turin-Lyons railway: 442
Turkey: 4, 6, 8, 12, 14, 15, 17, 18, 24, 43, 44, 436
Tusa ridge: 318, 321, 322
Tusa River: 318, 321
Tyrol. *See* South Tyrol.
Tyrrhenian coast: 67
Tyrrhenian islands: 14
Tyrrhenian Sea: 45

Ulich, Col. Max: 318, 322
Unconditional surrender: 239, 277, 279, 298, 447, 448, 449, 458, 460, 462
    British view: 12
    for Italy: 11, 12, 19, 25, 39, 44, 51, 269, 271, 273, 274, 442, 443, 444, 445, 446, 447, 464, 484, 512, 542, 550. *See also* Long terms.
    Roosevelt's demand for: 11-12, 19
Union of Soviet Socialist Republics: 1, 2, 3, 5, 8, 21, 26, 29, 38, 44, 47, 464. *See also* Russo-German campaign.
    and Italy's peace efforts: 34, 38
    and strategic planning: 3-4, 23
Unit of fire. *See* Logistical operations, Allied; Maintenance, Allied.
United Kingdom. *See* Great Britain.
Ustica Island: 500
Utili, Generale di Brigata Umberto: 293, 440, 441, 515, 518, 519

V of V's formation: 101, 117, 175
Valetta Harbor: 549
Valguarnera: 233
*Valiant:* 533
Vandervoort, Maj. Benjamin H.: 168, 169
Vassallo, Major: 482
Vatican: 40, 41, 274, 278-79, 283, 468
Vatican City: 24, 26, 296, 475
Vehicles, German: 37, 320, 365, 398, 451. *See also* Tanks, German.
Vehicles, Italian: 493, 525

Vehicles, U.S.: 252, 409. *See also* Dukws; Half-tracks, U.S.; Tanks, U.S.
Velletri: 515
Venturi, Colonel: 191
Verlet, Capt. Guido: 340
Via Appia: 515
Via Cassia: 523
Via Claudia: 523
Via dell'Empero: 531
Via Laurentina: 515, 525
Via Ostiense: 515, 516, 525
Via Tiburtina: 516, 517, 518, 524
Vichy France: 32
Victor Emmanuel III, King: 28, 29, 270, 271, 273, 281, 283, 285, 286, 287, 297, 298, 306, 369, 371, 373, 440, 441, 453, 464, 467, 468, 474, 477, 483, 484, 493, 513, 514, 518, 519, 529, 532, 536, 539, 540, 544, 548, 552. *See also* Monarchy.
    and armistice: 441, 457, 466, 480, 510, 511, 512-13, 549
    and Badoglio government: 453, 481
    and Caviglia: 527, 531
    described by Mason-MacFarlane: 542
    and evacuation of Rome: 528
    and Germany alliance: 553
    and Government of Italy, postarmistice: 544, 546-48, 551
    and Grandi: 548, 549, 551
    and Mussolini's overthrow: 42-44, 239, 264, 265, 266-68
    peace efforts of: 239
    power of: 267, 281, 547-48
    and war declaration against Germany: 547, 549
Vietinghoff gennant Scheel, General der Panzertruppen Heinrich von: 470, 471
Villa San Giovanni: 376
Villach-Klagenfurt: 373
Villafrati: 300
Villarosa: 248, 249
Vitetti, Leonardo: 371
Vittoria: 100, 141, 142, 155, 163, 164, 168, 172, 418
*Vittorio Veneto:* 532-33
Vizzini: 96, 172, 202, 205, 207, 208, 209, 215, 219, 220, 224
Volturno River: 477, 552
VULCAN: 66

War criminals: 272, 274, 276
War Department, U.S.: 279
War Plans Division: 3
Warlimont, General der Artillerie Walter: 37, 50, 369, 371, 375
*Warspite:* 533
Wasten, Lt. Col. Charles N.: 426

# INDEX

Watkinson, Mr.: 299
Waybur, 1st Lt. David C.: 230n
Weapons, Allied: 553. *See also* Guns, U.S.; Weapons, U.S.
Weapons, German: 376, 377, 476. *See also* Guns, German.
   antitank: 377
   automatic: 358
Weapons, Italian: 476, 529. *See also* Guns, Italian.
Weapons, U.S.: 485. *See also* Guns, U.S.; Howitzers, U.S.; Mortars, U.S.
Weapons support, U.S.: 361, 394. *See also* Artillery support, U.S.
Weather conditions, and Sicilian invasion: 89, 108, 115, 123, 125, 139
Wedemeyer, Maj. Gen. Albert C.: 16n, 235, 436
*Wehrmacht:* 27, 473. *See also* German Army.
*Wehrmachtfuehrungsstag* (WFSt): 27, 368
Weichold, Vice Adm. Eberhard: 33n
Weizsaecker, Ernst von: 293
Welles, Sumner: 279
Wellington bombers, British: 278, 376, 379, 410, 411
Westphal, General der Artillerie Siegfried: 78, 375, 503, 510, 512, 513, 523, 525–26, 530
White, Col. I. D.: 158
Whiteley, General J. F. M.: 440
Wiart, de, Lt. Gen. Sir Adrian Carton: 454, 461, 463
Williams, Brig. Gen. Paul L.: 175n, 182
Wilson, General Sir Henry Maitland: 64, 436
Withdrawals, Axis. *See also Promemoria 2.*
   German, in Italy: 470, 552

Withdrawals, Axis—Continued
   Italian, to Tivoli: 516–19, 524–25, 529
   in Sicilian Campaign: 202–03, 205, 216–17, 217n, 219, 223–24, 233, 234, 238, 245, 314, 315, 325, 345–46, 357, 366, 404, 405. *See also* Evacuation of Sicily.
Wood's Hole beaches. *See* Green Beach; Red Beach; Yellow Beach.
World War I: 30, 551
Wyman, Col. Willard G.: 347

Yates, 1st Lt. Ralph J.: 416
Yellow Beach: 125, 133, 141, 144, 158, 159, 161
Yellow Beach 2: 136, 142, 144, 145
Yellow Line: 98, 99, 185–201, 206, 207, 208, 222, 223
York, Lt. Col. Robert H.: 187
Yugoslavia: 15, 17, 24, 37, 38, 261, 445

Zanussi, Generale Addetto al Capo di Stato Maggiore Giacomo: 440, 441, 453, 467, 477, 480, 484, 506, 512, 515, 517, 518, 520, 542, 552
   at Cassibile conference: 474, 475, 476, 478
   and Castellano: 455, 462, 463, 474, 478–79
   peace mission of: 454–55, 461–65, 466, 467
Zappulla River: 382, 388, 389, 401
Zeitzler, General der Infanterie Kurt: 294–95
Zingales, Generale di Corpo d'Armata Francesco: 84
*ZITADELLE:* 213
Zuckerman, Professor S.: 70n

## THE BATTLEGROUND AND THE ENEMY
### 10 July 1943

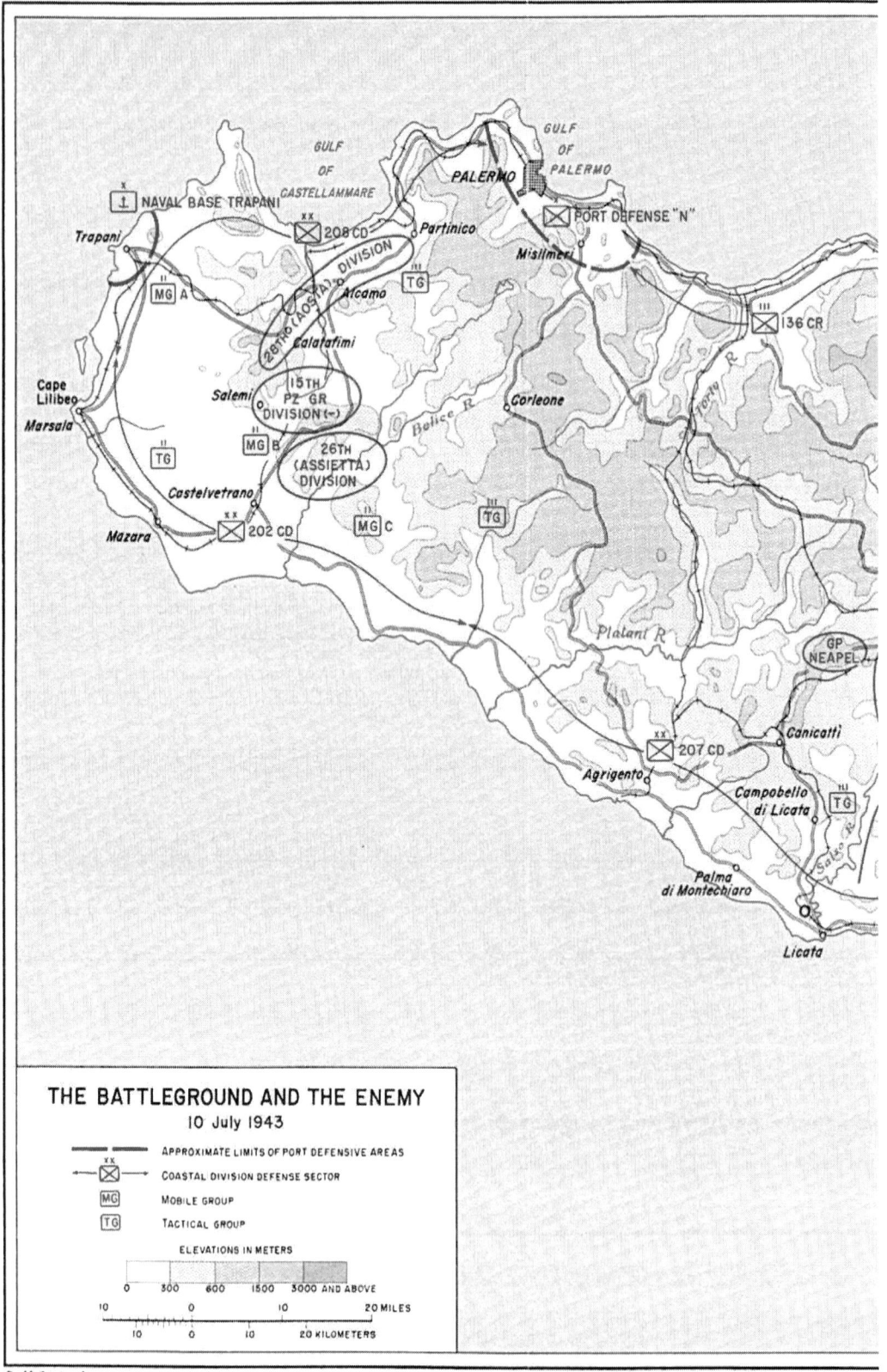

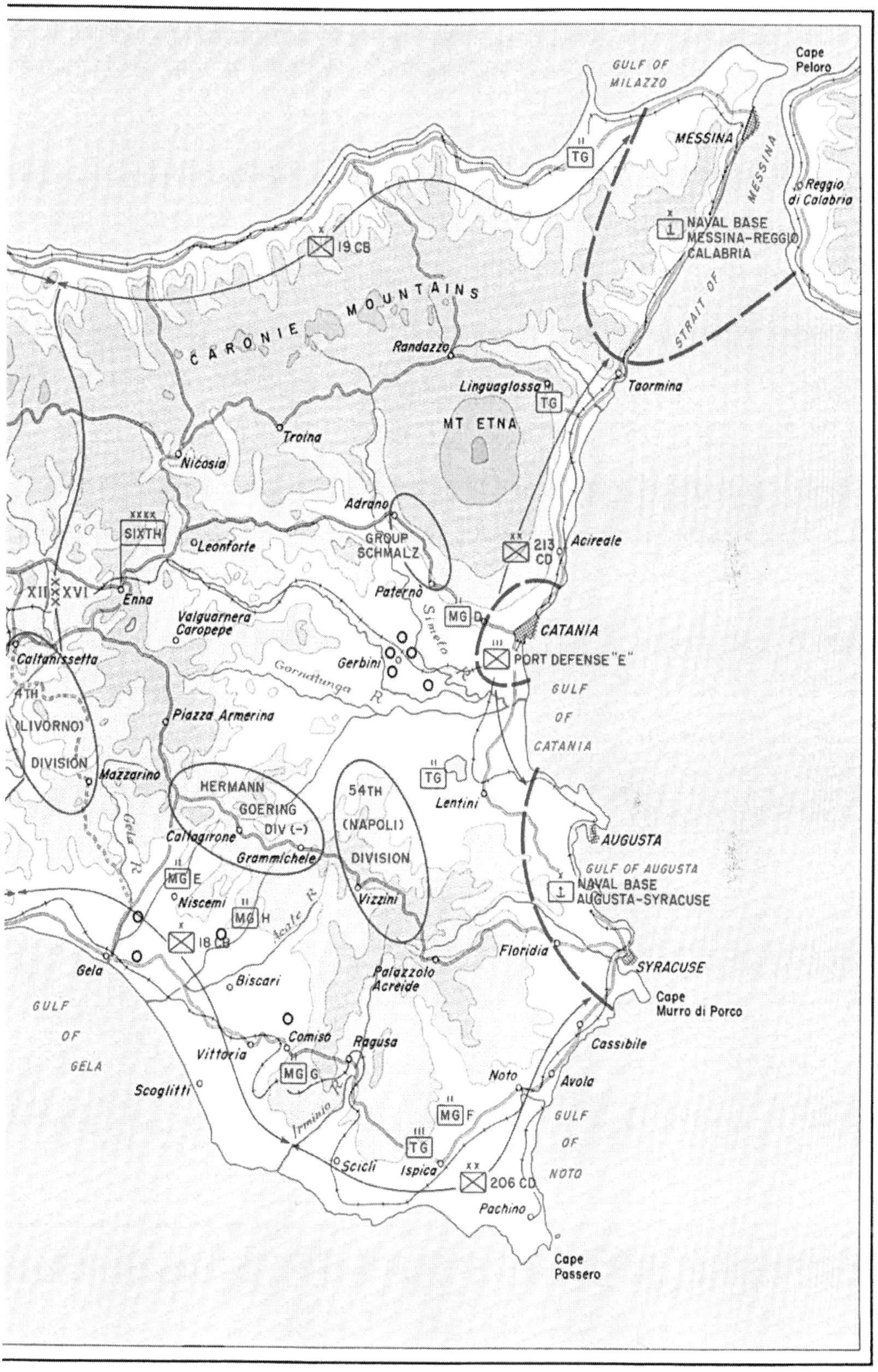

GULF OF MILAZZO
Cape Peloro
MESSINA
TG
Reggio di Calabria
MESSINA
NAVAL BASE MESSINA-REGGIO CALABRIA
19 CB
STRAIT OF
CARONIE MOUNTAINS
Randazzo
Taormina
Linguaglossa
TG
MT ETNA
Troina
Nicosia
Adrano
GROUP SCHMALZ
SIXTH
213 CD
Acireale
Leonforte
XII
XVI
Enna
Paternò
MG D
CATANIA
Valguarnera Caropepe
Simeto R
Caltanissetta
Gerbini
PORT DEFENSE "E"
Gornalunga R
GULF OF CATANIA
4TH (LIVORNO) DIVISION
Piazza Armerina
TG
Lentini
Mazzarino
HERMANN GOERING DIV (–)
54TH (NAPOLI) DIVISION
Caltagirone
AUGUSTA
Gela R
Grammichele
GULF OF AUGUSTA
MG E
NAVAL BASE AUGUSTA-SYRACUSE
Niscemi
MG H
Vizzini
18 CB
Floridia
Gela
Biscari
Palazzolo Acreide
SYRACUSE
Cape Murro di Porco
GULF OF GELA
Comiso
Ragusa
Cassibile
Vittoria
MG G
Noto
Avola
Scoglitti
MG F
GULF OF NOTO
TG
Scicli
Ispica
206 CD
Pachino
Cape Passero


MAP I

## THE FINAL LANDING PLAN

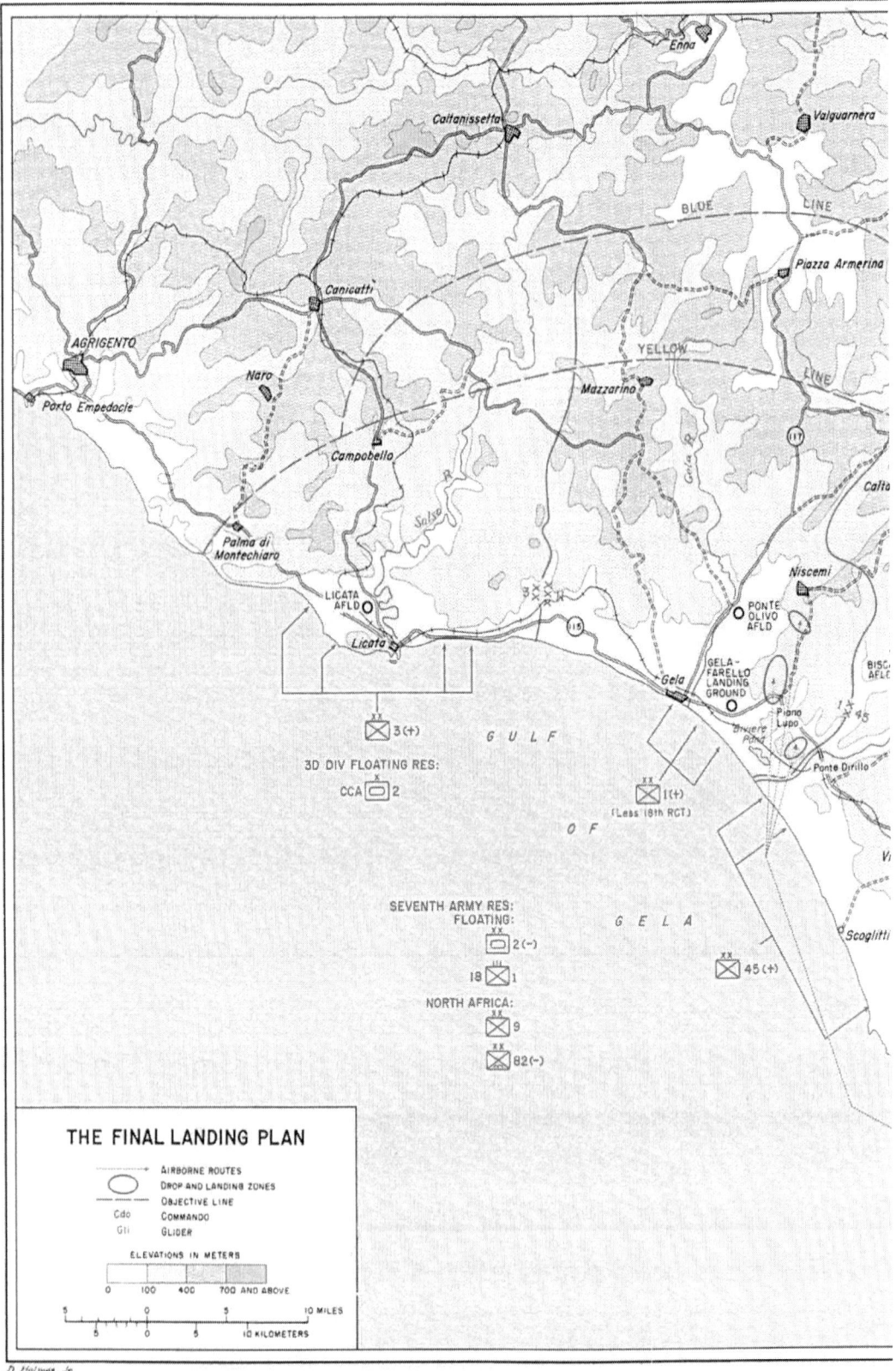

- AIRBORNE ROUTES
- DROP AND LANDING ZONES
- OBJECTIVE LINE
- Cdo   COMMANDO
- Gli   GLIDER

ELEVATIONS IN METERS
0   100   400   700 AND ABOVE

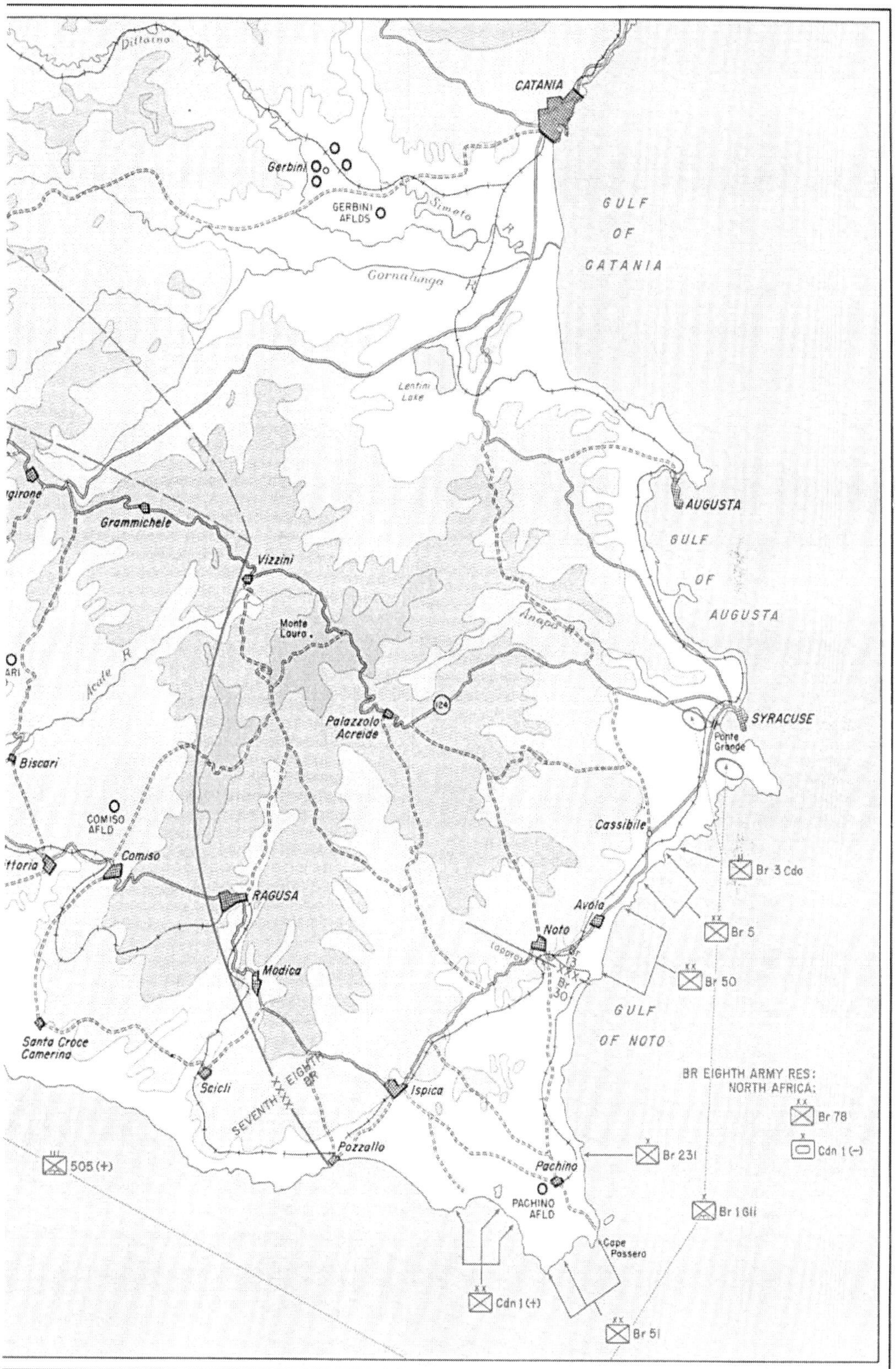

CATANIA
Gerbini
GERBINI AFLDS
Simeto R
Dittaino R
Gornalunga R
GULF OF CATANIA
Lentini Lake
AUGUSTA
GULF OF AUGUSTA
Grammichele
Vizzini
Monte Lauro
Anapo R
Acate R
124
Palazzolo Acreide
SYRACUSE
Ponte Grande
Biscari
COMISO AFLD
Comiso
RAGUSA
Cassibile
Br 3 Cdo
Avola
Noto
Br 5
Br 50
Modica
Br 13
Br 30
GULF OF NOTO
Santa Croce Camerina
Scicli
Ispica
SEVENTH
EIGHTH BR
BR EIGHTH ARMY RES: NORTH AFRICA:
Br 78
Cdn 1 (–)
Pozzallo
505 (+)
Br 231
Pachino
PACHINO AFLD
Br 1 Gli
Cape Passero
Cdn 1 (+)
Br 51

MAP II

SEVENTH ARMY GAINS
10 July 1943

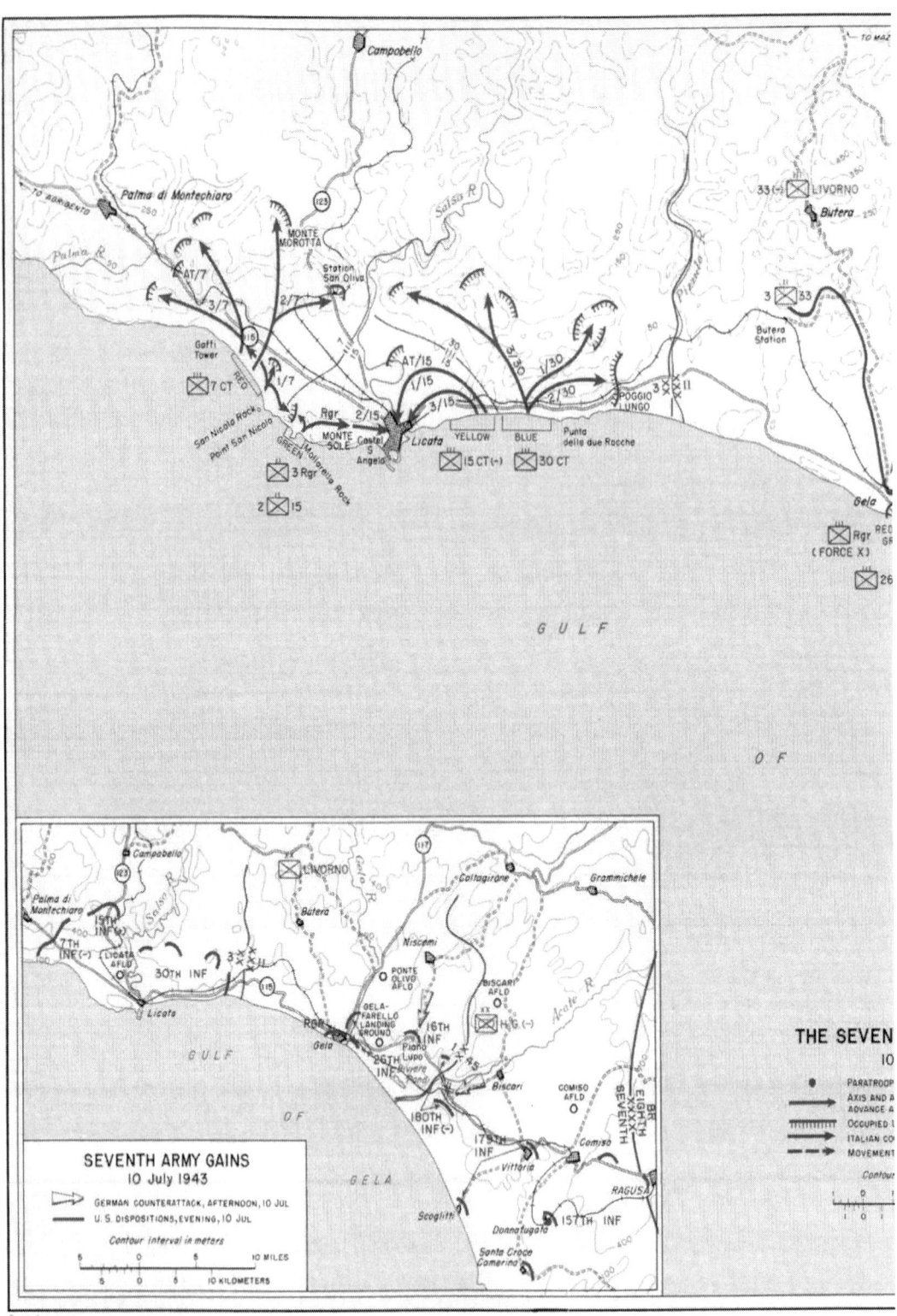

GERMAN COUNTERATTACK, AFTERNOON, 10 JUL
U.S. DISPOSITIONS, EVENING, 10 JUL

Contour Interval in meters

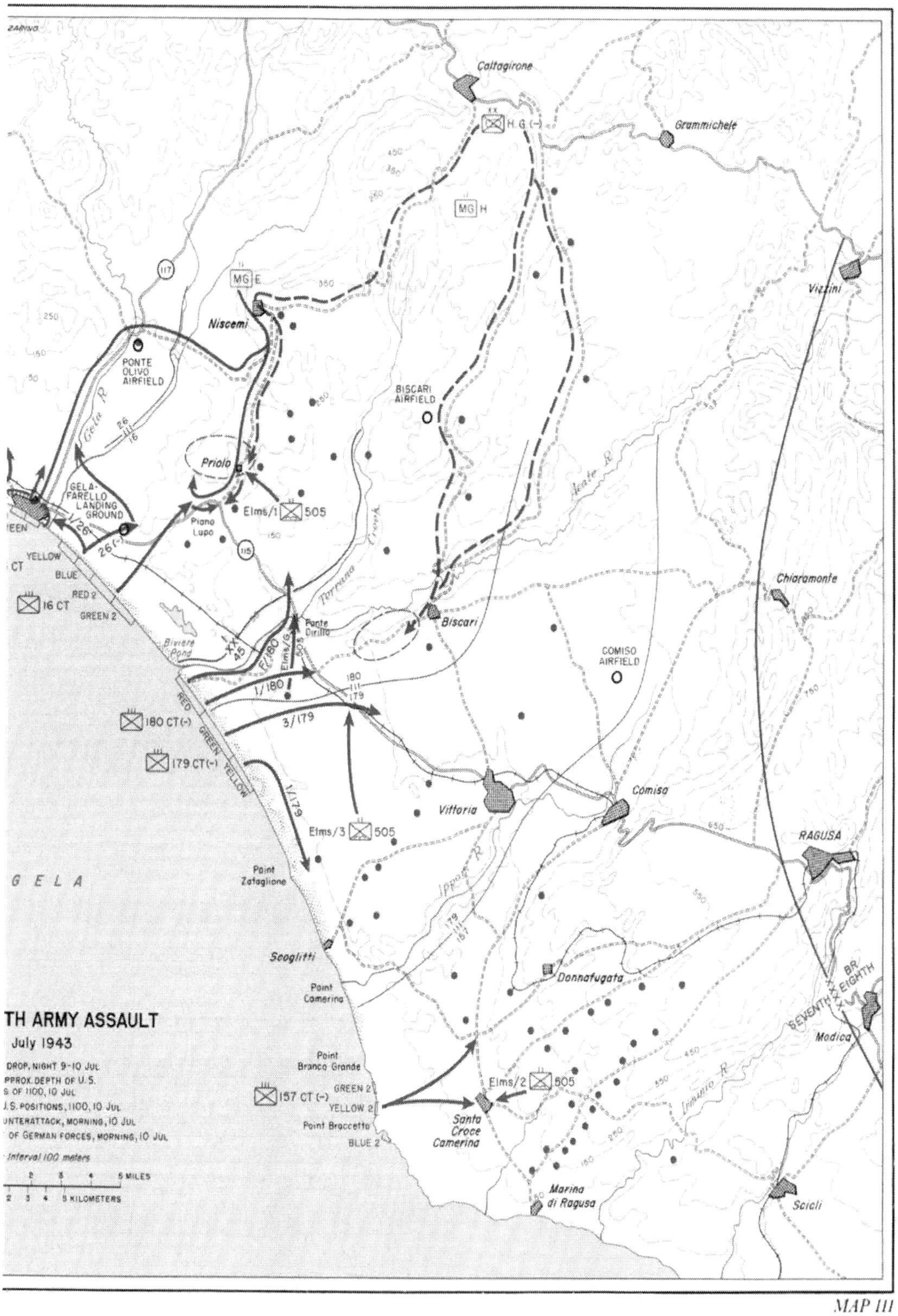
TH ARMY ASSAULT
July 1943
DROP, NIGHT 9-10 JUL
PPROX. DEPTH OF U.S.
S OF 1100, 10 JUL
J.S. POSITIONS, 1100, 10 JUL
UNTERATTACK, MORNING, 10 JUL
OF GERMAN FORCES, MORNING, 10 JUL
Interval 100 meters
2 3 4 5 MILES
2 3 4 5 KILOMETERS
Caltagirone
H.G (-)
Grammichele
MG H
MG E
Niscemi
PONTE OLIVO AIRFIELD
BISCARI AIRFIELD
Gela R
Priolo
GELA-FARELLO LANDING GROUND
Elms/1 505
Piano Lupo
1/26
26(-)
YELLOW
BLUE
RED 2
GREEN 2
16 CT
Biviere Pond
Ponte Dirillo
Biscari
Acate R
COMISO AIRFIELD
Chiaramonte
Vizzini
F/180
1/180
3/179
1/179
180 CT(-)
179 CT(-)
RED
GREEN
YELLOW
Elms/3 505
Vittoria
Comiso
RAGUSA
Point Zafaglione
G E L A
Ippari R
Scoglitti
Point Camerina
Donnafugata
SEVENTH
BR. EIGHTH
Modica
Point Branco Grande
157 CT (-)
GREEN 2
YELLOW 2
Point Braccetto
BLUE 2
Elms/2 505
Santa Croce Camerina
Irminio R
Marina di Ragusa
Scicli

MAP III

## COUNTERATTACK AT GELA
### 11 July 1943

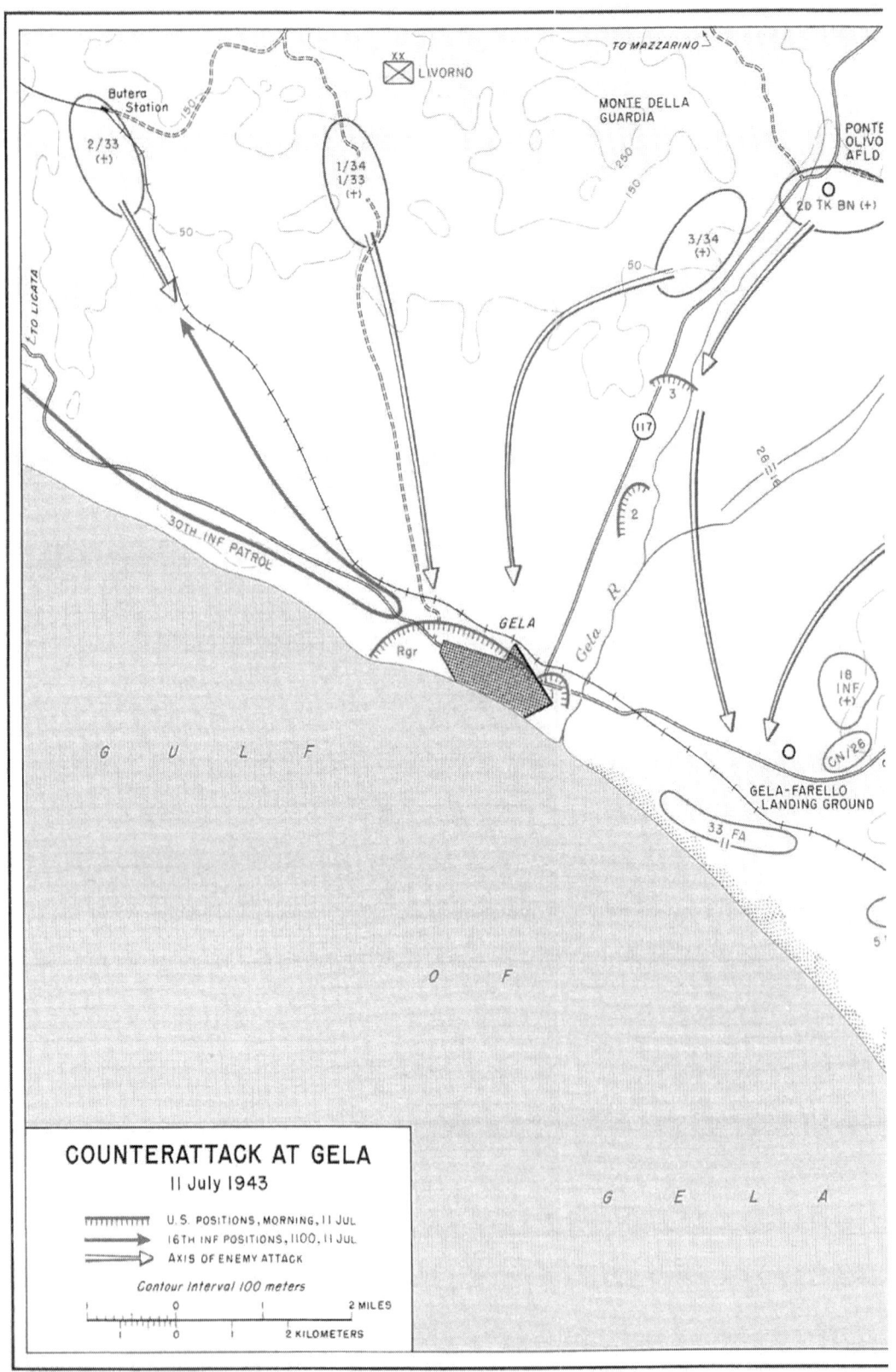

- U.S. POSITIONS, MORNING, 11 JUL
- 16TH INF POSITIONS, 1100, 11 JUL
- AXIS OF ENEMY ATTACK

*Contour Interval 100 meters*

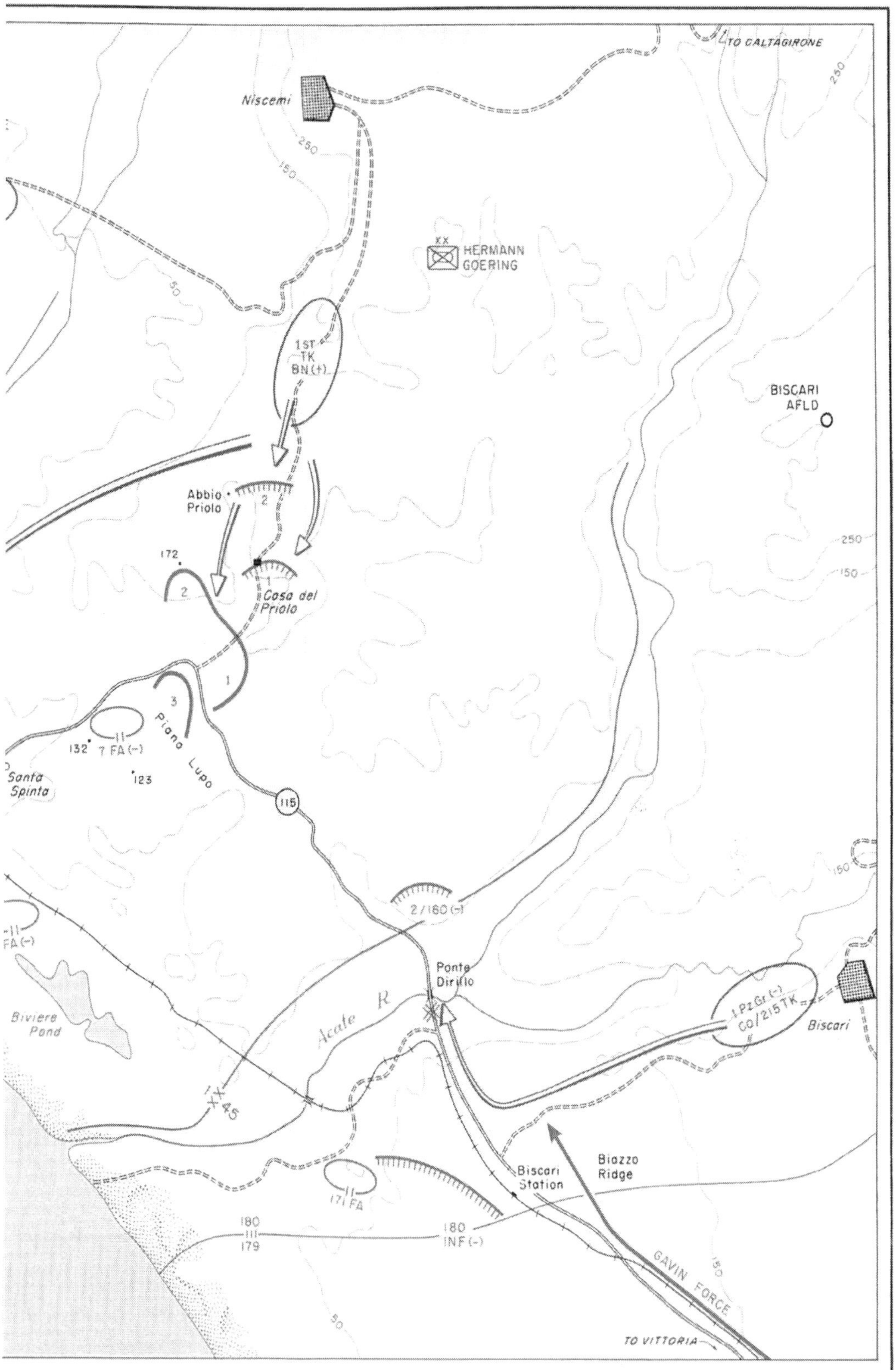
TO CALTAGIRONE
Niscemi
250
150
HERMANN GOERING
50
1ST TK BN(+)
BISCARI AFLD
Abbio Priolo
2
172
2
1
Casa del Priolo
1
3
Piano Lupo
7 FA(-)
132
123
Santa Spinta
115
250
150
150
2/160(-)
FA(-)
Ponte Dirillo
Acate R.
1 Pz Gr (-) CO/215 TK
Biscari
Biviere Pond
XX 45
Biscari Station
Biazzo Ridge
171 FA
180
179
180 INF(-)
GAVIN FORCE
150
50
TO VITTORIA

MAP IV

## SEVENTH ARMY ADVANCE
### 11-12 July 1943

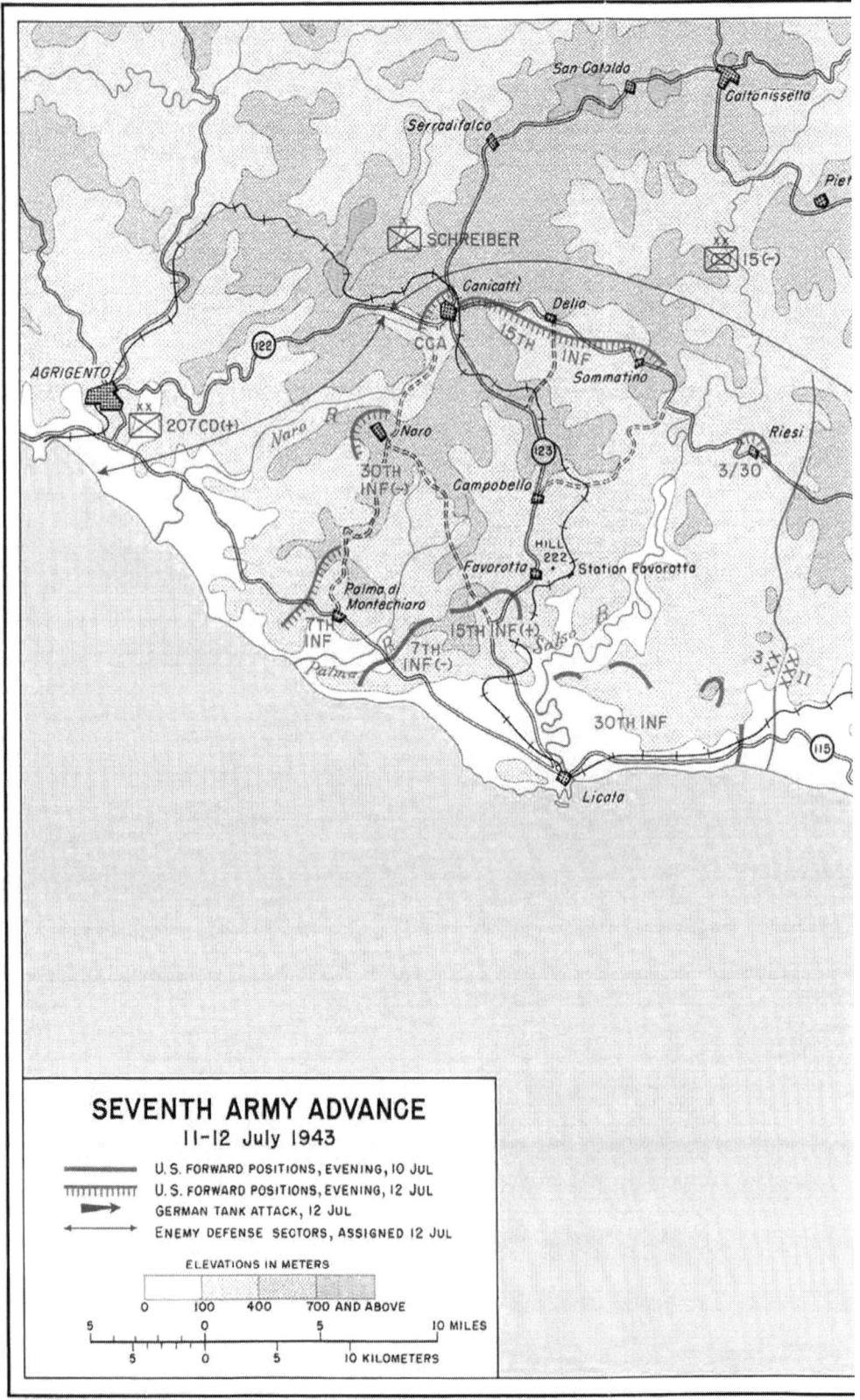

- U.S. FORWARD POSITIONS, EVENING, 10 JUL
- U.S. FORWARD POSITIONS, EVENING, 12 JUL
- GERMAN TANK ATTACK, 12 JUL
- ENEMY DEFENSE SECTORS, ASSIGNED 12 JUL

ELEVATIONS IN METERS: 0, 100, 400, 700 AND ABOVE

D. Holmes, Jr.

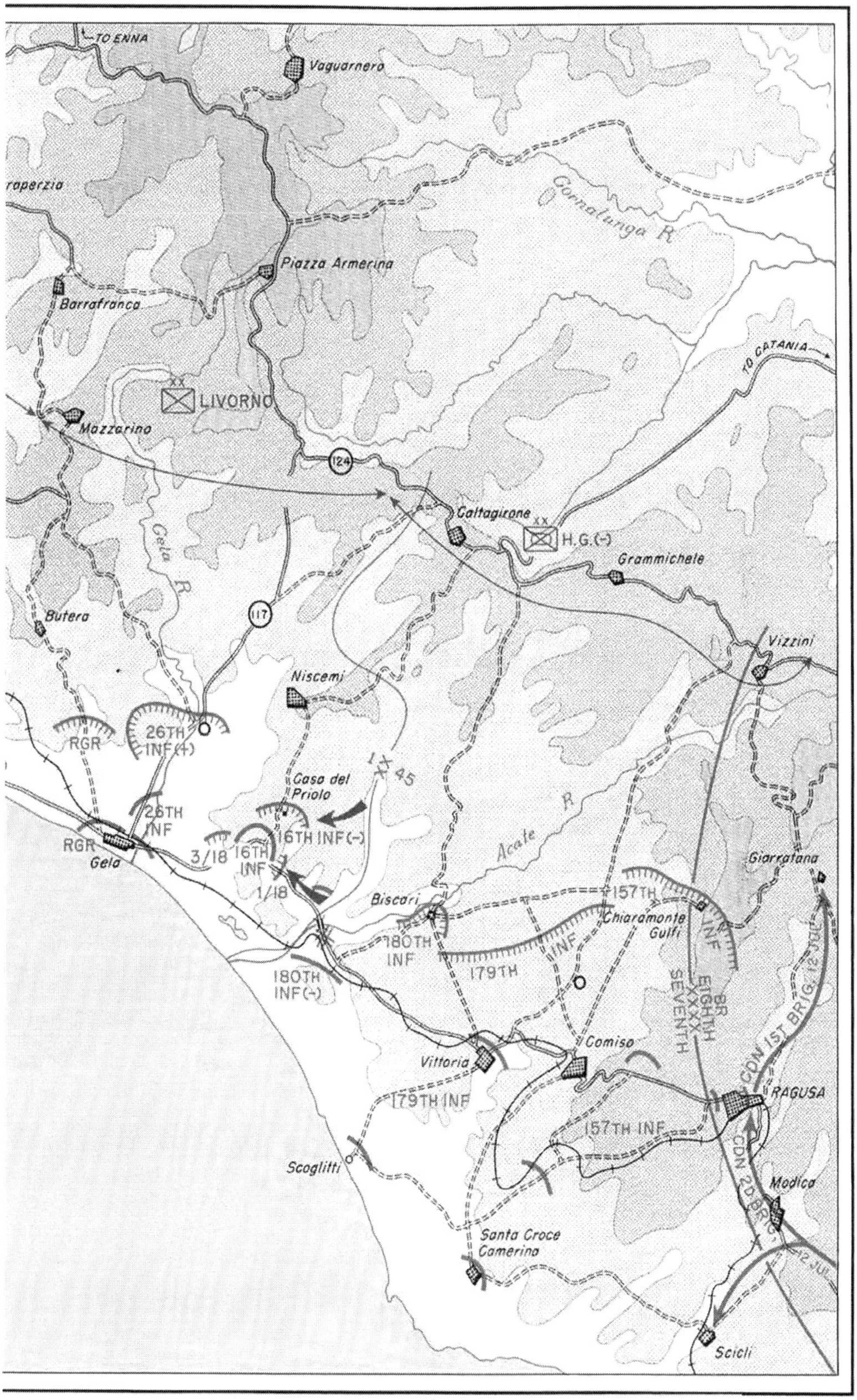
TO ENNA
Vaguarnero
raperzia
Gornalunga R.
Piazza Armerina
Barrafranca
TO CATANIA
LIVORNO
Mazzarino
124
Caltagirone
H.G.(-)
Gela R.
Grammichele
117
Butera
Vizzini
Niscemi
RGR
26TH INF(+)
Casa del Priolo
I X 45
Acate R.
26TH INF
16TH INF(-)
RGR
Gela
3/18
16TH INF
1/18
Giarratana
Biscari
157TH INF
Chiaramonte Gulfi
180TH INF
179TH INF
180TH INF(-)
BR EIGHTH
SEVENTH
Vittoria
Comiso
CDN 1ST BRIG 12 JUL
RAGUSA
179TH INF
157TH INF
Scoglitti
CDN 2D BRIG
Modica
Santa Croce Camerina
12 JUL
Scicli

MAP V

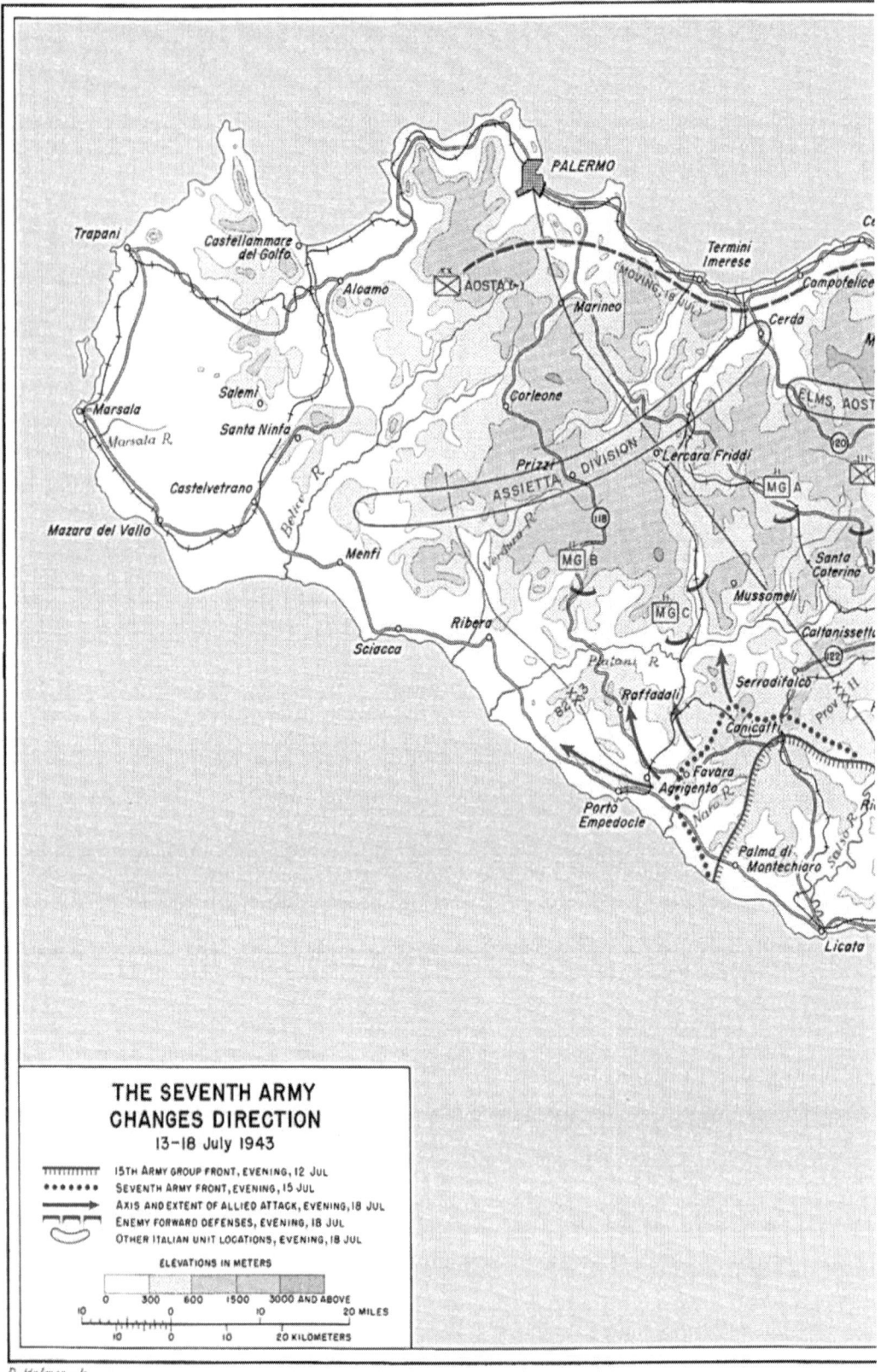

THE SEVENTH ARMY
CHANGES DIRECTION
13-18 July 1943

- 15TH ARMY GROUP FRONT, EVENING, 12 JUL
- SEVENTH ARMY FRONT, EVENING, 15 JUL
- AXIS AND EXTENT OF ALLIED ATTACK, EVENING, 18 JUL
- ENEMY FORWARD DEFENSES, EVENING, 18 JUL
- OTHER ITALIAN UNIT LOCATIONS, EVENING, 18 JUL

ELEVATIONS IN METERS
0   300   600   1500   3000 AND ABOVE

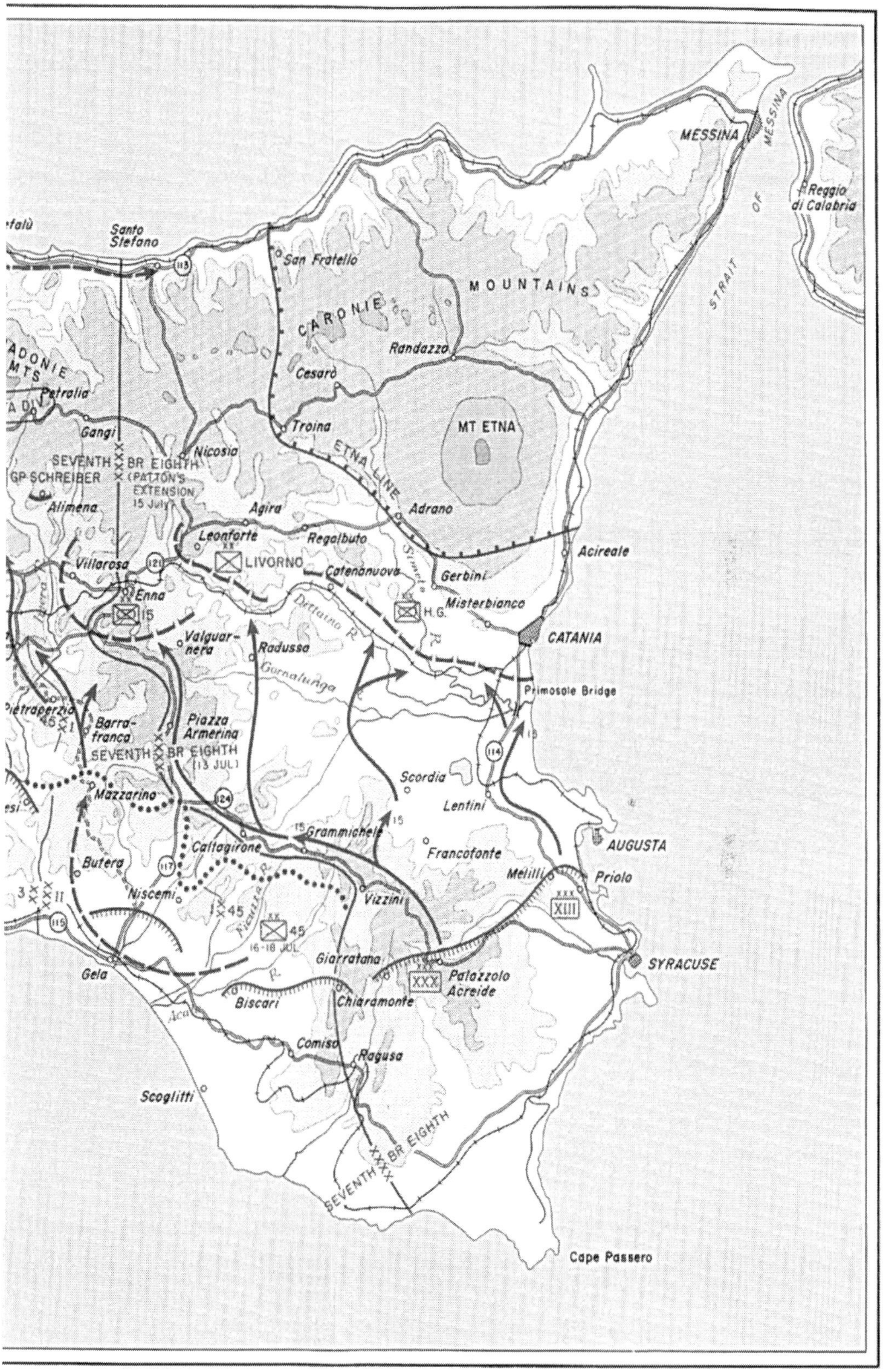
MESSINA
STRAIT OF MESSINA
Reggio di Calabria
Cefalù
Santo Stefano
San Fratello
CARONIE
MOUNTAINS
Randazzo
Cesarò
MADONIE MTS
Petralia
Troina
MT ETNA
Gangi
Nicosia
ETNA LINE
SEVENTH
BR EIGHTH
(PATTON'S EXTENSION 15 July)
GP SCHREIBER
Alimena
Agira
Adrano
Leonforte
Regalbuto
Acireale
LIVORNO
Villarosa
Catenanuova
Gerbini
Enna
15
Dittaino R
H.G.
Misterbianco
Valguarnera
Radussa
CATANIA
Gornalunga
Primosole Bridge
Pietraperzia
Barrafranca
Piazza Armerina
SEVENTH
BR EIGHTH
(13 JUL)
Scordia
Mazzarino
Lentini
Grammichele
AUGUSTA
Caltagirone
Francofonte
Butera
Melilli
Priolo
Niscemi
Vizzini
XIII
45
16-18 JUL
SYRACUSE
Gela
Giarratana
Palazzolo Acreide
XXX
Biscari
Chiaramonte
Comiso
Ragusa
Scoglitti
SEVENTH
BR EIGHTH
Cape Passero

MAP VI

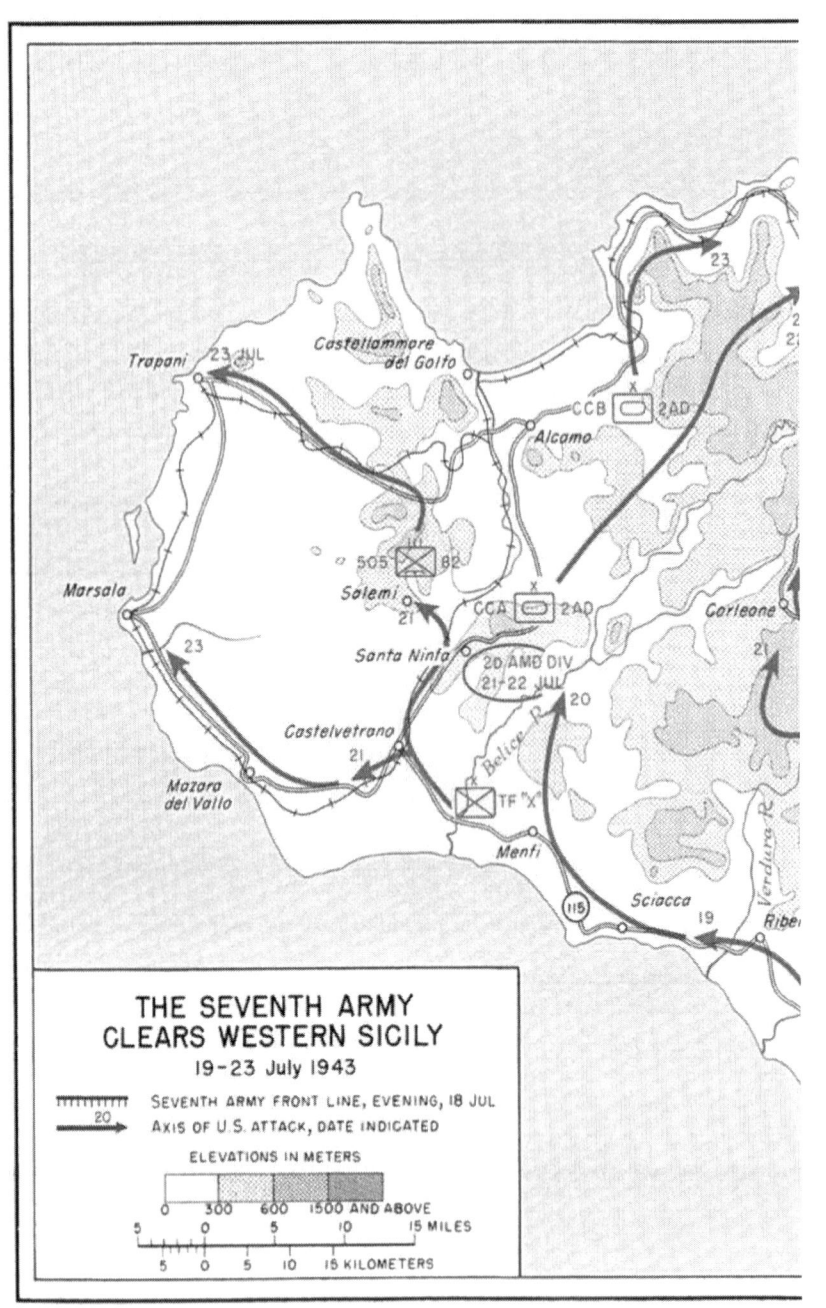

## THE SEVENTH ARMY CLEARS WESTERN SICILY
### 19–23 July 1943

SEVENTH ARMY FRONT LINE, EVENING, 18 JUL
AXIS OF U.S. ATTACK, DATE INDICATED

ELEVATIONS IN METERS
0   300   600   1500 AND ABOVE

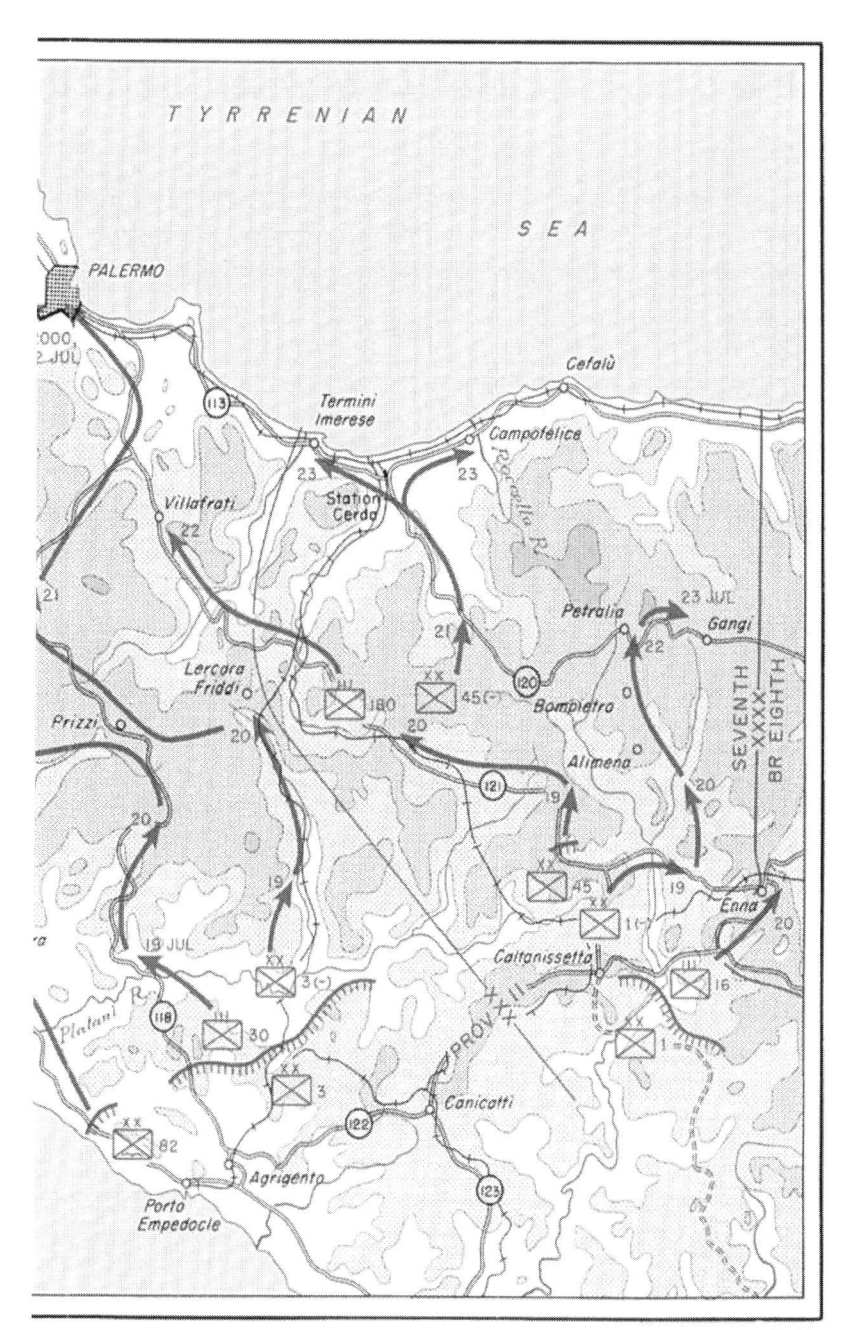

MAP VII

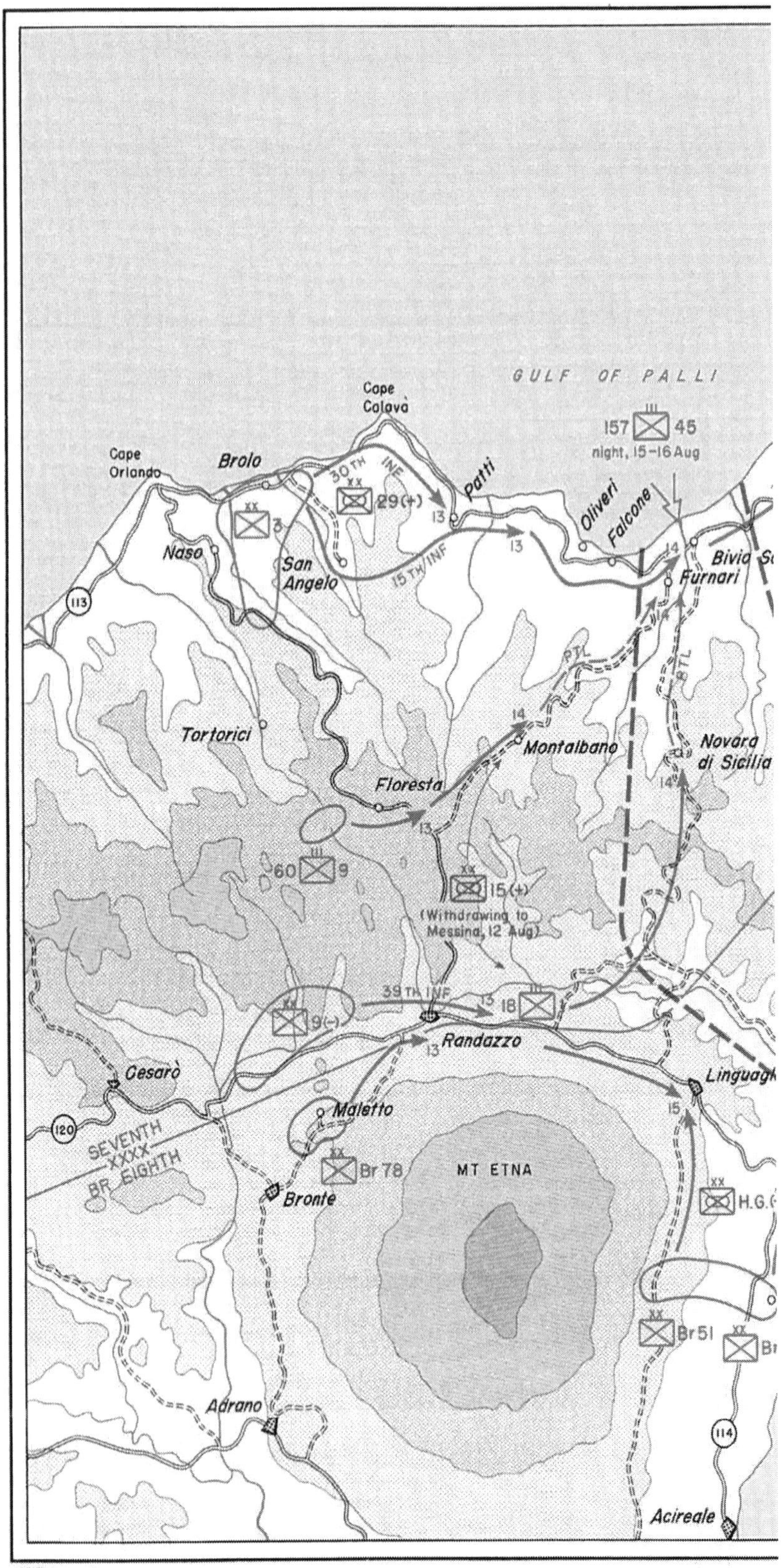
GULF OF PALLI
Cape Calavà
157 45
night, 15-16 Aug
Cape Orlando
Brolo
30TH INF
29(+)
Patti
Oliveri
Falcone
3
Naso
San Angelo
15TH INF
Bivio
Furnari
113
13
14
Tortorici
Montalbano
Novara di Sicilia
Floresta
60 9
15(+)
(Withdrawing to Messina, 12 Aug)
39TH INF
18
9(-)
Randazzo
Cesarò
Linguagl
Maletto
120
SEVENTH
XXXX
BR EIGHTH
Br 78
MT ETNA
Bronte
H.G.
Br51
Adrano
114
Acireale
H.C. Brewer, Jr

MAP VIII

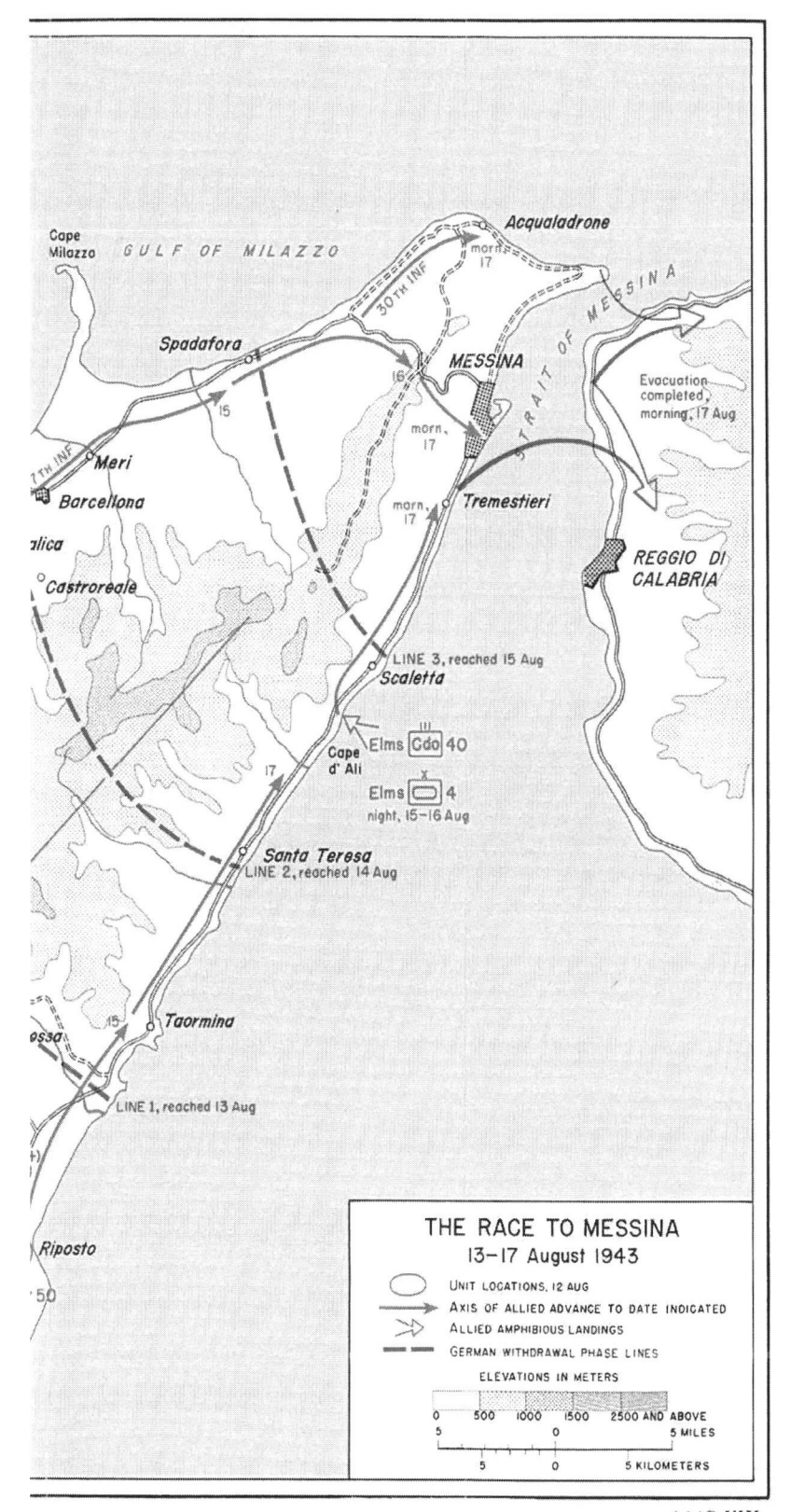

Printed in Great Britain
by Amazon